ASTRO BOY

OMNIBUS 5

by
OSAMU TEZUKA

Translation
FREDERIK L. SCHODT

Lettering and Retouch
DIGITAL CHAMELEON

D1126453

DARK HORSE MANGA

President and Publisher MIKE RICHARDSON

US Editor CHRIS WARNER

Assistant Editor JEMIAH JEFFERSON

Consulting Editor TOREN SMITH

Collection Designer JUSTIN COUCH

Digital Art Technician CONLEY SMITH

English-language version produced by
DARK HORSE MANGA

Dark Horse Manga, a division of Dark Horse Comics, Inc.
10956 SE Main Street, Milwaukie, OR 97222
DarkHorse.com

First edition: September 2016 | ISBN 978-1-50670-016-8

1 3 5 7 9 10 8 6 4 2
Printed in the United States of America

To find a comics shop in your area, call the Comic Shop Locator Service toll-free at 1-888-266-4226.

This volume collects stories previously published in *Astro Boy* Volumes 14, 15, 16, and 17,
published by Dark Horse Comics. The artwork of this volume has been produced
as a mirror image of the original Japanese edition.

Neil Hankerson, Executive Vice President; Tom Weddle, Chief Financial Officer; Randy Stradley, Vice President of
Publishing; Michael Martens, Vice President of Book Trade Sales; Matt Parkinson, Vice President of Marketing;
David Scroggy, Vice President of Product Development; Dale LaFountain, Vice President of Information
Technology; Cara Niece, Vice President of Production and Scheduling; Nick McWhorter, Vice President of Media
Licensing; Ken Lizzi, General Counsel; Dave Marshall, Editor in Chief; Davey Estrada, Editorial Director; Scott
Allie, Executive Senior Editor; Chris Warner, Senior Books Editor; Cary Grazzini, Director of Specialty Projects;
Lia Ribacchi, Art Director; Vanessa Todd, Director of Print Purchasing; Matt Dryer, Director of Digital Art and
Prepress; Mark Bernardi, Director of Digital Publishing; Sarah Robertson, Director of Product Sales; Michael
Gombos, Director of International Publishing and Licensing

A NOTE TO READERS

Many non-Japanese, including people from Africa and Southeast Asia, appear in Osamu Tezuka's works. Sometimes these people are depicted very differently from the way they actually are, in a manner that exaggerates a time long past, or shows them to be from extremely undeveloped lands. Some feel that such images contribute to racial discrimination, especially against people of African descent. This was never Osamu Tezuka's intent, but we believe that as long as there are people who feel insulted or demeaned by these drawings, we must not ignore their feelings.

We are against all forms of discrimination and intend to continue to work for its elimination. Nonetheless, we do not believe it would be proper to revise these works. Tezuka is no longer with us, and we cannot erase what he has done, and to alter his work would only violate his rights as a creator. More importantly, stopping publication or changing the content of his work would do little to solve the problems of discrimination that exist in the world.

We are presenting Osamu Tezuka's work as it was originally created, without changes. We do this because we believe it is also important to promote the underlying themes in his work, such as love for mankind and the sacredness of life. We hope that when you, the reader, encounter this work, you will keep in mind the differences in attitudes toward discrimination when the work was created and those of today, and that this will contribute to an even greater awareness of such problems.

— Tezuka Productions and Dark Horse Comics

THE WHITE-HOT BEING

First serialized from January to March 1961
in *Shonen* magazine.

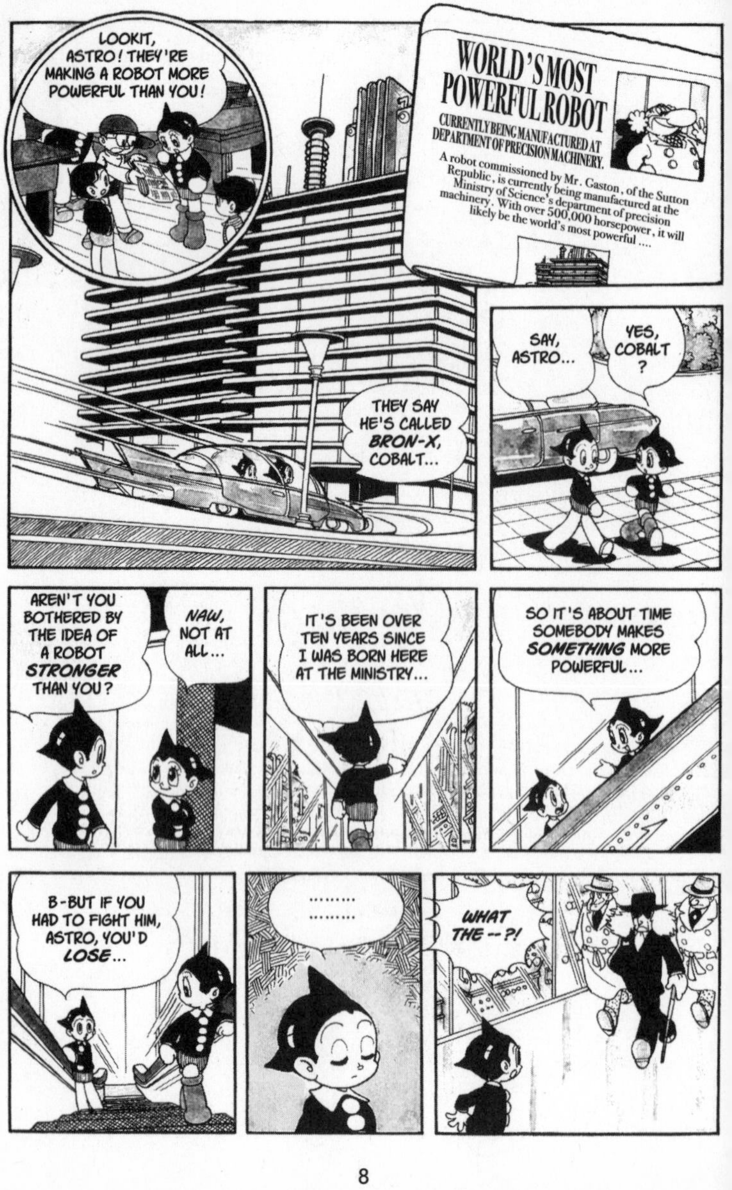
LOOKIT, ASTRO! THEY'RE MAKING A ROBOT MORE POWERFUL THAN YOU!
WORLD'S MOST POWERFUL ROBOT
CURRENTLY BEING MANUFACTURED AT DEPARTMENT OF PRECISION MACHINERY.
A robot commissioned by Mr. Gaston, of the Sutton Republic, is currently being manufactured at the Ministry of Science's department of precision machinery. With over 500,000 horsepower, it will likely be the world's most powerful ....
THEY SAY HE'S CALLED *BRON-X*, COBALT...
SAY, ASTRO...
YES, COBALT?
AREN'T YOU BOTHERED BY THE IDEA OF A ROBOT *STRONGER* THAN YOU?
NAW, NOT AT ALL...
IT'S BEEN OVER TEN YEARS SINCE I WAS BORN HERE AT THE MINISTRY...
SO IT'S ABOUT TIME SOMEBODY MAKES *SOMETHING* MORE POWERFUL...
B-BUT IF YOU HAD TO FIGHT HIM, ASTRO, YOU'D *LOSE*...
....
....
WHAT THE--?!

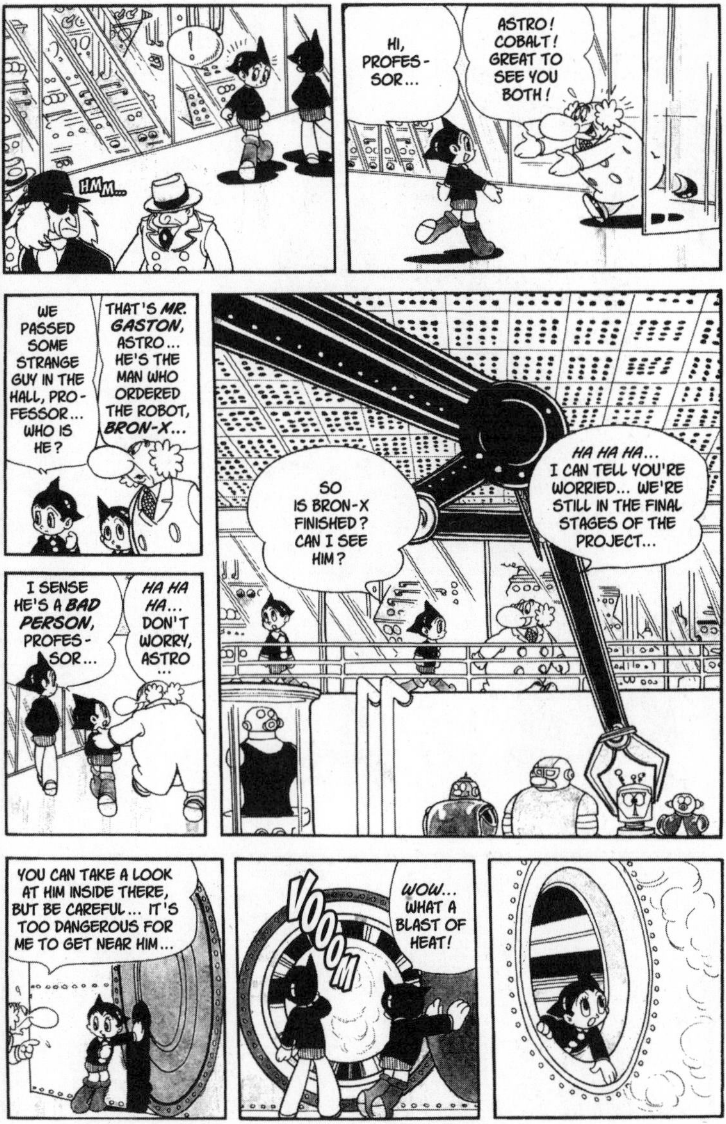
!
HMM...
HI, PROFES-SOR...
ASTRO! COBALT! GREAT TO SEE YOU BOTH!
WE PASSED SOME STRANGE GUY IN THE HALL, PRO-FESSOR... WHO IS HE?
THAT'S MR. GASTON, ASTRO... HE'S THE MAN WHO ORDERED THE ROBOT, BRON-X...
I SENSE HE'S A BAD PERSON, PROFES-SOR...
HA HA HA... DON'T WORRY, ASTRO...
SO IS BRON-X FINISHED? CAN I SEE HIM?
HA HA HA... I CAN TELL YOU'RE WORRIED... WE'RE STILL IN THE FINAL STAGES OF THE PROJECT...
YOU CAN TAKE A LOOK AT HIM INSIDE THERE, BUT BE CAREFUL... IT'S TOO DANGEROUS FOR ME TO GET NEAR HIM...
VOOOM
WOW... WHAT A BLAST OF HEAT!

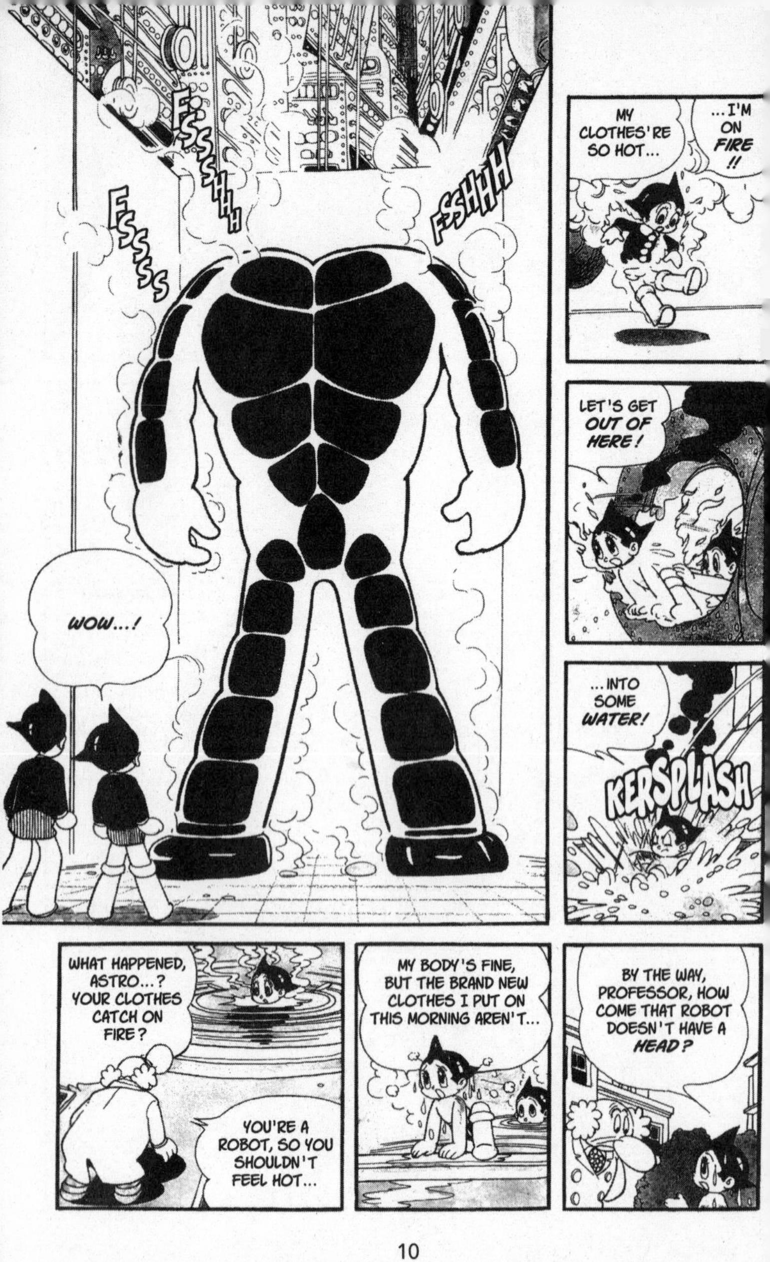
FSSSHHH
FSSSSS
FSHHHH
WOW...!
MY CLOTHES'RE SO HOT...
...I'M ON FIRE!!
LET'S GET OUT OF HERE!
...INTO SOME WATER!
KERSPLASH
WHAT HAPPENED, ASTRO...? YOUR CLOTHES CATCH ON FIRE?
YOU'RE A ROBOT, SO YOU SHOULDN'T FEEL HOT...
MY BODY'S FINE, BUT THE BRAND NEW CLOTHES I PUT ON THIS MORNING AREN'T...
BY THE WAY, PROFESSOR, HOW COME THAT ROBOT DOESN'T HAVE A HEAD?

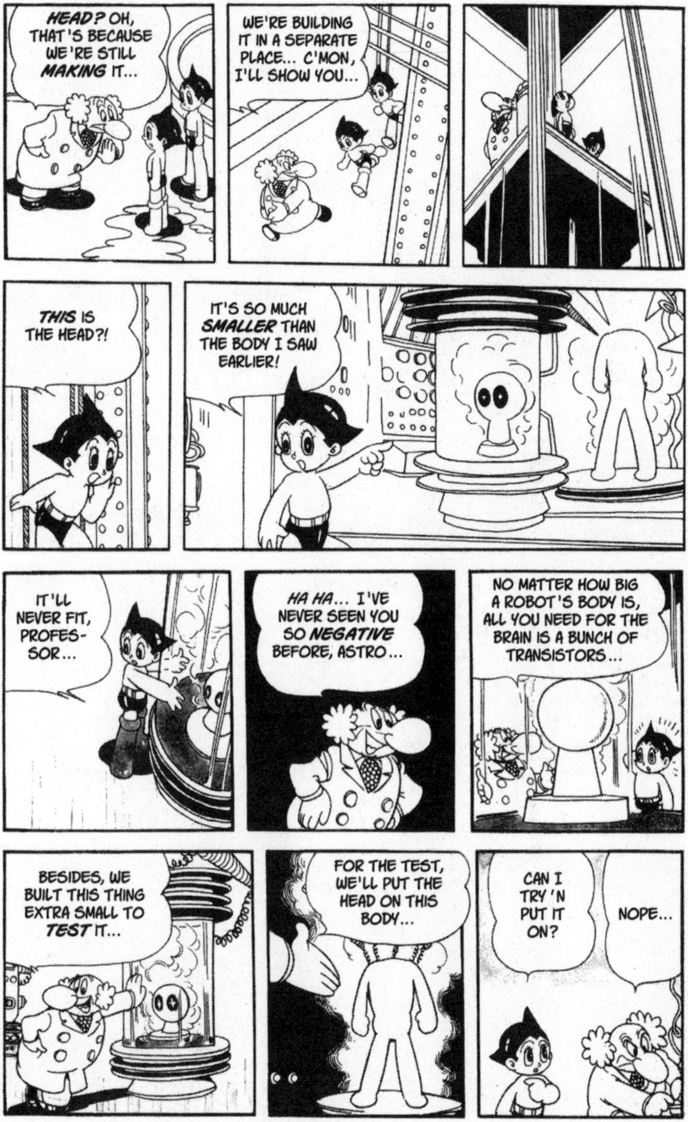
HEAD? OH, THAT'S BECAUSE WE'RE STILL MAKING IT...
WE'RE BUILDING IT IN A SEPARATE PLACE... C'MON, I'LL SHOW YOU...
THIS IS THE HEAD?!
IT'S SO MUCH SMALLER THAN THE BODY I SAW EARLIER!
IT'LL NEVER FIT, PROFES-SOR...
HA HA... I'VE NEVER SEEN YOU SO NEGATIVE BEFORE, ASTRO...
NO MATTER HOW BIG A ROBOT'S BODY IS, ALL YOU NEED FOR THE BRAIN IS A BUNCH OF TRANSISTORS...
BESIDES, WE BUILT THIS THING EXTRA SMALL TO TEST IT...
FOR THE TEST, WE'LL PUT THE HEAD ON THIS BODY...
CAN I TRY 'N PUT IT ON?
NOPE...

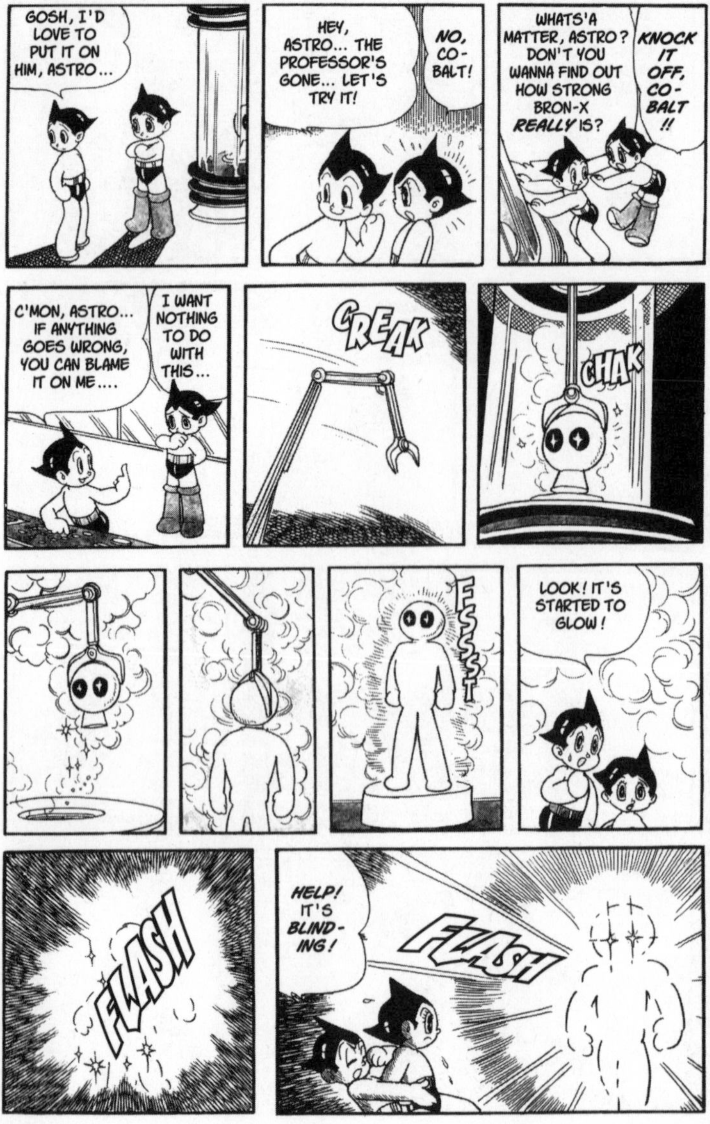
GOSH, I'D LOVE TO PUT IT ON HIM, ASTRO...
HEY, ASTRO... THE PROFESSOR'S GONE... LET'S TRY IT!
NO, CO-BALT!
WHATS'A MATTER, ASTRO? DON'T YOU WANNA FIND OUT HOW STRONG BRON-X REALLY IS?
KNOCK IT OFF, CO-BALT!!
C'MON, ASTRO... IF ANYTHING GOES WRONG, YOU CAN BLAME IT ON ME....
I WANT NOTHING TO DO WITH THIS...
CREAK
CHAK
FSSST
LOOK! IT'S STARTED TO GLOW!
FLASH
HELP! IT'S BLINDING!
FLASH

HELP, ASTRO! I CAN'T SEE!!

YOU'RE A ROBOT, COBALT, YOU'RE NOT SUPPOSED TO BE BLINDED....

WAIT A SEC'... I CAN'T SEE EITHER!

THIS IS TERRI-BLE...

GWA HA HA! WELL...IF IT ISN'T ASTRO AND HIS BROTHER COBALT!

∋UNGH?!?∈

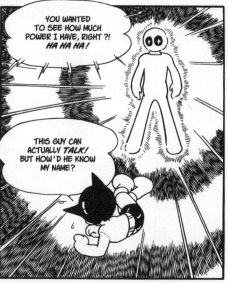

YOU WANTED TO SEE HOW MUCH POWER I HAVE, RIGHT?! HA HA HA!

THIS GUY CAN ACTUALLY TALK! BUT HOW'D HE KNOW MY NAME?

YOU'RE PROBABLY WONDERING HOW I KNOW YOUR NAMES...

C-CAN YOU READ MY MIND?

I CAN READ ANYONE'S MIND....

13

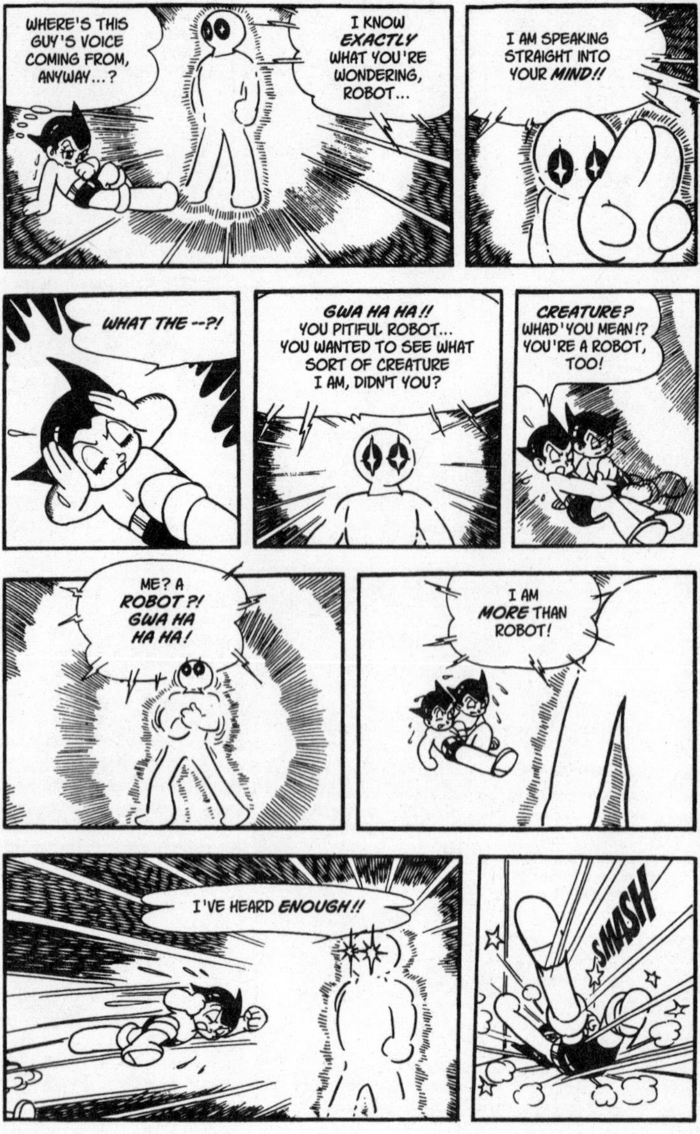
WHERE'S THIS GUY'S VOICE COMING FROM, ANYWAY...?
I KNOW *EXACTLY* WHAT YOU'RE WONDERING, ROBOT...
I AM SPEAKING STRAIGHT INTO YOUR *MIND!!*
WHAT THE --?!
GWA HA HA!! YOU PITIFUL ROBOT... YOU WANTED TO SEE WHAT SORT OF CREATURE I AM, DIDN'T YOU?
CREATURE? WHAD'YOU MEAN!? YOU'RE A ROBOT, TOO!
ME? A *ROBOT?! GWA HA HA HA!*
I AM *MORE* THAN ROBOT!
I'VE HEARD *ENOUGH!!*
SMASH

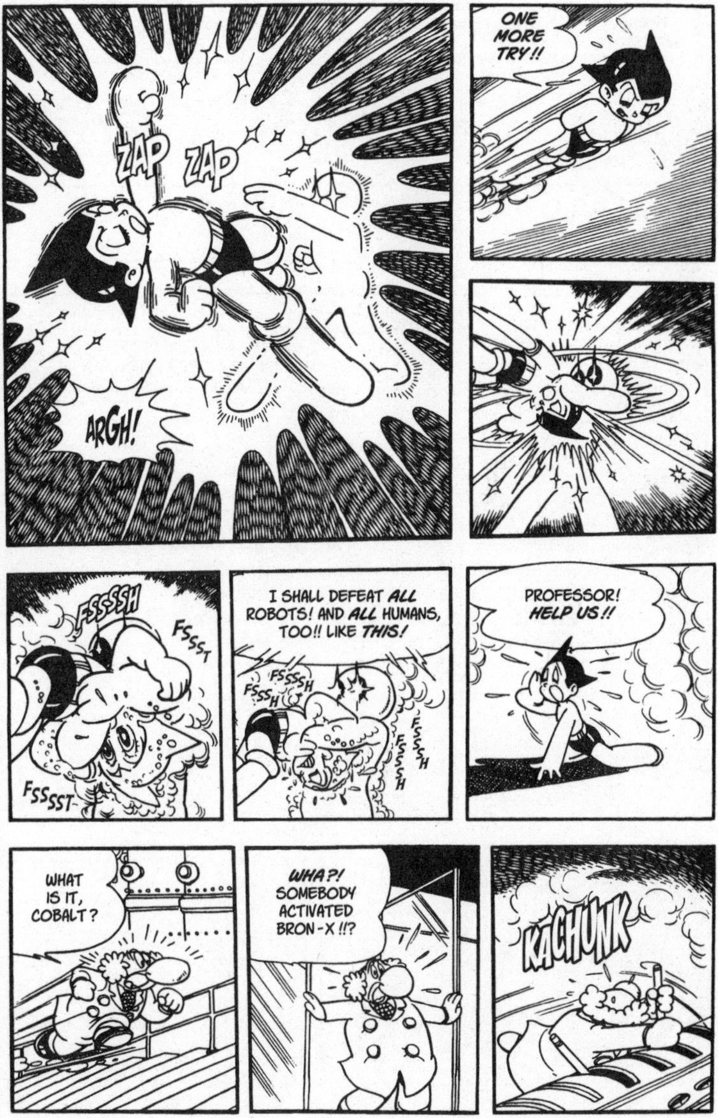
ZAP
ZAP
ARGH!
ONE MORE TRY!!
FSSSSH
FSSST
FSSSST
I SHALL DEFEAT ALL ROBOTS! AND ALL HUMANS, TOO!! LIKE THIS!
FSSSSH
FSSSH
FSSSH
FSSSH
PROFESSOR! HELP US!!
WHAT IS IT, COBALT?
WHA?! SOMEBODY ACTIVATED BRON-X!!?
KACHUNK

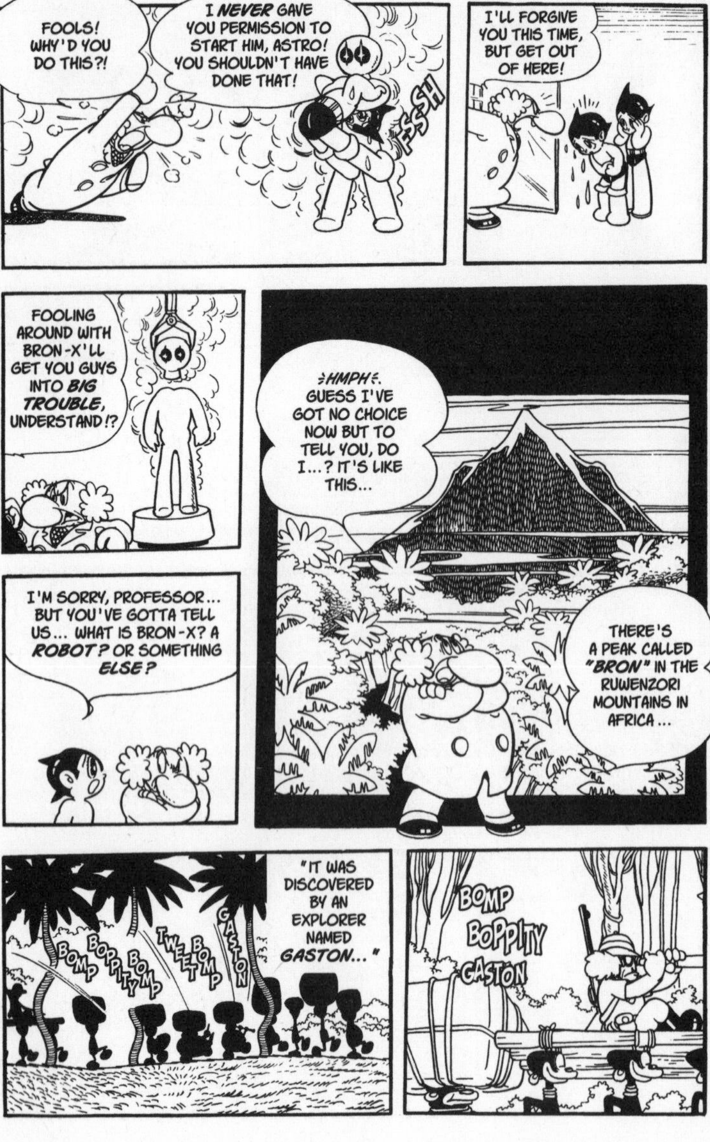
FOOLS! WHY'D YOU DO THIS?!
I NEVER GAVE YOU PERMISSION TO START HIM, ASTRO! YOU SHOULDN'T HAVE DONE THAT!
FSSH
I'LL FORGIVE YOU THIS TIME, BUT GET OUT OF HERE!
FOOLING AROUND WITH BRON-X'LL GET YOU GUYS INTO BIG TROUBLE, UNDERSTAND!?
I'M SORRY, PROFESSOR... BUT YOU'VE GOTTA TELL US... WHAT IS BRON-X? A ROBOT? OR SOMETHING ELSE?
HMPH. GUESS I'VE GOT NO CHOICE NOW BUT TO TELL YOU, DO I...? IT'S LIKE THIS...
THERE'S A PEAK CALLED "BRON" IN THE RUWENZORI MOUNTAINS IN AFRICA...
BOMP
BOPPITY
BOMP
TWEET
BOMP
GASTON
"IT WAS DISCOVERED BY AN EXPLORER NAMED GASTON..."
BOMP
BOPPITY
GASTON

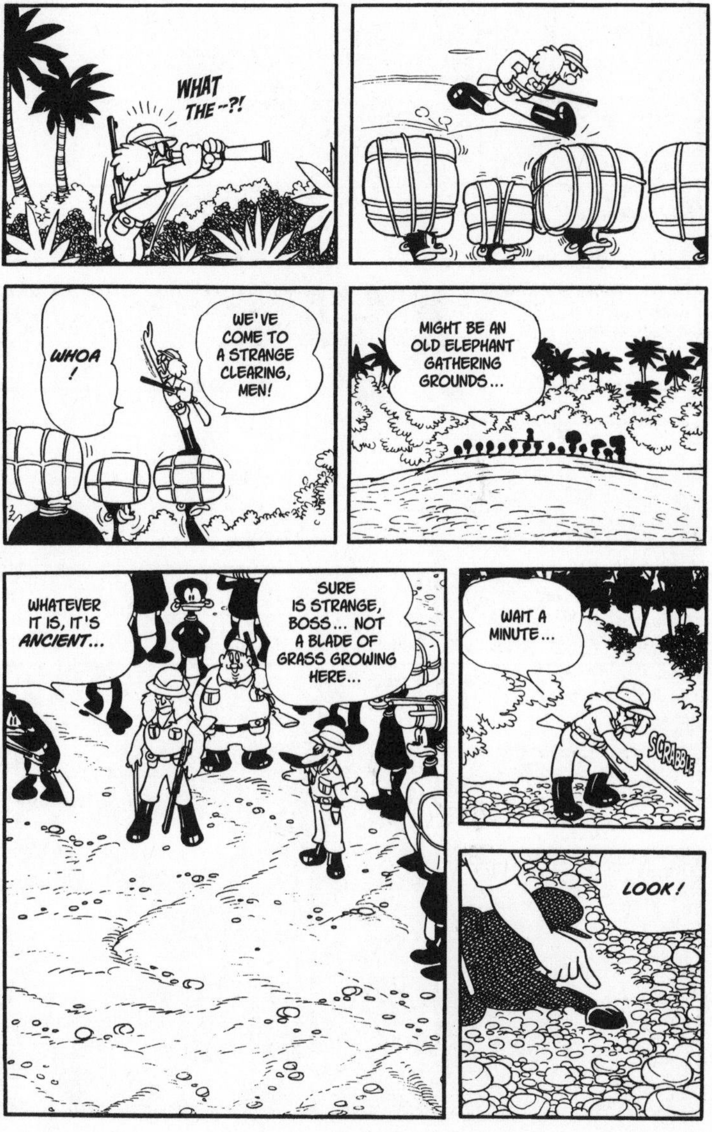
WHAT THE --?!
WHOA!
WE'VE COME TO A STRANGE CLEARING, MEN!
MIGHT BE AN OLD ELEPHANT GATHERING GROUNDS...
WHATEVER IT IS, IT'S *ANCIENT*...
SURE IS STRANGE, BOSS... NOT A BLADE OF GRASS GROWING HERE...
WAIT A MINUTE...
SCRABBLE
LOOK!

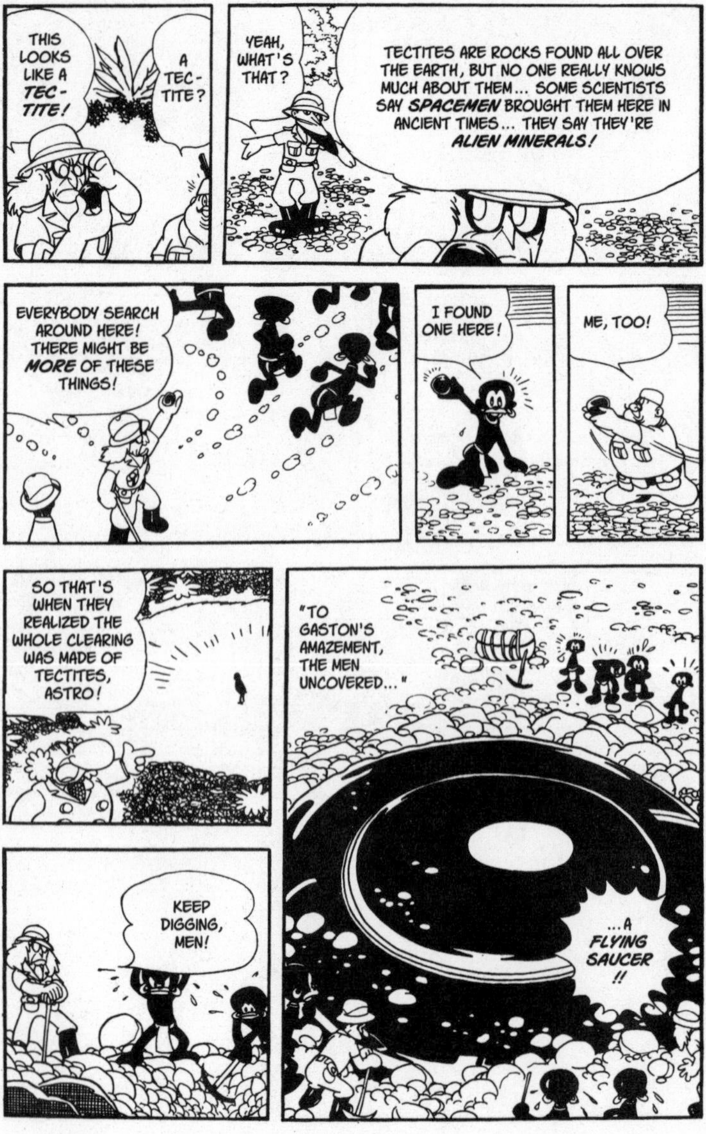
THIS LOOKS LIKE A *TEC-TITE!*
A TEC-TITE?
YEAH, WHAT'S THAT?
TECTITES ARE ROCKS FOUND ALL OVER THE EARTH, BUT NO ONE REALLY KNOWS MUCH ABOUT THEM... SOME SCIENTISTS SAY *SPACEMEN* BROUGHT THEM HERE IN ANCIENT TIMES... THEY SAY THEY'RE *ALIEN MINERALS!*
EVERYBODY SEARCH AROUND HERE! THERE MIGHT BE *MORE* OF THESE THINGS!
I FOUND ONE HERE!
ME, TOO!
SO THAT'S WHEN THEY REALIZED THE WHOLE CLEARING WAS MADE OF TECTITES, ASTRO!
"TO GASTON'S AMAZEMENT, THE MEN UNCOVERED..."
KEEP DIGGING, MEN!
...A *FLYING SAUCER* !!

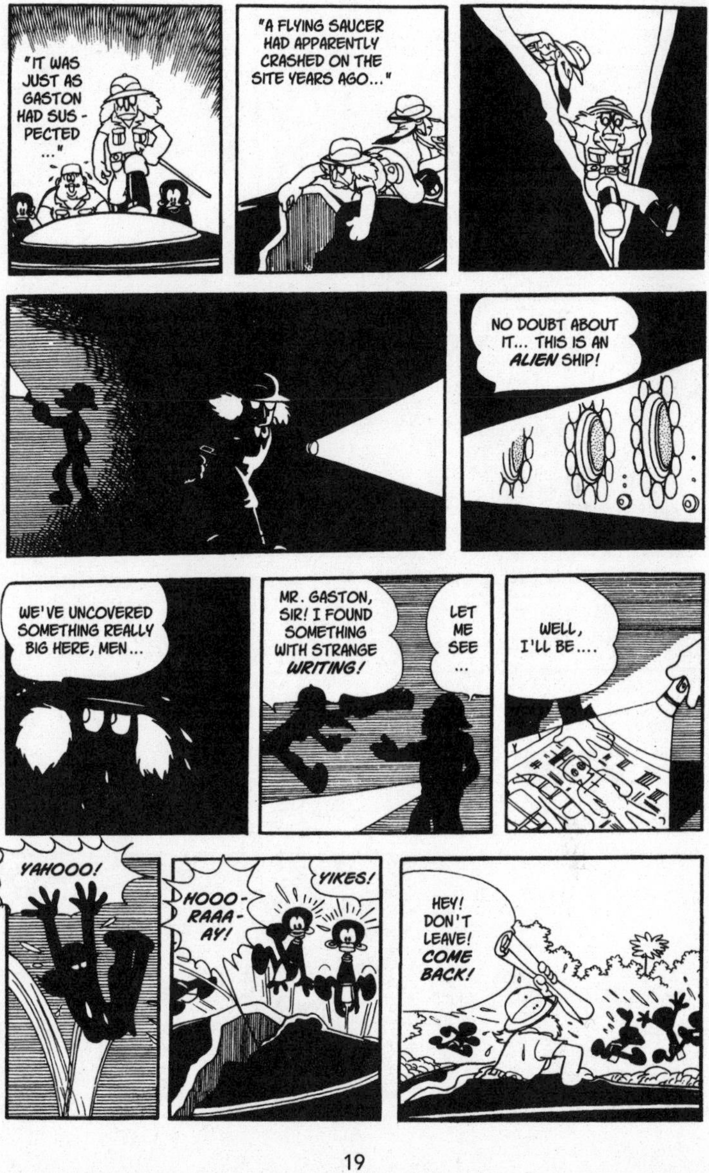

"IT WAS JUST AS GASTON HAD SUS-PECTED ..."
"A FLYING SAUCER HAD APPARENTLY CRASHED ON THE SITE YEARS AGO..."
NO DOUBT ABOUT IT... THIS IS AN ALIEN SHIP!
WE'VE UNCOVERED SOMETHING REALLY BIG HERE, MEN...
MR. GASTON, SIR! I FOUND SOMETHING WITH STRANGE WRITING!
LET ME SEE ...
WELL, I'LL BE....
YAHOOO!
HOOO-RAAA-AY!
YIKES!
HEY! DON'T LEAVE! COME BACK!

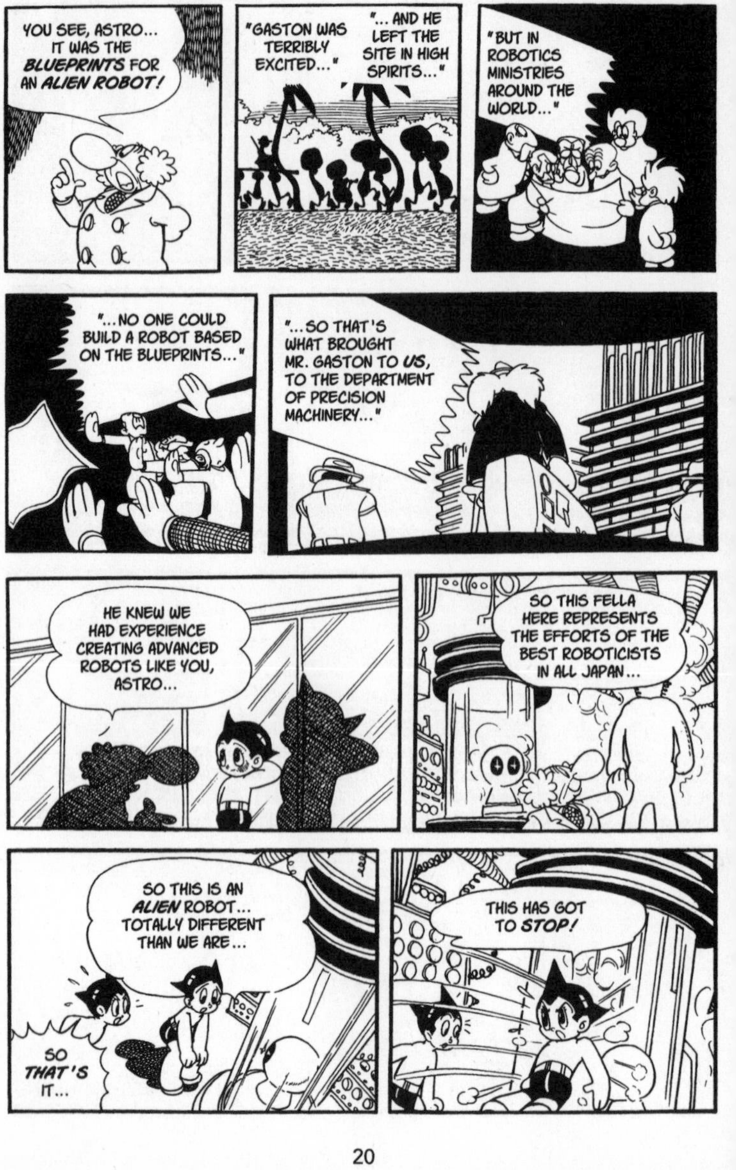
YOU SEE, ASTRO... IT WAS THE BLUEPRINTS FOR AN ALIEN ROBOT!
"GASTON WAS TERRIBLY EXCITED..."
"... AND HE LEFT THE SITE IN HIGH SPIRITS..."
"BUT IN ROBOTICS MINISTRIES AROUND THE WORLD..."
"...NO ONE COULD BUILD A ROBOT BASED ON THE BLUEPRINTS..."
"...SO THAT'S WHAT BROUGHT MR. GASTON TO US, TO THE DEPARTMENT OF PRECISION MACHINERY..."
HE KNEW WE HAD EXPERIENCE CREATING ADVANCED ROBOTS LIKE YOU, ASTRO...
SO THIS FELLA HERE REPRESENTS THE EFFORTS OF THE BEST ROBOTICISTS IN ALL JAPAN...
SO THIS IS AN ALIEN ROBOT... TOTALLY DIFFERENT THAN WE ARE...
SO THAT'S IT...
THIS HAS GOT TO STOP!

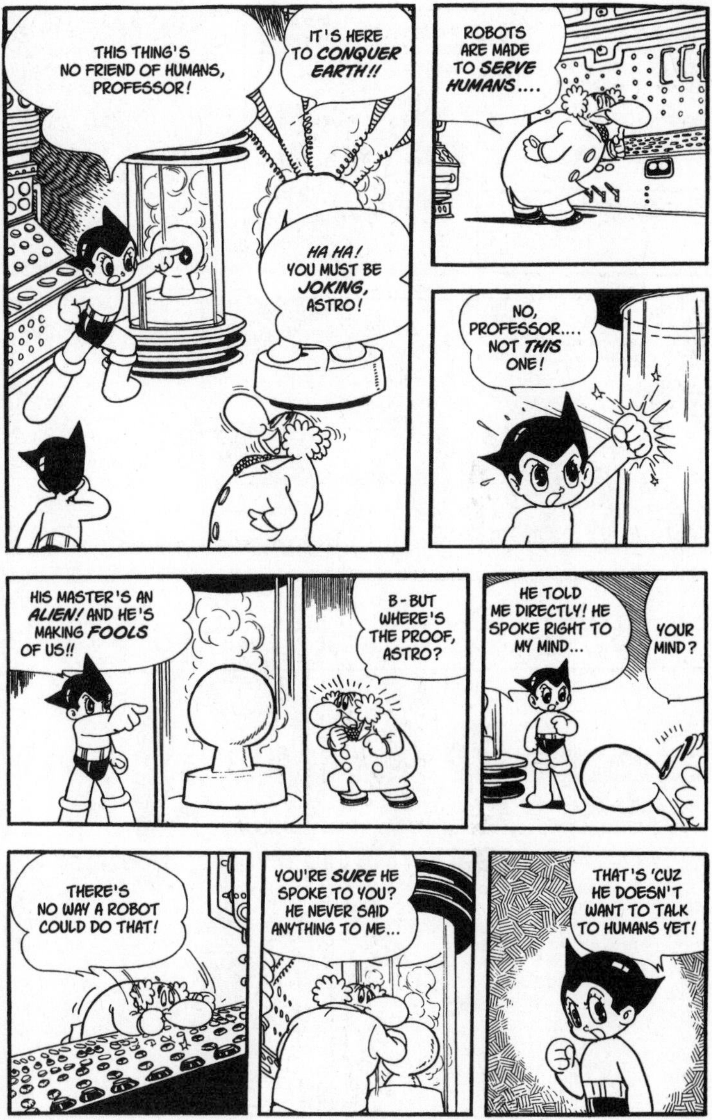
THIS THING'S NO FRIEND OF HUMANS, PROFESSOR!
IT'S HERE TO CONQUER EARTH!!
HA HA! YOU MUST BE JOKING, ASTRO!
ROBOTS ARE MADE TO SERVE HUMANS....
NO, PROFESSOR.... NOT THIS ONE!
HIS MASTER'S AN ALIEN! AND HE'S MAKING FOOLS OF US!!
B-BUT WHERE'S THE PROOF, ASTRO?
HE TOLD ME DIRECTLY! HE SPOKE RIGHT TO MY MIND...
YOUR MIND?
THERE'S NO WAY A ROBOT COULD DO THAT!
YOU'RE SURE HE SPOKE TO YOU? HE NEVER SAID ANYTHING TO ME...
THAT'S 'CUZ HE DOESN'T WANT TO TALK TO HUMANS YET!

I DON'T BELIEVE THIS!

BUT IT'S *TRUE*, PROFESSOR! I DON'T LIE!

I'M *BEGGING* YOU... *DON'T* COMPLETE HIM!

PLEASE DON'T, PROFESSOR...

BUT WHAT'LL MR. GASTON SAY?

I'LL GO TALK TO HIM!!

NO! STOP, ASTRO! YOU MUSTN'T TELL HIM WHAT I'VE TOLD YOU!!

YOU UNDER- STAND, ASTRO?!!

YES- SIR...

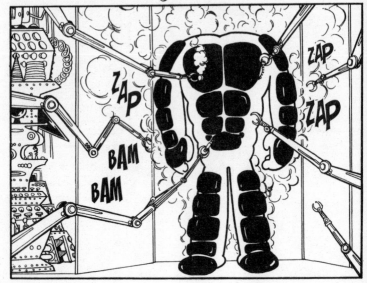

ZAP

ZAP

ZAP

BAM

BAM

22

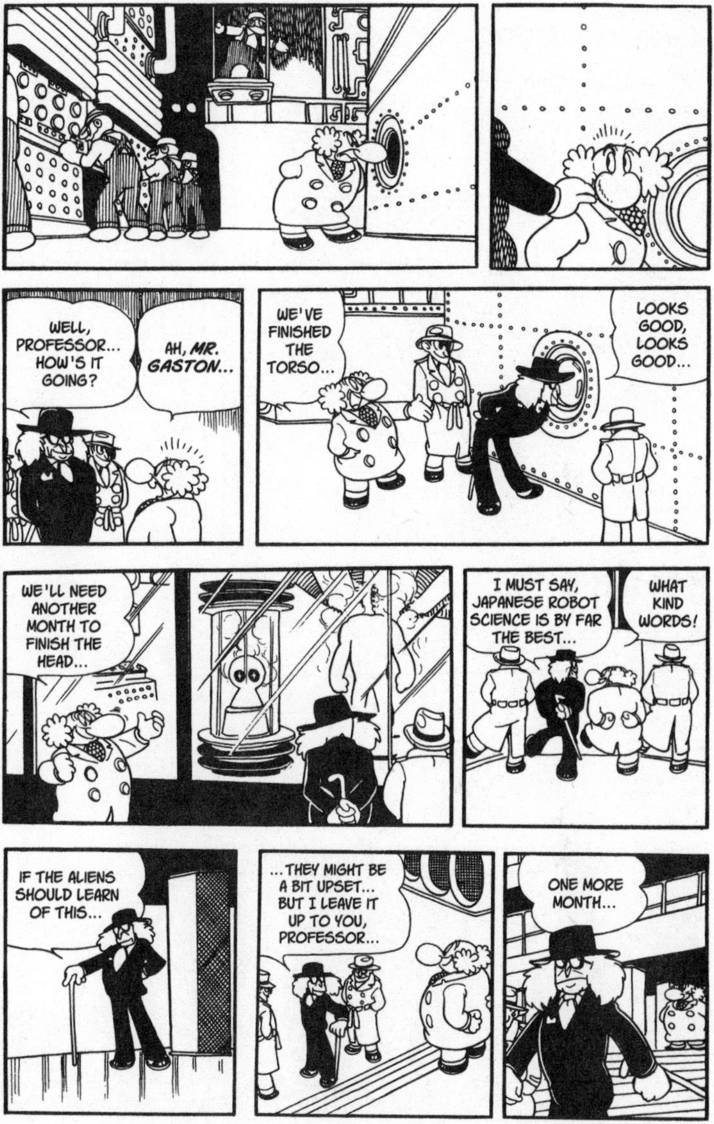
WELL, PROFESSOR... HOW'S IT GOING?
AH, MR. GASTON...
WE'VE FINISHED THE TORSO...
LOOKS GOOD, LOOKS GOOD...
WE'LL NEED ANOTHER MONTH TO FINISH THE HEAD...
I MUST SAY, JAPANESE ROBOT SCIENCE IS BY FAR THE BEST...
WHAT KIND WORDS!
IF THE ALIENS SHOULD LEARN OF THIS...
...THEY MIGHT BE A BIT UPSET... BUT I LEAVE IT UP TO YOU, PROFESSOR...
ONE MORE MONTH...

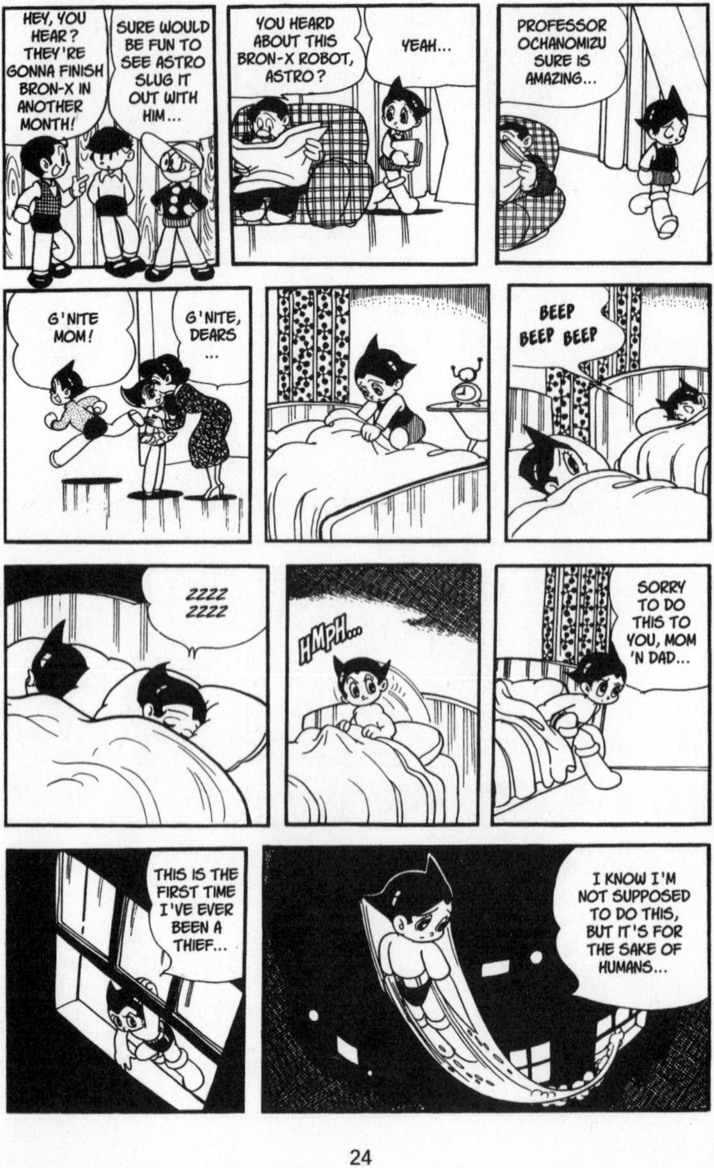
HEY, YOU HEAR? THEY'RE GONNA FINISH BRON-X IN ANOTHER MONTH!
SURE WOULD BE FUN TO SEE ASTRO SLUG IT OUT WITH HIM...
YOU HEARD ABOUT THIS BRON-X ROBOT, ASTRO?
YEAH...
PROFESSOR OCHANOMIZU SURE IS AMAZING...
G'NITE MOM!
G'NITE, DEARS ...
BEEP BEEP BEEP
ZZZZ ZZZZ
HMPH...
SORRY TO DO THIS TO YOU, MOM 'N DAD...
THIS IS THE FIRST TIME I'VE EVER BEEN A THIEF...
I KNOW I'M NOT SUPPOSED TO DO THIS, BUT IT'S FOR THE SAKE OF HUMANS...

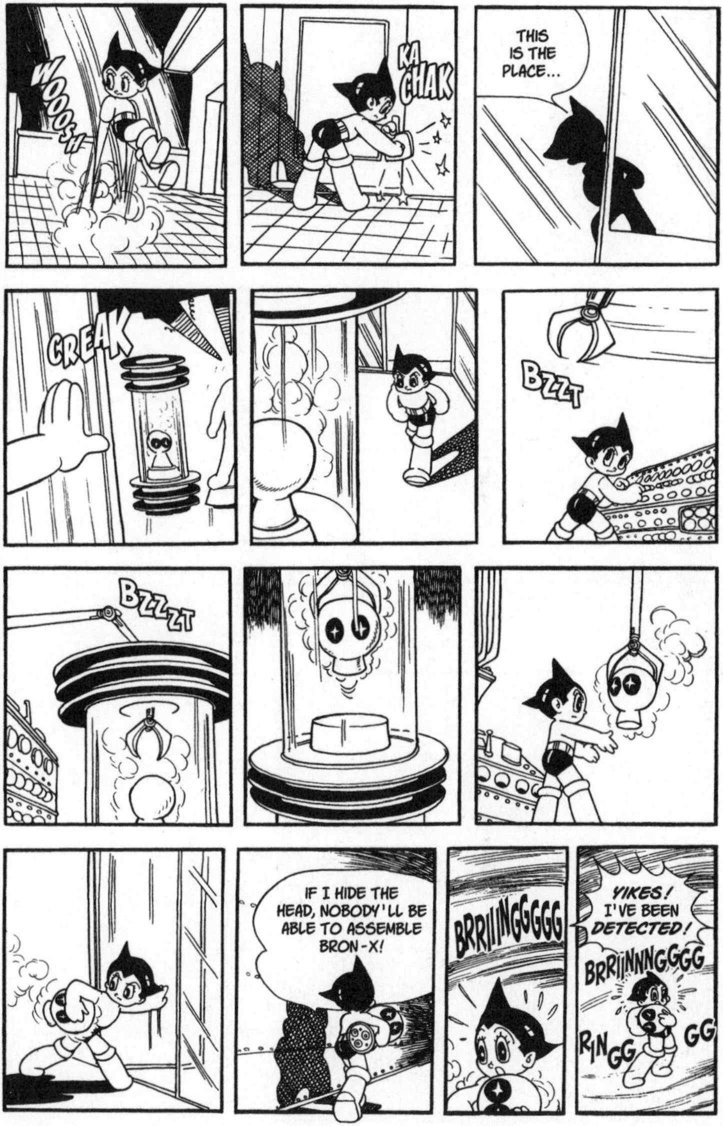
WOOOSH
KA CHAK
THIS IS THE PLACE...
CREAK
BZZZT
BZZZZT
IF I HIDE THE HEAD, NOBODY'LL BE ABLE TO ASSEMBLE BRON-X!
BRRIIINGGGGG
YIKES! I'VE BEEN DETECTED!
BRRIINNNGGGG
RINGG
GG

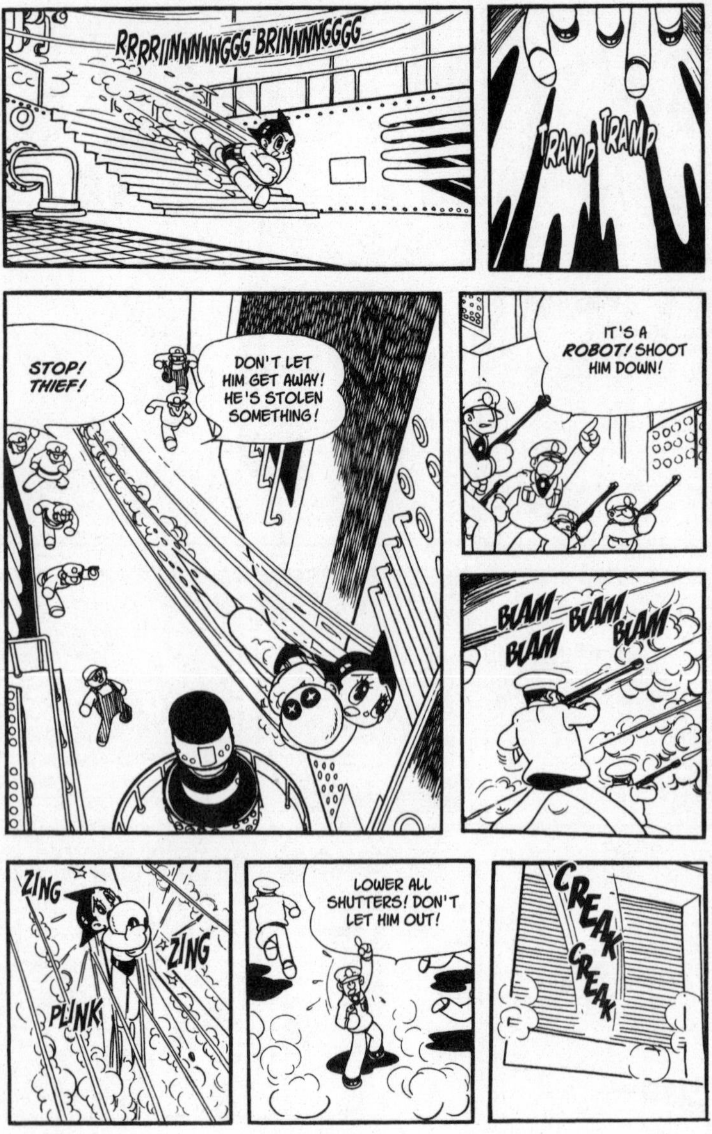
RRRRIINNNNNGGG BRINNNNGGGG
TRAMP TRAMP
STOP! THIEF!
DON'T LET HIM GET AWAY! HE'S STOLEN SOMETHING!
IT'S A ROBOT! SHOOT HIM DOWN!
BLAM BLAM BLAM BLAM BLAM
ZING
ZING
PLINK
LOWER ALL SHUTTERS! DON'T LET HIM OUT!
CREAK CREAK

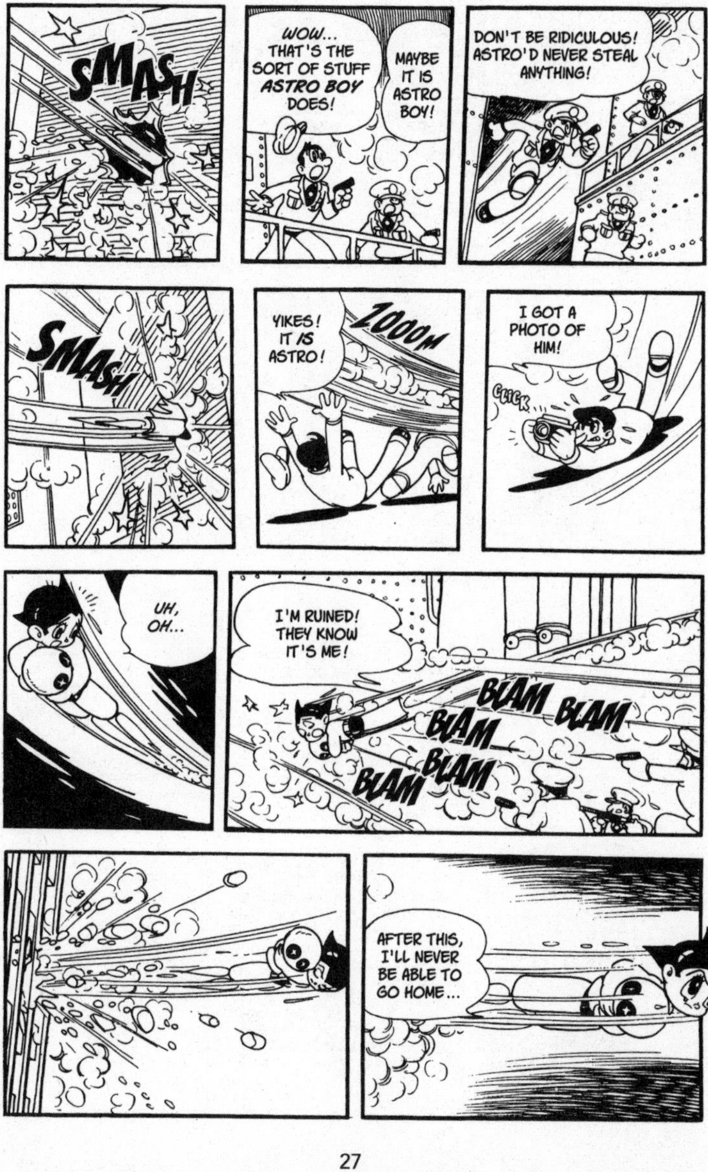
SMASH
WOW... THAT'S THE SORT OF STUFF ASTRO BOY DOES!
MAYBE IT IS ASTRO BOY!
DON'T BE RIDICULOUS! ASTRO'D NEVER STEAL ANYTHING!
SMASH
YIKES! IT IS ASTRO!
ZOOOM
I GOT A PHOTO OF HIM!
CLICK
UH, OH...
I'M RUINED! THEY KNOW IT'S ME!
BLAM
BLAM
BLAM
BLAM
BLAM
AFTER THIS, I'LL NEVER BE ABLE TO GO HOME...

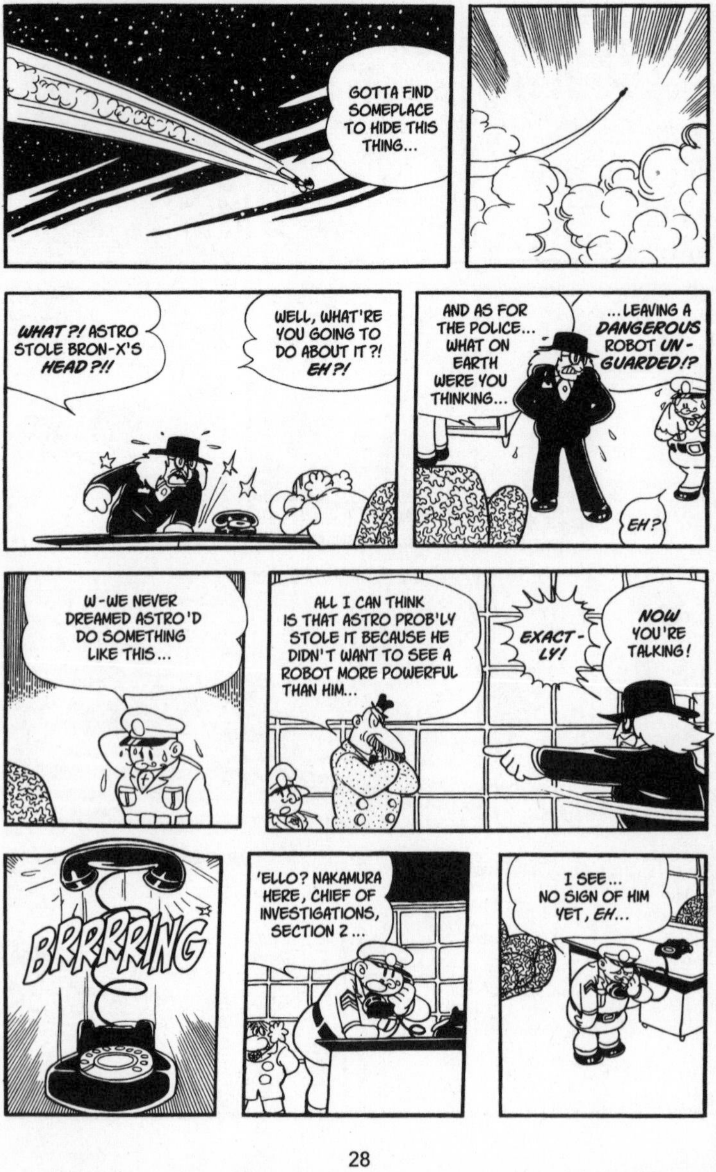
GOTTA FIND SOMEPLACE TO HIDE THIS THING...
WHAT?! ASTRO STOLE BRON-X'S *HEAD?!!*
WELL, WHAT'RE YOU GOING TO DO ABOUT IT?! *EH?!*
AND AS FOR THE POLICE... WHAT ON EARTH WERE YOU THINKING...
...LEAVING A *DANGEROUS* ROBOT *UN-GUARDED!?*
EH?
W-WE NEVER DREAMED ASTRO'D DO SOMETHING LIKE THIS...
ALL I CAN THINK IS THAT ASTRO PROB'LY STOLE IT BECAUSE HE DIDN'T WANT TO SEE A ROBOT MORE POWERFUL THAN HIM...
EXACT-LY!
NOW YOU'RE TALKING!
BRRRRING
'ELLO? NAKAMURA HERE, CHIEF OF INVESTIGATIONS, SECTION 2...
I SEE... NO SIGN OF HIM YET, *EH*...

THERE'S APPARENTLY NO TRACE OF ASTRO YET...

I'VE HAD ENOUGH!

IF THE POLICE CAN'T FIND HIM...

...I'LL HAVE TO TAKE MATTERS INTO MY *OWN* HANDS!

WHA--?

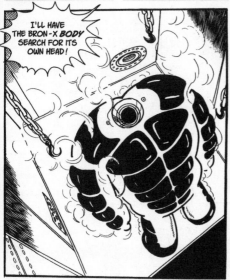
I'LL HAVE THE BRON-X *BODY* SEARCH FOR ITS OWN HEAD!

B-BUT THAT'S TOO DANGEROUS!!

DANGEROUS?! WHY? A ROBOT WITHOUT A HEAD'S JUST A MECHANICAL DOLL...

AND BESIDES, HIS BODY'S DESIGNED TO KNOW WHERE THE HEAD IS, USING RADIO WAVES... HE'LL FIND IT RIGHT AWAY...

AND MOREOVER, BRON-X'S *STRONGER* THAN ASTRO!!

29

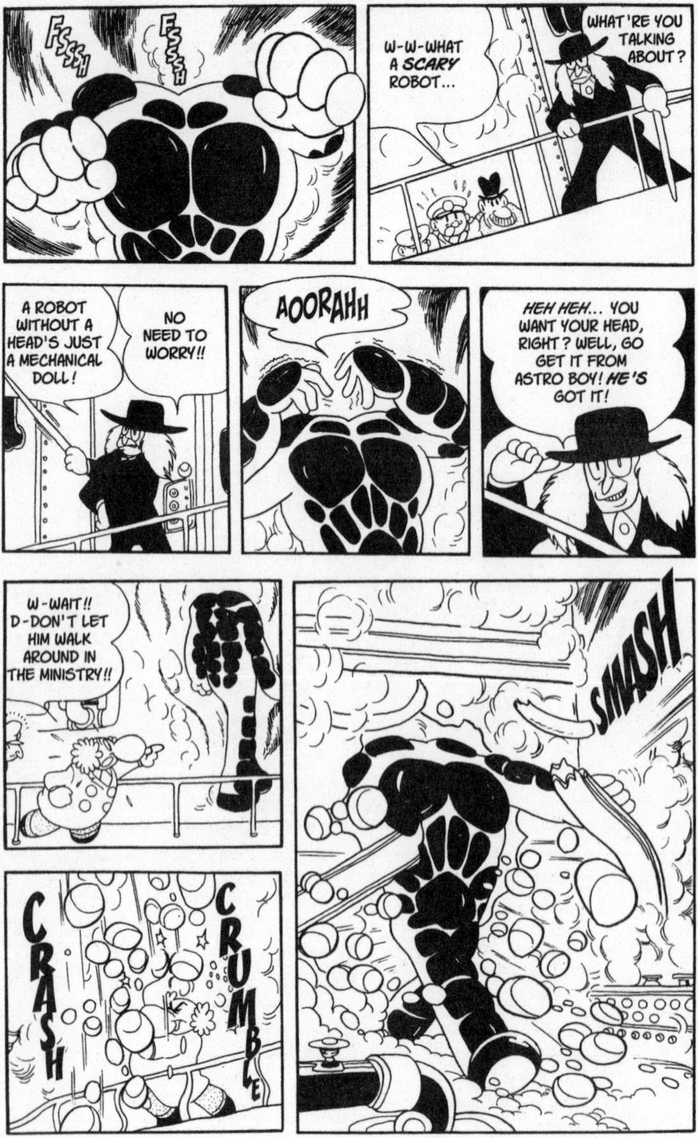
FSSSH
FSSSH
W-W-WHAT A *SCARY* ROBOT...
WHAT'RE YOU TALKING ABOUT?
A ROBOT WITHOUT A HEAD'S JUST A MECHANICAL DOLL!
NO NEED TO WORRY!!
AOORAHH
HEH HEH... YOU WANT YOUR HEAD, RIGHT? WELL, GO GET IT FROM ASTRO BOY! *HE'S* GOT IT!
W-WAIT!! D-DON'T LET HIM WALK AROUND IN THE MINISTRY!!
CRASH
CRUMBLE
SMASH

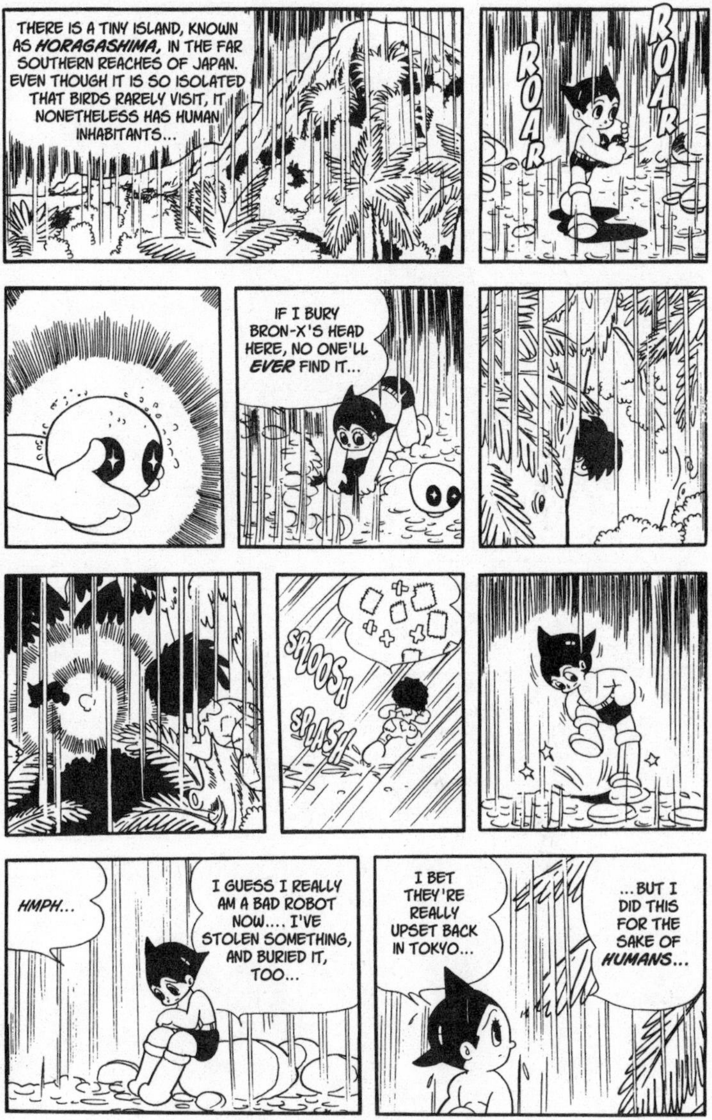

THERE IS A TINY ISLAND, KNOWN AS HORAGASHIMA, IN THE FAR SOUTHERN REACHES OF JAPAN. EVEN THOUGH IT IS SO ISOLATED THAT BIRDS RARELY VISIT, IT NONETHELESS HAS HUMAN INHABITANTS...
ROAR
ROAR
IF I BURY BRON-X'S HEAD HERE, NO ONE'LL EVER FIND IT...
SPLOOSH
SPLASH
HMPH...
I GUESS I REALLY AM A BAD ROBOT NOW.... I'VE STOLEN SOMETHING, AND BURIED IT, TOO...
I BET THEY'RE REALLY UPSET BACK IN TOKYO...
...BUT I DID THIS FOR THE SAKE OF HUMANS...

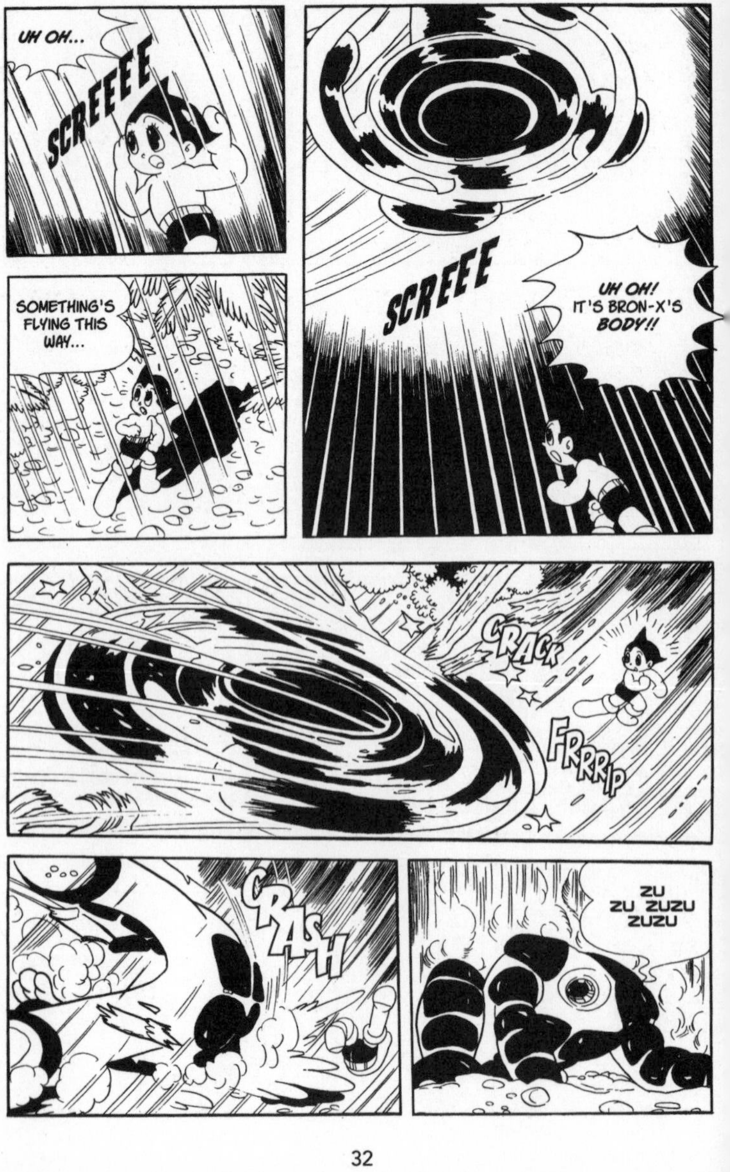
UH OH...
SCREEEE
SOMETHING'S FLYING THIS WAY...
SCREEE
UH OH! IT'S BRON-X'S BODY!!
CRACK
FRRRIP
CRASH
ZU ZU ZUZU ZUZU

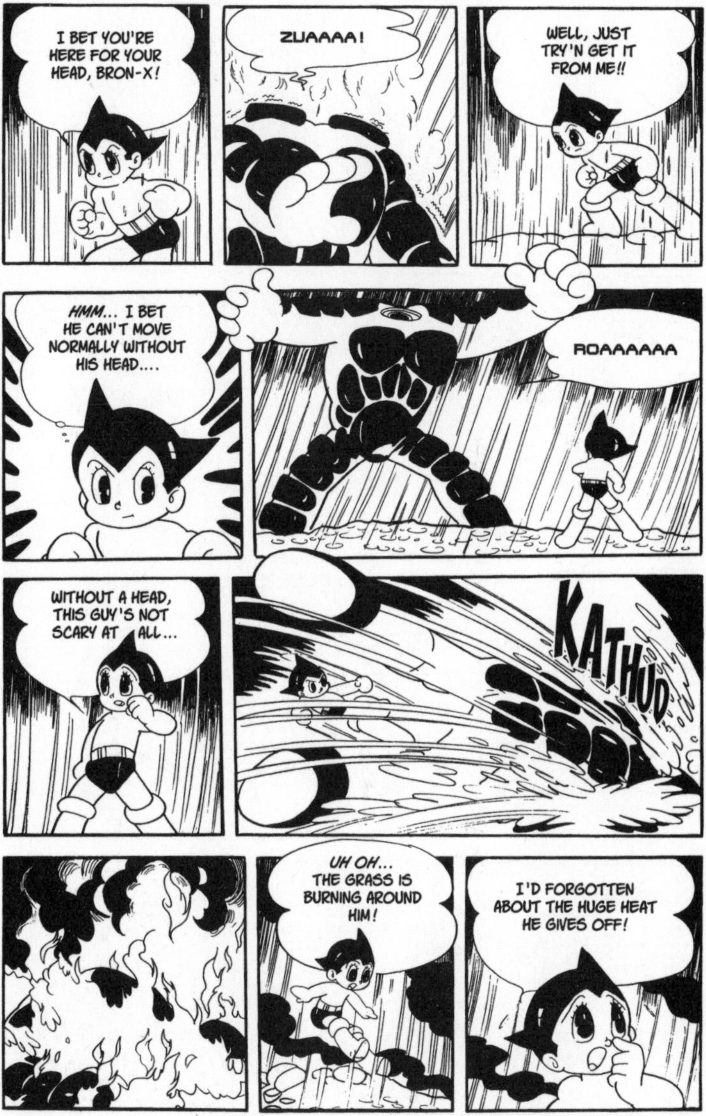
I BET YOU'RE HERE FOR YOUR HEAD, BRON-X!
ZUAAAA!
WELL, JUST TRY'N GET IT FROM ME!!
HMM... I BET HE CAN'T MOVE NORMALLY WITHOUT HIS HEAD....
ROAAAAAA
WITHOUT A HEAD, THIS GUY'S NOT SCARY AT ALL...
KATHUD
UH OH... THE GRASS IS BURNING AROUND HIM!
I'D FORGOTTEN ABOUT THE HUGE HEAT HE GIVES OFF!

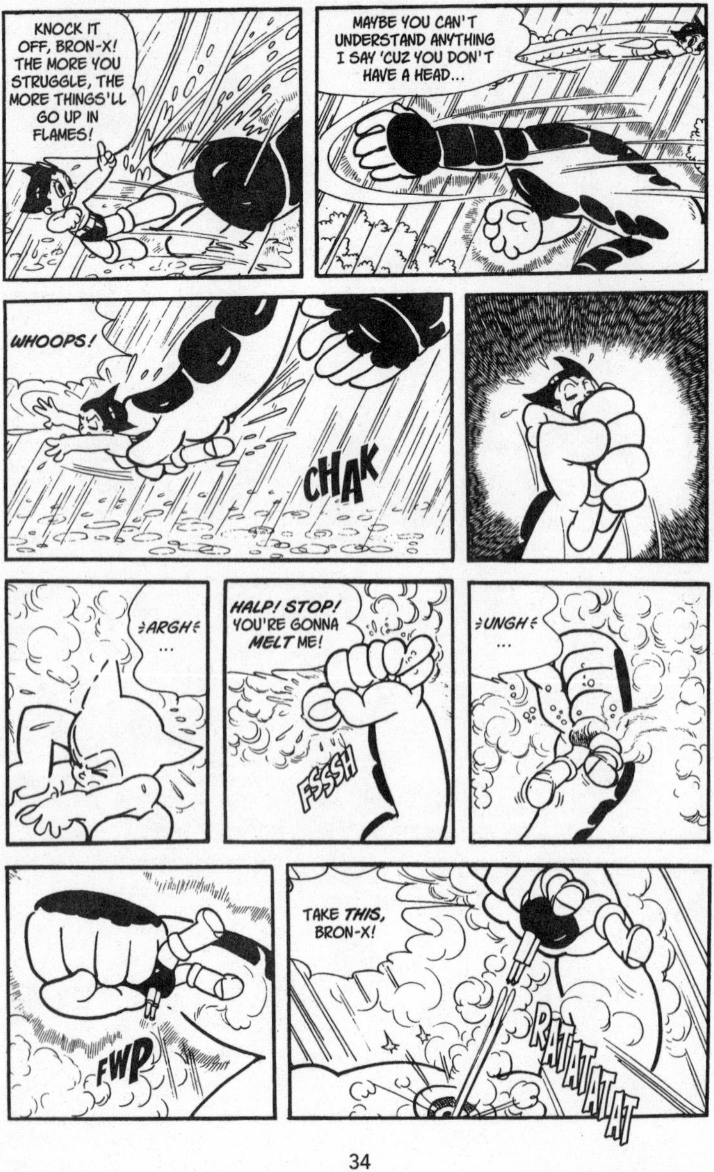
KNOCK IT OFF, BRON-X! THE MORE YOU STRUGGLE, THE MORE THINGS'LL GO UP IN FLAMES!
MAYBE YOU CAN'T UNDERSTAND ANYTHING I SAY 'CUZ YOU DON'T HAVE A HEAD...
WHOOPS!
CHAK
ARGH...
HALP! STOP! YOU'RE GONNA MELT ME!
FSSSH
UNGH...
FWP
TAKE THIS, BRON-X!
RATATATATAT

GAKKIII!

GAWA GA!

KERSPLOOSH

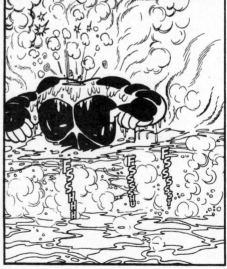

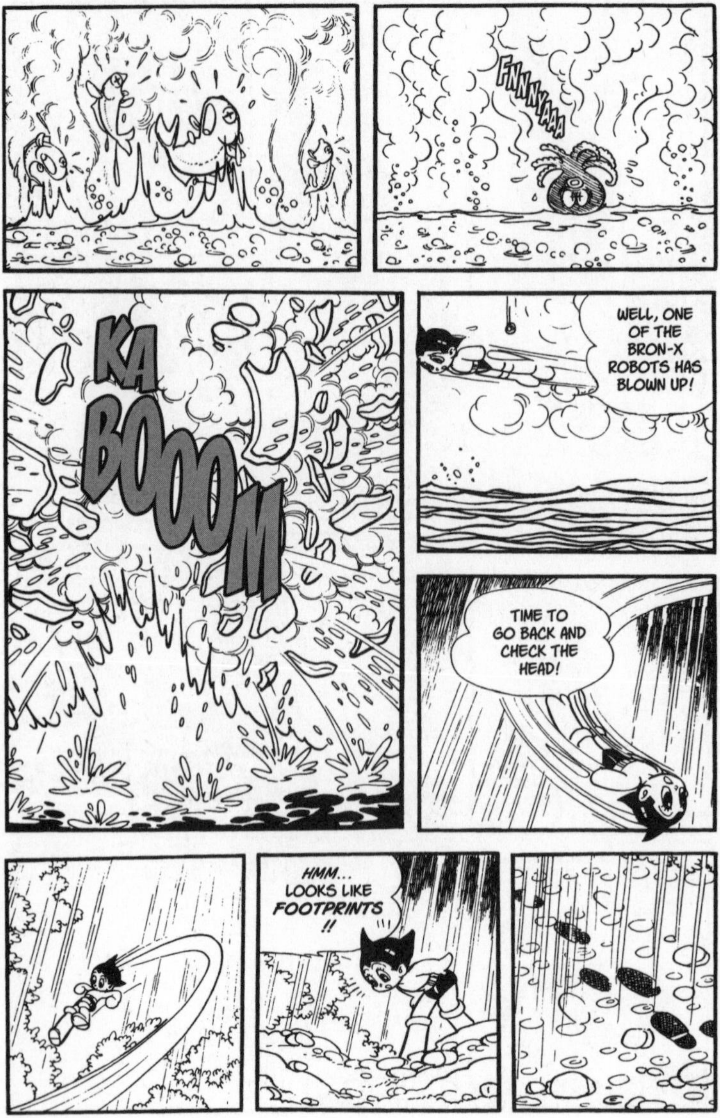
FNNNYAAA
KA BOOOM
WELL, ONE OF THE BRON-X ROBOTS HAS BLOWN UP!
TIME TO GO BACK AND CHECK THE HEAD!
HMM... LOOKS LIKE FOOTPRINTS !!

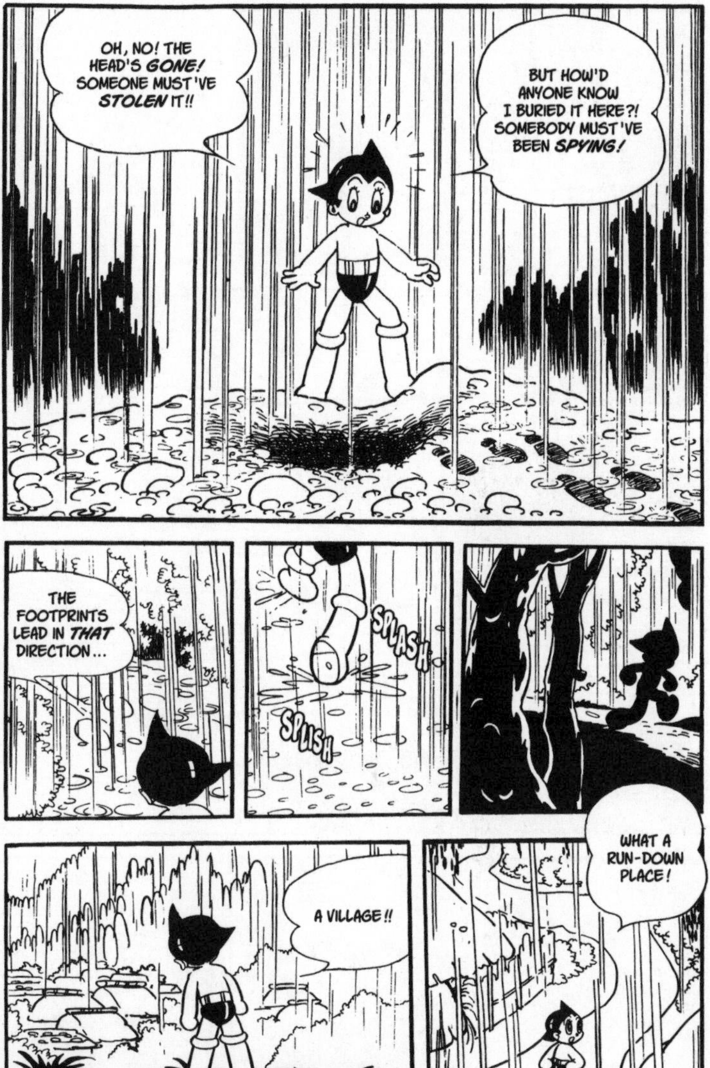
OH, NO! THE HEAD'S GONE! SOMEONE MUST'VE STOLEN IT!!
BUT HOW'D ANYONE KNOW I BURIED IT HERE?! SOMEBODY MUST'VE BEEN SPYING!
THE FOOTPRINTS LEAD IN THAT DIRECTION...
SPLASH
SPLISH
A VILLAGE!!
WHAT A RUN-DOWN PLACE!

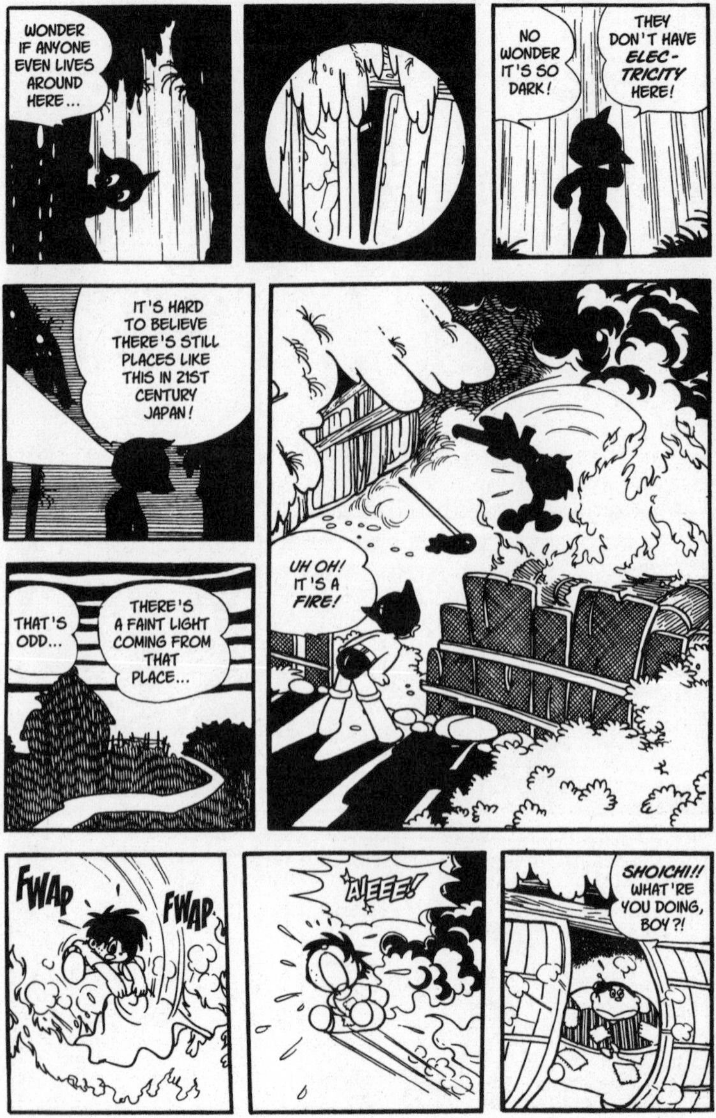
WONDER IF ANYONE EVEN LIVES AROUND HERE...
NO WONDER IT'S SO DARK!
THEY DON'T HAVE ELEC-TRICITY HERE!
IT'S HARD TO BELIEVE THERE'S STILL PLACES LIKE THIS IN 21ST CENTURY JAPAN!
THAT'S ODD...
THERE'S A FAINT LIGHT COMING FROM THAT PLACE...
UH OH! IT'S A FIRE!
FWAP
FWAP
AIEEE!
SHOICHI!! WHAT'RE YOU DOING, BOY?!

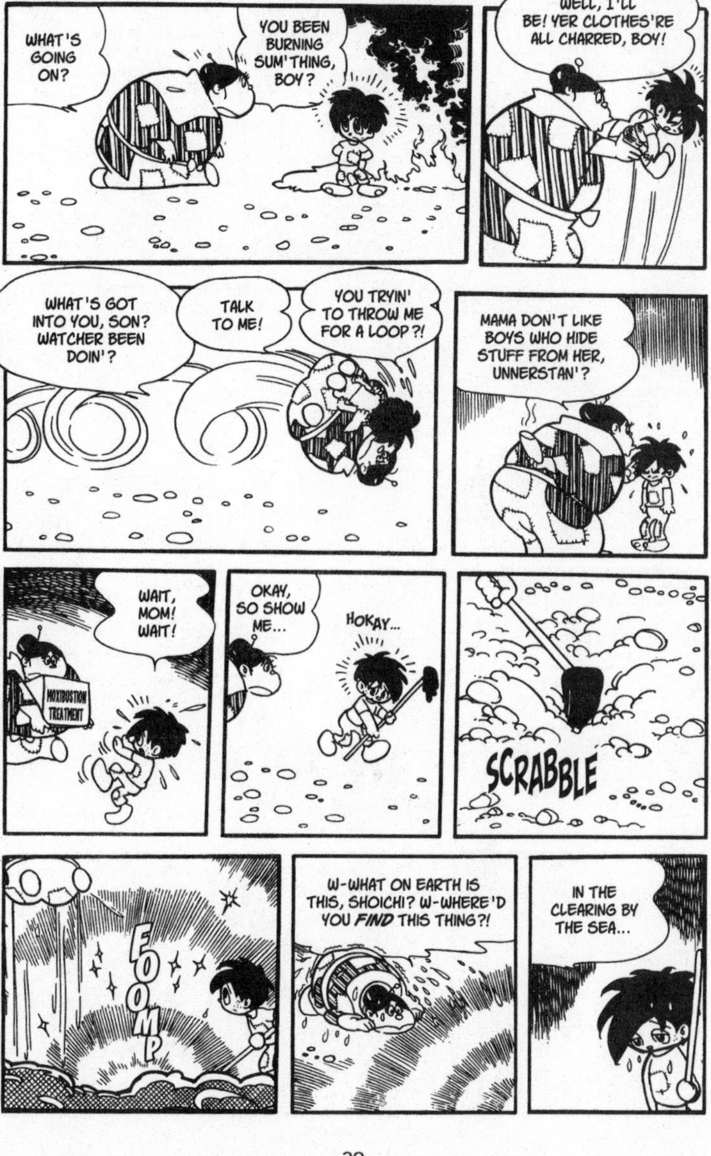
WHAT'S GOING ON?
YOU BEEN BURNING SUM'THING, BOY?
WELL, I'LL BE! YER CLOTHES'RE ALL CHARRED, BOY!
WHAT'S GOT INTO YOU, SON? WATCHER BEEN DOIN'?
TALK TO ME!
YOU TRYIN' TO THROW ME FOR A LOOP?!
MAMA DON'T LIKE BOYS WHO HIDE STUFF FROM HER, UNNERSTAN'?
WAIT, MOM! WAIT!
MOXIBUSTION TREATMENT
OKAY, SO SHOW ME...
HOKAY...
SCRABBLE
FOOMP
W-WHAT ON EARTH IS THIS, SHOICHI? W-WHERE'D YOU *FIND* THIS THING?!
IN THE CLEARING BY THE SEA...

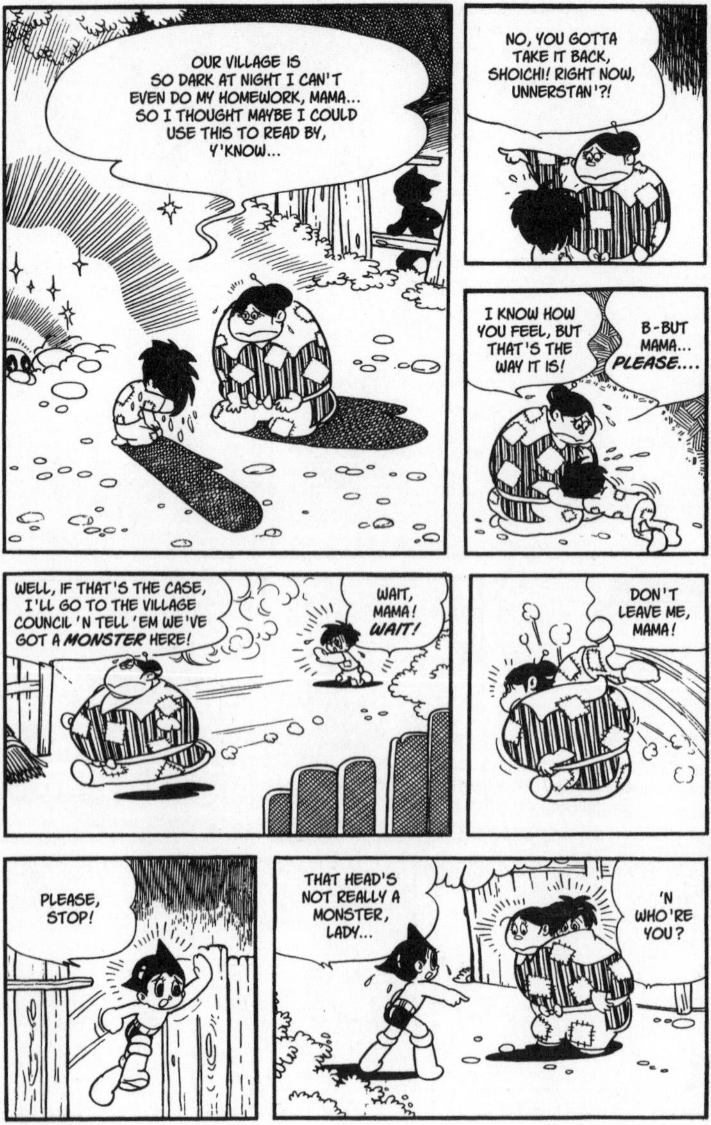
OUR VILLAGE IS SO DARK AT NIGHT I CAN'T EVEN DO MY HOMEWORK, MAMA... SO I THOUGHT MAYBE I COULD USE THIS TO READ BY, Y'KNOW...
NO, YOU GOTTA TAKE IT BACK, SHOICHI! RIGHT NOW, UNNERSTAN'?!
I KNOW HOW YOU FEEL, BUT THAT'S THE WAY IT IS!
B-BUT MAMA... PLEASE....
WELL, IF THAT'S THE CASE, I'LL GO TO THE VILLAGE COUNCIL 'N TELL 'EM WE'VE GOT A MONSTER HERE!
WAIT, MAMA! WAIT!
DON'T LEAVE ME, MAMA!
PLEASE, STOP!
THAT HEAD'S NOT REALLY A MONSTER, LADY...
'N WHO'RE YOU?

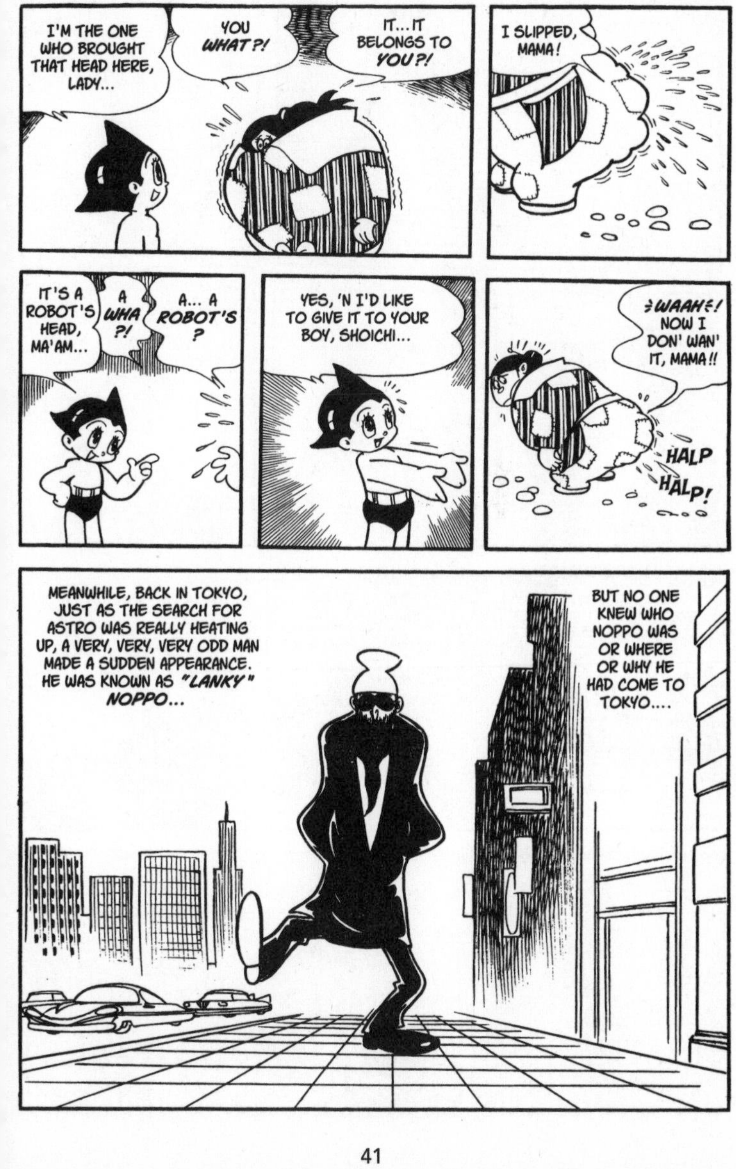
I'M THE ONE WHO BROUGHT THAT HEAD HERE, LADY...
YOU *WHAT?!*
IT... IT BELONGS TO *YOU?!*
I SLIPPED, MAMA!
IT'S A ROBOT'S HEAD, MA'AM...
A *WHA ?!*
A... A *ROBOT'S ?*
YES, 'N I'D LIKE TO GIVE IT TO YOUR BOY, SHOICHI...
WAAH! NOW I DON' WAN' IT, MAMA!!
HALP
HALP!
MEANWHILE, BACK IN TOKYO, JUST AS THE SEARCH FOR ASTRO WAS REALLY HEATING UP, A VERY, VERY, VERY ODD MAN MADE A SUDDEN APPEARANCE. HE WAS KNOWN AS *"LANKY" NOPPO...*
BUT NO ONE KNEW WHO NOPPO WAS OR WHERE OR WHY HE HAD COME TO TOKYO....

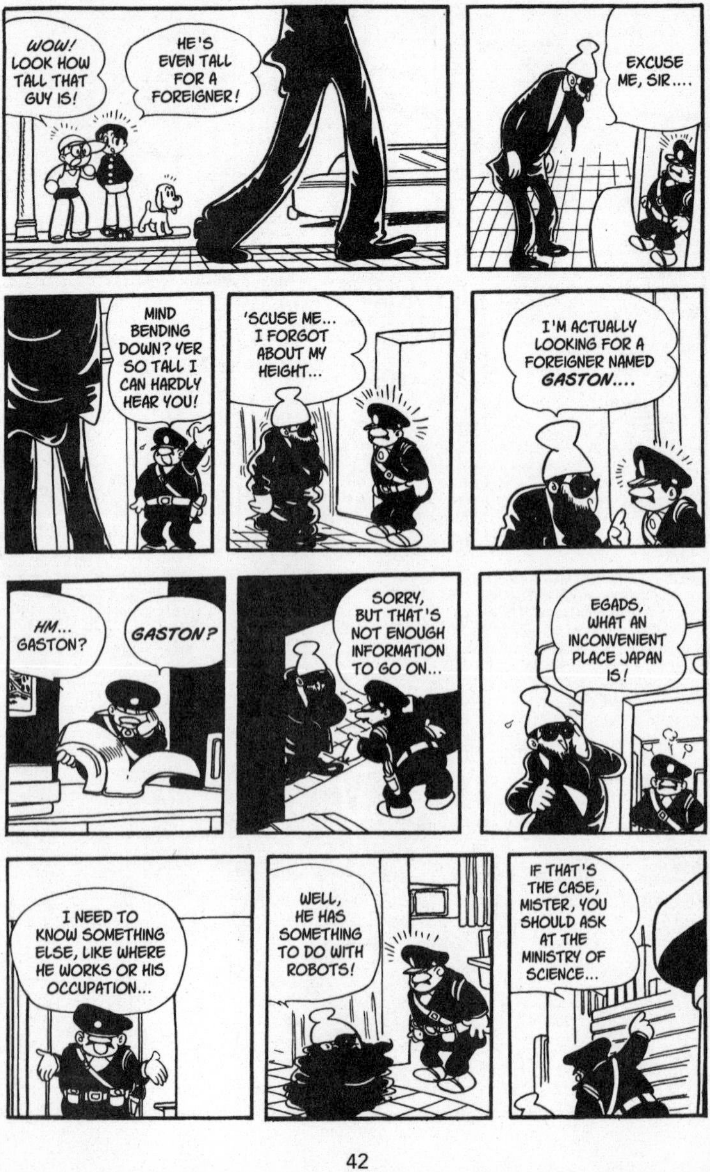
WOW! LOOK HOW TALL THAT GUY IS!
HE'S EVEN TALL FOR A FOREIGNER!
EXCUSE ME, SIR....
MIND BENDING DOWN? YER SO TALL I CAN HARDLY HEAR YOU!
'SCUSE ME... I FORGOT ABOUT MY HEIGHT...
I'M ACTUALLY LOOKING FOR A FOREIGNER NAMED GASTON....
HM... GASTON?
GASTON?
SORRY, BUT THAT'S NOT ENOUGH INFORMATION TO GO ON...
EGADS, WHAT AN INCONVENIENT PLACE JAPAN IS!
I NEED TO KNOW SOMETHING ELSE, LIKE WHERE HE WORKS OR HIS OCCUPATION...
WELL, HE HAS SOMETHING TO DO WITH ROBOTS!
IF THAT'S THE CASE, MISTER, YOU SHOULD ASK AT THE MINISTRY OF SCIENCE...

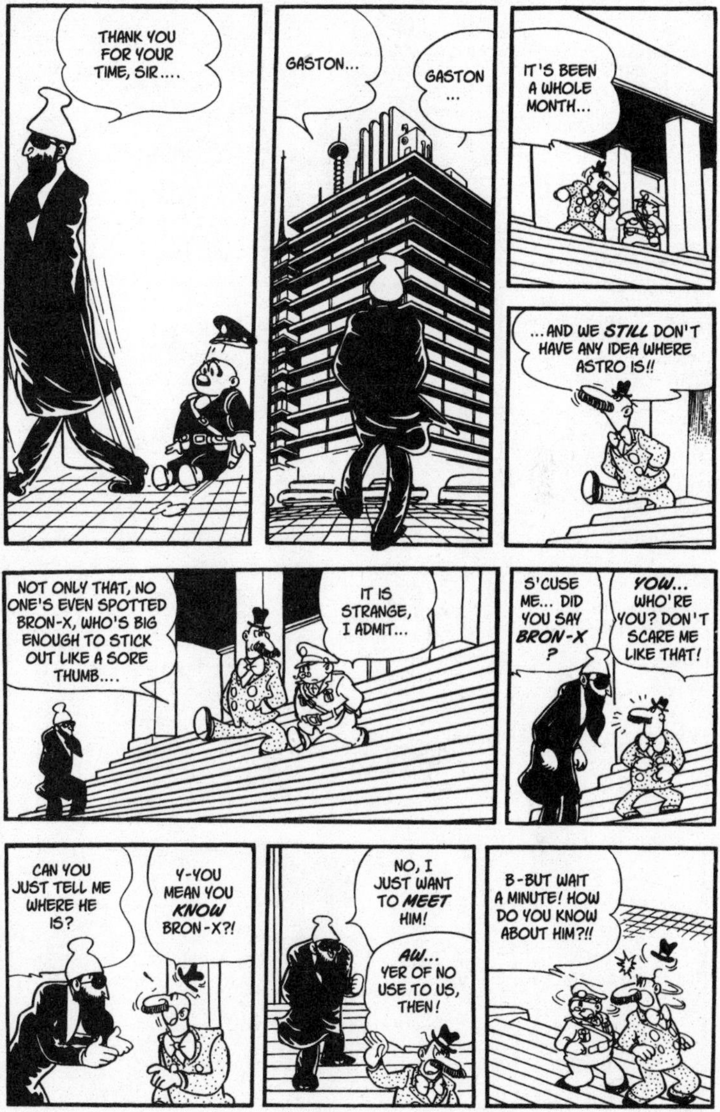
THANK YOU FOR YOUR TIME, SIR....
GASTON...
GASTON ...
IT'S BEEN A WHOLE MONTH...
...AND WE STILL DON'T HAVE ANY IDEA WHERE ASTRO IS!!
NOT ONLY THAT, NO ONE'S EVEN SPOTTED BRON-X, WHO'S BIG ENOUGH TO STICK OUT LIKE A SORE THUMB....
IT IS STRANGE, I ADMIT...
S'CUSE ME... DID YOU SAY BRON-X ?
YOW... WHO'RE YOU? DON'T SCARE ME LIKE THAT!
CAN YOU JUST TELL ME WHERE HE IS?
Y-YOU MEAN YOU KNOW BRON-X?!
NO, I JUST WANT TO MEET HIM!
AW... YER OF NO USE TO US, THEN!
B-BUT WAIT A MINUTE! HOW DO YOU KNOW ABOUT HIM?!!

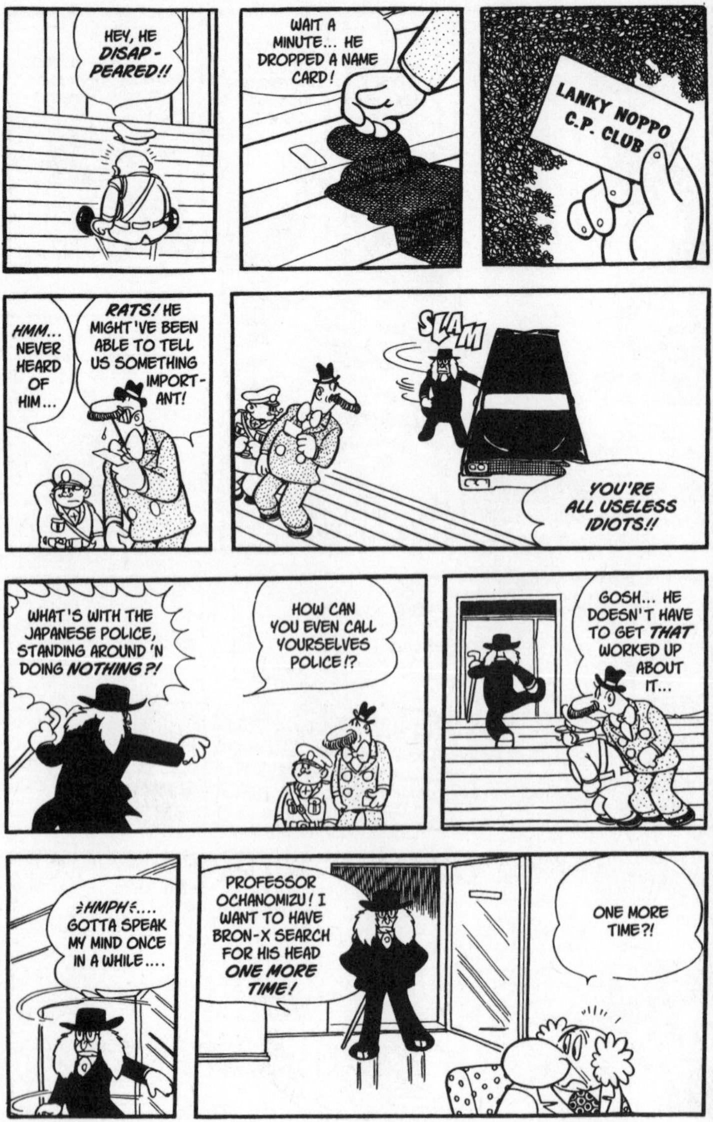
HEY, HE DISAP-PEARED!!
WAIT A MINUTE... HE DROPPED A NAME CARD!
LANKY NOPPO C.P. CLUB
HMM... NEVER HEARD OF HIM...
RATS! HE MIGHT'VE BEEN ABLE TO TELL US SOMETHING IMPORT-ANT!
SLAM
YOU'RE ALL USELESS IDIOTS!!
WHAT'S WITH THE JAPANESE POLICE, STANDING AROUND 'N DOING NOTHING?!
HOW CAN YOU EVEN CALL YOURSELVES POLICE!?
GOSH... HE DOESN'T HAVE TO GET THAT WORKED UP ABOUT IT...
HMPH.... GOTTA SPEAK MY MIND ONCE IN A WHILE....
PROFESSOR OCHANOMIZU! I WANT TO HAVE BRON-X SEARCH FOR HIS HEAD ONE MORE TIME!
ONE MORE TIME?!

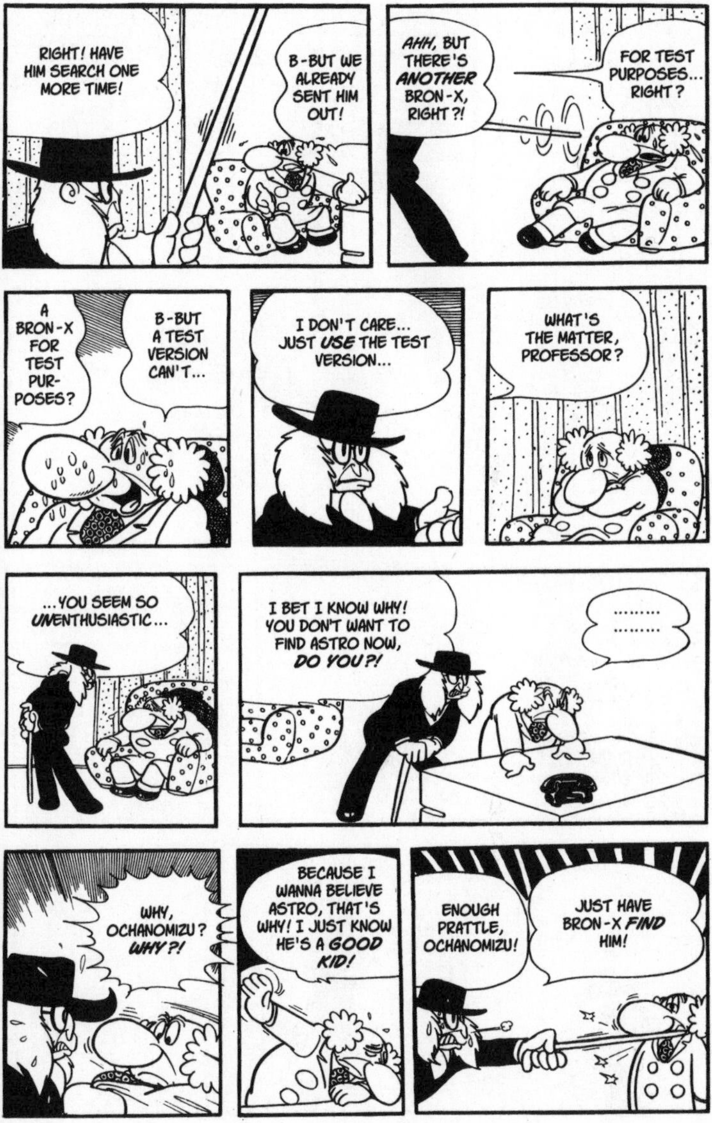
RIGHT! HAVE HIM SEARCH ONE MORE TIME!
B-BUT WE ALREADY SENT HIM OUT!
AHH, BUT THERE'S ANOTHER BRON-X, RIGHT?!
FOR TEST PURPOSES... RIGHT?
A BRON-X FOR TEST PUR-POSES?
B-BUT A TEST VERSION CAN'T...
I DON'T CARE... JUST USE THE TEST VERSION...
WHAT'S THE MATTER, PROFESSOR?
...YOU SEEM SO UNENTHUSIASTIC...
I BET I KNOW WHY! YOU DON'T WANT TO FIND ASTRO NOW, DO YOU?!
....
....
WHY, OCHANOMIZU? WHY?!
BECAUSE I WANNA BELIEVE ASTRO, THAT'S WHY! I JUST KNOW HE'S A GOOD KID!
ENOUGH PRATTLE, OCHANOMIZU!
JUST HAVE BRON-X FIND HIM!

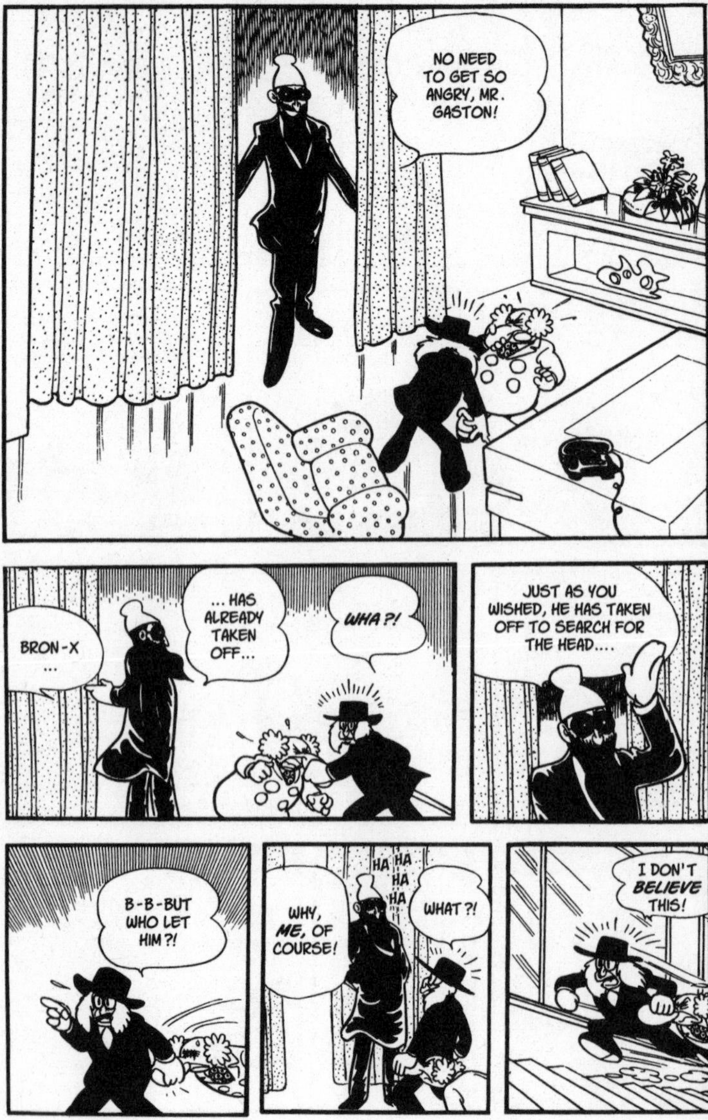
NO NEED TO GET SO ANGRY, MR. GASTON!
BRON-X ...
... HAS ALREADY TAKEN OFF...
WHA?!
JUST AS YOU WISHED, HE HAS TAKEN OFF TO SEARCH FOR THE HEAD....
B-B-BUT WHO LET HIM?!
WHY, ME, OF COURSE!
HA HA HA HA
WHAT?!
I DON'T BELIEVE THIS!

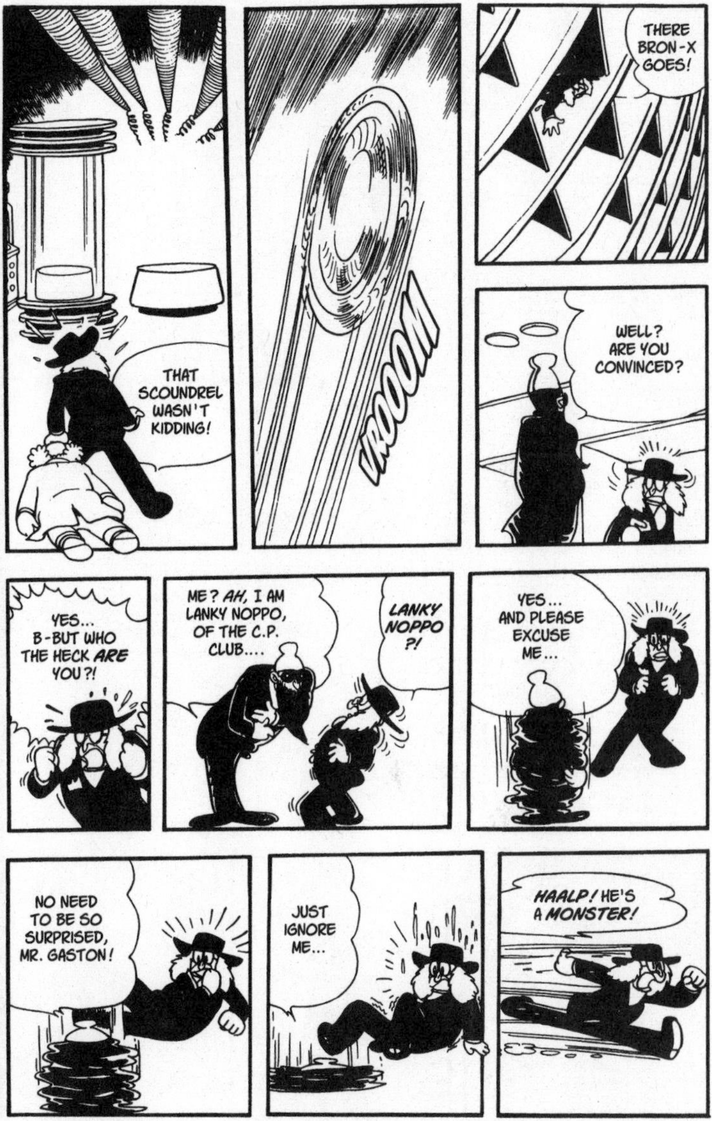
THAT SCOUNDREL WASN'T KIDDING!
VROOOM
THERE BRON-X GOES!
WELL? ARE YOU CONVINCED?
YES... B-BUT WHO THE HECK *ARE* YOU?!
ME? *AH,* I AM LANKY NOPPO, OF THE C.P. CLUB....
LANKY NOPPO ?!
YES... AND PLEASE EXCUSE ME...
NO NEED TO BE SO SURPRISED, MR. GASTON!
JUST IGNORE ME...
HAALP! HE'S A *MONSTER!*

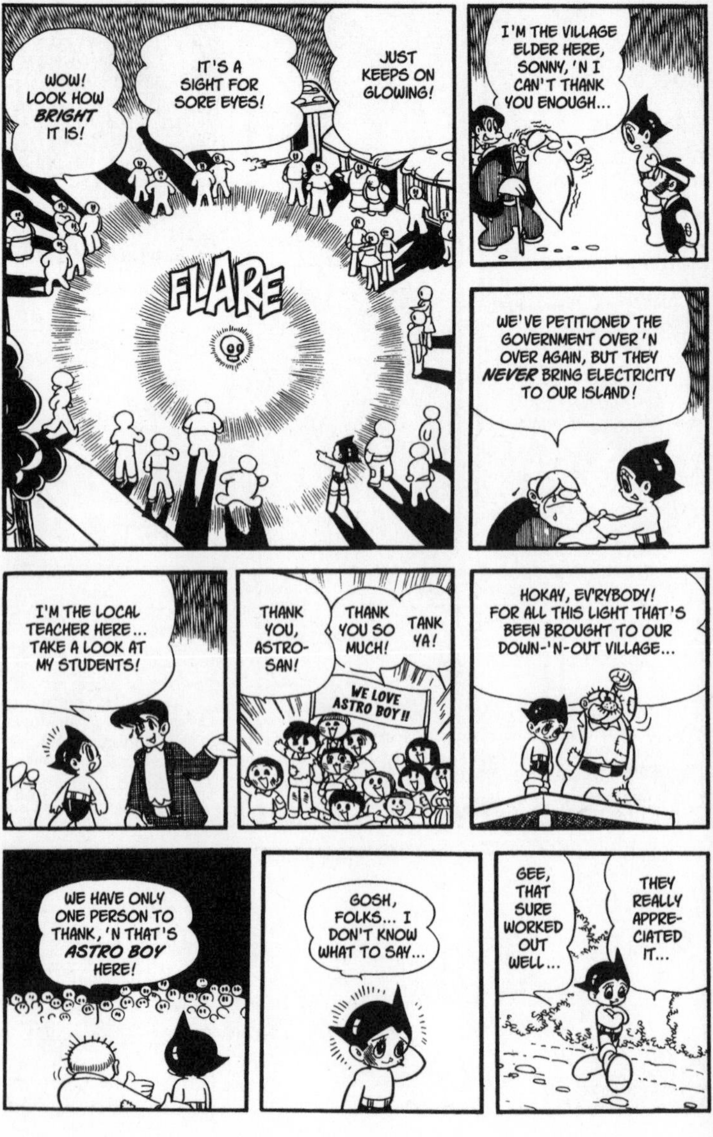
WOW! LOOK HOW *BRIGHT* IT IS!
IT'S A SIGHT FOR SORE EYES!
JUST KEEPS ON GLOWING!
FLARE
I'M THE VILLAGE ELDER HERE, SONNY, 'N I CAN'T THANK YOU ENOUGH...
WE'VE PETITIONED THE GOVERNMENT OVER 'N OVER AGAIN, BUT THEY *NEVER* BRING ELECTRICITY TO OUR ISLAND!
I'M THE LOCAL TEACHER HERE... TAKE A LOOK AT MY STUDENTS!
THANK YOU, ASTRO-SAN!
THANK YOU SO MUCH!
TANK YA!
WE LOVE ASTRO BOY!!
HOKAY, EV'RYBODY! FOR ALL THIS LIGHT THAT'S BEEN BROUGHT TO OUR DOWN-'N-OUT VILLAGE...
WE HAVE ONLY ONE PERSON TO THANK, 'N THAT'S *ASTRO BOY* HERE!
GOSH, FOLKS... I DON'T KNOW WHAT TO SAY...
GEE, THAT SURE WORKED OUT WELL...
THEY REALLY APPRECIATED IT...

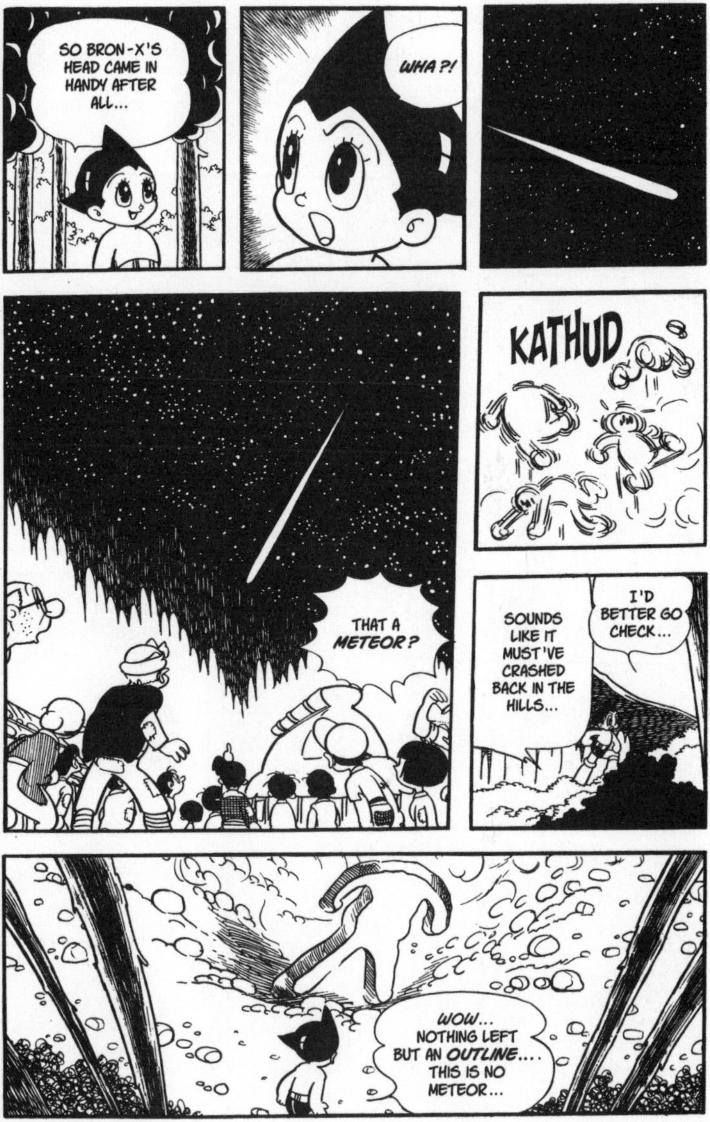
SO BRON-X'S HEAD CAME IN HANDY AFTER ALL...
WHA?!
THAT A METEOR?
KATHUD
SOUNDS LIKE IT MUST'VE CRASHED BACK IN THE HILLS...
I'D BETTER GO CHECK...
WOW... NOTHING LEFT BUT AN OUTLINE.... THIS IS NO METEOR...

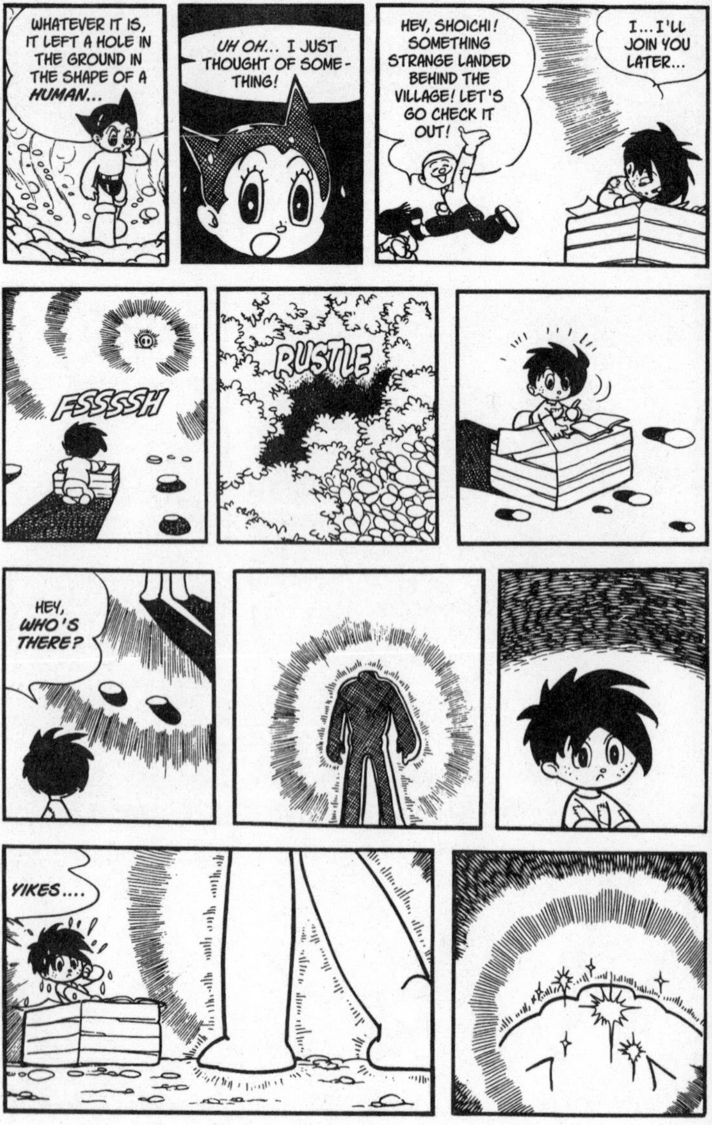
WHATEVER IT IS, IT LEFT A HOLE IN THE GROUND IN THE SHAPE OF A *HUMAN*...
UH OH... I JUST THOUGHT OF SOME-THING!
HEY, SHOICHI! SOMETHING STRANGE LANDED BEHIND THE VILLAGE! LET'S GO CHECK IT OUT!
I...I'LL JOIN YOU LATER...
FSSSSH
RUSTLE
HEY, *WHO'S THERE?*
YIKES....

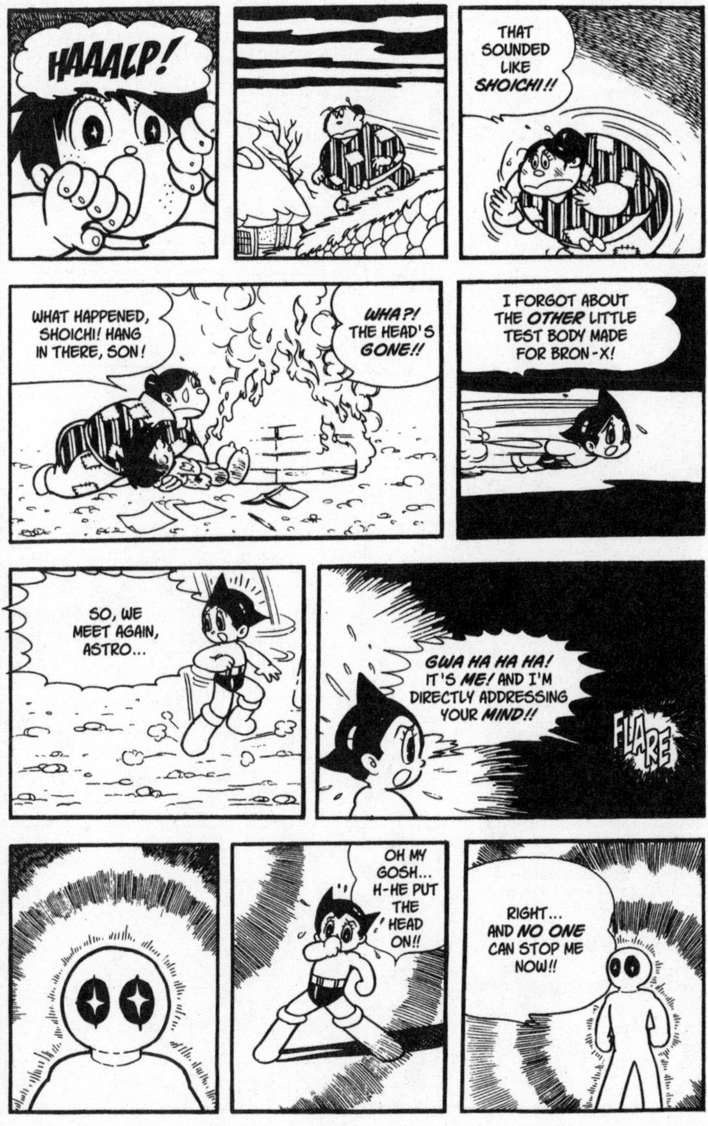

HAAALP!
THAT SOUNDED LIKE SHOICHI!!
WHAT HAPPENED, SHOICHI! HANG IN THERE, SON!
WHA?! THE HEAD'S GONE!!
I FORGOT ABOUT THE OTHER LITTLE TEST BODY MADE FOR BRON-X!
SO, WE MEET AGAIN, ASTRO...
GWA HA HA HA! IT'S ME! AND I'M DIRECTLY ADDRESSING YOUR MIND!!
FLARE
OH MY GOSH... H-HE PUT THE HEAD ON!!
RIGHT... AND NO ONE CAN STOP ME NOW!!

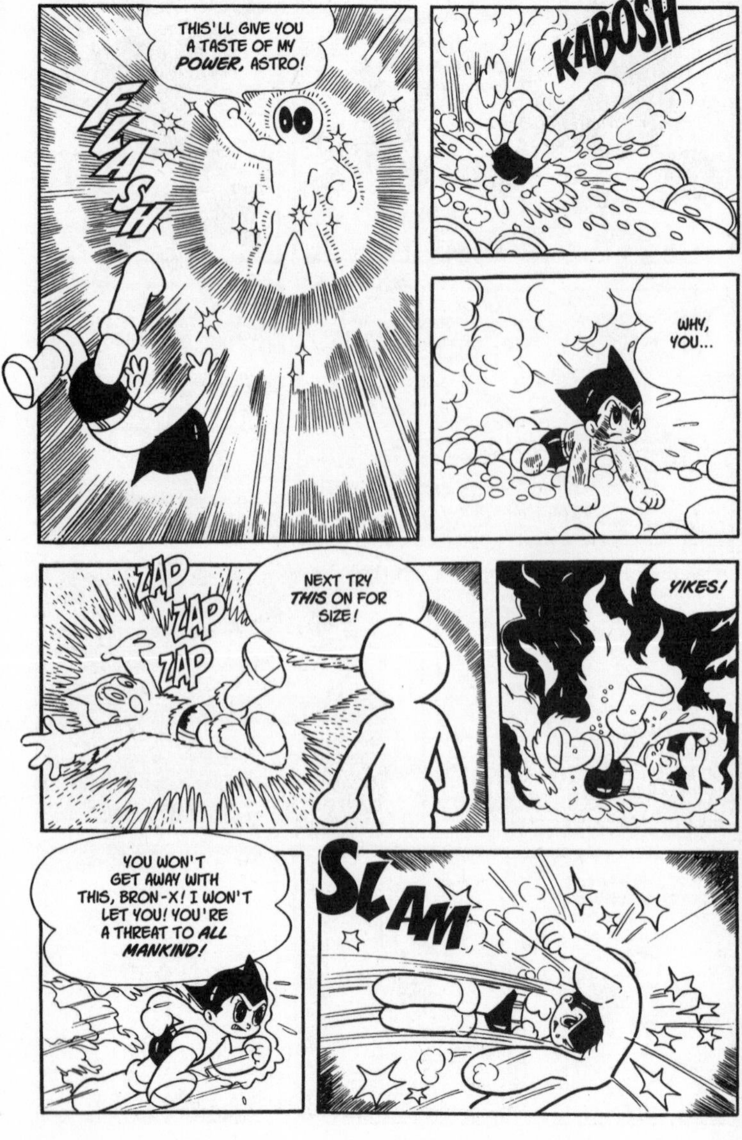
THIS'LL GIVE YOU A TASTE OF MY *POWER,* ASTRO!
FLASH
KABOSH
WHY, YOU...
ZAP ZAP ZAP
NEXT TRY *THIS* ON FOR SIZE!
YIKES!
YOU WON'T GET AWAY WITH THIS, BRON-X! I WON'T LET YOU! YOU'RE A THREAT TO *ALL MANKIND!*
SLAM

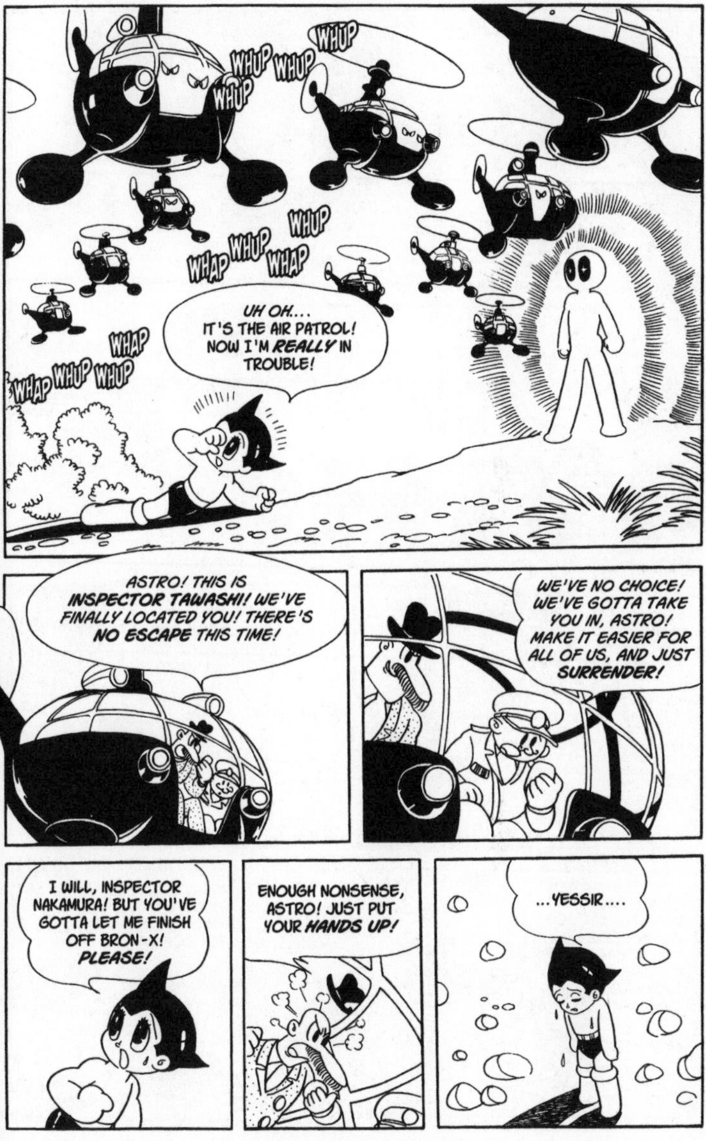
WHUP
WHUP WHUP
WHUP
WHUP
WHAP WHUP WHAP
UH OH....
IT'S THE AIR PATROL!
NOW I'M REALLY IN
TROUBLE!
WHAP
WHAP WHUP WHUP
ASTRO! THIS IS INSPECTOR TAWASHI! WE'VE FINALLY LOCATED YOU! THERE'S NO ESCAPE THIS TIME!
WE'VE NO CHOICE! WE'VE GOTTA TAKE YOU IN, ASTRO! MAKE IT EASIER FOR ALL OF US, AND JUST SURRENDER!
I WILL, INSPECTOR NAKAMURA! BUT YOU'VE GOTTA LET ME FINISH OFF BRON-X! PLEASE!
ENOUGH NONSENSE, ASTRO! JUST PUT YOUR HANDS UP!
...YESSIR....

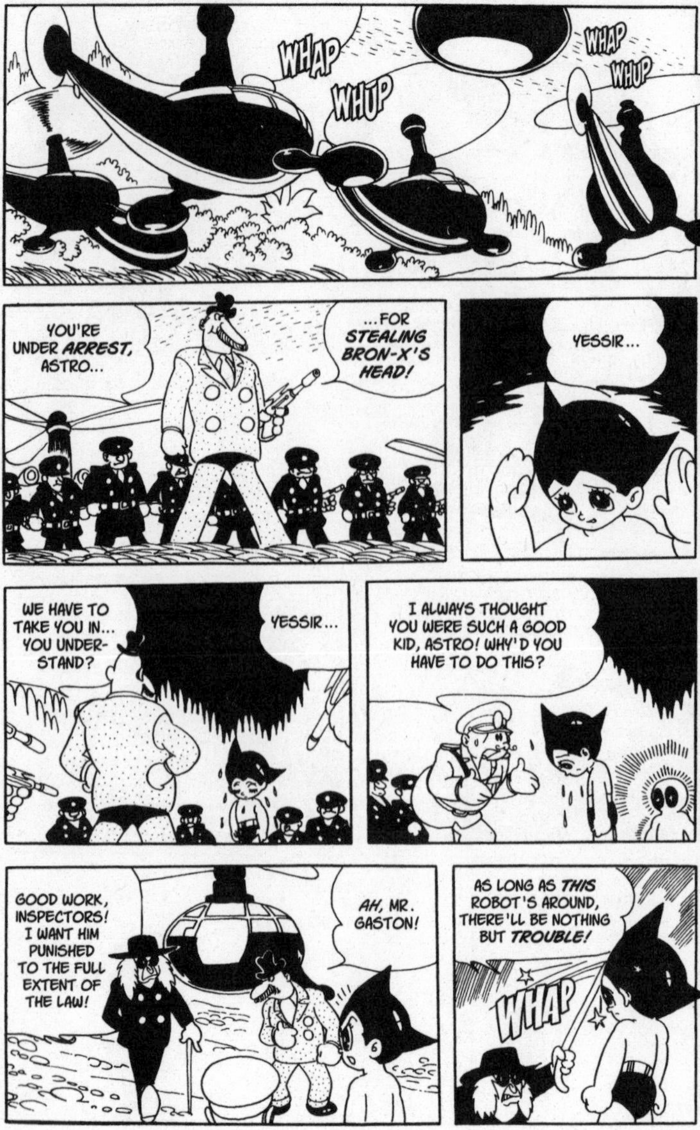
WHAP
WHUP
WHAP
WHUP
YOU'RE UNDER *ARREST*, ASTRO...
...FOR *STEALING BRON-X'S HEAD!*
YESSIR...
WE HAVE TO TAKE YOU IN... YOU UNDER-STAND?
YESSIR...
I ALWAYS THOUGHT YOU WERE SUCH A GOOD KID, ASTRO! WHY'D YOU HAVE TO DO THIS?
GOOD WORK, INSPECTORS! I WANT HIM PUNISHED TO THE FULL EXTENT OF THE LAW!
AH, MR. GASTON!
AS LONG AS *THIS* ROBOT'S AROUND, THERE'LL BE NOTHING BUT *TROUBLE!*
WHAP

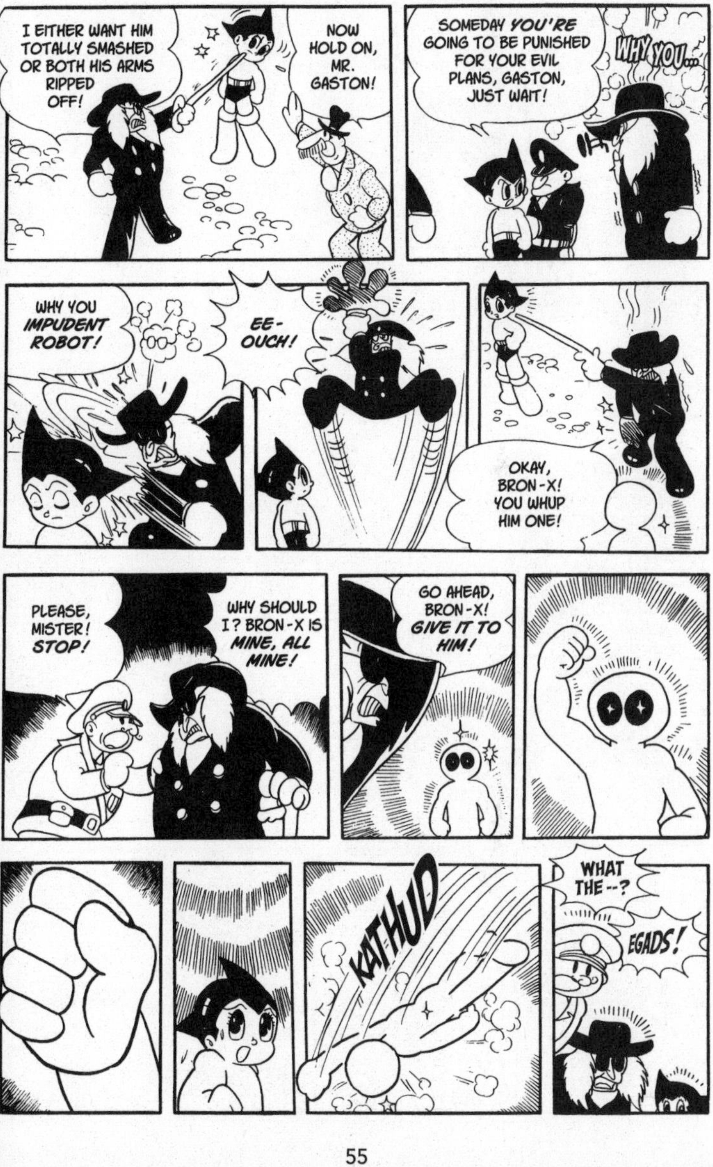
I EITHER WANT HIM TOTALLY SMASHED OR BOTH HIS ARMS RIPPED OFF!
NOW HOLD ON, MR. GASTON!
SOMEDAY *YOU'RE* GOING TO BE PUNISHED FOR YOUR EVIL PLANS, GASTON, JUST WAIT!
WHY YOU...
WHY YOU *IMPUDENT ROBOT!*
EE-OUCH!
OKAY, BRON-X! YOU WHUP HIM ONE!
PLEASE, MISTER! *STOP!*
WHY SHOULD I? BRON-X IS *MINE, ALL MINE!*
GO AHEAD, BRON-X! *GIVE IT TO HIM!*
KATHUD
WHAT THE--?
EGADS!

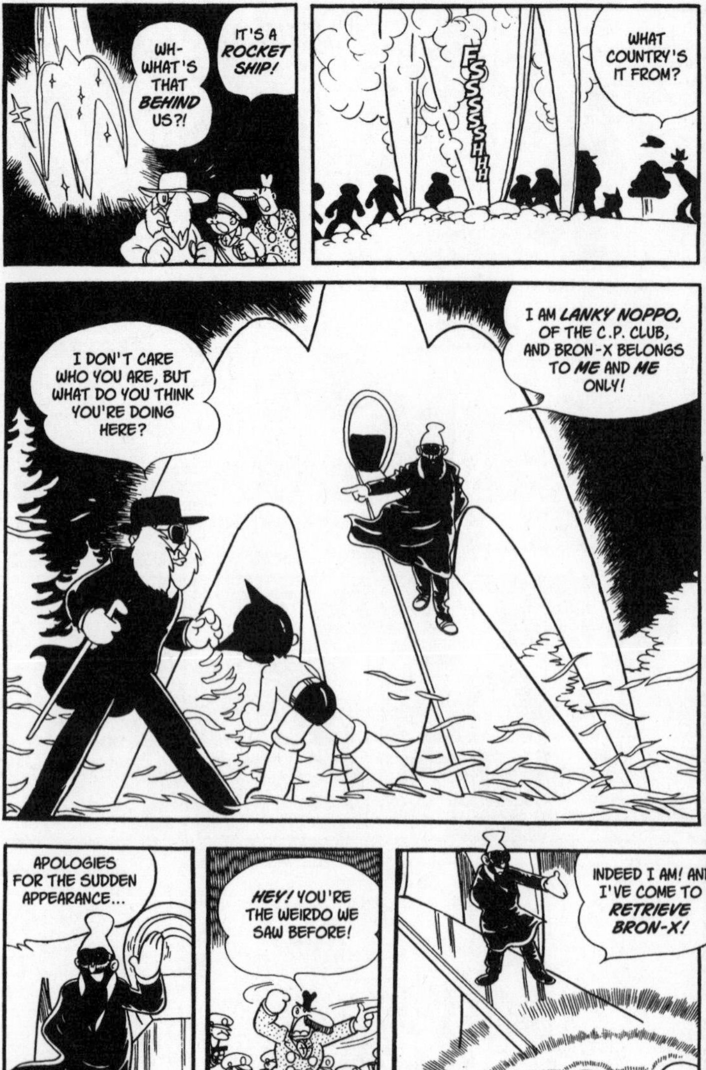
WH-WHAT'S THAT BEHIND US?!
IT'S A ROCKET SHIP!
FSSSSSHHH
WHAT COUNTRY'S IT FROM?
I DON'T CARE WHO YOU ARE, BUT WHAT DO YOU THINK YOU'RE DOING HERE?
I AM LANKY NOPPO, OF THE C.P. CLUB, AND BRON-X BELONGS TO ME AND ME ONLY!
APOLOGIES FOR THE SUDDEN APPEARANCE...
HEY! YOU'RE THE WEIRDO WE SAW BEFORE!
INDEED I AM! AND I'VE COME TO RETRIEVE BRON-X!

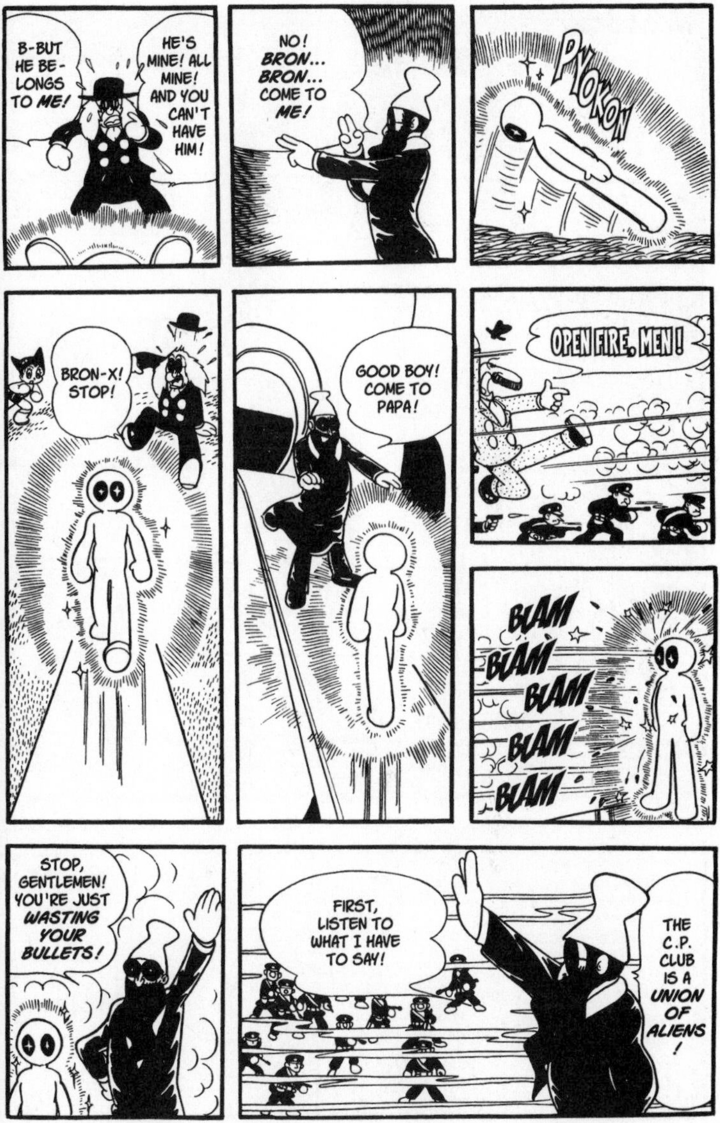
B-BUT HE BE-LONGS TO ME!
HE'S MINE! ALL MINE! AND YOU CAN'T HAVE HIM!
NO! BRON... BRON... COME TO ME!
PYOKON
BRON-X! STOP!
GOOD BOY! COME TO PAPA!
OPEN FIRE, MEN!
BLAM
BLAM
BLAM
BLAM
BLAM
STOP, GENTLEMEN! YOU'RE JUST WASTING YOUR BULLETS!
FIRST, LISTEN TO WHAT I HAVE TO SAY!
THE C.P. CLUB IS A UNION OF ALIENS!

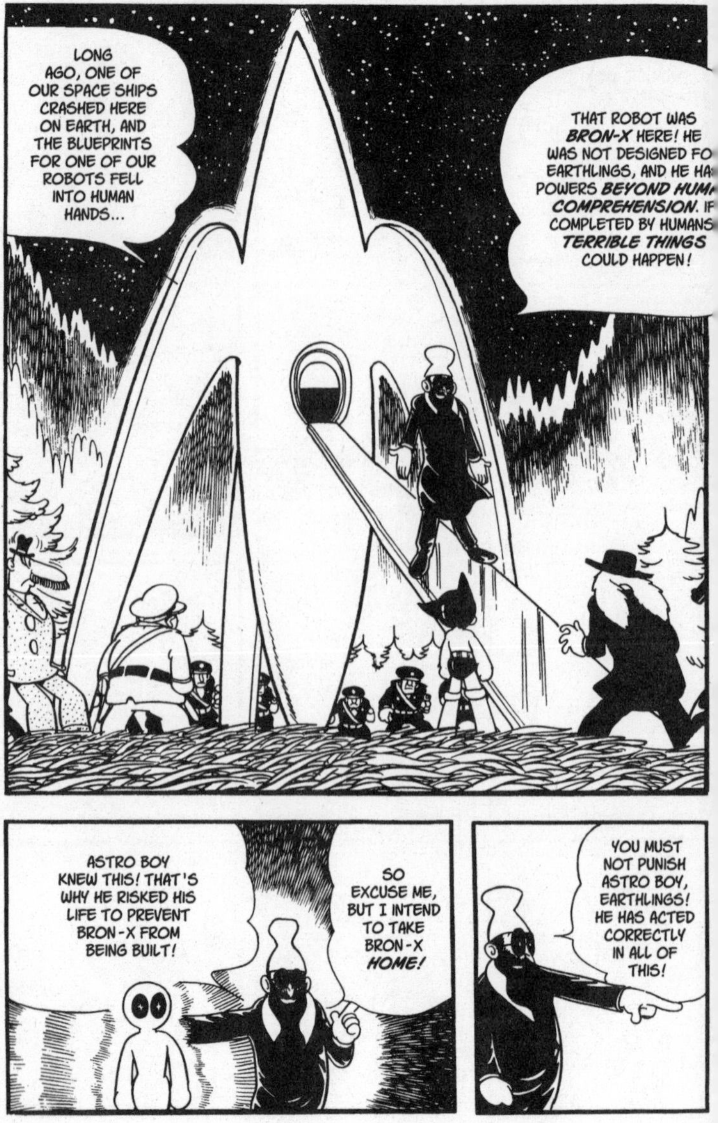
LONG AGO, ONE OF OUR SPACE SHIPS CRASHED HERE ON EARTH, AND THE BLUEPRINTS FOR ONE OF OUR ROBOTS FELL INTO HUMAN HANDS...
THAT ROBOT WAS BRON-X HERE! HE WAS NOT DESIGNED FO EARTHLINGS, AND HE HA POWERS BEYOND HUM COMPREHENSION. IF COMPLETED BY HUMANS TERRIBLE THINGS COULD HAPPEN!
ASTRO BOY KNEW THIS! THAT'S WHY HE RISKED HIS LIFE TO PREVENT BRON-X FROM BEING BUILT!
SO EXCUSE ME, BUT I INTEND TO TAKE BRON-X HOME!
YOU MUST NOT PUNISH ASTRO BOY, EARTHLINGS! HE HAS ACTED CORRECTLY IN ALL OF THIS!

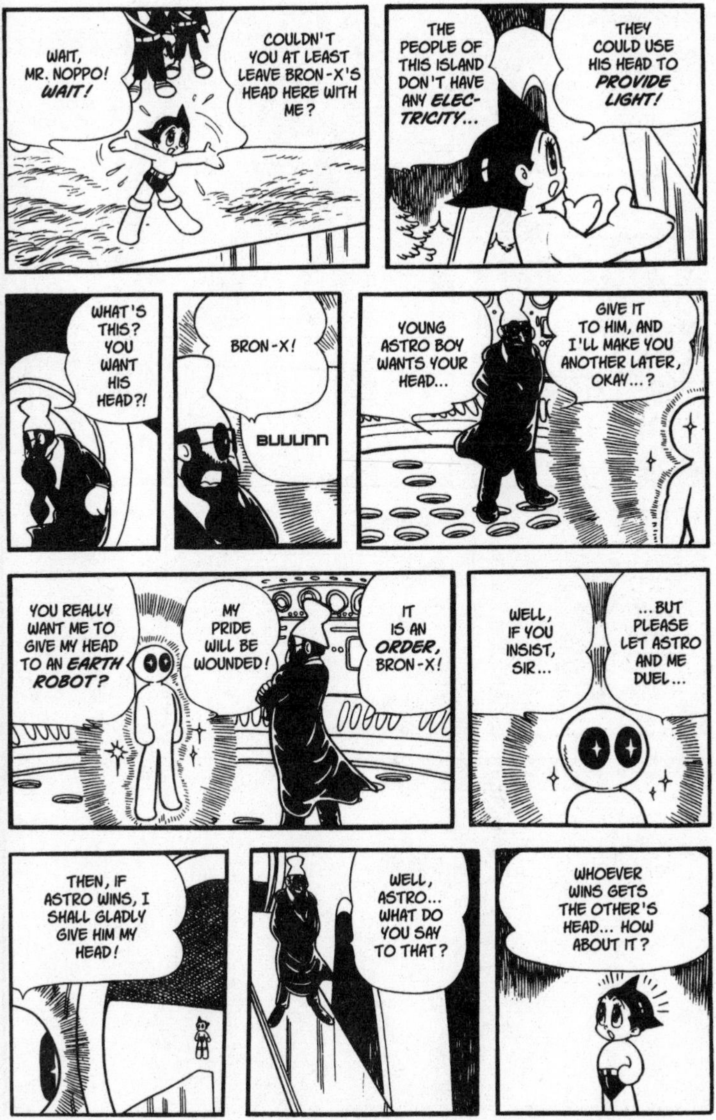
WAIT, MR. NOPPO! WAIT!
COULDN'T YOU AT LEAST LEAVE BRON-X'S HEAD HERE WITH ME?
THE PEOPLE OF THIS ISLAND DON'T HAVE ANY ELECTRICITY...
THEY COULD USE HIS HEAD TO PROVIDE LIGHT!
WHAT'S THIS? YOU WANT HIS HEAD?!
BRON-X!
BUUUNN
YOUNG ASTRO BOY WANTS YOUR HEAD...
GIVE IT TO HIM, AND I'LL MAKE YOU ANOTHER LATER, OKAY...?
YOU REALLY WANT ME TO GIVE MY HEAD TO AN EARTH ROBOT?
MY PRIDE WILL BE WOUNDED!
IT IS AN ORDER, BRON-X!
WELL, IF YOU INSIST, SIR...
...BUT PLEASE LET ASTRO AND ME DUEL...
THEN, IF ASTRO WINS, I SHALL GLADLY GIVE HIM MY HEAD!
WELL, ASTRO... WHAT DO YOU SAY TO THAT?
WHOEVER WINS GETS THE OTHER'S HEAD... HOW ABOUT IT?

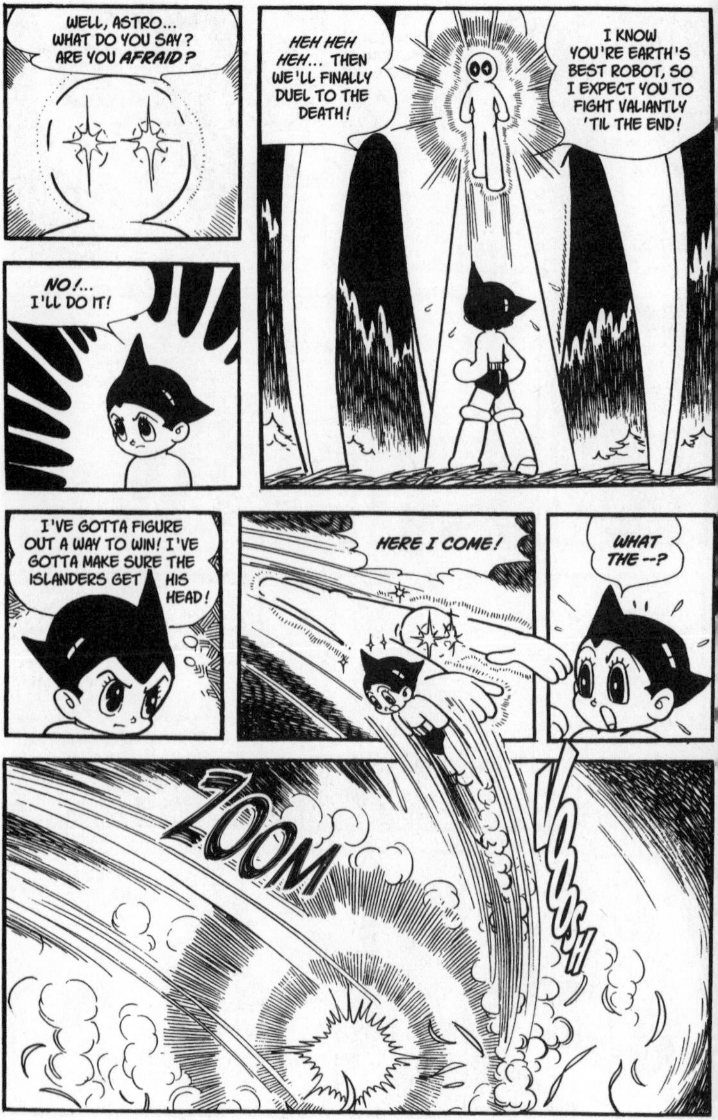
WELL, ASTRO... WHAT DO YOU SAY? ARE YOU *AFRAID?*
HEH HEH HEH... THEN WE'LL FINALLY DUEL TO THE DEATH!
I KNOW YOU'RE EARTH'S BEST ROBOT, SO I EXPECT YOU TO FIGHT VALIANTLY 'TIL THE END!
NO!... I'LL DO IT!
I'VE GOTTA FIGURE OUT A WAY TO WIN! I'VE GOTTA MAKE SURE THE ISLANDERS GET HIS HEAD!
HERE I COME!
WHAT THE --?
ZOOM
VOOOSH

TAKE TO THE SKY, WILL YOU?! YOU COWARD!

OH MY GOSH... LOOK AT THEM!

I'M NOT TRYING TO ESCAPE, BRON-X! THIS IS PART OF MY STRATEGY!

I KNOW YOU'D WIN IN A FRONTAL ASSAULT!

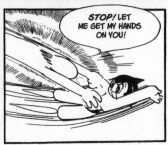

STOP! LET ME GET MY HANDS ON YOU!

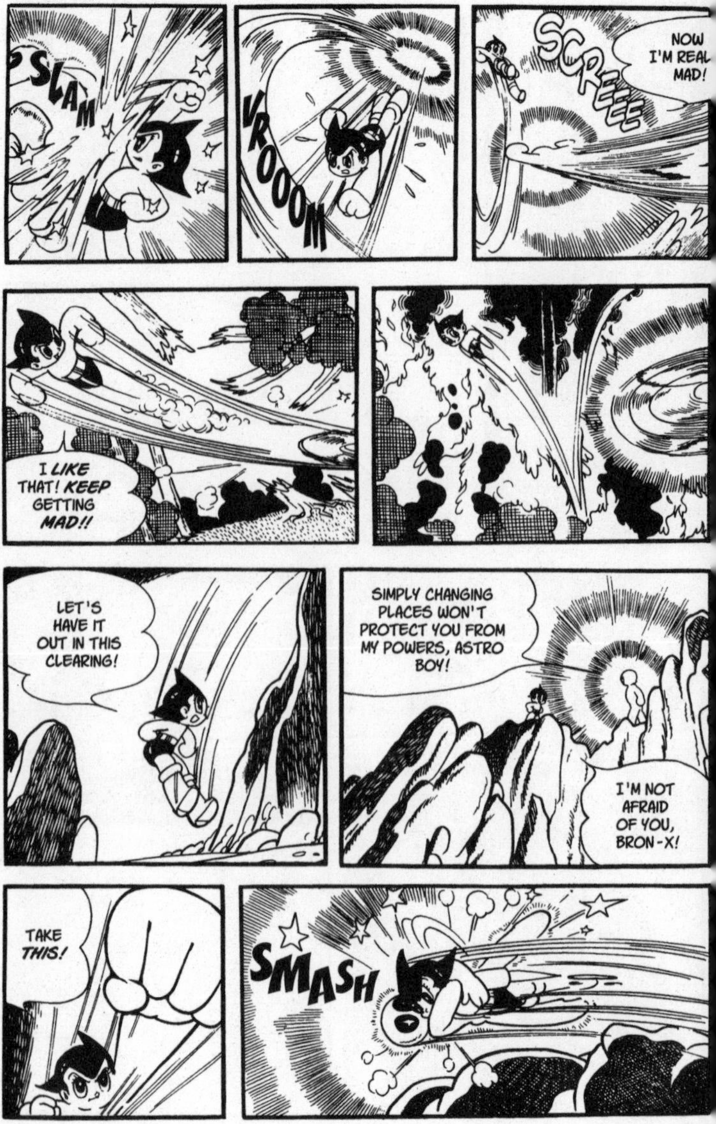
SLAM
VROOOM
SCREEE
NOW I'M REAL MAD!
I LIKE THAT! KEEP GETTING MAD!!
LET'S HAVE IT OUT IN THIS CLEARING!
SIMPLY CHANGING PLACES WON'T PROTECT YOU FROM MY POWERS, ASTRO BOY!
I'M NOT AFRAID OF YOU, BRON-X!
TAKE THIS!
SMASH

KASPLOOSH
SHLA
BUB
FSSSH
BUUUn
U UUUU UU
CRACK
POP
SNAP

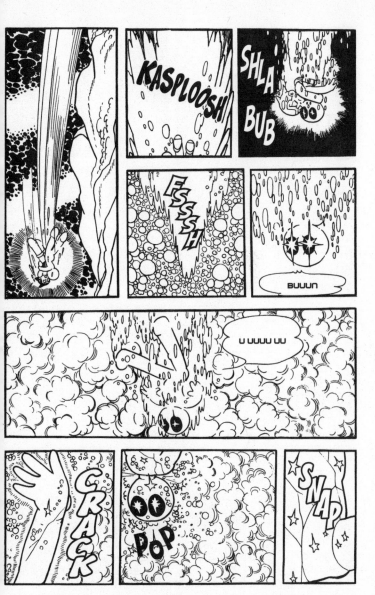

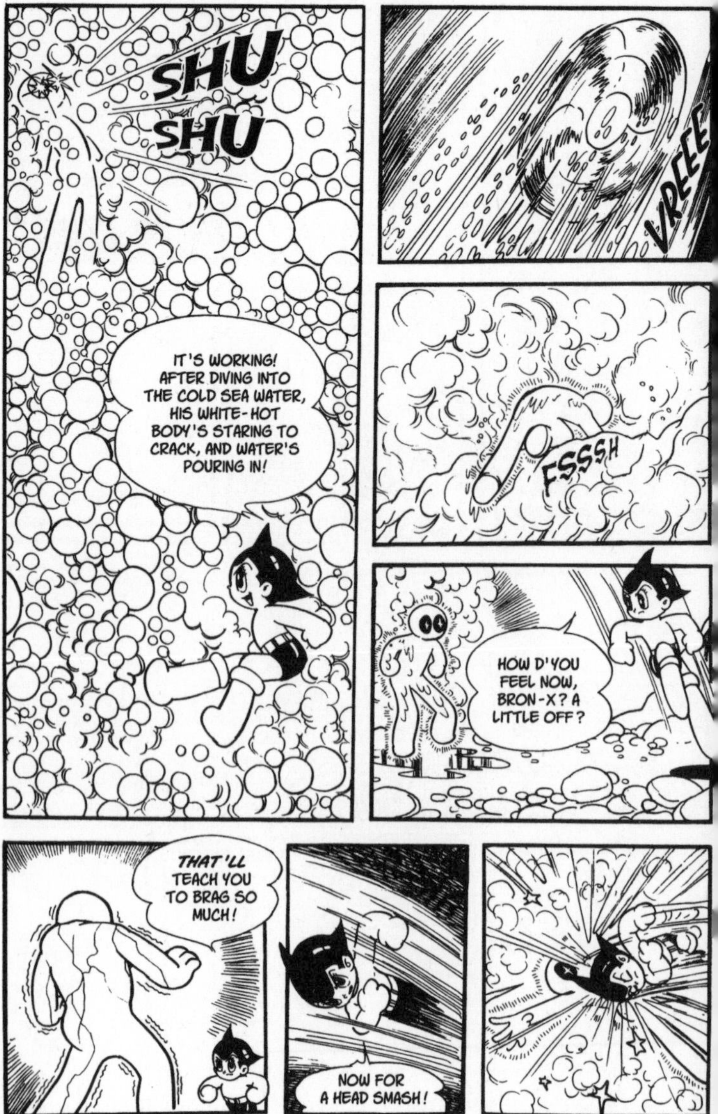
SHU
SHU
IT'S WORKING! AFTER DIVING INTO THE COLD SEA WATER, HIS WHITE-HOT BODY'S STARING TO CRACK, AND WATER'S POURING IN!
VREEE
FSSSH
HOW D'YOU FEEL NOW, BRON-X? A LITTLE OFF?
THAT'LL TEACH YOU TO BRAG SO MUCH!
NOW FOR A HEAD SMASH!

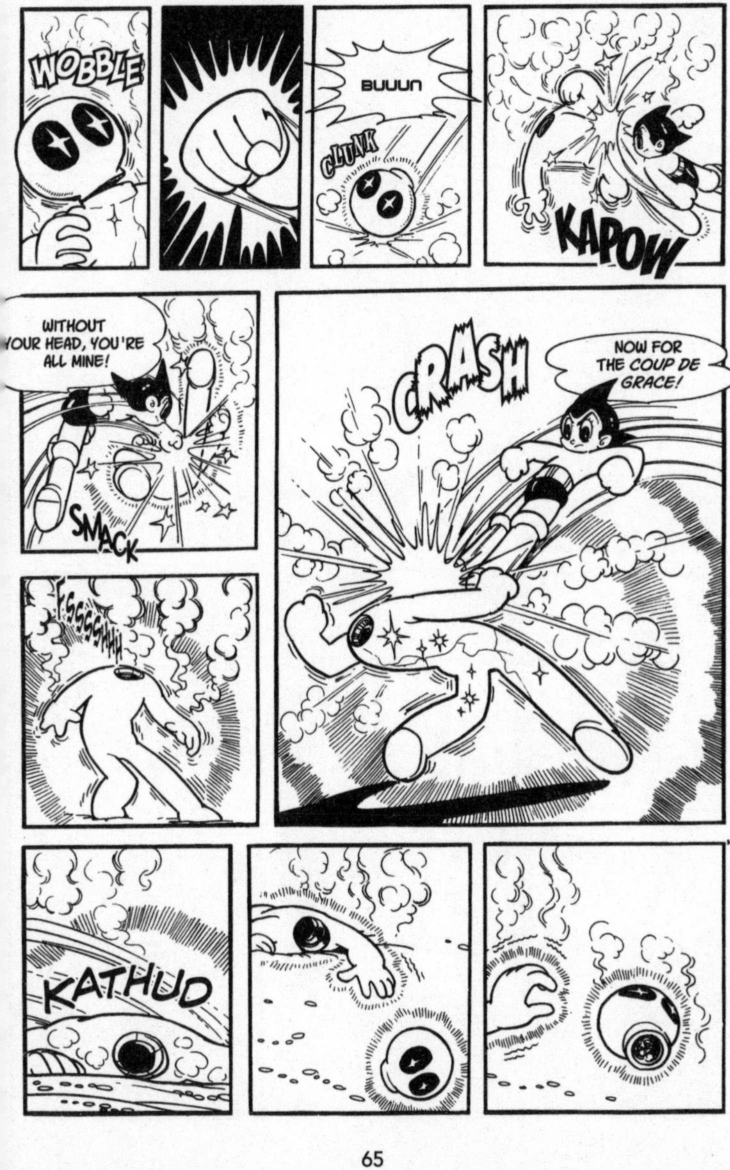
WOBBLE
BUUUn
CLUNK
KAPOW
WITHOUT YOUR HEAD, YOU'RE ALL MINE!
SMACK
CRASH
NOW FOR THE COUP DE GRACE!
FSSSSSHHH
KATHUD

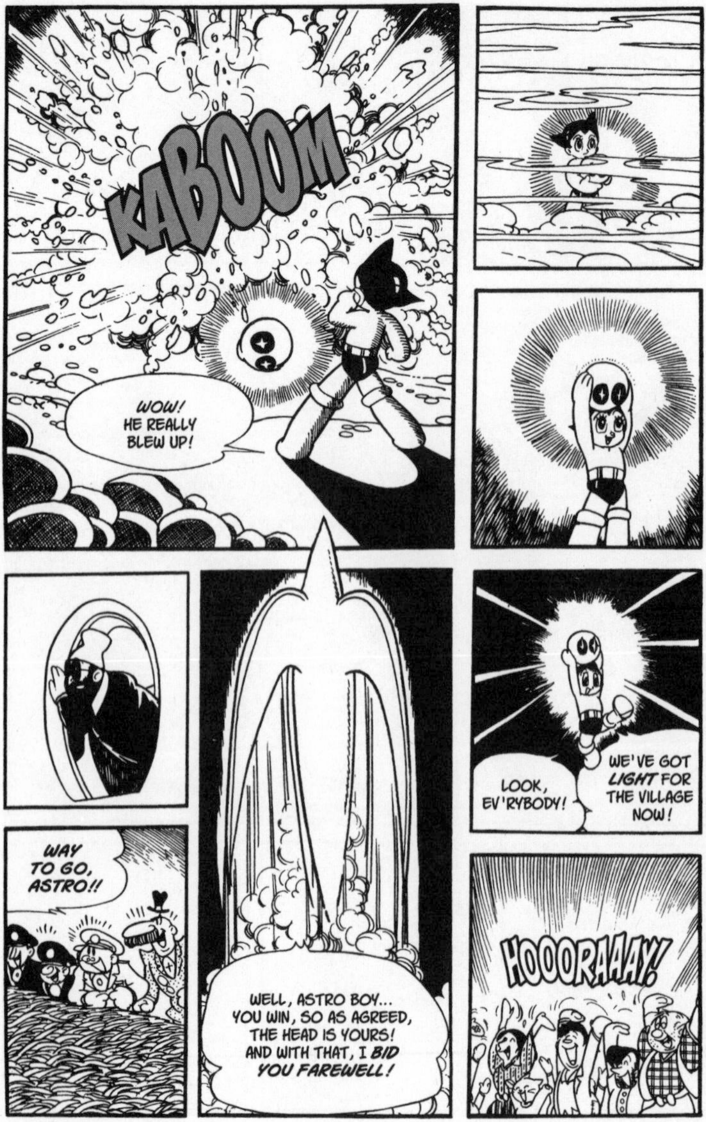
KABOOM
WOW! HE REALLY BLEW UP!
WAY TO GO, ASTRO!!
WELL, ASTRO BOY... YOU WIN, SO AS AGREED, THE HEAD IS YOURS! AND WITH THAT, I BID YOU FAREWELL!
LOOK, EV'RYBODY!
WE'VE GOT LIGHT FOR THE VILLAGE NOW!
HOOORAAAY!

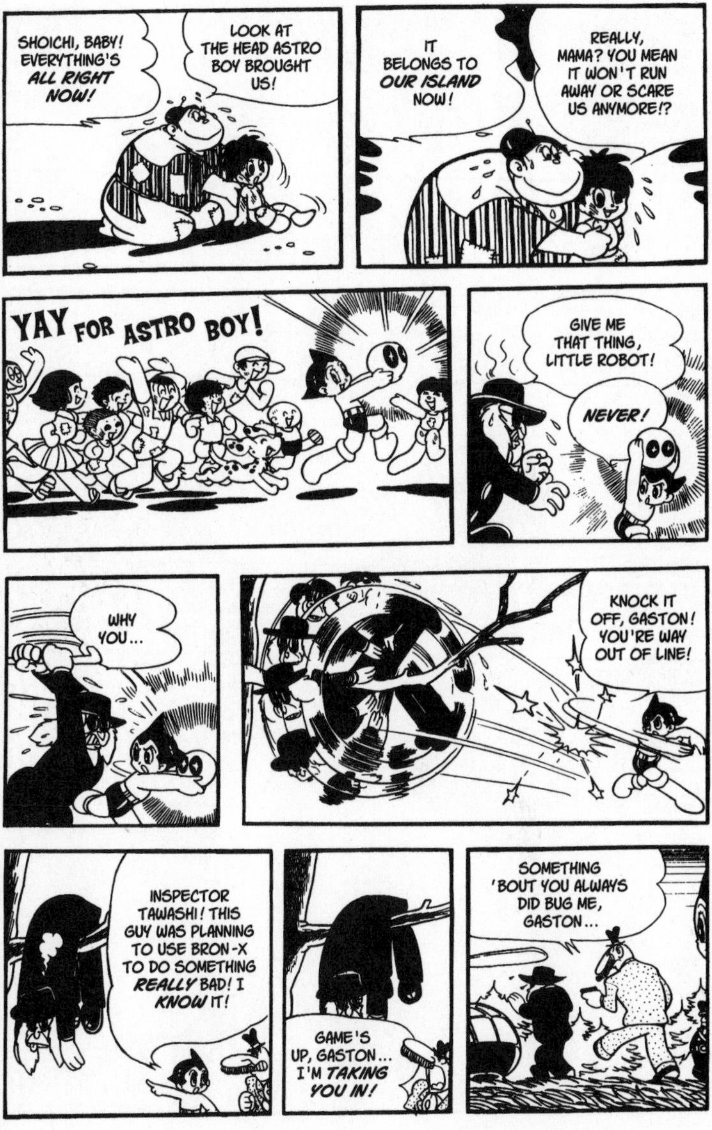
SHOICHI, BABY! EVERYTHING'S ALL RIGHT NOW!
LOOK AT THE HEAD ASTRO BOY BROUGHT US!
IT BELONGS TO OUR ISLAND NOW!
REALLY, MAMA? YOU MEAN IT WON'T RUN AWAY OR SCARE US ANYMORE!?
YAY FOR ASTRO BOY!
GIVE ME THAT THING, LITTLE ROBOT!
NEVER!
WHY YOU...
KNOCK IT OFF, GASTON! YOU'RE WAY OUT OF LINE!
INSPECTOR TAWASHI! THIS GUY WAS PLANNING TO USE BRON-X TO DO SOMETHING REALLY BAD! I KNOW IT!
GAME'S UP, GASTON... I'M TAKING YOU IN!
SOMETHING 'BOUT YOU ALWAYS DID BUG ME, GASTON...

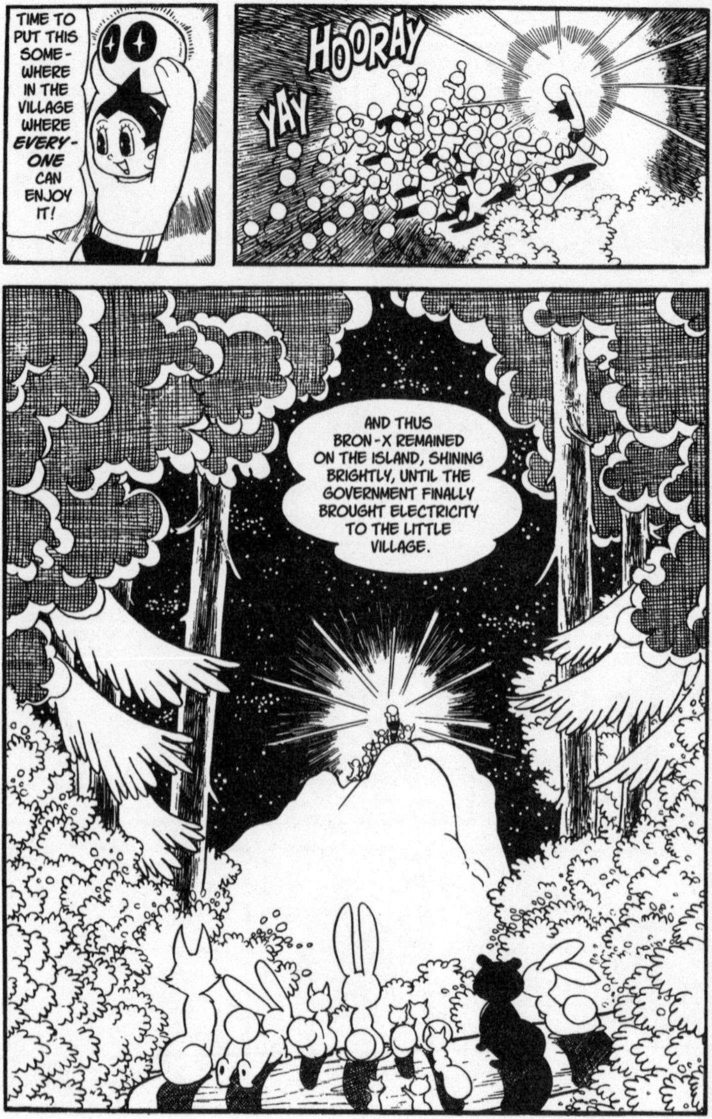
TIME TO PUT THIS SOME-WHERE IN THE VILLAGE WHERE *EVERY-ONE* CAN ENJOY IT!
HOORAY
YAY
AND THUS BRON-X REMAINED ON THE ISLAND, SHINING BRIGHTLY, UNTIL THE GOVERNMENT FINALLY BROUGHT ELECTRICITY TO THE LITTLE VILLAGE.

U R A N

First serialized in August and September 1960
in *Shonen* magazine.

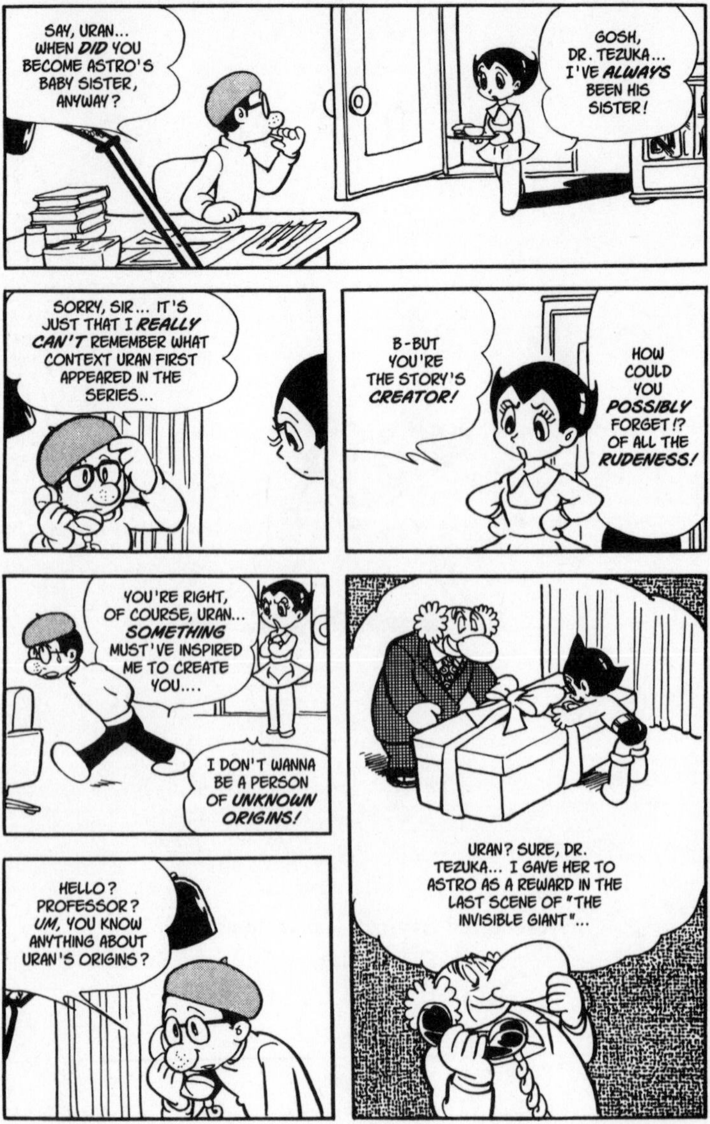
SAY, URAN... WHEN DID YOU BECOME ASTRO'S BABY SISTER, ANYWAY?
GOSH, DR. TEZUKA... I'VE ALWAYS BEEN HIS SISTER!
SORRY, SIR... IT'S JUST THAT I REALLY CAN'T REMEMBER WHAT CONTEXT URAN FIRST APPEARED IN THE SERIES...
B-BUT YOU'RE THE STORY'S CREATOR!
HOW COULD YOU POSSIBLY FORGET!? OF ALL THE RUDENESS!
YOU'RE RIGHT, OF COURSE, URAN... SOMETHING MUST'VE INSPIRED ME TO CREATE YOU....
I DON'T WANNA BE A PERSON OF UNKNOWN ORIGINS!
HELLO? PROFESSOR? UM, YOU KNOW ANYTHING ABOUT URAN'S ORIGINS?
URAN? SURE, DR. TEZUKA... I GAVE HER TO ASTRO AS A REWARD IN THE LAST SCENE OF "THE INVISIBLE GIANT"...

HELLO? THIS ASTRO'S PARENTS? *UM, ABOUT URAN...*

UM, RIGHT... URAN WAS CREATED AT THE MINISTRY OF SCIENCE'S DEPARTMENT OF PRECISION MACHINERY. HER DESIGN WAS BASED ON ASTRO'S, AND SHE WAS SENT HERE FROM THE DEPARTMENT...

...IN A REGISTERED MAIL PACKAGE!

WHAT?! YOU WANT TO KNOW ABOUT *URAN?!*

IT WAS A FLAWED IMPLEMENTATION OF ASTRO'S DESIGN... I SOLD THE ROBOT AFTER DEVELOPING IT, AND THEN SOMEONE AT THE DEPARTMENT MODIFIED IT INTO A LITTLE GIRL MODEL...

URAN? HMM... DON'T REMEMBER TOO WELL, BUT ON THE TV SHOW, I'M PRETTY SURE SHE WAS RETRIEVED FROM THE BOTTOM OF THE OCEAN...

NAW, IT WASN'T THE BOTTOM OF THE OCEAN, IT WAS FROM THE TRASH DUMP!

HMM...

BUT WHAT'S THE *REAL* TRUTH HERE?

HEY! WHAT'S GOING?! IF YOU DON'T TREAT ME WITH A LITTLE MORE *RESPECT,* I'M GONNA THROW A *FIT!!*

SO HOW'S ASTRO GETTING ALONG WITH THE BROTHER 'N SISTER WE MADE FOR HIM?

WELL, HE'S SHOWING THEM AROUND TOKYO NOW...

...ACTING LIKE A GOOD BROTHER SHOULD!

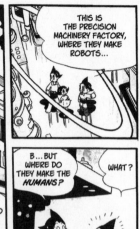

THIS IS THE PRECISION MACHINERY FACTORY, WHERE THEY MAKE ROBOTS...

B...BUT WHERE DO THEY MAKE THE *HUMANS*?

WHAT?

HA HA! ACTUALLY, HUMANS COME FROM INSIDE THEIR MOTHER'S TUMMIES, COBALT...

GEE, I DON'T GET IT...

DON'T WORRY, COBALT...

...IT'LL ALL MAKE SENSE SOME DAY.

THIS IS AN ATOMIC REACTOR...

WHERE ARE WE? SURE IS BUSY...

WE'RE DOWNTOWN, COBALT... THERE'S LOTS OF STORES HERE...

WOW... THIS IS NEAT...

MAYBE I'LL TAKE THIS...

HEY! YOU GOTTA PAY FOR THAT STUFF, SONNY!!

72

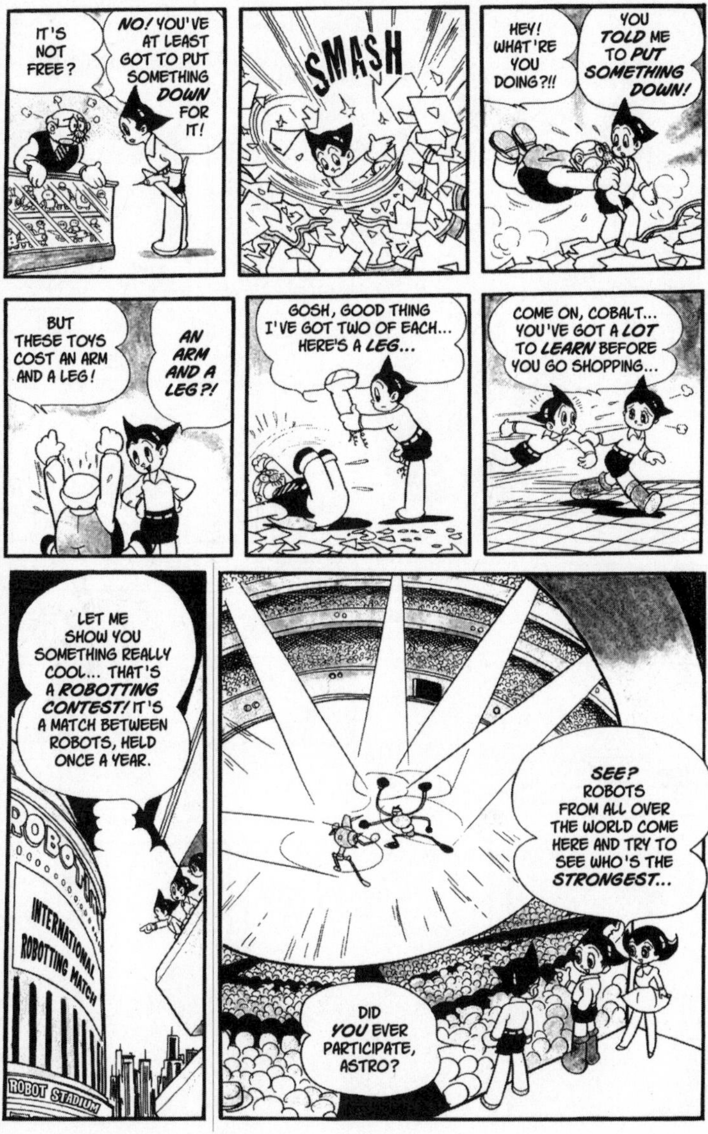
IT'S NOT FREE?
NO! YOU'VE AT LEAST GOT TO PUT SOMETHING DOWN FOR IT!
SMASH
HEY! WHAT'RE YOU DOING?!!
YOU TOLD ME TO PUT SOMETHING DOWN!
BUT THESE TOYS COST AN ARM AND A LEG!
AN ARM AND A LEG?!
GOSH, GOOD THING I'VE GOT TWO OF EACH... HERE'S A LEG...
COME ON, COBALT... YOU'VE GOT A LOT TO LEARN BEFORE YOU GO SHOPPING...
LET ME SHOW YOU SOMETHING REALLY COOL... THAT'S A ROBOTTING CONTEST! IT'S A MATCH BETWEEN ROBOTS, HELD ONCE A YEAR.
INTERNATIONAL ROBOTTING MATCH
ROBOT STADIUM
SEE? ROBOTS FROM ALL OVER THE WORLD COME HERE AND TRY TO SEE WHO'S THE STRONGEST...
DID YOU EVER PARTICIPATE, ASTRO?

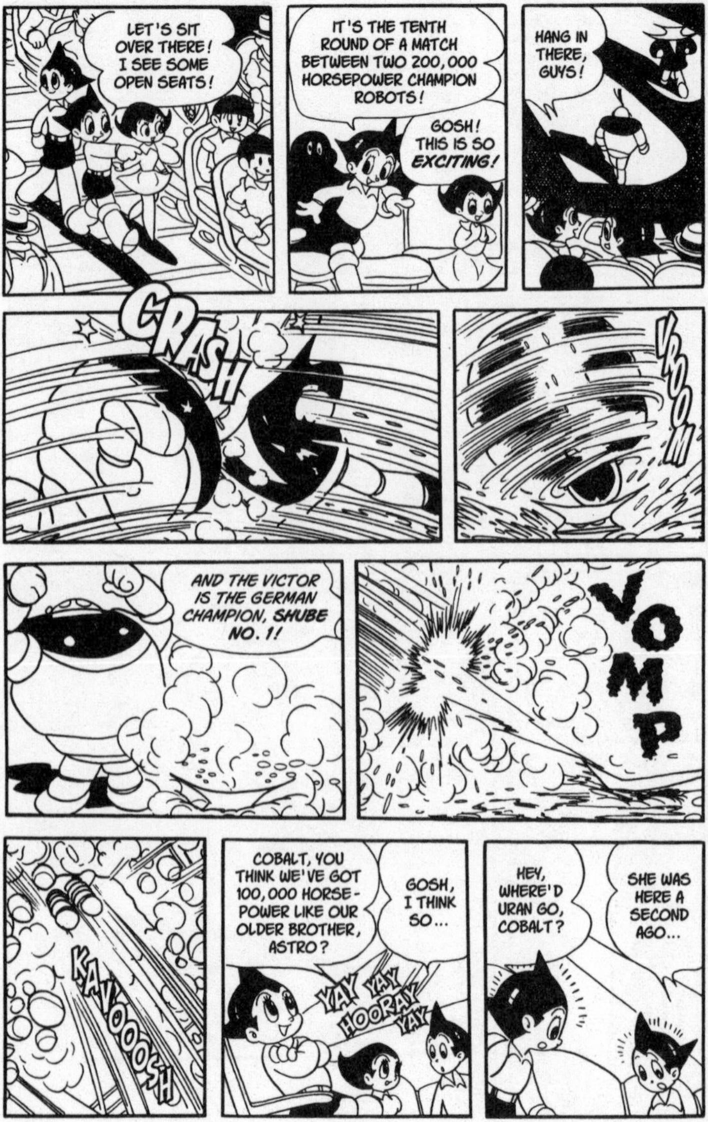
LET'S SIT OVER THERE! I SEE SOME OPEN SEATS!
IT'S THE TENTH ROUND OF A MATCH BETWEEN TWO 200,000 HORSEPOWER CHAMPION ROBOTS!
GOSH! THIS IS SO *EXCITING!*
HANG IN THERE, GUYS!
CRASH
VROOOM
AND THE VICTOR IS THE GERMAN CHAMPION, ***SHUBE NO. 1!***
VOMP
KAVOOOOSH
COBALT, YOU THINK WE'VE GOT 100,000 HORSE-POWER LIKE OUR OLDER BROTHER, ASTRO?
GOSH, I THINK SO...
YAY YAY HOORAY YAY
HEY, WHERE'D URAN GO, COBALT?
SHE WAS HERE A SECOND AGO...

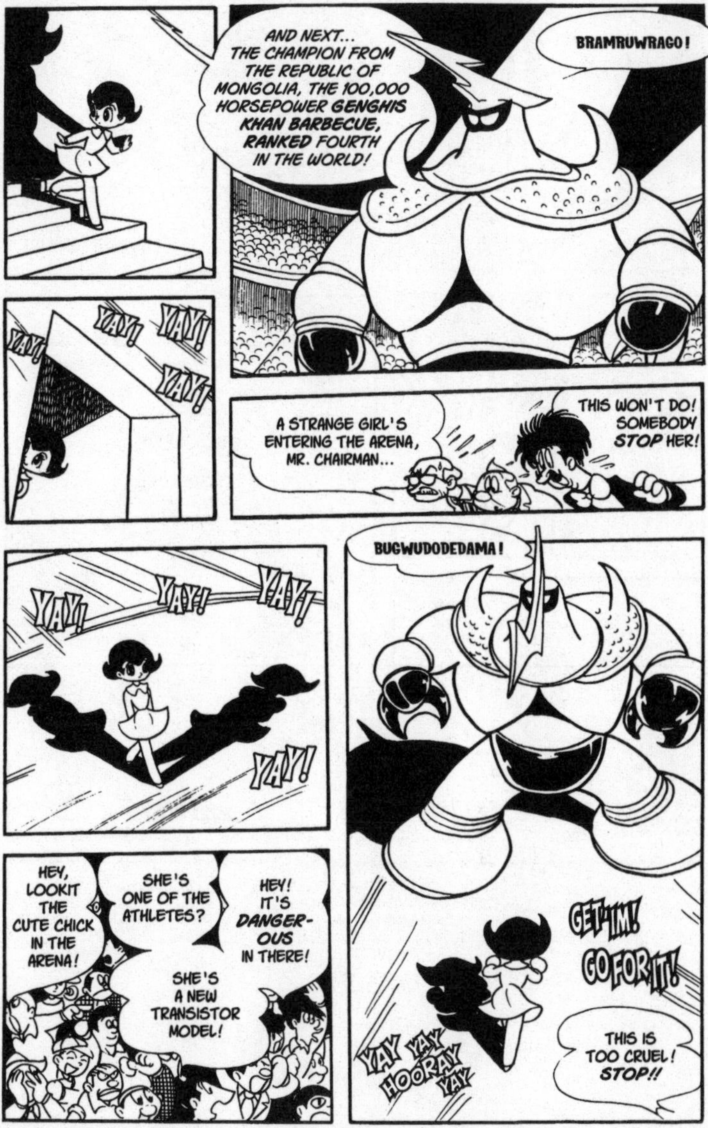
AND NEXT... THE CHAMPION FROM THE REPUBLIC OF MONGOLIA, THE 100,000 HORSEPOWER GENGHIS KHAN BARBECUE, RANKED FOURTH IN THE WORLD!
BRAMRUWRAGO!
YAY! YAY! YAY! YAY!
A STRANGE GIRL'S ENTERING THE ARENA, MR. CHAIRMAN...
THIS WON'T DO! SOMEBODY STOP HER!
YAY! YAY! YAY! YAY!
BUGWUDODEDAMA!
HEY, LOOKIT THE CUTE CHICK IN THE ARENA!
SHE'S ONE OF THE ATHLETES?
HEY! IT'S DANGEROUS IN THERE!
SHE'S A NEW TRANSISTOR MODEL!
GET 'IM! GO FOR IT!
YAY YAY HOORAY YAY
THIS IS TOO CRUEL! STOP!!

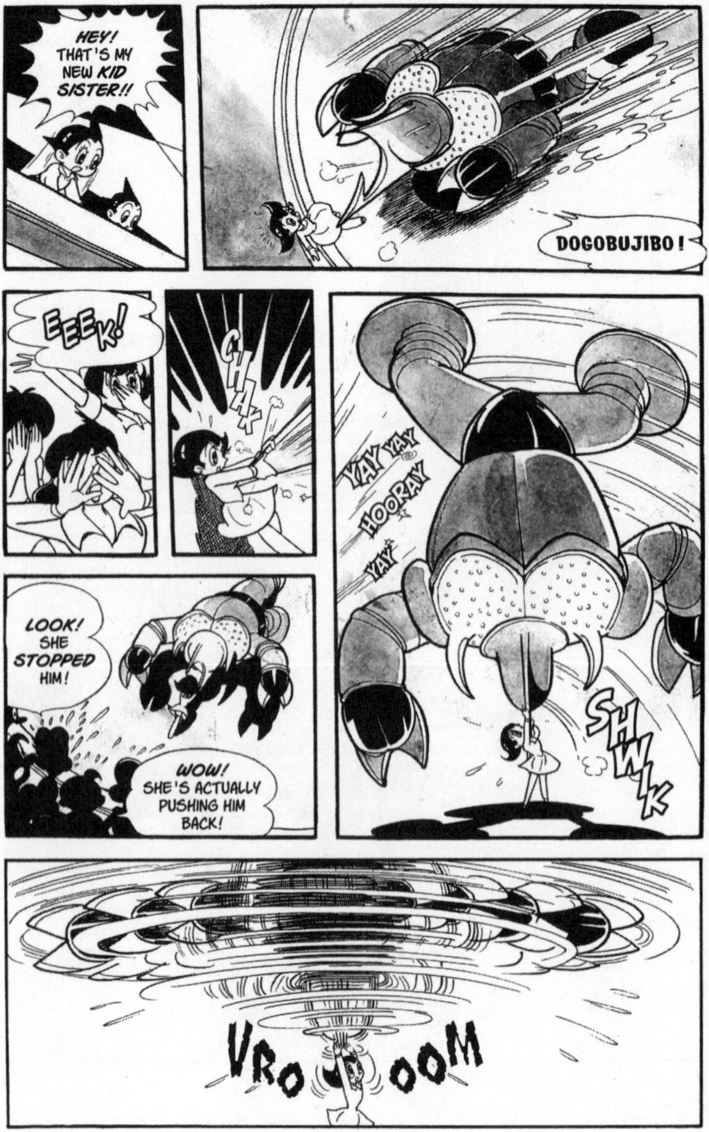

HEY! THAT'S MY NEW KID SISTER!!
DOGOBUJIBO!
EEEK!
CHAK
YAY YAY
HOORAY
YAY
SHWIK
LOOK! SHE STOPPED HIM!
WOW! SHE'S ACTUALLY PUSHING HIM BACK!
VROOOM

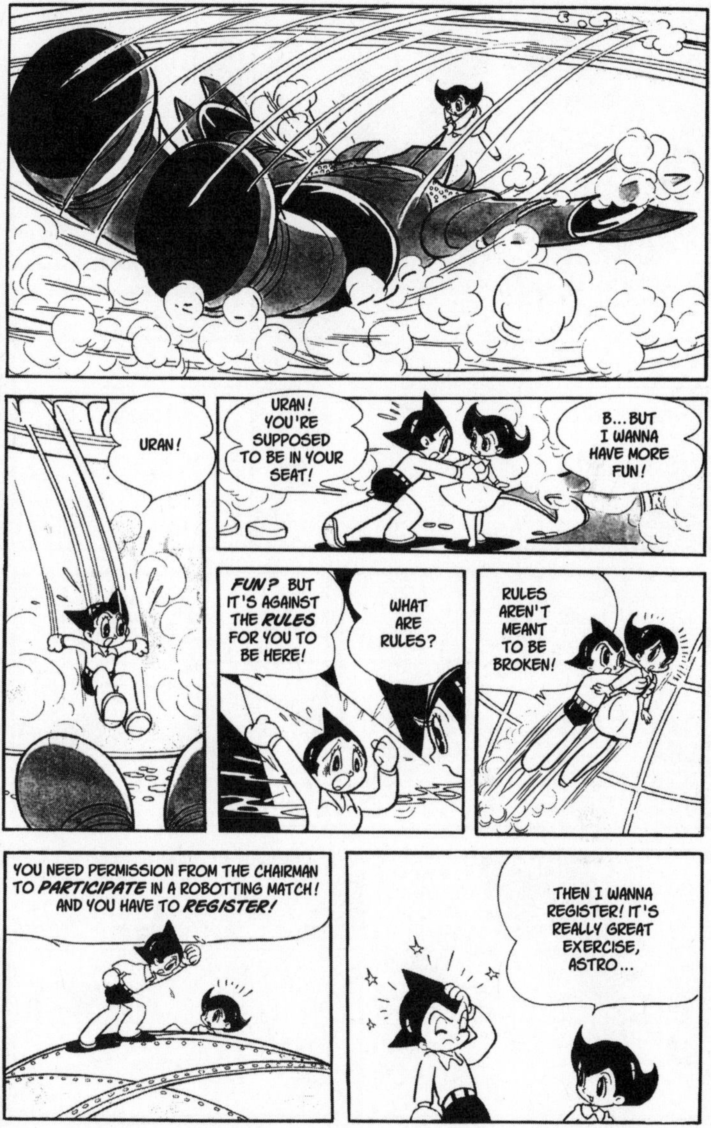
URAN!
URAN! YOU'RE SUPPOSED TO BE IN YOUR SEAT!
B...BUT I WANNA HAVE MORE FUN!
FUN? BUT IT'S AGAINST THE RULES FOR YOU TO BE HERE!
WHAT ARE RULES?
RULES AREN'T MEANT TO BE BROKEN!
YOU NEED PERMISSION FROM THE CHAIRMAN TO PARTICIPATE IN A ROBOTTING MATCH! AND YOU HAVE TO REGISTER!
THEN I WANNA REGISTER! IT'S REALLY GREAT EXERCISE, ASTRO...

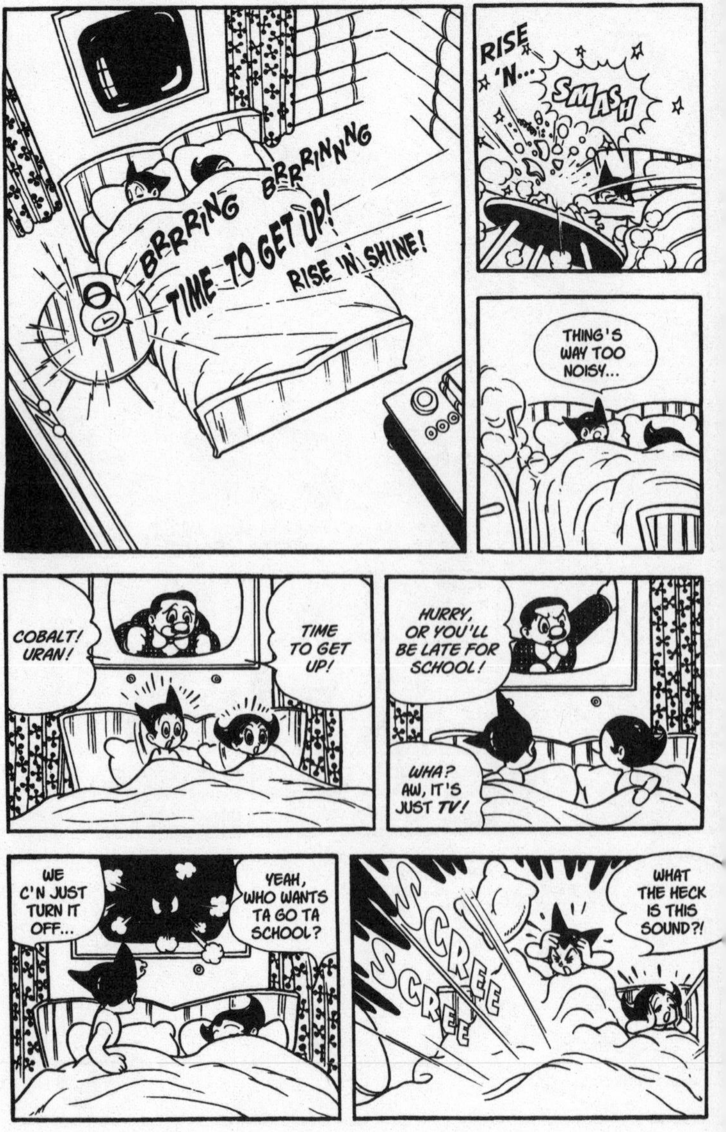
BRRRING BRRRINNNG
TIME TO GET UP!
RISE 'N SHINE!
RISE 'N...
SMASH
THING'S WAY TOO NOISY...
COBALT! URAN!
TIME TO GET UP!
HURRY, OR YOU'LL BE LATE FOR SCHOOL!
WHA? AW, IT'S JUST TV!
WE C'N JUST TURN IT OFF...
YEAH, WHO WANTS TA GO TA SCHOOL?
SCREE
SCREE
WHAT THE HECK IS THIS SOUND?!

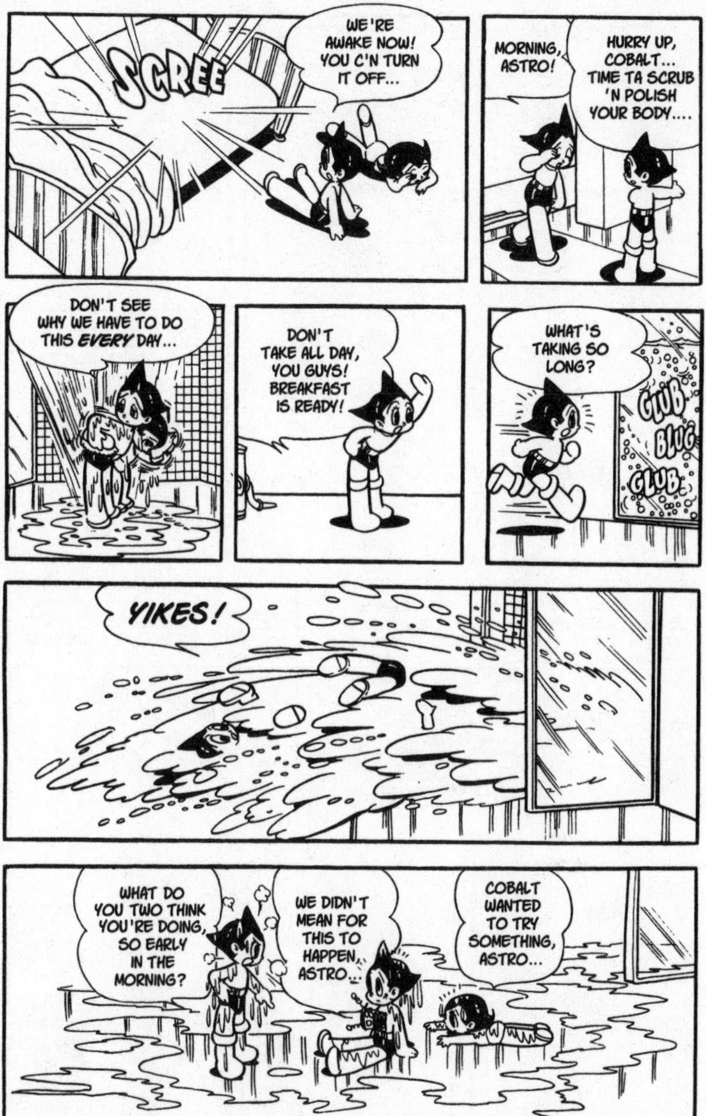
SCREE
WE'RE AWAKE NOW! YOU C'N TURN IT OFF...
MORNING, ASTRO!
HURRY UP, COBALT... TIME TA SCRUB 'N POLISH YOUR BODY....
DON'T SEE WHY WE HAVE TO DO THIS EVERY DAY...
DON'T TAKE ALL DAY, YOU GUYS! BREAKFAST IS READY!
WHAT'S TAKING SO LONG?
GLUB
BLUG
GLUB
YIKES!
WHAT DO YOU TWO THINK YOU'RE DOING, SO EARLY IN THE MORNING?
WE DIDN'T MEAN FOR THIS TO HAPPEN, ASTRO...
COBALT WANTED TO TRY SOMETHING, ASTRO...

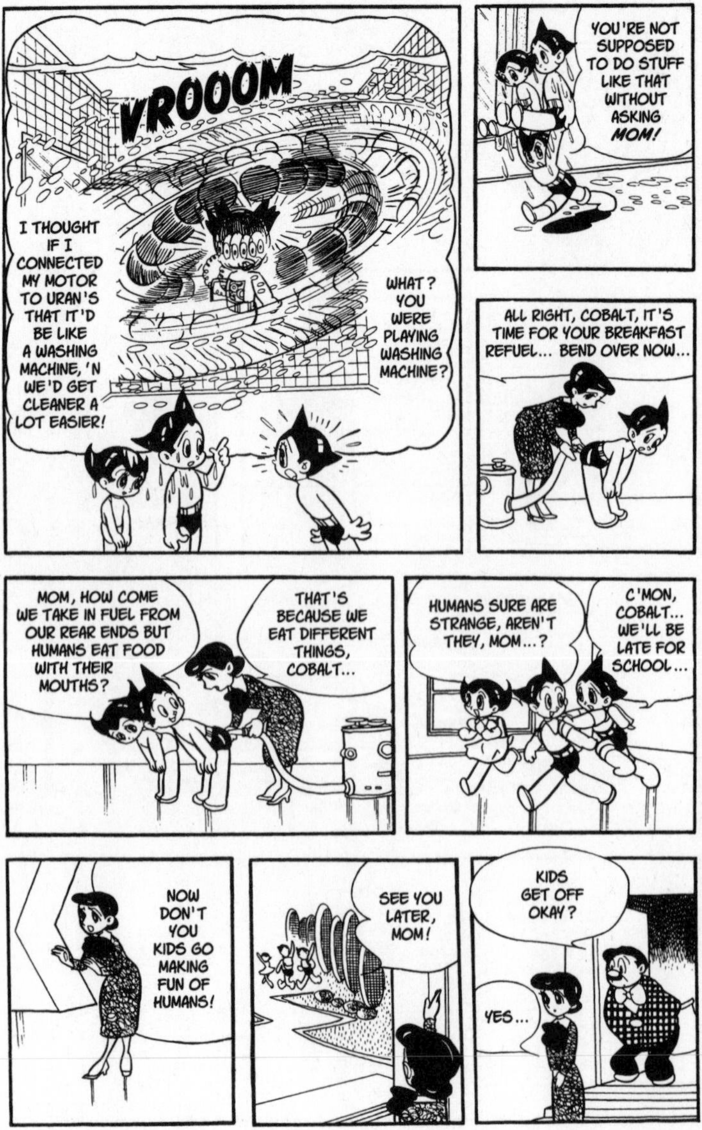
VROOOM
I THOUGHT IF I CONNECTED MY MOTOR TO URAN'S THAT IT'D BE LIKE A WASHING MACHINE, 'N WE'D GET CLEANER A LOT EASIER!
WHAT? YOU WERE PLAYING WASHING MACHINE?
YOU'RE NOT SUPPOSED TO DO STUFF LIKE THAT WITHOUT ASKING MOM!
ALL RIGHT, COBALT, IT'S TIME FOR YOUR BREAKFAST REFUEL... BEND OVER NOW...
MOM, HOW COME WE TAKE IN FUEL FROM OUR REAR ENDS BUT HUMANS EAT FOOD WITH THEIR MOUTHS?
THAT'S BECAUSE WE EAT DIFFERENT THINGS, COBALT...
HUMANS SURE ARE STRANGE, AREN'T THEY, MOM...?
C'MON, COBALT... WE'LL BE LATE FOR SCHOOL...
NOW DON'T YOU KIDS GO MAKING FUN OF HUMANS!
SEE YOU LATER, MOM!
KIDS GET OFF OKAY?
YES...

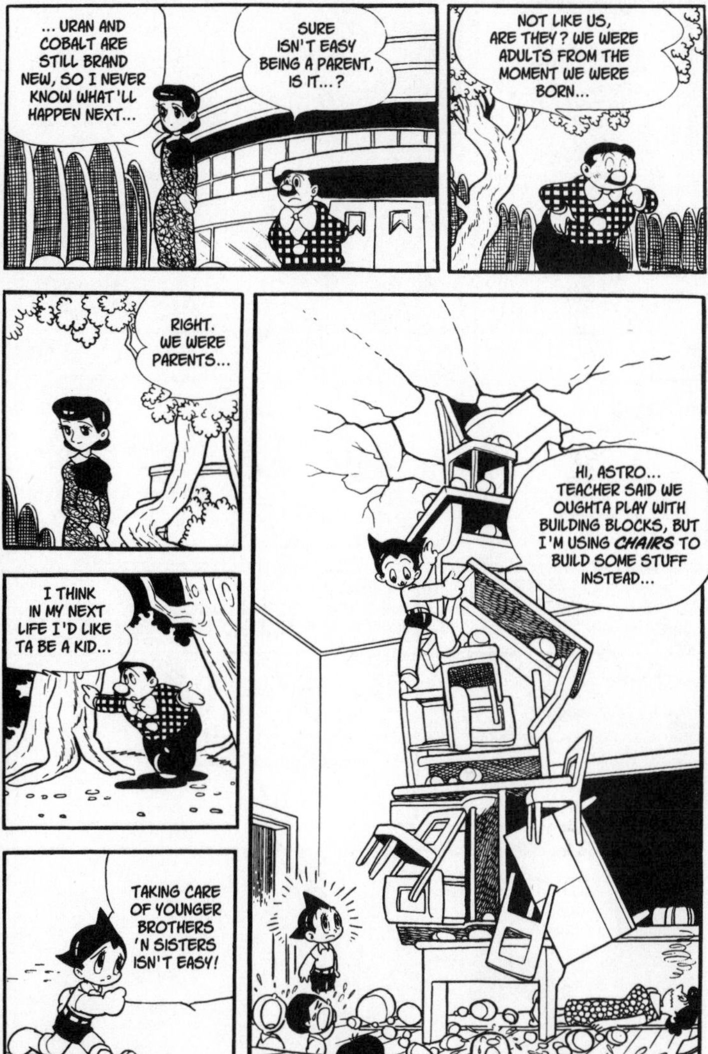
... URAN AND COBALT ARE STILL BRAND NEW, SO I NEVER KNOW WHAT'LL HAPPEN NEXT...
SURE ISN'T EASY BEING A PARENT, IS IT...?
NOT LIKE US, ARE THEY? WE WERE ADULTS FROM THE MOMENT WE WERE BORN...
RIGHT. WE WERE PARENTS...
I THINK IN MY NEXT LIFE I'D LIKE TA BE A KID...
TAKING CARE OF YOUNGER BROTHERS 'N SISTERS ISN'T EASY!
HI, ASTRO... TEACHER SAID WE OUGHTA PLAY WITH BUILDING BLOCKS, BUT I'M USING *CHAIRS* TO BUILD SOME STUFF INSTEAD...

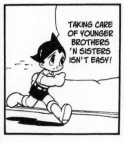

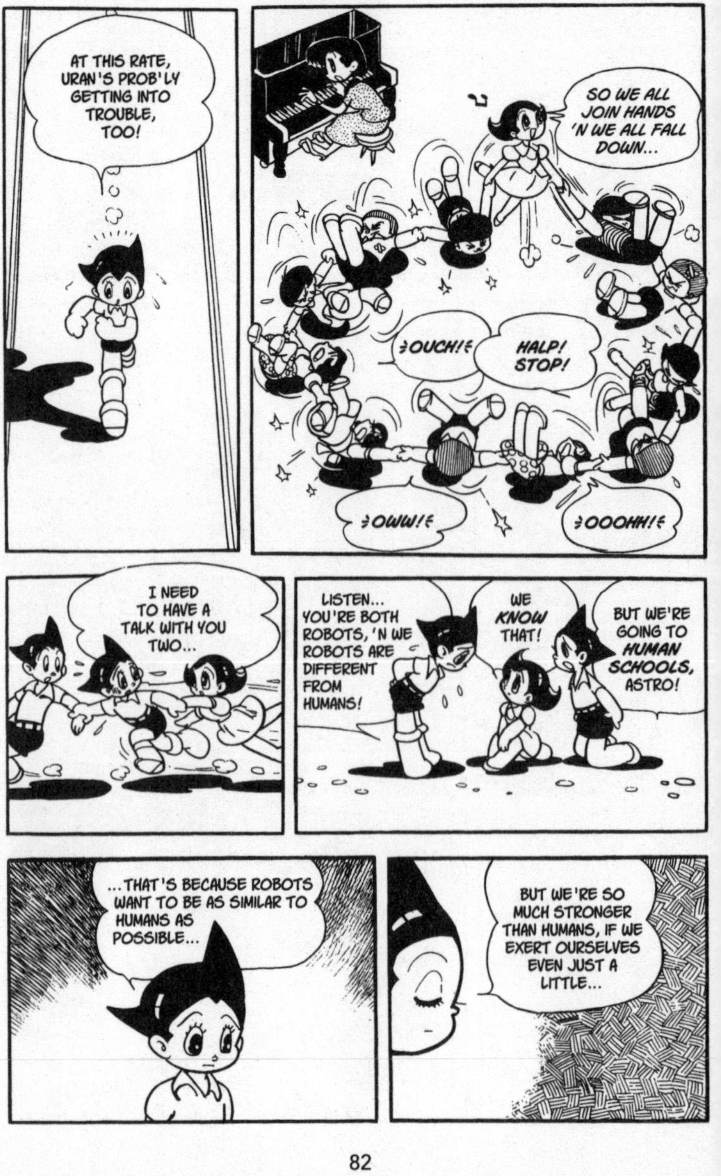
AT THIS RATE, URAN'S PROB'LY GETTING INTO TROUBLE, TOO!
SO WE ALL JOIN HANDS 'N WE ALL FALL DOWN...
OUCH!
HALP! STOP!
OWW!
OOOHH!
I NEED TO HAVE A TALK WITH YOU TWO...
LISTEN... YOU'RE BOTH ROBOTS, 'N WE ROBOTS ARE DIFFERENT FROM HUMANS!
WE *KNOW* THAT!
BUT WE'RE GOING TO *HUMAN SCHOOLS,* ASTRO!
...THAT'S BECAUSE ROBOTS WANT TO BE AS SIMILAR TO HUMANS AS POSSIBLE...
BUT WE'RE SO MUCH STRONGER THAN HUMANS, IF WE EXERT OURSELVES EVEN JUST A LITTLE...

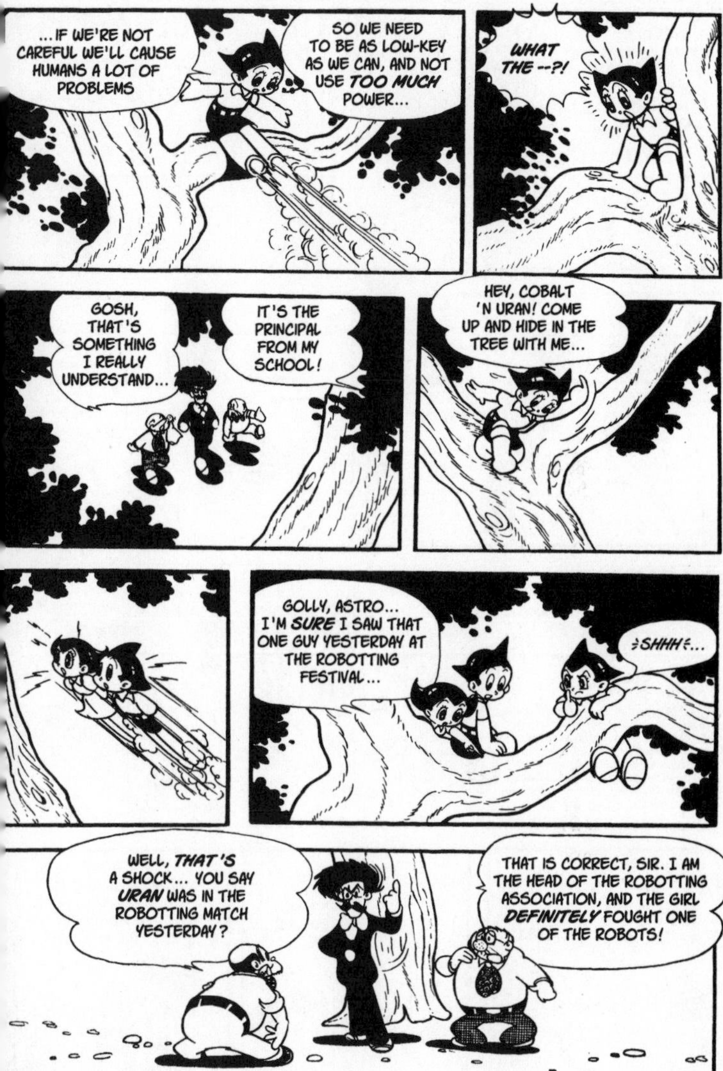
...IF WE'RE NOT CAREFUL WE'LL CAUSE HUMANS A LOT OF PROBLEMS
SO WE NEED TO BE AS LOW-KEY AS WE CAN, AND NOT USE *TOO MUCH* POWER...
WHAT THE --?!
GOSH, THAT'S SOMETHING I REALLY UNDERSTAND...
IT'S THE PRINCIPAL FROM MY SCHOOL!
HEY, COBALT 'N URAN! COME UP AND HIDE IN THE TREE WITH ME...
GOLLY, ASTRO... I'M *SURE* I SAW THAT ONE GUY YESTERDAY AT THE ROBOTTING FESTIVAL...
SHHH...
WELL, *THAT'S* A SHOCK... YOU SAY *URAN* WAS IN THE ROBOTTING MATCH YESTERDAY?
THAT IS CORRECT, SIR. I AM THE HEAD OF THE ROBOTTING ASSOCIATION, AND THE GIRL *DEFINITELY* FOUGHT ONE OF THE ROBOTS!

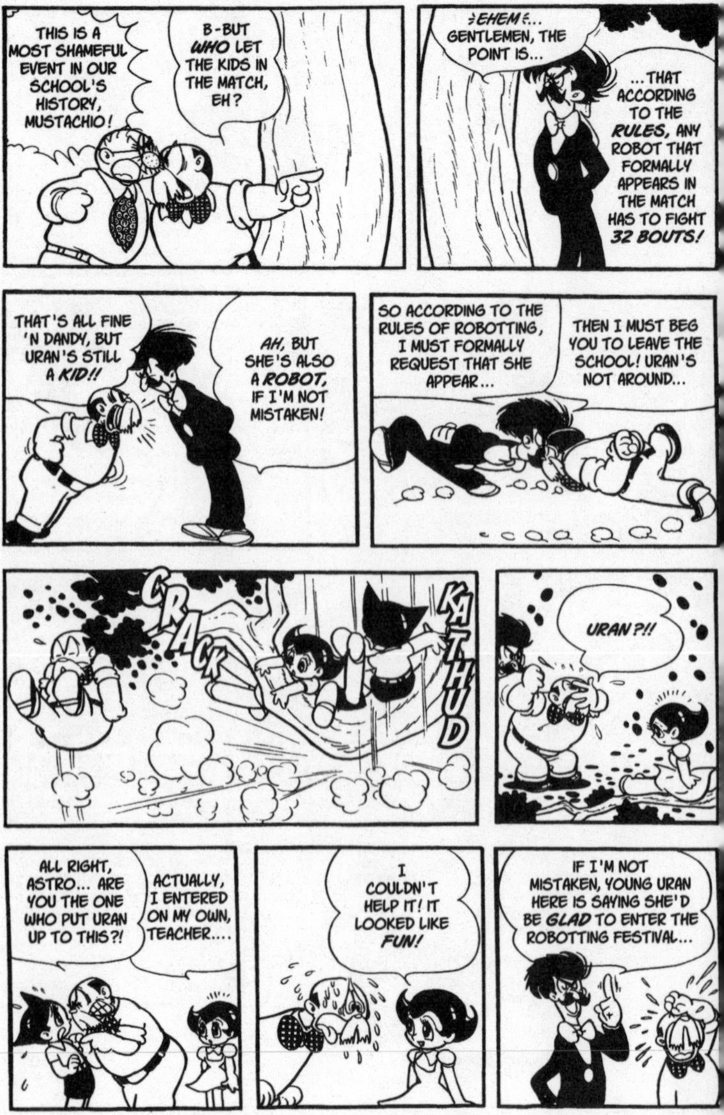
THIS IS A MOST SHAMEFUL EVENT IN OUR SCHOOL'S HISTORY, MUSTACHIO!
B-BUT *WHO* LET THE KIDS IN THE MATCH, EH?
≷EHEM≶... GENTLEMEN, THE POINT IS...
...THAT ACCORDING TO THE *RULES,* ANY ROBOT THAT FORMALLY APPEARS IN THE MATCH HAS TO FIGHT *32 BOUTS!*
THAT'S ALL FINE 'N DANDY, BUT URAN'S STILL A *KID!!*
AH, BUT SHE'S ALSO A *ROBOT,* IF I'M NOT MISTAKEN!
SO ACCORDING TO THE RULES OF ROBOTTING, I MUST FORMALLY REQUEST THAT SHE APPEAR...
THEN I MUST BEG YOU TO LEAVE THE SCHOOL! URAN'S NOT AROUND...
CRACK
KATHUD
URAN?!!
ALL RIGHT, ASTRO... ARE YOU THE ONE WHO PUT URAN UP TO THIS?!
ACTUALLY, I ENTERED ON MY OWN, TEACHER....
I COULDN'T HELP IT! IT LOOKED LIKE *FUN!*
IF I'M NOT MISTAKEN, YOUNG URAN HERE IS SAYING SHE'D BE *GLAD* TO ENTER THE ROBOTTING FESTIVAL...

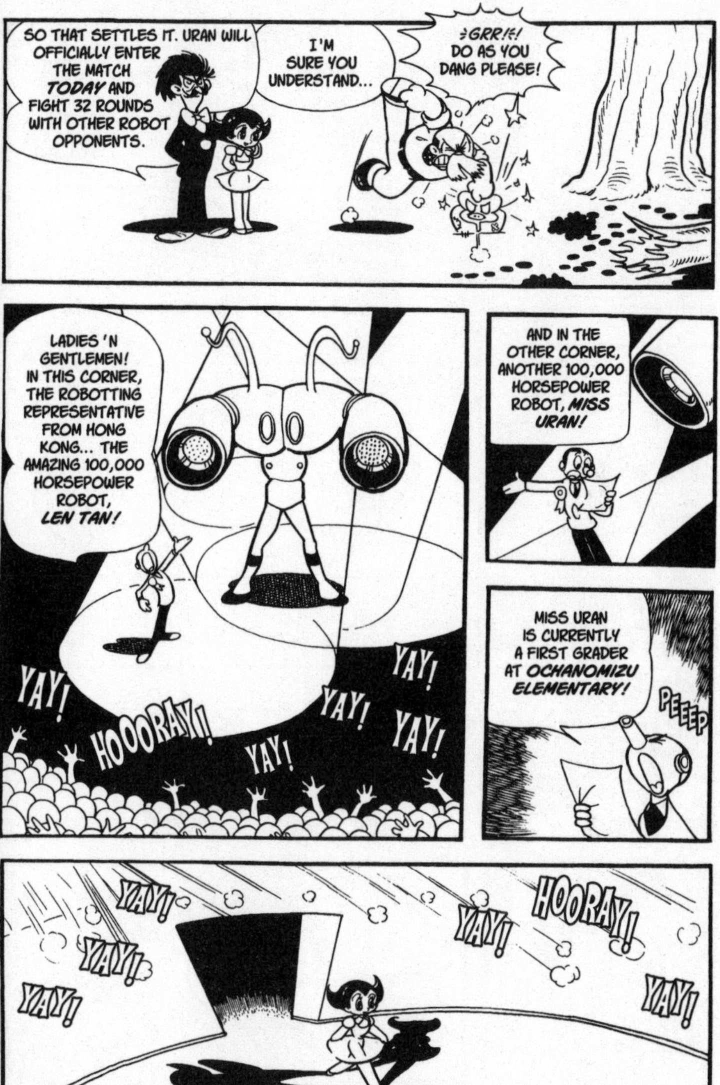
SO THAT SETTLES IT. URAN WILL OFFICIALLY ENTER THE MATCH *TODAY* AND FIGHT 32 ROUNDS WITH OTHER ROBOT OPPONENTS.
I'M SURE YOU UNDERSTAND...
GRR! DO AS YOU DANG PLEASE!
LADIES 'N GENTLEMEN! IN THIS CORNER, THE ROBOTTING REPRESENTATIVE FROM HONG KONG... THE AMAZING 100,000 HORSEPOWER ROBOT, *LEN TAN!*
YAY!
HOOORAY!!
YAY!
YAY!
YAY!
YAY!
AND IN THE OTHER CORNER, ANOTHER 100,000 HORSEPOWER ROBOT, *MISS URAN!*
MISS URAN IS CURRENTLY A FIRST GRADER AT *OCHANOMIZU ELEMENTARY!*
PEEEP
YAY!
YAY!
YAY!
YAY!
HOORAY!
YAY!

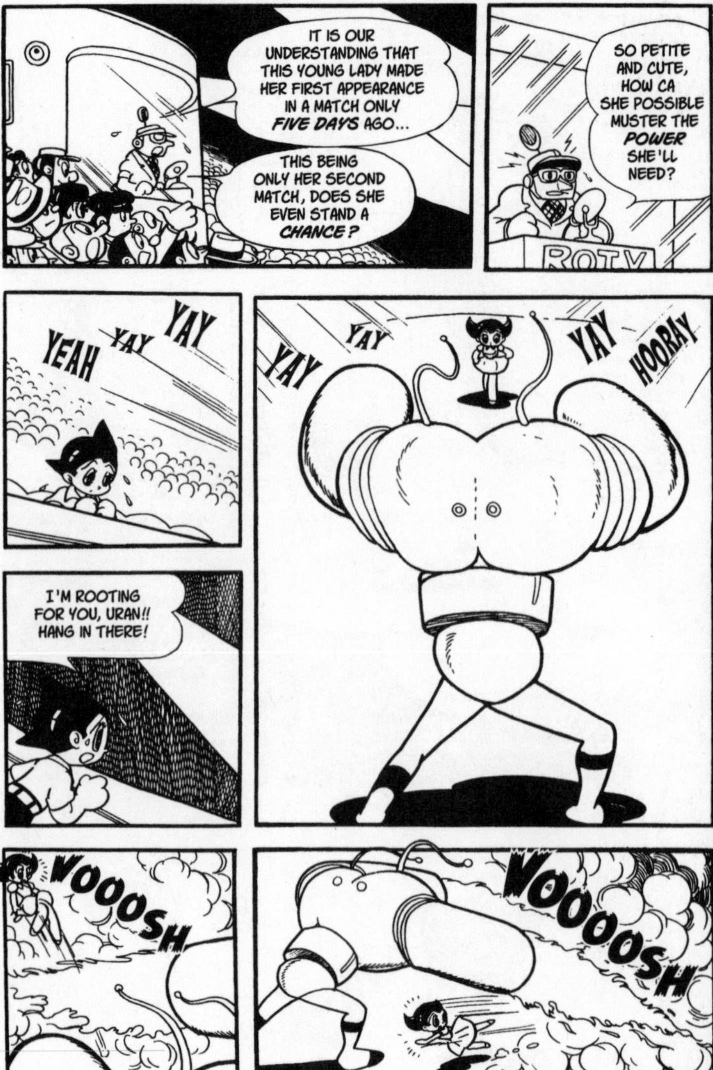
IT IS OUR UNDERSTANDING THAT THIS YOUNG LADY MADE HER FIRST APPEARANCE IN A MATCH ONLY FIVE DAYS AGO...
THIS BEING ONLY HER SECOND MATCH, DOES SHE EVEN STAND A CHANCE?
SO PETITE AND CUTE, HOW CA SHE POSSIBLE MUSTER THE POWER SHE'LL NEED?
ROTV
YEAH
YAY
YAY
I'M ROOTING FOR YOU, URAN!! HANG IN THERE!
YAY
YAY
YAY
HOORAY
VOOOOSH
VOOOOSH

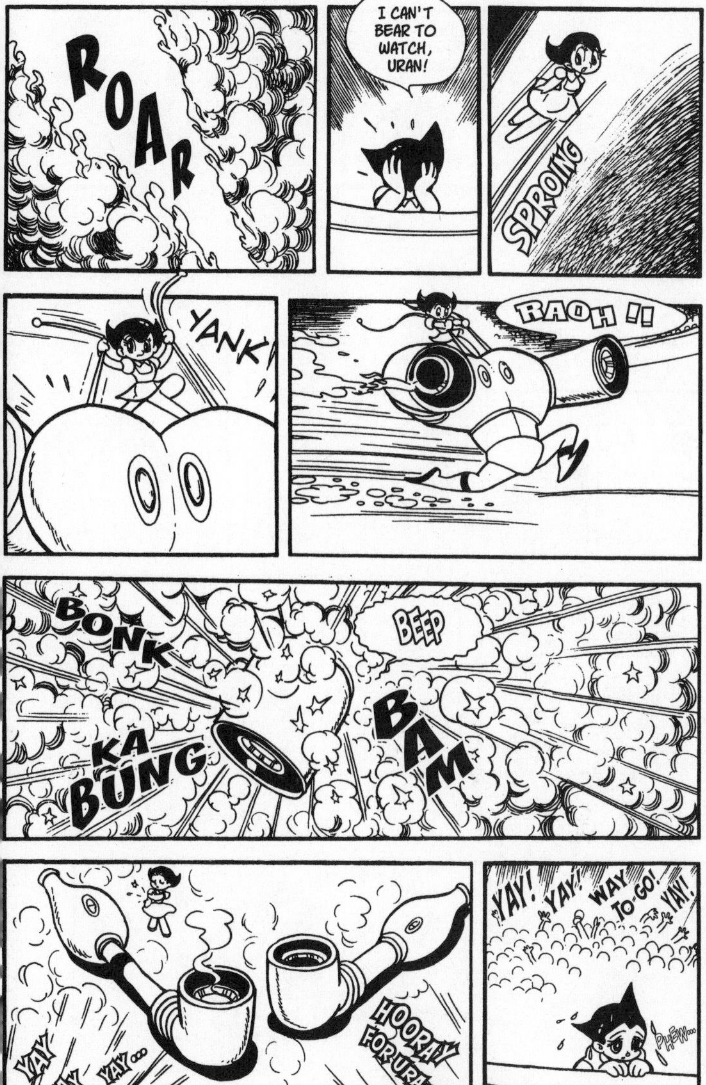
ROAR
I CAN'T BEAR TO WATCH, URAN!
SPROING
YANK
RAOH !!
BONK
BEEP
KA BUNG
BAM
YAY YAY YAY...
HOORAY FOR URAN!
YAY! YAY! WAY TO GO! YAY!
PHEW...

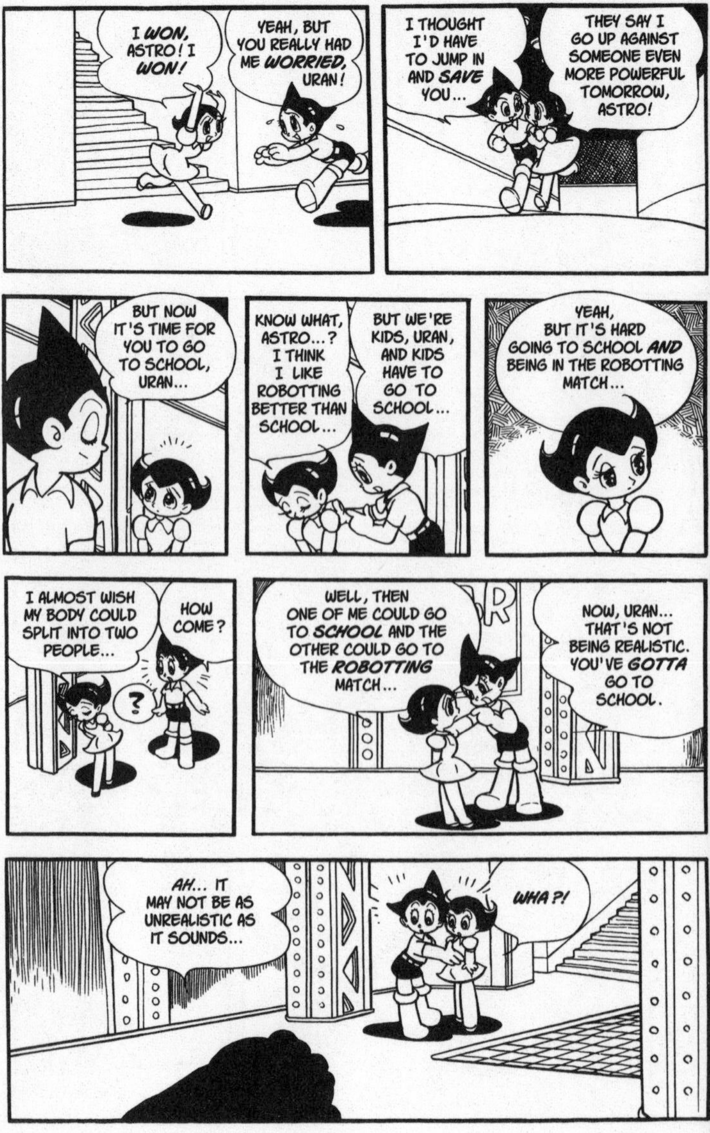
I WON, ASTRO! I WON!
YEAH, BUT YOU REALLY HAD ME WORRIED, URAN!
I THOUGHT I'D HAVE TO JUMP IN AND SAVE YOU...
THEY SAY I GO UP AGAINST SOMEONE EVEN MORE POWERFUL TOMORROW, ASTRO!
BUT NOW IT'S TIME FOR YOU TO GO TO SCHOOL, URAN...
KNOW WHAT, ASTRO...? I THINK I LIKE ROBOTTING BETTER THAN SCHOOL...
BUT WE'RE KIDS, URAN, AND KIDS HAVE TO GO TO SCHOOL...
YEAH, BUT IT'S HARD GOING TO SCHOOL AND BEING IN THE ROBOTTING MATCH...
I ALMOST WISH MY BODY COULD SPLIT INTO TWO PEOPLE...
HOW COME?
?
WELL, THEN ONE OF ME COULD GO TO SCHOOL AND THE OTHER COULD GO TO THE ROBOTTING MATCH...
NOW, URAN... THAT'S NOT BEING REALISTIC. YOU'VE GOTTA GO TO SCHOOL.
AH... IT MAY NOT BE AS UNREALISTIC AS IT SOUNDS...
WHA?!

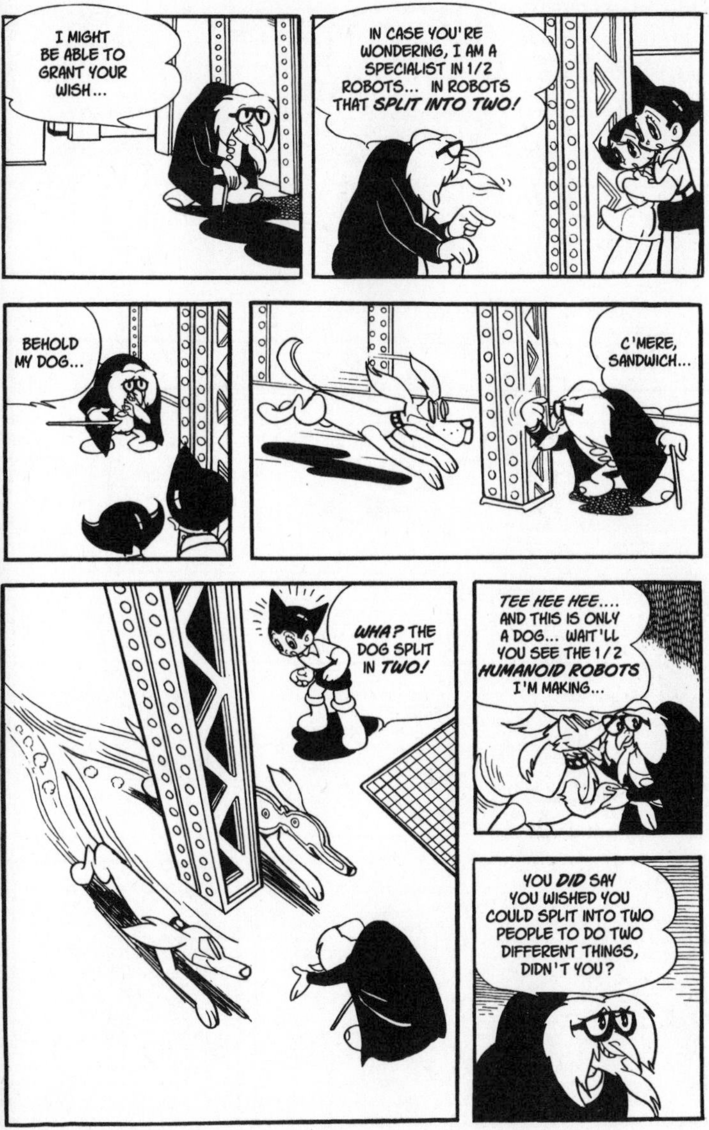

I MIGHT BE ABLE TO GRANT YOUR WISH...
IN CASE YOU'RE WONDERING, I AM A SPECIALIST IN 1/2 ROBOTS... IN ROBOTS THAT *SPLIT INTO TWO!*
BEHOLD MY DOG...
C'MERE, SANDWICH...
WHA? THE DOG SPLIT IN *TWO!*
TEE HEE HEE.... AND THIS IS ONLY A DOG... WAIT'LL YOU SEE THE 1/2 *HUMANOID ROBOTS* I'M MAKING...
YOU *DID* SAY YOU WISHED YOU COULD SPLIT INTO TWO PEOPLE TO DO TWO DIFFERENT THINGS, DIDN'T YOU?

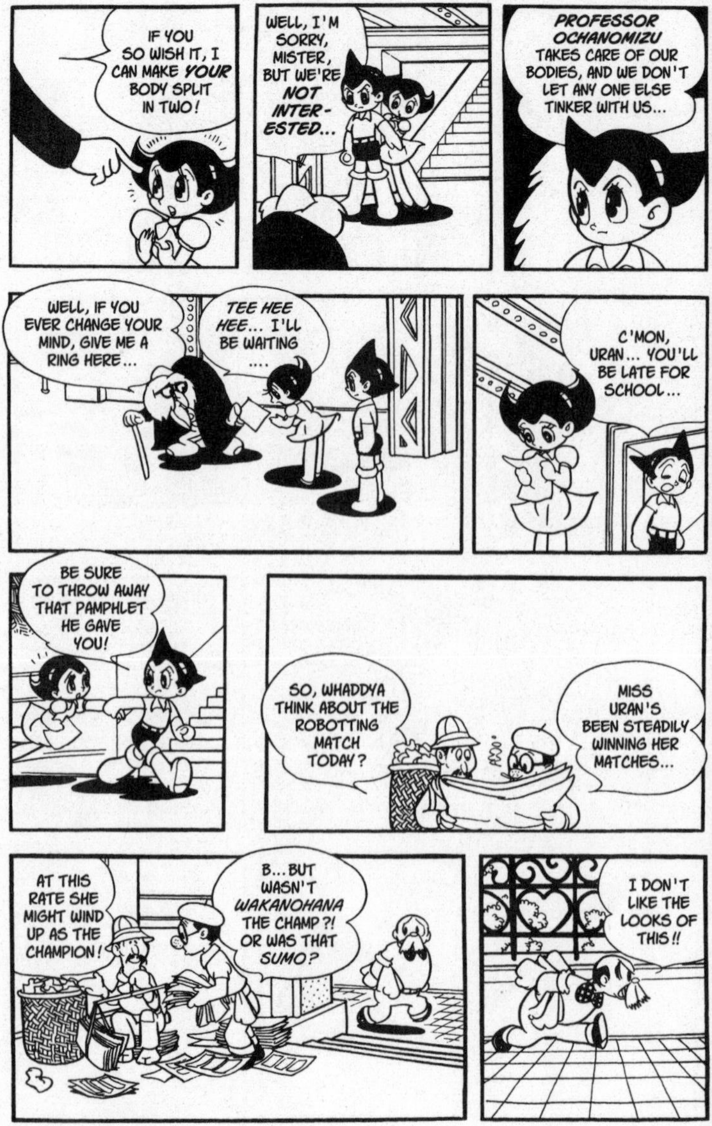
IF YOU SO WISH IT, I CAN MAKE *YOUR* BODY SPLIT IN TWO!
WELL, I'M SORRY, MISTER, BUT WE'RE *NOT INTERESTED*...
PROFESSOR OCHANOMIZU TAKES CARE OF OUR BODIES, AND WE DON'T LET ANY ONE ELSE TINKER WITH US...
WELL, IF YOU EVER CHANGE YOUR MIND, GIVE ME A RING HERE...
TEE HEE HEE... I'LL BE WAITING ....
C'MON, URAN... YOU'LL BE LATE FOR SCHOOL...
BE SURE TO THROW AWAY THAT PAMPHLET HE GAVE YOU!
SO, WHADDYA THINK ABOUT THE ROBOTTING MATCH TODAY?
MISS URAN'S BEEN STEADILY WINNING HER MATCHES...
AT THIS RATE SHE MIGHT WIND UP AS THE CHAMPION!
B... BUT WASN'T *WAKANOHANA* THE CHAMP?! OR WAS THAT *SUMO*?
I DON'T LIKE THE LOOKS OF THIS!!

COULD BE A *PROBLEM*...

HEY, URAN! URAN!

CAN WE HAVE YOUR AUTO-GRAPH?

UM, I DON'T KNOW HOW TO WRITE YET...

HI, URAN! WE'RE ROOTING FOR YOU TODAY...

DON'T WORRY... I'LL WIN...

URAN!!

GOSH, ALL OF A SUDDEN SHE'S SO *POPULAR*...

BEFORE I KNOW IT, SHE'LL BE FEATURED IN ONE OF THOSE WEEKLY IDOL MAGAZINES FOR GIRLS...

'N THAT WOULDN'T BE GOOD FOR URAN...

EVEN MORE WORRISOME...

... IS THAT SHE'LL LIKE FIGHTING MORE THAN STUDYING!!

TODAY'S ROBOTTING MATCH AGAIN STARS MISS URAN! THE HALL'S PACKED WITH HER FANS!

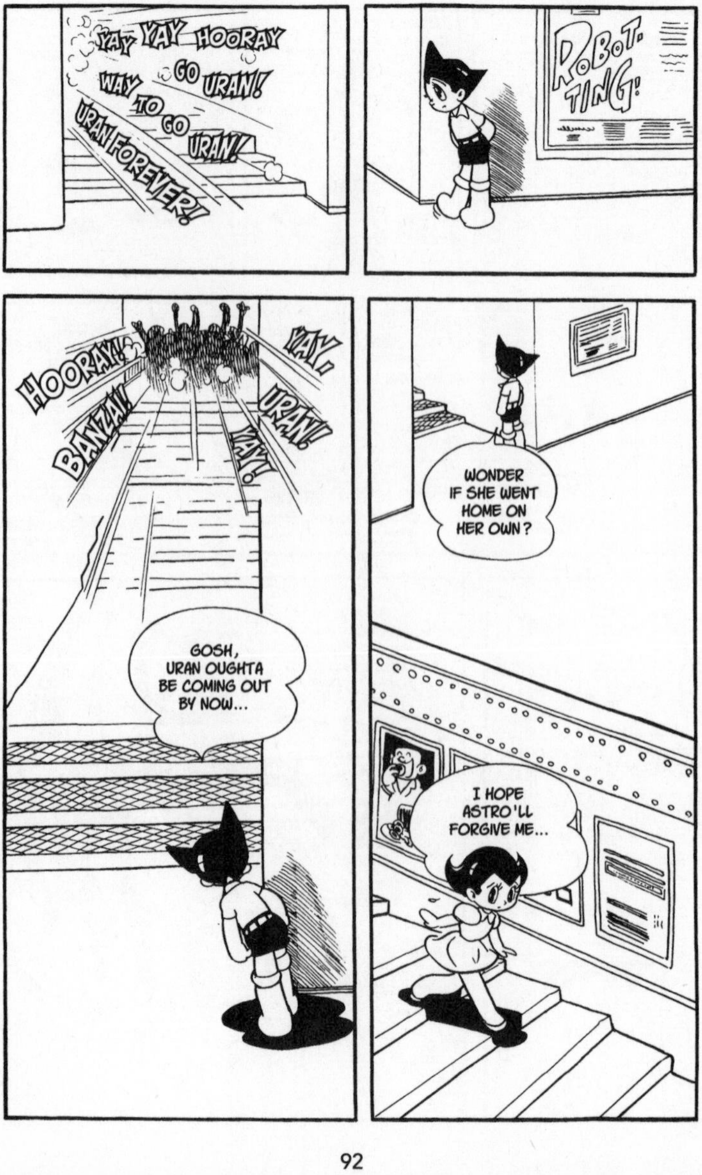

YAY YAY HOORAY
WAY TO GO URAN!
GO URAN!
URAN FOREVER!
ROBOT-TING!
HOORAY!
BANZAI!
YAY.
URAN!
YAY!
GOSH, URAN OUGHTA BE COMING OUT BY NOW...
WONDER IF SHE WENT HOME ON HER OWN?
I HOPE ASTRO'LL FORGIVE ME...

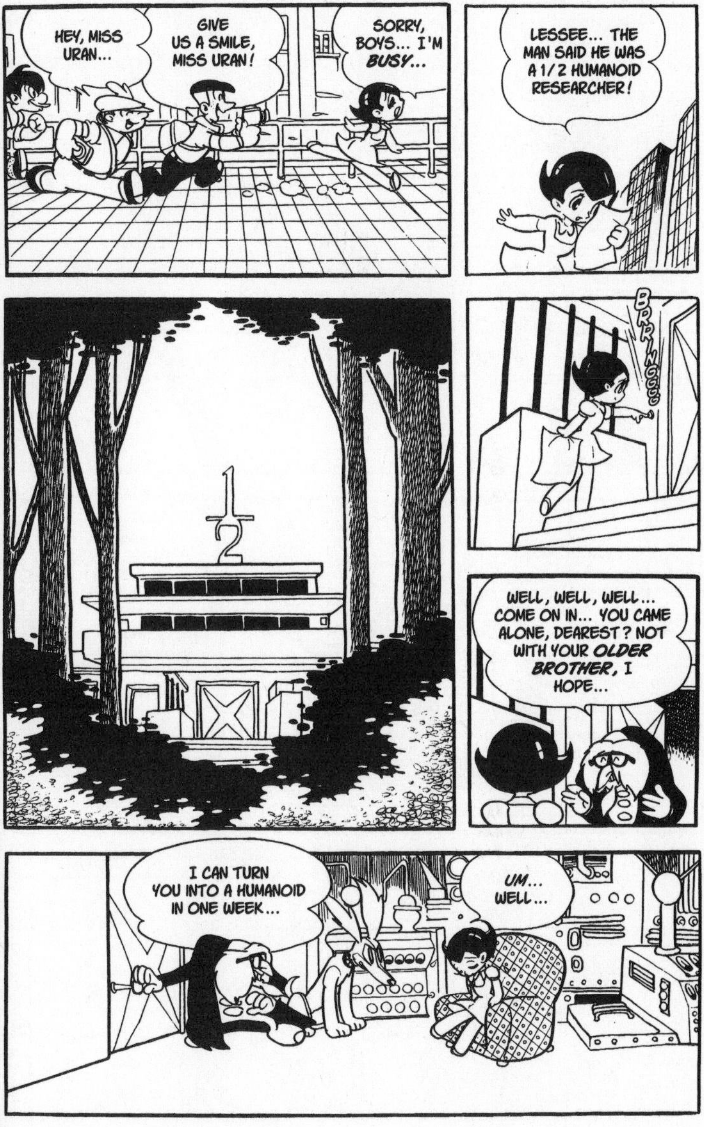
HEY, MISS URAN...
GIVE US A SMILE, MISS URAN!
SORRY, BOYS... I'M *BUSY*...
LESSEE... THE MAN SAID HE WAS A 1/2 HUMANOID RESEARCHER!
BRRINGGGG
WELL, WELL, WELL... COME ON IN... YOU CAME ALONE, DEAREST? NOT WITH YOUR *OLDER BROTHER*, I HOPE...
I CAN TURN YOU INTO A HUMANOID IN ONE WEEK...
UM... WELL...

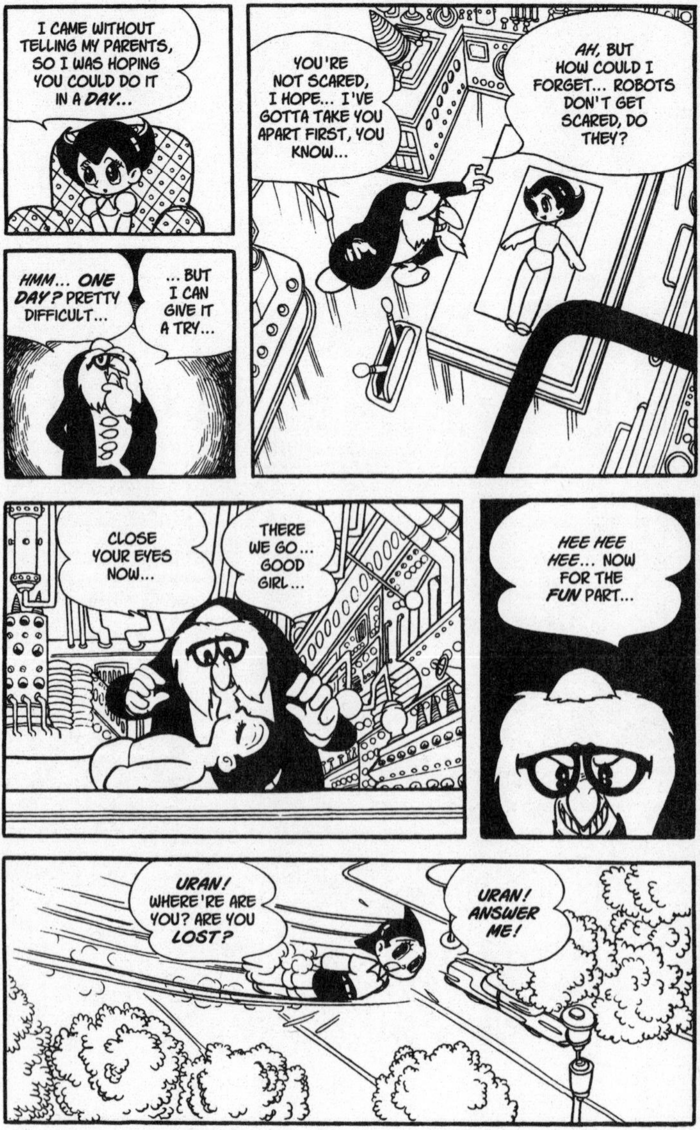
I CAME WITHOUT TELLING MY PARENTS, SO I WAS HOPING YOU COULD DO IT IN A *DAY*...
YOU'RE NOT SCARED, I HOPE... I'VE GOTTA TAKE YOU APART FIRST, YOU KNOW...
AH, BUT HOW COULD I FORGET... ROBOTS DON'T GET SCARED, DO THEY?
HMM... ONE DAY? PRETTY DIFFICULT...
... BUT I CAN GIVE IT A TRY...
CLOSE YOUR EYES NOW...
THERE WE GO... GOOD GIRL...
HEE HEE HEE... NOW FOR THE *FUN* PART...
URAN! WHERE'RE ARE YOU? ARE YOU *LOST?*
URAN! ANSWER ME!

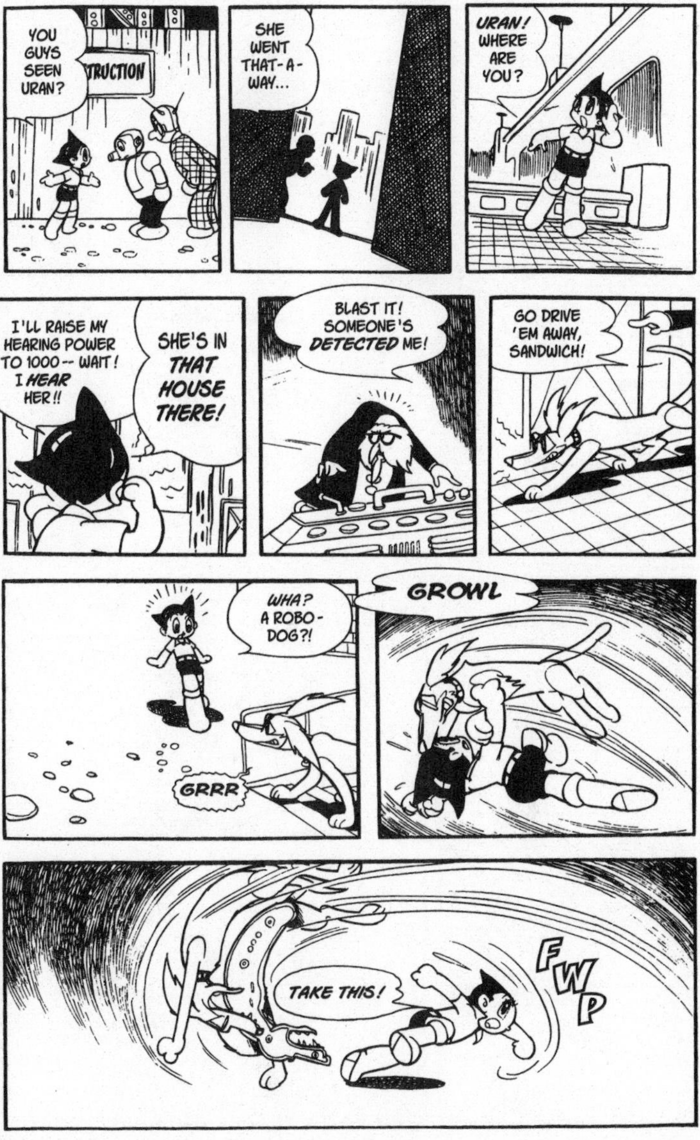
YOU GUYS SEEN URAN?
STRUCTION
SHE WENT THAT-A-WAY...
URAN! WHERE ARE YOU?
I'LL RAISE MY HEARING POWER TO 1000-- WAIT! I HEAR HER!!
SHE'S IN THAT HOUSE THERE!
BLAST IT! SOMEONE'S DETECTED ME!
GO DRIVE 'EM AWAY, SANDWICH!
WHA? A ROBO-DOG?!
GRRR
GROWL
TAKE THIS!
FWP

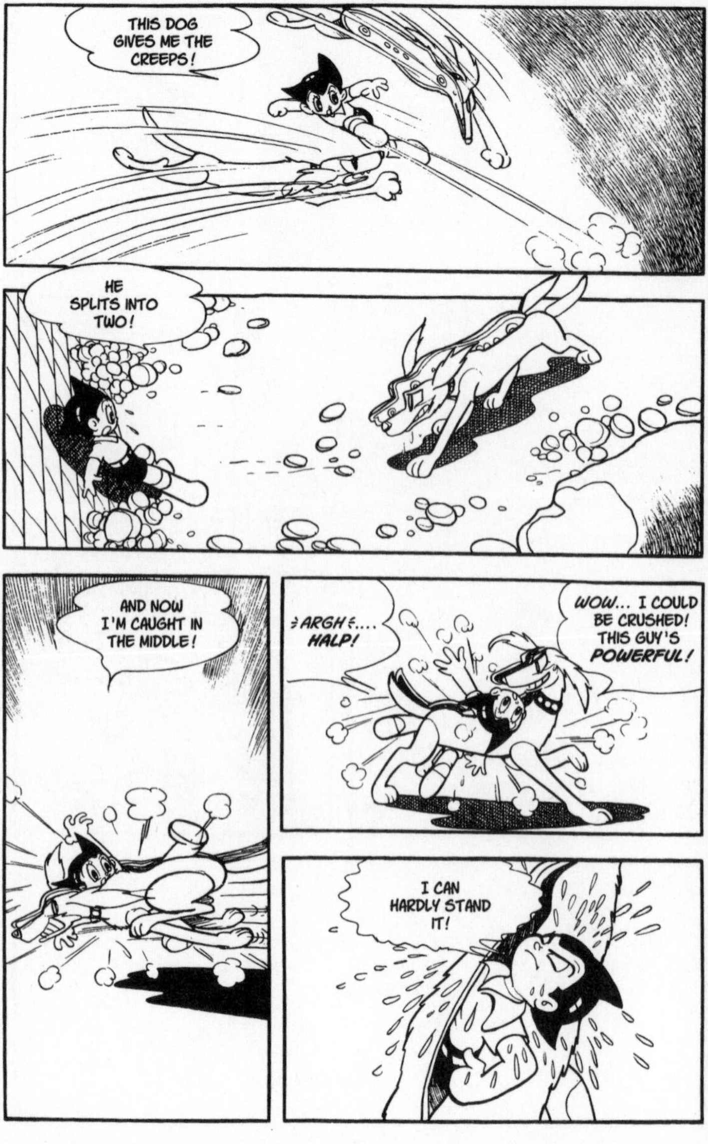
THIS DOG GIVES ME THE CREEPS!
HE SPLITS INTO TWO!
AND NOW I'M CAUGHT IN THE MIDDLE!
≉ARGH≉.... HALP!
WOW... I COULD BE CRUSHED! THIS GUY'S POWERFUL!
I CAN HARDLY STAND IT!

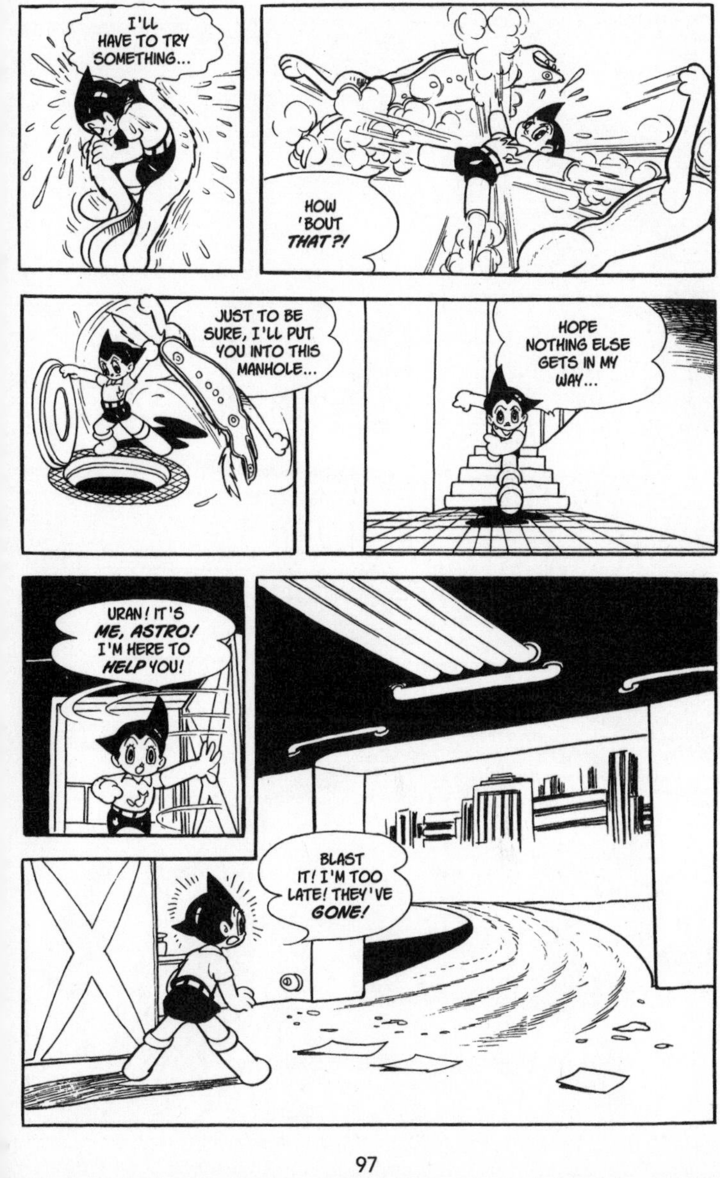
I'LL HAVE TO TRY SOMETHING...
HOW 'BOUT *THAT?!*
JUST TO BE SURE, I'LL PUT YOU INTO THIS MANHOLE...
HOPE NOTHING ELSE GETS IN MY WAY...
URAN! IT'S *ME, ASTRO!* I'M HERE TO *HELP* YOU!
BLAST IT! I'M TOO LATE! THEY'VE *GONE!*

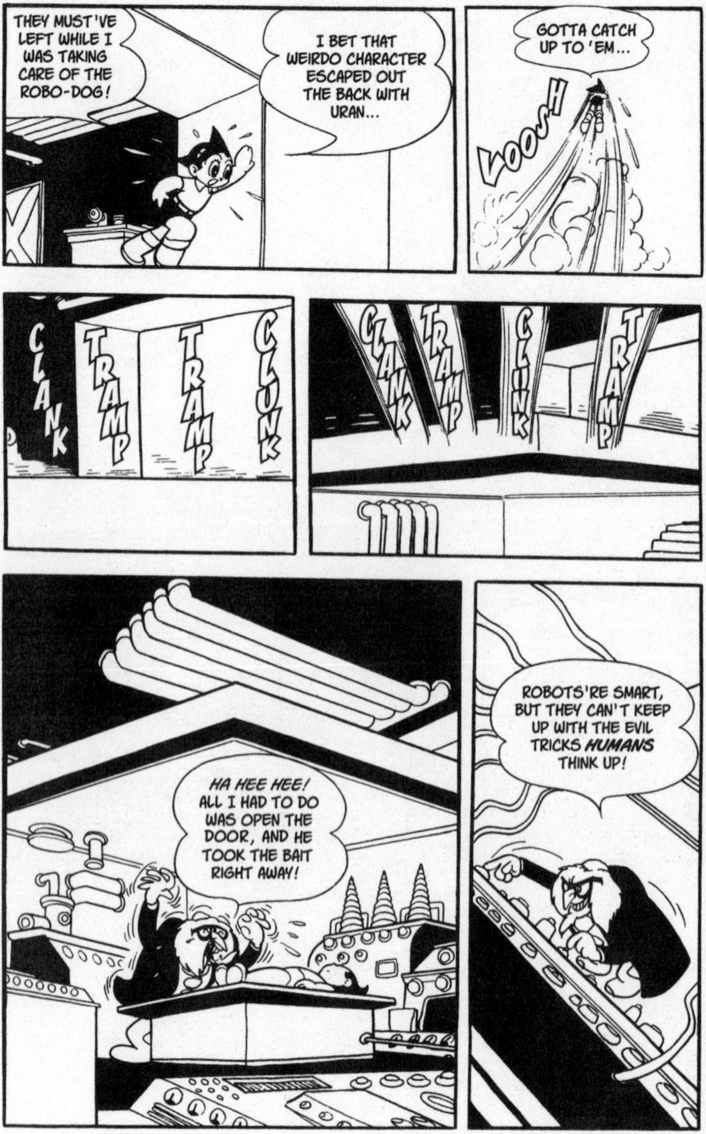
THEY MUST'VE LEFT WHILE I WAS TAKING CARE OF THE ROBO-DOG!
I BET THAT WEIRDO CHARACTER ESCAPED OUT THE BACK WITH URAN...
GOTTA CATCH UP TO 'EM...
VOOSH
CLANK
TRAMP
TRAMP
CLUNK
CLANK
TRAMP
CLINK
TRAMP
HA HEE HEE! ALL I HAD TO DO WAS OPEN THE DOOR, AND HE TOOK THE BAIT RIGHT AWAY!
ROBOTS'RE SMART, BUT THEY CAN'T KEEP UP WITH THE EVIL TRICKS *HUMANS* THINK UP!

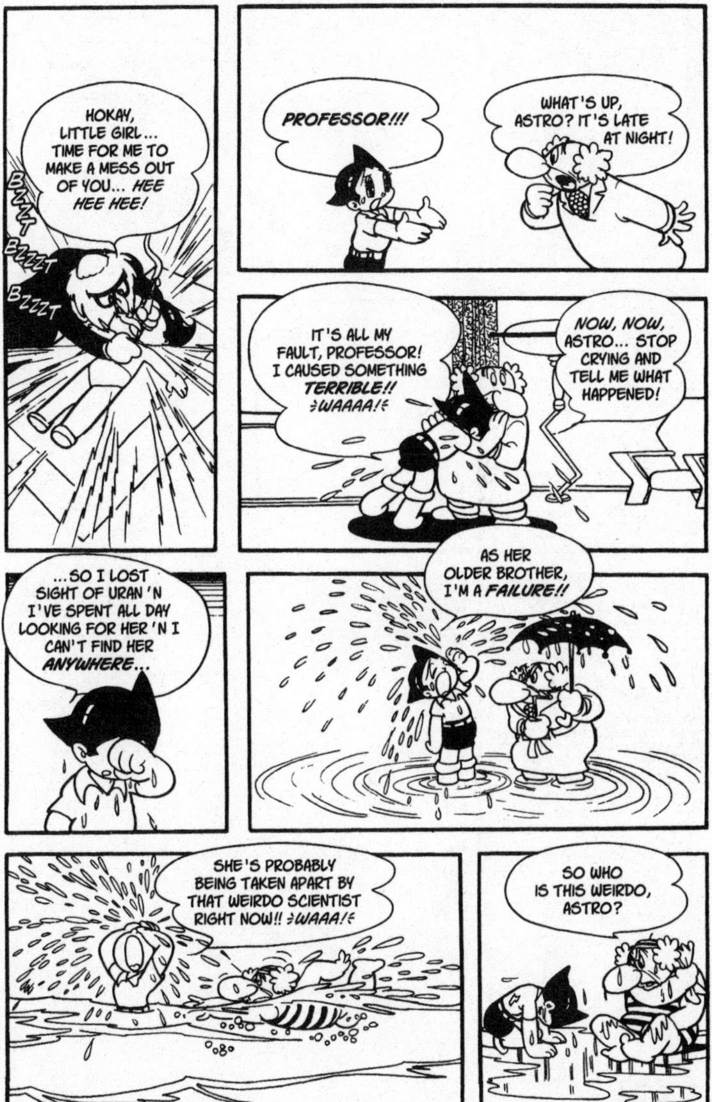

HOKAY, LITTLE GIRL... TIME FOR ME TO MAKE A MESS OUT OF YOU... HEE HEE HEE!
BZZZT BZZZZT BZZZZT
PROFESSOR!!!
WHAT'S UP, ASTRO? IT'S LATE AT NIGHT!
IT'S ALL MY FAULT, PROFESSOR! I CAUSED SOMETHING TERRIBLE!! WAAAA!
NOW, NOW, ASTRO... STOP CRYING AND TELL ME WHAT HAPPENED!
...SO I LOST SIGHT OF URAN 'N I'VE SPENT ALL DAY LOOKING FOR HER 'N I CAN'T FIND HER ANYWHERE...
AS HER OLDER BROTHER, I'M A FAILURE!!
SHE'S PROBABLY BEING TAKEN APART BY THAT WEIRDO SCIENTIST RIGHT NOW!! WAAA!
SO WHO IS THIS WEIRDO, ASTRO?

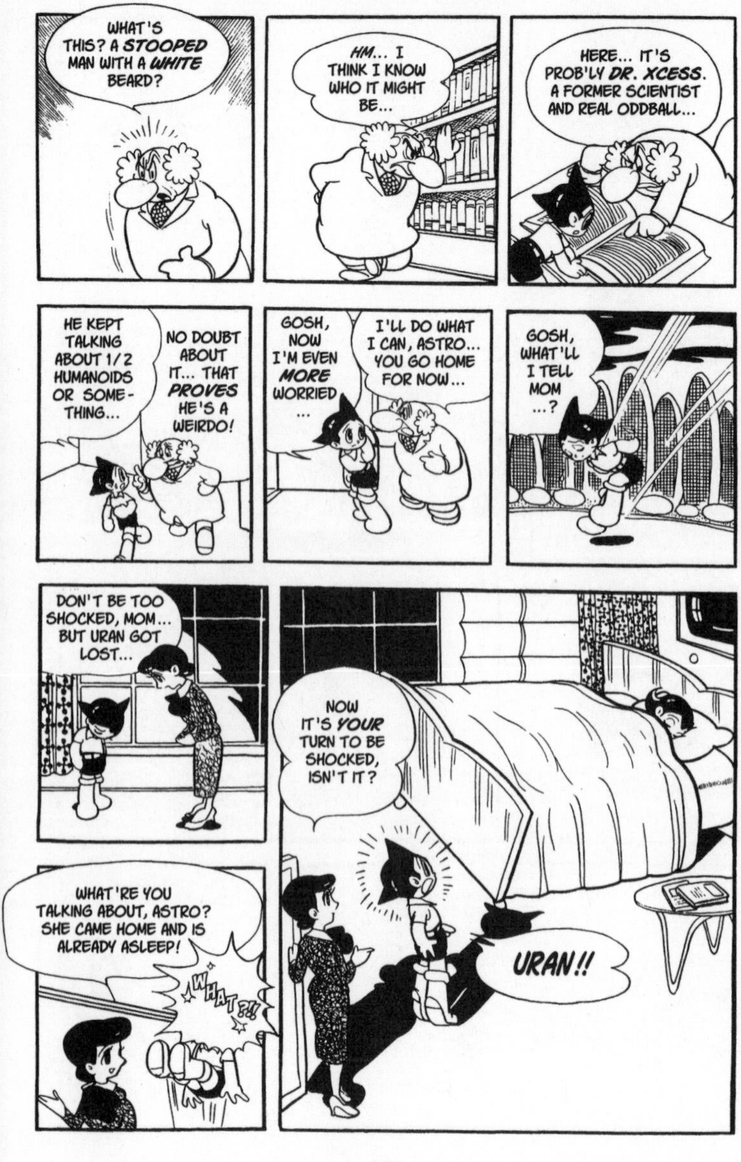
WHAT'S THIS? A STOOPED MAN WITH A WHITE BEARD?
HM... I THINK I KNOW WHO IT MIGHT BE...
HERE... IT'S PROB'LY DR. XCESS. A FORMER SCIENTIST AND REAL ODDBALL...
HE KEPT TALKING ABOUT 1/2 HUMANOIDS OR SOME-THING...
NO DOUBT ABOUT IT... THAT PROVES HE'S A WEIRDO!
GOSH, NOW I'M EVEN MORE WORRIED ...
I'LL DO WHAT I CAN, ASTRO... YOU GO HOME FOR NOW...
GOSH, WHAT'LL I TELL MOM ...?
DON'T BE TOO SHOCKED, MOM... BUT URAN GOT LOST...
WHAT'RE YOU TALKING ABOUT, ASTRO? SHE CAME HOME AND IS ALREADY ASLEEP!
WHAT?!!
NOW IT'S YOUR TURN TO BE SHOCKED, ISN'T IT?
URAN!!

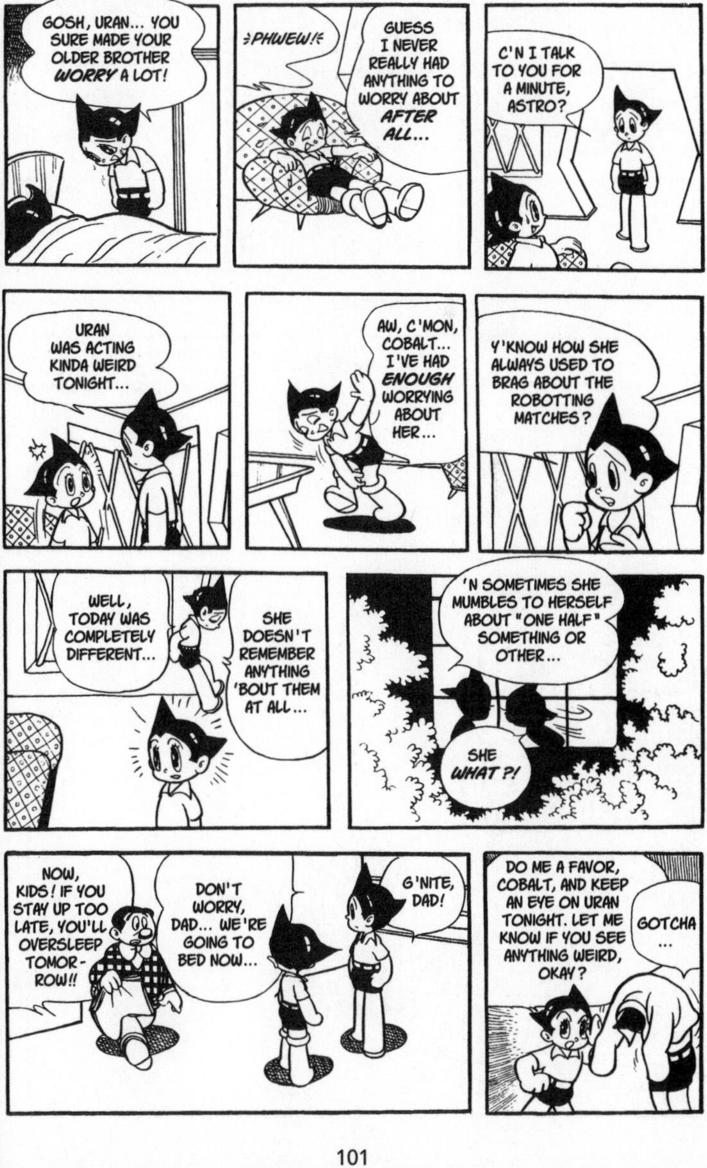
GOSH, URAN... YOU SURE MADE YOUR OLDER BROTHER WORRY A LOT!
PHWEW!
GUESS I NEVER REALLY HAD ANYTHING TO WORRY ABOUT AFTER ALL...
C'N I TALK TO YOU FOR A MINUTE, ASTRO?
URAN WAS ACTING KINDA WEIRD TONIGHT...
AW, C'MON, COBALT... I'VE HAD ENOUGH WORRYING ABOUT HER...
Y'KNOW HOW SHE ALWAYS USED TO BRAG ABOUT THE ROBOTTING MATCHES?
WELL, TODAY WAS COMPLETELY DIFFERENT...
SHE DOESN'T REMEMBER ANYTHING 'BOUT THEM AT ALL...
'N SOMETIMES SHE MUMBLES TO HERSELF ABOUT "ONE HALF" SOMETHING OR OTHER...
SHE WHAT?!
NOW, KIDS! IF YOU STAY UP TOO LATE, YOU'LL OVERSLEEP TOMOR-ROW!!
DON'T WORRY, DAD... WE'RE GOING TO BED NOW...
G'NITE, DAD!
DO ME A FAVOR, COBALT, AND KEEP AN EYE ON URAN TONIGHT. LET ME KNOW IF YOU SEE ANYTHING WEIRD, OKAY?
GOTCHA...

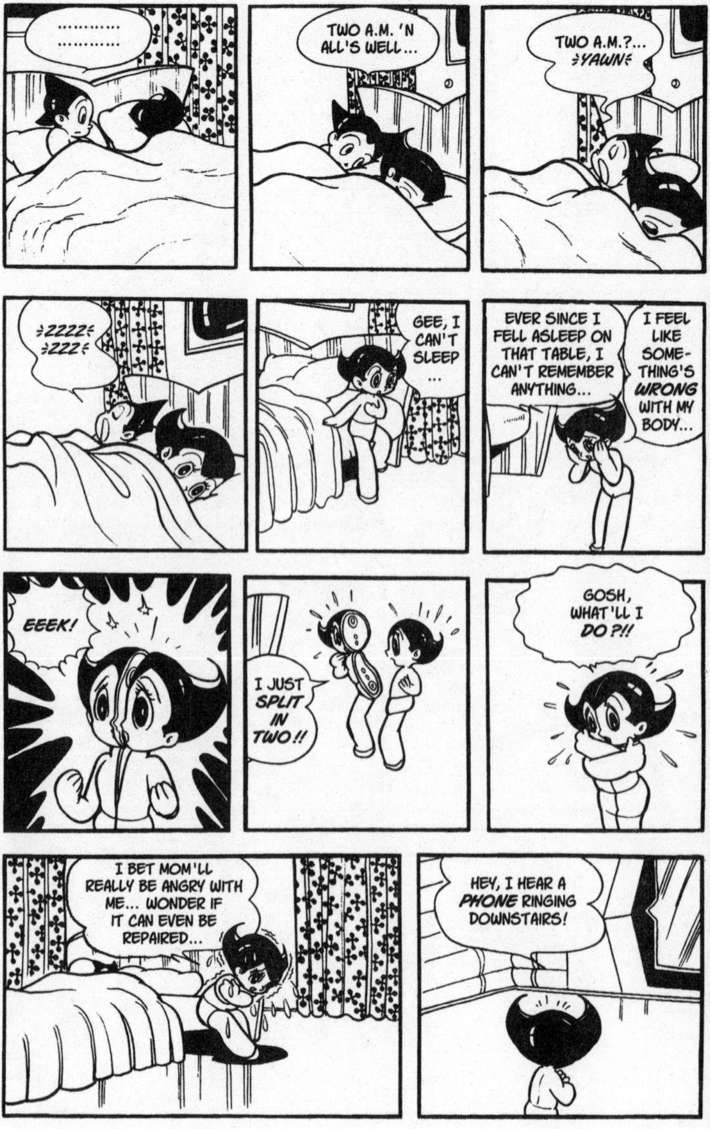

....
....
TWO A.M. 'N ALL'S WELL...
TWO A.M.?... YAWN
ZZZZ ZZZ
GEE, I CAN'T SLEEP ...
EVER SINCE I FELL ASLEEP ON THAT TABLE, I CAN'T REMEMBER ANYTHING...
I FEEL LIKE SOME-THING'S WRONG WITH MY BODY...
EEEK!
I JUST SPLIT IN TWO!!
GOSH, WHAT'LL I DO?!!
I BET MOM'LL REALLY BE ANGRY WITH ME... WONDER IF IT CAN EVEN BE REPAIRED...
HEY, I HEAR A PHONE RINGING DOWNSTAIRS!

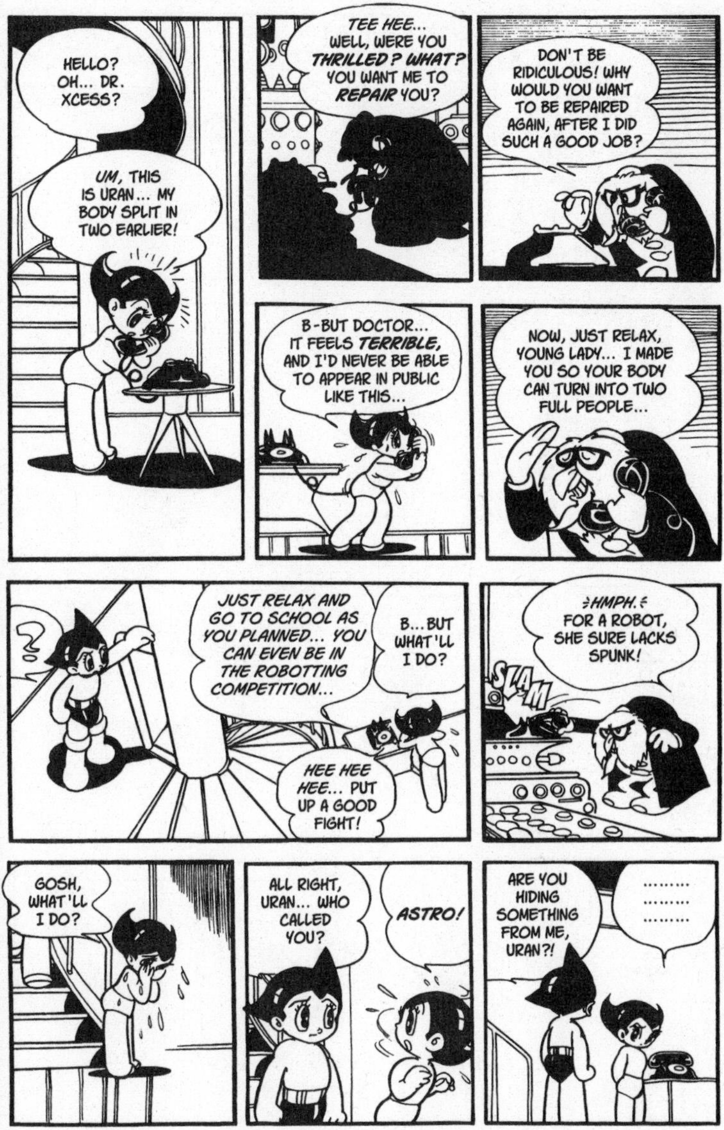
HELLO? OH... DR. XCESS?
UM, THIS IS URAN... MY BODY SPLIT IN TWO EARLIER!
TEE HEE... WELL, WERE YOU THRILLED? WHAT? YOU WANT ME TO REPAIR YOU?
DON'T BE RIDICULOUS! WHY WOULD YOU WANT TO BE REPAIRED AGAIN, AFTER I DID SUCH A GOOD JOB?
B-BUT DOCTOR... IT FEELS TERRIBLE, AND I'D NEVER BE ABLE TO APPEAR IN PUBLIC LIKE THIS...
NOW, JUST RELAX, YOUNG LADY... I MADE YOU SO YOUR BODY CAN TURN INTO TWO FULL PEOPLE...
JUST RELAX AND GO TO SCHOOL AS YOU PLANNED... YOU CAN EVEN BE IN THE ROBOTTING COMPETITION...
B... BUT WHAT'LL I DO?
HEE HEE HEE... PUT UP A GOOD FIGHT!
SLAM
HMPH. FOR A ROBOT, SHE SURE LACKS SPUNK!
GOSH, WHAT'LL I DO?
ALL RIGHT, URAN... WHO CALLED YOU?
ASTRO!
ARE YOU HIDING SOMETHING FROM ME, URAN?!
....
....
....

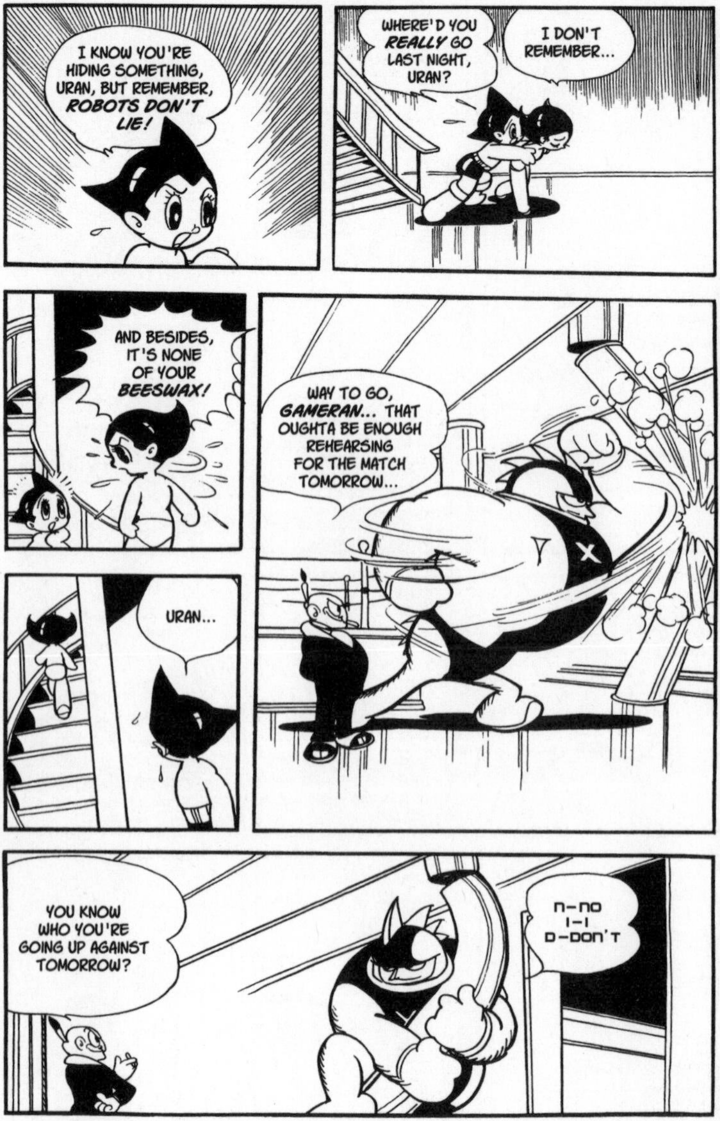

I KNOW YOU'RE HIDING SOMETHING, URAN, BUT REMEMBER, ***ROBOTS DON'T LIE!***
WHERE'D YOU ***REALLY*** GO LAST NIGHT, URAN?
I DON'T REMEMBER...
AND BESIDES, IT'S NONE OF YOUR ***BEESWAX!***
URAN...
WAY TO GO, ***GAMERAN...*** THAT OUGHTA BE ENOUGH REHEARSING FOR THE MATCH TOMORROW...
YOU KNOW WHO YOU'RE GOING UP AGAINST TOMORROW?
N-NO I-I D-DON'T

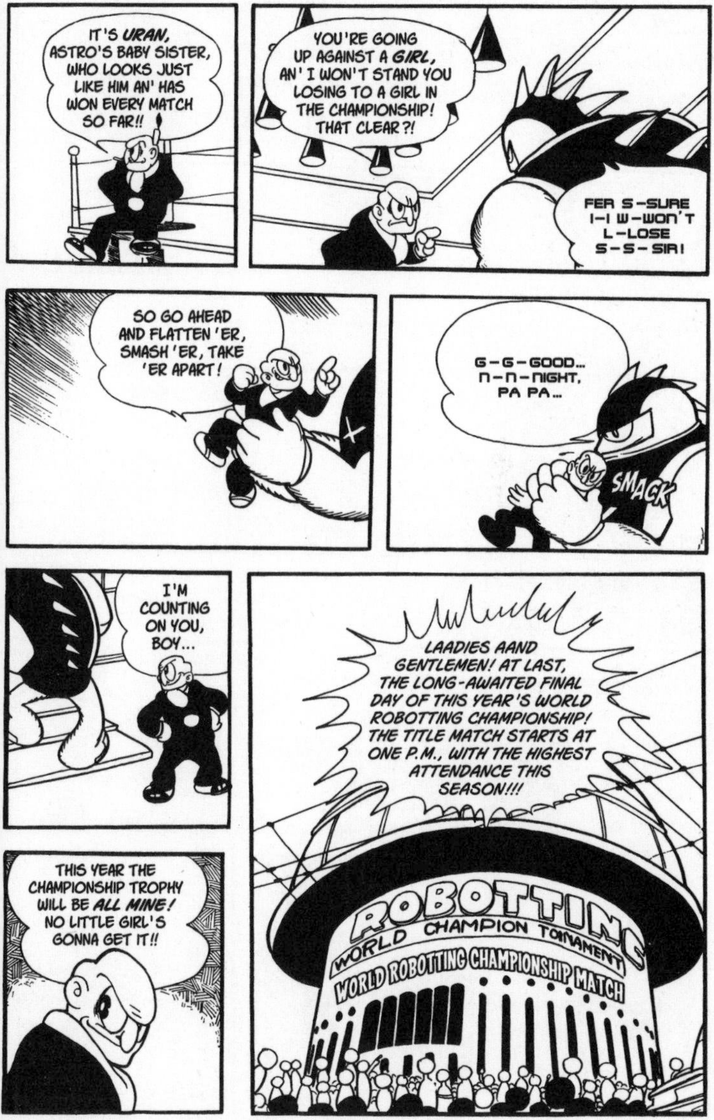

IT'S URAN, ASTRO'S BABY SISTER, WHO LOOKS JUST LIKE HIM AN' HAS WON EVERY MATCH SO FAR!!
YOU'RE GOING UP AGAINST A GIRL, AN' I WON'T STAND YOU LOSING TO A GIRL IN THE CHAMPIONSHIP! THAT CLEAR?!
FER S-SURE I-I W-WON'T L-LOSE S-S-SIR!
SO GO AHEAD AND FLATTEN 'ER, SMASH 'ER, TAKE 'ER APART!
G-G-GOOD... N-N-NIGHT, PA PA...
SMACK
I'M COUNTING ON YOU, BOY...
THIS YEAR THE CHAMPIONSHIP TROPHY WILL BE ALL MINE! NO LITTLE GIRL'S GONNA GET IT!!
LAADIES AAND GENTLEMEN! AT LAST, THE LONG-AWAITED FINAL DAY OF THIS YEAR'S WORLD ROBOTTING CHAMPIONSHIP! THE TITLE MATCH STARTS AT ONE P.M., WITH THE HIGHEST ATTENDANCE THIS SEASON!!!
ROBOTTING
WORLD CHAMPION TORNAMENT
WORLD ROBOTTING CHAMPIONSHIP MATCH

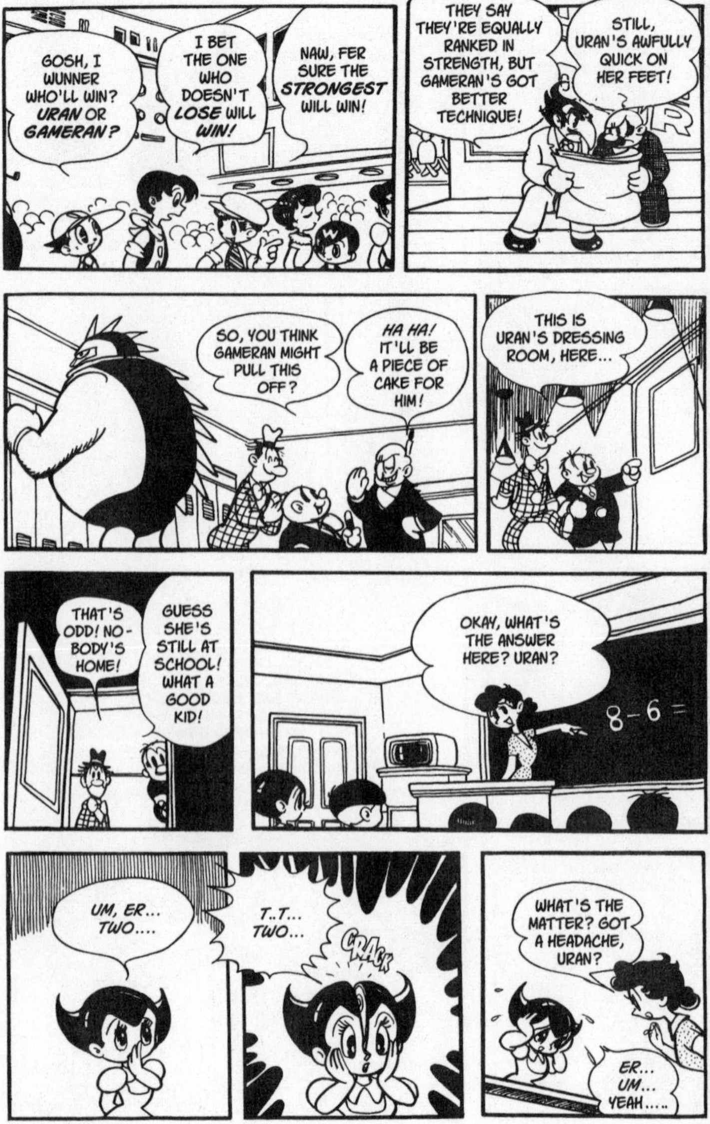
GOSH, I WUNNER WHO'LL WIN? URAN OR GAMERAN?
I BET THE ONE WHO DOESN'T LOSE WILL WIN!
NAW, FER SURE THE STRONGEST WILL WIN!
THEY SAY THEY'RE EQUALLY RANKED IN STRENGTH, BUT GAMERAN'S GOT BETTER TECHNIQUE!
STILL, URAN'S AWFULLY QUICK ON HER FEET!
SO, YOU THINK GAMERAN MIGHT PULL THIS OFF?
HA HA! IT'LL BE A PIECE OF CAKE FOR HIM!
THIS IS URAN'S DRESSING ROOM, HERE...
THAT'S ODD! NO-BODY'S HOME!
GUESS SHE'S STILL AT SCHOOL! WHAT A GOOD KID!
OKAY, WHAT'S THE ANSWER HERE? URAN?
8-6=
UM, ER... TWO....
T..T... TWO...
CRACK
WHAT'S THE MATTER? GOT A HEADACHE, URAN?
ER... UM... YEAH.....

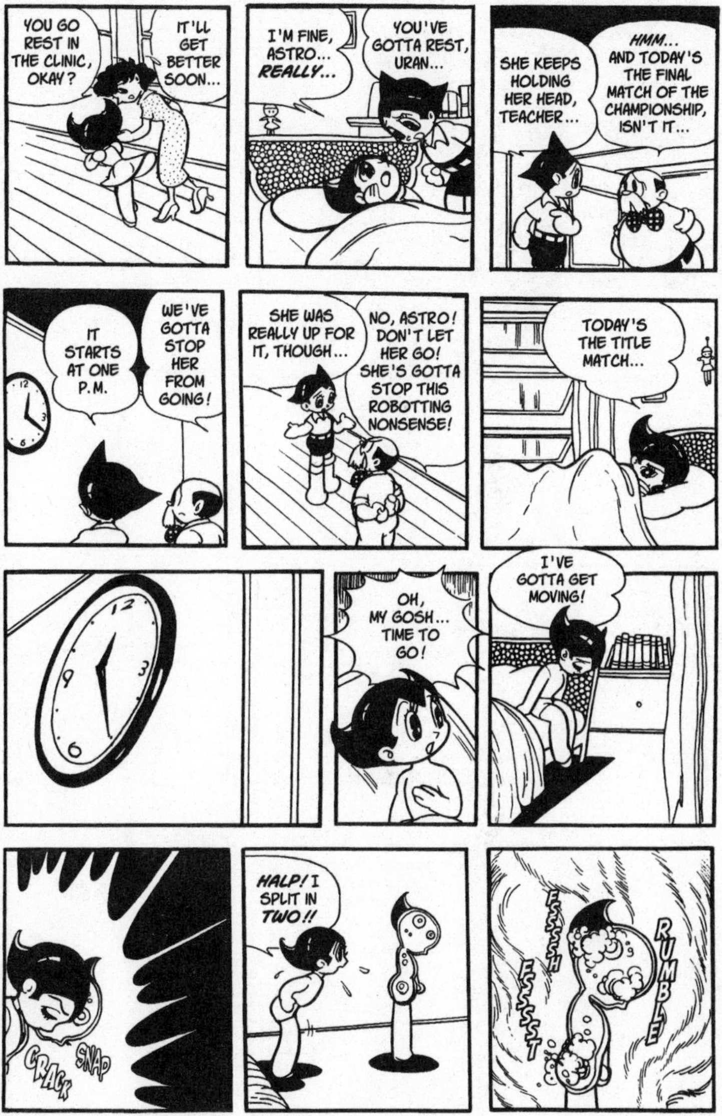
YOU GO REST IN THE CLINIC, OKAY?
IT'LL GET BETTER SOON...
I'M FINE, ASTRO... *REALLY*...
YOU'VE GOTTA REST, URAN...
SHE KEEPS HOLDING HER HEAD, TEACHER...
HMM... AND TODAY'S THE FINAL MATCH OF THE CHAMPIONSHIP, ISN'T IT...
IT STARTS AT ONE P.M.
WE'VE GOTTA STOP HER FROM GOING!
SHE WAS REALLY UP FOR IT, THOUGH...
NO, ASTRO! DON'T LET HER GO! SHE'S GOTTA STOP THIS ROBOTTING NONSENSE!
TODAY'S THE TITLE MATCH...
OH, MY GOSH... TIME TO GO!
I'VE GOTTA GET MOVING!
CRACK
SNAP
HALP! I SPLIT IN *TWO*!!
FSSSH
FSSST
RUMBLE

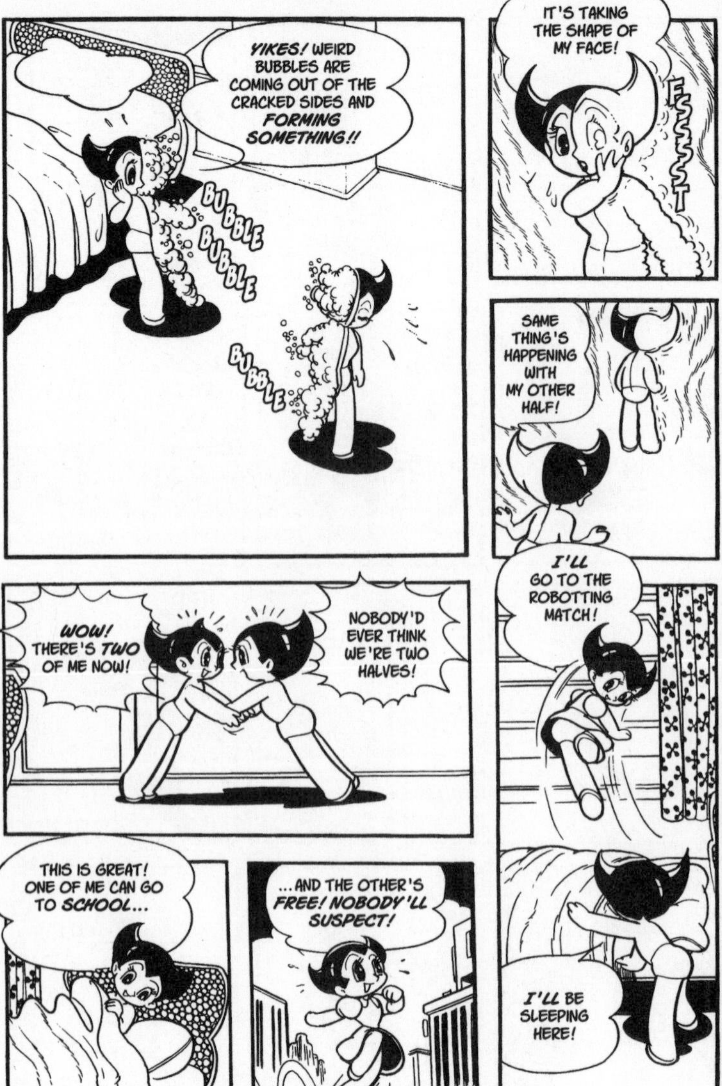
YIKES! WEIRD BUBBLES ARE COMING OUT OF THE CRACKED SIDES AND FORMING SOMETHING!!
BUBBLE
BUBBLE
BUBBLE
IT'S TAKING THE SHAPE OF MY FACE!
FSSSST
SAME THING'S HAPPENING WITH MY OTHER HALF!
WOW! THERE'S TWO OF ME NOW!
NOBODY'D EVER THINK WE'RE TWO HALVES!
THIS IS GREAT! ONE OF ME CAN GO TO SCHOOL...
...AND THE OTHER'S FREE! NOBODY'LL SUSPECT!
I'LL GO TO THE ROBOTTING MATCH!
I'LL BE SLEEPING HERE!

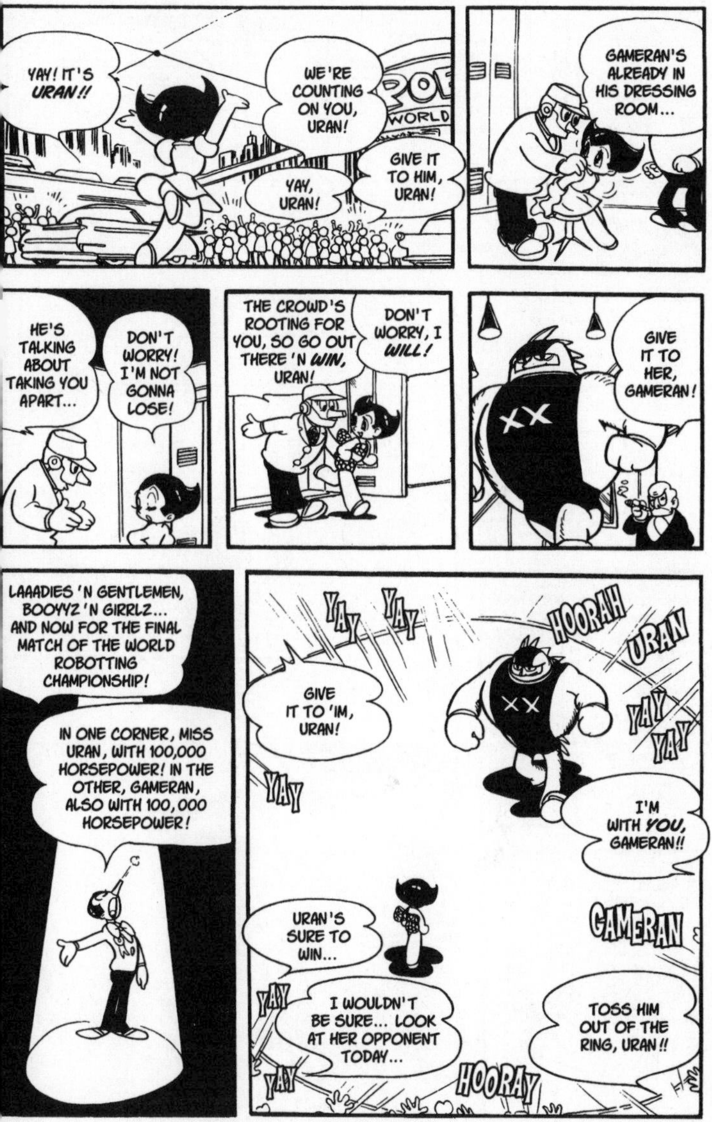
YAY! IT'S URAN!!
WE'RE COUNTING ON YOU, URAN!
YAY, URAN!
GIVE IT TO HIM, URAN!
GAMERAN'S ALREADY IN HIS DRESSING ROOM...
HE'S TALKING ABOUT TAKING YOU APART...
DON'T WORRY! I'M NOT GONNA LOSE!
THE CROWD'S ROOTING FOR YOU, SO GO OUT THERE 'N WIN, URAN!
DON'T WORRY, I WILL!
GIVE IT TO HER, GAMERAN!
LAAADIES 'N GENTLEMEN, BOOYYZ 'N GIRRLZ... AND NOW FOR THE FINAL MATCH OF THE WORLD ROBOTTING CHAMPIONSHIP!
IN ONE CORNER, MISS URAN, WITH 100,000 HORSEPOWER! IN THE OTHER, GAMERAN, ALSO WITH 100,000 HORSEPOWER!
YAY
YAY
HOORAH
URAN
GIVE IT TO 'IM, URAN!
YAY
YAY
YAY
I'M WITH YOU, GAMERAN!!
GAMERAN
URAN'S SURE TO WIN...
YAY
I WOULDN'T BE SURE... LOOK AT HER OPPONENT TODAY...
TOSS HIM OUT OF THE RING, URAN!!
YAY
HOORAY

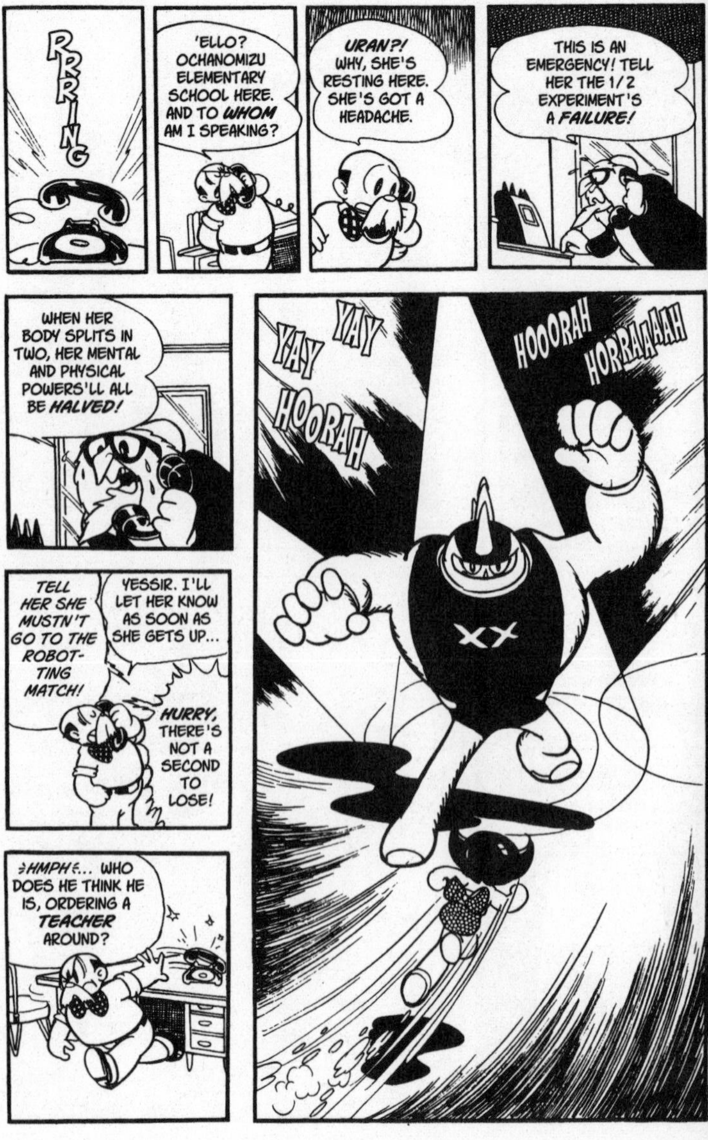
RRRING
'ELLO? OCHANOMIZU ELEMENTARY SCHOOL HERE. AND TO WHOM AM I SPEAKING?
URAN?! WHY, SHE'S RESTING HERE. SHE'S GOT A HEADACHE.
THIS IS AN EMERGENCY! TELL HER THE 1/2 EXPERIMENT'S A FAILURE!
WHEN HER BODY SPLITS IN TWO, HER MENTAL AND PHYSICAL POWERS'LL ALL BE HALVED!
TELL HER SHE MUSTN'T GO TO THE ROBOT-TING MATCH!
YESSIR. I'LL LET HER KNOW AS SOON AS SHE GETS UP...
HURRY, THERE'S NOT A SECOND TO LOSE!
HMPH... WHO DOES HE THINK HE IS, ORDERING A TEACHER AROUND?
YAY
YAY
HOOORAH
HORRAAAAH
HOORAH
XX

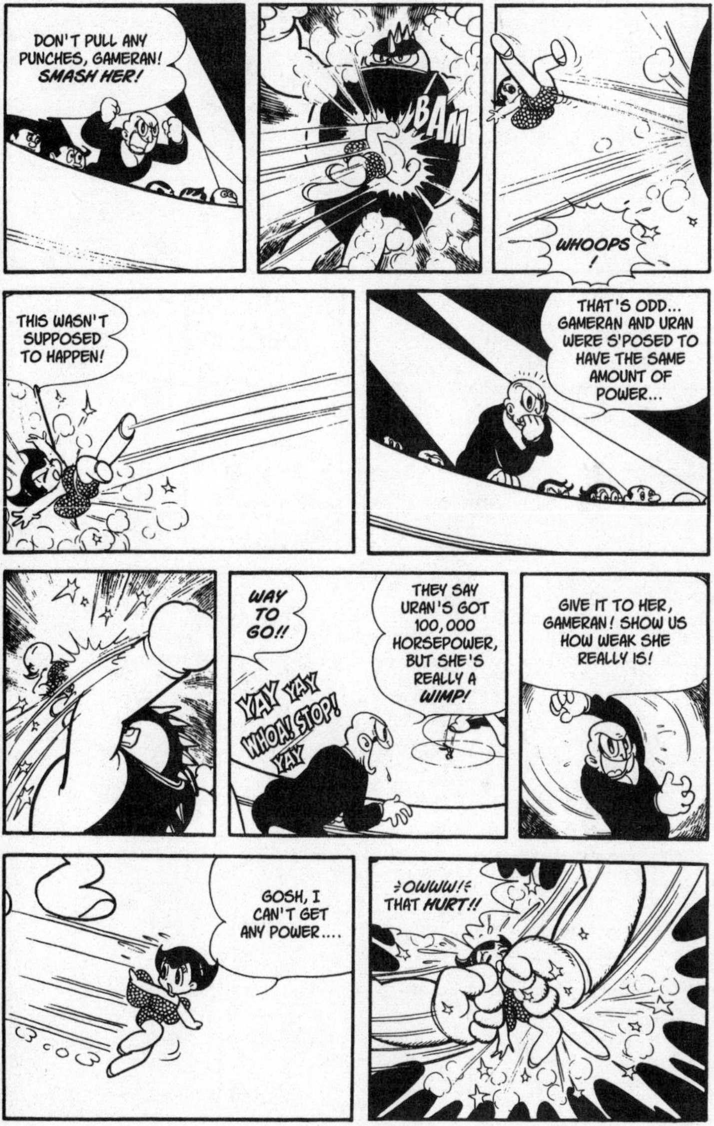
DON'T PULL ANY PUNCHES, GAMERAN! SMASH HER!
BAM
WHOOPS!
THIS WASN'T SUPPOSED TO HAPPEN!
THAT'S ODD... GAMERAN AND URAN WERE S'POSED TO HAVE THE SAME AMOUNT OF POWER...
WAY TO GO!!
YAY YAY
WHOA! STOP!
YAY
THEY SAY URAN'S GOT 100,000 HORSEPOWER, BUT SHE'S REALLY A WIMP!
GIVE IT TO HER, GAMERAN! SHOW US HOW WEAK SHE REALLY IS!
GOSH, I CAN'T GET ANY POWER....
OWWW!
THAT HURT!!

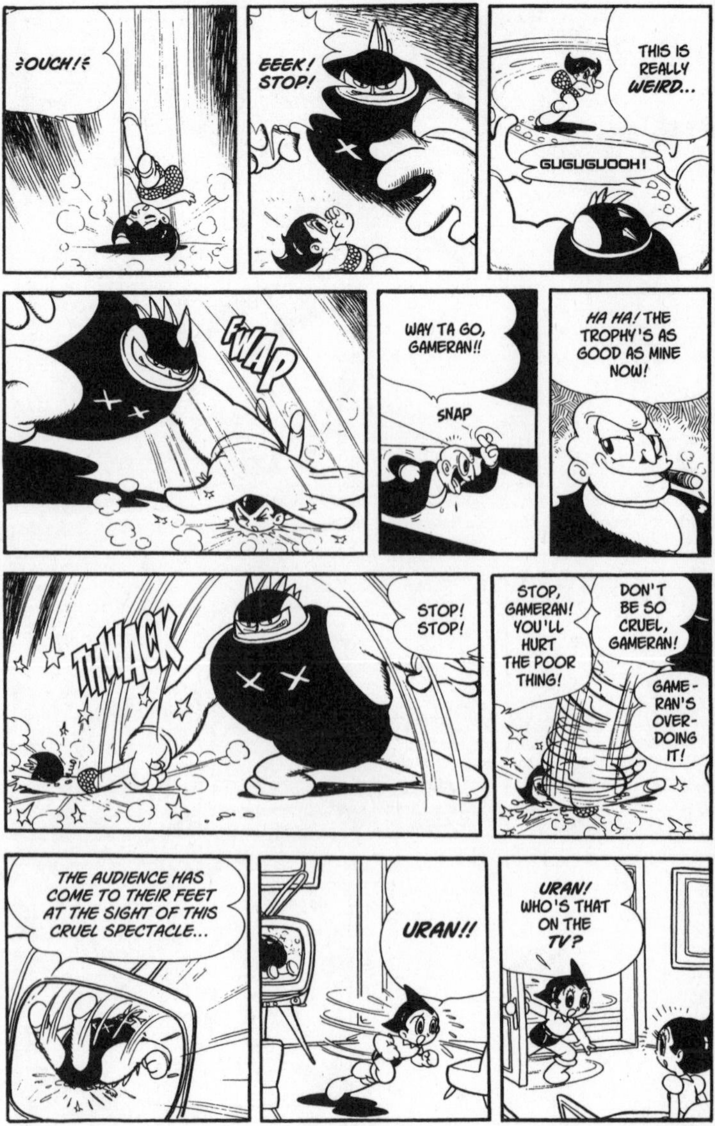

OUCH!
EEEK! STOP!
THIS IS REALLY WEIRD...
GUGUGUOOH!
FWAP
WAY TA GO, GAMERAN!!
SNAP
HA HA! THE TROPHY'S AS GOOD AS MINE NOW!
THWACK
STOP! STOP!
STOP, GAMERAN! YOU'LL HURT THE POOR THING!
DON'T BE SO CRUEL, GAMERAN!
GAME-RAN'S OVER-DOING IT!
THE AUDIENCE HAS COME TO THEIR FEET AT THE SIGHT OF THIS CRUEL SPECTACLE...
URAN!!
URAN! WHO'S THAT ON THE TV?

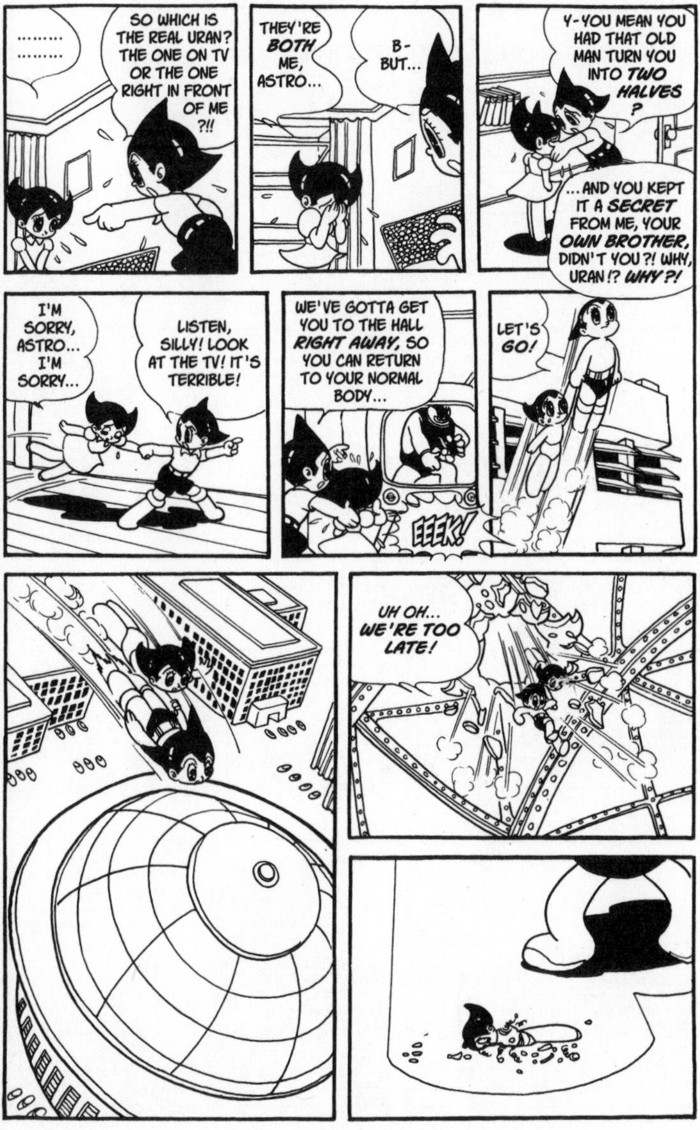
....
....
SO WHICH IS THE REAL URAN? THE ONE ON TV OR THE ONE RIGHT IN FRONT OF ME ?!!
THEY'RE BOTH ME, ASTRO...
B-BUT...
Y-YOU MEAN YOU HAD THAT OLD MAN TURN YOU INTO TWO HALVES ?
...AND YOU KEPT IT A SECRET FROM ME, YOUR OWN BROTHER, DIDN'T YOU?! WHY, URAN!? WHY?!
I'M SORRY, ASTRO... I'M SORRY...
LISTEN, SILLY! LOOK AT THE TV! IT'S TERRIBLE!
WE'VE GOTTA GET YOU TO THE HALL RIGHT AWAY, SO YOU CAN RETURN TO YOUR NORMAL BODY...
EEEK!
LET'S GO!
UH OH... WE'RE TOO LATE!

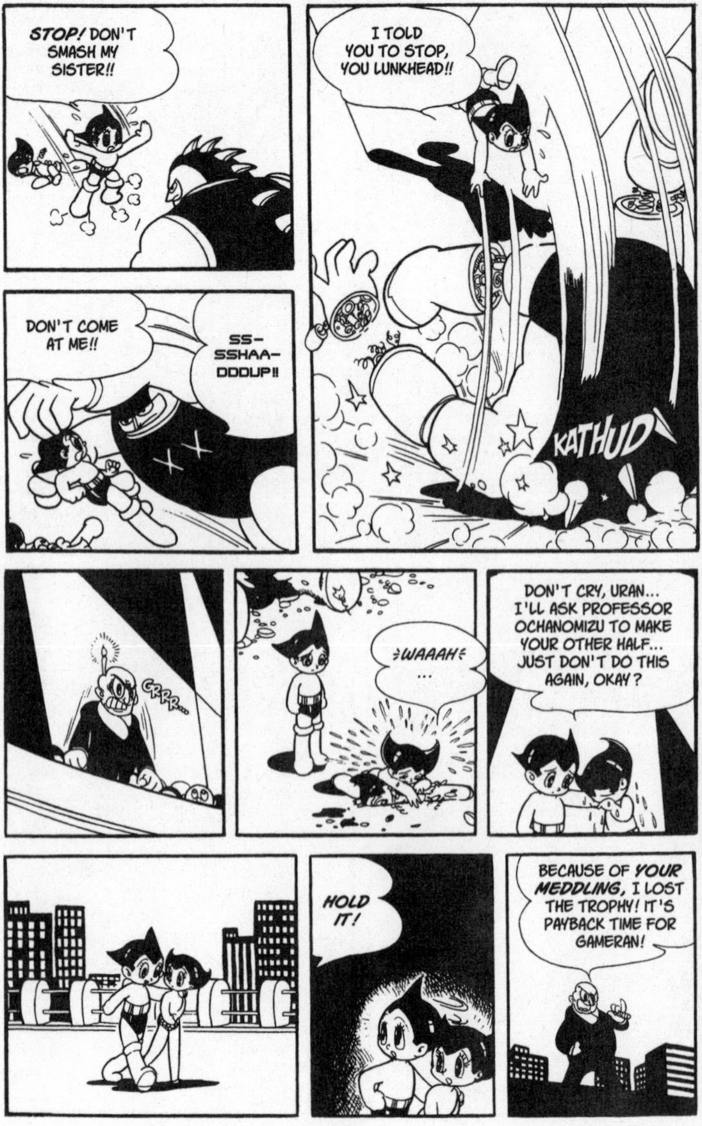

STOP! DON'T SMASH MY SISTER!!
I TOLD YOU TO STOP, YOU LUNKHEAD!!
DON'T COME AT ME!!
SS-SSHAA-DDDUP!!
KATHUD
GRRR...
≶WAAAH≶ ...
DON'T CRY, URAN... I'LL ASK PROFESSOR OCHANOMIZU TO MAKE YOUR OTHER HALF... JUST DON'T DO THIS AGAIN, OKAY?
HOLD IT!
BECAUSE OF YOUR MEDDLING, I LOST THE TROPHY! IT'S PAYBACK TIME FOR GAMERAN!

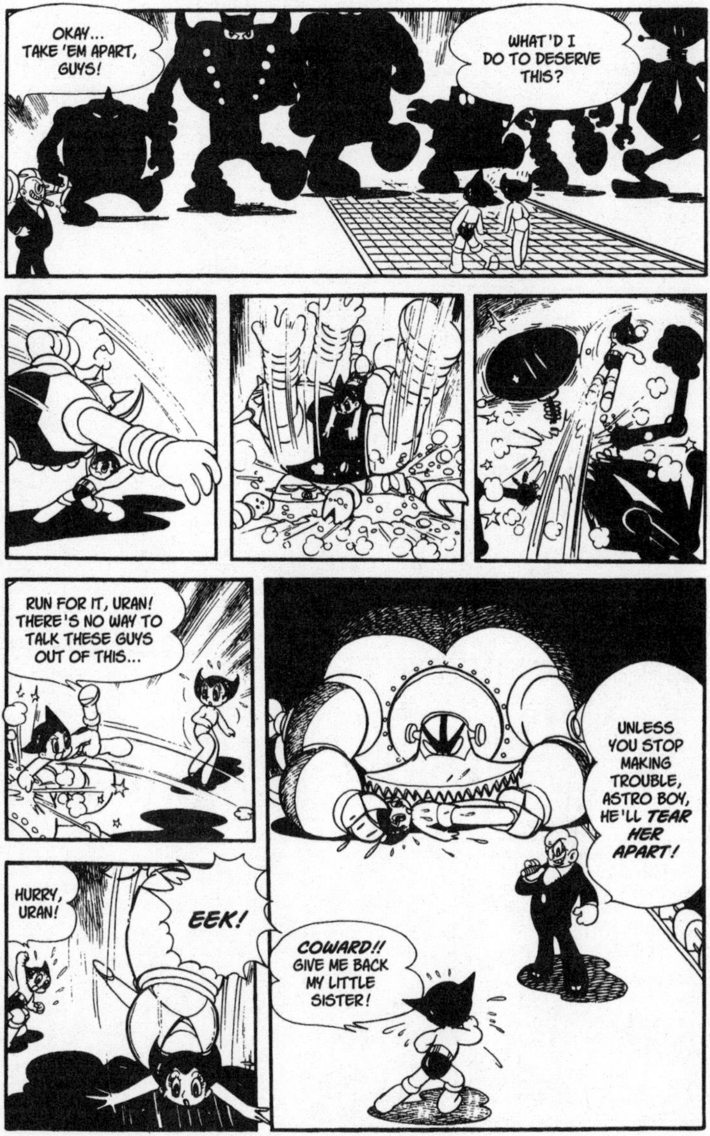
OKAY... TAKE 'EM APART, GUYS!
WHAT'D I DO TO DESERVE THIS?
RUN FOR IT, URAN! THERE'S NO WAY TO TALK THESE GUYS OUT OF THIS...
UNLESS YOU STOP MAKING TROUBLE, ASTRO BOY, HE'LL *TEAR HER APART!*
HURRY, URAN!
EEK!
COWARD!! GIVE ME BACK MY LITTLE SISTER!

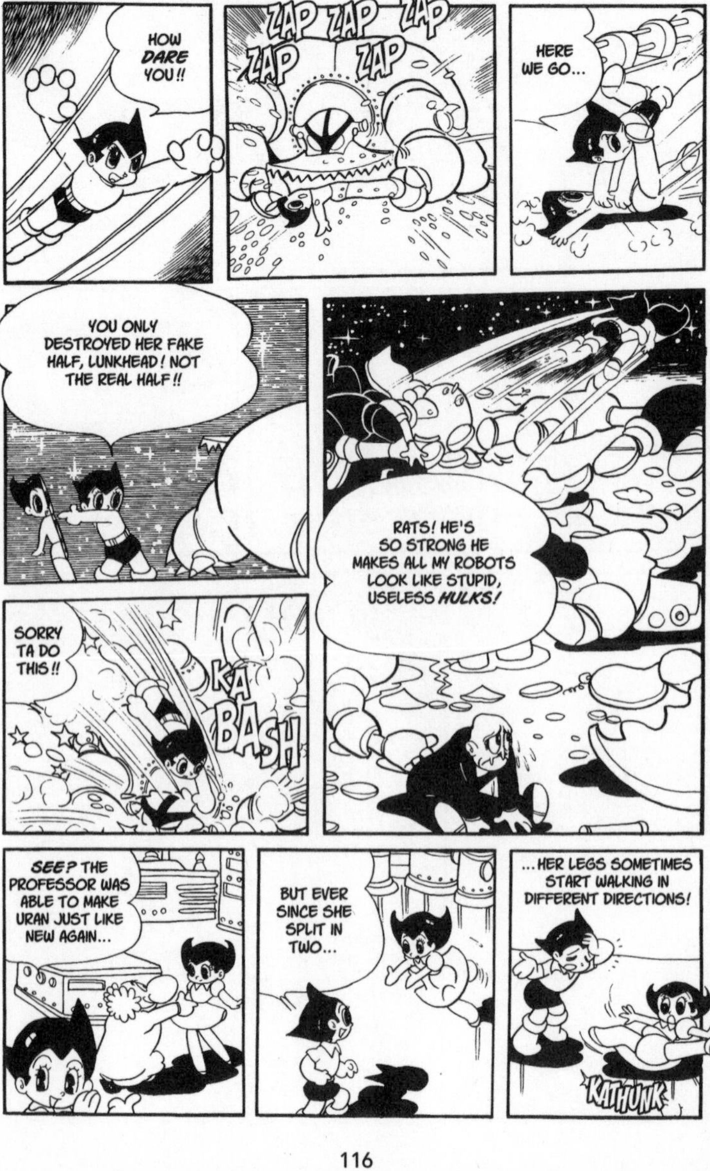
HOW DARE YOU!!
ZAP ZAP ZAP ZAP ZAP
HERE WE GO...
YOU ONLY DESTROYED HER FAKE HALF, LUNKHEAD! NOT THE REAL HALF!!
SORRY TA DO THIS!!
KA BASH
RATS! HE'S SO STRONG HE MAKES ALL MY ROBOTS LOOK LIKE STUPID, USELESS HULKS!
SEE? THE PROFESSOR WAS ABLE TO MAKE URAN JUST LIKE NEW AGAIN...
BUT EVER SINCE SHE SPLIT IN TWO...
...HER LEGS SOMETIMES START WALKING IN DIFFERENT DIRECTIONS!
KATHUNK

D E M O N
B E E S

First serialized from March to June 1963
in *Shonen* magazine.

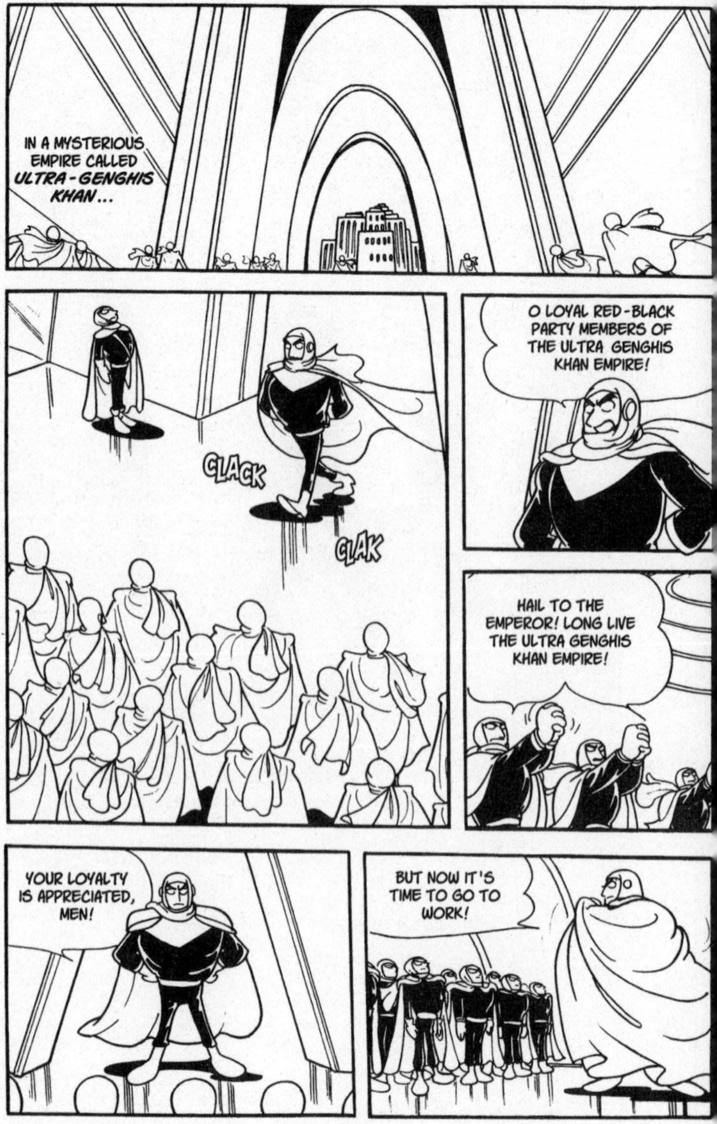
IN A MYSTERIOUS EMPIRE CALLED *ULTRA-GENGHIS KHAN*...
CLACK
CLAK
O LOYAL RED-BLACK PARTY MEMBERS OF THE ULTRA GENGHIS KHAN EMPIRE!
HAIL TO THE EMPEROR! LONG LIVE THE ULTRA GENGHIS KHAN EMPIRE!
YOUR LOYALTY IS APPRECIATED, MEN!
BUT NOW IT'S TIME TO GO TO WORK!

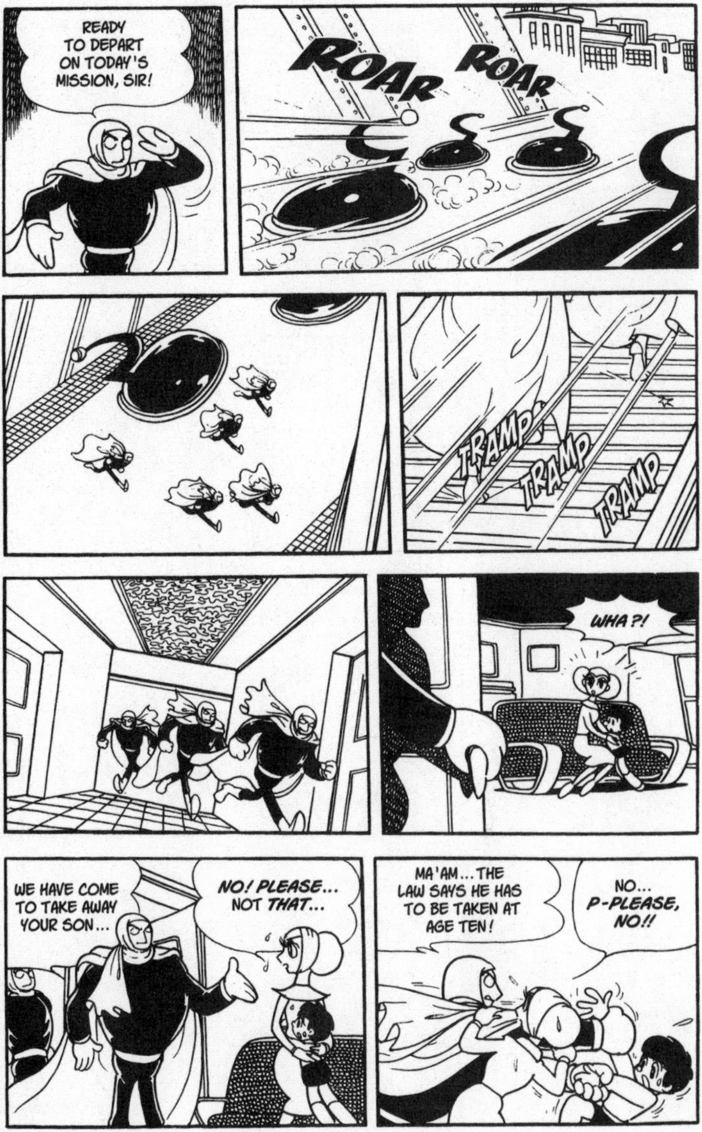
READY TO DEPART ON TODAY'S MISSION, SIR!
ROAR ROAR
TRAMP TRAMP TRAMP
WHA?!
WE HAVE COME TO TAKE AWAY YOUR SON...
NO! PLEASE... NOT THAT...
MA'AM... THE LAW SAYS HE HAS TO BE TAKEN AT AGE TEN!
NO... P-PLEASE, NO!!

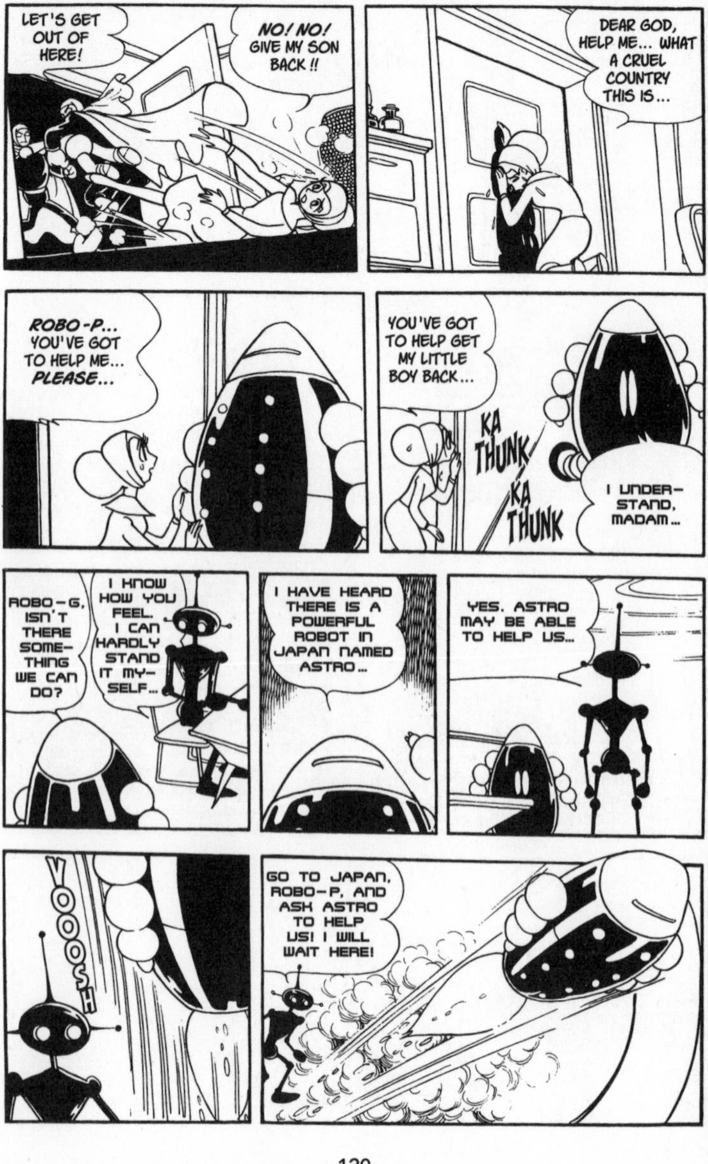
LET'S GET OUT OF HERE!
NO! NO! GIVE MY SON BACK !!
DEAR GOD, HELP ME... WHAT A CRUEL COUNTRY THIS IS...
ROBO-P... YOU'VE GOT TO HELP ME... PLEASE...
YOU'VE GOT TO HELP GET MY LITTLE BOY BACK...
KA THUNK KA THUNK
I UNDER-STAND, MADAM...
ROBO-G, ISN'T THERE SOME-THING WE CAN DO?
I KNOW HOW YOU FEEL. I CAN HARDLY STAND IT MY-SELF...
I HAVE HEARD THERE IS A POWERFUL ROBOT IN JAPAN NAMED ASTRO...
YES. ASTRO MAY BE ABLE TO HELP US...
VOOOSH
GO TO JAPAN, ROBO-P, AND ASK ASTRO TO HELP US! I WILL WAIT HERE!

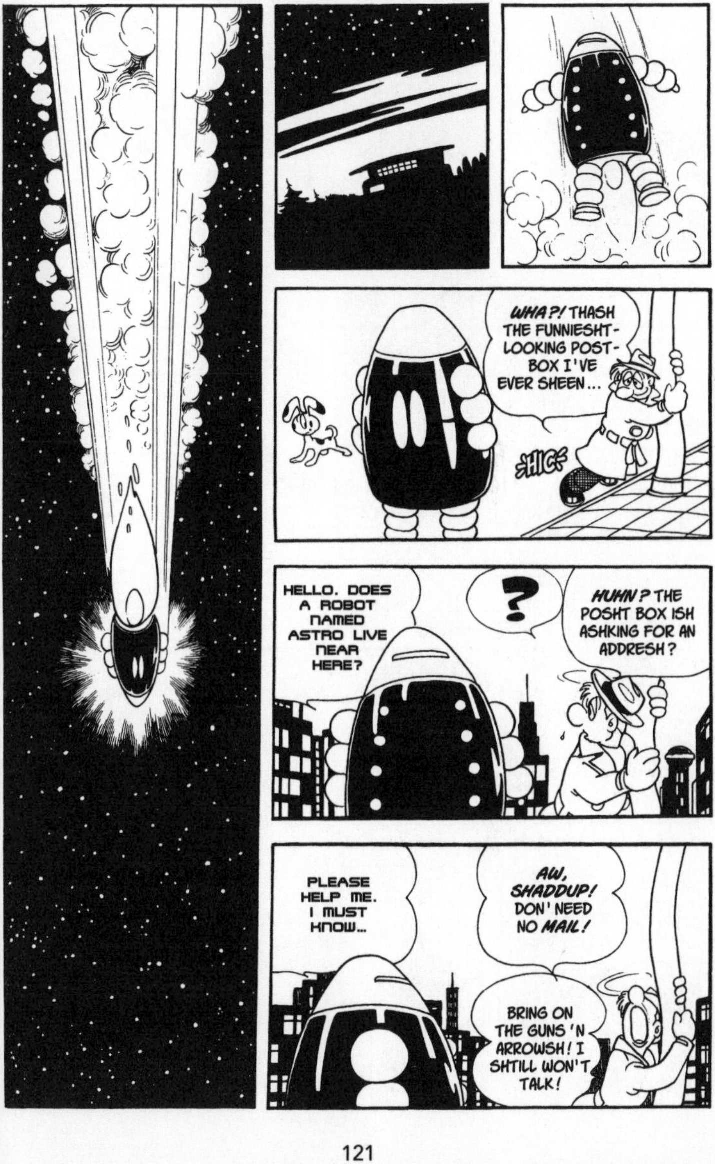

WHA?! THASH THE FUNNIESHT-LOOKING POST-BOX I'VE EVER SHEEN...
HIC
HELLO. DOES A ROBOT NAMED ASTRO LIVE NEAR HERE?
?
HUHN? THE POSHT BOX ISH ASHKING FOR AN ADDRESH?
PLEASE HELP ME. I MUST KNOW...
AW, SHADDUP! DON' NEED NO MAIL!
BRING ON THE GUNS 'N ARROWSH! I SHTILL WON'T TALK!

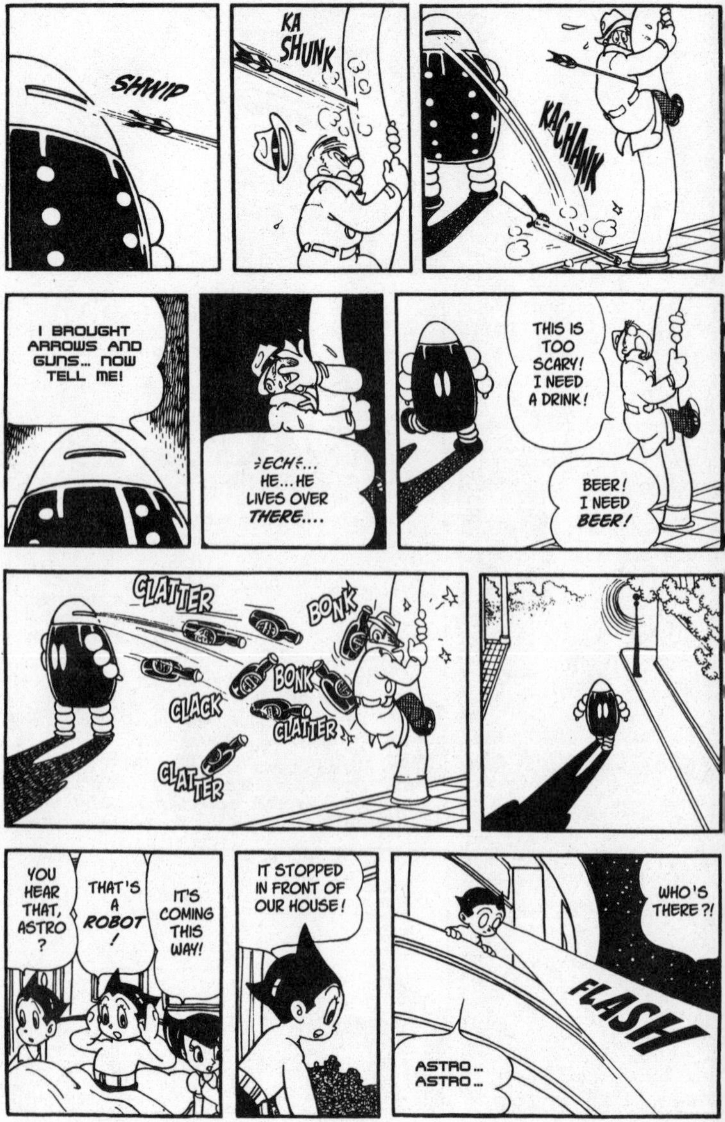
SHWIP
KA SHUNK
KACHANK
I BROUGHT ARROWS AND GUNS... NOW TELL ME!
ECH... HE... HE LIVES OVER THERE....
THIS IS TOO SCARY! I NEED A DRINK!
BEER! I NEED BEER!
CLATTER
BONK
BONK
CLACK
CLATTER
CLATTER
YOU HEAR THAT, ASTRO?
THAT'S A ROBOT!
IT'S COMING THIS WAY!
IT STOPPED IN FRONT OF OUR HOUSE!
WHO'S THERE?!
FLASH
ASTRO... ASTRO...

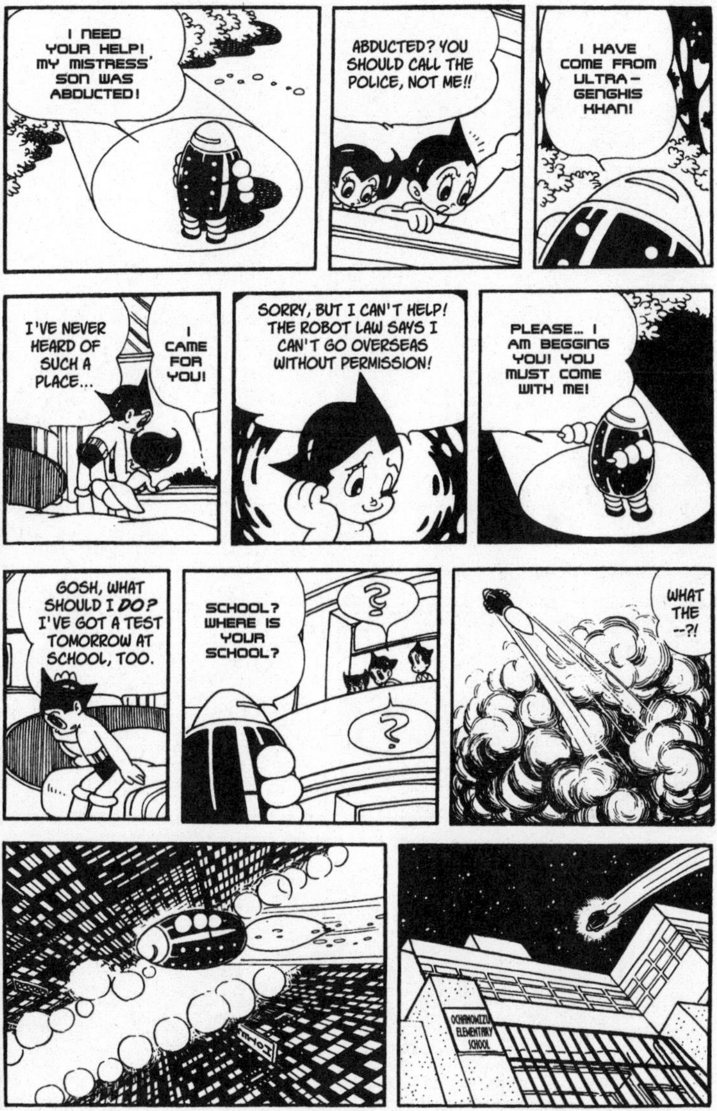
I NEED YOUR HELP! MY MISTRESS' SON WAS ABDUCTED!
ABDUCTED? YOU SHOULD CALL THE POLICE, NOT ME!!
I HAVE COME FROM ULTRA-GENGHIS KHAN!
I'VE NEVER HEARD OF SUCH A PLACE...
I CAME FOR YOU!
SORRY, BUT I CAN'T HELP! THE ROBOT LAW SAYS I CAN'T GO OVERSEAS WITHOUT PERMISSION!
PLEASE... I AM BEGGING YOU! YOU MUST COME WITH ME!
GOSH, WHAT SHOULD I DO? I'VE GOT A TEST TOMORROW AT SCHOOL, TOO.
SCHOOL? WHERE IS YOUR SCHOOL?
?
?
WHAT THE --?!
OCHANOMIZU ELEMENTARY SCHOOL

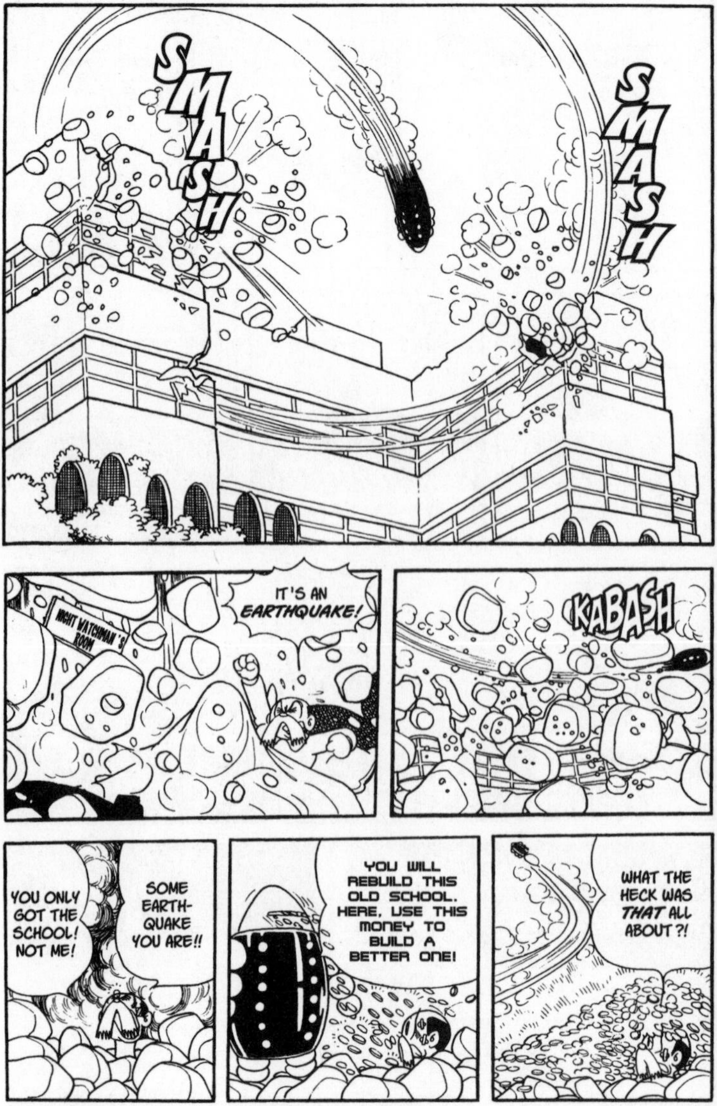
SMASH
SMASH
NIGHT WATCHMAN'S ROOM
IT'S AN EARTHQUAKE!
KABASH
YOU ONLY GOT THE SCHOOL! NOT ME!
SOME EARTH-QUAKE YOU ARE!!
YOU WILL REBUILD THIS OLD SCHOOL. HERE, USE THIS MONEY TO BUILD A BETTER ONE!
WHAT THE HECK WAS THAT ALL ABOUT?!

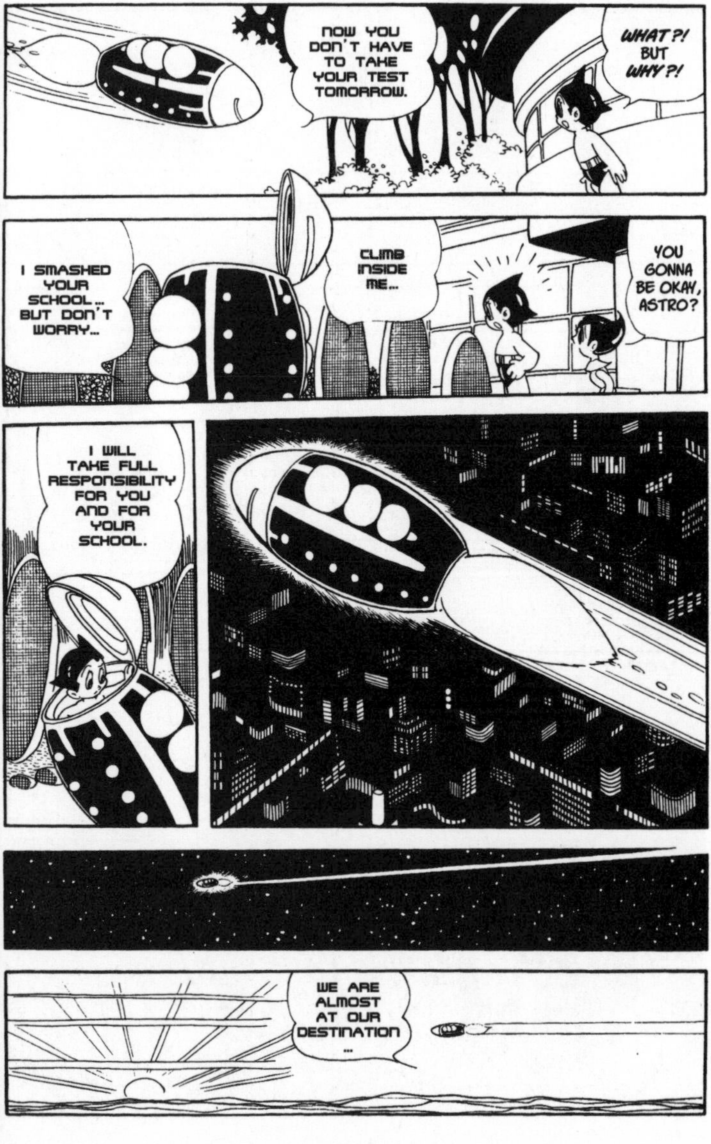
NOW YOU DON'T HAVE TO TAKE YOUR TEST TOMORROW.
WHAT?! BUT WHY?!
I SMASHED YOUR SCHOOL... BUT DON'T WORRY...
CLIMB INSIDE ME...
YOU GONNA BE OKAY, ASTRO?
I WILL TAKE FULL RESPONSIBILITY FOR YOU AND FOR YOUR SCHOOL.
WE ARE ALMOST AT OUR DESTINATION ...

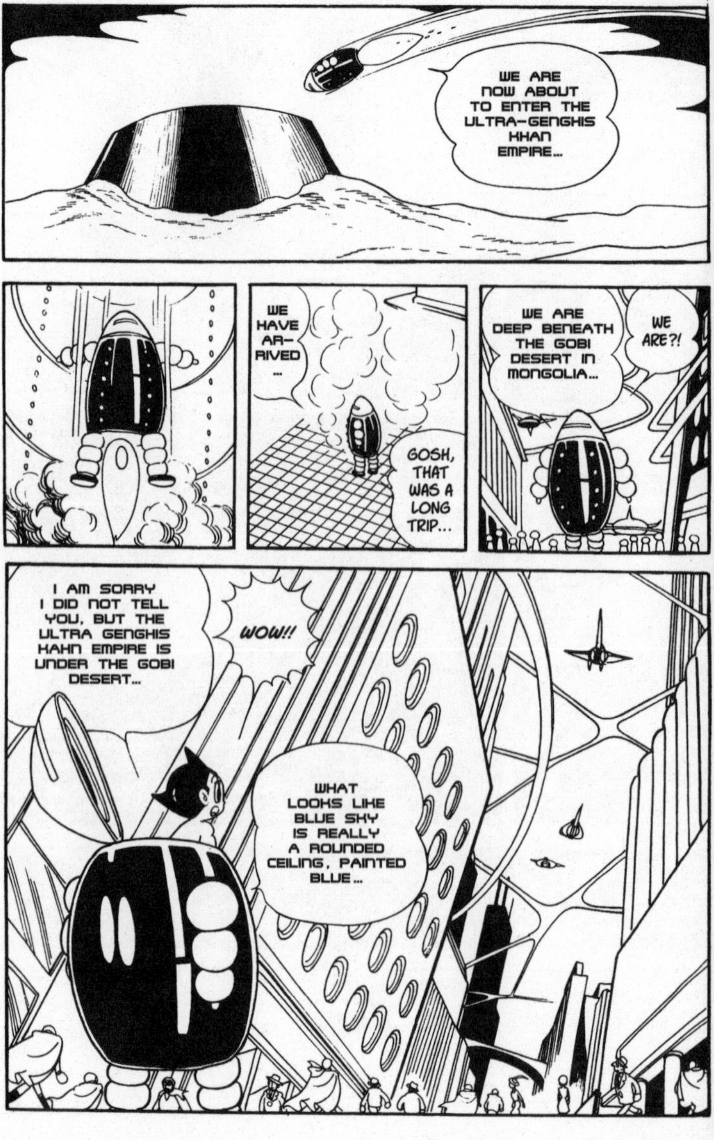

WE ARE NOW ABOUT TO ENTER THE ULTRA-GENGHIS KHAN EMPIRE...
WE HAVE AR-RIVED ...
GOSH, THAT WAS A LONG TRIP...
WE ARE DEEP BENEATH THE GOBI DESERT IN MONGOLIA...
WE ARE?!
I AM SORRY I DID NOT TELL YOU, BUT THE ULTRA GENGHIS KAHN EMPIRE IS UNDER THE GOBI DESERT...
WOW!!
WHAT LOOKS LIKE BLUE SKY IS REALLY A ROUNDED CEILING, PAINTED BLUE...

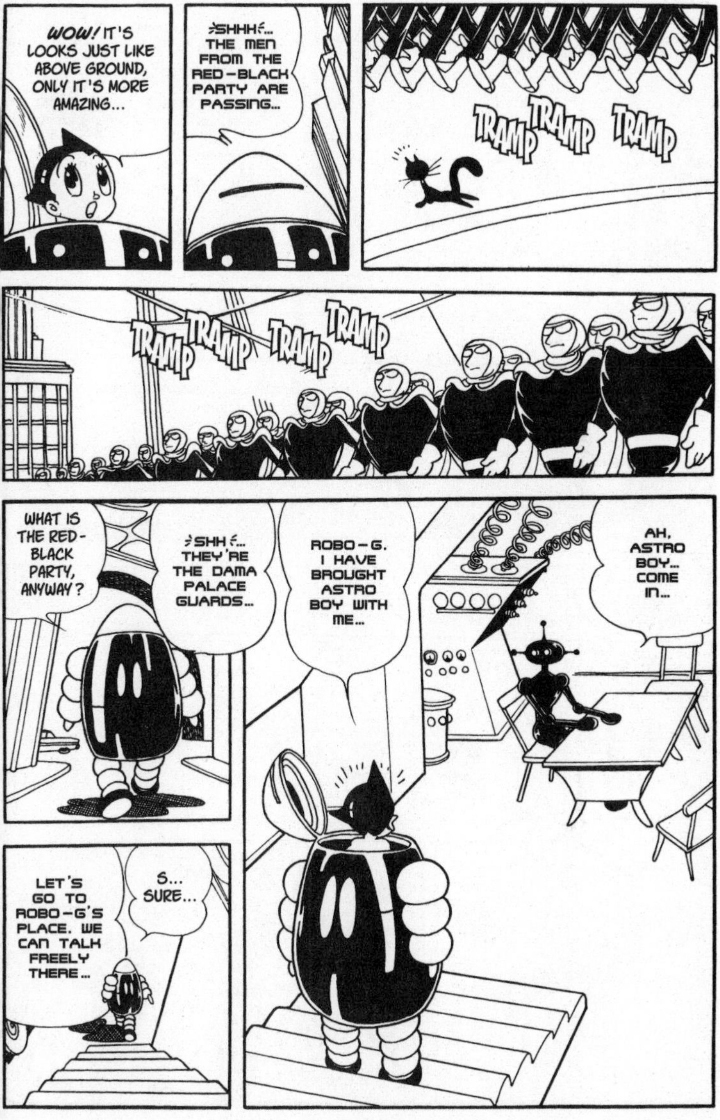
WOW! IT'S LOOKS JUST LIKE ABOVE GROUND, ONLY IT'S MORE AMAZING...
SHHH... THE MEN FROM THE RED-BLACK PARTY ARE PASSING...
TRAMP TRAMP TRAMP
TRAMP TRAMP TRAMP TRAMP
WHAT IS THE RED-BLACK PARTY, ANYWAY?
SHH... THEY'RE THE DAMA PALACE GUARDS...
LET'S GO TO ROBO-G'S PLACE. WE CAN TALK FREELY THERE...
S... SURE...
ROBO-G. I HAVE BROUGHT ASTRO BOY WITH ME...
AH, ASTRO BOY... COME IN...

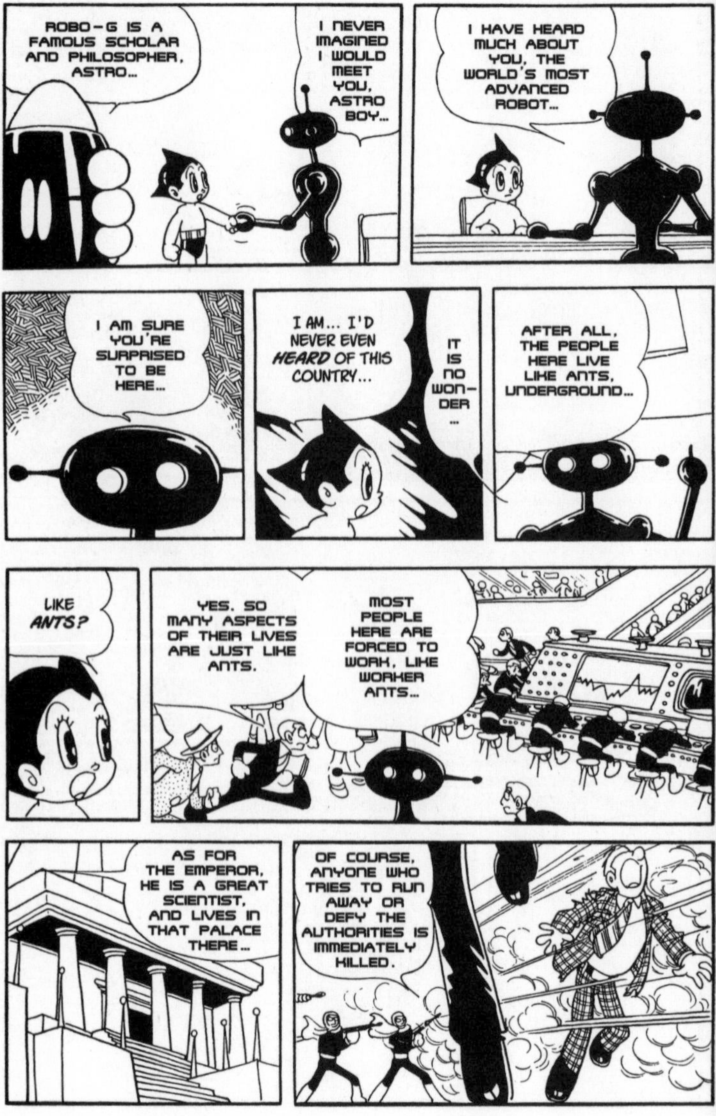
ROBO-G IS A FAMOUS SCHOLAR AND PHILOSOPHER, ASTRO...
I NEVER IMAGINED I WOULD MEET YOU, ASTRO BOY...
I HAVE HEARD MUCH ABOUT YOU, THE WORLD'S MOST ADVANCED ROBOT...
I AM SURE YOU'RE SURPRISED TO BE HERE...
I AM... I'D NEVER EVEN *HEARD* OF THIS COUNTRY...
IT IS NO WON-DER ...
AFTER ALL, THE PEOPLE HERE LIVE LIKE ANTS, UNDERGROUND...
LIKE *ANTS?*
YES. SO MANY ASPECTS OF THEIR LIVES ARE JUST LIKE ANTS.
MOST PEOPLE HERE ARE FORCED TO WORK, LIKE WORKER ANTS...
AS FOR THE EMPEROR, HE IS A GREAT SCIENTIST, AND LIVES IN THAT PALACE THERE...
OF COURSE, ANYONE WHO TRIES TO RUN AWAY OR DEFY THE AUTHORITIES IS IMMEDIATELY KILLED.

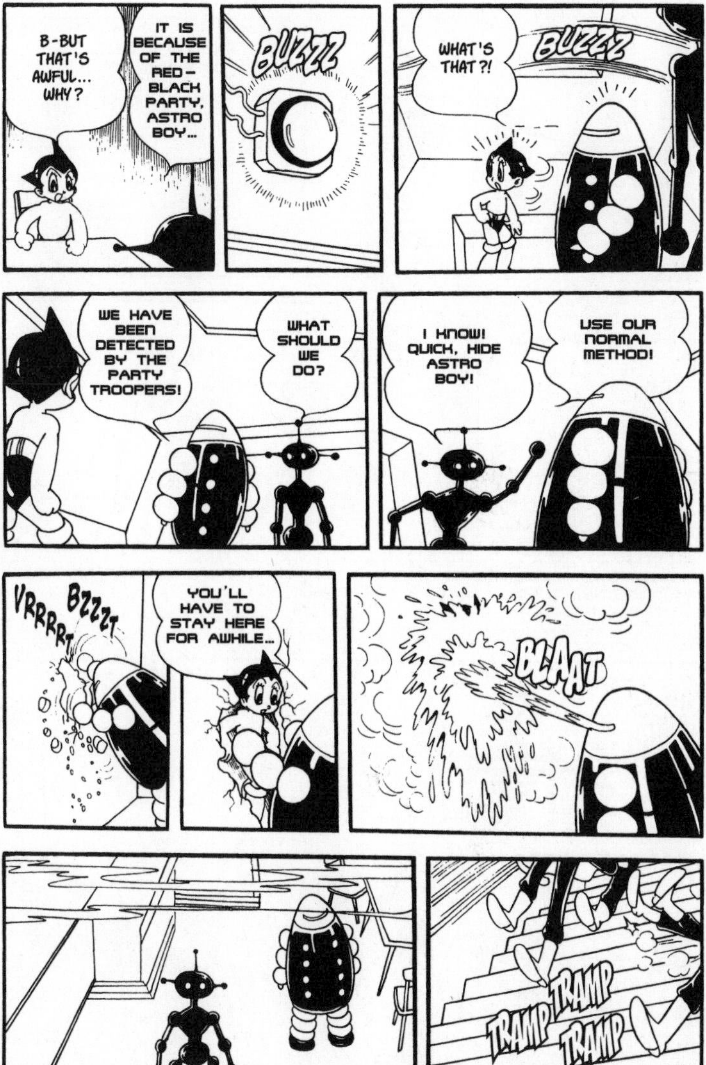
B-BUT THAT'S AWFUL... WHY?
IT IS BECAUSE OF THE RED-BLACK PARTY, ASTRO BOY...
BUZZZ
WHAT'S THAT?!
BUZZZ
WE HAVE BEEN DETECTED BY THE PARTY TROOPERS!
WHAT SHOULD WE DO?
I KNOW! QUICK, HIDE ASTRO BOY!
USE OUR NORMAL METHOD!
VRRRRRT
BZZZZT
YOU'LL HAVE TO STAY HERE FOR AWHILE...
BLAAAT
TRAMP TRAMP
TRAMP

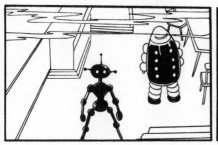

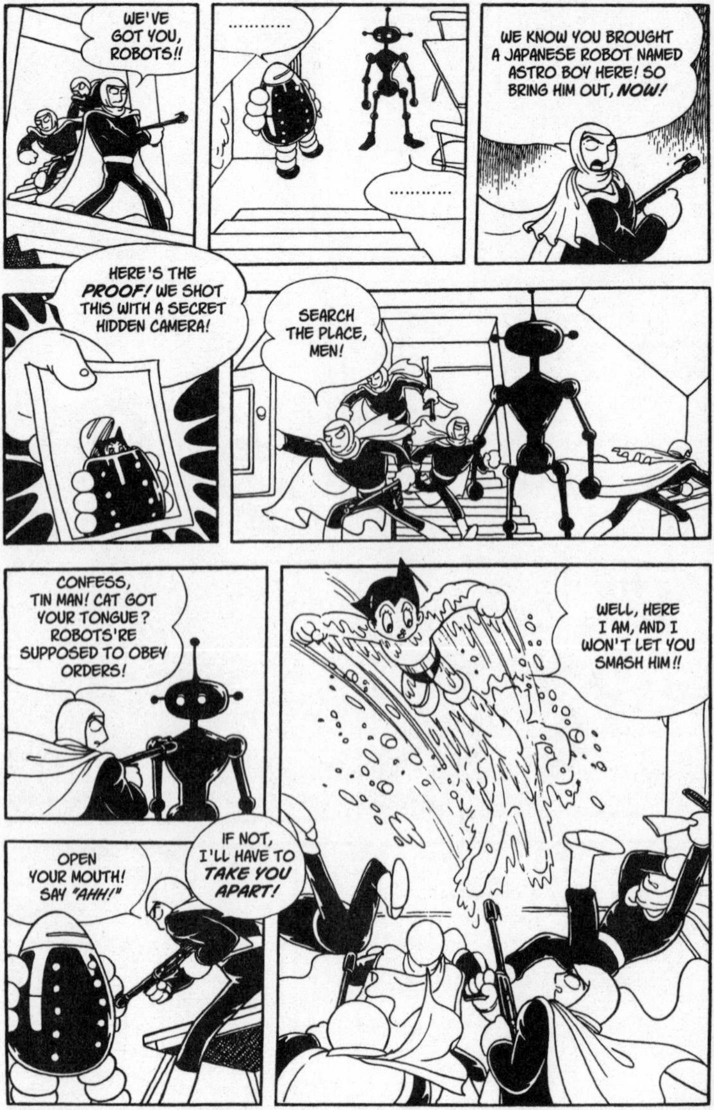
WE'VE GOT YOU, ROBOTS!!
....
....
WE KNOW YOU BROUGHT A JAPANESE ROBOT NAMED ASTRO BOY HERE! SO BRING HIM OUT, NOW!
HERE'S THE PROOF! WE SHOT THIS WITH A SECRET HIDDEN CAMERA!
SEARCH THE PLACE, MEN!
CONFESS, TIN MAN! CAT GOT YOUR TONGUE? ROBOTS'RE SUPPOSED TO OBEY ORDERS!
OPEN YOUR MOUTH! SAY "AHH!"
IF NOT, I'LL HAVE TO TAKE YOU APART!
WELL, HERE I AM, AND I WON'T LET YOU SMASH HIM!!

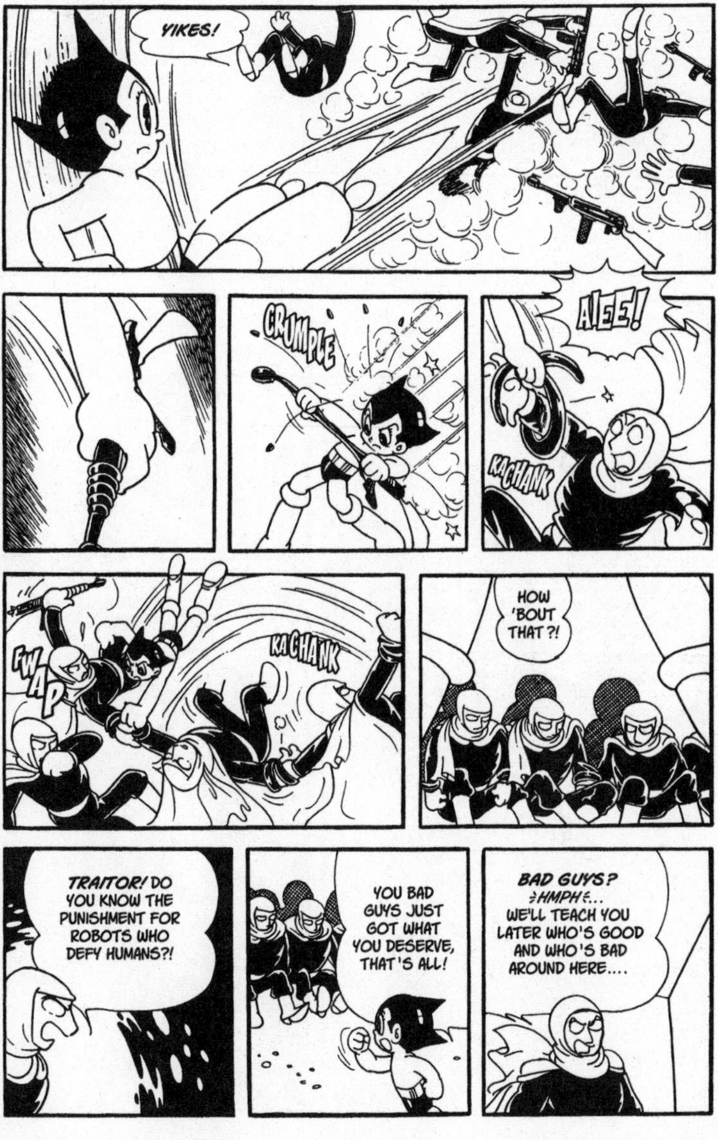
YIKES!
CRUMPLE
AIEE!
KACHANK
FWAP
KACHANK
HOW 'BOUT THAT?!
TRAITOR! DO YOU KNOW THE PUNISHMENT FOR ROBOTS WHO DEFY HUMANS?!
YOU BAD GUYS JUST GOT WHAT YOU DESERVE, THAT'S ALL!
BAD GUYS? HMPH... WE'LL TEACH YOU LATER WHO'S GOOD AND WHO'S BAD AROUND HERE....

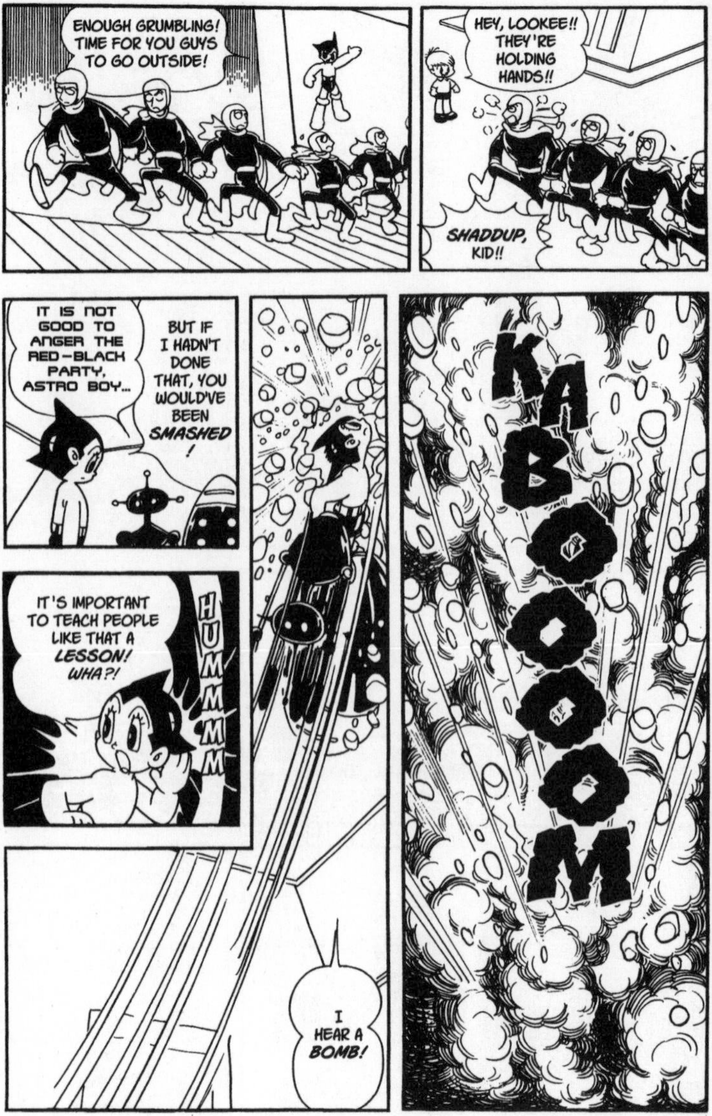
ENOUGH GRUMBLING! TIME FOR YOU GUYS TO GO OUTSIDE!
HEY, LOOKEE!! THEY'RE HOLDING HANDS!!
SHADDUP, KID!!
IT IS NOT GOOD TO ANGER THE RED-BLACK PARTY, ASTRO BOY...
BUT IF I HADN'T DONE THAT, YOU WOULD'VE BEEN SMASHED!
IT'S IMPORTANT TO TEACH PEOPLE LIKE THAT A LESSON! WHA?!
HUMMMMMM
I HEAR A BOMB!
KABOOOOOM

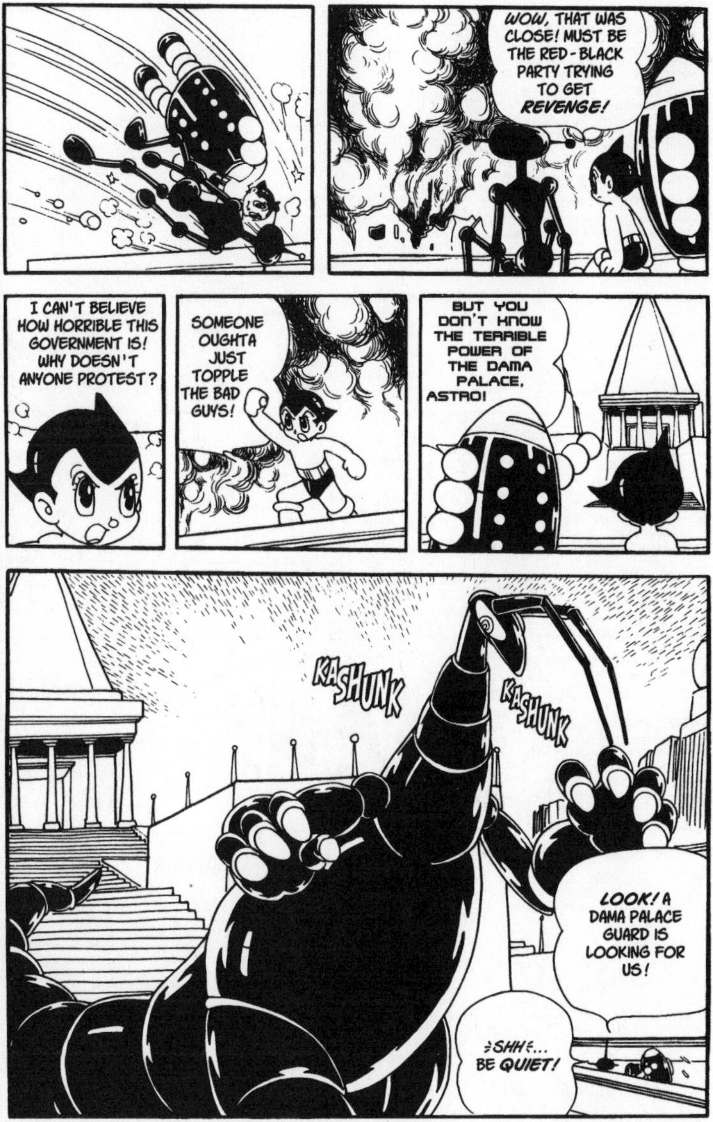
WOW, THAT WAS CLOSE! MUST BE THE RED-BLACK PARTY TRYING TO GET REVENGE!
I CAN'T BELIEVE HOW HORRIBLE THIS GOVERNMENT IS! WHY DOESN'T ANYONE PROTEST?
SOMEONE OUGHTA JUST TOPPLE THE BAD GUYS!
BUT YOU DON'T KNOW THE TERRIBLE POWER OF THE DAMA PALACE, ASTRO!
KASHUNK
KASHUNK
LOOK! A DAMA PALACE GUARD IS LOOKING FOR US!
SHH... BE QUIET!

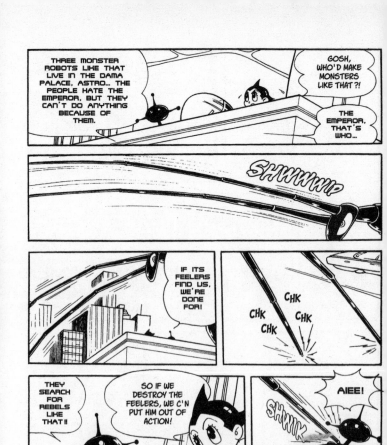

THREE MONSTER ROBOTS LIKE THAT LIVE IN THE DAMA PALACE, ASTRO... THE PEOPLE HATE THE EMPEROR, BUT THEY CAN'T DO ANYTHING BECAUSE OF THEM.

GOSH, WHO'D MAKE MONSTERS LIKE THAT?!

THE EMPEROR, THAT'S WHO...

SHWWWIP

IF ITS FEELERS FIND US, WE'RE DONE FOR!

CHK CHK CHK CHK

THEY SEARCH FOR REBELS LIKE THAT!!

SO IF WE DESTROY THE FEELERS, WE C'N PUT HIM OUT OF ACTION!

AIEE!

SHWWK

OH, NO YOU DON'T!

WATCH OUT, ASTRO!

SHWOOP

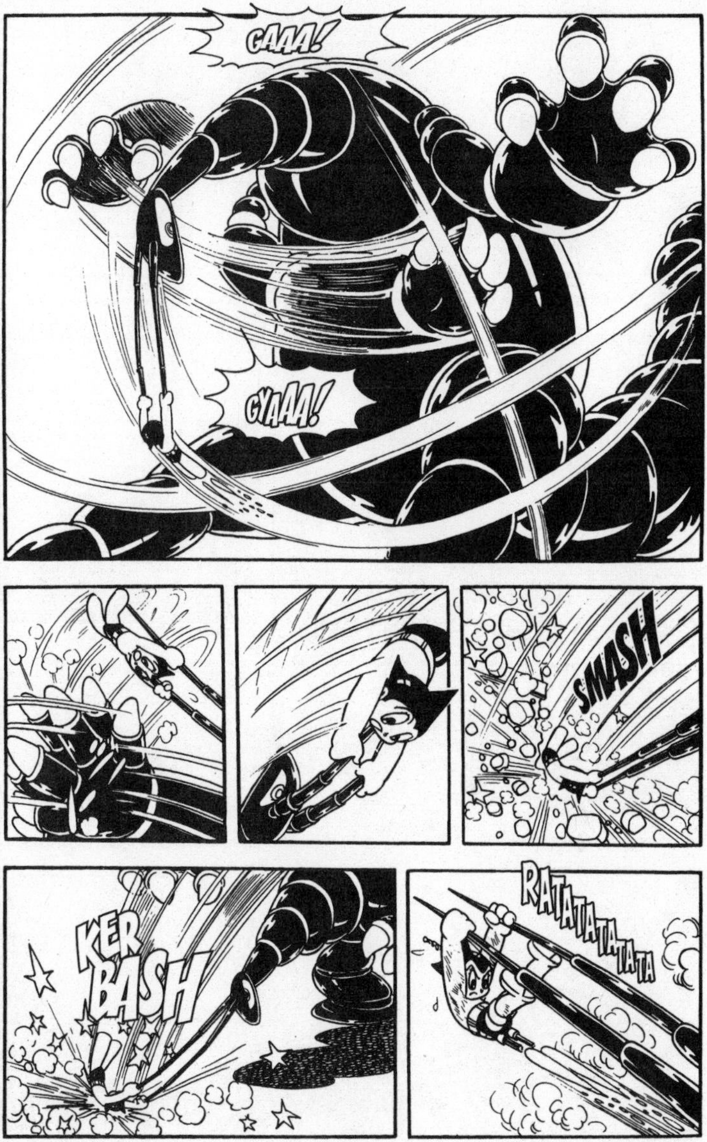
GAAA!
GYAAA!
SMASH
KER BASH
RATATATATATATA

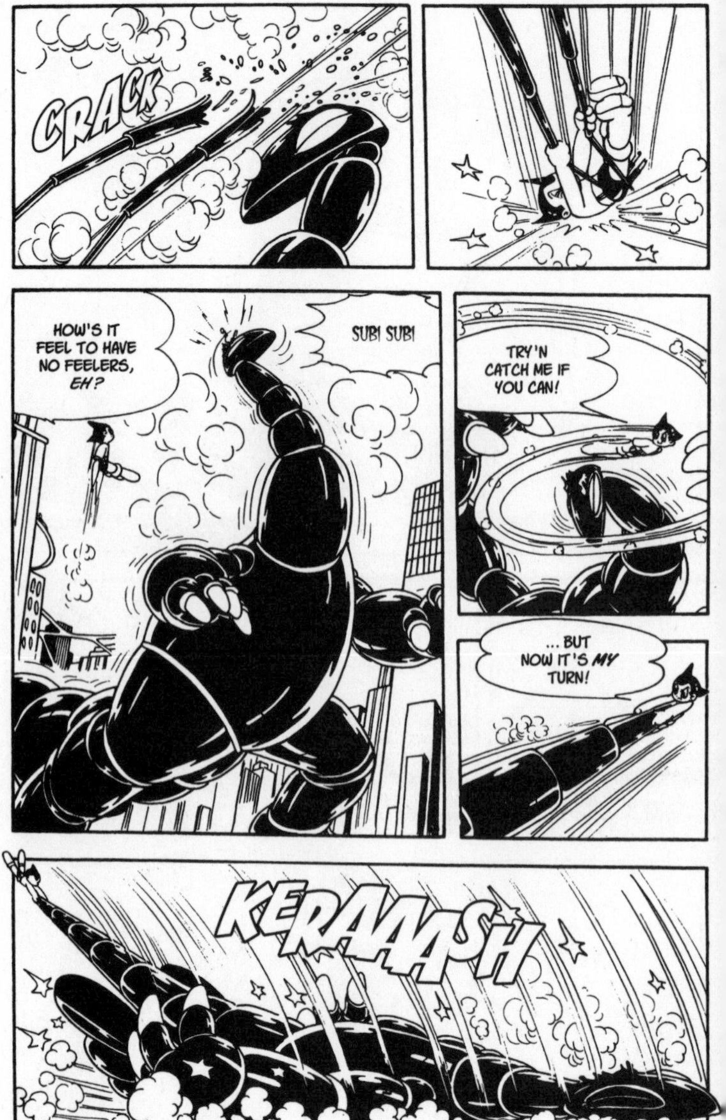
CRACK
HOW'S IT FEEL TO HAVE NO FEELERS, *EH?*
SUBI SUBI
TRY'N CATCH ME IF YOU CAN!
... BUT NOW IT'S *MY* TURN!
KERAAASH

UH OH...

THE OTHER GUARD ROBOTS'RE COMING OUT NOW, ASTRO!

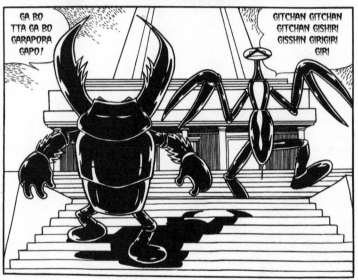

GA BO TTA GA BO GARAPORA GAPO!

GITCHAN GITCHAN GITCHAN GISHIRI GISSHIN GIRIGIRI GIRI

UH OH... I FORGOT THERE WERE *MORE* OF 'EM!

HOPE I HAVE ENOUGH *ENERGY!*

GABORA GABORA GABORA

137

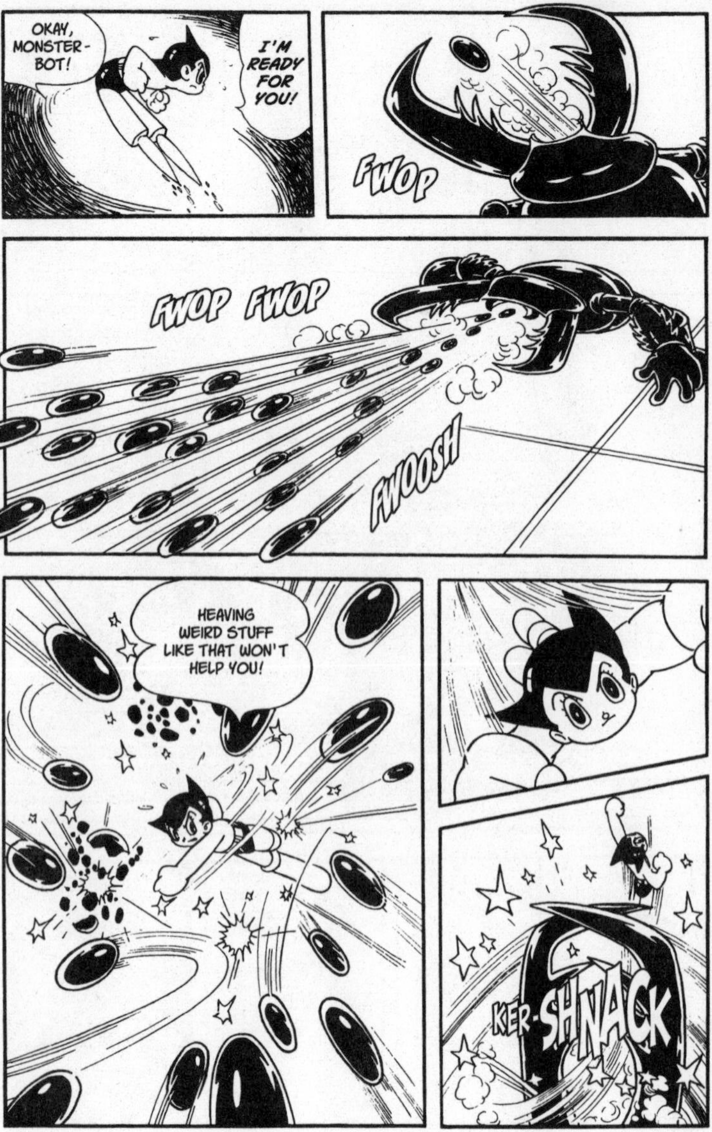
OKAY, MONSTER-BOT!
I'M READY FOR YOU!
FWOP
FWOP FWOP
FWOOSH
HEAVING WEIRD STUFF LIKE THAT WON'T HELP YOU!
KER-SHNACK

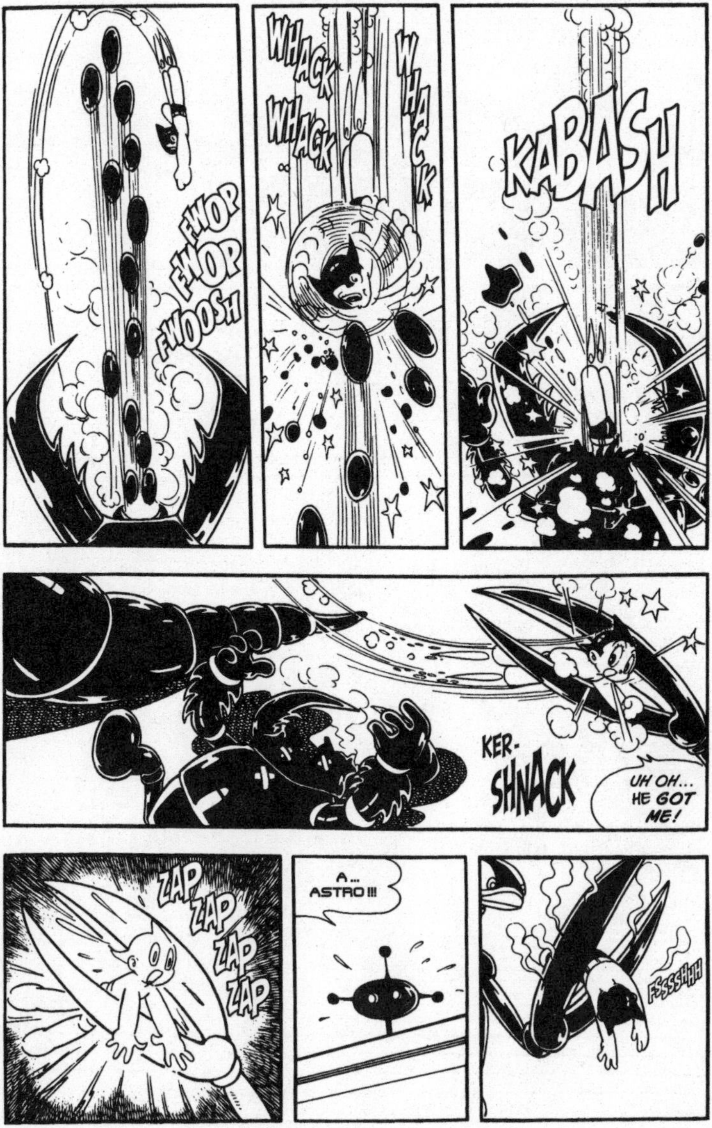
FWOP
FWOP
FWOOSH
WHACK
WHACK
WHACK
KABASH
KER-
SHNACK
UH OH... HE GOT ME!
ZAP
ZAP
ZAP
ZAP
A... ASTRO !!!
FSSSSHHH

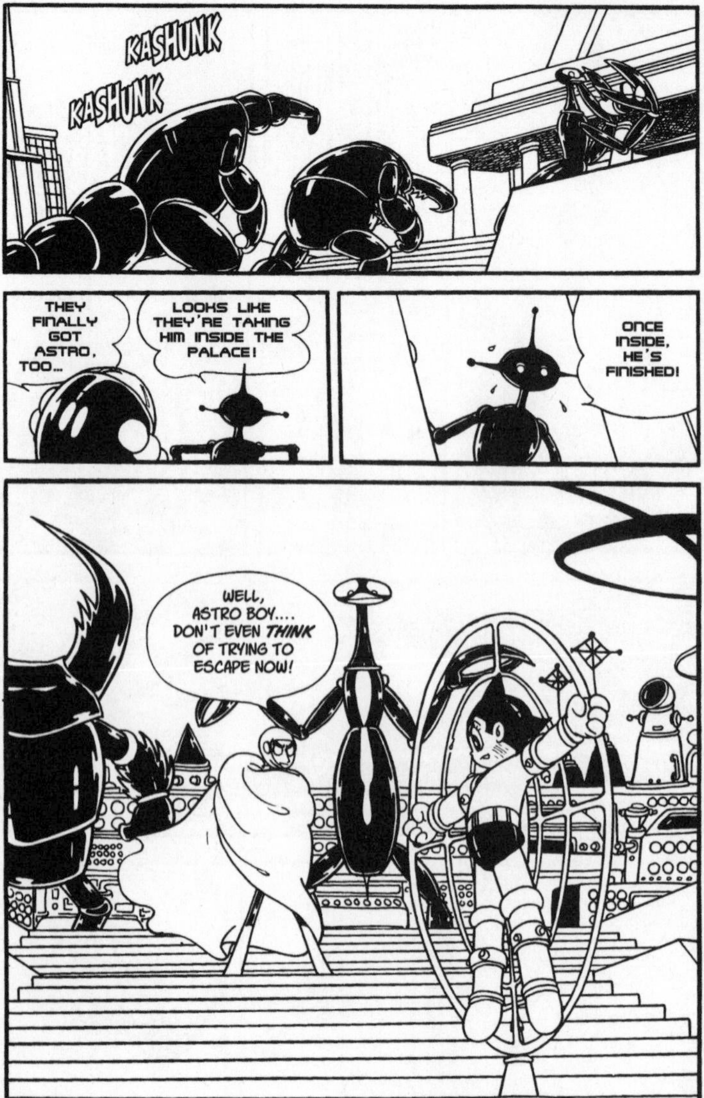
KASHUNK
KASHUNK
THEY FINALLY GOT ASTRO, TOO...
LOOKS LIKE THEY'RE TAKING HIM INSIDE THE PALACE!
ONCE INSIDE, HE'S FINISHED!
WELL, ASTRO BOY.... DON'T EVEN *THINK* OF TRYING TO ESCAPE NOW!

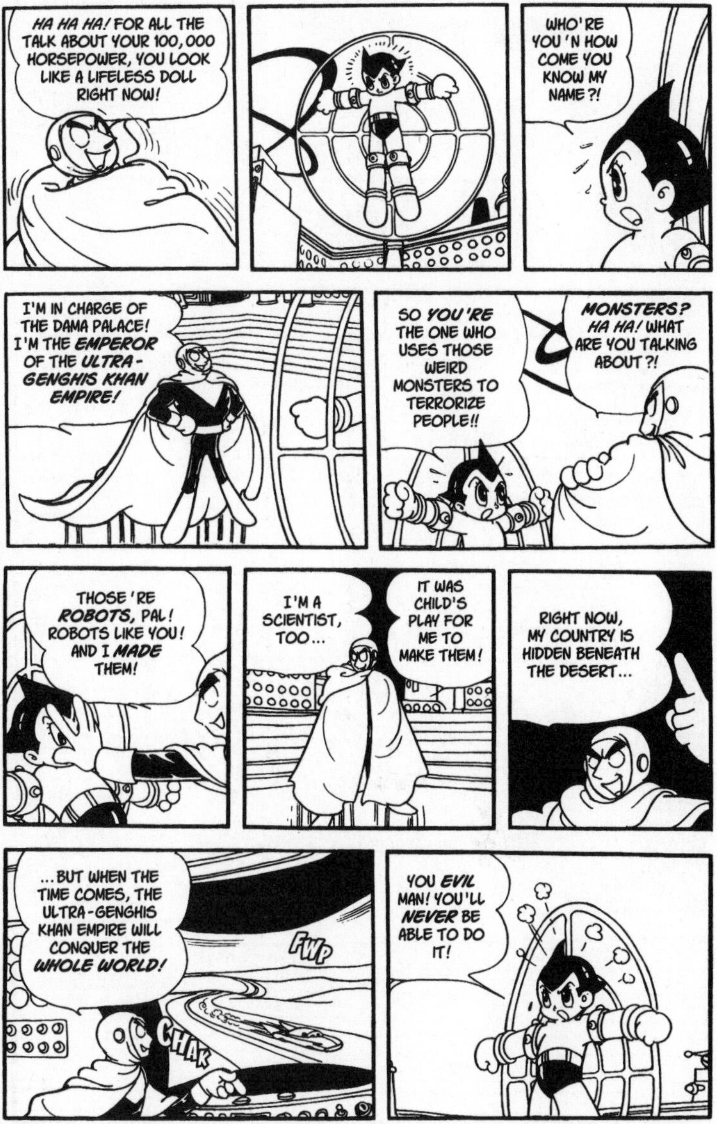
HA HA HA! FOR ALL THE TALK ABOUT YOUR 100,000 HORSEPOWER, YOU LOOK LIKE A LIFELESS DOLL RIGHT NOW!
WHO'RE YOU 'N HOW COME YOU KNOW MY NAME?!
I'M IN CHARGE OF THE DAMA PALACE! I'M THE EMPEROR OF THE ULTRA-GENGHIS KHAN EMPIRE!
SO YOU'RE THE ONE WHO USES THOSE WEIRD MONSTERS TO TERRORIZE PEOPLE!!
MONSTERS? HA HA! WHAT ARE YOU TALKING ABOUT?!
THOSE'RE ROBOTS, PAL! ROBOTS LIKE YOU! AND I MADE THEM!
I'M A SCIENTIST, TOO...
IT WAS CHILD'S PLAY FOR ME TO MAKE THEM!
RIGHT NOW, MY COUNTRY IS HIDDEN BENEATH THE DESERT...
...BUT WHEN THE TIME COMES, THE ULTRA-GENGHIS KHAN EMPIRE WILL CONQUER THE WHOLE WORLD!
FWP
CHAK
YOU EVIL MAN! YOU'LL NEVER BE ABLE TO DO IT!

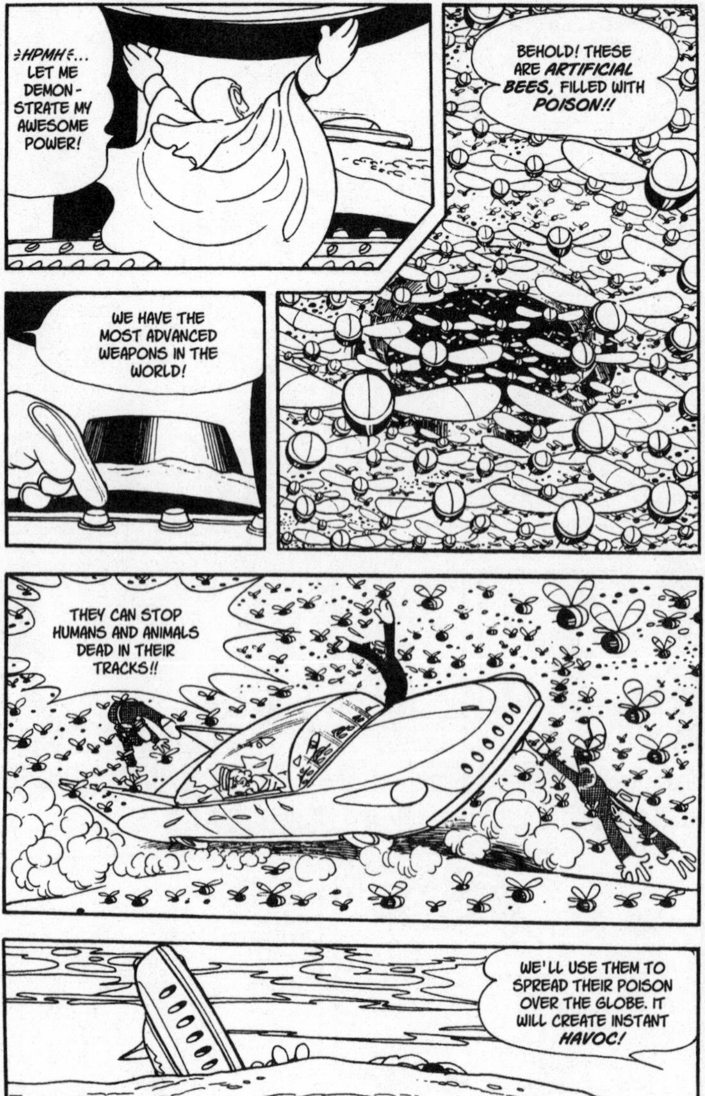

≡HPMH≡... LET ME DEMON-STRATE MY AWESOME POWER!
BEHOLD! THESE ARE ***ARTIFICIAL BEES,*** FILLED WITH ***POISON!!***
WE HAVE THE MOST ADVANCED WEAPONS IN THE WORLD!
THEY CAN STOP HUMANS AND ANIMALS DEAD IN THEIR TRACKS!!
WE'LL USE THEM TO SPREAD THEIR POISON OVER THE GLOBE. IT WILL CREATE INSTANT ***HAVOC!***

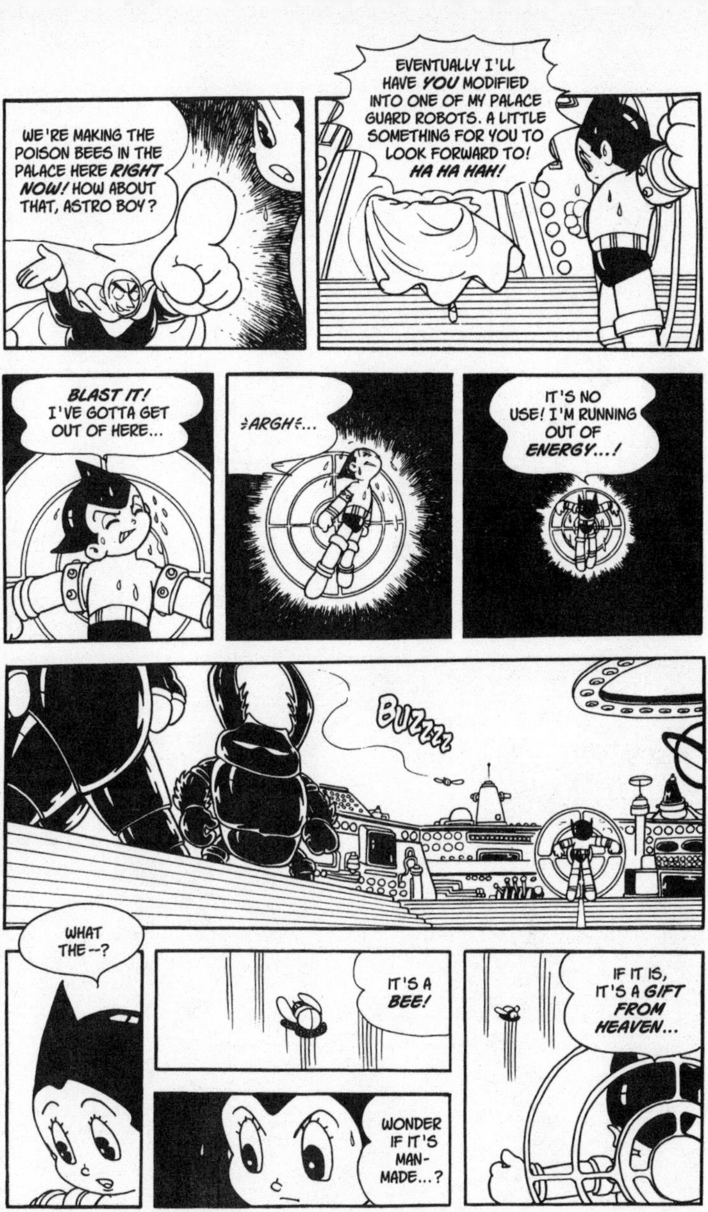
WE'RE MAKING THE POISON BEES IN THE PALACE HERE RIGHT NOW! HOW ABOUT THAT, ASTRO BOY?
EVENTUALLY I'LL HAVE YOU MODIFIED INTO ONE OF MY PALACE GUARD ROBOTS. A LITTLE SOMETHING FOR YOU TO LOOK FORWARD TO! HA HA HAH!
BLAST IT! I'VE GOTTA GET OUT OF HERE...
ARGH...
IT'S NO USE! I'M RUNNING OUT OF ENERGY...!
BUZZZZ
WHAT THE--?
IT'S A BEE!
WONDER IF IT'S MAN-MADE...?
IF IT IS, IT'S A GIFT FROM HEAVEN...

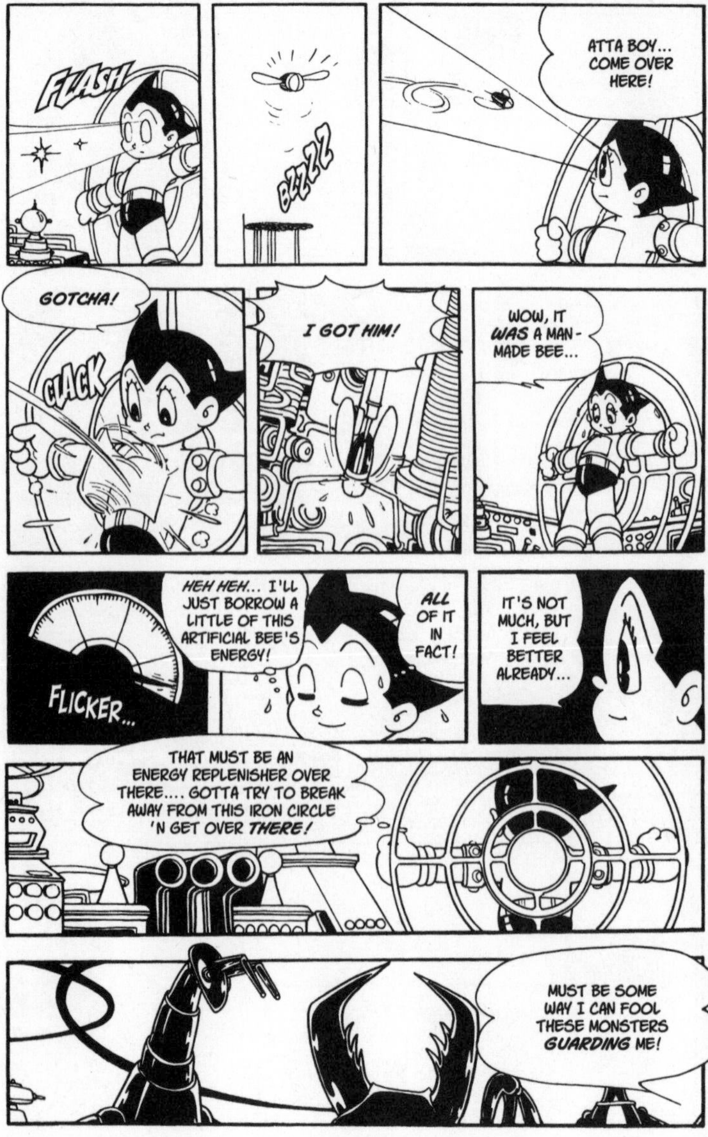
FLASH
BZZZZ
ATTA BOY... COME OVER HERE!
GOTCHA!
CLACK
I GOT HIM!
WOW, IT *WAS* A MAN-MADE BEE...
FLICKER...
HEH HEH... I'LL JUST BORROW A LITTLE OF THIS ARTIFICIAL BEE'S ENERGY!
ALL OF IT IN FACT!
IT'S NOT MUCH, BUT I FEEL BETTER ALREADY...
THAT MUST BE AN ENERGY REPLENISHER OVER THERE.... GOTTA TRY TO BREAK AWAY FROM THIS IRON CIRCLE 'N GET OVER *THERE!*
MUST BE SOME WAY I CAN FOOL THESE MONSTERS *GUARDING* ME!

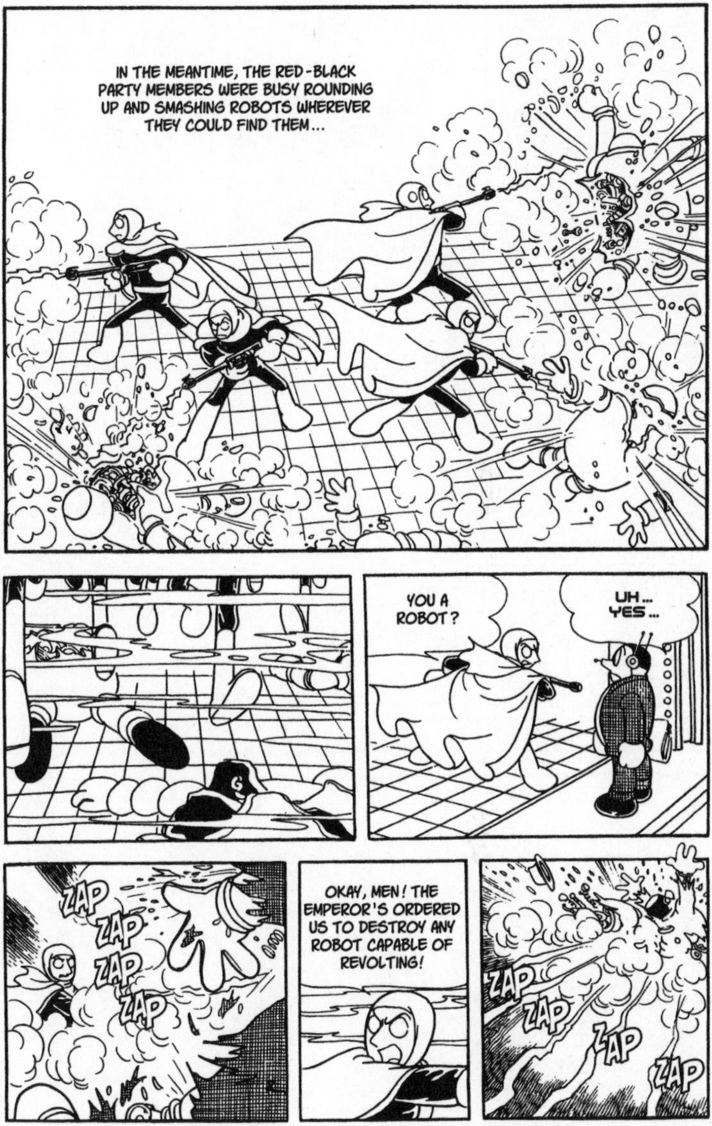
IN THE MEANTIME, THE RED-BLACK PARTY MEMBERS WERE BUSY ROUNDING UP AND SMASHING ROBOTS WHEREVER THEY COULD FIND THEM...
YOU A ROBOT?
UH... YES...
ZAP
ZAP
ZAP
ZAP
OKAY, MEN! THE EMPEROR'S ORDERED US TO DESTROY ANY ROBOT CAPABLE OF REVOLTING!
ZAP
ZAP
ZAP
ZAP

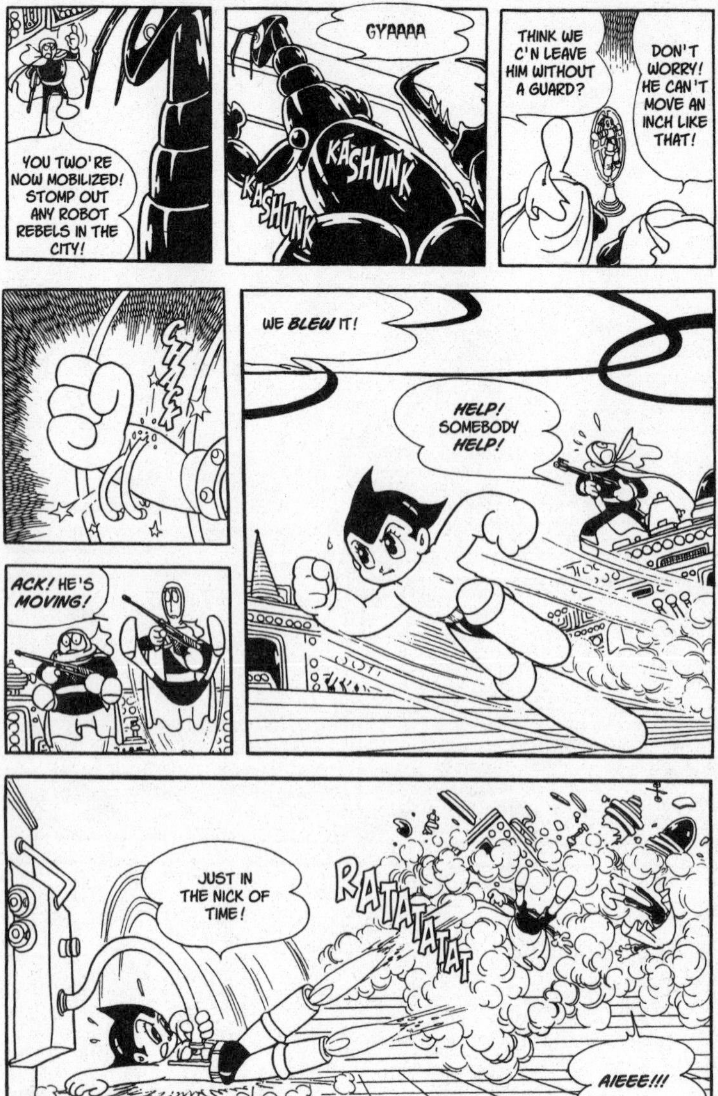
YOU TWO'RE NOW MOBILIZED! STOMP OUT ANY ROBOT REBELS IN THE CITY!
GYAAAA
KASHUNK
KASHUNK
THINK WE C'N LEAVE HIM WITHOUT A GUARD?
DON'T WORRY! HE CAN'T MOVE AN INCH LIKE THAT!
CHACK
ACK! HE'S MOVING!
WE BLEW IT!
HELP! SOMEBODY HELP!
JUST IN THE NICK OF TIME!
RATATATATAT
AIEEE!!!

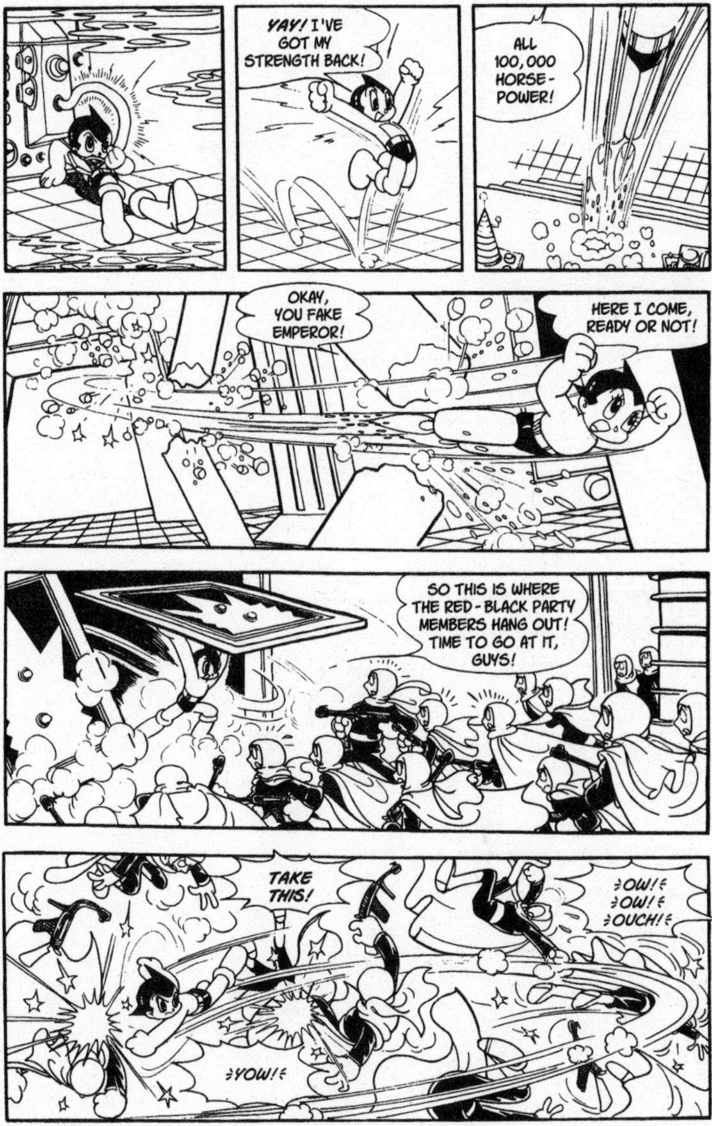
YAY! I'VE GOT MY STRENGTH BACK!
ALL 100,000 HORSE-POWER!
OKAY, YOU FAKE EMPEROR!
HERE I COME, READY OR NOT!
SO THIS IS WHERE THE RED-BLACK PARTY MEMBERS HANG OUT! TIME TO GO AT IT, GUYS!
TAKE THIS!
OW! OW! OUCH!
YOW!

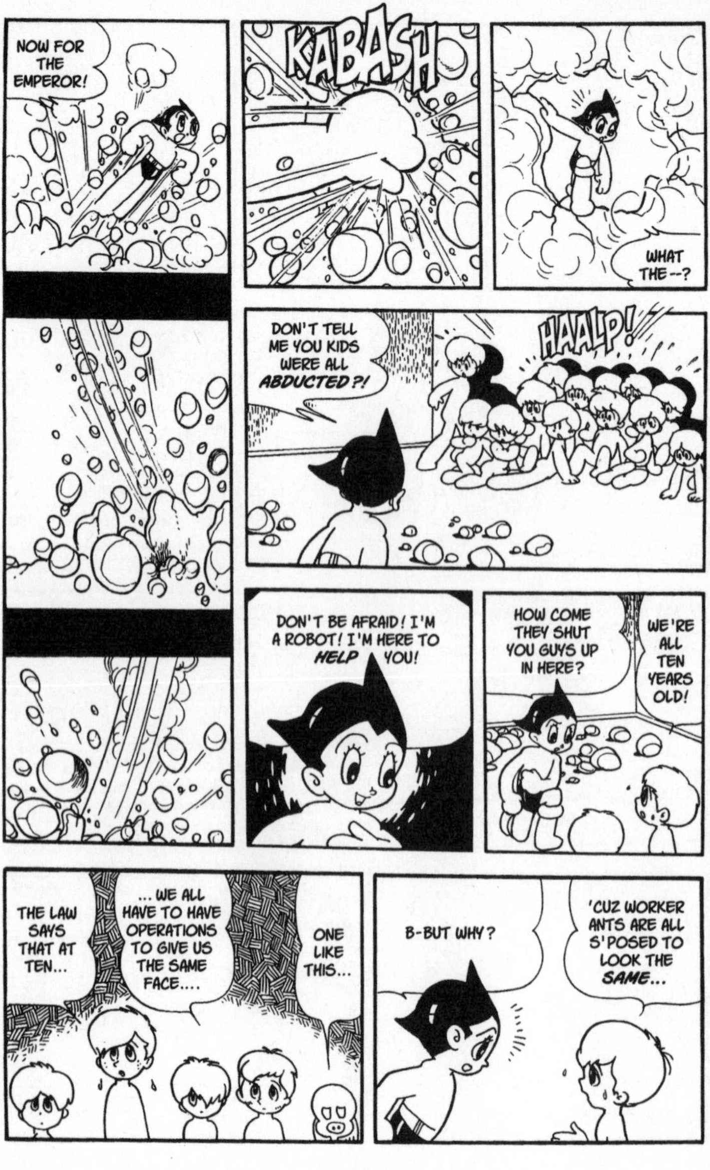
NOW FOR THE EMPEROR!
KABASH
WHAT THE--?
DON'T TELL ME YOU KIDS WERE ALL ABDUCTED?!
HAALP!
DON'T BE AFRAID! I'M A ROBOT! I'M HERE TO HELP YOU!
HOW COME THEY SHUT YOU GUYS UP IN HERE?
WE'RE ALL TEN YEARS OLD!
THE LAW SAYS THAT AT TEN...
... WE ALL HAVE TO HAVE OPERATIONS TO GIVE US THE SAME FACE....
ONE LIKE THIS...
B-BUT WHY?
'CUZ WORKER ANTS ARE ALL S'POSED TO LOOK THE SAME...

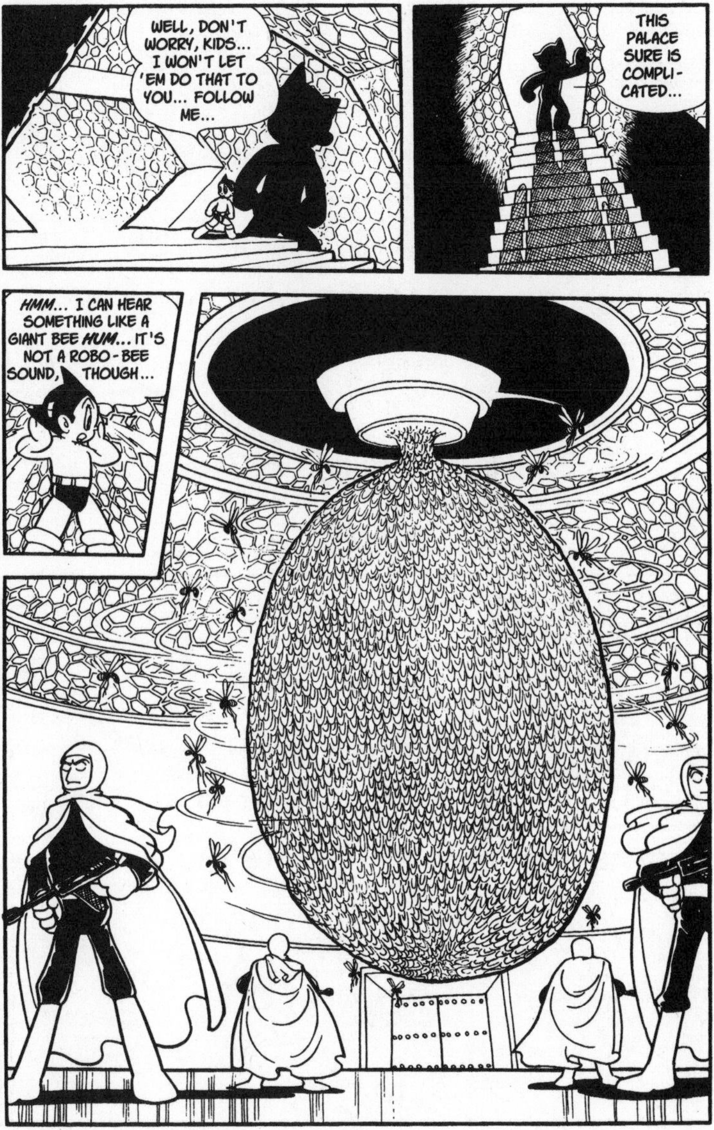
WELL, DON'T WORRY, KIDS... I WON'T LET 'EM DO THAT TO YOU... FOLLOW ME...
THIS PALACE SURE IS COMPLI-CATED...
HMM... I CAN HEAR SOMETHING LIKE A GIANT BEE *HUM*... IT'S NOT A ROBO-BEE SOUND, THOUGH...

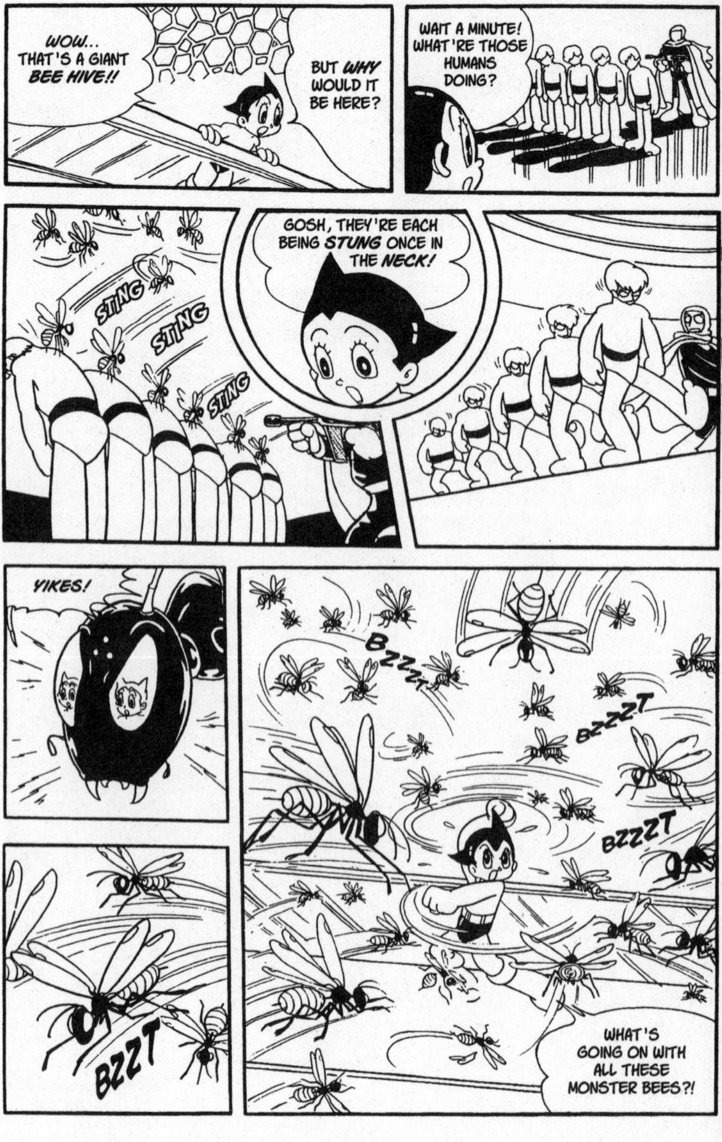
WOW... THAT'S A GIANT BEE HIVE!!
BUT WHY WOULD IT BE HERE?
WAIT A MINUTE! WHAT'RE THOSE HUMANS DOING?
STING
STING
STING
GOSH, THEY'RE EACH BEING STUNG ONCE IN THE NECK!
YIKES!
BZZT
BZZZT
BZZZZT
BZZZT
WHAT'S GOING ON WITH ALL THESE MONSTER BEES?!

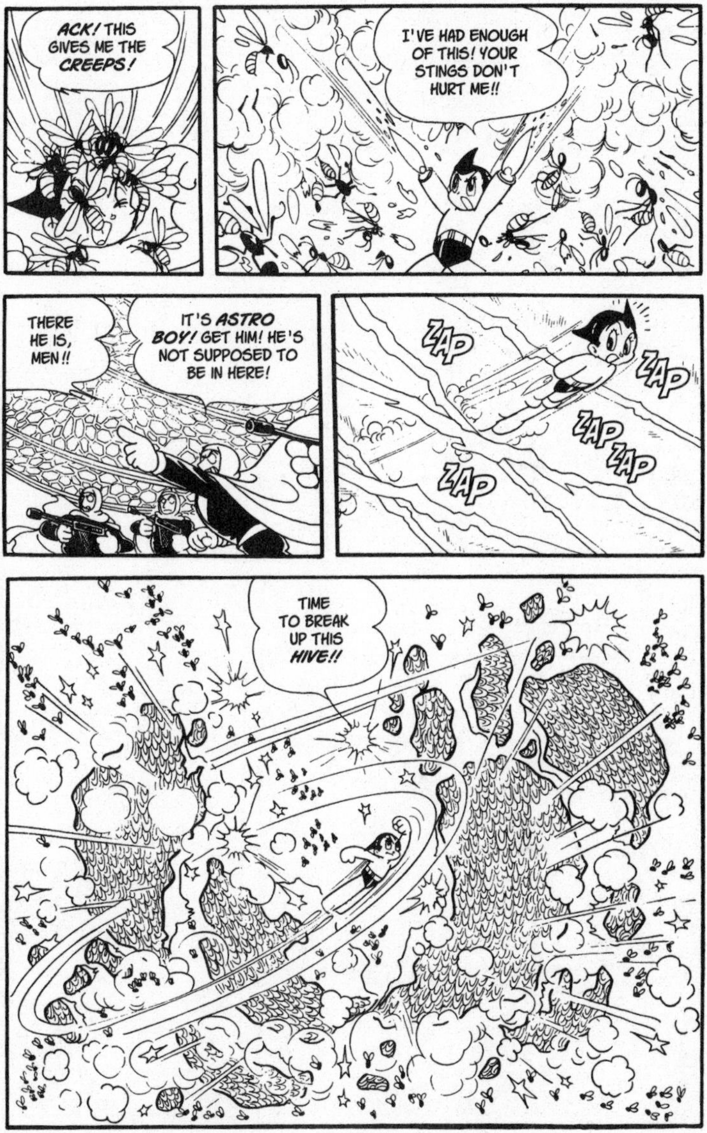
ACK! THIS GIVES ME THE CREEPS!
I'VE HAD ENOUGH OF THIS! YOUR STINGS DON'T HURT ME!!
THERE HE IS, MEN!!
IT'S ASTRO BOY! GET HIM! HE'S NOT SUPPOSED TO BE IN HERE!
ZAP
ZAP
ZAP ZAP
ZAP
TIME TO BREAK UP THIS HIVE!!

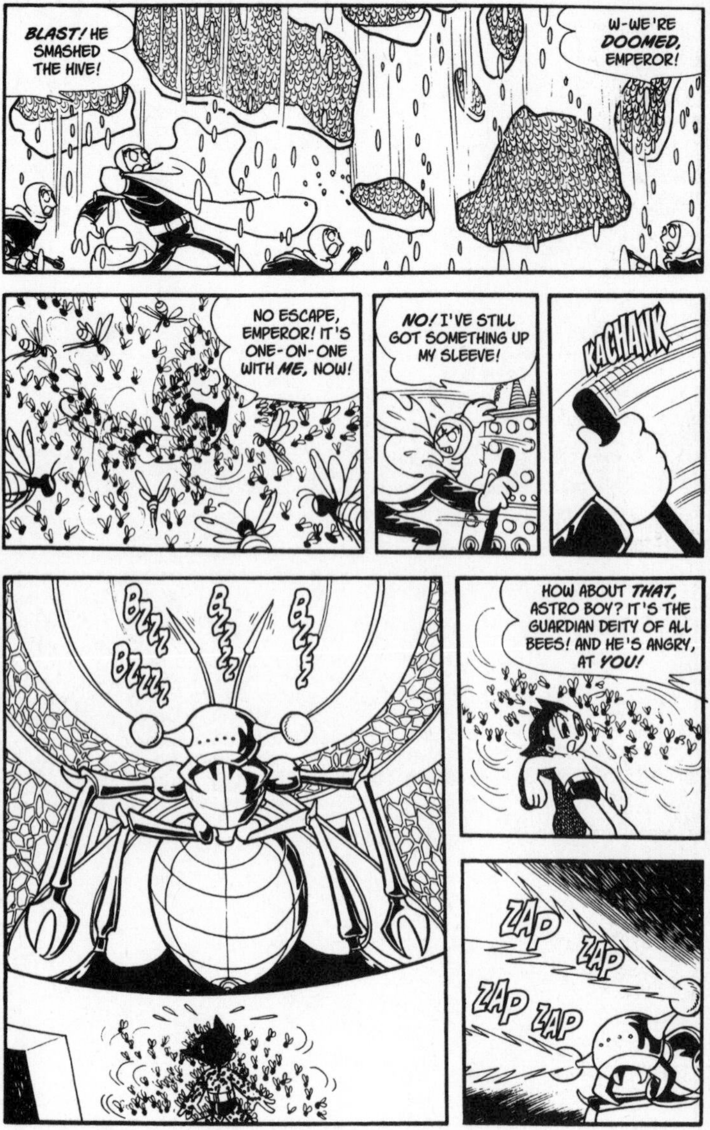
BLAST! HE SMASHED THE HIVE!
W-WE'RE DOOMED, EMPEROR!
NO ESCAPE, EMPEROR! IT'S ONE-ON-ONE WITH ME, NOW!
NO! I'VE STILL GOT SOMETHING UP MY SLEEVE!
KACHANK
BZZZZ
BZZZZ
BZZZ
BZZZ
HOW ABOUT THAT, ASTRO BOY? IT'S THE GUARDIAN DEITY OF ALL BEES! AND HE'S ANGRY, AT YOU!
ZAP
ZAP
ZAP
ZAP

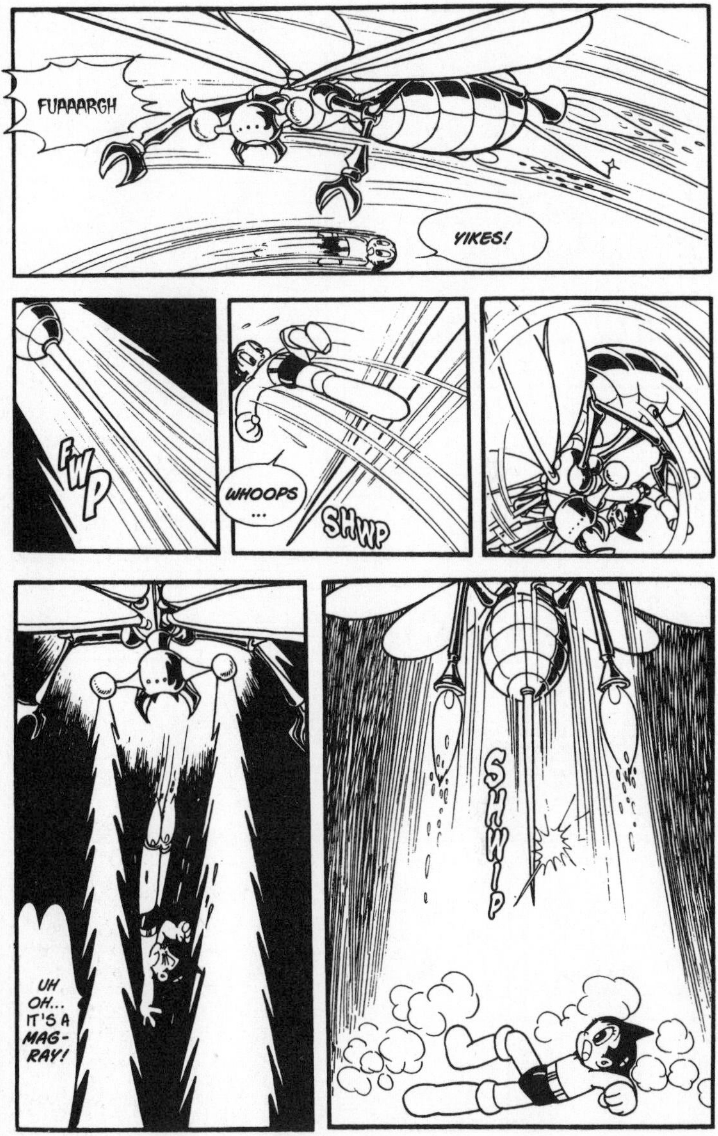
FUAAARGH
YIKES!
FWP
WHOOPS ...
SHWP
UH OH... IT'S A MAG-RAY!
SHWIP

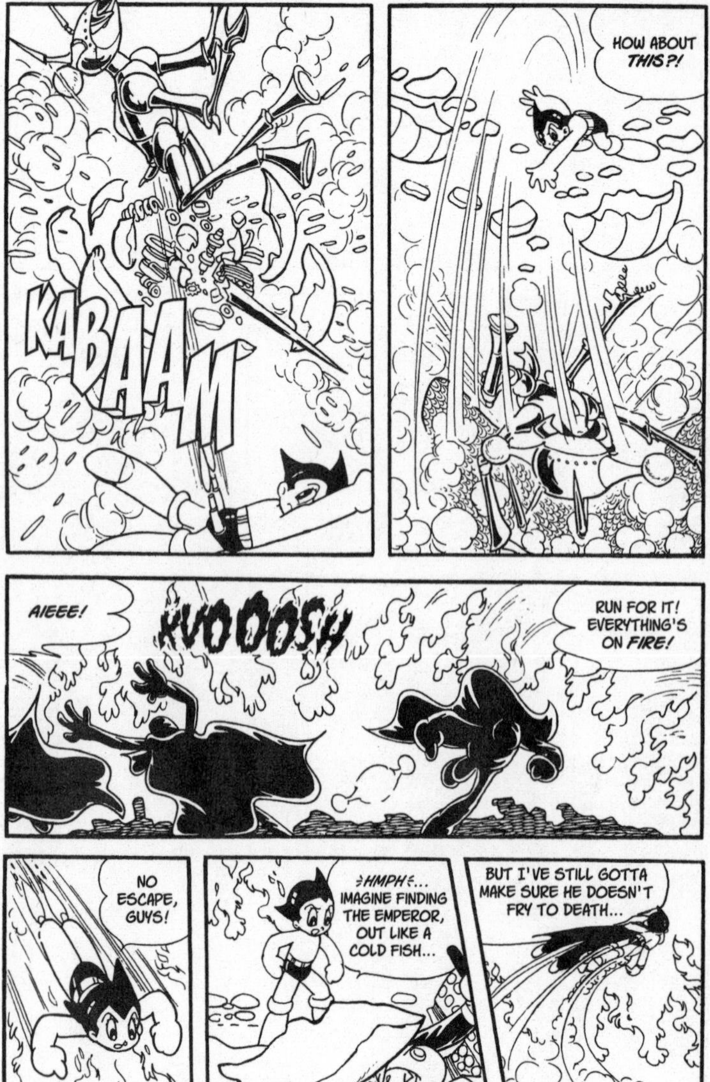
KABAAM
HOW ABOUT THIS?!
AIEEE!
KVOOOSH
RUN FOR IT! EVERYTHING'S ON FIRE!
NO ESCAPE, GUYS!
HMPH... IMAGINE FINDING THE EMPEROR, OUT LIKE A COLD FISH...
BUT I'VE STILL GOTTA MAKE SURE HE DOESN'T FRY TO DEATH...

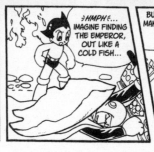

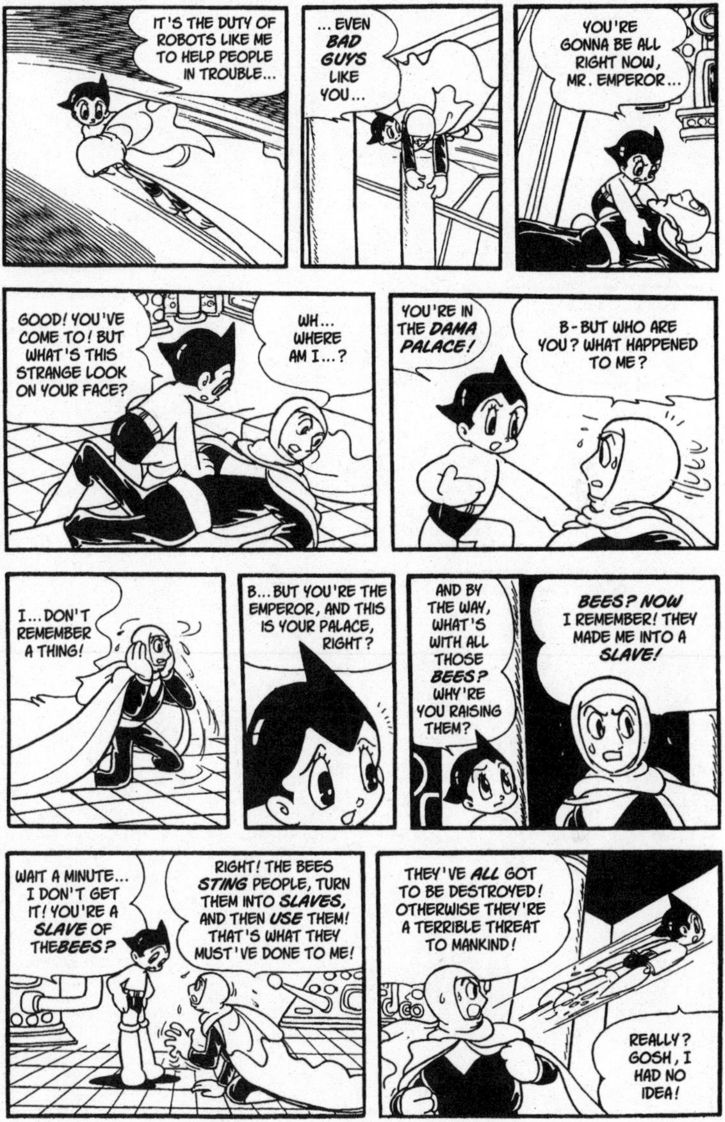
IT'S THE DUTY OF ROBOTS LIKE ME TO HELP PEOPLE IN TROUBLE...
... EVEN BAD GUYS LIKE YOU...
YOU'RE GONNA BE ALL RIGHT NOW, MR. EMPEROR...
GOOD! YOU'VE COME TO! BUT WHAT'S THIS STRANGE LOOK ON YOUR FACE?
WH... WHERE AM I...?
YOU'RE IN THE DAMA PALACE!
B-BUT WHO ARE YOU? WHAT HAPPENED TO ME?
I... DON'T REMEMBER A THING!
B... BUT YOU'RE THE EMPEROR, AND THIS IS YOUR PALACE, RIGHT?
AND BY THE WAY, WHAT'S WITH ALL THOSE BEES? WHY'RE YOU RAISING THEM?
BEES? NOW I REMEMBER! THEY MADE ME INTO A SLAVE!
WAIT A MINUTE... I DON'T GET IT! YOU'RE A SLAVE OF THEBEES?
RIGHT! THE BEES STING PEOPLE, TURN THEM INTO SLAVES, AND THEN USE THEM! THAT'S WHAT THEY MUST'VE DONE TO ME!
THEY'VE ALL GOT TO BE DESTROYED! OTHERWISE THEY'RE A TERRIBLE THREAT TO MANKIND!
REALLY? GOSH, I HAD NO IDEA!

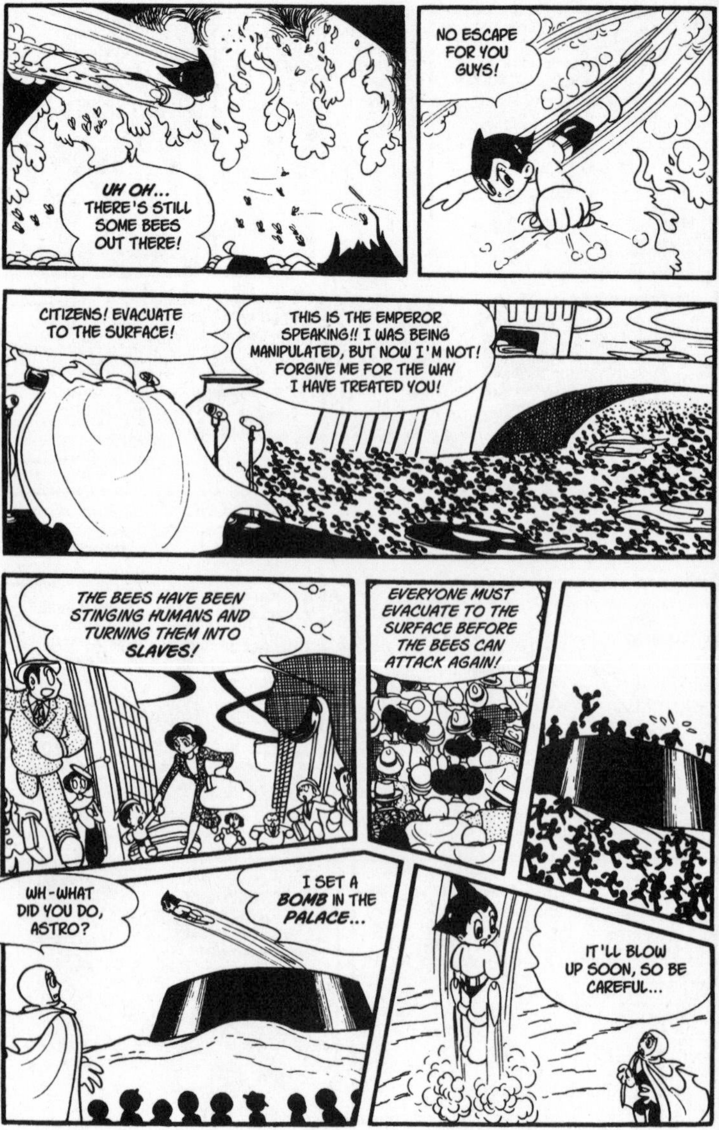
UH OH...
THERE'S STILL SOME BEES OUT THERE!
NO ESCAPE FOR YOU GUYS!
CITIZENS! EVACUATE TO THE SURFACE!
THIS IS THE EMPEROR SPEAKING!! I WAS BEING MANIPULATED, BUT NOW I'M NOT! FORGIVE ME FOR THE WAY I HAVE TREATED YOU!
THE BEES HAVE BEEN STINGING HUMANS AND TURNING THEM INTO SLAVES!
EVERYONE MUST EVACUATE TO THE SURFACE BEFORE THE BEES CAN ATTACK AGAIN!
WH-WHAT DID YOU DO, ASTRO?
I SET A BOMB IN THE PALACE...
IT'LL BLOW UP SOON, SO BE CAREFUL...

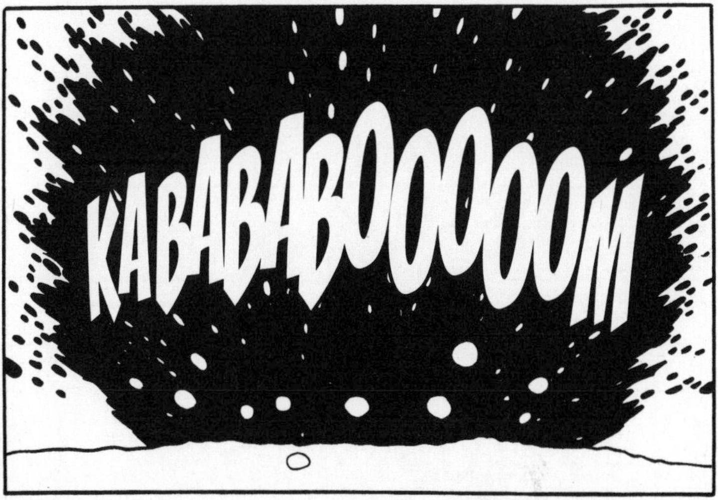
KABABABOOOOOM

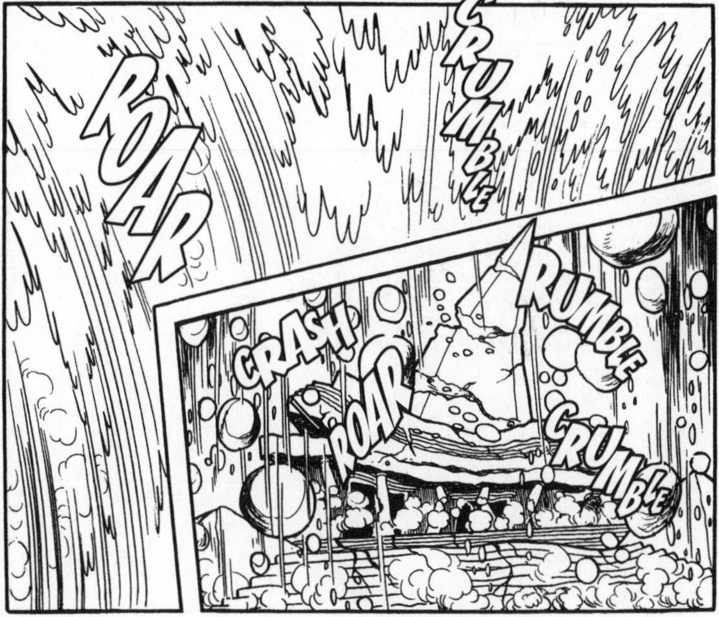
ROAR
CRUMBLE
CRASH
ROAR
RUMBLE
CRUMBLE

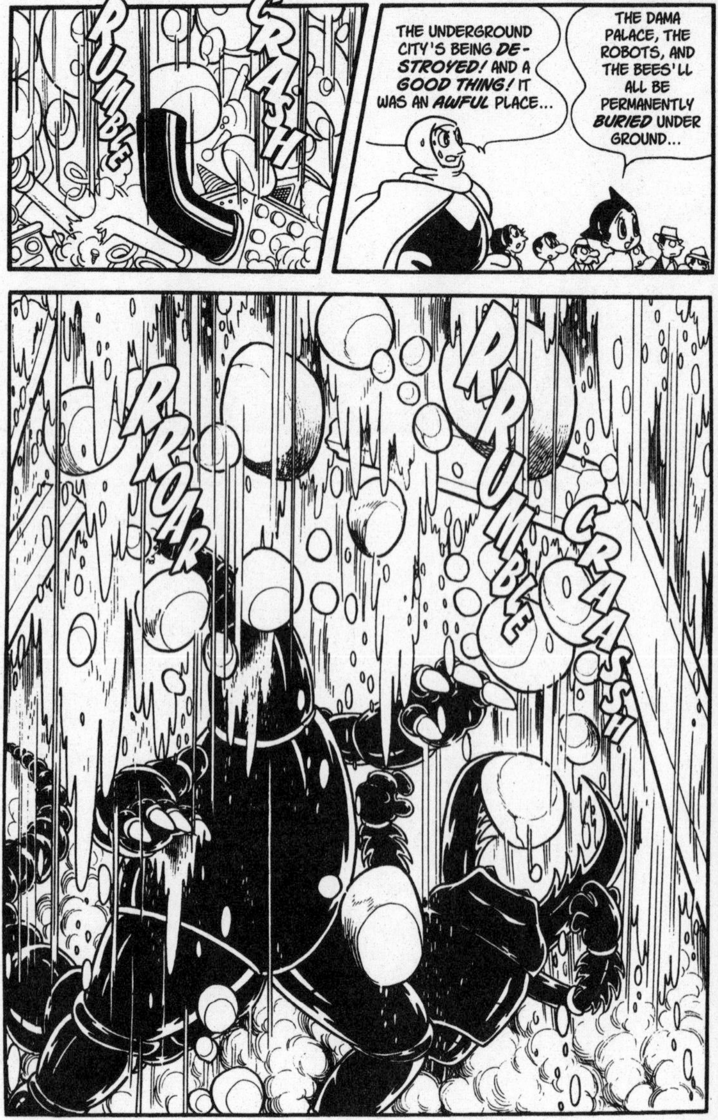
RUMBLE
CRASH
THE UNDERGROUND CITY'S BEING DE-STROYED! AND A GOOD THING! IT WAS AN AWFUL PLACE...
THE DAMA PALACE, THE ROBOTS, AND THE BEES'LL ALL BE PERMANENTLY BURIED UNDER GROUND...
RROAR
RRUMBLE
CRASSH

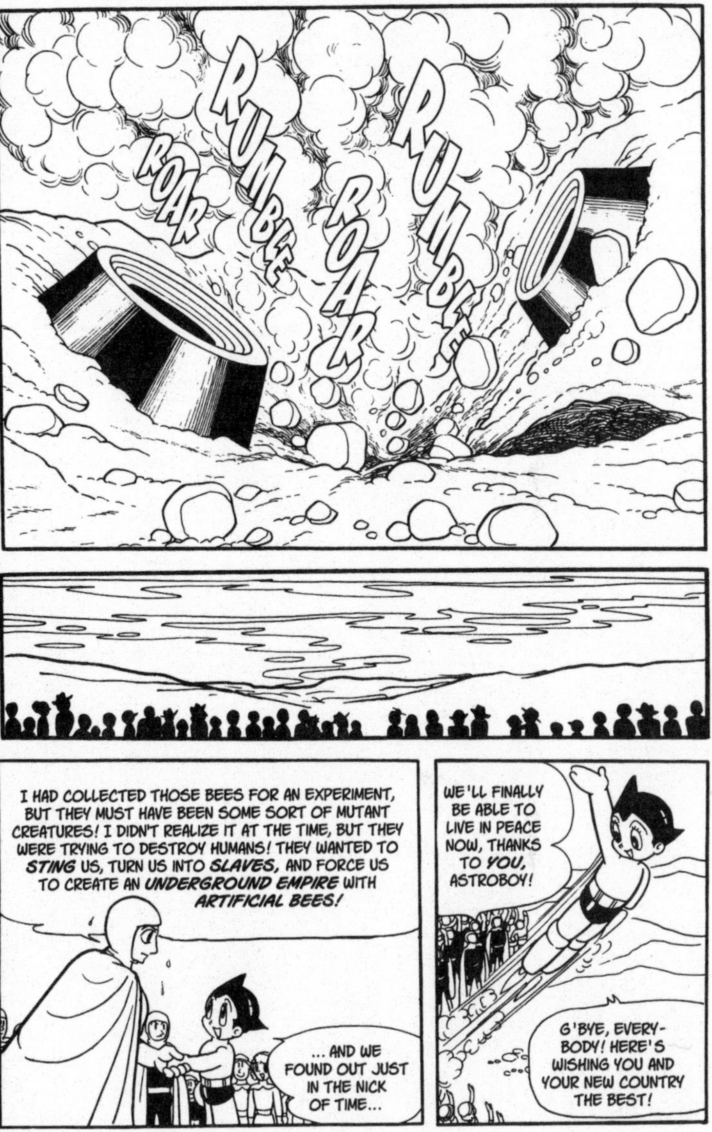
ROAR
RUMBLE
RUMBLE
ROAR
I HAD COLLECTED THOSE BEES FOR AN EXPERIMENT, BUT THEY MUST HAVE BEEN SOME SORT OF MUTANT CREATURES! I DIDN'T REALIZE IT AT THE TIME, BUT THEY WERE TRYING TO DESTROY HUMANS! THEY WANTED TO STING US, TURN US INTO SLAVES, AND FORCE US TO CREATE AN UNDERGROUND EMPIRE WITH ARTIFICIAL BEES!
... AND WE FOUND OUT JUST IN THE NICK OF TIME...
WE'LL FINALLY BE ABLE TO LIVE IN PEACE NOW, THANKS TO YOU, ASTROBOY!
G'BYE, EVERY-BODY! HERE'S WISHING YOU AND YOUR NEW COUNTRY THE BEST!

FORTRESS
OF THE
CENTAURS

First serialized in May and June 1958
in *Shonen* magazine.

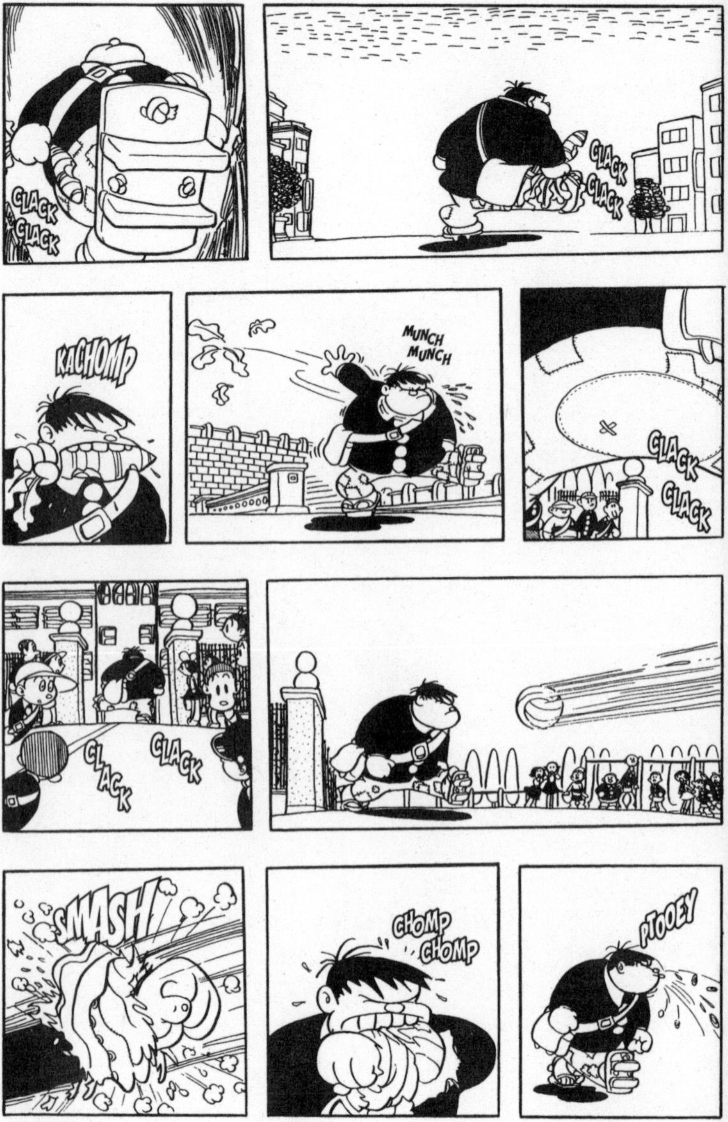
CLACK
CLACK
CLACK
CLACK
KACHOMP
MUNCH
MUNCH
CLACK
CLACK
CLACK
CLACK
SMASH!
CHOMP
CHOMP
PTOOEY

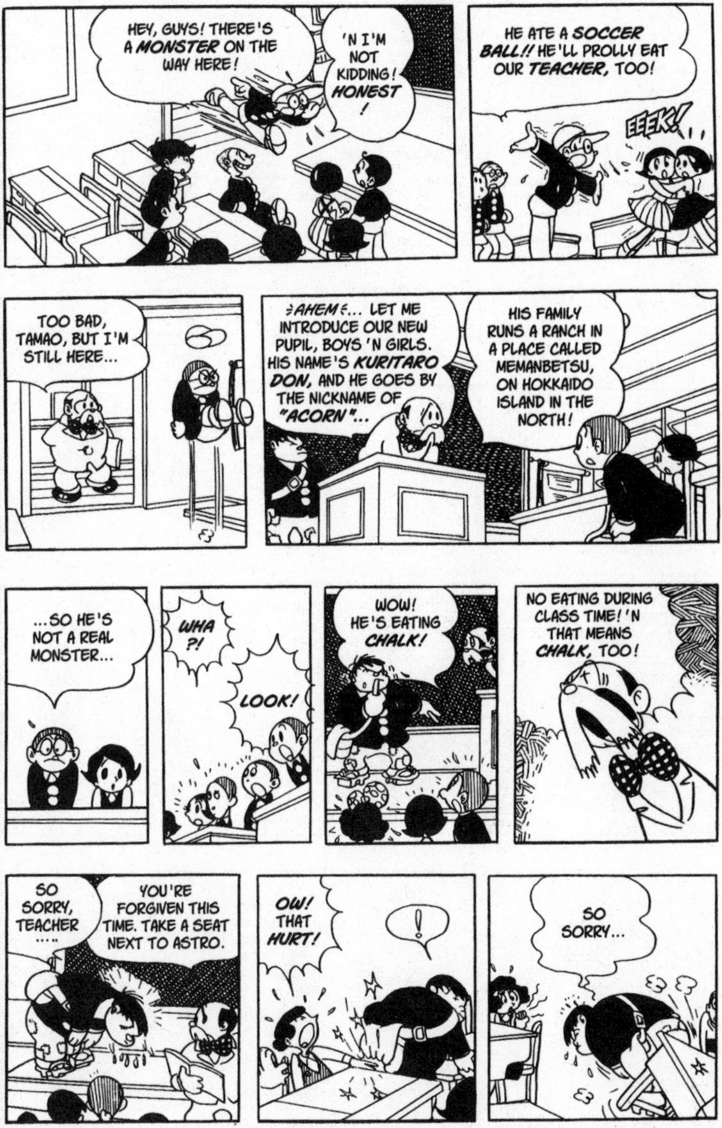
HEY, GUYS! THERE'S A MONSTER ON THE WAY HERE!
'N I'M NOT KIDDING! HONEST!
HE ATE A SOCCER BALL!! HE'LL PROLLY EAT OUR TEACHER, TOO!
EEEK!
TOO BAD, TAMAO, BUT I'M STILL HERE...
≠AHEM≠... LET ME INTRODUCE OUR NEW PUPIL, BOYS 'N GIRLS. HIS NAME'S KURITARO DON, AND HE GOES BY THE NICKNAME OF "ACORN"...
HIS FAMILY RUNS A RANCH IN A PLACE CALLED MEMANBETSU, ON HOKKAIDO ISLAND IN THE NORTH!
...SO HE'S NOT A REAL MONSTER...
WHA?!
LOOK!
WOW! HE'S EATING CHALK!
NO EATING DURING CLASS TIME! 'N THAT MEANS CHALK, TOO!
SO SORRY, TEACHER.....
YOU'RE FORGIVEN THIS TIME. TAKE A SEAT NEXT TO ASTRO.
OW! THAT HURT!
!
SO SORRY...

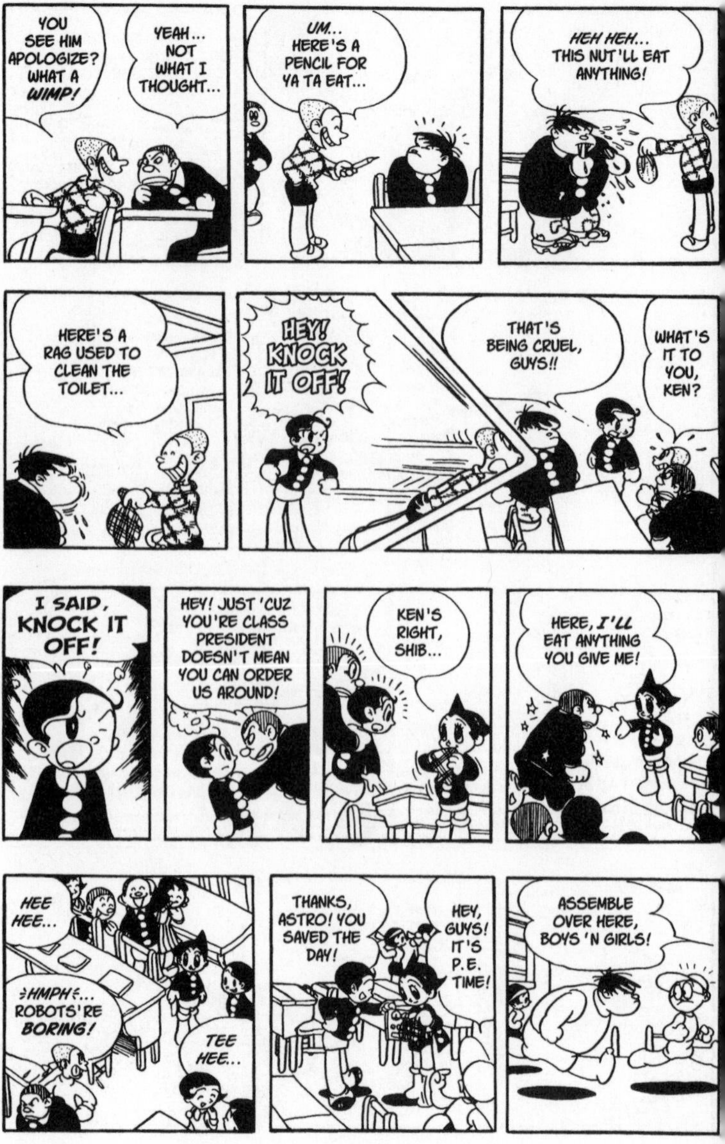
YOU SEE HIM APOLOGIZE? WHAT A WIMP!
YEAH... NOT WHAT I THOUGHT...
UM... HERE'S A PENCIL FOR YA TA EAT...
HEH HEH... THIS NUT'LL EAT ANYTHING!
HERE'S A RAG USED TO CLEAN THE TOILET...
HEY! KNOCK IT OFF!
THAT'S BEING CRUEL, GUYS!!
WHAT'S IT TO YOU, KEN?
I SAID, KNOCK IT OFF!
HEY! JUST 'CUZ YOU'RE CLASS PRESIDENT DOESN'T MEAN YOU CAN ORDER US AROUND!
KEN'S RIGHT, SHIB...
HERE, I'LL EAT ANYTHING YOU GIVE ME!
HEE HEE...
HMPH... ROBOTS'RE BORING!
TEE HEE...
THANKS, ASTRO! YOU SAVED THE DAY!
HEY, GUYS! IT'S P.E. TIME!
ASSEMBLE OVER HERE, BOYS 'N GIRLS!

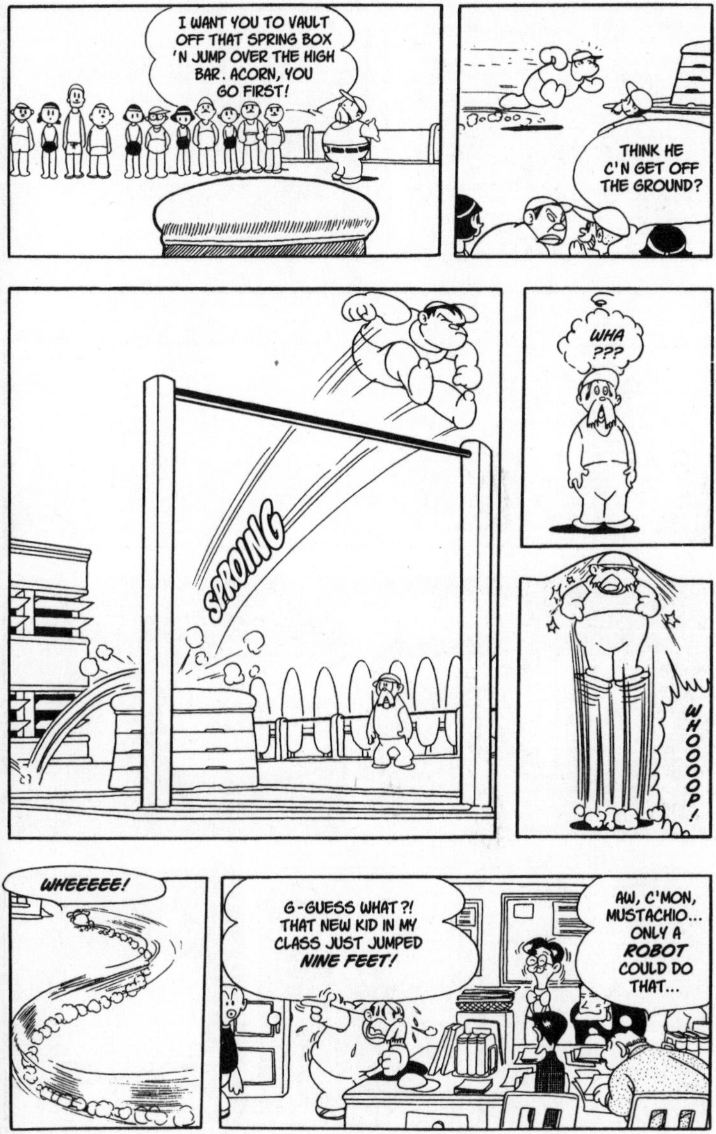

I WANT YOU TO VAULT OFF THAT SPRING BOX 'N JUMP OVER THE HIGH BAR. ACORN, YOU GO FIRST!
THINK HE C'N GET OFF THE GROUND?
SPROING
WHA ???
WHOOOOOP!
WHEEEEE!
G-GUESS WHAT?! THAT NEW KID IN MY CLASS JUST JUMPED NINE FEET!
AW, C'MON, MUSTACHIO... ONLY A ROBOT COULD DO THAT...

DID HE HAVE A PHYSICAL EXAM?

HEY! I *KNOW* HE'S A *HUMAN*, OKAY?

B-BUT NO HUMAN COULD DO THAT!

WELL, COME ALONG WITH ME THEN TO SEE!!

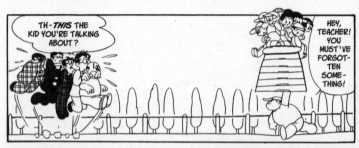

TH-*THIS* THE KID YOU'RE TALKING ABOUT?

HEY, TEACHER! YOU MUST'VE FORGOTTEN SOMETHING!

'ELLO? REALLY? THAT *IS* AN ODD KID...

...BUT A REALLY TRAINED HUMAN MIGHT BE ABLE TO JUMP THAT HIGH...

UM, WAIT A SEC, MUSTACHIO...

I HEAR STRANGE FOOTSTEPS...

CLIP CLOP CLIP CLIP

CLIP CLOP CLIP CLOP

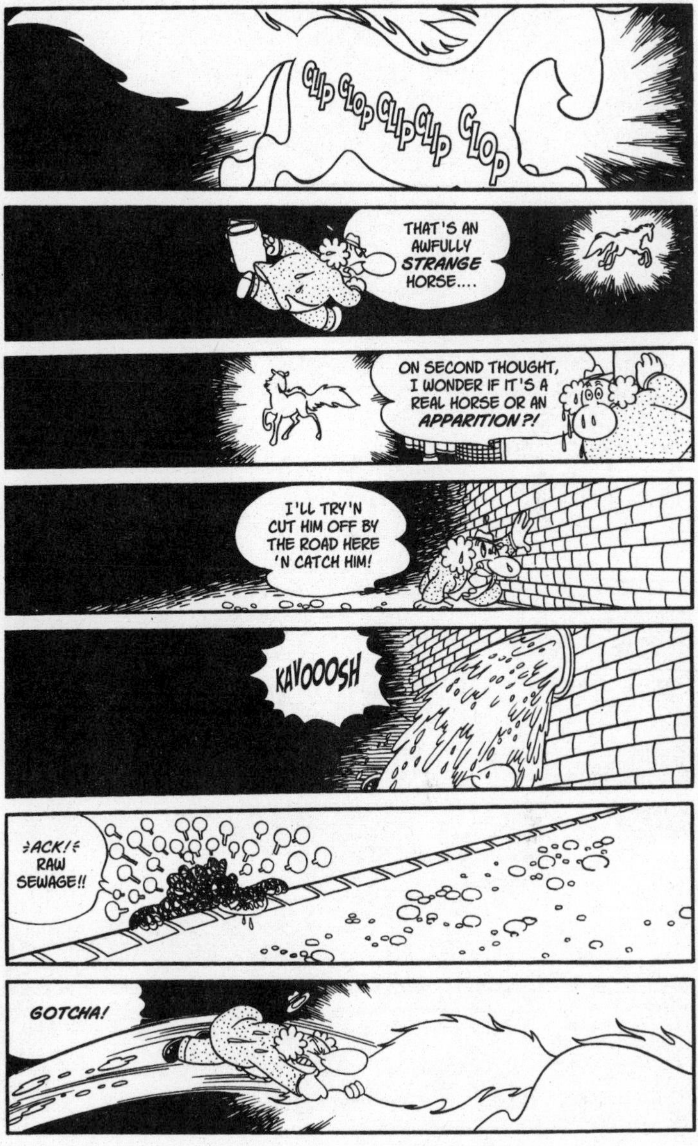
CLIP CLOP CLIP CLIP CLOP
THAT'S AN AWFULLY STRANGE HORSE....
ON SECOND THOUGHT, I WONDER IF IT'S A REAL HORSE OR AN APPARITION?!
I'LL TRY'N CUT HIM OFF BY THE ROAD HERE 'N CATCH HIM!
KAVOOOSH
ACK! RAW SEWAGE!!
GOTCHA!

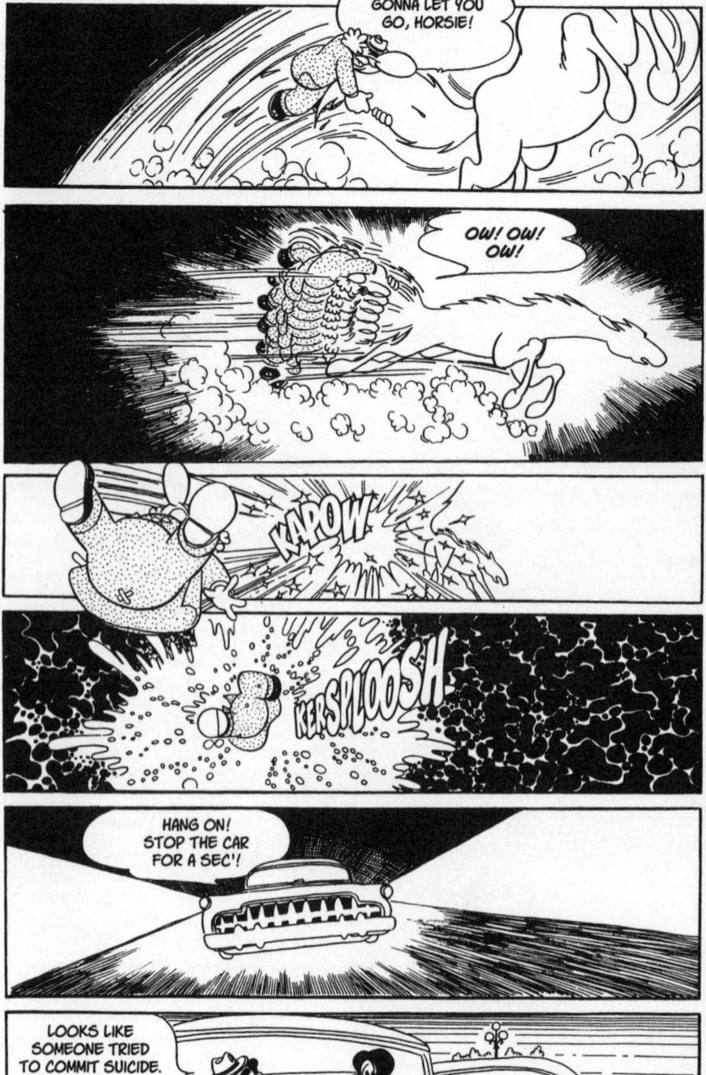
I'M NOT GONNA LET YOU GO, HORSIE!
OW! OW! OW!
KAPOW
KERSPLOOSH
HANG ON! STOP THE CAR FOR A SEC'!
LOOKS LIKE SOMEONE TRIED TO COMMIT SUICIDE. LET'S HELP THE POOR GUY OUT...

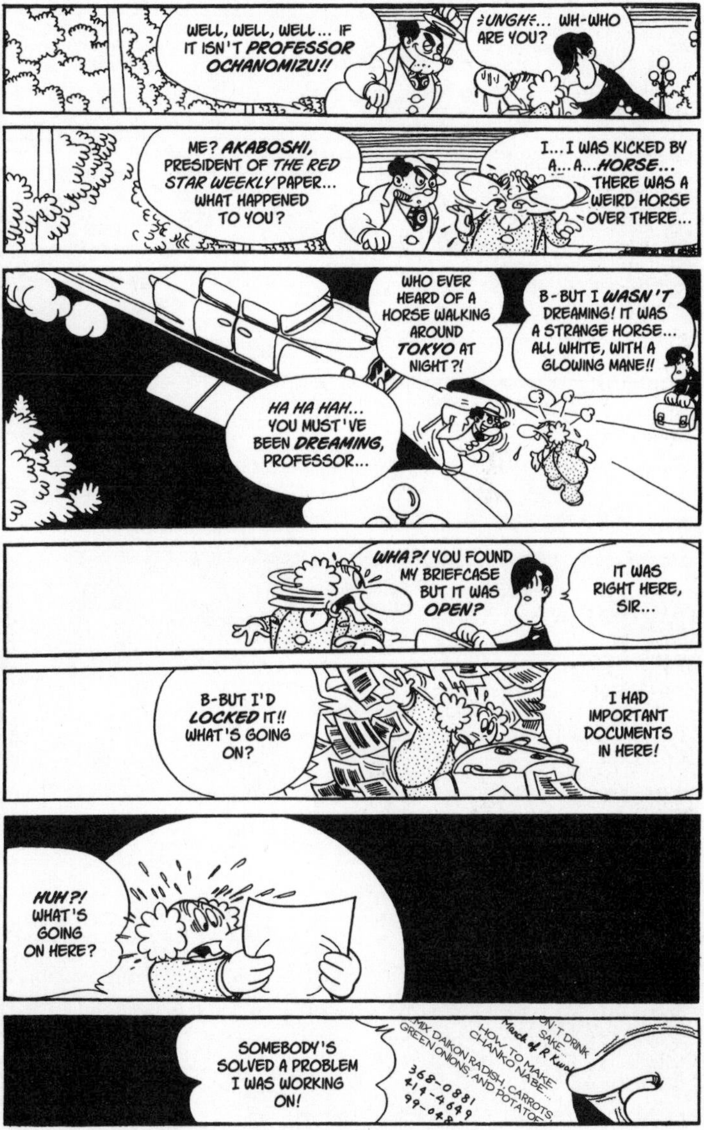
WELL, WELL, WELL... IF IT ISN'T PROFESSOR OCHANOMIZU!!
UNGH... WH-WHO ARE YOU?
ME? AKABOSHI, PRESIDENT OF THE RED STAR WEEKLY PAPER... WHAT HAPPENED TO YOU?
I... I WAS KICKED BY A... A... HORSE... THERE WAS A WEIRD HORSE OVER THERE...
WHO EVER HEARD OF A HORSE WALKING AROUND TOKYO AT NIGHT?!
B-BUT I WASN'T DREAMING! IT WAS A STRANGE HORSE... ALL WHITE, WITH A GLOWING MANE!!
HA HA HAH... YOU MUST'VE BEEN DREAMING, PROFESSOR...
WHA?! YOU FOUND MY BRIEFCASE BUT IT WAS OPEN?
IT WAS RIGHT HERE, SIR...
B-BUT I'D LOCKED IT!! WHAT'S GOING ON?
I HAD IMPORTANT DOCUMENTS IN HERE!
HUH?! WHAT'S GOING ON HERE?
SOMEBODY'S SOLVED A PROBLEM I WAS WORKING ON!
SAKE...
HOW TO MAKE CHANKO NABE...
368-0881
414-4649

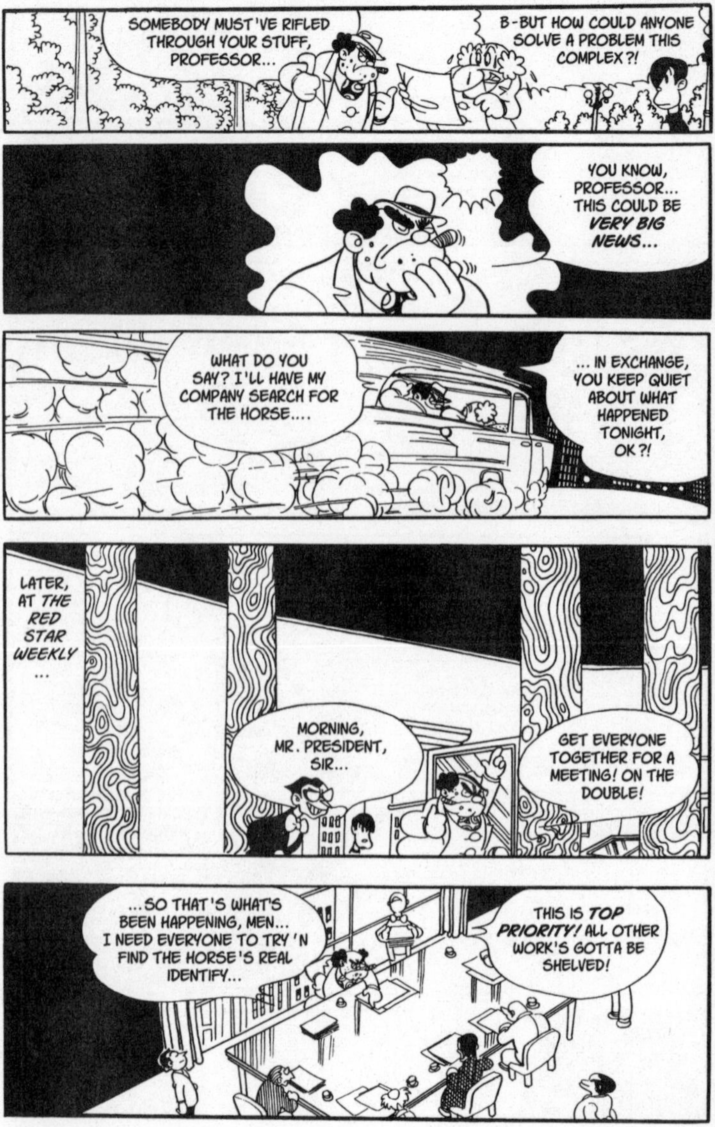
SOMEBODY MUST'VE RIFLED THROUGH YOUR STUFF, PROFESSOR...
B-BUT HOW COULD ANYONE SOLVE A PROBLEM THIS COMPLEX?!
YOU KNOW, PROFESSOR... THIS COULD BE *VERY BIG NEWS*...
WHAT DO YOU SAY? I'LL HAVE MY COMPANY SEARCH FOR THE HORSE....
... IN EXCHANGE, YOU KEEP QUIET ABOUT WHAT HAPPENED TONIGHT, OK?!
LATER, AT *THE RED STAR WEEKLY* ...
MORNING, MR. PRESIDENT, SIR...
GET EVERYONE TOGETHER FOR A MEETING! ON THE DOUBLE!
...SO THAT'S WHAT'S BEEN HAPPENING, MEN... I NEED EVERYONE TO TRY 'N FIND THE HORSE'S REAL IDENTIFY...
THIS IS *TOP PRIORITY!* ALL OTHER WORK'S GOTTA BE SHELVED!

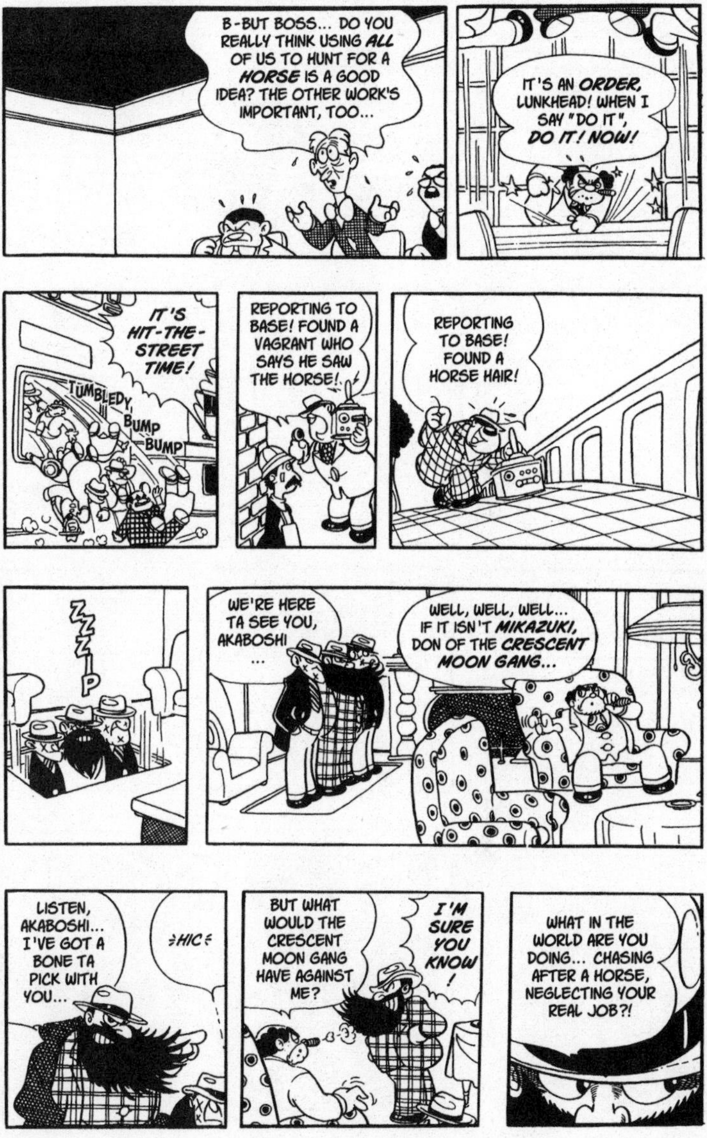
B-BUT BOSS... DO YOU REALLY THINK USING ALL OF US TO HUNT FOR A HORSE IS A GOOD IDEA? THE OTHER WORK'S IMPORTANT, TOO...
IT'S AN ORDER, LUNKHEAD! WHEN I SAY "DO IT", DO IT! NOW!
IT'S HIT-THE-STREET TIME!
TUMBLEDY, BUMP BUMP
REPORTING TO BASE! FOUND A VAGRANT WHO SAYS HE SAW THE HORSE!
REPORTING TO BASE! FOUND A HORSE HAIR!
ZZZIP
WE'RE HERE TA SEE YOU, AKABOSHI ...
WELL, WELL, WELL... IF IT ISN'T MIKAZUKI, DON OF THE CRESCENT MOON GANG...
LISTEN, AKABOSHI... I'VE GOT A BONE TA PICK WITH YOU...
HIC
BUT WHAT WOULD THE CRESCENT MOON GANG HAVE AGAINST ME?
I'M SURE YOU KNOW!
WHAT IN THE WORLD ARE YOU DOING... CHASING AFTER A HORSE, NEGLECTING YOUR REAL JOB?!

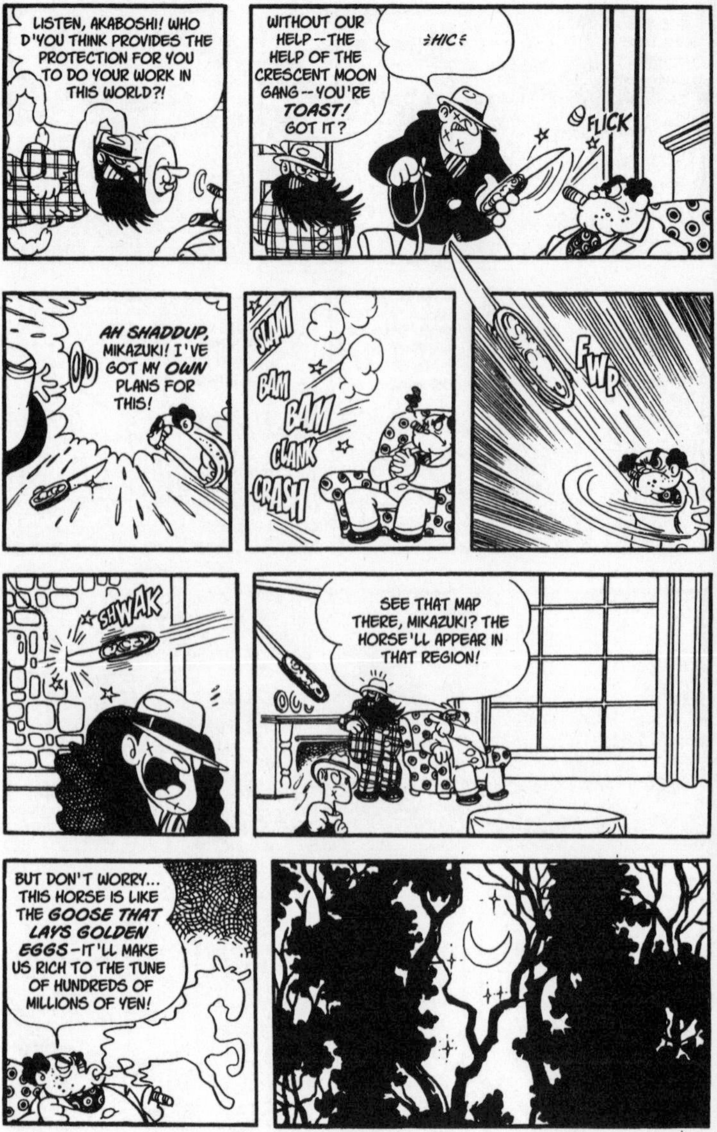
LISTEN, AKABOSHI! WHO D'YOU THINK PROVIDES THE PROTECTION FOR YOU TO DO YOUR WORK IN THIS WORLD?!
WITHOUT OUR HELP--THE HELP OF THE CRESCENT MOON GANG--YOU'RE TOAST! GOT IT?
HIC
FLICK
AH SHADDUP, MIKAZUKI! I'VE GOT MY OWN PLANS FOR THIS!
SLAM
BAM
BAM
CLANK
CRASH
FWP
SHWAK
SEE THAT MAP THERE, MIKAZUKI? THE HORSE'LL APPEAR IN THAT REGION!
BUT DON'T WORRY... THIS HORSE IS LIKE THE GOOSE THAT LAYS GOLDEN EGGS--IT'LL MAKE US RICH TO THE TUNE OF HUNDREDS OF MILLIONS OF YEN!

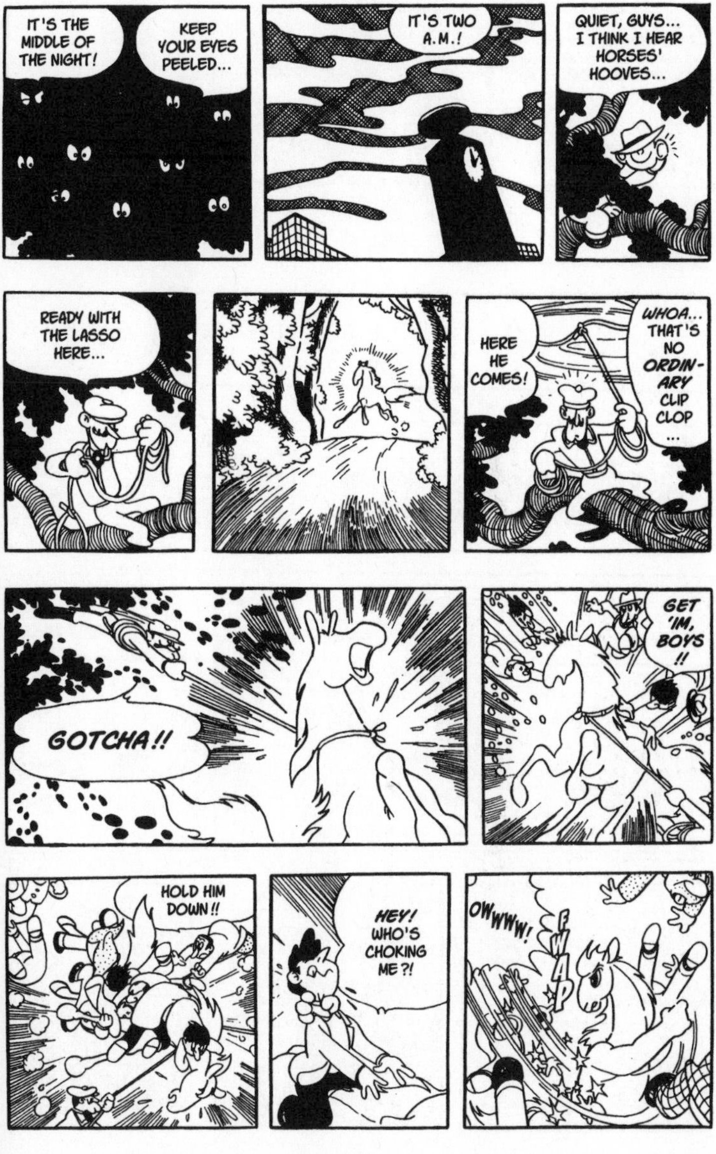
IT'S THE MIDDLE OF THE NIGHT!
KEEP YOUR EYES PEELED...
IT'S TWO A.M.!
QUIET, GUYS... I THINK I HEAR HORSES' HOOVES...
READY WITH THE LASSO HERE...
HERE HE COMES!
WHOA... THAT'S NO ORDINARY CLIP CLOP ...
GOTCHA!!
GET 'IM, BOYS !!
HOLD HIM DOWN!!
HEY! WHO'S CHOKING ME?!
OWWWW!
FWAP

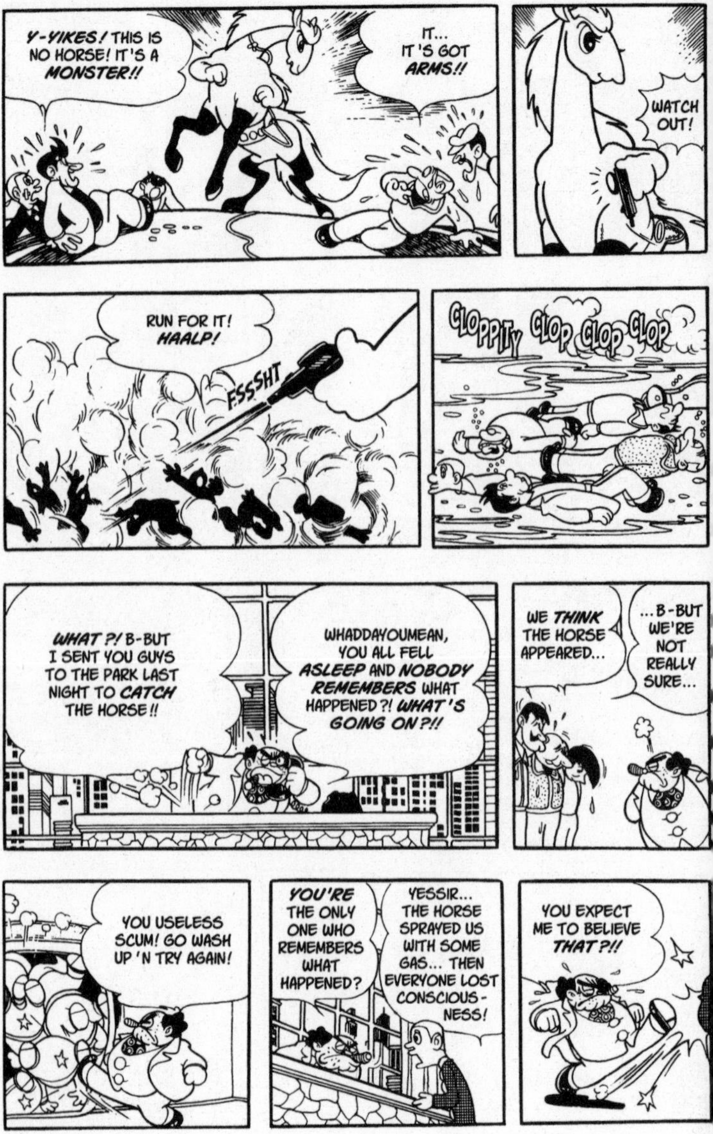
Y-YIKES! THIS IS NO HORSE! IT'S A MONSTER!!
IT... IT'S GOT ARMS!!
WATCH OUT!
RUN FOR IT! HAALP!
FSSSHT
CLOPPITY CLOP CLOP CLOP
WHAT?! B-BUT I SENT YOU GUYS TO THE PARK LAST NIGHT TO CATCH THE HORSE!!
WHADDAYOUMEAN, YOU ALL FELL ASLEEP AND NOBODY REMEMBERS WHAT HAPPENED?! WHAT'S GOING ON?!!
WE THINK THE HORSE APPEARED...
...B-BUT WE'RE NOT REALLY SURE...
YOU USELESS SCUM! GO WASH UP 'N TRY AGAIN!
YOU'RE THE ONLY ONE WHO REMEMBERS WHAT HAPPENED?
YESSIR... THE HORSE SPRAYED US WITH SOME GAS... THEN EVERYONE LOST CONSCIOUS-NESS!
YOU EXPECT ME TO BELIEVE THAT?!!

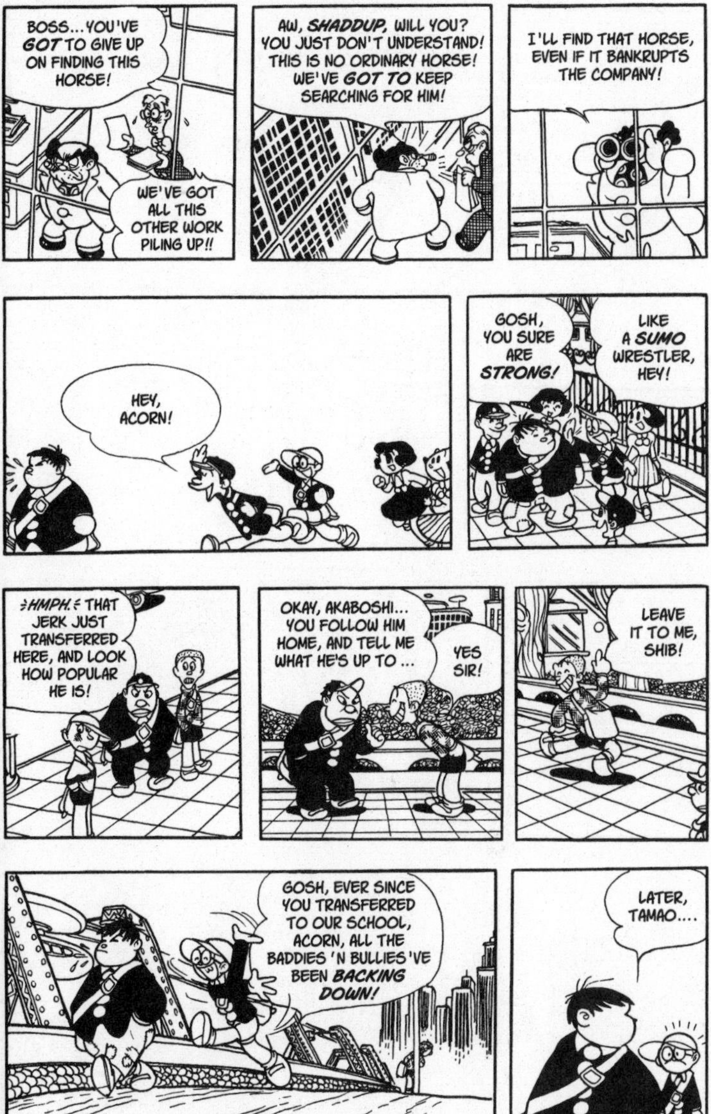
BOSS...YOU'VE GOT TO GIVE UP ON FINDING THIS HORSE!
WE'VE GOT ALL THIS OTHER WORK PILING UP!!
AW, SHADDUP, WILL YOU? YOU JUST DON'T UNDERSTAND! THIS IS NO ORDINARY HORSE! WE'VE GOT TO KEEP SEARCHING FOR HIM!
I'LL FIND THAT HORSE, EVEN IF IT BANKRUPTS THE COMPANY!
HEY, ACORN!
GOSH, YOU SURE ARE STRONG!
LIKE A SUMO WRESTLER, HEY!
HMPH. THAT JERK JUST TRANSFERRED HERE, AND LOOK HOW POPULAR HE IS!
OKAY, AKABOSHI... YOU FOLLOW HIM HOME, AND TELL ME WHAT HE'S UP TO ...
YES SIR!
LEAVE IT TO ME, SHIB!
GOSH, EVER SINCE YOU TRANSFERRED TO OUR SCHOOL, ACORN, ALL THE BADDIES 'N BULLIES 'VE BEEN BACKING DOWN!
LATER, TAMAO....

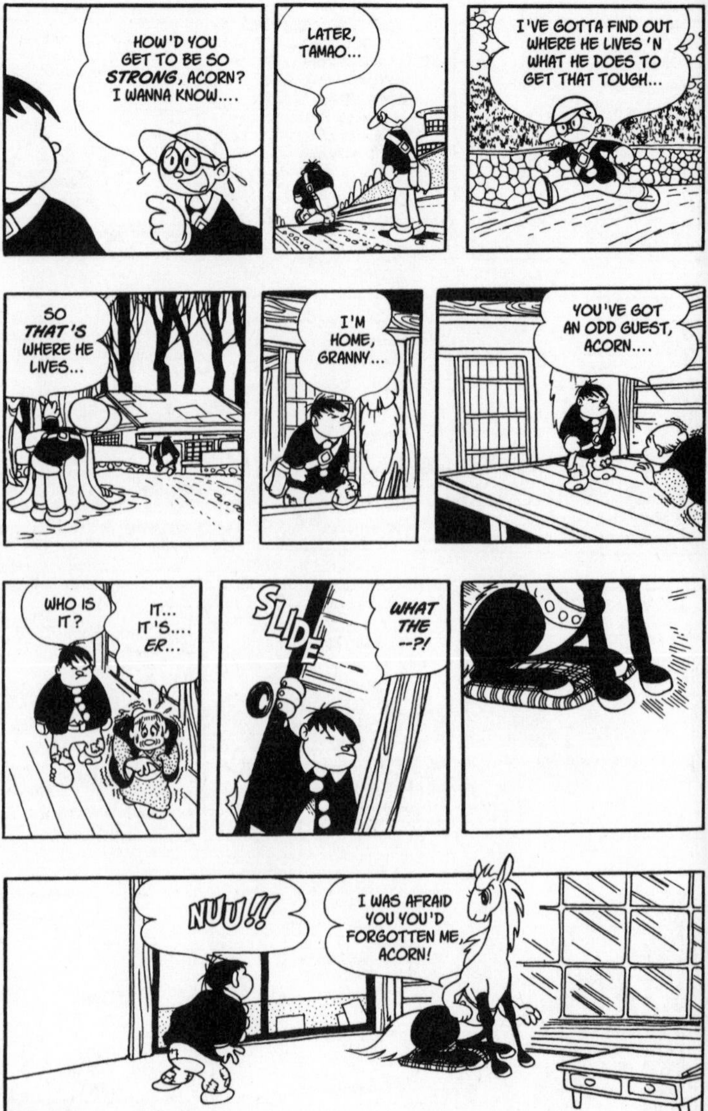
HOW'D YOU GET TO BE SO STRONG, ACORN? I WANNA KNOW....
LATER, TAMAO...
I'VE GOTTA FIND OUT WHERE HE LIVES 'N WHAT HE DOES TO GET THAT TOUGH...
SO THAT'S WHERE HE LIVES...
I'M HOME, GRANNY...
YOU'VE GOT AN ODD GUEST, ACORN....
WHO IS IT?
IT... IT'S.... ER...
SLIDE
WHAT THE --?!
NUU!!
I WAS AFRAID YOU YOU'D FORGOTTEN ME, ACORN!

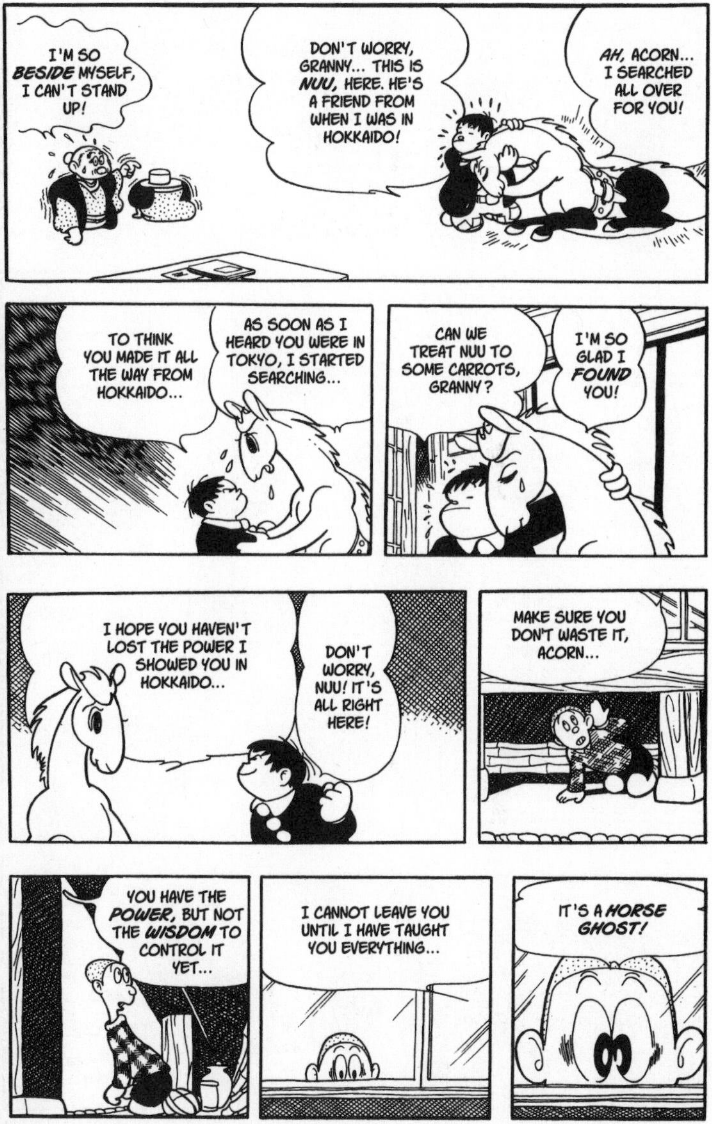
I'M SO *BESIDE* MYSELF, I CAN'T STAND UP!
DON'T WORRY, GRANNY... THIS IS *NUU,* HERE. HE'S A FRIEND FROM WHEN I WAS IN HOKKAIDO!
AH, ACORN... I SEARCHED ALL OVER FOR YOU!
TO THINK YOU MADE IT ALL THE WAY FROM HOKKAIDO...
AS SOON AS I HEARD YOU WERE IN TOKYO, I STARTED SEARCHING...
CAN WE TREAT NUU TO SOME CARROTS, GRANNY?
I'M SO GLAD I *FOUND* YOU!
I HOPE YOU HAVEN'T LOST THE POWER I SHOWED YOU IN HOKKAIDO...
DON'T WORRY, NUU! IT'S ALL RIGHT HERE!
MAKE SURE YOU DON'T WASTE IT, ACORN...
YOU HAVE THE *POWER,* BUT NOT THE *WISDOM* TO CONTROL IT YET...
I CANNOT LEAVE YOU UNTIL I HAVE TAUGHT YOU EVERYTHING...
IT'S A *HORSE GHOST!*

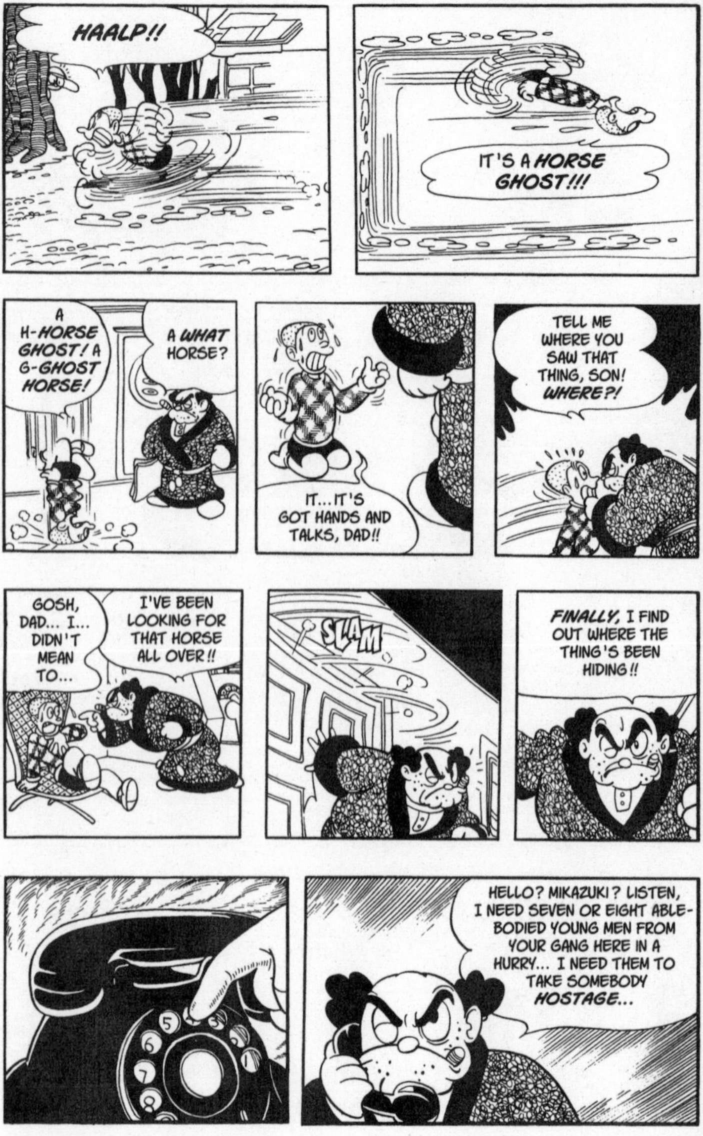
HAALP!!
IT'S A HORSE GHOST!!!
A H-HORSE GHOST! A G-GHOST HORSE!
A WHAT HORSE?
IT... IT'S GOT HANDS AND TALKS, DAD!!
TELL ME WHERE YOU SAW THAT THING, SON! WHERE?!
GOSH, DAD... I... DIDN'T MEAN TO...
I'VE BEEN LOOKING FOR THAT HORSE ALL OVER!!
SLAM
FINALLY, I FIND OUT WHERE THE THING'S BEEN HIDING!!
HELLO? MIKAZUKI? LISTEN, I NEED SEVEN OR EIGHT ABLE-BODIED YOUNG MEN FROM YOUR GANG HERE IN A HURRY... I NEED THEM TO TAKE SOMEBODY HOSTAGE...

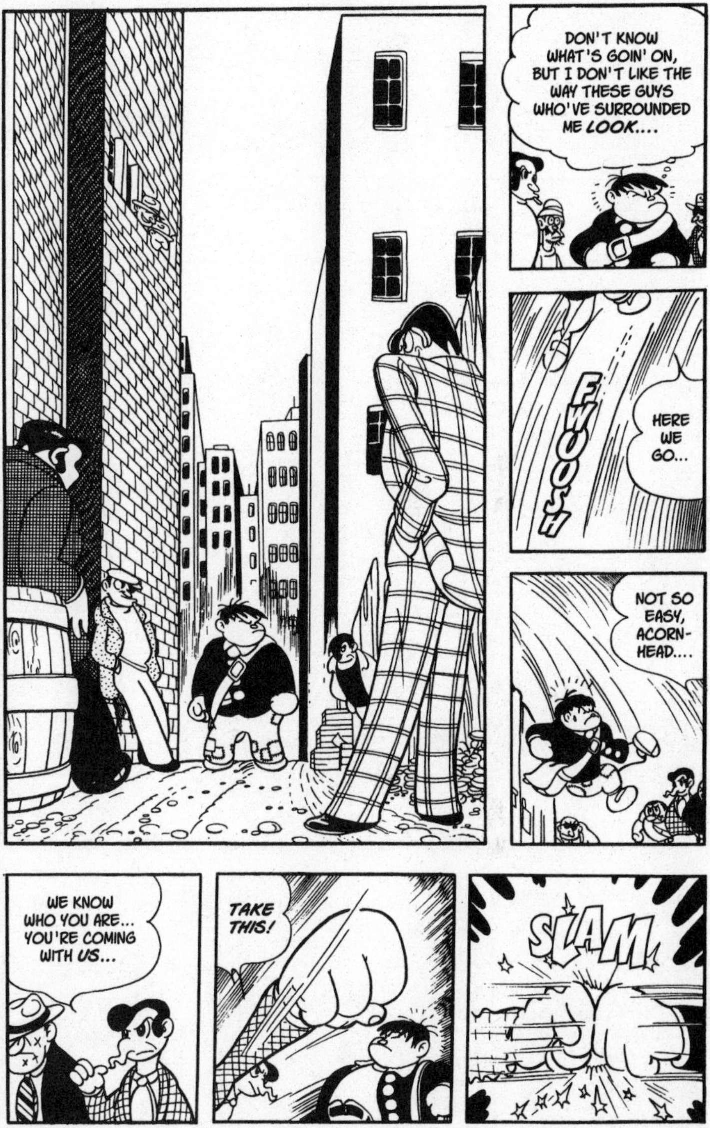
DON'T KNOW WHAT'S GOIN' ON, BUT I DON'T LIKE THE WAY THESE GUYS WHO'VE SURROUNDED ME LOOK....
FWOOOSH
HERE WE GO...
NOT SO EASY, ACORN-HEAD....
WE KNOW WHO YOU ARE... YOU'RE COMING WITH US...
TAKE THIS!
SLAM

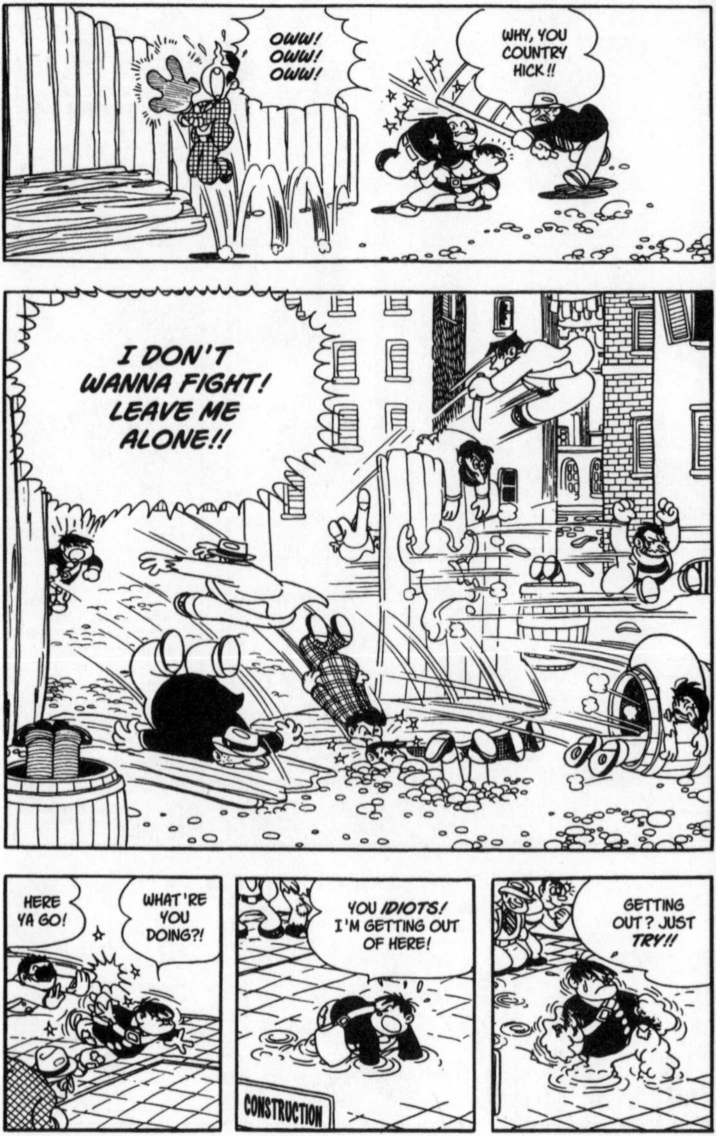
OWW! OWW! OWW!
WHY, YOU COUNTRY HICK!!
I DON'T WANNA FIGHT! LEAVE ME ALONE!!
HERE YA GO!
WHAT'RE YOU DOING?!
YOU IDIOTS! I'M GETTING OUT OF HERE!
CONSTRUCTION
GETTING OUT? JUST TRY!!

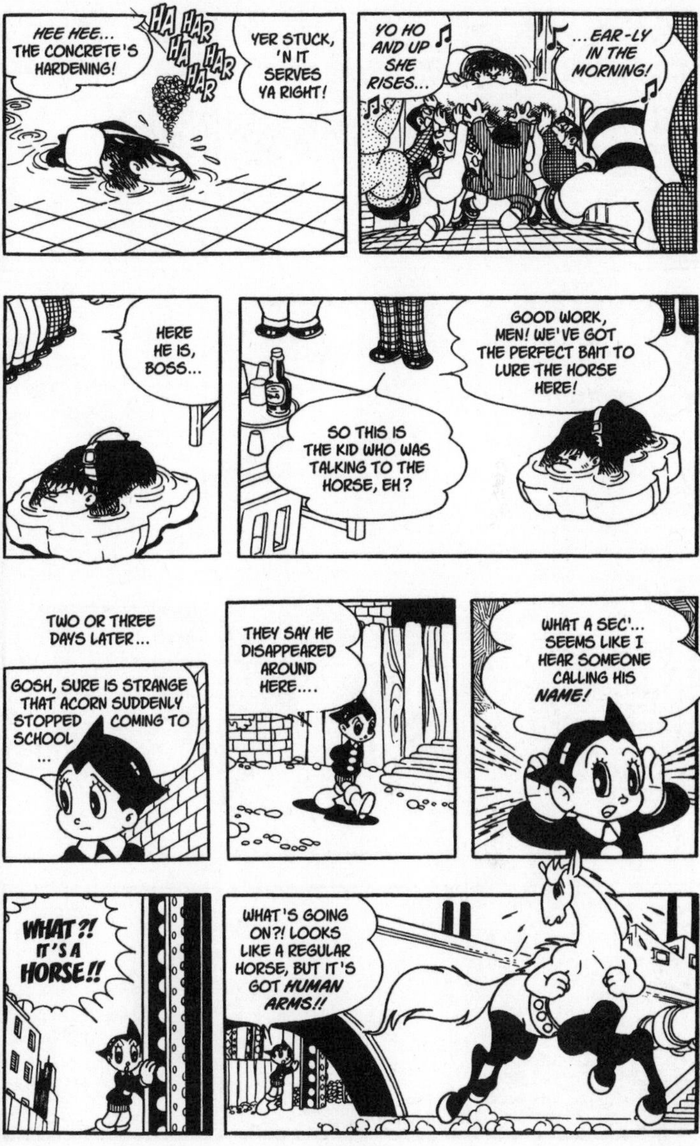
HEE HEE... THE CONCRETE'S HARDENING!
HA HAR HA HAR HAR
YER STUCK, 'N IT SERVES YA RIGHT!
YO HO AND UP SHE RISES...
...EAR-LY IN THE MORNING!
HERE HE IS, BOSS...
GOOD WORK, MEN! WE'VE GOT THE PERFECT BAIT TO LURE THE HORSE HERE!
SO THIS IS THE KID WHO WAS TALKING TO THE HORSE, EH?
TWO OR THREE DAYS LATER...
GOSH, SURE IS STRANGE THAT ACORN SUDDENLY STOPPED COMING TO SCHOOL ...
THEY SAY HE DISAPPEARED AROUND HERE....
WHAT A SEC'... SEEMS LIKE I HEAR SOMEONE CALLING HIS NAME!
WHAT?! IT'S A HORSE!!
WHAT'S GOING ON?! LOOKS LIKE A REGULAR HORSE, BUT IT'S GOT HUMAN ARMS!!

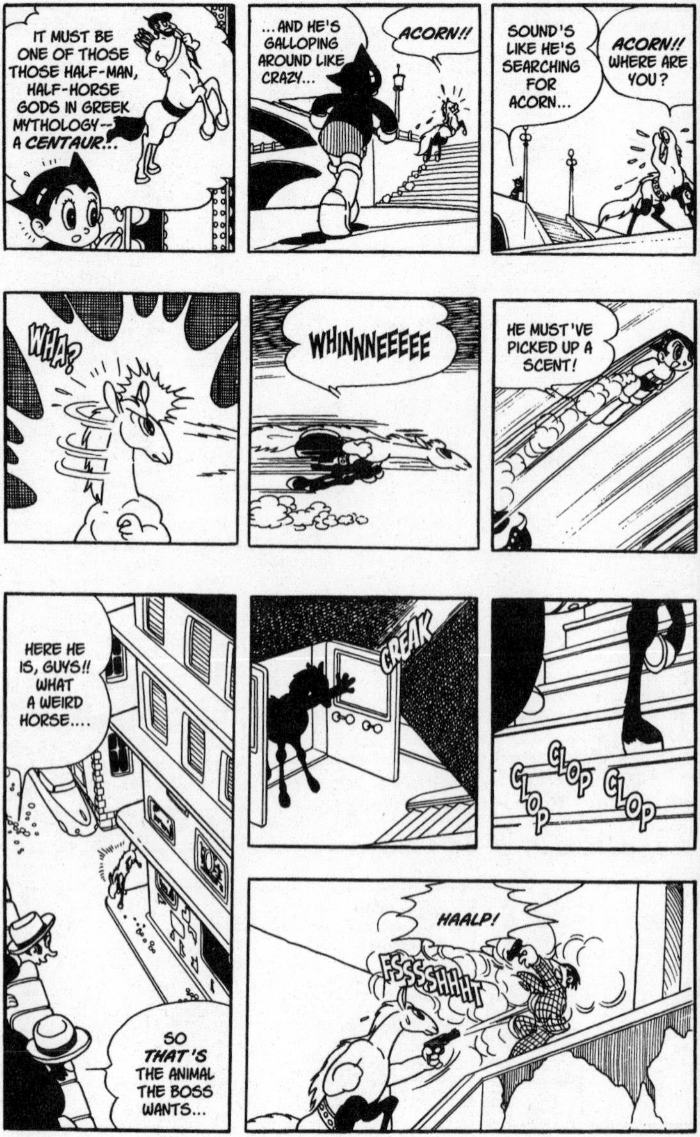
IT MUST BE ONE OF THOSE THOSE HALF-MAN, HALF-HORSE GODS IN GREEK MYTHOLOGY-- A *CENTAUR*...
...AND HE'S GALLOPING AROUND LIKE CRAZY...
ACORN!!
SOUND'S LIKE HE'S SEARCHING FOR ACORN...
ACORN!! WHERE ARE YOU?
WHA?
WHINNNEEEEE
HE MUST'VE PICKED UP A SCENT!
HERE HE IS, GUYS!! WHAT A WEIRD HORSE....
SO *THAT'S* THE ANIMAL THE BOSS WANTS...
CREAK
CLOP CLOP CLOP
HAALP!
FSSSSHHHT

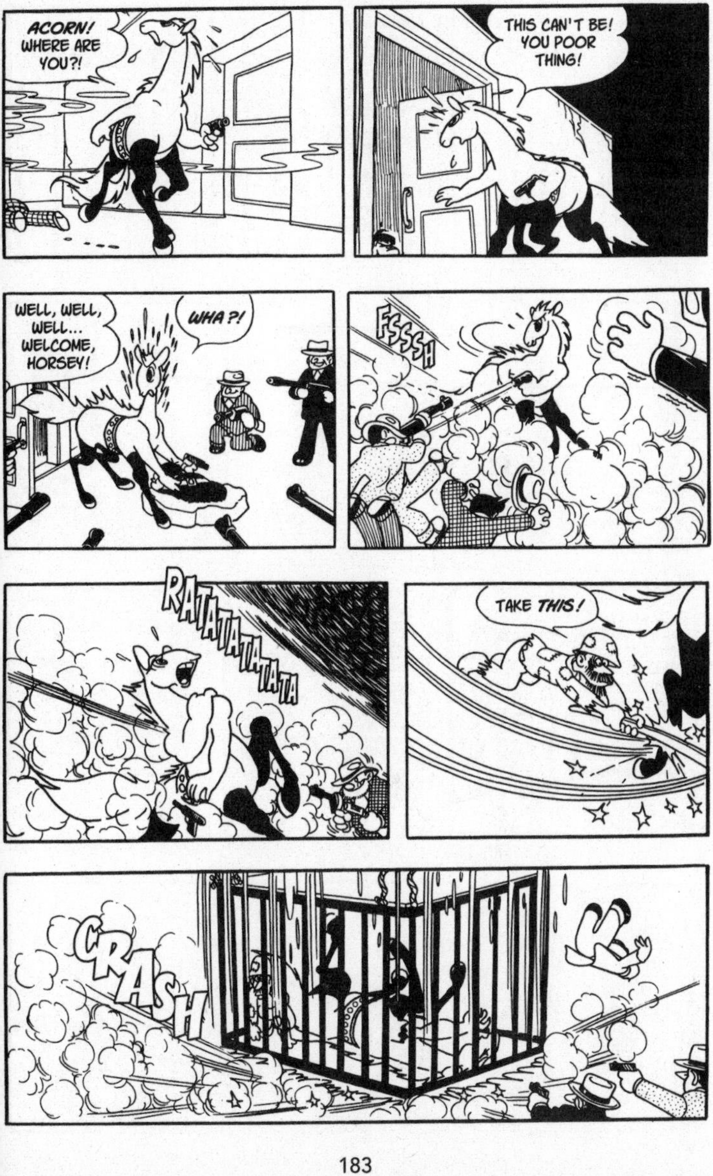
ACORN! WHERE ARE YOU?!
THIS CAN'T BE! YOU POOR THING!
WELL, WELL, WELL... WELCOME, HORSEY!
WHA?!
FSSSH
RATATATATATATA
TAKE THIS!
CRASH

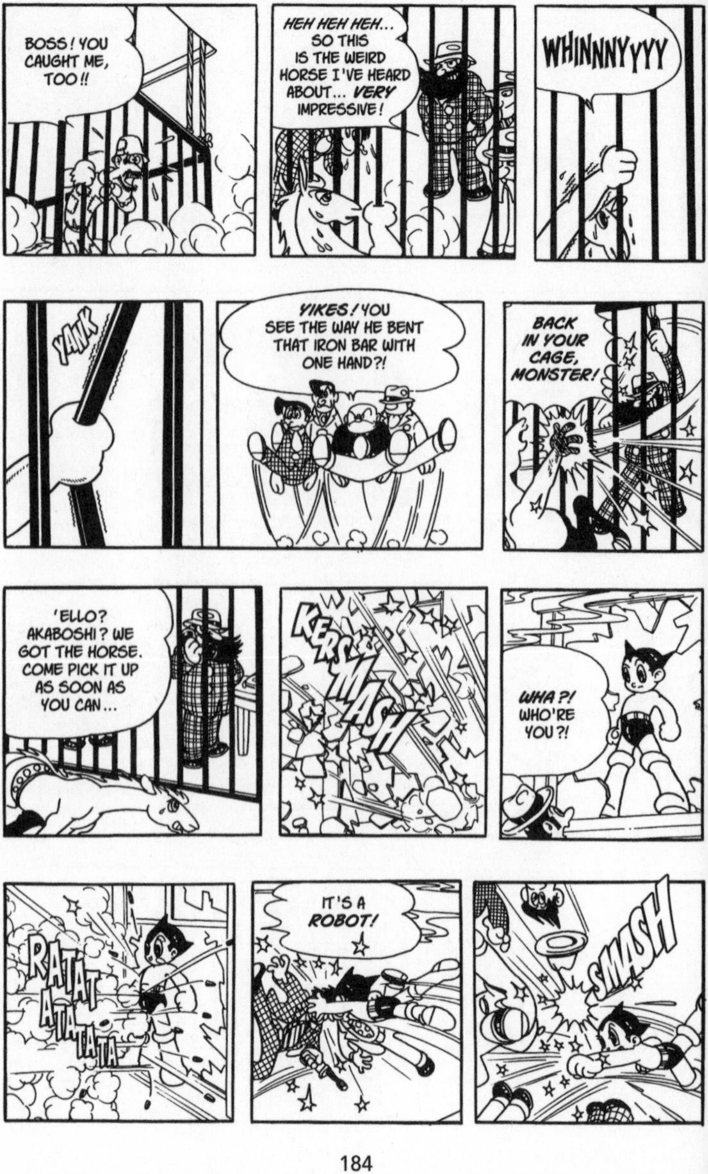
BOSS! YOU CAUGHT ME, TOO!!
HEH HEH HEH... SO THIS IS THE WEIRD HORSE I'VE HEARD ABOUT... VERY IMPRESSIVE!
WHINNNYYYY
YANK
YIKES! YOU SEE THE WAY HE BENT THAT IRON BAR WITH ONE HAND?!
BACK IN YOUR CAGE, MONSTER!
'ELLO? AKABOSHI? WE GOT THE HORSE. COME PICK IT UP AS SOON AS YOU CAN...
KERSMASH
WHA?! WHO'RE YOU?!
RATATATATATATA
IT'S A ROBOT!
SMASH

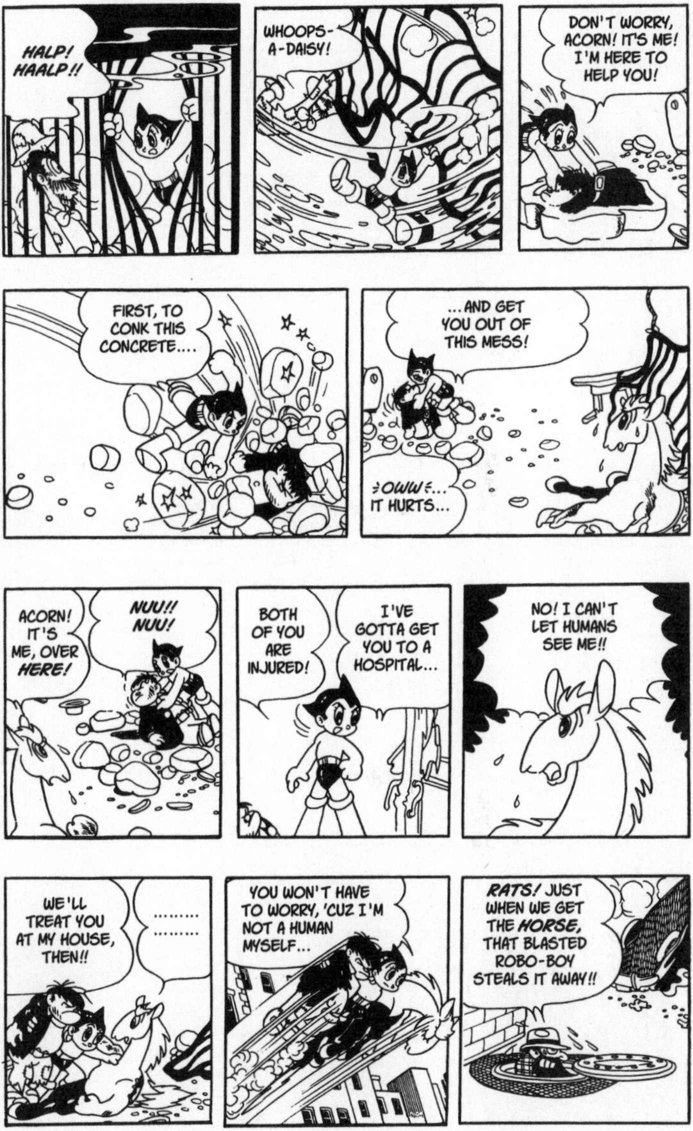
HALP! HAALP!!
WHOOPS-A-DAISY!
DON'T WORRY, ACORN! IT'S ME! I'M HERE TO HELP YOU!
FIRST, TO CONK THIS CONCRETE....
...AND GET YOU OUT OF THIS MESS!
OWW... IT HURTS...
ACORN! IT'S ME, OVER HERE!
NUU!! NUU!
BOTH OF YOU ARE INJURED!
I'VE GOTTA GET YOU TO A HOSPITAL...
NO! I CAN'T LET HUMANS SEE ME!!
WE'LL TREAT YOU AT MY HOUSE, THEN!!
....
....
YOU WON'T HAVE TO WORRY, 'CUZ I'M NOT A HUMAN MYSELF...
RATS! JUST WHEN WE GET THE HORSE, THAT BLASTED ROBO-BOY STEALS IT AWAY!!

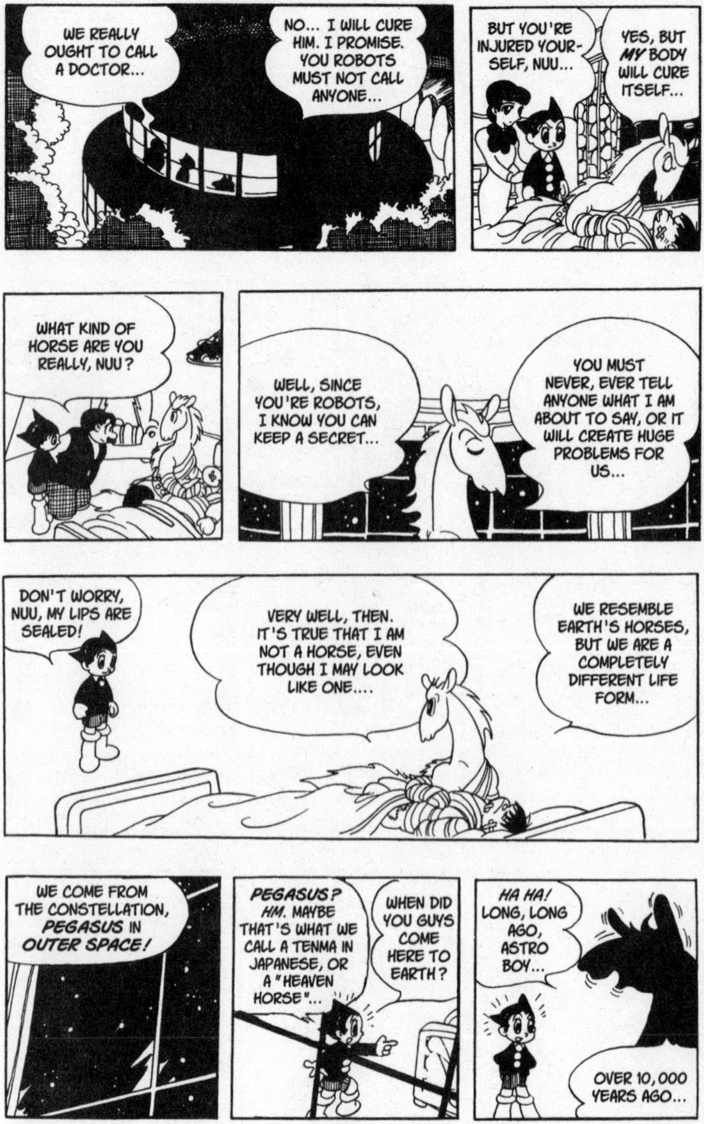
WE REALLY OUGHT TO CALL A DOCTOR...
NO... I WILL CURE HIM. I PROMISE. YOU ROBOTS MUST NOT CALL ANYONE...
BUT YOU'RE INJURED YOURSELF, NUU...
YES, BUT *MY* BODY WILL CURE ITSELF...
WHAT KIND OF HORSE ARE YOU REALLY, NUU?
WELL, SINCE YOU'RE ROBOTS, I KNOW YOU CAN KEEP A SECRET...
YOU MUST NEVER, EVER TELL ANYONE WHAT I AM ABOUT TO SAY, OR IT WILL CREATE HUGE PROBLEMS FOR US...
DON'T WORRY, NUU, MY LIPS ARE SEALED!
VERY WELL, THEN. IT'S TRUE THAT I AM NOT A HORSE, EVEN THOUGH I MAY LOOK LIKE ONE....
WE RESEMBLE EARTH'S HORSES, BUT WE ARE A COMPLETELY DIFFERENT LIFE FORM...
WE COME FROM THE CONSTELLATION, *PEGASUS* IN *OUTER SPACE!*
PEGASUS? HM. MAYBE THAT'S WHAT WE CALL A TENMA IN JAPANESE, OR A "HEAVEN HORSE"...
WHEN DID YOU GUYS COME HERE TO EARTH?
HA HA! LONG, LONG AGO, ASTRO BOY...
OVER 10,000 YEARS AGO...

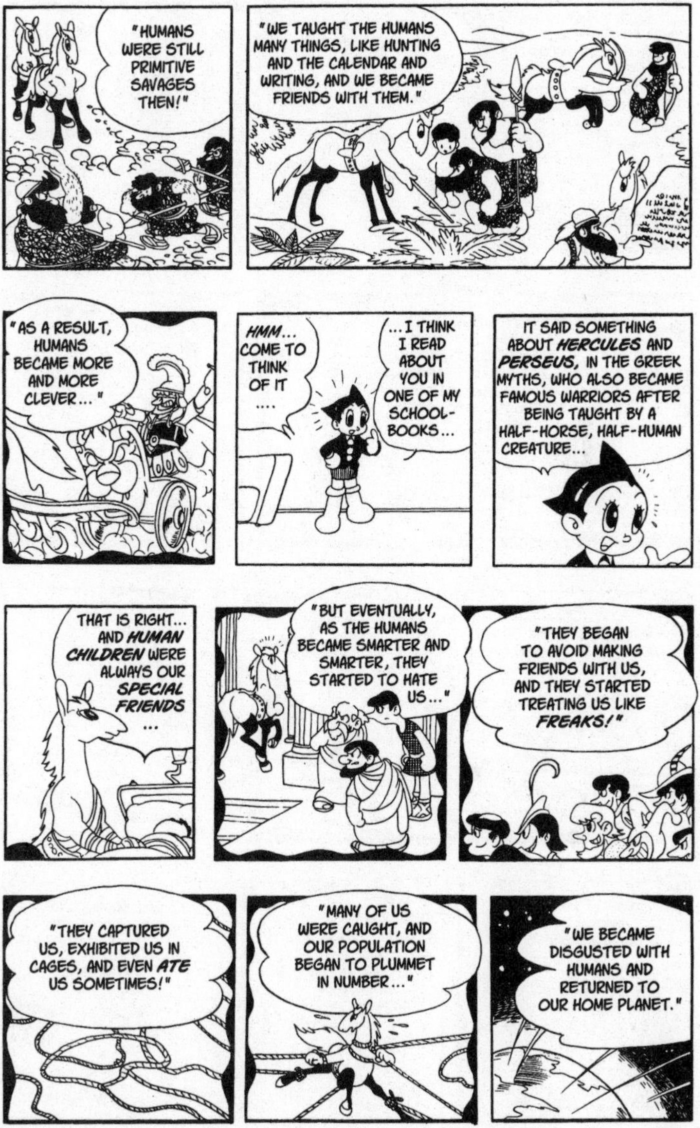
"HUMANS WERE STILL PRIMITIVE SAVAGES THEN!"
"WE TAUGHT THE HUMANS MANY THINGS, LIKE HUNTING AND THE CALENDAR AND WRITING, AND WE BECAME FRIENDS WITH THEM."
"AS A RESULT, HUMANS BECAME MORE AND MORE CLEVER..."
HMM... COME TO THINK OF IT ....
...I THINK I READ ABOUT YOU IN ONE OF MY SCHOOL-BOOKS...
IT SAID SOMETHING ABOUT HERCULES AND PERSEUS, IN THE GREEK MYTHS, WHO ALSO BECAME FAMOUS WARRIORS AFTER BEING TAUGHT BY A HALF-HORSE, HALF-HUMAN CREATURE...
THAT IS RIGHT... AND HUMAN CHILDREN WERE ALWAYS OUR SPECIAL FRIENDS ...
"BUT EVENTUALLY, AS THE HUMANS BECAME SMARTER AND SMARTER, THEY STARTED TO HATE US..."
"THEY BEGAN TO AVOID MAKING FRIENDS WITH US, AND THEY STARTED TREATING US LIKE FREAKS!"
"THEY CAPTURED US, EXHIBITED US IN CAGES, AND EVEN ATE US SOMETIMES!"
"MANY OF US WERE CAUGHT, AND OUR POPULATION BEGAN TO PLUMMET IN NUMBER..."
"WE BECAME DISGUSTED WITH HUMANS AND RETURNED TO OUR HOME PLANET."

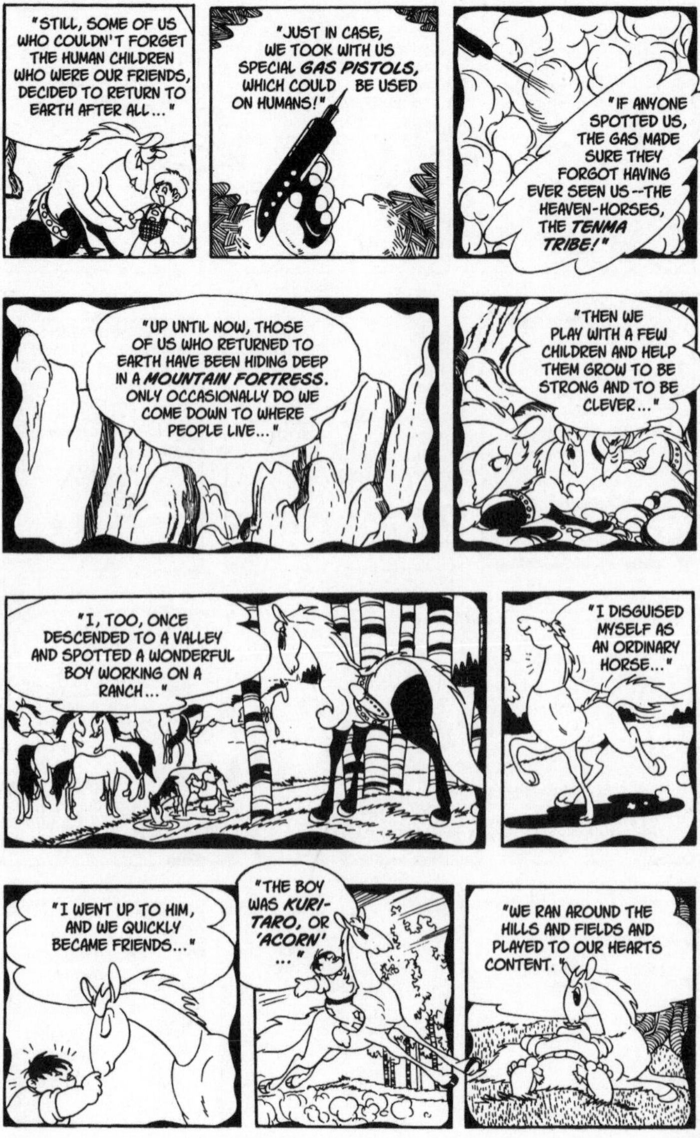
"STILL, SOME OF US WHO COULDN'T FORGET THE HUMAN CHILDREN WHO WERE OUR FRIENDS, DECIDED TO RETURN TO EARTH AFTER ALL..."
"JUST IN CASE, WE TOOK WITH US SPECIAL GAS PISTOLS, WHICH COULD BE USED ON HUMANS!"
"IF ANYONE SPOTTED US, THE GAS MADE SURE THEY FORGOT HAVING EVER SEEN US--THE HEAVEN-HORSES, THE TENMA TRIBE!"
"UP UNTIL NOW, THOSE OF US WHO RETURNED TO EARTH HAVE BEEN HIDING DEEP IN A MOUNTAIN FORTRESS. ONLY OCCASIONALLY DO WE COME DOWN TO WHERE PEOPLE LIVE..."
"THEN WE PLAY WITH A FEW CHILDREN AND HELP THEM GROW TO BE STRONG AND TO BE CLEVER..."
"I, TOO, ONCE DESCENDED TO A VALLEY AND SPOTTED A WONDERFUL BOY WORKING ON A RANCH..."
"I DISGUISED MYSELF AS AN ORDINARY HORSE..."
"I WENT UP TO HIM, AND WE QUICKLY BECAME FRIENDS..."
"THE BOY WAS KURI-TARO, OR 'ACORN'..."
"WE RAN AROUND THE HILLS AND FIELDS AND PLAYED TO OUR HEARTS CONTENT."

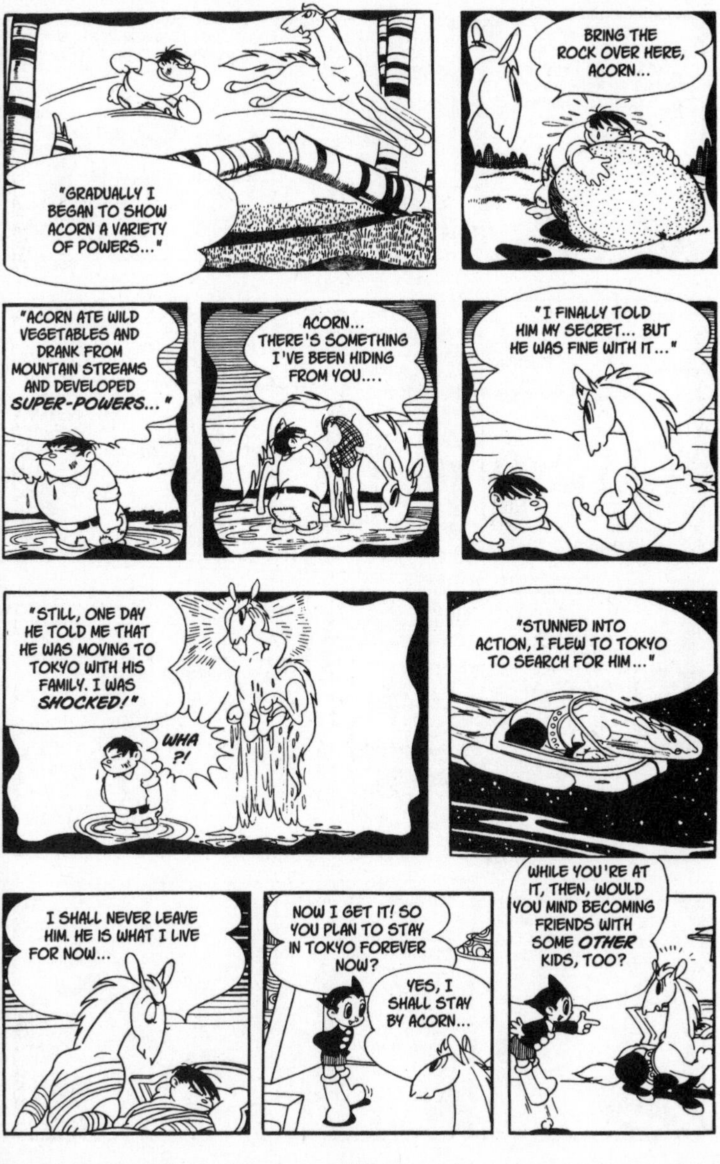
"GRADUALLY I BEGAN TO SHOW ACORN A VARIETY OF POWERS..."
BRING THE ROCK OVER HERE, ACORN...
"ACORN ATE WILD VEGETABLES AND DRANK FROM MOUNTAIN STREAMS AND DEVELOPED *SUPER-POWERS...*"
ACORN... THERE'S SOMETHING I'VE BEEN HIDING FROM YOU....
"I FINALLY TOLD HIM MY SECRET... BUT HE WAS FINE WITH IT..."
"STILL, ONE DAY HE TOLD ME THAT HE WAS MOVING TO TOKYO WITH HIS FAMILY. I WAS *SHOCKED!*"
WHA ?!
"STUNNED INTO ACTION, I FLEW TO TOKYO TO SEARCH FOR HIM..."
I SHALL NEVER LEAVE HIM. HE IS WHAT I LIVE FOR NOW...
NOW I GET IT! SO YOU PLAN TO STAY IN TOKYO FOREVER NOW?
YES, I SHALL STAY BY ACORN...
WHILE YOU'RE AT IT, THEN, WOULD YOU MIND BECOMING FRIENDS WITH SOME *OTHER* KIDS, TOO?

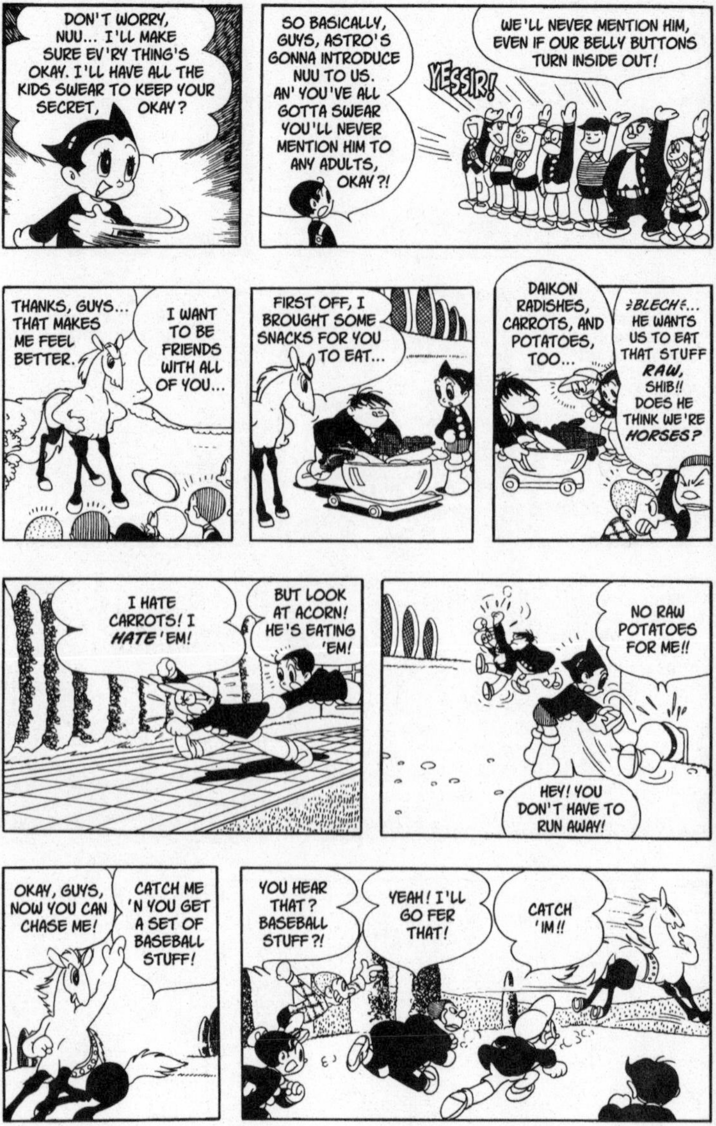
DON'T WORRY, NUU... I'LL MAKE SURE EV'RY THING'S OKAY. I'LL HAVE ALL THE KIDS SWEAR TO KEEP YOUR SECRET, OKAY?
SO BASICALLY, GUYS, ASTRO'S GONNA INTRODUCE NUU TO US. AN' YOU'VE ALL GOTTA SWEAR YOU'LL NEVER MENTION HIM TO ANY ADULTS, OKAY?!
YESSIR!
WE'LL NEVER MENTION HIM, EVEN IF OUR BELLY BUTTONS TURN INSIDE OUT!
THANKS, GUYS... THAT MAKES ME FEEL BETTER.
I WANT TO BE FRIENDS WITH ALL OF YOU...
FIRST OFF, I BROUGHT SOME SNACKS FOR YOU TO EAT...
DAIKON RADISHES, CARROTS, AND POTATOES, TOO...
BLECH... HE WANTS US TO EAT THAT STUFF RAW, SHIB!! DOES HE THINK WE'RE HORSES?
I HATE CARROTS! I HATE 'EM!
BUT LOOK AT ACORN! HE'S EATING 'EM!
NO RAW POTATOES FOR ME!!
HEY! YOU DON'T HAVE TO RUN AWAY!
OKAY, GUYS, NOW YOU CAN CHASE ME!
CATCH ME 'N YOU GET A SET OF BASEBALL STUFF!
YOU HEAR THAT? BASEBALL STUFF?!
YEAH! I'LL GO FER THAT!
CATCH 'IM!!

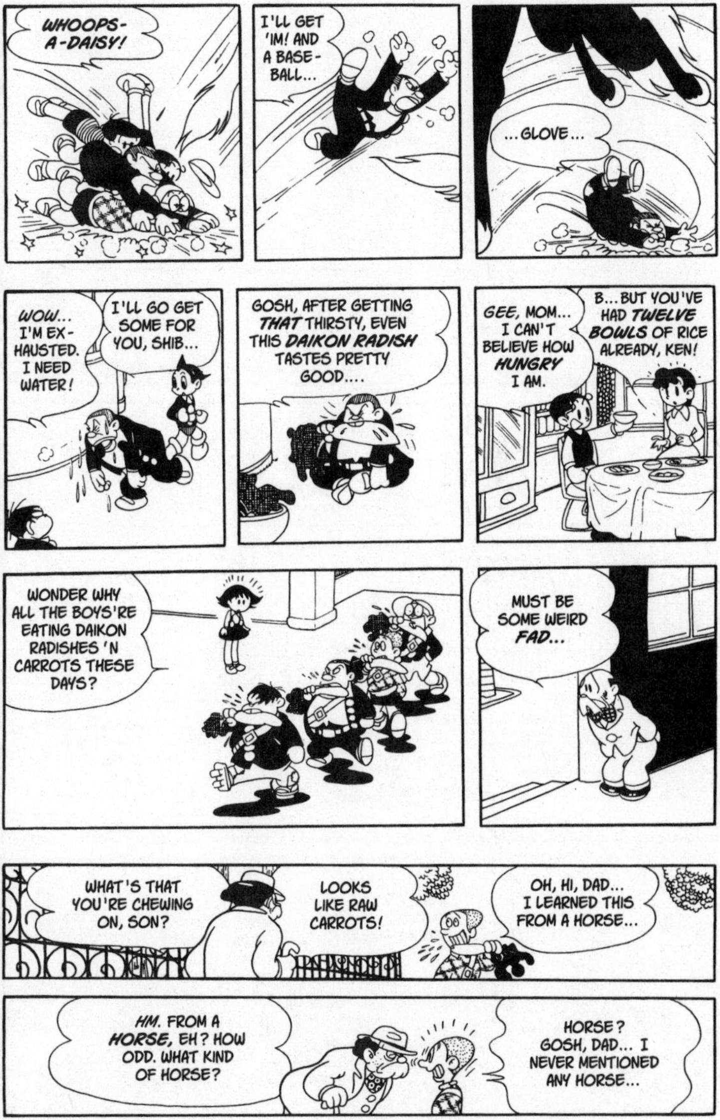
WHOOPS-A-DAISY!
I'LL GET 'IM! AND A BASE-BALL...
...GLOVE...
WOW... I'M EX-HAUSTED. I NEED WATER!
I'LL GO GET SOME FOR YOU, SHIB...
GOSH, AFTER GETTING THAT THIRSTY, EVEN THIS DAIKON RADISH TASTES PRETTY GOOD....
GEE, MOM... I CAN'T BELIEVE HOW HUNGRY I AM.
B... BUT YOU'VE HAD TWELVE BOWLS OF RICE ALREADY, KEN!
WONDER WHY ALL THE BOYS'RE EATING DAIKON RADISHES 'N CARROTS THESE DAYS?
MUST BE SOME WEIRD FAD...
WHAT'S THAT YOU'RE CHEWING ON, SON?
LOOKS LIKE RAW CARROTS!
OH, HI, DAD... I LEARNED THIS FROM A HORSE...
HM. FROM A HORSE, EH? HOW ODD. WHAT KIND OF HORSE?
HORSE? GOSH, DAD... I NEVER MENTIONED ANY HORSE...

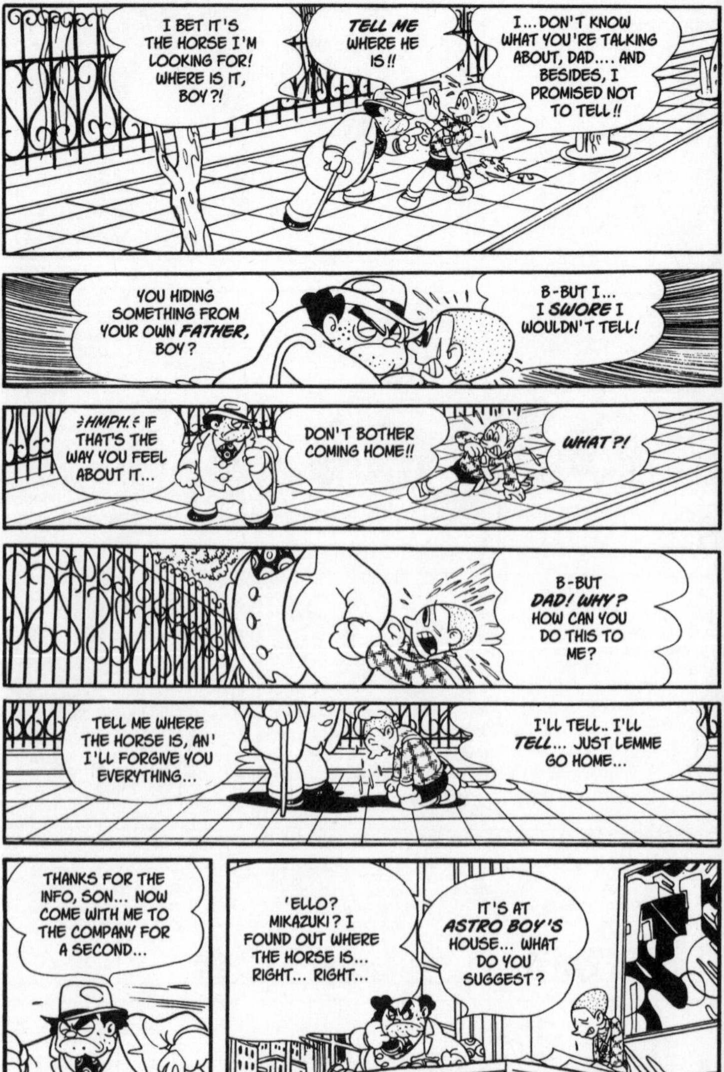
I BET IT'S THE HORSE I'M LOOKING FOR! WHERE IS IT, BOY?!
TELL ME WHERE HE IS!!
I... DON'T KNOW WHAT YOU'RE TALKING ABOUT, DAD.... AND BESIDES, I PROMISED NOT TO TELL!!
YOU HIDING SOMETHING FROM YOUR OWN FATHER, BOY?
B-BUT I... I SWORE I WOULDN'T TELL!
HMPH. IF THAT'S THE WAY YOU FEEL ABOUT IT...
DON'T BOTHER COMING HOME!!
WHAT?!
B-BUT DAD! WHY? HOW CAN YOU DO THIS TO ME?
TELL ME WHERE THE HORSE IS, AN' I'LL FORGIVE YOU EVERYTHING...
I'LL TELL.. I'LL TELL... JUST LEMME GO HOME...
THANKS FOR THE INFO, SON... NOW COME WITH ME TO THE COMPANY FOR A SECOND...
'ELLO? MIKAZUKI? I FOUND OUT WHERE THE HORSE IS... RIGHT... RIGHT...
IT'S AT ASTRO BOY'S HOUSE... WHAT DO YOU SUGGEST?

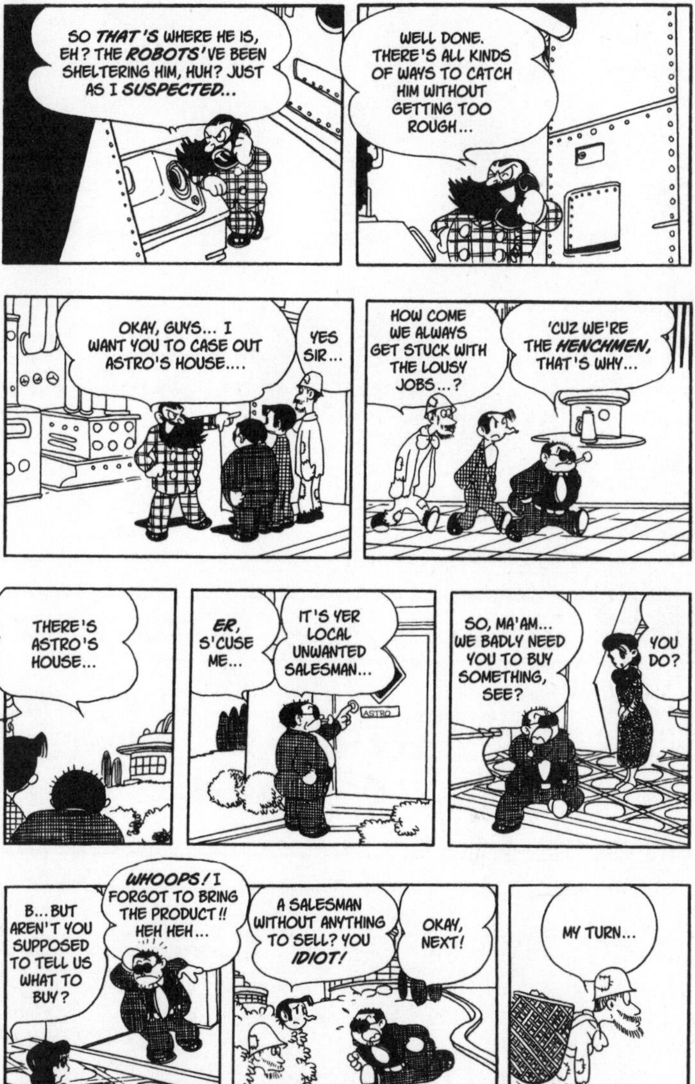
SO *THAT'S* WHERE HE IS, EH? THE *ROBOTS'* VE BEEN SHELTERING HIM, HUH? JUST AS I *SUSPECTED*...
WELL DONE. THERE'S ALL KINDS OF WAYS TO CATCH HIM WITHOUT GETTING TOO ROUGH...
OKAY, GUYS... I WANT YOU TO CASE OUT ASTRO'S HOUSE....
YES SIR...
HOW COME WE ALWAYS GET STUCK WITH THE LOUSY JOBS...?
'CUZ WE'RE THE *HENCHMEN*, THAT'S WHY...
THERE'S ASTRO'S HOUSE...
ER, S'CUSE ME...
IT'S YER LOCAL UNWANTED SALESMAN...
ASTRO
SO, MA'AM... WE BADLY NEED YOU TO BUY SOMETHING, SEE?
YOU DO?
B...BUT AREN'T YOU SUPPOSED TO TELL US WHAT TO BUY?
WHOOPS! I FORGOT TO BRING THE PRODUCT!! HEH HEH...
A SALESMAN WITHOUT ANYTHING TO SELL? YOU *IDIOT!*
OKAY, NEXT!
MY TURN...

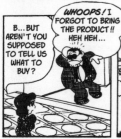

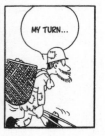

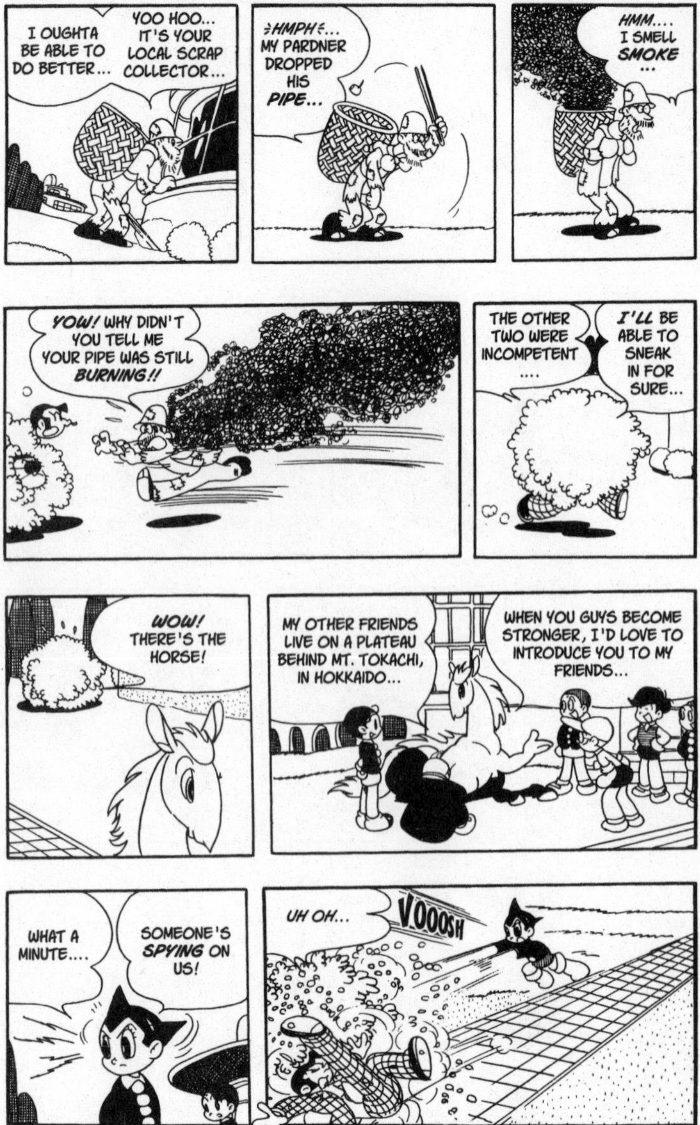
I OUGHTA BE ABLE TO DO BETTER...
YOO HOO... IT'S YOUR LOCAL SCRAP COLLECTOR...
HMPH... MY PARDNER DROPPED HIS PIPE...
HMM.... I SMELL SMOKE ...
YOW! WHY DIDN'T YOU TELL ME YOUR PIPE WAS STILL BURNING!!
THE OTHER TWO WERE INCOMPETENT ....
I'LL BE ABLE TO SNEAK IN FOR SURE...
WOW! THERE'S THE HORSE!
MY OTHER FRIENDS LIVE ON A PLATEAU BEHIND MT. TOKACHI, IN HOKKAIDO...
WHEN YOU GUYS BECOME STRONGER, I'D LOVE TO INTRODUCE YOU TO MY FRIENDS...
WHAT A MINUTE....
SOMEONE'S SPYING ON US!
UH OH...
VOOOSH

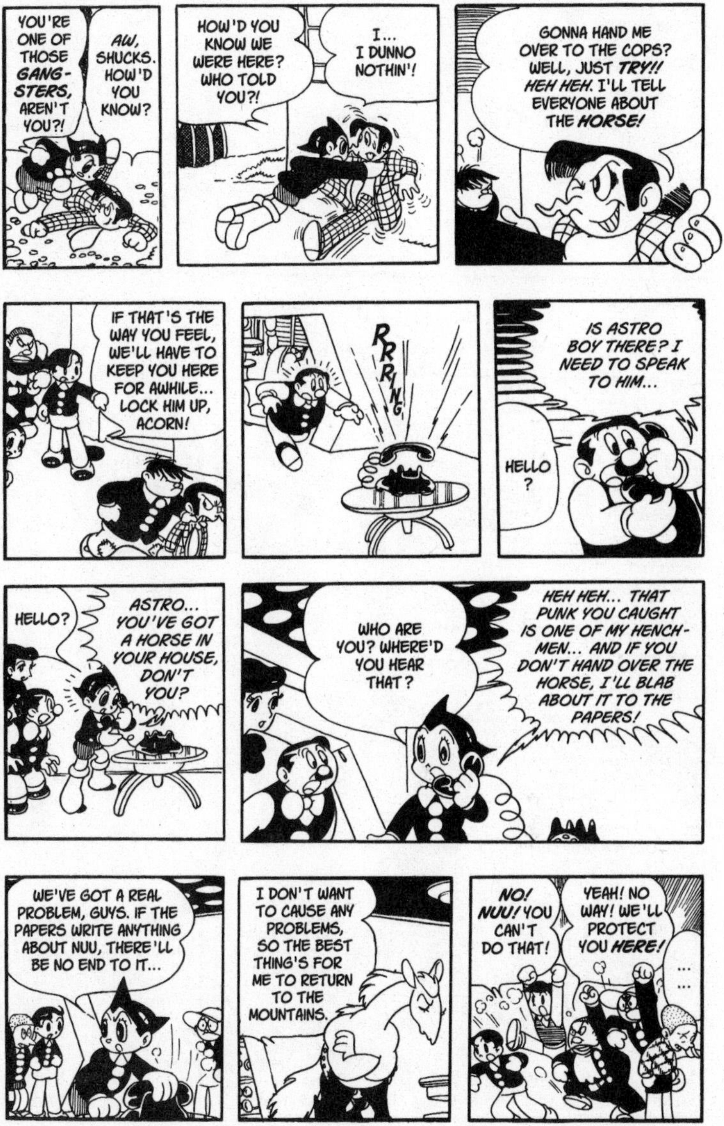
YOU'RE ONE OF THOSE GANGSTERS, AREN'T YOU?!
AW, SHUCKS. HOW'D YOU KNOW?
HOW'D YOU KNOW WE WERE HERE? WHO TOLD YOU?!
I... I DUNNO NOTHIN'!
GONNA HAND ME OVER TO THE COPS? WELL, JUST TRY!! HEH HEH. I'LL TELL EVERYONE ABOUT THE HORSE!
IF THAT'S THE WAY YOU FEEL, WE'LL HAVE TO KEEP YOU HERE FOR AWHILE... LOCK HIM UP, ACORN!
RRRING
IS ASTRO BOY THERE? I NEED TO SPEAK TO HIM...
HELLO?
HELLO?
ASTRO... YOU'VE GOT A HORSE IN YOUR HOUSE, DON'T YOU?
WHO ARE YOU? WHERE'D YOU HEAR THAT?
HEH HEH... THAT PUNK YOU CAUGHT IS ONE OF MY HENCHMEN... AND IF YOU DON'T HAND OVER THE HORSE, I'LL BLAB ABOUT IT TO THE PAPERS!
WE'VE GOT A REAL PROBLEM, GUYS. IF THE PAPERS WRITE ANYTHING ABOUT NUU, THERE'LL BE NO END TO IT...
I DON'T WANT TO CAUSE ANY PROBLEMS, SO THE BEST THING'S FOR ME TO RETURN TO THE MOUNTAINS.
NO! NUU! YOU CAN'T DO THAT!
YEAH! NO WAY! WE'LL PROTECT YOU HERE!
... ...

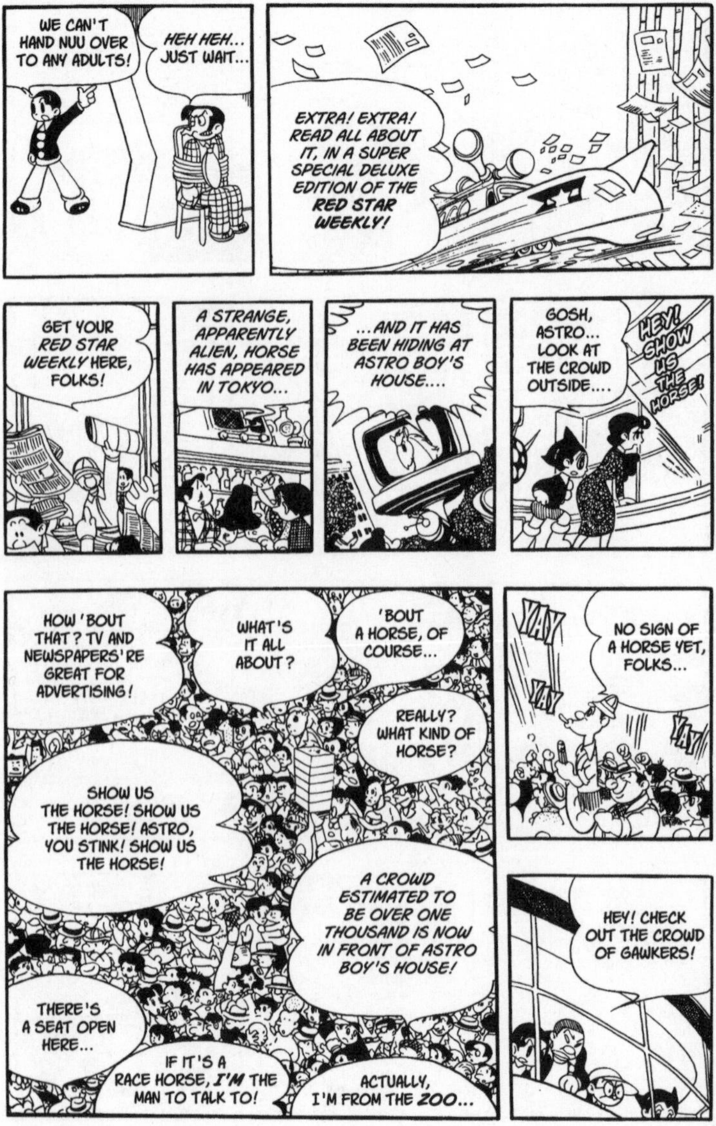
WE CAN'T HAND NUU OVER TO ANY ADULTS!
HEH HEH... JUST WAIT...
EXTRA! EXTRA! READ ALL ABOUT IT, IN A SUPER SPECIAL DELUXE EDITION OF THE RED STAR WEEKLY!
GET YOUR RED STAR WEEKLY HERE, FOLKS!
A STRANGE, APPARENTLY ALIEN, HORSE HAS APPEARED IN TOKYO...
...AND IT HAS BEEN HIDING AT ASTRO BOY'S HOUSE....
GOSH, ASTRO... LOOK AT THE CROWD OUTSIDE....
HEY! SHOW US THE HORSE!
HOW 'BOUT THAT? TV AND NEWSPAPERS'RE GREAT FOR ADVERTISING!
WHAT'S IT ALL ABOUT?
'BOUT A HORSE, OF COURSE...
REALLY? WHAT KIND OF HORSE?
SHOW US THE HORSE! SHOW US THE HORSE! ASTRO, YOU STINK! SHOW US THE HORSE!
A CROWD ESTIMATED TO BE OVER ONE THOUSAND IS NOW IN FRONT OF ASTRO BOY'S HOUSE!
THERE'S A SEAT OPEN HERE...
IF IT'S A RACE HORSE, I'M THE MAN TO TALK TO!
ACTUALLY, I'M FROM THE ZOO...
YAY
YAY
NO SIGN OF A HORSE YET, FOLKS...
YAY
HEY! CHECK OUT THE CROWD OF GAWKERS!

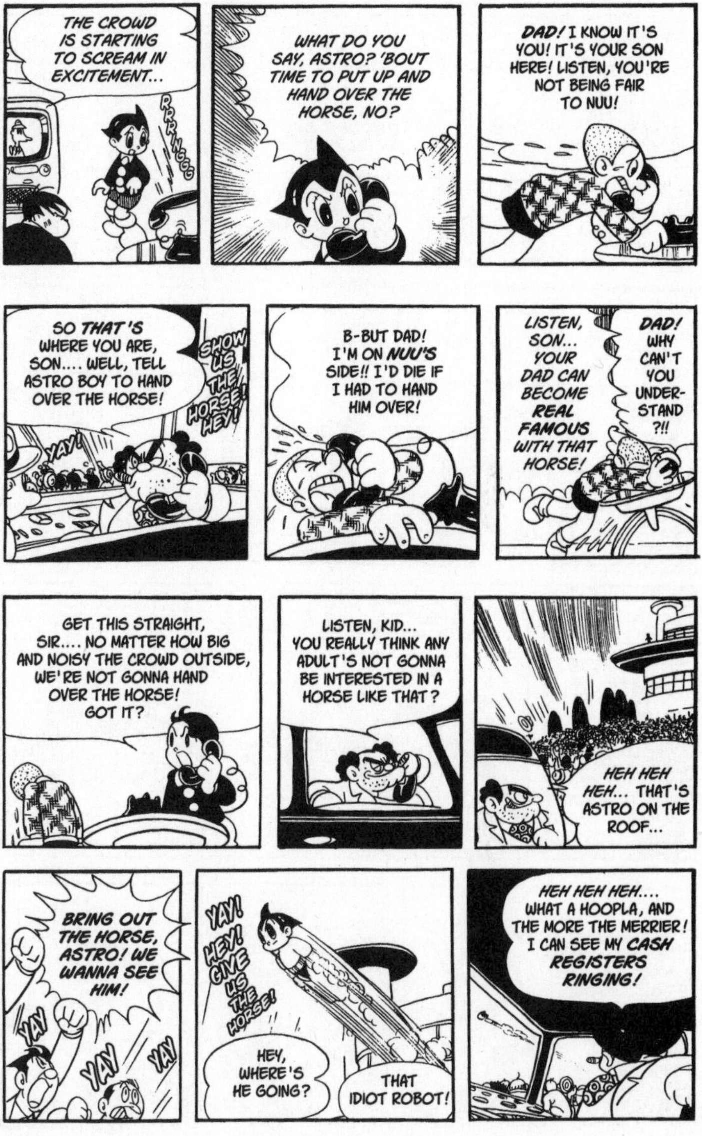
THE CROWD IS STARTING TO SCREAM IN EXCITEMENT...
RRRINGGG
WHAT DO YOU SAY, ASTRO? 'BOUT TIME TO PUT UP AND HAND OVER THE HORSE, NO?
DAD! I KNOW IT'S YOU! IT'S YOUR SON HERE! LISTEN, YOU'RE NOT BEING FAIR TO NUU!
SO THAT'S WHERE YOU ARE, SON.... WELL, TELL ASTRO BOY TO HAND OVER THE HORSE!
SHOW US THE HORSE! HEY!
YAY!
B-BUT DAD! I'M ON NUU'S SIDE!! I'D DIE IF I HAD TO HAND HIM OVER!
LISTEN, SON... YOUR DAD CAN BECOME REAL FAMOUS WITH THAT HORSE!
DAD! WHY CAN'T YOU UNDER-STAND?!!
GET THIS STRAIGHT, SIR.... NO MATTER HOW BIG AND NOISY THE CROWD OUTSIDE, WE'RE NOT GONNA HAND OVER THE HORSE! GOT IT?
LISTEN, KID... YOU REALLY THINK ANY ADULT'S NOT GONNA BE INTERESTED IN A HORSE LIKE THAT?
HEH HEH HEH... THAT'S ASTRO ON THE ROOF...
BRING OUT THE HORSE, ASTRO! WE WANNA SEE HIM!
YAY
YAY
YAY
YAY! HEY! GIVE US THE HORSE!
HEY, WHERE'S HE GOING?
THAT IDIOT ROBOT!
HEH HEH HEH.... WHAT A HOOPLA, AND THE MORE THE MERRIER! I CAN SEE MY CASH REGISTERS RINGING!

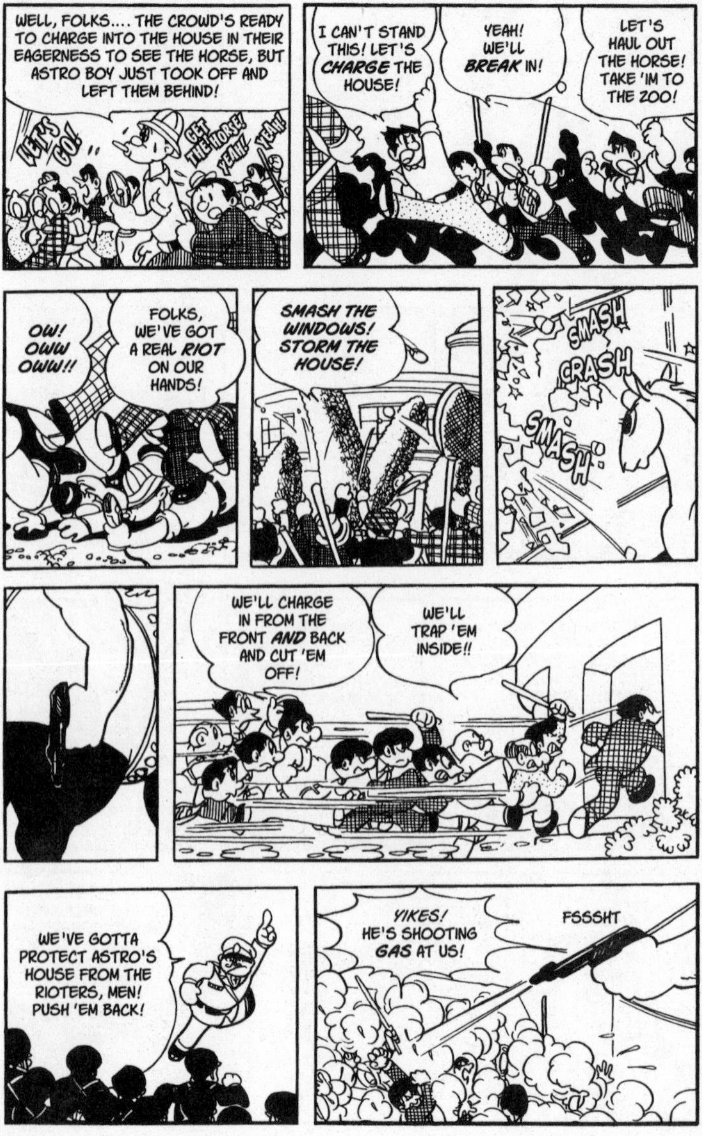
WELL, FOLKS.... THE CROWD'S READY TO CHARGE INTO THE HOUSE IN THEIR EAGERNESS TO SEE THE HORSE, BUT ASTRO BOY JUST TOOK OFF AND LEFT THEM BEHIND!
LET'S GO!
GET THE HORSE!
YEAH!
YEAH!
I CAN'T STAND THIS! LET'S *CHARGE* THE HOUSE!
YEAH! WE'LL *BREAK* IN!
LET'S HAUL OUT THE HORSE! TAKE 'IM TO THE ZOO!
OW! OWW OWW!!
FOLKS, WE'VE GOT A REAL *RIOT* ON OUR HANDS!
SMASH THE WINDOWS! STORM THE HOUSE!
SMASH
CRASH
SMASH
WE'LL CHARGE IN FROM THE FRONT *AND* BACK AND CUT 'EM OFF!
WE'LL TRAP 'EM INSIDE!!
WE'VE GOTTA PROTECT ASTRO'S HOUSE FROM THE RIOTERS, MEN! PUSH 'EM BACK!
YIKES! HE'S SHOOTING *GAS* AT US!
FSSSHT

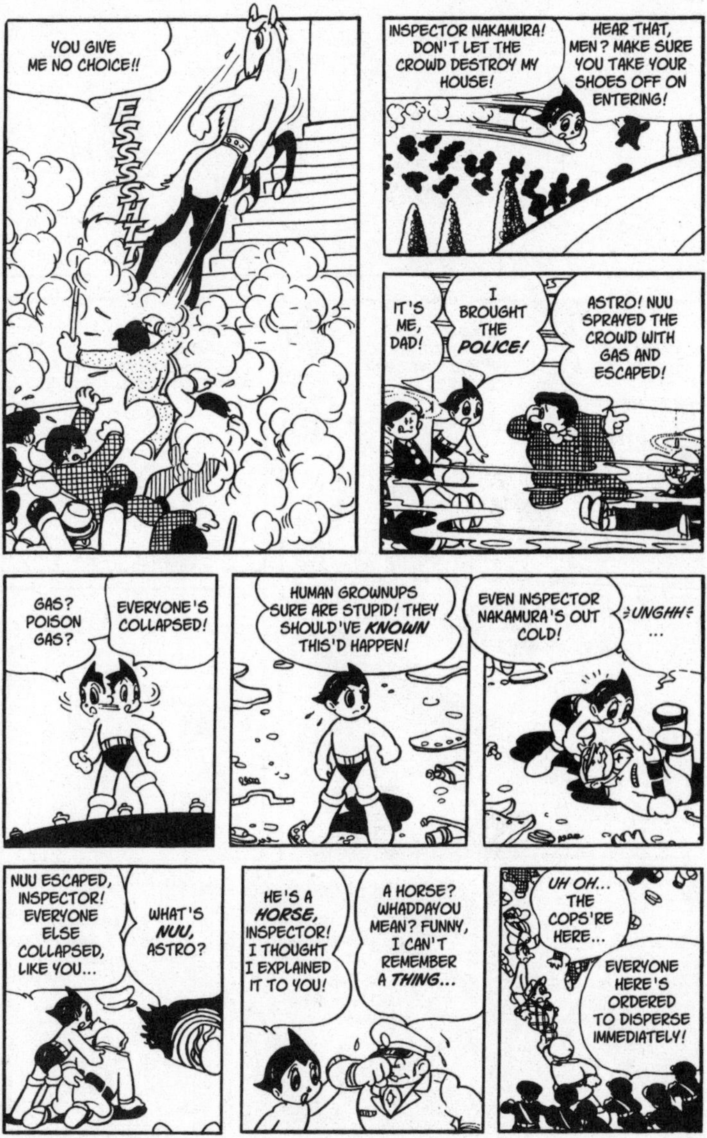
YOU GIVE ME NO CHOICE!!
FSSSSHTT
INSPECTOR NAKAMURA! DON'T LET THE CROWD DESTROY MY HOUSE!
HEAR THAT, MEN? MAKE SURE YOU TAKE YOUR SHOES OFF ON ENTERING!
IT'S ME, DAD!
I BROUGHT THE *POLICE!*
ASTRO! NUU SPRAYED THE CROWD WITH GAS AND ESCAPED!
GAS? POISON GAS?
EVERYONE'S COLLAPSED!
HUMAN GROWNUPS SURE ARE STUPID! THEY SHOULD'VE *KNOWN* THIS'D HAPPEN!
EVEN INSPECTOR NAKAMURA'S OUT COLD!
UNGHH ...
NUU ESCAPED, INSPECTOR! EVERYONE ELSE COLLAPSED, LIKE YOU...
WHAT'S *NUU,* ASTRO?
HE'S A *HORSE,* INSPECTOR! I THOUGHT I EXPLAINED IT TO YOU!
A HORSE? WHADDAYOU MEAN? FUNNY, I CAN'T REMEMBER A *THING...*
UH OH... THE COPS'RE HERE...
EVERYONE HERE'S ORDERED TO DISPERSE IMMEDIATELY!

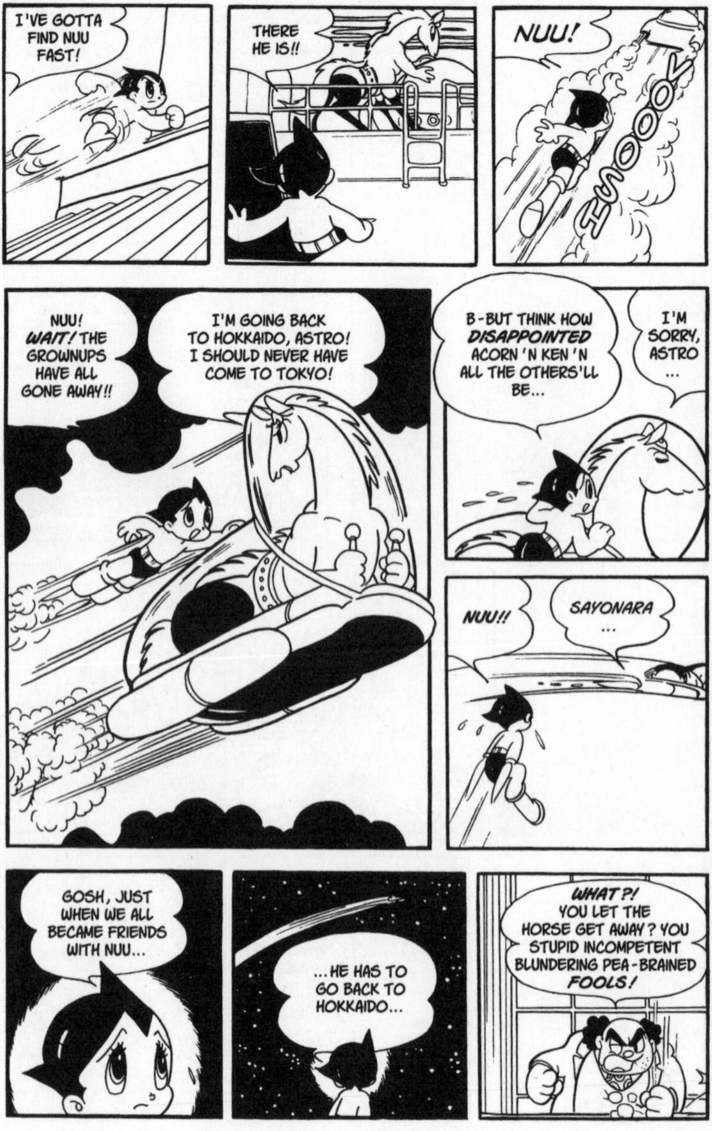
I'VE GOTTA FIND NUU FAST!
THERE HE IS!!
NUU!
VOOOSH
NUU! WAIT! THE GROWNUPS HAVE ALL GONE AWAY!!
I'M GOING BACK TO HOKKAIDO, ASTRO! I SHOULD NEVER HAVE COME TO TOKYO!
B-BUT THINK HOW DISAPPOINTED ACORN 'N KEN 'N ALL THE OTHERS'LL BE...
I'M SORRY, ASTRO ...
NUU!!
SAYONARA ...
GOSH, JUST WHEN WE ALL BECAME FRIENDS WITH NUU...
...HE HAS TO GO BACK TO HOKKAIDO...
WHAT?! YOU LET THE HORSE GET AWAY? YOU STUPID INCOMPETENT BLUNDERING PEA-BRAINED FOOLS!

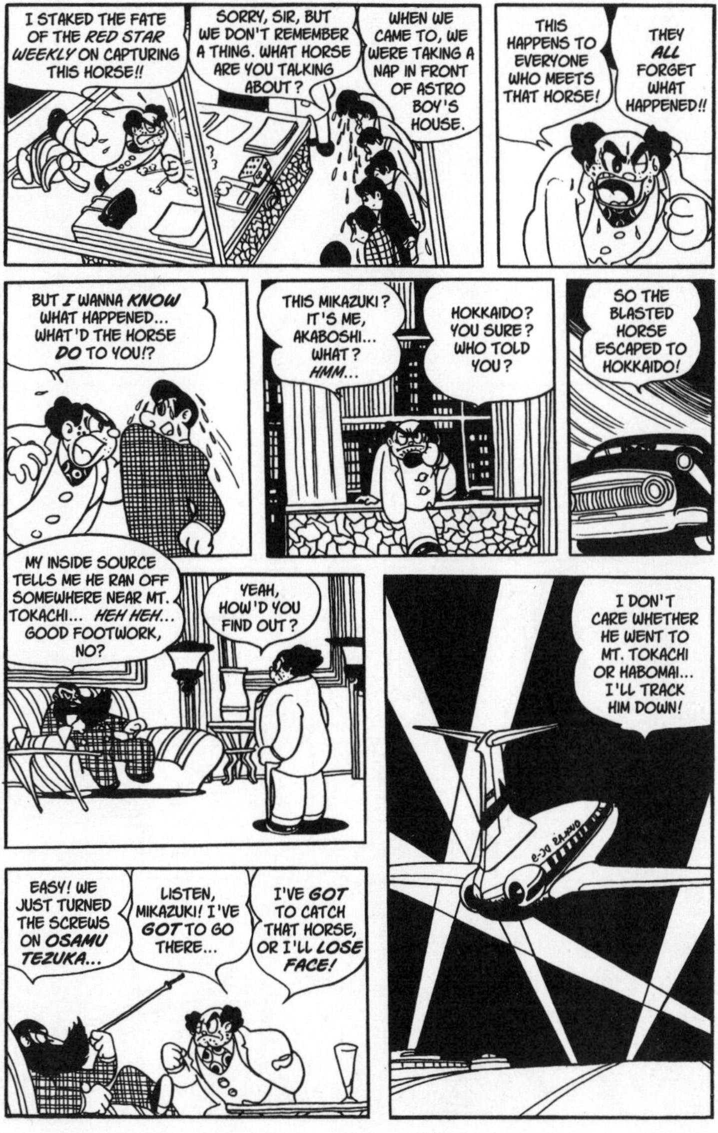
I STAKED THE FATE OF THE RED STAR WEEKLY ON CAPTURING THIS HORSE!!
SORRY, SIR, BUT WE DON'T REMEMBER A THING. WHAT HORSE ARE YOU TALKING ABOUT?
WHEN WE CAME TO, WE WERE TAKING A NAP IN FRONT OF ASTRO BOY'S HOUSE.
THIS HAPPENS TO EVERYONE WHO MEETS THAT HORSE!
THEY ALL FORGET WHAT HAPPENED!!
BUT I WANNA KNOW WHAT HAPPENED... WHAT'D THE HORSE DO TO YOU!?
THIS MIKAZUKI? IT'S ME, AKABOSHI... WHAT? HMM...
HOKKAIDO? YOU SURE? WHO TOLD YOU?
SO THE BLASTED HORSE ESCAPED TO HOKKAIDO!
MY INSIDE SOURCE TELLS ME HE RAN OFF SOMEWHERE NEAR MT. TOKACHI... HEH HEH... GOOD FOOTWORK, NO?
YEAH, HOW'D YOU FIND OUT?
EASY! WE JUST TURNED THE SCREWS ON OSAMU TEZUKA...
LISTEN, MIKAZUKI! I'VE GOT TO GO THERE...
I'VE GOT TO CATCH THAT HORSE, OR I'LL LOSE FACE!
I DON'T CARE WHETHER HE WENT TO MT. TOKACHI OR HABOMAI... I'LL TRACK HIM DOWN!

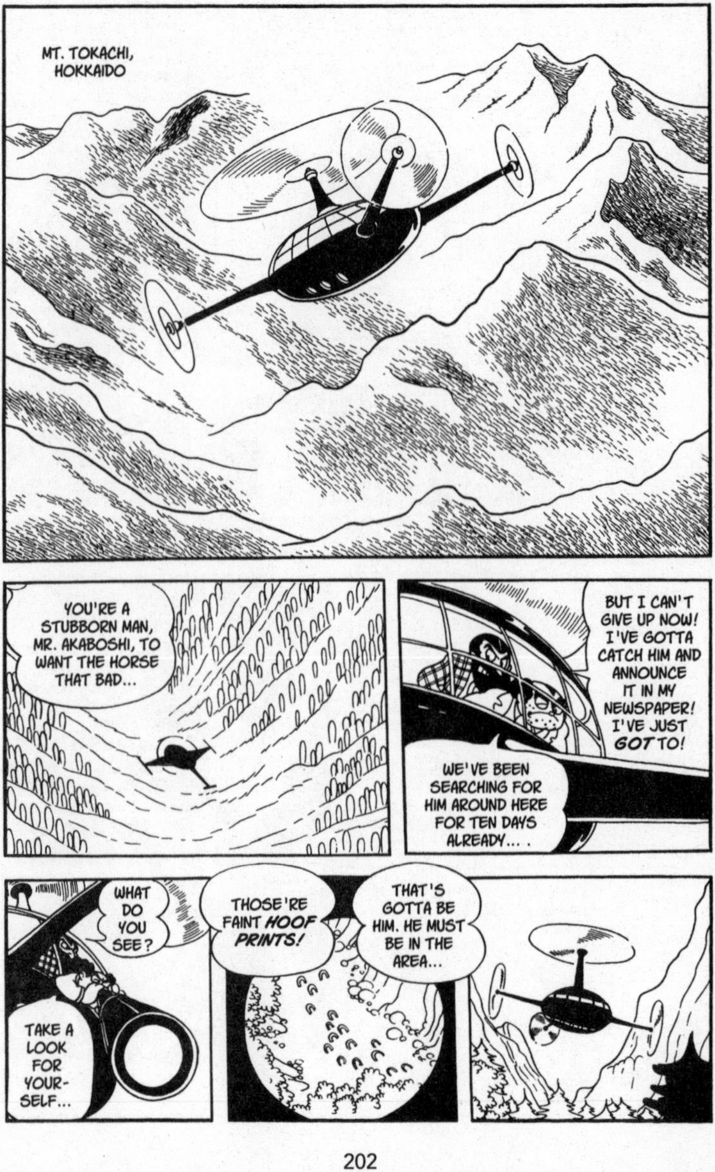
MT. TOKACHI, HOKKAIDO
YOU'RE A STUBBORN MAN, MR. AKABOSHI, TO WANT THE HORSE THAT BAD...
BUT I CAN'T GIVE UP NOW! I'VE GOTTA CATCH HIM AND ANNOUNCE IT IN MY NEWSPAPER! I'VE JUST GOT TO!
WE'VE BEEN SEARCHING FOR HIM AROUND HERE FOR TEN DAYS ALREADY... .
WHAT DO YOU SEE?
TAKE A LOOK FOR YOURSELF...
THOSE'RE FAINT HOOF PRINTS!
THAT'S GOTTA BE HIM. HE MUST BE IN THE AREA...

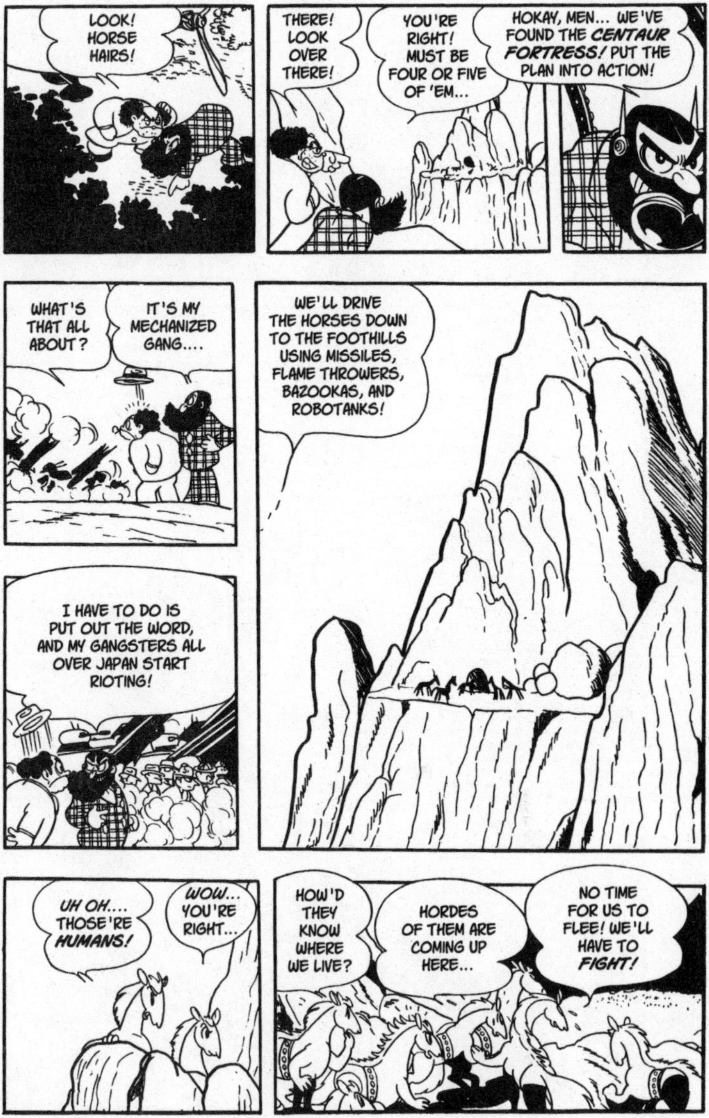
LOOK! HORSE HAIRS!
THERE! LOOK OVER THERE!
YOU'RE RIGHT! MUST BE FOUR OR FIVE OF 'EM...
HOKAY, MEN... WE'VE FOUND THE *CENTAUR FORTRESS!* PUT THE PLAN INTO ACTION!
WHAT'S THAT ALL ABOUT?
IT'S MY MECHANIZED GANG....
I HAVE TO DO IS PUT OUT THE WORD, AND MY GANGSTERS ALL OVER JAPAN START RIOTING!
WE'LL DRIVE THE HORSES DOWN TO THE FOOTHILLS USING MISSILES, FLAME THROWERS, BAZOOKAS, AND ROBOTANKS!
UH OH.... THOSE'RE *HUMANS!*
WOW... YOU'RE RIGHT...
HOW'D THEY KNOW WHERE WE LIVE?
HORDES OF THEM ARE COMING UP HERE...
NO TIME FOR US TO FLEE! WE'LL HAVE TO *FIGHT!*

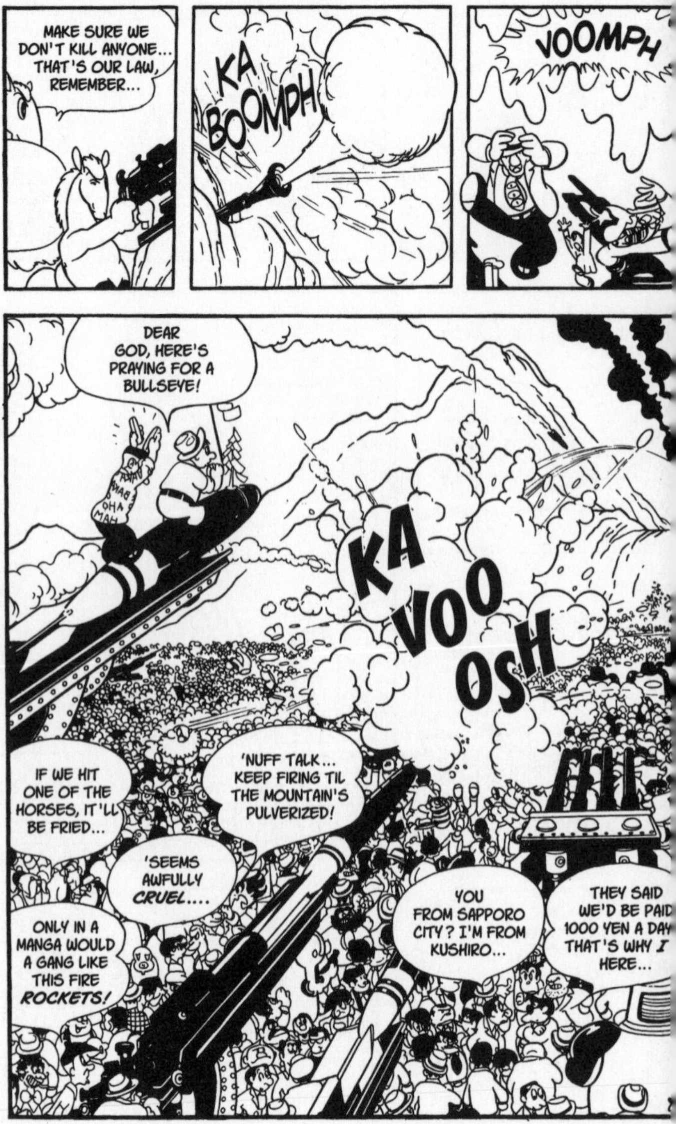
MAKE SURE WE DON'T KILL ANYONE... THAT'S OUR LAW, REMEMBER...
KA BOOMPH
VOOMPH
DEAR GOD, HERE'S PRAYING FOR A BULLSEYE!
OHA MAH
KA VOO OSH
IF WE HIT ONE OF THE HORSES, IT'LL BE FRIED...
'NUFF TALK... KEEP FIRING TIL THE MOUNTAIN'S PULVERIZED!
'SEEMS AWFULLY CRUEL....
ONLY IN A MANGA WOULD A GANG LIKE THIS FIRE ROCKETS!
YOU FROM SAPPORO CITY? I'M FROM KUSHIRO...
THEY SAID WE'D BE PAID 1000 YEN A DAY THAT'S WHY I HERE...

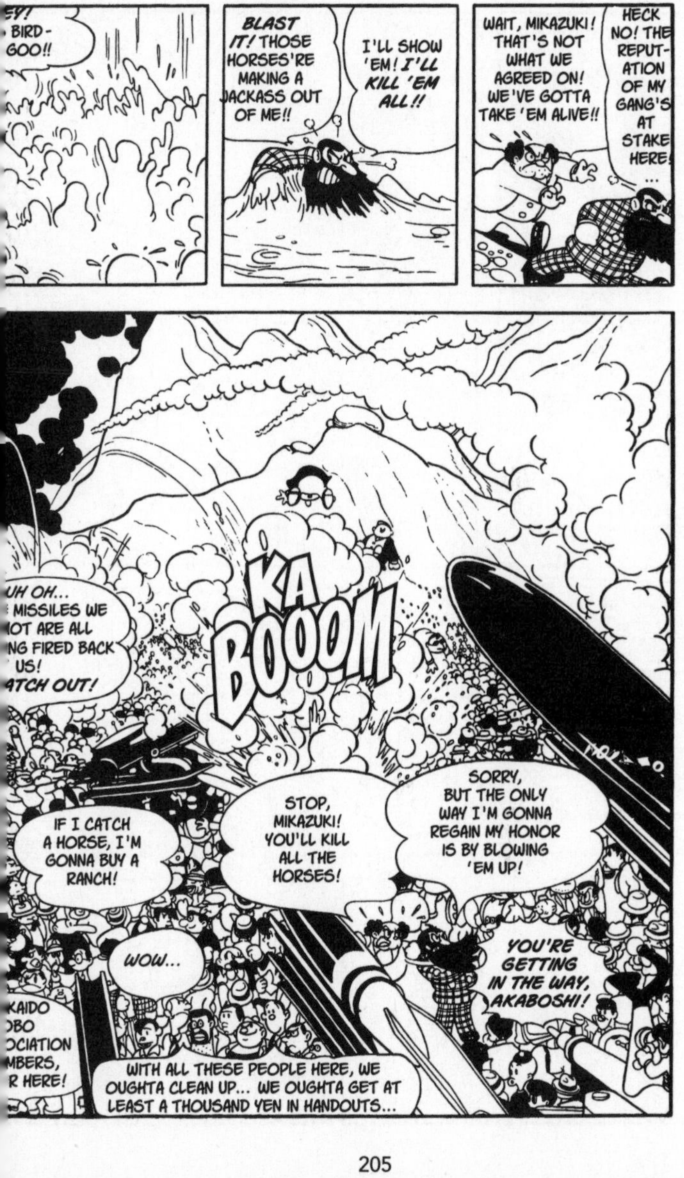
EY!
BIRD-
GOO!!
BLAST IT! THOSE HORSES'RE MAKING A JACKASS OUT OF ME!!
I'LL SHOW 'EM! I'LL KILL 'EM ALL!!
WAIT, MIKAZUKI! THAT'S NOT WHAT WE AGREED ON! WE'VE GOTTA TAKE 'EM ALIVE!!
HECK NO! THE REPUT-ATION OF MY GANG'S AT STAKE HERE! ...
UH OH... MISSILES WE OT ARE ALL NG FIRED BACK US! ATCH OUT!
KA BOOOM
IF I CATCH A HORSE, I'M GONNA BUY A RANCH!
STOP, MIKAZUKI! YOU'LL KILL ALL THE HORSES!
SORRY, BUT THE ONLY WAY I'M GONNA REGAIN MY HONOR IS BY BLOWING 'EM UP!
WOW...
YOU'RE GETTING IN THE WAY, AKABOSHI!
KAIDO OBO OCIATION MBERS, R HERE!
WITH ALL THESE PEOPLE HERE, WE OUGHTA CLEAN UP... WE OUGHTA GET AT LEAST A THOUSAND YEN IN HANDOUTS...

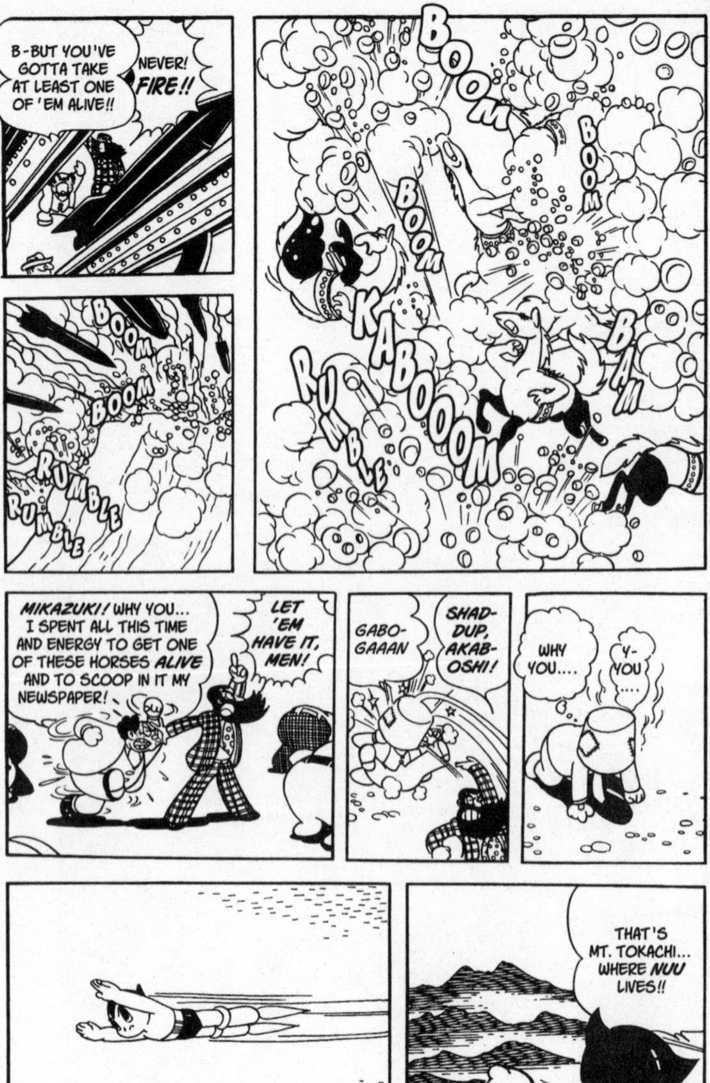
B-BUT YOU'VE GOTTA TAKE AT LEAST ONE OF 'EM ALIVE!!
NEVER! FIRE!!
BOOM
BOOM
RUMBLE
RUMBLE
BOOM
BOOM
BOOM
KABOOOOM
RUMBLE
BAM
MIKAZUKI! WHY YOU... I SPENT ALL THIS TIME AND ENERGY TO GET ONE OF THESE HORSES ALIVE AND TO SCOOP IN IT MY NEWSPAPER!
LET 'EM HAVE IT, MEN!
GABO-GAAAN
SHAD-DUP, AKAB-OSHI!
WHY YOU....
Y-YOU ....
THAT'S MT. TOKACHI... WHERE NUU LIVES!!

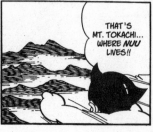

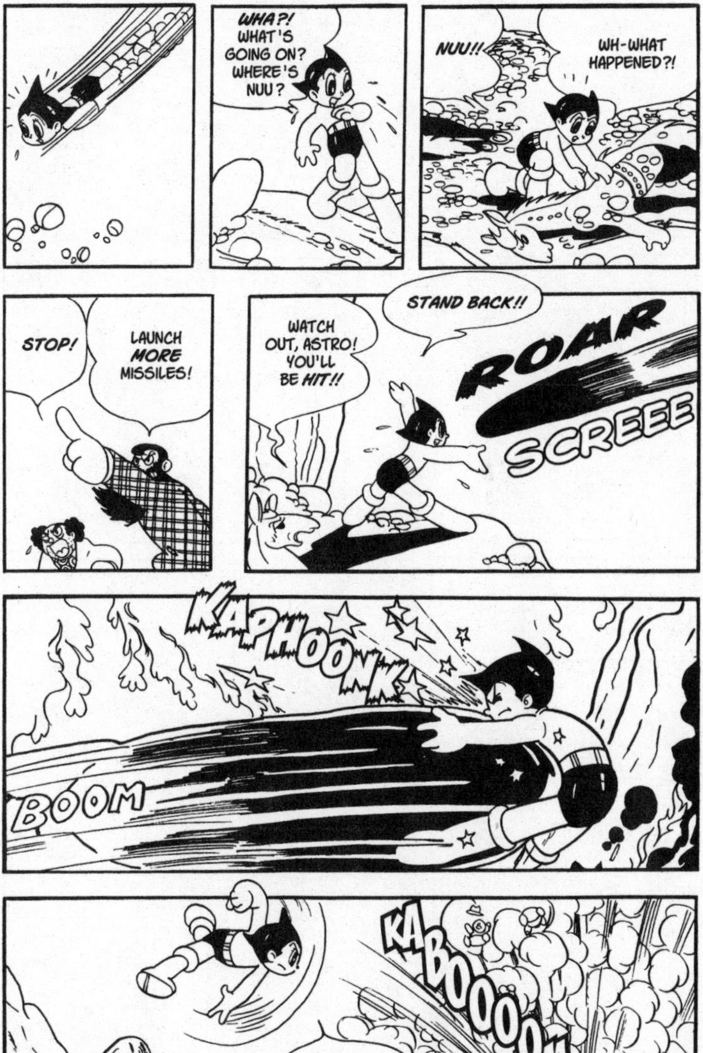

WHA?! WHAT'S GOING ON? WHERE'S NUU?
NUU!!
WH-WHAT HAPPENED?!
STOP!
LAUNCH MORE MISSILES!
WATCH OUT, ASTRO! YOU'LL BE HIT!!
STAND BACK!!
ROAR
SCREEE
KAPHOOONK
BOOM
KABOOOOOM
TIME FOR A RETURN TRIP!

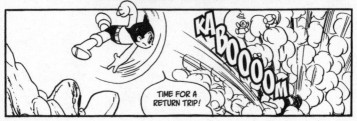

UH OH... THE ROBOTS ARE ATTACKING NEXT, ASTRO!

LEAVE THEM TO ME!

GA GA BEEEP

I *WON'T* LET YOU PASS!!

GAAN GON

YOU GUYS AREN'T REAL ROBOTS! YOU'RE *FAKES!*

OWWW OWWW!!

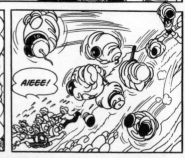

AIEEE!

THESE ROBO-SUITS'RE CHEAPOS!

NAW... IT'S THE OTHER WAY AROUND! ASTRO'S TOO WELL-MADE...

PANT GASP
GASP
PANT PUFF

BLAST IT! IT'S ALL UP TO *ME* NOW!

ASTRO...

IF THEY KEEP THIS UP, THEY'LL JUST RUIN THIS BEAUTIFUL MOUNTAIN...

LET'S GO BACK TO TOKYO, NUU!

NO, ASTRO... WE'VE DECIDED TO GO BACK TO OUR *OWN* PLANET...

YOUR *OWN PLANET?*

RIGHT. TO OUR *HOME*...

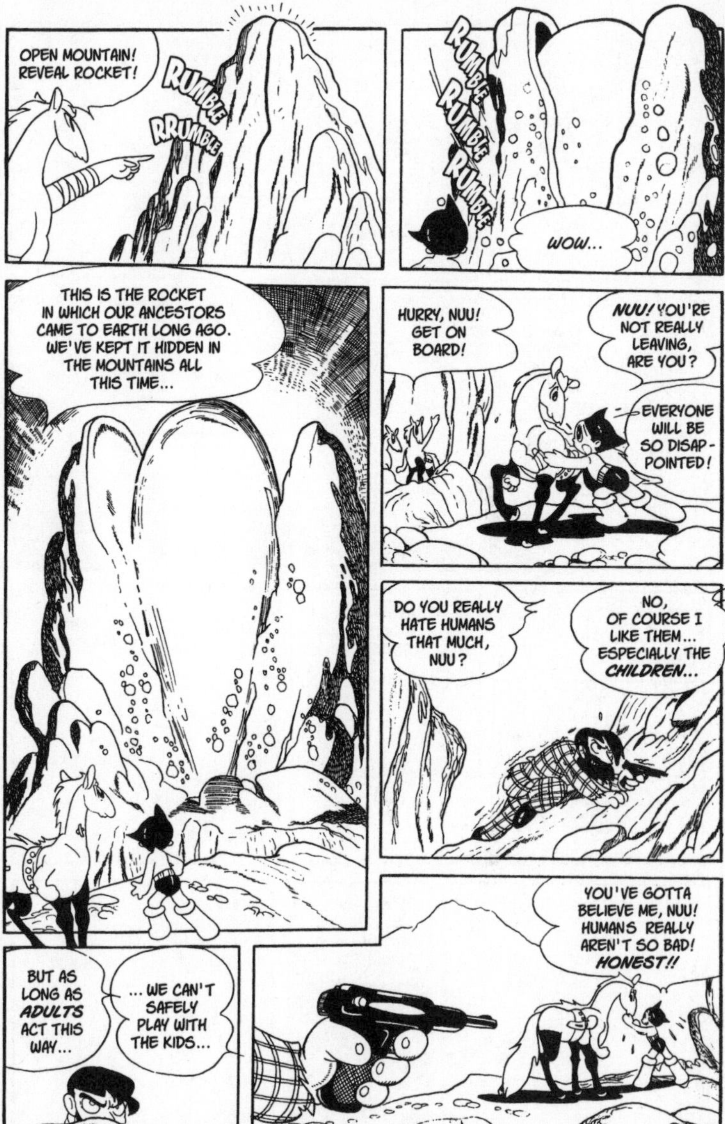
OPEN MOUNTAIN! REVEAL ROCKET!
RUMBLE
RRUMBLE
RUMBLE RUMBLE RUMBLE
WOW...
THIS IS THE ROCKET IN WHICH OUR ANCESTORS CAME TO EARTH LONG AGO. WE'VE KEPT IT HIDDEN IN THE MOUNTAINS ALL THIS TIME...
HURRY, NUU! GET ON BOARD!
NUU! YOU'RE NOT REALLY LEAVING, ARE YOU?
EVERYONE WILL BE SO DISAP-POINTED!
DO YOU REALLY HATE HUMANS THAT MUCH, NUU?
NO, OF COURSE I LIKE THEM... ESPECIALLY THE CHILDREN...
BUT AS LONG AS ADULTS ACT THIS WAY...
... WE CAN'T SAFELY PLAY WITH THE KIDS...
YOU'VE GOTTA BELIEVE ME, NUU! HUMANS REALLY AREN'T SO BAD! HONEST!!

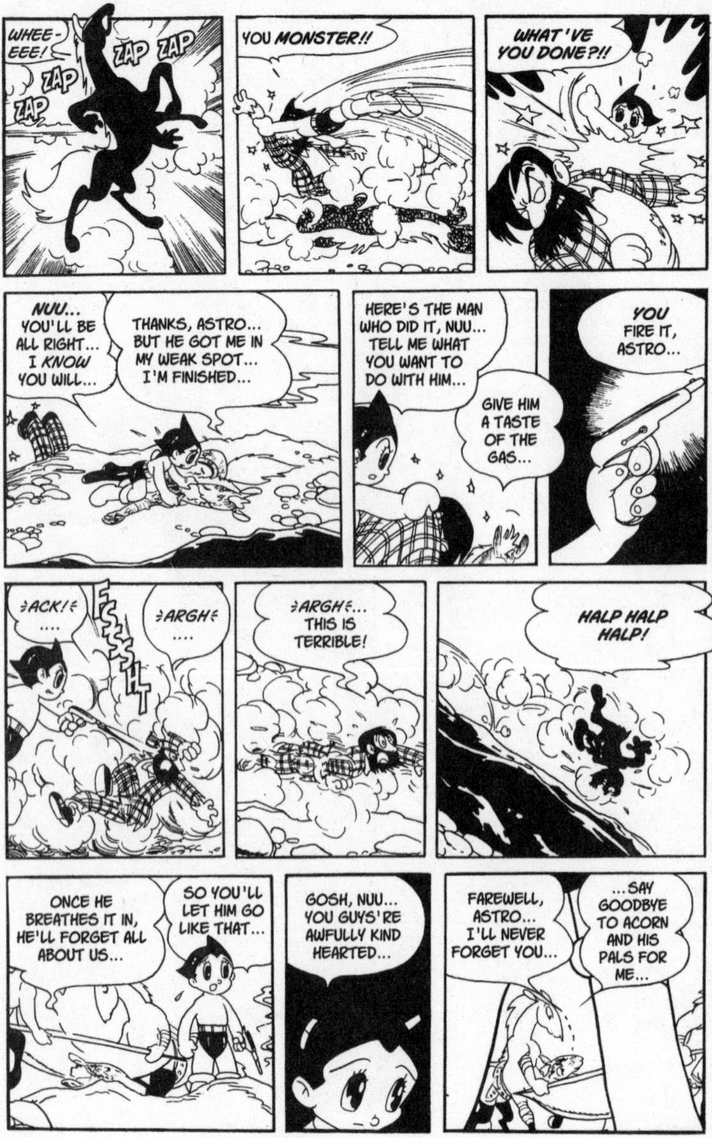
WHEE-EEE!
ZAP ZAP
ZAP
ZAP
YOU MONSTER!!
WHAT'VE YOU DONE?!!
NUU... YOU'LL BE ALL RIGHT... I KNOW YOU WILL...
THANKS, ASTRO... BUT HE GOT ME IN MY WEAK SPOT... I'M FINISHED...
HERE'S THE MAN WHO DID IT, NUU... TELL ME WHAT YOU WANT TO DO WITH HIM...
GIVE HIM A TASTE OF THE GAS...
YOU FIRE IT, ASTRO...
ACK! ....
FSSSHT
ARGH ....
ARGH... THIS IS TERRIBLE!
HALP HALP HALP!
ONCE HE BREATHES IT IN, HE'LL FORGET ALL ABOUT US...
SO YOU'LL LET HIM GO LIKE THAT...
GOSH, NUU... YOU GUYS'RE AWFULLY KIND HEARTED...
FAREWELL, ASTRO... I'LL NEVER FORGET YOU...
...SAY GOODBYE TO ACORN AND HIS PALS FOR ME...

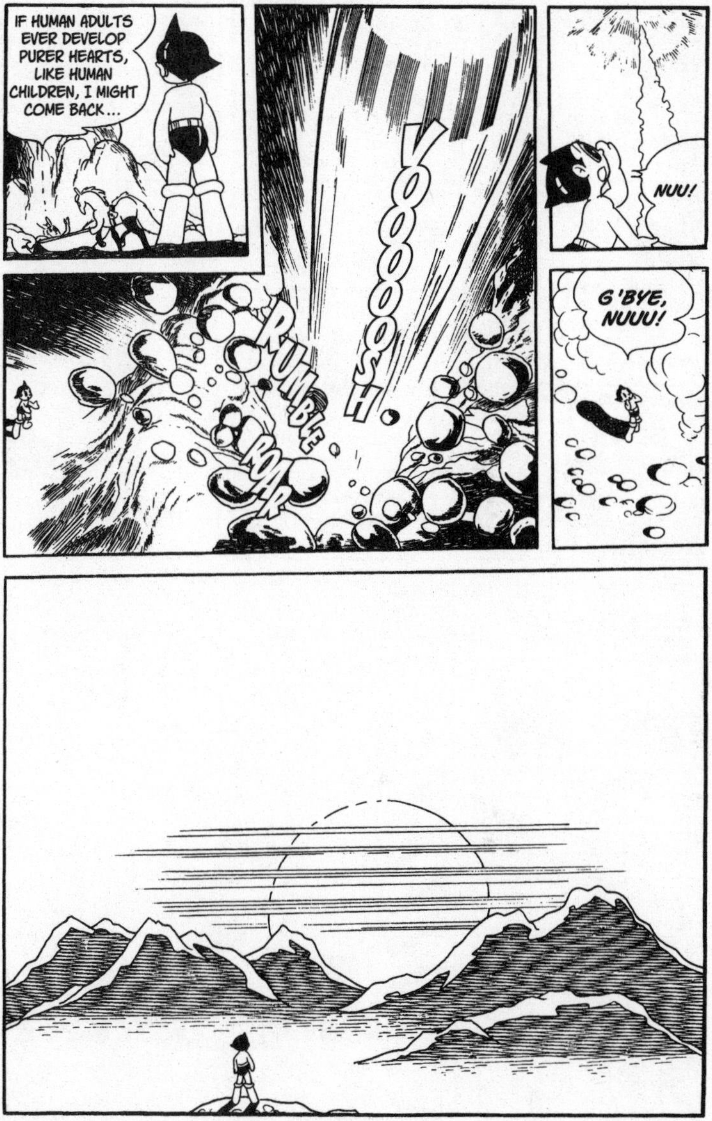
IF HUMAN ADULTS EVER DEVELOP PURER HEARTS, LIKE HUMAN CHILDREN, I MIGHT COME BACK...
VOOOOOOSH
RUMBLE
ROAR
NUU!
G'BYE, NUUU!

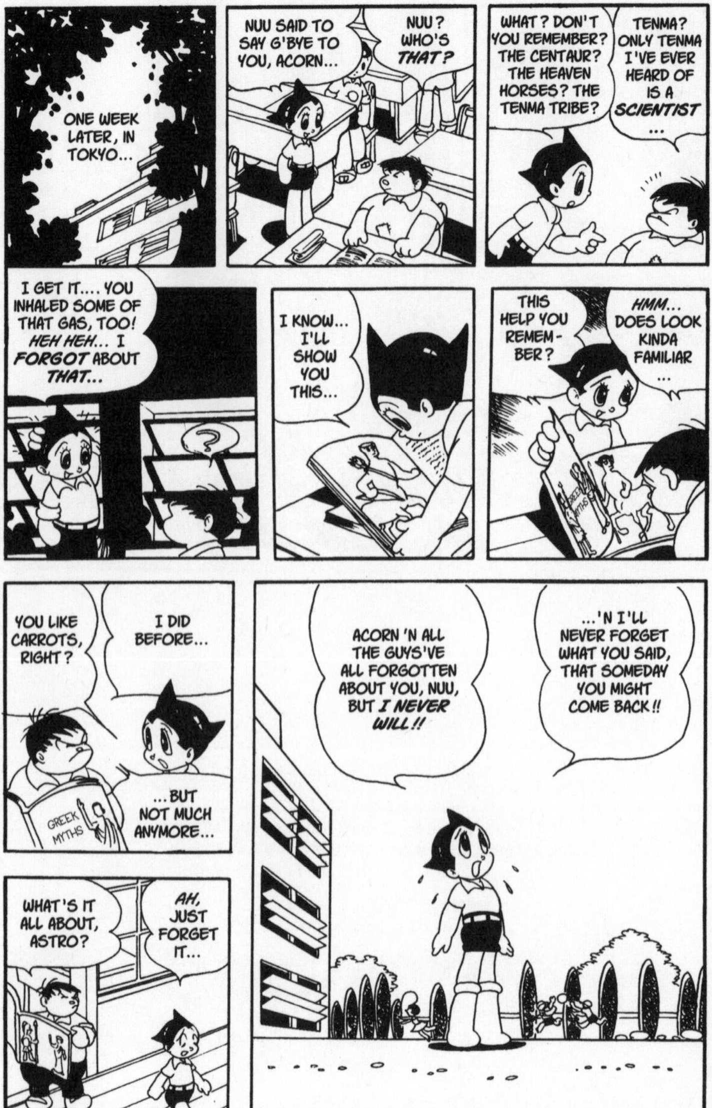
ONE WEEK LATER, IN TOKYO...
NUU SAID TO SAY G'BYE TO YOU, ACORN...
NUU? WHO'S *THAT?*
WHAT? DON'T YOU REMEMBER? THE CENTAUR? THE HEAVEN HORSES? THE TENMA TRIBE?
TENMA? ONLY TENMA I'VE EVER HEARD OF IS A *SCIENTIST* ...
I GET IT.... YOU INHALED SOME OF THAT GAS, TOO! *HEH HEH*... I *FORGOT* ABOUT *THAT*...
I KNOW... I'LL SHOW YOU THIS...
THIS HELP YOU REMEM-BER?
HMM... DOES LOOK KINDA FAMILIAR ...
GREEK MYTHS
YOU LIKE CARROTS, RIGHT?
I DID BEFORE...
...BUT NOT MUCH ANYMORE...
GREEK MYTHS
WHAT'S IT ALL ABOUT, ASTRO?
AH, JUST FORGET IT...
ACORN 'N ALL THE GUYS'VE ALL FORGOTTEN ABOUT YOU, NUU, BUT *I NEVER WILL!!*
...'N I'LL NEVER FORGET WHAT YOU SAID, THAT SOMEDAY YOU MIGHT COME BACK!!

GERNICA

First appeared in the special expanded New Year's
edition of *Shonen* magazine.

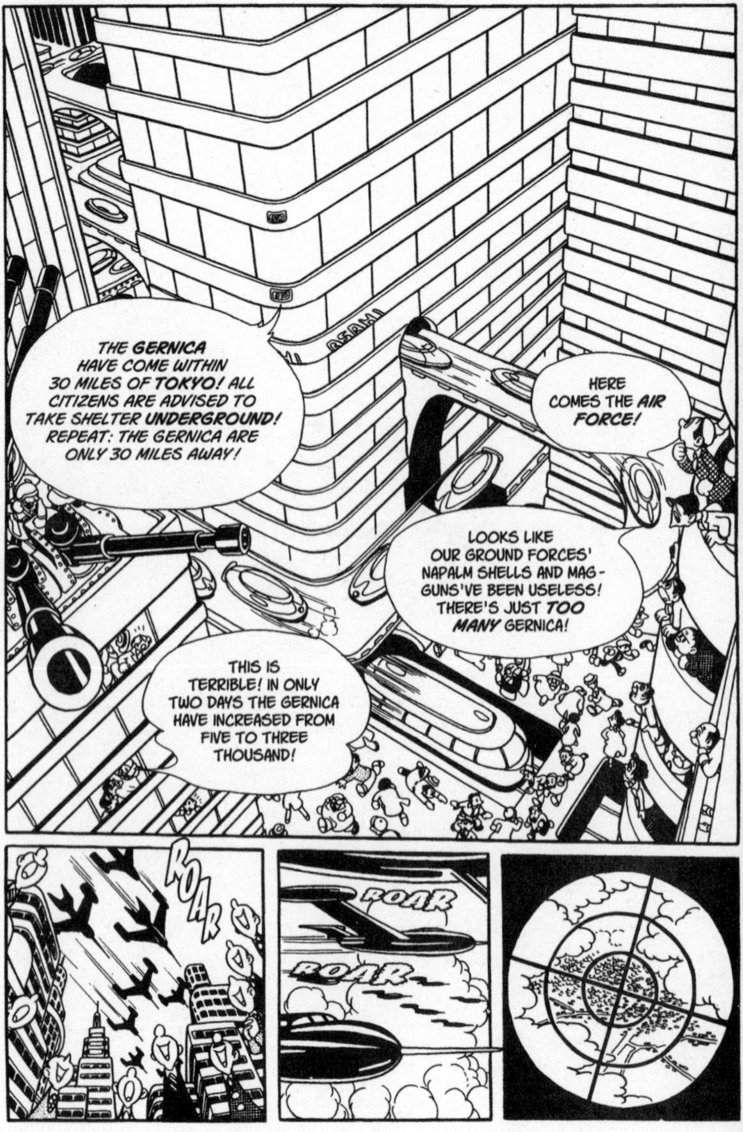
THE GERNICA HAVE COME WITHIN 30 MILES OF TOKYO! ALL CITIZENS ARE ADVISED TO TAKE SHELTER UNDERGROUND! REPEAT: THE GERNICA ARE ONLY 30 MILES AWAY!
HERE COMES THE AIR FORCE!
LOOKS LIKE OUR GROUND FORCES' NAPALM SHELLS AND MAG-GUNS'VE BEEN USELESS! THERE'S JUST TOO MANY GERNICA!
THIS IS TERRIBLE! IN ONLY TWO DAYS THE GERNICA HAVE INCREASED FROM FIVE TO THREE THOUSAND!
ROAR
ROAR
ROAR

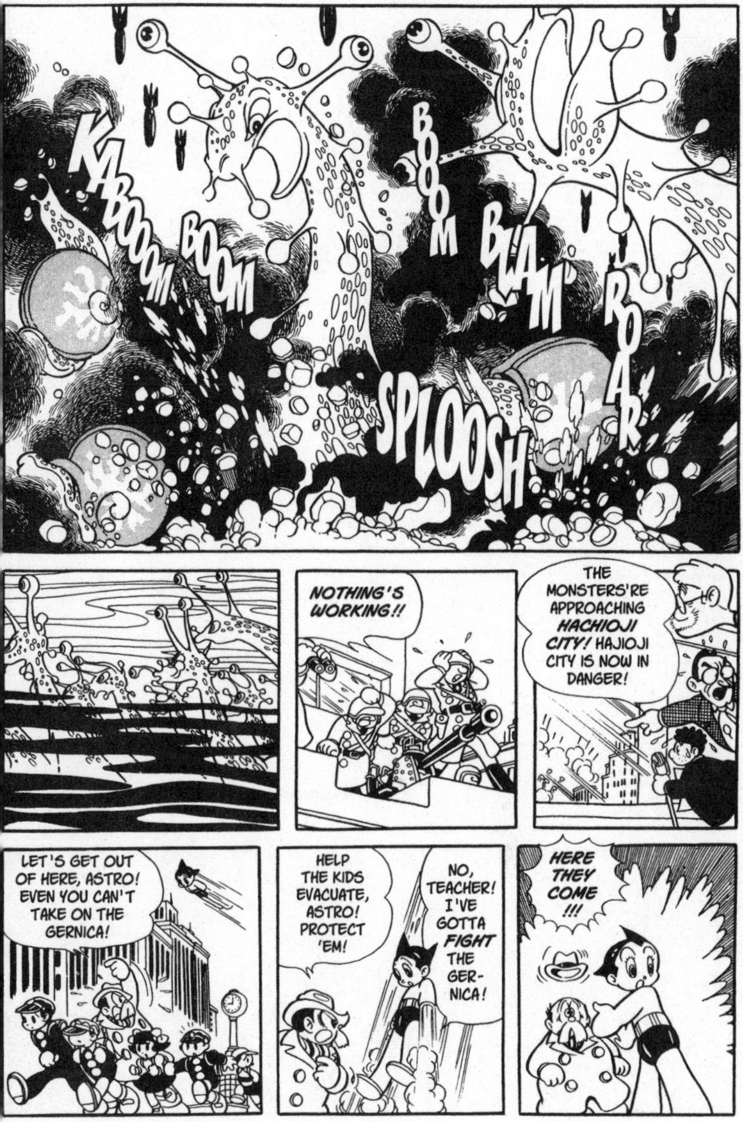
KABOOOM
BOOOM
BOOOM
BLAM
ROAR
SPLOOSH
NOTHING'S WORKING!!
THE MONSTERS'RE APPROACHING HACHIOJI CITY! HAJIOJI CITY IS NOW IN DANGER!
LET'S GET OUT OF HERE, ASTRO! EVEN YOU CAN'T TAKE ON THE GERNICA!
HELP THE KIDS EVACUATE, ASTRO! PROTECT 'EM!
NO, TEACHER! I'VE GOTTA FIGHT THE GER-NICA!
HERE THEY COME!!!

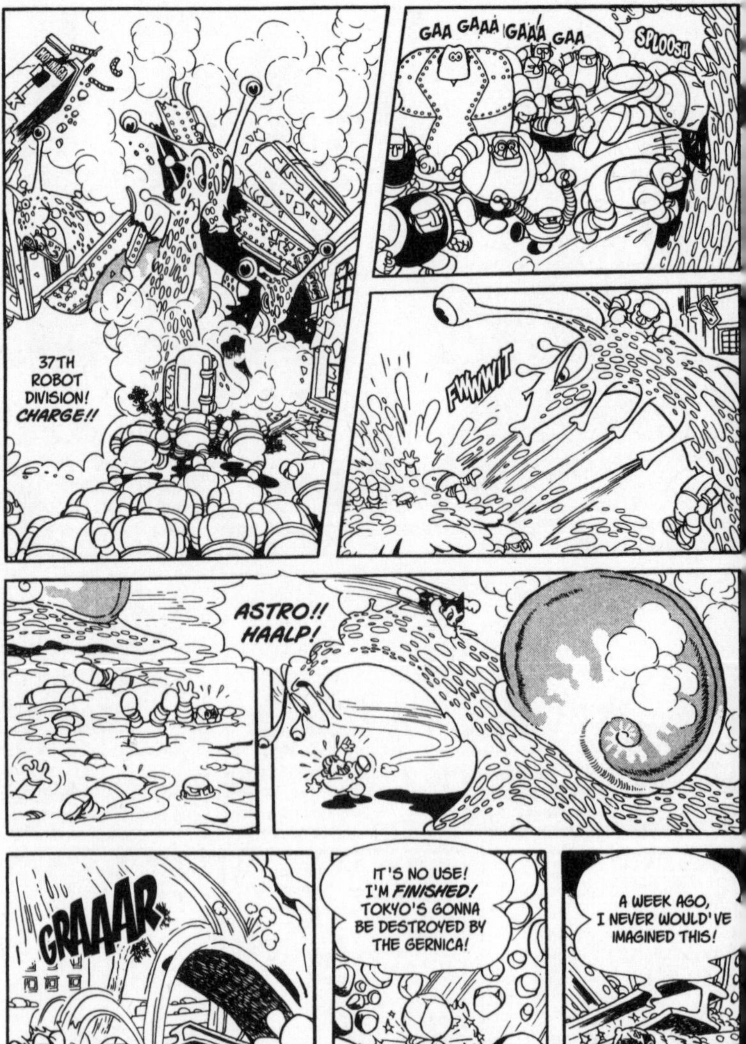
37TH ROBOT DIVISION! CHARGE!!
GAA GAAA GAAA GAA
SPLOOSH
FWWWIT
ASTRO!! HAALP!
GRAAAR
IT'S NO USE! I'M FINISHED! TOKYO'S GONNA BE DESTROYED BY THE GERNICA!
A WEEK AGO, I NEVER WOULD'VE IMAGINED THIS!

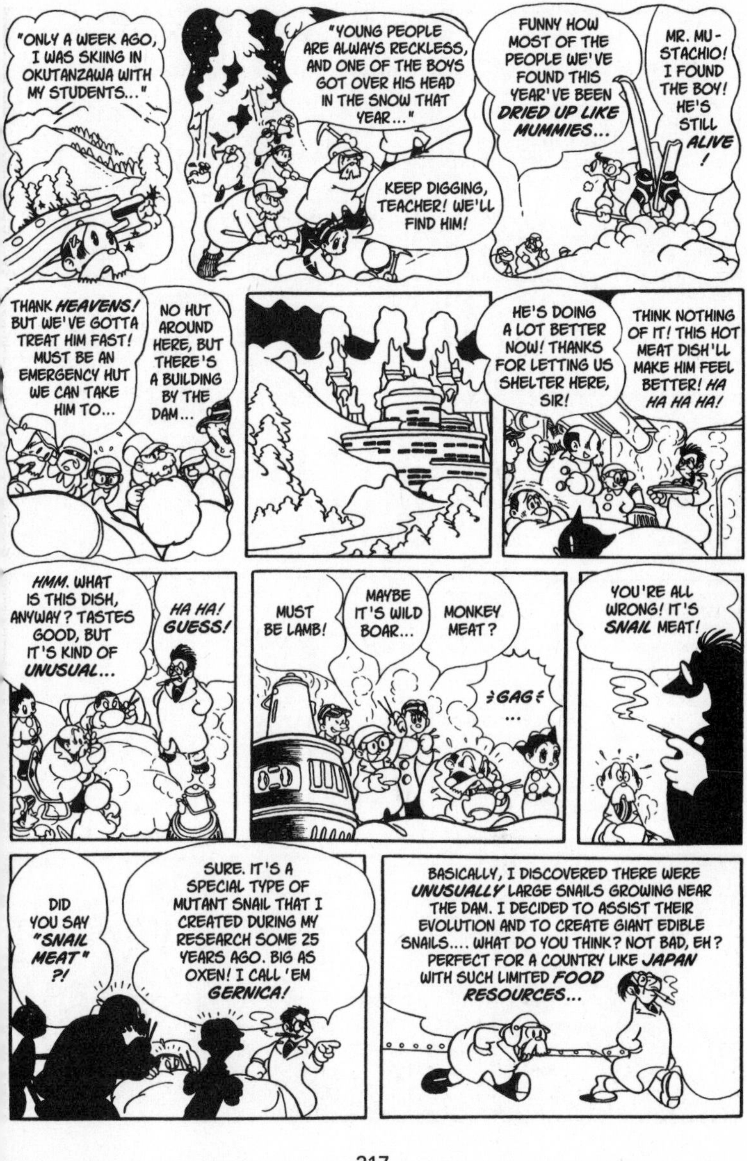
"ONLY A WEEK AGO, I WAS SKIING IN OKUTANZAWA WITH MY STUDENTS..."
"YOUNG PEOPLE ARE ALWAYS RECKLESS, AND ONE OF THE BOYS GOT OVER HIS HEAD IN THE SNOW THAT YEAR..."
KEEP DIGGING, TEACHER! WE'LL FIND HIM!
FUNNY HOW MOST OF THE PEOPLE WE'VE FOUND THIS YEAR'VE BEEN *DRIED UP LIKE MUMMIES*...
MR. MUSTACHIO! I FOUND THE BOY! HE'S STILL *ALIVE*!
THANK *HEAVENS!* BUT WE'VE GOTTA TREAT HIM FAST! MUST BE AN EMERGENCY HUT WE CAN TAKE HIM TO...
NO HUT AROUND HERE, BUT THERE'S A BUILDING BY THE DAM...
HE'S DOING A LOT BETTER NOW! THANKS FOR LETTING US SHELTER HERE, SIR!
THINK NOTHING OF IT! THIS HOT MEAT DISH'LL MAKE HIM FEEL BETTER! *HA HA HA HA!*
HMM. WHAT IS THIS DISH, ANYWAY? TASTES GOOD, BUT IT'S KIND OF *UNUSUAL*...
HA HA! GUESS!
MUST BE LAMB!
MAYBE IT'S WILD BOAR...
MONKEY MEAT?
GAG ...
YOU'RE ALL WRONG! IT'S *SNAIL* MEAT!
DID YOU SAY *"SNAIL MEAT"* ?!
SURE. IT'S A SPECIAL TYPE OF MUTANT SNAIL THAT I CREATED DURING MY RESEARCH SOME 25 YEARS AGO. BIG AS OXEN! I CALL 'EM *GERNICA!*
BASICALLY, I DISCOVERED THERE WERE *UNUSUALLY* LARGE SNAILS GROWING NEAR THE DAM. I DECIDED TO ASSIST THEIR EVOLUTION AND TO CREATE GIANT EDIBLE SNAILS.... WHAT DO YOU THINK? NOT BAD, EH? PERFECT FOR A COUNTRY LIKE *JAPAN* WITH SUCH LIMITED *FOOD RESOURCES*...

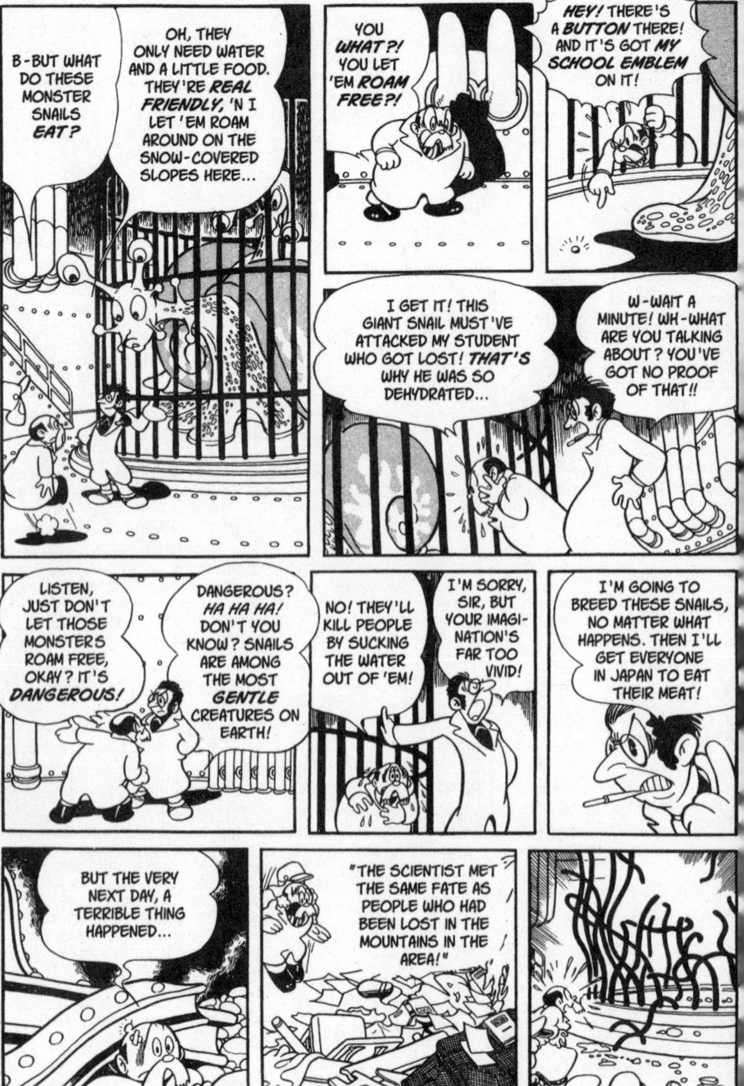
B-BUT WHAT DO THESE MONSTER SNAILS EAT?
OH, THEY ONLY NEED WATER AND A LITTLE FOOD. THEY'RE REAL FRIENDLY, 'N I LET 'EM ROAM AROUND ON THE SNOW-COVERED SLOPES HERE...
YOU WHAT?! YOU LET 'EM ROAM FREE?!
HEY! THERE'S A BUTTON THERE! AND IT'S GOT MY SCHOOL EMBLEM ON IT!
I GET IT! THIS GIANT SNAIL MUST'VE ATTACKED MY STUDENT WHO GOT LOST! THAT'S WHY HE WAS SO DEHYDRATED...
W-WAIT A MINUTE! WH-WHAT ARE YOU TALKING ABOUT? YOU'VE GOT NO PROOF OF THAT!!
LISTEN, JUST DON'T LET THOSE MONSTERS ROAM FREE, OKAY? IT'S DANGEROUS!
DANGEROUS? HA HA HA! DON'T YOU KNOW? SNAILS ARE AMONG THE MOST GENTLE CREATURES ON EARTH!
NO! THEY'LL KILL PEOPLE BY SUCKING THE WATER OUT OF 'EM!
I'M SORRY, SIR, BUT YOUR IMAGI-NATION'S FAR TOO VIVID!
I'M GOING TO BREED THESE SNAILS, NO MATTER WHAT HAPPENS. THEN I'LL GET EVERYONE IN JAPAN TO EAT THEIR MEAT!
BUT THE VERY NEXT DAY, A TERRIBLE THING HAPPENED...
"THE SCIENTIST MET THE SAME FATE AS PEOPLE WHO HAD BEEN LOST IN THE MOUNTAINS IN THE AREA!"

THERE'S NO MORE WATER IN THE DAM!

THOSE MONSTER SNAILS MUST'VE SUCKED UP EVERY LAST DROP!!

THESE'RE *GERNICA* TRACKS! THEY LOOK LIKE *TIRE TRACKS*!

"UNABLE TO WITHSTAND THE COLD, THE GERNICA EVENTUALLY BEGAN MIGRATING TO LOWER AND LOWER GROUND..."

...WHICH BRINGS US TO THE PRESENT...

TEACHER! TEACHER!

THANK GOD *YOU'RE* OKAY, ASTRO...

DON'T WORRY, I'LL FREE YOU, TEACHER! THE GERNICA HAVE GONE THROUGH THIS VILLAGE 'N ARE SWARMING AROUND TACHIKAWA CITY...

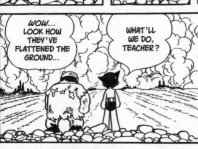

WOW... LOOK HOW THEY'VE FLATTENED THE GROUND...

WHAT'LL WE DO, TEACHER?

I DUNNO... THEY'RE TOO CLOSE FOR COMFORT TO TOKYO NOW... 'N WE CAN'T USE POISON GAS THERE...

HEH HEH... HAH HAH... HAH HAH HAH....

THIS IS REALLY *FUNNY*, COME TO THINK OF IT. MAN MAKES SNAILS FOR FOOD, AND THE SNAILS TURN MAN INTO FOOD....

WE BRING YOU AN EMERGENCY ANNOUNCEMENT. THE CITY OF TACHIKAWA HAS BEEN WIPED OUT! THE GERNICA ARE NOW WITHIN TWELVE MILES OF TOKYO...

219

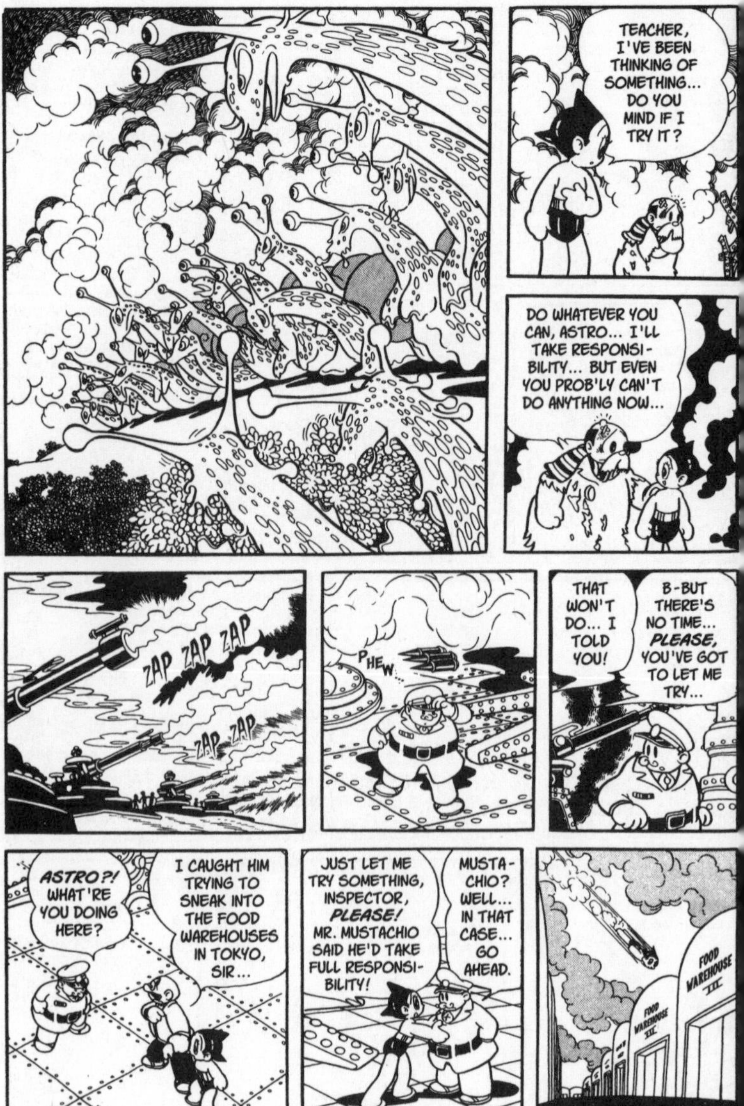
TEACHER, I'VE BEEN THINKING OF SOMETHING... DO YOU MIND IF I TRY IT?
DO WHATEVER YOU CAN, ASTRO... I'LL TAKE RESPONSI-BILITY... BUT EVEN YOU PROB'LY CAN'T DO ANYTHING NOW...
ZAP ZAP ZAP
ZAP ZAP
PHEW...
THAT WON'T DO... I TOLD YOU!
B-BUT THERE'S NO TIME... *PLEASE,* YOU'VE GOT TO LET ME TRY...
ASTRO?! WHAT'RE YOU DOING HERE?
I CAUGHT HIM TRYING TO SNEAK INTO THE FOOD WAREHOUSES IN TOKYO, SIR...
JUST LET ME TRY SOMETHING, INSPECTOR, *PLEASE!* MR. MUSTACHIO SAID HE'D TAKE FULL RESPONSI-BILITY!
MUSTA-CHIO? WELL... IN THAT CASE... GO AHEAD.
FOOD WAREHOUSE III
FOOD WAREHOUSE II

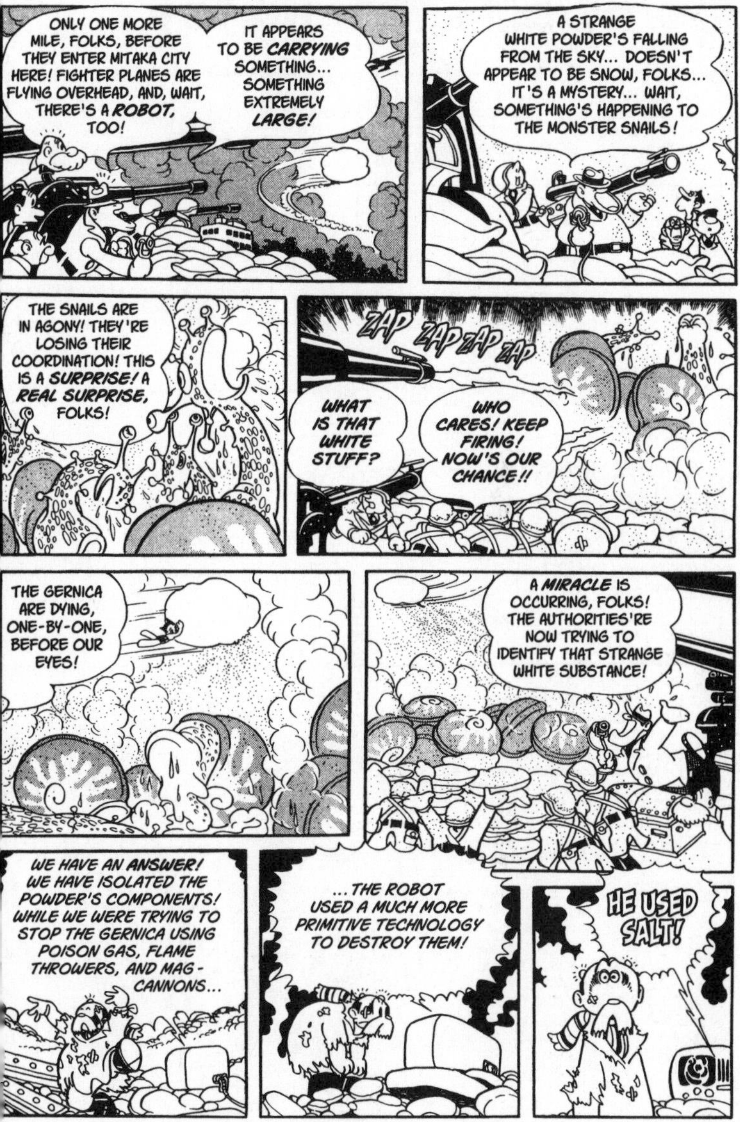
ONLY ONE MORE MILE, FOLKS, BEFORE THEY ENTER MITAKA CITY HERE! FIGHTER PLANES ARE FLYING OVERHEAD, AND, WAIT, THERE'S A *ROBOT,* TOO!
IT APPEARS TO BE *CARRYING* SOMETHING... SOMETHING EXTREMELY *LARGE!*
A STRANGE WHITE POWDER'S FALLING FROM THE SKY... DOESN'T APPEAR TO BE SNOW, FOLKS... IT'S A MYSTERY... WAIT, SOMETHING'S HAPPENING TO THE MONSTER SNAILS!
THE SNAILS ARE IN AGONY! THEY'RE LOSING THEIR COORDINATION! THIS IS A *SURPRISE!* A *REAL SURPRISE,* FOLKS!
ZAP ZAP ZAP ZAP
WHAT IS THAT WHITE STUFF?
WHO CARES! KEEP FIRING! NOW'S OUR CHANCE!!
THE GERNICA ARE DYING, ONE-BY-ONE, BEFORE OUR EYES!
A *MIRACLE* IS OCCURRING, FOLKS! THE AUTHORITIES'RE NOW TRYING TO IDENTIFY THAT STRANGE WHITE SUBSTANCE!
WE HAVE AN **ANSWER!** WE HAVE ISOLATED THE POWDER'S COMPONENTS! WHILE WE WERE TRYING TO STOP THE GERNICA USING POISON GAS, FLAME THROWERS, AND MAG-CANNONS...
...THE ROBOT USED A MUCH MORE PRIMITIVE TECHNOLOGY TO DESTROY THEM!
HE USED SALT!

ASTRO BOY'S ORIGINS AND HISTORY
PART 2

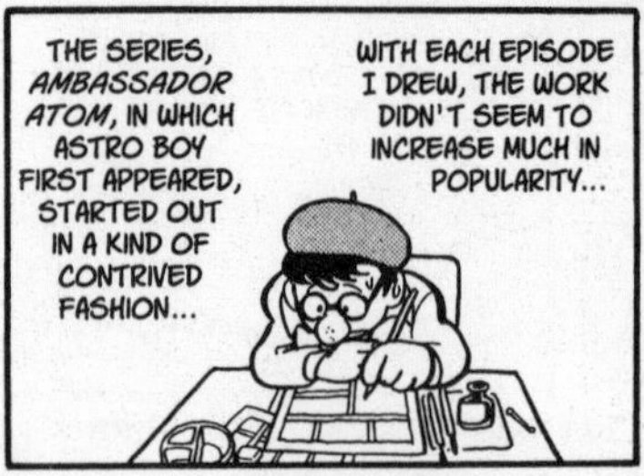
THE SERIES, *AMBASSADOR ATOM*, IN WHICH ASTRO BOY FIRST APPEARED, STARTED OUT IN A KIND OF CONTRIVED FASHION...
WITH EACH EPISODE I DREW, THE WORK DIDN'T SEEM TO INCREASE MUCH IN POPULARITY...

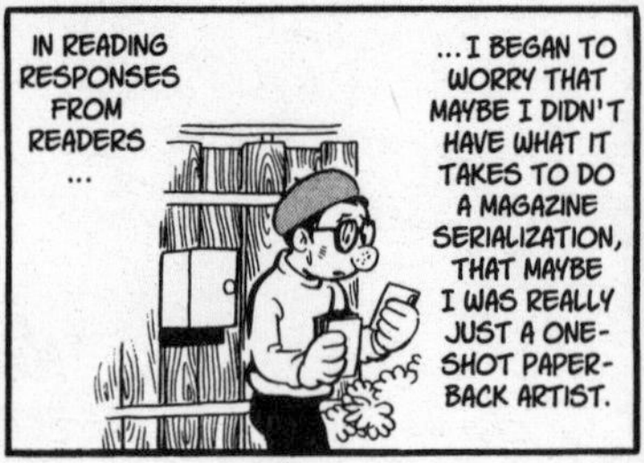
IN READING RESPONSES FROM READERS ...
...I BEGAN TO WORRY THAT MAYBE I DIDN'T HAVE WHAT IT TAKES TO DO A MAGAZINE SERIALIZATION, THAT MAYBE I WAS REALLY JUST A ONE-SHOT PAPER-BACK ARTIST.

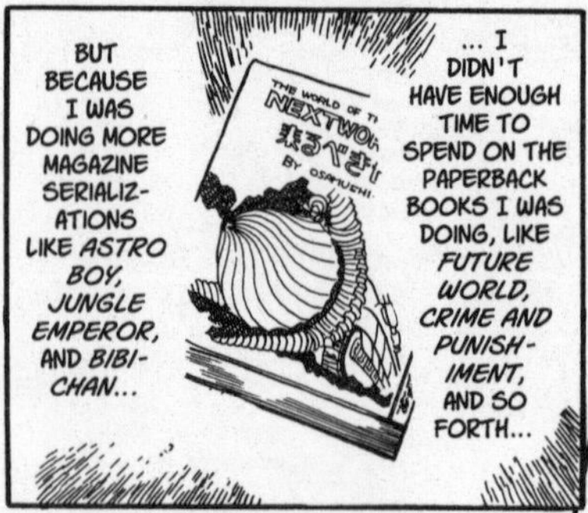
BUT BECAUSE I WAS DOING MORE MAGAZINE SERIALIZ-ATIONS LIKE *ASTRO BOY, JUNGLE EMPEROR*, AND *BIBI-CHAN*...
... I DIDN'T HAVE ENOUGH TIME TO SPEND ON THE PAPERBACK BOOKS I WAS DOING, LIKE *FUTURE WORLD, CRIME AND PUNISH-IMENT*, AND SO FORTH...

I CREATED THE NEW YEAR'S CARD AT RIGHT IN 1952. IT SHOWS THE CHARACTERS FROM THE FOLLOWING WORKS:
[1+2] *BIBICHAN* ("LITTLE BIBI," THEN SERIALIZED IN *OMOSHIRO BOOK*).
[3+4] *JUNGLE EMPEROR* (KNOWN AS *"KIMBA, THE WHITE LION"* IN AMERICA, SERIALIZED IN *MANGA SHONEN*)
[5+6] *DEKOBOKO SERIES ("UNEVEN SERIES"* N *MANGA TO YOMIMONO*)
[7] *SABOTEN-KUN* ("CACTUS KID," IN *SHONEN GAHO*)
[8] *BOKU NO SONGOKU* ("MY MONKEY KING," THEN SCHEDULED FOR SERIALIZATION IN *MANGA-O*).
[9] *BOKENKYO JIDAI* ("THE AGE OF ADVENTURES," IN *BOKEN-O*).
[10+11] *AMBASSADOR ATOM*.
NOTE THAT THE CHARACTER ATOM (OR ASTRO), DOESN'T APPEAR ANYWHERE. IN OTHER WORDS, IN 1952 ASTRO WAS STILL A BIT-PART PLAYER!

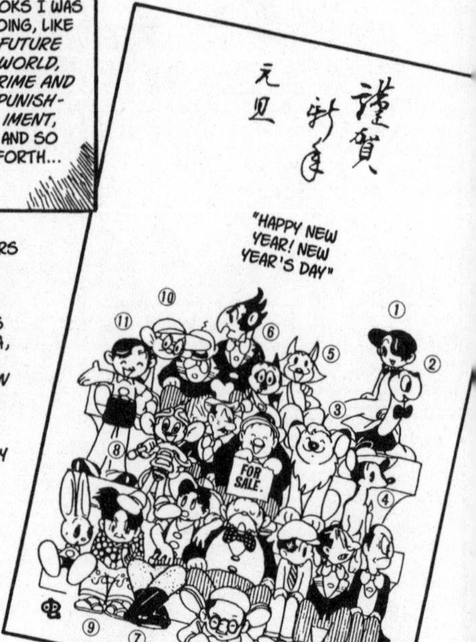
謹賀新年
元旦
"HAPPY NEW YEAR! NEW YEAR'S DAY"
FOR SALE.

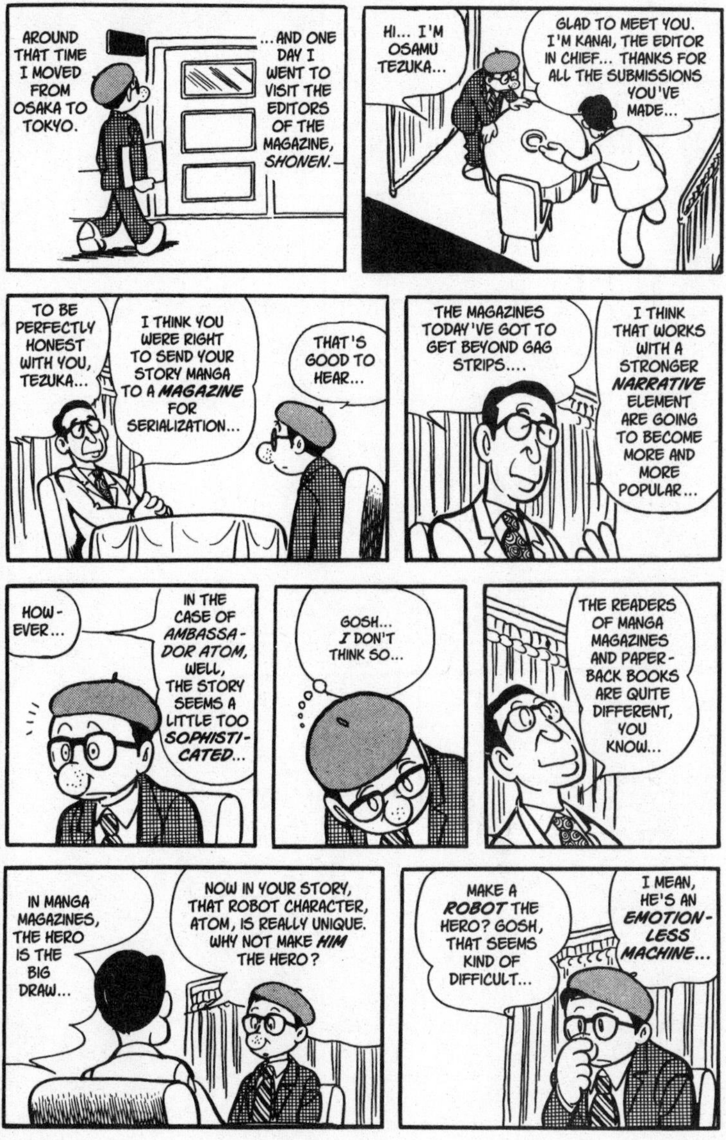

AROUND THAT TIME I MOVED FROM OSAKA TO TOKYO.
...AND ONE DAY I WENT TO VISIT THE EDITORS OF THE MAGAZINE, SHONEN.
HI... I'M OSAMU TEZUKA...
GLAD TO MEET YOU. I'M KANAI, THE EDITOR IN CHIEF... THANKS FOR ALL THE SUBMISSIONS YOU'VE MADE...
TO BE PERFECTLY HONEST WITH YOU, TEZUKA...
I THINK YOU WERE RIGHT TO SEND YOUR STORY MANGA TO A MAGAZINE FOR SERIALIZATION...
THAT'S GOOD TO HEAR...
THE MAGAZINES TODAY'VE GOT TO GET BEYOND GAG STRIPS....
I THINK THAT WORKS WITH A STRONGER NARRATIVE ELEMENT ARE GOING TO BECOME MORE AND MORE POPULAR...
HOW-EVER...
IN THE CASE OF AMBASSA-DOR ATOM, WELL, THE STORY SEEMS A LITTLE TOO SOPHISTI-CATED...
GOSH... I DON'T THINK SO...
THE READERS OF MANGA MAGAZINES AND PAPER-BACK BOOKS ARE QUITE DIFFERENT, YOU KNOW...
IN MANGA MAGAZINES, THE HERO IS THE BIG DRAW...
NOW IN YOUR STORY, THAT ROBOT CHARACTER, ATOM, IS REALLY UNIQUE. WHY NOT MAKE HIM THE HERO?
MAKE A ROBOT THE HERO? GOSH, THAT SEEMS KIND OF DIFFICULT...
I MEAN, HE'S AN EMOTION-LESS MACHINE...

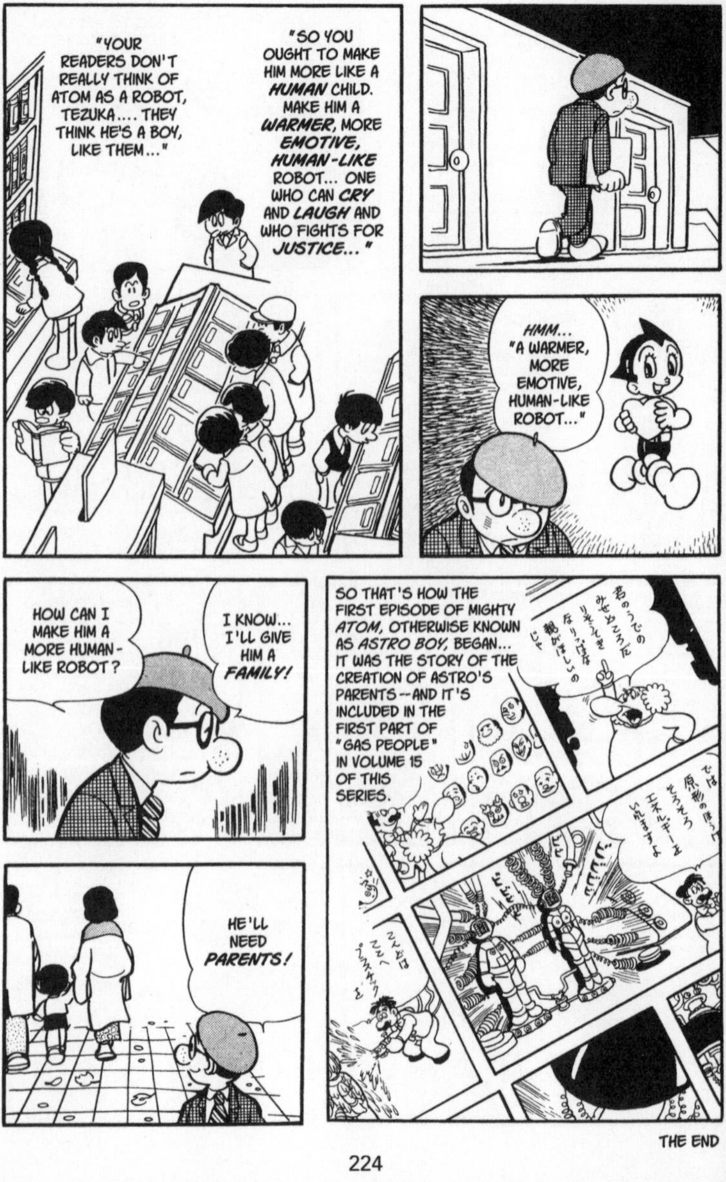
"YOUR READERS DON'T REALLY THINK OF ATOM AS A ROBOT, TEZUKA.... THEY THINK HE'S A BOY, LIKE THEM..."
"SO YOU OUGHT TO MAKE HIM MORE LIKE A *HUMAN* CHILD. MAKE HIM A *WARMER*, MORE *EMOTIVE, HUMAN-LIKE* ROBOT... ONE WHO CAN *CRY* AND *LAUGH* AND WHO FIGHTS FOR *JUSTICE...*"
HMM... "A WARMER, MORE EMOTIVE, HUMAN-LIKE ROBOT..."
HOW CAN I MAKE HIM A MORE HUMAN-LIKE ROBOT?
I KNOW... I'LL GIVE HIM A *FAMILY!*
HE'LL NEED *PARENTS!*
SO THAT'S HOW THE FIRST EPISODE OF MIGHTY *ATOM,* OTHERWISE KNOWN AS *ASTRO BOY,* BEGAN... IT WAS THE STORY OF THE CREATION OF ASTRO'S PARENTS--AND IT'S INCLUDED IN THE FIRST PART OF "GAS PEOPLE" IN VOLUME 15 OF THIS SERIES.
君のうでのみせどころだ りそうてきなりっぱな親がほしいのじゃ
では原形のほうにそろそろエネルギーをいれますよ

THE END

ELECTRO

First appeared in the January 1955 supplement
of *Shonen* magazine.

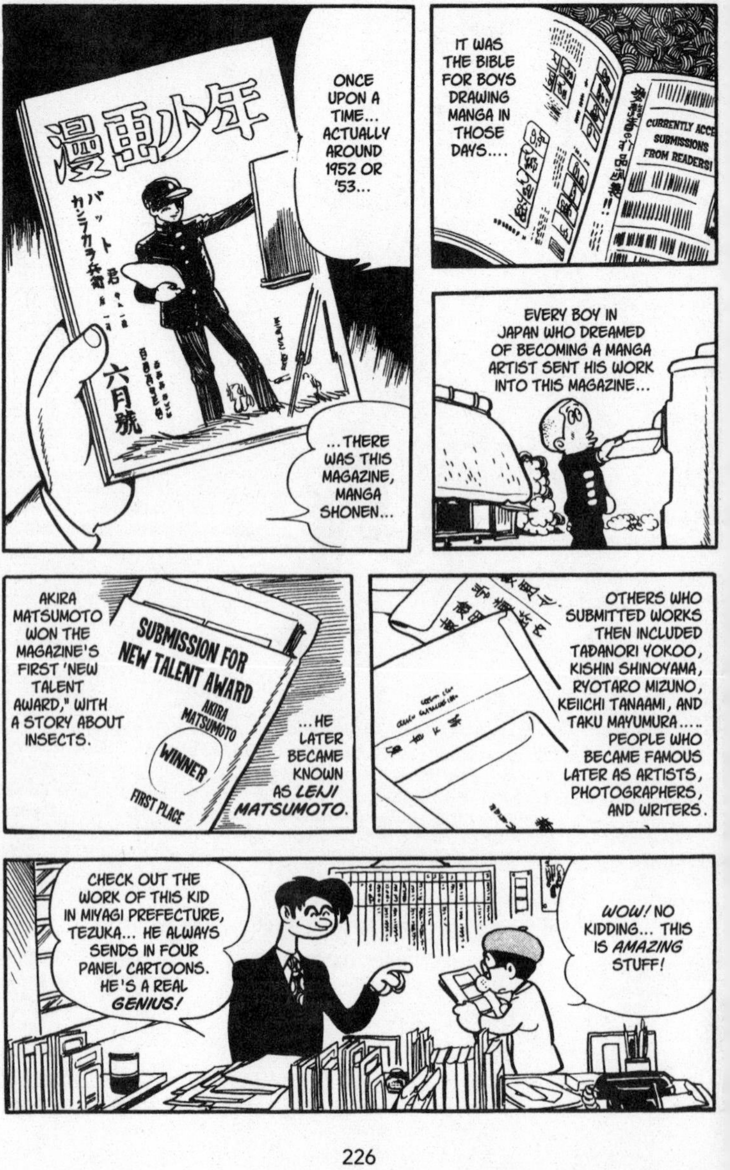

漫画少年
バット君
カンラカラ兵衛
六月號
ONCE UPON A TIME... ACTUALLY AROUND 1952 OR '53...
...THERE WAS THIS MAGAZINE, MANGA SHONEN...
IT WAS THE BIBLE FOR BOYS DRAWING MANGA IN THOSE DAYS....
CURRENTLY ACCE SUBMISSIONS FROM READERS!
EVERY BOY IN JAPAN WHO DREAMED OF BECOMING A MANGA ARTIST SENT HIS WORK INTO THIS MAGAZINE...
AKIRA MATSUMOTO WON THE MAGAZINE'S FIRST 'NEW TALENT AWARD," WITH A STORY ABOUT INSECTS.
SUBMISSION FOR NEW TALENT AWARD
AKIRA MATSUMOTO
WINNER
FIRST PLACE
...HE LATER BECAME KNOWN AS *LEIJI MATSUMOTO*.
OTHERS WHO SUBMITTED WORKS THEN INCLUDED TADANORI YOKOO, KISHIN SHINOYAMA, RYOTARO MIZUNO, KEIICHI TANAAMI, AND TAKU MAYUMURA..... PEOPLE WHO BECAME FAMOUS LATER AS ARTISTS, PHOTOGRAPHERS, AND WRITERS.
CHECK OUT THE WORK OF THIS KID IN MIYAGI PREFECTURE, TEZUKA... HE ALWAYS SENDS IN FOUR PANEL CARTOONS. HE'S A REAL *GENIUS!*
WOW! NO KIDDING... THIS IS *AMAZING* STUFF!

WISH I COULD GET HIM TO HELP ME OUT WITH *MY* MANGA...

HIS NAME'S *ONODERA* ...

HE'S APPARENTLY THE PRESIDENT OF A BIG MANGA STUDY GROUP IN EASTERN JAPAN...

I'LL SEND HIM A TELEGRAM ...

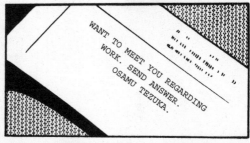

WANT TO MEET YOU REGARDING WORK. SEND ANSWER. OSAMU TEZUKA.

HI. I'M *ONODERA* ...

SO *YOU'RE* ONODERA!

LOOKS A BIT LIKE A POTATO..."

I'VE GOTTA TELL YOU.... YOUR DRAWINGS ARE *FANTASTIC!*

227

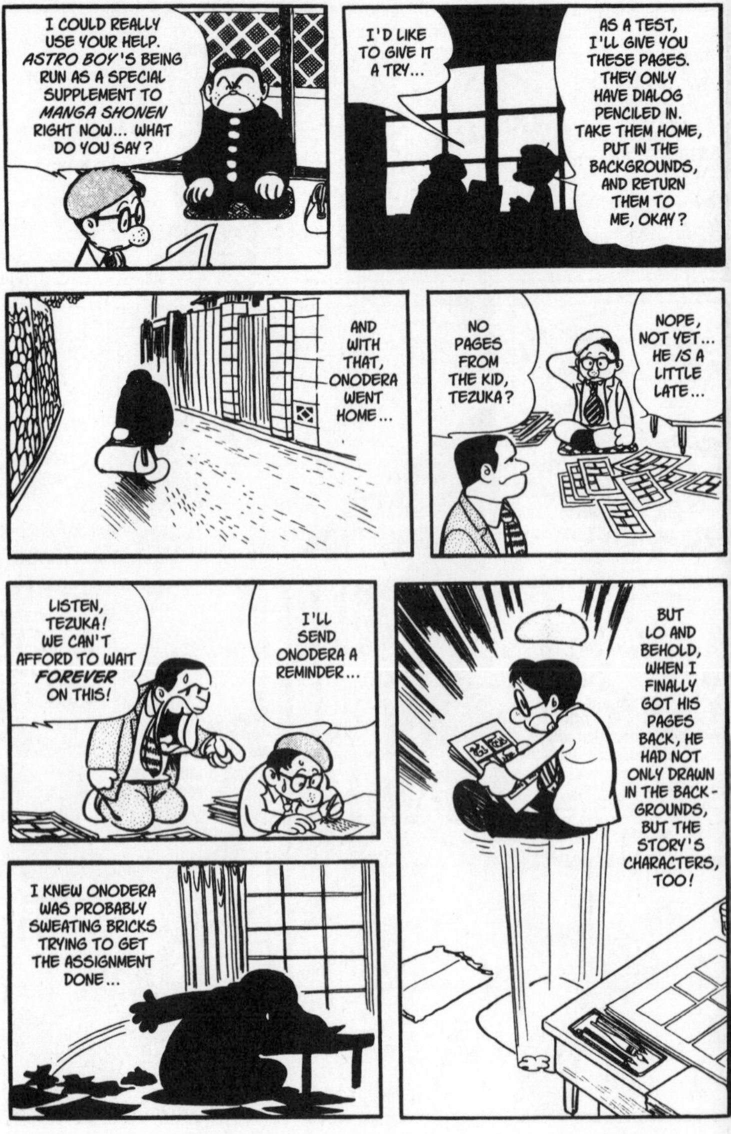
I COULD REALLY USE YOUR HELP. *ASTRO BOY*'S BEING RUN AS A SPECIAL SUPPLEMENT TO *MANGA SHONEN* RIGHT NOW... WHAT DO YOU SAY?
I'D LIKE TO GIVE IT A TRY...
AS A TEST, I'LL GIVE YOU THESE PAGES. THEY ONLY HAVE DIALOG PENCILED IN. TAKE THEM HOME, PUT IN THE BACKGROUNDS, AND RETURN THEM TO ME, OKAY?
AND WITH THAT, ONODERA WENT HOME...
NO PAGES FROM THE KID, TEZUKA?
NOPE, NOT YET... HE *IS* A LITTLE LATE...
LISTEN, TEZUKA! WE CAN'T AFFORD TO WAIT ***FOREVER*** ON THIS!
I'LL SEND ONODERA A REMINDER...
I KNEW ONODERA WAS PROBABLY SWEATING BRICKS TRYING TO GET THE ASSIGNMENT DONE...
BUT LO AND BEHOLD, WHEN I FINALLY GOT HIS PAGES BACK, HE HAD NOT ONLY DRAWN IN THE BACKGROUNDS, BUT THE STORY'S CHARACTERS, TOO!

SO THAT'S HOW THIS STORY, *ELECTRO*, CAME TO BE...

ONODERA DREW THE INTERIORS OF MUSTACHIO'S HOUSE, THE PART WHERE ELECTRO'S STOLEN AND A COMMOTION ENSUES, AND THE FIRST MEETING BETWEEN ASTRO AND ELECTRO....

WHAT?! ELECTRO'S *MISSING?!*

MUST BE AROUND HERE SOMEWHERE.... DON'T TRIP OVER HIM!

MAYBE HE WAS AFRAID OF GETTING THE GRAND PRIX AWARD AND RAN AWAY?

THINK HE WAS *ABDUCTED?*

JUST LIKE IN THIS SCENE....

ONODERA EVEN DREW CROSS-HATCHED BACK-GROUNDS LIKE THIS...

OF COURSE, ONODERA WENT ON TO CREATE HIS OWN DEBUT WORK, TITLED *NIKYU-TENSHI*, OR "SECOND-CLASS ANGEL." IT REALLY WOWED ALL THE OTHER KIDS WHO HAD BEEN SUBMITTING TO *MANGA SHONEN*...

EVENTUALLY ONODERA MOVED TO TOKYO AND BEGAN LIVING AS A MANGA ARTIST...

...USING THE PEN NAME OF *SHOTARO ISHIMORI*...

229

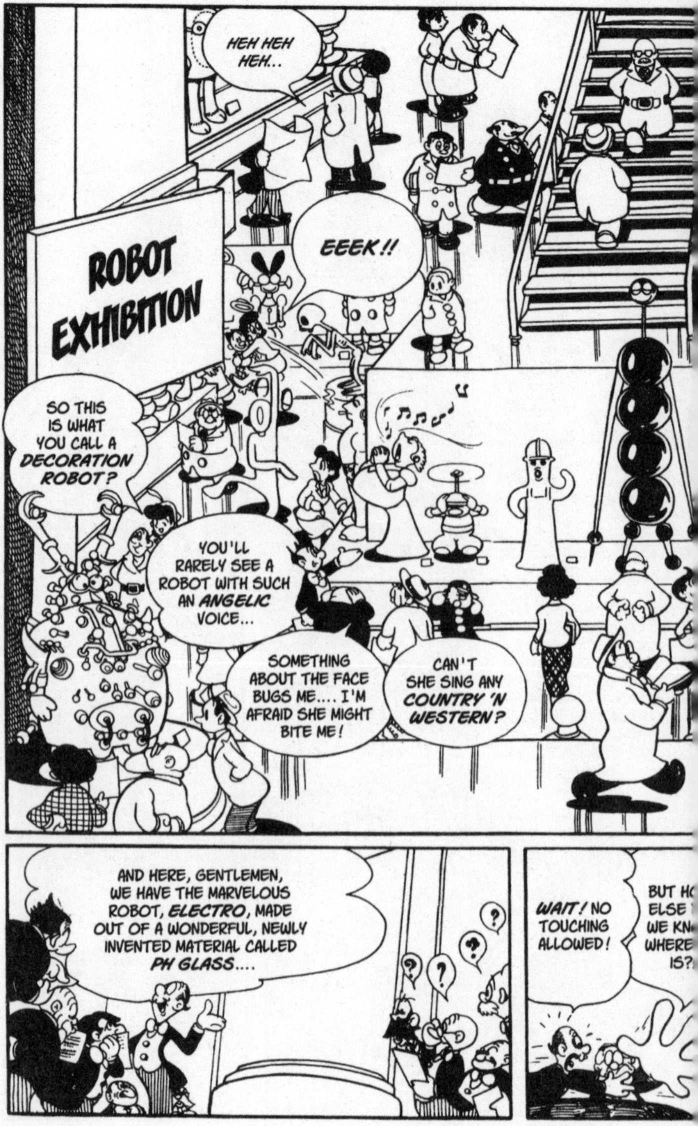

HEH HEH HEH...
ROBOT EXHIBITION
EEEK!!
SO THIS IS WHAT YOU CALL A *DECORATION ROBOT?*
YOU'LL RARELY SEE A ROBOT WITH SUCH AN *ANGELIC* VOICE...
SOMETHING ABOUT THE FACE BUGS ME.... I'M AFRAID SHE MIGHT BITE ME!
CAN'T SHE SING ANY *COUNTRY 'N WESTERN?*
AND HERE, GENTLEMEN, WE HAVE THE MARVELOUS ROBOT, *ELECTRO*, MADE OUT OF A WONDERFUL, NEWLY INVENTED MATERIAL CALLED *PH GLASS....*
?
?
?
?
WAIT! NO TOUCHING ALLOWED!

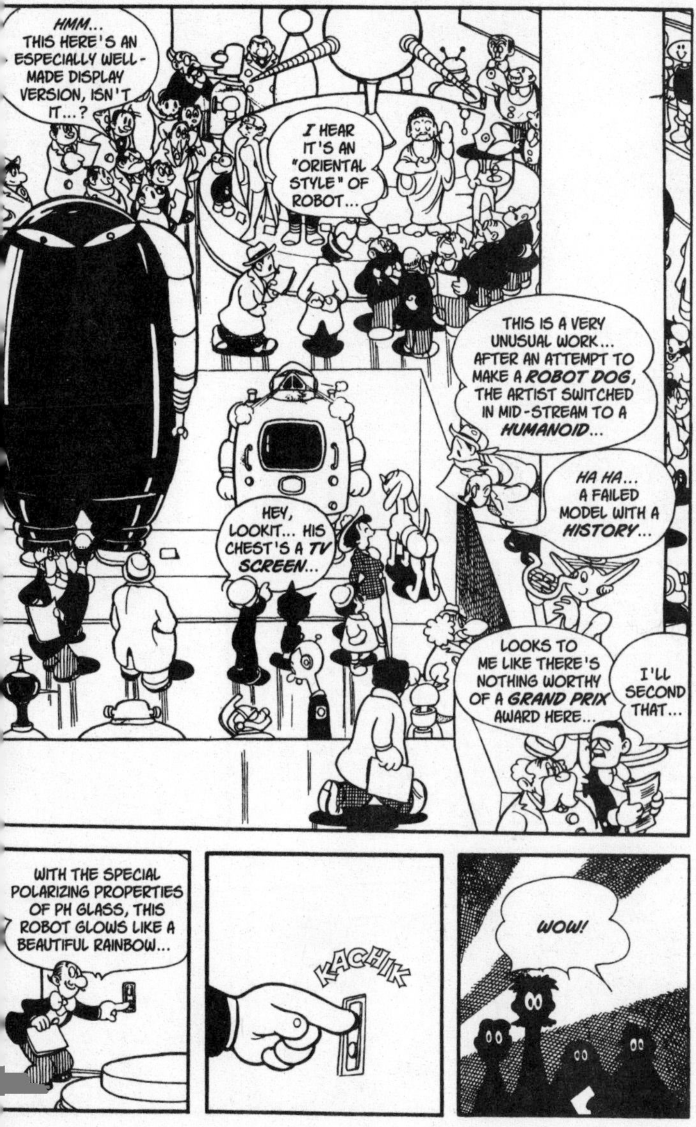
HMM... THIS HERE'S AN ESPECIALLY WELL-MADE DISPLAY VERSION, ISN'T IT...?
I HEAR IT'S AN "ORIENTAL STYLE" OF ROBOT...
THIS IS A VERY UNUSUAL WORK... AFTER AN ATTEMPT TO MAKE A ROBOT DOG, THE ARTIST SWITCHED IN MID-STREAM TO A HUMANOID...
HA HA... A FAILED MODEL WITH A HISTORY...
HEY, LOOKIT... HIS CHEST'S A TV SCREEN...
LOOKS TO ME LIKE THERE'S NOTHING WORTHY OF A GRAND PRIX AWARD HERE...
I'LL SECOND THAT...
WITH THE SPECIAL POLARIZING PROPERTIES OF PH GLASS, THIS ROBOT GLOWS LIKE A BEAUTIFUL RAINBOW...
KACHIK
WOW!

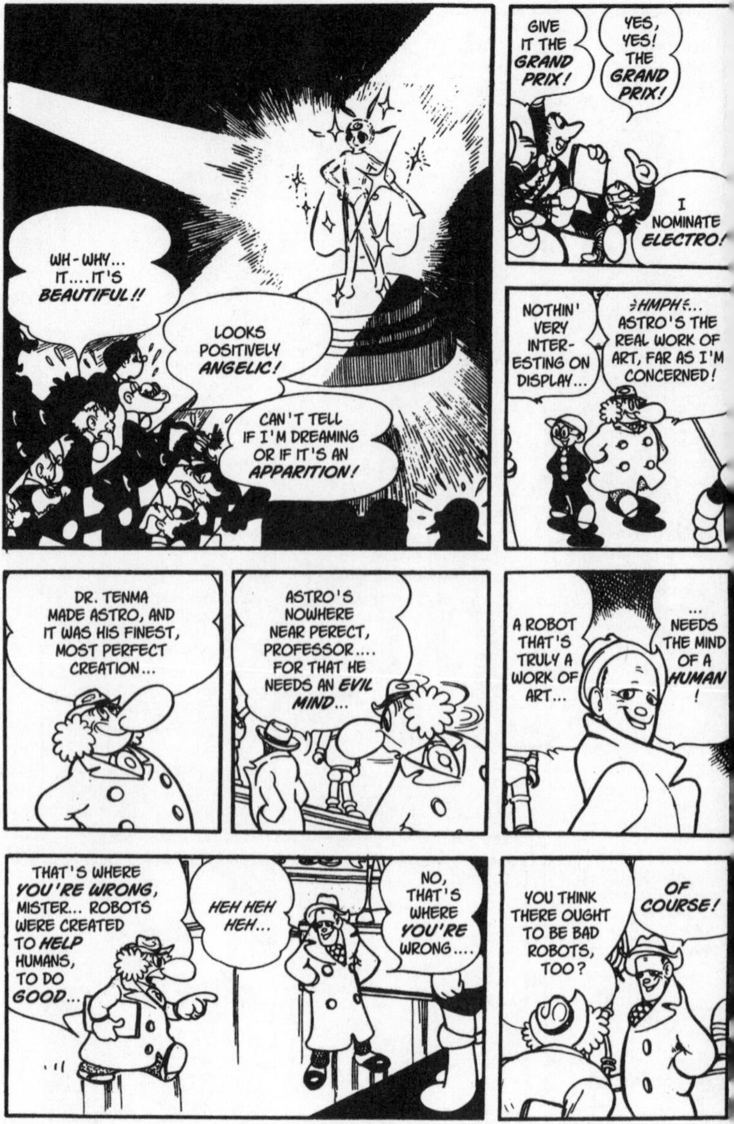

WH-WHY... IT.... IT'S BEAUTIFUL!!
LOOKS POSITIVELY ANGELIC!
CAN'T TELL IF I'M DREAMING OR IF IT'S AN APPARITION!
GIVE IT THE GRAND PRIX!
YES, YES! THE GRAND PRIX!
I NOMINATE ELECTRO!
NOTHIN' VERY INTER-ESTING ON DISPLAY...
HMPH... ASTRO'S THE REAL WORK OF ART, FAR AS I'M CONCERNED!
DR. TENMA MADE ASTRO, AND IT WAS HIS FINEST, MOST PERFECT CREATION...
ASTRO'S NOWHERE NEAR PERECT, PROFESSOR.... FOR THAT HE NEEDS AN EVIL MIND...
A ROBOT THAT'S TRULY A WORK OF ART...
... NEEDS THE MIND OF A HUMAN!
THAT'S WHERE YOU'RE WRONG, MISTER... ROBOTS WERE CREATED TO HELP HUMANS, TO DO GOOD...
HEH HEH HEH...
NO, THAT'S WHERE YOU'RE WRONG....
YOU THINK THERE OUGHT TO BE BAD ROBOTS, TOO?
OF COURSE!

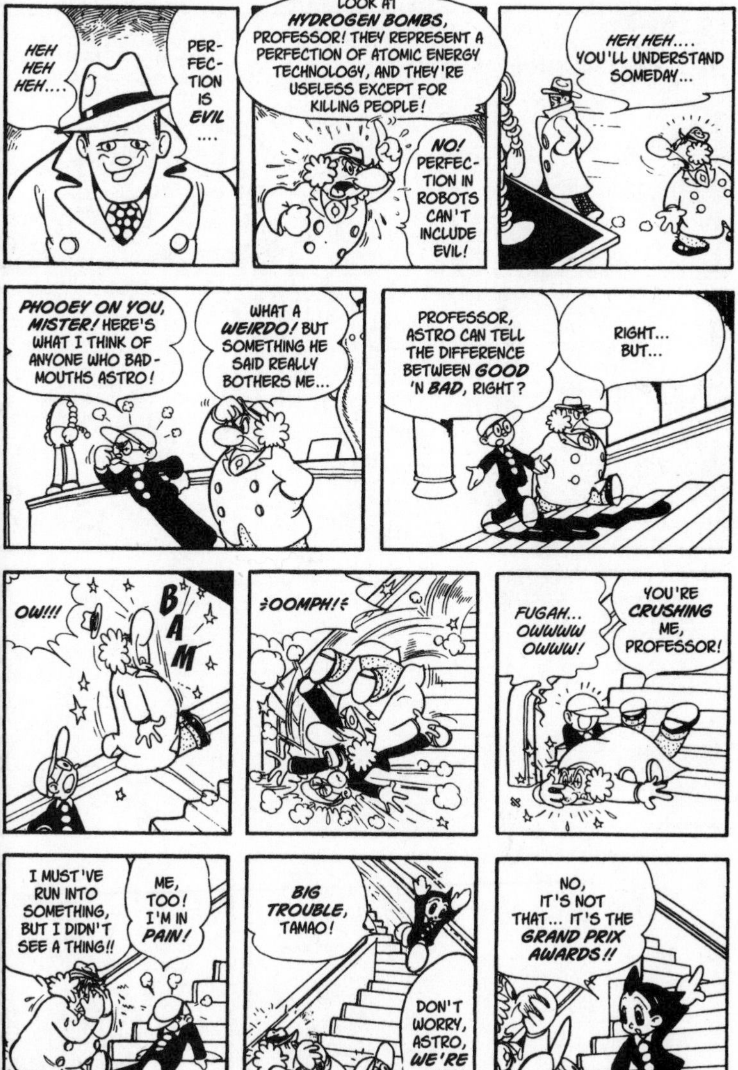

HEH HEH HEH....
PERFECTION IS EVIL ....
LOOK AT HYDROGEN BOMBS, PROFESSOR! THEY REPRESENT A PERFECTION OF ATOMIC ENERGY TECHNOLOGY, AND THEY'RE USELESS EXCEPT FOR KILLING PEOPLE!
NO! PERFECTION IN ROBOTS CAN'T INCLUDE EVIL!
HEH HEH.... YOU'LL UNDERSTAND SOMEDAY...
PHOOEY ON YOU, MISTER! HERE'S WHAT I THINK OF ANYONE WHO BAD-MOUTHS ASTRO!
WHAT A WEIRDO! BUT SOMETHING HE SAID REALLY BOTHERS ME...
PROFESSOR, ASTRO CAN TELL THE DIFFERENCE BETWEEN GOOD 'N BAD, RIGHT?
RIGHT... BUT...
OW!!!
BAM
OOMPH!
FUGAH... OWWWW OWWW!
YOU'RE CRUSHING ME, PROFESSOR!
I MUST'VE RUN INTO SOMETHING, BUT I DIDN'T SEE A THING!!
ME, TOO! I'M IN PAIN!
BIG TROUBLE, TAMAO!
DON'T WORRY, ASTRO, WE'RE OKAY!
NO, IT'S NOT THAT... IT'S THE GRAND PRIX AWARDS!!

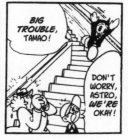

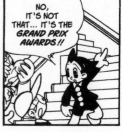

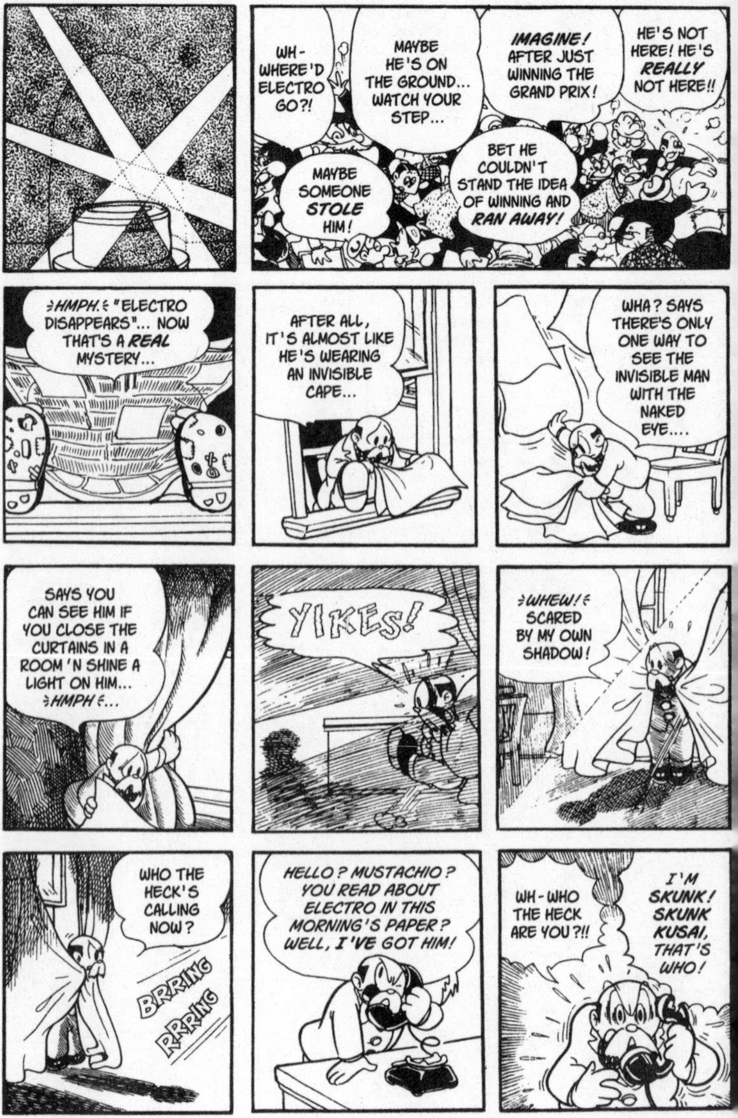
WH-WHERE'D ELECTRO GO?!
MAYBE HE'S ON THE GROUND... WATCH YOUR STEP...
IMAGINE! AFTER JUST WINNING THE GRAND PRIX!
HE'S NOT HERE! HE'S REALLY NOT HERE!!
MAYBE SOMEONE STOLE HIM!
BET HE COULDN'T STAND THE IDEA OF WINNING AND RAN AWAY!
HMPH. "ELECTRO DISAPPEARS"... NOW THAT'S A REAL MYSTERY...
AFTER ALL, IT'S ALMOST LIKE HE'S WEARING AN INVISIBLE CAPE...
WHA? SAYS THERE'S ONLY ONE WAY TO SEE THE INVISIBLE MAN WITH THE NAKED EYE....
SAYS YOU CAN SEE HIM IF YOU CLOSE THE CURTAINS IN A ROOM 'N SHINE A LIGHT ON HIM... HMPH...
YIKES!
WHEW! SCARED BY MY OWN SHADOW!
WHO THE HECK'S CALLING NOW?
BRRING
RRRING
HELLO? MUSTACHIO? YOU READ ABOUT ELECTRO IN THIS MORNING'S PAPER? WELL, I'VE GOT HIM!
WH-WHO THE HECK ARE YOU?!!
I'M SKUNK! SKUNK KUSAI, THAT'S WHO!

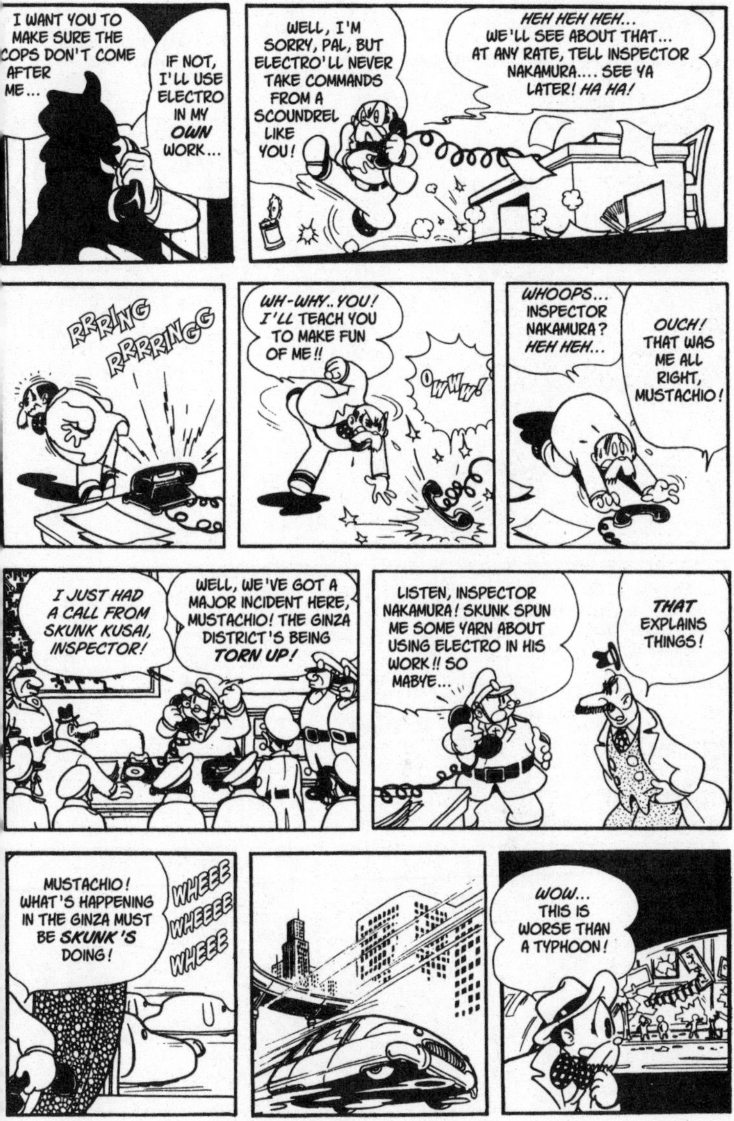
I WANT YOU TO MAKE SURE THE COPS DON'T COME AFTER ME...
IF NOT, I'LL USE ELECTRO IN MY *OWN* WORK...
WELL, I'M SORRY, PAL, BUT ELECTRO'LL NEVER TAKE COMMANDS FROM A SCOUNDREL LIKE YOU!
HEH HEH HEH... WE'LL SEE ABOUT THAT... AT ANY RATE, TELL INSPECTOR NAKAMURA.... SEE YA LATER! *HA HA!*
RRRING
RRRRINGG
WH-WHY..YOU! I'LL TEACH YOU TO MAKE FUN OF ME!!
OWWW!
WHOOPS... INSPECTOR NAKAMURA? HEH HEH...
OUCH! THAT WAS ME ALL RIGHT, MUSTACHIO!
I JUST HAD A CALL FROM SKUNK KUSAI, INSPECTOR!
WELL, WE'VE GOT A MAJOR INCIDENT HERE, MUSTACHIO! THE GINZA DISTRICT'S BEING *TORN UP!*
LISTEN, INSPECTOR NAKAMURA! SKUNK SPUN ME SOME YARN ABOUT USING ELECTRO IN HIS WORK!! SO MABYE...
THAT EXPLAINS THINGS!
MUSTACHIO! WHAT'S HAPPENING IN THE GINZA MUST BE *SKUNK'S* DOING!
WHEEE
WHEEEE
WHEEE
WOW... THIS IS WORSE THAN A TYPHOON!

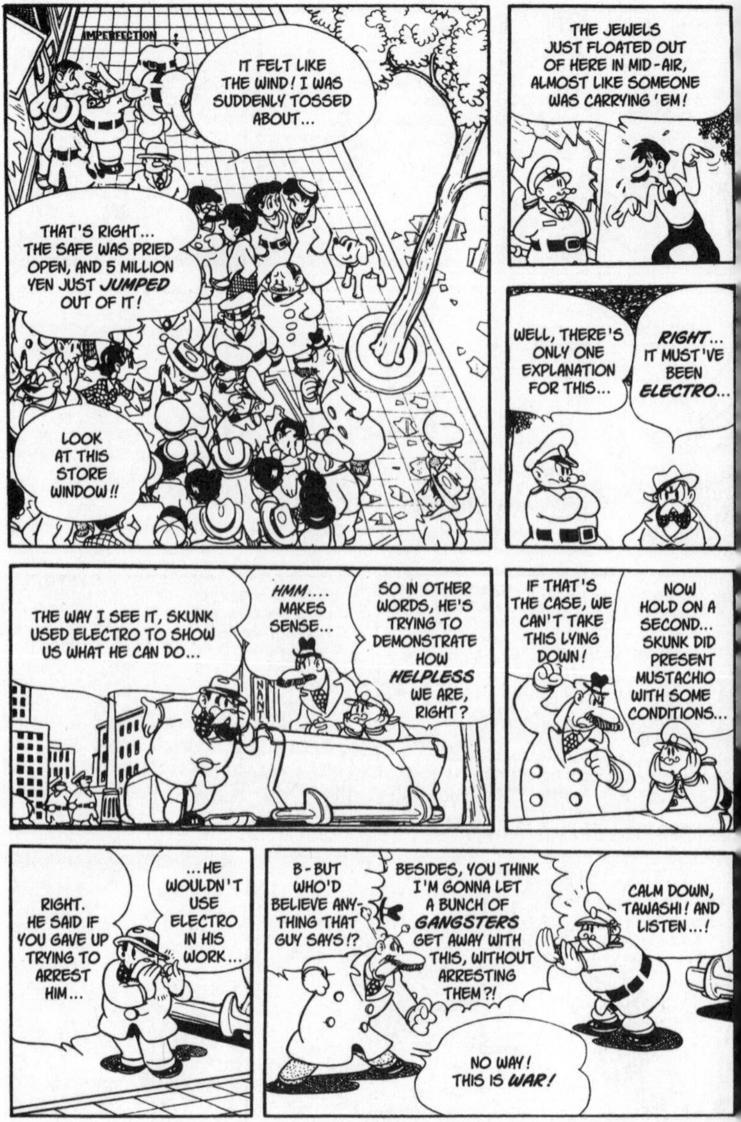
IMPERFECTION
IT FELT LIKE THE WIND! I WAS SUDDENLY TOSSED ABOUT...
THAT'S RIGHT... THE SAFE WAS PRIED OPEN, AND 5 MILLION YEN JUST *JUMPED* OUT OF IT!
LOOK AT THIS STORE WINDOW!!
THE JEWELS JUST FLOATED OUT OF HERE IN MID-AIR, ALMOST LIKE SOMEONE WAS CARRYING 'EM!
WELL, THERE'S ONLY ONE EXPLANATION FOR THIS...
RIGHT... IT MUST'VE BEEN *ELECTRO*...
THE WAY I SEE IT, SKUNK USED ELECTRO TO SHOW US WHAT HE CAN DO...
HMM.... MAKES SENSE...
SO IN OTHER WORDS, HE'S TRYING TO DEMONSTRATE HOW *HELPLESS* WE ARE, RIGHT?
IF THAT'S THE CASE, WE CAN'T TAKE THIS LYING DOWN!
NOW HOLD ON A SECOND... SKUNK DID PRESENT MUSTACHIO WITH SOME CONDITIONS...
RIGHT. HE SAID IF YOU GAVE UP TRYING TO ARREST HIM...
...HE WOULDN'T USE ELECTRO IN HIS WORK...
B-BUT WHO'D BELIEVE ANY-THING THAT GUY SAYS!?
BESIDES, YOU THINK I'M GONNA LET A BUNCH OF *GANGSTERS* GET AWAY WITH THIS, WITHOUT ARRESTING THEM?!
CALM DOWN, TAWASHI! AND LISTEN...!
NO WAY! THIS IS *WAR!*

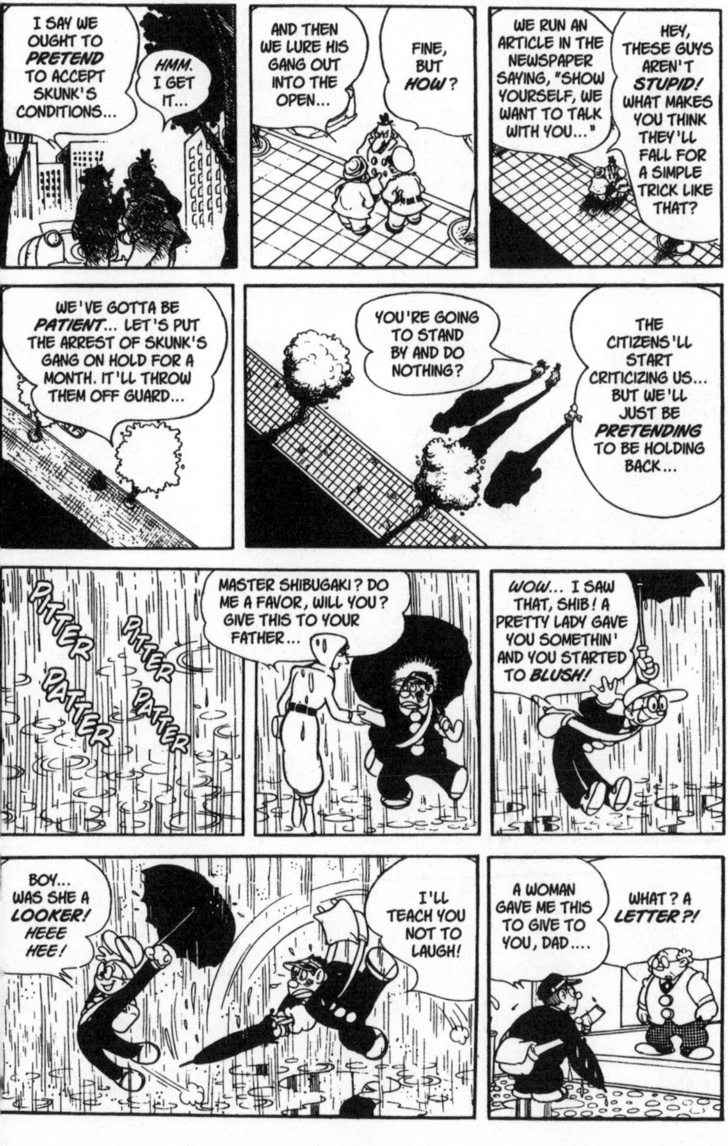
I SAY WE OUGHT TO PRETEND TO ACCEPT SKUNK'S CONDITIONS...
HMM. I GET IT...
AND THEN WE LURE HIS GANG OUT INTO THE OPEN...
FINE, BUT HOW?
WE RUN AN ARTICLE IN THE NEWSPAPER SAYING, "SHOW YOURSELF, WE WANT TO TALK WITH YOU..."
HEY, THESE GUYS AREN'T STUPID! WHAT MAKES YOU THINK THEY'LL FALL FOR A SIMPLE TRICK LIKE THAT?
WE'VE GOTTA BE PATIENT... LET'S PUT THE ARREST OF SKUNK'S GANG ON HOLD FOR A MONTH. IT'LL THROW THEM OFF GUARD...
YOU'RE GOING TO STAND BY AND DO NOTHING?
THE CITIZENS'LL START CRITICIZING US... BUT WE'LL JUST BE PRETENDING TO BE HOLDING BACK...
PITTER PATTER
PITTER PATTER
MASTER SHIBUGAKI? DO ME A FAVOR, WILL YOU? GIVE THIS TO YOUR FATHER...
WOW... I SAW THAT, SHIB! A PRETTY LADY GAVE YOU SOMETHIN' AND YOU STARTED TO BLUSH!
BOY... WAS SHE A LOOKER! HEEE HEE!
I'LL TEACH YOU NOT TO LAUGH!
A WOMAN GAVE ME THIS TO GIVE TO YOU, DAD....
WHAT? A LETTER?!

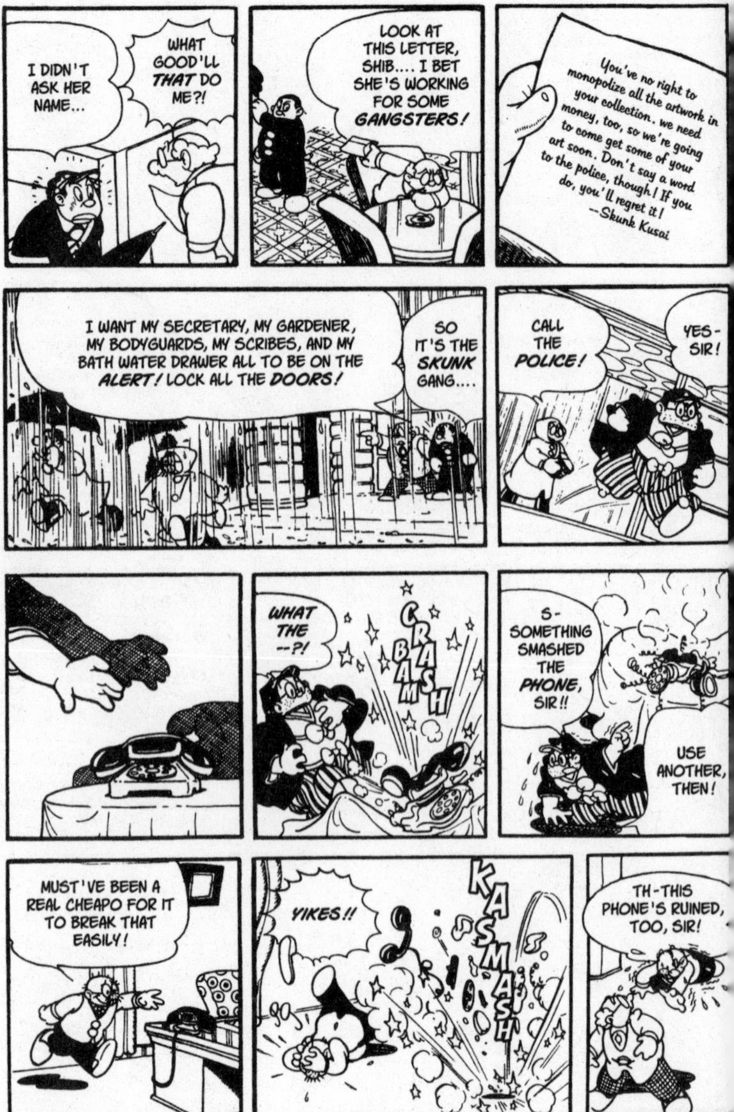
I DIDN'T ASK HER NAME...
WHAT GOOD'LL *THAT* DO ME?!
LOOK AT THIS LETTER, SHIB.... I BET SHE'S WORKING FOR SOME *GANGSTERS!*
You've no right to monopolize all the artwork in your collection. we need money, too, so we're going to come get some of your art soon. Don't say a word to the police, though! If you do, you'll regret it!
--Skunk Kusai
I WANT MY SECRETARY, MY GARDENER, MY BODYGUARDS, MY SCRIBES, AND MY BATH WATER DRAWER ALL TO BE ON THE *ALERT!* LOCK ALL THE *DOORS!*
SO IT'S THE *SKUNK* GANG....
CALL THE *POLICE!*
YES-SIR!
WHAT THE --?!
CRASH
BAM
S-SOMETHING SMASHED THE *PHONE*, SIR!!
USE ANOTHER, THEN!
MUST'VE BEEN A REAL CHEAPO FOR IT TO BREAK THAT EASILY!
YIKES!!
KASMASH
TH-THIS PHONE'S RUINED, TOO, SIR!

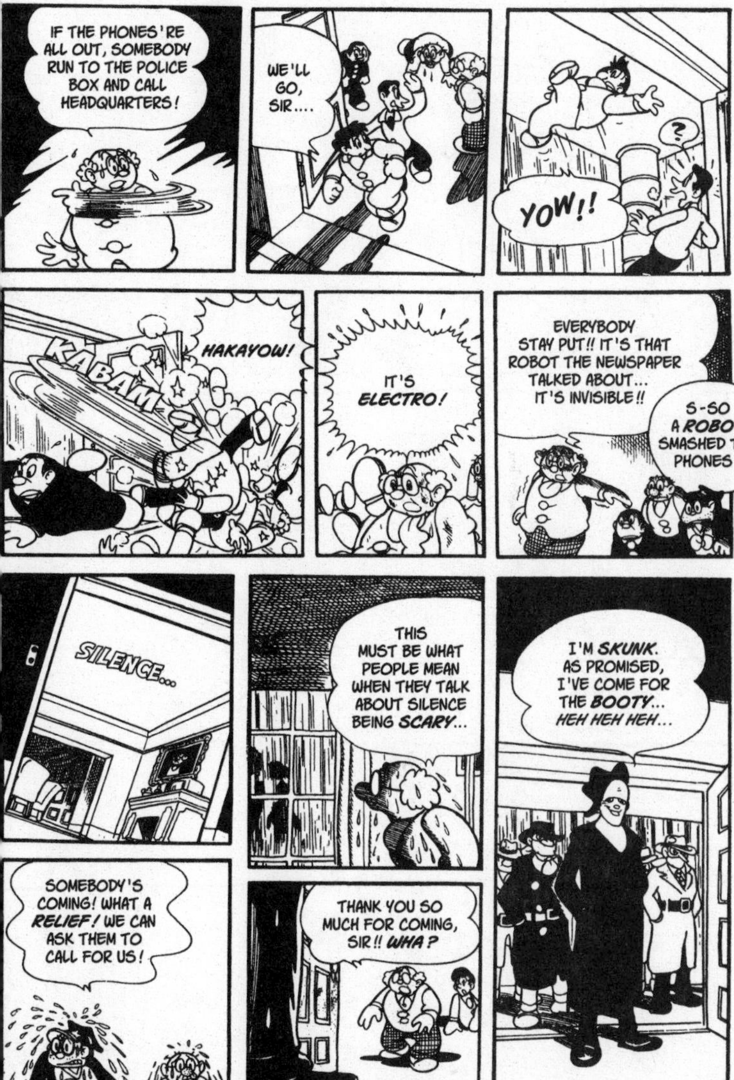
IF THE PHONES'RE ALL OUT, SOMEBODY RUN TO THE POLICE BOX AND CALL HEADQUARTERS!
WE'LL GO, SIR....
?
YOW!!
KABAM
HAKAYOW!
IT'S ELECTRO!
EVERYBODY STAY PUT!! IT'S THAT ROBOT THE NEWSPAPER TALKED ABOUT... IT'S INVISIBLE!!
S-SO A ROBOT SMASHED THE PHONES?!!
SILENCE...
THIS MUST BE WHAT PEOPLE MEAN WHEN THEY TALK ABOUT SILENCE BEING SCARY...
SOMEBODY'S COMING! WHAT A RELIEF! WE CAN ASK THEM TO CALL FOR US!
THANK YOU SO MUCH FOR COMING, SIR!! WHA?
I'M SKUNK. AS PROMISED, I'VE COME FOR THE BOOTY... HEH HEH HEH...

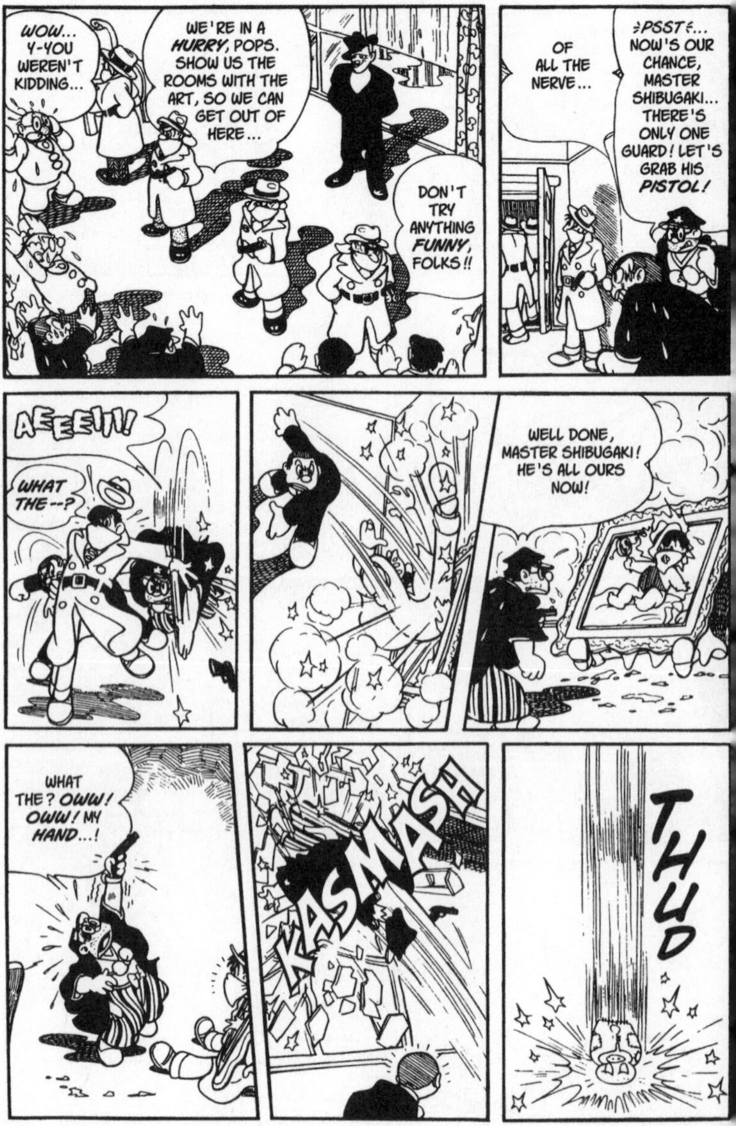
WOW... Y-YOU WEREN'T KIDDING...
WE'RE IN A HURRY, POPS. SHOW US THE ROOMS WITH THE ART, SO WE CAN GET OUT OF HERE...
DON'T TRY ANYTHING FUNNY, FOLKS!!
OF ALL THE NERVE...
PSST... NOW'S OUR CHANCE, MASTER SHIBUGAKI... THERE'S ONLY ONE GUARD! LET'S GRAB HIS PISTOL!
AEEEIII!
WHAT THE--?
WELL DONE, MASTER SHIBUGAKI! HE'S ALL OURS NOW!
WHAT THE? OWW! OWW! MY HAND...!
KASMASH
THUD

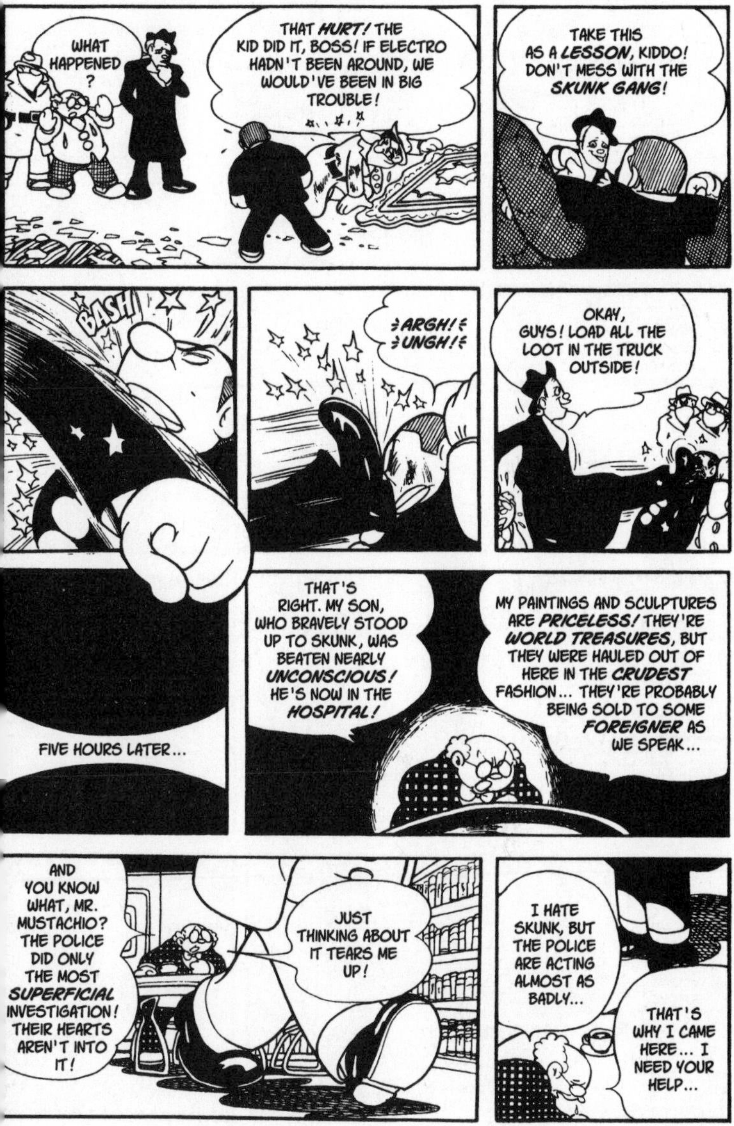
WHAT HAPPENED ?
THAT HURT! THE KID DID IT, BOSS! IF ELECTRO HADN'T BEEN AROUND, WE WOULD'VE BEEN IN BIG TROUBLE!
TAKE THIS AS A LESSON, KIDDO! DON'T MESS WITH THE SKUNK GANG!
BASH
ARGH! UNGH!
OKAY, GUYS! LOAD ALL THE LOOT IN THE TRUCK OUTSIDE!
FIVE HOURS LATER...
THAT'S RIGHT. MY SON, WHO BRAVELY STOOD UP TO SKUNK, WAS BEATEN NEARLY UNCONSCIOUS! HE'S NOW IN THE HOSPITAL!
MY PAINTINGS AND SCULPTURES ARE PRICELESS! THEY'RE WORLD TREASURES, BUT THEY WERE HAULED OUT OF HERE IN THE CRUDEST FASHION... THEY'RE PROBABLY BEING SOLD TO SOME FOREIGNER AS WE SPEAK...
AND YOU KNOW WHAT, MR. MUSTACHIO? THE POLICE DID ONLY THE MOST SUPERFICIAL INVESTIGATION! THEIR HEARTS AREN'T INTO IT!
JUST THINKING ABOUT IT TEARS ME UP!
I HATE SKUNK, BUT THE POLICE ARE ACTING ALMOST AS BADLY...
THAT'S WHY I CAME HERE... I NEED YOUR HELP...

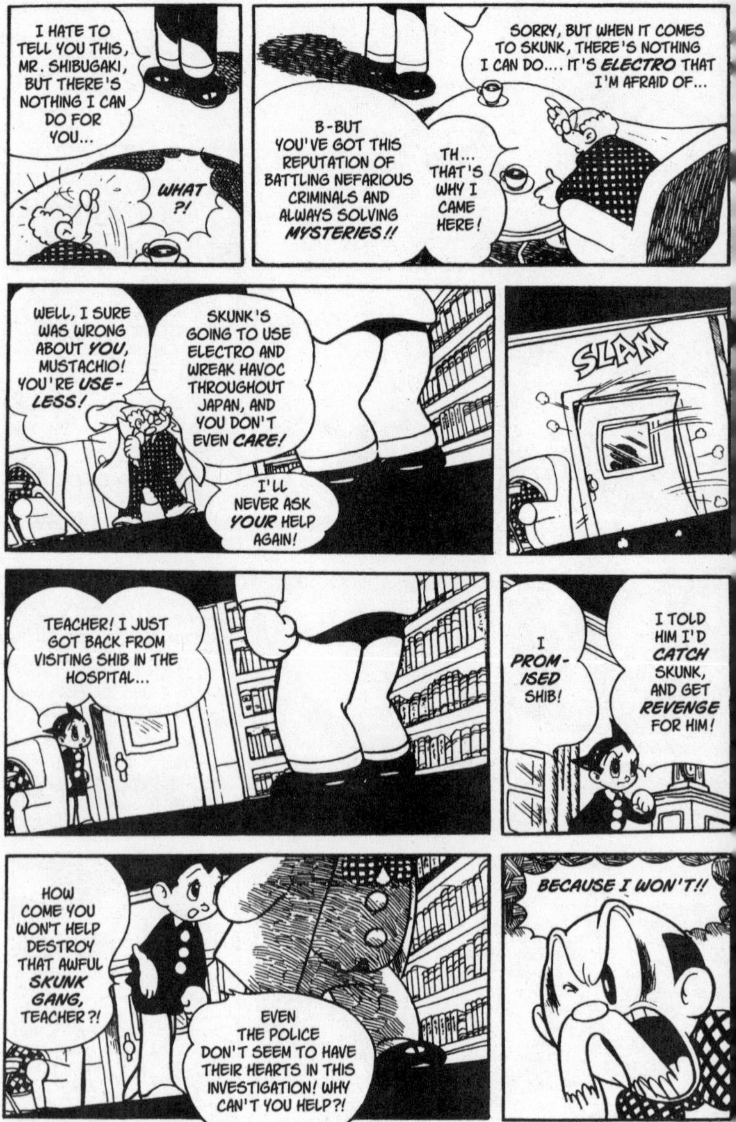

I HATE TO TELL YOU THIS, MR. SHIBUGAKI, BUT THERE'S NOTHING I CAN DO FOR YOU...
WHAT ?!
SORRY, BUT WHEN IT COMES TO SKUNK, THERE'S NOTHING I CAN DO.... IT'S ELECTRO THAT I'M AFRAID OF...
B-BUT YOU'VE GOT THIS REPUTATION OF BATTLING NEFARIOUS CRIMINALS AND ALWAYS SOLVING MYSTERIES!!
TH... THAT'S WHY I CAME HERE!
WELL, I SURE WAS WRONG ABOUT YOU, MUSTACHIO! YOU'RE USE-LESS!
SKUNK'S GOING TO USE ELECTRO AND WREAK HAVOC THROUGHOUT JAPAN, AND YOU DON'T EVEN CARE!
I'LL NEVER ASK YOUR HELP AGAIN!
SLAM
TEACHER! I JUST GOT BACK FROM VISITING SHIB IN THE HOSPITAL...
I PROM-ISED SHIB!
I TOLD HIM I'D CATCH SKUNK, AND GET REVENGE FOR HIM!
HOW COME YOU WON'T HELP DESTROY THAT AWFUL SKUNK GANG, TEACHER?!
EVEN THE POLICE DON'T SEEM TO HAVE THEIR HEARTS IN THIS INVESTIGATION! WHY CAN'T YOU HELP?!
BECAUSE I WON'T!!

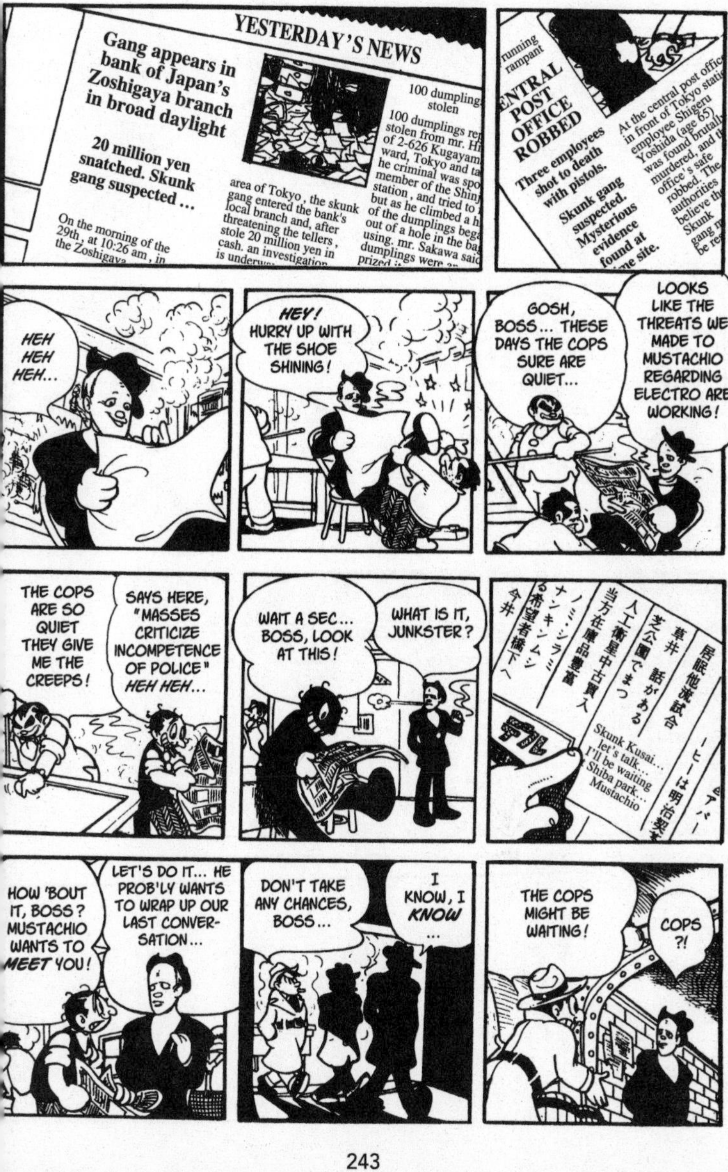

YESTERDAY'S NEWS
Gang appears in bank of Japan's Zoshigaya branch in broad daylight
20 million yen snatched. Skunk gang suspected …
On the morning of the 29th, at 10:26 am, in the Zoshigaya
area of Tokyo, the skunk gang entered the bank's local branch and, after threatening the tellers, stole 20 million yen in cash. an investigation
100 dumplings stolen
100 dumplings
stolen from mr.
of 2-626 Kugayam
ward, Tokyo and
he criminal was
member of the
station, and tried to
but as he climbed a
of the dumplings
out of a hole in the
using. mr. Sakawa said
dumplings were
running rampant
POST OFFICE ROBBED
Three employees shot to death with pistols.
Skunk gang suspected. Mysterious evidence found at
site.
At the central post
in front of Tokyo
employee Shigeru
Yoshida (age 65)
was found
murdered, and
office's safe
robbed. The
authorities
believe
Skunk
gang
HEH HEH HEH…
HEY! HURRY UP WITH THE SHOE SHINING!
GOSH, BOSS… THESE DAYS THE COPS SURE ARE QUIET…
LOOKS LIKE THE THREATS WE MADE TO MUSTACHIO REGARDING ELECTRO ARE WORKING!
THE COPS ARE SO QUIET THEY GIVE ME THE CREEPS!
SAYS HERE, "MASSES CRITICIZE INCOMPETENCE OF POLICE" HEH HEH…
WAIT A SEC… BOSS, LOOK AT THIS!
WHAT IS IT, JUNKSTER?
居眠他流試合
草井 話がある
芝公園でまつ
人工衛星中古買入
当方在庫品豊富
ノミ・シラミ
ナンキンムシ
希望者橋下へ
今井
Skunk Kusai… let's talk… I'll be waiting Shiba park… Mustachio
HOW 'BOUT IT, BOSS? MUSTACHIO WANTS TO MEET YOU!
LET'S DO IT… HE PROB'LY WANTS TO WRAP UP OUR LAST CONVER-SATION…
DON'T TAKE ANY CHANCES, BOSS…
I KNOW, I KNOW…
THE COPS MIGHT BE WAITING!
COPS?!

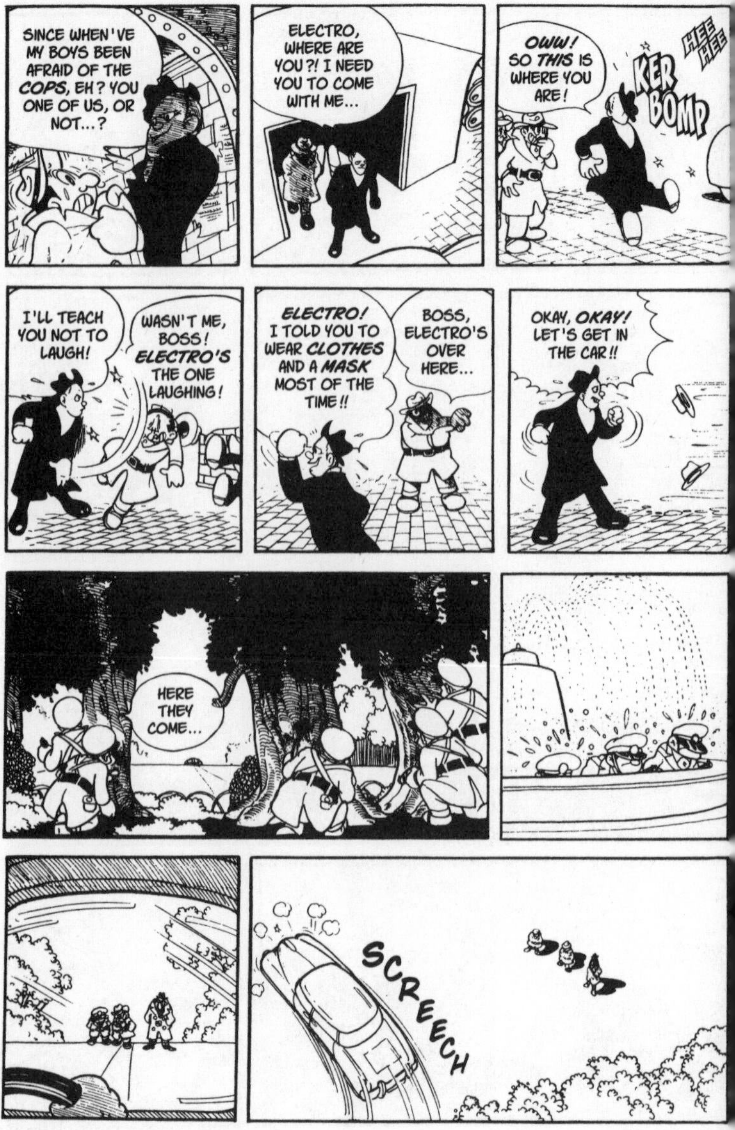
SINCE WHEN'VE MY BOYS BEEN AFRAID OF THE COPS, EH? YOU ONE OF US, OR NOT...?
ELECTRO, WHERE ARE YOU?! I NEED YOU TO COME WITH ME...
OWW! SO THIS IS WHERE YOU ARE!
KER BOMP
HEE HEE
I'LL TEACH YOU NOT TO LAUGH!
WASN'T ME, BOSS! ELECTRO'S THE ONE LAUGHING!
ELECTRO! I TOLD YOU TO WEAR CLOTHES AND A MASK MOST OF THE TIME!!
BOSS, ELECTRO'S OVER HERE...
OKAY, OKAY! LET'S GET IN THE CAR!!
HERE THEY COME...
SCREECH

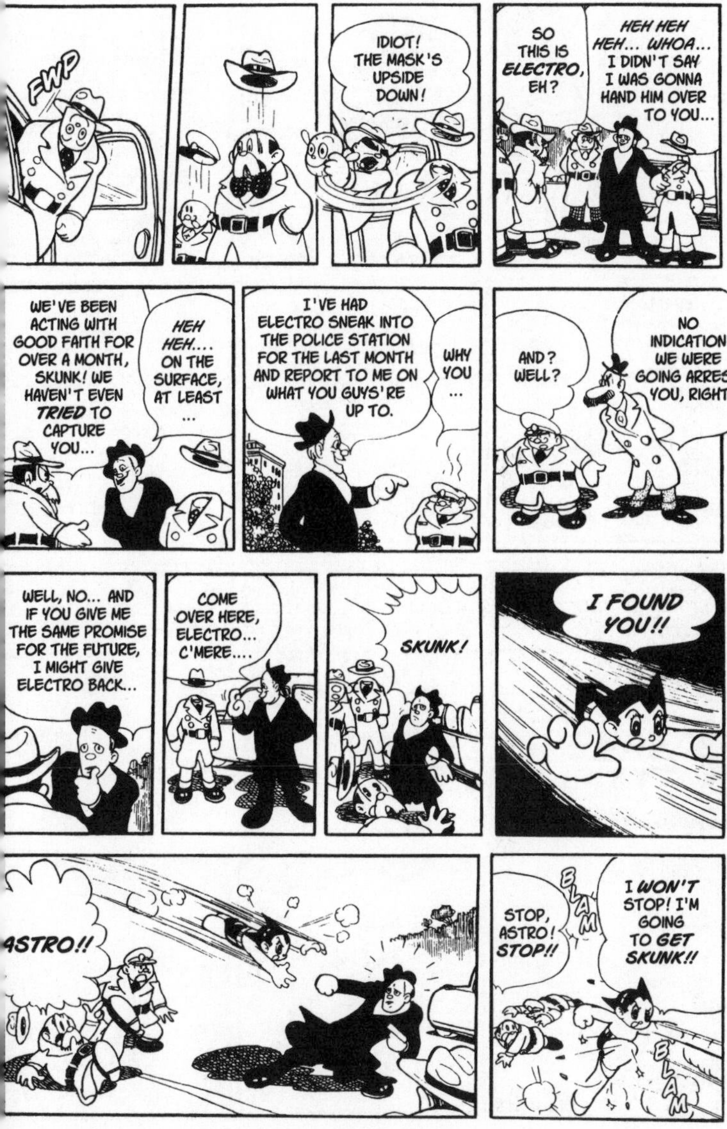
FWP
IDIOT! THE MASK'S UPSIDE DOWN!
SO THIS IS ELECTRO, EH?
HEH HEH HEH... WHOA... I DIDN'T SAY I WAS GONNA HAND HIM OVER TO YOU...
WE'VE BEEN ACTING WITH GOOD FAITH FOR OVER A MONTH, SKUNK! WE HAVEN'T EVEN TRIED TO CAPTURE YOU...
HEH HEH.... ON THE SURFACE, AT LEAST ...
I'VE HAD ELECTRO SNEAK INTO THE POLICE STATION FOR THE LAST MONTH AND REPORT TO ME ON WHAT YOU GUYS'RE UP TO.
WHY YOU ...
AND? WELL?
NO INDICATION WE WERE GOING ARREST YOU, RIGHT?
WELL, NO... AND IF YOU GIVE ME THE SAME PROMISE FOR THE FUTURE, I MIGHT GIVE ELECTRO BACK...
COME OVER HERE, ELECTRO... C'MERE....
SKUNK!
I FOUND YOU!!
ASTRO!!
STOP, ASTRO! STOP!!
BLAM
I WON'T STOP! I'M GOING TO GET SKUNK!!
BLAM

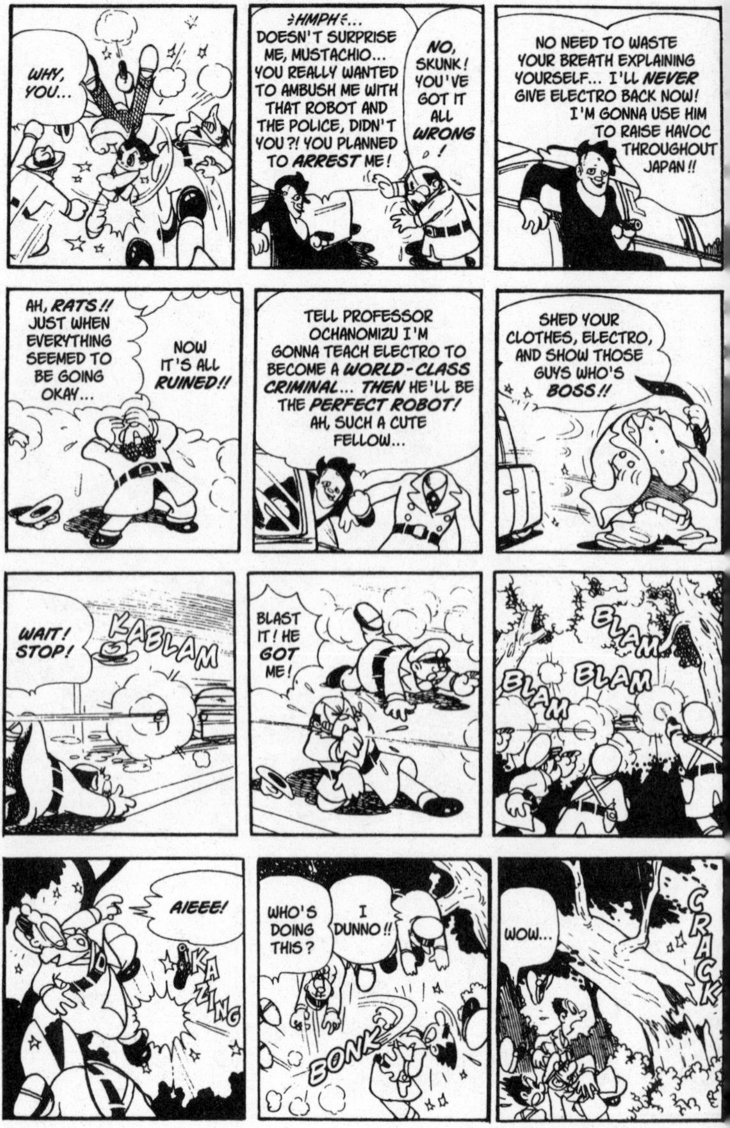

WHY, YOU...
⇉HMPH⇇... DOESN'T SURPRISE ME, MUSTACHIO... YOU REALLY WANTED TO AMBUSH ME WITH THAT ROBOT AND THE POLICE, DIDN'T YOU?! YOU PLANNED TO ARREST ME!
NO, SKUNK! YOU'VE GOT IT ALL WRONG!
NO NEED TO WASTE YOUR BREATH EXPLAINING YOURSELF... I'LL NEVER GIVE ELECTRO BACK NOW! I'M GONNA USE HIM TO RAISE HAVOC THROUGHOUT JAPAN!!
AH, RATS!! JUST WHEN EVERYTHING SEEMED TO BE GOING OKAY...
NOW IT'S ALL RUINED!!
TELL PROFESSOR OCHANOMIZU I'M GONNA TEACH ELECTRO TO BECOME A WORLD-CLASS CRIMINAL... THEN HE'LL BE THE PERFECT ROBOT! AH, SUCH A CUTE FELLOW...
SHED YOUR CLOTHES, ELECTRO, AND SHOW THOSE GUYS WHO'S BOSS!!
WAIT! STOP!
KABLAM
BLAST IT! HE GOT ME!
BLAM
BLAM
BLAM
AIEEE!
KAZING
WHO'S DOING THIS?
I DUNNO!!
BONK
WOW...
CRACK

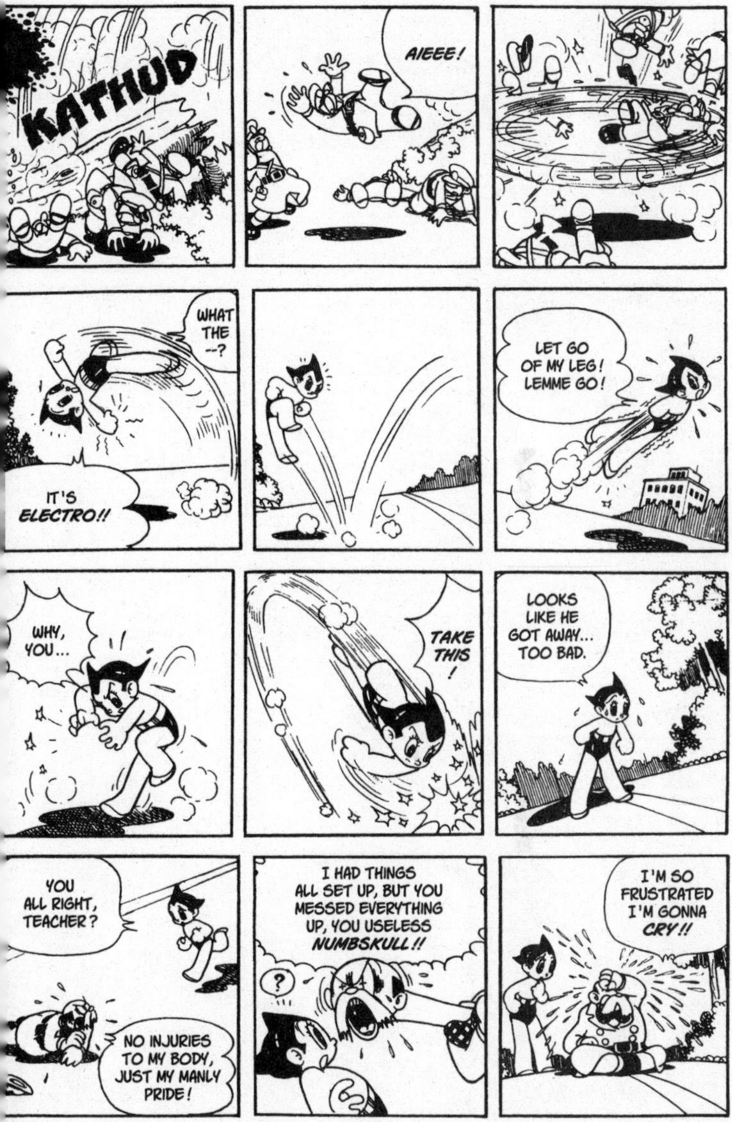
KATHUD
AIEEE!
WHAT THE --?
IT'S ELECTRO!!
LET GO OF MY LEG! LEMME GO!
WHY, YOU...
TAKE THIS!
LOOKS LIKE HE GOT AWAY... TOO BAD.
YOU ALL RIGHT, TEACHER?
NO INJURIES TO MY BODY, JUST MY MANLY PRIDE!
I HAD THINGS ALL SET UP, BUT YOU MESSED EVERYTHING UP, YOU USELESS NUMBSKULL!!
?
I'M SO FRUSTRATED I'M GONNA CRY!!

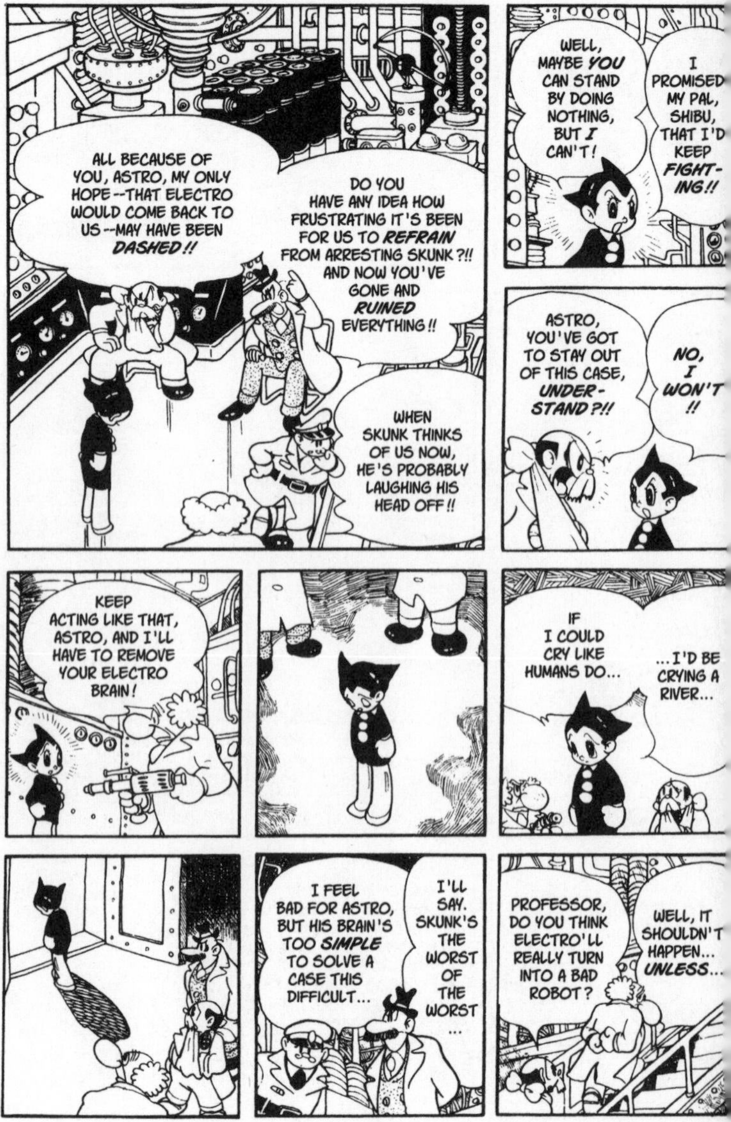
ALL BECAUSE OF YOU, ASTRO, MY ONLY HOPE--THAT ELECTRO WOULD COME BACK TO US--MAY HAVE BEEN DASHED!!
DO YOU HAVE ANY IDEA HOW FRUSTRATING IT'S BEEN FOR US TO REFRAIN FROM ARRESTING SKUNK?!! AND NOW YOU'VE GONE AND RUINED EVERYTHING!!
WHEN SKUNK THINKS OF US NOW, HE'S PROBABLY LAUGHING HIS HEAD OFF!!
WELL, MAYBE YOU CAN STAND BY DOING NOTHING, BUT I CAN'T!
I PROMISED MY PAL, SHIBU, THAT I'D KEEP FIGHTING!!
ASTRO, YOU'VE GOT TO STAY OUT OF THIS CASE, UNDERSTAND?!!
NO, I WON'T!!
KEEP ACTING LIKE THAT, ASTRO, AND I'LL HAVE TO REMOVE YOUR ELECTRO BRAIN!
IF I COULD CRY LIKE HUMANS DO...
...I'D BE CRYING A RIVER...
I FEEL BAD FOR ASTRO, BUT HIS BRAIN'S TOO SIMPLE TO SOLVE A CASE THIS DIFFICULT...
I'LL SAY. SKUNK'S THE WORST OF THE WORST...
PROFESSOR, DO YOU THINK ELECTRO'LL REALLY TURN INTO A BAD ROBOT?
WELL, IT SHOULDN'T HAPPEN... UNLESS...

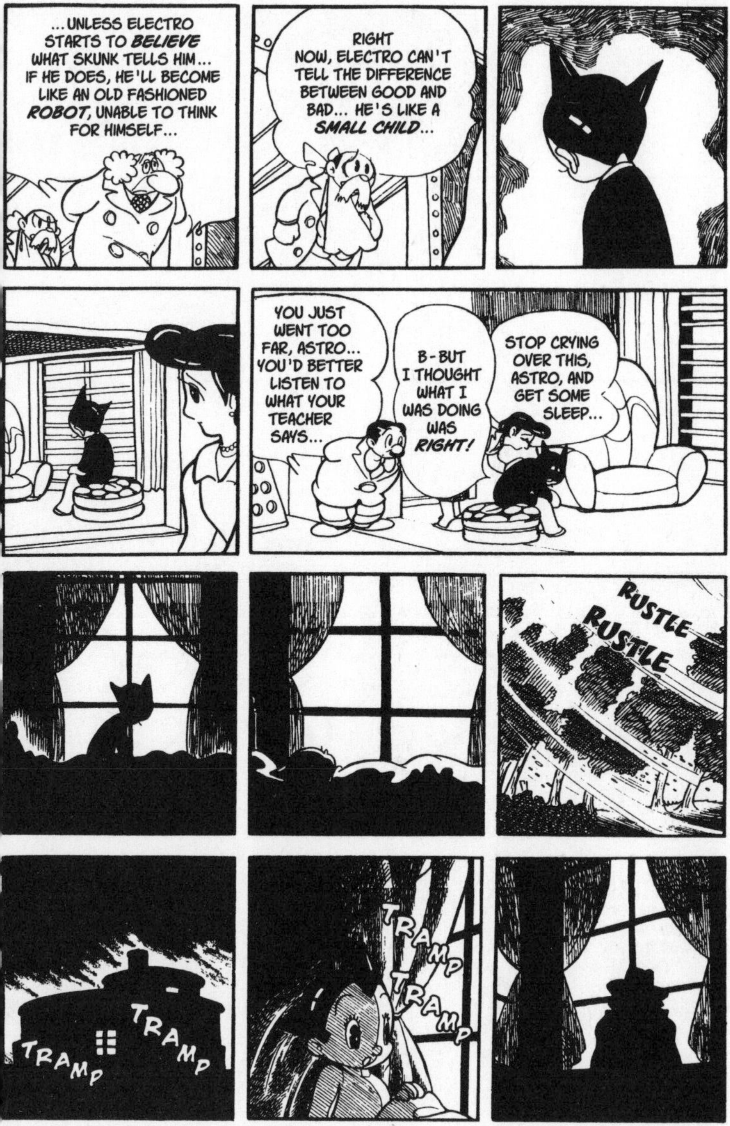
...UNLESS ELECTRO STARTS TO BELIEVE WHAT SKUNK TELLS HIM... IF HE DOES, HE'LL BECOME LIKE AN OLD FASHIONED ROBOT, UNABLE TO THINK FOR HIMSELF...
RIGHT NOW, ELECTRO CAN'T TELL THE DIFFERENCE BETWEEN GOOD AND BAD... HE'S LIKE A SMALL CHILD...
YOU JUST WENT TOO FAR, ASTRO... YOU'D BETTER LISTEN TO WHAT YOUR TEACHER SAYS...
B-BUT I THOUGHT WHAT I WAS DOING WAS RIGHT!
STOP CRYING OVER THIS, ASTRO, AND GET SOME SLEEP...
RUSTLE
RUSTLE
TRAMP
TRAMP
TRAMP
TRAMP

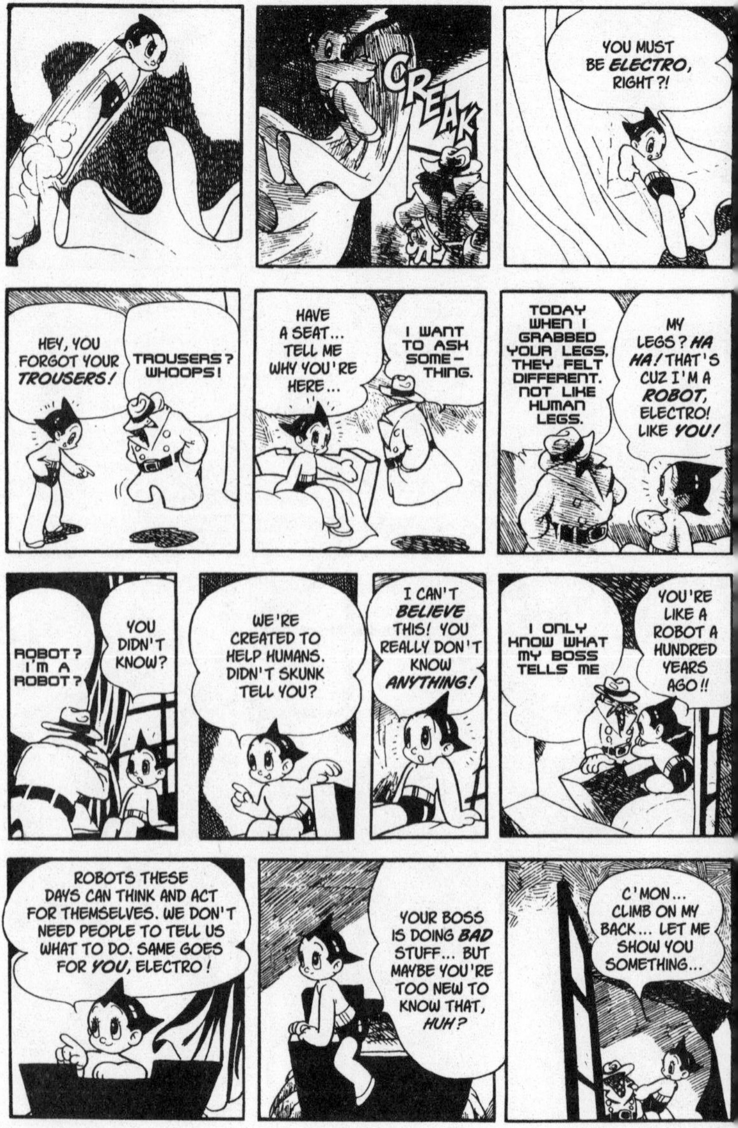
CREAK
YOU MUST BE *ELECTRO*, RIGHT ?!
HEY, YOU FORGOT YOUR *TROUSERS!*
TROUSERS? WHOOPS!
HAVE A SEAT... TELL ME WHY YOU'RE HERE...
I WANT TO ASK SOME-THING.
TODAY WHEN I GRABBED YOUR LEGS, THEY FELT DIFFERENT. NOT LIKE HUMAN LEGS.
MY LEGS? *HA HA!* THAT'S CUZ I'M A *ROBOT*, ELECTRO! LIKE *YOU!*
ROBOT? I'M A ROBOT?
YOU DIDN'T KNOW?
WE'RE CREATED TO HELP HUMANS. DIDN'T SKUNK TELL YOU?
I CAN'T *BELIEVE* THIS! YOU REALLY DON'T KNOW *ANYTHING!*
I ONLY KNOW WHAT MY BOSS TELLS ME
YOU'RE LIKE A ROBOT A HUNDRED YEARS AGO!!
ROBOTS THESE DAYS CAN THINK AND ACT FOR THEMSELVES. WE DON'T NEED PEOPLE TO TELL US WHAT TO DO. SAME GOES FOR *YOU*, ELECTRO!
YOUR BOSS IS DOING *BAD* STUFF... BUT MAYBE YOU'RE TOO NEW TO KNOW THAT, *HUH?*
C'MON... CLIMB ON MY BACK... LET ME SHOW YOU SOMETHING...

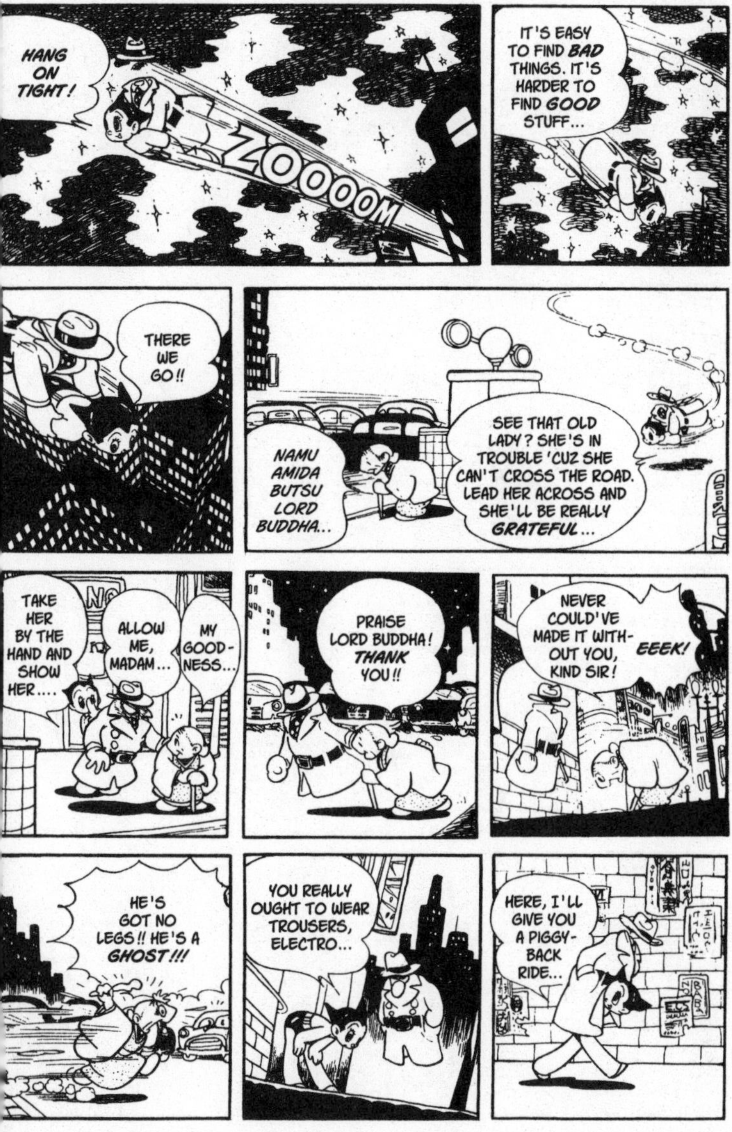
HANG ON TIGHT!
ZOOOOM
IT'S EASY TO FIND BAD THINGS. IT'S HARDER TO FIND GOOD STUFF...
THERE WE GO!!
NAMU AMIDA BUTSU LORD BUDDHA...
SEE THAT OLD LADY? SHE'S IN TROUBLE 'CUZ SHE CAN'T CROSS THE ROAD. LEAD HER ACROSS AND SHE'LL BE REALLY GRATEFUL...
TAKE HER BY THE HAND AND SHOW HER....
ALLOW ME, MADAM...
MY GOOD-NESS...
PRAISE LORD BUDDHA! THANK YOU!!
NEVER COULD'VE MADE IT WITH-OUT YOU, KIND SIR!
EEEK!
HE'S GOT NO LEGS!! HE'S A GHOST!!!
YOU REALLY OUGHT TO WEAR TROUSERS, ELECTRO...
HERE, I'LL GIVE YOU A PIGGY-BACK RIDE...

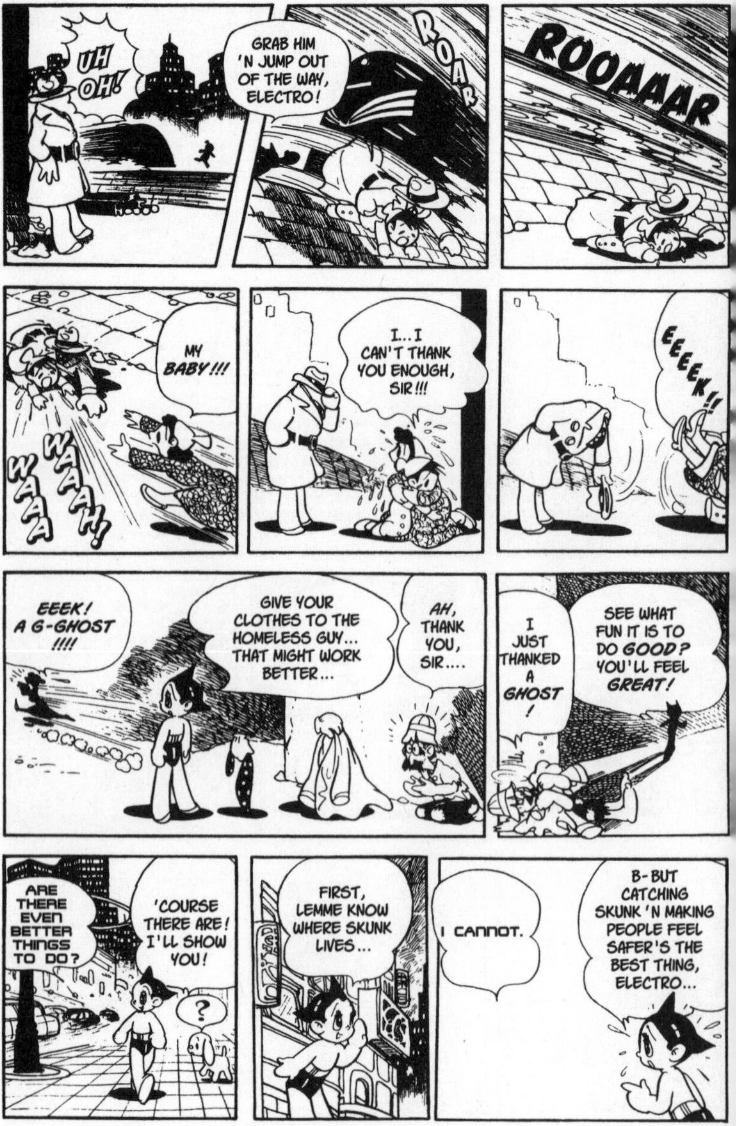
UH OH!
GRAB HIM 'N JUMP OUT OF THE WAY, ELECTRO!
ROAR
ROOAAAR
MY BABY!!!
WAAAAH!
WAAA
I...I CAN'T THANK YOU ENOUGH, SIR!!!
EEEEK!!
EEEK! A G-GHOST!!!!
GIVE YOUR CLOTHES TO THE HOMELESS GUY... THAT MIGHT WORK BETTER...
AH, THANK YOU, SIR....
I JUST THANKED A GHOST!
SEE WHAT FUN IT IS TO DO GOOD? YOU'LL FEEL GREAT!
ARE THERE EVEN BETTER THINGS TO DO?
'COURSE THERE ARE! I'LL SHOW YOU!
?
FIRST, LEMME KNOW WHERE SKUNK LIVES...
I CANNOT.
B-BUT CATCHING SKUNK 'N MAKING PEOPLE FEEL SAFER'S THE BEST THING, ELECTRO...

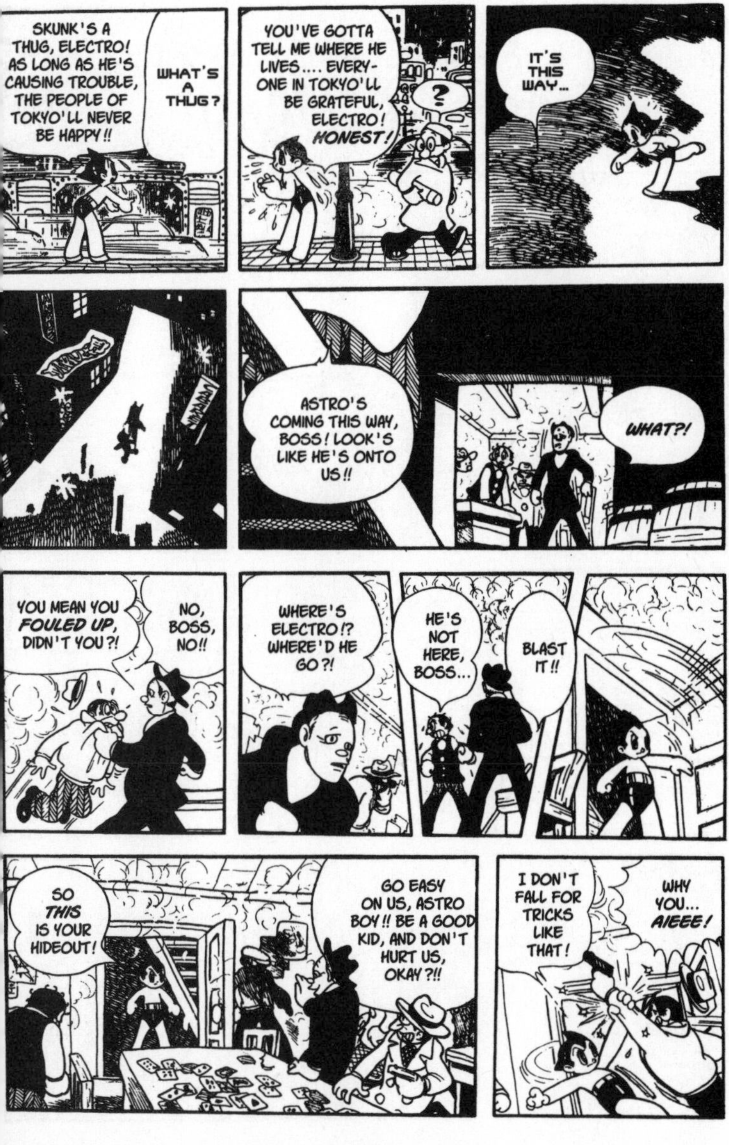

SKUNK'S A THUG, ELECTRO! AS LONG AS HE'S CAUSING TROUBLE, THE PEOPLE OF TOKYO'LL NEVER BE HAPPY!!
WHAT'S A THUG?
YOU'VE GOTTA TELL ME WHERE HE LIVES.... EVERY-ONE IN TOKYO'LL BE GRATEFUL, ELECTRO! *HONEST!*
?
IT'S THIS WAY...
ASTRO'S COMING THIS WAY, BOSS! LOOK'S LIKE HE'S ONTO US!!
WHAT?!
YOU MEAN YOU *FOULED UP*, DIDN'T YOU?!
NO, BOSS, NO!!
WHERE'S ELECTRO!? WHERE'D HE GO?!
HE'S NOT HERE, BOSS...
BLAST IT!!
SO *THIS* IS YOUR HIDEOUT!
GO EASY ON US, ASTRO BOY!! BE A GOOD KID, AND DON'T HURT US, OKAY?!!
I DON'T FALL FOR TRICKS LIKE THAT!
WHY YOU... *AIEEE!*

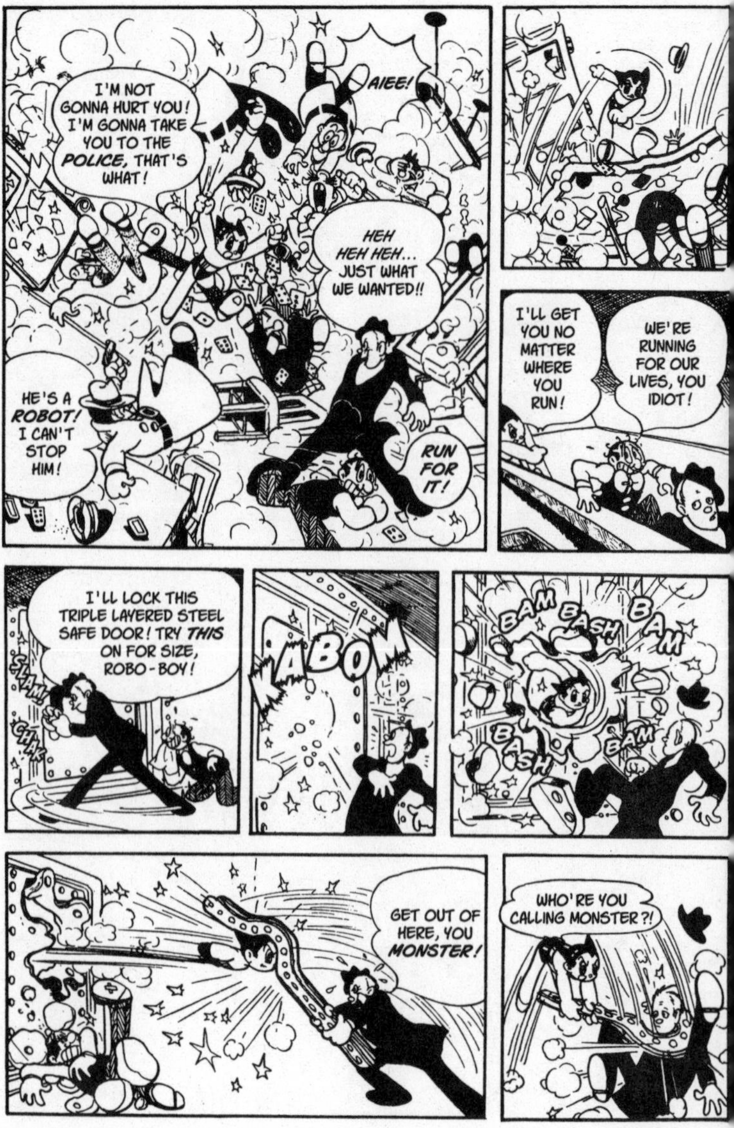
I'M NOT GONNA HURT YOU! I'M GONNA TAKE YOU TO THE *POLICE,* THAT'S WHAT!
AIEE!
HEH HEH HEH... JUST WHAT WE WANTED!!
HE'S A *ROBOT!* I CAN'T STOP HIM!
RUN FOR IT!
I'LL GET YOU NO MATTER WHERE YOU RUN!
WE'RE RUNNING FOR OUR LIVES, YOU IDIOT!
I'LL LOCK THIS TRIPLE LAYERED STEEL SAFE DOOR! TRY *THIS* ON FOR SIZE, ROBO-BOY!
SLAM
CHAK
KABOM
BAM
BASH
BAM
BASH
BAM
GET OUT OF HERE, YOU *MONSTER!*
WHO'RE YOU CALLING MONSTER?!

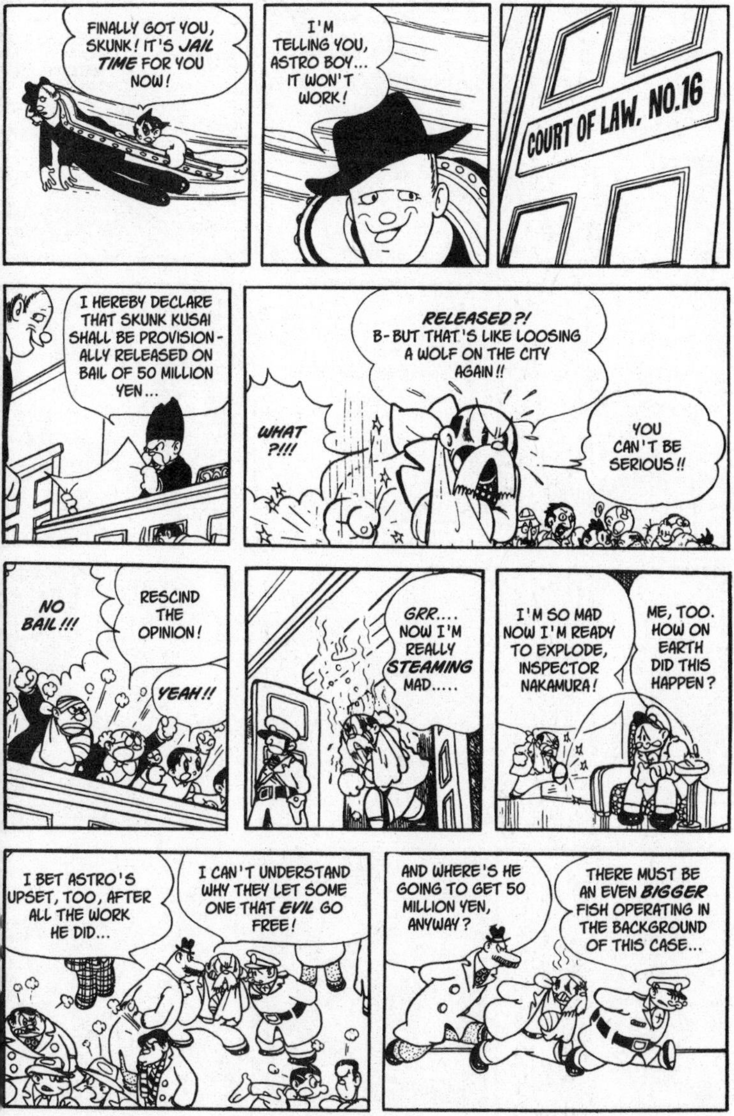
FINALLY GOT YOU, SKUNK! IT'S JAIL TIME FOR YOU NOW!
I'M TELLING YOU, ASTRO BOY... IT WON'T WORK!
COURT OF LAW, NO.16
I HEREBY DECLARE THAT SKUNK KUSAI SHALL BE PROVISION-ALLY RELEASED ON BAIL OF 50 MILLION YEN...
WHAT ?!!!
RELEASED?! B-BUT THAT'S LIKE LOOSING A WOLF ON THE CITY AGAIN!!
YOU CAN'T BE SERIOUS!!
NO BAIL!!!
RESCIND THE OPINION!
YEAH!!
GRR.... NOW I'M REALLY STEAMING MAD.....
I'M SO MAD NOW I'M READY TO EXPLODE, INSPECTOR NAKAMURA!
ME, TOO. HOW ON EARTH DID THIS HAPPEN?
I BET ASTRO'S UPSET, TOO, AFTER ALL THE WORK HE DID...
I CAN'T UNDERSTAND WHY THEY LET SOME ONE THAT EVIL GO FREE!
AND WHERE'S HE GOING TO GET 50 MILLION YEN, ANYWAY?
THERE MUST BE AN EVEN BIGGER FISH OPERATING IN THE BACKGROUND OF THIS CASE...

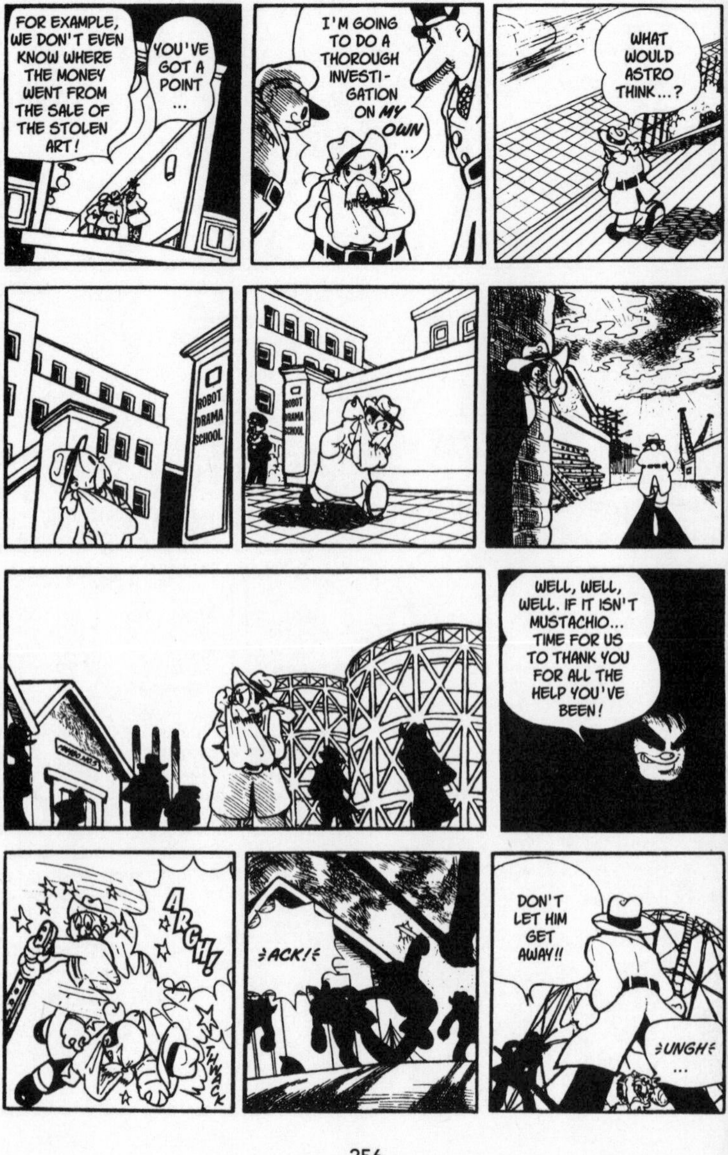
FOR EXAMPLE, WE DON'T EVEN KNOW WHERE THE MONEY WENT FROM THE SALE OF THE STOLEN ART!
YOU'VE GOT A POINT ...
I'M GOING TO DO A THOROUGH INVESTI-GATION ON MY OWN ...
WHAT WOULD ASTRO THINK...?
ROBOT DRAMA SCHOOL
ROBOT DRAMA SCHOOL
WELL, WELL, WELL. IF IT ISN'T MUSTACHIO... TIME FOR US TO THANK YOU FOR ALL THE HELP YOU'VE BEEN!
ARGH!
THWACK
ACK!
DON'T LET HIM GET AWAY!!
UNGH ...

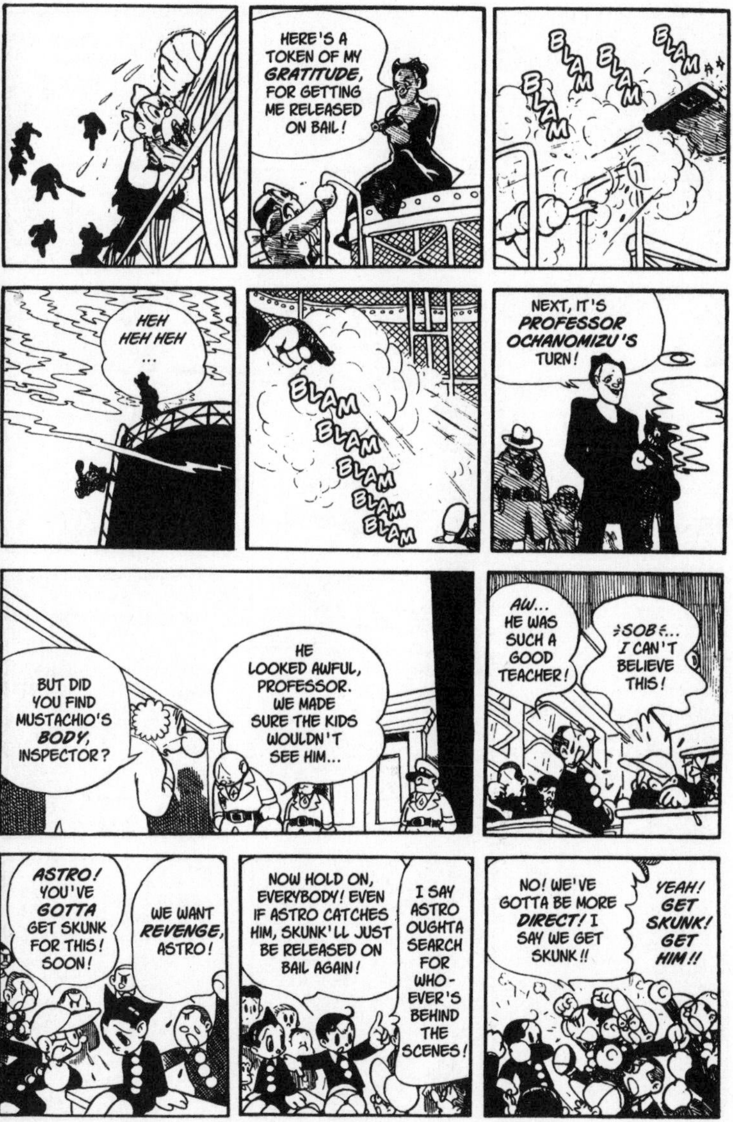
HERE'S A TOKEN OF MY GRATITUDE, FOR GETTING ME RELEASED ON BAIL!
BLAM BLAM BLAM BLAM
HEH HEH HEH ...
BLAM BLAM BLAM BLAM BLAM
NEXT, IT'S PROFESSOR OCHANOMIZU'S TURN!
BUT DID YOU FIND MUSTACHIO'S BODY, INSPECTOR?
HE LOOKED AWFUL, PROFESSOR. WE MADE SURE THE KIDS WOULDN'T SEE HIM...
AW... HE WAS SUCH A GOOD TEACHER!
SOB... I CAN'T BELIEVE THIS!
ASTRO! YOU'VE GOTTA GET SKUNK FOR THIS! SOON!
WE WANT REVENGE, ASTRO!
NOW HOLD ON, EVERYBODY! EVEN IF ASTRO CATCHES HIM, SKUNK'LL JUST BE RELEASED ON BAIL AGAIN!
I SAY ASTRO OUGHTA SEARCH FOR WHO-EVER'S BEHIND THE SCENES!
NO! WE'VE GOTTA BE MORE DIRECT! I SAY WE GET SKUNK!!
YEAH! GET SKUNK! GET HIM!!

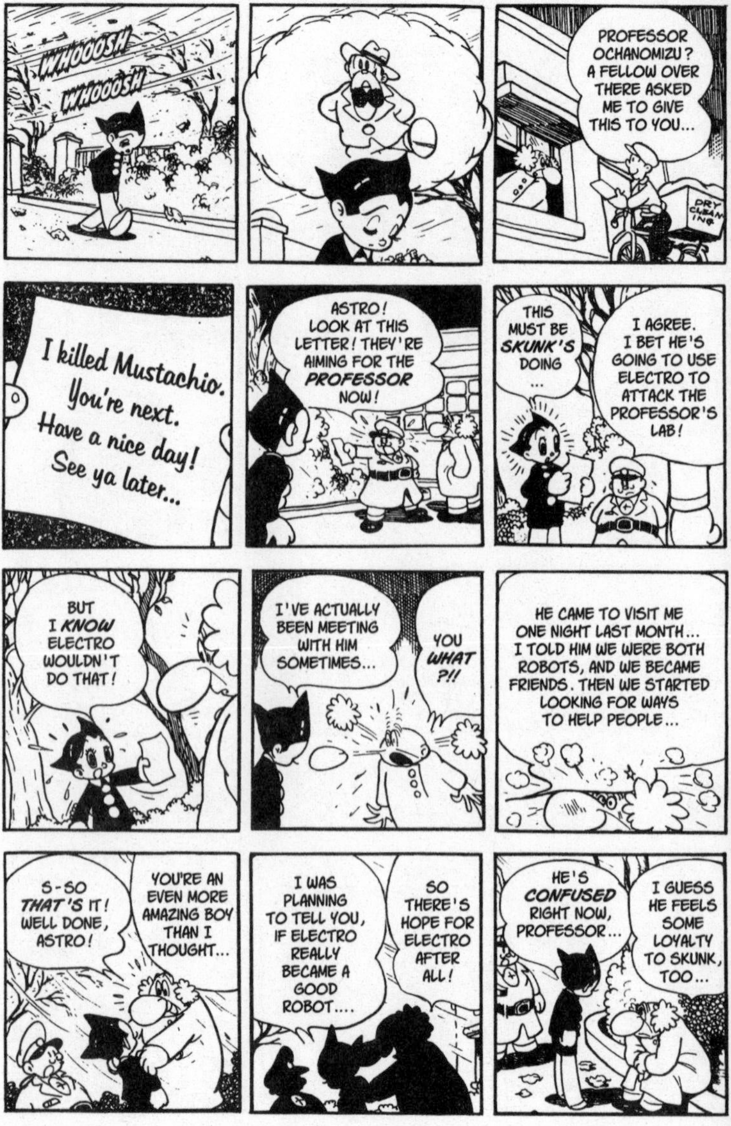
WHOOOSH
WHOOOSH
PROFESSOR OCHANOMIZU? A FELLOW OVER THERE ASKED ME TO GIVE THIS TO YOU...
DRY CLEANING
I killed Mustachio. You're next. Have a nice day! See ya later...
ASTRO! LOOK AT THIS LETTER! THEY'RE AIMING FOR THE *PROFESSOR* NOW!
THIS MUST BE *SKUNK'S* DOING ...
I AGREE. I BET HE'S GOING TO USE ELECTRO TO ATTACK THE PROFESSOR'S LAB!
BUT I *KNOW* ELECTRO WOULDN'T DO THAT!
I'VE ACTUALLY BEEN MEETING WITH HIM SOMETIMES...
YOU *WHAT* ?!!
HE CAME TO VISIT ME ONE NIGHT LAST MONTH... I TOLD HIM WE WERE BOTH ROBOTS, AND WE BECAME FRIENDS. THEN WE STARTED LOOKING FOR WAYS TO HELP PEOPLE...
S-SO *THAT'S* IT! WELL DONE, ASTRO!
YOU'RE AN EVEN MORE AMAZING BOY THAN I THOUGHT...
I WAS PLANNING TO TELL YOU, IF ELECTRO REALLY BECAME A GOOD ROBOT....
SO THERE'S HOPE FOR ELECTRO AFTER ALL!
HE'S *CONFUSED* RIGHT NOW, PROFESSOR...
I GUESS HE FEELS SOME LOYALTY TO SKUNK, TOO...

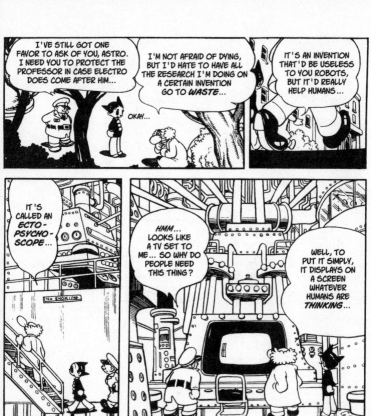

I'VE STILL GOT ONE FAVOR TO ASK OF YOU, ASTRO. I NEED YOU TO PROTECT THE PROFESSOR IN CASE ELECTRO DOES COME AFTER HIM...

OKAY...

I'M NOT AFRAID OF DYING, BUT I'D HATE TO HAVE ALL THE RESEARCH I'M DOING ON A CERTAIN INVENTION GO TO *WASTE*...

IT'S AN INVENTION THAT'D BE USELESS TO YOU ROBOTS, BUT IT'D REALLY HELP HUMANS...

IT'S CALLED AN *ECTO-PSYCHO-SCOPE*...

HMM... LOOKS LIKE A TV SET TO ME... SO WHY DO PEOPLE NEED THIS THING?

WELL, TO PUT IT SIMPLY, IT DISPLAYS ON A SCREEN WHATEVER HUMANS ARE *THINKING*...

IT USES A COMPLEX EMOTION SENSOR TO SHOW YOU, RIGHT HERE, WHAT PEOPLE ARE THINKING -- EVEN THEIR MEMORIES...

WOW... VERY IMPRES-SIVE...

HERE, INSPECTOR NAKAMURA... TRY THESE ON!

WHO? ME?

≠ACK≠... I'VE BECOME A *GUINEA PIG!*

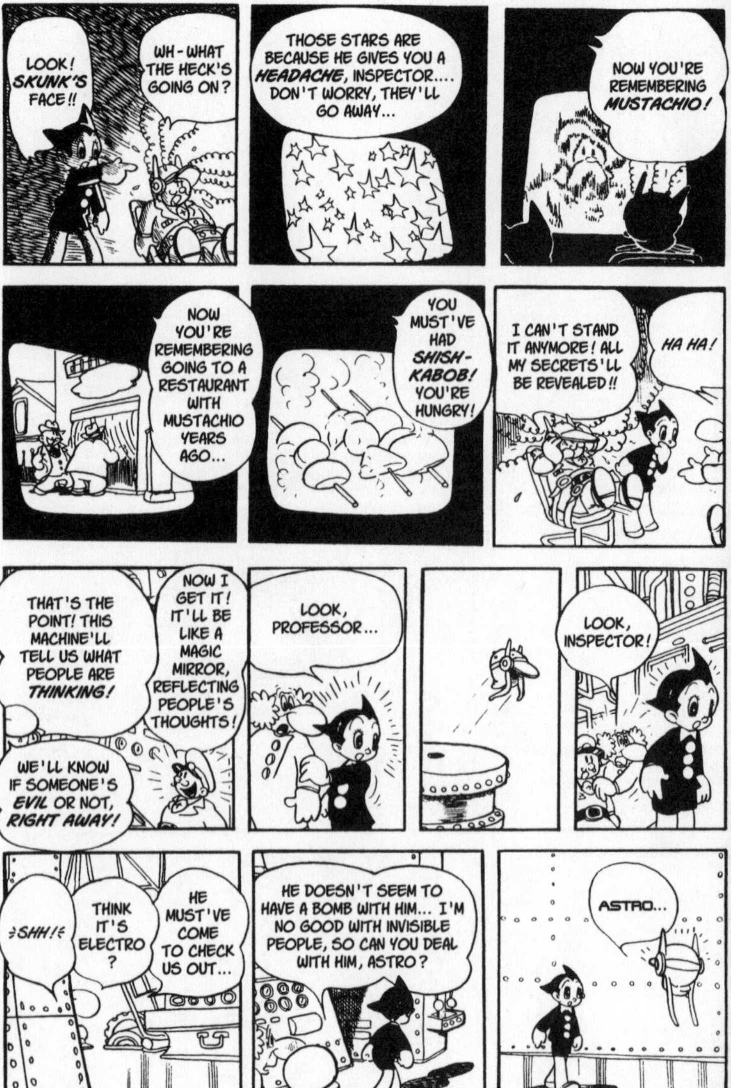
LOOK! SKUNK'S FACE!!
WH-WHAT THE HECK'S GOING ON?
THOSE STARS ARE BECAUSE HE GIVES YOU A HEADACHE, INSPECTOR.... DON'T WORRY, THEY'LL GO AWAY...
NOW YOU'RE REMEMBERING MUSTACHIO!
NOW YOU'RE REMEMBERING GOING TO A RESTAURANT WITH MUSTACHIO YEARS AGO...
YOU MUST'VE HAD SHISH-KABOB! YOU'RE HUNGRY!
I CAN'T STAND IT ANYMORE! ALL MY SECRETS'LL BE REVEALED!!
HA HA!
THAT'S THE POINT! THIS MACHINE'LL TELL US WHAT PEOPLE ARE THINKING!
NOW I GET IT! IT'LL BE LIKE A MAGIC MIRROR, REFLECTING PEOPLE'S THOUGHTS!
WE'LL KNOW IF SOMEONE'S EVIL OR NOT, RIGHT AWAY!
LOOK, PROFESSOR...
LOOK, INSPECTOR!
SHH!
THINK IT'S ELECTRO?
HE MUST'VE COME TO CHECK US OUT...
HE DOESN'T SEEM TO HAVE A BOMB WITH HIM... I'M NO GOOD WITH INVISIBLE PEOPLE, SO CAN YOU DEAL WITH HIM, ASTRO?
ASTRO...

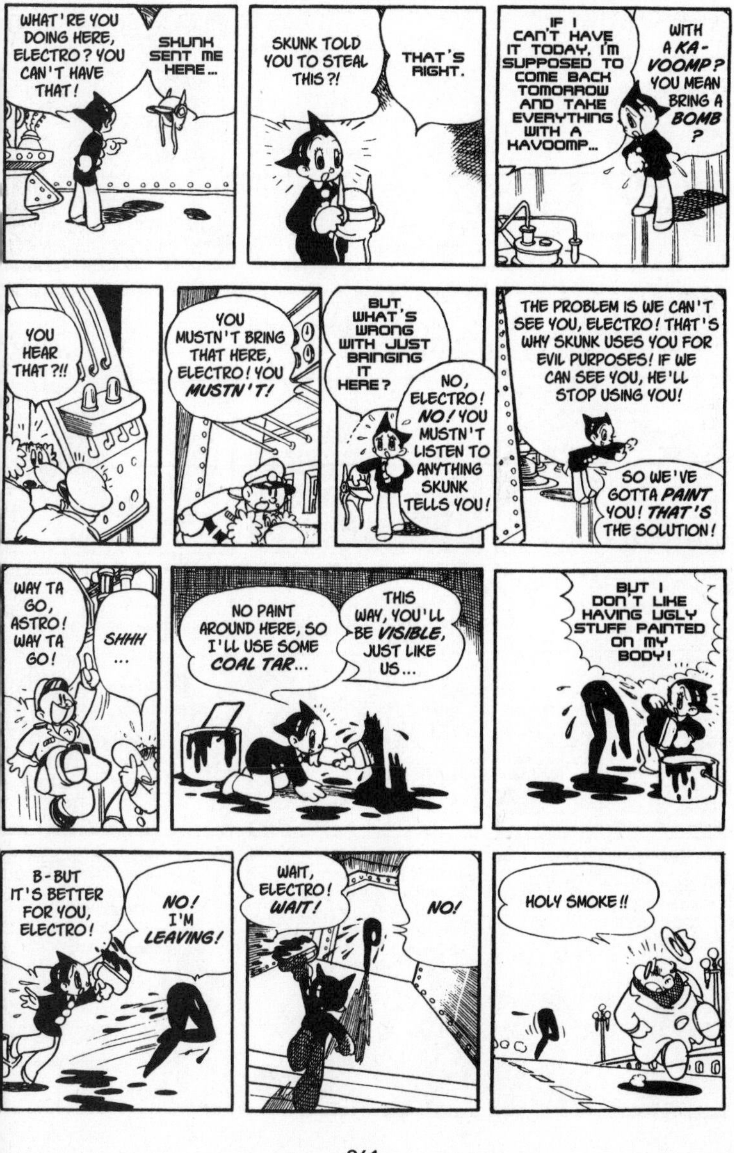
WHAT'RE YOU DOING HERE, ELECTRO? YOU CAN'T HAVE THAT!
SHUNK SENT ME HERE...
SKUNK TOLD YOU TO STEAL THIS?!
THAT'S RIGHT.
IF I CAN'T HAVE IT TODAY, I'M SUPPOSED TO COME BACK TOMORROW AND TAKE EVERYTHING WITH A KAVOOMP...
WITH A KA-VOOMP? YOU MEAN BRING A BOMB?
YOU HEAR THAT?!!
YOU MUSTN'T BRING THAT HERE, ELECTRO! YOU MUSTN'T!
BUT, WHAT'S WRONG WITH JUST BRINGING IT HERE?
NO, ELECTRO! NO! YOU MUSTN'T LISTEN TO ANYTHING SKUNK TELLS YOU!
THE PROBLEM IS WE CAN'T SEE YOU, ELECTRO! THAT'S WHY SKUNK USES YOU FOR EVIL PURPOSES! IF WE CAN SEE YOU, HE'LL STOP USING YOU!
SO WE'VE GOTTA PAINT YOU! THAT'S THE SOLUTION!
WAY TA GO, ASTRO! WAY TA GO!
SHHH...
NO PAINT AROUND HERE, SO I'LL USE SOME COAL TAR...
THIS WAY, YOU'LL BE VISIBLE, JUST LIKE US...
BUT I DON'T LIKE HAVING UGLY STUFF PAINTED ON MY BODY!
B-BUT IT'S BETTER FOR YOU, ELECTRO!
NO! I'M LEAVING!
WAIT, ELECTRO! WAIT!
NO!
HOLY SMOKE!!

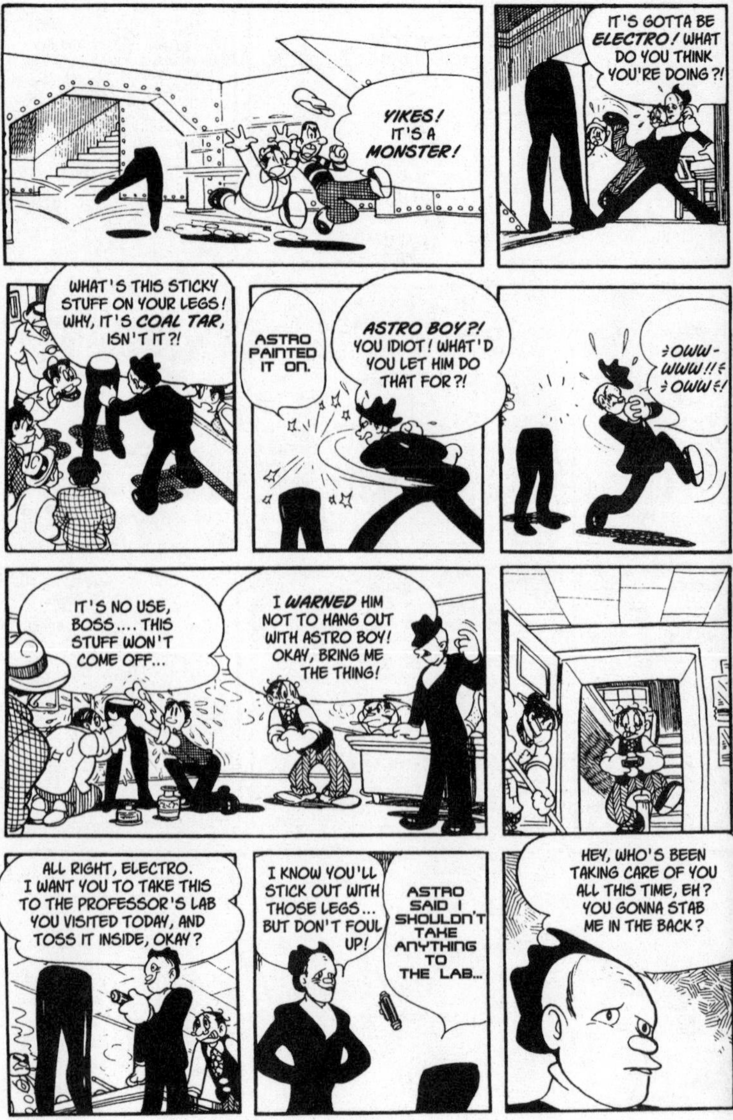
YIKES! IT'S A MONSTER!
IT'S GOTTA BE ELECTRO! WHAT DO YOU THINK YOU'RE DOING?!
WHAT'S THIS STICKY STUFF ON YOUR LEGS! WHY, IT'S COAL TAR, ISN'T IT?!
ASTRO PAINTED IT ON.
ASTRO BOY?! YOU IDIOT! WHAT'D YOU LET HIM DO THAT FOR?!
OWW-WWW!! OWW!
IT'S NO USE, BOSS.... THIS STUFF WON'T COME OFF...
I WARNED HIM NOT TO HANG OUT WITH ASTRO BOY! OKAY, BRING ME THE THING!
ALL RIGHT, ELECTRO. I WANT YOU TO TAKE THIS TO THE PROFESSOR'S LAB YOU VISITED TODAY, AND TOSS IT INSIDE, OKAY?
I KNOW YOU'LL STICK OUT WITH THOSE LEGS... BUT DON'T FOUL UP!
ASTRO SAID I SHOULDN'T TAKE ANYTHING TO THE LAB...
HEY, WHO'S BEEN TAKING CARE OF YOU ALL THIS TIME, EH? YOU GONNA STAB ME IN THE BACK?

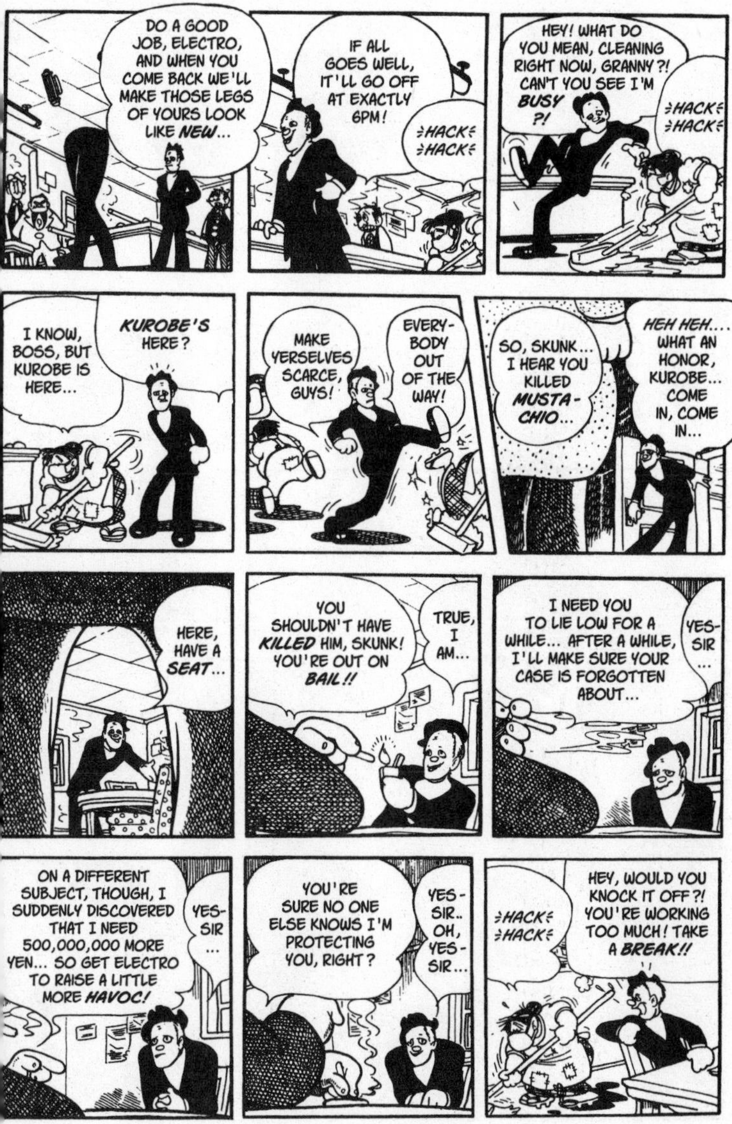

DO A GOOD JOB, ELECTRO, AND WHEN YOU COME BACK WE'LL MAKE THOSE LEGS OF YOURS LOOK LIKE NEW...
IF ALL GOES WELL, IT'LL GO OFF AT EXACTLY 6PM!
HACK HACK
HEY! WHAT DO YOU MEAN, CLEANING RIGHT NOW, GRANNY?! CAN'T YOU SEE I'M BUSY?!
HACK HACK
I KNOW, BOSS, BUT KUROBE IS HERE...
KUROBE'S HERE?
MAKE YERSELVES SCARCE, GUYS!
EVERY-BODY OUT OF THE WAY!
SO, SKUNK... I HEAR YOU KILLED MUSTA-CHIO...
HEH HEH.... WHAT AN HONOR, KUROBE... COME IN, COME IN...
HERE, HAVE A SEAT...
YOU SHOULDN'T HAVE KILLED HIM, SKUNK! YOU'RE OUT ON BAIL!!
TRUE, I AM...
I NEED YOU TO LIE LOW FOR A WHILE... AFTER A WHILE, I'LL MAKE SURE YOUR CASE IS FORGOTTEN ABOUT...
YES-SIR...
ON A DIFFERENT SUBJECT, THOUGH, I SUDDENLY DISCOVERED THAT I NEED 500,000,000 MORE YEN... SO GET ELECTRO TO RAISE A LITTLE MORE HAVOC!
YES-SIR...
YOU'RE SURE NO ONE ELSE KNOWS I'M PROTECTING YOU, RIGHT?
YES-SIR.. OH, YES-SIR...
HACK HACK
HEY, WOULD YOU KNOCK IT OFF?! YOU'RE WORKING TOO MUCH! TAKE A BREAK!!

SILENCE....

PROFESSOR
OCHANOMIZU
RESEARCH LABORATORY

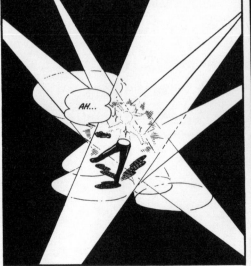

AH...

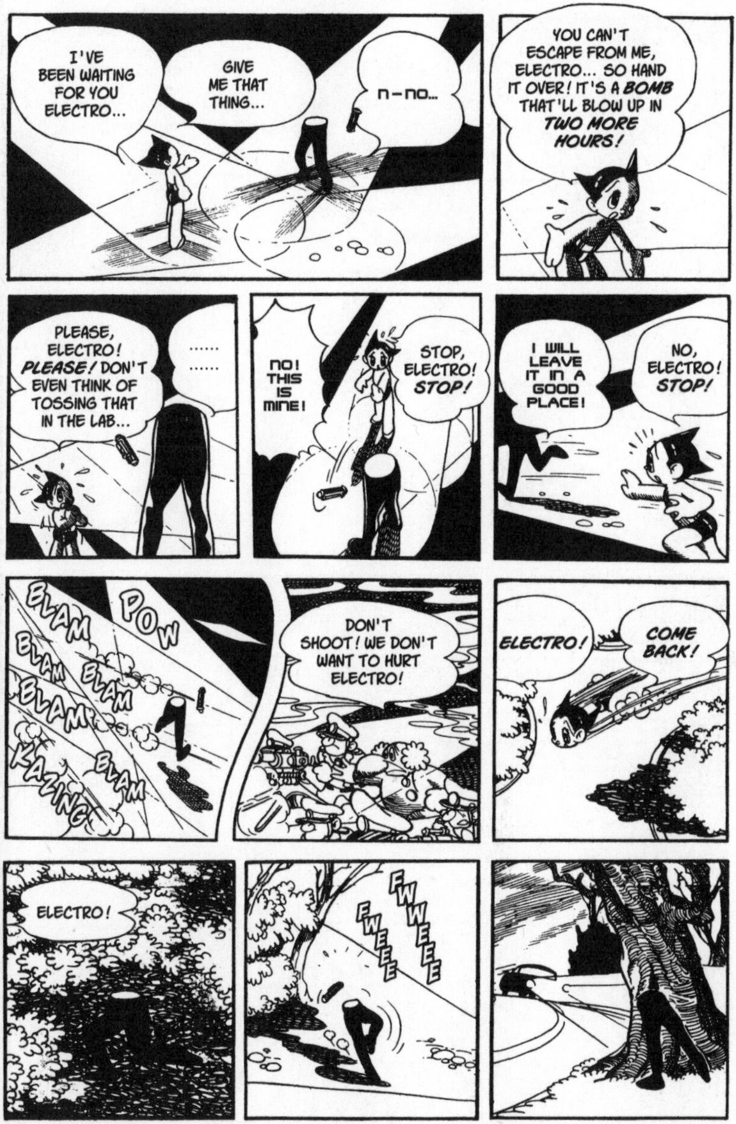
I'VE BEEN WAITING FOR YOU ELECTRO...
GIVE ME THAT THING...
n-no...
YOU CAN'T ESCAPE FROM ME, ELECTRO... SO HAND IT OVER! IT'S A BOMB THAT'LL BLOW UP IN TWO MORE HOURS!
PLEASE, ELECTRO! PLEASE! DON'T EVEN THINK OF TOSSING THAT IN THE LAB...
......
......
NO! THIS IS MINE!
STOP, ELECTRO! STOP!
I WILL LEAVE IT IN A GOOD PLACE!
NO, ELECTRO! STOP!
BLAM
POW
BLAM BLAM
BLAM
BLAM
KAZING
DON'T SHOOT! WE DON'T WANT TO HURT ELECTRO!
ELECTRO!
COME BACK!
ELECTRO!
FWEEE
FWWEEE

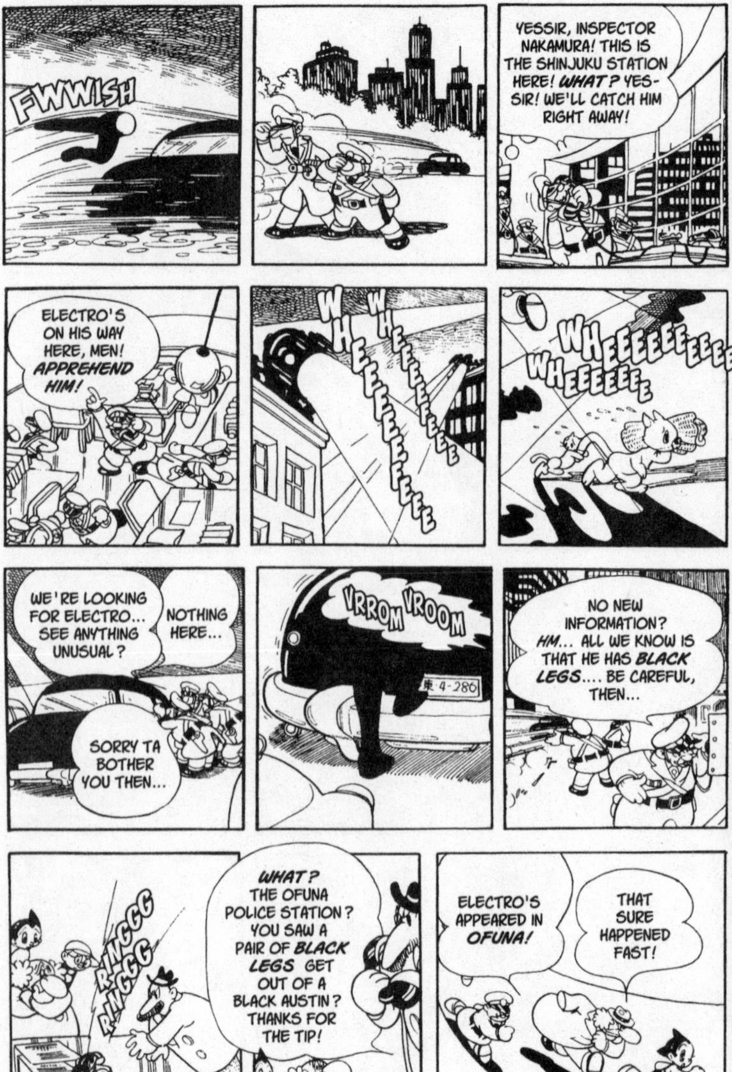
FWWISH
YESSIR, INSPECTOR NAKAMURA! THIS IS THE SHINJUKU STATION HERE! WHAT? YES-SIR! WE'LL CATCH HIM RIGHT AWAY!
ELECTRO'S ON HIS WAY HERE, MEN! APPREHEND HIM!
WHEEEEEEEEE
WHEEEEEEEEEEE
WHEEEEEEEEEE
WHEEEEEEE
WE'RE LOOKING FOR ELECTRO... SEE ANYTHING UNUSUAL?
NOTHING HERE...
SORRY TA BOTHER YOU THEN...
VRROOM VROOM
東 4-286
NO NEW INFORMATION? HM... ALL WE KNOW IS THAT HE HAS BLACK LEGS.... BE CAREFUL, THEN...
RINGGG RINGGG
WHAT? THE OFUNA POLICE STATION? YOU SAW A PAIR OF BLACK LEGS GET OUT OF A BLACK AUSTIN? THANKS FOR THE TIP!
ELECTRO'S APPEARED IN OFUNA!
THAT SURE HAPPENED FAST!

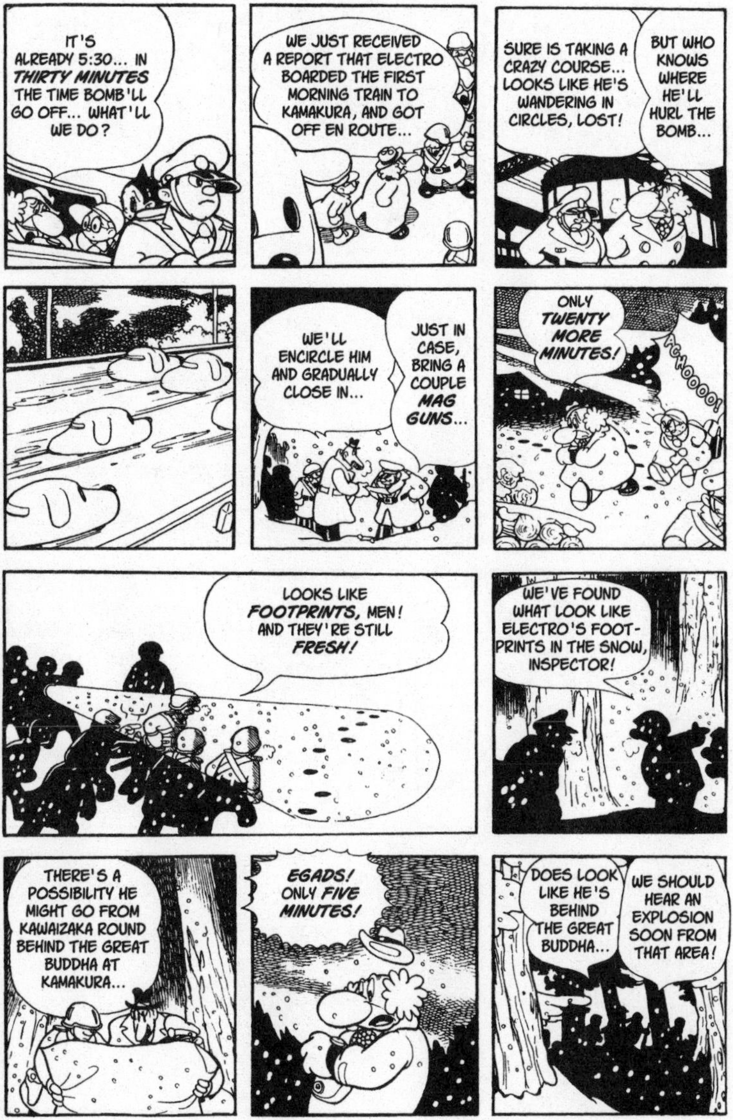
IT'S ALREADY 5:30... IN *THIRTY MINUTES* THE TIME BOMB'LL GO OFF... WHAT'LL WE DO?
WE JUST RECEIVED A REPORT THAT ELECTRO BOARDED THE FIRST MORNING TRAIN TO KAMAKURA, AND GOT OFF EN ROUTE...
SURE IS TAKING A CRAZY COURSE... LOOKS LIKE HE'S WANDERING IN CIRCLES, LOST!
BUT WHO KNOWS WHERE HE'LL HURL THE BOMB...
WE'LL ENCIRCLE HIM AND GRADUALLY CLOSE IN...
JUST IN CASE, BRING A COUPLE *MAG GUNS*...
ONLY *TWENTY MORE MINUTES!*
ACHOOOOO!
LOOKS LIKE *FOOTPRINTS,* MEN! AND THEY'RE STILL *FRESH!*
WE'VE FOUND WHAT LOOK LIKE ELECTRO'S FOOT-PRINTS IN THE SNOW, INSPECTOR!
THERE'S A POSSIBILITY HE MIGHT GO FROM KAWAIZAKA ROUND BEHIND THE GREAT BUDDHA AT KAMAKURA...
EGADS! ONLY *FIVE MINUTES!*
DOES LOOK LIKE HE'S BEHIND THE GREAT BUDDHA...
WE SHOULD HEAR AN EXPLOSION SOON FROM THAT AREA!

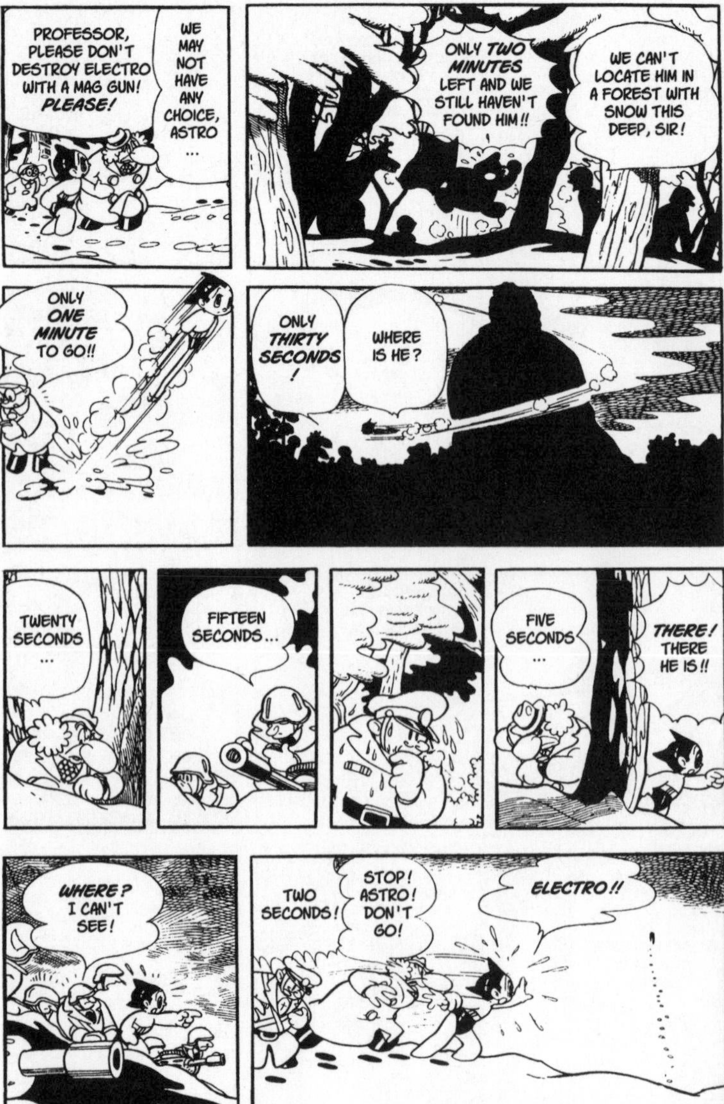

PROFESSOR, PLEASE DON'T DESTROY ELECTRO WITH A MAG GUN! PLEASE!
WE MAY NOT HAVE ANY CHOICE, ASTRO ...
ONLY TWO MINUTES LEFT AND WE STILL HAVEN'T FOUND HIM!!
WE CAN'T LOCATE HIM IN A FOREST WITH SNOW THIS DEEP, SIR!
ONLY ONE MINUTE TO GO!!
ONLY THIRTY SECONDS!
WHERE IS HE?
TWENTY SECONDS ...
FIFTEEN SECONDS...
FIVE SECONDS ...
THERE! THERE HE IS!!
WHERE? I CAN'T SEE!
TWO SECONDS!
STOP! ASTRO! DON'T GO!
ELECTRO!!

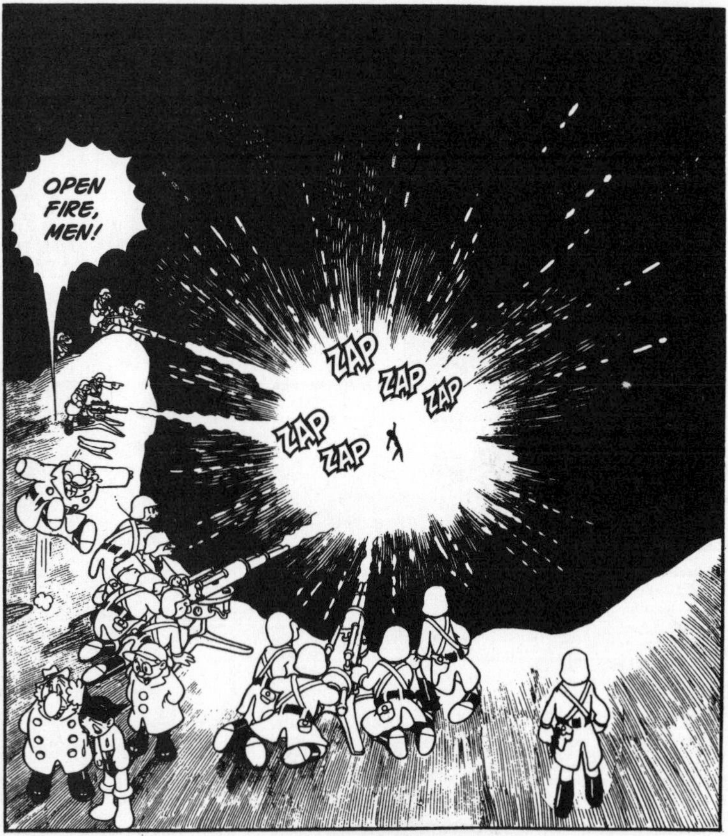
OPEN FIRE, MEN!
ZAP
ZAP
ZAP
ZAP
ZAP
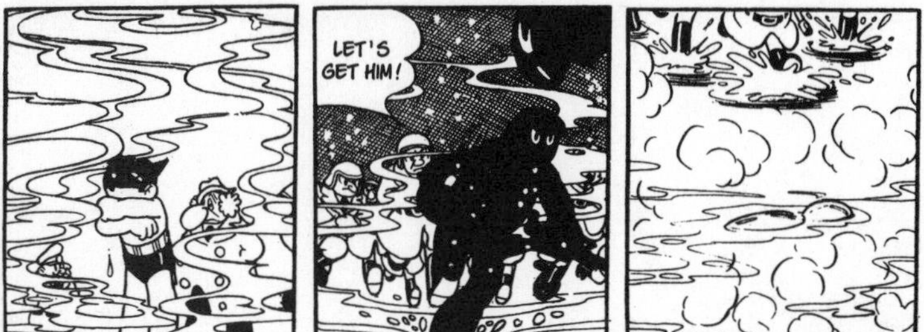
LET'S GET HIM!

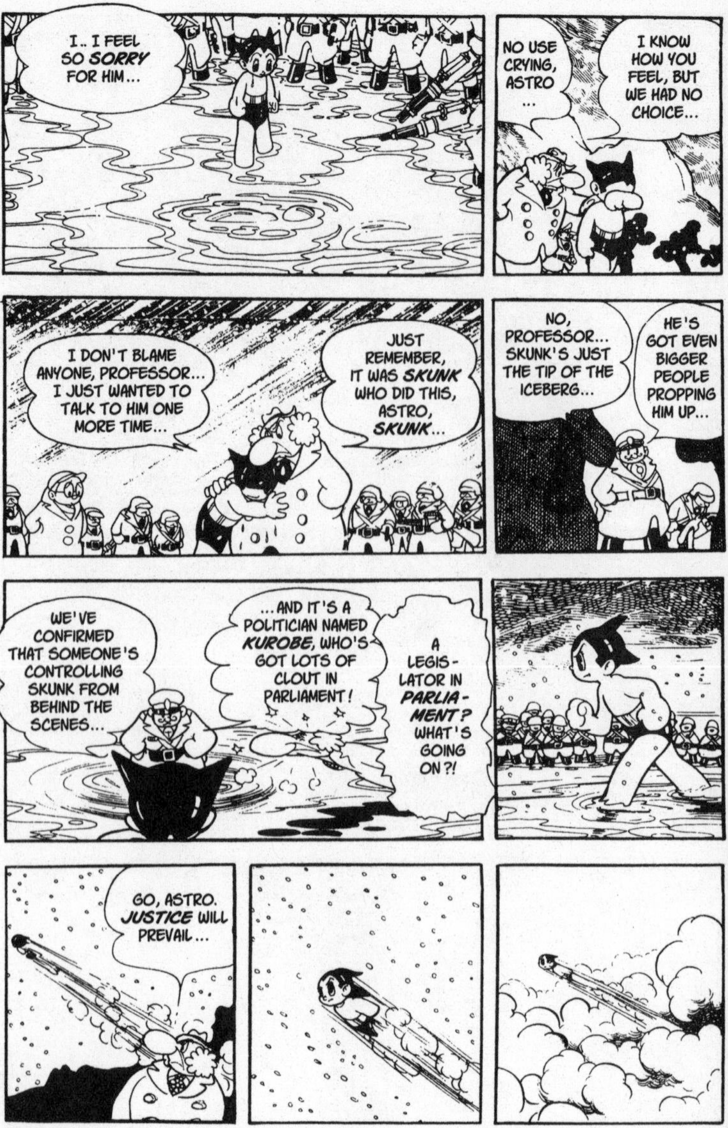
I.. I FEEL SO SORRY FOR HIM...
NO USE CRYING, ASTRO ...
I KNOW HOW YOU FEEL, BUT WE HAD NO CHOICE...
I DON'T BLAME ANYONE, PROFESSOR... I JUST WANTED TO TALK TO HIM ONE MORE TIME...
JUST REMEMBER, IT WAS SKUNK WHO DID THIS, ASTRO, SKUNK...
NO, PROFESSOR... SKUNK'S JUST THE TIP OF THE ICEBERG...
HE'S GOT EVEN BIGGER PEOPLE PROPPING HIM UP...
WE'VE CONFIRMED THAT SOMEONE'S CONTROLLING SKUNK FROM BEHIND THE SCENES...
...AND IT'S A POLITICIAN NAMED KUROBE, WHO'S GOT LOTS OF CLOUT IN PARLIAMENT!
A LEGIS-LATOR IN PARLIA-MENT? WHAT'S GOING ON?!
GO, ASTRO. JUSTICE WILL PREVAIL...

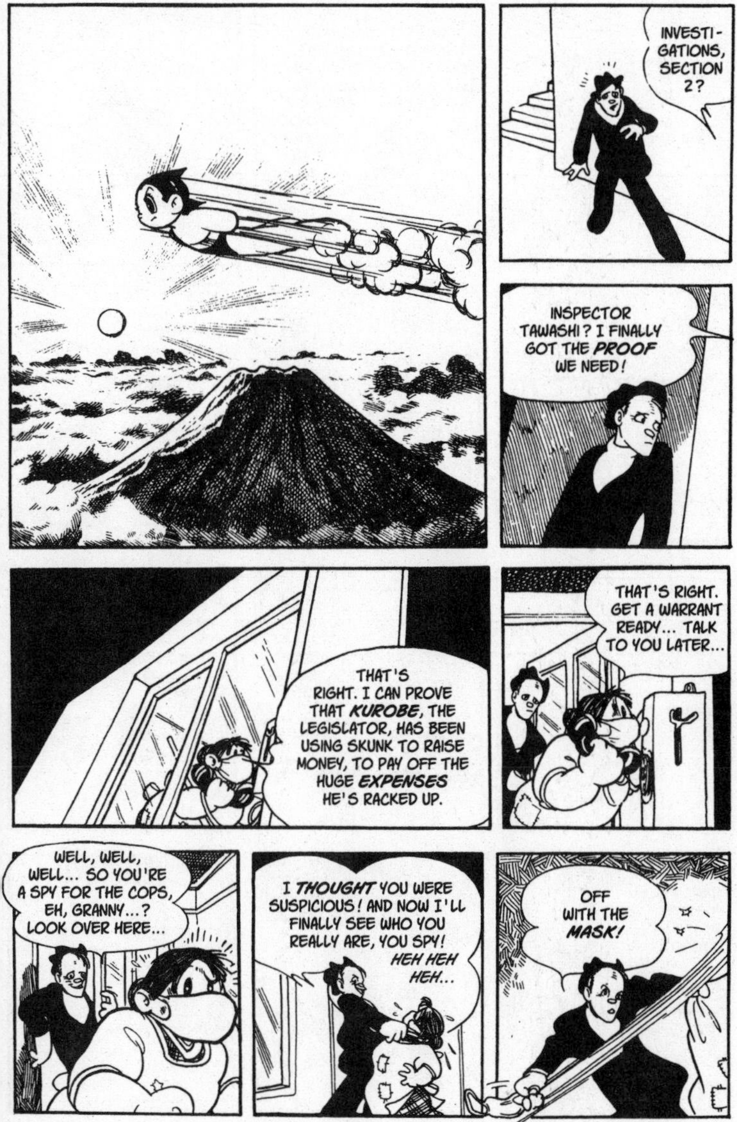
INVESTI-GATIONS, SECTION 2?
INSPECTOR TAWASHI? I FINALLY GOT THE PROOF WE NEED!
THAT'S RIGHT. I CAN PROVE THAT KUROBE, THE LEGISLATOR, HAS BEEN USING SKUNK TO RAISE MONEY, TO PAY OFF THE HUGE EXPENSES HE'S RACKED UP.
THAT'S RIGHT. GET A WARRANT READY... TALK TO YOU LATER...
WELL, WELL, WELL... SO YOU'RE A SPY FOR THE COPS, EH, GRANNY...? LOOK OVER HERE...
I THOUGHT YOU WERE SUSPICIOUS! AND NOW I'LL FINALLY SEE WHO YOU REALLY ARE, YOU SPY! HEH HEH HEH...
OFF WITH THE MASK!

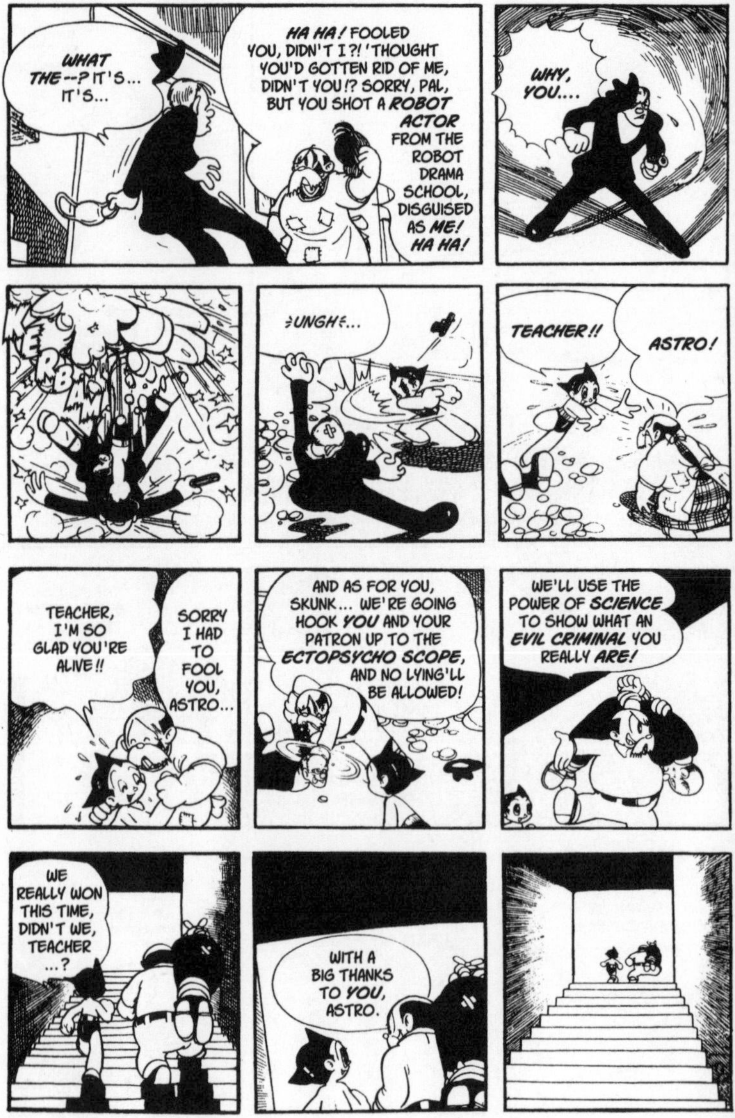
WHAT THE--? IT'S... IT'S...
HA HA! FOOLED YOU, DIDN'T I?! 'THOUGHT YOU'D GOTTEN RID OF ME, DIDN'T YOU!? SORRY, PAL, BUT YOU SHOT A ROBOT ACTOR FROM THE ROBOT DRAMA SCHOOL, DISGUISED AS ME! HA HA!
WHY, YOU....
KERBAM!
UNGH...
TEACHER!!
ASTRO!
TEACHER, I'M SO GLAD YOU'RE ALIVE!!
SORRY I HAD TO FOOL YOU, ASTRO...
AND AS FOR YOU, SKUNK... WE'RE GOING HOOK YOU AND YOUR PATRON UP TO THE ECTOPSYCHO SCOPE, AND NO LYING'LL BE ALLOWED!
WE'LL USE THE POWER OF SCIENCE TO SHOW WHAT AN EVIL CRIMINAL YOU REALLY ARE!
WE REALLY WON THIS TIME, DIDN'T WE, TEACHER ...?
WITH A BIG THANKS TO YOU, ASTRO.

B L A C K
L U X

First appeared in the September 1957 supplement
of *Shonen* magazine.

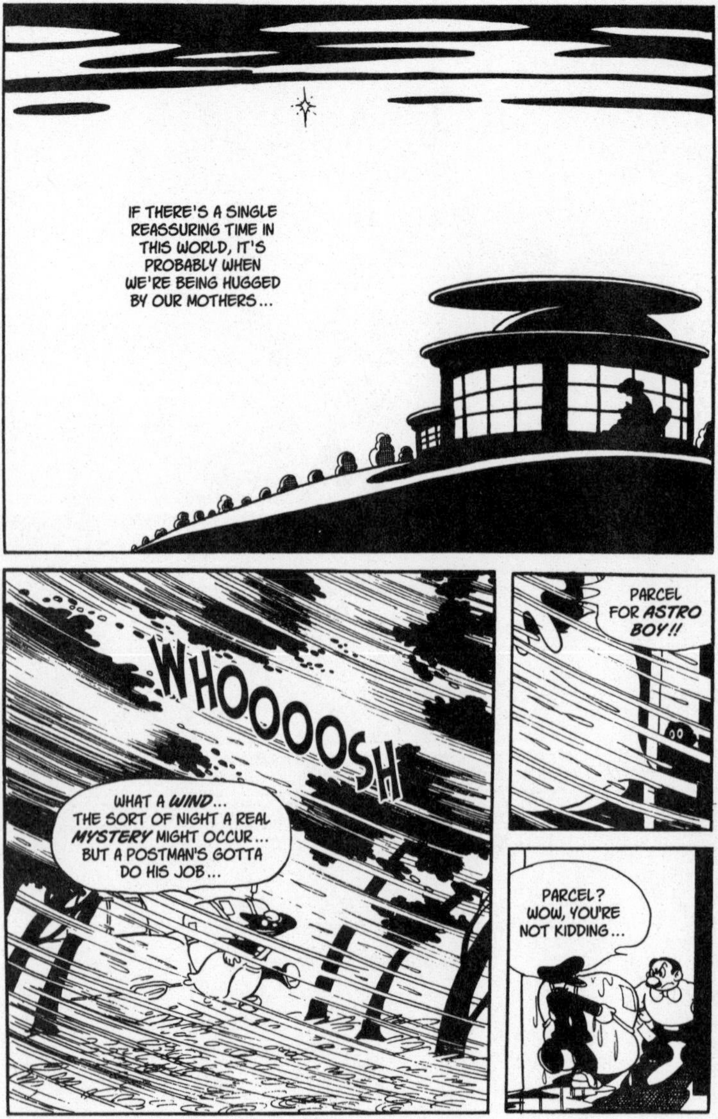
IF THERE'S A SINGLE REASSURING TIME IN THIS WORLD, IT'S PROBABLY WHEN WE'RE BEING HUGGED BY OUR MOTHERS...
WHOOOOSH
WHAT A WIND... THE SORT OF NIGHT A REAL MYSTERY MIGHT OCCUR... BUT A POSTMAN'S GOTTA DO HIS JOB...
PARCEL FOR ASTRO BOY!!
PARCEL? WOW, YOU'RE NOT KIDDING...

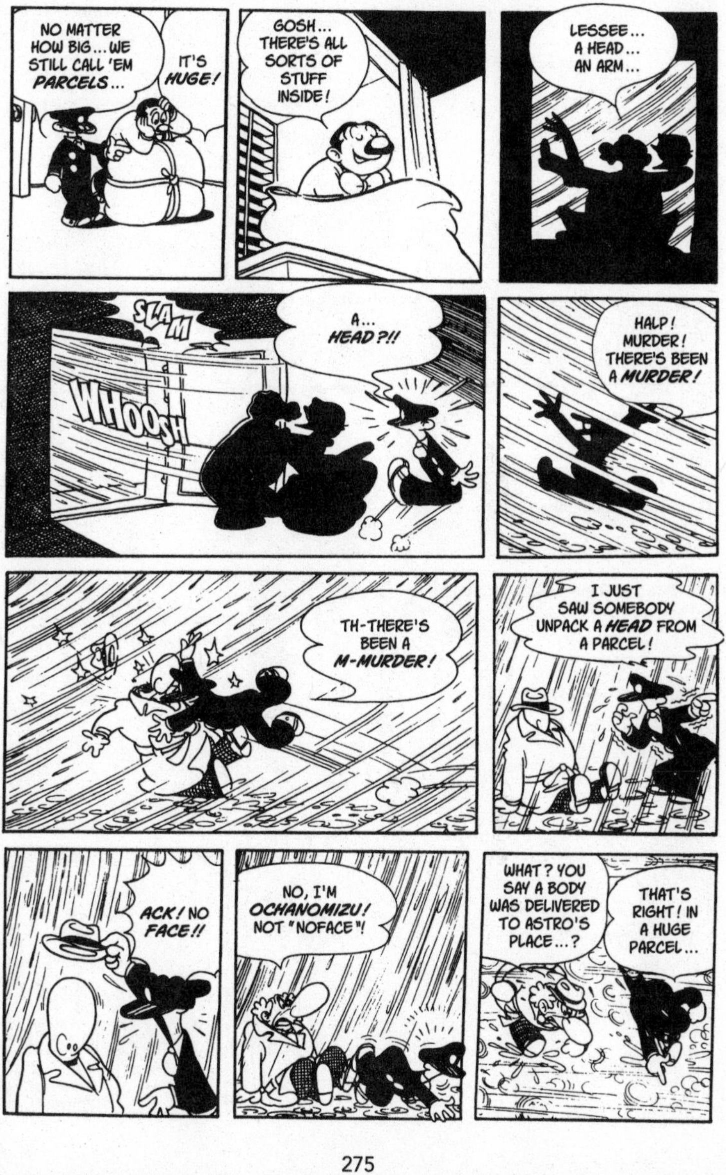
NO MATTER HOW BIG... WE STILL CALL 'EM PARCELS...
IT'S HUGE!
GOSH... THERE'S ALL SORTS OF STUFF INSIDE!
LESSEE... A HEAD... AN ARM...
SLAM
WHOOSH
A... HEAD?!!
HALP! MURDER! THERE'S BEEN A MURDER!
TH-THERE'S BEEN A M-MURDER!
I JUST SAW SOMEBODY UNPACK A HEAD FROM A PARCEL!
ACK! NO FACE!!
NO, I'M OCHANOMIZU! NOT "NOFACE"!
WHAT? YOU SAY A BODY WAS DELIVERED TO ASTRO'S PLACE...?
THAT'S RIGHT! IN A HUGE PARCEL...

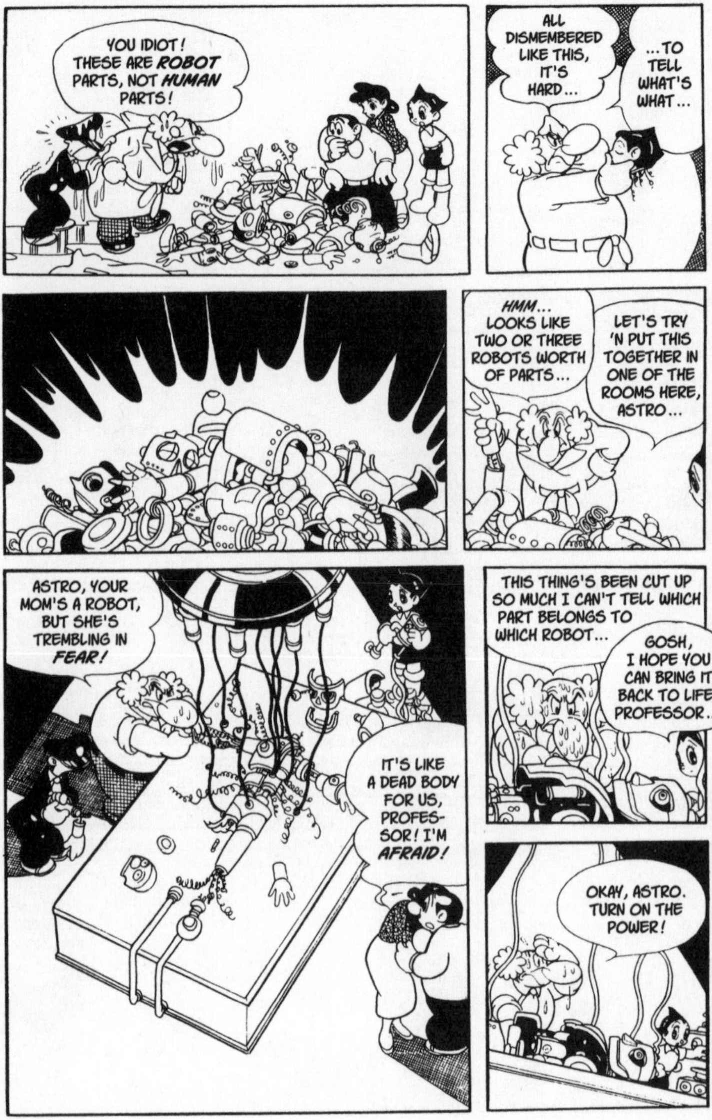
YOU IDIOT! THESE ARE *ROBOT* PARTS, NOT *HUMAN* PARTS!
ALL DISMEMBERED LIKE THIS, IT'S HARD...
...TO TELL WHAT'S WHAT...
HMM... LOOKS LIKE TWO OR THREE ROBOTS WORTH OF PARTS...
LET'S TRY 'N PUT THIS TOGETHER IN ONE OF THE ROOMS HERE, ASTRO...
ASTRO, YOUR MOM'S A ROBOT, BUT SHE'S TREMBLING IN *FEAR!*
IT'S LIKE A DEAD BODY FOR US, PROFES-SOR! I'M *AFRAID!*
THIS THING'S BEEN CUT UP SO MUCH I CAN'T TELL WHICH PART BELONGS TO WHICH ROBOT...
GOSH, I HOPE YOU CAN BRING IT BACK TO LIFE, PROFESSOR...
OKAY, ASTRO. TURN ON THE POWER!

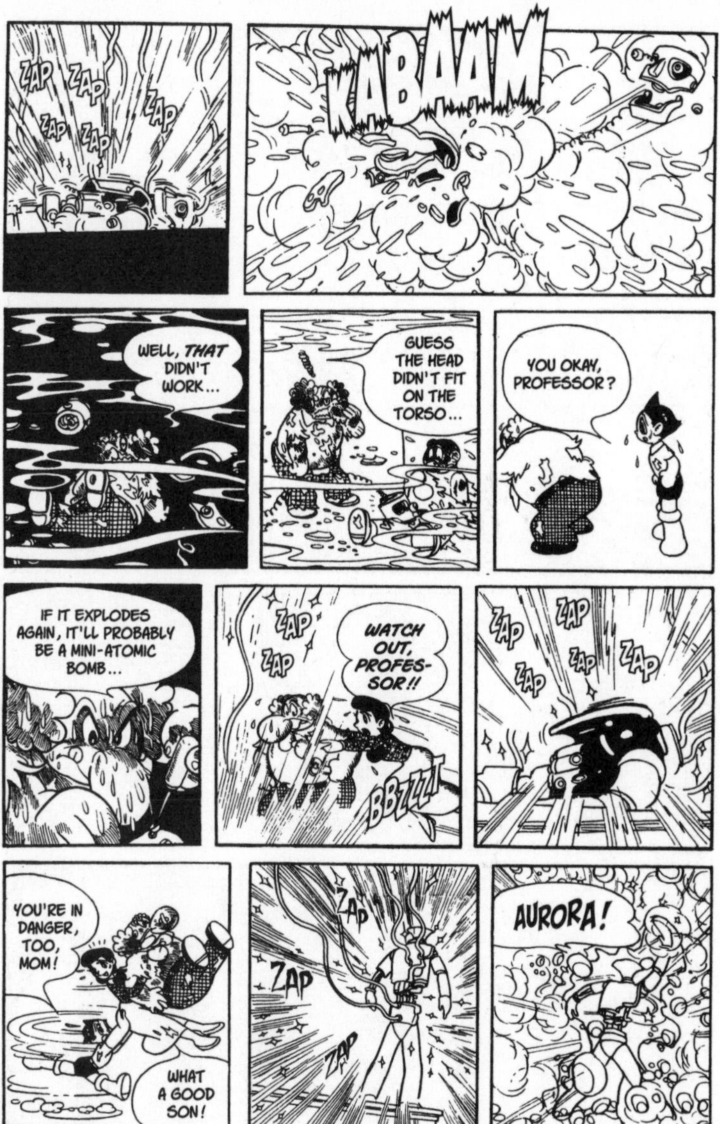
ZAP ZAP ZAP ZAP ZAP
KABAAM
WELL, THAT DIDN'T WORK...
GUESS THE HEAD DIDN'T FIT ON THE TORSO...
YOU OKAY, PROFESSOR?
IF IT EXPLODES AGAIN, IT'LL PROBABLY BE A MINI-ATOMIC BOMB...
ZAP
ZAP
WATCH OUT, PROFES- SOR!!
BBZZZT
ZAP ZAP ZAP ZAP ZAP
YOU'RE IN DANGER, TOO, MOM!
WHAT A GOOD SON!
ZAP
ZAP
ZAP
AURORA!

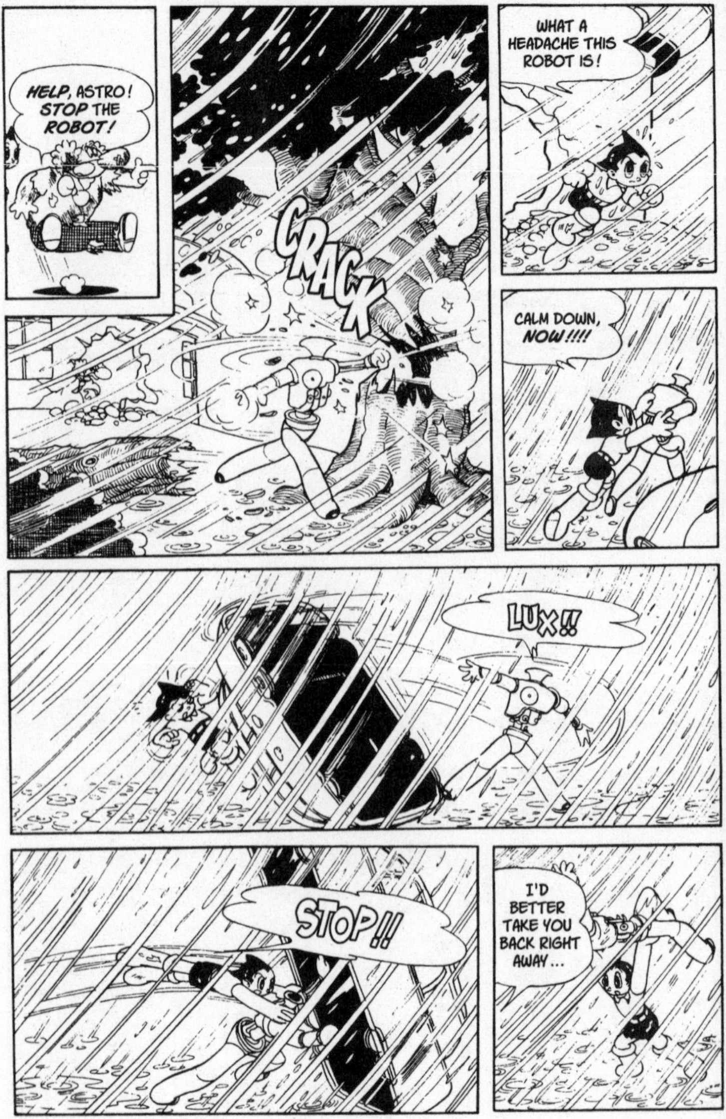
HELP, ASTRO! STOP THE ROBOT!
CRACK
WHAT A HEADACHE THIS ROBOT IS!
CALM DOWN, NOW!!!!
LUX!!
STOP!!
I'D BETTER TAKE YOU BACK RIGHT AWAY...

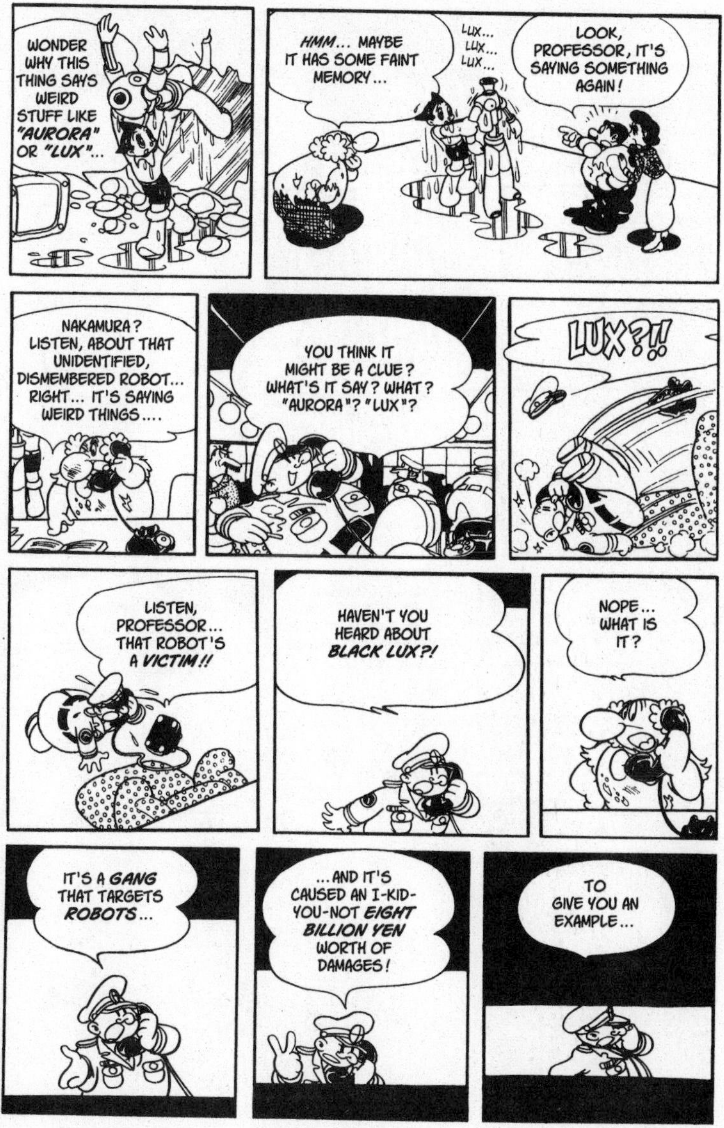
WONDER WHY THIS THING SAYS WEIRD STUFF LIKE "AURORA" OR "LUX"...
HMM... MAYBE IT HAS SOME FAINT MEMORY...
LUX... LUX... LUX...
LOOK, PROFESSOR, IT'S SAYING SOMETHING AGAIN!
NAKAMURA? LISTEN, ABOUT THAT UNIDENTIFIED, DISMEMBERED ROBOT... RIGHT... IT'S SAYING WEIRD THINGS....
YOU THINK IT MIGHT BE A CLUE? WHAT'S IT SAY? WHAT? "AURORA"? "LUX"?
LUX?!!
LISTEN, PROFESSOR... THAT ROBOT'S A VICTIM!!
HAVEN'T YOU HEARD ABOUT BLACK LUX?!
NOPE... WHAT IS IT?
IT'S A GANG THAT TARGETS ROBOTS...
...AND IT'S CAUSED AN I-KID-YOU-NOT EIGHT BILLION YEN WORTH OF DAMAGES!
TO GIVE YOU AN EXAMPLE...

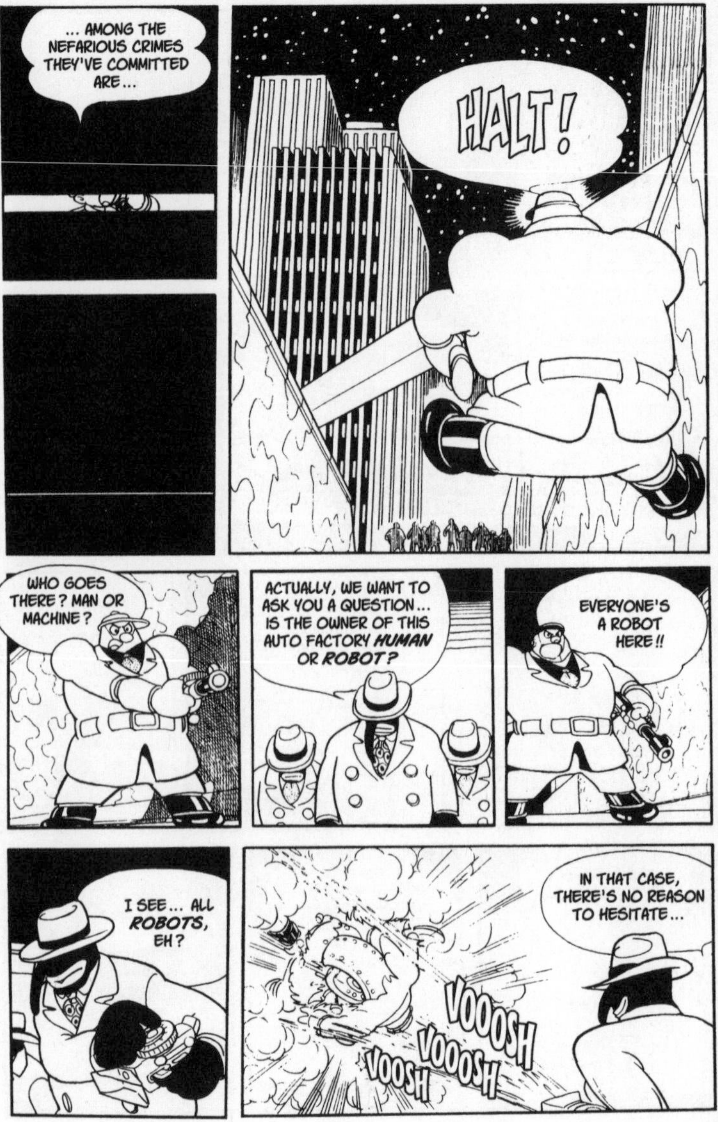
... AMONG THE NEFARIOUS CRIMES THEY'VE COMMITTED ARE...
HALT!
WHO GOES THERE? MAN OR MACHINE?
ACTUALLY, WE WANT TO ASK YOU A QUESTION... IS THE OWNER OF THIS AUTO FACTORY *HUMAN* OR *ROBOT?*
EVERYONE'S A ROBOT HERE!!
I SEE... ALL *ROBOTS,* EH?
IN THAT CASE, THERE'S NO REASON TO HESITATE...
VOOOSH
VOOOSH
VOOSH

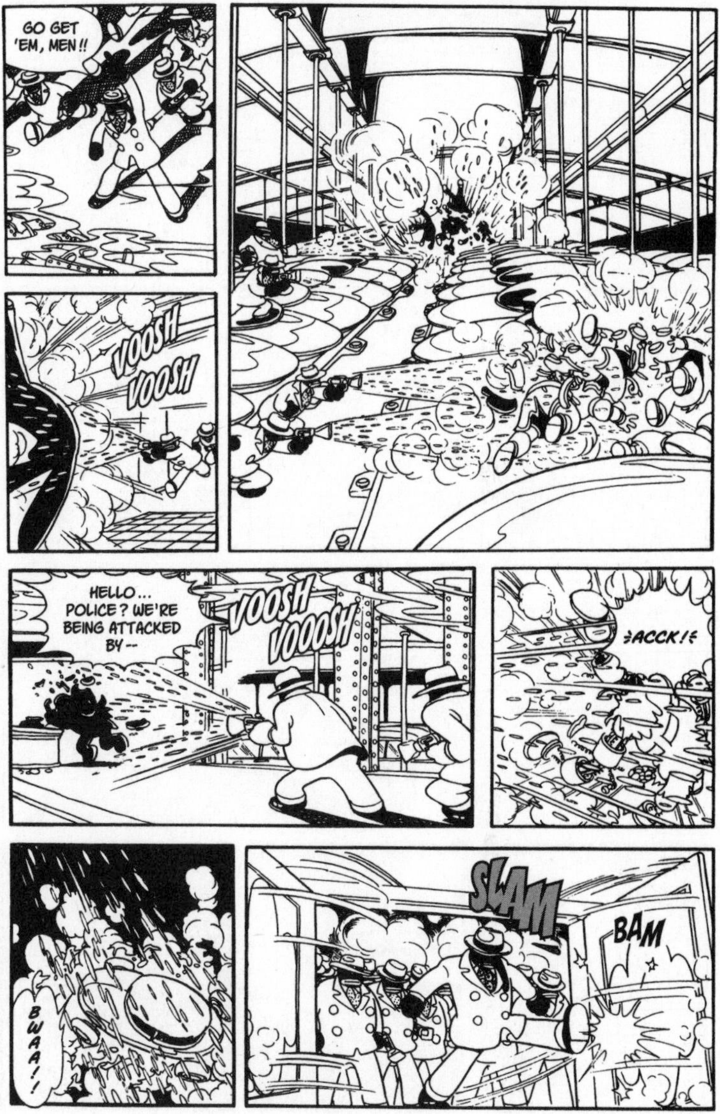
GO GET 'EM, MEN!!
VOOSH
VOOSH
HELLO... POLICE? WE'RE BEING ATTACKED BY--
VOOSH
VOOOSH
ACCK!
BWAAA!!
SLAM
BAM

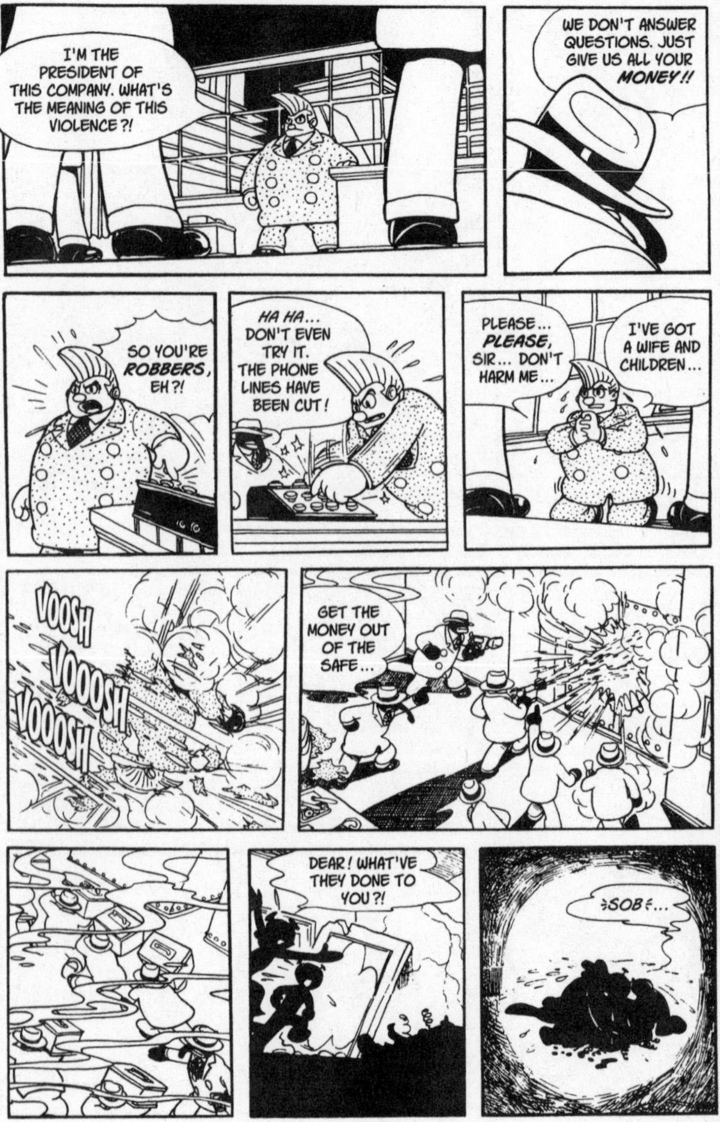
I'M THE PRESIDENT OF THIS COMPANY. WHAT'S THE MEANING OF THIS VIOLENCE?!
WE DON'T ANSWER QUESTIONS. JUST GIVE US ALL YOUR MONEY!!
SO YOU'RE ROBBERS, EH?!
HA HA... DON'T EVEN TRY IT. THE PHONE LINES HAVE BEEN CUT!
PLEASE... PLEASE, SIR... DON'T HARM ME...
I'VE GOT A WIFE AND CHILDREN...
VOOSH
VOOOSH
VOOOSH
GET THE MONEY OUT OF THE SAFE...
DEAR! WHAT'VE THEY DONE TO YOU?!
SOB...

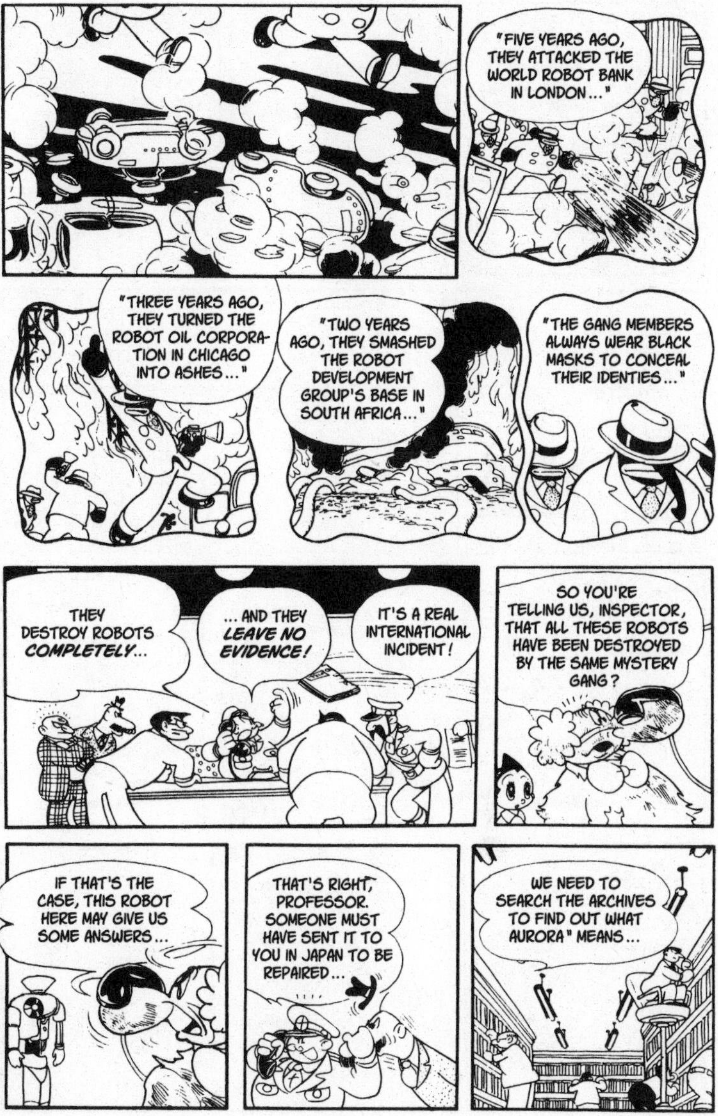
"FIVE YEARS AGO, THEY ATTACKED THE WORLD ROBOT BANK IN LONDON..."
"THREE YEARS AGO, THEY TURNED THE ROBOT OIL CORPORA-TION IN CHICAGO INTO ASHES..."
"TWO YEARS AGO, THEY SMASHED THE ROBOT DEVELOPMENT GROUP'S BASE IN SOUTH AFRICA..."
"THE GANG MEMBERS ALWAYS WEAR BLACK MASKS TO CONCEAL THEIR IDENTIES..."
THEY DESTROY ROBOTS *COMPLETELY*...
... AND THEY *LEAVE NO EVIDENCE!*
IT'S A REAL INTERNATIONAL INCIDENT!
SO YOU'RE TELLING US, INSPECTOR, THAT ALL THESE ROBOTS HAVE BEEN DESTROYED BY THE SAME MYSTERY GANG?
IF THAT'S THE CASE, THIS ROBOT HERE MAY GIVE US SOME ANSWERS...
THAT'S RIGHT, PROFESSOR. SOMEONE MUST HAVE SENT IT TO YOU IN JAPAN TO BE REPAIRED...
WE NEED TO SEARCH THE ARCHIVES TO FIND OUT WHAT AURORA" MEANS...

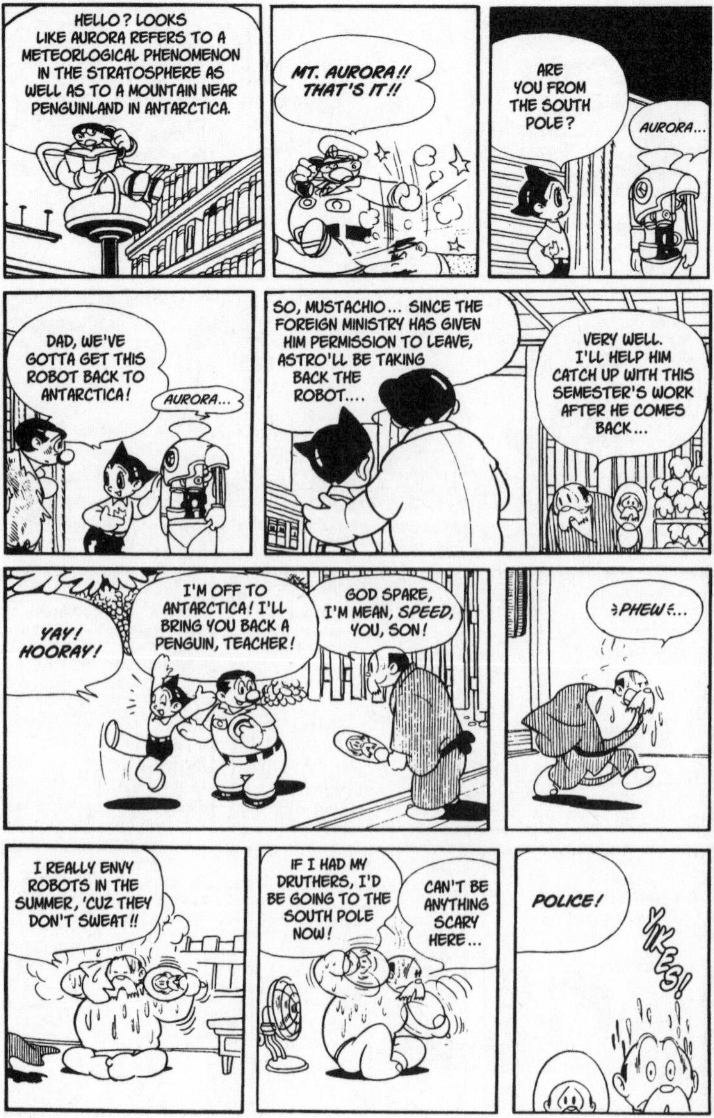
HELLO? LOOKS LIKE AURORA REFERS TO A METEORLOGICAL PHENOMENON IN THE STRATOSPHERE AS WELL AS TO A MOUNTAIN NEAR PENGUINLAND IN ANTARCTICA.
MT. AURORA!! THAT'S IT!!
ARE YOU FROM THE SOUTH POLE?
AURORA...
DAD, WE'VE GOTTA GET THIS ROBOT BACK TO ANTARCTICA!
AURORA...
SO, MUSTACHIO... SINCE THE FOREIGN MINISTRY HAS GIVEN HIM PERMISSION TO LEAVE, ASTRO'LL BE TAKING BACK THE ROBOT....
VERY WELL. I'LL HELP HIM CATCH UP WITH THIS SEMESTER'S WORK AFTER HE COMES BACK...
YAY! HOORAY!
I'M OFF TO ANTARCTICA! I'LL BRING YOU BACK A PENGUIN, TEACHER!
GOD SPARE, I'M MEAN, SPEED, YOU, SON!
PHEW...
I REALLY ENVY ROBOTS IN THE SUMMER, 'CUZ THEY DON'T SWEAT!!
IF I HAD MY DRUTHERS, I'D BE GOING TO THE SOUTH POLE NOW!
CAN'T BE ANYTHING SCARY HERE...
POLICE!
YIKES!

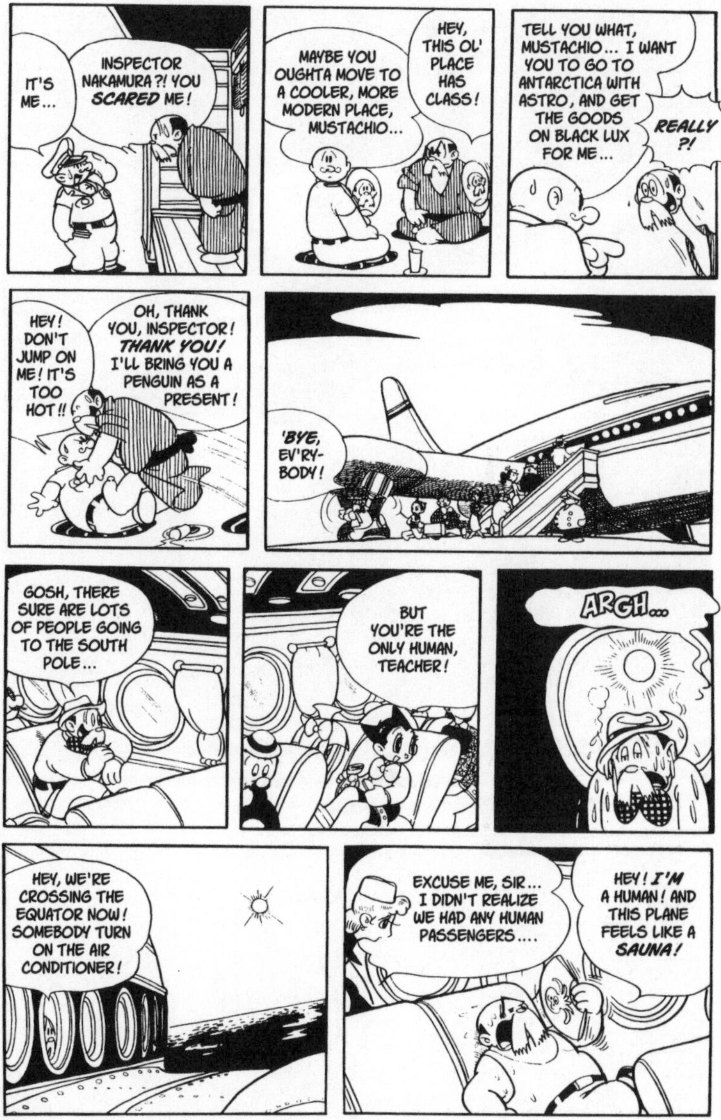
IT'S ME...
INSPECTOR NAKAMURA?! YOU SCARED ME!
MAYBE YOU OUGHTA MOVE TO A COOLER, MORE MODERN PLACE, MUSTACHIO...
HEY, THIS OL' PLACE HAS CLASS!
TELL YOU WHAT, MUSTACHIO... I WANT YOU TO GO TO ANTARCTICA WITH ASTRO, AND GET THE GOODS ON BLACK LUX FOR ME...
REALLY?!
HEY! DON'T JUMP ON ME! IT'S TOO HOT!!
OH, THANK YOU, INSPECTOR! THANK YOU! I'LL BRING YOU A PENGUIN AS A PRESENT!
'BYE, EV'RY-BODY!
GOSH, THERE SURE ARE LOTS OF PEOPLE GOING TO THE SOUTH POLE...
BUT YOU'RE THE ONLY HUMAN, TEACHER!
ARGH...
HEY, WE'RE CROSSING THE EQUATOR NOW! SOMEBODY TURN ON THE AIR CONDITIONER!
EXCUSE ME, SIR... I DIDN'T REALIZE WE HAD ANY HUMAN PASSENGERS....
HEY! I'M A HUMAN! AND THIS PLANE FEELS LIKE A SAUNA!

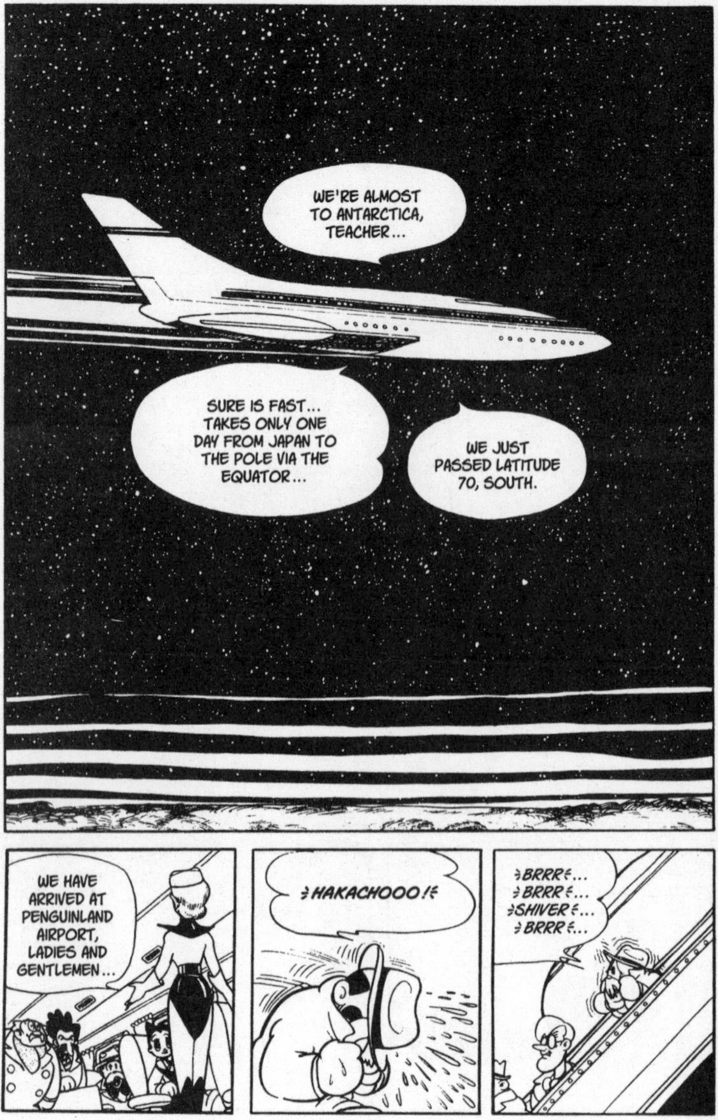
WE'RE ALMOST TO ANTARCTICA, TEACHER...
SURE IS FAST... TAKES ONLY ONE DAY FROM JAPAN TO THE POLE VIA THE EQUATOR...
WE JUST PASSED LATITUDE 70, SOUTH.
WE HAVE ARRIVED AT PENGUINLAND AIRPORT, LADIES AND GENTLEMEN...
HAKACHOOO!
BRRR... BRRR... SHIVER... BRRR...

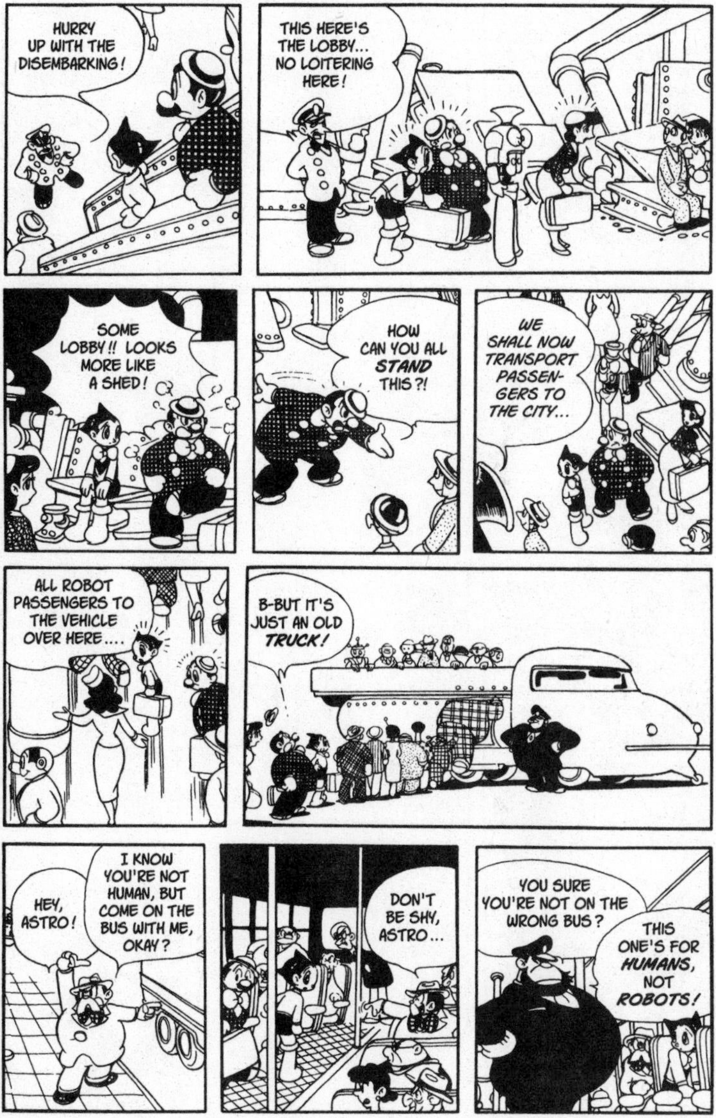
HURRY UP WITH THE DISEMBARKING!
THIS HERE'S THE LOBBY... NO LOITERING HERE!
SOME LOBBY!! LOOKS MORE LIKE A SHED!
HOW CAN YOU ALL *STAND* THIS?!
WE SHALL NOW TRANSPORT PASSEN-GERS TO THE CITY...
ALL ROBOT PASSENGERS TO THE VEHICLE OVER HERE....
B-BUT IT'S JUST AN OLD *TRUCK!*
HEY, ASTRO!
I KNOW YOU'RE NOT HUMAN, BUT COME ON THE BUS WITH ME, OKAY?
DON'T BE SHY, ASTRO...
YOU SURE YOU'RE NOT ON THE WRONG BUS?
THIS ONE'S FOR *HUMANS*, NOT *ROBOTS!*

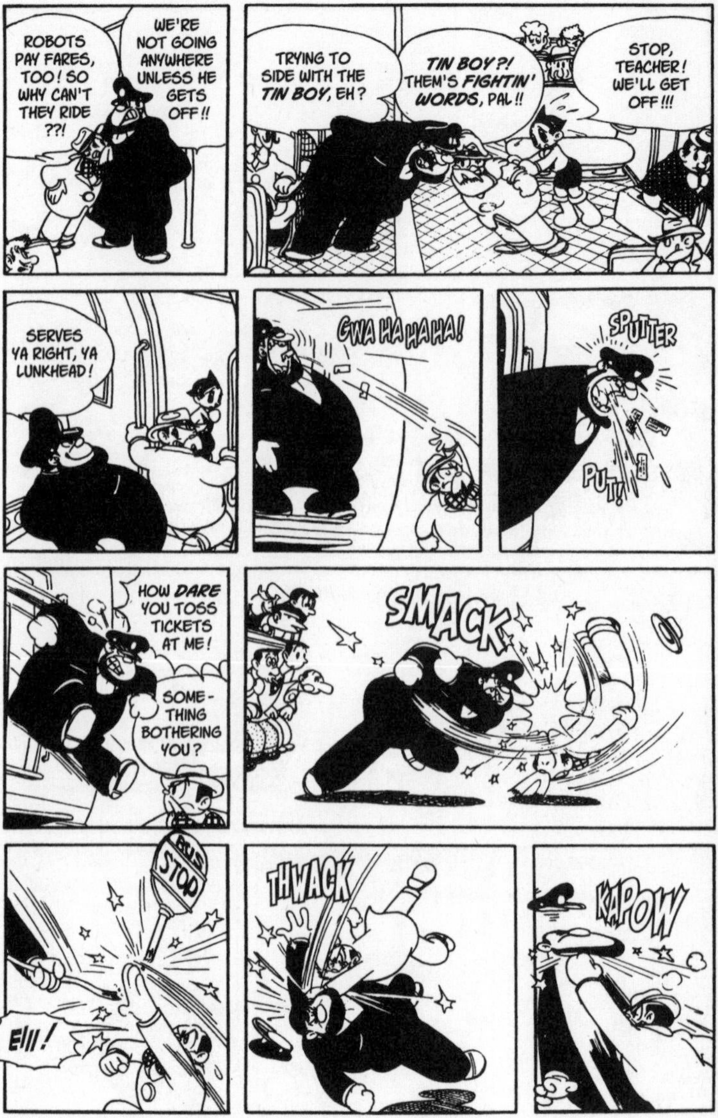
ROBOTS PAY FARES, TOO! SO WHY CAN'T THEY RIDE ??!
WE'RE NOT GOING ANYWHERE UNLESS HE GETS OFF!!
TRYING TO SIDE WITH THE *TIN BOY*, EH?
TIN BOY?! THEM'S *FIGHTIN' WORDS*, PAL!!
STOP, TEACHER! WE'LL GET OFF!!!
SERVES YA RIGHT, YA LUNKHEAD!
GWA HA HA HA!
SPUTTER
PUT!
HOW *DARE* YOU TOSS TICKETS AT ME!
SOME-THING BOTHERING YOU?
SMACK
BUS STOP
EIII!
THWACK
KAPOW

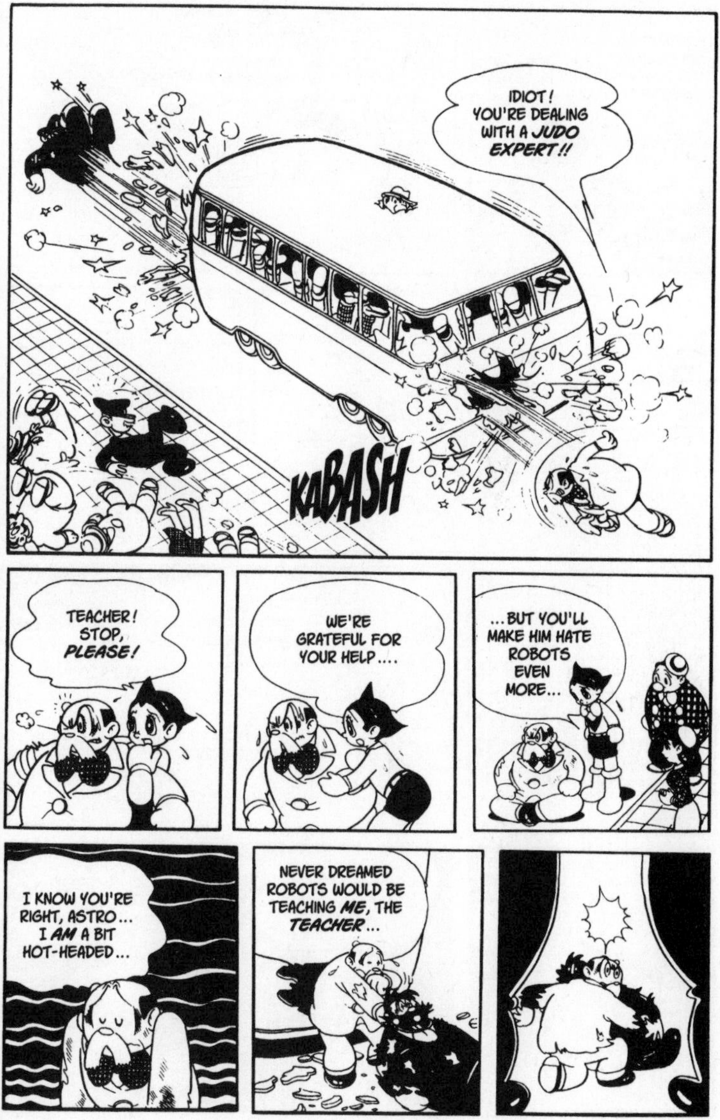
IDIOT! YOU'RE DEALING WITH A JUDO EXPERT!!
KABASH
TEACHER! STOP, PLEASE!
WE'RE GRATEFUL FOR YOUR HELP....
...BUT YOU'LL MAKE HIM HATE ROBOTS EVEN MORE...
I KNOW YOU'RE RIGHT, ASTRO... I AM A BIT HOT-HEADED...
NEVER DREAMED ROBOTS WOULD BE TEACHING ME, THE TEACHER...

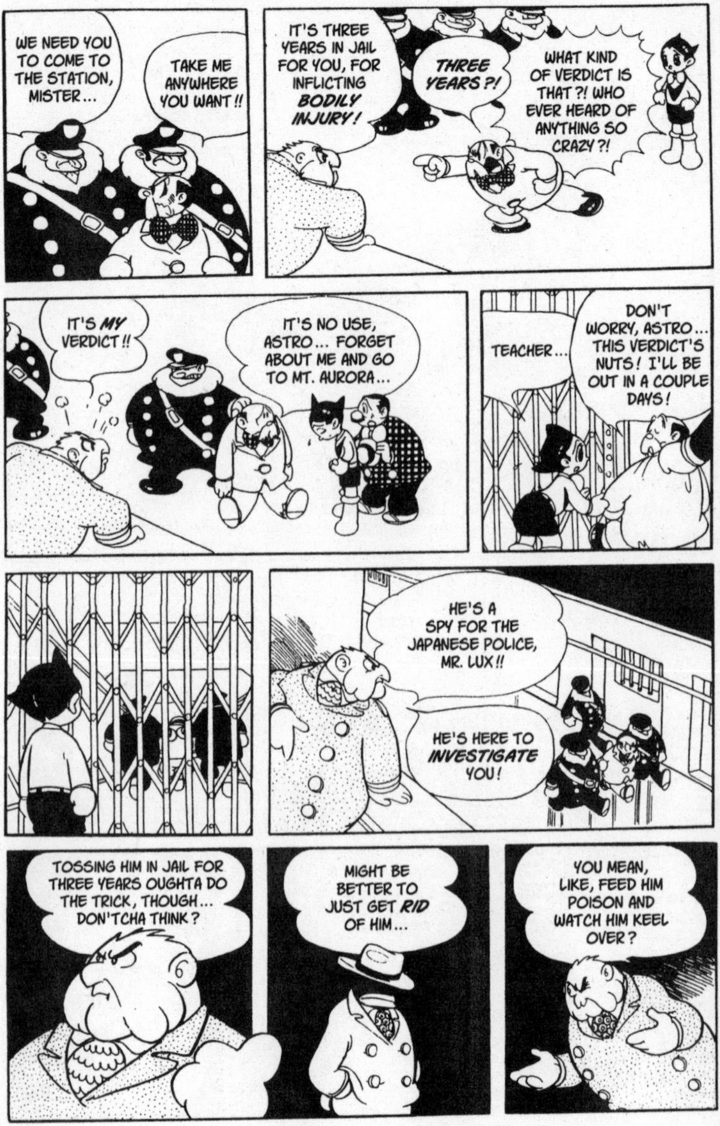
WE NEED YOU TO COME TO THE STATION, MISTER...
TAKE ME ANYWHERE YOU WANT!!
IT'S THREE YEARS IN JAIL FOR YOU, FOR INFLICTING BODILY INJURY!
THREE YEARS?!
WHAT KIND OF VERDICT IS THAT?! WHO EVER HEARD OF ANYTHING SO CRAZY?!
IT'S MY VERDICT!!
IT'S NO USE, ASTRO... FORGET ABOUT ME AND GO TO MT. AURORA...
TEACHER...
DON'T WORRY, ASTRO... THIS VERDICT'S NUTS! I'LL BE OUT IN A COUPLE DAYS!
HE'S A SPY FOR THE JAPANESE POLICE, MR. LUX!!
HE'S HERE TO INVESTIGATE YOU!
TOSSING HIM IN JAIL FOR THREE YEARS OUGHTA DO THE TRICK, THOUGH... DON'TCHA THINK?
MIGHT BE BETTER TO JUST GET RID OF HIM...
YOU MEAN, LIKE, FEED HIM POISON AND WATCH HIM KEEL OVER?

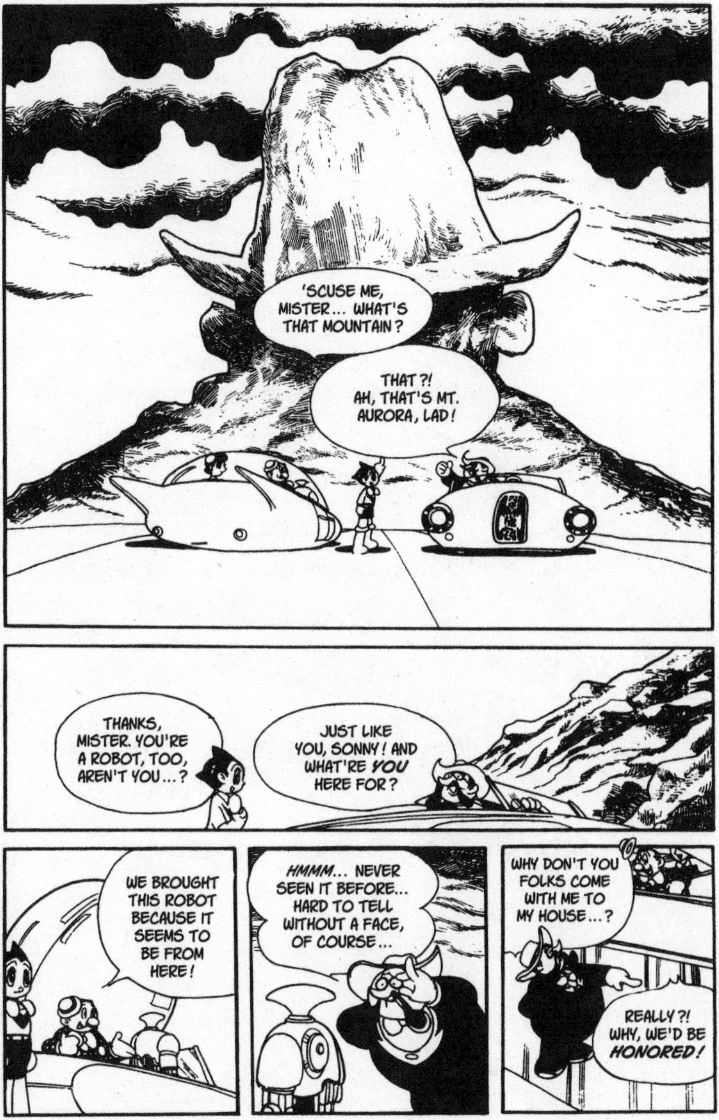
'SCUSE ME, MISTER... WHAT'S THAT MOUNTAIN?
THAT?! AH, THAT'S MT. AURORA, LAD!
THANKS, MISTER. YOU'RE A ROBOT, TOO, AREN'T YOU...?
JUST LIKE YOU, SONNY! AND WHAT'RE *YOU* HERE FOR?
WE BROUGHT THIS ROBOT BECAUSE IT SEEMS TO BE FROM HERE!
HMMM... NEVER SEEN IT BEFORE... HARD TO TELL WITHOUT A FACE, OF COURSE...
WHY DON'T YOU FOLKS COME WITH ME TO MY HOUSE...?
REALLY?! WHY, WE'D BE ***HONORED!***

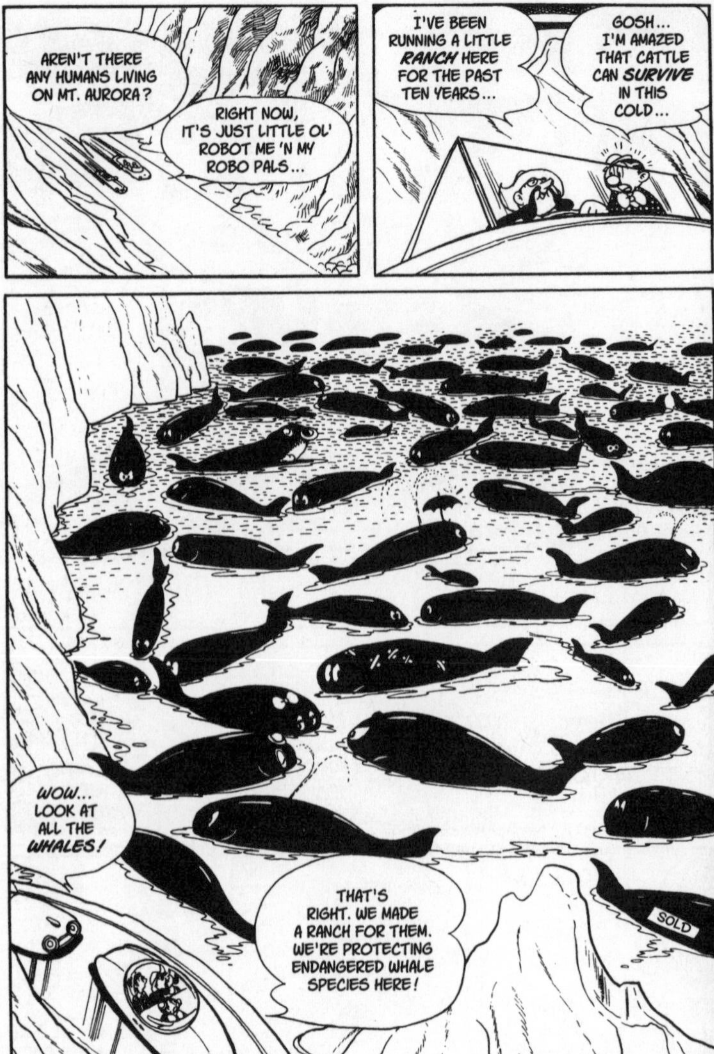
AREN'T THERE ANY HUMANS LIVING ON MT. AURORA?
RIGHT NOW, IT'S JUST LITTLE OL' ROBOT ME 'N MY ROBO PALS...
I'VE BEEN RUNNING A LITTLE *RANCH* HERE FOR THE PAST TEN YEARS...
GOSH... I'M AMAZED THAT CATTLE CAN *SURVIVE* IN THIS COLD...
WOW... LOOK AT ALL THE *WHALES!*
THAT'S RIGHT. WE MADE A RANCH FOR THEM. WE'RE PROTECTING ENDANGERED WHALE SPECIES HERE!
SOLD

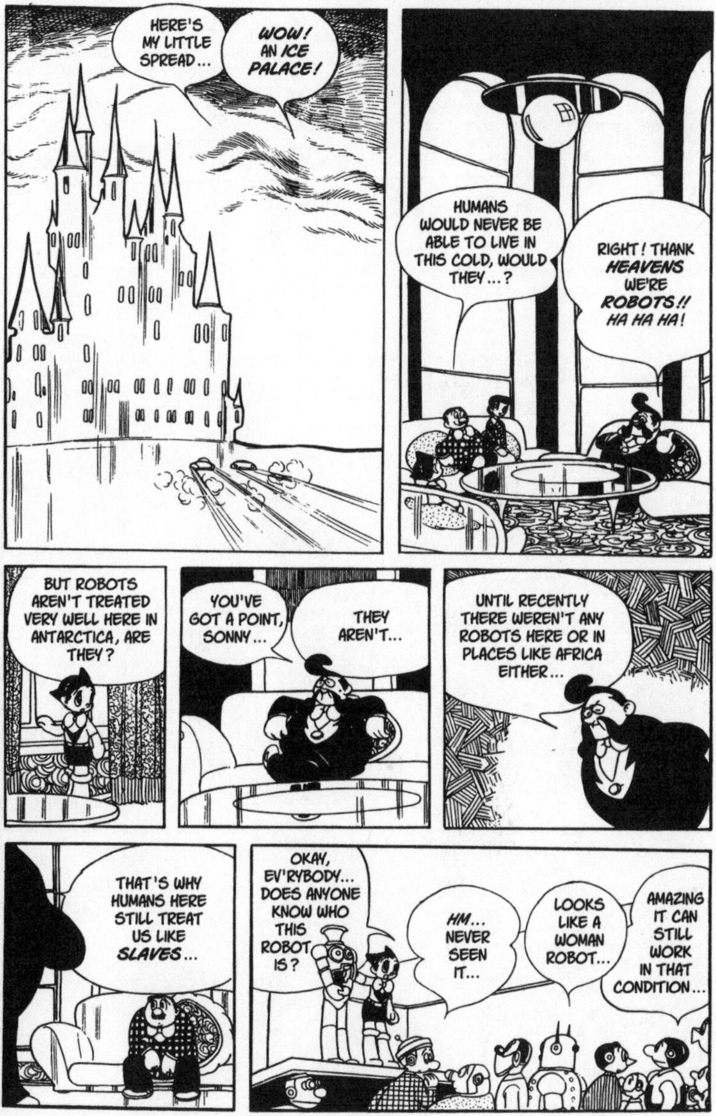

HERE'S MY LITTLE SPREAD...
WOW! AN ICE PALACE!
HUMANS WOULD NEVER BE ABLE TO LIVE IN THIS COLD, WOULD THEY...?
RIGHT! THANK HEAVENS WE'RE ROBOTS!! HA HA HA!
BUT ROBOTS AREN'T TREATED VERY WELL HERE IN ANTARCTICA, ARE THEY?
YOU'VE GOT A POINT, SONNY...
THEY AREN'T...
UNTIL RECENTLY THERE WEREN'T ANY ROBOTS HERE OR IN PLACES LIKE AFRICA EITHER...
THAT'S WHY HUMANS HERE STILL TREAT US LIKE SLAVES...
OKAY, EV'RYBODY... DOES ANYONE KNOW WHO THIS ROBOT IS?
HM... NEVER SEEN IT...
LOOKS LIKE A WOMAN ROBOT...
AMAZING IT CAN STILL WORK IN THAT CONDITION...

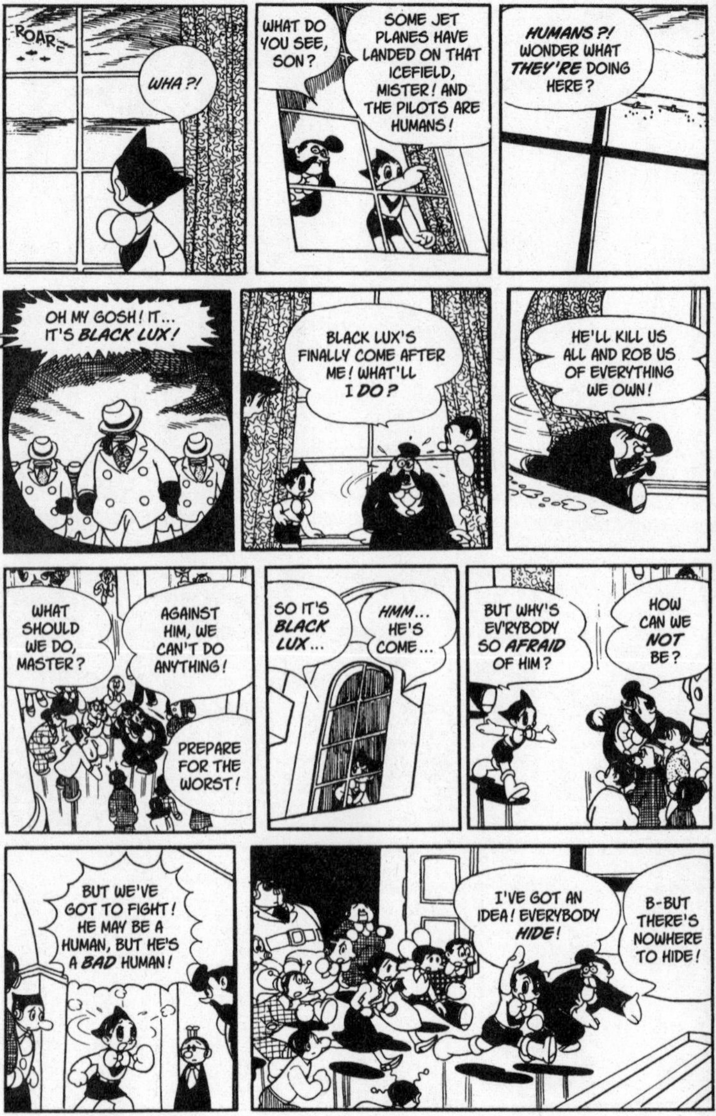
ROAR
WHA?!
WHAT DO YOU SEE, SON?
SOME JET PLANES HAVE LANDED ON THAT ICEFIELD, MISTER! AND THE PILOTS ARE HUMANS!
HUMANS?! WONDER WHAT THEY'RE DOING HERE?
OH MY GOSH! IT... IT'S BLACK LUX!
BLACK LUX'S FINALLY COME AFTER ME! WHAT'LL I DO?
HE'LL KILL US ALL AND ROB US OF EVERYTHING WE OWN!
WHAT SHOULD WE DO, MASTER?
AGAINST HIM, WE CAN'T DO ANYTHING!
PREPARE FOR THE WORST!
SO IT'S BLACK LUX...
HMM... HE'S COME...
BUT WHY'S EV'RYBODY SO AFRAID OF HIM?
HOW CAN WE NOT BE?
BUT WE'VE GOT TO FIGHT! HE MAY BE A HUMAN, BUT HE'S A BAD HUMAN!
I'VE GOT AN IDEA! EVERYBODY HIDE!
B-BUT THERE'S NOWHERE TO HIDE!

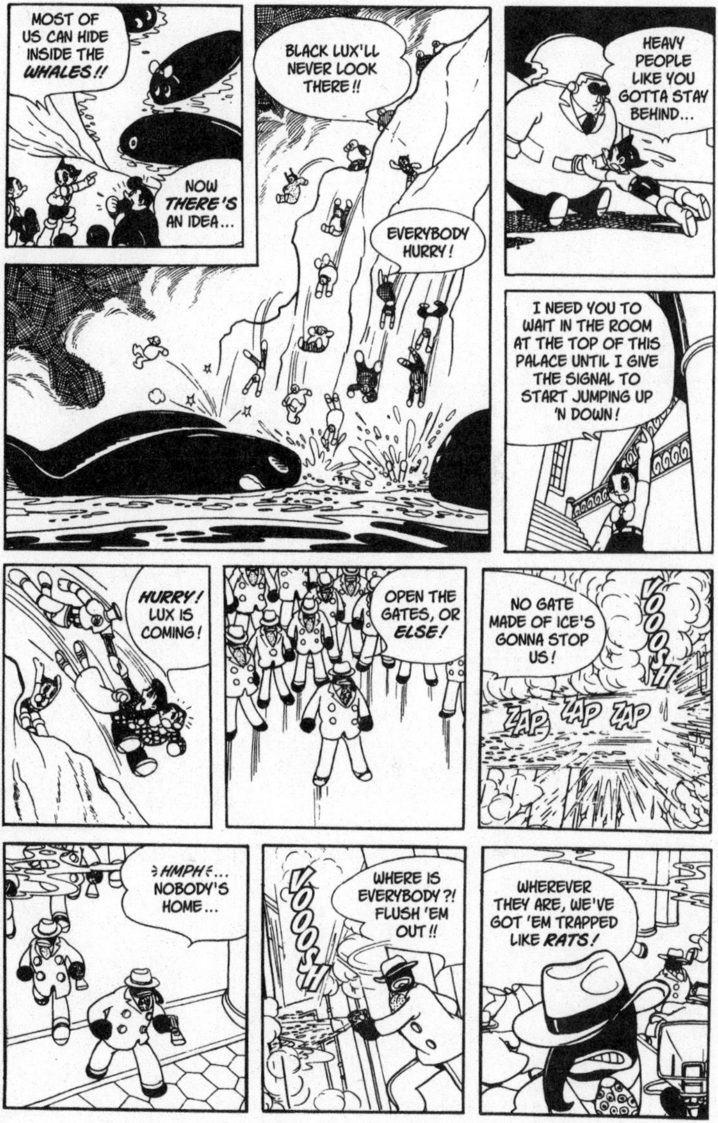
MOST OF US CAN HIDE INSIDE THE WHALES!!
NOW THERE'S AN IDEA...
BLACK LUX'LL NEVER LOOK THERE!!
EVERYBODY HURRY!
HEAVY PEOPLE LIKE YOU GOTTA STAY BEHIND...
I NEED YOU TO WAIT IN THE ROOM AT THE TOP OF THIS PALACE UNTIL I GIVE THE SIGNAL TO START JUMPING UP 'N DOWN!
HURRY! LUX IS COMING!
OPEN THE GATES, OR ELSE!
NO GATE MADE OF ICE'S GONNA STOP US!
VOOOSH
ZAP ZAP ZAP
HMPH... NOBODY'S HOME...
VOOOSH
WHERE IS EVERYBODY?! FLUSH 'EM OUT!!
WHEREVER THEY ARE, WE'VE GOT 'EM TRAPPED LIKE RATS!

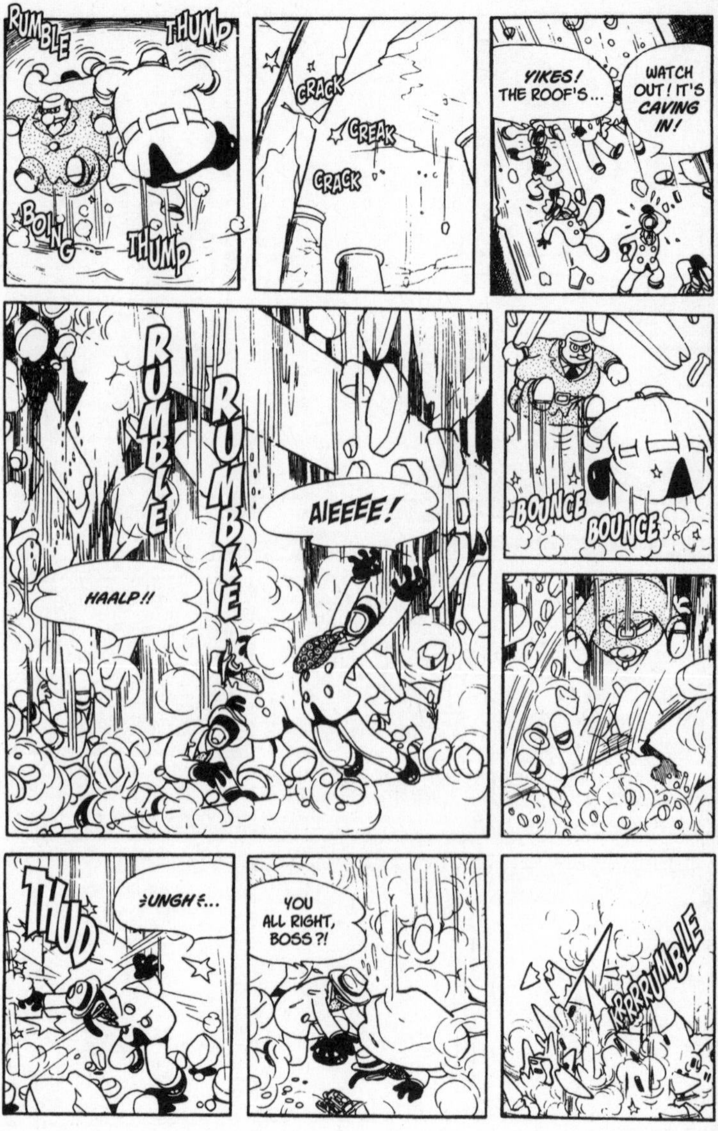
RUMBLE
THUMP
BOING
THUMP
CRACK
CREAK
CRACK
YIKES! THE ROOF'S...
WATCH OUT! IT'S CAVING IN!
RUMBLE
RUMBLE
AIEEEE!
HAALP!!
BOUNCE
BOUNCE
THUD
UNGH...
YOU ALL RIGHT, BOSS?!
RRRRUMBLE

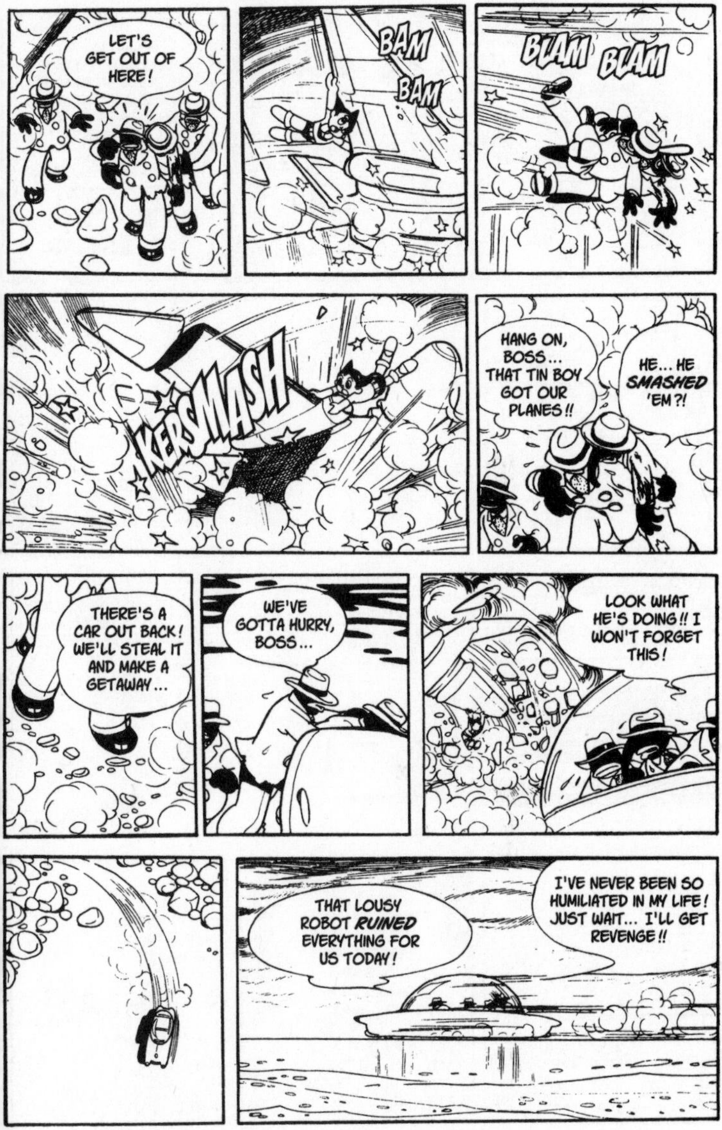
LET'S GET OUT OF HERE!
BAM
BAM
BLAM BLAM
KERSMASH
HANG ON, BOSS... THAT TIN BOY GOT OUR PLANES!!
HE... HE SMASHED 'EM?!
THERE'S A CAR OUT BACK! WE'LL STEAL IT AND MAKE A GETAWAY...
WE'VE GOTTA HURRY, BOSS...
LOOK WHAT HE'S DOING!! I WON'T FORGET THIS!
THAT LOUSY ROBOT RUINED EVERYTHING FOR US TODAY!
I'VE NEVER BEEN SO HUMILIATED IN MY LIFE! JUST WAIT... I'LL GET REVENGE!!

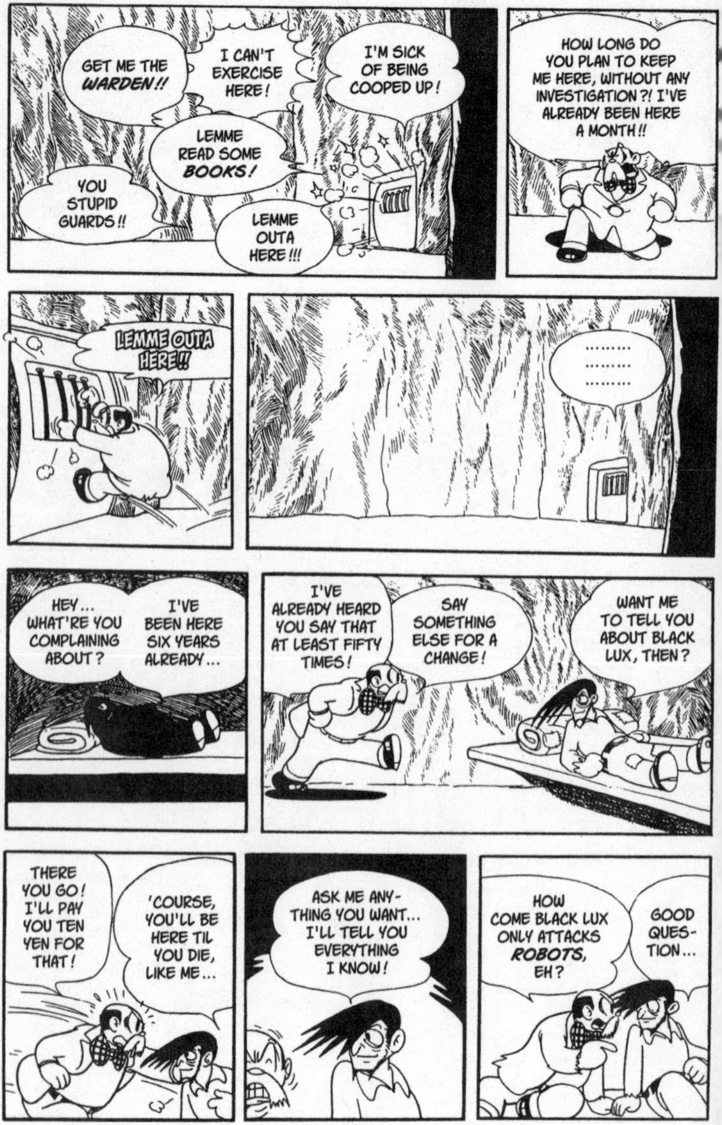
GET ME THE WARDEN!!
I CAN'T EXERCISE HERE!
I'M SICK OF BEING COOPED UP!
LEMME READ SOME BOOKS!
YOU STUPID GUARDS!!
LEMME OUTA HERE!!!
HOW LONG DO YOU PLAN TO KEEP ME HERE, WITHOUT ANY INVESTIGATION?! I'VE ALREADY BEEN HERE A MONTH!!
LEMME OUTA HERE!!
....
....
....
HEY... WHAT'RE YOU COMPLAINING ABOUT?
I'VE BEEN HERE SIX YEARS ALREADY...
I'VE ALREADY HEARD YOU SAY THAT AT LEAST FIFTY TIMES!
SAY SOMETHING ELSE FOR A CHANGE!
WANT ME TO TELL YOU ABOUT BLACK LUX, THEN?
THERE YOU GO! I'LL PAY YOU TEN YEN FOR THAT!
'COURSE, YOU'LL BE HERE TIL YOU DIE, LIKE ME...
ASK ME ANY-THING YOU WANT... I'LL TELL YOU EVERYTHING I KNOW!
HOW COME BLACK LUX ONLY ATTACKS ROBOTS, EH?
GOOD QUES-TION...

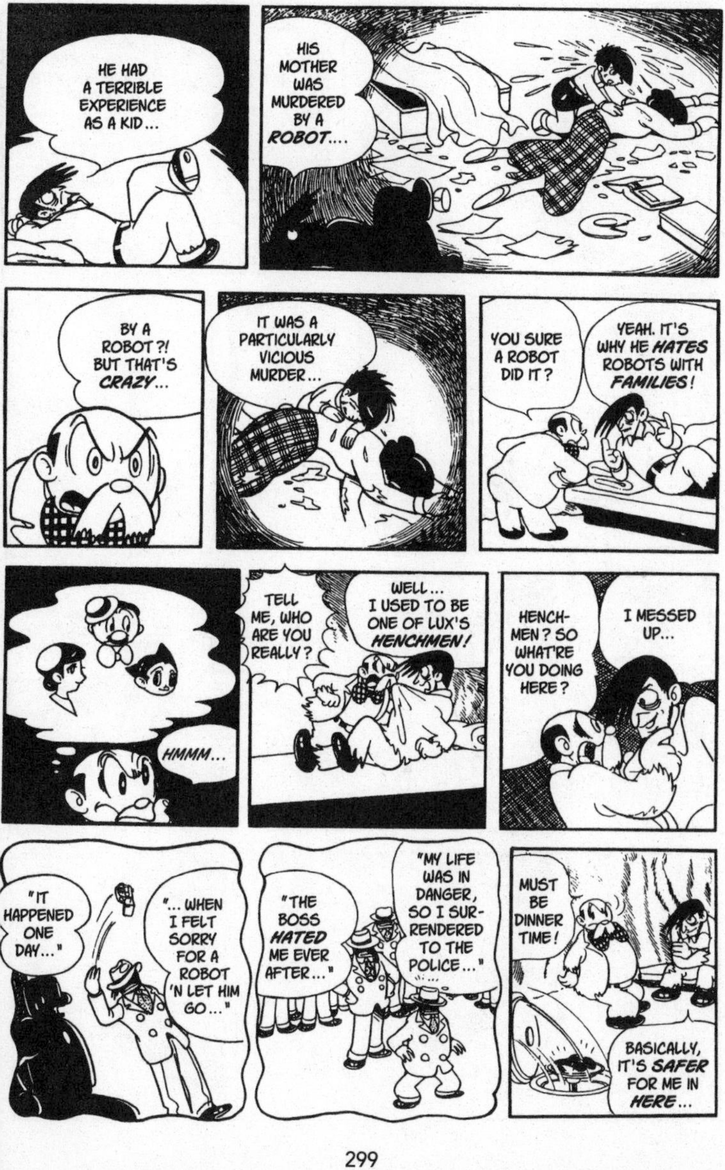
HE HAD A TERRIBLE EXPERIENCE AS A KID...
HIS MOTHER WAS MURDERED BY A ROBOT....
BY A ROBOT?! BUT THAT'S CRAZY...
IT WAS A PARTICULARLY VICIOUS MURDER...
YOU SURE A ROBOT DID IT?
YEAH. IT'S WHY HE HATES ROBOTS WITH FAMILIES!
HMMM...
TELL ME, WHO ARE YOU REALLY?
WELL... I USED TO BE ONE OF LUX'S HENCHMEN!
HENCH-MEN? SO WHAT'RE YOU DOING HERE?
I MESSED UP...
"IT HAPPENED ONE DAY..."
"...WHEN I FELT SORRY FOR A ROBOT 'N LET HIM GO..."
"THE BOSS HATED ME EVER AFTER..."
"MY LIFE WAS IN DANGER, SO I SUR-RENDERED TO THE POLICE..."
MUST BE DINNER TIME!
BASICALLY, IT'S SAFER FOR ME IN HERE...

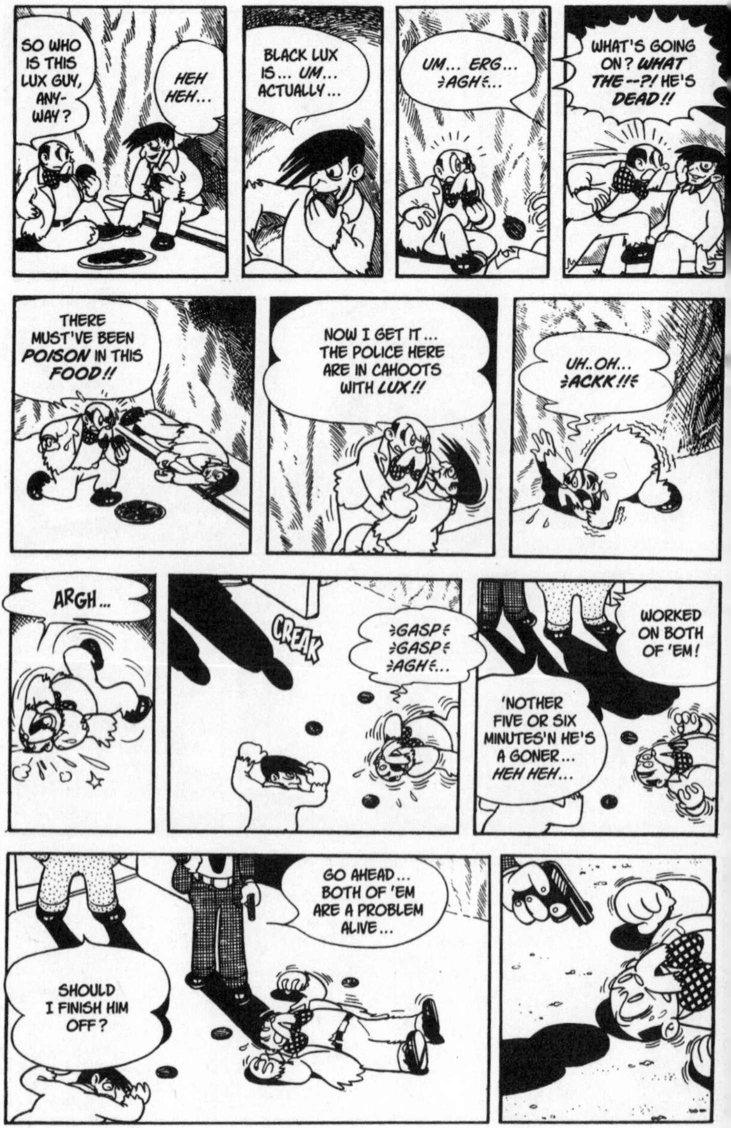
SO WHO IS THIS LUX GUY, ANYWAY?
HEH HEH...
BLACK LUX IS... UM... ACTUALLY...
UM... ERG... AGH...
WHAT'S GOING ON? WHAT THE--?! HE'S DEAD!!
THERE MUST'VE BEEN POISON IN THIS FOOD!!
NOW I GET IT... THE POLICE HERE ARE IN CAHOOTS WITH LUX!!
UH..OH... ACKK!!
ARGH...
CREAK
GASP GASP AGH...
WORKED ON BOTH OF 'EM!
'NOTHER FIVE OR SIX MINUTES'N HE'S A GONER... HEH HEH...
SHOULD I FINISH HIM OFF?
GO AHEAD... BOTH OF 'EM ARE A PROBLEM ALIVE...

AIEEE!

BLAM

HEH HEH! YOU FELL FOR MY LITTLE ACT, 'N THE TABLES'RE TURNED NOW, GUYS!!

IMAGINE, EVEN THE CHIEF OF POLICE ACTING THIS WAY...

SO WHAT *WAS* THE IDEA OF TRYING TO POISON ME, EH?

SORRY, PAL...

...BUT WE HAD OUR *REASONS*....

WELL, I WANNA *KNOW* THE REASONS!!

〈HMPH〉... I JUST DON'T GET IT...

HAVEN'T YOU SEARCHED MY PAPERS ENOUGH, ALREADY?!

COME TO THINK OF IT... THERE'S *ONE* PLACE I STILL HAVEN'T SEARCHED YET...

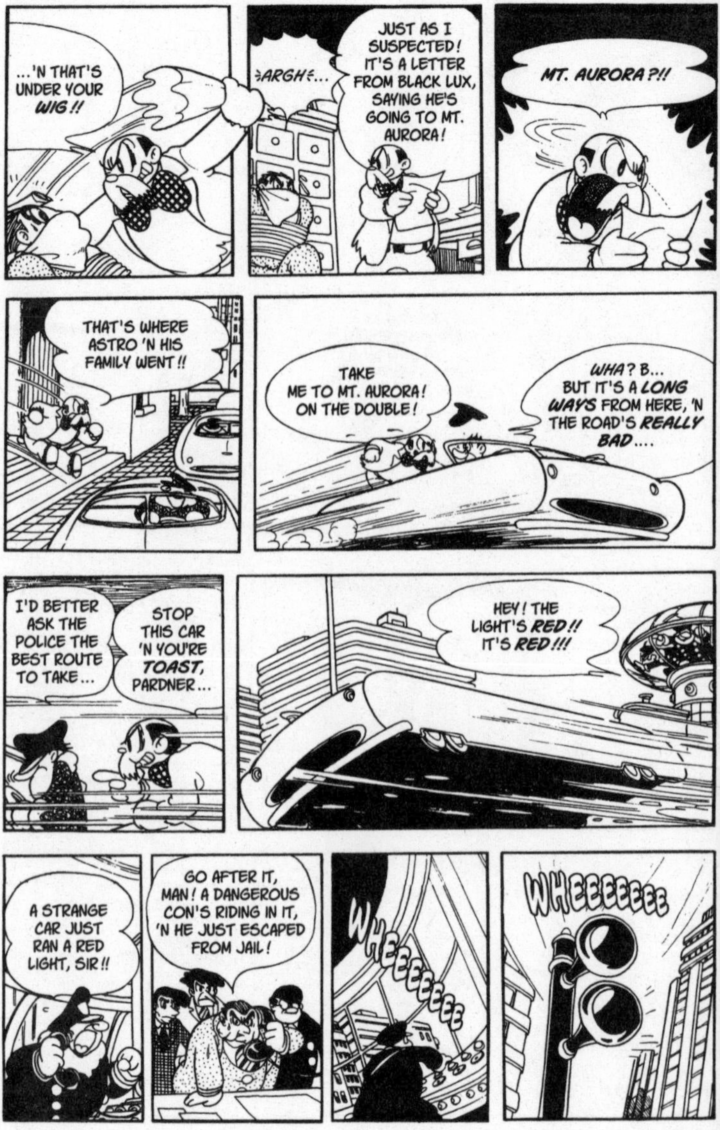
...'N THAT'S UNDER YOUR WIG!!
≯ARGH≮...
JUST AS I SUSPECTED! IT'S A LETTER FROM BLACK LUX, SAYING HE'S GOING TO MT. AURORA!
MT. AURORA?!!
THAT'S WHERE ASTRO 'N HIS FAMILY WENT!!
TAKE ME TO MT. AURORA! ON THE DOUBLE!
WHA? B... BUT IT'S A LONG WAYS FROM HERE, 'N THE ROAD'S REALLY BAD....
I'D BETTER ASK THE POLICE THE BEST ROUTE TO TAKE...
STOP THIS CAR 'N YOU'RE TOAST, PARDNER...
HEY! THE LIGHT'S RED!! IT'S RED!!!
A STRANGE CAR JUST RAN A RED LIGHT, SIR!!
GO AFTER IT, MAN! A DANGEROUS CON'S RIDING IN IT, 'N HE JUST ESCAPED FROM JAIL!
WHEEEEEEEE
WHEEEEEEEE

THE CAR'S HEADED SOUTH, OUTSIDE THE CITY...

WHEEEE

ƒARGH!ƒ WHY'D PENGUINS HAVE TO GET IN MY WAY?!

CAN'T THEY JUST LET US PASS?

I KNOW YOU'RE SHORT-TEMPERED, MISTER...

...BUT YOU'RE AN ALRIGHT TYPE....

'COURSE I AM! I'M A TRUE-BLUE TOKYO-ITE!

YOU'RE JAPANESE? WHAT'S A JAPANESE ESCAPED CON DOING HERE?

WHO'RE YOU CALLING AN ESCAPED CON? WATCH YOUR LANGUAGE, PAL!

ROAR

303

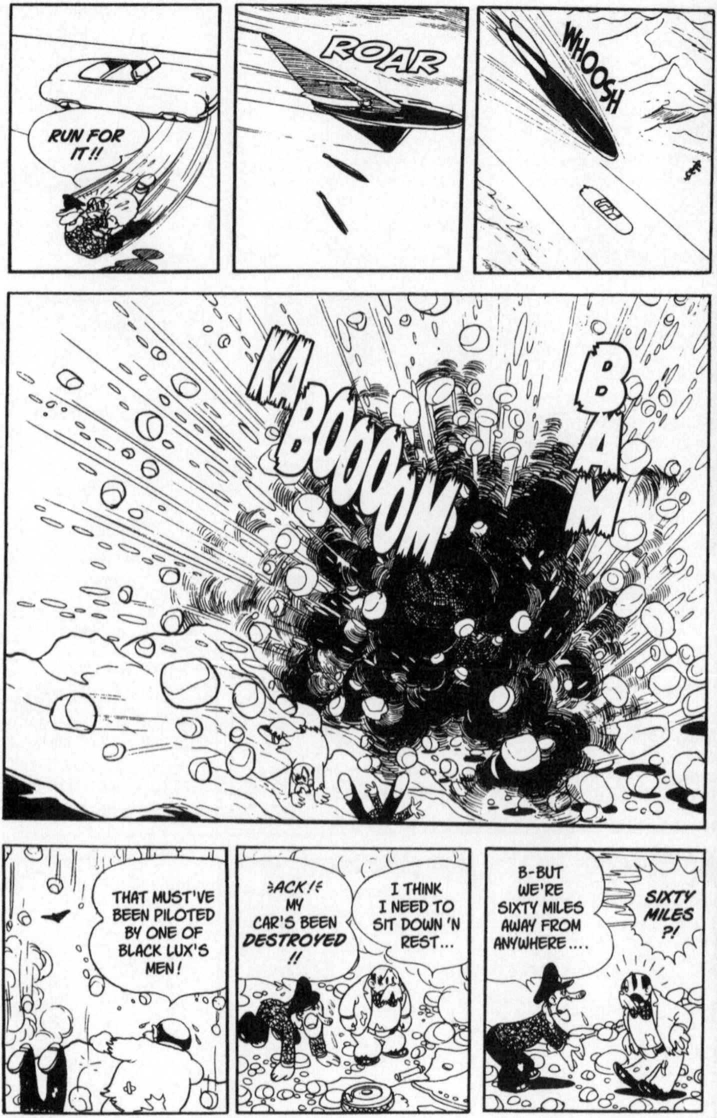

RUN FOR IT!!
ROAR
WHOOSH
KA BOOOOM
BAM
THAT MUST'VE BEEN PILOTED BY ONE OF BLACK LUX'S MEN!
ACK! MY CAR'S BEEN DESTROYED!!
I THINK I NEED TO SIT DOWN 'N REST...
B-BUT WE'RE SIXTY MILES AWAY FROM ANYWHERE....
SIXTY MILES?!

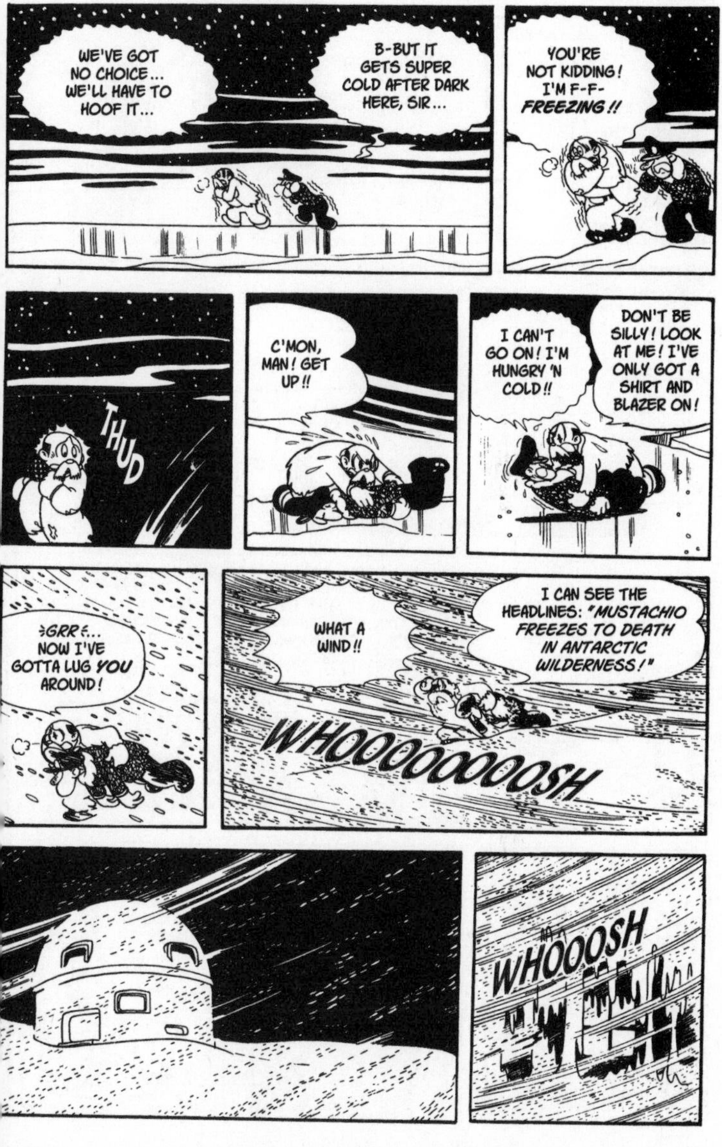
WE'VE GOT NO CHOICE... WE'LL HAVE TO HOOF IT...
B-BUT IT GETS SUPER COLD AFTER DARK HERE, SIR...
YOU'RE NOT KIDDING! I'M F-F-FREEZING!!
THUD
C'MON, MAN! GET UP!!
I CAN'T GO ON! I'M HUNGRY 'N COLD!!
DON'T BE SILLY! LOOK AT ME! I'VE ONLY GOT A SHIRT AND BLAZER ON!
GRR... NOW I'VE GOTTA LUG YOU AROUND!
WHAT A WIND!!
I CAN SEE THE HEADLINES: "MUSTACHIO FREEZES TO DEATH IN ANTARCTIC WILDERNESS!"
WHOOOOOOOOOSH
WHOOOSH

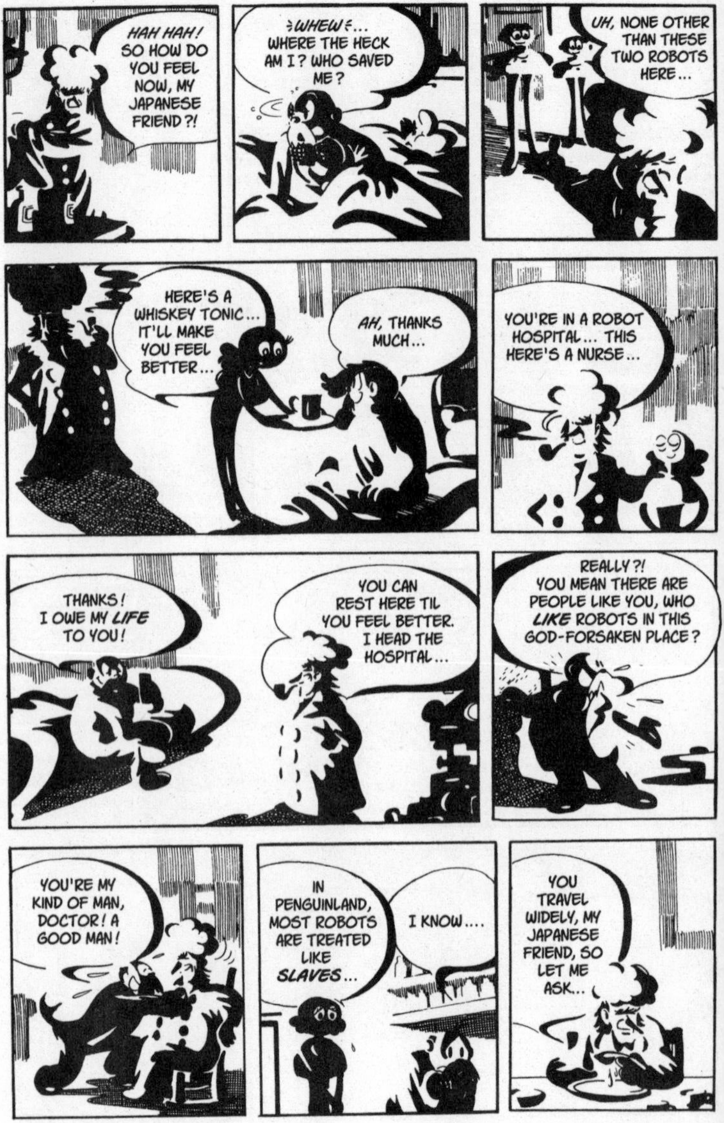
HAH HAH! SO HOW DO YOU FEEL NOW, MY JAPANESE FRIEND?!
≑WHEW≑... WHERE THE HECK AM I? WHO SAVED ME?
UH, NONE OTHER THAN THESE TWO ROBOTS HERE...
HERE'S A WHISKEY TONIC... IT'LL MAKE YOU FEEL BETTER...
AH, THANKS MUCH...
YOU'RE IN A ROBOT HOSPITAL... THIS HERE'S A NURSE...
THANKS! I OWE MY LIFE TO YOU!
YOU CAN REST HERE TIL YOU FEEL BETTER. I HEAD THE HOSPITAL...
REALLY?! YOU MEAN THERE ARE PEOPLE LIKE YOU, WHO LIKE ROBOTS IN THIS GOD-FORSAKEN PLACE?
YOU'RE MY KIND OF MAN, DOCTOR! A GOOD MAN!
IN PENGUINLAND, MOST ROBOTS ARE TREATED LIKE SLAVES...
I KNOW....
YOU TRAVEL WIDELY, MY JAPANESE FRIEND, SO LET ME ASK...

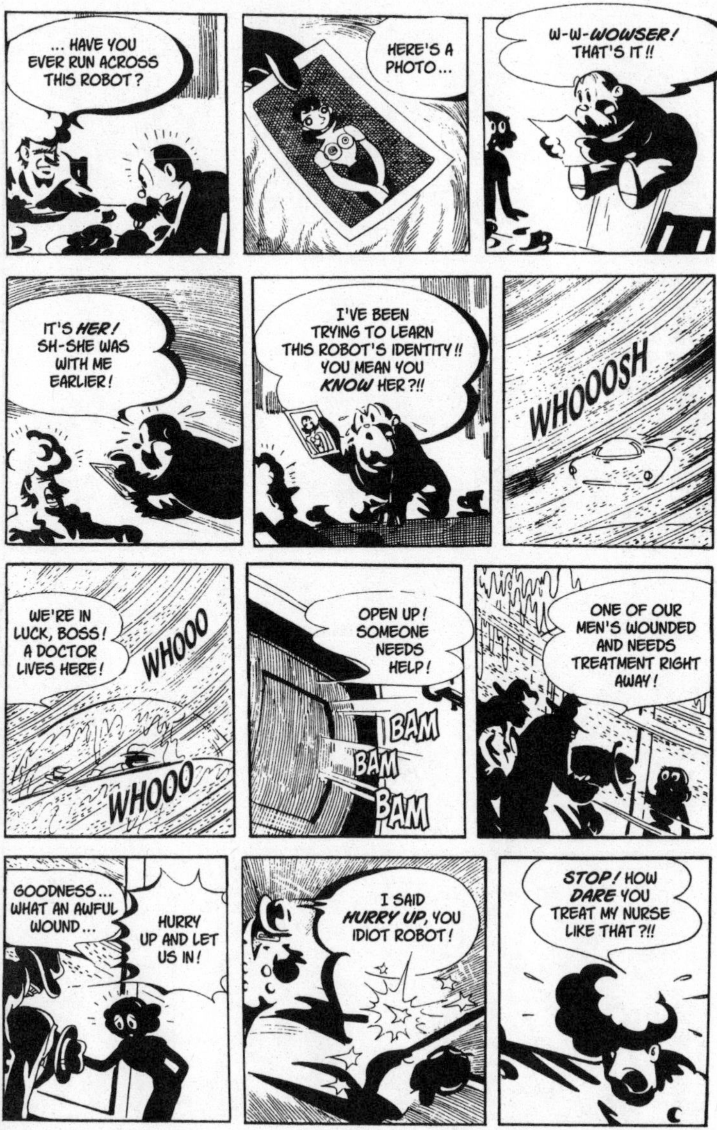
... HAVE YOU EVER RUN ACROSS THIS ROBOT?
HERE'S A PHOTO...
W-W-WOWSER! THAT'S IT!!
IT'S HER! SH-SHE WAS WITH ME EARLIER!
I'VE BEEN TRYING TO LEARN THIS ROBOT'S IDENTITY!! YOU MEAN YOU KNOW HER?!!
WHOOOSH
WE'RE IN LUCK, BOSS! A DOCTOR LIVES HERE!
WHOOO
WHOOO
OPEN UP! SOMEONE NEEDS HELP!
BAM
BAM
BAM
ONE OF OUR MEN'S WOUNDED AND NEEDS TREATMENT RIGHT AWAY!
GOODNESS... WHAT AN AWFUL WOUND...
HURRY UP AND LET US IN!
I SAID HURRY UP, YOU IDIOT ROBOT!
STOP! HOW DARE YOU TREAT MY NURSE LIKE THAT?!!

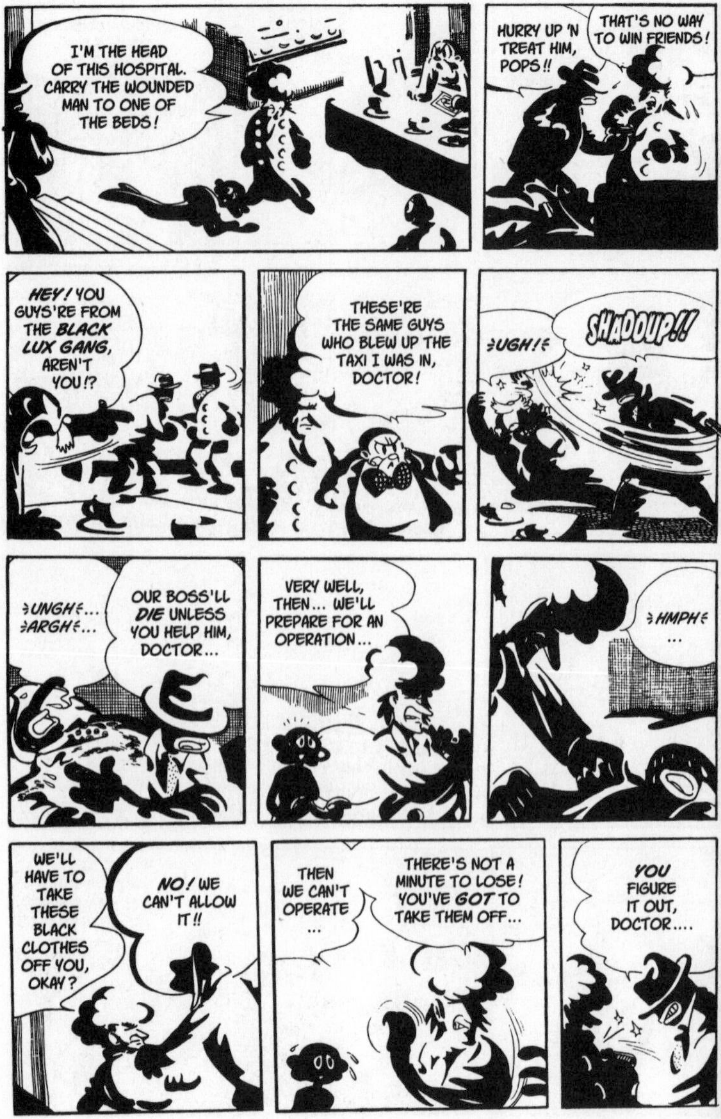
I'M THE HEAD OF THIS HOSPITAL. CARRY THE WOUNDED MAN TO ONE OF THE BEDS!
HURRY UP 'N TREAT HIM, POPS!!
THAT'S NO WAY TO WIN FRIENDS!
HEY! YOU GUYS'RE FROM THE BLACK LUX GANG, AREN'T YOU!?
THESE'RE THE SAME GUYS WHO BLEW UP THE TAXI I WAS IN, DOCTOR!
SHADDUP!!
UGH!
UNGH... ARGH...
OUR BOSS'LL DIE UNLESS YOU HELP HIM, DOCTOR...
VERY WELL, THEN... WE'LL PREPARE FOR AN OPERATION...
HMPH ...
WE'LL HAVE TO TAKE THESE BLACK CLOTHES OFF YOU, OKAY?
NO! WE CAN'T ALLOW IT!!
THEN WE CAN'T OPERATE ...
THERE'S NOT A MINUTE TO LOSE! YOU'VE GOT TO TAKE THEM OFF...
YOU FIGURE IT OUT, DOCTOR....

WE'LL TAKE OFF HIS CLOTHES 'N WORK IN THE *DARK!!*

TURN OFF THE ROOM LIGHTS, NURSE...

EVERYONE, *QUIET!* I'M STARTING THE *OPERATION!*

TWEEZERS...

GAUZE...

THAT'S IT...

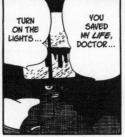

TURN ON THE LIGHTS... YOU SAVED MY *LIFE,* DOCTOR...

BUT YOU SAW MY *FACE,* DIDN'T YOU!? WAIT, YOU MUSTN'T MOVE YET!

NO ONE IS ALLOWED TO SEE MY FACE!! WH-WHAT DO YOU MEAN?

KEEP YOUR HANDS OFF THE DOCTOR!

VOOSH VOOSH

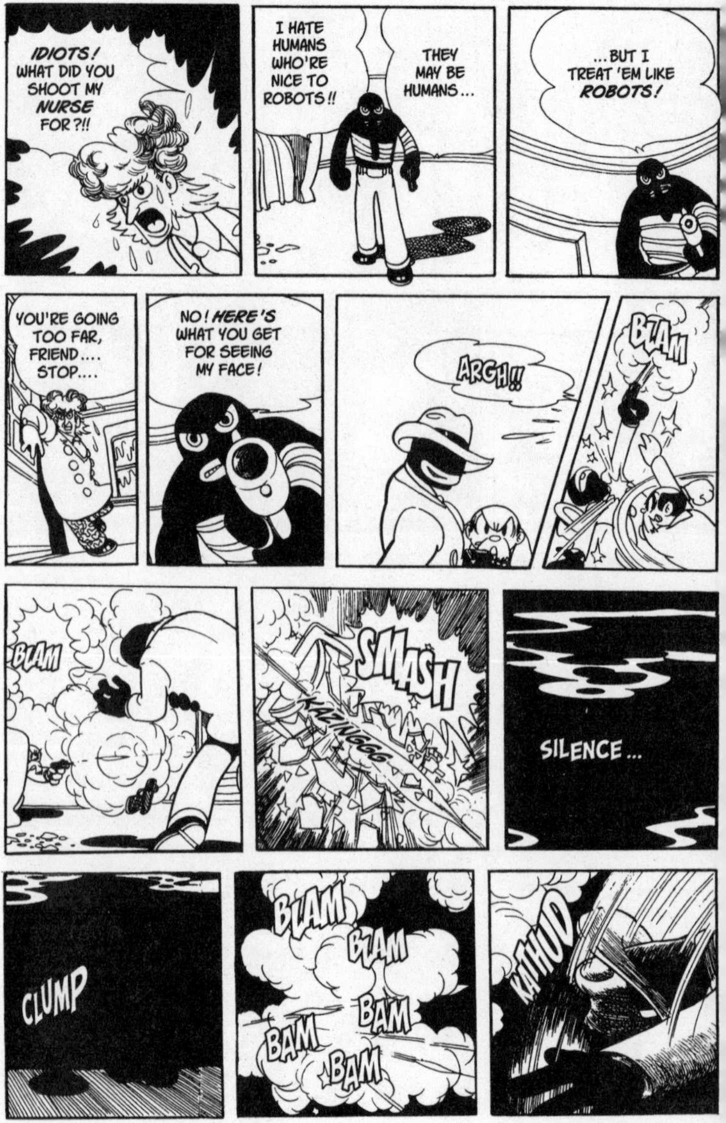
IDIOTS! WHAT DID YOU SHOOT MY NURSE FOR?!!
I HATE HUMANS WHO'RE NICE TO ROBOTS!!
THEY MAY BE HUMANS...
...BUT I TREAT 'EM LIKE ROBOTS!
YOU'RE GOING TOO FAR, FRIEND.... STOP....
NO! HERE'S WHAT YOU GET FOR SEEING MY FACE!
ARGH!!
BLAM
BLAM
SMASH
KAZINGGG
SILENCE...
CLUMP
BLAM
BLAM
BAM
BAM
BAM
KATHUD

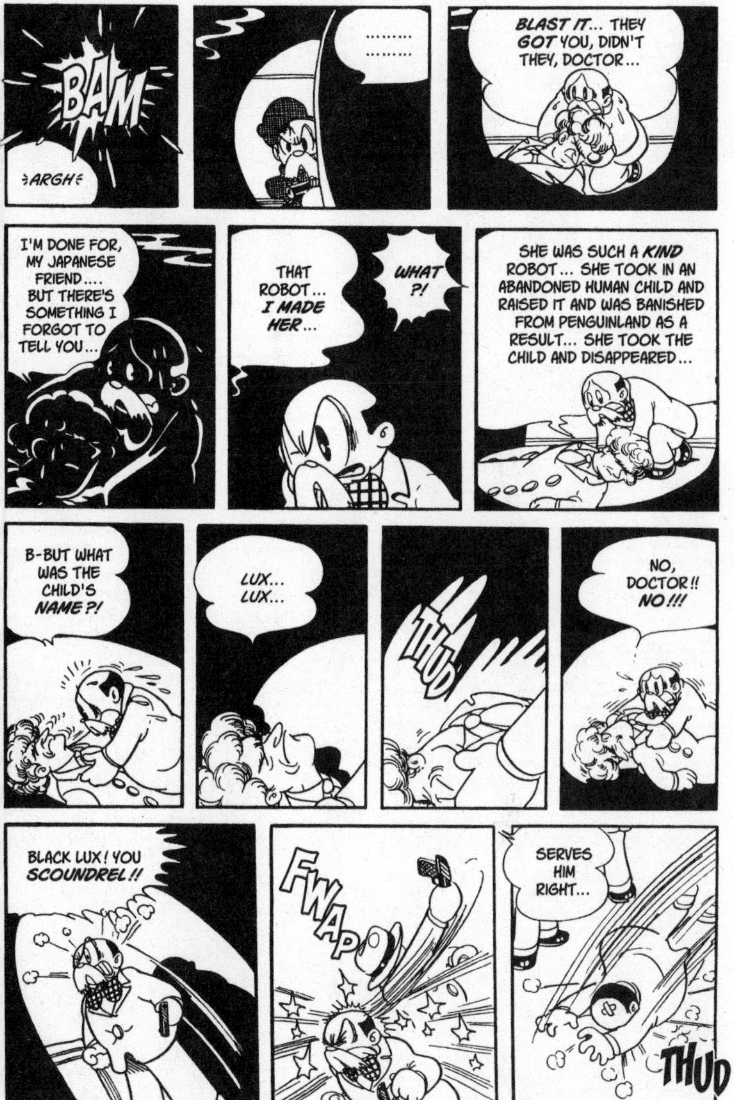
BAM
ARGH
....
....
BLAST IT... THEY GOT YOU, DIDN'T THEY, DOCTOR...
I'M DONE FOR, MY JAPANESE FRIEND.... BUT THERE'S SOMETHING I FORGOT TO TELL YOU...
THAT ROBOT... I MADE HER...
WHAT ?!
SHE WAS SUCH A KIND ROBOT... SHE TOOK IN AN ABANDONED HUMAN CHILD AND RAISED IT AND WAS BANISHED FROM PENGUINLAND AS A RESULT... SHE TOOK THE CHILD AND DISAPPEARED...
B-BUT WHAT WAS THE CHILD'S NAME ?!
LUX... LUX...
THUD
NO, DOCTOR!! NO!!!
BLACK LUX! YOU SCOUNDREL!!
FWAP
SERVES HIM RIGHT...
THUD

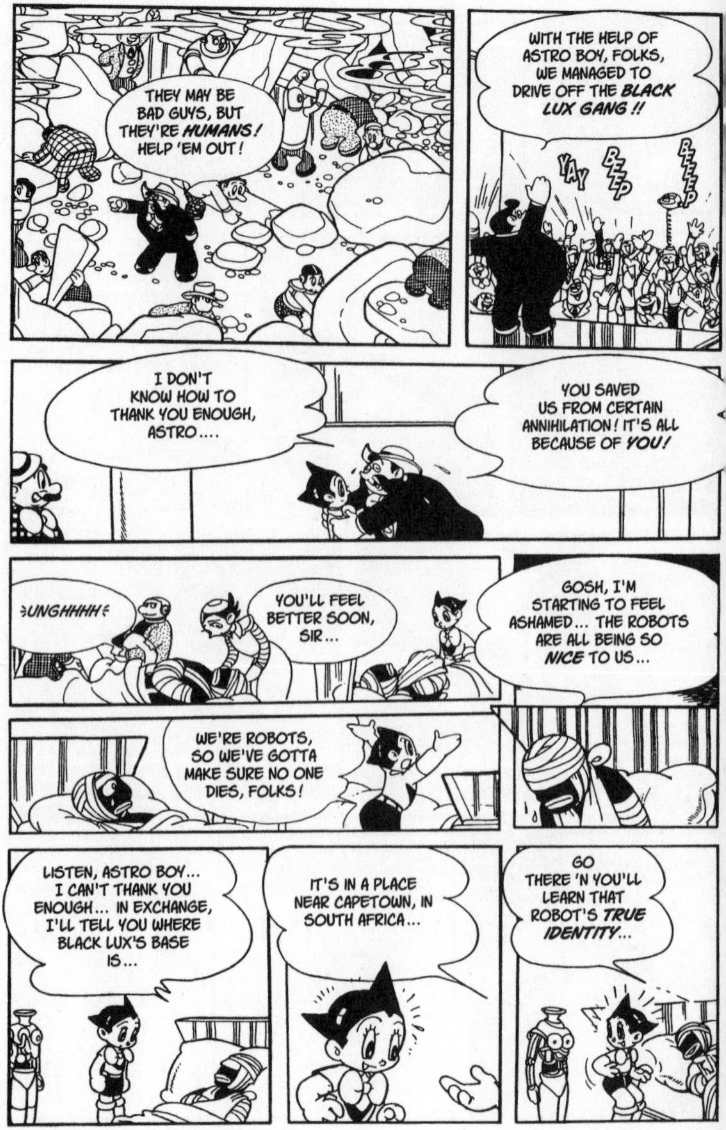
THEY MAY BE BAD GUYS, BUT THEY'RE HUMANS! HELP 'EM OUT!
WITH THE HELP OF ASTRO BOY, FOLKS, WE MANAGED TO DRIVE OFF THE BLACK LUX GANG!!
YAY
BEEP
BEEEP
I DON'T KNOW HOW TO THANK YOU ENOUGH, ASTRO....
YOU SAVED US FROM CERTAIN ANNIHILATION! IT'S ALL BECAUSE OF YOU!
UNGHHHH
YOU'LL FEEL BETTER SOON, SIR...
GOSH, I'M STARTING TO FEEL ASHAMED... THE ROBOTS ARE ALL BEING SO NICE TO US...
WE'RE ROBOTS, SO WE'VE GOTTA MAKE SURE NO ONE DIES, FOLKS!
LISTEN, ASTRO BOY... I CAN'T THANK YOU ENOUGH... IN EXCHANGE, I'LL TELL YOU WHERE BLACK LUX'S BASE IS...
IT'S IN A PLACE NEAR CAPETOWN, IN SOUTH AFRICA...
GO THERE 'N YOU'LL LEARN THAT ROBOT'S TRUE IDENTITY...

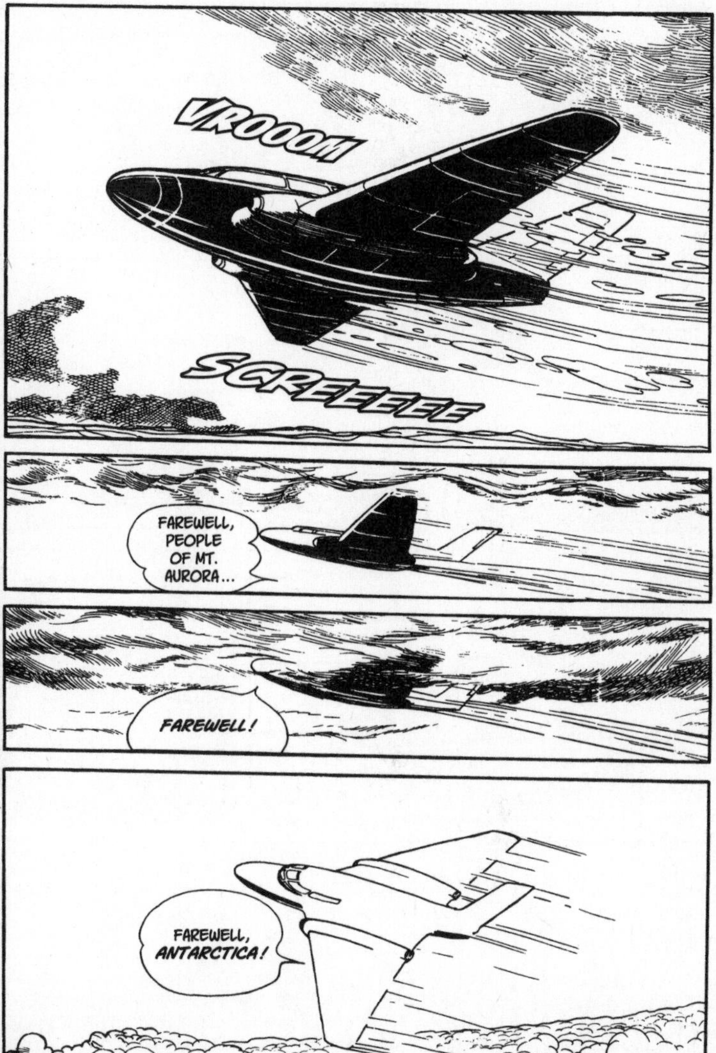
VROOOM
SCREEEEEE
FAREWELL, PEOPLE OF MT. AURORA...
FAREWELL!
FAREWELL, ANTARCTICA!

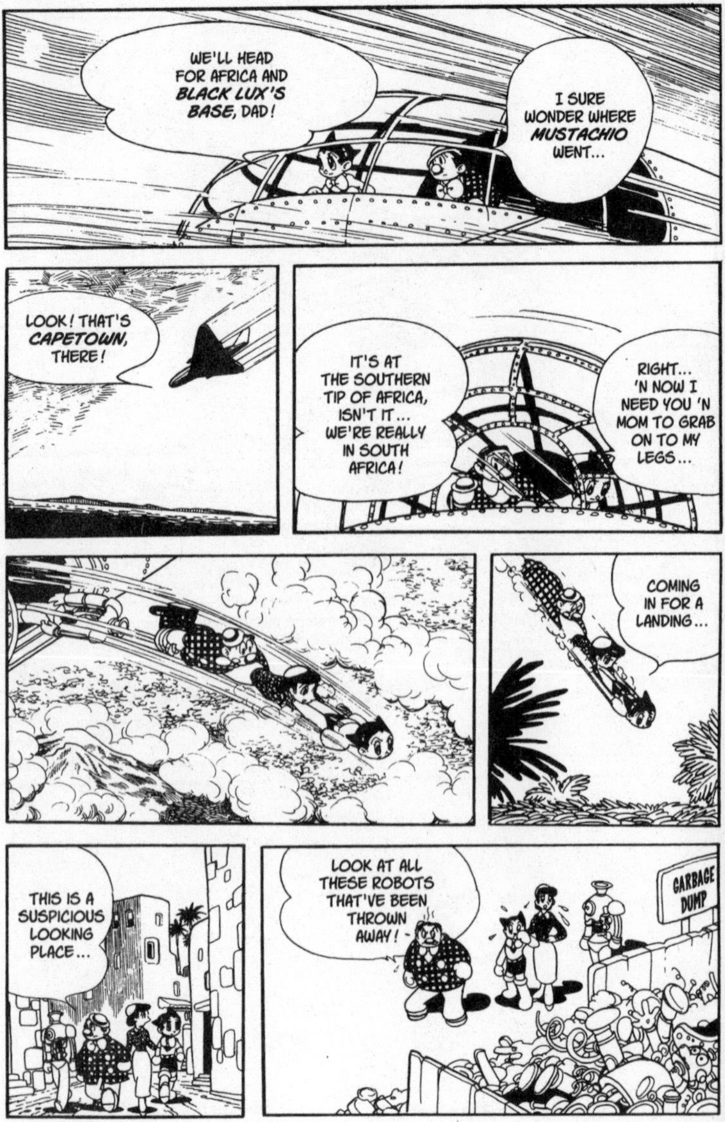
WE'LL HEAD FOR AFRICA AND *BLACK LUX'S BASE*, DAD!
I SURE WONDER WHERE *MUSTACHIO* WENT...
LOOK! THAT'S *CAPETOWN*, THERE!
IT'S AT THE SOUTHERN TIP OF AFRICA, ISN'T IT... WE'RE REALLY IN SOUTH AFRICA!
RIGHT... 'N NOW I NEED YOU 'N MOM TO GRAB ON TO MY LEGS...
COMING IN FOR A LANDING...
THIS IS A SUSPICIOUS LOOKING PLACE...
LOOK AT ALL THESE ROBOTS THAT'VE BEEN THROWN AWAY!
GARBAGE DUMP

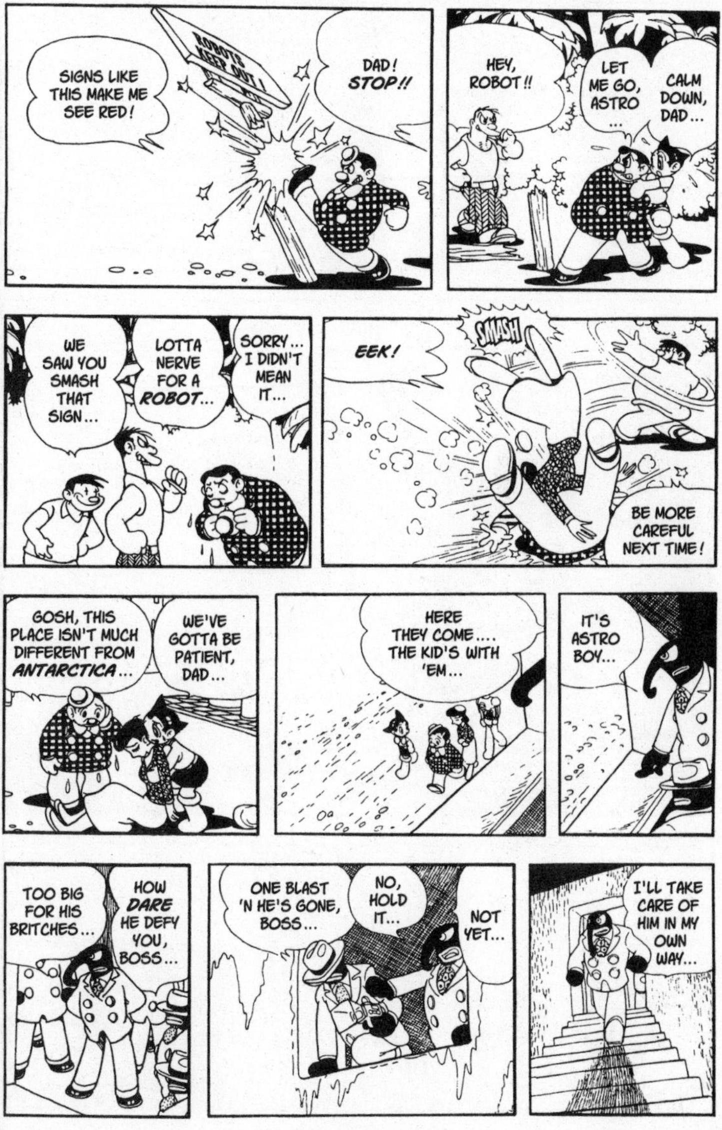
SIGNS LIKE THIS MAKE ME SEE RED!
ROBOTS KEEP OUT!
DAD! STOP!!
HEY, ROBOT!!
LET ME GO, ASTRO...
CALM DOWN, DAD...
WE SAW YOU SMASH THAT SIGN...
LOTTA NERVE FOR A ROBOT...
SORRY... I DIDN'T MEAN IT...
EEK!
SMASH
BE MORE CAREFUL NEXT TIME!
GOSH, THIS PLACE ISN'T MUCH DIFFERENT FROM ANTARCTICA...
WE'VE GOTTA BE PATIENT, DAD...
HERE THEY COME.... THE KID'S WITH 'EM...
IT'S ASTRO BOY...
TOO BIG FOR HIS BRITCHES...
HOW DARE HE DEFY YOU, BOSS...
ONE BLAST 'N HE'S GONE, BOSS...
NO, HOLD IT...
NOT YET...
I'LL TAKE CARE OF HIM IN MY OWN WAY...

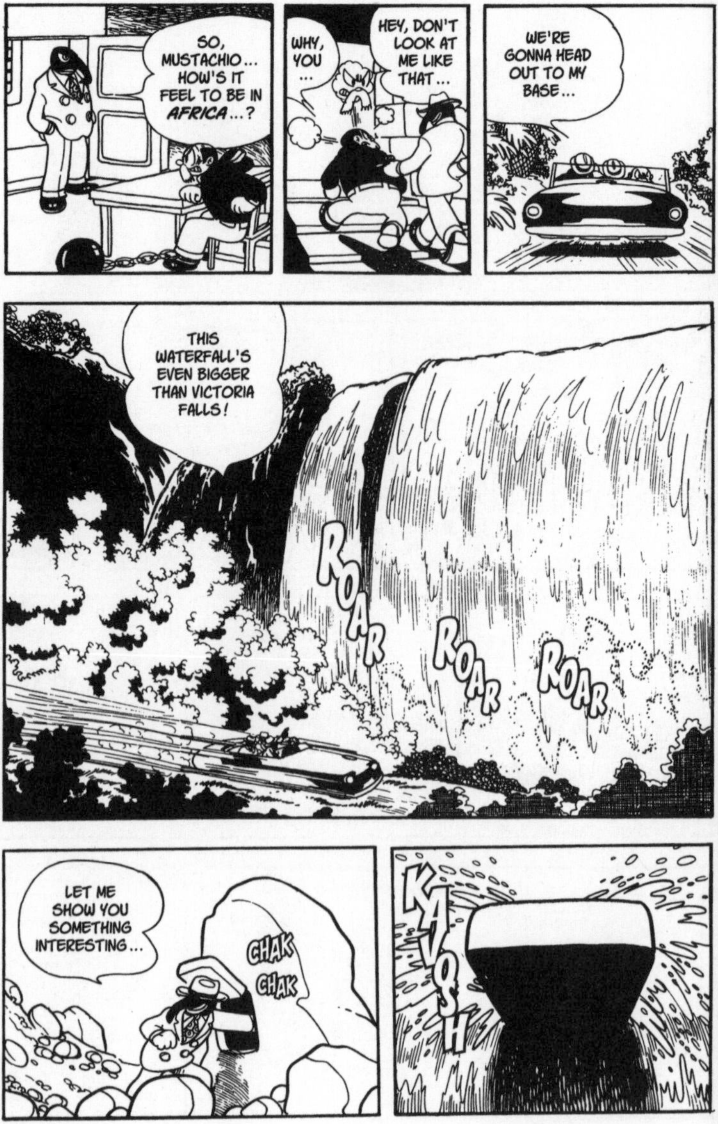
SO, MUSTACHIO... HOW'S IT FEEL TO BE IN *AFRICA*...?
WHY, YOU ...
HEY, DON'T LOOK AT ME LIKE THAT...
WE'RE GONNA HEAD OUT TO MY BASE...
THIS WATERFALL'S EVEN BIGGER THAN VICTORIA FALLS!
ROAR
ROAR
ROAR
LET ME SHOW YOU SOMETHING INTERESTING...
CHAK
CHAK
KAVOSH

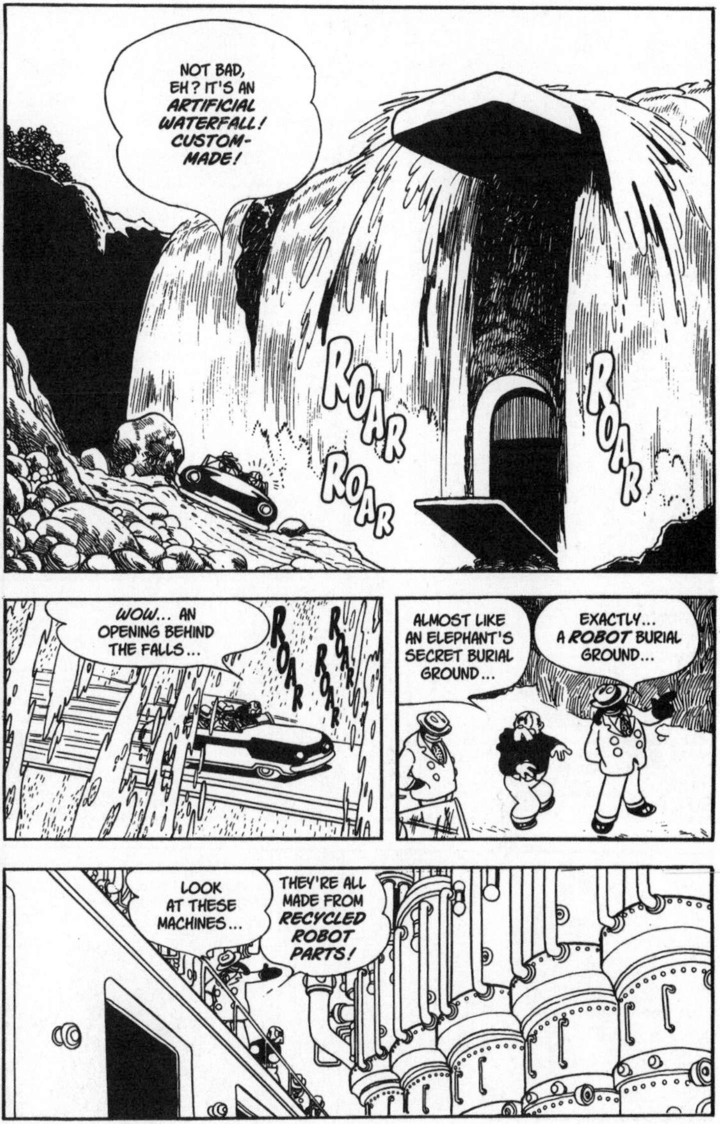
NOT BAD, EH? IT'S AN ARTIFICIAL WATERFALL! CUSTOM-MADE!
ROAR
ROAR
ROAR
WOW... AN OPENING BEHIND THE FALLS...
ROAR
ROAR
ROAR
ALMOST LIKE AN ELEPHANT'S SECRET BURIAL GROUND...
EXACTLY... A ROBOT BURIAL GROUND...
LOOK AT THESE MACHINES...
THEY'RE ALL MADE FROM RECYCLED ROBOT PARTS!

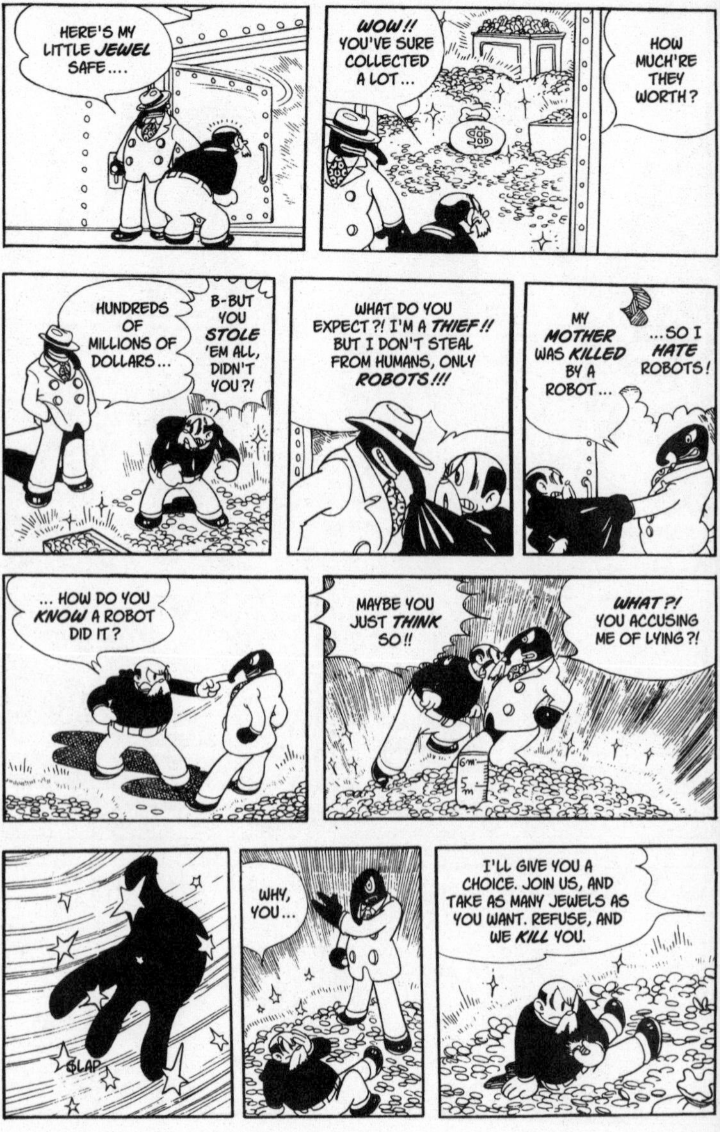
HERE'S MY LITTLE JEWEL SAFE....
WOW!! YOU'VE SURE COLLECTED A LOT...
HOW MUCH'RE THEY WORTH?
HUNDREDS OF MILLIONS OF DOLLARS...
B-BUT YOU STOLE 'EM ALL, DIDN'T YOU?!
WHAT DO YOU EXPECT?! I'M A THIEF!! BUT I DON'T STEAL FROM HUMANS, ONLY ROBOTS!!!
MY MOTHER WAS KILLED BY A ROBOT...
...SO I HATE ROBOTS!
... HOW DO YOU KNOW A ROBOT DID IT?
MAYBE YOU JUST THINK SO!!
WHAT?! YOU ACCUSING ME OF LYING?!
SLAP
WHY, YOU...
I'LL GIVE YOU A CHOICE. JOIN US, AND TAKE AS MANY JEWELS AS YOU WANT. REFUSE, AND WE KILL YOU.

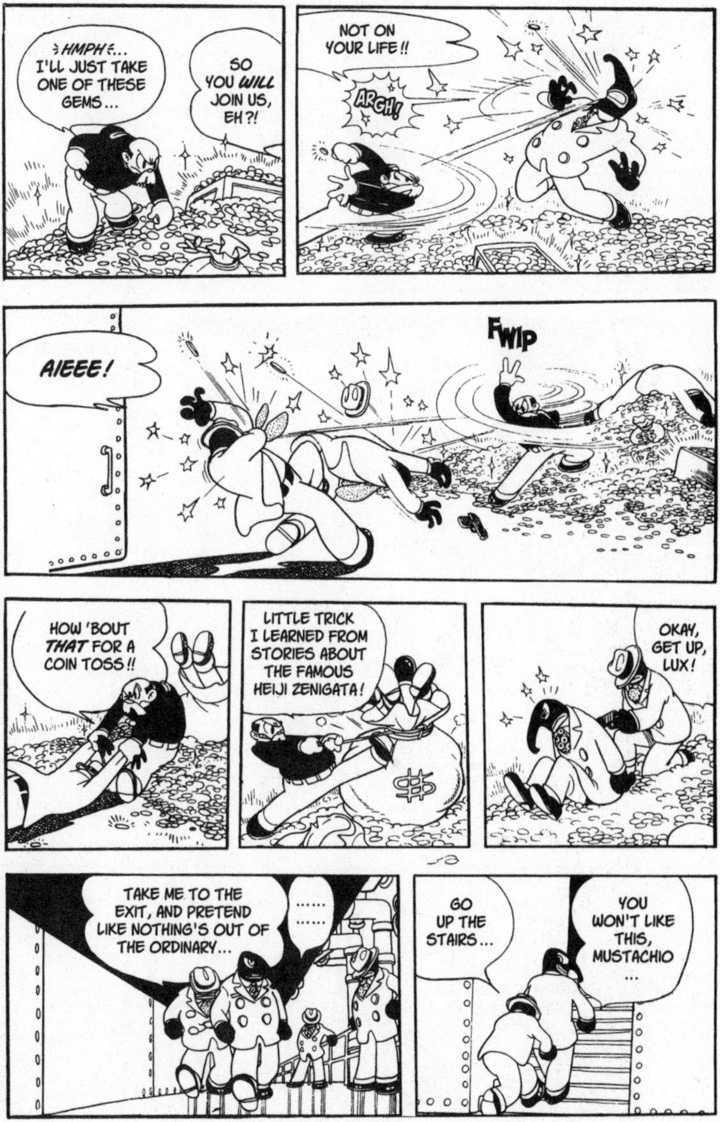

HMPH... I'LL JUST TAKE ONE OF THESE GEMS...
SO YOU *WILL* JOIN US, EH?!
NOT ON YOUR LIFE!!
ARGH!
AIEEE!
FWIP
HOW 'BOUT *THAT* FOR A COIN TOSS!!
LITTLE TRICK I LEARNED FROM STORIES ABOUT THE FAMOUS HEIJI ZENIGATA!
OKAY, GET UP, LUX!
TAKE ME TO THE EXIT, AND PRETEND LIKE NOTHING'S OUT OF THE ORDINARY...
......
......
GO UP THE STAIRS...
YOU WON'T LIKE THIS, MUSTACHIO ...

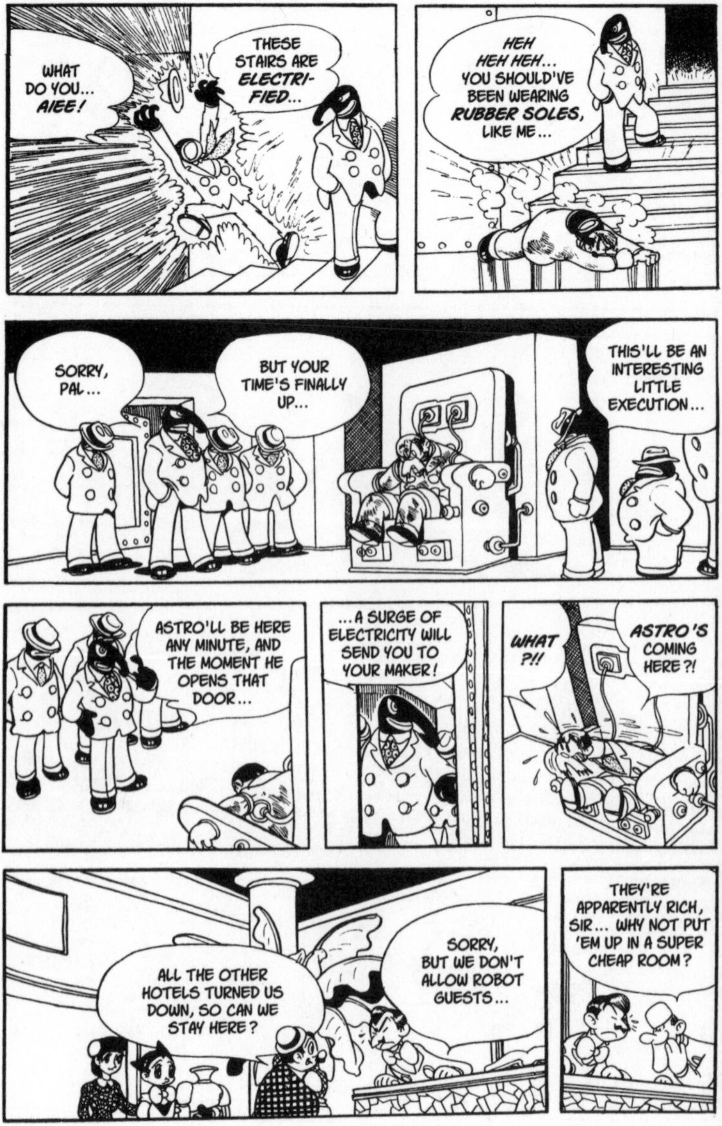
WHAT DO YOU... AIEE!
THESE STAIRS ARE ELECTRI-FIED...
HEH HEH HEH... YOU SHOULD'VE BEEN WEARING RUBBER SOLES, LIKE ME...
SORRY, PAL...
BUT YOUR TIME'S FINALLY UP...
THIS'LL BE AN INTERESTING LITTLE EXECUTION...
ASTRO'LL BE HERE ANY MINUTE, AND THE MOMENT HE OPENS THAT DOOR...
...A SURGE OF ELECTRICITY WILL SEND YOU TO YOUR MAKER!
WHAT ?!!
ASTRO'S COMING HERE ?!
ALL THE OTHER HOTELS TURNED US DOWN, SO CAN WE STAY HERE?
SORRY, BUT WE DON'T ALLOW ROBOT GUESTS...
THEY'RE APPARENTLY RICH, SIR... WHY NOT PUT 'EM UP IN A SUPER CHEAP ROOM?

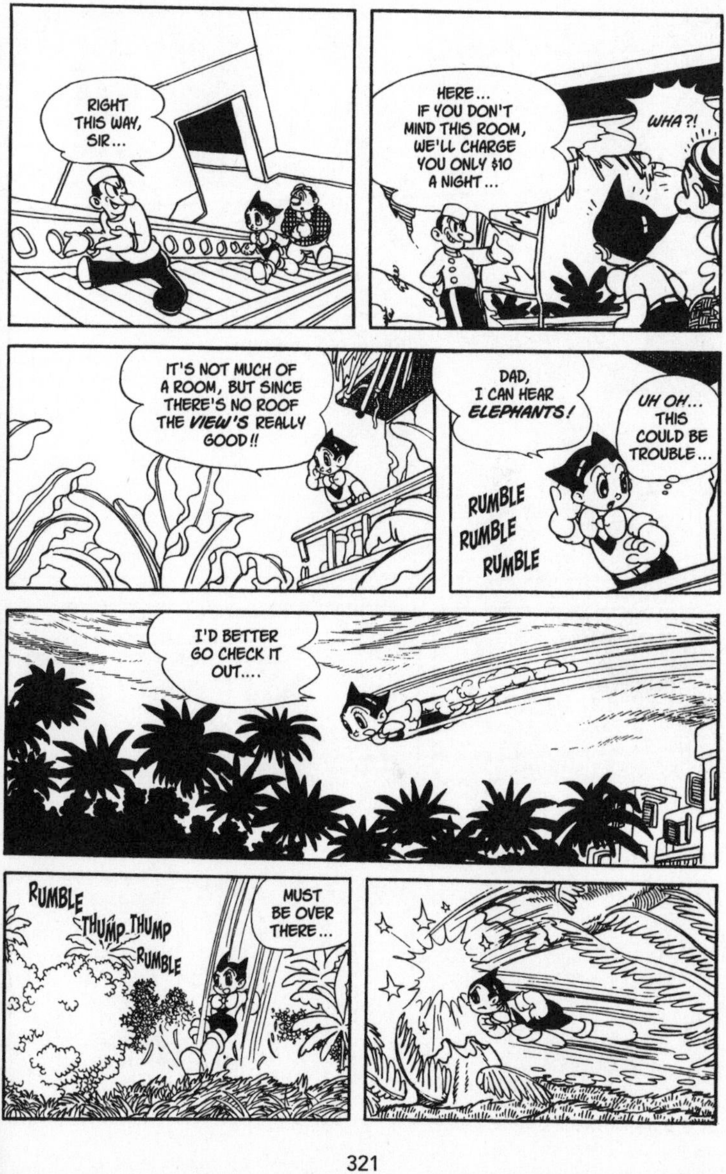
RIGHT THIS WAY, SIR...
HERE... IF YOU DON'T MIND THIS ROOM, WE'LL CHARGE YOU ONLY $10 A NIGHT...
WHA?!
IT'S NOT MUCH OF A ROOM, BUT SINCE THERE'S NO ROOF THE VIEW'S REALLY GOOD!!
DAD, I CAN HEAR ELEPHANTS!
UH OH... THIS COULD BE TROUBLE...
RUMBLE
RUMBLE
RUMBLE
I'D BETTER GO CHECK IT OUT....
RUMBLE
THUMP THUMP
RUMBLE
MUST BE OVER THERE...

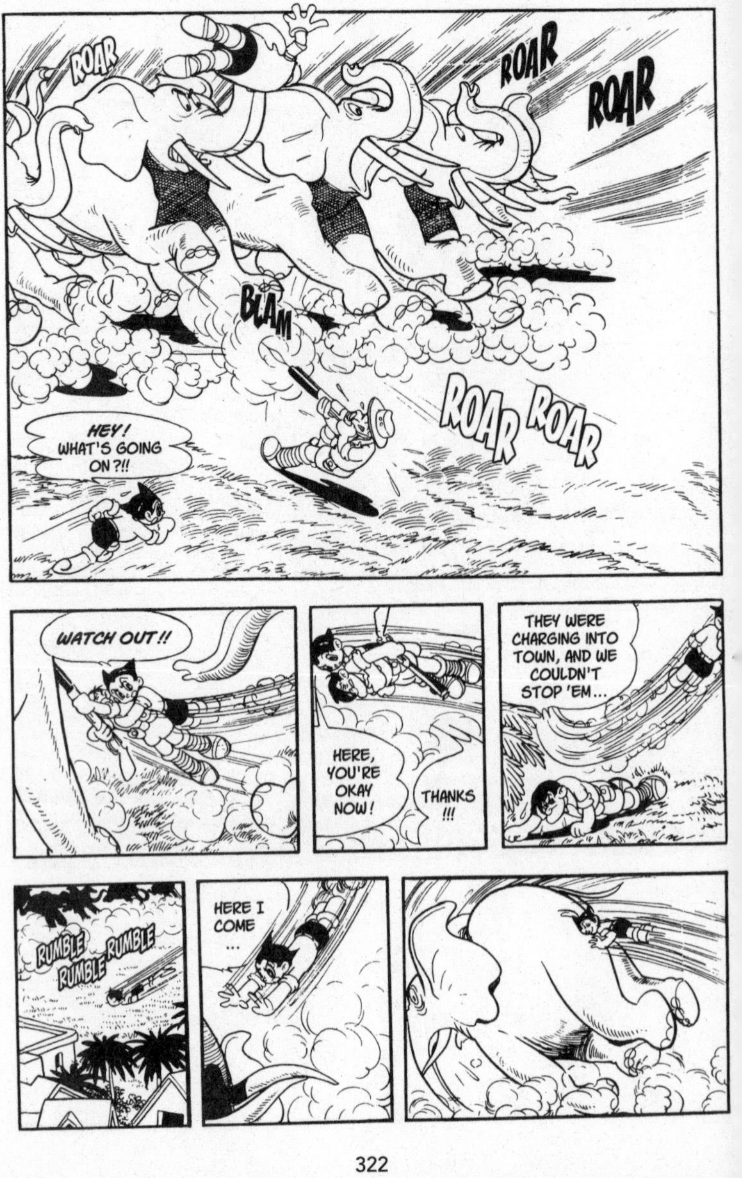
ROAR
ROAR
ROAR
BLAM
ROAR
ROAR
HEY! WHAT'S GOING ON?!!
WATCH OUT!!
HERE, YOU'RE OKAY NOW!
THANKS !!!
THEY WERE CHARGING INTO TOWN, AND WE COULDN'T STOP 'EM...
RUMBLE RUMBLE RUMBLE
HERE I COME ...

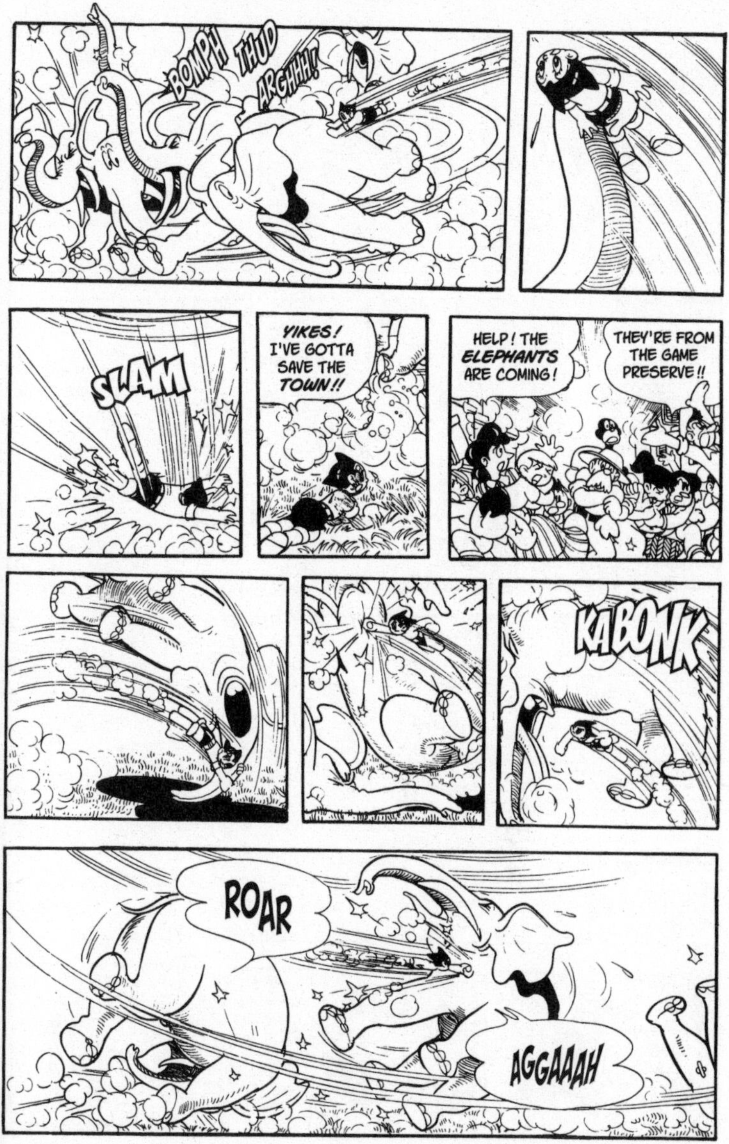
BOMPH
THUD
ARGHHH!
SLAM
YIKES! I'VE GOTTA SAVE THE TOWN!!
HELP! THE ELEPHANTS ARE COMING!
THEY'RE FROM THE GAME PRESERVE!!
KABONK
ROAR
AGGAAAH

WOW! YOU SEE THAT? A SINGLE *ROBOT* SAVED US!

SPUTTER SPUT
SPUT

ARROOO!

GET 'EM, MR. ROBOT! GET 'EM!

EEEK!

CRASH

HELP THE ROBOT! *OPEN FIRE*, MEN!

BLAM

BLAM

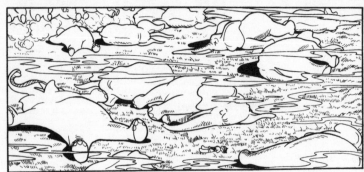

ASTRO ...

HI, MOM....

IT'S THE TOWNSPEOPLE, ASTRO ...

WE JUST WANT TO *THANK* YOU, SON ...

324

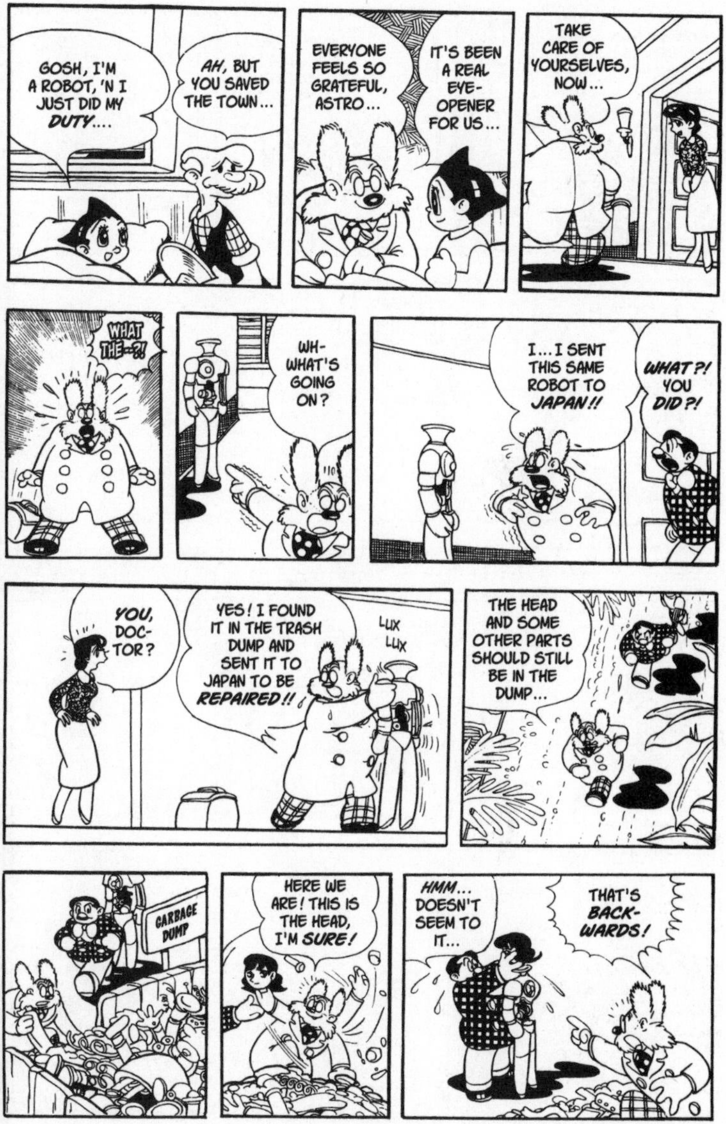
GOSH, I'M A ROBOT, 'N I JUST DID MY DUTY....
AH, BUT YOU SAVED THE TOWN...
EVERYONE FEELS SO GRATEFUL, ASTRO...
IT'S BEEN A REAL EYE-OPENER FOR US...
TAKE CARE OF YOURSELVES, NOW...
WHAT THE--?!
WH-WHAT'S GOING ON?
I...I SENT THIS SAME ROBOT TO JAPAN!!
WHAT?! YOU DID?!
YOU, DOCTOR?
YES! I FOUND IT IN THE TRASH DUMP AND SENT IT TO JAPAN TO BE REPAIRED!!
LUX LUX
THE HEAD AND SOME OTHER PARTS SHOULD STILL BE IN THE DUMP...
GARBAGE DUMP
HERE WE ARE! THIS IS THE HEAD, I'M SURE!
HMM... DOESN'T SEEM TO IT...
THAT'S BACKWARDS!

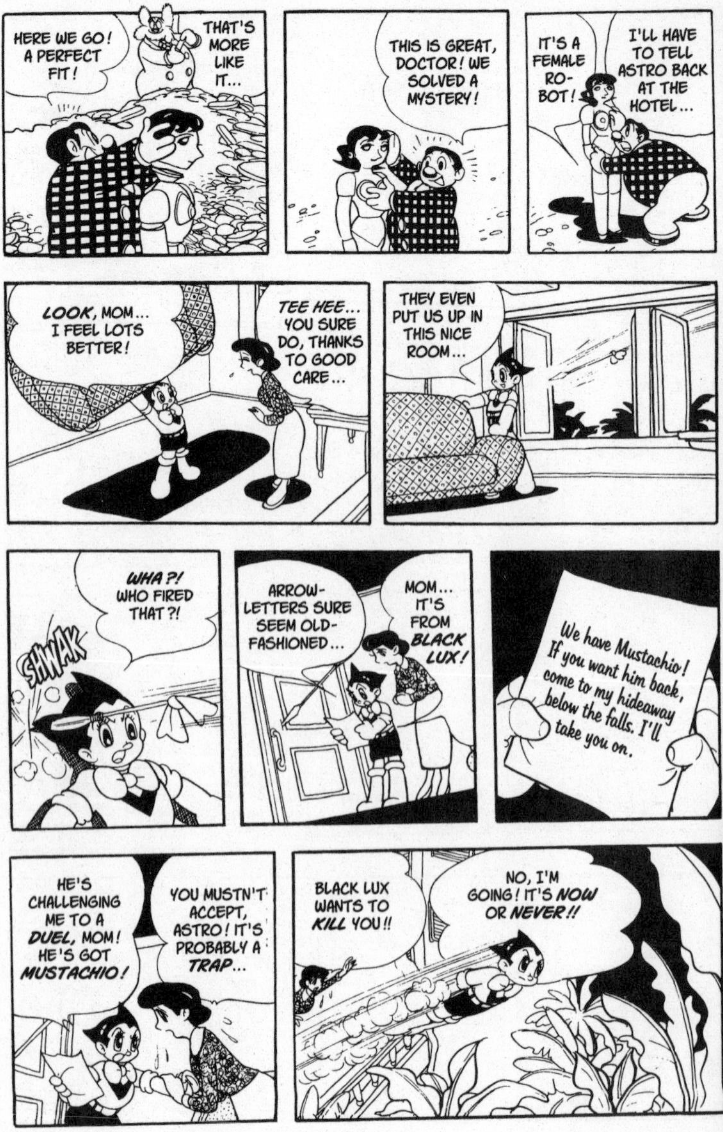
HERE WE GO! A PERFECT FIT!
THAT'S MORE LIKE IT...
THIS IS GREAT, DOCTOR! WE SOLVED A MYSTERY!
IT'S A FEMALE RO-BOT!
I'LL HAVE TO TELL ASTRO BACK AT THE HOTEL...
LOOK, MOM... I FEEL LOTS BETTER!
TEE HEE... YOU SURE DO, THANKS TO GOOD CARE...
THEY EVEN PUT US UP IN THIS NICE ROOM...
WHA?! WHO FIRED THAT?!
SHWAK
ARROW-LETTERS SURE SEEM OLD-FASHIONED...
MOM... IT'S FROM BLACK LUX!
We have Mustachio! If you want him back, come to my hideaway below the falls. I'll take you on.
HE'S CHALLENGING ME TO A DUEL, MOM! HE'S GOT MUSTACHIO!
YOU MUSTN'T ACCEPT, ASTRO! IT'S PROBABLY A TRAP...
BLACK LUX WANTS TO KILL YOU!!
NO, I'M GOING! IT'S NOW OR NEVER!!

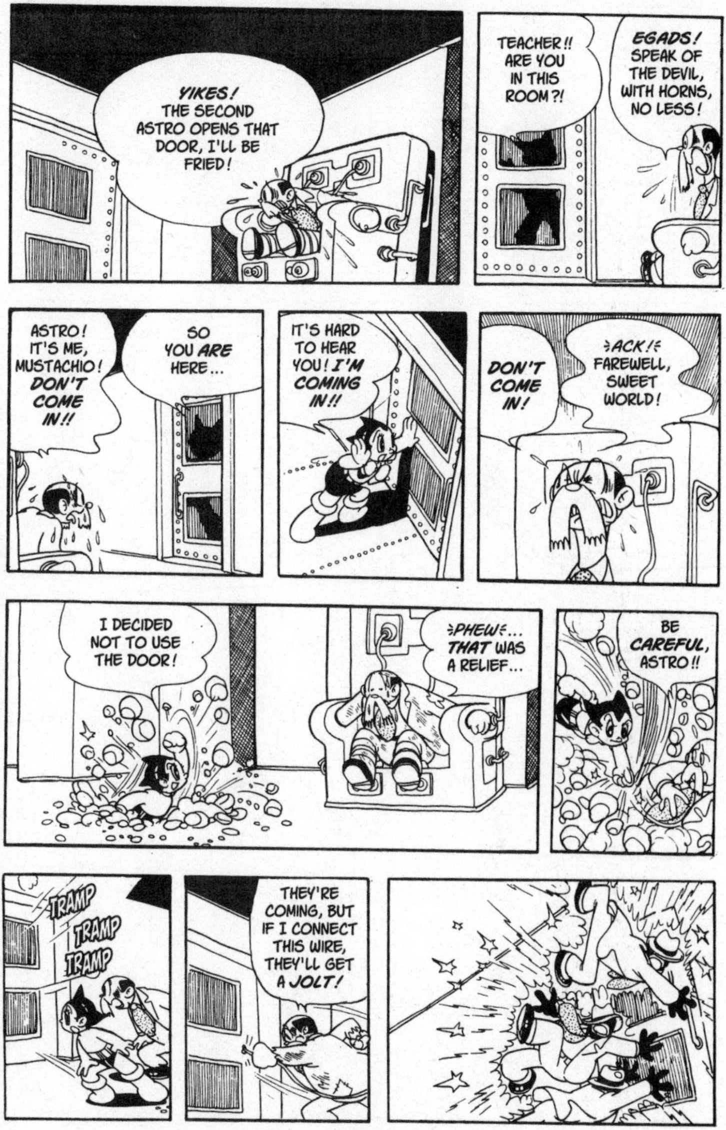
YIKES! THE SECOND ASTRO OPENS THAT DOOR, I'LL BE FRIED!
TEACHER!! ARE YOU IN THIS ROOM?!
EGADS! SPEAK OF THE DEVIL, WITH HORNS, NO LESS!
ASTRO! IT'S ME, MUSTACHIO! DON'T COME IN!!
SO YOU ARE HERE...
IT'S HARD TO HEAR YOU! I'M COMING IN!!
DON'T COME IN!
ACK! FAREWELL, SWEET WORLD!
I DECIDED NOT TO USE THE DOOR!
PHEW... THAT WAS A RELIEF...
BE CAREFUL, ASTRO!!
TRAMP
TRAMP
TRAMP
THEY'RE COMING, BUT IF I CONNECT THIS WIRE, THEY'LL GET A JOLT!

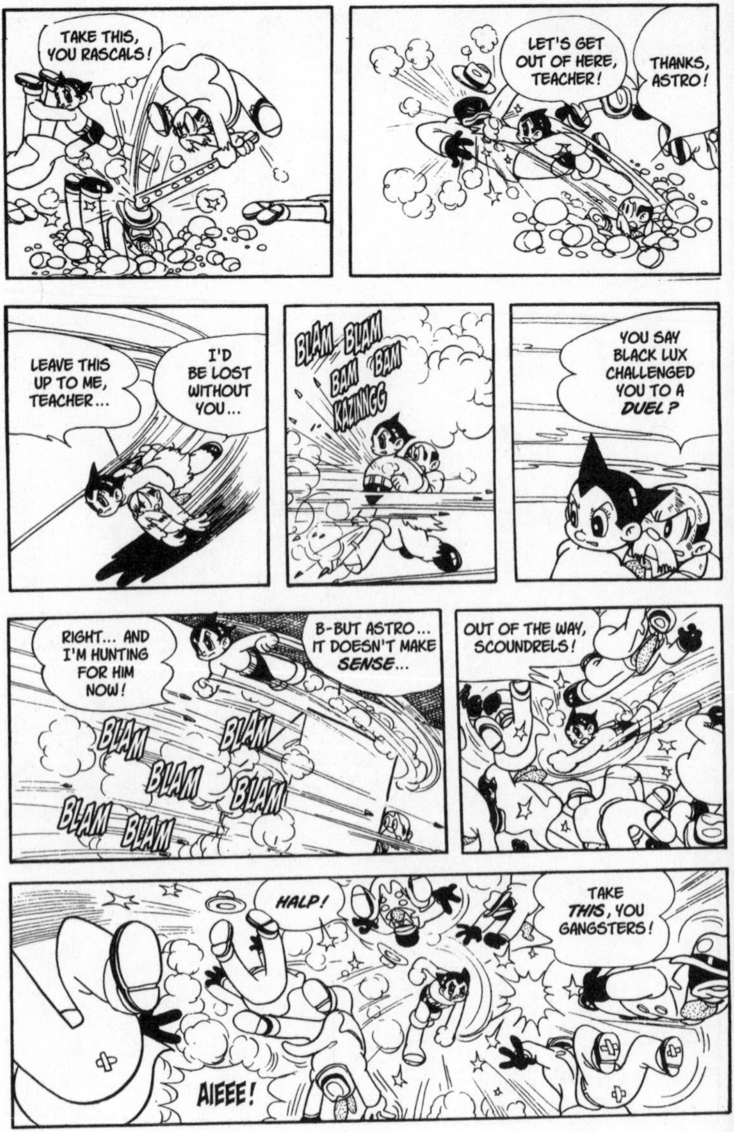
TAKE THIS, YOU RASCALS!
LET'S GET OUT OF HERE, TEACHER!
THANKS, ASTRO!
LEAVE THIS UP TO ME, TEACHER...
I'D BE LOST WITHOUT YOU...
BLAM BLAM BAM BAM KAZINNGG
YOU SAY BLACK LUX CHALLENGED YOU TO A *DUEL?*
RIGHT... AND I'M HUNTING FOR HIM NOW!
B-BUT ASTRO... IT DOESN'T MAKE *SENSE*...
BLAM BLAM BLAM BLAM BLAM BLAM
OUT OF THE WAY, SCOUNDRELS!
HALP!
TAKE *THIS*, YOU GANGSTERS!
AIEEE!

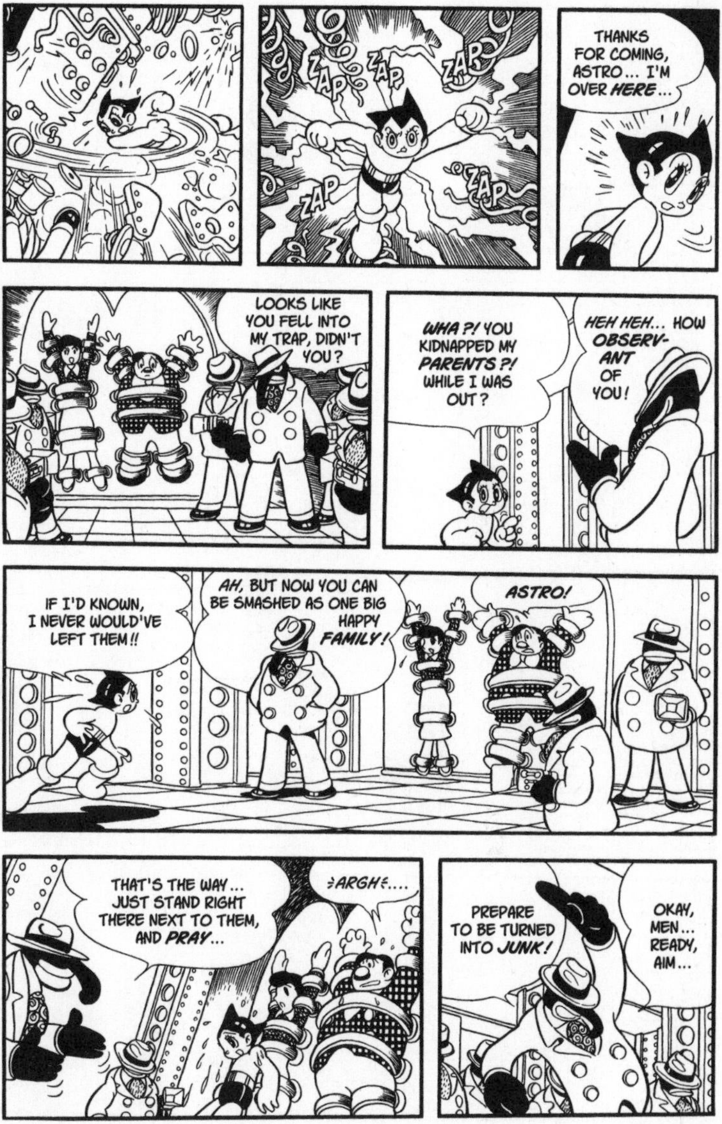
ZAP
ZAP
ZAP
ZAP
ZAP
THANKS FOR COMING, ASTRO... I'M OVER HERE...
LOOKS LIKE YOU FELL INTO MY TRAP, DIDN'T YOU?
WHA?! YOU KIDNAPPED MY PARENTS?! WHILE I WAS OUT?
HEH HEH... HOW OBSERV-ANT OF YOU!
IF I'D KNOWN, I NEVER WOULD'VE LEFT THEM!!
AH, BUT NOW YOU CAN BE SMASHED AS ONE BIG HAPPY FAMILY!
ASTRO!
THAT'S THE WAY... JUST STAND RIGHT THERE NEXT TO THEM, AND PRAY...
ARGH....
PREPARE TO BE TURNED INTO JUNK!
OKAY, MEN... READY, AIM...

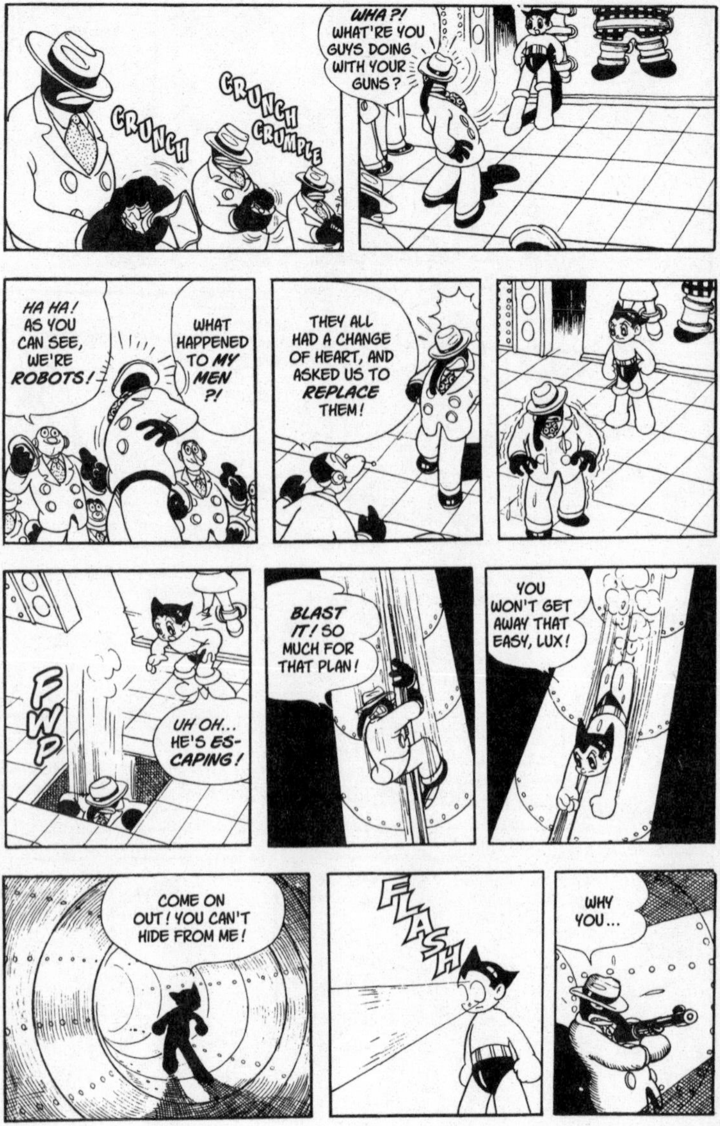
CRUNCH
CRUNCH
CRUMPLE
WHA?! WHAT'RE YOU GUYS DOING WITH YOUR GUNS?
HA HA! AS YOU CAN SEE, WE'RE ROBOTS!
WHAT HAPPENED TO MY MEN?!
THEY ALL HAD A CHANGE OF HEART, AND ASKED US TO REPLACE THEM!
FWP
UH OH... HE'S ES-CAPING!
BLAST IT! SO MUCH FOR THAT PLAN!
YOU WON'T GET AWAY THAT EASY, LUX!
COME ON OUT! YOU CAN'T HIDE FROM ME!
FLASH
WHY YOU...

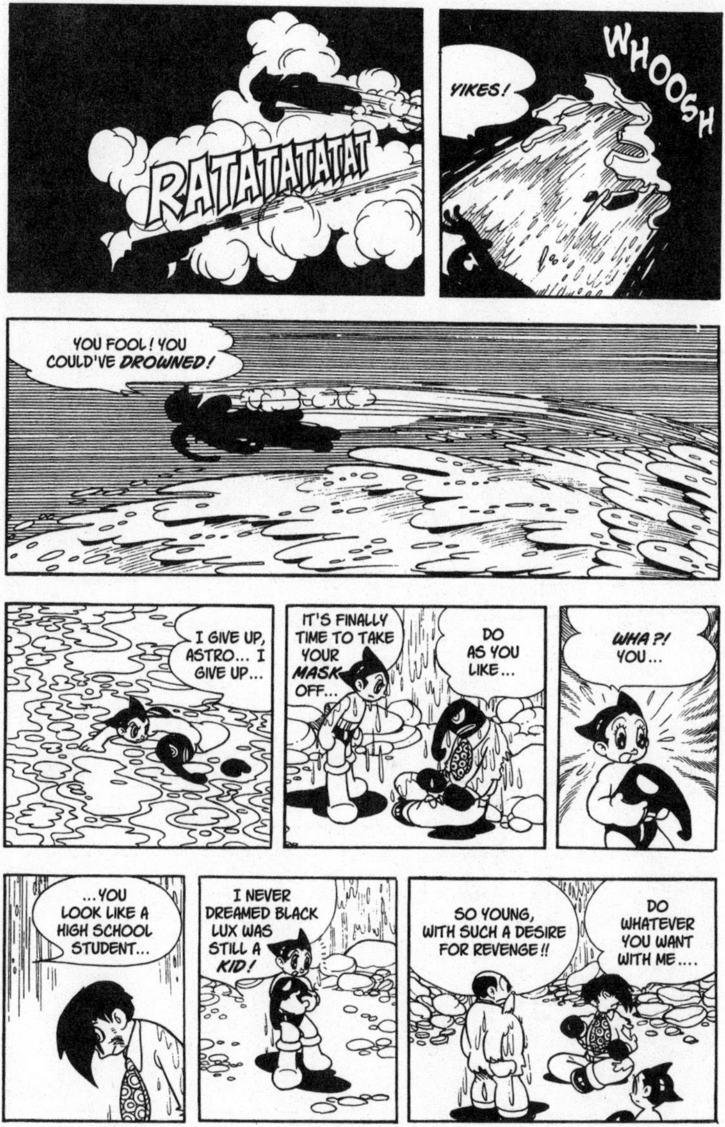

RATATATATAT
YIKES!
WHOOSH
YOU FOOL! YOU COULD'VE DROWNED!
I GIVE UP, ASTRO... I GIVE UP...
IT'S FINALLY TIME TO TAKE YOUR MASK OFF...
DO AS YOU LIKE...
WHA?! YOU...
...YOU LOOK LIKE A HIGH SCHOOL STUDENT...
I NEVER DREAMED BLACK LUX WAS STILL A KID!
SO YOUNG, WITH SUCH A DESIRE FOR REVENGE!!
DO WHATEVER YOU WANT WITH ME....

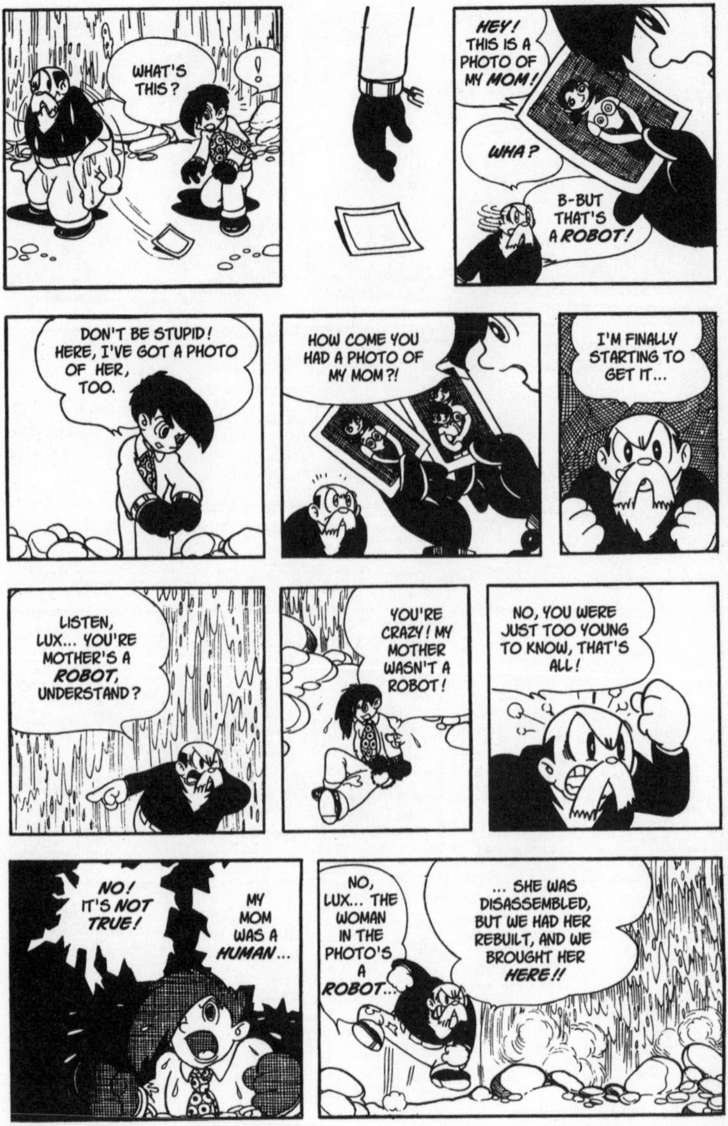
WHAT'S THIS?
!
HEY! THIS IS A PHOTO OF MY MOM!
WHA?
B-BUT THAT'S A ROBOT!
DON'T BE STUPID! HERE, I'VE GOT A PHOTO OF HER, TOO.
HOW COME YOU HAD A PHOTO OF MY MOM?!
I'M FINALLY STARTING TO GET IT...
LISTEN, LUX... YOU'RE MOTHER'S A ROBOT, UNDERSTAND?
YOU'RE CRAZY! MY MOTHER WASN'T A ROBOT!
NO, YOU WERE JUST TOO YOUNG TO KNOW, THAT'S ALL!
NO! IT'S NOT TRUE!
MY MOM WAS A HUMAN...
NO, LUX... THE WOMAN IN THE PHOTO'S A ROBOT...
... SHE WAS DISASSEMBLED, BUT WE HAD HER REBUILT, AND WE BROUGHT HER HERE!!

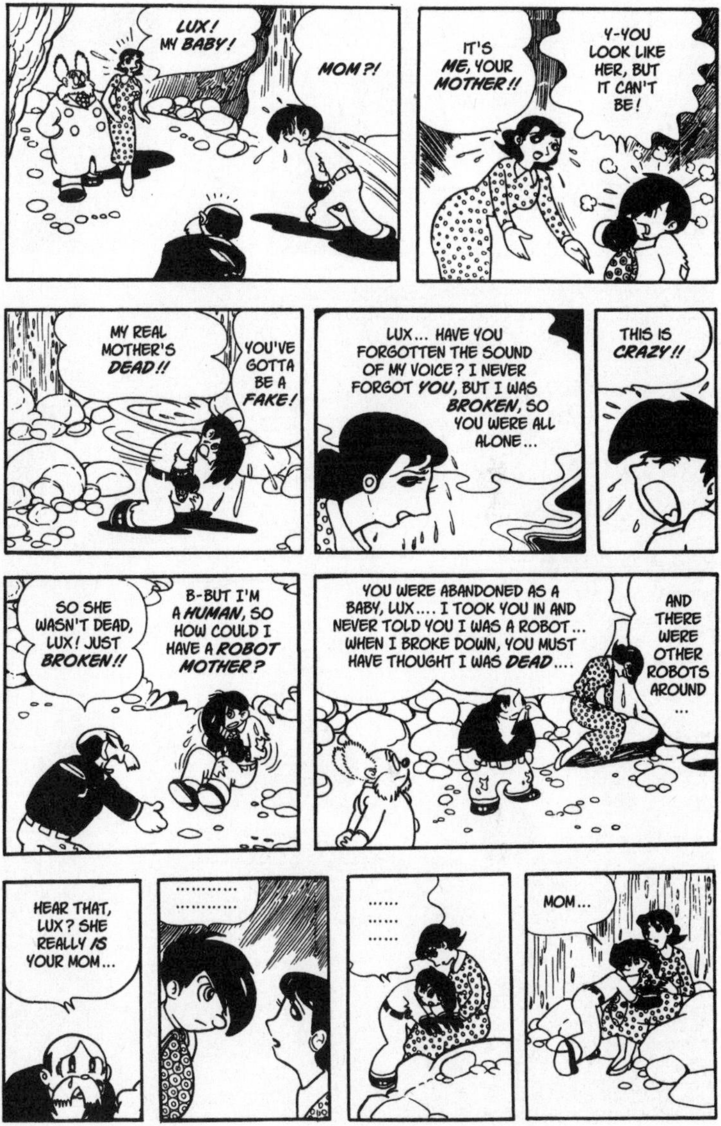
LUX! MY BABY!
MOM?!
IT'S ME, YOUR MOTHER!!
Y-YOU LOOK LIKE HER, BUT IT CAN'T BE!
MY REAL MOTHER'S DEAD!!
YOU'VE GOTTA BE A FAKE!
LUX... HAVE YOU FORGOTTEN THE SOUND OF MY VOICE? I NEVER FORGOT YOU, BUT I WAS BROKEN, SO YOU WERE ALL ALONE...
THIS IS CRAZY!!
SO SHE WASN'T DEAD, LUX! JUST BROKEN!!
B-BUT I'M A HUMAN, SO HOW COULD I HAVE A ROBOT MOTHER?
YOU WERE ABANDONED AS A BABY, LUX.... I TOOK YOU IN AND NEVER TOLD YOU I WAS A ROBOT... WHEN I BROKE DOWN, YOU MUST HAVE THOUGHT I WAS DEAD....
AND THERE WERE OTHER ROBOTS AROUND ...
HEAR THAT, LUX? SHE REALLY IS YOUR MOM...
....
....
MOM...

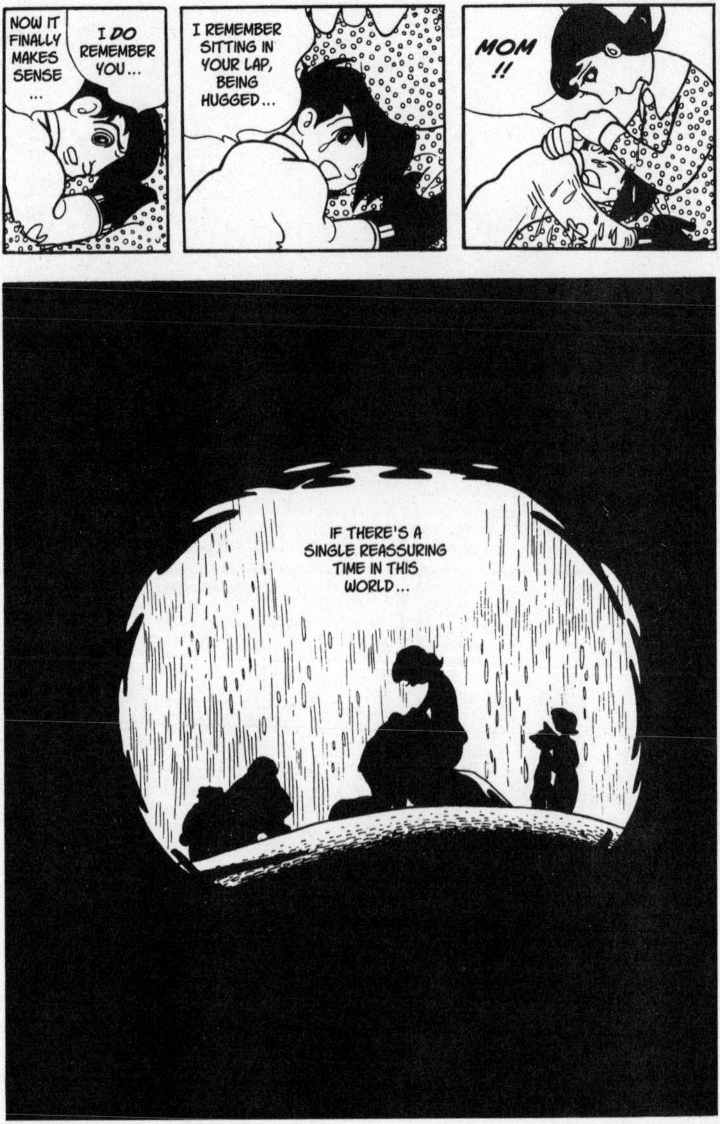
NOW IT FINALLY MAKES SENSE ...
I *DO* REMEMBER YOU...
I REMEMBER SITTING IN YOUR LAP, BEING HUGGED...
MOM !!
IF THERE'S A SINGLE REASSURING TIME IN THIS WORLD...

AMBASSADOR ATOM

First serialized from April 1951 to March 1952
in *Shonen* magazine.

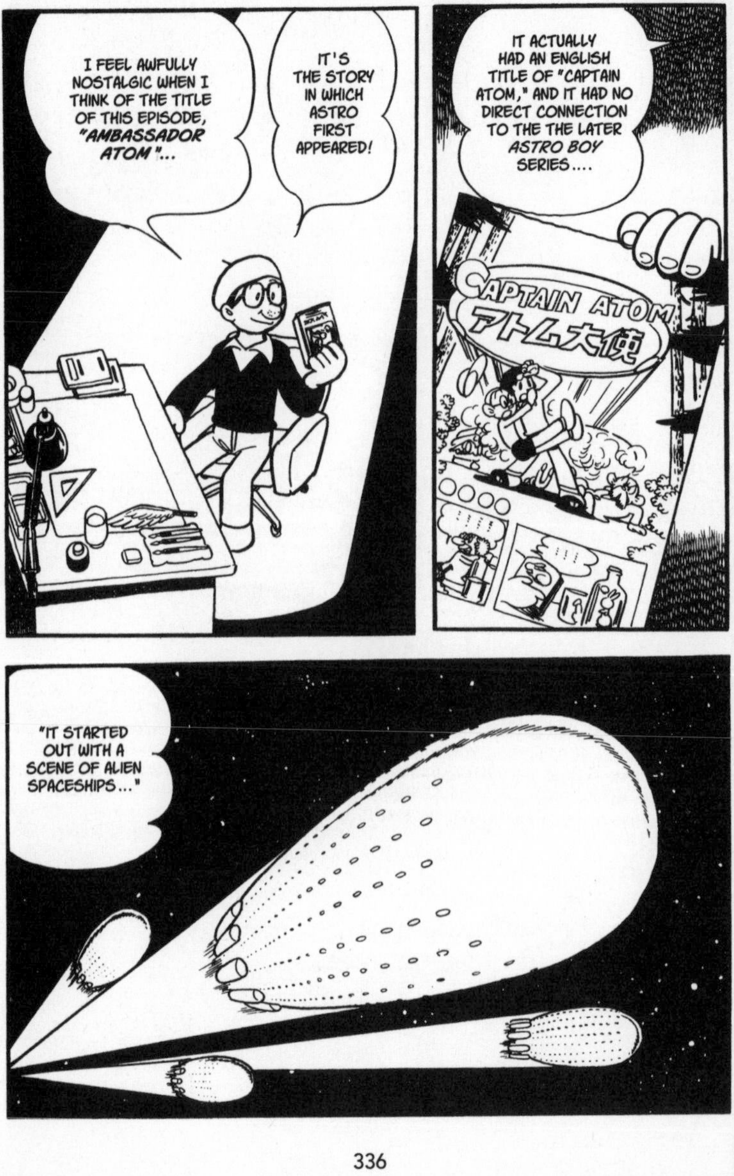
I FEEL AWFULLY NOSTALGIC WHEN I THINK OF THE TITLE OF THIS EPISODE, *"AMBASSADOR ATOM"*...
IT'S THE STORY IN WHICH ASTRO FIRST APPEARED!
IT ACTUALLY HAD AN ENGLISH TITLE OF "CAPTAIN ATOM," AND IT HAD NO DIRECT CONNECTION TO THE THE LATER *ASTRO BOY* SERIES....
CAPTAIN ATOM
アトム大使
"IT STARTED OUT WITH A SCENE OF ALIEN SPACESHIPS..."

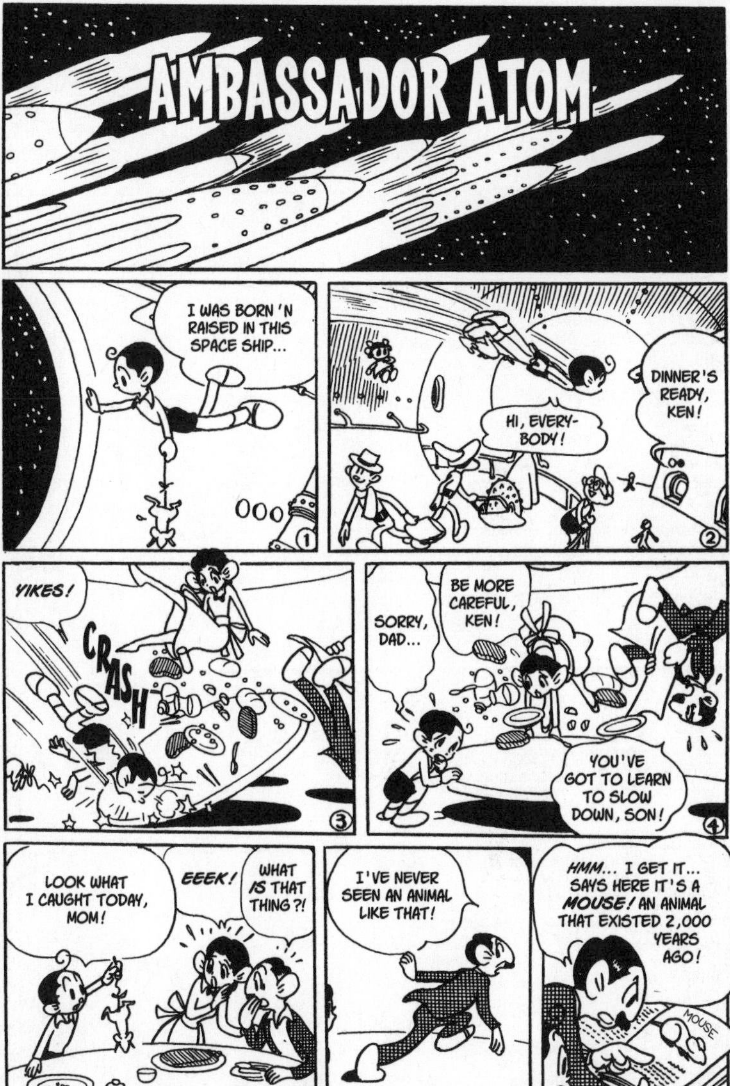
AMBASSADOR ATOM
I WAS BORN 'N RAISED IN THIS SPACE SHIP...
HI, EVERY-BODY!
DINNER'S READY, KEN!
YIKES!
CRASH
SORRY, DAD...
BE MORE CAREFUL, KEN!
YOU'VE GOT TO LEARN TO SLOW DOWN, SON!
LOOK WHAT I CAUGHT TODAY, MOM!
EEEK!
WHAT *IS* THAT THING?!
I'VE NEVER SEEN AN ANIMAL LIKE THAT!
HMM... I GET IT... SAYS HERE IT'S A *MOUSE!* AN ANIMAL THAT EXISTED 2,000 YEARS AGO!
MOUSE

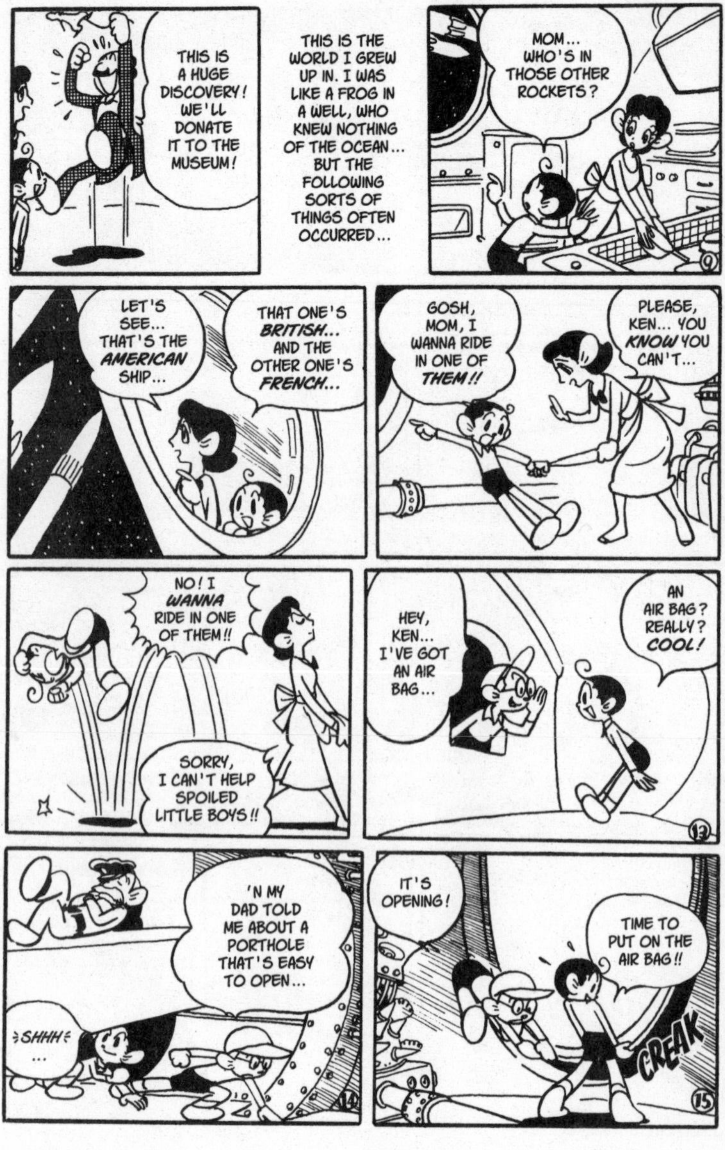
THIS IS A HUGE DISCOVERY! WE'LL DONATE IT TO THE MUSEUM!
THIS IS THE WORLD I GREW UP IN. I WAS LIKE A FROG IN A WELL, WHO KNEW NOTHING OF THE OCEAN... BUT THE FOLLOWING SORTS OF THINGS OFTEN OCCURRED...
MOM... WHO'S IN THOSE OTHER ROCKETS?
LET'S SEE... THAT'S THE AMERICAN SHIP...
THAT ONE'S BRITISH... AND THE OTHER ONE'S FRENCH...
GOSH, MOM, I WANNA RIDE IN ONE OF THEM!!
PLEASE, KEN... YOU KNOW YOU CAN'T...
NO! I WANNA RIDE IN ONE OF THEM!!
SORRY, I CAN'T HELP SPOILED LITTLE BOYS!!
HEY, KEN... I'VE GOT AN AIR BAG...
AN AIR BAG? REALLY? COOL!
'N MY DAD TOLD ME ABOUT A PORTHOLE THAT'S EASY TO OPEN...
SHHH ...
IT'S OPENING!
TIME TO PUT ON THE AIR BAG!!
CREAK

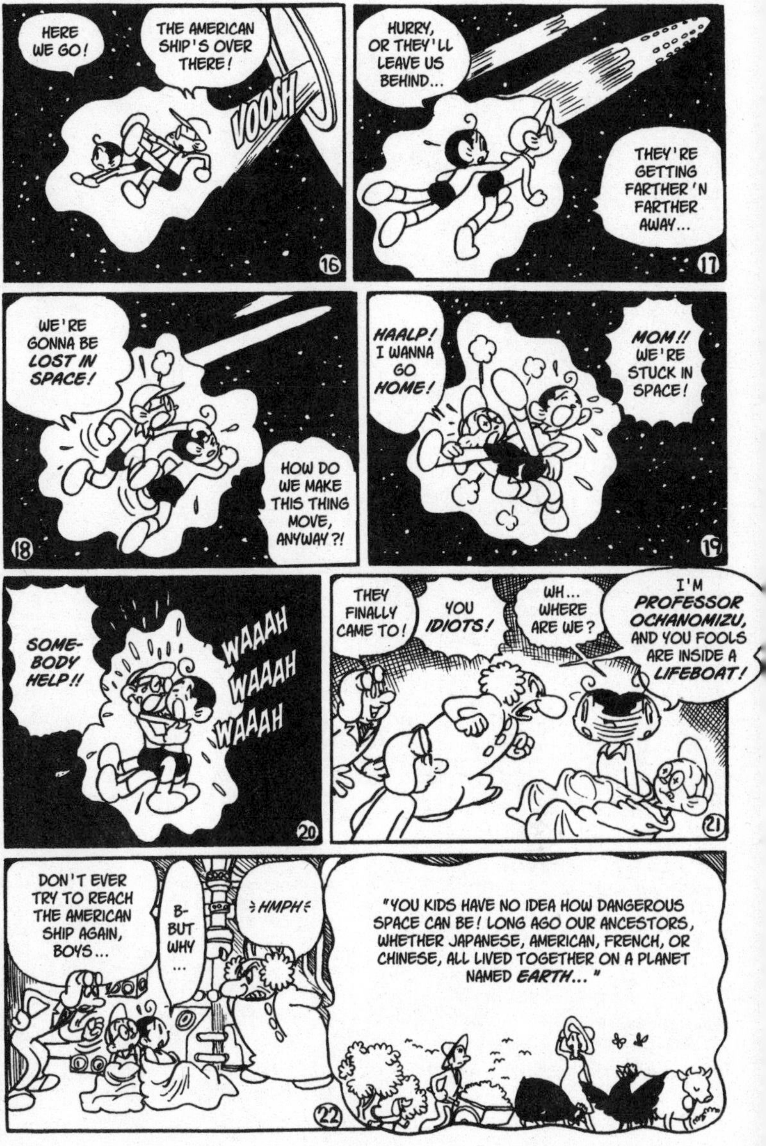
HERE WE GO!
THE AMERICAN SHIP'S OVER THERE!
VOOSH
HURRY, OR THEY'LL LEAVE US BEHIND...
THEY'RE GETTING FARTHER 'N FARTHER AWAY...
WE'RE GONNA BE LOST IN SPACE!
HOW DO WE MAKE THIS THING MOVE, ANYWAY?!
HAALP! I WANNA GO HOME!
MOM!! WE'RE STUCK IN SPACE!
SOME-BODY HELP!!
WAAAH
WAAAH
WAAAH
THEY FINALLY CAME TO!
YOU IDIOTS!
WH... WHERE ARE WE?
I'M PROFESSOR OCHANOMIZU, AND YOU FOOLS ARE INSIDE A LIFEBOAT!
DON'T EVER TRY TO REACH THE AMERICAN SHIP AGAIN, BOYS...
B-BUT WHY ...
HMPH
"YOU KIDS HAVE NO IDEA HOW DANGEROUS SPACE CAN BE! LONG AGO OUR ANCESTORS, WHETHER JAPANESE, AMERICAN, FRENCH, OR CHINESE, ALL LIVED TOGETHER ON A PLANET NAMED EARTH..."

YOU MEAN PEOPLE COULD GO TO AMERICA?

TO *ANY* COUNTRY!

"BUT ONE DAY EARTH CAME TO AN END... SO PEOPLE BUILT A ROCKET AND ESCAPED INTO SPACE..."

EVER SINCE THEN, WE'VE BEEN WANDERING SPACE FOR TWO THOUSAND YEARS, SEARCHING FOR A NEW PLANET TO LIVE ON...

AND YOU BOYS'LL PROBABLY SPEND YOUR WHOLE LIVES ON THIS SHIP...

PANTIORUS

GORT

METROSRAP

COLONEL ANTI ANT

THE LACK OF GRAVITY'S ONE OF THE REASONS PEOPLE'S BODIES ARE DIFFERENT NOW...

SO AS LONG AS WE'RE SEARCHING FOR A NEW PLANET, YOU BOYS CAN'T GO OUTSIDE!!

WHAT? ARE YOU *SERIOUS*?

PROFESSOR!! *BIG NEWS!!* THERE APPEARS TO BE AN OBJECT IN SPACE IN FRONT OF US WITH AN *ATMOSPHERE!*

NO DOUBT ABOUT IT! JUST GOT WORD FROM THE MOTHER SHIP!

BRAVO!!

YOU BOYS'RE *LUCKY!* YOU'LL BE ABLE TO GO *OUTSIDE!*

SMACK

340

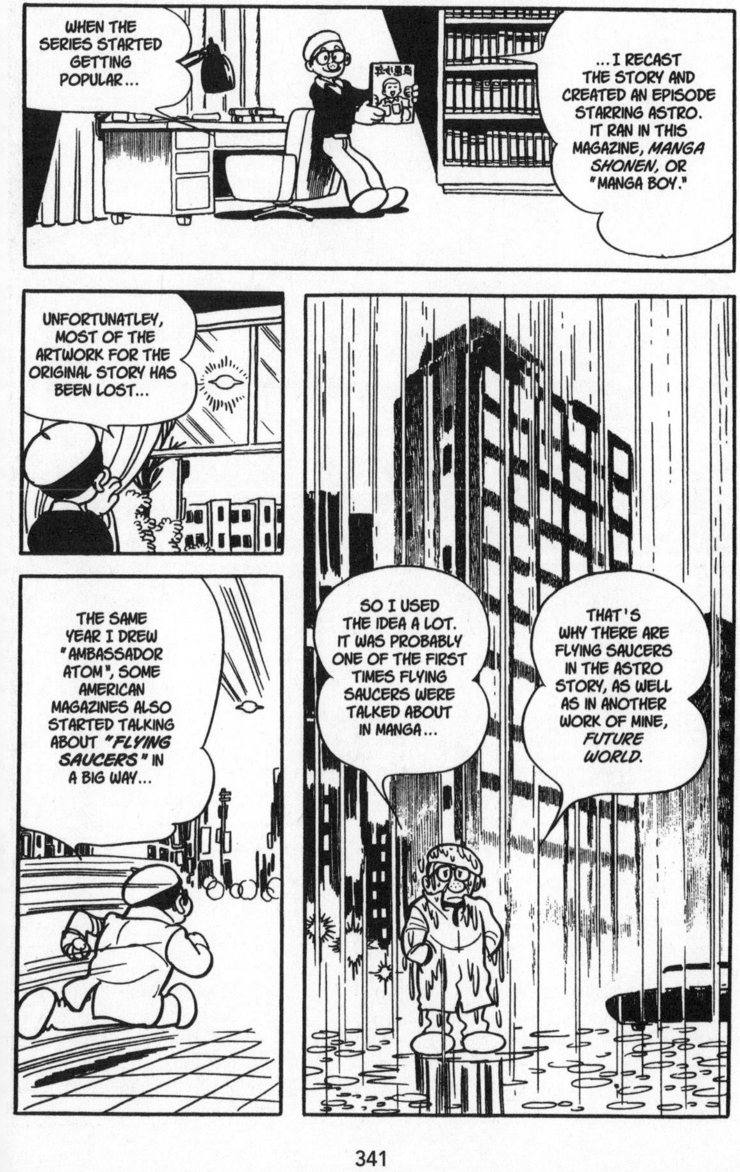
WHEN THE SERIES STARTED GETTING POPULAR...
...I RECAST THE STORY AND CREATED AN EPISODE STARRING ASTRO. IT RAN IN THIS MAGAZINE, *MANGA SHONEN*, OR "MANGA BOY."
UNFORTUNATLEY, MOST OF THE ARTWORK FOR THE ORIGINAL STORY HAS BEEN LOST...
THE SAME YEAR I DREW "AMBASSADOR ATOM", SOME AMERICAN MAGAZINES ALSO STARTED TALKING ABOUT *"FLYING SAUCERS"* IN A BIG WAY...
SO I USED THE IDEA A LOT. IT WAS PROBABLY ONE OF THE FIRST TIMES FLYING SAUCERS WERE TALKED ABOUT IN MANGA...
THAT'S WHY THERE ARE FLYING SAUCERS IN THE ASTRO STORY, AS WELL AS IN ANOTHER WORK OF MINE, *FUTURE WORLD*.

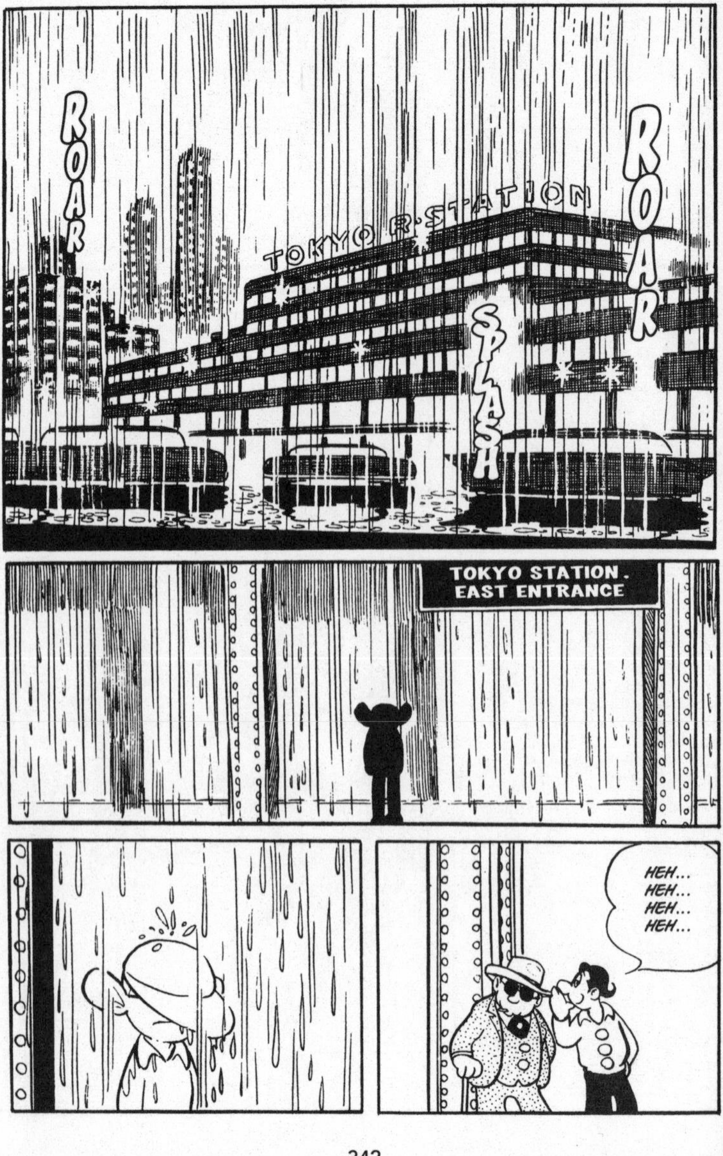
ROAR
TOKYO R STATION
ROAR
SPLASH
TOKYO STATION.
EAST ENTRANCE
HEH...
HEH...
HEH...
HEH...

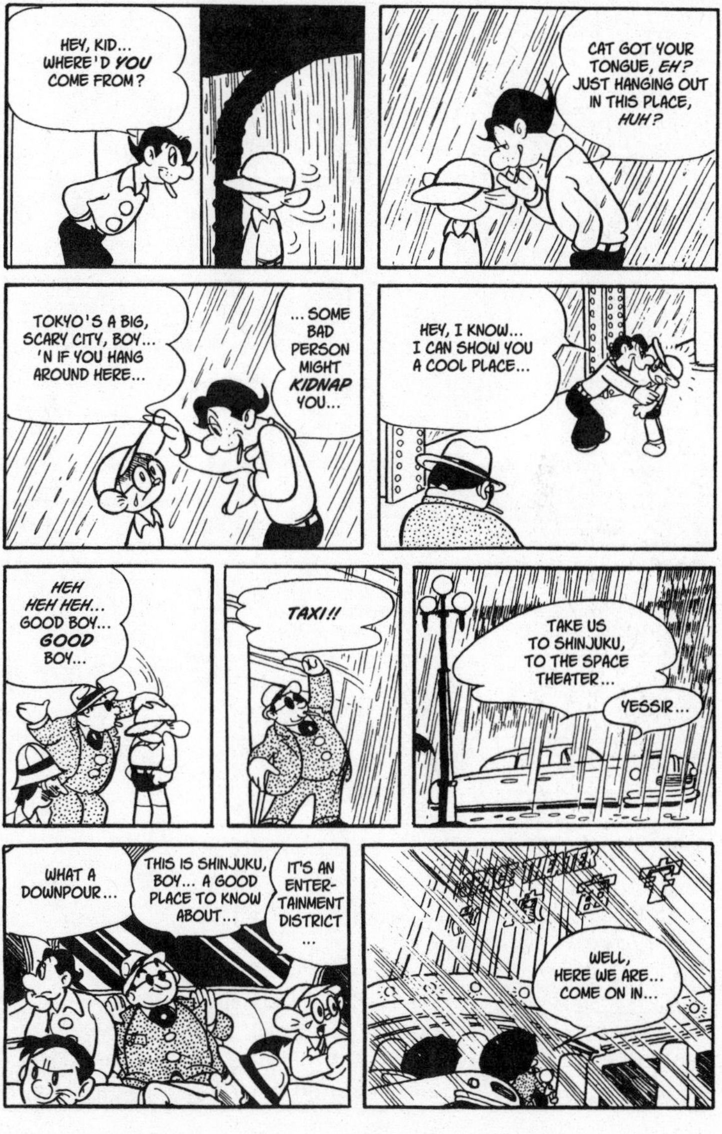
HEY, KID... WHERE'D *YOU* COME FROM?
CAT GOT YOUR TONGUE, *EH?* JUST HANGING OUT IN THIS PLACE, *HUH?*
TOKYO'S A BIG, SCARY CITY, BOY... 'N IF YOU HANG AROUND HERE...
... SOME BAD PERSON MIGHT *KIDNAP* YOU...
HEY, I KNOW... I CAN SHOW YOU A COOL PLACE...
HEH HEH HEH... GOOD BOY... *GOOD* BOY...
TAXI!!
TAKE US TO SHINJUKU, TO THE SPACE THEATER...
YESSIR...
WHAT A DOWNPOUR...
THIS IS SHINJUKU, BOY... A GOOD PLACE TO KNOW ABOUT...
IT'S AN ENTER-TAINMENT DISTRICT ...
WELL, HERE WE ARE... COME ON IN...

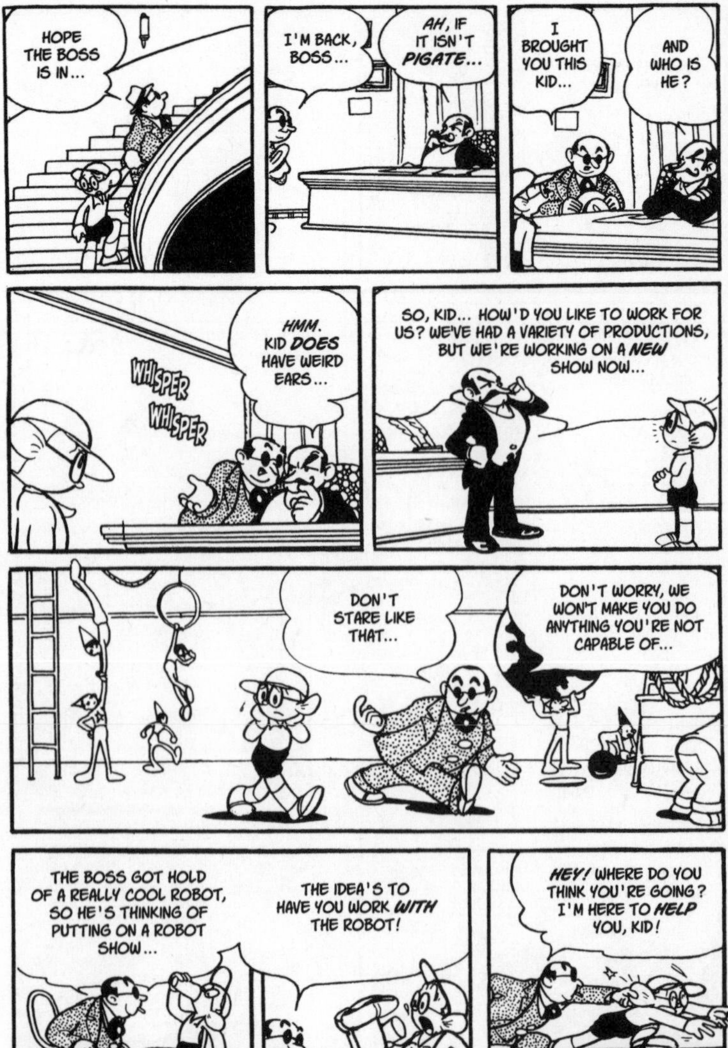
HOPE THE BOSS IS IN...
I'M BACK, BOSS...
AH, IF IT ISN'T PIGATE...
I BROUGHT YOU THIS KID...
AND WHO IS HE?
WHISPER
WHISPER
HMM. KID DOES HAVE WEIRD EARS...
SO, KID... HOW'D YOU LIKE TO WORK FOR US? WE'VE HAD A VARIETY OF PRODUCTIONS, BUT WE'RE WORKING ON A NEW SHOW NOW...
DON'T STARE LIKE THAT...
DON'T WORRY, WE WON'T MAKE YOU DO ANYTHING YOU'RE NOT CAPABLE OF...
THE BOSS GOT HOLD OF A REALLY COOL ROBOT, SO HE'S THINKING OF PUTTING ON A ROBOT SHOW...
THE IDEA'S TO HAVE YOU WORK WITH THE ROBOT!
HEY! WHERE DO YOU THINK YOU'RE GOING? I'M HERE TO HELP YOU, KID!

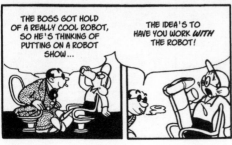

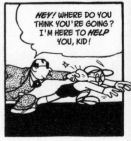

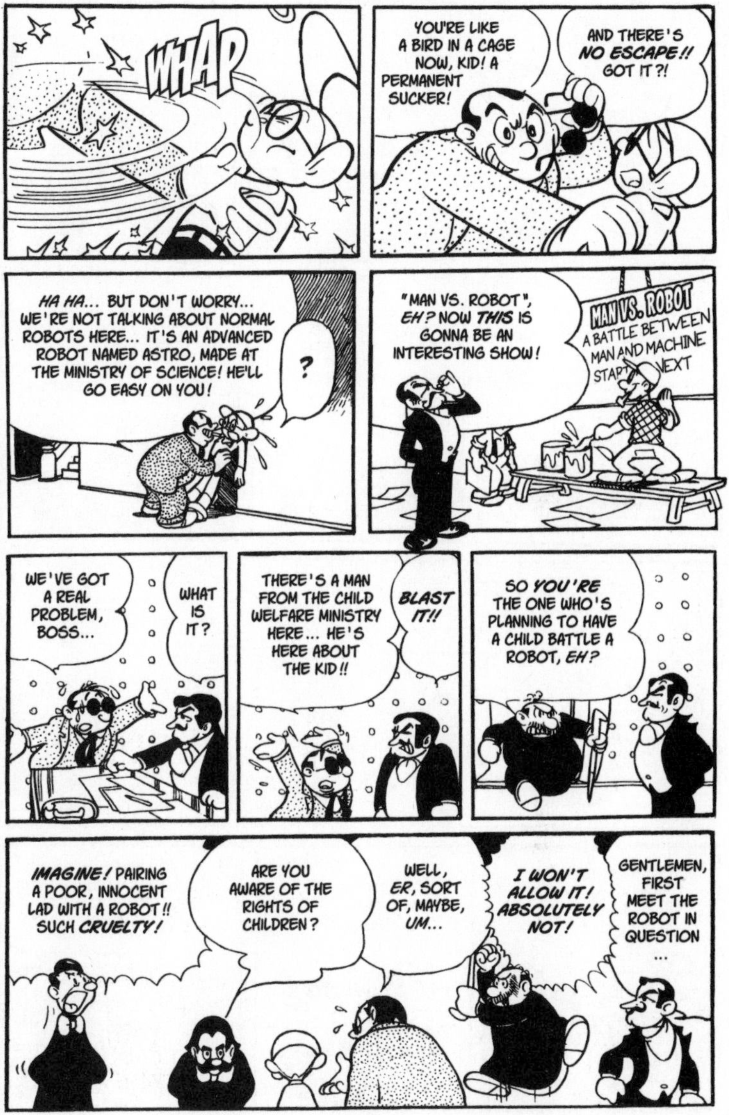
WHAP
YOU'RE LIKE A BIRD IN A CAGE NOW, KID! A PERMANENT SUCKER!
AND THERE'S *NO ESCAPE!!* GOT IT?!
HA HA... BUT DON'T WORRY... WE'RE NOT TALKING ABOUT NORMAL ROBOTS HERE... IT'S AN ADVANCED ROBOT NAMED ASTRO, MADE AT THE MINISTRY OF SCIENCE! HE'LL GO EASY ON YOU!
?
"MAN VS. ROBOT", *EH?* NOW *THIS* IS GONNA BE AN INTERESTING SHOW!
MAN VS. ROBOT
A BATTLE BETWEEN MAN AND MACHINE
WE'VE GOT A REAL PROBLEM, BOSS...
WHAT IS IT?
THERE'S A MAN FROM THE CHILD WELFARE MINISTRY HERE... HE'S HERE ABOUT THE KID!!
BLAST IT!!
SO *YOU'RE* THE ONE WHO'S PLANNING TO HAVE A CHILD BATTLE A ROBOT, *EH?*
IMAGINE! PAIRING A POOR, INNOCENT LAD WITH A ROBOT!! SUCH *CRUELTY!*
ARE YOU AWARE OF THE RIGHTS OF CHILDREN?
WELL, *ER*, SORT OF, MAYBE, *UM*...
I WON'T ALLOW IT! ABSOLUTELY NOT!
GENTLEMEN, FIRST MEET THE ROBOT IN QUESTION ...

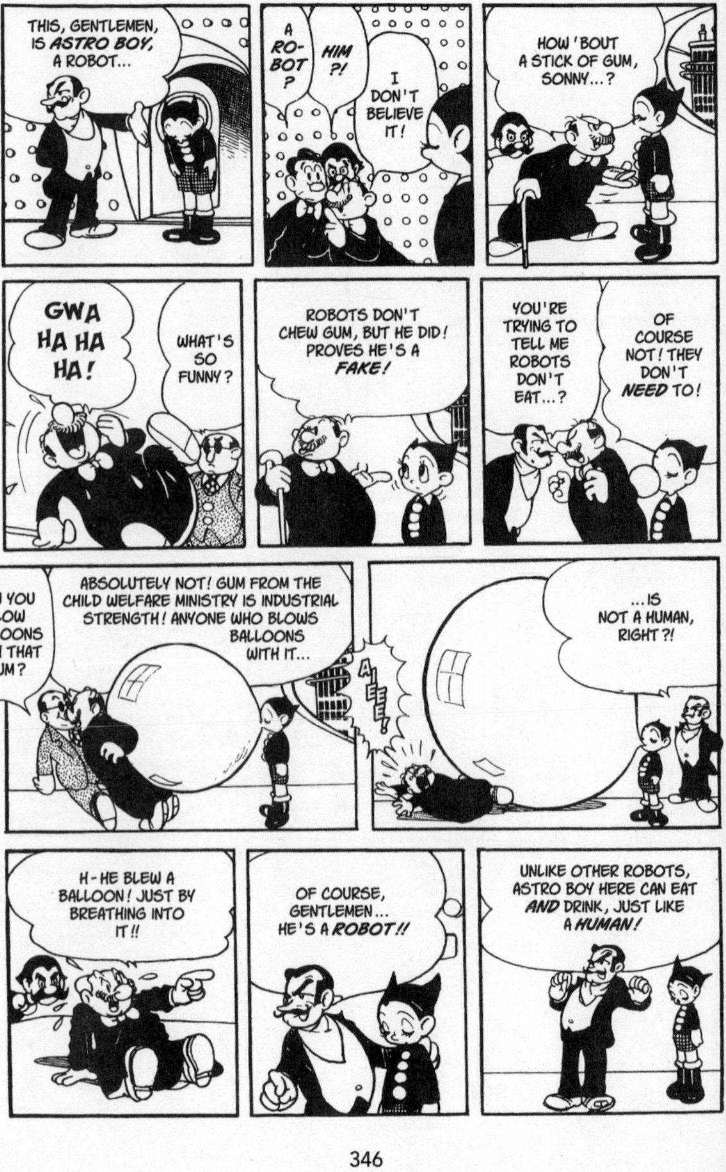
THIS, GENTLEMEN, IS ASTRO BOY, A ROBOT...
A RO-BOT?
HIM ?!
I DON'T BELIEVE IT!
HOW 'BOUT A STICK OF GUM, SONNY...?
GWA HA HA HA!
WHAT'S SO FUNNY?
ROBOTS DON'T CHEW GUM, BUT HE DID! PROVES HE'S A FAKE!
YOU'RE TRYING TO TELL ME ROBOTS DON'T EAT...?
OF COURSE NOT! THEY DON'T NEED TO!
C'N YOU BLOW BALLOONS WITH THAT GUM?
ABSOLUTELY NOT! GUM FROM THE CHILD WELFARE MINISTRY IS INDUSTRIAL STRENGTH! ANYONE WHO BLOWS BALLOONS WITH IT...
AIEEE!
...IS NOT A HUMAN, RIGHT?!
H-HE BLEW A BALLOON! JUST BY BREATHING INTO IT!!
OF COURSE, GENTLEMEN... HE'S A ROBOT!!
UNLIKE OTHER ROBOTS, ASTRO BOY HERE CAN EAT AND DRINK, JUST LIKE A HUMAN!

ALLOW ME TO EXPLAIN, GENTLEMEN, ABOUT THIS ROBOT AND HOW HE CAME INTO MY POSSESSION...

ASTRO IS A *WORK OF ART*, CREATED AT THE MINISTRY OF SCIENCE BY *DR. TENMA.*

THAT, OVER THERE, IS THE ADVANCED FACTORY WHERE HE WAS MANUFACTURED!

DR. TENMA ?! BUT ISN'T HE THE HEAD OF THE MINISTRY OF SCIENCE ?

DR. TENMA:

BORN INTO A LONG LINE OF HORSE RADISH FARMERS, IN THE PARTICULARLY UNLUCKY YEAR OF THE HORSE, IN GUNMA ("HORSE HERD") PREFECTURE. REAL NAME IS TARO UMA ("HORSE"). GRADUATED FROM THE UNIVERSITY OF NERIMA ("WALKING HORSE"), AND THOUGH A COMPLETE DARK HORSE, THROUGH AN AMAZING DEMONSTRATION OF INTELLECTUAL HORSEPOWER ROSE TO BE THE HEAD OF THE MINISTRY OF SCIENCE -- IN AN AREA OF TOKYO KNOWN AS TAKADANOBABA, WHICH LOOSELY TRANSLATES INTO A "HIGH PASTURE FOR HORSES." AMONG THOSE WISHING TO UNSEAT HIM, HE IS KNOWN AS A REAL HORSE OF A DIFFERENT COLOR.

"THIS DR. TENMA HAD A SON OF HIS OWN, NAMED *TOBIO*..."

"... AND HE LOVED HIS SON *DEEPLY*... "

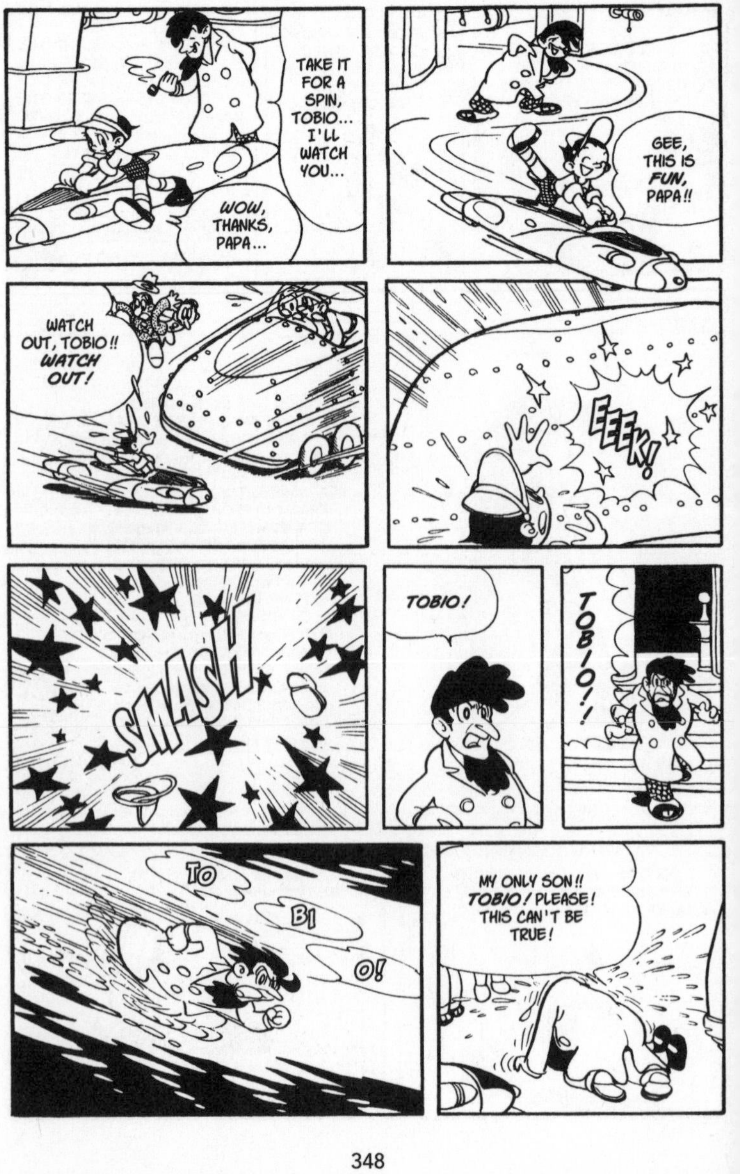
TAKE IT FOR A SPIN, TOBIO... I'LL WATCH YOU...
WOW, THANKS, PAPA...
GEE, THIS IS FUN, PAPA!!
WATCH OUT, TOBIO!! WATCH OUT!
EEEK!
SMASH
TOBIO!
TOBIO!!
TO
BI
O!
MY ONLY SON!! TOBIO! PLEASE! THIS CAN'T BE TRUE!

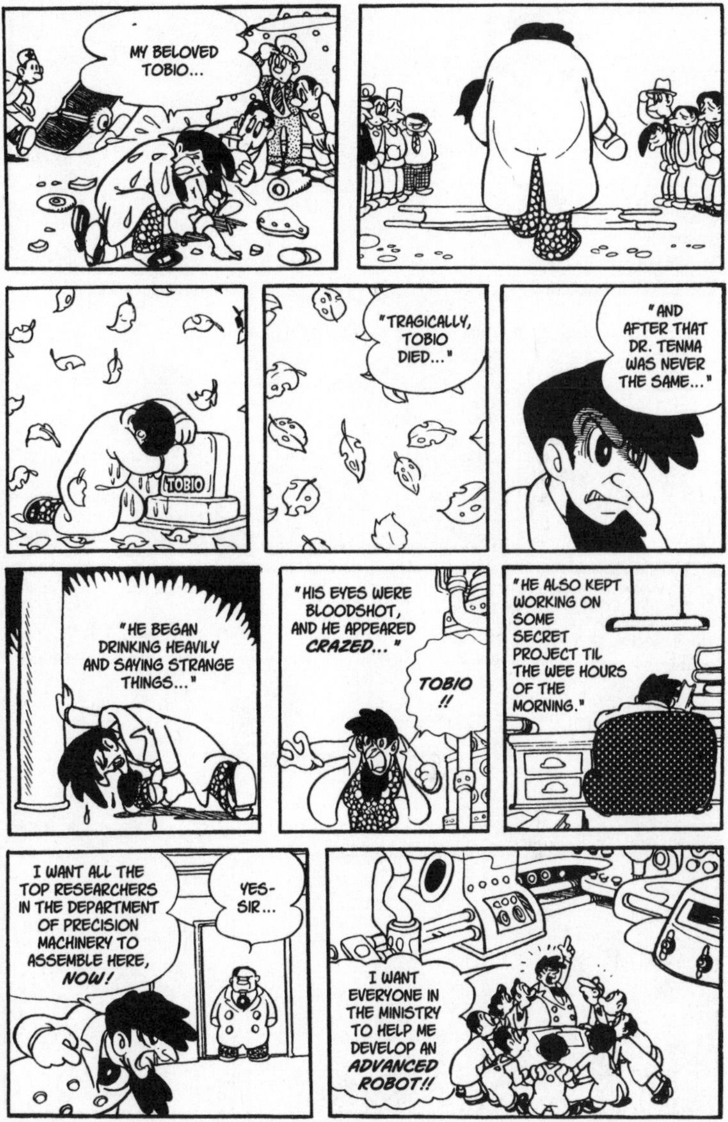
MY BELOVED TOBIO...
"TRAGICALLY, TOBIO DIED..."
"AND AFTER THAT DR. TENMA WAS NEVER THE SAME..."
TOBIO
"HE BEGAN DRINKING HEAVILY AND SAYING STRANGE THINGS..."
"HIS EYES WERE BLOODSHOT, AND HE APPEARED *CRAZED*..."
TOBIO !!
"HE ALSO KEPT WORKING ON SOME SECRET PROJECT TIL THE WEE HOURS OF THE MORNING."
I WANT ALL THE TOP RESEARCHERS IN THE DEPARTMENT OF PRECISION MACHINERY TO ASSEMBLE HERE, *NOW!*
YES-SIR...
I WANT EVERYONE IN THE MINISTRY TO HELP ME DEVELOP AN *ADVANCED ROBOT!!*

"DR. TENMA WAS DETERMINED TO REPLICATE HIS SON TOBIO, AS A *ROBOT*..."

"HE TOOK ADVANTAGE OF THE WORLD'S MOST ADVANCED TECHNOLOGY..."

"A NEW, HIGHLY ELASTIC PLASTIC WAS USED TO COVER THE ROBOT'S BODY..."

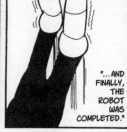

"...AND FINALLY, THE ROBOT WAS COMPLETED."

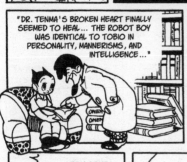

"DR. TENMA'S BROKEN HEART FINALLY SEEMED TO HEAL... THE ROBOT BOY WAS IDENTICAL TO TOBIO IN PERSONALITY, MANNERISMS, AND INTELLIGENCE..."

"BUT THEN..."

"...TENMA DISCOVERED A TERRIBLE *FLAW* IN HIS CREATION..."

HOW COME YOU NEVER *GROW* ?!!!

YOU'RE NOT TOBIO !! YOU'RE A JUST A *ROBOT* AFTER ALL !!

YOU'RE *USELESS* ...!!

350

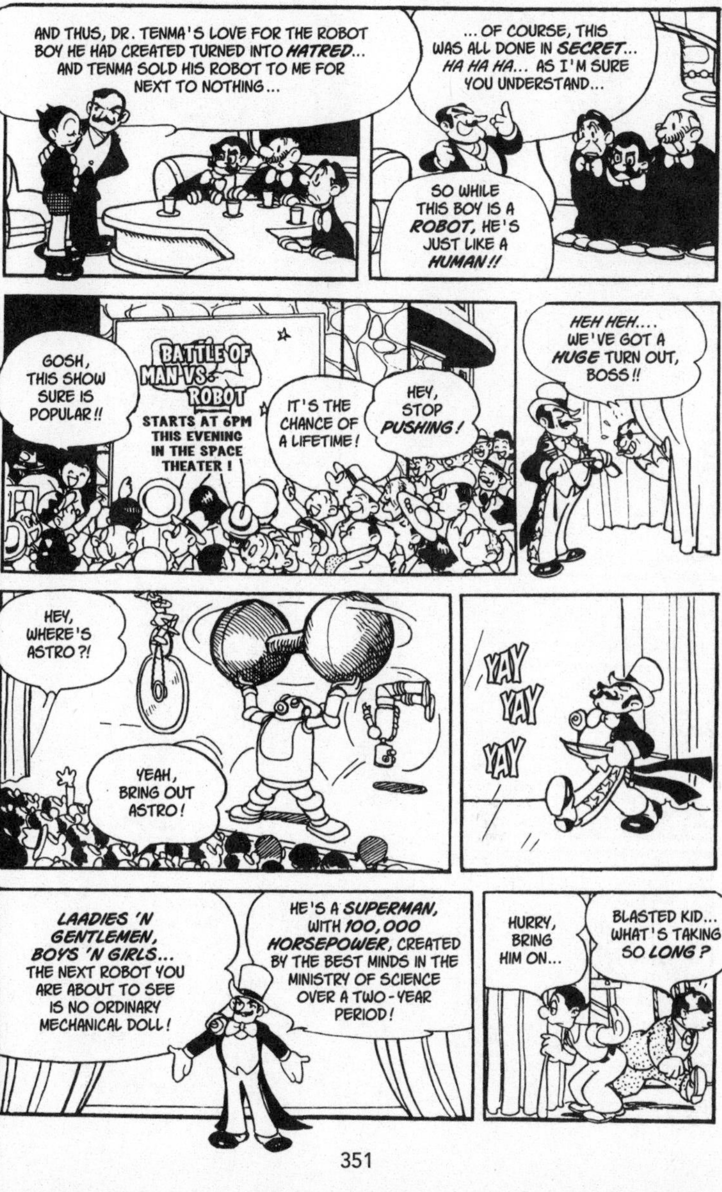
AND THUS, DR. TENMA'S LOVE FOR THE ROBOT BOY HE HAD CREATED TURNED INTO HATRED... AND TENMA SOLD HIS ROBOT TO ME FOR NEXT TO NOTHING...
... OF COURSE, THIS WAS ALL DONE IN SECRET... HA HA HA... AS I'M SURE YOU UNDERSTAND...
SO WHILE THIS BOY IS A ROBOT, HE'S JUST LIKE A HUMAN!!
GOSH, THIS SHOW SURE IS POPULAR!!
BATTLE OF MAN VS. ROBOT
STARTS AT 6PM THIS EVENING IN THE SPACE THEATER!
IT'S THE CHANCE OF A LIFETIME!
HEY, STOP PUSHING!
HEH HEH.... WE'VE GOT A HUGE TURN OUT, BOSS!!
HEY, WHERE'S ASTRO?!
YEAH, BRING OUT ASTRO!
YAY
YAY
YAY
LAADIES 'N GENTLEMEN, BOYS 'N GIRLS... THE NEXT ROBOT YOU ARE ABOUT TO SEE IS NO ORDINARY MECHANICAL DOLL!
HE'S A SUPERMAN, WITH 100,000 HORSEPOWER, CREATED BY THE BEST MINDS IN THE MINISTRY OF SCIENCE OVER A TWO-YEAR PERIOD!
HURRY, BRING HIM ON...
BLASTED KID... WHAT'S TAKING SO LONG?

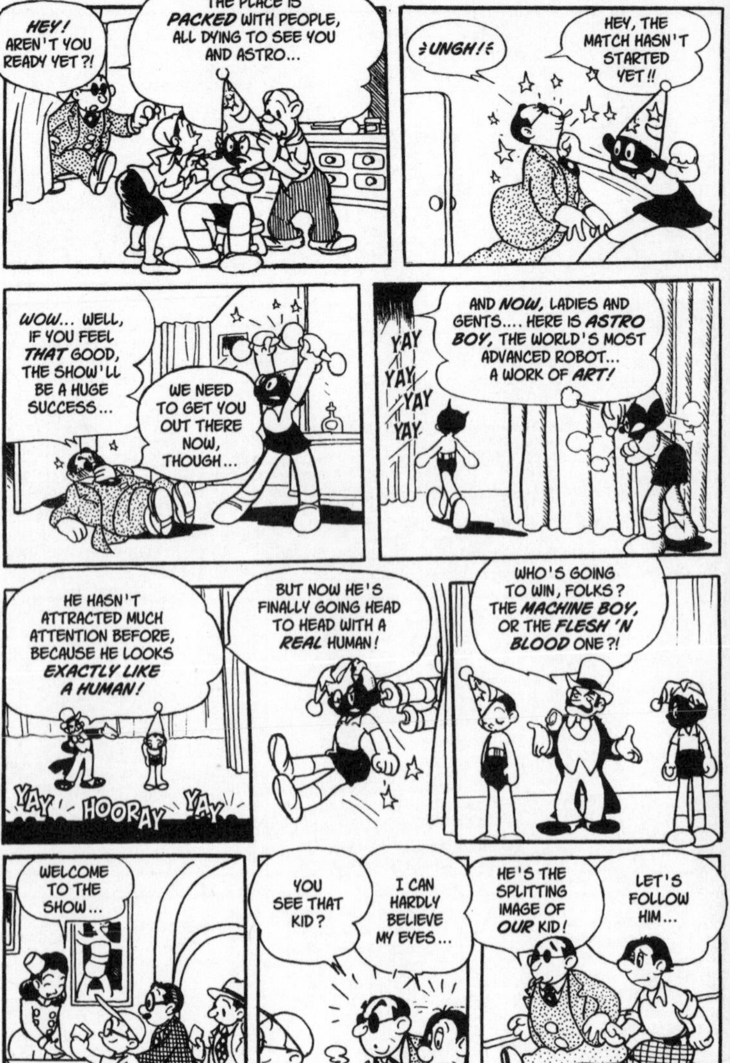
HEY! AREN'T YOU READY YET?!
THE PLACE IS PACKED WITH PEOPLE, ALL DYING TO SEE YOU AND ASTRO...
UNGH!
HEY, THE MATCH HASN'T STARTED YET!!
WOW... WELL, IF YOU FEEL THAT GOOD, THE SHOW'LL BE A HUGE SUCCESS...
WE NEED TO GET YOU OUT THERE NOW, THOUGH...
YAY
YAY
YAY
YAY
AND NOW, LADIES AND GENTS.... HERE IS ASTRO BOY, THE WORLD'S MOST ADVANCED ROBOT... A WORK OF ART!
HE HASN'T ATTRACTED MUCH ATTENTION BEFORE, BECAUSE HE LOOKS EXACTLY LIKE A HUMAN!
YAY HOORAY YAY
BUT NOW HE'S FINALLY GOING HEAD TO HEAD WITH A REAL HUMAN!
WHO'S GOING TO WIN, FOLKS? THE MACHINE BOY, OR THE FLESH 'N BLOOD ONE?!
WELCOME TO THE SHOW...
YOU SEE THAT KID?
I CAN HARDLY BELIEVE MY EYES...
HE'S THE SPLITTING IMAGE OF OUR KID!
LET'S FOLLOW HIM...

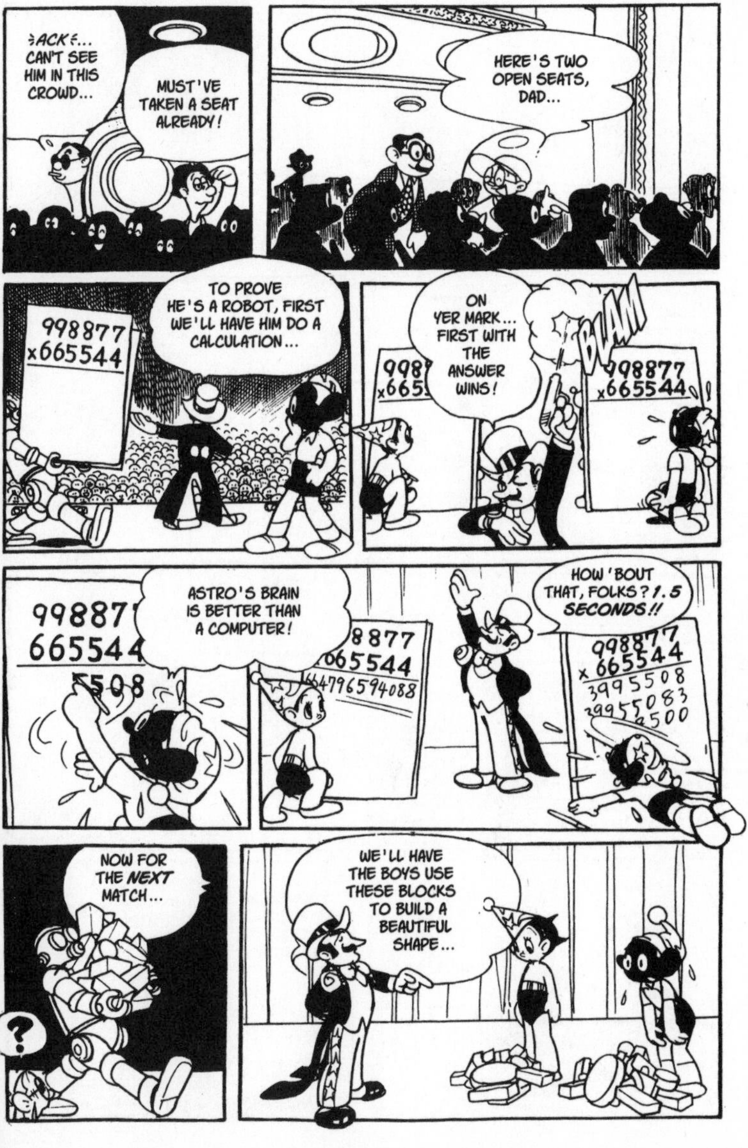

ACK...
CAN'T SEE HIM IN THIS CROWD...
MUST'VE TAKEN A SEAT ALREADY!
HERE'S TWO OPEN SEATS, DAD...
998877
x665544
TO PROVE HE'S A ROBOT, FIRST WE'LL HAVE HIM DO A CALCULATION...
ON YER MARK... FIRST WITH THE ANSWER WINS!
BLAM
998877
x665544
998877
665544
ASTRO'S BRAIN IS BETTER THAN A COMPUTER!
8877
665544
664796594088
HOW 'BOUT THAT, FOLKS? 1.5 SECONDS!!
998877
x 665544
3995508
NOW FOR THE NEXT MATCH...
?
WE'LL HAVE THE BOYS USE THESE BLOCKS TO BUILD A BEAUTIFUL SHAPE...

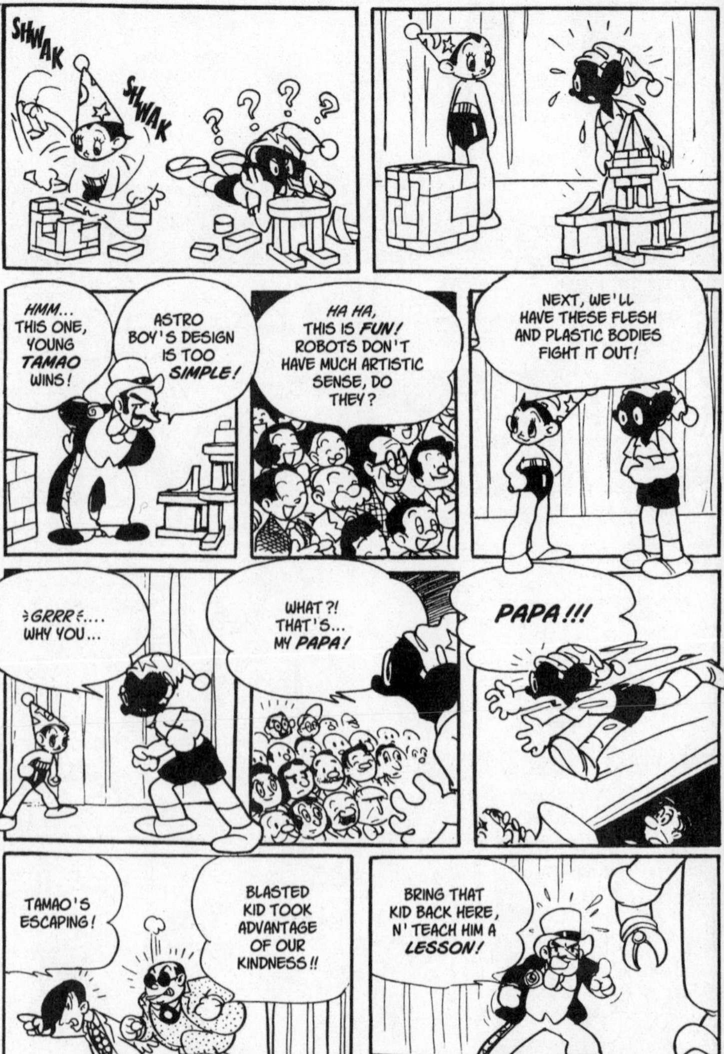
SHWAK
SHWAK
HMM... THIS ONE, YOUNG TAMAO WINS!
ASTRO BOY'S DESIGN IS TOO SIMPLE!
HA HA, THIS IS FUN! ROBOTS DON'T HAVE MUCH ARTISTIC SENSE, DO THEY?
NEXT, WE'LL HAVE THESE FLESH AND PLASTIC BODIES FIGHT IT OUT!
GRRR.... WHY YOU...
WHAT?! THAT'S... MY PAPA!
PAPA!!!
TAMAO'S ESCAPING!
BLASTED KID TOOK ADVANTAGE OF OUR KINDNESS!!
BRING THAT KID BACK HERE, N' TEACH HIM A LESSON!

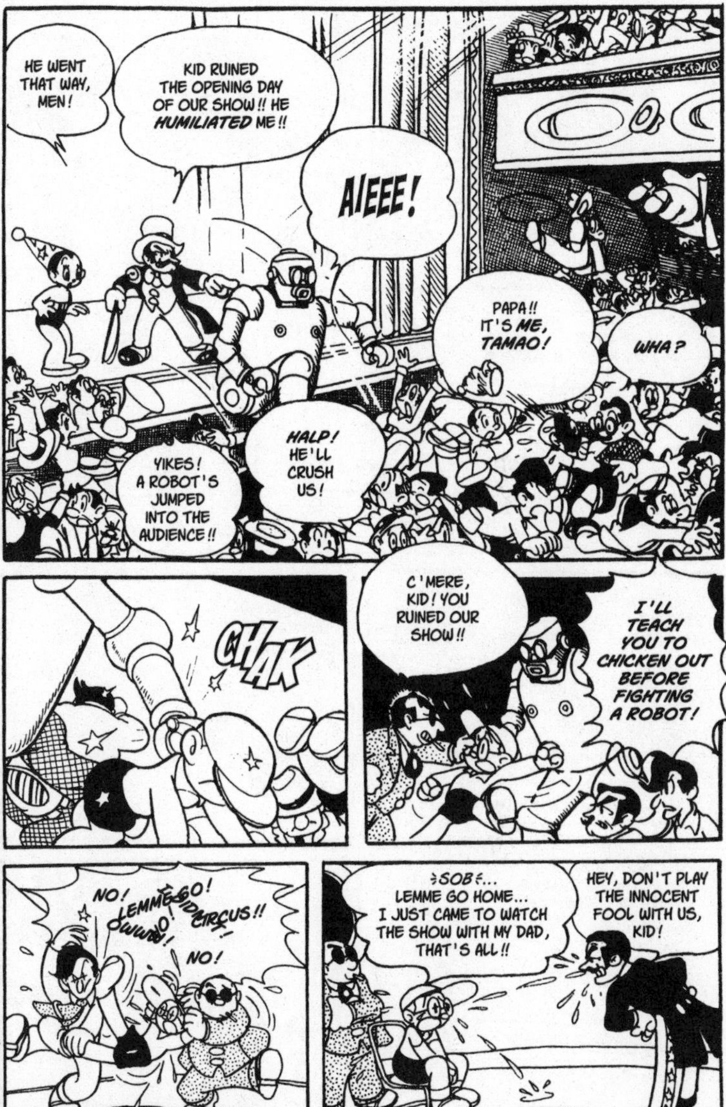
HE WENT THAT WAY, MEN!
KID RUINED THE OPENING DAY OF OUR SHOW!! HE ***HUMILIATED*** ME!!
AIEEE!
PAPA!! IT'S ***ME, TAMAO!***
WHA?
YIKES! A ROBOT'S JUMPED INTO THE AUDIENCE!!
HALP! HE'LL CRUSH US!
CHAK
C'MERE, KID! YOU RUINED OUR SHOW!!
I'LL TEACH YOU TO CHICKEN OUT BEFORE FIGHTING A ROBOT!
NO!
LEMME GO!
OWWW!
CIRCUS!!
NO!
SOB... LEMME GO HOME... I JUST CAME TO WATCH THE SHOW WITH MY DAD, THAT'S ALL!!
HEY, DON'T PLAY THE INNOCENT FOOL WITH US, KID!

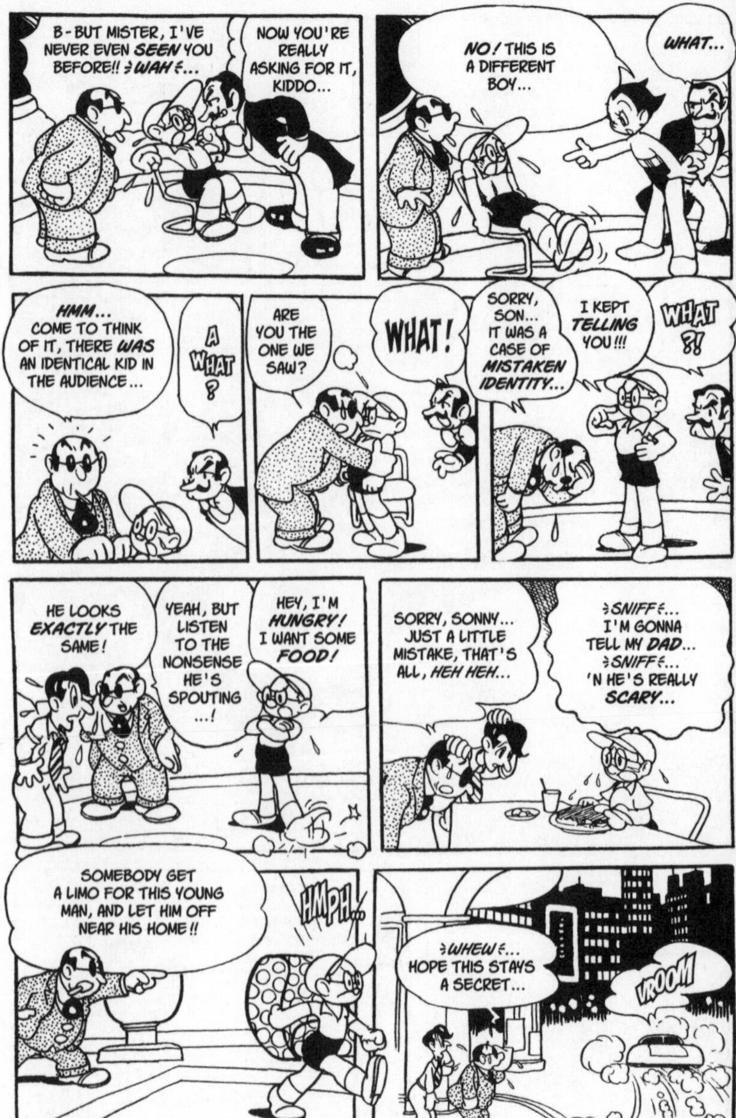
B-BUT MISTER, I'VE NEVER EVEN SEEN YOU BEFORE!! »WAH«...
NOW YOU'RE REALLY ASKING FOR IT, KIDDO...
NO! THIS IS A DIFFERENT BOY...
WHAT...
HMM... COME TO THINK OF IT, THERE WAS AN IDENTICAL KID IN THE AUDIENCE...
A WHAT?
ARE YOU THE ONE WE SAW?
WHAT!
SORRY, SON... IT WAS A CASE OF MISTAKEN IDENTITY...
I KEPT TELLING YOU!!!
WHAT?!
HE LOOKS EXACTLY THE SAME!
YEAH, BUT LISTEN TO THE NONSENSE HE'S SPOUTING...!
HEY, I'M HUNGRY! I WANT SOME FOOD!
SORRY, SONNY... JUST A LITTLE MISTAKE, THAT'S ALL, HEH HEH...
»SNIFF«... I'M GONNA TELL MY DAD... »SNIFF«... 'N HE'S REALLY SCARY...
SOMEBODY GET A LIMO FOR THIS YOUNG MAN, AND LET HIM OFF NEAR HIS HOME!!
HMPH...
»WHEW«... HOPE THIS STAYS A SECRET...
VROOM

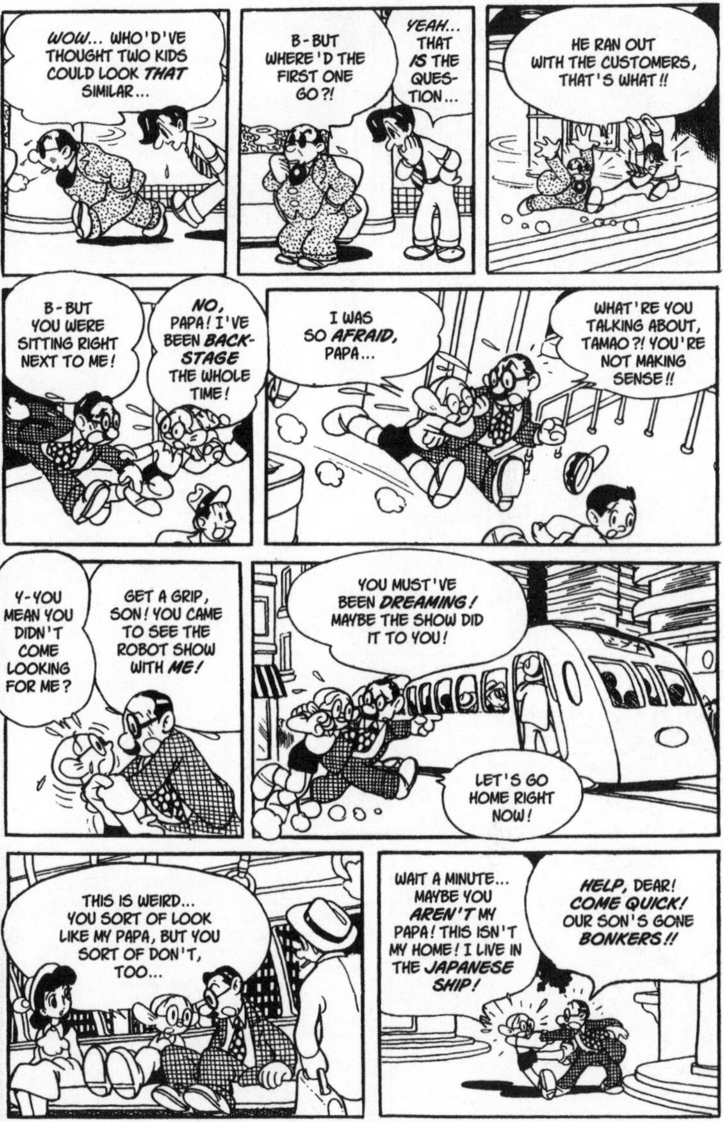
WOW... WHO'D'VE THOUGHT TWO KIDS COULD LOOK THAT SIMILAR...
B-BUT WHERE'D THE FIRST ONE GO?!
YEAH... THAT IS THE QUES-TION...
HE RAN OUT WITH THE CUSTOMERS, THAT'S WHAT!!
B-BUT YOU WERE SITTING RIGHT NEXT TO ME!
NO, PAPA! I'VE BEEN BACK-STAGE THE WHOLE TIME!
I WAS SO AFRAID, PAPA...
WHAT'RE YOU TALKING ABOUT, TAMAO?! YOU'RE NOT MAKING SENSE!!
Y-YOU MEAN YOU DIDN'T COME LOOKING FOR ME?
GET A GRIP, SON! YOU CAME TO SEE THE ROBOT SHOW WITH ME!
YOU MUST'VE BEEN DREAMING! MAYBE THE SHOW DID IT TO YOU!
LET'S GO HOME RIGHT NOW!
THIS IS WEIRD... YOU SORT OF LOOK LIKE MY PAPA, BUT YOU SORT OF DON'T, TOO...
WAIT A MINUTE... MAYBE YOU AREN'T MY PAPA! THIS ISN'T MY HOME! I LIVE IN THE JAPANESE SHIP!
HELP, DEAR! COME QUICK! OUR SON'S GONE BONKERS!!

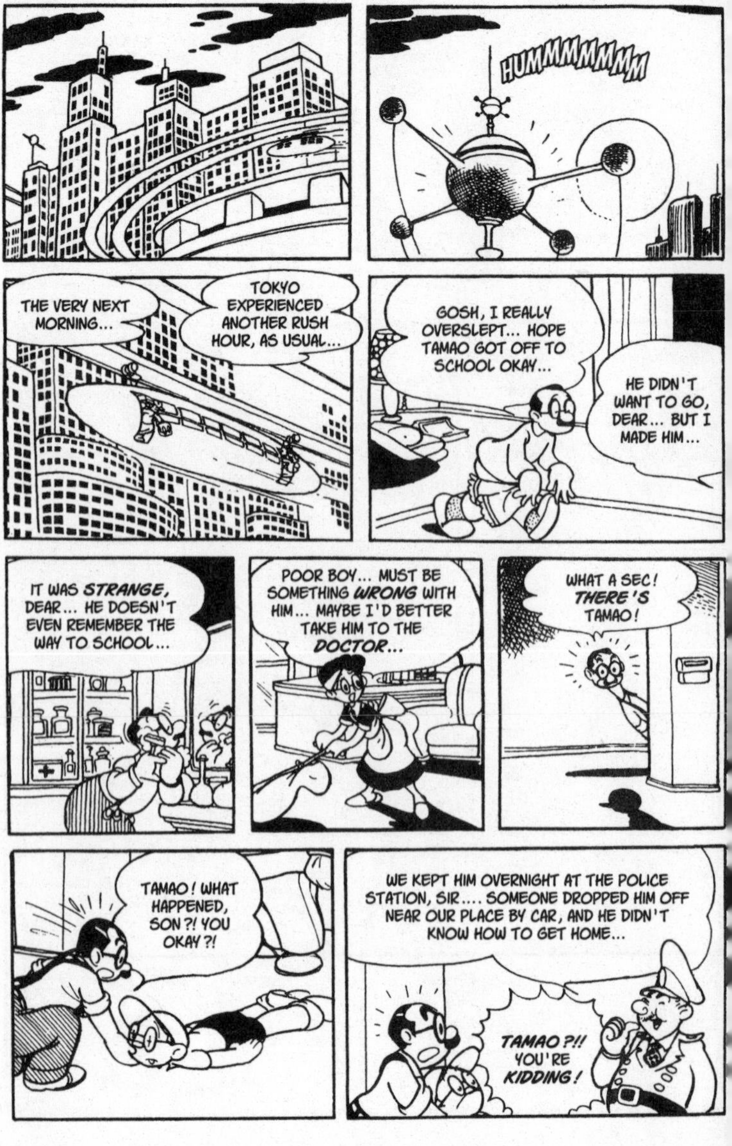
HUMMMMMMM
THE VERY NEXT MORNING...
TOKYO EXPERIENCED ANOTHER RUSH HOUR, AS USUAL...
GOSH, I REALLY OVERSLEPT... HOPE TAMAO GOT OFF TO SCHOOL OKAY...
HE DIDN'T WANT TO GO, DEAR... BUT I MADE HIM...
IT WAS ***STRANGE,*** DEAR... HE DOESN'T EVEN REMEMBER THE WAY TO SCHOOL...
POOR BOY... MUST BE SOMETHING ***WRONG*** WITH HIM... MAYBE I'D BETTER TAKE HIM TO THE ***DOCTOR...***
WHAT A SEC! ***THERE'S*** TAMAO!
TAMAO! WHAT HAPPENED, SON?! YOU OKAY?!
WE KEPT HIM OVERNIGHT AT THE POLICE STATION, SIR.... SOMEONE DROPPED HIM OFF NEAR OUR PLACE BY CAR, AND HE DIDN'T KNOW HOW TO GET HOME...
TAMAO?!! YOU'RE ***KIDDING!***

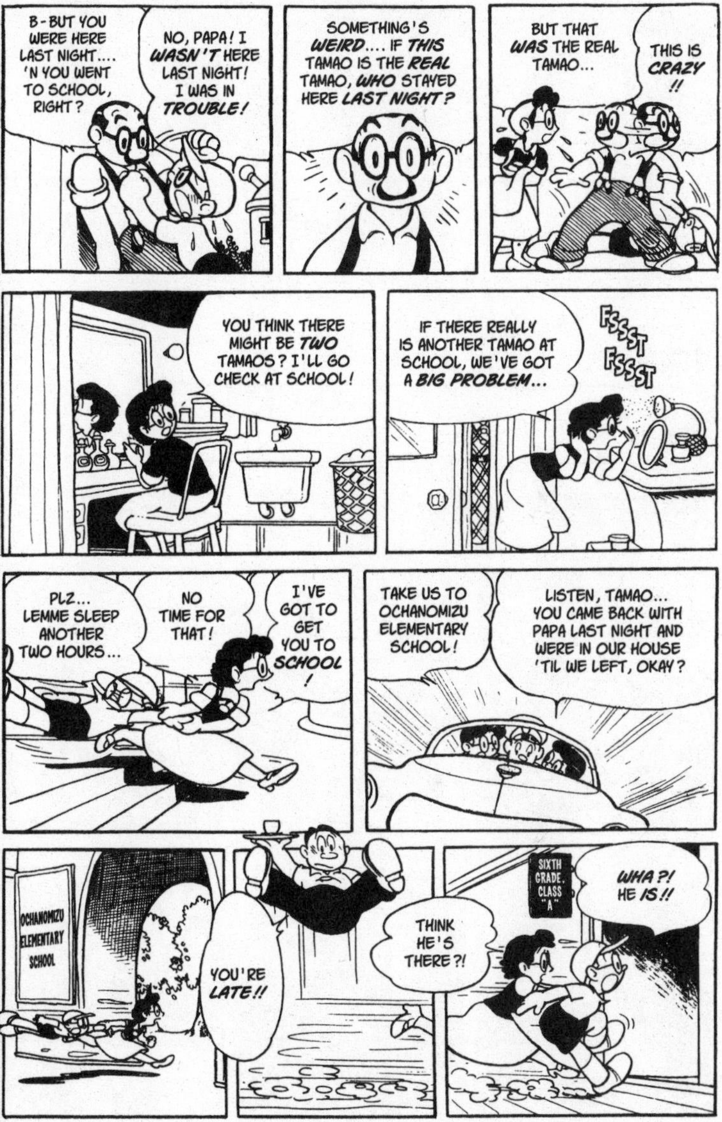
B-BUT YOU WERE HERE LAST NIGHT.... 'N YOU WENT TO SCHOOL, RIGHT?
NO, PAPA! I WASN'T HERE LAST NIGHT! I WAS IN TROUBLE!
SOMETHING'S WEIRD.... IF THIS TAMAO IS THE REAL TAMAO, WHO STAYED HERE LAST NIGHT?
BUT THAT WAS THE REAL TAMAO...
THIS IS CRAZY !!
YOU THINK THERE MIGHT BE TWO TAMAOS? I'LL GO CHECK AT SCHOOL!
IF THERE REALLY IS ANOTHER TAMAO AT SCHOOL, WE'VE GOT A BIG PROBLEM...
FSSST FSSST
PLZ... LEMME SLEEP ANOTHER TWO HOURS...
NO TIME FOR THAT!
I'VE GOT TO GET YOU TO SCHOOL!
TAKE US TO OCHANOMIZU ELEMENTARY SCHOOL!
LISTEN, TAMAO... YOU CAME BACK WITH PAPA LAST NIGHT AND WERE IN OUR HOUSE 'TIL WE LEFT, OKAY?
OCHANOMIZU ELEMENTARY SCHOOL
YOU'RE LATE!!
THINK HE'S THERE?!
SIXTH GRADE, CLASS "A"
WHA?! HE IS!!

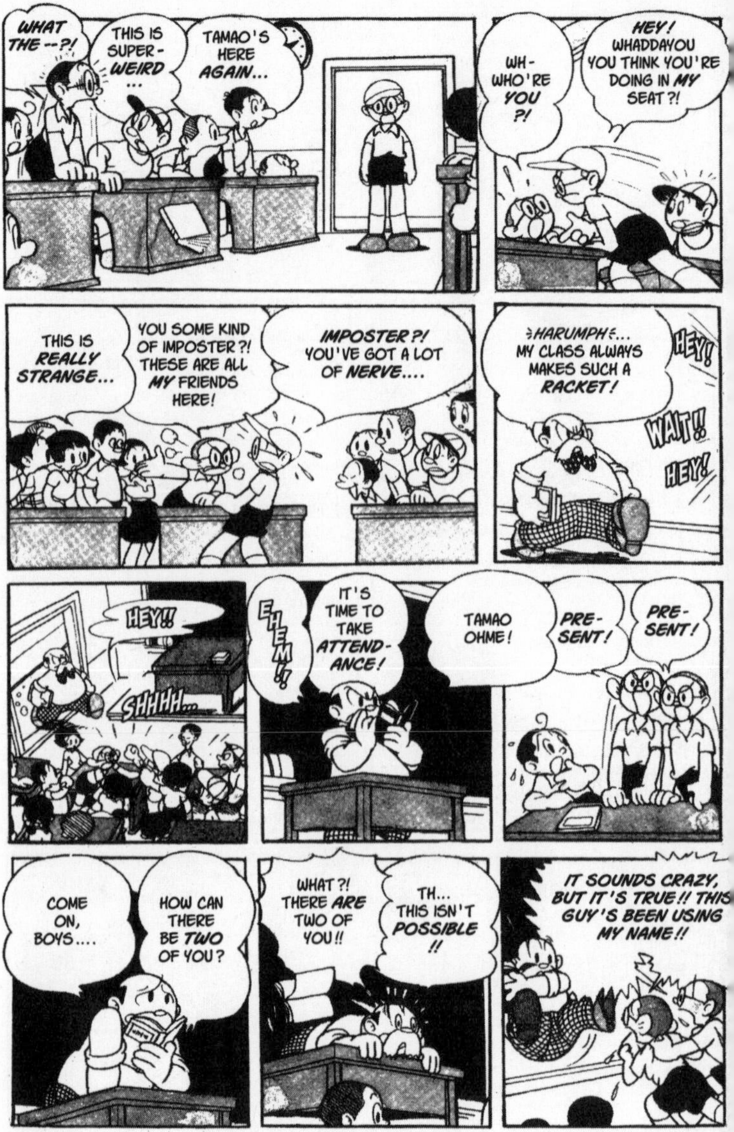
WHAT THE --?!
THIS IS SUPER-WEIRD ...
TAMAO'S HERE AGAIN...
WH-WHO'RE YOU ?!
HEY! WHADDAYOU YOU THINK YOU'RE DOING IN MY SEAT?!
THIS IS REALLY STRANGE...
YOU SOME KIND OF IMPOSTER?! THESE ARE ALL MY FRIENDS HERE!
IMPOSTER?! YOU'VE GOT A LOT OF NERVE....
HARUMPH... MY CLASS ALWAYS MAKES SUCH A RACKET!
HEY!
WAIT!!
HEY!
HEY!!
SHHHH...
EHEM!!
IT'S TIME TO TAKE ATTENDANCE!
TAMAO OHME!
PRE-SENT!
PRE-SENT!
COME ON, BOYS....
HOW CAN THERE BE TWO OF YOU?
WHAT?! THERE ARE TWO OF YOU!!
TH... THIS ISN'T POSSIBLE !!
IT SOUNDS CRAZY, BUT IT'S TRUE!! THIS GUY'S BEEN USING MY NAME!!

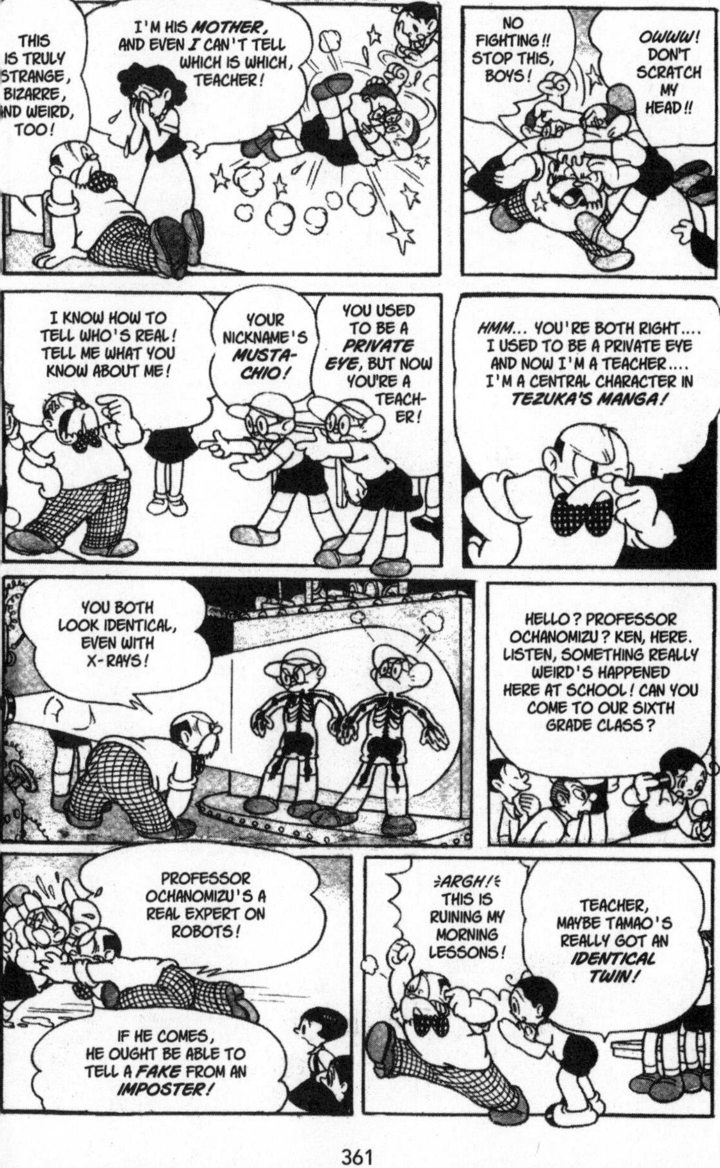
THIS IS TRULY STRANGE, BIZARRE, AND WEIRD, TOO!
I'M HIS MOTHER, AND EVEN I CAN'T TELL WHICH IS WHICH, TEACHER!
NO FIGHTING!! STOP THIS, BOYS!
OWWW! DON'T SCRATCH MY HEAD!!
I KNOW HOW TO TELL WHO'S REAL! TELL ME WHAT YOU KNOW ABOUT ME!
YOUR NICKNAME'S MUSTA-CHIO!
YOU USED TO BE A PRIVATE EYE, BUT NOW YOU'RE A TEACH-ER!
HMM... YOU'RE BOTH RIGHT.... I USED TO BE A PRIVATE EYE AND NOW I'M A TEACHER.... I'M A CENTRAL CHARACTER IN TEZUKA'S MANGA!
YOU BOTH LOOK IDENTICAL, EVEN WITH X-RAYS!
HELLO? PROFESSOR OCHANOMIZU? KEN, HERE. LISTEN, SOMETHING REALLY WEIRD'S HAPPENED HERE AT SCHOOL! CAN YOU COME TO OUR SIXTH GRADE CLASS?
PROFESSOR OCHANOMIZU'S A REAL EXPERT ON ROBOTS!
IF HE COMES, HE OUGHT BE ABLE TO TELL A FAKE FROM AN IMPOSTER!
ARGH! THIS IS RUINING MY MORNING LESSONS!
TEACHER, MAYBE TAMAO'S REALLY GOT AN IDENTICAL TWIN!

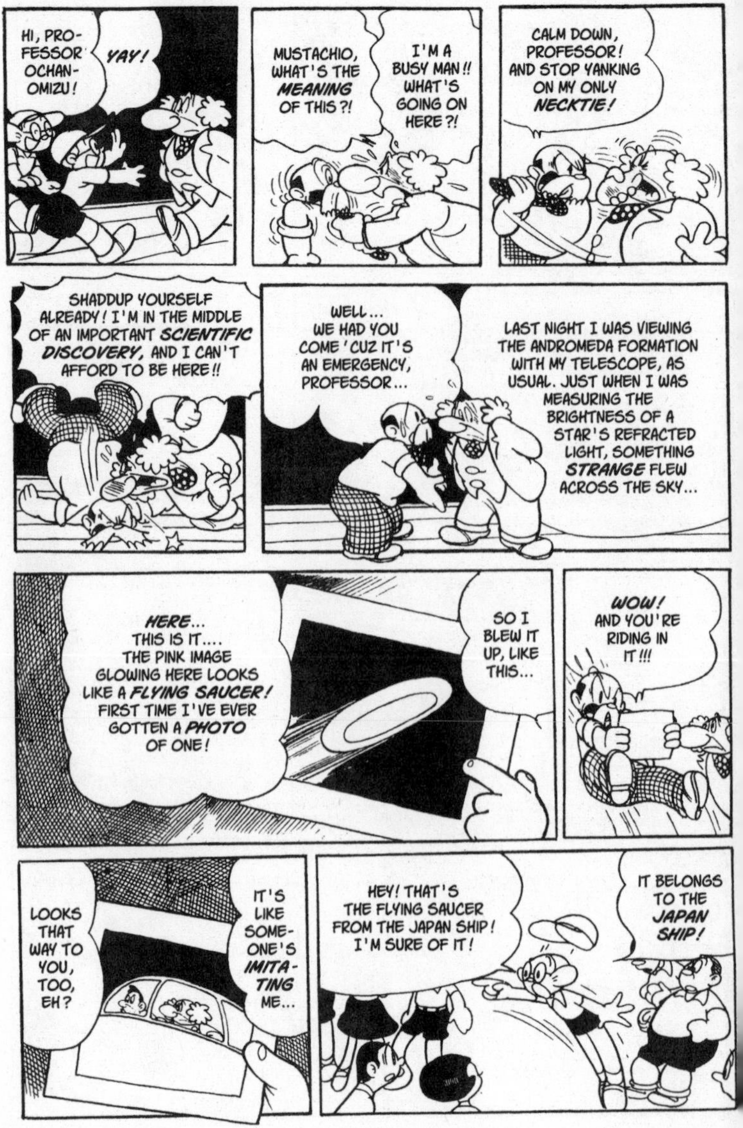
HI, PROFESSOR OCHANOMIZU!
YAY!
MUSTACHIO, WHAT'S THE MEANING OF THIS?!
I'M A BUSY MAN!! WHAT'S GOING ON HERE?!
CALM DOWN, PROFESSOR! AND STOP YANKING ON MY ONLY NECKTIE!
SHADDUP YOURSELF ALREADY! I'M IN THE MIDDLE OF AN IMPORTANT SCIENTIFIC DISCOVERY, AND I CAN'T AFFORD TO BE HERE!!
WELL... WE HAD YOU COME 'CUZ IT'S AN EMERGENCY, PROFESSOR...
LAST NIGHT I WAS VIEWING THE ANDROMEDA FORMATION WITH MY TELESCOPE, AS USUAL. JUST WHEN I WAS MEASURING THE BRIGHTNESS OF A STAR'S REFRACTED LIGHT, SOMETHING STRANGE FLEW ACROSS THE SKY...
HERE... THIS IS IT.... THE PINK IMAGE GLOWING HERE LOOKS LIKE A FLYING SAUCER! FIRST TIME I'VE EVER GOTTEN A PHOTO OF ONE!
SO I BLEW IT UP, LIKE THIS...
WOW! AND YOU'RE RIDING IN IT!!!
LOOKS THAT WAY TO YOU, TOO, EH?
IT'S LIKE SOMEONE'S IMITATING ME...
HEY! THAT'S THE FLYING SAUCER FROM THE JAPAN SHIP! I'M SURE OF IT!
IT BELONGS TO THE JAPAN SHIP!

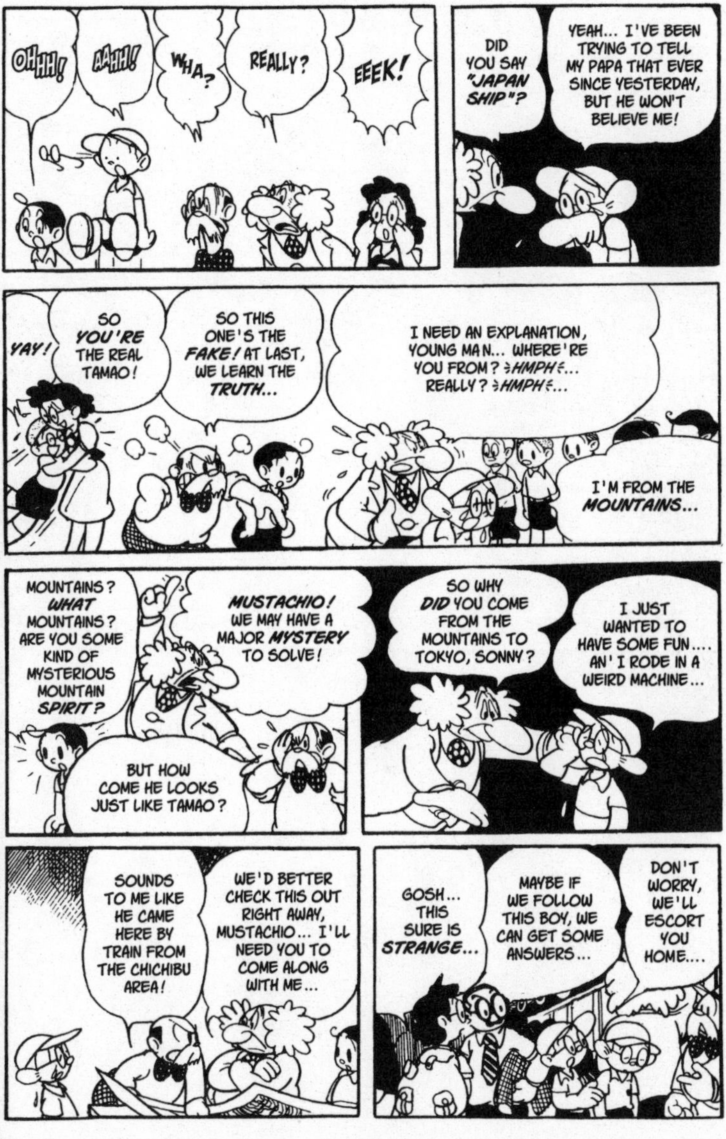
OHHH!
AAHH!
WHA?
REALLY?
EEEK!
DID YOU SAY "JAPAN SHIP"?
YEAH... I'VE BEEN TRYING TO TELL MY PAPA THAT EVER SINCE YESTERDAY, BUT HE WON'T BELIEVE ME!
YAY!
SO *YOU'RE* THE REAL TAMAO!
SO THIS ONE'S THE *FAKE!* AT LAST, WE LEARN THE *TRUTH*...
I NEED AN EXPLANATION, YOUNG MAN... WHERE'RE YOU FROM? ≥HMPH≤... REALLY? ≥HMPH≤...
I'M FROM THE *MOUNTAINS*...
MOUNTAINS? *WHAT* MOUNTAINS? ARE YOU SOME KIND OF MYSTERIOUS MOUNTAIN *SPIRIT?*
MUSTACHIO! WE MAY HAVE A MAJOR *MYSTERY* TO SOLVE!
BUT HOW COME HE LOOKS JUST LIKE TAMAO?
SO WHY *DID* YOU COME FROM THE MOUNTAINS TO TOKYO, SONNY?
I JUST WANTED TO HAVE SOME FUN.... AN' I RODE IN A WEIRD MACHINE...
SOUNDS TO ME LIKE HE CAME HERE BY TRAIN FROM THE CHICHIBU AREA!
WE'D BETTER CHECK THIS OUT RIGHT AWAY, MUSTACHIO... I'LL NEED YOU TO COME ALONG WITH ME...
GOSH... THIS SURE IS *STRANGE*...
MAYBE IF WE FOLLOW THIS BOY, WE CAN GET SOME ANSWERS...
DON'T WORRY, WE'LL ESCORT YOU HOME....

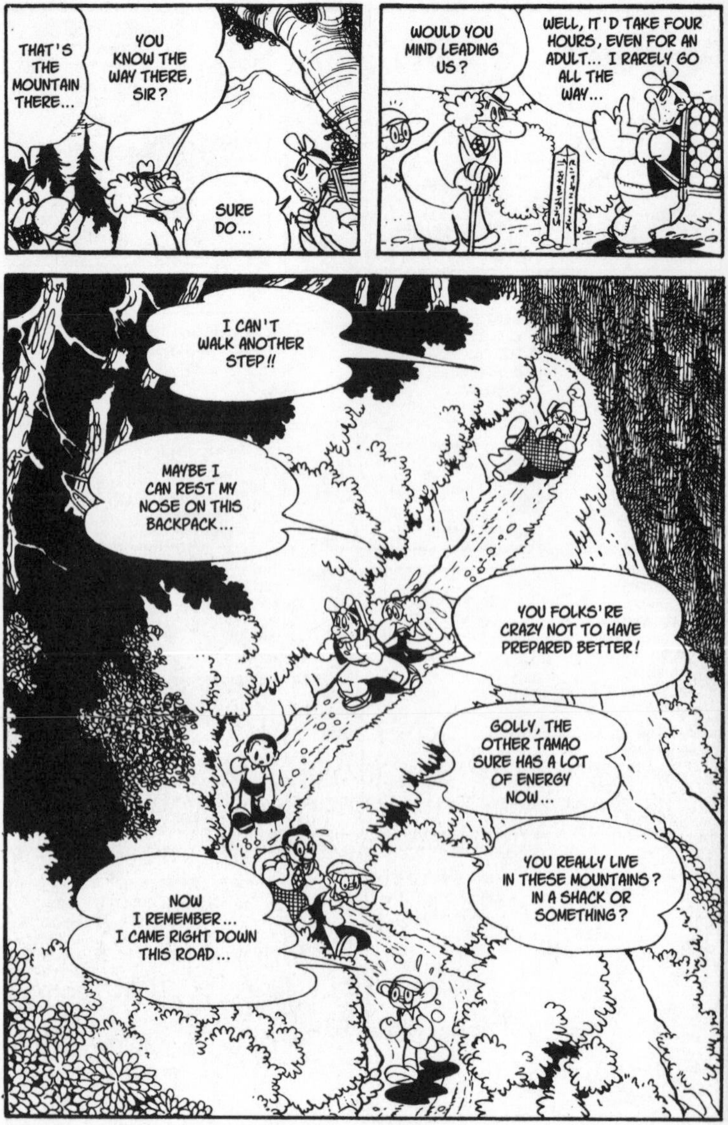
THAT'S THE MOUNTAIN THERE...
YOU KNOW THE WAY THERE, SIR?
SURE DO...
WOULD YOU MIND LEADING US?
WELL, IT'D TAKE FOUR HOURS, EVEN FOR AN ADULT... I RARELY GO ALL THE WAY...
I CAN'T WALK ANOTHER STEP!!
MAYBE I CAN REST MY NOSE ON THIS BACKPACK...
YOU FOLKS'RE CRAZY NOT TO HAVE PREPARED BETTER!
GOLLY, THE OTHER TAMAO SURE HAS A LOT OF ENERGY NOW...
NOW I REMEMBER... I CAME RIGHT DOWN THIS ROAD...
YOU REALLY LIVE IN THESE MOUNTAINS? IN A SHACK OR SOMETHING?

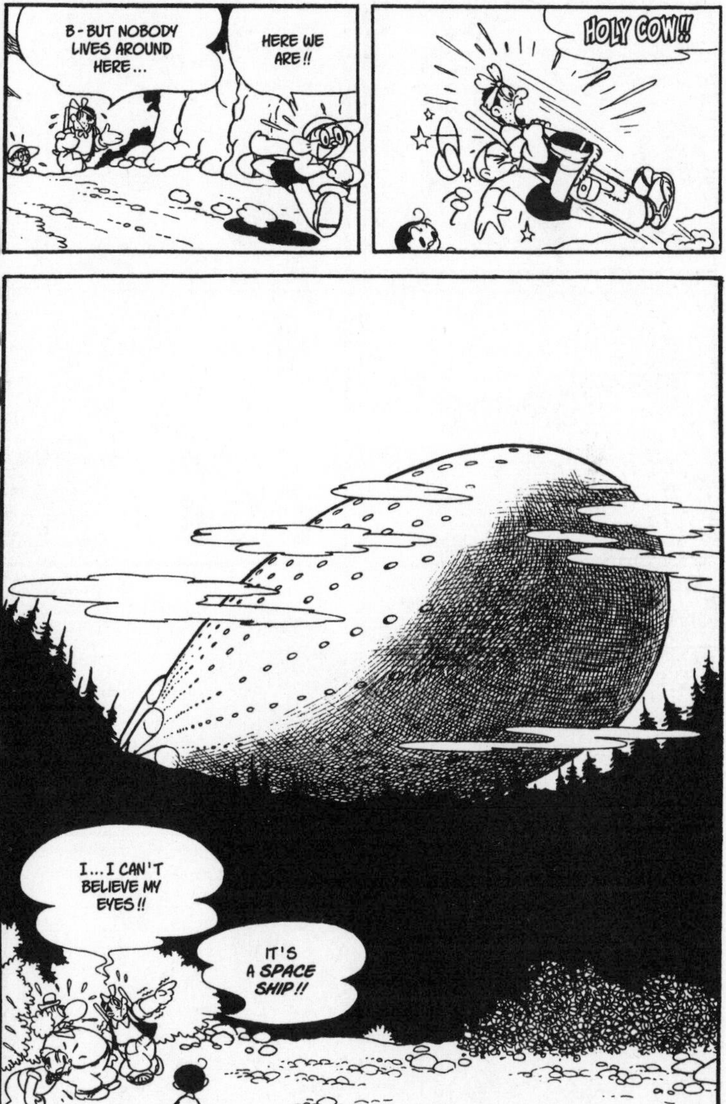
B-BUT NOBODY LIVES AROUND HERE...
HERE WE ARE!!
HOLY COW!!
I...I CAN'T BELIEVE MY EYES!!
IT'S A SPACE SHIP!!

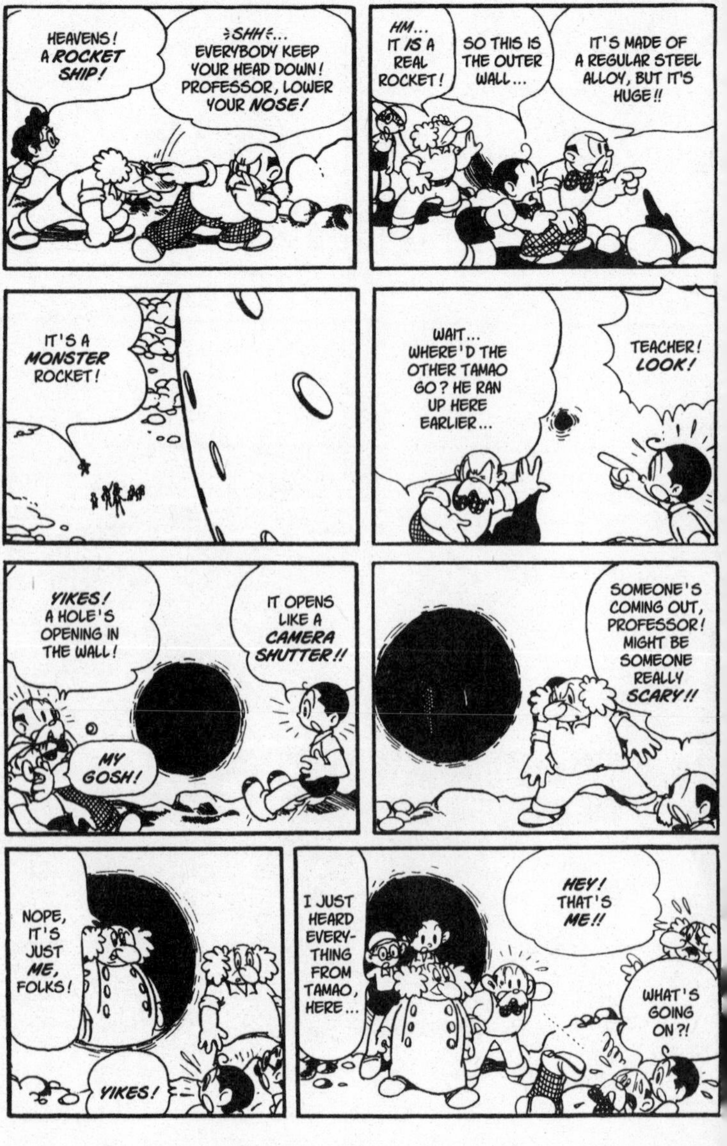
HEAVENS! A ROCKET SHIP!
SHH... EVERYBODY KEEP YOUR HEAD DOWN! PROFESSOR, LOWER YOUR NOSE!
HM... IT IS A REAL ROCKET!
SO THIS IS THE OUTER WALL...
IT'S MADE OF A REGULAR STEEL ALLOY, BUT IT'S HUGE!!
IT'S A MONSTER ROCKET!
WAIT... WHERE'D THE OTHER TAMAO GO? HE RAN UP HERE EARLIER...
TEACHER! LOOK!
YIKES! A HOLE'S OPENING IN THE WALL!
MY GOSH!
IT OPENS LIKE A CAMERA SHUTTER!!
SOMEONE'S COMING OUT, PROFESSOR! MIGHT BE SOMEONE REALLY SCARY!!
NOPE, IT'S JUST ME, FOLKS!
YIKES!
I JUST HEARD EVERYTHING FROM TAMAO, HERE...
HEY! THAT'S ME!!
WHAT'S GOING ON?!

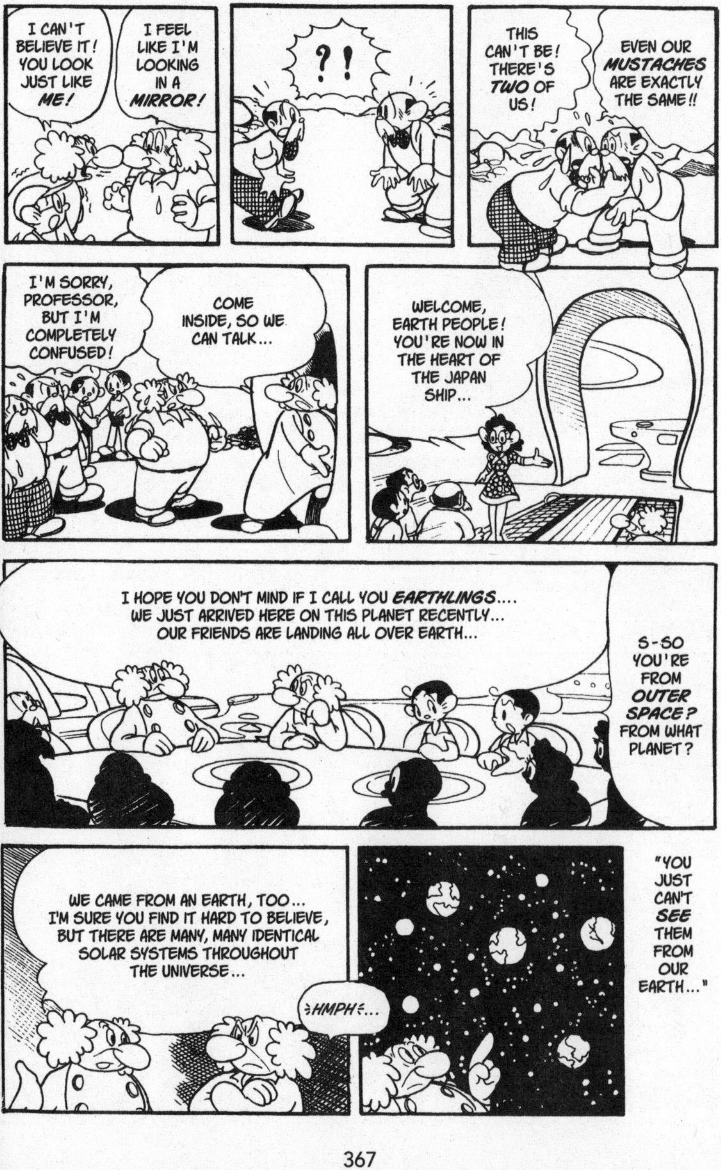

I CAN'T BELIEVE IT! YOU LOOK JUST LIKE ***ME!***
I FEEL LIKE I'M LOOKING IN A ***MIRROR!***
? !
THIS CAN'T BE! THERE'S ***TWO*** OF US!
EVEN OUR ***MUSTACHES*** ARE EXACTLY THE SAME!!
I'M SORRY, PROFESSOR, BUT I'M COMPLETELY CONFUSED!
COME INSIDE, SO WE CAN TALK...
WELCOME, EARTH PEOPLE! YOU'RE NOW IN THE HEART OF THE JAPAN SHIP...
I HOPE YOU DON'T MIND IF I CALL YOU ***EARTHLINGS***.... WE JUST ARRIVED HERE ON THIS PLANET RECENTLY... OUR FRIENDS ARE LANDING ALL OVER EARTH...
S-SO YOU'RE FROM ***OUTER SPACE?*** FROM WHAT PLANET?
WE CAME FROM AN EARTH, TOO... I'M SURE YOU FIND IT HARD TO BELIEVE, BUT THERE ARE MANY, MANY IDENTICAL SOLAR SYSTEMS THROUGHOUT THE UNIVERSE...
HMPH...
"YOU JUST CAN'T ***SEE*** THEM FROM OUR EARTH..."

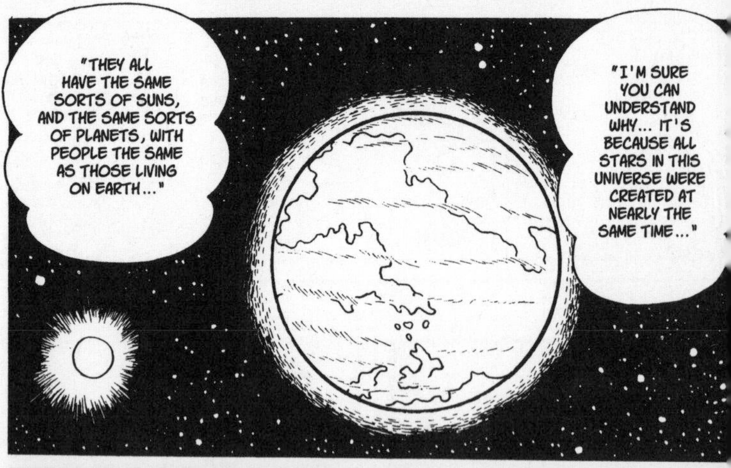
"THEY ALL HAVE THE SAME SORTS OF SUNS, AND THE SAME SORTS OF PLANETS, WITH PEOPLE THE SAME AS THOSE LIVING ON EARTH..."
"I'M SURE YOU CAN UNDERSTAND WHY... IT'S BECAUSE ALL STARS IN THIS UNIVERSE WERE CREATED AT NEARLY THE SAME TIME..."
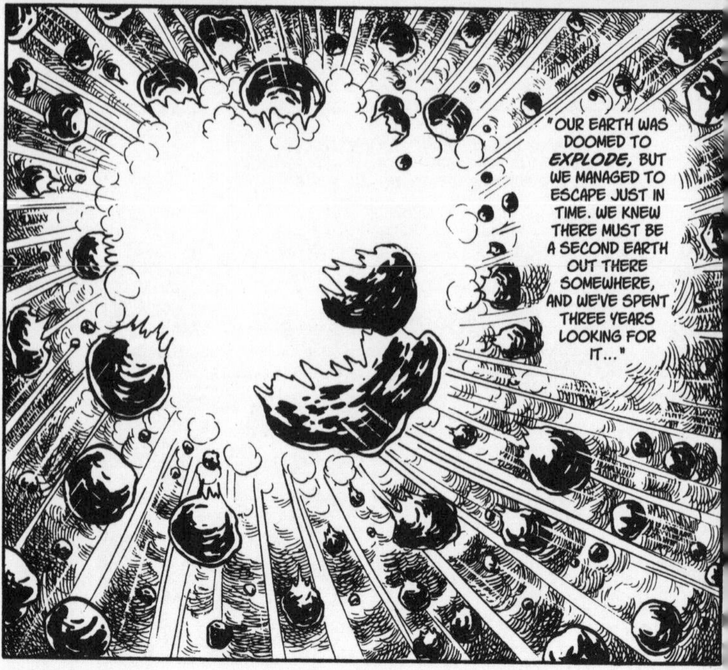
"OUR EARTH WAS DOOMED TO EXPLODE, BUT WE MANAGED TO ESCAPE JUST IN TIME. WE KNEW THERE MUST BE A SECOND EARTH OUT THERE SOMEWHERE, AND WE'VE SPENT THREE YEARS LOOKING FOR IT..."

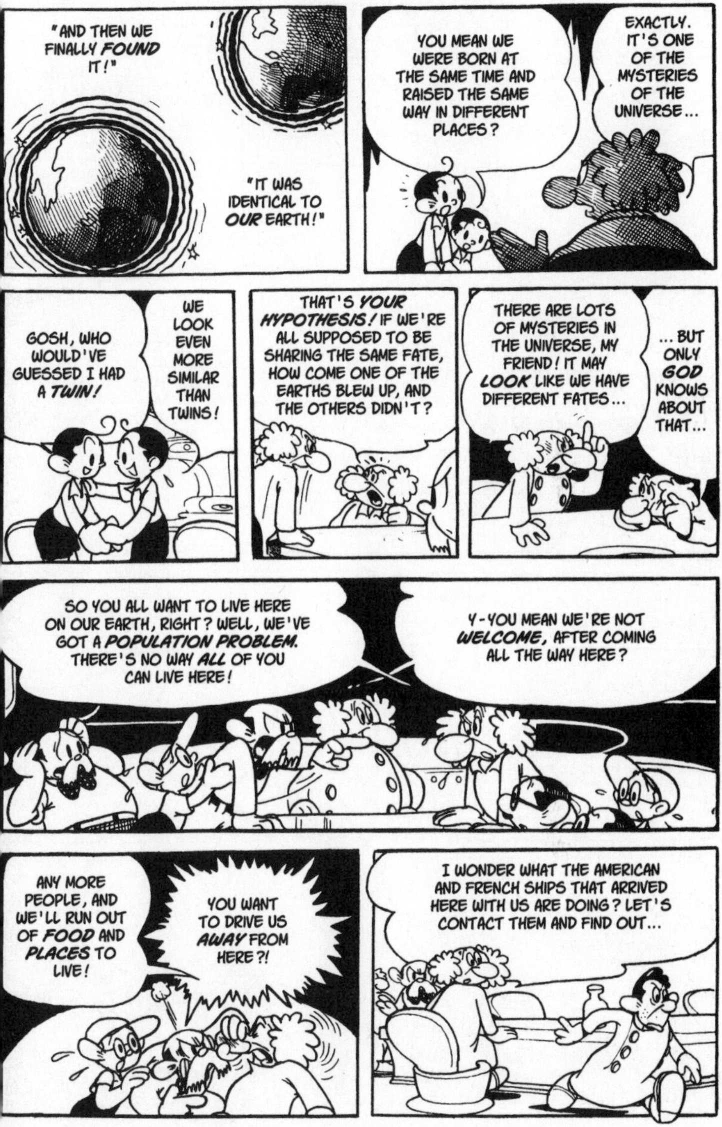
"AND THEN WE FINALLY *FOUND* IT!"
"IT WAS IDENTICAL TO *OUR* EARTH!"
YOU MEAN WE WERE BORN AT THE SAME TIME AND RAISED THE SAME WAY IN DIFFERENT PLACES?
EXACTLY. IT'S ONE OF THE MYSTERIES OF THE UNIVERSE...
GOSH, WHO WOULD'VE GUESSED I HAD A *TWIN!*
WE LOOK EVEN MORE SIMILAR THAN TWINS!
THAT'S *YOUR HYPOTHESIS!* IF WE'RE ALL SUPPOSED TO BE SHARING THE SAME FATE, HOW COME ONE OF THE EARTHS BLEW UP, AND THE OTHERS DIDN'T?
THERE ARE LOTS OF MYSTERIES IN THE UNIVERSE, MY FRIEND! IT MAY *LOOK* LIKE WE HAVE DIFFERENT FATES...
... BUT ONLY *GOD* KNOWS ABOUT THAT...!
SO YOU ALL WANT TO LIVE HERE ON OUR EARTH, RIGHT? WELL, WE'VE GOT A *POPULATION PROBLEM.* THERE'S NO WAY *ALL* OF YOU CAN LIVE HERE!
Y-YOU MEAN WE'RE NOT *WELCOME,* AFTER COMING ALL THE WAY HERE?
ANY MORE PEOPLE, AND WE'LL RUN OUT OF *FOOD* AND *PLACES* TO LIVE!
YOU WANT TO DRIVE US *AWAY* FROM HERE?!
I WONDER WHAT THE AMERICAN AND FRENCH SHIPS THAT ARRIVED HERE WITH US ARE DOING? LET'S CONTACT THEM AND FIND OUT...

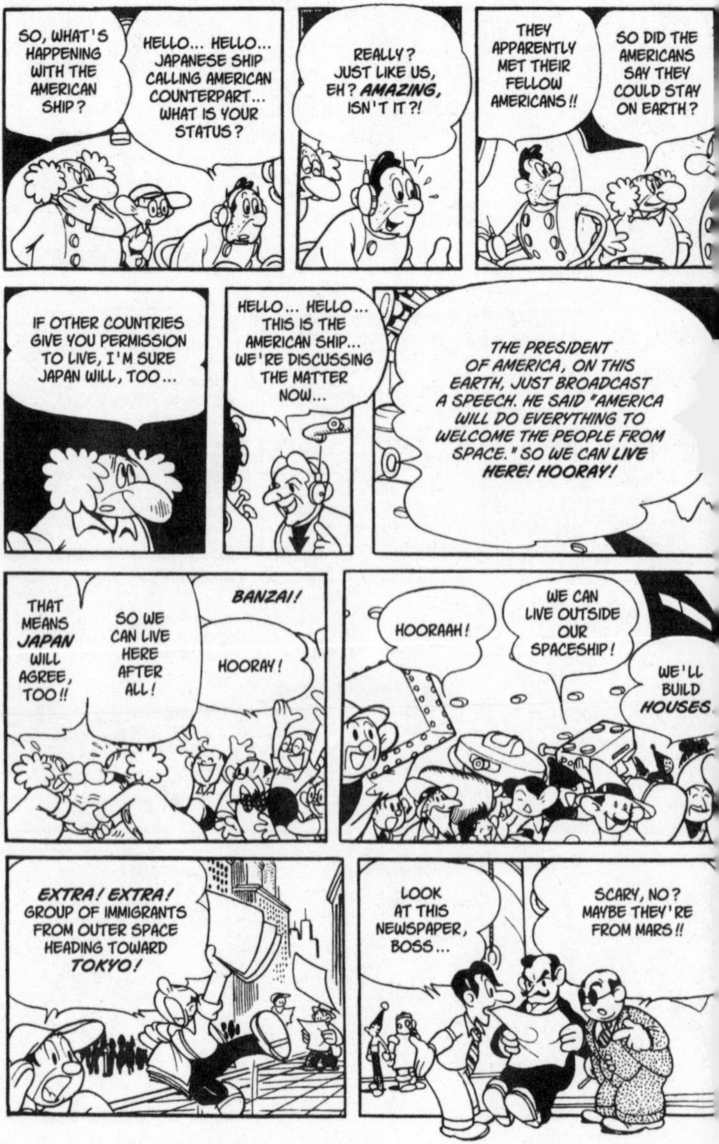
SO, WHAT'S HAPPENING WITH THE AMERICAN SHIP?
HELLO... HELLO... JAPANESE SHIP CALLING AMERICAN COUNTERPART... WHAT IS YOUR STATUS?
REALLY? JUST LIKE US, EH? AMAZING, ISN'T IT?!
THEY APPARENTLY MET THEIR FELLOW AMERICANS!!
SO DID THE AMERICANS SAY THEY COULD STAY ON EARTH?
IF OTHER COUNTRIES GIVE YOU PERMISSION TO LIVE, I'M SURE JAPAN WILL, TOO...
HELLO... HELLO... THIS IS THE AMERICAN SHIP... WE'RE DISCUSSING THE MATTER NOW...
THE PRESIDENT OF AMERICA, ON THIS EARTH, JUST BROADCAST A SPEECH. HE SAID "AMERICA WILL DO EVERYTHING TO WELCOME THE PEOPLE FROM SPACE." SO WE CAN LIVE HERE! HOORAY!
THAT MEANS JAPAN WILL AGREE, TOO!!
SO WE CAN LIVE HERE AFTER ALL!
BANZAI!
HOORAY!
HOORAAH!
WE CAN LIVE OUTSIDE OUR SPACESHIP!
WE'LL BUILD HOUSES
EXTRA! EXTRA! GROUP OF IMMIGRANTS FROM OUTER SPACE HEADING TOWARD TOKYO!
LOOK AT THIS NEWSPAPER, BOSS...
SCARY, NO? MAYBE THEY'RE FROM MARS!!

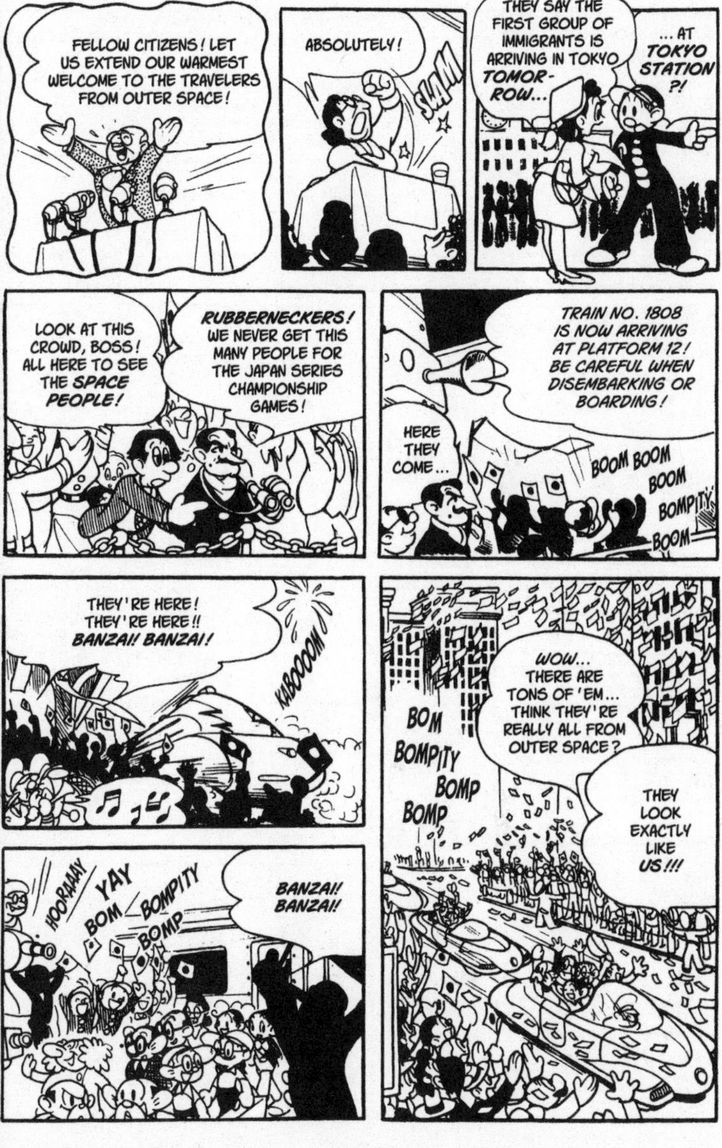
FELLOW CITIZENS! LET US EXTEND OUR WARMEST WELCOME TO THE TRAVELERS FROM OUTER SPACE!
ABSOLUTELY!
SLAM
THEY SAY THE FIRST GROUP OF IMMIGRANTS IS ARRIVING IN TOKYO TOMORROW...
... AT TOKYO STATION ?!
LOOK AT THIS CROWD, BOSS! ALL HERE TO SEE THE SPACE PEOPLE!
RUBBERNECKERS! WE NEVER GET THIS MANY PEOPLE FOR THE JAPAN SERIES CHAMPIONSHIP GAMES!
TRAIN NO. 1808 IS NOW ARRIVING AT PLATFORM 12! BE CAREFUL WHEN DISEMBARKING OR BOARDING!
HERE THEY COME...
BOOM BOOM BOOM BOMPITY BOOM
THEY'RE HERE! THEY'RE HERE!! BANZAI! BANZAI!
KABOOOOM
HOORAAAY
YAY
BOM BOMPITY BOMP
BANZAI! BANZAI!
BOM BOMPITY BOMP BOMP
WOW... THERE ARE TONS OF 'EM... THINK THEY'RE REALLY ALL FROM OUTER SPACE?
THEY LOOK EXACTLY LIKE US!!!

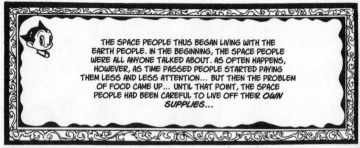

THE SPACE PEOPLE THUS BEGAN LIVING WITH THE EARTH PEOPLE. IN THE BEGINNING, THE SPACE PEOPLE WERE ALL ANYONE TALKED ABOUT. AS OFTEN HAPPENS, HOWEVER, AS TIME PASSED PEOPLE STARTED PAYING THEM LESS AND LESS ATTENTION... BUT THEN THE PROBLEM OF FOOD CAME UP... UNTIL THAT POINT, THE SPACE PEOPLE HAD BEEN CAREFUL TO LIVE OFF THEIR *OWN* SUPPLIES...

BLAM

HEY! YOU THREW MY AIM OFF!!

B-BUT WHY'RE YOU KILLING THEM?

WHY?

TO HAVE SOMETHING TO EAT, THAT'S WHY!

BUT I FEEL SORRY FOR THE BIRDS...

WHAT'RE WE HUMANS S'POSED TO EAT, THEN?!

YIKES!!

YOU'RE BEING SO CRUEL!

KNOCK IT OFF, WILL YOU? SO WHAT'RE YOU SPACE GUYS EATING, ANYWAY?

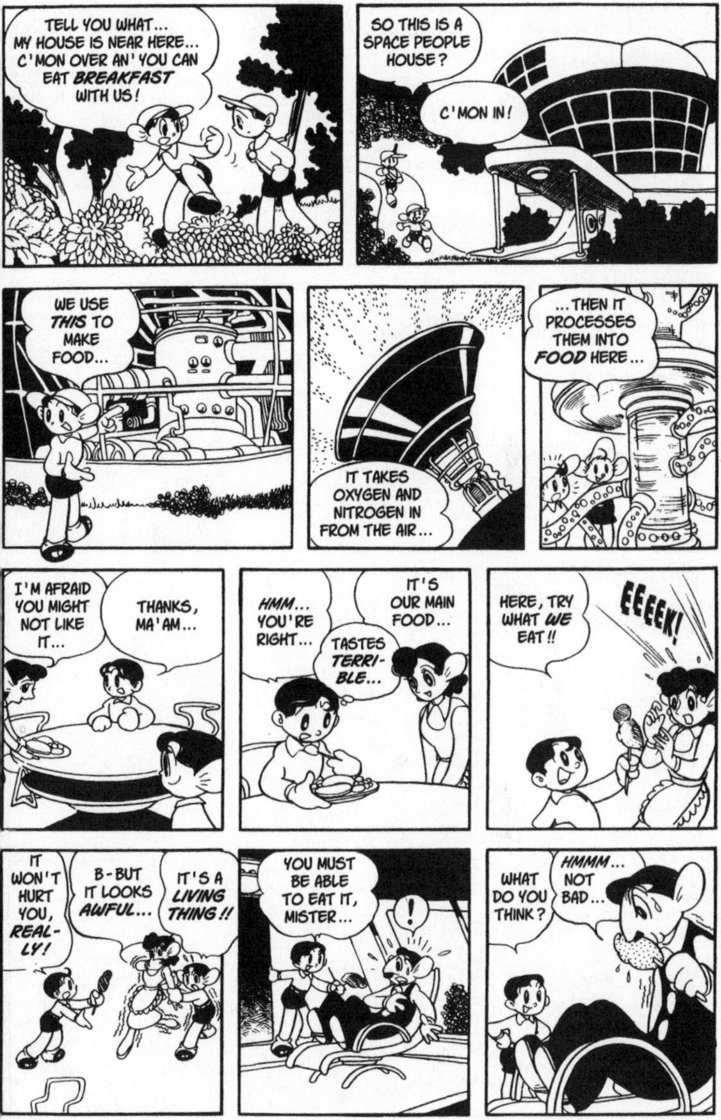

TELL YOU WHAT... MY HOUSE IS NEAR HERE... C'MON OVER AN' YOU CAN EAT BREAKFAST WITH US!
SO THIS IS A SPACE PEOPLE HOUSE?
C'MON IN!
WE USE THIS TO MAKE FOOD...
IT TAKES OXYGEN AND NITROGEN IN FROM THE AIR...
...THEN IT PROCESSES THEM INTO FOOD HERE...
I'M AFRAID YOU MIGHT NOT LIKE IT...
THANKS, MA'AM...
HMM... YOU'RE RIGHT...
IT'S OUR MAIN FOOD...
TASTES TERRI-BLE...
HERE, TRY WHAT WE EAT!!
EEEEK!
IT WON'T HURT YOU, REAL-LY!
B-BUT IT LOOKS AWFUL...
IT'S A LIVING THING!!
YOU MUST BE ABLE TO EAT IT, MISTER...
!
WHAT DO YOU THINK?
HMMM... NOT BAD...

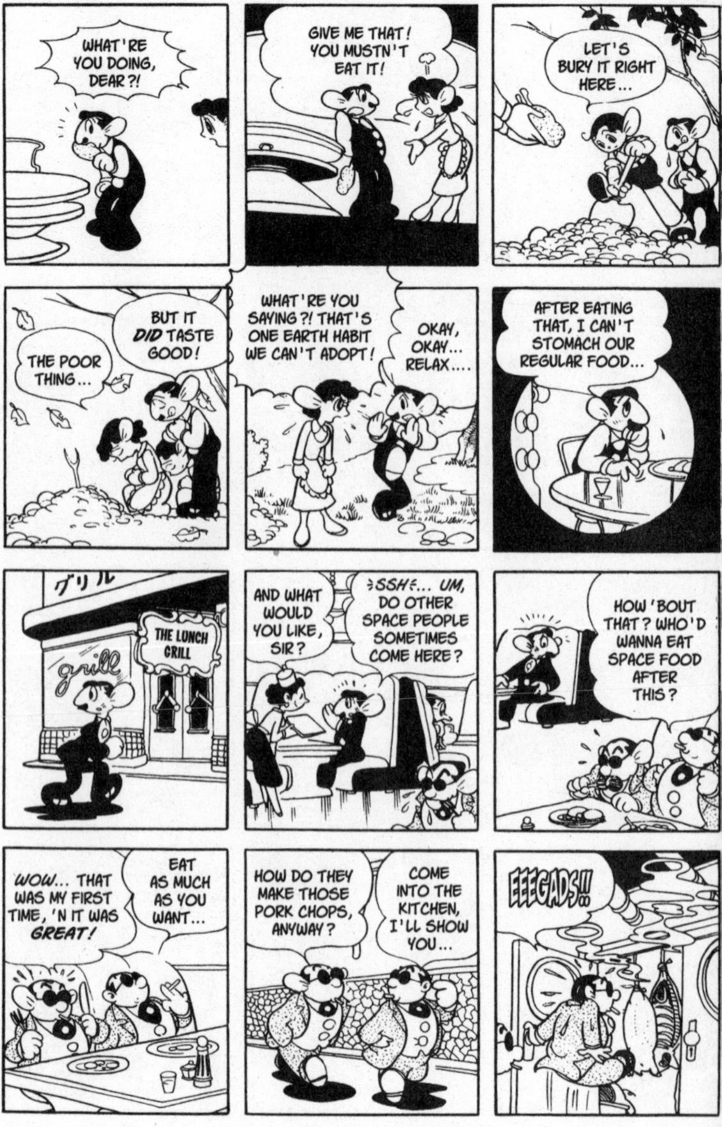
WHAT'RE YOU DOING, DEAR?!
GIVE ME THAT! YOU MUSTN'T EAT IT!
LET'S BURY IT RIGHT HERE...
THE POOR THING...
BUT IT DID TASTE GOOD!
WHAT'RE YOU SAYING?! THAT'S ONE EARTH HABIT WE CAN'T ADOPT!
OKAY, OKAY... RELAX....
AFTER EATING THAT, I CAN'T STOMACH OUR REGULAR FOOD...
グリル
THE LUNCH GRILL
grill
AND WHAT WOULD YOU LIKE, SIR?
≶SSH≶... UM, DO OTHER SPACE PEOPLE SOMETIMES COME HERE?
HOW 'BOUT THAT? WHO'D WANNA EAT SPACE FOOD AFTER THIS?
WOW... THAT WAS MY FIRST TIME, 'N IT WAS GREAT!
EAT AS MUCH AS YOU WANT...
HOW DO THEY MAKE THOSE PORK CHOPS, ANYWAY?
COME INTO THE KITCHEN, I'LL SHOW YOU...
EEEGADS!!

WHAT'S THE MATTER?

¡GAG!
...!

THAT'S *TERRIFYING!* YOU MADE ME EAT ANIMAL FLESH!! YOU'RE *CRUEL!!*

DR. TENMA, THE EARTHLING, IS HERE TO SEE YOU, SIR...

GO AHEAD, SHOW HIM IN...

IT'S AN HONOR TO MEET YOU...

LIKEWISE...

EARTHLINGS AND SPACE PEOPLE REALLY *SHOULD* SHARE TECHNOLOGY.

I'LL SECOND THAT...

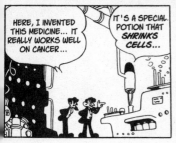

HERE, I INVENTED THIS MEDICINE... IT REALLY WORKS WELL ON CANCER...

IT'S A SPECIAL POTION THAT *SHRINKS* CELLS...

WOW... IT *SHRINKS* CELLS?!

THAT'S RIGHT.... AND IT WORKS ON ALL LIVING CREATURES!

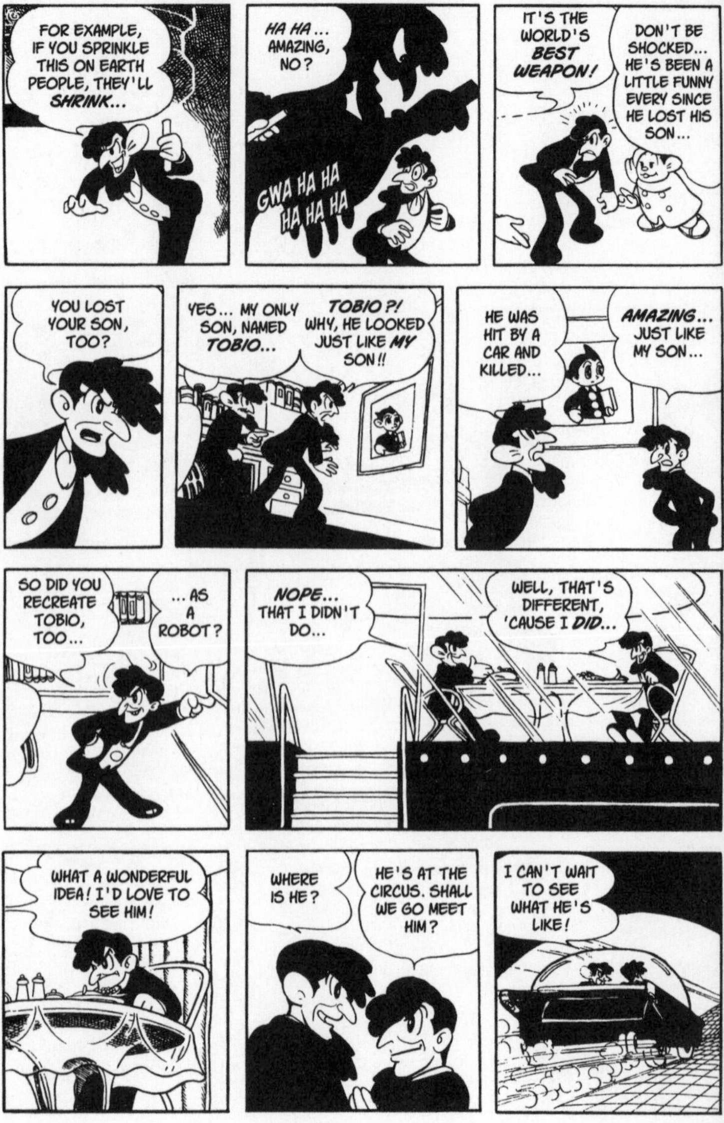
FOR EXAMPLE, IF YOU SPRINKLE THIS ON EARTH PEOPLE, THEY'LL *SHRINK*...
HA HA... AMAZING, NO?
GWA HA HA HA HA HA
IT'S THE WORLD'S *BEST WEAPON!*
DON'T BE SHOCKED... HE'S BEEN A LITTLE FUNNY EVERY SINCE HE LOST HIS SON...
YOU LOST YOUR SON, TOO?
YES... MY ONLY SON, NAMED *TOBIO*...
TOBIO?! WHY, HE LOOKED JUST LIKE *MY* SON!!
HE WAS HIT BY A CAR AND KILLED...
AMAZING... JUST LIKE MY SON...
SO DID YOU RECREATE TOBIO, TOO...
... AS A ROBOT?
NOPE... THAT I DIDN'T DO...
WELL, THAT'S DIFFERENT, 'CAUSE I *DID*...
WHAT A WONDERFUL IDEA! I'D LOVE TO SEE HIM!
WHERE IS HE?
HE'S AT THE CIRCUS. SHALL WE GO MEET HIM?
I CAN'T WAIT TO SEE WHAT HE'S LIKE!

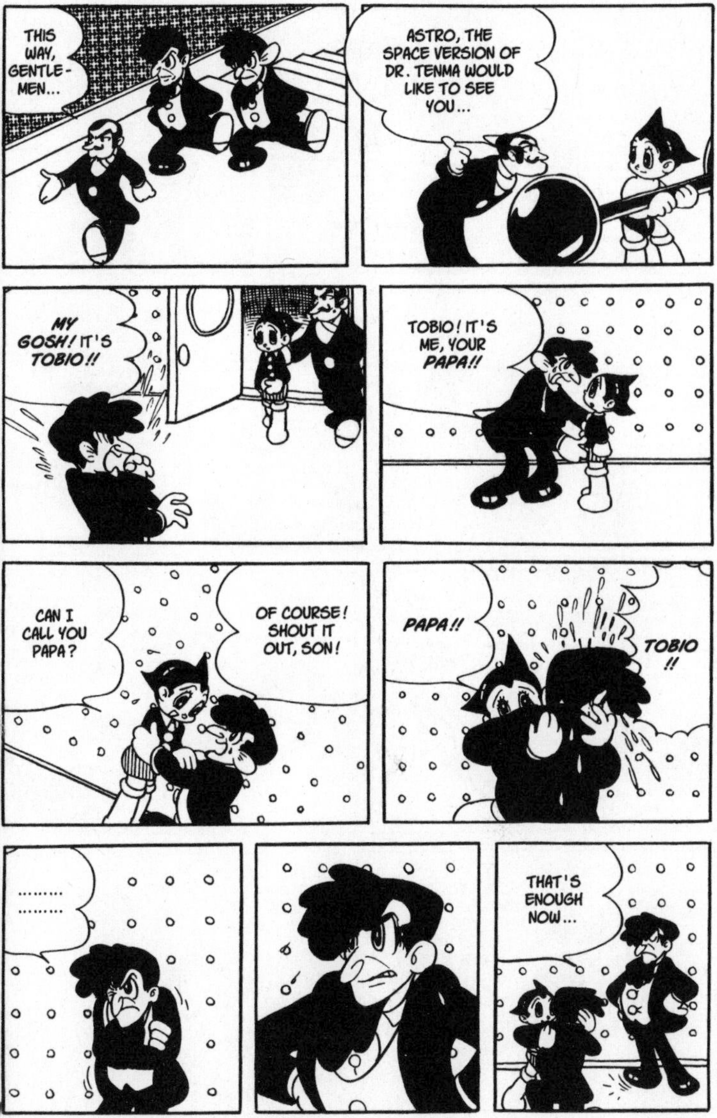
THIS WAY, GENTLE-MEN...
ASTRO, THE SPACE VERSION OF DR. TENMA WOULD LIKE TO SEE YOU...
MY GOSH! IT'S TOBIO!!
TOBIO! IT'S ME, YOUR PAPA!!
CAN I CALL YOU PAPA?
OF COURSE! SHOUT IT OUT, SON!
PAPA!!
TOBIO!!
....
....
THAT'S ENOUGH NOW...

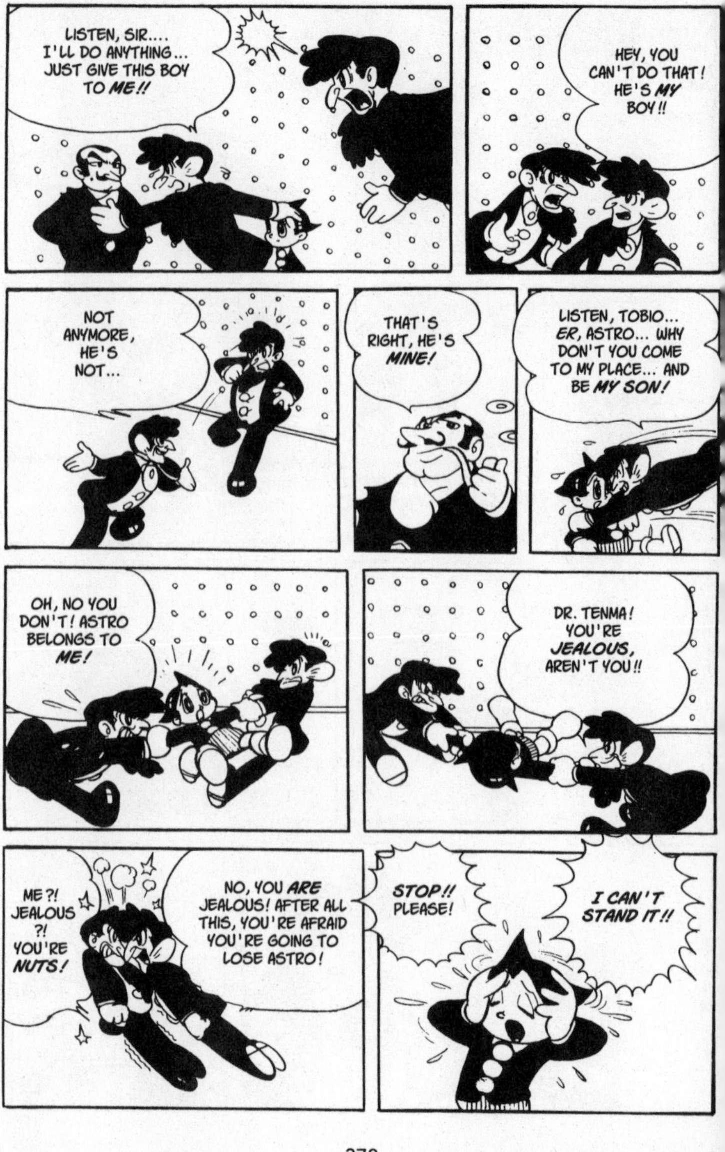
LISTEN, SIR.... I'LL DO ANYTHING... JUST GIVE THIS BOY TO *ME!!*
HEY, YOU CAN'T DO THAT! HE'S *MY* BOY!!
NOT ANYMORE, HE'S NOT...
THAT'S RIGHT, HE'S *MINE!*
LISTEN, TOBIO... *ER,* ASTRO... WHY DON'T YOU COME TO MY PLACE... AND BE *MY SON!*
OH, NO YOU DON'T! ASTRO BELONGS TO *ME!*
DR. TENMA! YOU'RE *JEALOUS,* AREN'T YOU!!
ME?! JEALOUS?! YOU'RE *NUTS!*
NO, YOU *ARE* JEALOUS! AFTER ALL THIS, YOU'RE AFRAID YOU'RE GOING TO LOSE ASTRO!
STOP!! PLEASE!
I CAN'T STAND IT!!

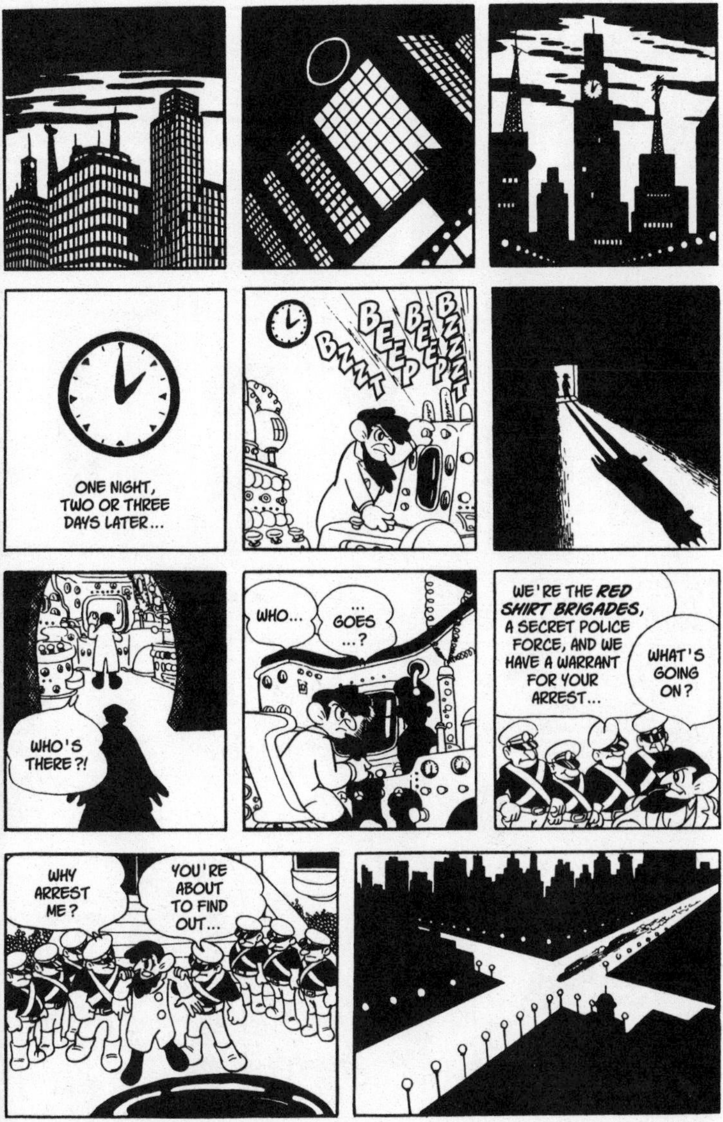
ONE NIGHT, TWO OR THREE DAYS LATER...
BZZZT BEEP BEEP BZZZT
WHO'S THERE?!
WHO...
... GOES ...?
WE'RE THE ***RED SHIRT BRIGADES***, A SECRET POLICE FORCE, AND WE HAVE A WARRANT FOR YOUR ARREST...
WHAT'S GOING ON?
WHY ARREST ME?
YOU'RE ABOUT TO FIND OUT...

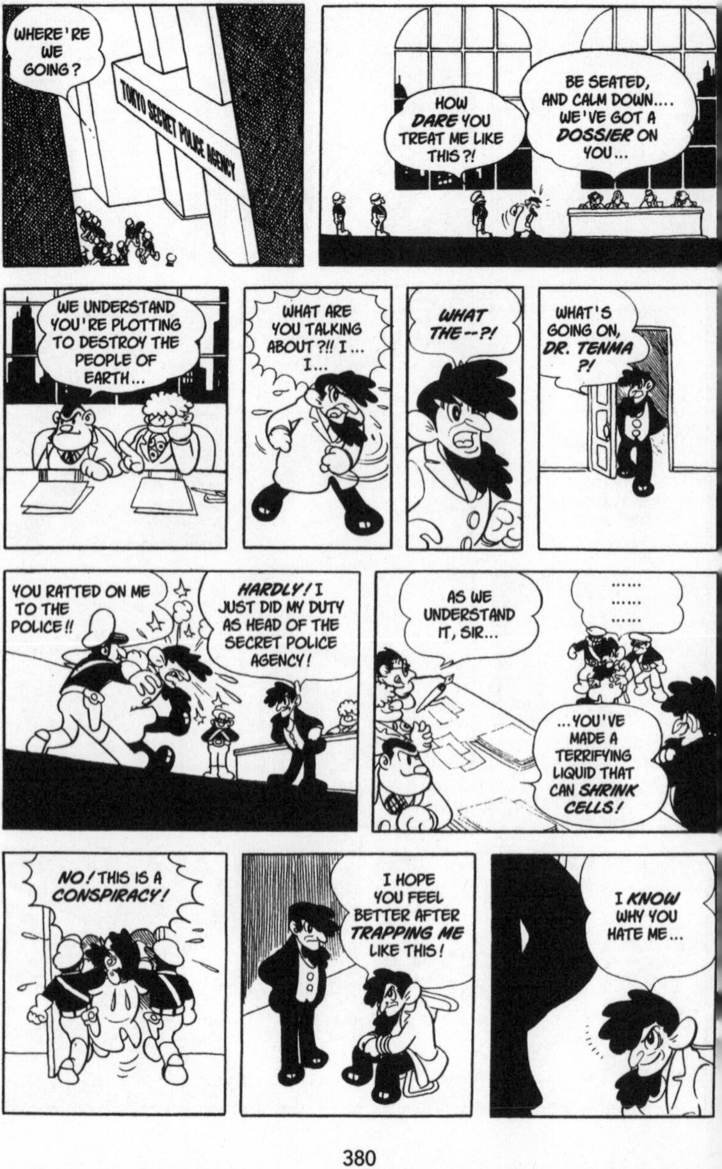
WHERE'RE WE GOING?
TOKYO SECRET POLICE AGENCY
HOW DARE YOU TREAT ME LIKE THIS?!
BE SEATED, AND CALM DOWN.... WE'VE GOT A DOSSIER ON YOU...
WE UNDERSTAND YOU'RE PLOTTING TO DESTROY THE PEOPLE OF EARTH...
WHAT ARE YOU TALKING ABOUT?!! I... I...
WHAT THE--?!
WHAT'S GOING ON, DR. TENMA ?!
YOU RATTED ON ME TO THE POLICE!!
HARDLY! I JUST DID MY DUTY AS HEAD OF THE SECRET POLICE AGENCY!
AS WE UNDERSTAND IT, SIR...
....
...YOU'VE MADE A TERRIFYING LIQUID THAT CAN SHRINK CELLS!
NO! THIS IS A CONSPIRACY!
I HOPE YOU FEEL BETTER AFTER TRAPPING ME LIKE THIS!
I KNOW WHY YOU HATE ME...

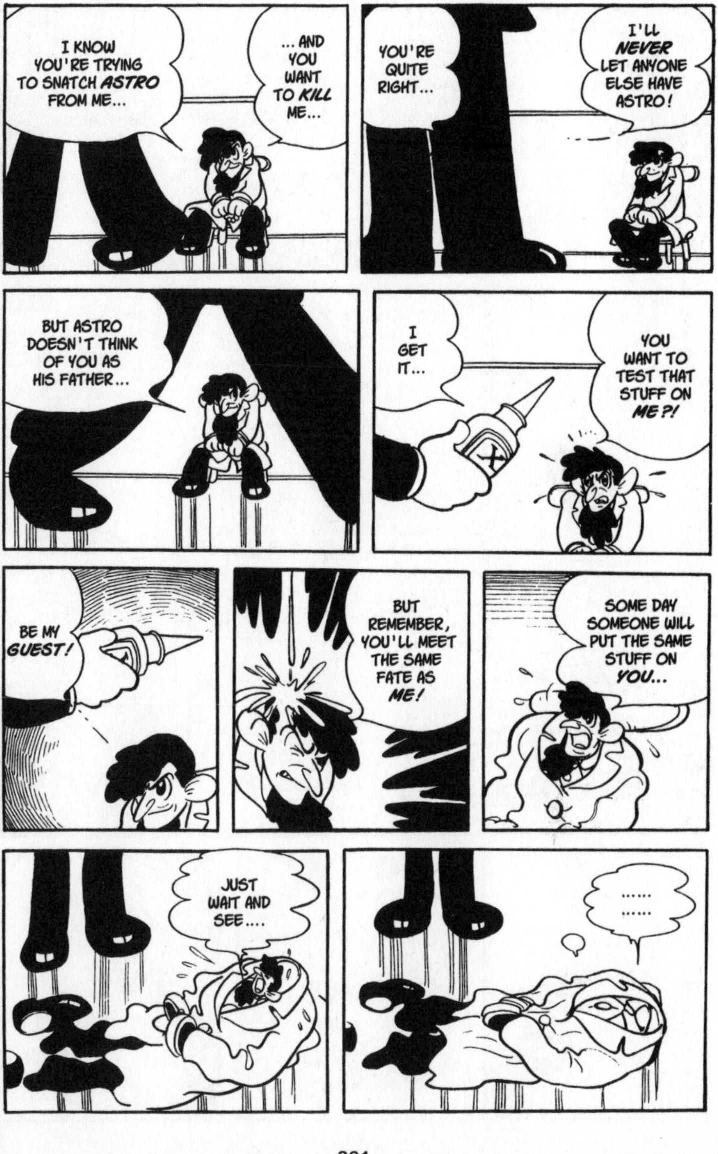
I KNOW YOU'RE TRYING TO SNATCH *ASTRO* FROM ME...
... AND YOU WANT TO *KILL* ME...
YOU'RE QUITE RIGHT...
I'LL *NEVER* LET ANYONE ELSE HAVE ASTRO!
BUT ASTRO DOESN'T THINK OF YOU AS HIS FATHER...
I GET IT...
YOU WANT TO TEST THAT STUFF ON *ME?!*
BE MY *GUEST!*
BUT REMEMBER, YOU'LL MEET THE SAME FATE AS *ME!*
SOME DAY SOMEONE WILL PUT THE SAME STUFF ON *YOU*...
JUST WAIT AND SEE....
......
......

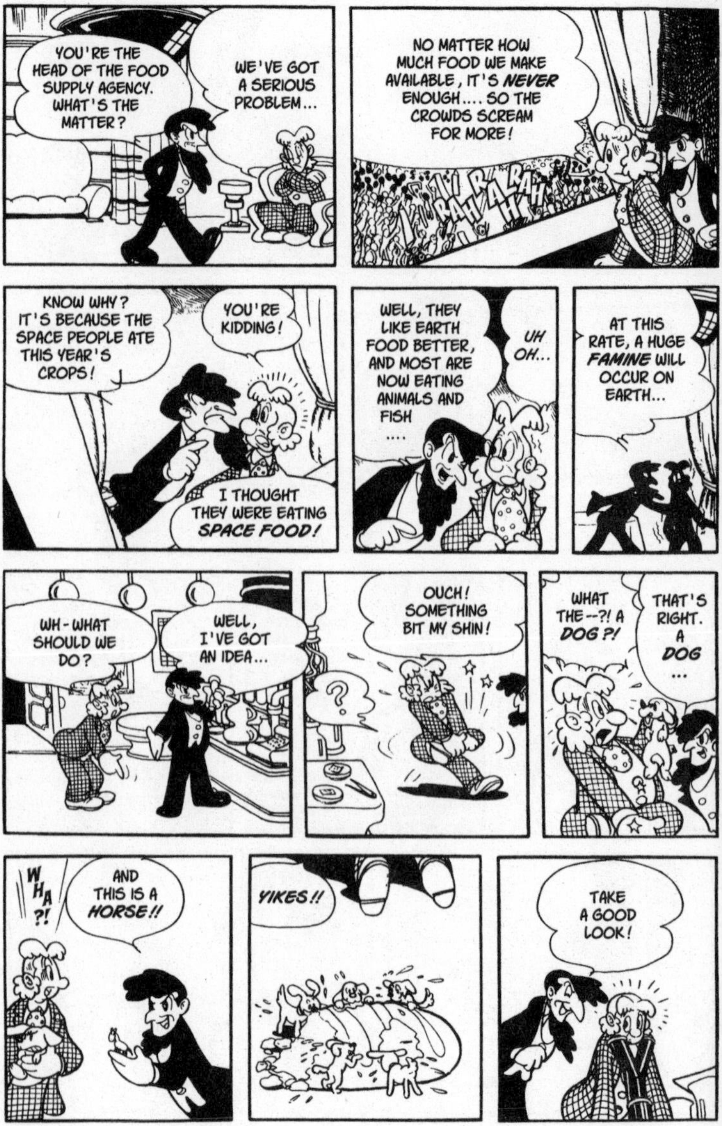
YOU'RE THE HEAD OF THE FOOD SUPPLY AGENCY. WHAT'S THE MATTER?
WE'VE GOT A SERIOUS PROBLEM...
NO MATTER HOW MUCH FOOD WE MAKE AVAILABLE, IT'S NEVER ENOUGH.... SO THE CROWDS SCREAM FOR MORE!
RAH RAH
KNOW WHY? IT'S BECAUSE THE SPACE PEOPLE ATE THIS YEAR'S CROPS!
YOU'RE KIDDING!
I THOUGHT THEY WERE EATING SPACE FOOD!
WELL, THEY LIKE EARTH FOOD BETTER, AND MOST ARE NOW EATING ANIMALS AND FISH ....
UH OH...
AT THIS RATE, A HUGE FAMINE WILL OCCUR ON EARTH...
WH-WHAT SHOULD WE DO?
WELL, I'VE GOT AN IDEA...
?
OUCH! SOMETHING BIT MY SHIN!
WHAT THE--?! A DOG?!
THAT'S RIGHT. A DOG ...
WHA ?!
AND THIS IS A HORSE!!
YIKES!!
TAKE A GOOD LOOK!

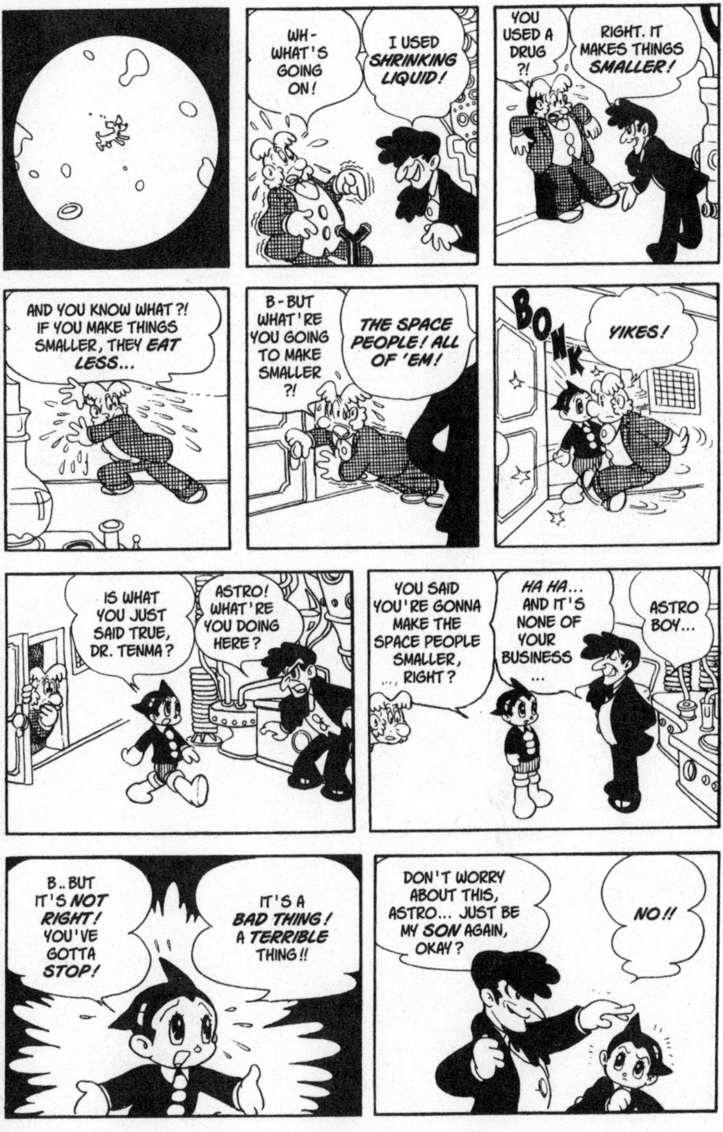
WH-WHAT'S GOING ON!
I USED *SHRINKING LIQUID!*
YOU USED A DRUG ?!
RIGHT. IT MAKES THINGS *SMALLER!*
AND YOU KNOW WHAT ?! IF YOU MAKE THINGS SMALLER, THEY *EAT LESS...*
B-BUT WHAT'RE YOU GOING TO MAKE SMALLER ?!
THE SPACE PEOPLE! ALL OF 'EM!
BONK
YIKES!
IS WHAT YOU JUST SAID TRUE, DR. TENMA?
ASTRO! WHAT'RE YOU DOING HERE?
YOU SAID YOU'RE GONNA MAKE THE SPACE PEOPLE SMALLER, RIGHT?
HA HA... AND IT'S NONE OF YOUR BUSINESS ...
ASTRO BOY...
B..BUT IT'S *NOT RIGHT!* YOU'VE GOTTA *STOP!*
IT'S A *BAD THING!* A *TERRIBLE* THING!!
DON'T WORRY ABOUT THIS, ASTRO... JUST BE MY *SON* AGAIN, OKAY?
NO!!

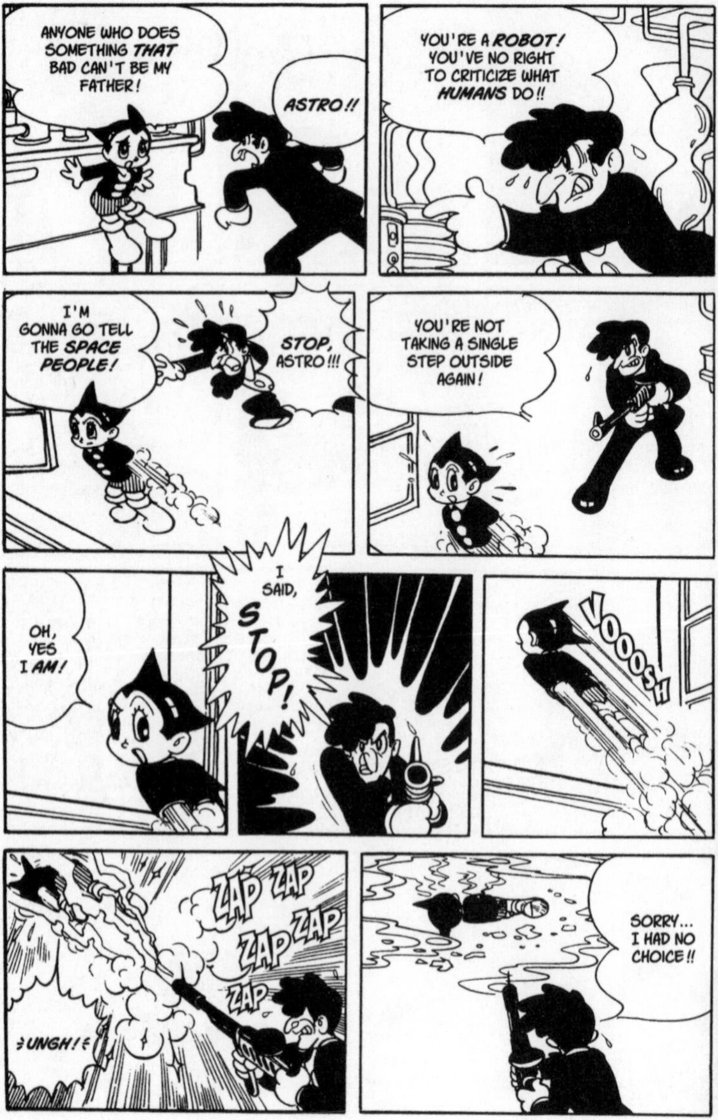

ANYONE WHO DOES SOMETHING *THAT* BAD CAN'T BE MY FATHER!
ASTRO!!
YOU'RE A *ROBOT!* YOU'VE NO RIGHT TO CRITICIZE WHAT *HUMANS* DO!!
I'M GONNA GO TELL THE *SPACE PEOPLE!*
STOP, ASTRO!!!
YOU'RE NOT TAKING A SINGLE STEP OUTSIDE AGAIN!
OH, YES I *AM!*
I SAID, STOP!
VOOOSH
ZAP ZAP
ZAP ZAP
ZAP
UNGH!
SORRY... I HAD NO CHOICE!!

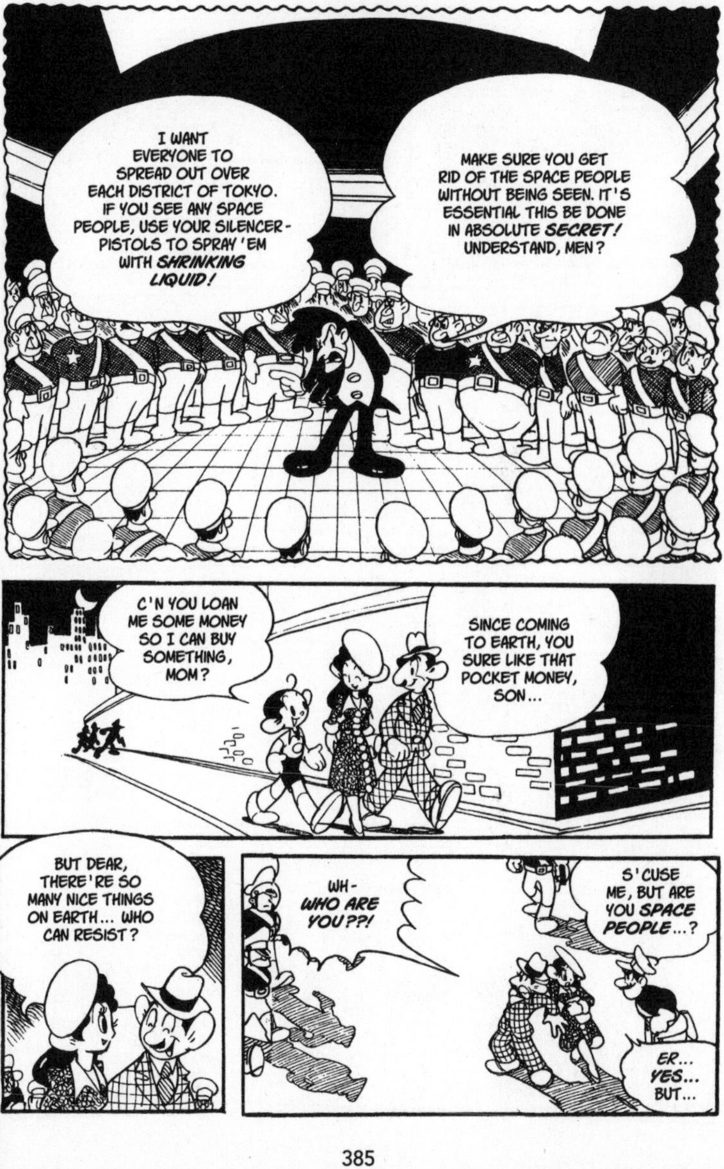
I WANT EVERYONE TO SPREAD OUT OVER EACH DISTRICT OF TOKYO. IF YOU SEE ANY SPACE PEOPLE, USE YOUR SILENCER-PISTOLS TO SPRAY 'EM WITH *SHRINKING LIQUID!*
MAKE SURE YOU GET RID OF THE SPACE PEOPLE WITHOUT BEING SEEN. IT'S ESSENTIAL THIS BE DONE IN ABSOLUTE *SECRET!* UNDERSTAND, MEN?
C'N YOU LOAN ME SOME MONEY SO I CAN BUY SOMETHING, MOM?
SINCE COMING TO EARTH, YOU SURE LIKE THAT POCKET MONEY, SON...
BUT DEAR, THERE'RE SO MANY NICE THINGS ON EARTH... WHO CAN RESIST?
WH- *WHO ARE YOU??!*
S'CUSE ME, BUT ARE YOU *SPACE PEOPLE*...?
ER... YES... BUT...

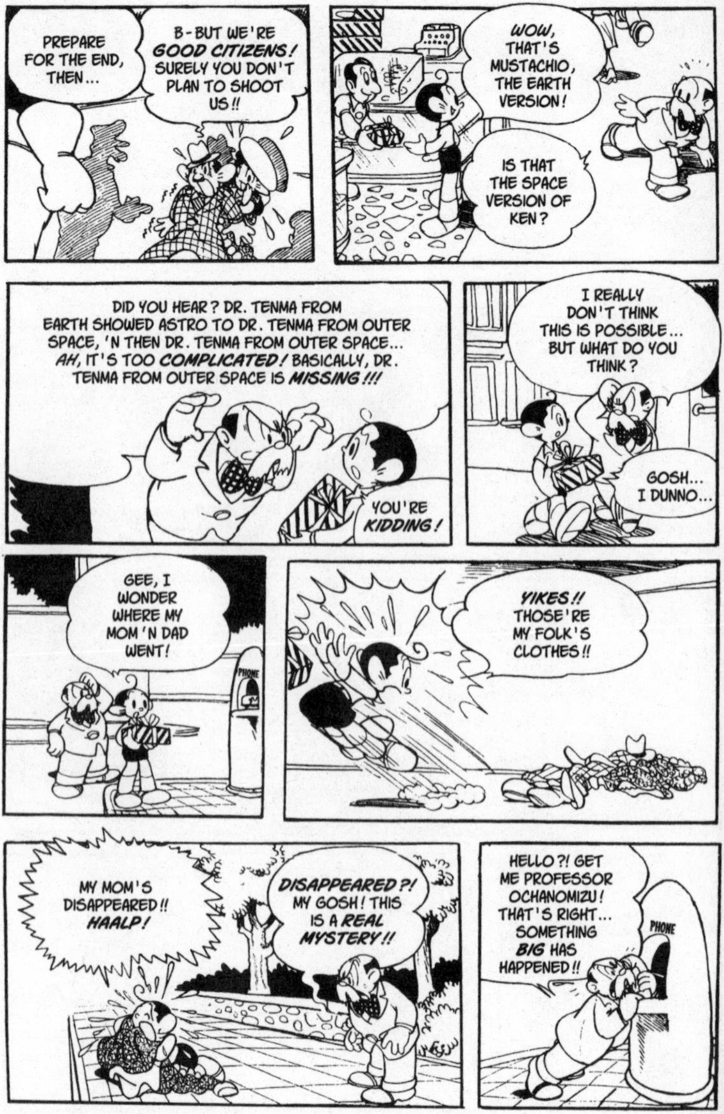
PREPARE FOR THE END, THEN...
B-BUT WE'RE GOOD CITIZENS! SURELY YOU DON'T PLAN TO SHOOT US!!
WOW, THAT'S MUSTACHIO, THE EARTH VERSION!
IS THAT THE SPACE VERSION OF KEN?
DID YOU HEAR? DR. TENMA FROM EARTH SHOWED ASTRO TO DR. TENMA FROM OUTER SPACE, 'N THEN DR. TENMA FROM OUTER SPACE... AH, IT'S TOO COMPLICATED! BASICALLY, DR. TENMA FROM OUTER SPACE IS MISSING!!!
YOU'RE KIDDING!
I REALLY DON'T THINK THIS IS POSSIBLE... BUT WHAT DO YOU THINK?
GOSH... I DUNNO...
GEE, I WONDER WHERE MY MOM 'N DAD WENT!
PHONE
YIKES!! THOSE'RE MY FOLK'S CLOTHES!!
MY MOM'S DISAPPEARED!! HAALP!
DISAPPEARED?! MY GOSH! THIS IS A REAL MYSTERY!!
HELLO?! GET ME PROFESSOR OCHANOMIZU! THAT'S RIGHT... SOMETHING BIG HAS HAPPENED!!
PHONE

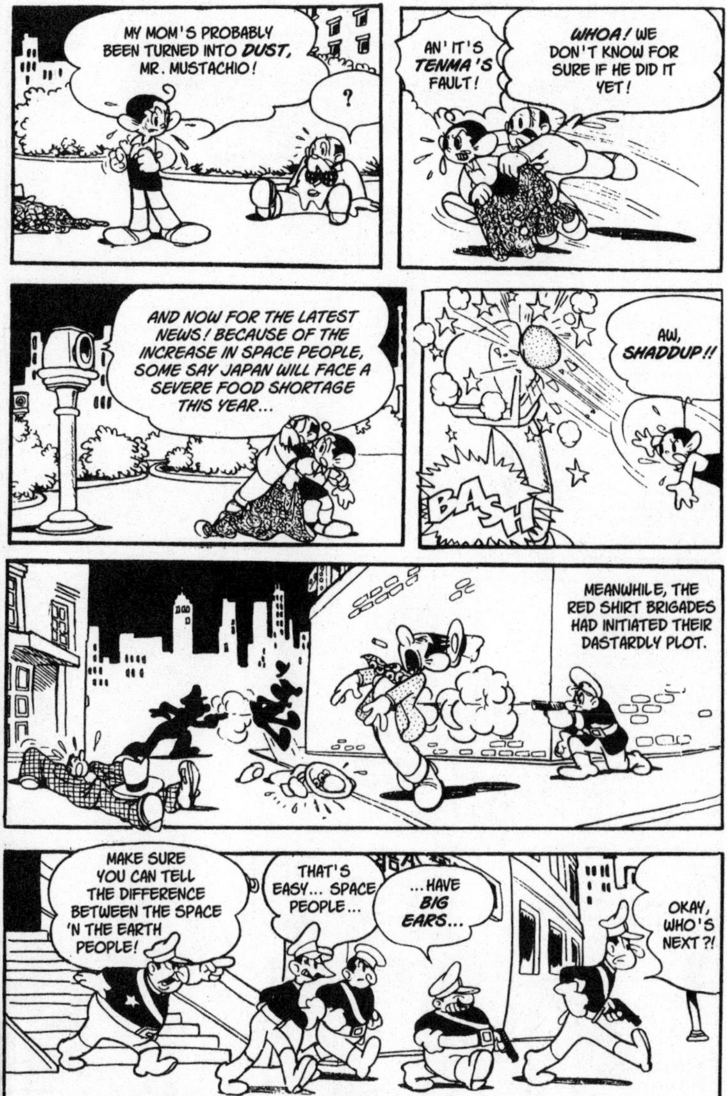
MY MOM'S PROBABLY BEEN TURNED INTO DUST, MR. MUSTACHIO!
?
AN' IT'S TENMA'S FAULT!
WHOA! WE DON'T KNOW FOR SURE IF HE DID IT YET!
AND NOW FOR THE LATEST NEWS! BECAUSE OF THE INCREASE IN SPACE PEOPLE, SOME SAY JAPAN WILL FACE A SEVERE FOOD SHORTAGE THIS YEAR...
AW, SHADDUP!!
BASH
MEANWHILE, THE RED SHIRT BRIGADES HAD INITIATED THEIR DASTARDLY PLOT.
MAKE SURE YOU CAN TELL THE DIFFERENCE BETWEEN THE SPACE 'N THE EARTH PEOPLE!
THAT'S EASY... SPACE PEOPLE...
...HAVE BIG EARS...
OKAY, WHO'S NEXT?!

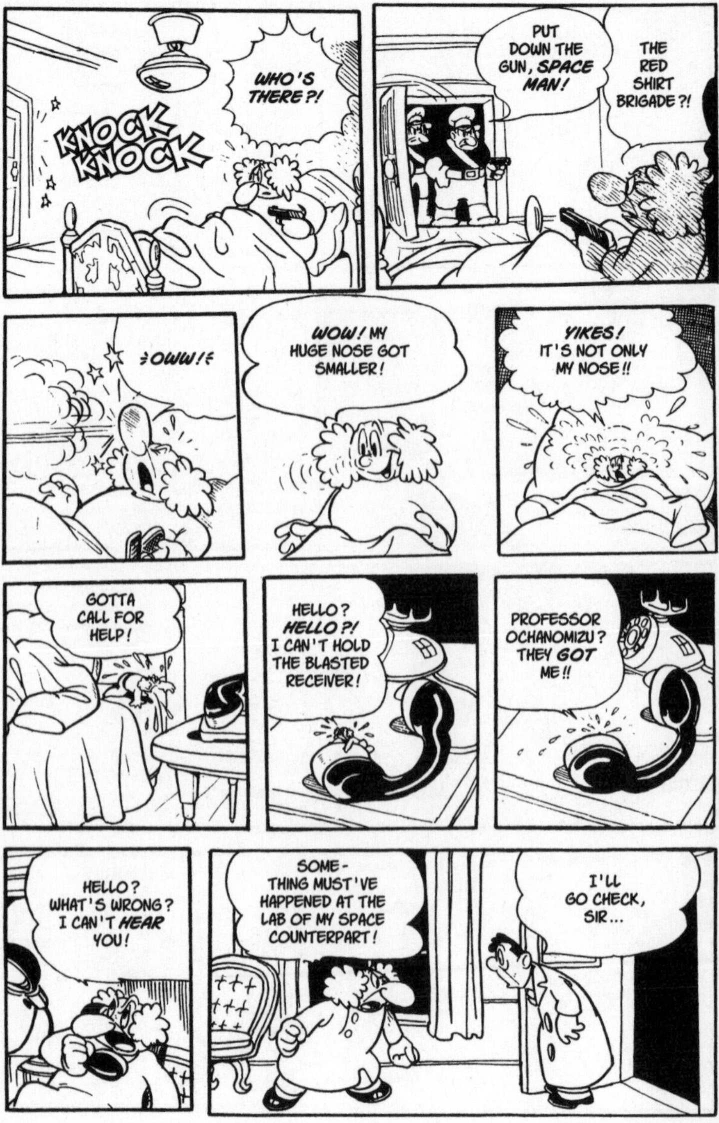
WHO'S THERE?!
KNOCK KNOCK
PUT DOWN THE GUN, SPACE MAN!
THE RED SHIRT BRIGADE?!
OWW!
WOW! MY HUGE NOSE GOT SMALLER!
YIKES! IT'S NOT ONLY MY NOSE!!
GOTTA CALL FOR HELP!
HELLO? HELLO?! I CAN'T HOLD THE BLASTED RECEIVER!
PROFESSOR OCHANOMIZU? THEY GOT ME!!
HELLO? WHAT'S WRONG? I CAN'T HEAR YOU!
SOME-THING MUST'VE HAPPENED AT THE LAB OF MY SPACE COUNTERPART!
I'LL GO CHECK, SIR...

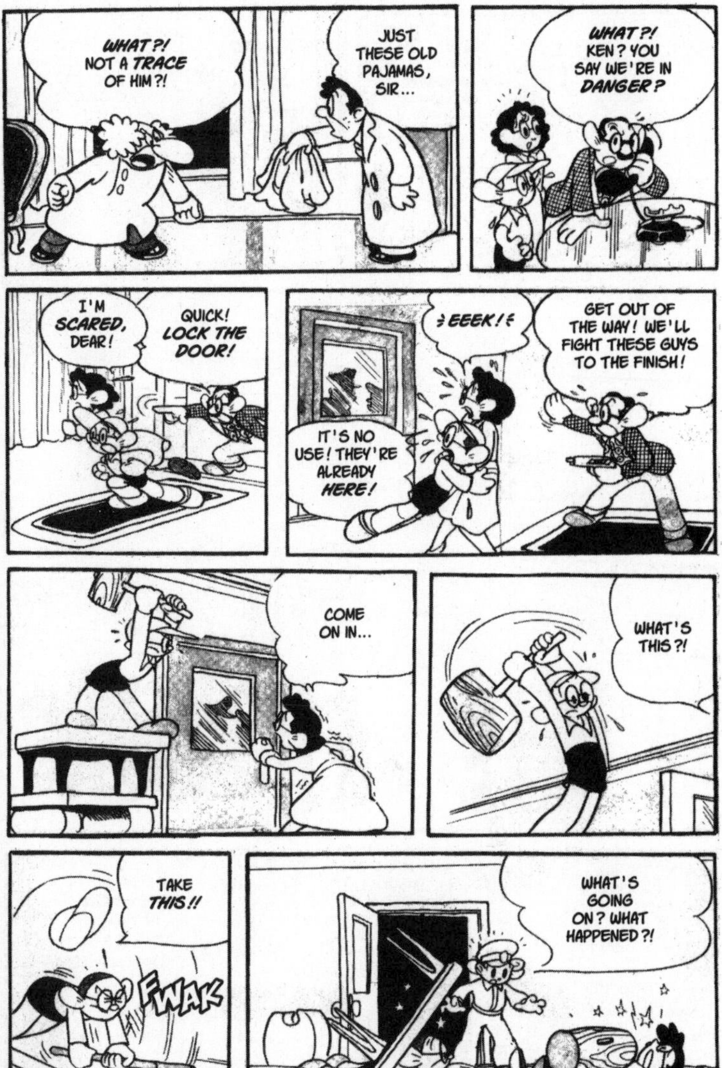
WHAT?! NOT A TRACE OF HIM?!
JUST THESE OLD PAJAMAS, SIR...
WHAT?! KEN? YOU SAY WE'RE IN DANGER?
I'M SCARED, DEAR!
QUICK! LOCK THE DOOR!
EEEK!
GET OUT OF THE WAY! WE'LL FIGHT THESE GUYS TO THE FINISH!
IT'S NO USE! THEY'RE ALREADY HERE!
COME ON IN...
WHAT'S THIS?!
TAKE THIS!!
FWAK
WHAT'S GOING ON? WHAT HAPPENED?!

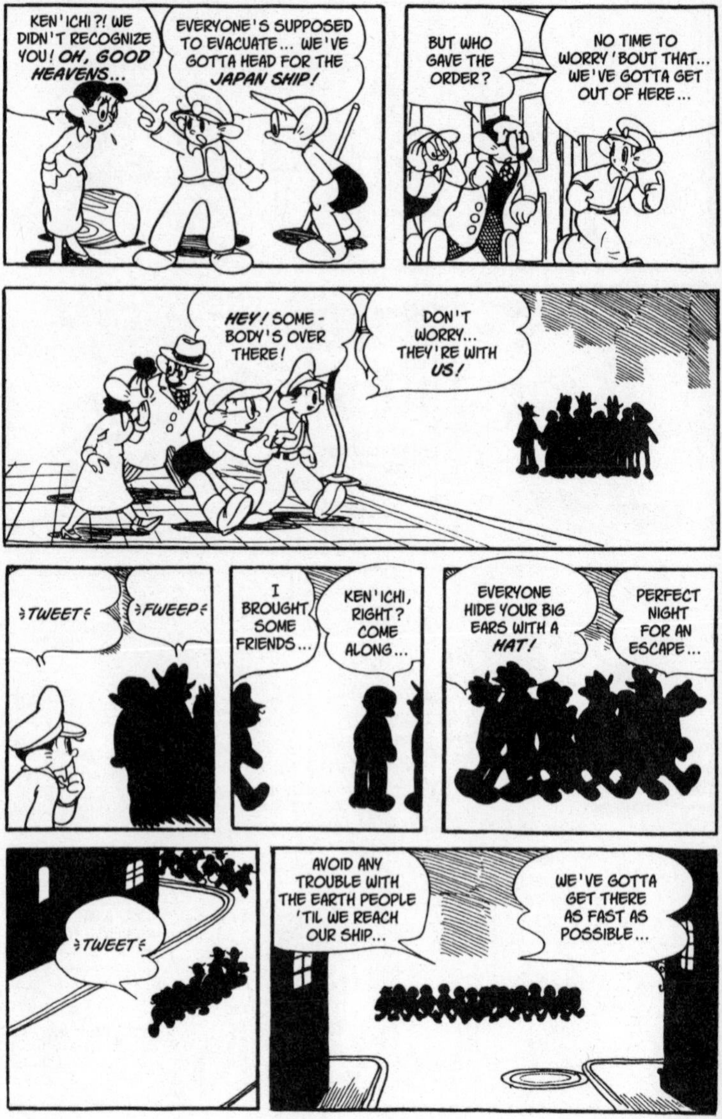
KEN'ICHI?! WE DIDN'T RECOGNIZE YOU! OH, GOOD HEAVENS...
EVERYONE'S SUPPOSED TO EVACUATE... WE'VE GOTTA HEAD FOR THE JAPAN SHIP!
BUT WHO GAVE THE ORDER?
NO TIME TO WORRY 'BOUT THAT... WE'VE GOTTA GET OUT OF HERE...
HEY! SOMEBODY'S OVER THERE!
DON'T WORRY... THEY'RE WITH US!
TWEET
FWEEP
I BROUGHT SOME FRIENDS...
KEN'ICHI, RIGHT? COME ALONG...
EVERYONE HIDE YOUR BIG EARS WITH A HAT!
PERFECT NIGHT FOR AN ESCAPE...
TWEET
AVOID ANY TROUBLE WITH THE EARTH PEOPLE 'TIL WE REACH OUR SHIP...
WE'VE GOTTA GET THERE AS FAST AS POSSIBLE...

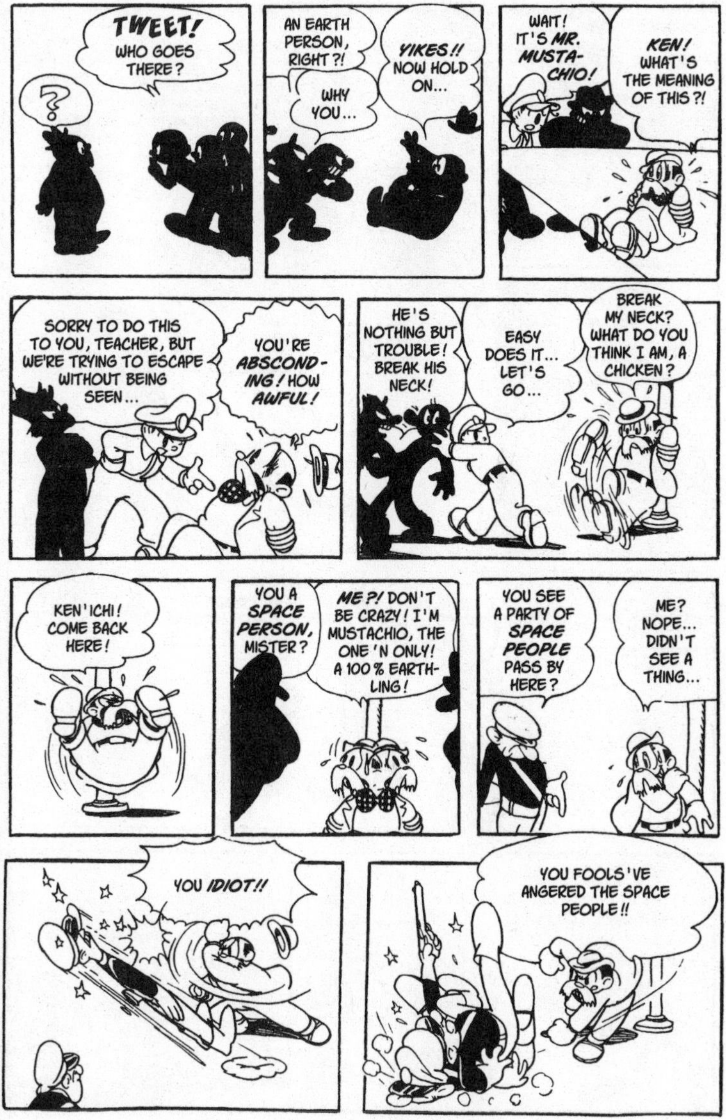
TWEET! WHO GOES THERE?
?
AN EARTH PERSON, RIGHT?!
WHY YOU...
YIKES!! NOW HOLD ON...
WAIT! IT'S MR. MUSTACHIO!
KEN! WHAT'S THE MEANING OF THIS?!
SORRY TO DO THIS TO YOU, TEACHER, BUT WE'RE TRYING TO ESCAPE WITHOUT BEING SEEN...
YOU'RE ABSCONDING! HOW AWFUL!
HE'S NOTHING BUT TROUBLE! BREAK HIS NECK!
EASY DOES IT... LET'S GO...
BREAK MY NECK? WHAT DO YOU THINK I AM, A CHICKEN?
KEN'ICHI! COME BACK HERE!
YOU A SPACE PERSON, MISTER?
ME?! DON'T BE CRAZY! I'M MUSTACHIO, THE ONE 'N ONLY! A 100% EARTHLING!
YOU SEE A PARTY OF SPACE PEOPLE PASS BY HERE?
ME? NOPE... DIDN'T SEE A THING...
YOU IDIOT!!
YOU FOOLS'VE ANGERED THE SPACE PEOPLE!!

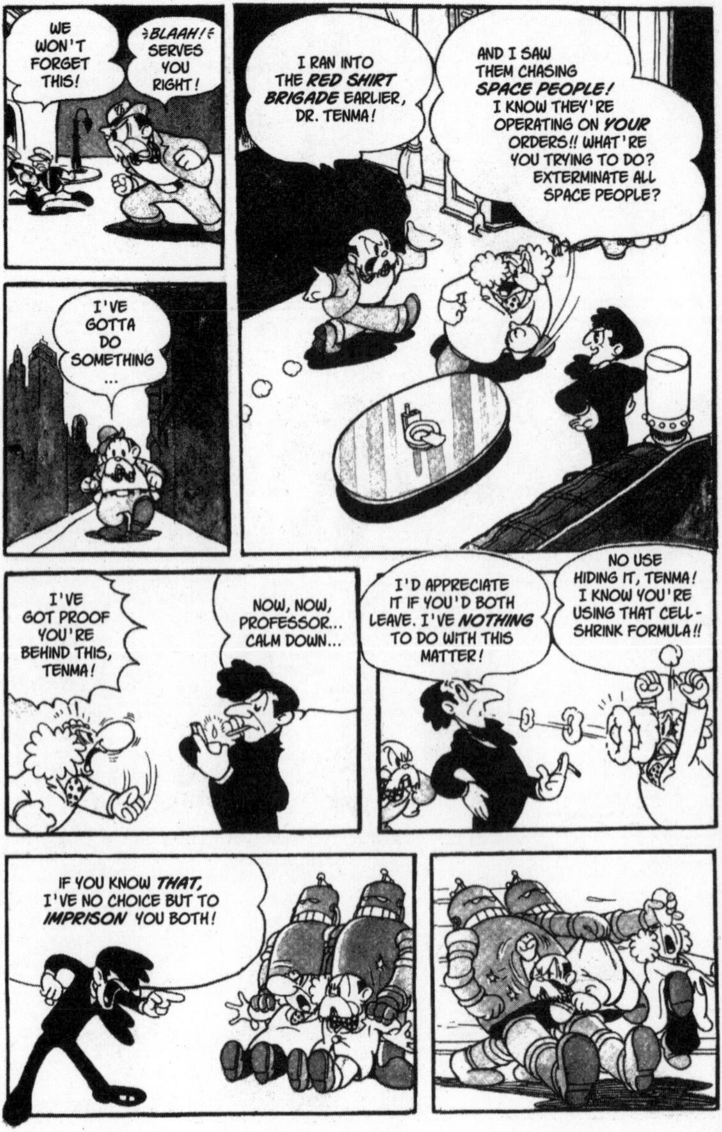
WE WON'T FORGET THIS!
⚡BLAAH!⚡ SERVES YOU RIGHT!
I'VE GOTTA DO SOMETHING ...
I RAN INTO THE RED SHIRT BRIGADE EARLIER, DR. TENMA!
AND I SAW THEM CHASING SPACE PEOPLE! I KNOW THEY'RE OPERATING ON YOUR ORDERS!! WHAT'RE YOU TRYING TO DO? EXTERMINATE ALL SPACE PEOPLE?
I'VE GOT PROOF YOU'RE BEHIND THIS, TENMA!
NOW, NOW, PROFESSOR... CALM DOWN...
I'D APPRECIATE IT IF YOU'D BOTH LEAVE. I'VE NOTHING TO DO WITH THIS MATTER!
NO USE HIDING IT, TENMA! I KNOW YOU'RE USING THAT CELL-SHRINK FORMULA!!
IF YOU KNOW THAT, I'VE NO CHOICE BUT TO IMPRISON YOU BOTH!

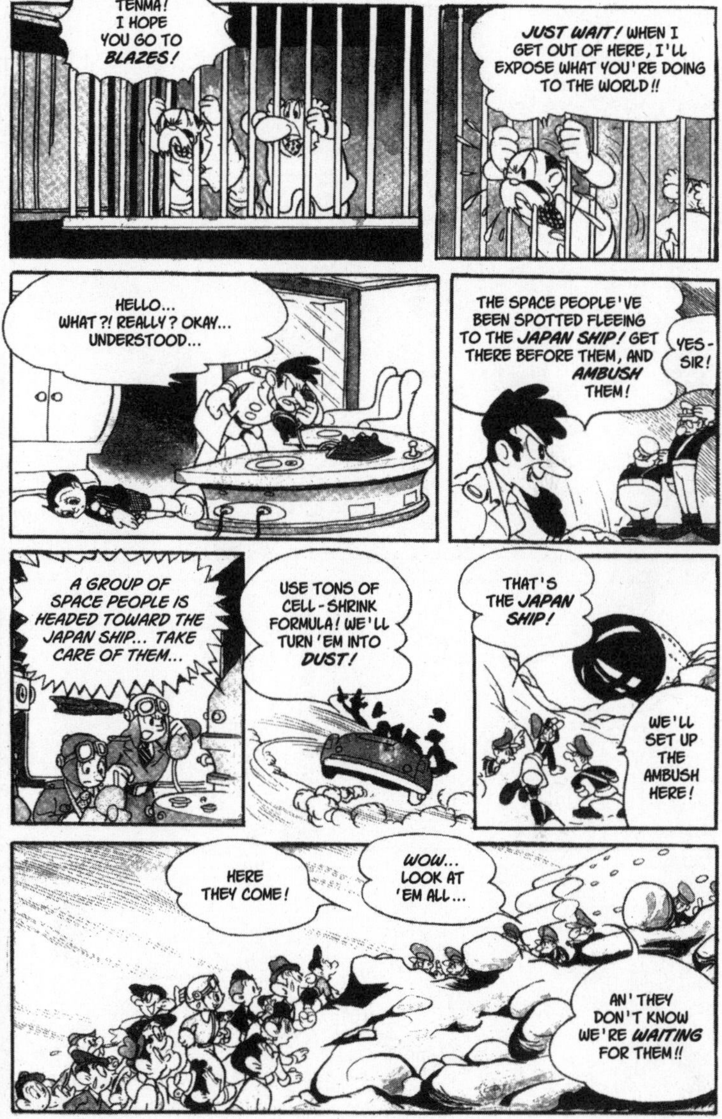
TENMA! I HOPE YOU GO TO BLAZES!
JUST WAIT! WHEN I GET OUT OF HERE, I'LL EXPOSE WHAT YOU'RE DOING TO THE WORLD!!
HELLO... WHAT?! REALLY? OKAY... UNDERSTOOD...
THE SPACE PEOPLE'VE BEEN SPOTTED FLEEING TO THE JAPAN SHIP! GET THERE BEFORE THEM, AND AMBUSH THEM!
YES-SIR!
A GROUP OF SPACE PEOPLE IS HEADED TOWARD THE JAPAN SHIP... TAKE CARE OF THEM...
USE TONS OF CELL-SHRINK FORMULA! WE'LL TURN 'EM INTO DUST!
THAT'S THE JAPAN SHIP!
WE'LL SET UP THE AMBUSH HERE!
HERE THEY COME!
WOW... LOOK AT 'EM ALL...
AN' THEY DON'T KNOW WE'RE WAITING FOR THEM!!

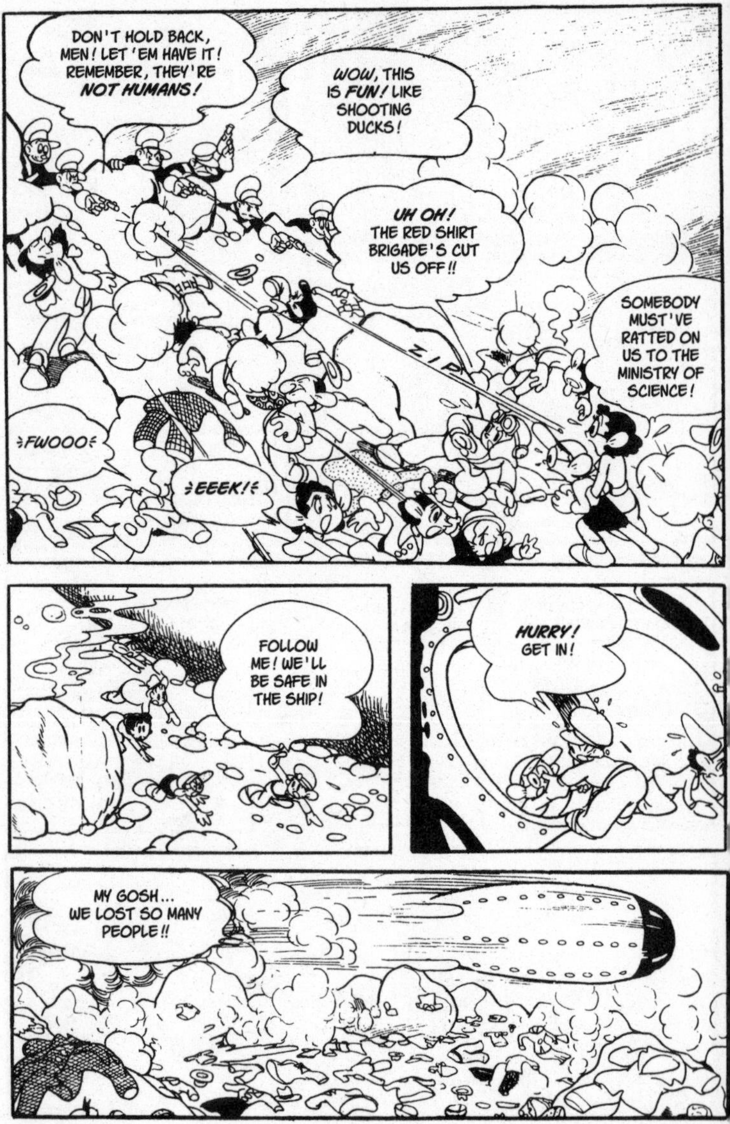
DON'T HOLD BACK, MEN! LET 'EM HAVE IT! REMEMBER, THEY'RE NOT HUMANS!
WOW, THIS IS FUN! LIKE SHOOTING DUCKS!
UH OH! THE RED SHIRT BRIGADE'S CUT US OFF!!
ZIP
SOMEBODY MUST'VE RATTED ON US TO THE MINISTRY OF SCIENCE!
FWOOO
EEEK!
FOLLOW ME! WE'LL BE SAFE IN THE SHIP!
HURRY! GET IN!
MY GOSH... WE LOST SO MANY PEOPLE!!

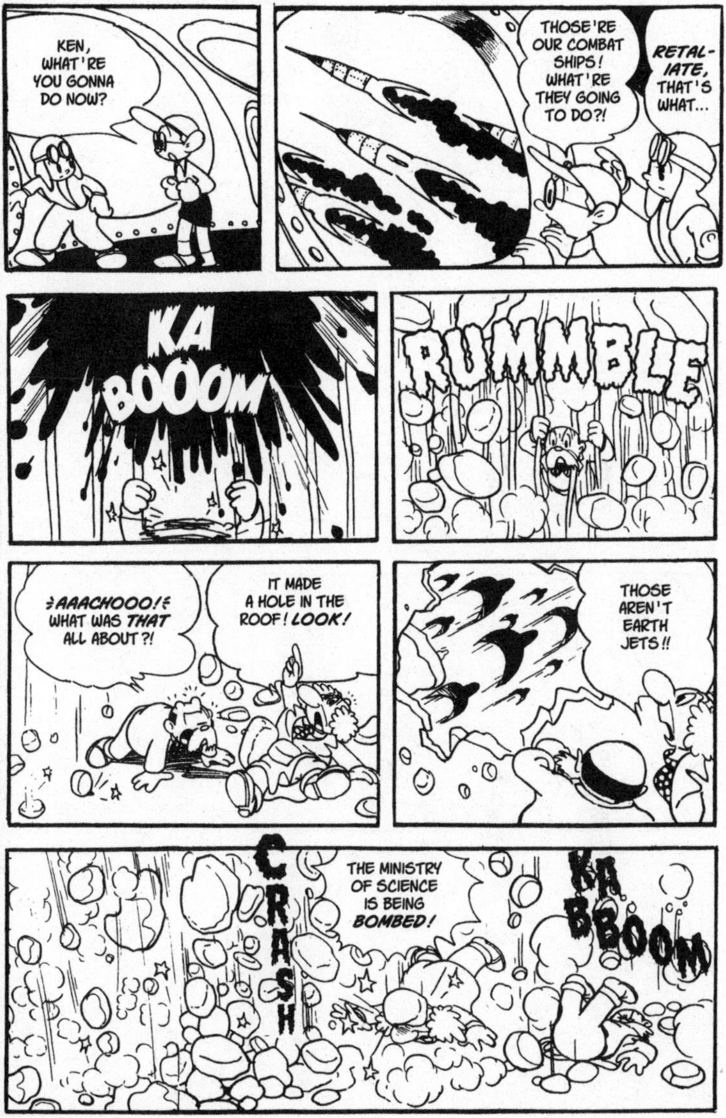
KEN, WHAT'RE YOU GONNA DO NOW?
THOSE'RE OUR COMBAT SHIPS! WHAT'RE THEY GOING TO DO?!
RETAL-IATE, THAT'S WHAT...
KA BOOOM
RUMMBLE
AAACHOOO! WHAT WAS THAT ALL ABOUT?!
IT MADE A HOLE IN THE ROOF! LOOK!
THOSE AREN'T EARTH JETS!!
CRASH
THE MINISTRY OF SCIENCE IS BEING BOMBED!
KA BBOOM

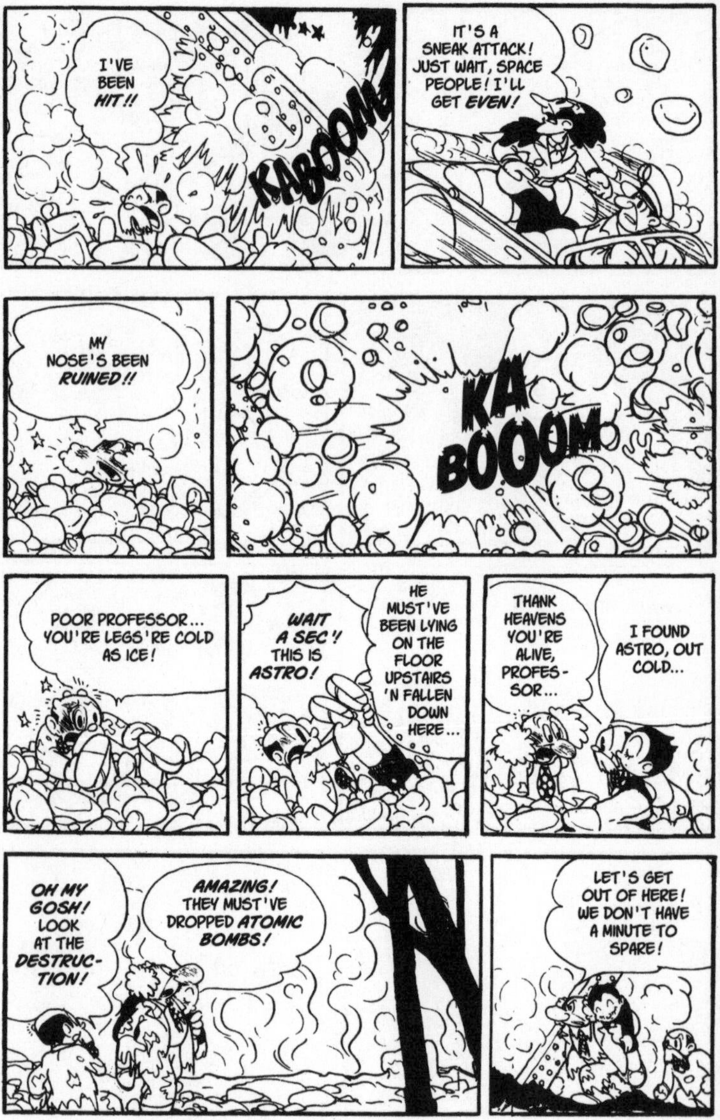
I'VE BEEN HIT!!
KABOOM
IT'S A SNEAK ATTACK! JUST WAIT, SPACE PEOPLE! I'LL GET EVEN!
MY NOSE'S BEEN RUINED!!
KA BOOOM
POOR PROFESSOR... YOU'RE LEGS'RE COLD AS ICE!
WAIT A SEC'! THIS IS ASTRO!
HE MUST'VE BEEN LYING ON THE FLOOR UPSTAIRS 'N FALLEN DOWN HERE...
THANK HEAVENS YOU'RE ALIVE, PROFES-SOR...
I FOUND ASTRO, OUT COLD...
OH MY GOSH! LOOK AT THE DESTRUC-TION!
AMAZING! THEY MUST'VE DROPPED ATOMIC BOMBS!
LET'S GET OUT OF HERE! WE DON'T HAVE A MINUTE TO SPARE!

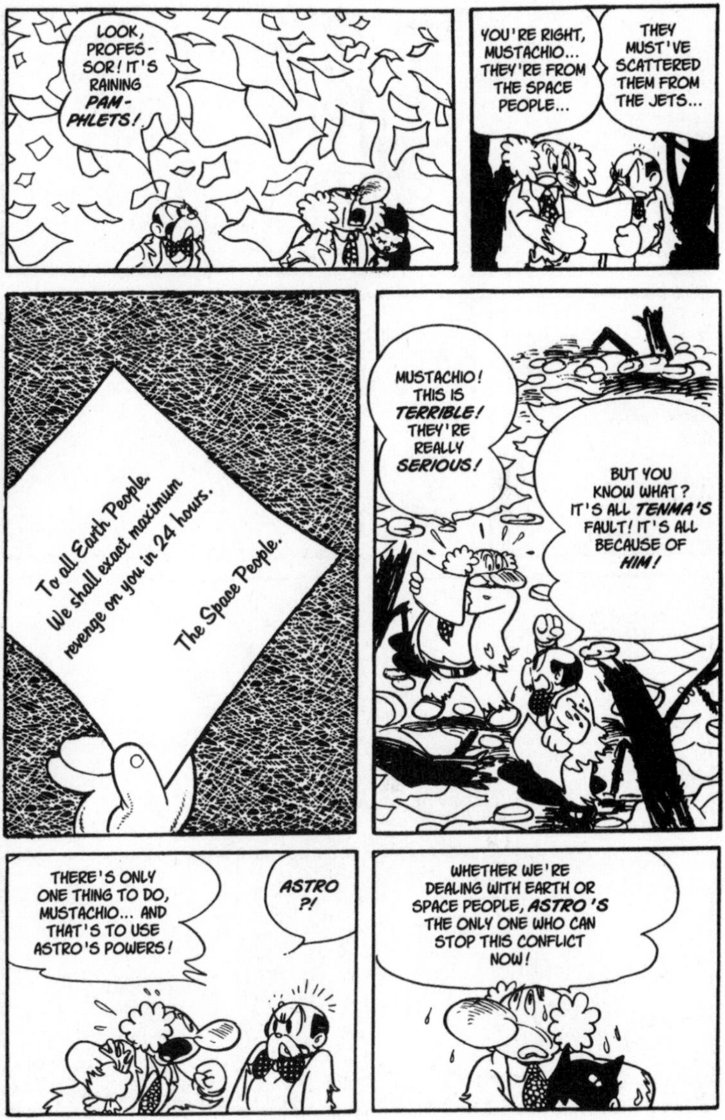
LOOK, PROFES-SOR! IT'S RAINING PAM-PHLETS!
YOU'RE RIGHT, MUSTACHIO... THEY'RE FROM THE SPACE PEOPLE...
THEY MUST'VE SCATTERED THEM FROM THE JETS...
To all Earth People.
We shall exact maximum revenge on you in 24 hours.
The Space People.
MUSTACHIO! THIS IS TERRIBLE! THEY'RE REALLY SERIOUS!
BUT YOU KNOW WHAT? IT'S ALL TENMA'S FAULT! IT'S ALL BECAUSE OF HIM!
THERE'S ONLY ONE THING TO DO, MUSTACHIO... AND THAT'S TO USE ASTRO'S POWERS!
ASTRO?!
WHETHER WE'RE DEALING WITH EARTH OR SPACE PEOPLE, ASTRO'S THE ONLY ONE WHO CAN STOP THIS CONFLICT NOW!

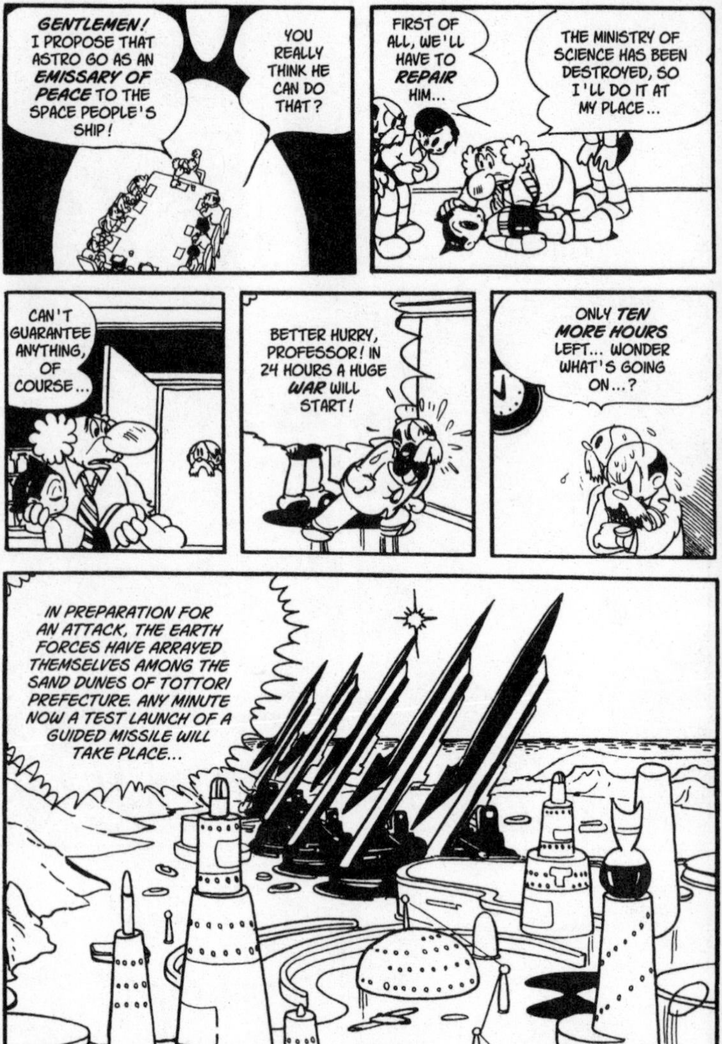
GENTLEMEN! I PROPOSE THAT ASTRO GO AS AN EMISSARY OF PEACE TO THE SPACE PEOPLE'S SHIP!
YOU REALLY THINK HE CAN DO THAT?
FIRST OF ALL, WE'LL HAVE TO REPAIR HIM...
THE MINISTRY OF SCIENCE HAS BEEN DESTROYED, SO I'LL DO IT AT MY PLACE...
CAN'T GUARANTEE ANYTHING, OF COURSE...
BETTER HURRY, PROFESSOR! IN 24 HOURS A HUGE WAR WILL START!
ONLY TEN MORE HOURS LEFT... WONDER WHAT'S GOING ON...?
IN PREPARATION FOR AN ATTACK, THE EARTH FORCES HAVE ARRAYED THEMSELVES AMONG THE SAND DUNES OF TOTTORI PREFECTURE. ANY MINUTE NOW A TEST LAUNCH OF A GUIDED MISSILE WILL TAKE PLACE...

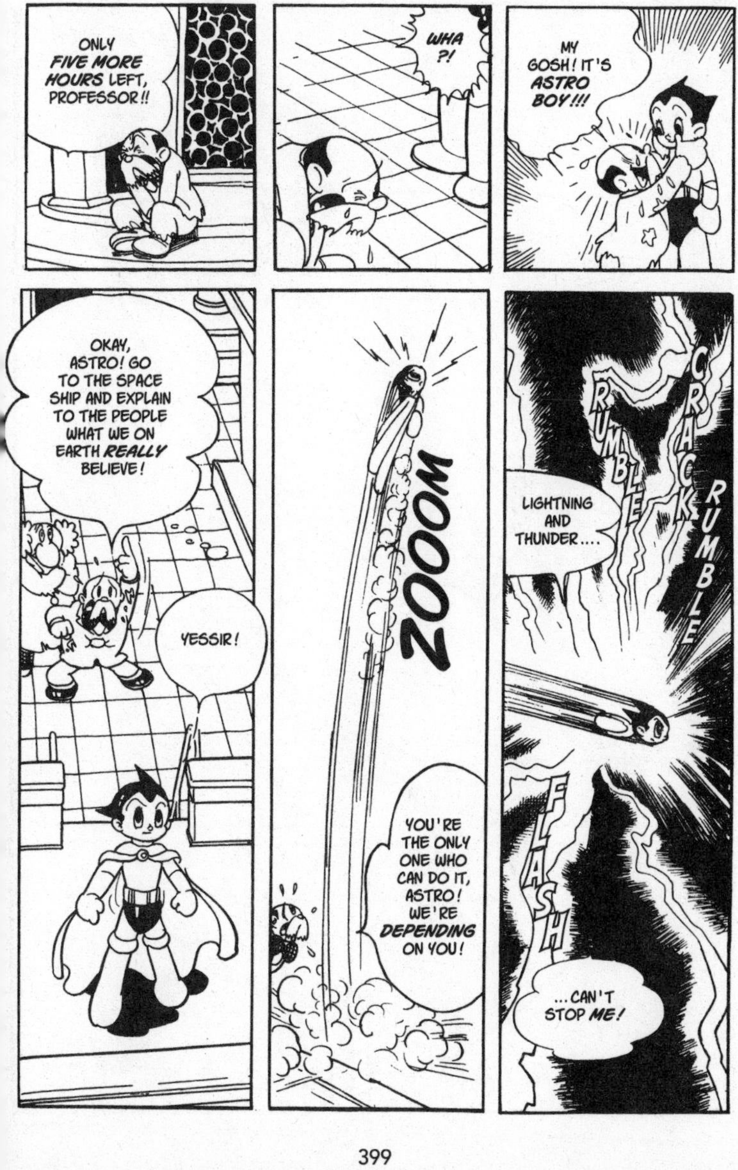
ONLY FIVE MORE HOURS LEFT, PROFESSOR!!
WHA ?!
MY GOSH! IT'S ASTRO BOY!!!
OKAY, ASTRO! GO TO THE SPACE SHIP AND EXPLAIN TO THE PEOPLE WHAT WE ON EARTH REALLY BELIEVE!
YESSIR!
ZOOOM
YOU'RE THE ONLY ONE WHO CAN DO IT, ASTRO! WE'RE DEPENDING ON YOU!
RUMBLE
CRACK
RUMBLE
LIGHTNING AND THUNDER....
FLASH
...CAN'T STOP ME!

LOOK! IT'S ASTRO BOY!
WHAT DO YOU WANT?!

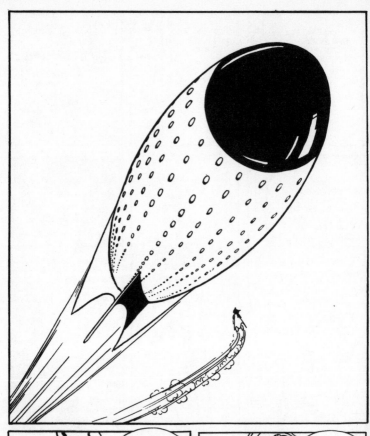

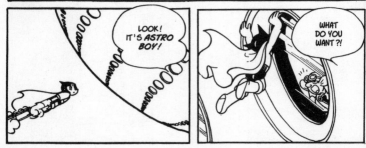

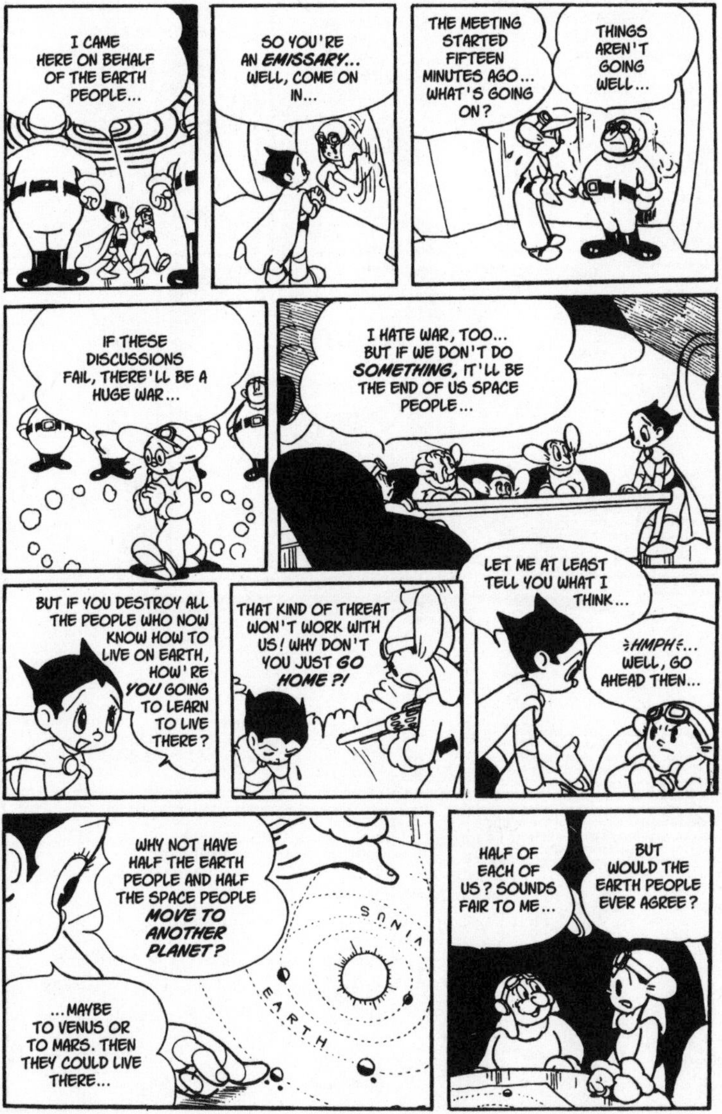
I CAME HERE ON BEHALF OF THE EARTH PEOPLE...
SO YOU'RE AN EMISSARY... WELL, COME ON IN...
THE MEETING STARTED FIFTEEN MINUTES AGO... WHAT'S GOING ON?
THINGS AREN'T GOING WELL...
IF THESE DISCUSSIONS FAIL, THERE'LL BE A HUGE WAR...
I HATE WAR, TOO... BUT IF WE DON'T DO SOMETHING, IT'LL BE THE END OF US SPACE PEOPLE...
BUT IF YOU DESTROY ALL THE PEOPLE WHO NOW KNOW HOW TO LIVE ON EARTH, HOW'RE YOU GOING TO LEARN TO LIVE THERE?
THAT KIND OF THREAT WON'T WORK WITH US! WHY DON'T YOU JUST GO HOME?!
LET ME AT LEAST TELL YOU WHAT I THINK...
HMPH... WELL, GO AHEAD THEN...
WHY NOT HAVE HALF THE EARTH PEOPLE AND HALF THE SPACE PEOPLE MOVE TO ANOTHER PLANET?
VENUS
EARTH
...MAYBE TO VENUS OR TO MARS. THEN THEY COULD LIVE THERE...
HALF OF EACH OF US? SOUNDS FAIR TO ME...
BUT WOULD THE EARTH PEOPLE EVER AGREE?

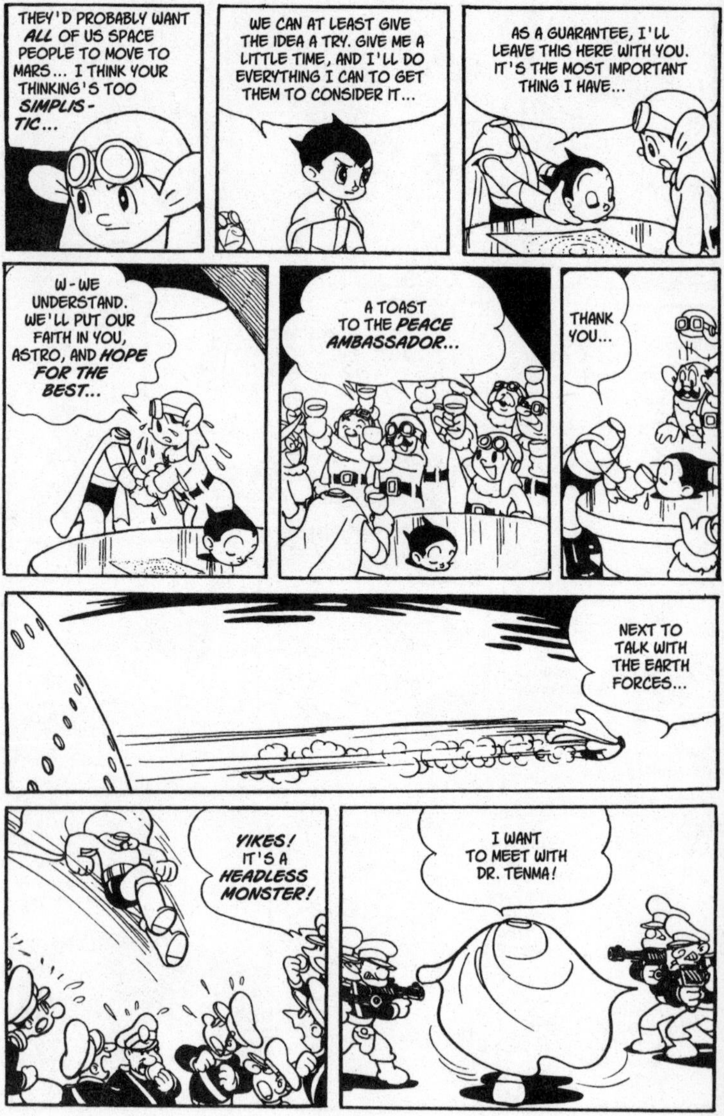
THEY'D PROBABLY WANT ALL OF US SPACE PEOPLE TO MOVE TO MARS... I THINK YOUR THINKING'S TOO SIMPLISTIC...
WE CAN AT LEAST GIVE THE IDEA A TRY. GIVE ME A LITTLE TIME, AND I'LL DO EVERYTHING I CAN TO GET THEM TO CONSIDER IT...
AS A GUARANTEE, I'LL LEAVE THIS HERE WITH YOU. IT'S THE MOST IMPORTANT THING I HAVE...
W-WE UNDERSTAND. WE'LL PUT OUR FAITH IN YOU, ASTRO, AND HOPE FOR THE BEST...
A TOAST TO THE PEACE AMBASSADOR...
THANK YOU...
NEXT TO TALK WITH THE EARTH FORCES...
YIKES! IT'S A HEADLESS MONSTER!
I WANT TO MEET WITH DR. TENMA!

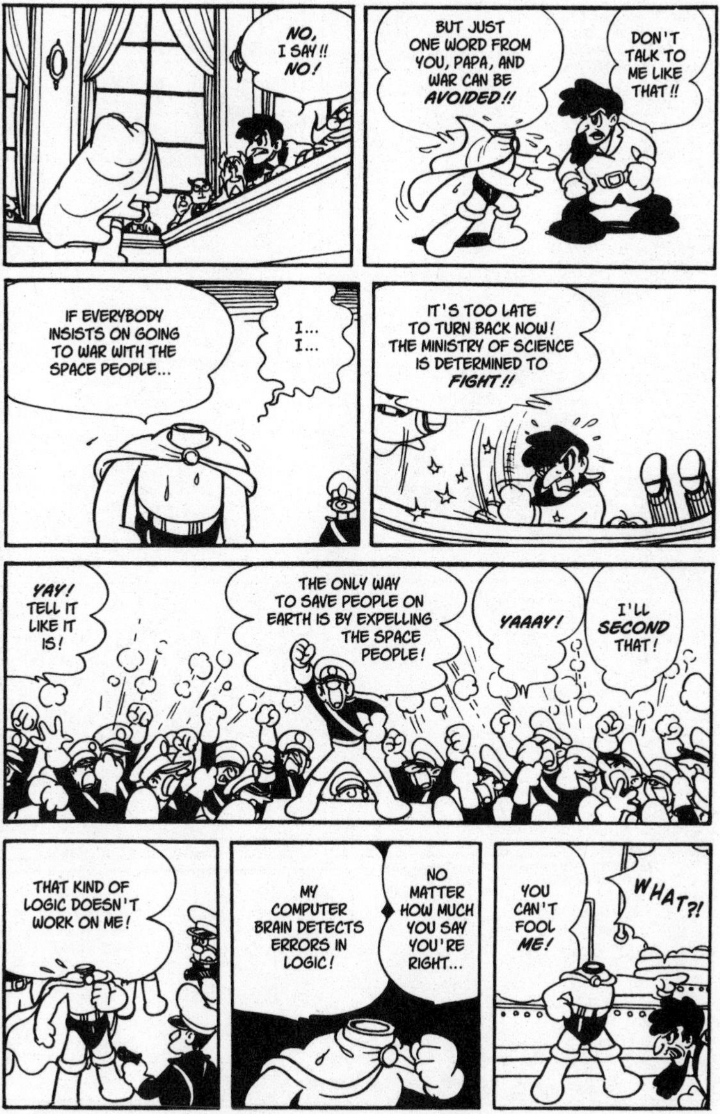
NO, I SAY!! NO!
BUT JUST ONE WORD FROM YOU, PAPA, AND WAR CAN BE AVOIDED!!
DON'T TALK TO ME LIKE THAT!!
IF EVERYBODY INSISTS ON GOING TO WAR WITH THE SPACE PEOPLE...
I... I...
IT'S TOO LATE TO TURN BACK NOW! THE MINISTRY OF SCIENCE IS DETERMINED TO FIGHT!!
YAY! TELL IT LIKE IT IS!
THE ONLY WAY TO SAVE PEOPLE ON EARTH IS BY EXPELLING THE SPACE PEOPLE!
YAAAY!
I'LL SECOND THAT!
THAT KIND OF LOGIC DOESN'T WORK ON ME!
MY COMPUTER BRAIN DETECTS ERRORS IN LOGIC!
NO MATTER HOW MUCH YOU SAY YOU'RE RIGHT...
YOU CAN'T FOOL ME!
WHAT?!

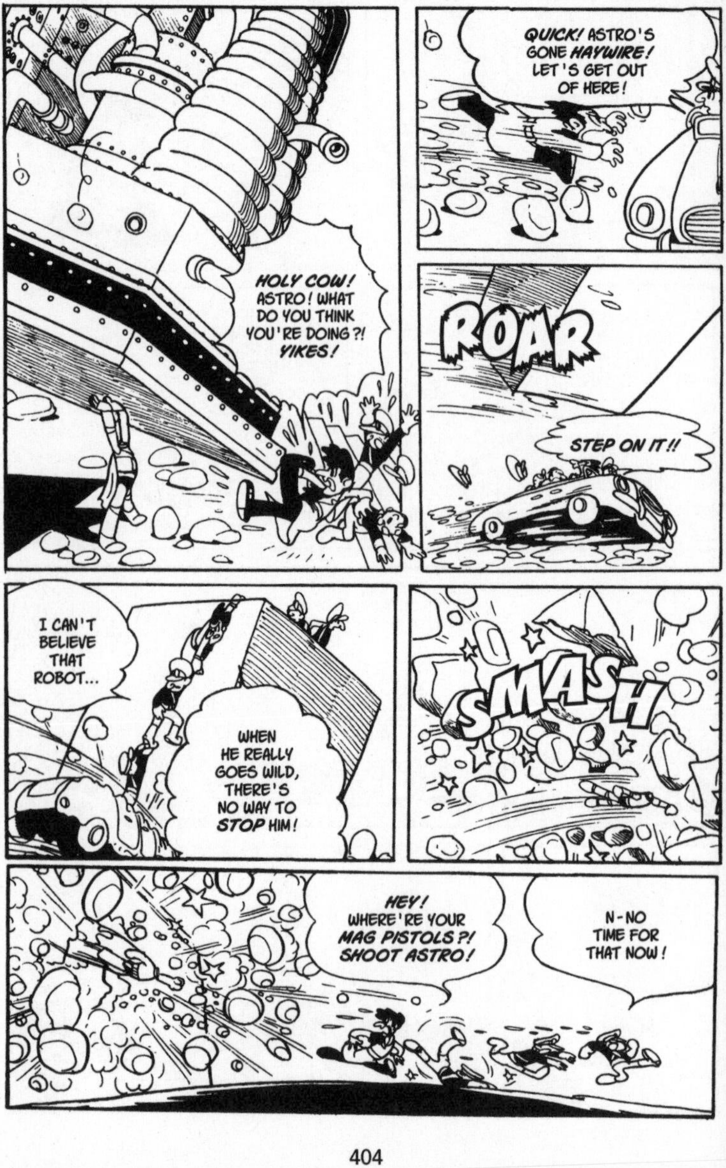
HOLY COW! ASTRO! WHAT DO YOU THINK YOU'RE DOING?! YIKES!
QUICK! ASTRO'S GONE HAYWIRE! LET'S GET OUT OF HERE!
ROAR
STEP ON IT!!
I CAN'T BELIEVE THAT ROBOT...
WHEN HE REALLY GOES WILD, THERE'S NO WAY TO STOP HIM!
SMASH
HEY! WHERE'RE YOUR MAG PISTOLS?! SHOOT ASTRO!
N-NO TIME FOR THAT NOW!

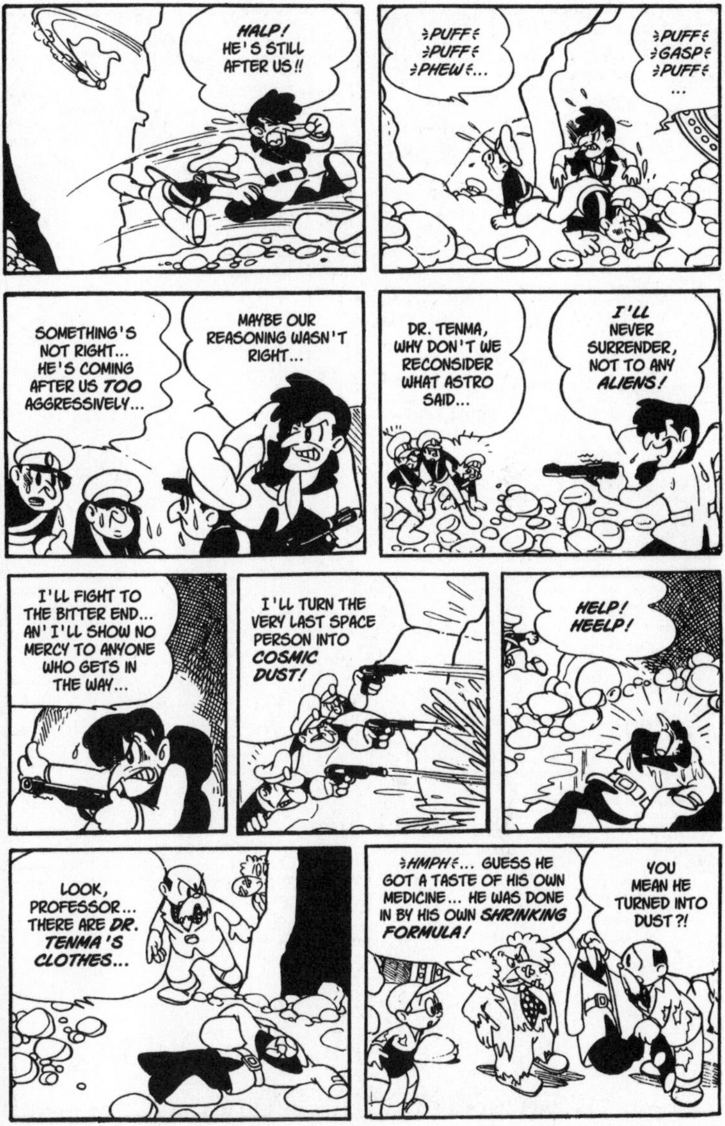
HALP! HE'S STILL AFTER US!!
PUFF PUFF PHEW...
PUFF GASP PUFF ...
SOMETHING'S NOT RIGHT... HE'S COMING AFTER US TOO AGGRESSIVELY...
MAYBE OUR REASONING WASN'T RIGHT...
DR. TENMA, WHY DON'T WE RECONSIDER WHAT ASTRO SAID...
I'LL NEVER SURRENDER, NOT TO ANY ALIENS!
I'LL FIGHT TO THE BITTER END... AN' I'LL SHOW NO MERCY TO ANYONE WHO GETS IN THE WAY...
I'LL TURN THE VERY LAST SPACE PERSON INTO COSMIC DUST!
HELP! HEELP!
LOOK, PROFESSOR... THERE ARE DR. TENMA'S CLOTHES...
HMPH... GUESS HE GOT A TASTE OF HIS OWN MEDICINE... HE WAS DONE IN BY HIS OWN SHRINKING FORMULA!
YOU MEAN HE TURNED INTO DUST?!

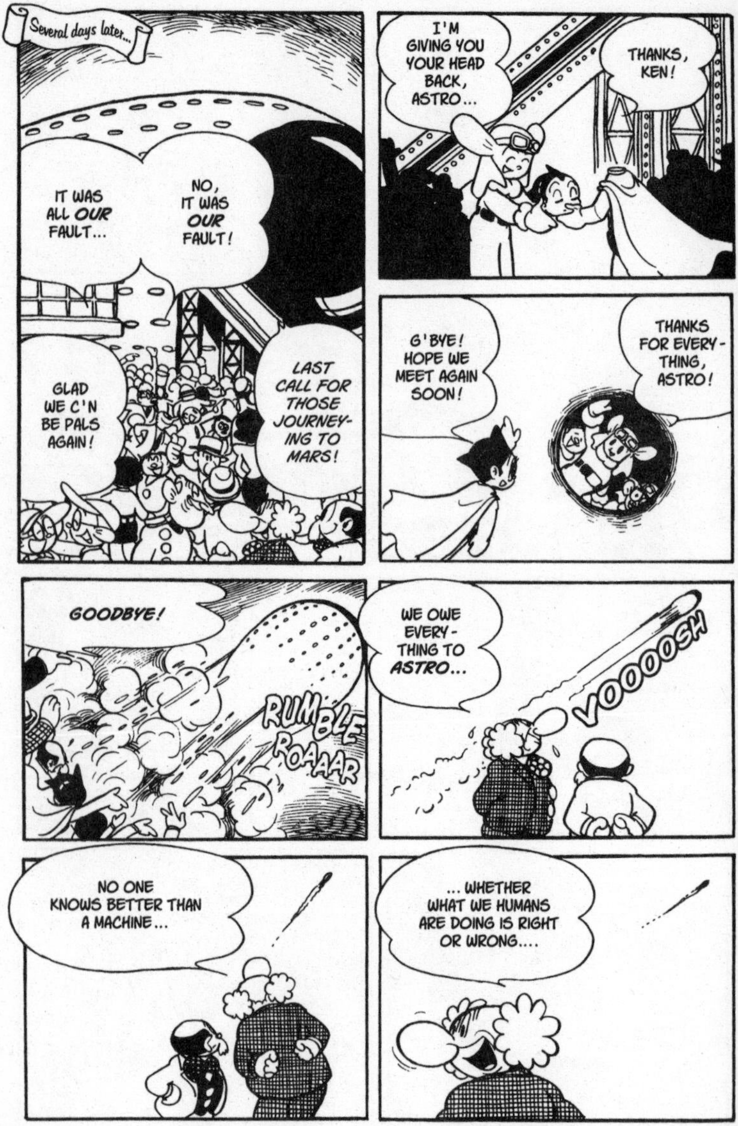
Several days later...
IT WAS ALL OUR FAULT...
NO, IT WAS OUR FAULT!
GLAD WE C'N BE PALS AGAIN!
LAST CALL FOR THOSE JOURNEY-ING TO MARS!
I'M GIVING YOU YOUR HEAD BACK, ASTRO...
THANKS, KEN!
G'BYE! HOPE WE MEET AGAIN SOON!
THANKS FOR EVERY-THING, ASTRO!
GOODBYE!
RUMBLE
ROAAAR
WE OWE EVERY-THING TO ASTRO...
VOOOOSH
NO ONE KNOWS BETTER THAN A MACHINE...
... WHETHER WHAT WE HUMANS ARE DOING IS RIGHT OR WRONG....

GAS
PEOPLE

First serialized from April to October 1952
in *Shonen* magazine.

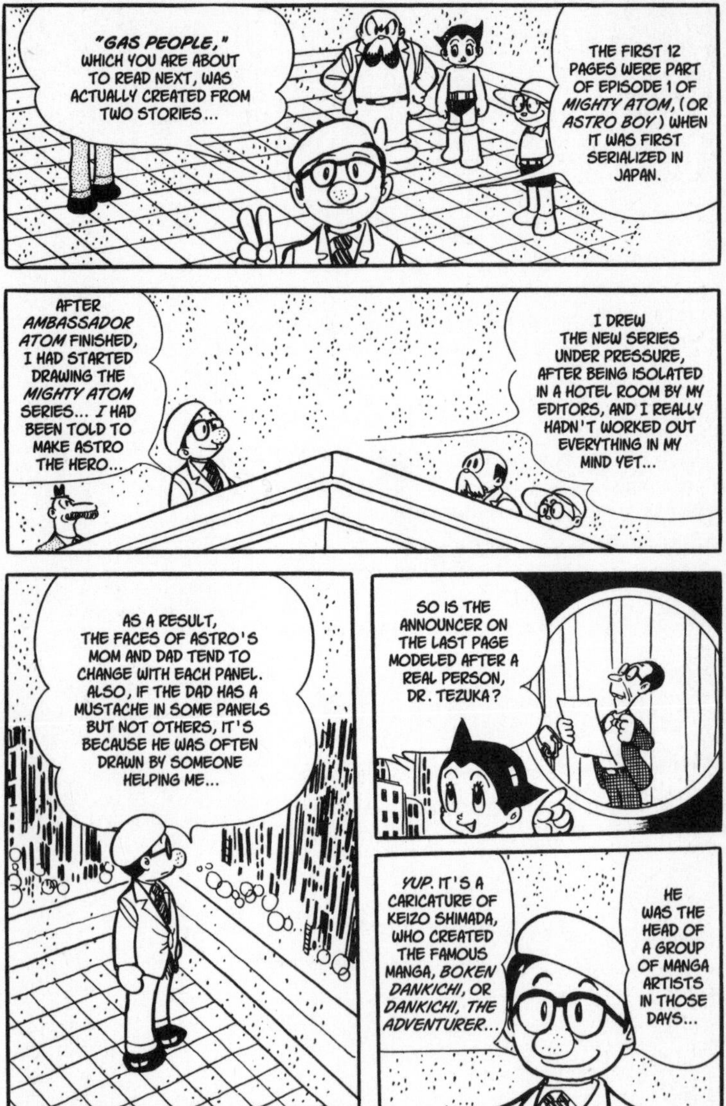
"GAS PEOPLE," WHICH YOU ARE ABOUT TO READ NEXT, WAS ACTUALLY CREATED FROM TWO STORIES...
THE FIRST 12 PAGES WERE PART OF EPISODE 1 OF MIGHTY ATOM, (OR ASTRO BOY) WHEN IT WAS FIRST SERIALIZED IN JAPAN.
AFTER AMBASSADOR ATOM FINISHED, I HAD STARTED DRAWING THE MIGHTY ATOM SERIES... I HAD BEEN TOLD TO MAKE ASTRO THE HERO...
I DREW THE NEW SERIES UNDER PRESSURE, AFTER BEING ISOLATED IN A HOTEL ROOM BY MY EDITORS, AND I REALLY HADN'T WORKED OUT EVERYTHING IN MY MIND YET...
AS A RESULT, THE FACES OF ASTRO'S MOM AND DAD TEND TO CHANGE WITH EACH PANEL. ALSO, IF THE DAD HAS A MUSTACHE IN SOME PANELS BUT NOT OTHERS, IT'S BECAUSE HE WAS OFTEN DRAWN BY SOMEONE HELPING ME...
SO IS THE ANNOUNCER ON THE LAST PAGE MODELED AFTER A REAL PERSON, DR. TEZUKA?
YUP. IT'S A CARICATURE OF KEIZO SHIMADA, WHO CREATED THE FAMOUS MANGA, BOKEN DANKICHI, OR DANKICHI, THE ADVENTURER...
HE WAS THE HEAD OF A GROUP OF MANGA ARTISTS IN THOSE DAYS...

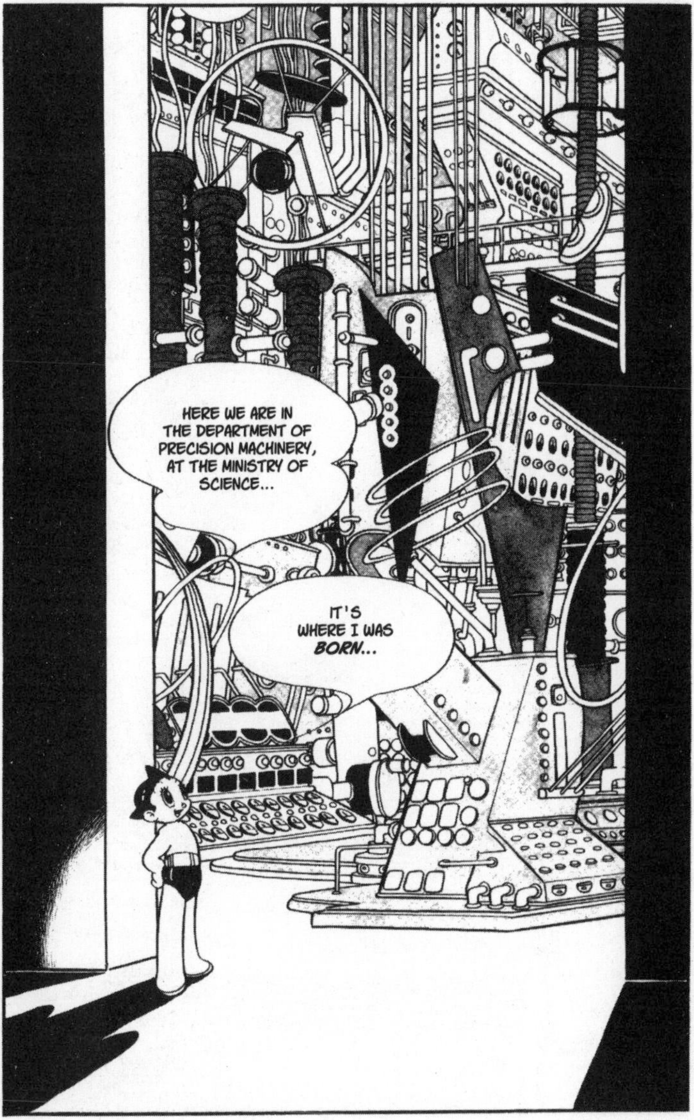
HERE WE ARE IN THE DEPARTMENT OF PRECISION MACHINERY, AT THE MINISTRY OF SCIENCE...
IT'S WHERE I WAS *BORN*...

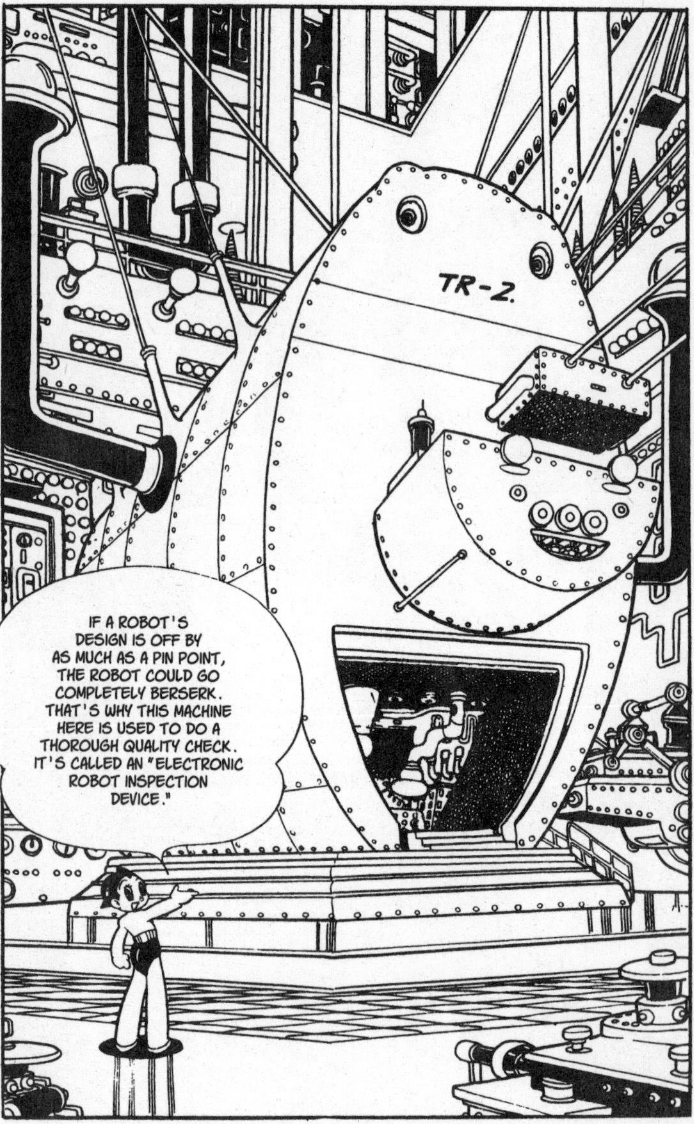
TR-2.
IF A ROBOT'S DESIGN IS OFF BY AS MUCH AS A PIN POINT, THE ROBOT COULD GO COMPLETELY BERSERK. THAT'S WHY THIS MACHINE HERE IS USED TO DO A THOROUGH QUALITY CHECK. IT'S CALLED AN "ELECTRONIC ROBOT INSPECTION DEVICE."

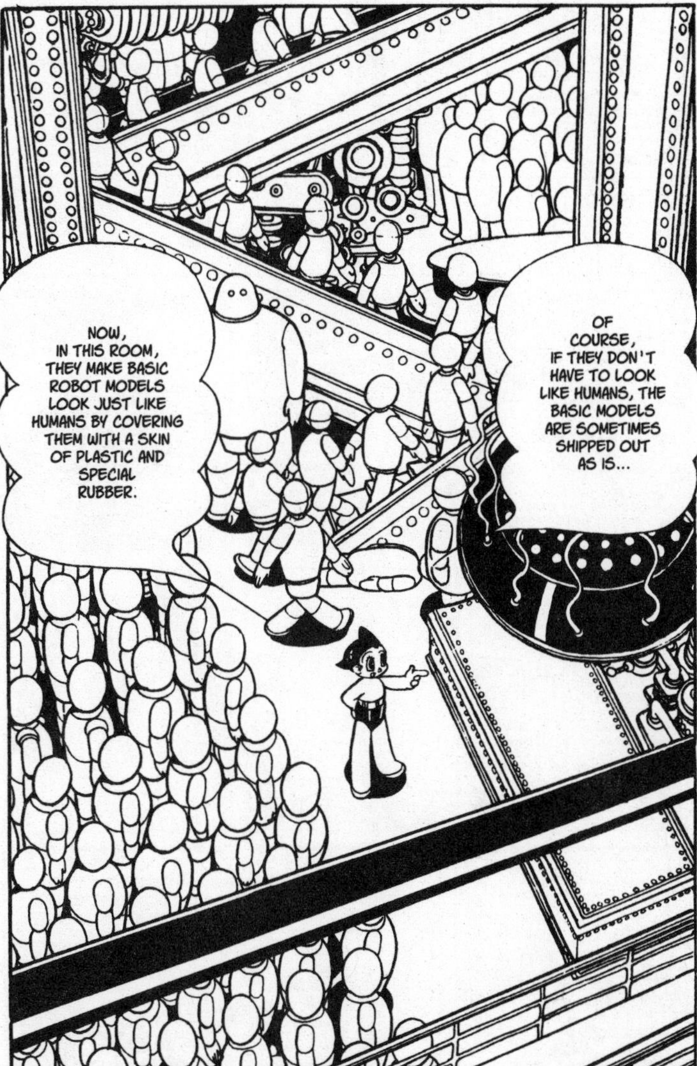
NOW, IN THIS ROOM, THEY MAKE BASIC ROBOT MODELS LOOK JUST LIKE HUMANS BY COVERING THEM WITH A SKIN OF PLASTIC AND SPECIAL RUBBER.
OF COURSE, IF THEY DON'T HAVE TO LOOK LIKE HUMANS, THE BASIC MODELS ARE SOMETIMES SHIPPED OUT AS IS...

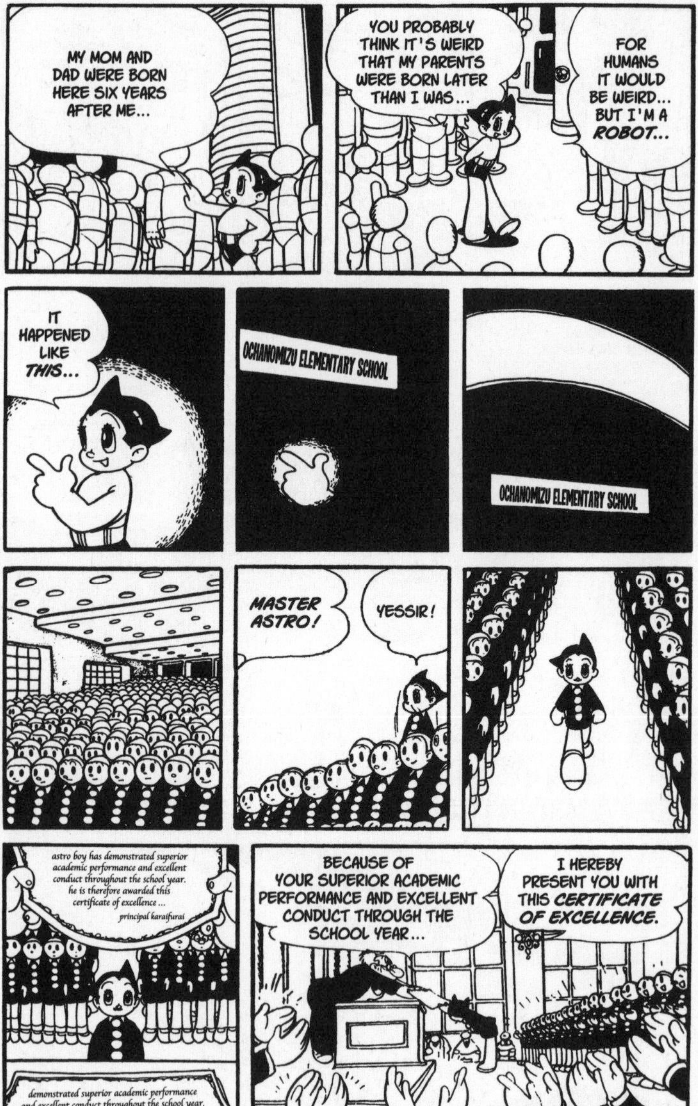
MY MOM AND DAD WERE BORN HERE SIX YEARS AFTER ME...
YOU PROBABLY THINK IT'S WEIRD THAT MY PARENTS WERE BORN LATER THAN I WAS...
FOR HUMANS IT WOULD BE WEIRD... BUT I'M A *ROBOT*...
IT HAPPENED LIKE *THIS*...
OCHANOMIZU ELEMENTARY SCHOOL
OCHANOMIZU ELEMENTARY SCHOOL
MASTER ASTRO!
YESSIR!
astro boy has demonstrated superior academic performance and excellent conduct throughout the school year. he is therefore awarded this certificate of excellence ...
principal karaifurai
demonstrated superior academic performance and excellent conduct throughout the school year.
BECAUSE OF YOUR SUPERIOR ACADEMIC PERFORMANCE AND EXCELLENT CONDUCT THROUGH THE SCHOOL YEAR...
I HEREBY PRESENT YOU WITH THIS *CERTIFICATE OF EXCELLENCE.*

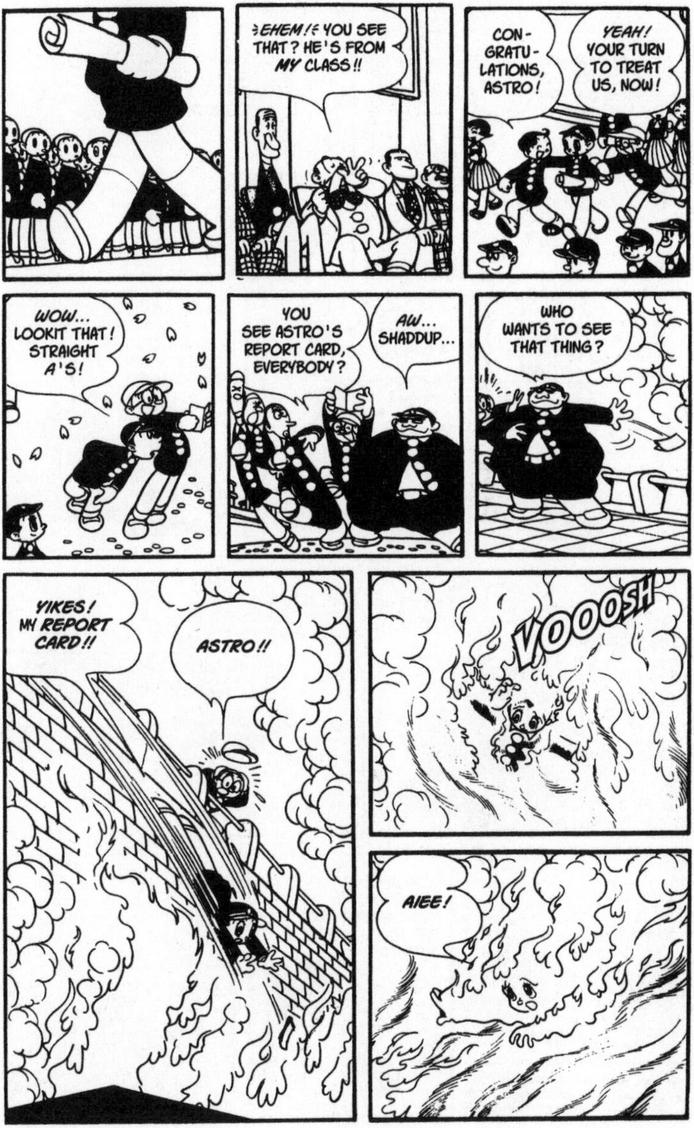

EHEM! YOU SEE THAT? HE'S FROM MY CLASS!!
CON-GRATU-LATIONS, ASTRO!
YEAH! YOUR TURN TO TREAT US, NOW!
WOW... LOOKIT THAT! STRAIGHT A'S!
YOU SEE ASTRO'S REPORT CARD, EVERYBODY?
AW... SHADDUP...
WHO WANTS TO SEE THAT THING?
YIKES! MY REPORT CARD!!
ASTRO!!
VOOOSH
AIEE!

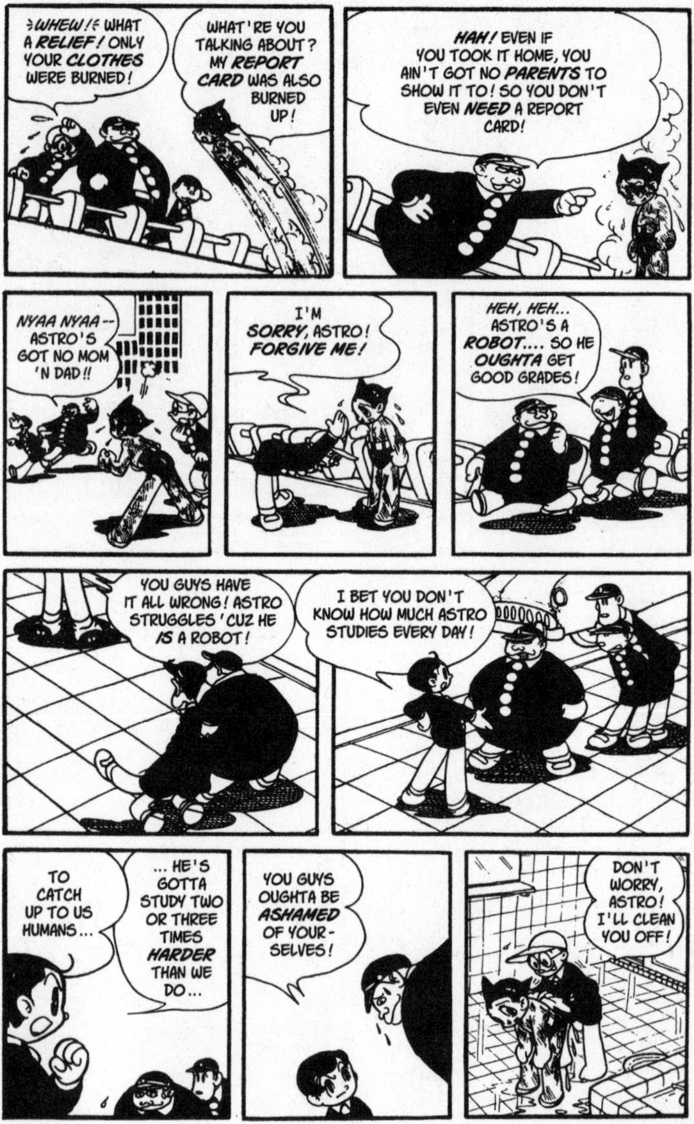

≑WHEW!≑ WHAT A RELIEF! ONLY YOUR CLOTHES WERE BURNED!
WHAT'RE YOU TALKING ABOUT? MY REPORT CARD WAS ALSO BURNED UP!
HAH! EVEN IF YOU TOOK IT HOME, YOU AIN'T GOT NO PARENTS TO SHOW IT TO! SO YOU DON'T EVEN NEED A REPORT CARD!
NYAA NYAA -- ASTRO'S GOT NO MOM 'N DAD!!
I'M SORRY, ASTRO! FORGIVE ME!
HEH, HEH... ASTRO'S A ROBOT.... SO HE OUGHTA GET GOOD GRADES!
YOU GUYS HAVE IT ALL WRONG! ASTRO STRUGGLES 'CUZ HE IS A ROBOT!
I BET YOU DON'T KNOW HOW MUCH ASTRO STUDIES EVERY DAY!
TO CATCH UP TO US HUMANS...
... HE'S GOTTA STUDY TWO OR THREE TIMES HARDER THAN WE DO...
YOU GUYS OUGHTA BE ASHAMED OF YOURSELVES!
DON'T WORRY, ASTRO! I'LL CLEAN YOU OFF!

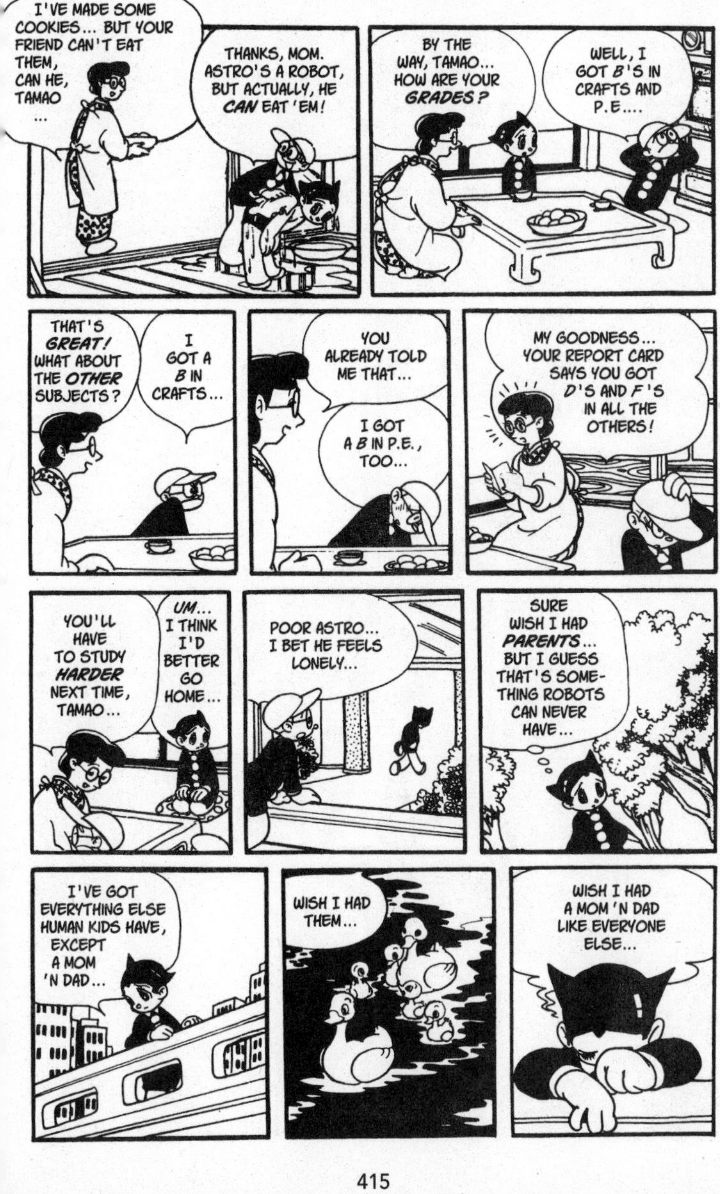
I'VE MADE SOME COOKIES... BUT YOUR FRIEND CAN'T EAT THEM, CAN HE, TAMAO ...
THANKS, MOM. ASTRO'S A ROBOT, BUT ACTUALLY, HE CAN EAT 'EM!
BY THE WAY, TAMAO... HOW ARE YOUR GRADES?
WELL, I GOT B'S IN CRAFTS AND P.E....
THAT'S GREAT! WHAT ABOUT THE OTHER SUBJECTS?
I GOT A B IN CRAFTS...
YOU ALREADY TOLD ME THAT...
I GOT A B IN P.E., TOO...
MY GOODNESS... YOUR REPORT CARD SAYS YOU GOT D'S AND F'S IN ALL THE OTHERS!
YOU'LL HAVE TO STUDY HARDER NEXT TIME, TAMAO...
UM... I THINK I'D BETTER GO HOME...
POOR ASTRO... I BET HE FEELS LONELY...
SURE WISH I HAD PARENTS... BUT I GUESS THAT'S SOME-THING ROBOTS CAN NEVER HAVE...
I'VE GOT EVERYTHING ELSE HUMAN KIDS HAVE, EXCEPT A MOM 'N DAD...
WISH I HAD THEM...
WISH I HAD A MOM 'N DAD LIKE EVERYONE ELSE...

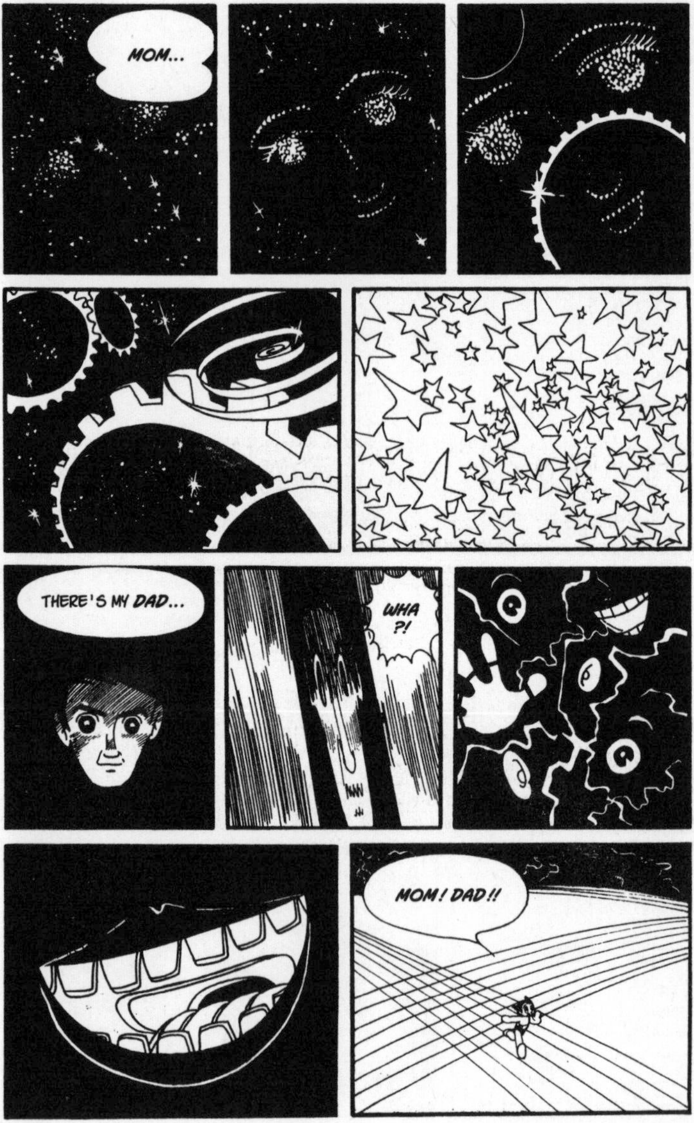
MOM...
THERE'S MY DAD...
WHA ?!
MOM! DAD!!

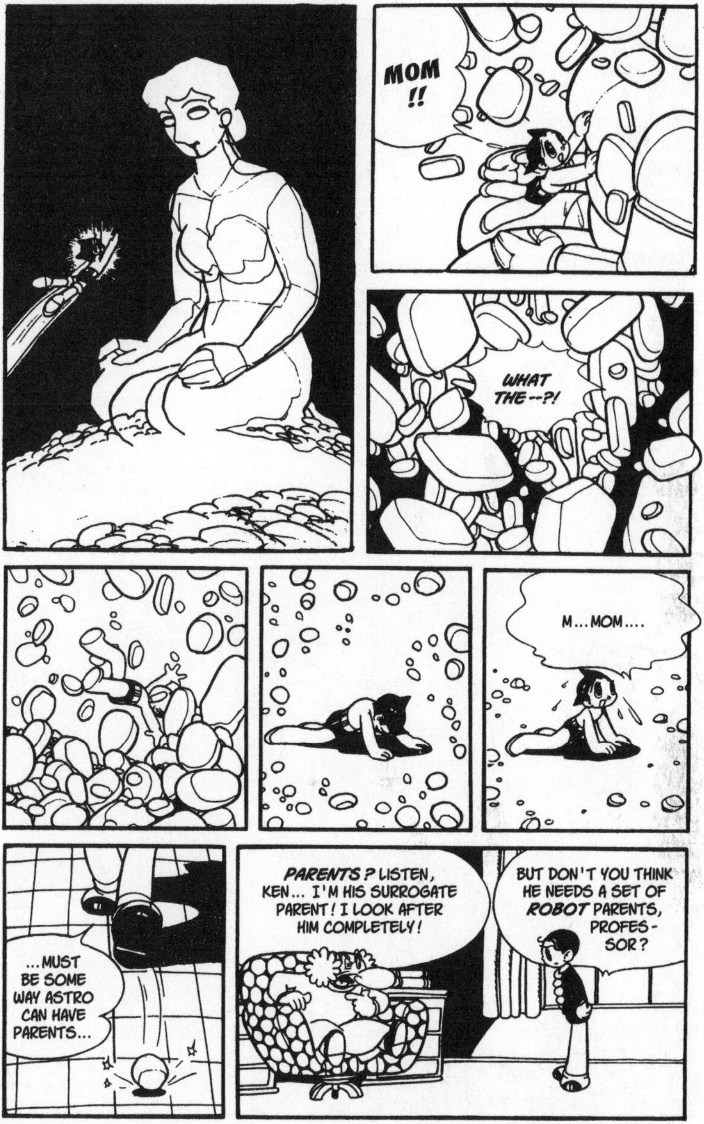
MOM !!
WHAT THE--?!
M...MOM....
...MUST BE SOME WAY ASTRO CAN HAVE PARENTS...
PARENTS? LISTEN, KEN... I'M HIS SURROGATE PARENT! I LOOK AFTER HIM COMPLETELY!
BUT DON'T YOU THINK HE NEEDS A SET OF ROBOT PARENTS, PROFES-SOR?

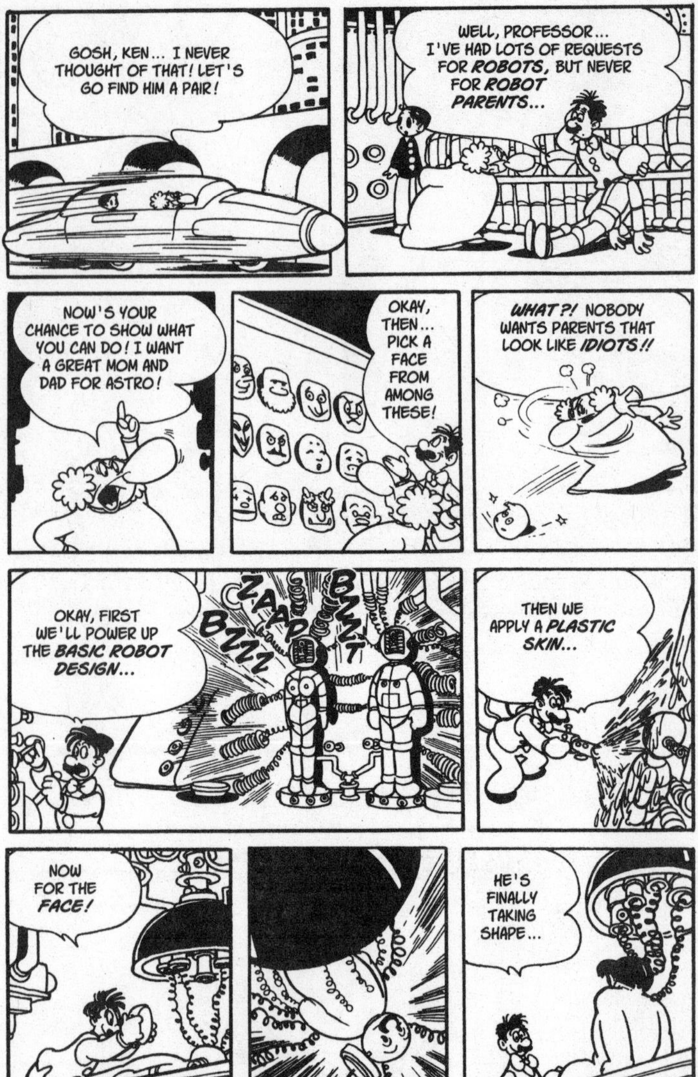
GOSH, KEN... I NEVER THOUGHT OF THAT! LET'S GO FIND HIM A PAIR!
WELL, PROFESSOR... I'VE HAD LOTS OF REQUESTS FOR *ROBOTS,* BUT NEVER FOR *ROBOT PARENTS...*
NOW'S YOUR CHANCE TO SHOW WHAT YOU CAN DO! I WANT A GREAT MOM AND DAD FOR ASTRO!
OKAY, THEN... PICK A FACE FROM AMONG THESE!
WHAT?! NOBODY WANTS PARENTS THAT LOOK LIKE *IDIOTS!!*
OKAY, FIRST WE'LL POWER UP THE *BASIC ROBOT DESIGN...*
ZAAAP
BZZZZ
BZZZT
THEN WE APPLY A *PLASTIC SKIN...*
NOW FOR THE *FACE!*
HE'S FINALLY TAKING SHAPE...

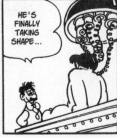

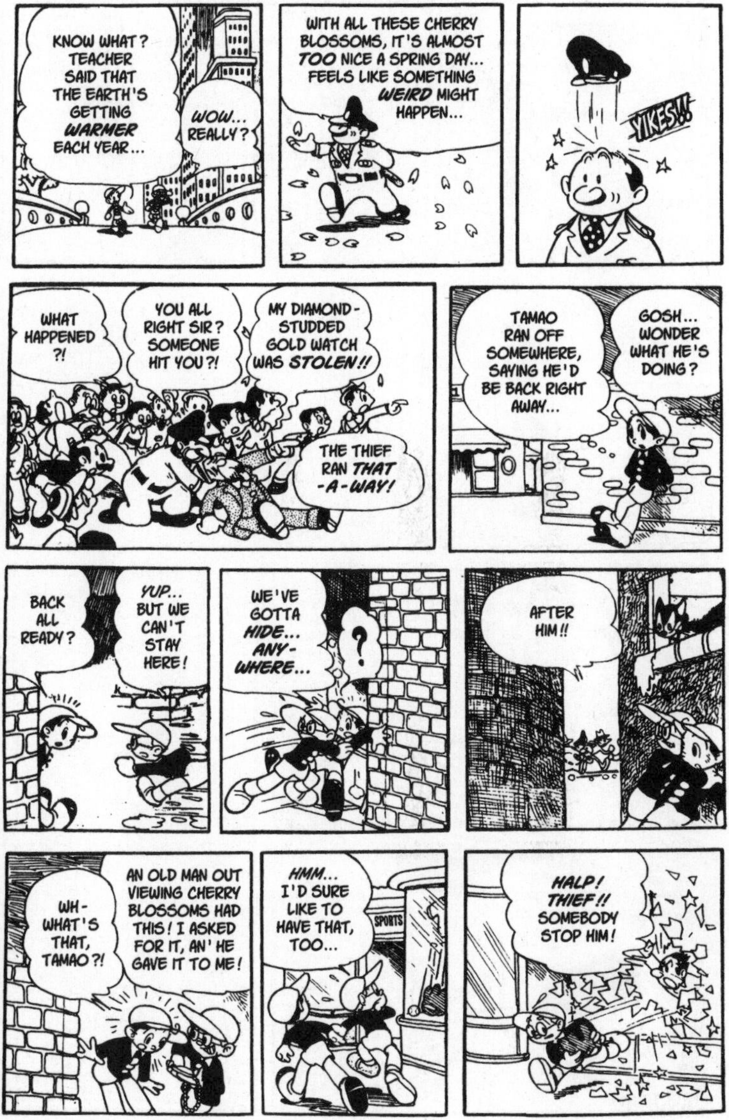
KNOW WHAT? TEACHER SAID THAT THE EARTH'S GETTING WARMER EACH YEAR...
WOW... REALLY?
WITH ALL THESE CHERRY BLOSSOMS, IT'S ALMOST TOO NICE A SPRING DAY... FEELS LIKE SOMETHING WEIRD MIGHT HAPPEN...
YIKES!!
WHAT HAPPENED ?!
YOU ALL RIGHT SIR? SOMEONE HIT YOU?!
MY DIAMOND-STUDDED GOLD WATCH WAS STOLEN!!
THE THIEF RAN THAT-A-WAY!
TAMAO RAN OFF SOMEWHERE, SAYING HE'D BE BACK RIGHT AWAY...
GOSH... WONDER WHAT HE'S DOING?
BACK ALL READY?
YUP... BUT WE CAN'T STAY HERE!
WE'VE GOTTA HIDE... ANY-WHERE...
?
AFTER HIM!!
WH-WHAT'S THAT, TAMAO?!
AN OLD MAN OUT VIEWING CHERRY BLOSSOMS HAD THIS! I ASKED FOR IT, AN' HE GAVE IT TO ME!
HMM... I'D SURE LIKE TO HAVE THAT, TOO...
SPORTS
HALP! THIEF!! SOMEBODY STOP HIM!

YOU TOOK THAT, TOO?
EVER SEE SUCH A COOL GLOVE?
I DON'T BELIEVE THIS, BUT TAMAO SURE SEEMS LIKE HE'S GONE WEIRD...
OWWW!
OWW! OWW! MY HEAD'S SPLITTING!!
HANG ON, TAMAO... HANG ON... WE'LL GET HELP!
WHAT?! YOU SAY TAMAO'S GONE NEUROTIC? HE NEEDS TO REST!
CALM DOWN, BOY, CALM DOWN...
REST A WHILE HERE 'N YOU'LL FEEL BETTER...
MUST BE THE SPRING WEATHER... HE'LL BE BETTER SOON...
I CAN HARDLY BELIEVE IT, BUT IT SEEMS LIKE HE'S BEEN STEALING, PROFES-SOR!
THAT MUST BE BECAUSE OF THE WEATHER, TOO... WHA?!
HALP! THIEF!!!
HE STOLE ALL THE DOCUMENTS OUT OF MY SAFE!! WHAT THE--?! THERE HE IS!

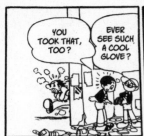

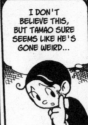

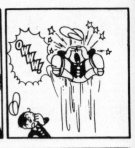

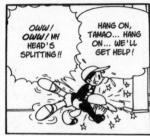

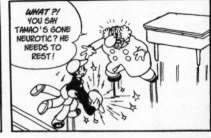

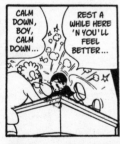

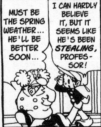

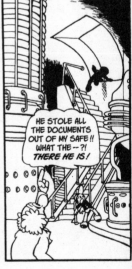

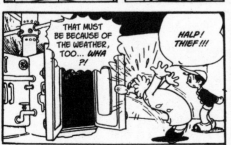

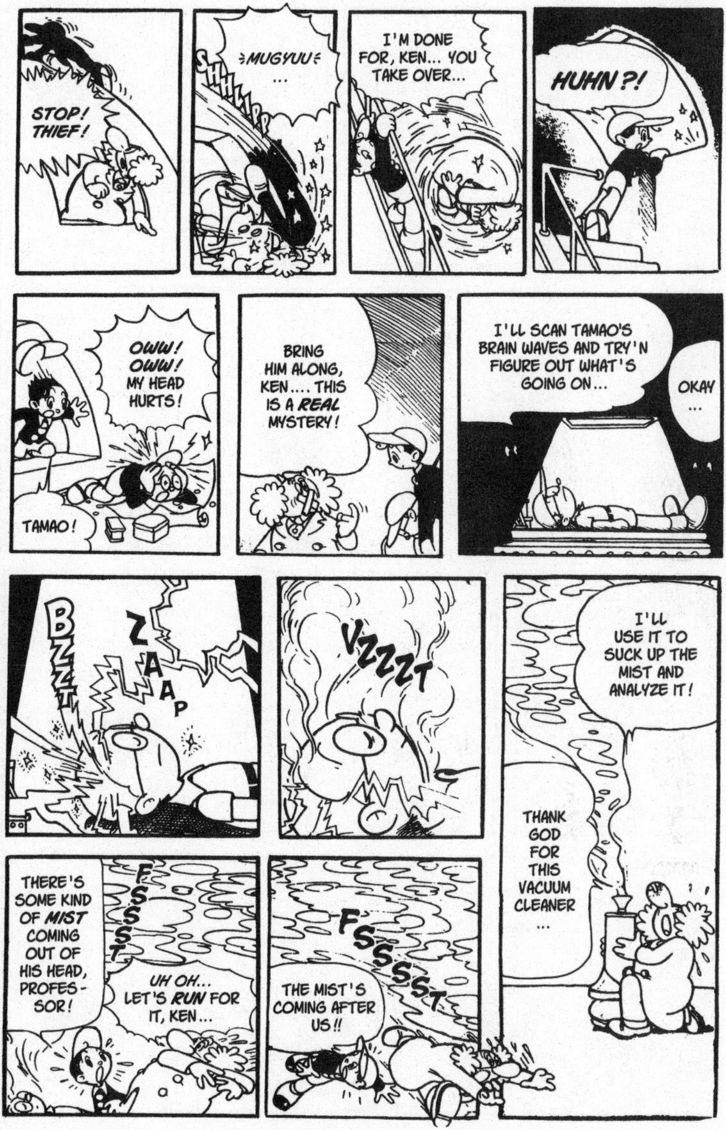
STOP! THIEF!
SHHHLIPP
MUGYUU ...
I'M DONE FOR, KEN... YOU TAKE OVER...
HUHN?!
OWW! OWW! MY HEAD HURTS!
TAMAO!
BRING HIM ALONG, KEN.... THIS IS A REAL MYSTERY!
I'LL SCAN TAMAO'S BRAIN WAVES AND TRY'N FIGURE OUT WHAT'S GOING ON...
OKAY ...
BZZZT
ZAAP
VZZZZT
I'LL USE IT TO SUCK UP THE MIST AND ANALYZE IT!
THANK GOD FOR THIS VACUUM CLEANER ...
THERE'S SOME KIND OF MIST COMING OUT OF HIS HEAD, PROFES-SOR!
FSSST
UH OH... LET'S RUN FOR IT, KEN...
FSSSSST
THE MIST'S COMING AFTER US!!

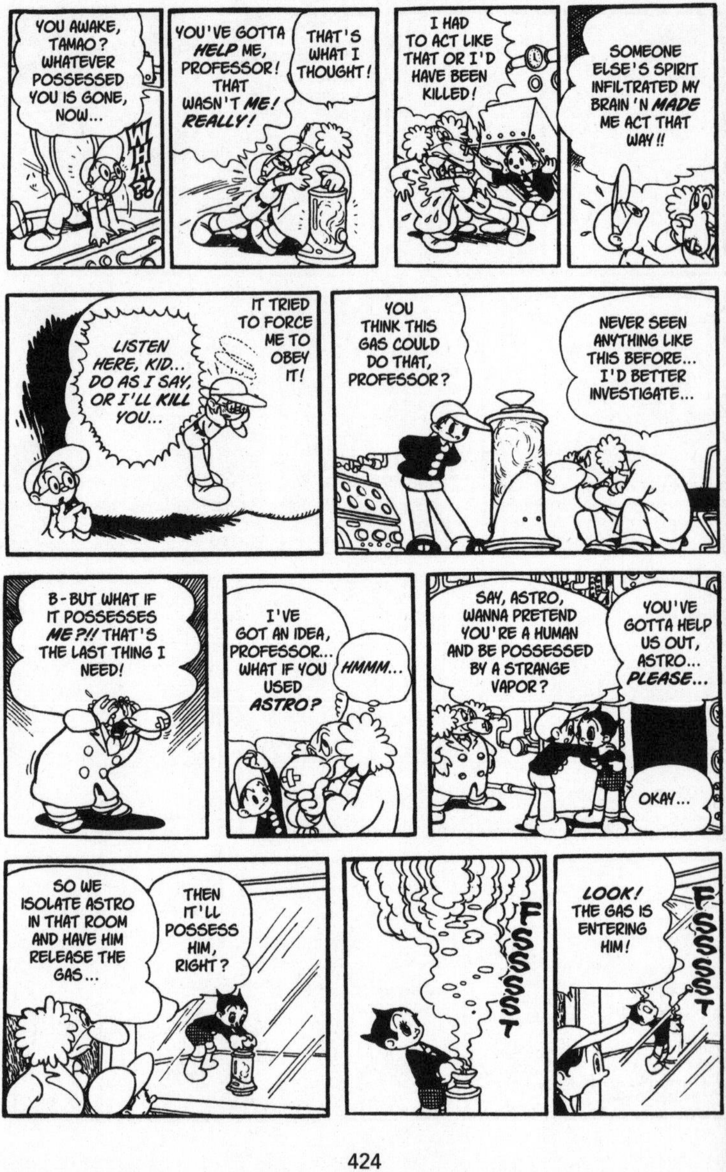
YOU AWAKE, TAMAO? WHATEVER POSSESSED YOU IS GONE, NOW...
WHA?!
YOU'VE GOTTA HELP ME, PROFESSOR! THAT WASN'T ME! REALLY!
THAT'S WHAT I THOUGHT!
I HAD TO ACT LIKE THAT OR I'D HAVE BEEN KILLED!
SOMEONE ELSE'S SPIRIT INFILTRATED MY BRAIN 'N MADE ME ACT THAT WAY!!
LISTEN HERE, KID... DO AS I SAY, OR I'LL KILL YOU...
IT TRIED TO FORCE ME TO OBEY IT!
YOU THINK THIS GAS COULD DO THAT, PROFESSOR?
NEVER SEEN ANYTHING LIKE THIS BEFORE... I'D BETTER INVESTIGATE...
B-BUT WHAT IF IT POSSESSES ME?!! THAT'S THE LAST THING I NEED!
I'VE GOT AN IDEA, PROFESSOR... WHAT IF YOU USED ASTRO?
HMMM...
SAY, ASTRO, WANNA PRETEND YOU'RE A HUMAN AND BE POSSESSED BY A STRANGE VAPOR?
YOU'VE GOTTA HELP US OUT, ASTRO... PLEASE...
OKAY...
SO WE ISOLATE ASTRO IN THAT ROOM AND HAVE HIM RELEASE THE GAS...
THEN IT'LL POSSESS HIM, RIGHT?
FSSSST
LOOK! THE GAS IS ENTERING HIM!
FSSSST

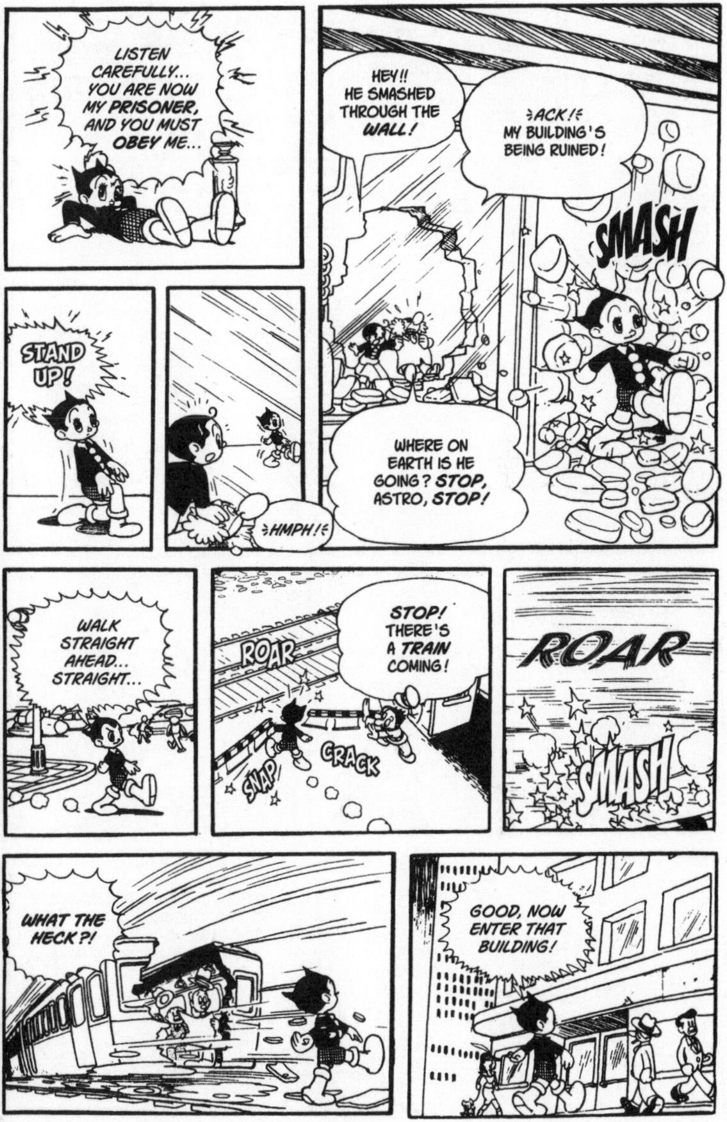

LISTEN CAREFULLY... YOU ARE NOW MY PRISONER, AND YOU MUST OBEY ME...
HEY!! HE SMASHED THROUGH THE WALL!
ACK! MY BUILDING'S BEING RUINED!
SMASH
STAND UP!
HMPH!
WHERE ON EARTH IS HE GOING? STOP, ASTRO, STOP!
WALK STRAIGHT AHEAD... STRAIGHT...
ROAR
STOP! THERE'S A TRAIN COMING!
SNAP
CRACK
ROAR
SMASH
WHAT THE HECK?!
GOOD, NOW ENTER THAT BUILDING!

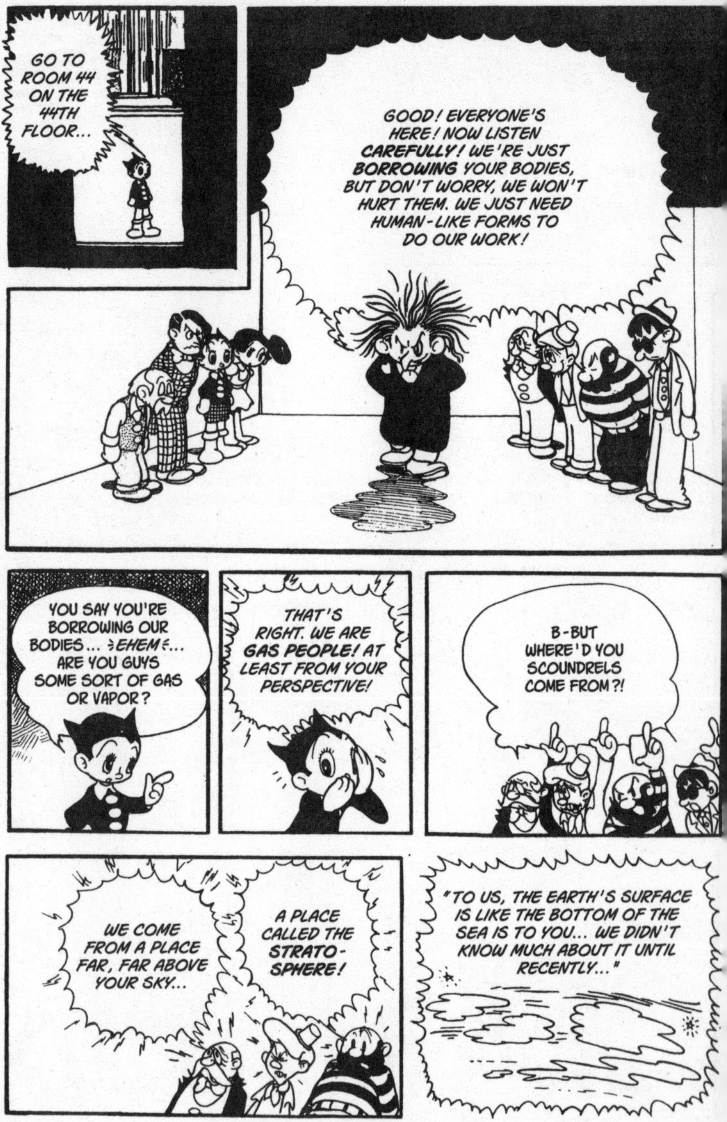
GO TO ROOM 44 ON THE 44TH FLOOR...
GOOD! EVERYONE'S HERE! NOW LISTEN CAREFULLY! WE'RE JUST BORROWING YOUR BODIES, BUT DON'T WORRY, WE WON'T HURT THEM. WE JUST NEED HUMAN-LIKE FORMS TO DO OUR WORK!
YOU SAY YOU'RE BORROWING OUR BODIES... ≥EHEM≤... ARE YOU GUYS SOME SORT OF GAS OR VAPOR?
THAT'S RIGHT. WE ARE GAS PEOPLE! AT LEAST FROM YOUR PERSPECTIVE!
B-BUT WHERE'D YOU SCOUNDRELS COME FROM?!
WE COME FROM A PLACE FAR, FAR ABOVE YOUR SKY...
A PLACE CALLED THE STRATO-SPHERE!
"TO US, THE EARTH'S SURFACE IS LIKE THE BOTTOM OF THE SEA IS TO YOU... WE DIDN'T KNOW MUCH ABOUT IT UNTIL RECENTLY..."

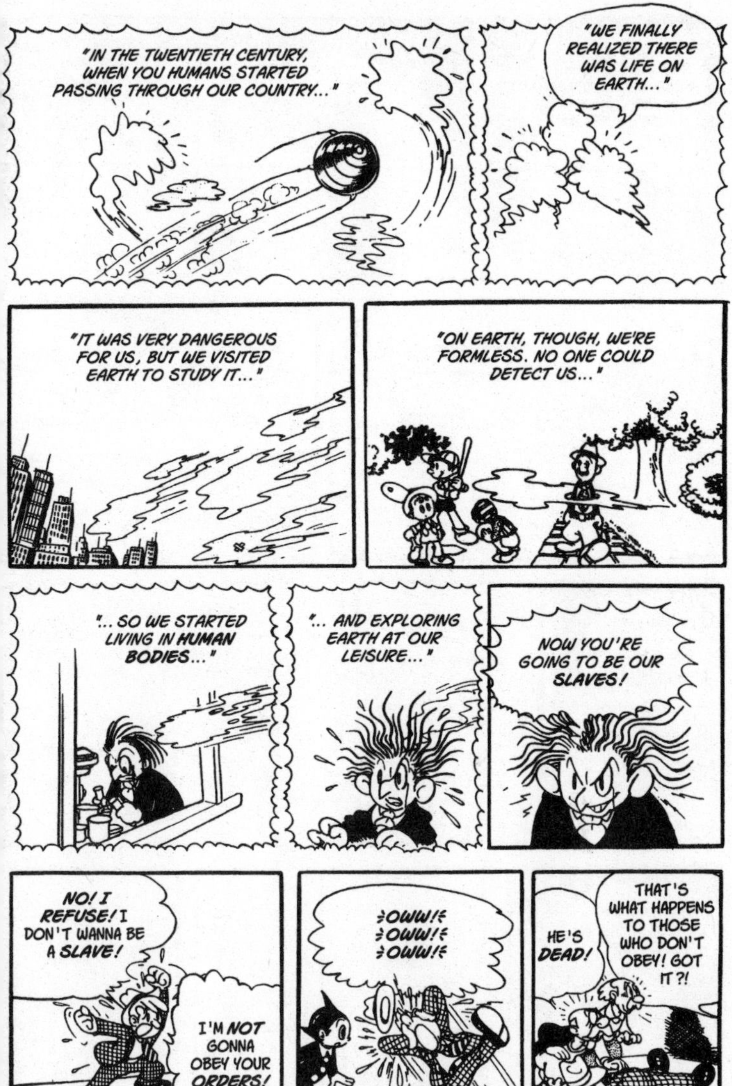

"IN THE TWENTIETH CENTURY, WHEN YOU HUMANS STARTED PASSING THROUGH OUR COUNTRY..."
"WE FINALLY REALIZED THERE WAS LIFE ON EARTH..."
"IT WAS VERY DANGEROUS FOR US, BUT WE VISITED EARTH TO STUDY IT..."
"ON EARTH, THOUGH, WE'RE FORMLESS. NO ONE COULD DETECT US..."
"... SO WE STARTED LIVING IN HUMAN BODIES..."
"... AND EXPLORING EARTH AT OUR LEISURE..."
NOW YOU'RE GOING TO BE OUR SLAVES!
NO! I REFUSE! I DON'T WANNA BE A SLAVE!
I'M NOT GONNA OBEY YOUR ORDERS!
OWW! OWW! OWW!
HE'S DEAD!
THAT'S WHAT HAPPENS TO THOSE WHO DON'T OBEY! GOT IT?!

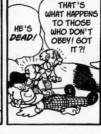

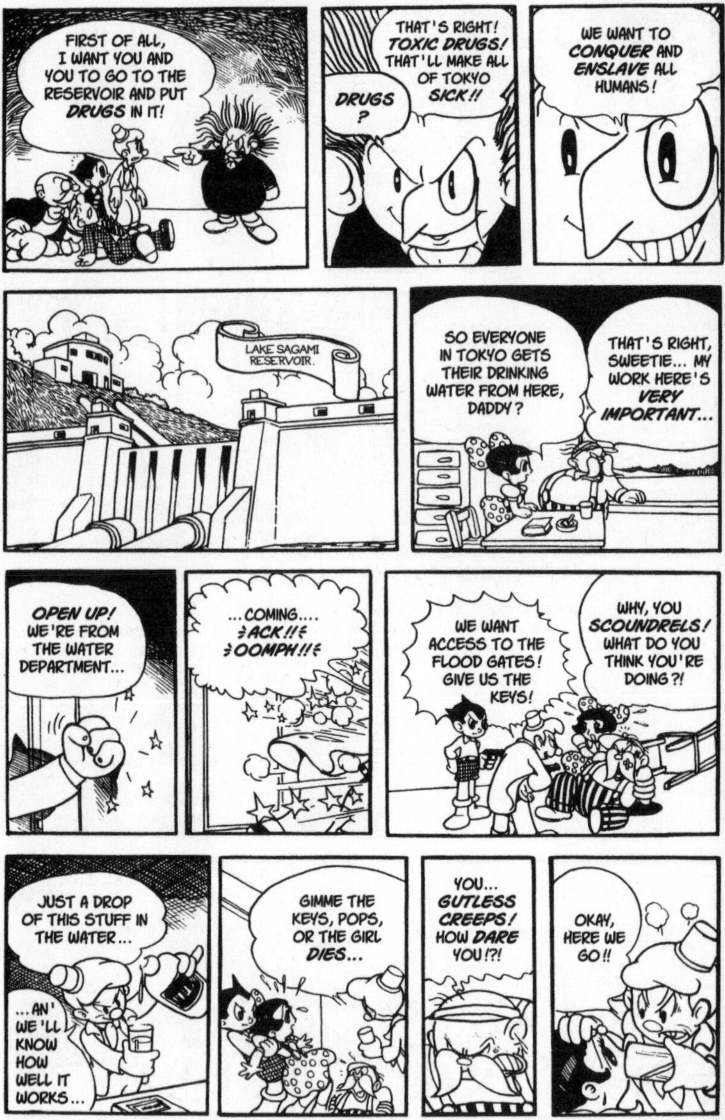
FIRST OF ALL, I WANT YOU AND YOU TO GO TO THE RESERVOIR AND PUT DRUGS IN IT!
DRUGS ?
THAT'S RIGHT! TOXIC DRUGS! THAT'LL MAKE ALL OF TOKYO SICK!!
WE WANT TO CONQUER AND ENSLAVE ALL HUMANS!
LAKE SAGAMI RESERVOIR.
SO EVERYONE IN TOKYO GETS THEIR DRINKING WATER FROM HERE, DADDY?
THAT'S RIGHT, SWEETIE... MY WORK HERE'S VERY IMPORTANT...
OPEN UP! WE'RE FROM THE WATER DEPARTMENT...
...COMING....
ACK!!
OOMPH!!
WE WANT ACCESS TO THE FLOOD GATES! GIVE US THE KEYS!
WHY, YOU SCOUNDRELS! WHAT DO YOU THINK YOU'RE DOING?!
JUST A DROP OF THIS STUFF IN THE WATER...
...AN' WE'LL KNOW HOW WELL IT WORKS...
GIMME THE KEYS, POPS, OR THE GIRL DIES...
YOU... GUTLESS CREEPS! HOW DARE YOU!?!
OKAY, HERE WE GO!!

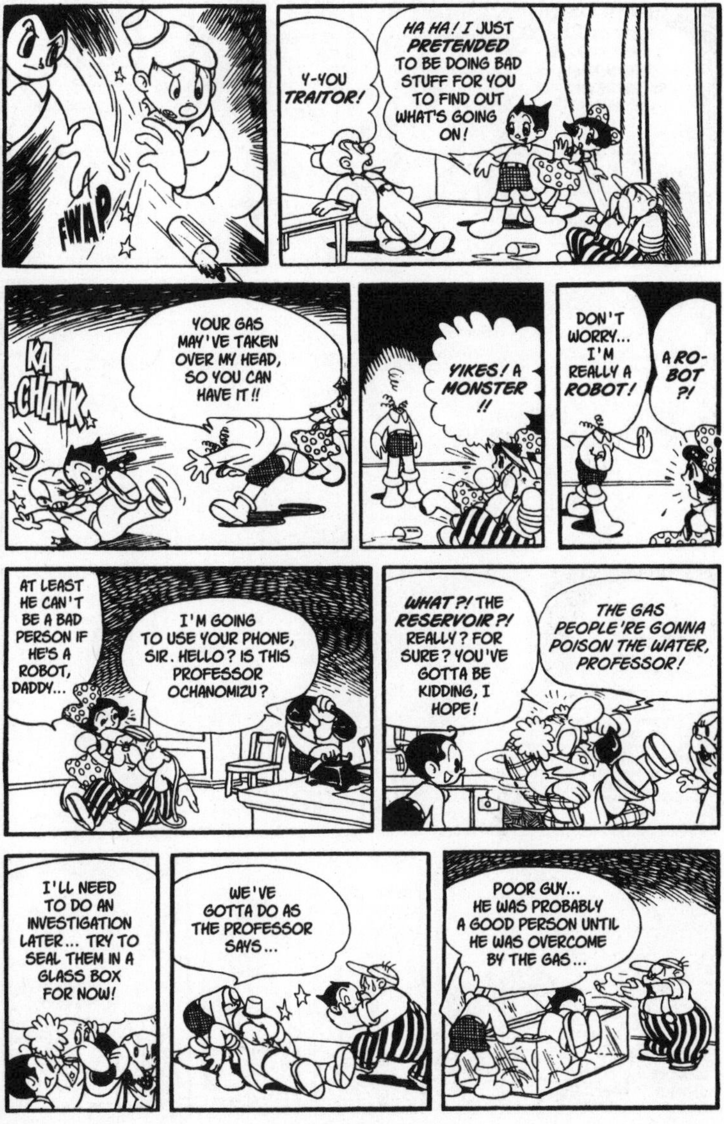
FWAP
Y-YOU TRAITOR!
HA HA! I JUST PRETENDED TO BE DOING BAD STUFF FOR YOU TO FIND OUT WHAT'S GOING ON!
KA CHANK
YOUR GAS MAY'VE TAKEN OVER MY HEAD, SO YOU CAN HAVE IT!!
YIKES! A MONSTER!!
DON'T WORRY... I'M REALLY A ROBOT!
A RO-BOT?!
AT LEAST HE CAN'T BE A BAD PERSON IF HE'S A ROBOT, DADDY...
I'M GOING TO USE YOUR PHONE, SIR. HELLO? IS THIS PROFESSOR OCHANOMIZU?
WHAT?! THE RESERVOIR?! REALLY? FOR SURE? YOU'VE GOTTA BE KIDDING, I HOPE!
THE GAS PEOPLE'RE GONNA POISON THE WATER, PROFESSOR!
I'LL NEED TO DO AN INVESTIGATION LATER... TRY TO SEAL THEM IN A GLASS BOX FOR NOW!
WE'VE GOTTA DO AS THE PROFESSOR SAYS...
POOR GUY... HE WAS PROBABLY A GOOD PERSON UNTIL HE WAS OVERCOME BY THE GAS...

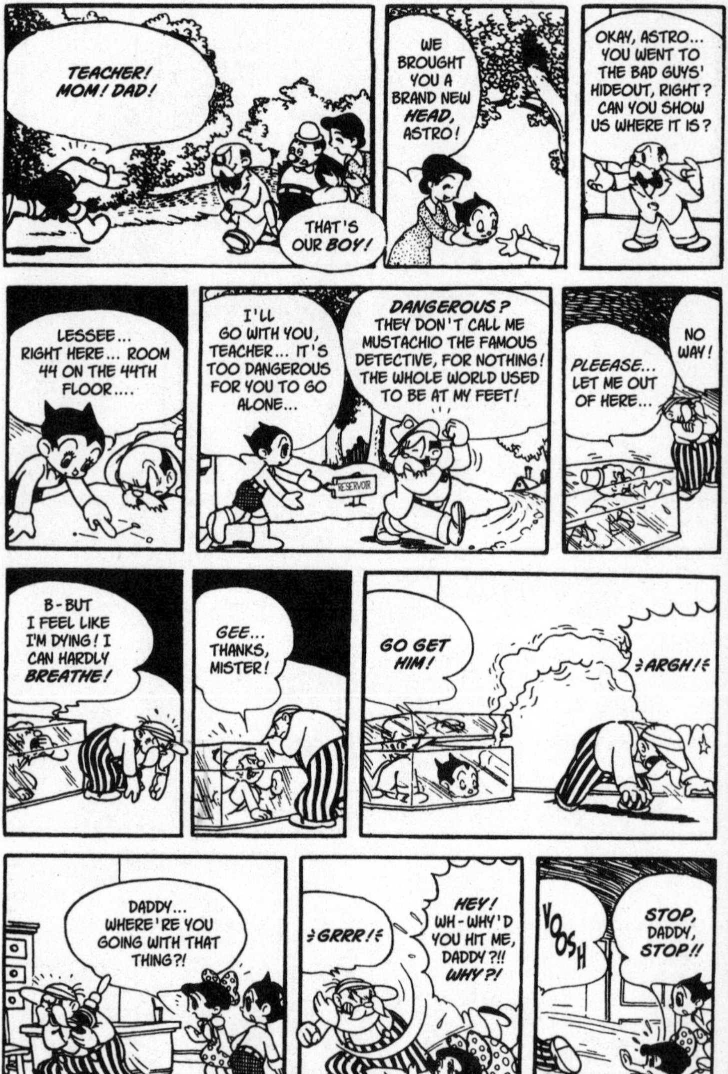
TEACHER! MOM! DAD!
THAT'S OUR BOY!
WE BROUGHT YOU A BRAND NEW HEAD, ASTRO!
OKAY, ASTRO... YOU WENT TO THE BAD GUYS' HIDEOUT, RIGHT? CAN YOU SHOW US WHERE IT IS?
LESSEE... RIGHT HERE... ROOM 44 ON THE 44TH FLOOR....
I'LL GO WITH YOU, TEACHER... IT'S TOO DANGEROUS FOR YOU TO GO ALONE...
RESERVOIR
DANGEROUS? THEY DON'T CALL ME MUSTACHIO THE FAMOUS DETECTIVE, FOR NOTHING! THE WHOLE WORLD USED TO BE AT MY FEET!
PLEEASE... LET ME OUT OF HERE...
NO WAY!
B-BUT I FEEL LIKE I'M DYING! I CAN HARDLY BREATHE!
GEE... THANKS, MISTER!
GO GET HIM!
ARGH!
DADDY... WHERE'RE YOU GOING WITH THAT THING?!
GRRR!
HEY! WH-WHY'D YOU HIT ME, DADDY?!! WHY?!
VOOSH
STOP, DADDY, STOP!!

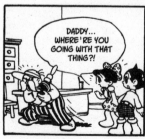

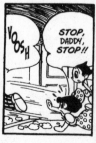

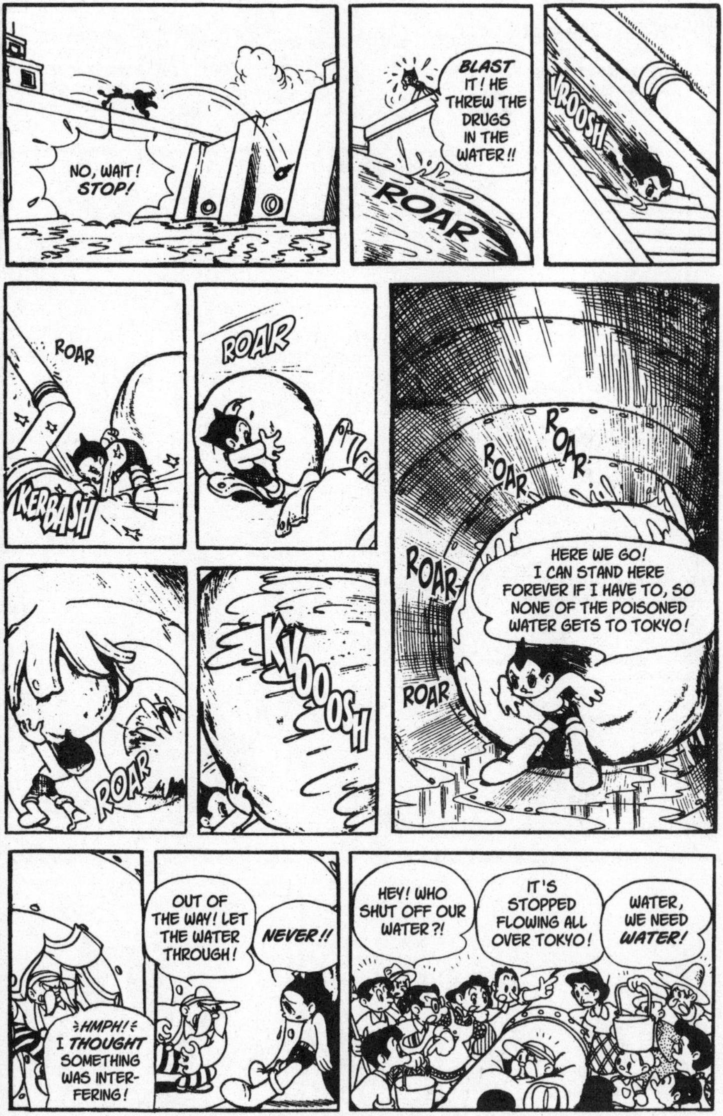
NO, WAIT! STOP!
BLAST IT! HE THREW THE DRUGS IN THE WATER!!
ROAR
VROOSH
ROAR
KERBASH
ROAR
ROAR
ROAR
ROAR
HERE WE GO! I CAN STAND HERE FOREVER IF I HAVE TO, SO NONE OF THE POISONED WATER GETS TO TOKYO!
ROAR
ROAR
KVOOOOSH
HMPH! I THOUGHT SOMETHING WAS INTER-FERING!
OUT OF THE WAY! LET THE WATER THROUGH!
NEVER!!
HEY! WHO SHUT OFF OUR WATER?!
IT'S STOPPED FLOWING ALL OVER TOKYO!
WATER, WE NEED WATER!

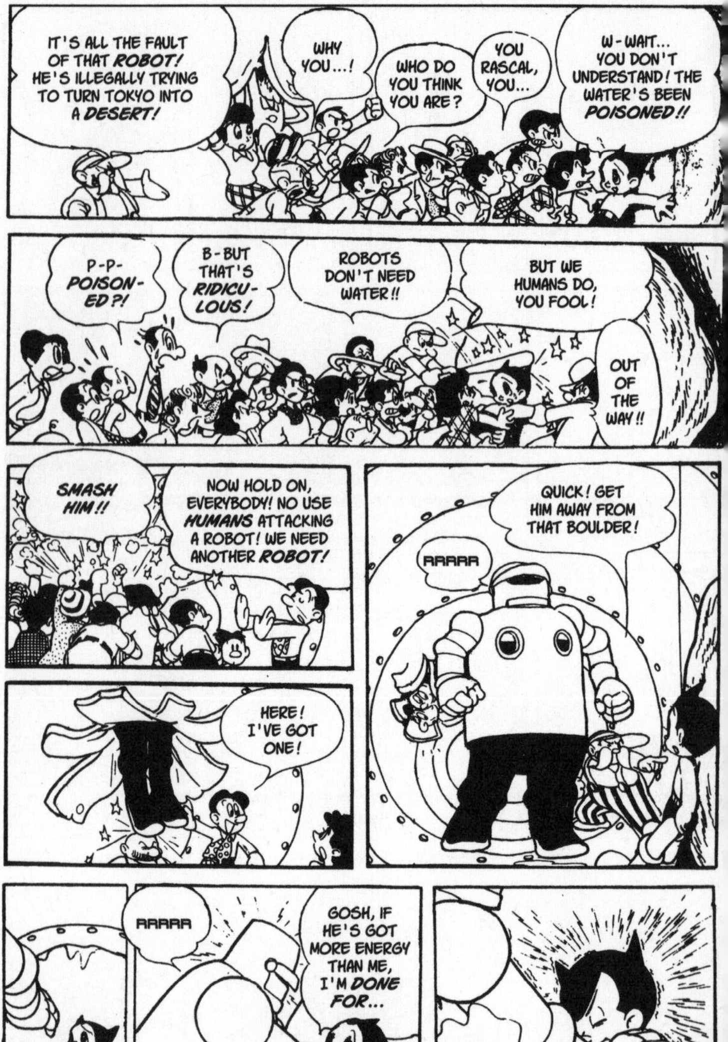
IT'S ALL THE FAULT OF THAT ROBOT! HE'S ILLEGALLY TRYING TO TURN TOKYO INTO A DESERT!
WHY YOU...!
WHO DO YOU THINK YOU ARE?
YOU RASCAL, YOU...
W-WAIT... YOU DON'T UNDERSTAND! THE WATER'S BEEN POISONED!!
P-P-POISON-ED?!
B-BUT THAT'S RIDICU-LOUS!
ROBOTS DON'T NEED WATER!!
BUT WE HUMANS DO, YOU FOOL!
OUT OF THE WAY!!
SMASH HIM!!
NOW HOLD ON, EVERYBODY! NO USE HUMANS ATTACKING A ROBOT! WE NEED ANOTHER ROBOT!
HERE! I'VE GOT ONE!
QUICK! GET HIM AWAY FROM THAT BOULDER!
RRRRR
RRRRR
GOSH, IF HE'S GOT MORE ENERGY THAN ME, I'M DONE FOR...
HERE, TAKE THIS!

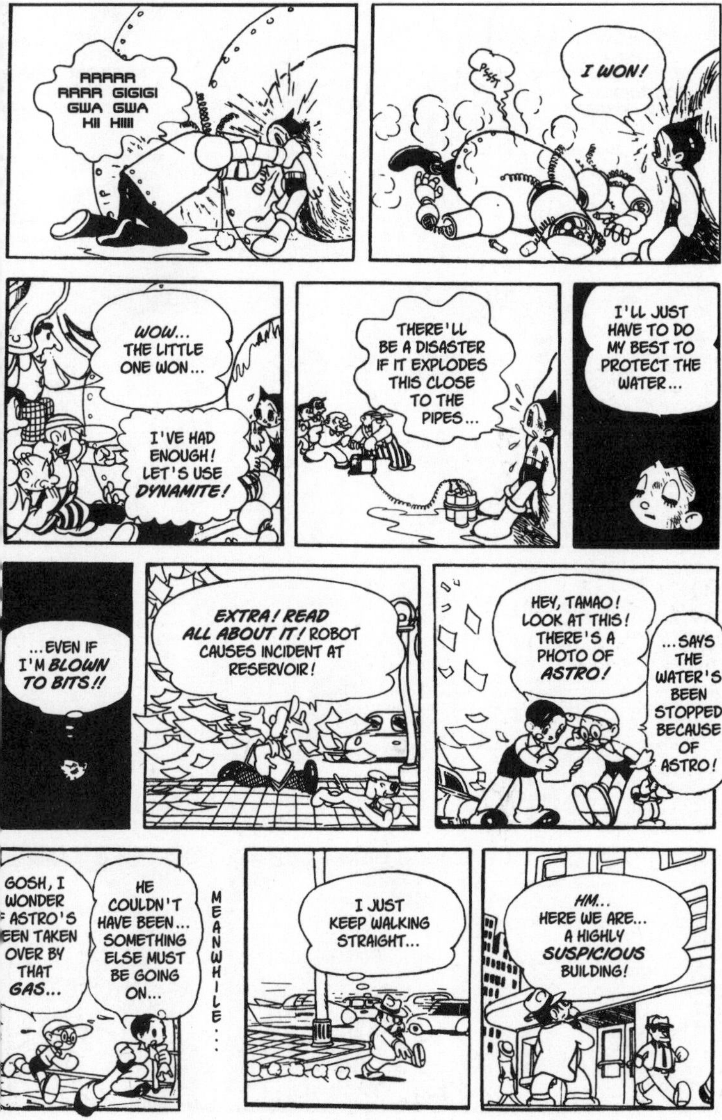
RRRRR RRRR GIGIGI GWA GWA HII HIIII
PSSST
I WON!
WOW... THE LITTLE ONE WON...
I'VE HAD ENOUGH! LET'S USE DYNAMITE!
THERE'LL BE A DISASTER IF IT EXPLODES THIS CLOSE TO THE PIPES...
I'LL JUST HAVE TO DO MY BEST TO PROTECT THE WATER...
...EVEN IF I'M BLOWN TO BITS!!
EXTRA! READ ALL ABOUT IT! ROBOT CAUSES INCIDENT AT RESERVOIR!
HEY, TAMAO! LOOK AT THIS! THERE'S A PHOTO OF ASTRO!
...SAYS THE WATER'S BEEN STOPPED BECAUSE OF ASTRO!
GOSH, I WONDER IF ASTRO'S BEEN TAKEN OVER BY THAT GAS...
HE COULDN'T HAVE BEEN... SOMETHING ELSE MUST BE GOING ON...
MEANWHILE...
I JUST KEEP WALKING STRAIGHT...
HM... HERE WE ARE... A HIGHLY SUSPICIOUS BUILDING!

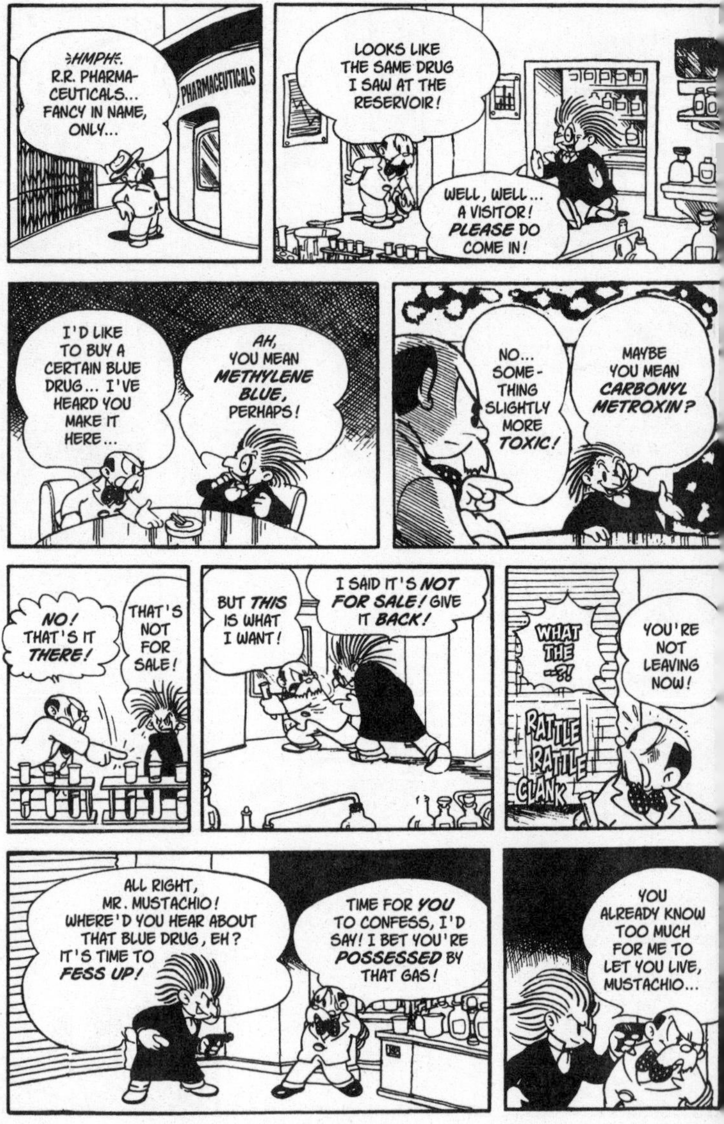

HMPH. R.R. PHARMA-CEUTICALS... FANCY IN NAME, ONLY...
PHARMACEUTICALS
LOOKS LIKE THE SAME DRUG I SAW AT THE RESERVOIR!
WELL, WELL... A VISITOR! PLEASE DO COME IN!
I'D LIKE TO BUY A CERTAIN BLUE DRUG... I'VE HEARD YOU MAKE IT HERE...
AH, YOU MEAN METHYLENE BLUE, PERHAPS!
NO... SOME-THING SLIGHTLY MORE TOXIC!
MAYBE YOU MEAN CARBONYL METROXIN?
NO! THAT'S IT THERE!
THAT'S NOT FOR SALE!
BUT THIS IS WHAT I WANT!
I SAID IT'S NOT FOR SALE! GIVE IT BACK!
WHAT THE --?!
RATTLE RATTLE CLANK
YOU'RE NOT LEAVING NOW!
ALL RIGHT, MR. MUSTACHIO! WHERE'D YOU HEAR ABOUT THAT BLUE DRUG, EH? IT'S TIME TO FESS UP!
TIME FOR YOU TO CONFESS, I'D SAY! I BET YOU'RE POSSESSED BY THAT GAS!
YOU ALREADY KNOW TOO MUCH FOR ME TO LET YOU LIVE, MUSTACHIO...

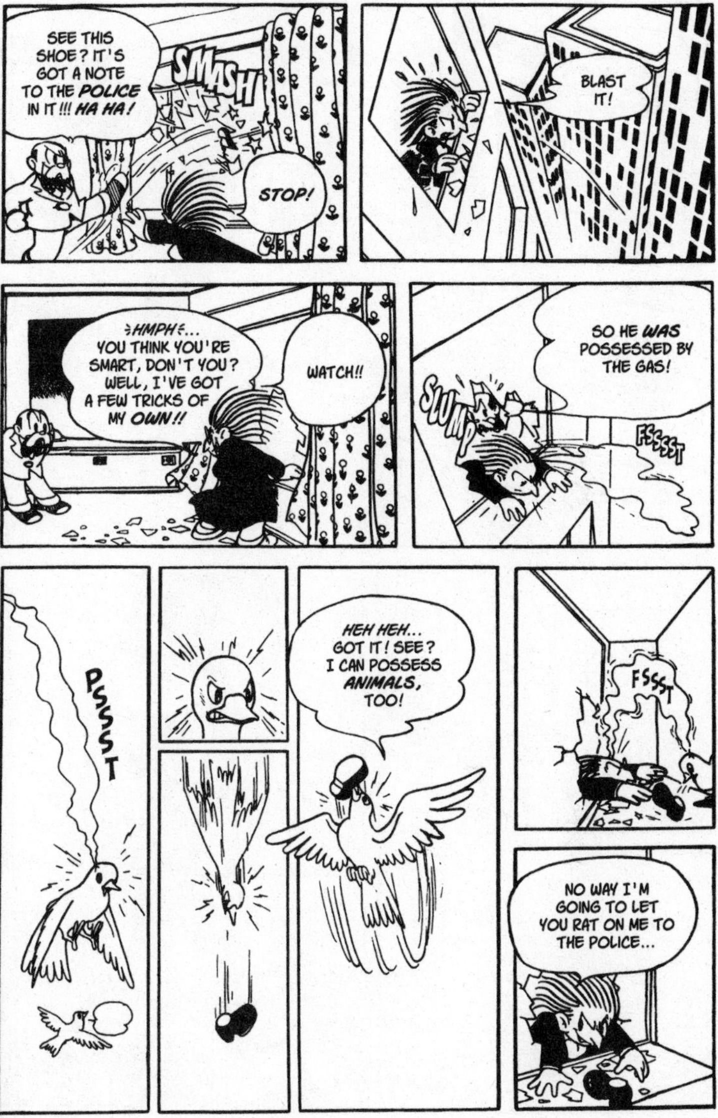
SEE THIS SHOE? IT'S GOT A NOTE TO THE *POLICE* IN IT!!! *HA HA!*
SMASH
STOP!
BLAST IT!
HMPH... YOU THINK YOU'RE SMART, DON'T YOU? WELL, I'VE GOT A FEW TRICKS OF MY *OWN!!*
WATCH!!
SO HE *WAS* POSSESSED BY THE GAS!
SLUMP
FSSSST
PSSST
HEH HEH... GOT IT! SEE? I CAN POSSESS *ANIMALS,* TOO!
FSSST
NO WAY I'M GOING TO LET YOU RAT ON ME TO THE POLICE...

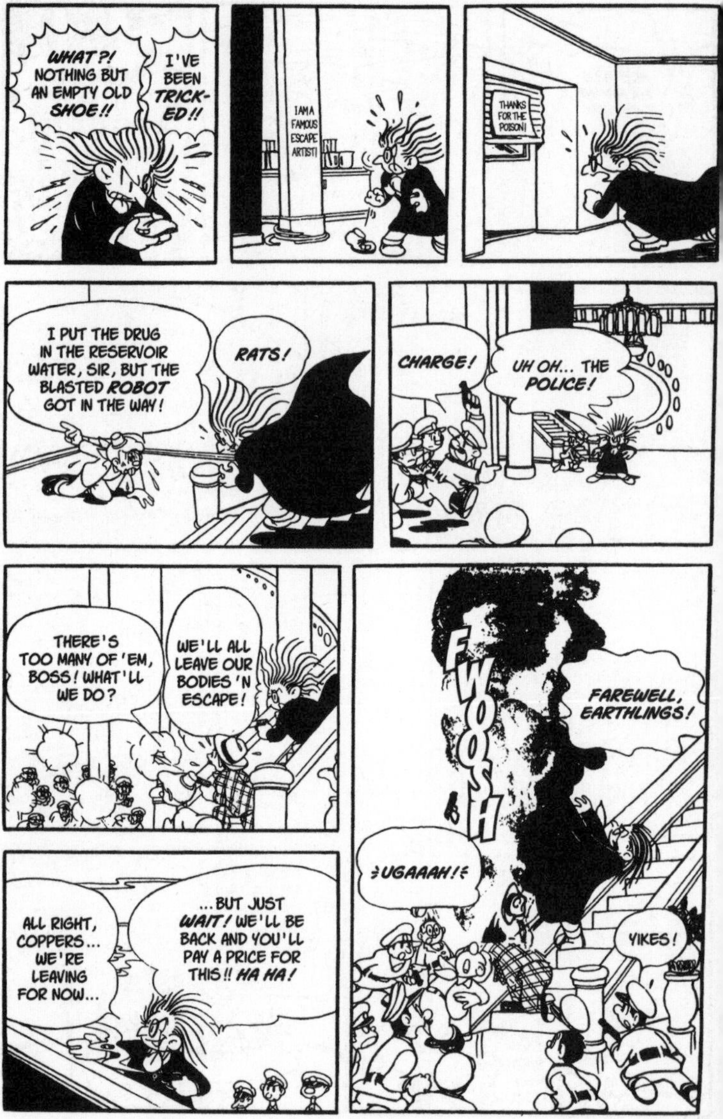
WHAT?! NOTHING BUT AN EMPTY OLD SHOE!!
I'VE BEEN TRICK-ED!!
I AM A FAMOUS ESCAPE ARTIST!
THANKS FOR THE POISON!
I PUT THE DRUG IN THE RESERVOIR WATER, SIR, BUT THE BLASTED ROBOT GOT IN THE WAY!
RATS!
CHARGE!
UH OH... THE POLICE!
THERE'S TOO MANY OF 'EM, BOSS! WHAT'LL WE DO?
WE'LL ALL LEAVE OUR BODIES 'N ESCAPE!
FWOOSH
FAREWELL, EARTHLINGS!
UGAAAH!
YIKES!
ALL RIGHT, COPPERS... WE'RE LEAVING FOR NOW...
...BUT JUST WAIT! WE'LL BE BACK AND YOU'LL PAY A PRICE FOR THIS!! HA HA!

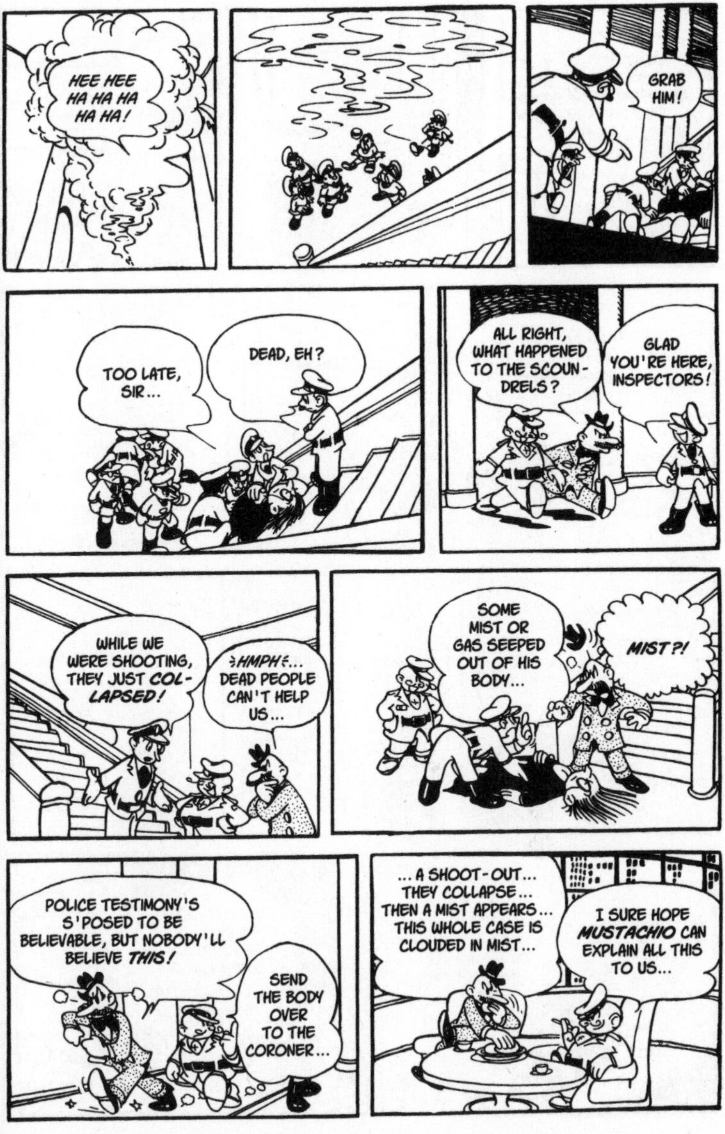
HEE HEE HA HA HA HA HA!
GRAB HIM!
TOO LATE, SIR...
DEAD, EH?
ALL RIGHT, WHAT HAPPENED TO THE SCOUN-DRELS?
GLAD YOU'RE HERE, INSPECTORS!
WHILE WE WERE SHOOTING, THEY JUST COL-LAPSED!
HMPH... DEAD PEOPLE CAN'T HELP US...
SOME MIST OR GAS SEEPED OUT OF HIS BODY...
MIST?!
POLICE TESTIMONY'S S'POSED TO BE BELIEVABLE, BUT NOBODY'LL BELIEVE THIS!
SEND THE BODY OVER TO THE CORONER...
... A SHOOT-OUT... THEY COLLAPSE... THEN A MIST APPEARS... THIS WHOLE CASE IS CLOUDED IN MIST...
I SURE HOPE MUSTACHIO CAN EXPLAIN ALL THIS TO US...

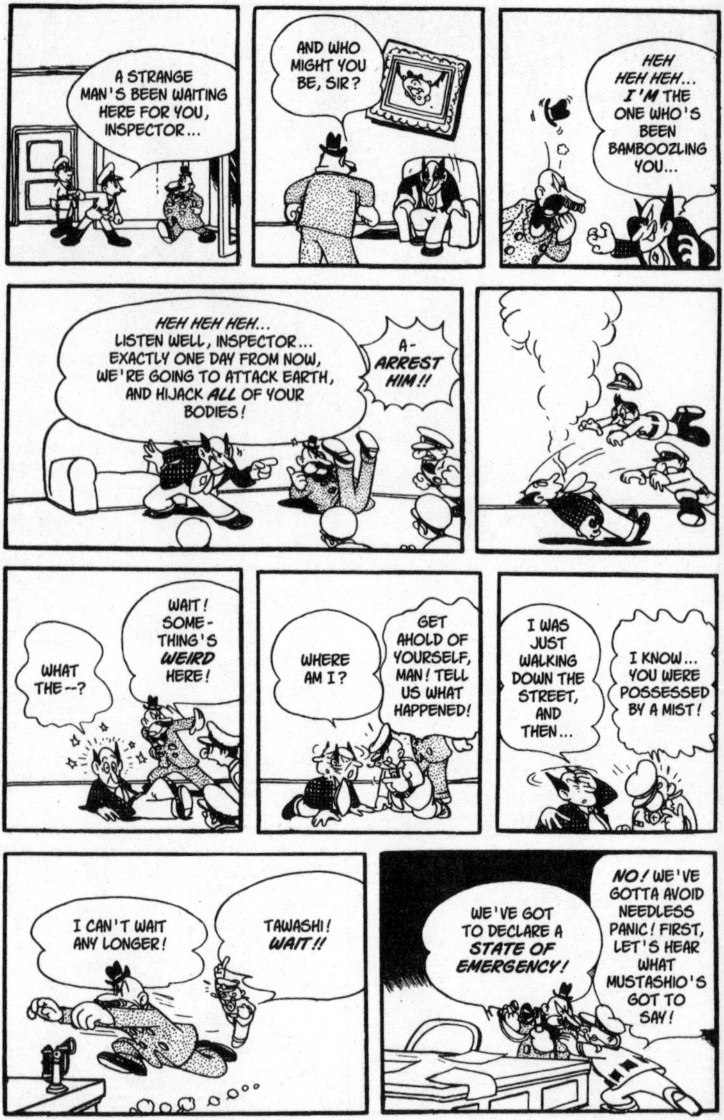
A STRANGE MAN'S BEEN WAITING HERE FOR YOU, INSPECTOR...
AND WHO MIGHT YOU BE, SIR?
HEH HEH HEH... I'M THE ONE WHO'S BEEN BAMBOOZLING YOU...
HEH HEH HEH... LISTEN WELL, INSPECTOR... EXACTLY ONE DAY FROM NOW, WE'RE GOING TO ATTACK EARTH, AND HIJACK ALL OF YOUR BODIES!
A- ARREST HIM!!
WHAT THE--?
WAIT! SOME-THING'S WEIRD HERE!
WHERE AM I?
GET AHOLD OF YOURSELF, MAN! TELL US WHAT HAPPENED!
I WAS JUST WALKING DOWN THE STREET, AND THEN...
I KNOW... YOU WERE POSSESSED BY A MIST!
I CAN'T WAIT ANY LONGER!
TAWASHI! WAIT!!
WE'VE GOT TO DECLARE A STATE OF EMERGENCY!
NO! WE'VE GOTTA AVOID NEEDLESS PANIC! FIRST, LET'S HEAR WHAT MUSTASHIO'S GOT TO SAY!

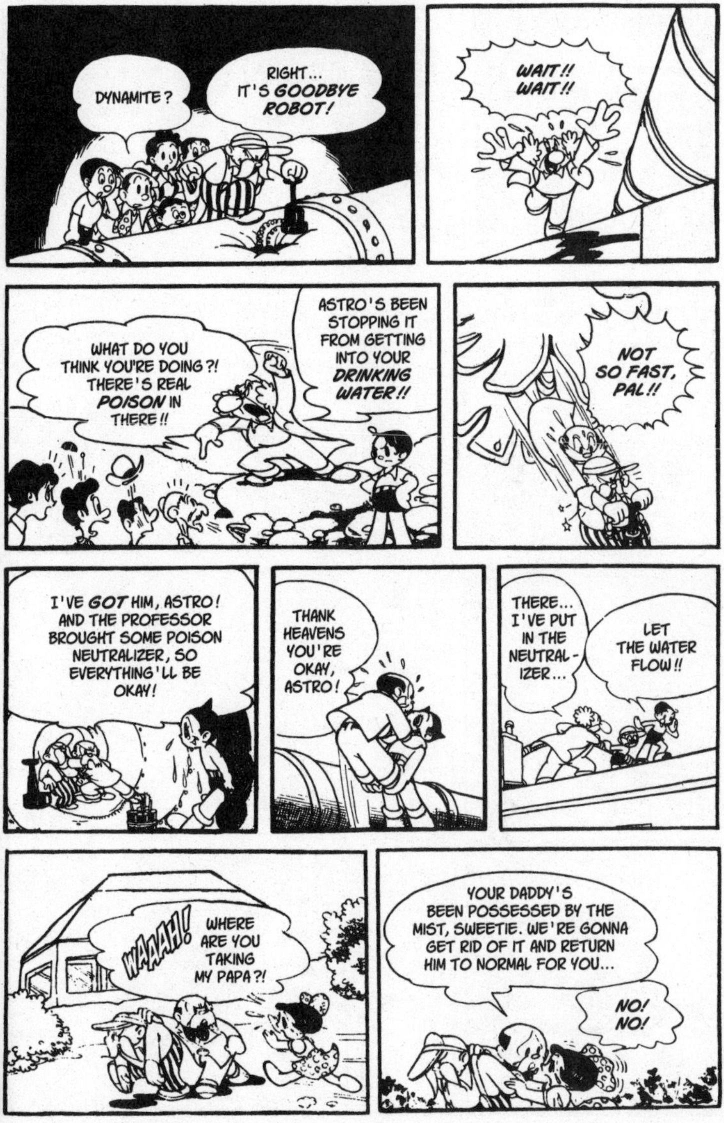
DYNAMITE?
RIGHT... IT'S GOODBYE ROBOT!
WAIT!! WAIT!!
WHAT DO YOU THINK YOU'RE DOING?! THERE'S REAL POISON IN THERE!!
ASTRO'S BEEN STOPPING IT FROM GETTING INTO YOUR DRINKING WATER!!
NOT SO FAST, PAL!!
I'VE GOT HIM, ASTRO! AND THE PROFESSOR BROUGHT SOME POISON NEUTRALIZER, SO EVERYTHING'LL BE OKAY!
THANK HEAVENS YOU'RE OKAY, ASTRO!
THERE... I'VE PUT IN THE NEUTRAL-IZER...
LET THE WATER FLOW!!
WAAAH!
WHERE ARE YOU TAKING MY PAPA?!
YOUR DADDY'S BEEN POSSESSED BY THE MIST, SWEETIE. WE'RE GONNA GET RID OF IT AND RETURN HIM TO NORMAL FOR YOU...
NO! NO!

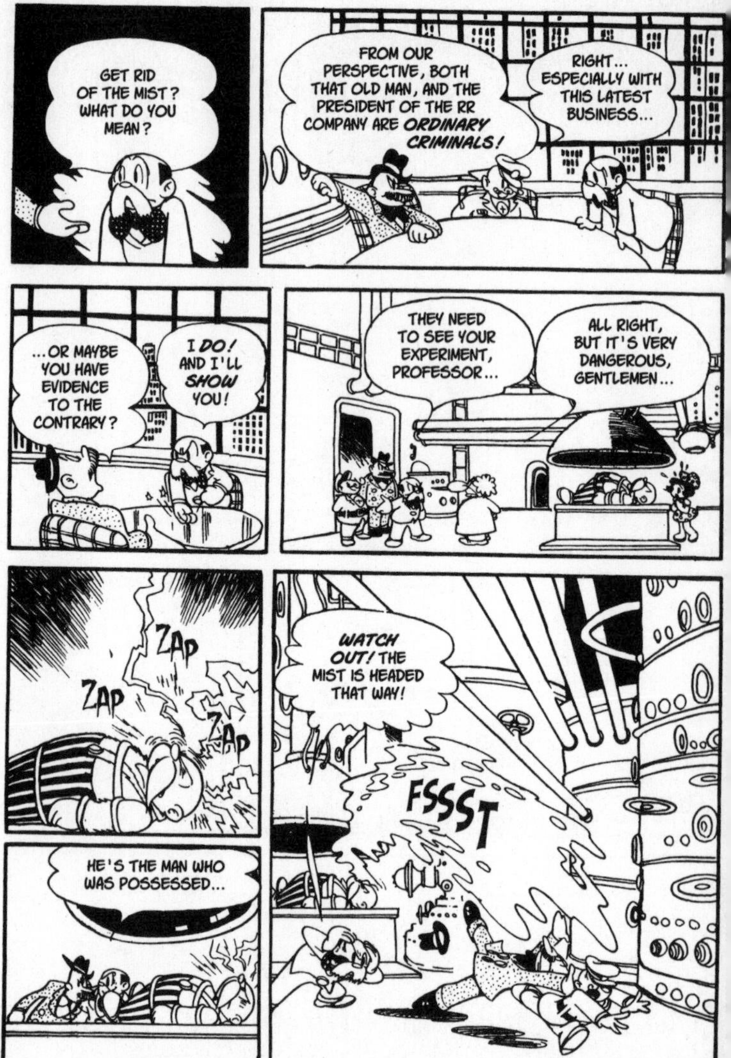
GET RID OF THE MIST? WHAT DO YOU MEAN?
FROM OUR PERSPECTIVE, BOTH THAT OLD MAN, AND THE PRESIDENT OF THE RR COMPANY ARE ***ORDINARY CRIMINALS!***
RIGHT... ESPECIALLY WITH THIS LATEST BUSINESS...
...OR MAYBE YOU HAVE EVIDENCE TO THE CONTRARY?
I ***DO!*** AND I'LL ***SHOW*** YOU!
THEY NEED TO SEE YOUR EXPERIMENT, PROFESSOR...
ALL RIGHT, BUT IT'S VERY DANGEROUS, GENTLEMEN...
ZAP
ZAP
ZAP
HE'S THE MAN WHO WAS POSSESSED...
WATCH OUT! THE MIST IS HEADED THAT WAY!
FSSST

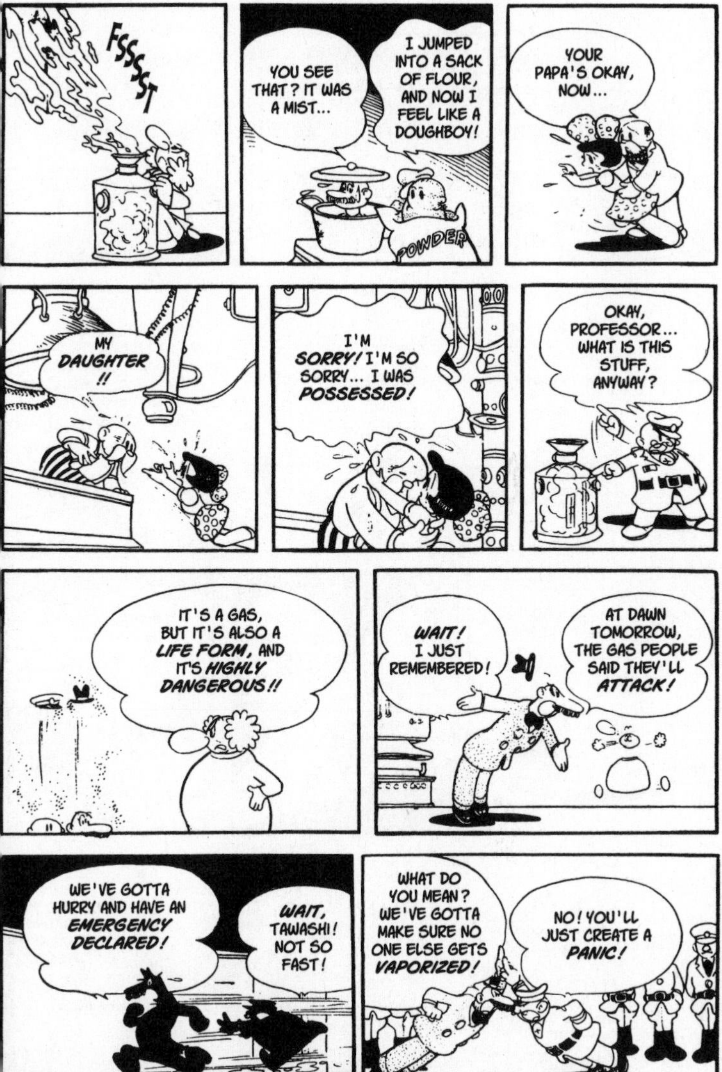
FSSSST
YOU SEE THAT? IT WAS A MIST...
I JUMPED INTO A SACK OF FLOUR, AND NOW I FEEL LIKE A DOUGHBOY!
POWDER
YOUR PAPA'S OKAY, NOW...
MY DAUGHTER !!
I'M SORRY! I'M SO SORRY... I WAS POSSESSED!
OKAY, PROFESSOR... WHAT IS THIS STUFF, ANYWAY?
IT'S A GAS, BUT IT'S ALSO A LIFE FORM, AND IT'S HIGHLY DANGEROUS!!
WAIT! I JUST REMEMBERED!
AT DAWN TOMORROW, THE GAS PEOPLE SAID THEY'LL ATTACK!
WE'VE GOTTA HURRY AND HAVE AN EMERGENCY DECLARED!
WAIT, TAWASHI! NOT SO FAST!
WHAT DO YOU MEAN? WE'VE GOTTA MAKE SURE NO ONE ELSE GETS VAPORIZED!
NO! YOU'LL JUST CREATE A PANIC!

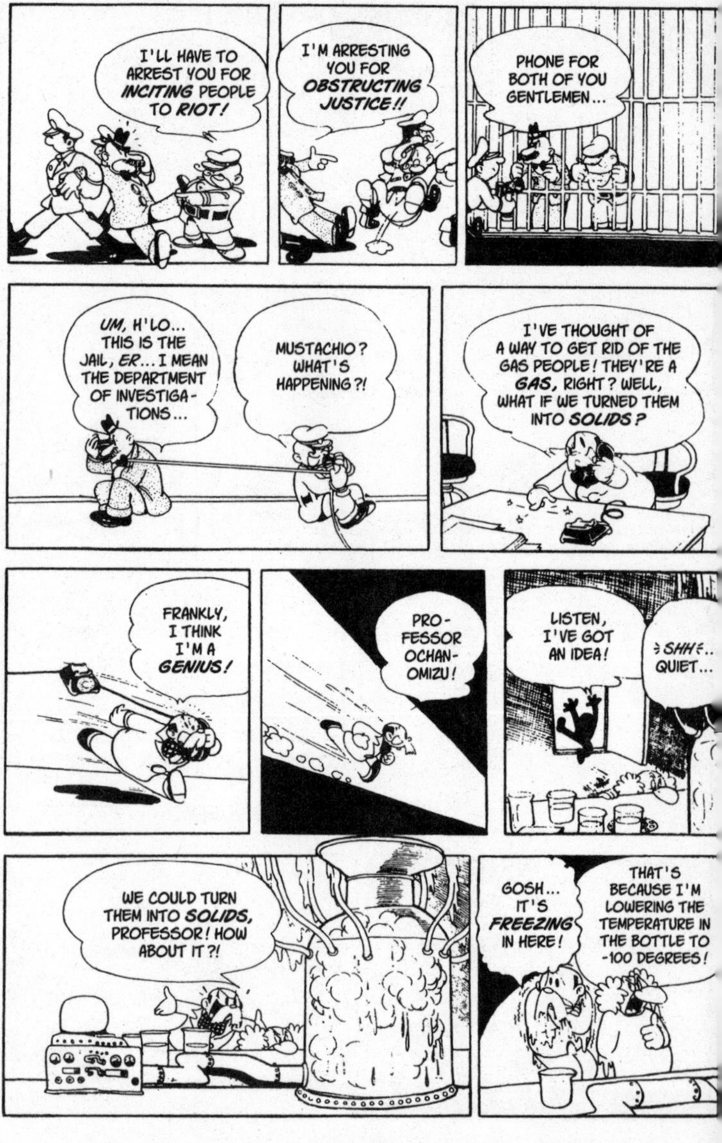
I'LL HAVE TO ARREST YOU FOR INCITING PEOPLE TO RIOT!
I'M ARRESTING YOU FOR OBSTRUCTING JUSTICE!!
PHONE FOR BOTH OF YOU GENTLEMEN...
UM, H'LO... THIS IS THE JAIL, ER... I MEAN THE DEPARTMENT OF INVESTIGA-TIONS...
MUSTACHIO? WHAT'S HAPPENING?!
I'VE THOUGHT OF A WAY TO GET RID OF THE GAS PEOPLE! THEY'RE A GAS, RIGHT? WELL, WHAT IF WE TURNED THEM INTO SOLIDS?
FRANKLY, I THINK I'M A GENIUS!
PRO-FESSOR OCHAN-OMIZU!
LISTEN, I'VE GOT AN IDEA!
SHH... QUIET...
WE COULD TURN THEM INTO SOLIDS, PROFESSOR! HOW ABOUT IT?!
GOSH... IT'S FREEZING IN HERE!
THAT'S BECAUSE I'M LOWERING THE TEMPERATURE IN THE BOTTLE TO -100 DEGREES!

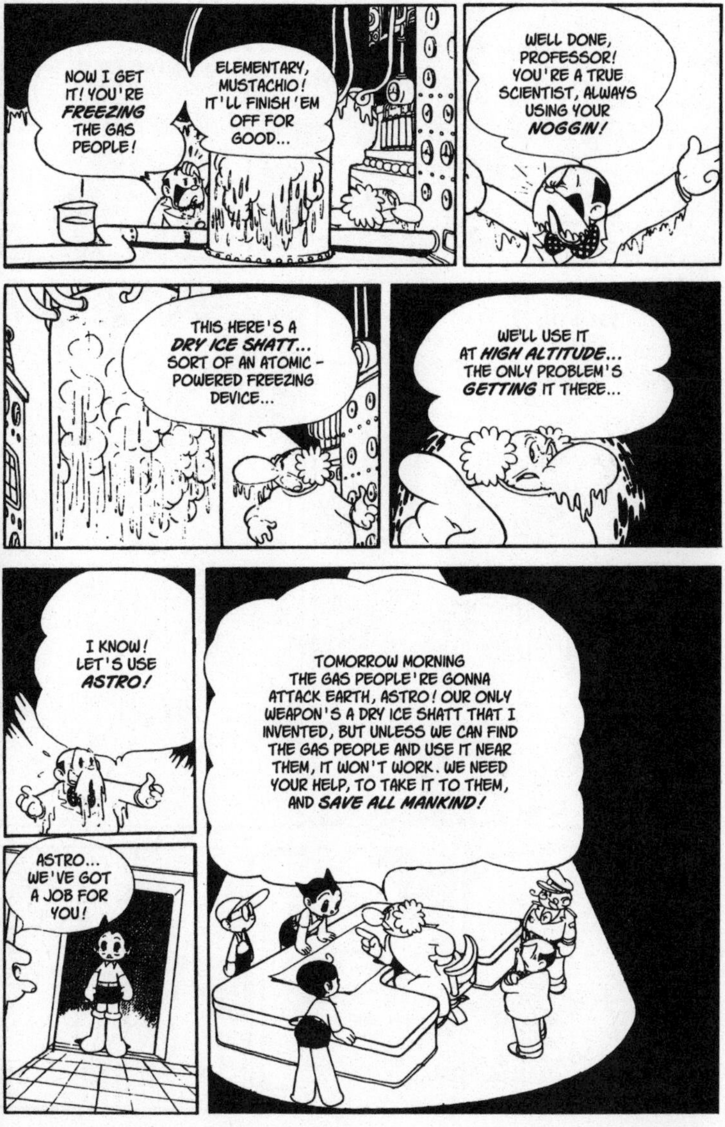
NOW I GET IT! YOU'RE FREEZING THE GAS PEOPLE!
ELEMENTARY, MUSTACHIO! IT'LL FINISH 'EM OFF FOR GOOD...
WELL DONE, PROFESSOR! YOU'RE A TRUE SCIENTIST, ALWAYS USING YOUR NOGGIN!
THIS HERE'S A DRY ICE SHATT... SORT OF AN ATOMIC-POWERED FREEZING DEVICE...
WE'LL USE IT AT HIGH ALTITUDE... THE ONLY PROBLEM'S GETTING IT THERE...
I KNOW! LET'S USE ASTRO!
ASTRO... WE'VE GOT A JOB FOR YOU!
TOMORROW MORNING THE GAS PEOPLE'RE GONNA ATTACK EARTH, ASTRO! OUR ONLY WEAPON'S A DRY ICE SHATT THAT I INVENTED, BUT UNLESS WE CAN FIND THE GAS PEOPLE AND USE IT NEAR THEM, IT WON'T WORK. WE NEED YOUR HELP, TO TAKE IT TO THEM, AND SAVE ALL MANKIND!

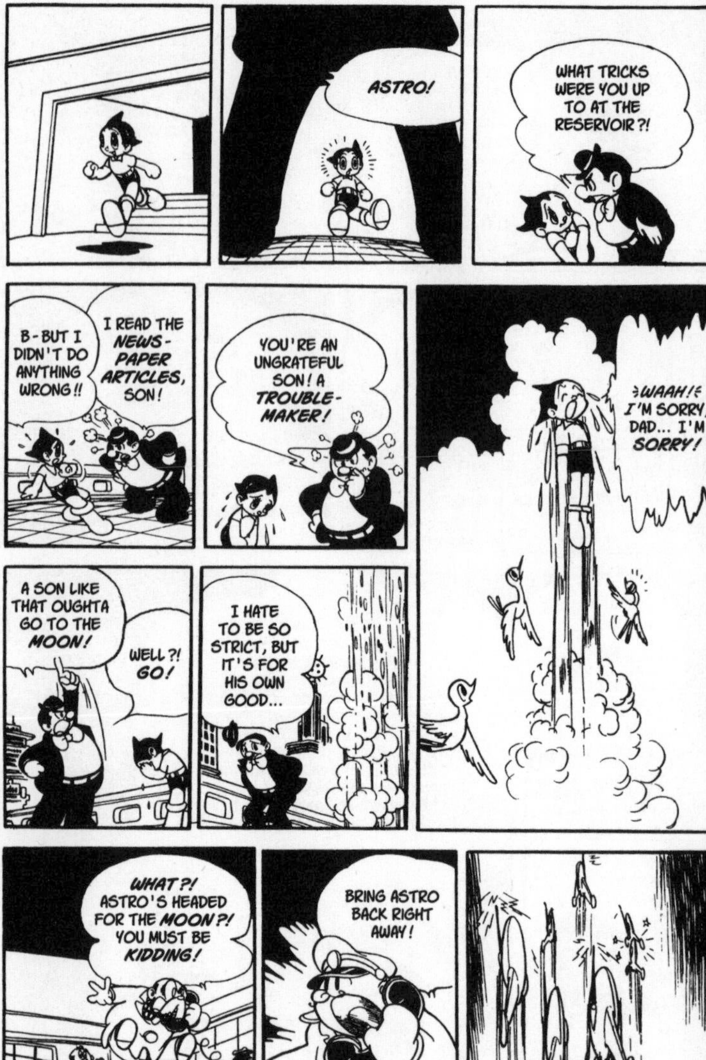
ASTRO!
WHAT TRICKS WERE YOU UP TO AT THE RESERVOIR?!
B-BUT I DIDN'T DO ANYTHING WRONG!!
I READ THE NEWS-PAPER ARTICLES, SON!
YOU'RE AN UNGRATEFUL SON! A TROUBLE-MAKER!
A SON LIKE THAT OUGHTA GO TO THE MOON!
WELL?! GO!
I HATE TO BE SO STRICT, BUT IT'S FOR HIS OWN GOOD...
WAAH! I'M SORRY, DAD... I'M SORRY!
WHAT?! ASTRO'S HEADED FOR THE MOON?! YOU MUST BE KIDDING!
BRING ASTRO BACK RIGHT AWAY!

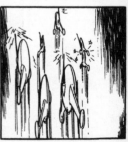

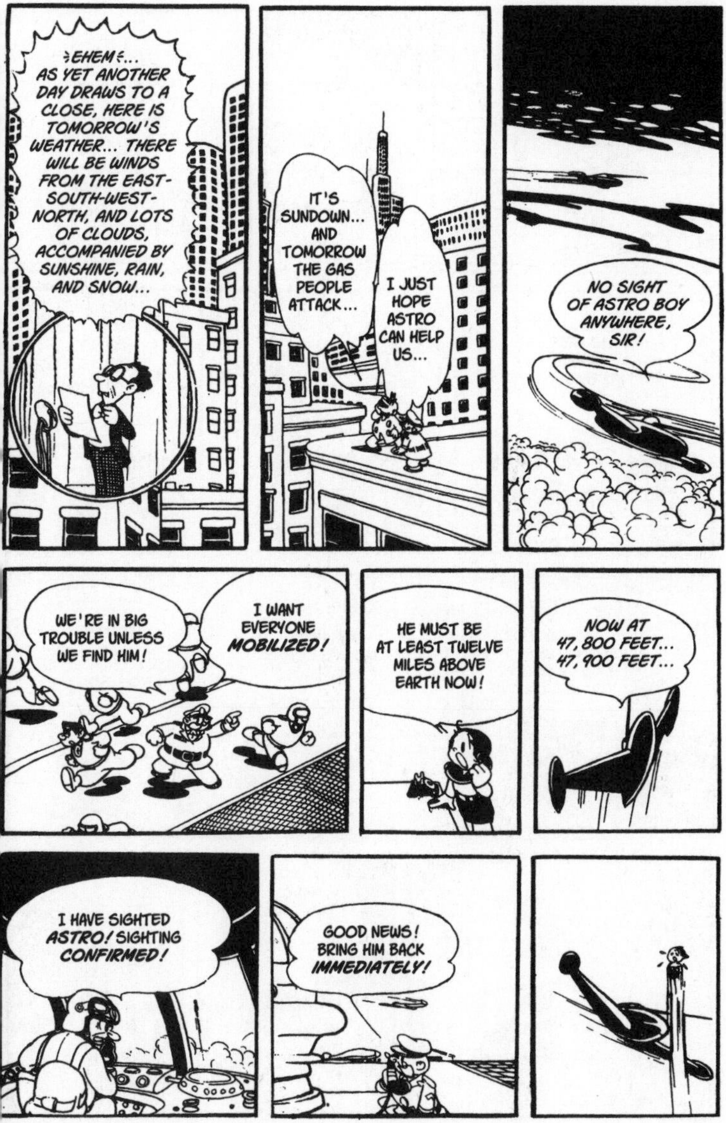

EHEM... AS YET ANOTHER DAY DRAWS TO A CLOSE, HERE IS TOMORROW'S WEATHER... THERE WILL BE WINDS FROM THE EAST-SOUTH-WEST-NORTH, AND LOTS OF CLOUDS, ACCOMPANIED BY SUNSHINE, RAIN, AND SNOW...
IT'S SUNDOWN... AND TOMORROW THE GAS PEOPLE ATTACK...
I JUST HOPE ASTRO CAN HELP US...
NO SIGHT OF ASTRO BOY ANYWHERE, SIR!
WE'RE IN BIG TROUBLE UNLESS WE FIND HIM!
I WANT EVERYONE MOBILIZED!
HE MUST BE AT LEAST TWELVE MILES ABOVE EARTH NOW!
NOW AT 47,800 FEET... 47,900 FEET...
I HAVE SIGHTED ASTRO! SIGHTING CONFIRMED!
GOOD NEWS! BRING HIM BACK IMMEDIATELY!

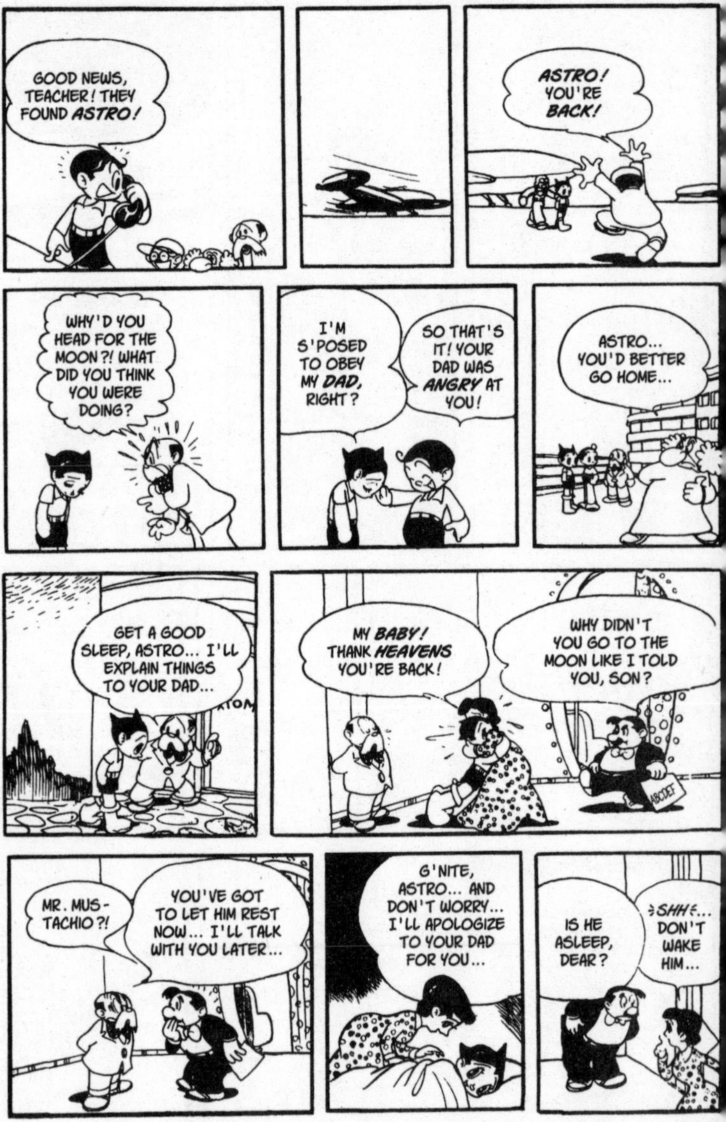
GOOD NEWS, TEACHER! THEY FOUND ASTRO!
ASTRO! YOU'RE BACK!
WHY'D YOU HEAD FOR THE MOON?! WHAT DID YOU THINK YOU WERE DOING?
I'M S'POSED TO OBEY MY DAD, RIGHT?
SO THAT'S IT! YOUR DAD WAS ANGRY AT YOU!
ASTRO... YOU'D BETTER GO HOME...
GET A GOOD SLEEP, ASTRO... I'LL EXPLAIN THINGS TO YOUR DAD...
MY BABY! THANK HEAVENS YOU'RE BACK!
WHY DIDN'T YOU GO TO THE MOON LIKE I TOLD YOU, SON?
ABCDEF
MR. MUS-TACHIO?!
YOU'VE GOT TO LET HIM REST NOW... I'LL TALK WITH YOU LATER...
G'NITE, ASTRO... AND DON'T WORRY... I'LL APOLOGIZE TO YOUR DAD FOR YOU...
IS HE ASLEEP, DEAR?
SHH... DON'T WAKE HIM...

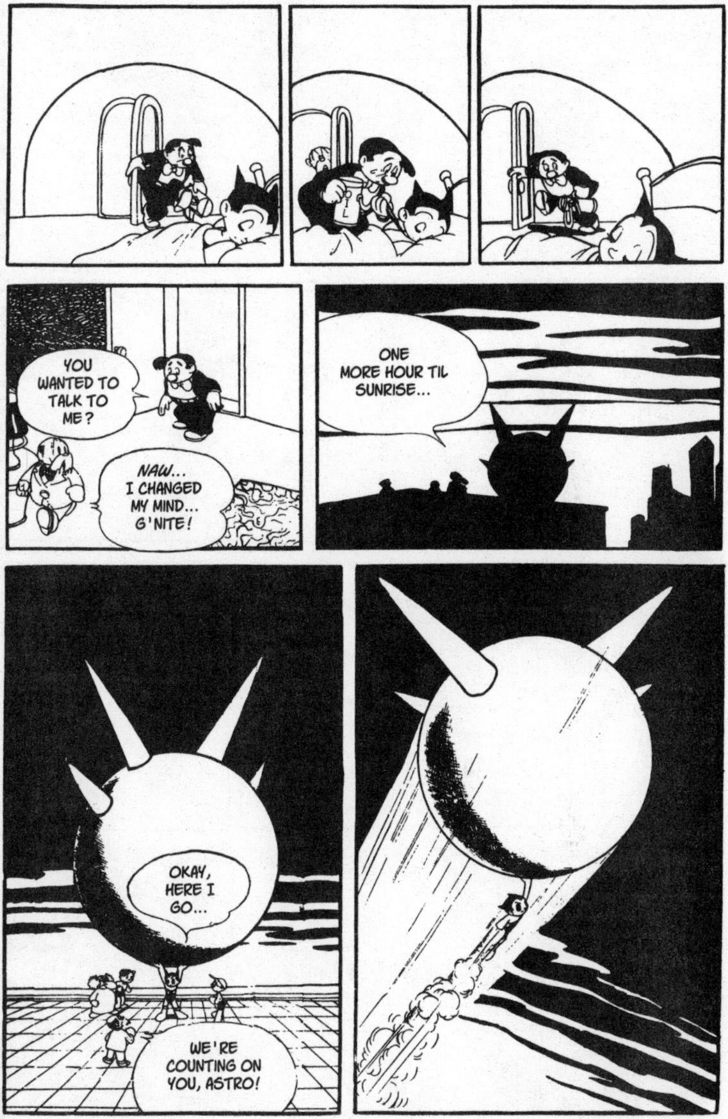
YOU WANTED TO TALK TO ME?
NAW... I CHANGED MY MIND... G'NITE!
ONE MORE HOUR TIL SUNRISE...
OKAY, HERE I GO...
WE'RE COUNTING ON YOU, ASTRO!

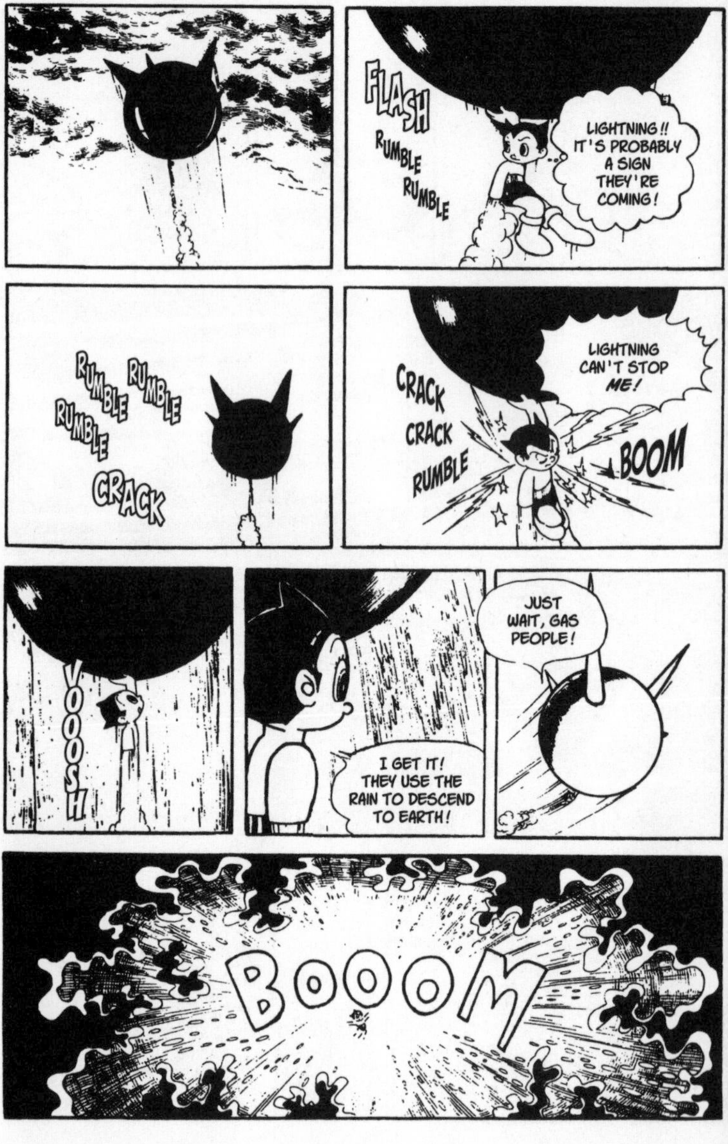

FLASH
RUMBLE
RUMBLE
LIGHTNING!! IT'S PROBABLY A SIGN THEY'RE COMING!
RUMBLE
RUMBLE
RUMBLE
CRACK
CRACK
CRACK
RUMBLE
LIGHTNING CAN'T STOP ME!
BOOM
VOOOSH
I GET IT! THEY USE THE RAIN TO DESCEND TO EARTH!
JUST WAIT, GAS PEOPLE!
BOOOM

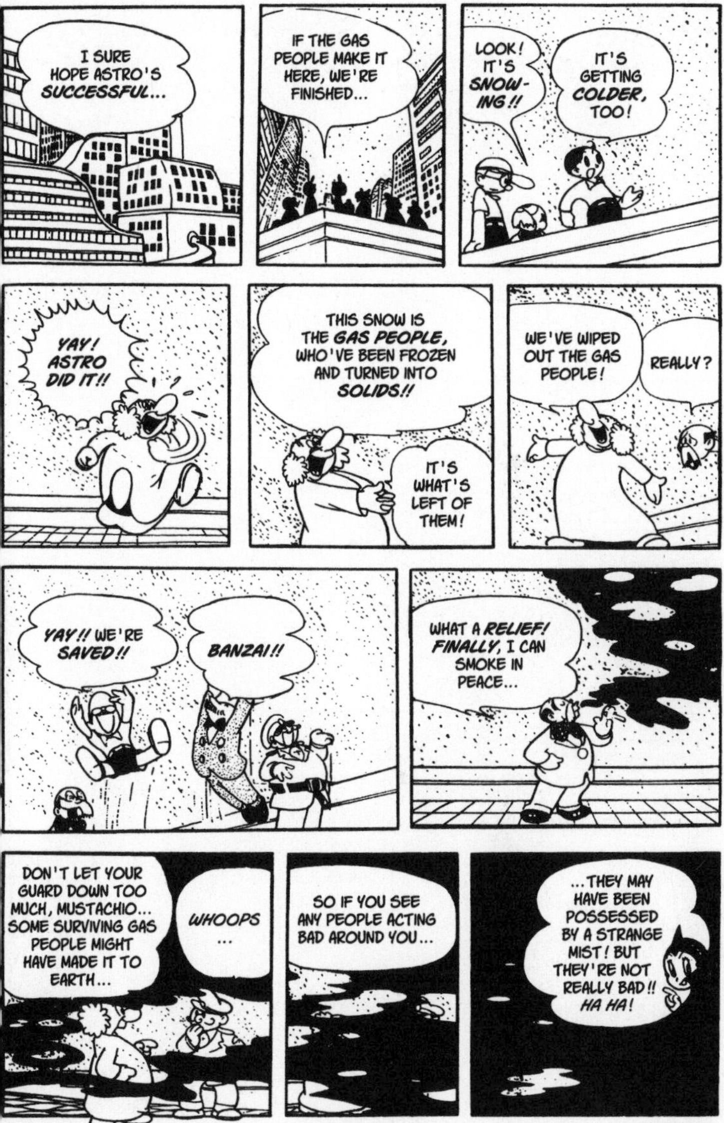
I SURE HOPE ASTRO'S SUCCESSFUL...
IF THE GAS PEOPLE MAKE IT HERE, WE'RE FINISHED...
LOOK! IT'S SNOW-ING!!
IT'S GETTING COLDER, TOO!
YAY! ASTRO DID IT!!
THIS SNOW IS THE GAS PEOPLE, WHO'VE BEEN FROZEN AND TURNED INTO SOLIDS!!
IT'S WHAT'S LEFT OF THEM!
WE'VE WIPED OUT THE GAS PEOPLE!
REALLY?
YAY!! WE'RE SAVED!!
BANZAI!!
WHAT A RELIEF! FINALLY, I CAN SMOKE IN PEACE...
DON'T LET YOUR GUARD DOWN TOO MUCH, MUSTACHIO... SOME SURVIVING GAS PEOPLE MIGHT HAVE MADE IT TO EARTH...
WHOOPS ...
SO IF YOU SEE ANY PEOPLE ACTING BAD AROUND YOU...
...THEY MAY HAVE BEEN POSSESSED BY A STRANGE MIST! BUT THEY'RE NOT REALLY BAD!! HA HA!

THE END

RED CAT

First serialized from May to November 1953
in *Shonen* magazine.

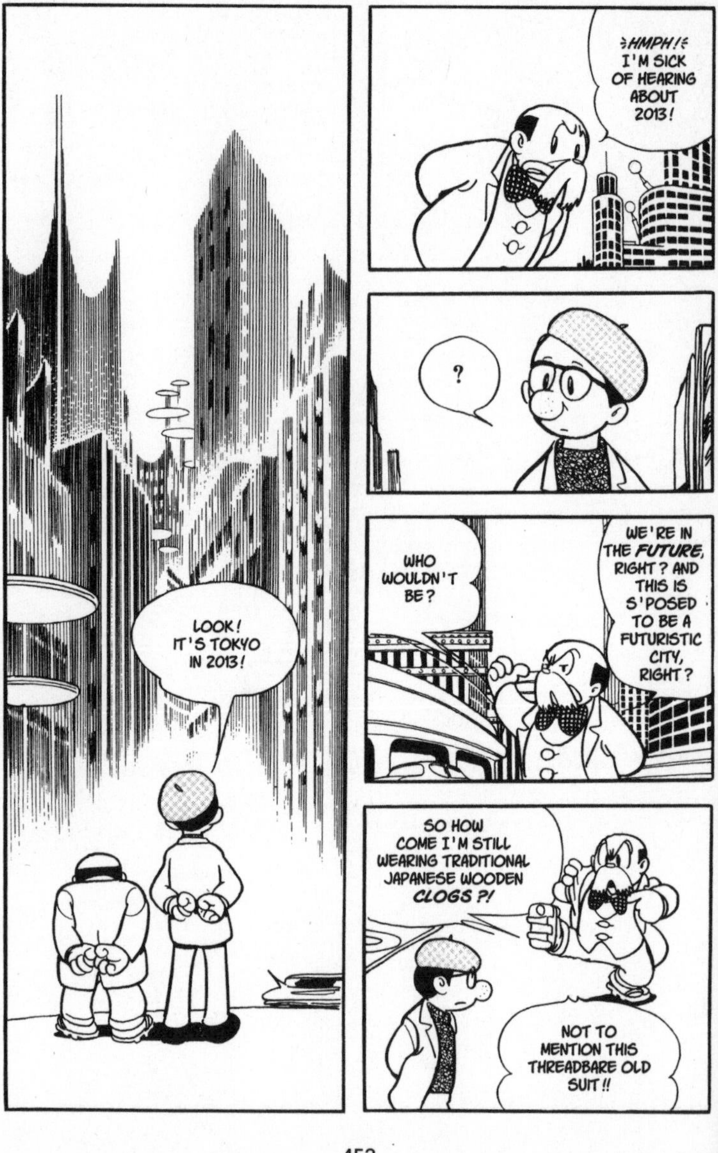
LOOK! IT'S TOKYO IN 2013!
HMPH! I'M SICK OF HEARING ABOUT 2013!
?
WHO WOULDN'T BE?
WE'RE IN THE FUTURE, RIGHT? AND THIS IS S'POSED TO BE A FUTURISTIC CITY, RIGHT?
SO HOW COME I'M STILL WEARING TRADITIONAL JAPANESE WOODEN CLOGS?!
NOT TO MENTION THIS THREADBARE OLD SUIT!!

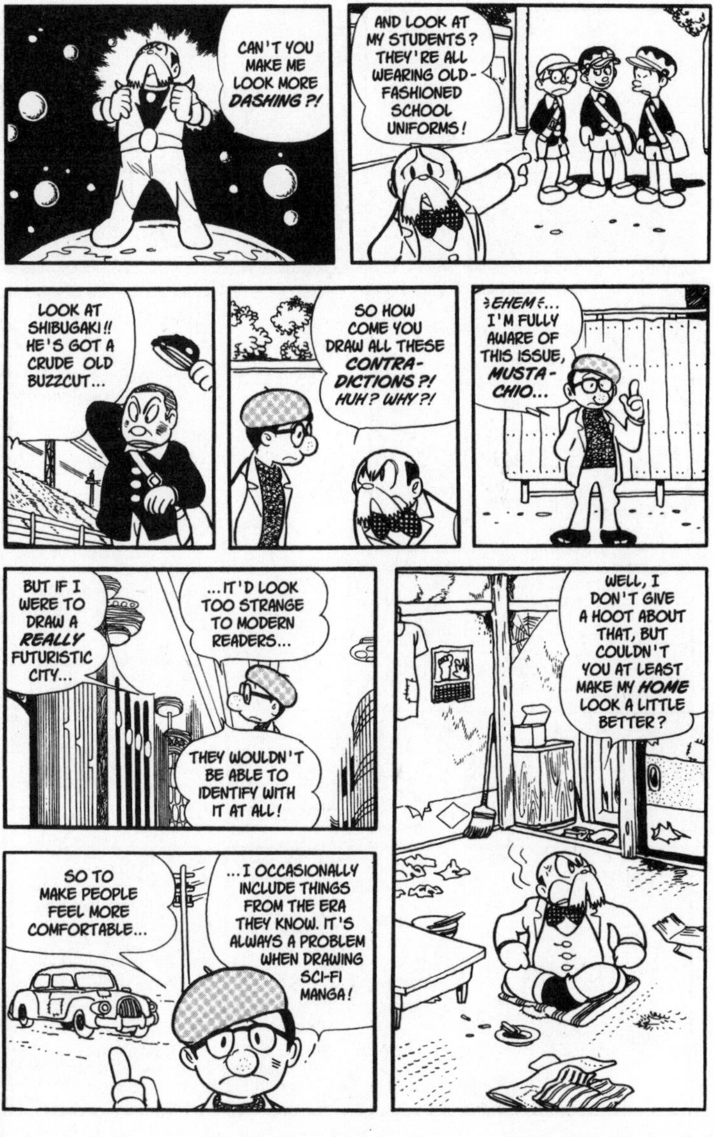

CAN'T YOU MAKE ME LOOK MORE DASHING?!
AND LOOK AT MY STUDENTS? THEY'RE ALL WEARING OLD-FASHIONED SCHOOL UNIFORMS!
LOOK AT SHIBUGAKI!! HE'S GOT A CRUDE OLD BUZZCUT...
SO HOW COME YOU DRAW ALL THESE CONTRADICTIONS?! HUH? WHY?!
EHEM... I'M FULLY AWARE OF THIS ISSUE, MUSTACHIO...
BUT IF I WERE TO DRAW A REALLY FUTURISTIC CITY...
...IT'D LOOK TOO STRANGE TO MODERN READERS...
THEY WOULDN'T BE ABLE TO IDENTIFY WITH IT AT ALL!
WELL, I DON'T GIVE A HOOT ABOUT THAT, BUT COULDN'T YOU AT LEAST MAKE MY HOME LOOK A LITTLE BETTER?
SO TO MAKE PEOPLE FEEL MORE COMFORTABLE...
...I OCCASIONALLY INCLUDE THINGS FROM THE ERA THEY KNOW. IT'S ALWAYS A PROBLEM WHEN DRAWING SCI-FI MANGA!

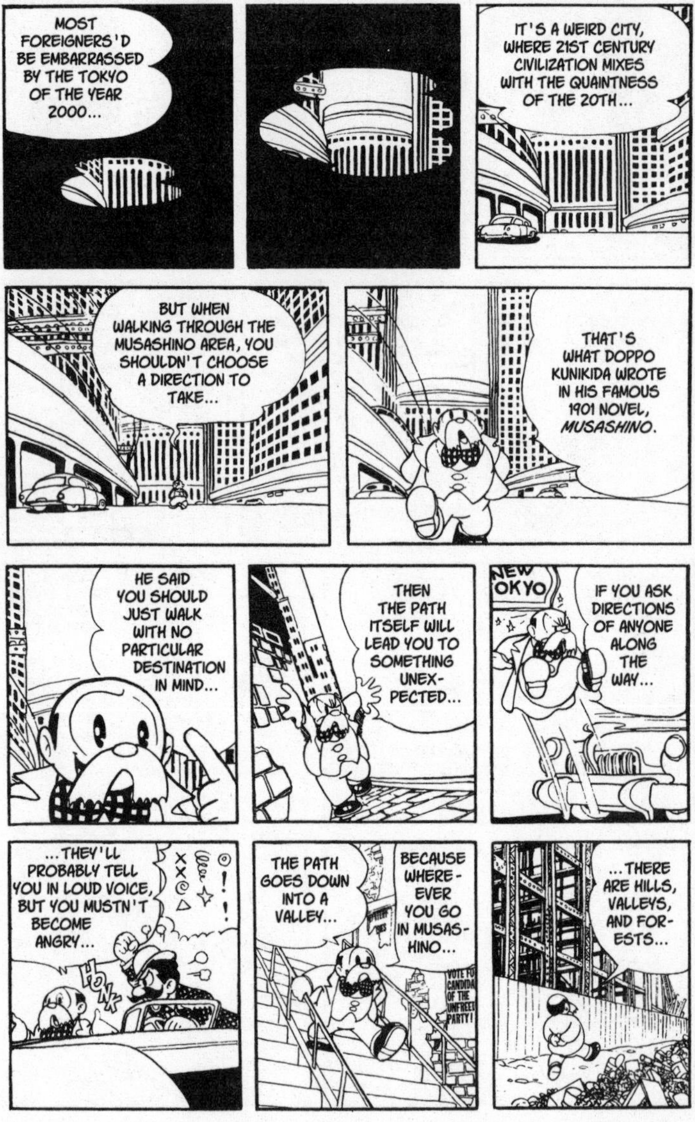
MOST FOREIGNERS'D BE EMBARRASSED BY THE TOKYO OF THE YEAR 2000...
IT'S A WEIRD CITY, WHERE 21ST CENTURY CIVILIZATION MIXES WITH THE QUAINTNESS OF THE 20TH...
BUT WHEN WALKING THROUGH THE MUSASHINO AREA, YOU SHOULDN'T CHOOSE A DIRECTION TO TAKE...
THAT'S WHAT DOPPO KUNIKIDA WROTE IN HIS FAMOUS 1901 NOVEL, *MUSASHINO*.
HE SAID YOU SHOULD JUST WALK WITH NO PARTICULAR DESTINATION IN MIND...
THEN THE PATH ITSELF WILL LEAD YOU TO SOMETHING UNEX-PECTED...
NEW
OKYO
IF YOU ASK DIRECTIONS OF ANYONE ALONG THE WAY...
...THEY'LL PROBABLY TELL YOU IN LOUD VOICE, BUT YOU MUSTN'T BECOME ANGRY...
HONK
THE PATH GOES DOWN INTO A VALLEY...
BECAUSE WHERE-EVER YOU GO IN MUSAS-HINO...
VOTE FO
CANDIDA
OF THE
UNFREE
PARTY!
...THERE ARE HILLS, VALLEYS, AND FOR-ESTS...

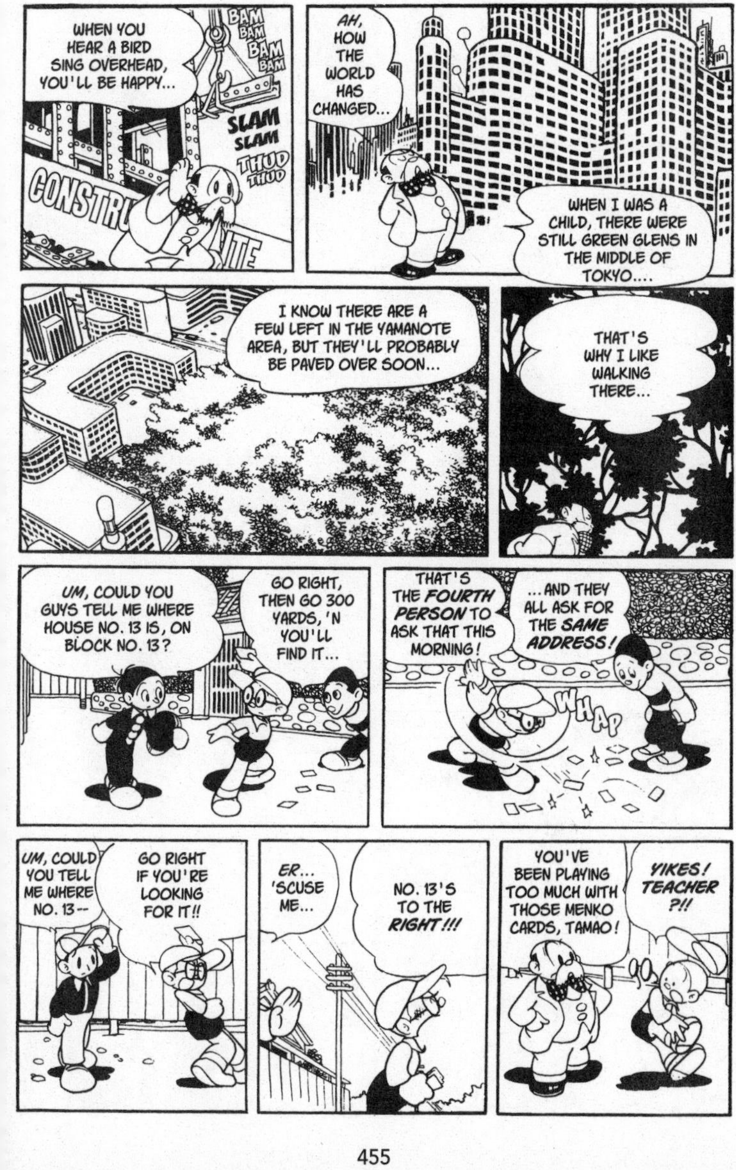
WHEN YOU HEAR A BIRD SING OVERHEAD, YOU'LL BE HAPPY...
BAM BAM BAM BAM
SLAM SLAM
THUD THUD
AH, HOW THE WORLD HAS CHANGED...
WHEN I WAS A CHILD, THERE WERE STILL GREEN GLENS IN THE MIDDLE OF TOKYO....
I KNOW THERE ARE A FEW LEFT IN THE YAMANOTE AREA, BUT THEY'LL PROBABLY BE PAVED OVER SOON...
THAT'S WHY I LIKE WALKING THERE...
UM, COULD YOU GUYS TELL ME WHERE HOUSE NO. 13 IS, ON BLOCK NO. 13?
GO RIGHT, THEN GO 300 YARDS, 'N YOU'LL FIND IT...
THAT'S THE FOURTH PERSON TO ASK THAT THIS MORNING!
...AND THEY ALL ASK FOR THE SAME ADDRESS!
WHAP
UM, COULD YOU TELL ME WHERE NO. 13--
GO RIGHT IF YOU'RE LOOKING FOR IT!!
ER... 'SCUSE ME...
NO. 13'S TO THE RIGHT!!!
YOU'VE BEEN PLAYING TOO MUCH WITH THOSE MENKO CARDS, TAMAO!
YIKES! TEACHER ?!!

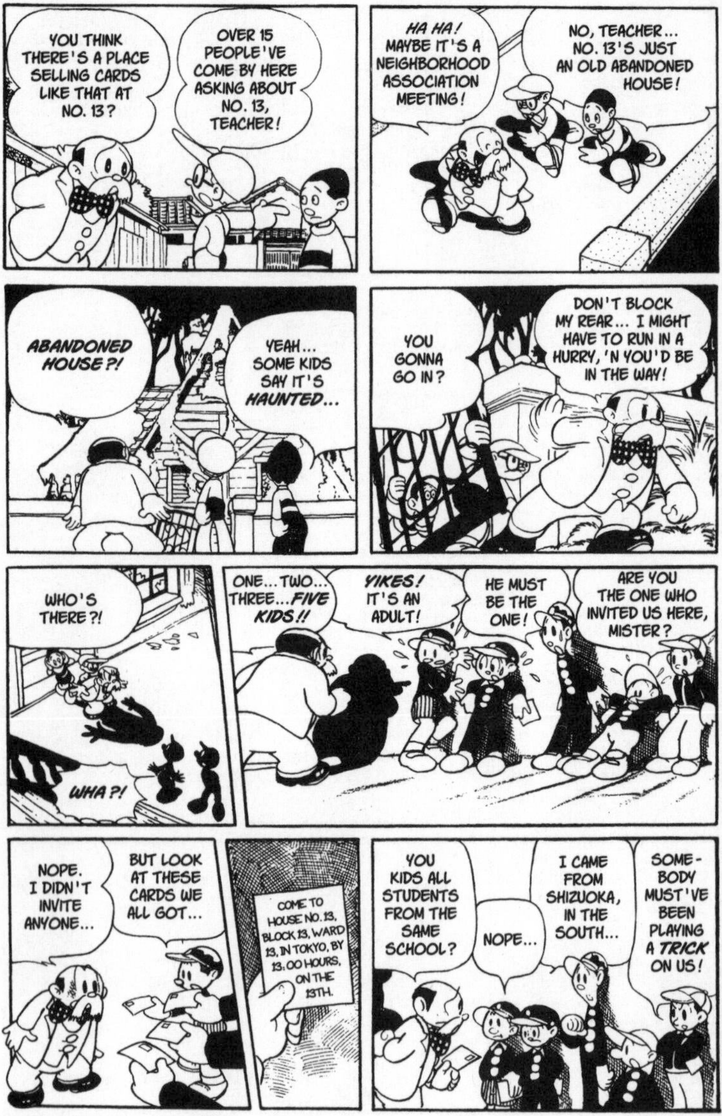
YOU THINK THERE'S A PLACE SELLING CARDS LIKE THAT AT NO. 13?
OVER 15 PEOPLE'VE COME BY HERE ASKING ABOUT NO. 13, TEACHER!
HA HA! MAYBE IT'S A NEIGHBORHOOD ASSOCIATION MEETING!
NO, TEACHER... NO. 13'S JUST AN OLD ABANDONED HOUSE!
ABANDONED HOUSE?!
YEAH... SOME KIDS SAY IT'S HAUNTED...
YOU GONNA GO IN?
DON'T BLOCK MY REAR... I MIGHT HAVE TO RUN IN A HURRY, 'N YOU'D BE IN THE WAY!
WHO'S THERE?!
WHA?!
ONE...TWO... THREE...FIVE KIDS!!
YIKES! IT'S AN ADULT!
HE MUST BE THE ONE!
ARE YOU THE ONE WHO INVITED US HERE, MISTER?
NOPE. I DIDN'T INVITE ANYONE...
BUT LOOK AT THESE CARDS WE ALL GOT...
COME TO HOUSE NO. 13, BLOCK 13, WARD 13, IN TOKYO, BY 13:00 HOURS, ON THE 13TH.
YOU KIDS ALL STUDENTS FROM THE SAME SCHOOL?
NOPE...
I CAME FROM SHIZUOKA, IN THE SOUTH...
SOME-BODY MUST'VE BEEN PLAYING A TRICK ON US!

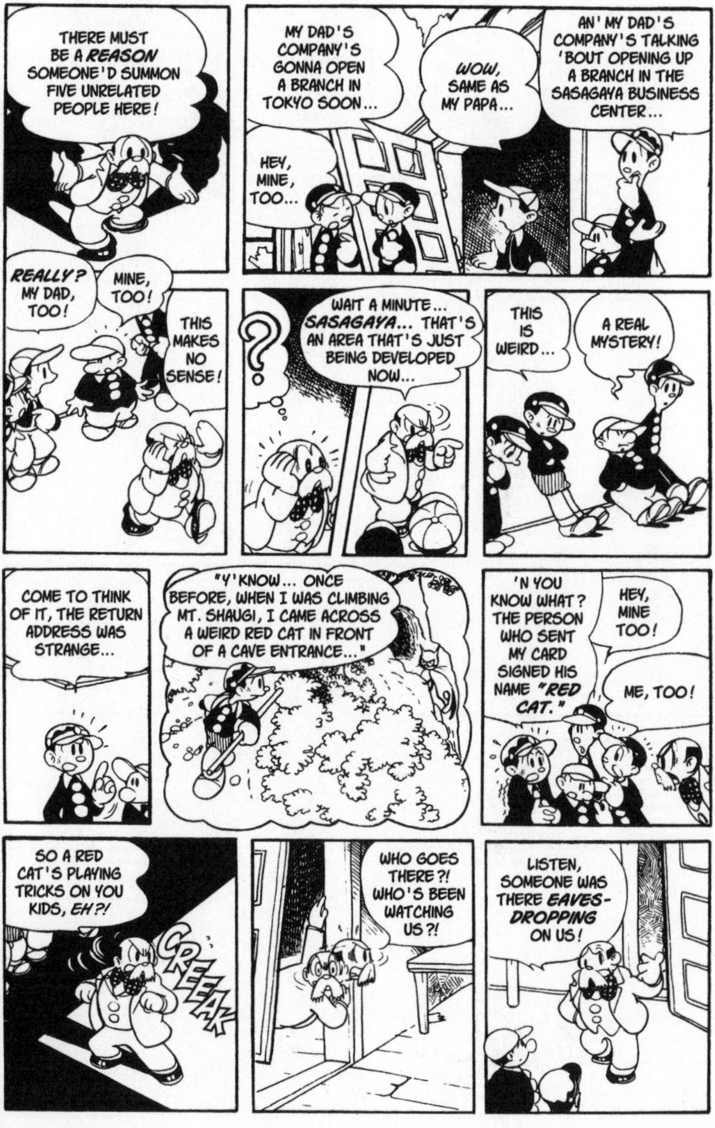
THERE MUST BE A *REASON* SOMEONE'D SUMMON FIVE UNRELATED PEOPLE HERE!
MY DAD'S COMPANY'S GONNA OPEN A BRANCH IN TOKYO SOON...
HEY, MINE, TOO...
WOW, SAME AS MY PAPA...
AN' MY DAD'S COMPANY'S TALKING 'BOUT OPENING UP A BRANCH IN THE SASAGAYA BUSINESS CENTER...
REALLY? MY DAD, TOO!
MINE, TOO!
THIS MAKES NO SENSE!
WAIT A MINUTE... *SASAGAYA*... THAT'S AN AREA THAT'S JUST BEING DEVELOPED NOW...
THIS IS WEIRD...
A REAL MYSTERY!
COME TO THINK OF IT, THE RETURN ADDRESS WAS STRANGE...
"Y'KNOW... ONCE BEFORE, WHEN I WAS CLIMBING MT. SHAUGI, I CAME ACROSS A WEIRD RED CAT IN FRONT OF A CAVE ENTRANCE..."
'N YOU KNOW WHAT? THE PERSON WHO SENT MY CARD SIGNED HIS NAME *"RED CAT."*
HEY, MINE TOO!
ME, TOO!
SO A RED CAT'S PLAYING TRICKS ON YOU KIDS, *EH?!*
CREEAK
WHO GOES THERE?! WHO'S BEEN WATCHING US?!
LISTEN, SOMEONE WAS THERE *EAVES-DROPPING* ON US!

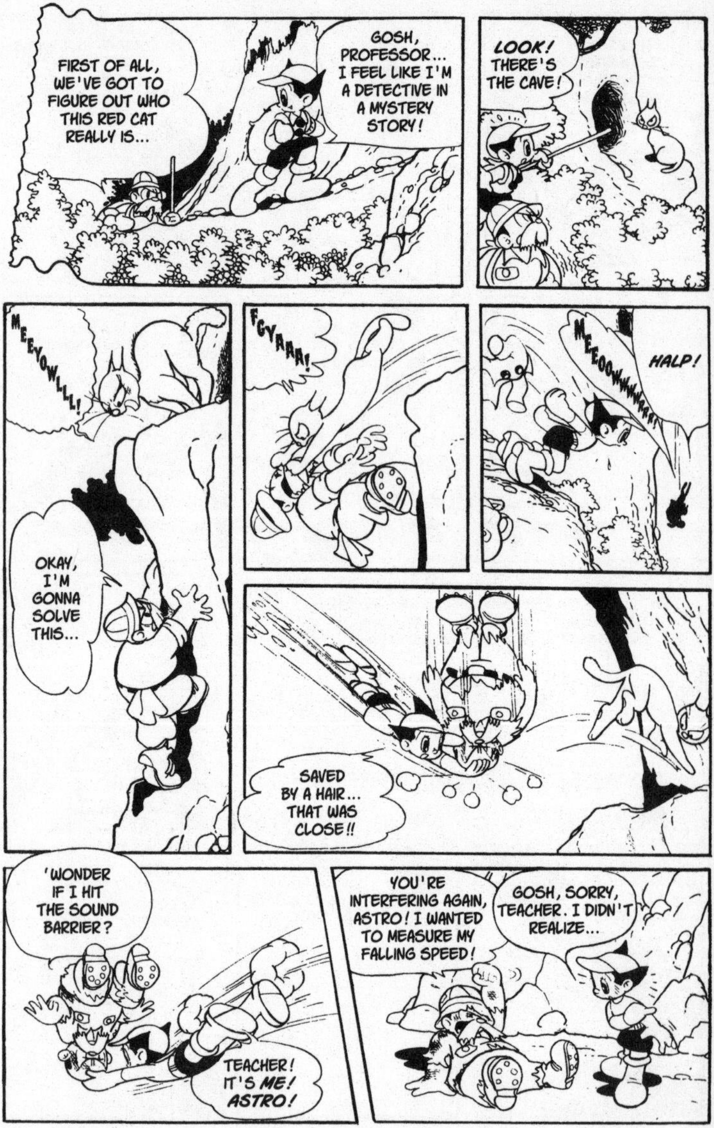
FIRST OF ALL, WE'VE GOT TO FIGURE OUT WHO THIS RED CAT REALLY IS...
GOSH, PROFESSOR... I FEEL LIKE I'M A DETECTIVE IN A MYSTERY STORY!
LOOK! THERE'S THE CAVE!
MEEYOWLLL!
OKAY, I'M GONNA SOLVE THIS...
FGYAAAA!
MEEOOWWWRR!
HALP!
SAVED BY A HAIR... THAT WAS CLOSE!!
'WONDER IF I HIT THE SOUND BARRIER?
TEACHER! IT'S ME! ASTRO!
YOU'RE INTERFERING AGAIN, ASTRO! I WANTED TO MEASURE MY FALLING SPEED!
GOSH, SORRY, TEACHER. I DIDN'T REALIZE...

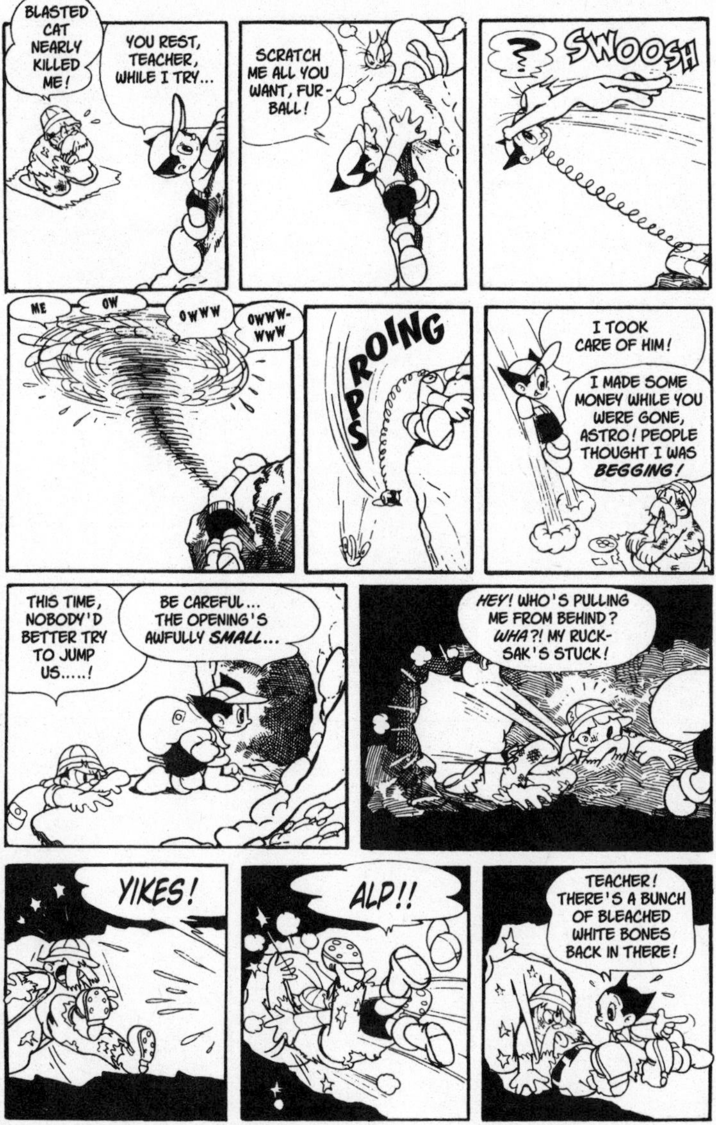
BLASTED CAT NEARLY KILLED ME!
YOU REST, TEACHER, WHILE I TRY...
SCRATCH ME ALL YOU WANT, FUR-BALL!
?
SWOOSH
ME
OW
OWWW
OWWW-WWW
SPROING
I TOOK CARE OF HIM!
I MADE SOME MONEY WHILE YOU WERE GONE, ASTRO! PEOPLE THOUGHT I WAS BEGGING!
THIS TIME, NOBODY'D BETTER TRY TO JUMP US.....!
BE CAREFUL... THE OPENING'S AWFULLY SMALL...
HEY! WHO'S PULLING ME FROM BEHIND? WHA?! MY RUCK-SAK'S STUCK!
YIKES!
ALP!!
TEACHER! THERE'S A BUNCH OF BLEACHED WHITE BONES BACK IN THERE!

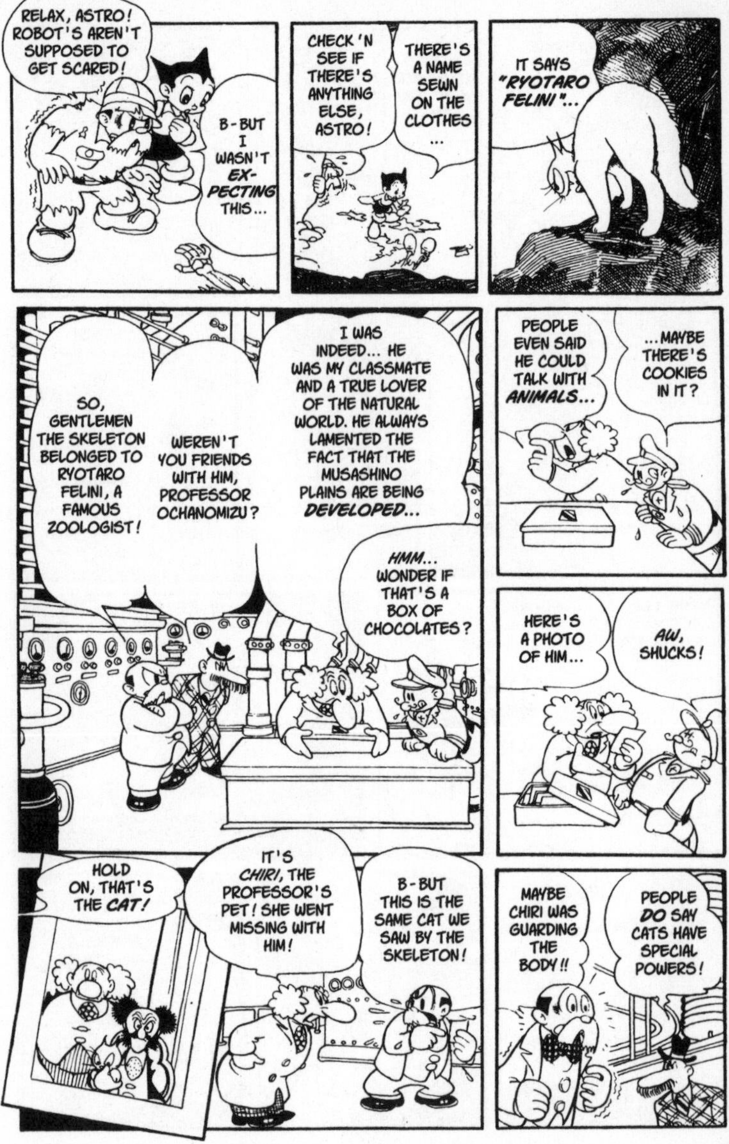
RELAX, ASTRO! ROBOT'S AREN'T SUPPOSED TO GET SCARED!
B-BUT I WASN'T EXPECTING THIS...
CHECK 'N SEE IF THERE'S ANYTHING ELSE, ASTRO!
THERE'S A NAME SEWN ON THE CLOTHES ...
IT SAYS "RYOTARO FELINI"...
SO, GENTLEMEN THE SKELETON BELONGED TO RYOTARO FELINI, A FAMOUS ZOOLOGIST!
WEREN'T YOU FRIENDS WITH HIM, PROFESSOR OCHANOMIZU?
I WAS INDEED... HE WAS MY CLASSMATE AND A TRUE LOVER OF THE NATURAL WORLD. HE ALWAYS LAMENTED THE FACT THAT THE MUSASHINO PLAINS ARE BEING DEVELOPED...
HMM... WONDER IF THAT'S A BOX OF CHOCOLATES?
PEOPLE EVEN SAID HE COULD TALK WITH ANIMALS...
...MAYBE THERE'S COOKIES IN IT?
HERE'S A PHOTO OF HIM...
AW, SHUCKS!
HOLD ON, THAT'S THE CAT!
IT'S CHIRI, THE PROFESSOR'S PET! SHE WENT MISSING WITH HIM!
B-BUT THIS IS THE SAME CAT WE SAW BY THE SKELETON!
MAYBE CHIRI WAS GUARDING THE BODY!!
PEOPLE DO SAY CATS HAVE SPECIAL POWERS!

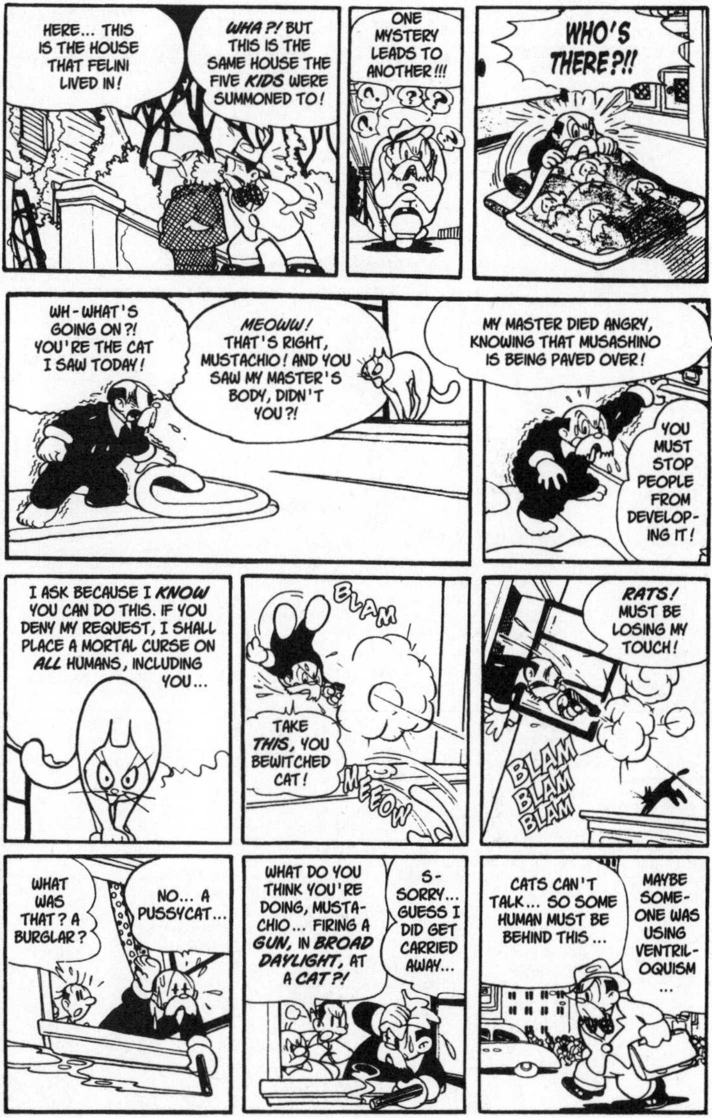

HERE... THIS IS THE HOUSE THAT FELINI LIVED IN!
WHA?! BUT THIS IS THE SAME HOUSE THE FIVE KIDS WERE SUMMONED TO!
ONE MYSTERY LEADS TO ANOTHER!!!
WHO'S THERE?!!
WH-WHAT'S GOING ON?! YOU'RE THE CAT I SAW TODAY!
MEOWW! THAT'S RIGHT, MUSTACHIO! AND YOU SAW MY MASTER'S BODY, DIDN'T YOU?!
MY MASTER DIED ANGRY, KNOWING THAT MUSASHINO IS BEING PAVED OVER!
YOU MUST STOP PEOPLE FROM DEVELOPING IT!
I ASK BECAUSE I KNOW YOU CAN DO THIS. IF YOU DENY MY REQUEST, I SHALL PLACE A MORTAL CURSE ON ALL HUMANS, INCLUDING YOU...
BLAM
TAKE THIS, YOU BEWITCHED CAT!
MEEOW
RATS! MUST BE LOSING MY TOUCH!
BLAM BLAM BLAM
WHAT WAS THAT? A BURGLAR?
NO... A PUSSYCAT...
WHAT DO YOU THINK YOU'RE DOING, MUSTACHIO... FIRING A GUN, IN BROAD DAYLIGHT, AT A CAT?!
S-SORRY... GUESS I DID GET CARRIED AWAY...
CATS CAN'T TALK... SO SOME HUMAN MUST BE BEHIND THIS...
MAYBE SOMEONE WAS USING VENTRILOQUISM...

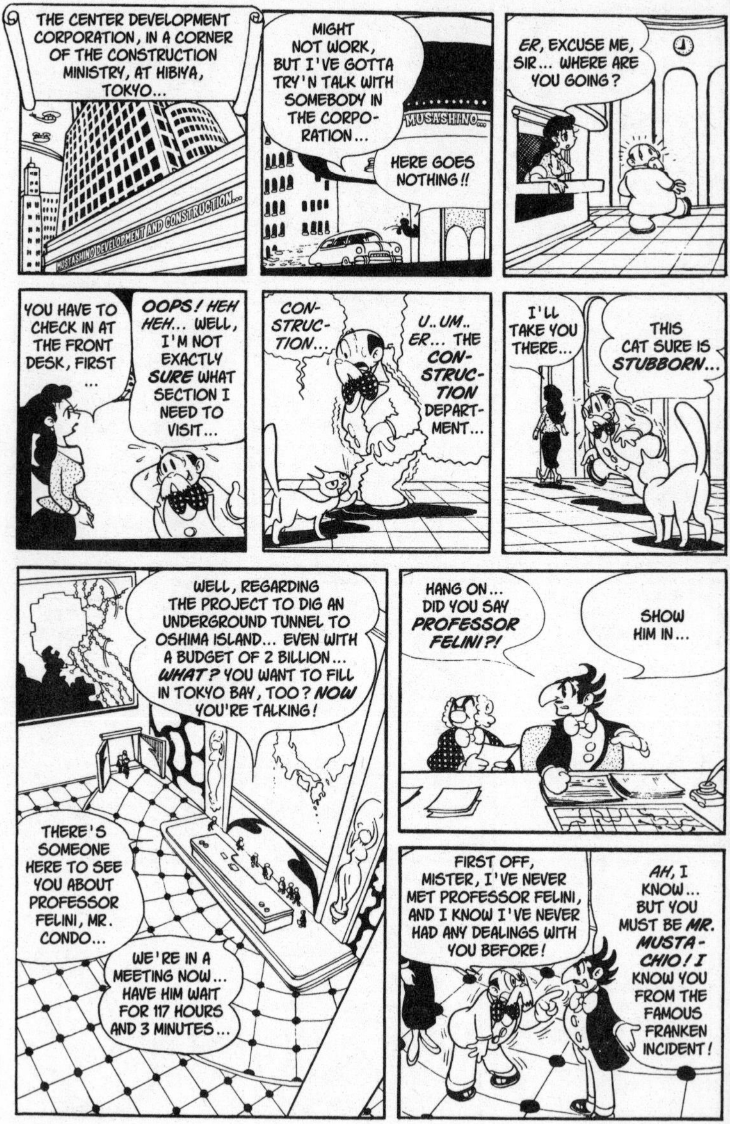
THE CENTER DEVELOPMENT CORPORATION, IN A CORNER OF THE CONSTRUCTION MINISTRY, AT HIBIYA, TOKYO...
MUSTASHINO DEVELOPMENT AND CONSTRUCTION...
MIGHT NOT WORK, BUT I'VE GOTTA TRY'N TALK WITH SOMEBODY IN THE CORPO- RATION...
MUSASHINO...
HERE GOES NOTHING!!
ER, EXCUSE ME, SIR... WHERE ARE YOU GOING?
YOU HAVE TO CHECK IN AT THE FRONT DESK, FIRST ...
OOPS! HEH HEH... WELL, I'M NOT EXACTLY SURE WHAT SECTION I NEED TO VISIT...
CON- STRUC- TION...
U.. UM.. ER... THE CON- STRUC- TION DEPART- MENT...
I'LL TAKE YOU THERE...
THIS CAT SURE IS STUBBORN...
WELL, REGARDING THE PROJECT TO DIG AN UNDERGROUND TUNNEL TO OSHIMA ISLAND... EVEN WITH A BUDGET OF 2 BILLION... WHAT? YOU WANT TO FILL IN TOKYO BAY, TOO? NOW YOU'RE TALKING!
THERE'S SOMEONE HERE TO SEE YOU ABOUT PROFESSOR FELINI, MR. CONDO...
WE'RE IN A MEETING NOW... HAVE HIM WAIT FOR 117 HOURS AND 3 MINUTES...
HANG ON... DID YOU SAY PROFESSOR FELINI?!
SHOW HIM IN...
FIRST OFF, MISTER, I'VE NEVER MET PROFESSOR FELINI, AND I KNOW I'VE NEVER HAD ANY DEALINGS WITH YOU BEFORE!
AH, I KNOW... BUT YOU MUST BE MR. MUSTA- CHIO! I KNOW YOU FROM THE FAMOUS FRANKEN INCIDENT!

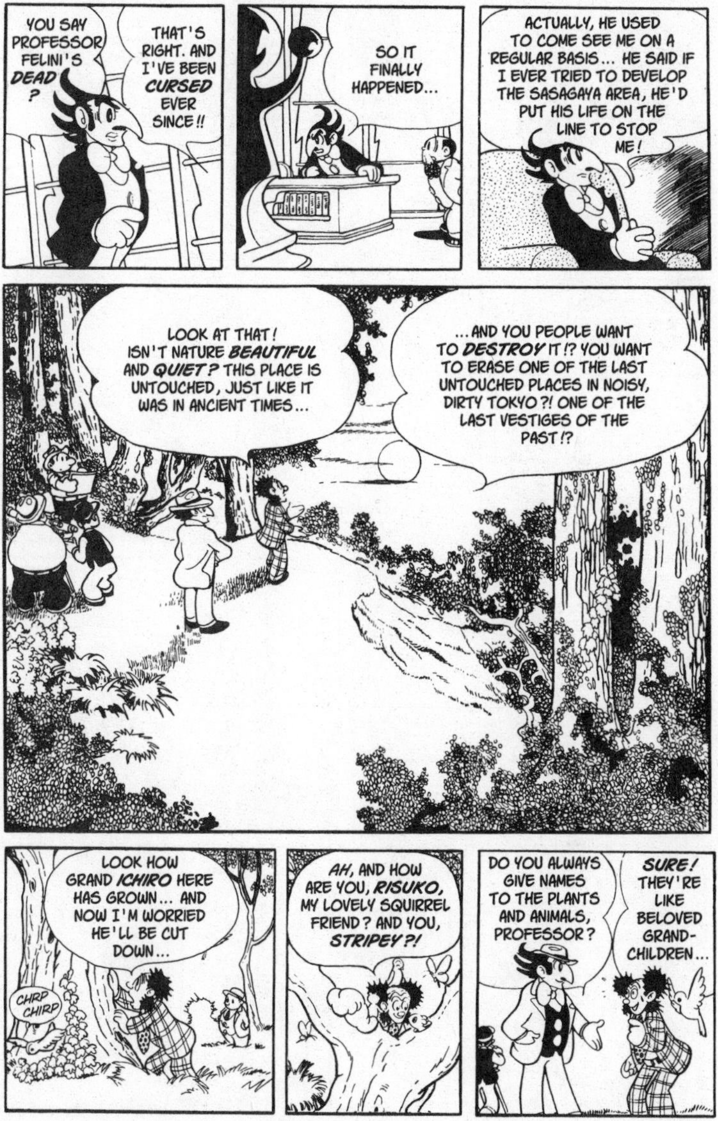
YOU SAY PROFESSOR FELINI'S *DEAD* ?
THAT'S RIGHT. AND I'VE BEEN *CURSED* EVER SINCE !!
SO IT FINALLY HAPPENED...
ACTUALLY, HE USED TO COME SEE ME ON A REGULAR BASIS... HE SAID IF I EVER TRIED TO DEVELOP THE SASAGAYA AREA, HE'D PUT HIS LIFE ON THE LINE TO STOP ME!
LOOK AT THAT! ISN'T NATURE *BEAUTIFUL* AND *QUIET?* THIS PLACE IS UNTOUCHED, JUST LIKE IT WAS IN ANCIENT TIMES...
...AND YOU PEOPLE WANT TO *DESTROY* IT !? YOU WANT TO ERASE ONE OF THE LAST UNTOUCHED PLACES IN NOISY, DIRTY TOKYO ?! ONE OF THE LAST VESTIGES OF THE PAST !?
LOOK HOW GRAND *ICHIRO* HERE HAS GROWN... AND NOW I'M WORRIED HE'LL BE CUT DOWN...
CHRP CHIRP
AH, AND HOW ARE YOU, *RISUKO*, MY LOVELY SQUIRREL FRIEND? AND YOU, *STRIPEY?!*
DO YOU ALWAYS GIVE NAMES TO THE PLANTS AND ANIMALS, PROFESSOR?
SURE! THEY'RE LIKE BELOVED GRAND-CHILDREN...

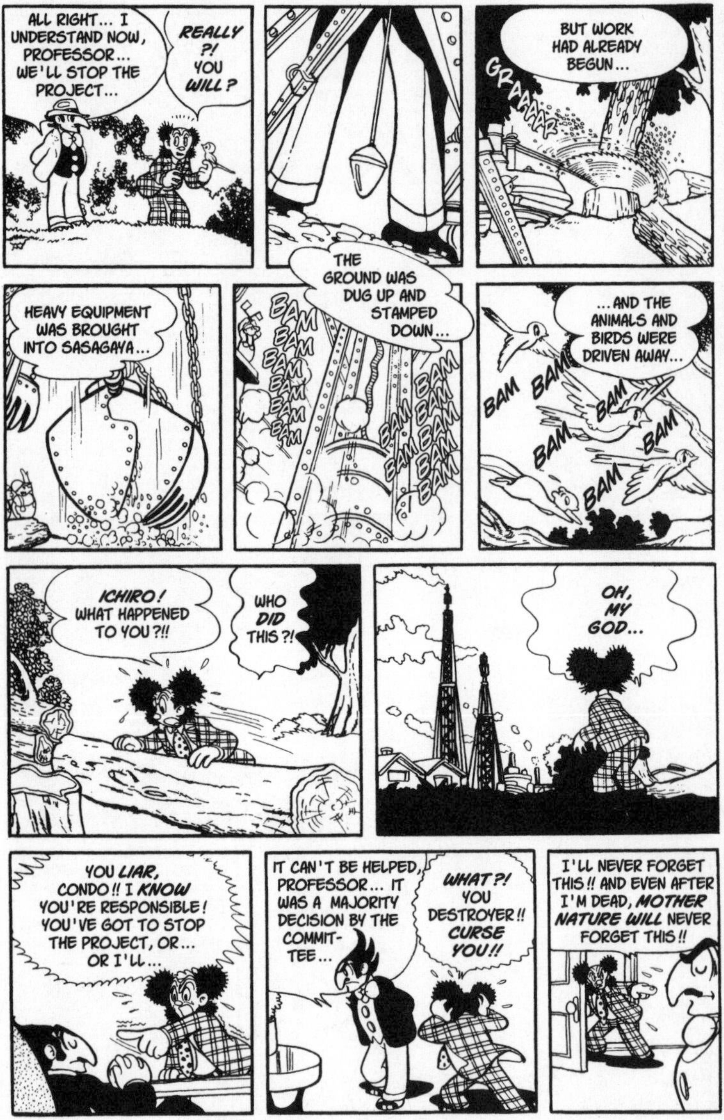

ALL RIGHT... I UNDERSTAND NOW, PROFESSOR... WE'LL STOP THE PROJECT...
REALLY ?! YOU WILL?
BUT WORK HAD ALREADY BEGUN...
GRAAAAAR
HEAVY EQUIPMENT WAS BROUGHT INTO SASAGAYA...
THE GROUND WAS DUG UP AND STAMPED DOWN...
BAM BAM BAM BAM BAM BAM BAM BAM
BAM BAM BAM BAM BAM BAM BAM BAM
...AND THE ANIMALS AND BIRDS WERE DRIVEN AWAY...
BAM BAM BAM BAM BAM BAM
ICHIRO! WHAT HAPPENED TO YOU?!!
WHO DID THIS?!
OH, MY GOD...
YOU LIAR, CONDO!! I KNOW YOU'RE RESPONSIBLE! YOU'VE GOT TO STOP THE PROJECT, OR... OR I'LL...
IT CAN'T BE HELPED, PROFESSOR... IT WAS A MAJORITY DECISION BY THE COMMIT-TEE...
WHAT?! YOU DESTROYER!! CURSE YOU!!
I'LL NEVER FORGET THIS!! AND EVEN AFTER I'M DEAD, MOTHER NATURE WILL NEVER FORGET THIS!!

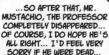

...SO AFTER THAT, MR. MUSTACHIO, THE PROFESSOR COMPLETELY DISAPPEARED... OF COURSE, I DO HOPE HE'S ALL RIGHT... I'D FEEL VERY SORRY IF HE WERE DEAD...

WELL, THE PROFESSOR'S PET CAT HAS BEEN POSSESSED, AND NOW IT'S RUNNING AROUND YELLING *MEEYOOWGO*...

YOU MEAN, YOU THINK HE'S TRYING TO GET REVENGE FOR HIS MASTER'S DEATH?

MAYBE HE TAKES AFTER THE POSSESSED CAT IN THE FAMOUS PLAY ABOUT PRINCE NABESHIMA...

≥HMPH≤... LOOKS LIKE CONSTRUCTION'S REALLY UNDERWAY NOW IN SASAGAYA...

MUSTACHIO! MAKE SURE YOU TELL YOUR PUPILS NOT TO GO NEAR THE CONSTRUCTION SITE, OKAY?

YAZ-ZIR...

BOYS AND GIRLS.... I KNOW YOU'RE FAMILIAR WITH THE *SASAGAYA* AREA... WELL, DANGEROUS CONSTRUCTION'S GOING ON THERE, SO LIKE THE SAYING GOES, DON'T BE THE FOOLS WHO RUSH IN, WHERE WISE MEN FEAR TO TREAD...

B-BUT TEACHER... THAT'S WHERE WE ALWAYS *PLAY*! THERE'S NOWHERE *ELSE* FOR US TO GO!

YEAH! TELL IT LIKE IT IS, SHIB!

I'M AGAINST THEM MAKING ANY BUILDINGS THERE!

YEAH-- ME, TOO! ME, TOO!

WE OUGHTA HAVE MORE RIGHTS TO THE PLACE THAN ANYONE ELSE!

ENOUGH, SHIBUGAKI! YOU'RE NOT THE ONLY ONE IN THE WORLD!

I'M *KING OF THE MOUNTAIN!*

NYA NYA! HEY, YOU'RE NOT KING ANYMORE, SHIB!

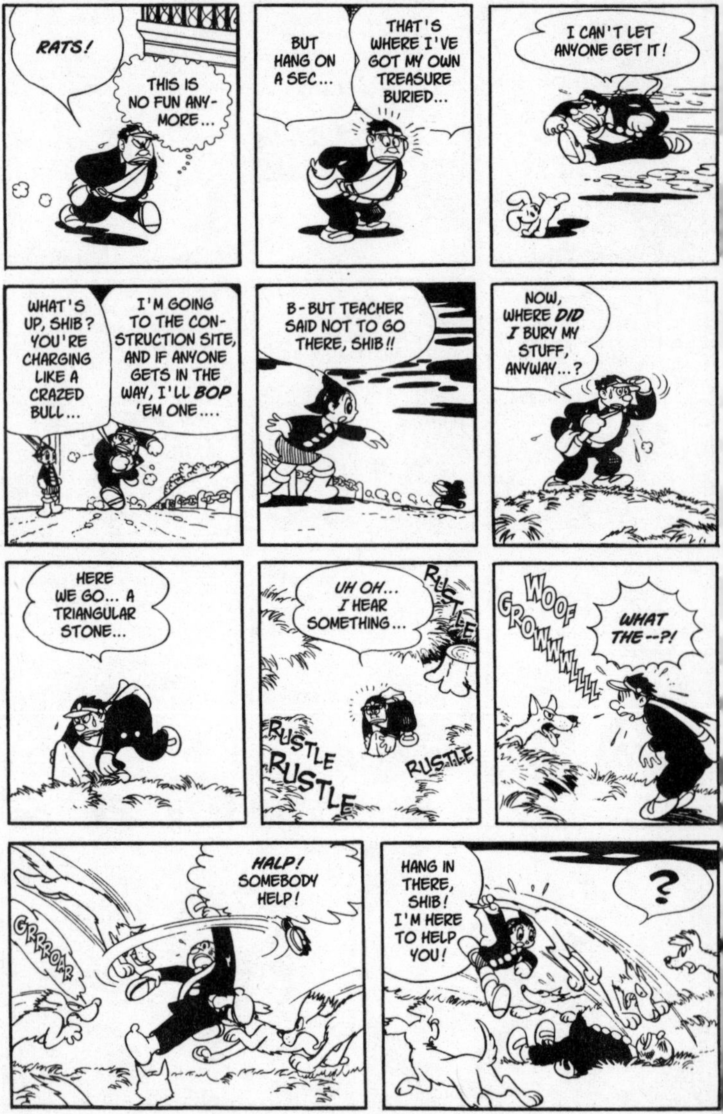
RATS!
THIS IS NO FUN ANY-MORE...
BUT HANG ON A SEC...
THAT'S WHERE I'VE GOT MY OWN TREASURE BURIED...
I CAN'T LET ANYONE GET IT!
WHAT'S UP, SHIB? YOU'RE CHARGING LIKE A CRAZED BULL...
I'M GOING TO THE CON-STRUCTION SITE, AND IF ANYONE GETS IN THE WAY, I'LL BOP 'EM ONE....
B-BUT TEACHER SAID NOT TO GO THERE, SHIB!!
NOW, WHERE DID I BURY MY STUFF, ANYWAY...?
HERE WE GO... A TRIANGULAR STONE...
UH OH... I HEAR SOMETHING...
RUSTLE
RUSTLE
RUSTLE
RUSTLE
WOOF
GROWWWLLLL
WHAT THE--?!
GRRROAR
HALP! SOMEBODY HELP!
HANG IN THERE, SHIB! I'M HERE TO HELP YOU!
?

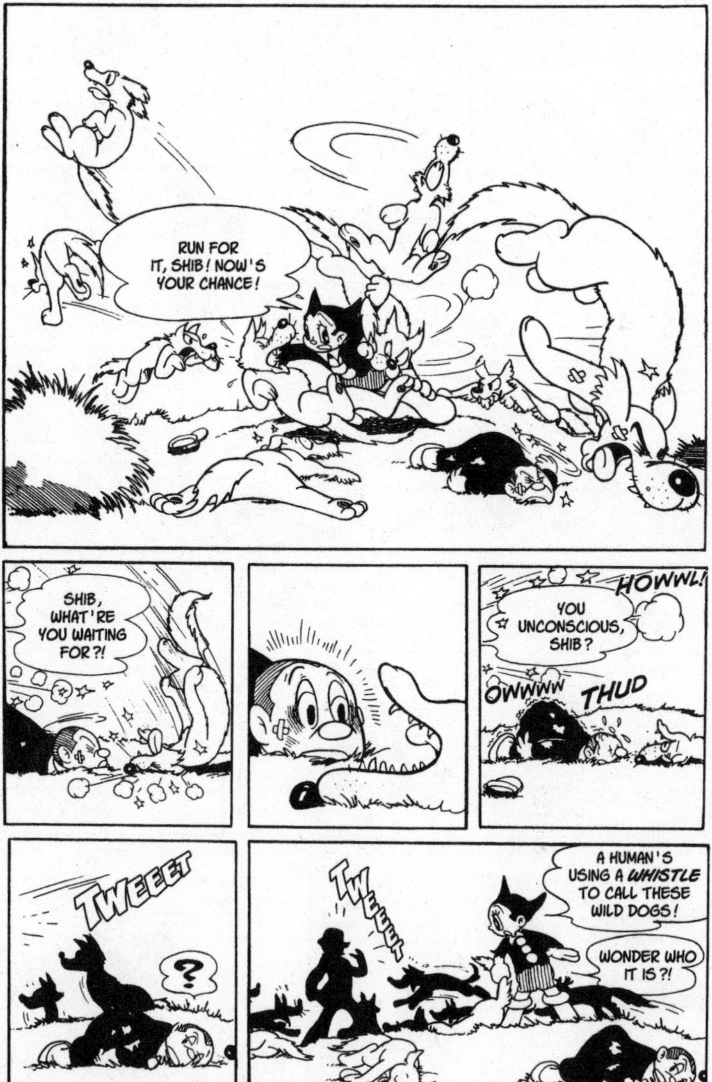
RUN FOR IT, SHIB! NOW'S YOUR CHANCE!
SHIB, WHAT'RE YOU WAITING FOR?!
YOU UNCONSCIOUS, SHIB?
HOWWL!
OWWWW
THUD
TWEEET
?
TWEEEET
A HUMAN'S USING A *WHISTLE* TO CALL THESE WILD DOGS!
WONDER WHO IT IS?!

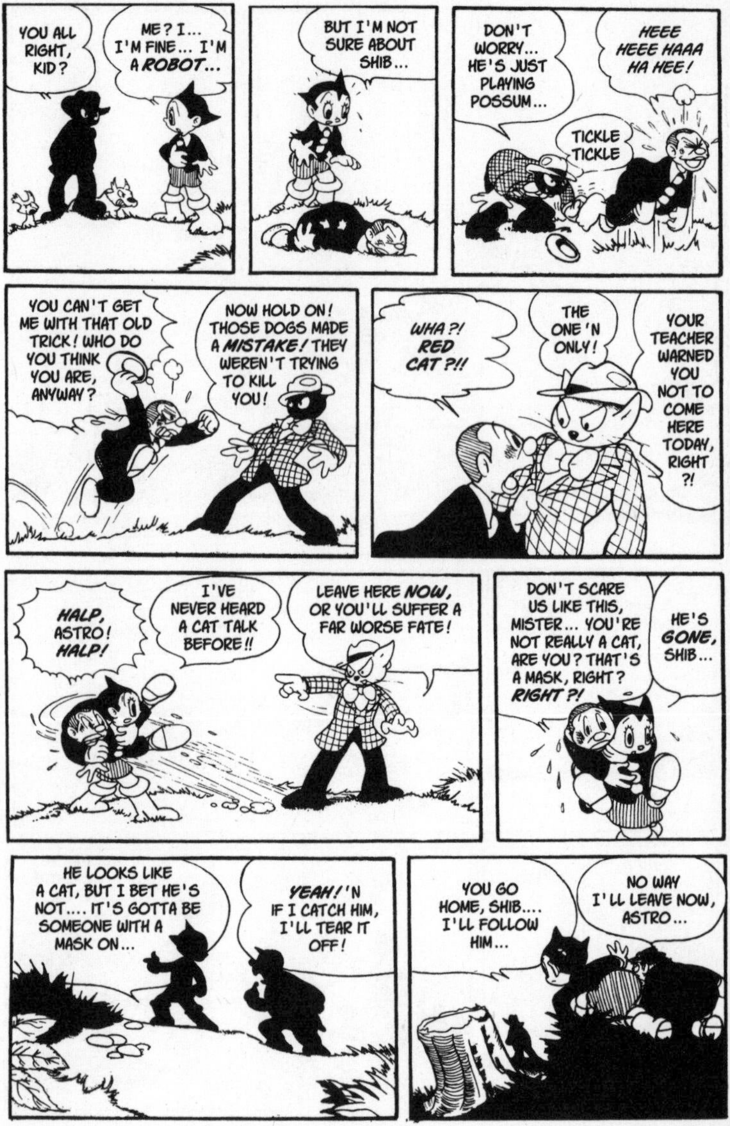
YOU ALL RIGHT, KID?
ME? I... I'M FINE... I'M A ROBOT...
BUT I'M NOT SURE ABOUT SHIB...
DON'T WORRY... HE'S JUST PLAYING POSSUM...
HEEE HEEE HAAA HA HEE!
TICKLE TICKLE
YOU CAN'T GET ME WITH THAT OLD TRICK! WHO DO YOU THINK YOU ARE, ANYWAY?
NOW HOLD ON! THOSE DOGS MADE A MISTAKE! THEY WEREN'T TRYING TO KILL YOU!
WHA?! RED CAT?!!
THE ONE 'N ONLY!
YOUR TEACHER WARNED YOU NOT TO COME HERE TODAY, RIGHT?!
HALP, ASTRO! HALP!
I'VE NEVER HEARD A CAT TALK BEFORE!!
LEAVE HERE NOW, OR YOU'LL SUFFER A FAR WORSE FATE!
DON'T SCARE US LIKE THIS, MISTER... YOU'RE NOT REALLY A CAT, ARE YOU? THAT'S A MASK, RIGHT? RIGHT?!
HE'S GONE, SHIB...
HE LOOKS LIKE A CAT, BUT I BET HE'S NOT.... IT'S GOTTA BE SOMEONE WITH A MASK ON...
YEAH! 'N IF I CATCH HIM, I'LL TEAR IT OFF!
YOU GO HOME, SHIB.... I'LL FOLLOW HIM...
NO WAY I'LL LEAVE NOW, ASTRO...

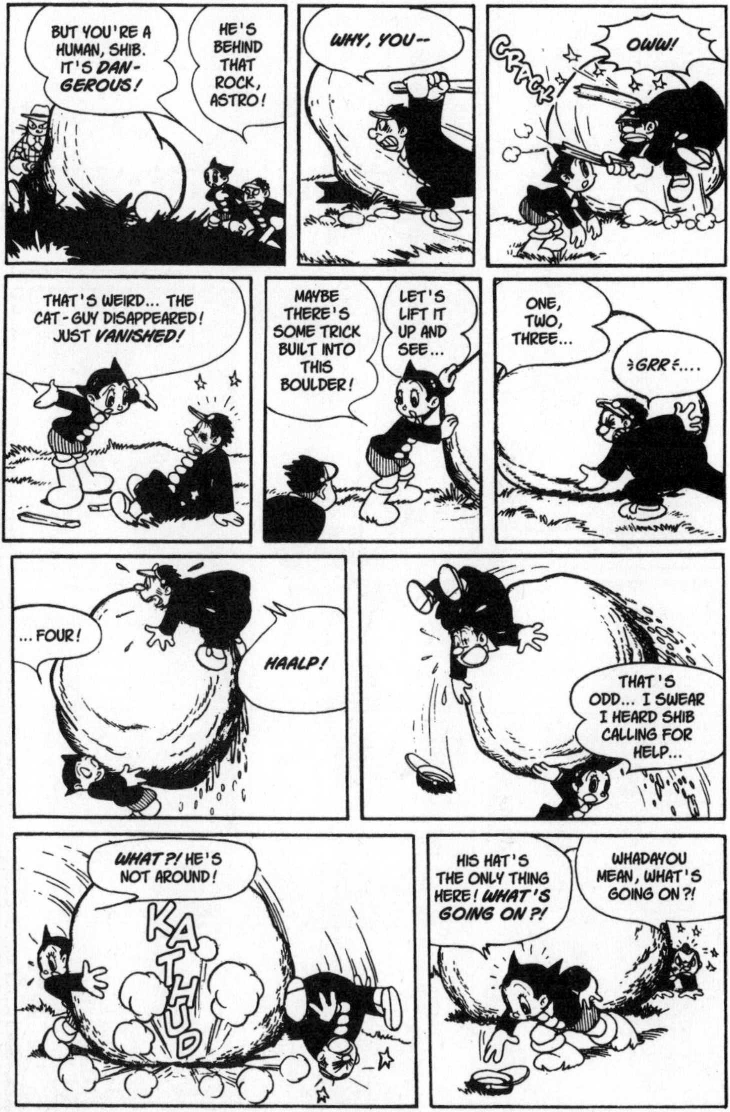
BUT YOU'RE A HUMAN, SHIB. IT'S *DANGEROUS!*
HE'S BEHIND THAT ROCK, ASTRO!
WHY, YOU--
CRACK
OWW!
THAT'S WEIRD... THE CAT-GUY DISAPPEARED! JUST *VANISHED!*
MAYBE THERE'S SOME TRICK BUILT INTO THIS BOULDER!
LET'S LIFT IT UP AND SEE...
ONE, TWO, THREE...
GRR....
... FOUR!
HAALP!
THAT'S ODD... I SWEAR I HEARD SHIB CALLING FOR HELP...
WHAT?! HE'S NOT AROUND!
KATHUD
HIS HAT'S THE ONLY THING HERE! *WHAT'S GOING ON?!*
WHADAYOU MEAN, WHAT'S GOING ON?!

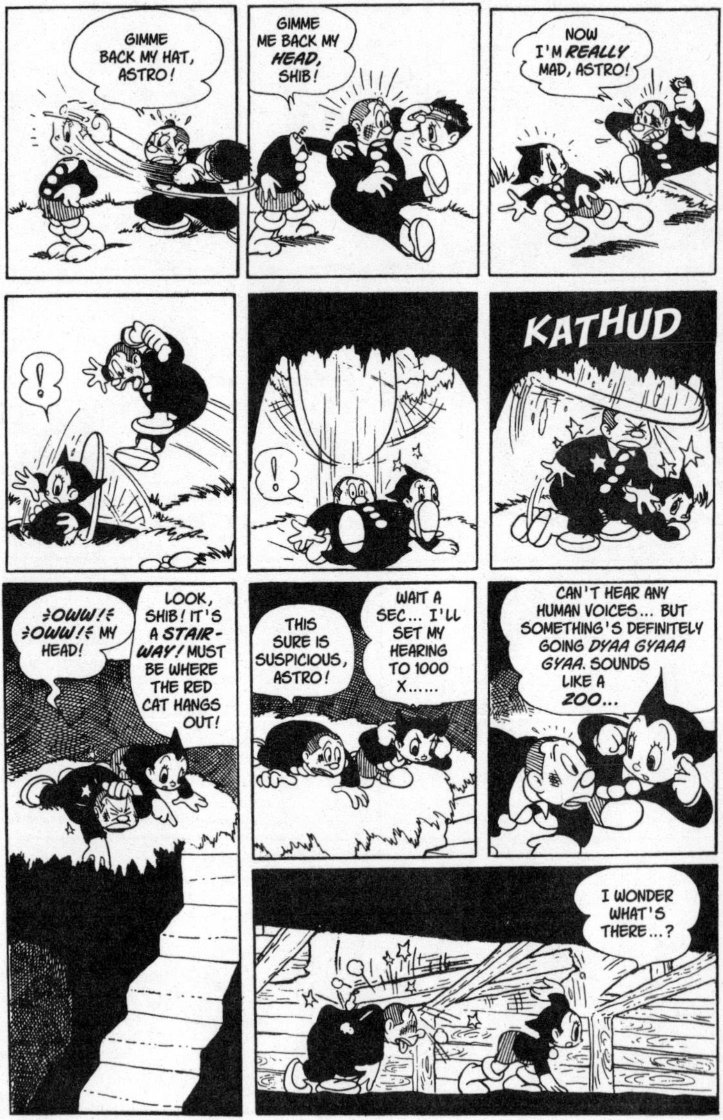
GIMME BACK MY HAT, ASTRO!
GIMME ME BACK MY HEAD, SHIB!
NOW I'M REALLY MAD, ASTRO!
!
!
KATHUD
OWW! OWW! MY HEAD!
LOOK, SHIB! IT'S A STAIRWAY! MUST BE WHERE THE RED CAT HANGS OUT!
THIS SURE IS SUSPICIOUS, ASTRO!
WAIT A SEC... I'LL SET MY HEARING TO 1000 X......
CAN'T HEAR ANY HUMAN VOICES... BUT SOMETHING'S DEFINITELY GOING DYAA GYAAA GYAA. SOUNDS LIKE A ZOO...
I WONDER WHAT'S THERE...?

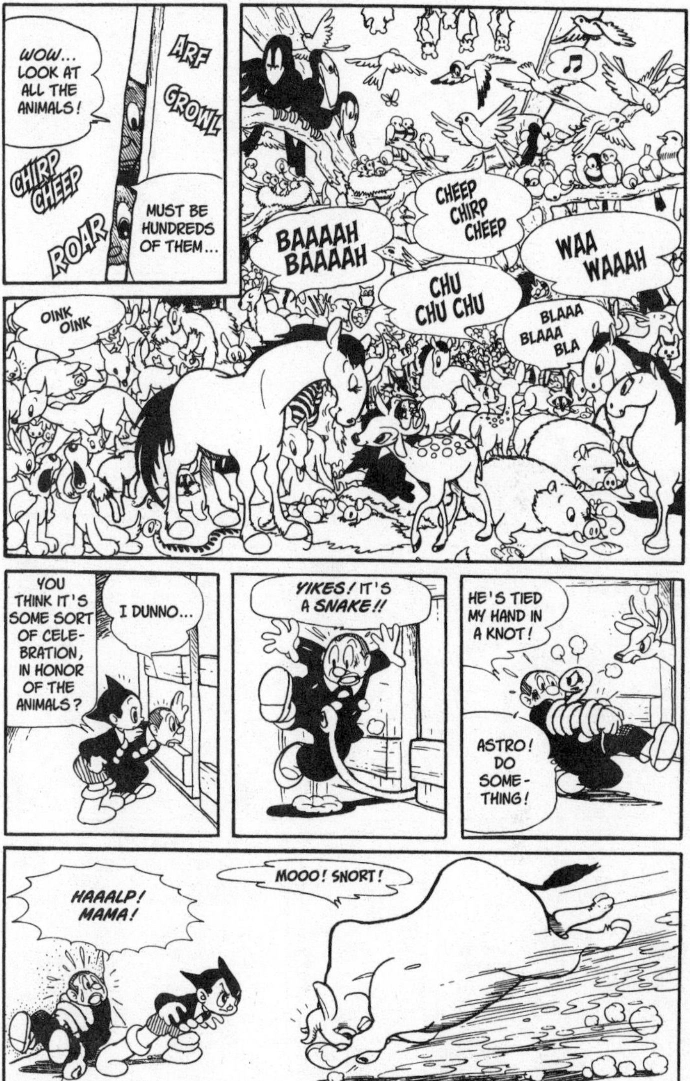
WOW... LOOK AT ALL THE ANIMALS!
ARF
GROWL
CHIRP CHEEP
ROAR
MUST BE HUNDREDS OF THEM...
♫
CHEEP CHIRP CHEEP
BAAAAH BAAAAH
WAA WAAAH
CHU CHU CHU
OINK OINK
BLAAA BLAAA BLA
YOU THINK IT'S SOME SORT OF CELE-BRATION, IN HONOR OF THE ANIMALS?
I DUNNO...
YIKES! IT'S A SNAKE!!
HE'S TIED MY HAND IN A KNOT!
ASTRO! DO SOME-THING!
HAAALP! MAMA!
MOOO! SNORT!

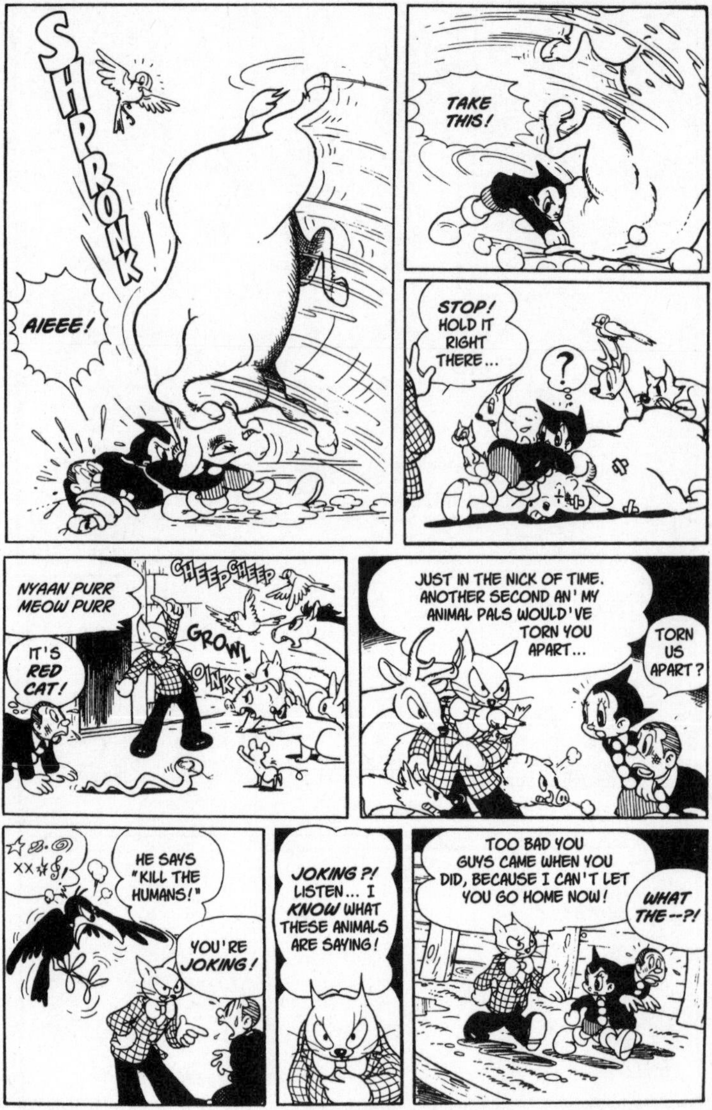
SHPRONK
AIEEE!
TAKE THIS!
STOP! HOLD IT RIGHT THERE...
?
NYAAN PURR MEOW PURR
CHEEP CHEEP
GROWL
OINK
IT'S RED CAT!
JUST IN THE NICK OF TIME. ANOTHER SECOND AN' MY ANIMAL PALS WOULD'VE TORN YOU APART...
TORN US APART?
HE SAYS "KILL THE HUMANS!"
YOU'RE JOKING!
JOKING?! LISTEN... I KNOW WHAT THESE ANIMALS ARE SAYING!
TOO BAD YOU GUYS CAME WHEN YOU DID, BECAUSE I CAN'T LET YOU GO HOME NOW!
WHAT THE--?!

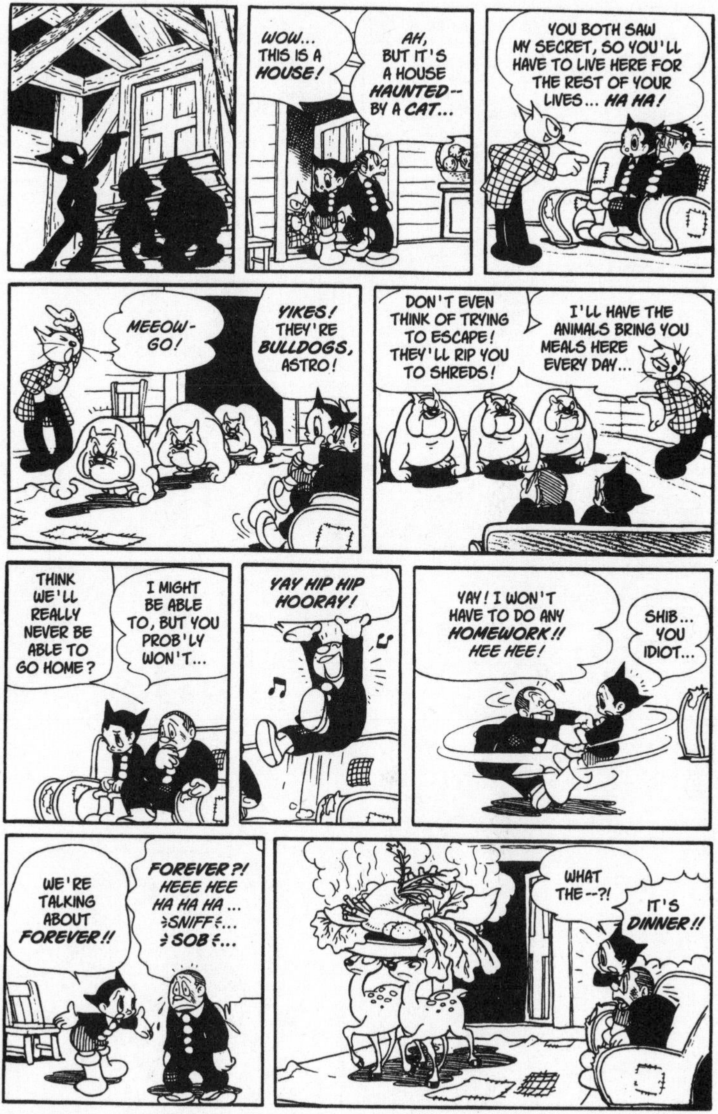
WOW... THIS IS A HOUSE!
AH, BUT IT'S A HOUSE HAUNTED-- BY A CAT...
YOU BOTH SAW MY SECRET, SO YOU'LL HAVE TO LIVE HERE FOR THE REST OF YOUR LIVES... HA HA!
MEEOW-GO!
YIKES! THEY'RE BULLDOGS, ASTRO!
DON'T EVEN THINK OF TRYING TO ESCAPE! THEY'LL RIP YOU TO SHREDS!
I'LL HAVE THE ANIMALS BRING YOU MEALS HERE EVERY DAY...
THINK WE'LL REALLY NEVER BE ABLE TO GO HOME?
I MIGHT BE ABLE TO, BUT YOU PROB'LY WON'T...
YAY HIP HIP HOORAY!
YAY! I WON'T HAVE TO DO ANY HOMEWORK!! HEE HEE!
SHIB... YOU IDIOT...
WE'RE TALKING ABOUT FOREVER!!
FOREVER?! HEEE HEE HA HA HA... ≷SNIFF≶... ≷SOB≶...
WHAT THE--?!
IT'S DINNER!!

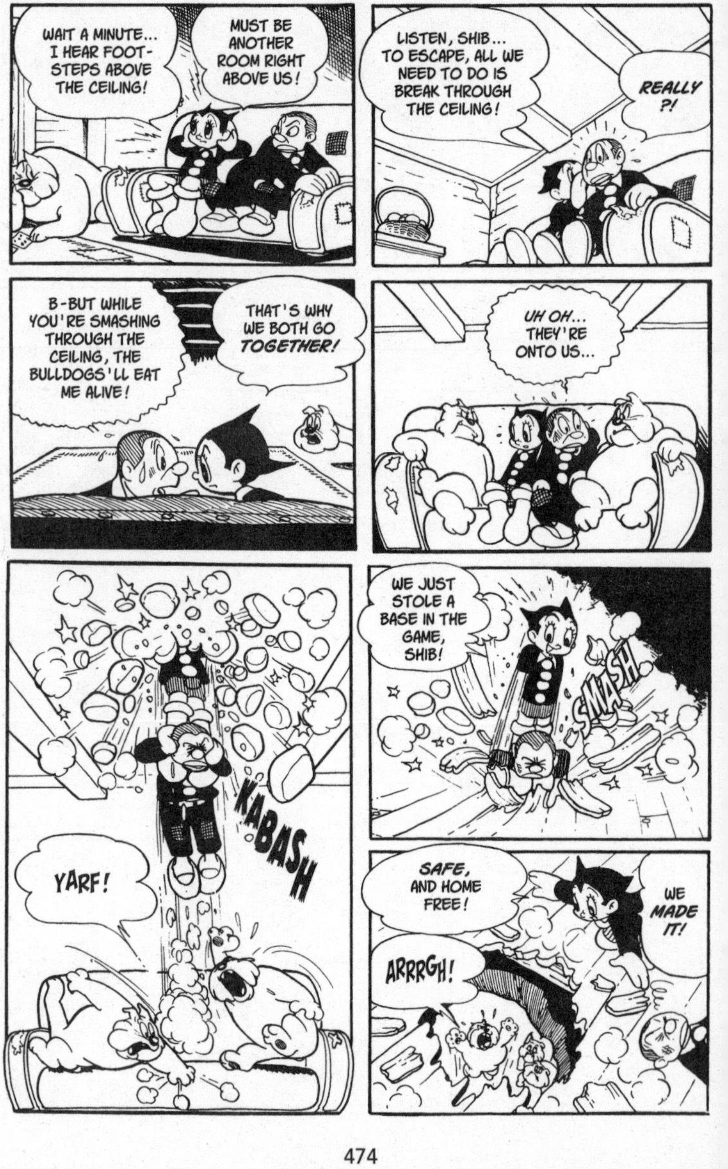
WAIT A MINUTE... I HEAR FOOT-STEPS ABOVE THE CEILING!
MUST BE ANOTHER ROOM RIGHT ABOVE US!
LISTEN, SHIB... TO ESCAPE, ALL WE NEED TO DO IS BREAK THROUGH THE CEILING!
REALLY?!
B-BUT WHILE YOU'RE SMASHING THROUGH THE CEILING, THE BULLDOGS'LL EAT ME ALIVE!
THAT'S WHY WE BOTH GO TOGETHER!
UH OH... THEY'RE ONTO US...
KABASH
YARF!
WE JUST STOLE A BASE IN THE GAME, SHIB!
SMASH
SAFE, AND HOME FREE!
WE MADE IT!
ARRRGH!

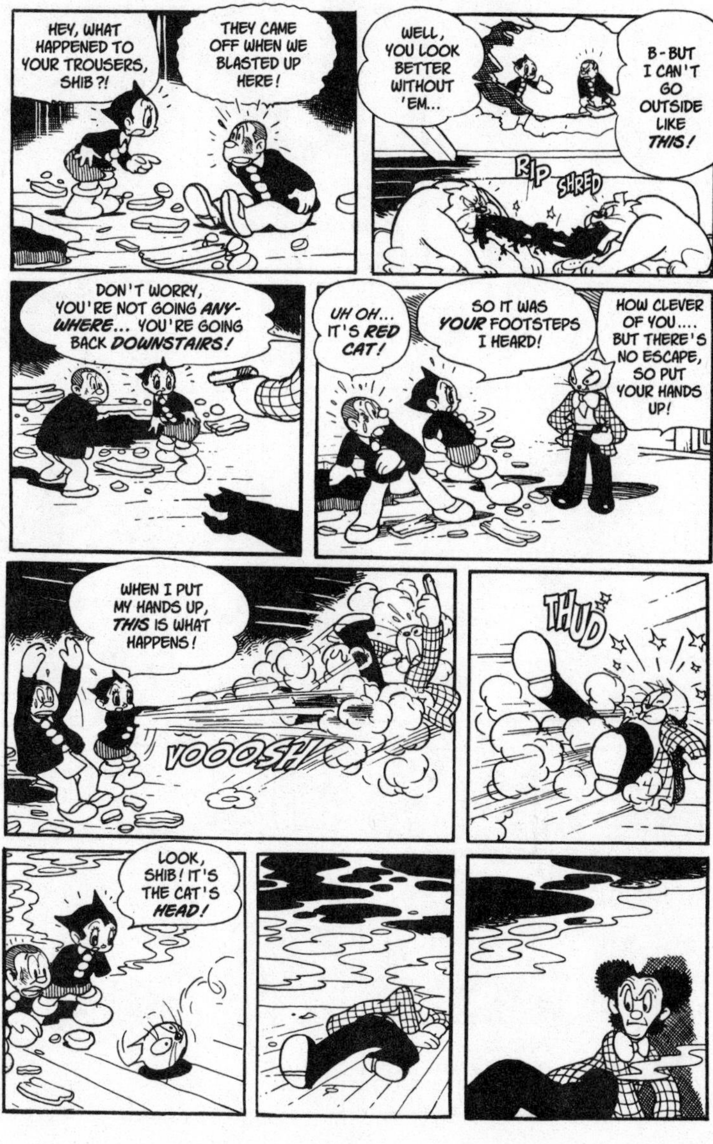
HEY, WHAT HAPPENED TO YOUR TROUSERS, SHIB ?!
THEY CAME OFF WHEN WE BLASTED UP HERE!
WELL, YOU LOOK BETTER WITHOUT 'EM...
B-BUT I CAN'T GO OUTSIDE LIKE THIS!
RIP
SHRED
DON'T WORRY, YOU'RE NOT GOING ANY-WHERE... YOU'RE GOING BACK DOWNSTAIRS!
UH OH... IT'S RED CAT!
SO IT WAS YOUR FOOTSTEPS I HEARD!
HOW CLEVER OF YOU.... BUT THERE'S NO ESCAPE, SO PUT YOUR HANDS UP!
WHEN I PUT MY HANDS UP, THIS IS WHAT HAPPENS!
VOOOSH
THUD
LOOK, SHIB! IT'S THE CAT'S HEAD!

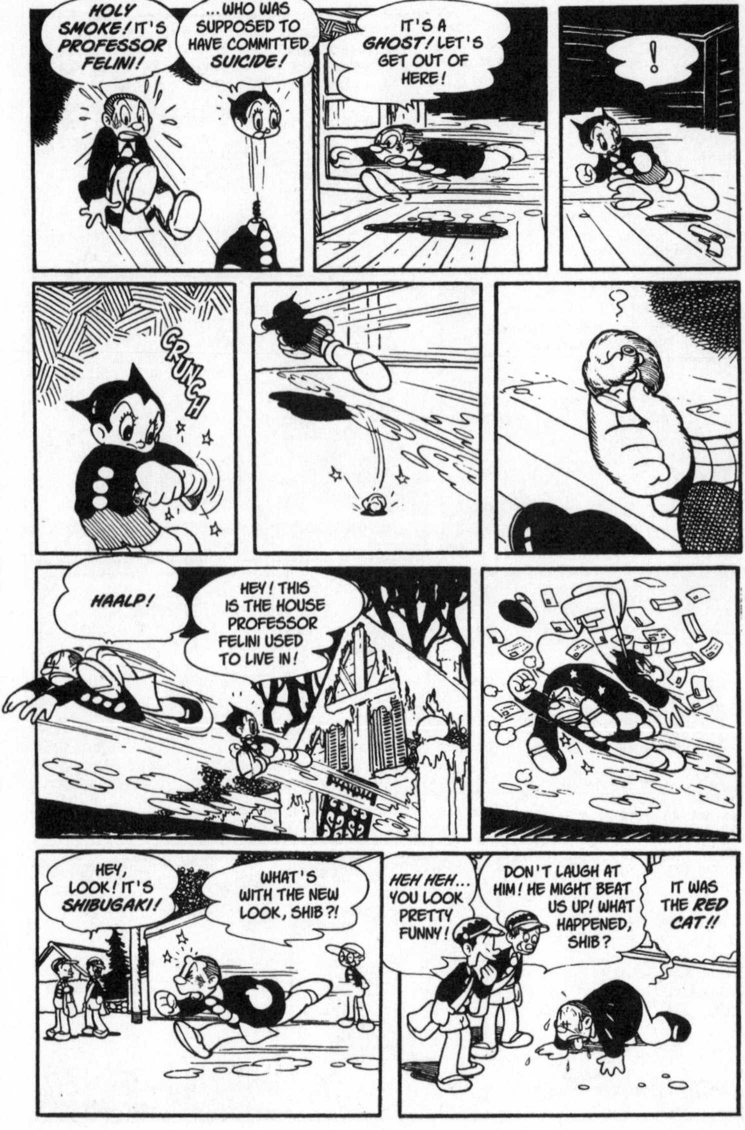
HOLY SMOKE! IT'S PROFESSOR FELINI!
...WHO WAS SUPPOSED TO HAVE COMMITTED SUICIDE!
IT'S A GHOST! LET'S GET OUT OF HERE!
!
CRUNCH
?
HAALP!
HEY! THIS IS THE HOUSE PROFESSOR FELINI USED TO LIVE IN!
HEY, LOOK! IT'S SHIBUGAKI!
WHAT'S WITH THE NEW LOOK, SHIB?!
HEH HEH... YOU LOOK PRETTY FUNNY!
DON'T LAUGH AT HIM! HE MIGHT BEAT US UP! WHAT HAPPENED, SHIB?
IT WAS THE RED CAT!!

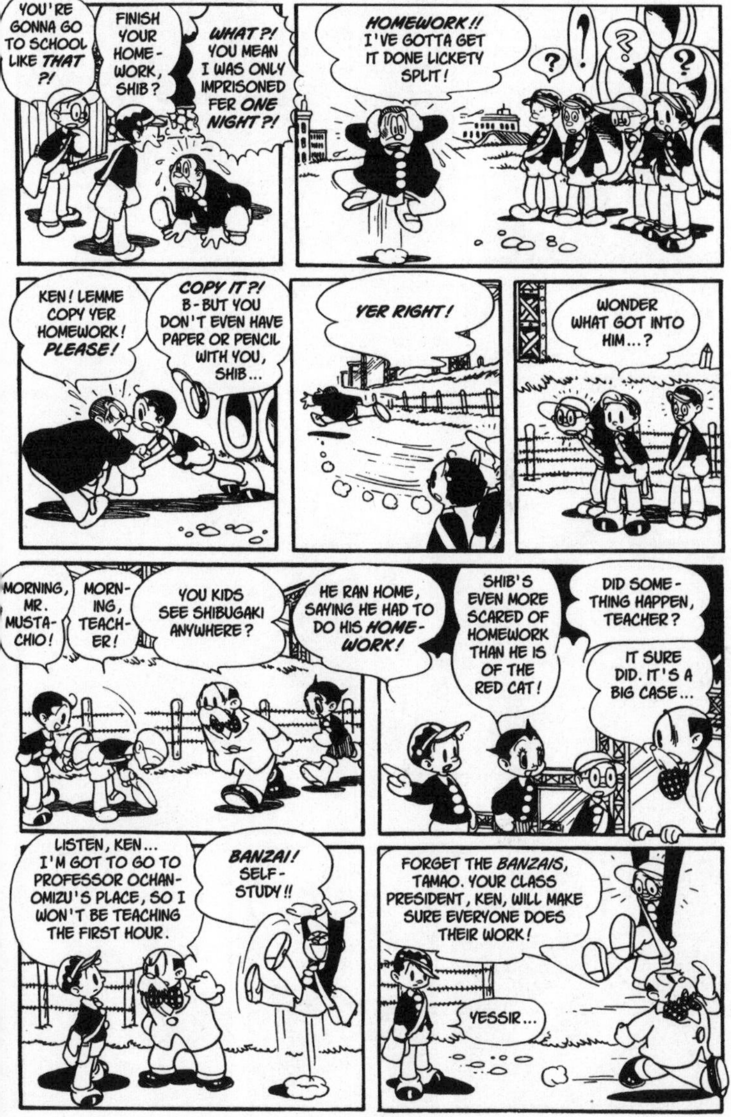

YOU'RE GONNA GO TO SCHOOL LIKE *THAT* ?!
FINISH YOUR HOME-WORK, SHIB?
WHAT?! YOU MEAN I WAS ONLY IMPRISONED FER *ONE NIGHT?!*
HOMEWORK!! I'VE GOTTA GET IT DONE LICKETY SPLIT!
?
!
?
?
KEN! LEMME COPY YER HOMEWORK! *PLEASE!*
COPY IT?! B-BUT YOU DON'T EVEN HAVE PAPER OR PENCIL WITH YOU, SHIB...
YER RIGHT!
WONDER WHAT GOT INTO HIM...?
MORNING, MR. MUSTA-CHIO!
MORN-ING, TEACH-ER!
YOU KIDS SEE SHIBUGAKI ANYWHERE?
HE RAN HOME, SAYING HE HAD TO DO HIS *HOME-WORK!*
SHIB'S EVEN MORE SCARED OF HOMEWORK THAN HE IS OF THE RED CAT!
DID SOME-THING HAPPEN, TEACHER?
IT SURE DID. IT'S A BIG CASE...
LISTEN, KEN... I'M GOT TO GO TO PROFESSOR OCHAN-OMIZU'S PLACE, SO I WON'T BE TEACHING THE FIRST HOUR.
BANZAI! SELF-STUDY!!
FORGET THE *BANZAIS*, TAMAO. YOUR CLASS PRESIDENT, KEN, WILL MAKE SURE EVERYONE DOES THEIR WORK!
YESSIR...

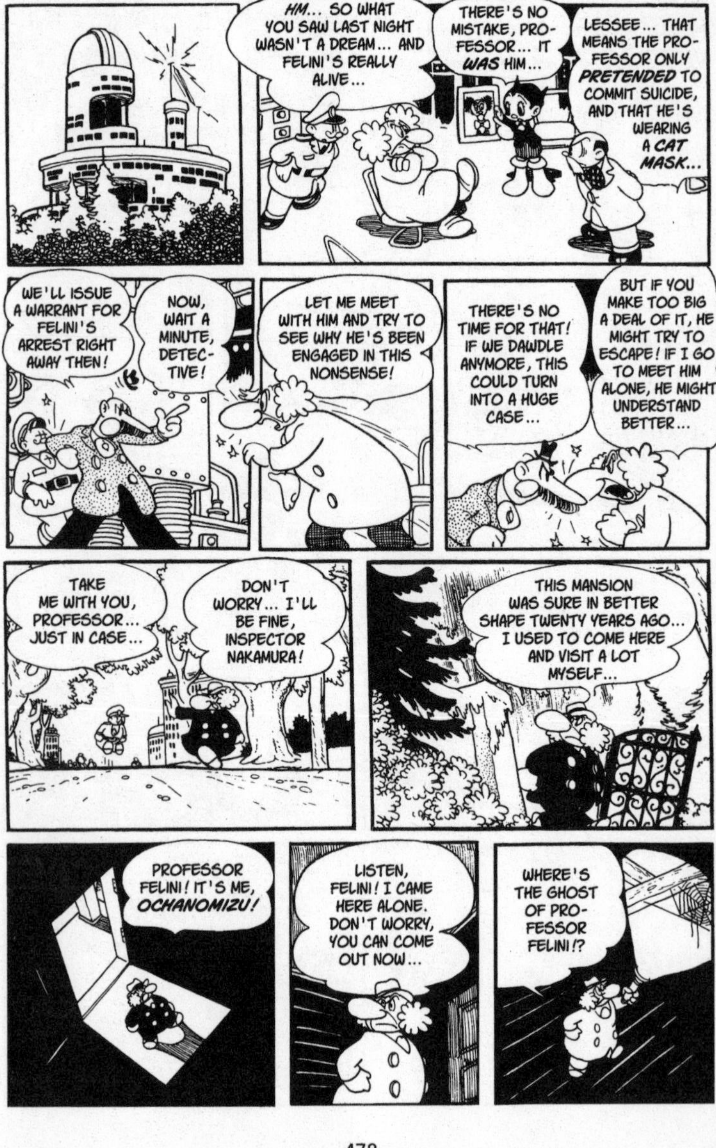
HM... SO WHAT YOU SAW LAST NIGHT WASN'T A DREAM... AND FELINI'S REALLY ALIVE...
THERE'S NO MISTAKE, PRO-FESSOR... IT WAS HIM...
LESSEE... THAT MEANS THE PRO-FESSOR ONLY PRETENDED TO COMMIT SUICIDE, AND THAT HE'S WEARING A CAT MASK...
WE'LL ISSUE A WARRANT FOR FELINI'S ARREST RIGHT AWAY THEN!
NOW, WAIT A MINUTE, DETEC-TIVE!
LET ME MEET WITH HIM AND TRY TO SEE WHY HE'S BEEN ENGAGED IN THIS NONSENSE!
THERE'S NO TIME FOR THAT! IF WE DAWDLE ANYMORE, THIS COULD TURN INTO A HUGE CASE...
BUT IF YOU MAKE TOO BIG A DEAL OF IT, HE MIGHT TRY TO ESCAPE! IF I GO TO MEET HIM ALONE, HE MIGHT UNDERSTAND BETTER...
TAKE ME WITH YOU, PROFESSOR... JUST IN CASE...
DON'T WORRY... I'LL BE FINE, INSPECTOR NAKAMURA!
THIS MANSION WAS SURE IN BETTER SHAPE TWENTY YEARS AGO... I USED TO COME HERE AND VISIT A LOT MYSELF...
PROFESSOR FELINI! IT'S ME, OCHANOMIZU!
LISTEN, FELINI! I CAME HERE ALONE. DON'T WORRY, YOU CAN COME OUT NOW...
WHERE'S THE GHOST OF PRO-FESSOR FELINI!?

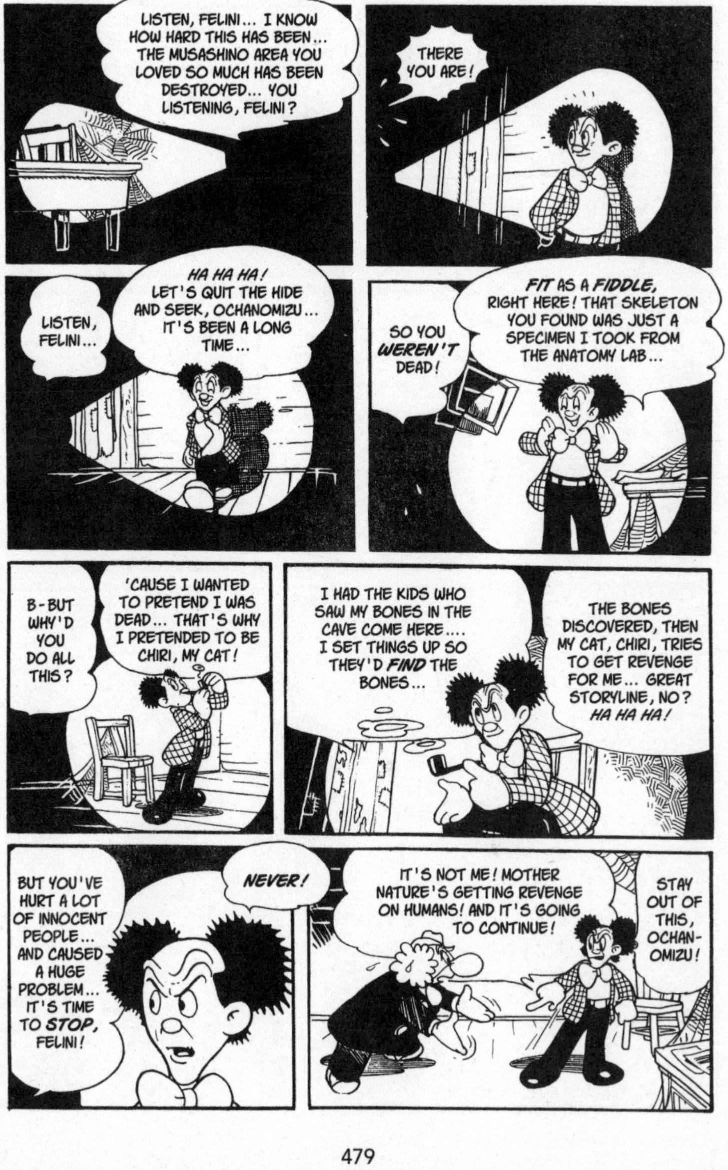
LISTEN, FELINI... I KNOW HOW HARD THIS HAS BEEN... THE MUSASHINO AREA YOU LOVED SO MUCH HAS BEEN DESTROYED... YOU LISTENING, FELINI?
THERE YOU ARE!
LISTEN, FELINI...
HA HA HA! LET'S QUIT THE HIDE AND SEEK, OCHANOMIZU... IT'S BEEN A LONG TIME...
SO YOU WEREN'T DEAD!
FIT AS A FIDDLE, RIGHT HERE! THAT SKELETON YOU FOUND WAS JUST A SPECIMEN I TOOK FROM THE ANATOMY LAB...
B-BUT WHY'D YOU DO ALL THIS?
'CAUSE I WANTED TO PRETEND I WAS DEAD... THAT'S WHY I PRETENDED TO BE CHIRI, MY CAT!
I HAD THE KIDS WHO SAW MY BONES IN THE CAVE COME HERE.... I SET THINGS UP SO THEY'D FIND THE BONES...
THE BONES DISCOVERED, THEN MY CAT, CHIRI, TRIES TO GET REVENGE FOR ME... GREAT STORYLINE, NO? HA HA HA!
BUT YOU'VE HURT A LOT OF INNOCENT PEOPLE... AND CAUSED A HUGE PROBLEM... IT'S TIME TO STOP, FELINI!
NEVER!
IT'S NOT ME! MOTHER NATURE'S GETTING REVENGE ON HUMANS! AND IT'S GOING TO CONTINUE!
STAY OUT OF THIS, OCHANOMIZU!

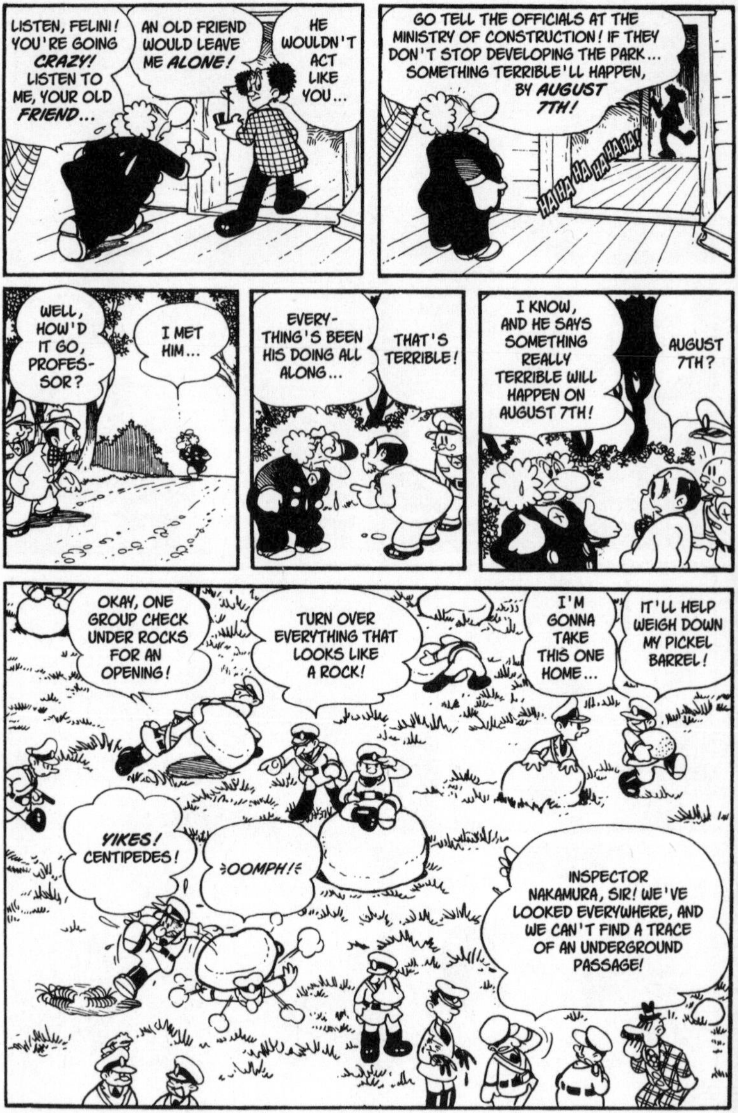
LISTEN, FELINI! YOU'RE GOING CRAZY! LISTEN TO ME, YOUR OLD FRIEND...
AN OLD FRIEND WOULD LEAVE ME ALONE!
HE WOULDN'T ACT LIKE YOU...
GO TELL THE OFFICIALS AT THE MINISTRY OF CONSTRUCTION! IF THEY DON'T STOP DEVELOPING THE PARK... SOMETHING TERRIBLE'LL HAPPEN, BY AUGUST 7TH!
HA HA HA HA HA HA!
WELL, HOW'D IT GO, PROFESSOR?
I MET HIM...
EVERYTHING'S BEEN HIS DOING ALL ALONG...
THAT'S TERRIBLE!
I KNOW, AND HE SAYS SOMETHING REALLY TERRIBLE WILL HAPPEN ON AUGUST 7TH!
AUGUST 7TH?
OKAY, ONE GROUP CHECK UNDER ROCKS FOR AN OPENING!
TURN OVER EVERYTHING THAT LOOKS LIKE A ROCK!
I'M GONNA TAKE THIS ONE HOME...
IT'LL HELP WEIGH DOWN MY PICKEL BARREL!
YIKES! CENTIPEDES!
OOMPH!
INSPECTOR NAKAMURA, SIR! WE'VE LOOKED EVERYWHERE, AND WE CAN'T FIND A TRACE OF AN UNDERGROUND PASSAGE!

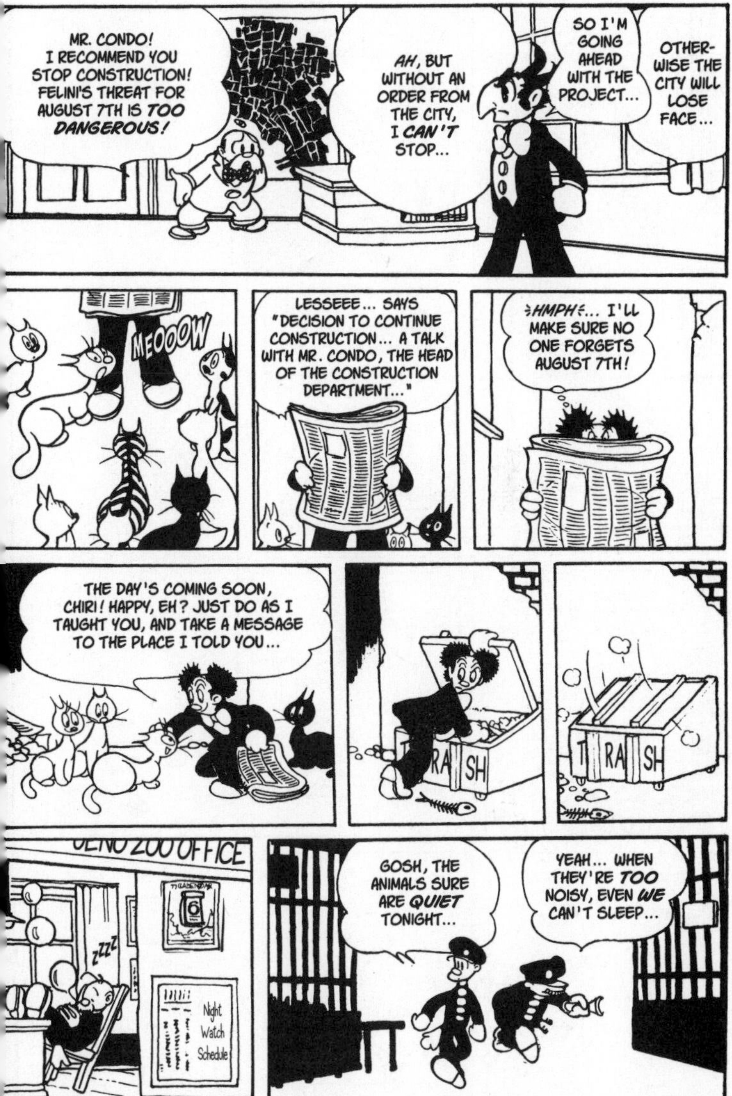
MR. CONDO! I RECOMMEND YOU STOP CONSTRUCTION! FELINI'S THREAT FOR AUGUST 7TH IS *TOO DANGEROUS!*
AH, BUT WITHOUT AN ORDER FROM THE CITY, I *CAN'T* STOP...
SO I'M GOING AHEAD WITH THE PROJECT...
OTHER-WISE THE CITY WILL LOSE FACE...
MEOOOW
LESSEEE... SAYS "DECISION TO CONTINUE CONSTRUCTION... A TALK WITH MR. CONDO, THE HEAD OF THE CONSTRUCTION DEPARTMENT..."
HMPH... I'LL MAKE SURE NO ONE FORGETS AUGUST 7TH!
THE DAY'S COMING SOON, CHIRI! HAPPY, EH? JUST DO AS I TAUGHT YOU, AND TAKE A MESSAGE TO THE PLACE I TOLD YOU...
TRASH
TRASH
UENO ZOO OFFICE
ZZZZ
Night Watch Schedule
GOSH, THE ANIMALS SURE ARE *QUIET* TONIGHT...
YEAH... WHEN THEY'RE *TOO* NOISY, EVEN *WE* CAN'T SLEEP...

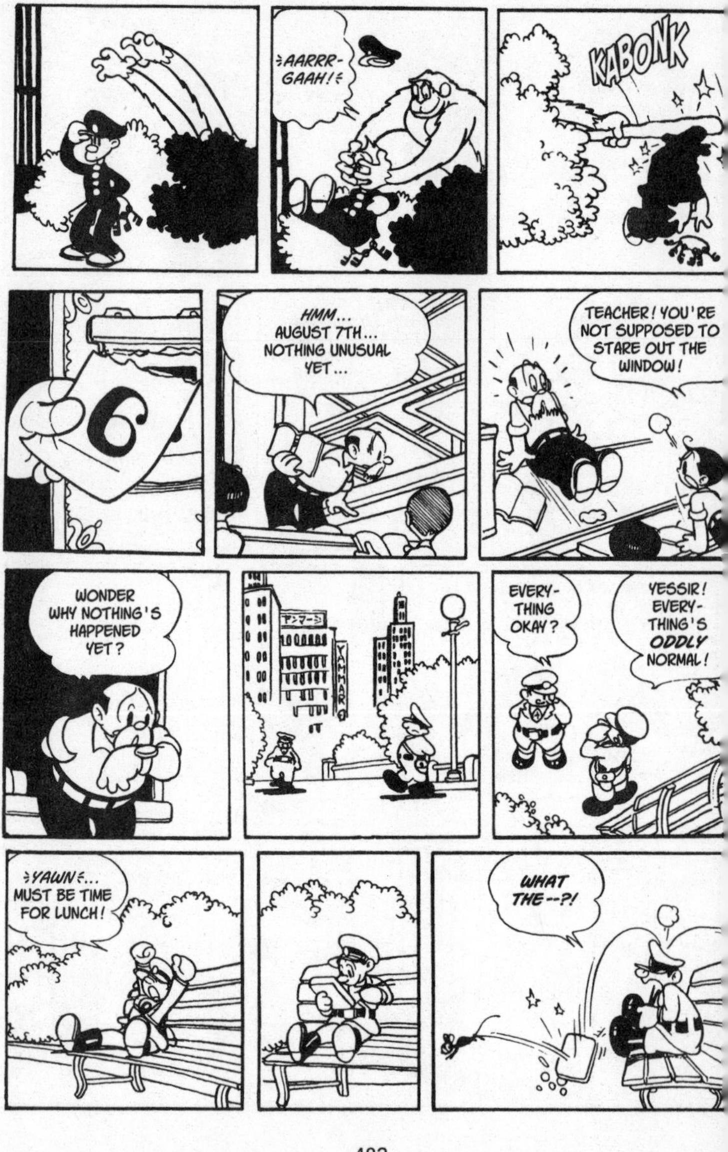
AARRR-GAAH!
KABONK
HMM... AUGUST 7TH... NOTHING UNUSUAL YET...
TEACHER! YOU'RE NOT SUPPOSED TO STARE OUT THE WINDOW!
WONDER WHY NOTHING'S HAPPENED YET?
YAMMAR
EVERY-THING OKAY?
YESSIR! EVERY-THING'S ODDLY NORMAL!
YAWN... MUST BE TIME FOR LUNCH!
WHAT THE--?!

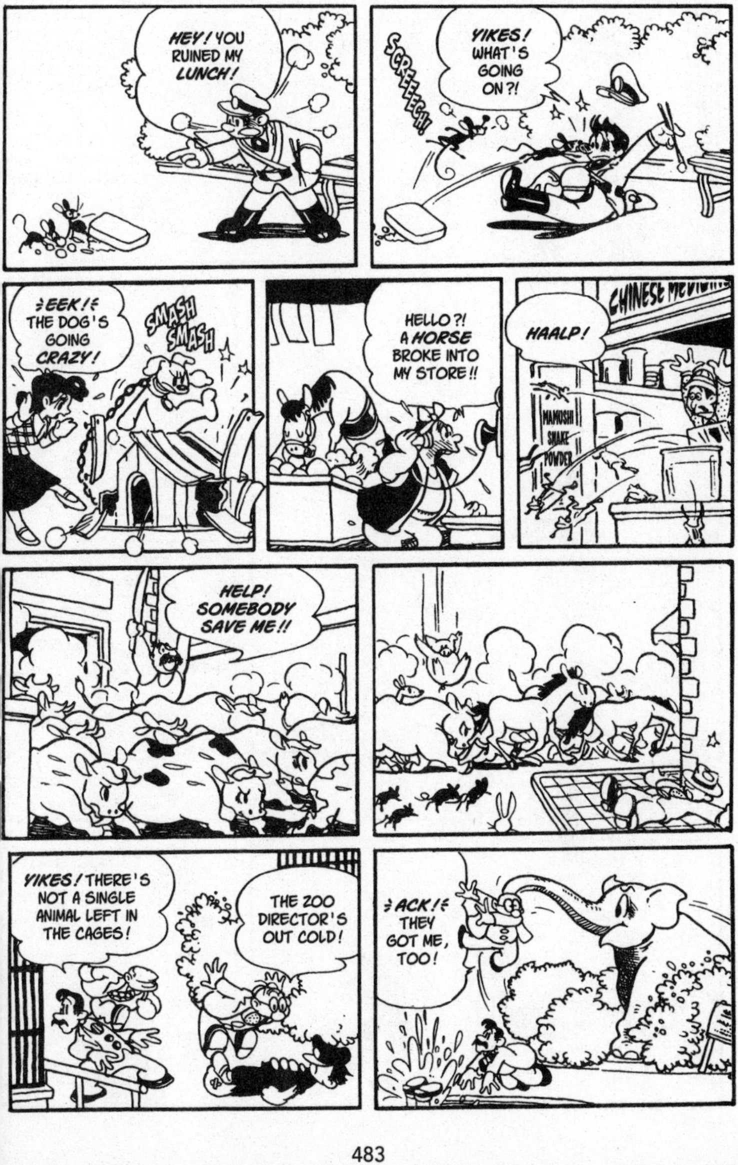
HEY! YOU RUINED MY LUNCH!
SCREEECH!
YIKES! WHAT'S GOING ON?!
EEK! THE DOG'S GOING CRAZY!
SMASH SMASH
HELLO?! A HORSE BROKE INTO MY STORE!!
CHINESE MEDICI
HAALP!
MAMUSHI SNAKE POWDER
HELP! SOMEBODY SAVE ME!!
YIKES! THERE'S NOT A SINGLE ANIMAL LEFT IN THE CAGES!
THE ZOO DIRECTOR'S OUT COLD!
ACK! THEY GOT ME, TOO!

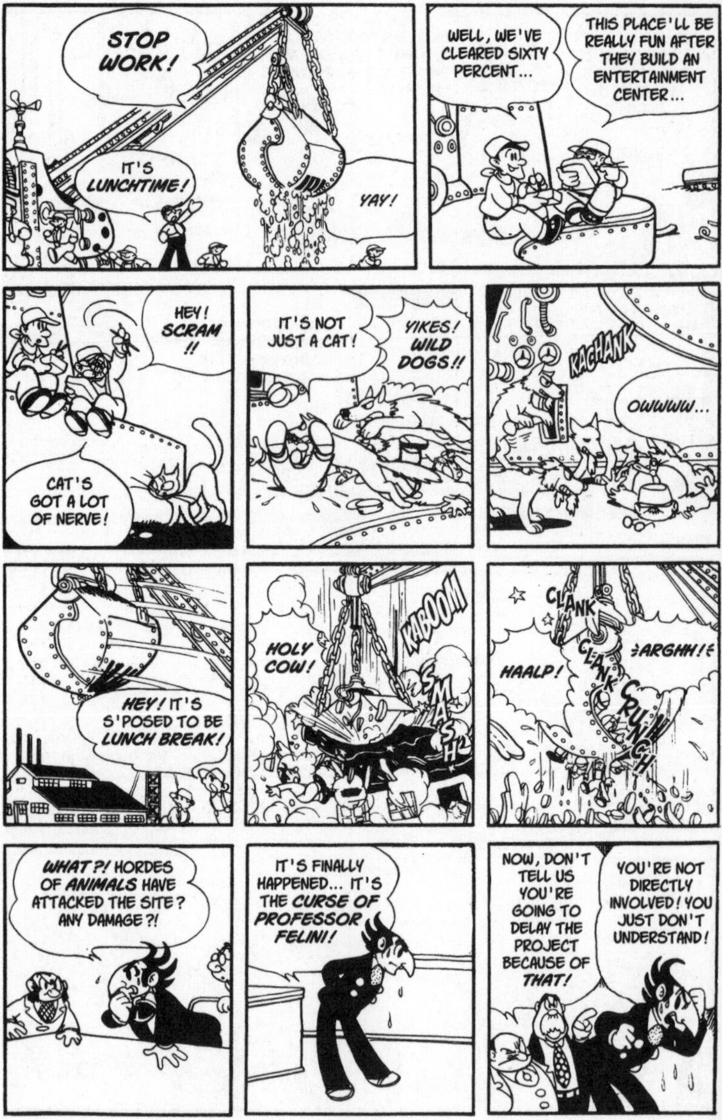
STOP WORK!
IT'S LUNCHTIME!
YAY!
WELL, WE'VE CLEARED SIXTY PERCENT...
THIS PLACE'LL BE REALLY FUN AFTER THEY BUILD AN ENTERTAINMENT CENTER...
HEY! SCRAM!!
CAT'S GOT A LOT OF NERVE!
IT'S NOT JUST A CAT!
YIKES! WILD DOGS!!
KACHANK
OWWWW...
HEY! IT'S S'POSED TO BE LUNCH BREAK!
HOLY COW!
KABOOM
SMASH
CLANK
HAALP!
CLANK
ARGHH!
CRUNCH
WHAT?! HORDES OF ANIMALS HAVE ATTACKED THE SITE? ANY DAMAGE?!
IT'S FINALLY HAPPENED... IT'S THE CURSE OF PROFESSOR FELINI!
NOW, DON'T TELL US YOU'RE GOING TO DELAY THE PROJECT BECAUSE OF THAT!
YOU'RE NOT DIRECTLY INVOLVED! YOU JUST DON'T UNDERSTAND!

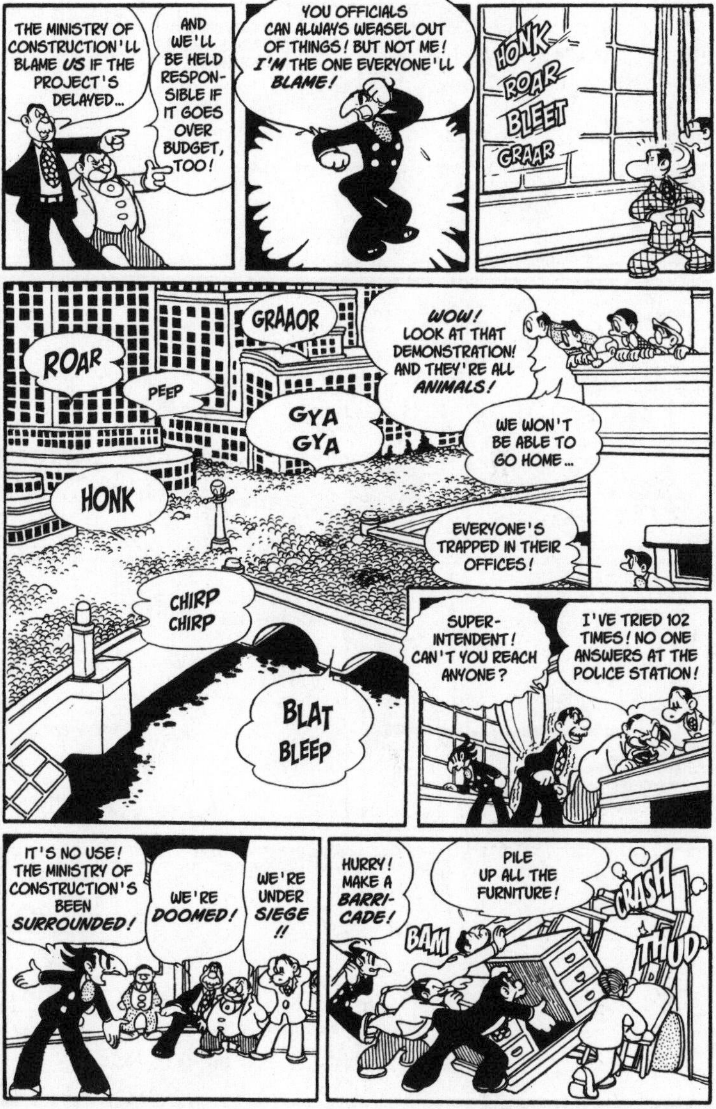

THE MINISTRY OF CONSTRUCTION'LL BLAME *US* IF THE PROJECT'S DELAYED...
AND WE'LL BE HELD RESPONSIBLE IF IT GOES OVER BUDGET, TOO!
YOU OFFICIALS CAN ALWAYS WEASEL OUT OF THINGS! BUT NOT ME! *I'M* THE ONE EVERYONE'LL *BLAME!*
HONK
ROAR
BLEET
GRAAR
ROAR
GRAAOR
PEEP
WOW! LOOK AT THAT DEMONSTRATION! AND THEY'RE ALL *ANIMALS!*
GYA GYA
WE WON'T BE ABLE TO GO HOME...
HONK
EVERYONE'S TRAPPED IN THEIR OFFICES!
CHIRP CHIRP
BLAT BLEEP
SUPER-INTENDENT! CAN'T YOU REACH ANYONE?
I'VE TRIED 102 TIMES! NO ONE ANSWERS AT THE POLICE STATION!
IT'S NO USE! THE MINISTRY OF CONSTRUCTION'S BEEN *SURROUNDED!*
WE'RE *DOOMED!*
WE'RE UNDER *SIEGE!!*
HURRY! MAKE A *BARRICADE!*
PILE UP ALL THE FURNITURE!
BAM
CRASH
THUD

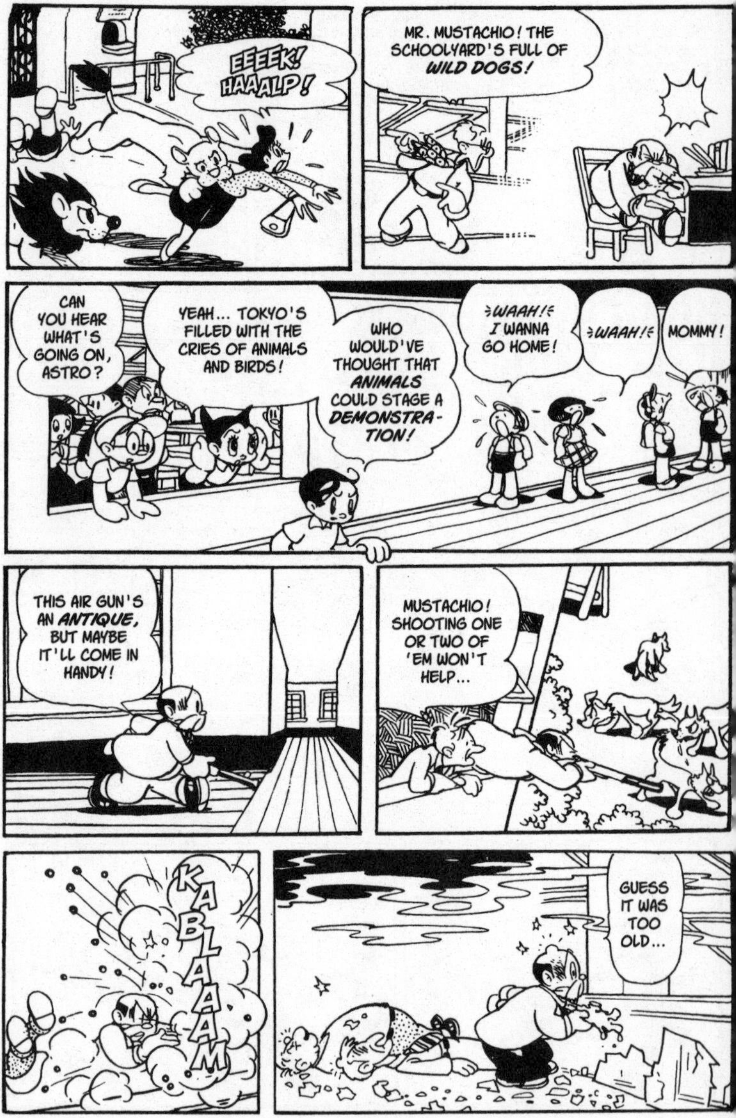
EEEEK! HAAALP!
MR. MUSTACHIO! THE SCHOOLYARD'S FULL OF WILD DOGS!
CAN YOU HEAR WHAT'S GOING ON, ASTRO?
YEAH... TOKYO'S FILLED WITH THE CRIES OF ANIMALS AND BIRDS!
WHO WOULD'VE THOUGHT THAT ANIMALS COULD STAGE A DEMONSTRATION!
WAAH! I WANNA GO HOME!
WAAH!
MOMMY!
THIS AIR GUN'S AN ANTIQUE, BUT MAYBE IT'LL COME IN HANDY!
MUSTACHIO! SHOOTING ONE OR TWO OF 'EM WON'T HELP...
KABLAAAAM
GUESS IT WAS TOO OLD...

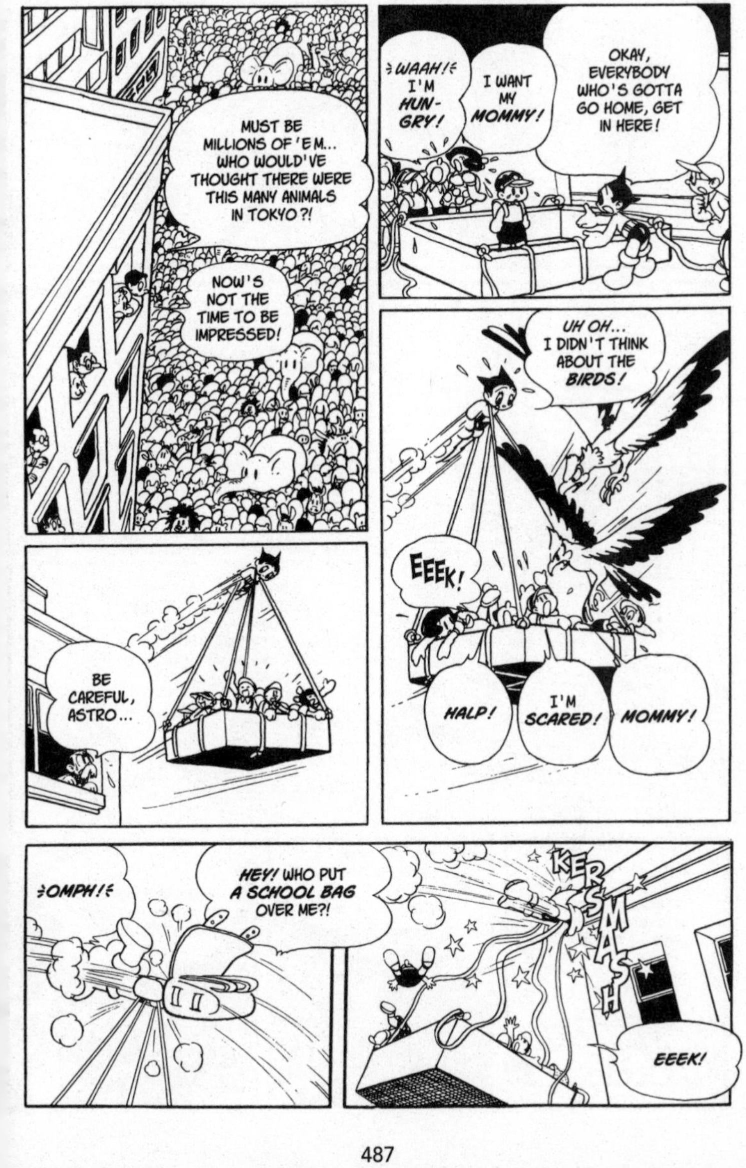
MUST BE MILLIONS OF 'EM... WHO WOULD'VE THOUGHT THERE WERE THIS MANY ANIMALS IN TOKYO?!
NOW'S NOT THE TIME TO BE IMPRESSED!
WAAH! I'M HUNGRY!
I WANT MY MOMMY!
OKAY, EVERYBODY WHO'S GOTTA GO HOME, GET IN HERE!
BE CAREFUL, ASTRO...
UH OH... I DIDN'T THINK ABOUT THE BIRDS!
EEEK!
HALP!
I'M SCARED!
MOMMY!
OMPH!
HEY! WHO PUT A SCHOOL BAG OVER ME?!
KERSMASH
EEEK!

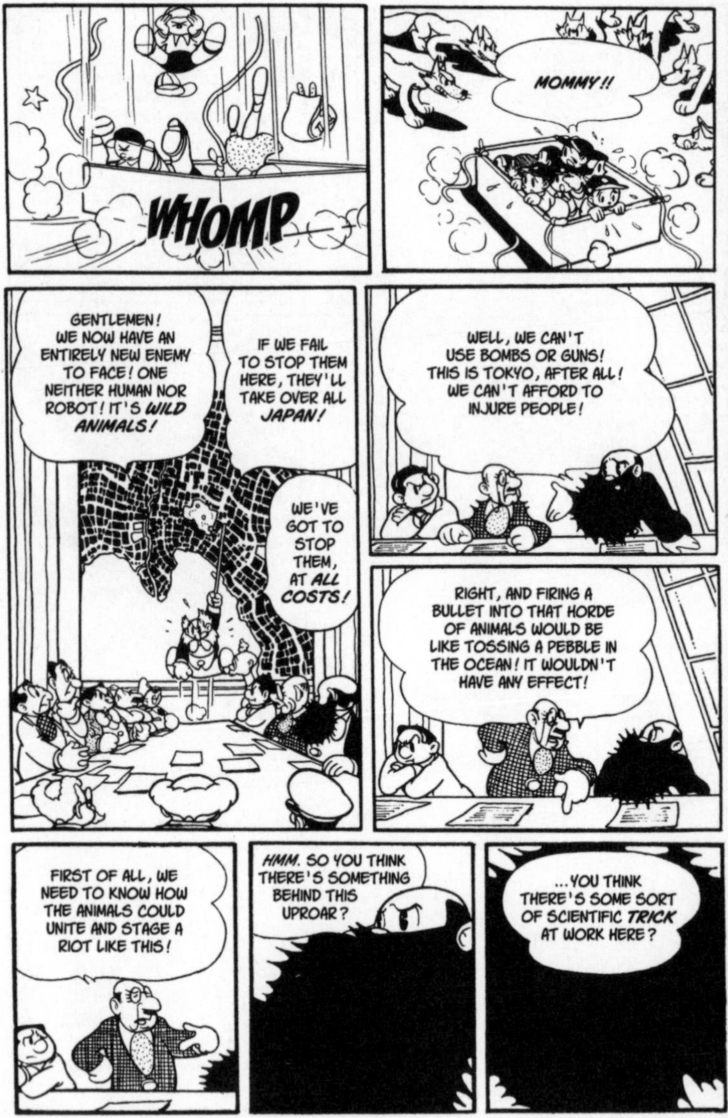
WHOMP
MOMMY!!
GENTLEMEN! WE NOW HAVE AN ENTIRELY NEW ENEMY TO FACE! ONE NEITHER HUMAN NOR ROBOT! IT'S WILD ANIMALS!
IF WE FAIL TO STOP THEM HERE, THEY'LL TAKE OVER ALL JAPAN!
WE'VE GOT TO STOP THEM, AT ALL COSTS!
WELL, WE CAN'T USE BOMBS OR GUNS! THIS IS TOKYO, AFTER ALL! WE CAN'T AFFORD TO INJURE PEOPLE!
RIGHT, AND FIRING A BULLET INTO THAT HORDE OF ANIMALS WOULD BE LIKE TOSSING A PEBBLE IN THE OCEAN! IT WOULDN'T HAVE ANY EFFECT!
FIRST OF ALL, WE NEED TO KNOW HOW THE ANIMALS COULD UNITE AND STAGE A RIOT LIKE THIS!
HMM. SO YOU THINK THERE'S SOMETHING BEHIND THIS UPROAR?
...YOU THINK THERE'S SOME SORT OF SCIENTIFIC TRICK AT WORK HERE?

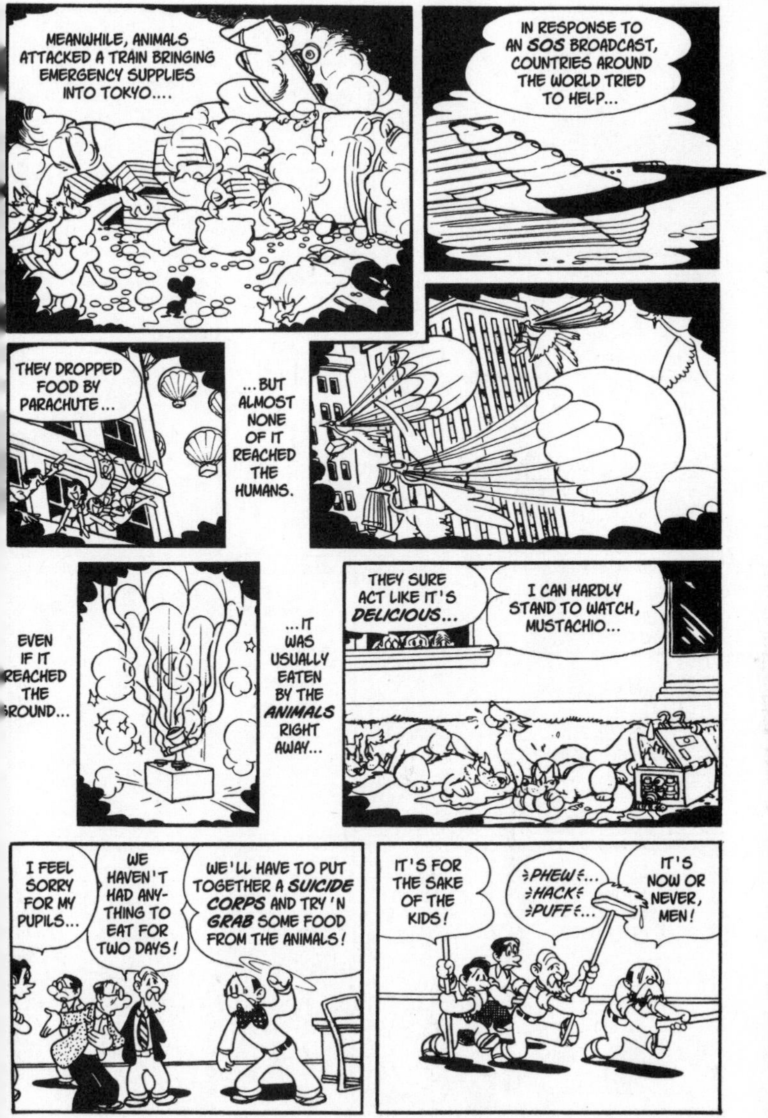

MEANWHILE, ANIMALS ATTACKED A TRAIN BRINGING EMERGENCY SUPPLIES INTO TOKYO....
IN RESPONSE TO AN SOS BROADCAST, COUNTRIES AROUND THE WORLD TRIED TO HELP...
THEY DROPPED FOOD BY PARACHUTE...
...BUT ALMOST NONE OF IT REACHED THE HUMANS.
EVEN IF IT REACHED THE GROUND...
...IT WAS USUALLY EATEN BY THE ANIMALS RIGHT AWAY...
THEY SURE ACT LIKE IT'S DELICIOUS...
I CAN HARDLY STAND TO WATCH, MUSTACHIO...
I FEEL SORRY FOR MY PUPILS...
WE HAVEN'T HAD ANY-THING TO EAT FOR TWO DAYS!
WE'LL HAVE TO PUT TOGETHER A SUICIDE CORPS AND TRY 'N GRAB SOME FOOD FROM THE ANIMALS!
IT'S FOR THE SAKE OF THE KIDS!
PHEW... HACK PUFF...
IT'S NOW OR NEVER, MEN!

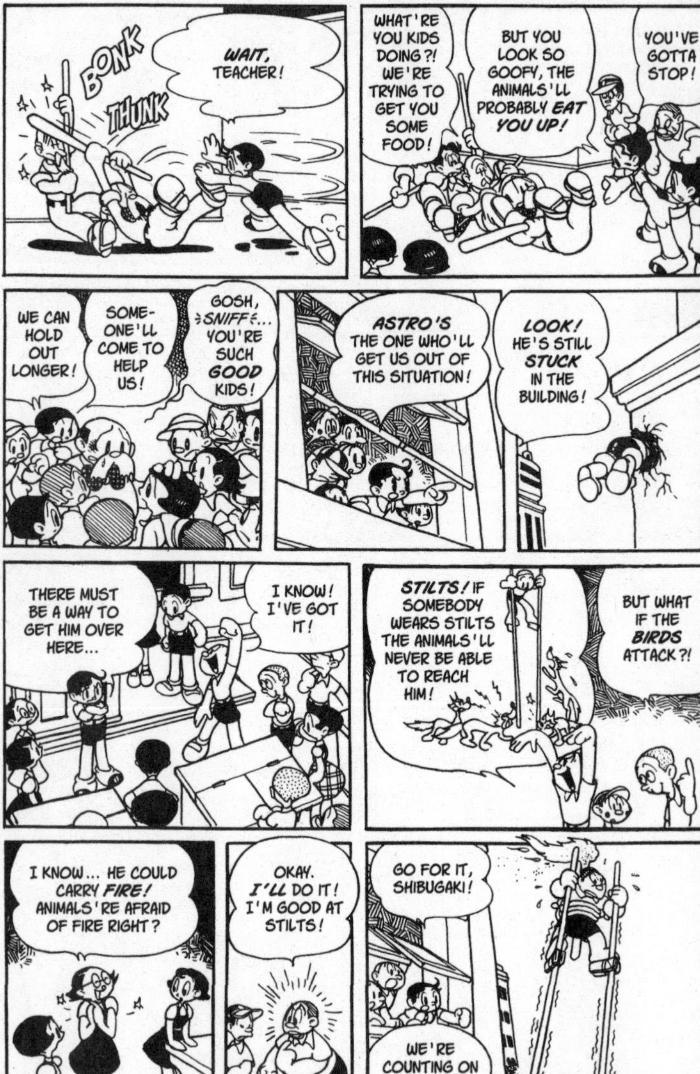
BONK
THUNK
WAIT, TEACHER!
WHAT'RE YOU KIDS DOING?! WE'RE TRYING TO GET YOU SOME FOOD!
BUT YOU LOOK SO GOOFY, THE ANIMALS'LL PROBABLY EAT YOU UP!
YOU'VE GOTTA STOP!
WE CAN HOLD OUT LONGER!
SOME-ONE'LL COME TO HELP US!
GOSH, SNIFF... YOU'RE SUCH GOOD KIDS!
ASTRO'S THE ONE WHO'LL GET US OUT OF THIS SITUATION!
LOOK! HE'S STILL STUCK IN THE BUILDING!
THERE MUST BE A WAY TO GET HIM OVER HERE...
I KNOW! I'VE GOT IT!
STILTS! IF SOMEBODY WEARS STILTS THE ANIMALS'LL NEVER BE ABLE TO REACH HIM!
BUT WHAT IF THE BIRDS ATTACK?!
I KNOW... HE COULD CARRY FIRE! ANIMALS'RE AFRAID OF FIRE RIGHT?
OKAY. I'LL DO IT! I'M GOOD AT STILTS!
GO FOR IT, SHIBUGAKI!
WE'RE COUNTING ON YOU, PAL!

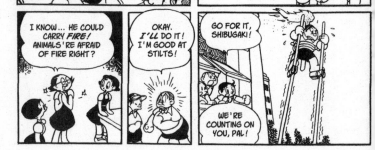

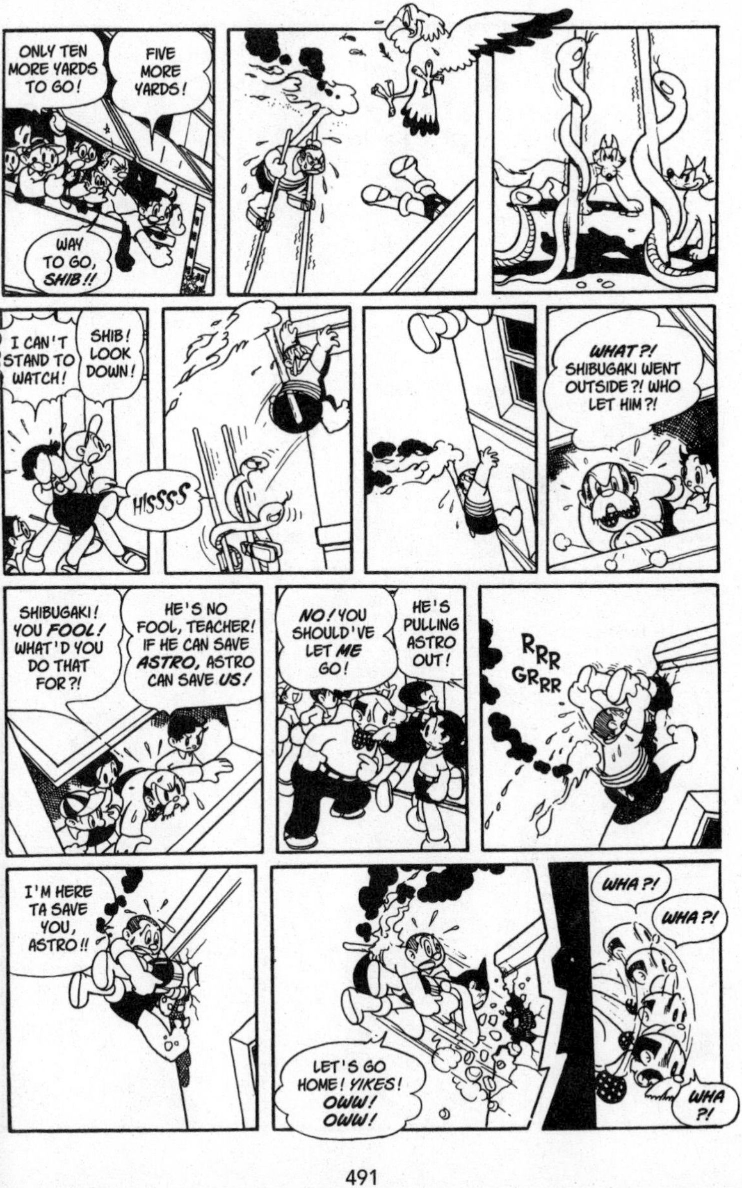
ONLY TEN MORE YARDS TO GO!
FIVE MORE YARDS!
WAY TO GO, SHIB!!
I CAN'T STAND TO WATCH!
SHIB! LOOK DOWN!
HISSSS
WHAT?! SHIBUGAKI WENT OUTSIDE?! WHO LET HIM?!
SHIBUGAKI! YOU FOOL! WHAT'D YOU DO THAT FOR?!
HE'S NO FOOL, TEACHER! IF HE CAN SAVE ASTRO, ASTRO CAN SAVE US!
NO! YOU SHOULD'VE LET ME GO!
HE'S PULLING ASTRO OUT!
RRR GRRR
I'M HERE TA SAVE YOU, ASTRO!!
LET'S GO HOME! YIKES! OWW! OWW!
WHA?!
WHA?!
WHA ?!

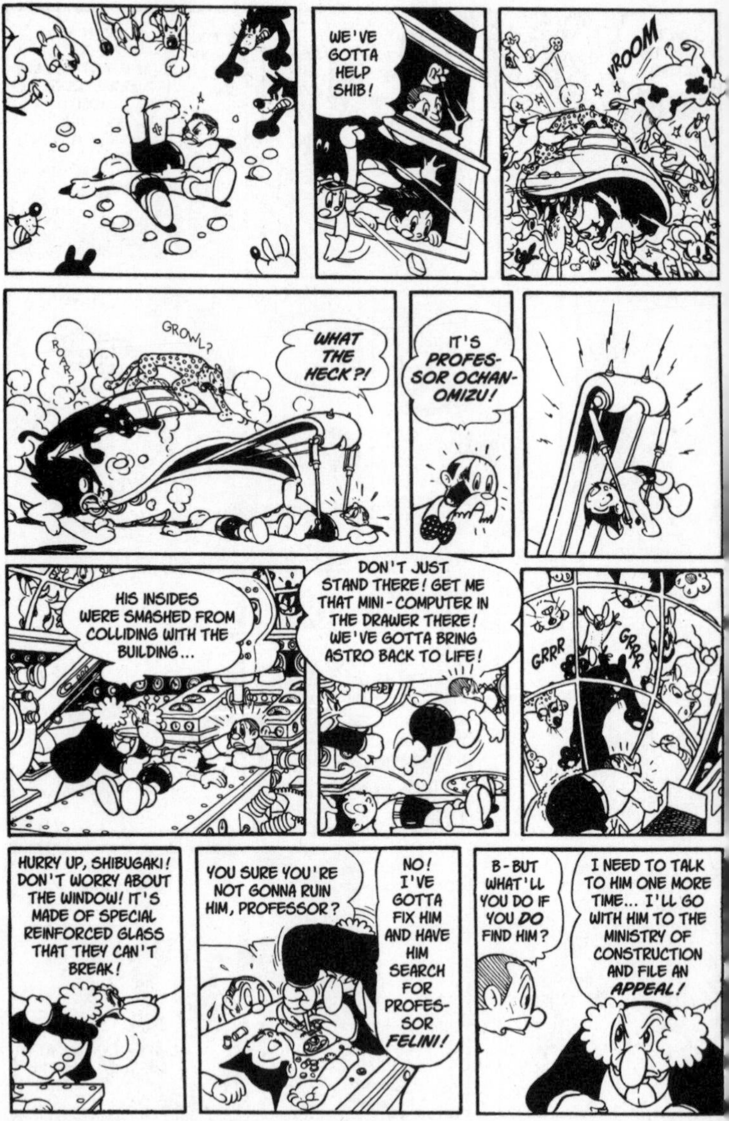
WE'VE GOTTA HELP SHIB!
VROOM
GROWL?
ROAR?
WHAT THE HECK?!
IT'S PROFESSOR OCHANOMIZU!
HIS INSIDES WERE SMASHED FROM COLLIDING WITH THE BUILDING...
DON'T JUST STAND THERE! GET ME THAT MINI-COMPUTER IN THE DRAWER THERE! WE'VE GOTTA BRING ASTRO BACK TO LIFE!
GRRR
GRRR
HURRY UP, SHIBUGAKI! DON'T WORRY ABOUT THE WINDOW! IT'S MADE OF SPECIAL REINFORCED GLASS THAT THEY CAN'T BREAK!
YOU SURE YOU'RE NOT GONNA RUIN HIM, PROFESSOR?
NO! I'VE GOTTA FIX HIM AND HAVE HIM SEARCH FOR PROFESSOR FELINI!
B-BUT WHAT'LL YOU DO IF YOU DO FIND HIM?
I NEED TO TALK TO HIM ONE MORE TIME... I'LL GO WITH HIM TO THE MINISTRY OF CONSTRUCTION AND FILE AN APPEAL!

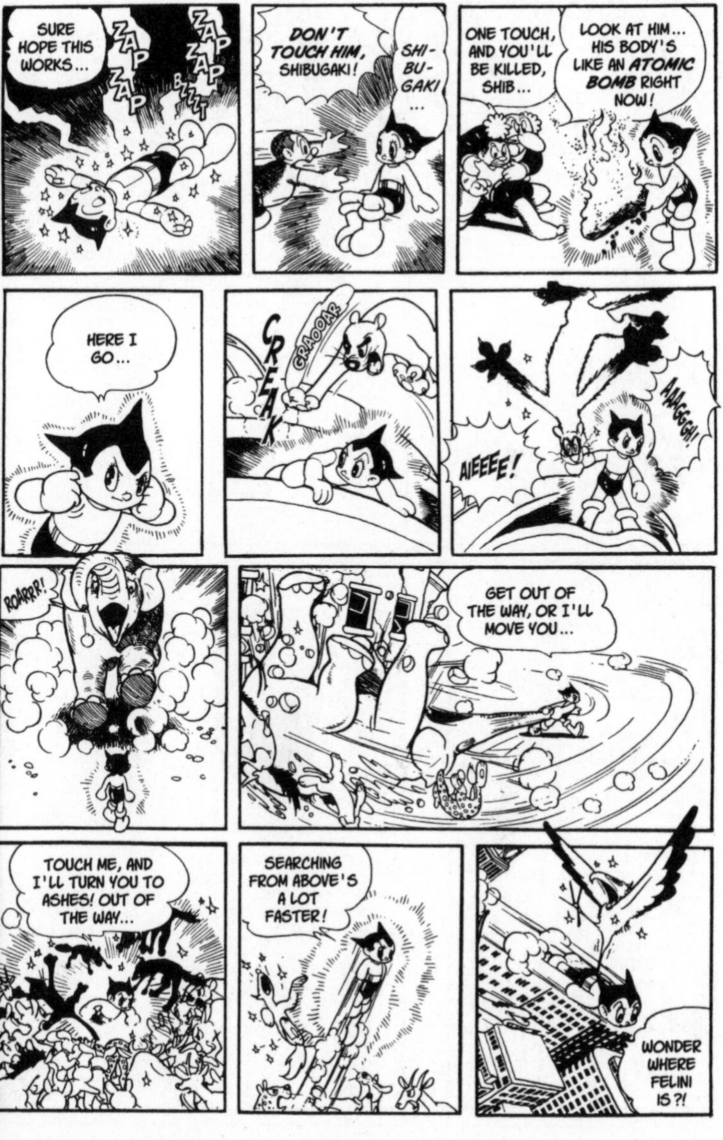
SURE HOPE THIS WORKS...
ZAP
ZAP
ZAP
ZAP
BZZZT
DON'T TOUCH HIM, SHIBUGAKI!
SHI-BU-GAKI...
ONE TOUCH, AND YOU'LL BE KILLED, SHIB...
LOOK AT HIM... HIS BODY'S LIKE AN ATOMIC BOMB RIGHT NOW!
HERE I GO...
CREAK
GRAOOAR
AAAGGGH!
AIEEEE!
ROARRR!
GET OUT OF THE WAY, OR I'LL MOVE YOU...
TOUCH ME, AND I'LL TURN YOU TO ASHES! OUT OF THE WAY...
SEARCHING FROM ABOVE'S A LOT FASTER!
WONDER WHERE FELINI IS?!

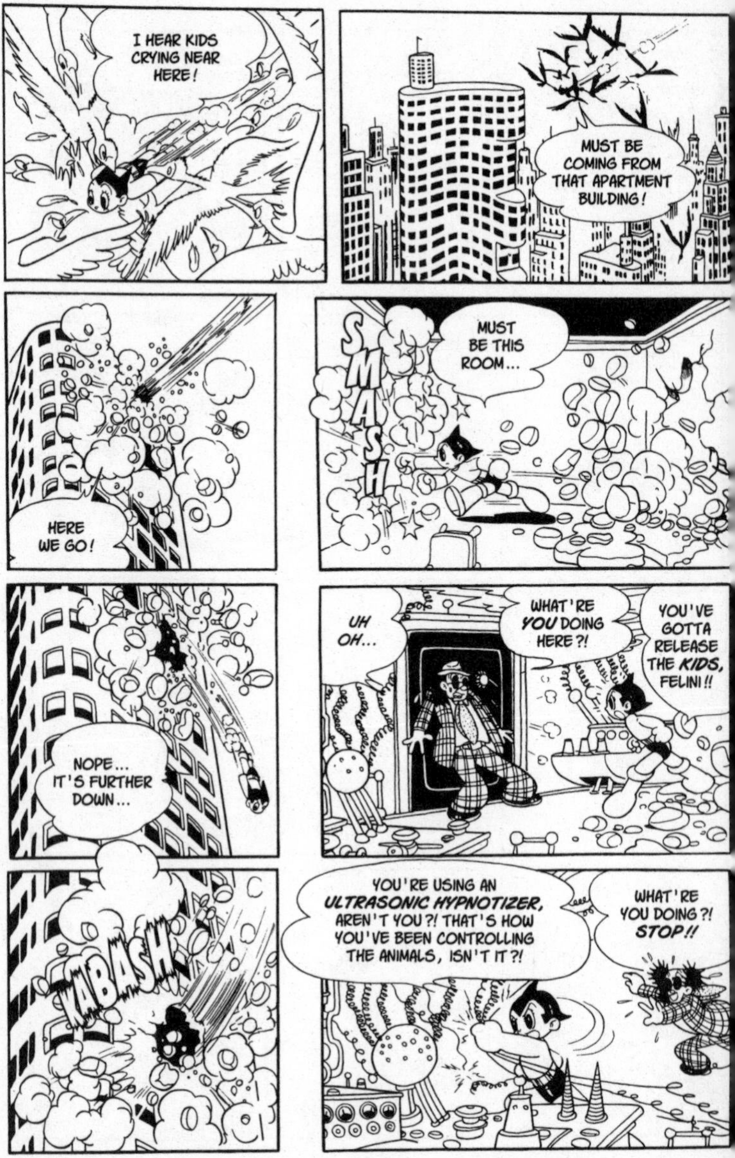
I HEAR KIDS CRYING NEAR HERE!
MUST BE COMING FROM THAT APARTMENT BUILDING!
HERE WE GO!
SMASH
MUST BE THIS ROOM...
NOPE... IT'S FURTHER DOWN...
UH OH...
WHAT'RE *YOU* DOING HERE?!
YOU'VE GOTTA RELEASE THE *KIDS*, FELINI!!
KABASH
YOU'RE USING AN ***ULTRASONIC HYPNOTIZER***, AREN'T YOU?! THAT'S HOW YOU'VE BEEN CONTROLLING THE ANIMALS, ISN'T IT?!
WHAT'RE YOU DOING?! ***STOP!!***

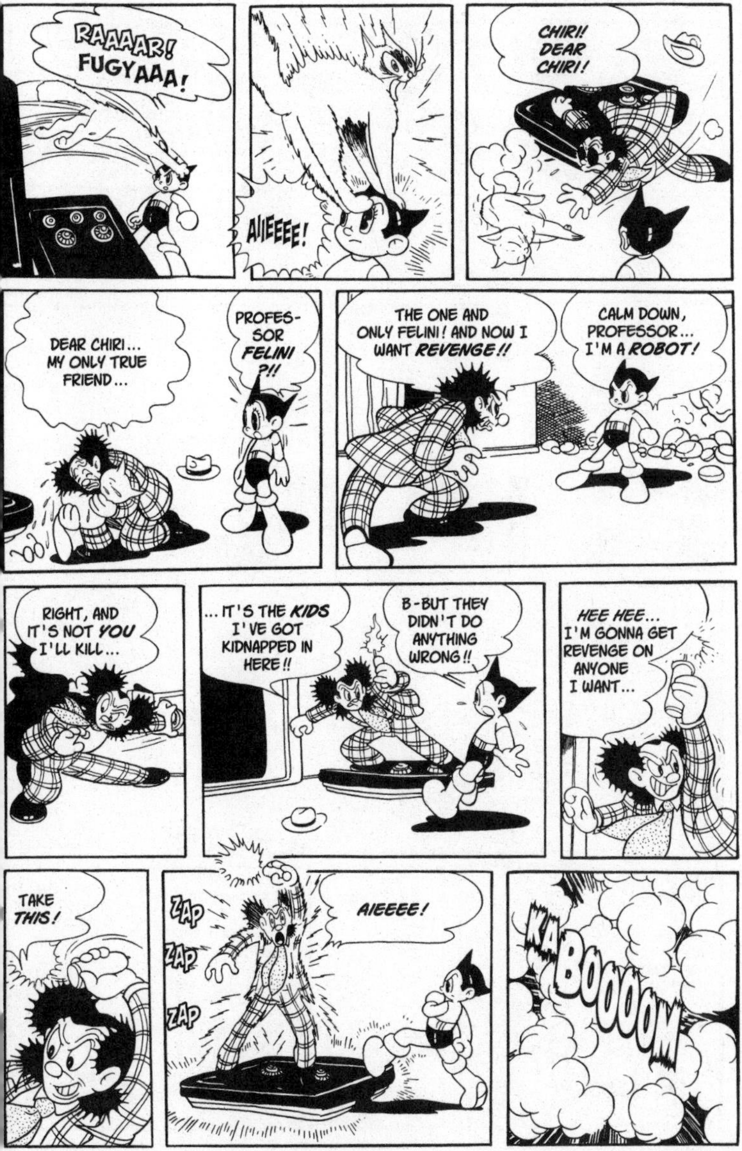

RAAAAR! FUGYAAA!
AIIEEEE!
CHIRI! DEAR CHIRI!
DEAR CHIRI... MY ONLY TRUE FRIEND...
PROFES-SOR FELINI ?!!
THE ONE AND ONLY FELINI! AND NOW I WANT REVENGE!!
CALM DOWN, PROFESSOR... I'M A ROBOT!
RIGHT, AND IT'S NOT YOU I'LL KILL...
... IT'S THE KIDS I'VE GOT KIDNAPPED IN HERE!!
B-BUT THEY DIDN'T DO ANYTHING WRONG!!
HEE HEE... I'M GONNA GET REVENGE ON ANYONE I WANT...
TAKE THIS!
ZAP
ZAP
ZAP
AIEEEE!
KABOOOOM

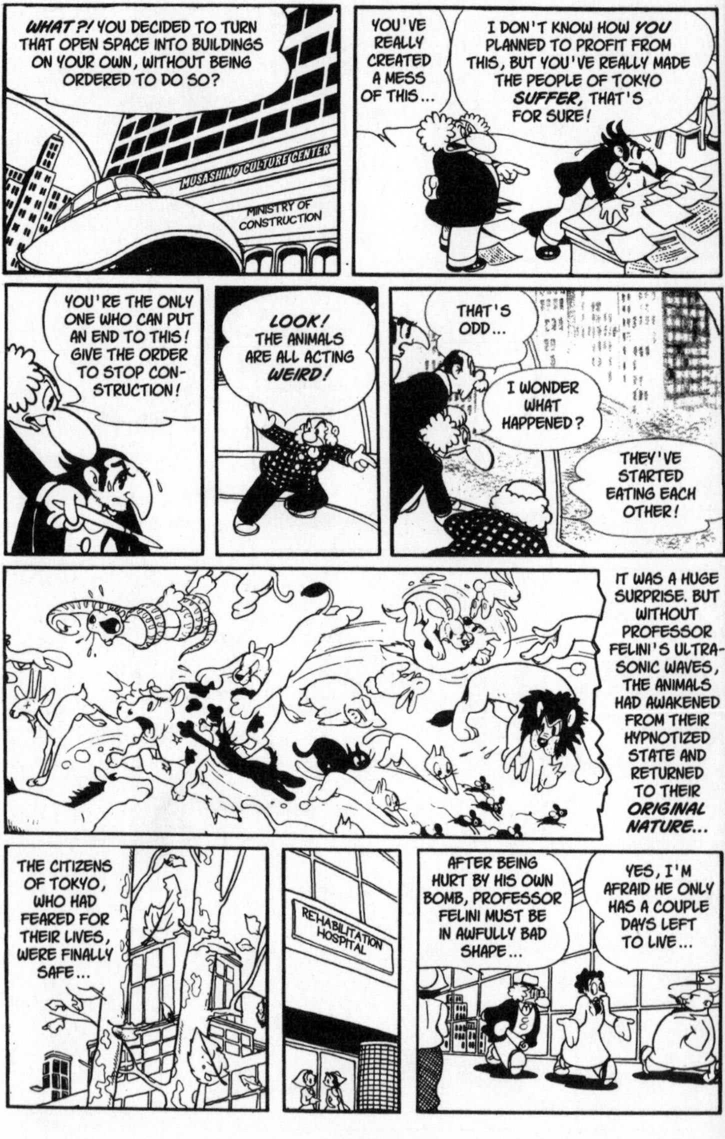
WHAT?! YOU DECIDED TO TURN THAT OPEN SPACE INTO BUILDINGS ON YOUR OWN, WITHOUT BEING ORDERED TO DO SO?
MUSASHINO CULTURE CENTER
MINISTRY OF CONSTRUCTION
YOU'VE REALLY CREATED A MESS OF THIS...
I DON'T KNOW HOW YOU PLANNED TO PROFIT FROM THIS, BUT YOU'VE REALLY MADE THE PEOPLE OF TOKYO SUFFER, THAT'S FOR SURE!
YOU'RE THE ONLY ONE WHO CAN PUT AN END TO THIS! GIVE THE ORDER TO STOP CONSTRUCTION!
LOOK! THE ANIMALS ARE ALL ACTING WEIRD!
THAT'S ODD...
I WONDER WHAT HAPPENED?
THEY'VE STARTED EATING EACH OTHER!
IT WAS A HUGE SURPRISE. BUT WITHOUT PROFESSOR FELINI'S ULTRASONIC WAVES, THE ANIMALS HAD AWAKENED FROM THEIR HYPNOTIZED STATE AND RETURNED TO THEIR ORIGINAL NATURE...
THE CITIZENS OF TOKYO, WHO HAD FEARED FOR THEIR LIVES, WERE FINALLY SAFE...
REHABILITATION HOSPITAL
AFTER BEING HURT BY HIS OWN BOMB, PROFESSOR FELINI MUST BE IN AWFULLY BAD SHAPE...
YES, I'M AFRAID HE ONLY HAS A COUPLE DAYS LEFT TO LIVE...

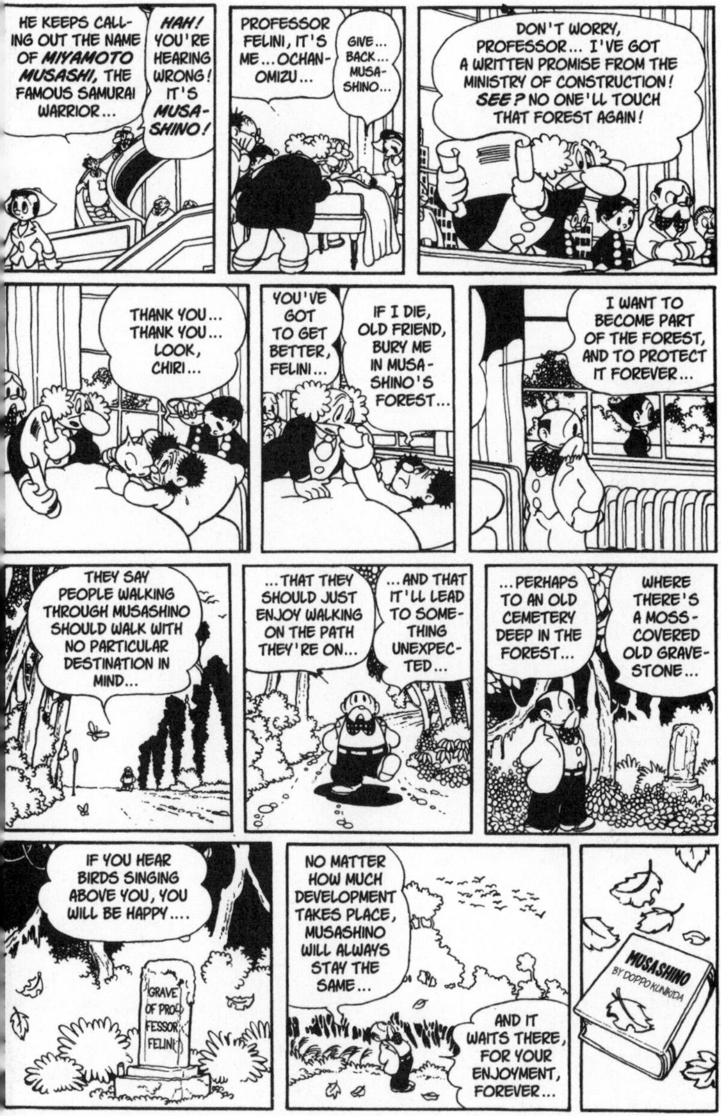
HE KEEPS CALLING OUT THE NAME OF MIYAMOTO MUSASHI, THE FAMOUS SAMURAI WARRIOR...
HAH! YOU'RE HEARING WRONG! IT'S MUSASHINO!
PROFESSOR FELINI, IT'S ME...OCHANOMIZU...
GIVE... BACK... MUSASHINO...
DON'T WORRY, PROFESSOR... I'VE GOT A WRITTEN PROMISE FROM THE MINISTRY OF CONSTRUCTION! SEE? NO ONE'LL TOUCH THAT FOREST AGAIN!
THANK YOU... THANK YOU... LOOK, CHIRI...
YOU'VE GOT TO GET BETTER, FELINI...
IF I DIE, OLD FRIEND, BURY ME IN MUSASHINO'S FOREST...
I WANT TO BECOME PART OF THE FOREST, AND TO PROTECT IT FOREVER...
THEY SAY PEOPLE WALKING THROUGH MUSASHINO SHOULD WALK WITH NO PARTICULAR DESTINATION IN MIND...
...THAT THEY SHOULD JUST ENJOY WALKING ON THE PATH THEY'RE ON...
...AND THAT IT'LL LEAD TO SOMETHING UNEXPECTED...
...PERHAPS TO AN OLD CEMETERY DEEP IN THE FOREST...
WHERE THERE'S A MOSS-COVERED OLD GRAVESTONE...
IF YOU HEAR BIRDS SINGING ABOVE YOU, YOU WILL BE HAPPY....
GRAVE OF PROFESSOR FELINI
NO MATTER HOW MUCH DEVELOPMENT TAKES PLACE, MUSASHINO WILL ALWAYS STAY THE SAME...
AND IT WAITS THERE, FOR YOUR ENJOYMENT, FOREVER...
MUSASHINO
BY DOPPO KUNIKIDA

THE MIDORO SWAMP

First serialized from August to November 1956
in *Shonen* magazine.

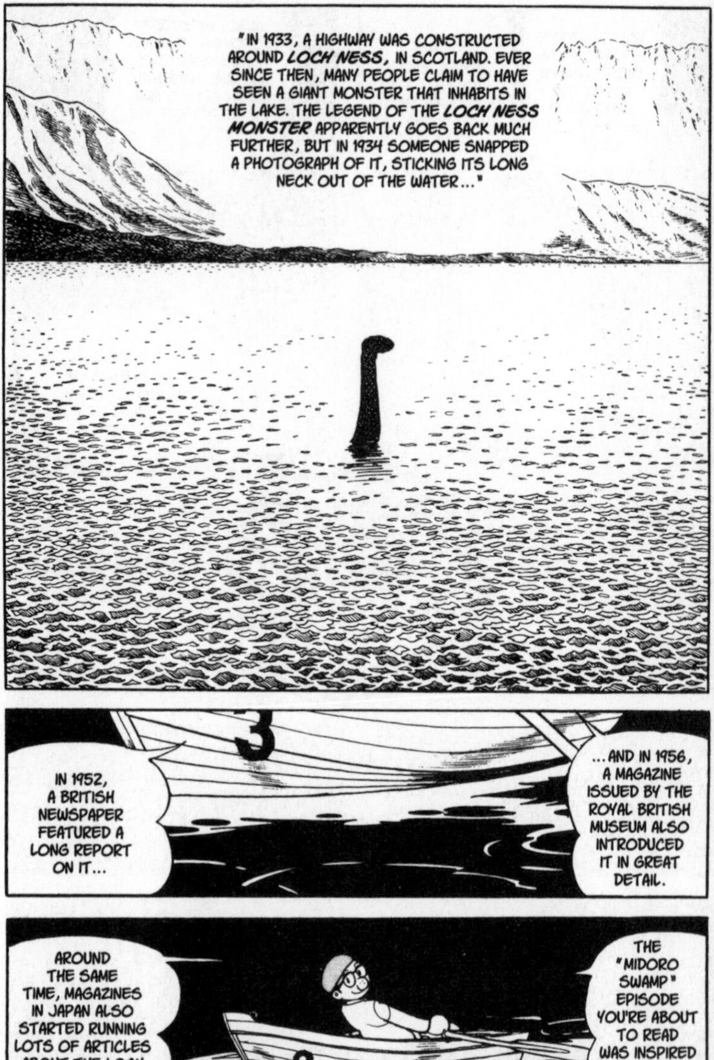
"IN 1933, A HIGHWAY WAS CONSTRUCTED AROUND LOCH NESS, IN SCOTLAND. EVER SINCE THEN, MANY PEOPLE CLAIM TO HAVE SEEN A GIANT MONSTER THAT INHABITS IN THE LAKE. THE LEGEND OF THE LOCH NESS MONSTER APPARENTLY GOES BACK MUCH FURTHER, BUT IN 1934 SOMEONE SNAPPED A PHOTOGRAPH OF IT, STICKING ITS LONG NECK OUT OF THE WATER..."
IN 1952, A BRITISH NEWSPAPER FEATURED A LONG REPORT ON IT...
...AND IN 1956, A MAGAZINE ISSUED BY THE ROYAL BRITISH MUSEUM ALSO INTRODUCED IT IN GREAT DETAIL.
AROUND THE SAME TIME, MAGAZINES IN JAPAN ALSO STARTED RUNNING LOTS OF ARTICLES ABOUT THE LOCH NESS MONSTER...
THE "MIDORO SWAMP" EPISODE YOU'RE ABOUT TO READ WAS INSPIRED BY THESE STORIES...

YOU'LL NOTICE A SCENE IN THE STORY WHERE INSPECTOR NAKAMURA IS EATING AN ICE CREAM...

I WAS INFLUENCED BY THE FACT THAT AROUND THAT TIME, SOFT ICE CREAM REALLY TOOK OFF IN JAPAN.

ALSO, MITSUTERU YOKOYAMA, FAMOUS FOR *GIGANTOR*, HAD JUST DEBUTED AS AN ARTIST, AND HE HELPED CREATE PART OF THIS STORY.

HE DREW THE SCENES OF WORKERS BEING ATTACKED BY THE LIZARDS...

ALSO, I SHOULD MENTION THAT THE FINAL SCENE IS DIFFERENT IN THE MAGAZINE AND BOOK VERSIONS.

IN THE MAGAZINE VERSION, COBALT DIES... HE DIES FIGHTING VALIANTLY, IN FACT...

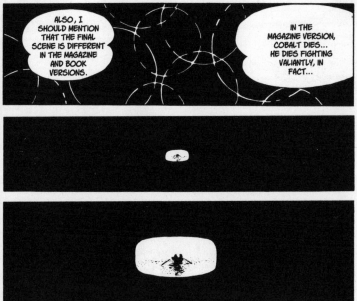

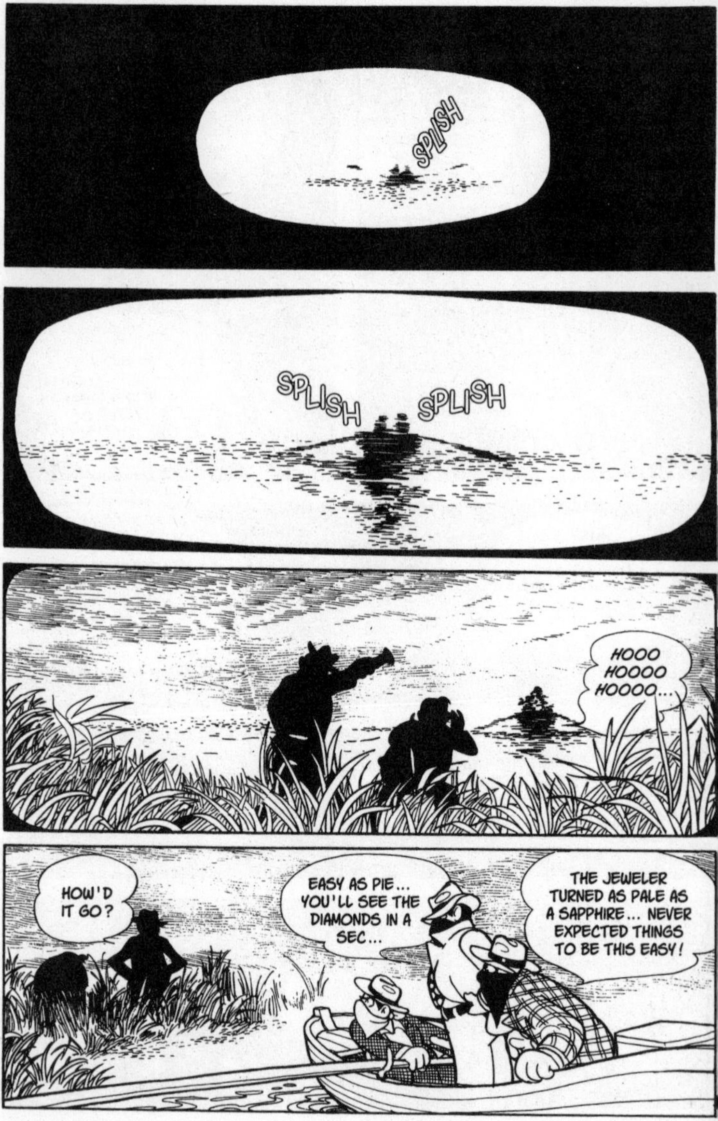
SPLISH
SPLISH
SPLISH
HOOO HOOOO HOOOO...
HOW'D IT GO?
EASY AS PIE... YOU'LL SEE THE DIAMONDS IN A SEC...
THE JEWELER TURNED AS PALE AS A SAPPHIRE... NEVER EXPECTED THINGS TO BE THIS EASY!

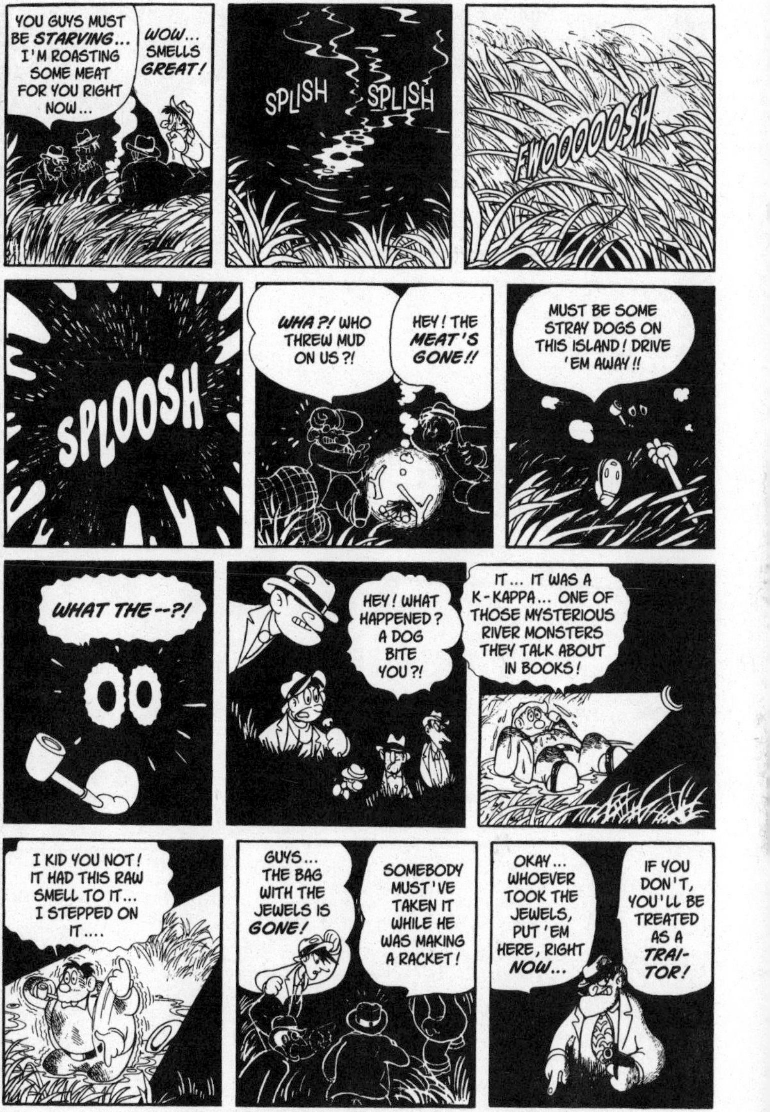
YOU GUYS MUST BE STARVING... I'M ROASTING SOME MEAT FOR YOU RIGHT NOW...
WOW... SMELLS GREAT!
SPLISH SPLISH
FWOOOOOSH
SPLOOSH
WHA?! WHO THREW MUD ON US?!
HEY! THE MEAT'S GONE!!
MUST BE SOME STRAY DOGS ON THIS ISLAND! DRIVE 'EM AWAY!!
WHAT THE--?!
HEY! WHAT HAPPENED? A DOG BITE YOU?!
IT... IT WAS A K-KAPPA... ONE OF THOSE MYSTERIOUS RIVER MONSTERS THEY TALK ABOUT IN BOOKS!
I KID YOU NOT! IT HAD THIS RAW SMELL TO IT... I STEPPED ON IT....
GUYS... THE BAG WITH THE JEWELS IS GONE!
SOMEBODY MUST'VE TAKEN IT WHILE HE WAS MAKING A RACKET!
OKAY... WHOEVER TOOK THE JEWELS, PUT 'EM HERE, RIGHT NOW...
IF YOU DON'T, YOU'LL BE TREATED AS A TRAITOR!

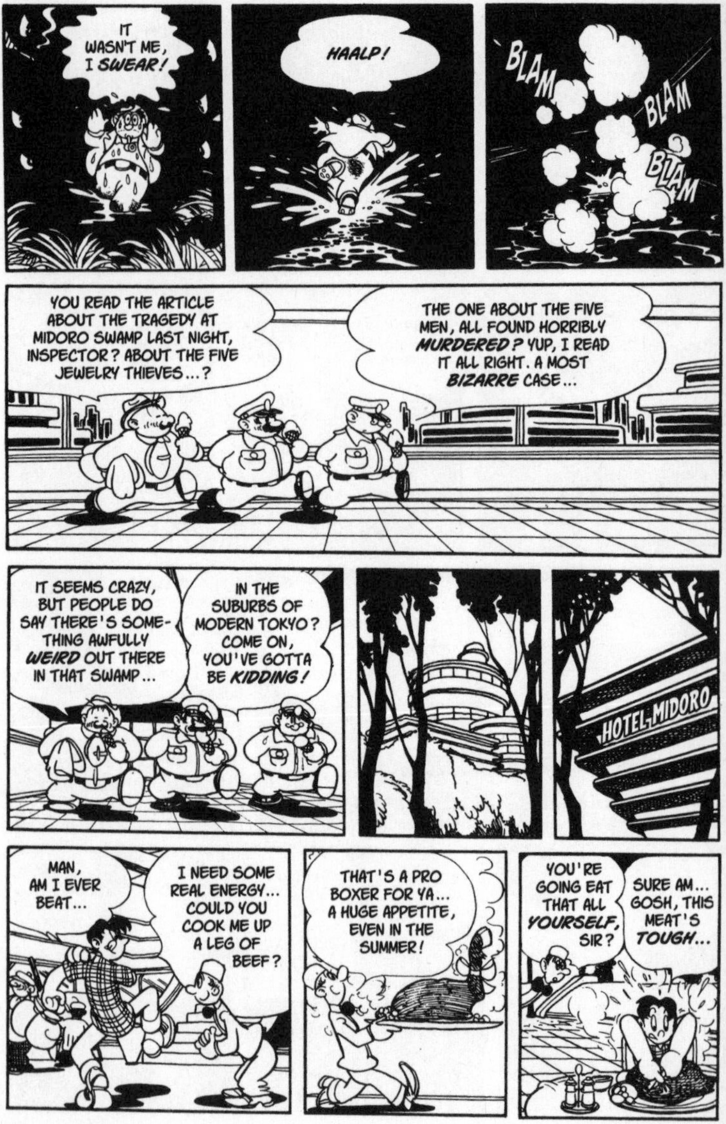
IT WASN'T ME, I SWEAR!
HAALP!
BLAM
BLAM
BLAM
YOU READ THE ARTICLE ABOUT THE TRAGEDY AT MIDORO SWAMP LAST NIGHT, INSPECTOR? ABOUT THE FIVE JEWELRY THIEVES...?
THE ONE ABOUT THE FIVE MEN, ALL FOUND HORRIBLY MURDERED? YUP, I READ IT ALL RIGHT. A MOST BIZARRE CASE...
IT SEEMS CRAZY, BUT PEOPLE DO SAY THERE'S SOMETHING AWFULLY WEIRD OUT THERE IN THAT SWAMP...
IN THE SUBURBS OF MODERN TOKYO? COME ON, YOU'VE GOTTA BE KIDDING!
HOTEL MIDORO
MAN, AM I EVER BEAT...
I NEED SOME REAL ENERGY... COULD YOU COOK ME UP A LEG OF BEEF?
THAT'S A PRO BOXER FOR YA... A HUGE APPETITE, EVEN IN THE SUMMER!
YOU'RE GOING EAT THAT ALL YOURSELF, SIR?
SURE AM... GOSH, THIS MEAT'S TOUGH...

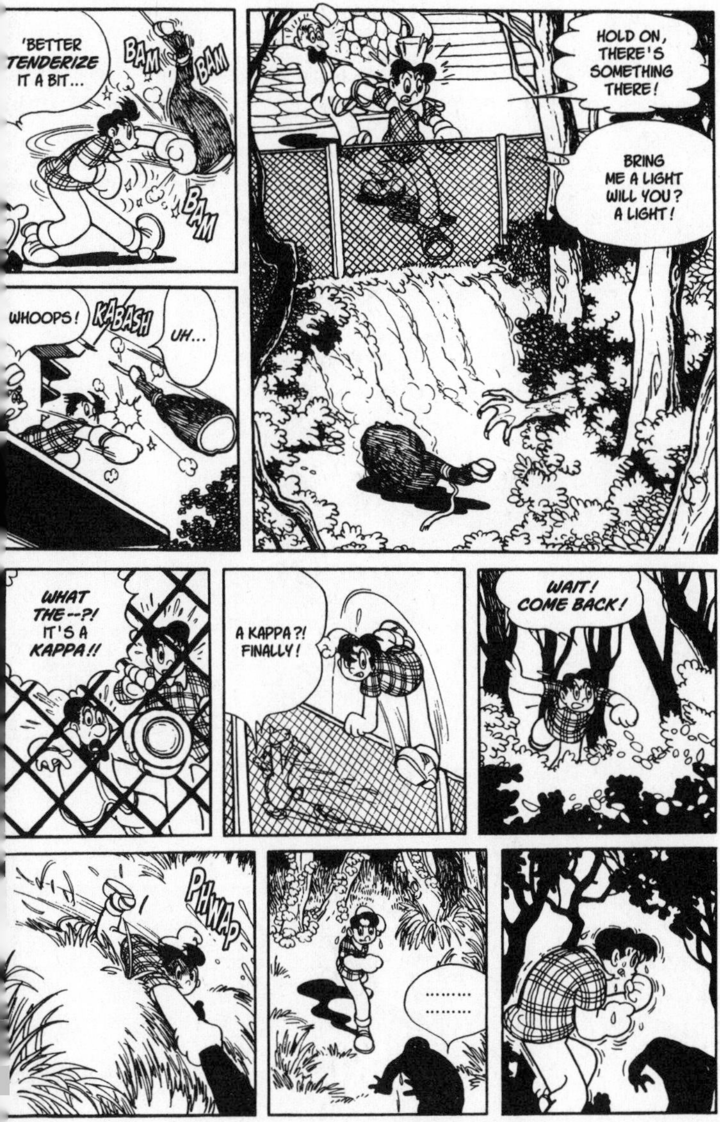
'BETTER TENDERIZE IT A BIT...
BAM
BAM
BAM
HOLD ON, THERE'S SOMETHING THERE!
BRING ME A LIGHT WILL YOU? A LIGHT!
WHOOPS!
KABASH
UH...
WHAT THE--?! IT'S A KAPPA!!
A KAPPA?! FINALLY!
WAIT! COME BACK!
PHWAP
....
....

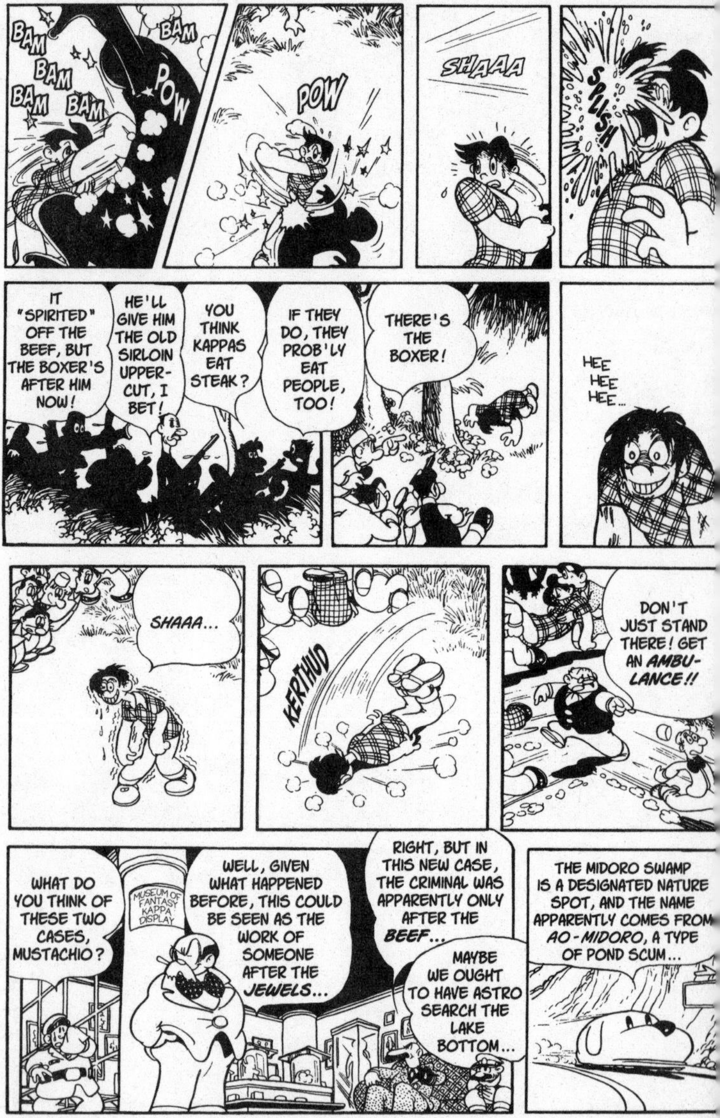
BAM
BAM
BAM
BAM
BAM
POW
POW
SHAAA
SPLUSH
IT "SPIRITED" OFF THE BEEF, BUT THE BOXER'S AFTER HIM NOW!
HE'LL GIVE HIM THE OLD SIRLOIN UPPER-CUT, I BET!
YOU THINK KAPPAS EAT STEAK?
IF THEY DO, THEY PROB'LY EAT PEOPLE, TOO!
THERE'S THE BOXER!
HEE HEE HEE...
SHAAA...
KERTHUD
DON'T JUST STAND THERE! GET AN *AMBU-LANCE!!*
WHAT DO YOU THINK OF THESE TWO CASES, MUSTACHIO?
MUSEUM OF FANTASY KAPPA DISPLAY
WELL, GIVEN WHAT HAPPENED BEFORE, THIS COULD BE SEEN AS THE WORK OF SOMEONE AFTER THE *JEWELS*...
RIGHT, BUT IN THIS NEW CASE, THE CRIMINAL WAS APPARENTLY ONLY AFTER THE *BEEF*...
MAYBE WE OUGHT TO HAVE ASTRO SEARCH THE LAKE BOTTOM...
THE MIDORO SWAMP IS A DESIGNATED NATURE SPOT, AND THE NAME APPARENTLY COMES FROM *AO-MIDORO*, A TYPE OF POND SCUM...

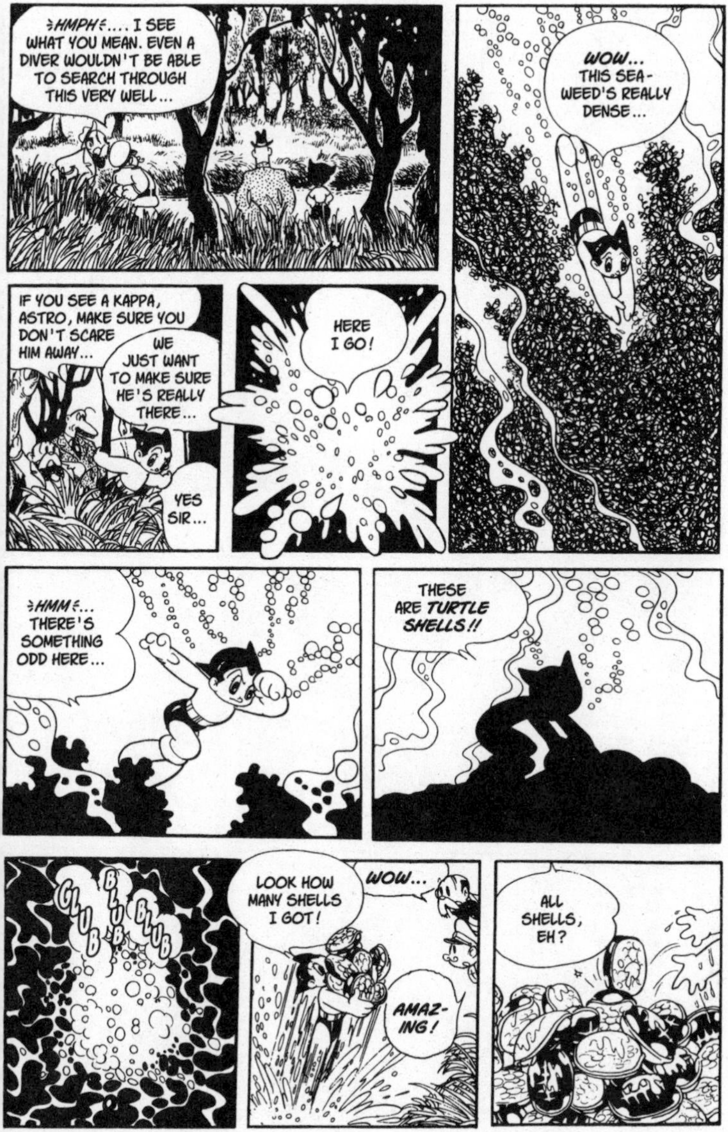
HMPH.... I SEE WHAT YOU MEAN. EVEN A DIVER WOULDN'T BE ABLE TO SEARCH THROUGH THIS VERY WELL...
IF YOU SEE A KAPPA, ASTRO, MAKE SURE YOU DON'T SCARE HIM AWAY...
WE JUST WANT TO MAKE SURE HE'S REALLY THERE...
YES SIR...
HERE I GO!
WOW... THIS SEA-WEED'S REALLY DENSE...
HMM... THERE'S SOMETHING ODD HERE...
THESE ARE TURTLE SHELLS!!
GLUB BLUB BLUB
LOOK HOW MANY SHELLS I GOT!
WOW...
AMAZ-ING!
ALL SHELLS, EH?

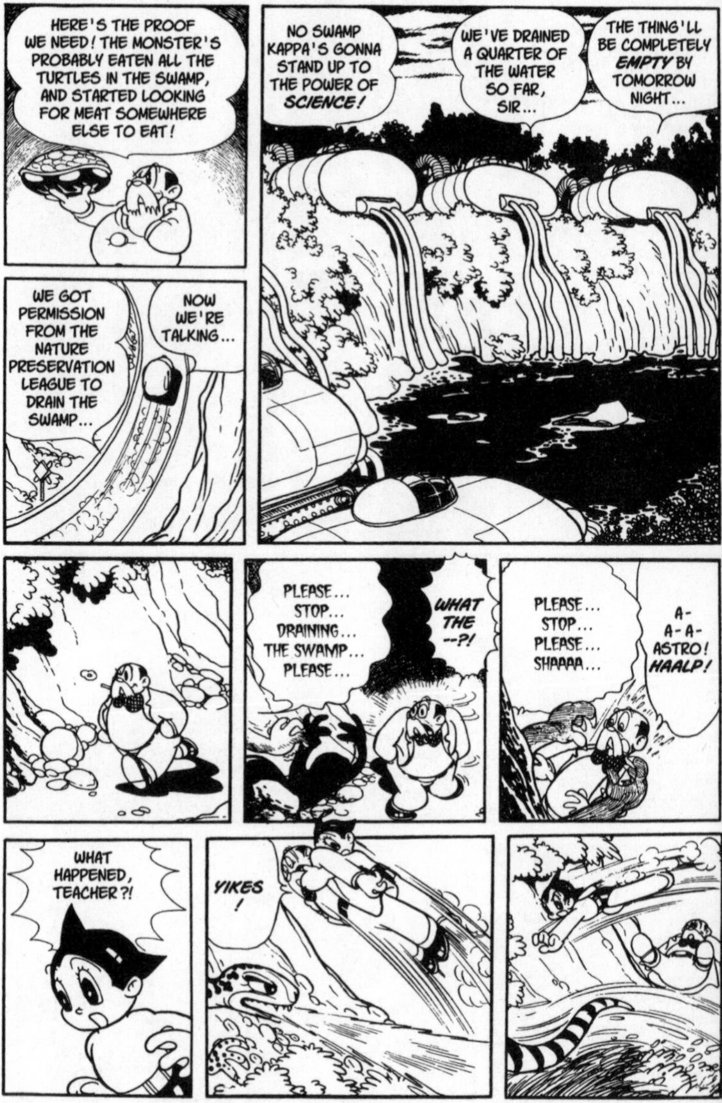
HERE'S THE PROOF WE NEED! THE MONSTER'S PROBABLY EATEN ALL THE TURTLES IN THE SWAMP, AND STARTED LOOKING FOR MEAT SOMEWHERE ELSE TO EAT!
NO SWAMP KAPPA'S GONNA STAND UP TO THE POWER OF *SCIENCE!*
WE'VE DRAINED A QUARTER OF THE WATER SO FAR, SIR...
THE THING'LL BE COMPLETELY *EMPTY* BY TOMORROW NIGHT...
WE GOT PERMISSION FROM THE NATURE PRESERVATION LEAGUE TO DRAIN THE SWAMP...
NOW WE'RE TALKING...
PLEASE... STOP... DRAINING... THE SWAMP... PLEASE...
WHAT THE --?!
PLEASE... STOP... PLEASE... SHAAAA...
A- A- A- ASTRO! *HAALP!*
WHAT HAPPENED, TEACHER?!
YIKES!

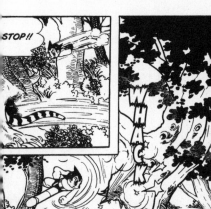

STOP!!

FWWISSH

POP

WHAM

RATS! HE GOT AWAY!

YOU ALL RIGHT, TEACHER?!

IF YOU HADN'T COME WHEN YOU DID, ASTRO, I'D BE A GONER... BUT THAT WAS NO *KAPPA*...

I KNOW... *LOOK*...

YIKES!! IT'S A TAIL!!

IN THE NOH PLAY, *RASHOMON*, WATANABE NO TSUNA CUTS OFF A DEMON'S ARM...

I'LL BET THE MONSTER COMES TO GET HIS TAIL BACK...

I'M TELLING YOU, PROFESSOR... IT SPOKE *HUMAN LANGUAGE*...

509

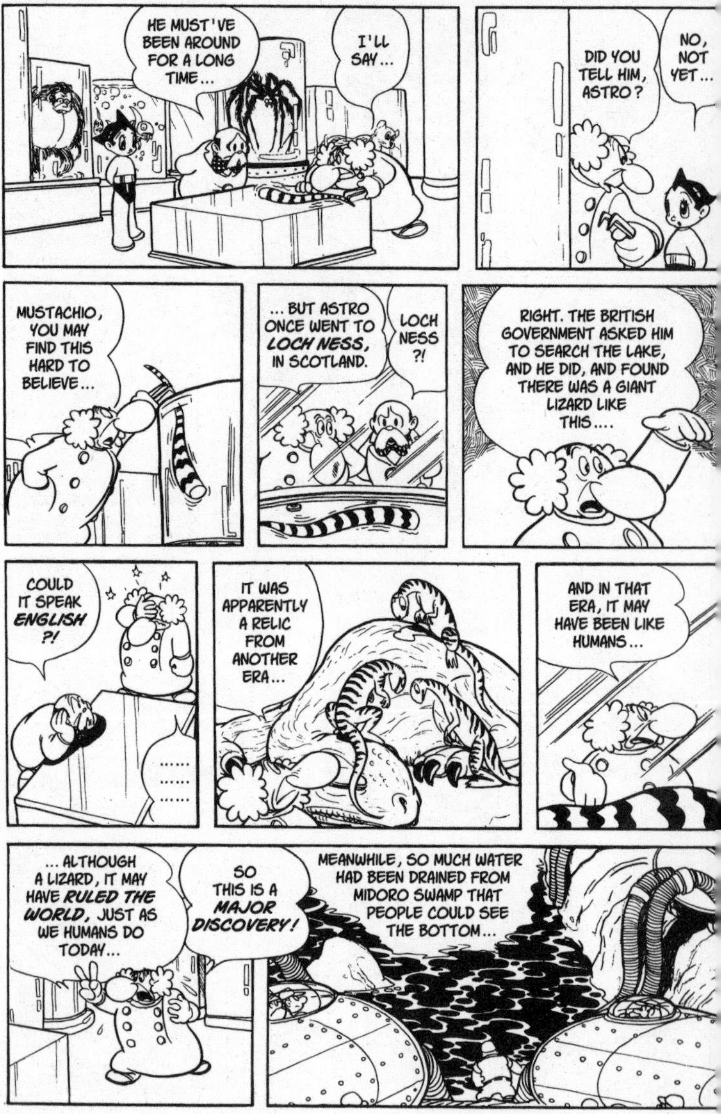
HE MUST'VE BEEN AROUND FOR A LONG TIME...
I'LL SAY...
DID YOU TELL HIM, ASTRO?
NO, NOT YET...
MUSTACHIO, YOU MAY FIND THIS HARD TO BELIEVE...
... BUT ASTRO ONCE WENT TO LOCH NESS, IN SCOTLAND.
LOCH NESS ?!
RIGHT. THE BRITISH GOVERNMENT ASKED HIM TO SEARCH THE LAKE, AND HE DID, AND FOUND THERE WAS A GIANT LIZARD LIKE THIS....
COULD IT SPEAK ENGLISH ?!
......
......
......
IT WAS APPARENTLY A RELIC FROM ANOTHER ERA...
AND IN THAT ERA, IT MAY HAVE BEEN LIKE HUMANS...
... ALTHOUGH A LIZARD, IT MAY HAVE RULED THE WORLD, JUST AS WE HUMANS DO TODAY...
SO THIS IS A MAJOR DISCOVERY!
MEANWHILE, SO MUCH WATER HAD BEEN DRAINED FROM MIDORO SWAMP THAT PEOPLE COULD SEE THE BOTTOM...

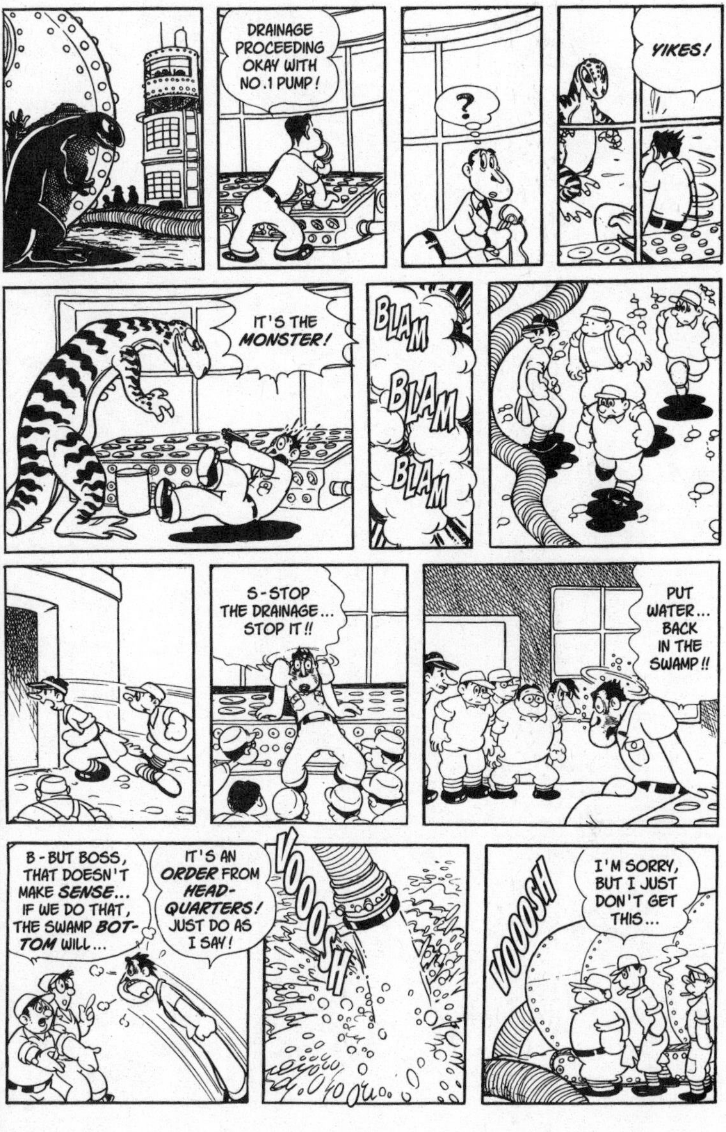
DRAINAGE PROCEEDING OKAY WITH NO.1 PUMP!
?
YIKES!
IT'S THE *MONSTER!*
BLAM
BLAM
BLAM
S-STOP THE DRAINAGE... STOP IT!!
PUT WATER... BACK IN THE SWAMP!!
B-BUT BOSS, THAT DOESN'T MAKE *SENSE*... IF WE DO THAT, THE SWAMP *BOTTOM* WILL...
IT'S AN *ORDER* FROM *HEADQUARTERS!* JUST DO AS I SAY!
VOOOOSH
VOOOSH
I'M SORRY, BUT I JUST DON'T GET THIS...

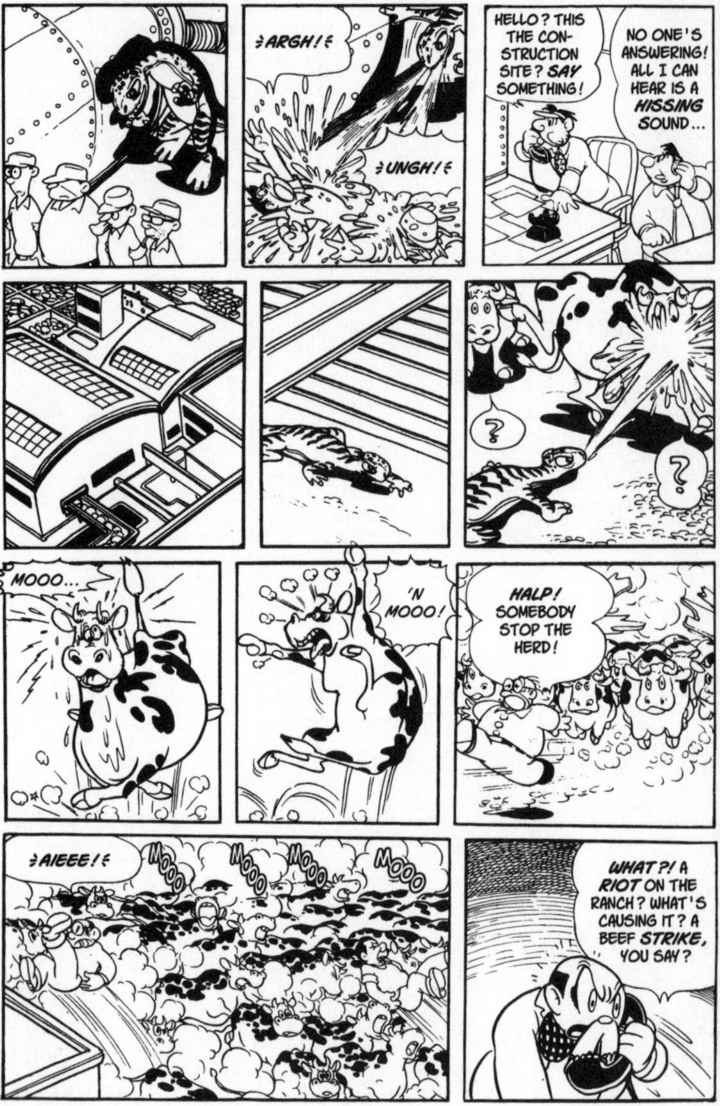

ARGH!
UNGH!
HELLO? THIS THE CON-STRUCTION SITE? SAY SOMETHING!
NO ONE'S ANSWERING! ALL I CAN HEAR IS A HISSING SOUND...
?
?
MOOO...
'N MOOO!
HALP! SOMEBODY STOP THE HERD!
AIEEE!
MOOO
MOOO
MOOO
MOOO
WHAT?! A RIOT ON THE RANCH? WHAT'S CAUSING IT? A BEEF STRIKE, YOU SAY?

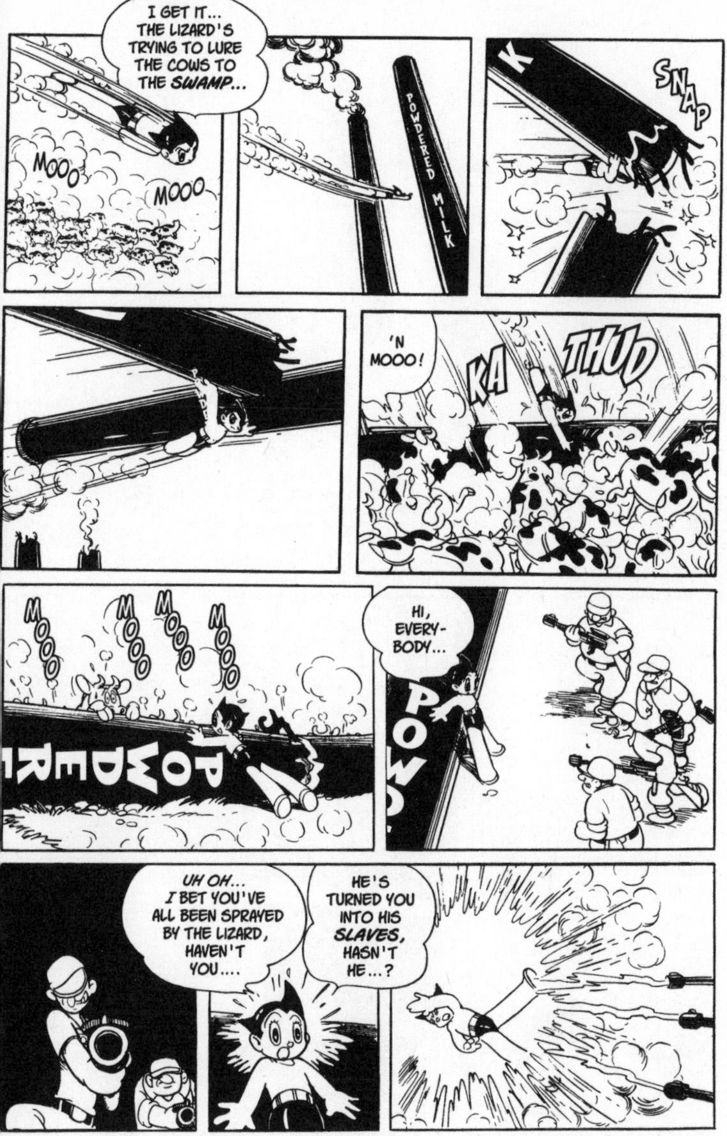
I GET IT... THE LIZARD'S TRYING TO LURE THE COWS TO THE *SWAMP*...
MOOO
MOOO
POWDERED MILK
K
SNAP
'N MOOO!
KA
THUD
MOOO
MOOO
MOOO
MOOO
HI, EVERY-BODY...
UH OH... *I* BET YOU'VE ALL BEEN SPRAYED BY THE LIZARD, HAVEN'T YOU....
HE'S TURNED YOU INTO HIS *SLAVES*, HASN'T HE...?

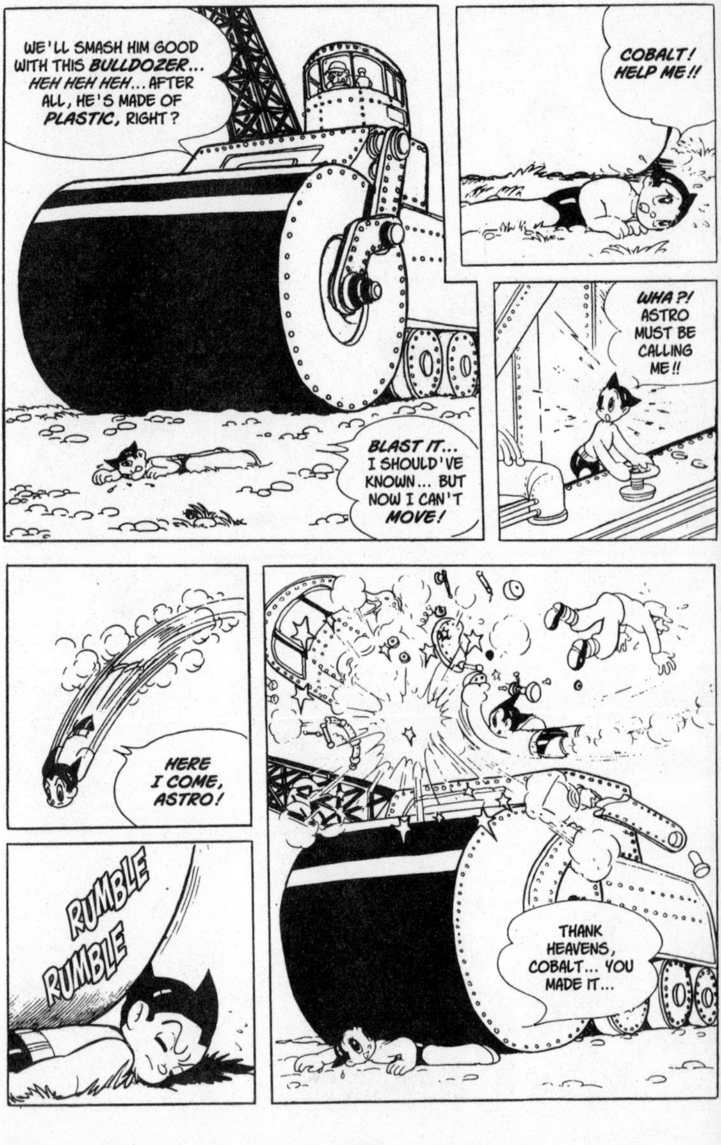
WE'LL SMASH HIM GOOD WITH THIS BULLDOZER... HEH HEH HEH... AFTER ALL, HE'S MADE OF PLASTIC, RIGHT?
BLAST IT... I SHOULD'VE KNOWN... BUT NOW I CAN'T MOVE!
COBALT! HELP ME!!
WHA?! ASTRO MUST BE CALLING ME!!
HERE I COME, ASTRO!
RUMBLE RUMBLE
THANK HEAVENS, COBALT... YOU MADE IT...

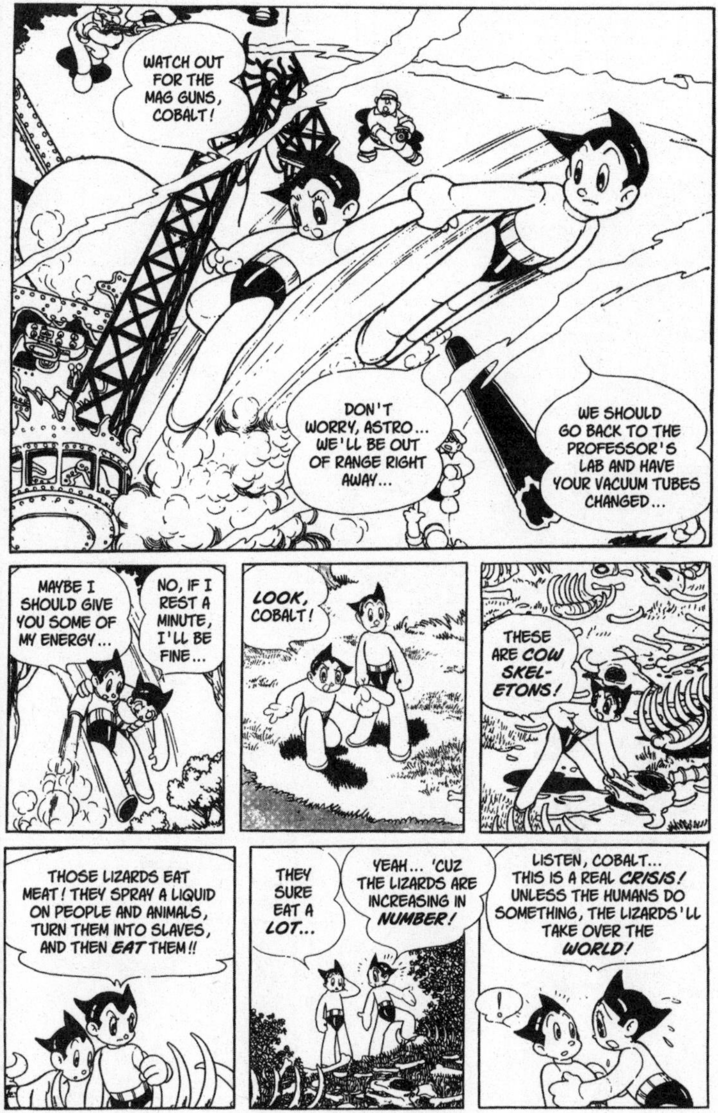

WATCH OUT FOR THE MAG GUNS, COBALT!
DON'T WORRY, ASTRO... WE'LL BE OUT OF RANGE RIGHT AWAY...
WE SHOULD GO BACK TO THE PROFESSOR'S LAB AND HAVE YOUR VACUUM TUBES CHANGED...
MAYBE I SHOULD GIVE YOU SOME OF MY ENERGY...
NO, IF I REST A MINUTE, I'LL BE FINE...
LOOK, COBALT!
THESE ARE COW SKEL-ETONS!
THOSE LIZARDS EAT MEAT! THEY SPRAY A LIQUID ON PEOPLE AND ANIMALS, TURN THEM INTO SLAVES, AND THEN EAT THEM!!
THEY SURE EAT A LOT...
YEAH... 'CUZ THE LIZARDS ARE INCREASING IN NUMBER!
LISTEN, COBALT... THIS IS A REAL CRISIS! UNLESS THE HUMANS DO SOMETHING, THE LIZARDS'LL TAKE OVER THE WORLD!
!

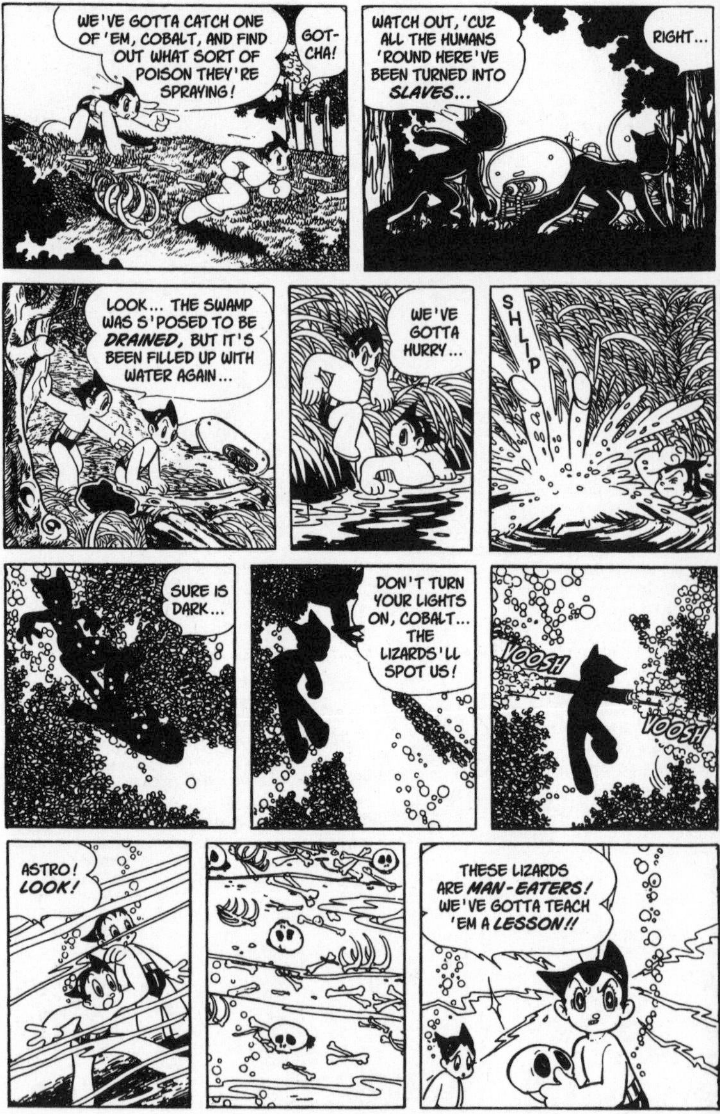

WE'VE GOTTA CATCH ONE OF 'EM, COBALT, AND FIND OUT WHAT SORT OF POISON THEY'RE SPRAYING!
GOT-CHA!
WATCH OUT, 'CUZ ALL THE HUMANS 'ROUND HERE'VE BEEN TURNED INTO SLAVES...
RIGHT...
LOOK... THE SWAMP WAS S'POSED TO BE DRAINED, BUT IT'S BEEN FILLED UP WITH WATER AGAIN...
WE'VE GOTTA HURRY...
SHLIP
SURE IS DARK...
DON'T TURN YOUR LIGHTS ON, COBALT... THE LIZARDS'LL SPOT US!
VOOSH
VOOSH
ASTRO! LOOK!
THESE LIZARDS ARE MAN-EATERS! WE'VE GOTTA TEACH 'EM A LESSON!!

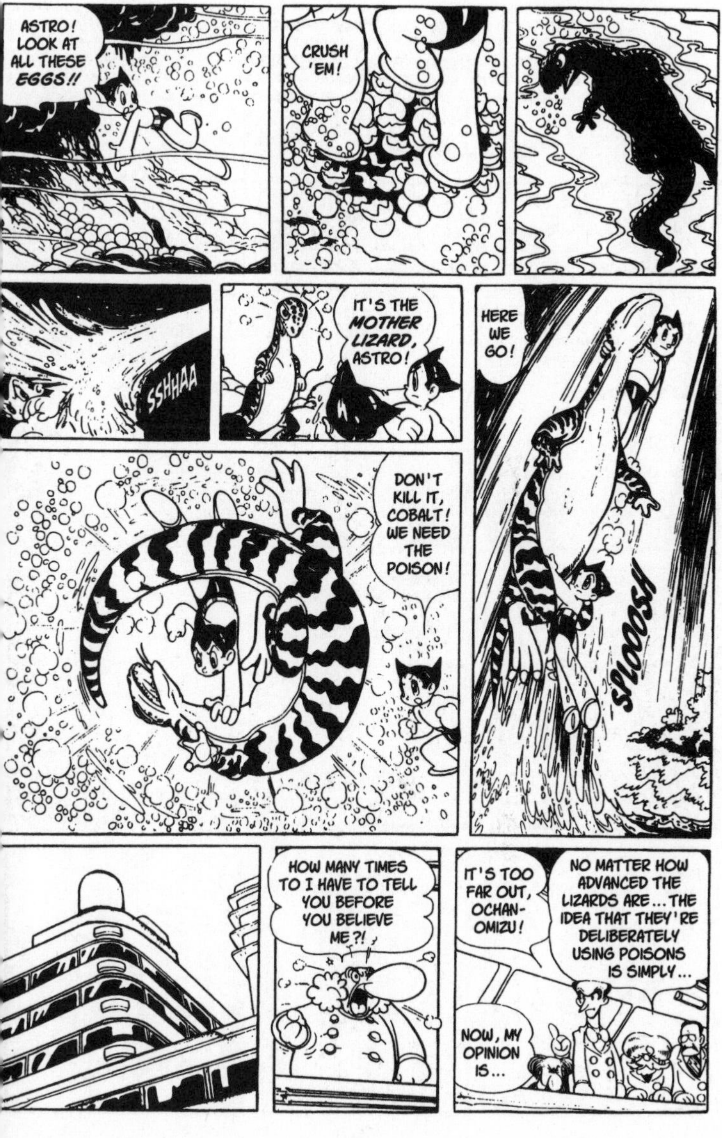

ASTRO! LOOK AT ALL THESE EGGS!!
CRUSH 'EM!
SSHHAA
IT'S THE MOTHER LIZARD, ASTRO!
DON'T KILL IT, COBALT! WE NEED THE POISON!
HERE WE GO!
SPLOOOSH
HOW MANY TIMES TO I HAVE TO TELL YOU BEFORE YOU BELIEVE ME?!
IT'S TOO FAR OUT, OCHANOMIZU!
NO MATTER HOW ADVANCED THE LIZARDS ARE... THE IDEA THAT THEY'RE DELIBERATELY USING POISONS IS SIMPLY...
NOW, MY OPINION IS...

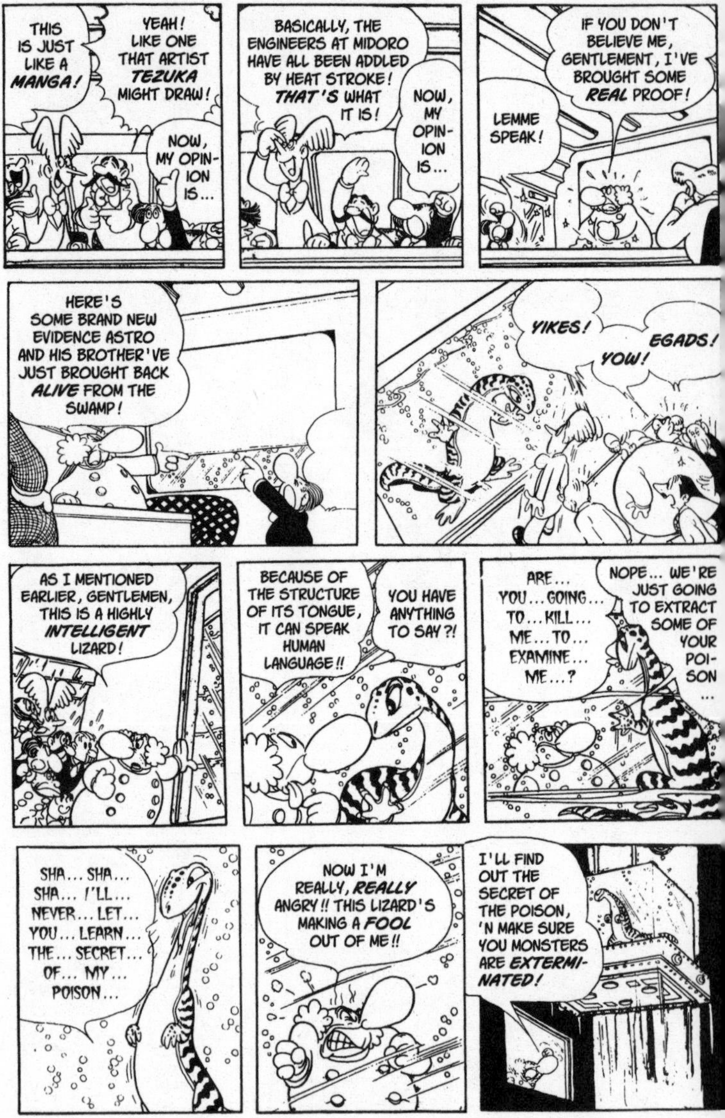

THIS IS JUST LIKE A *MANGA!*
YEAH! LIKE ONE THAT ARTIST *TEZUKA* MIGHT DRAW!
NOW, MY OPINION IS...
BASICALLY, THE ENGINEERS AT MIDORO HAVE ALL BEEN ADDLED BY HEAT STROKE! *THAT'S* WHAT IT IS!
NOW, MY OPINION IS...
LEMME SPEAK!
IF YOU DON'T BELIEVE ME, GENTLEMENT, I'VE BROUGHT SOME *REAL* PROOF!
HERE'S SOME BRAND NEW EVIDENCE ASTRO AND HIS BROTHER'VE JUST BROUGHT BACK *ALIVE* FROM THE SWAMP!
YIKES!
YOW!
EGADS!
AS I MENTIONED EARLIER, GENTLEMEN, THIS IS A HIGHLY *INTELLIGENT* LIZARD!
BECAUSE OF THE STRUCTURE OF ITS TONGUE, IT CAN SPEAK HUMAN LANGUAGE!!
YOU HAVE ANYTHING TO SAY?!
ARE... YOU... GOING... TO... KILL... ME... TO... EXAMINE... ME...?
NOPE... WE'RE JUST GOING TO EXTRACT SOME OF YOUR POISON...
SHA... SHA... SHA... I'LL... NEVER... LET... YOU... LEARN... THE... SECRET... OF... MY... POISON...
NOW I'M REALLY, *REALLY* ANGRY!! THIS LIZARD'S MAKING A *FOOL* OUT OF ME!!
I'LL FIND OUT THE SECRET OF THE POISON, 'N MAKE SURE YOU MONSTERS ARE *EXTERMINATED!*

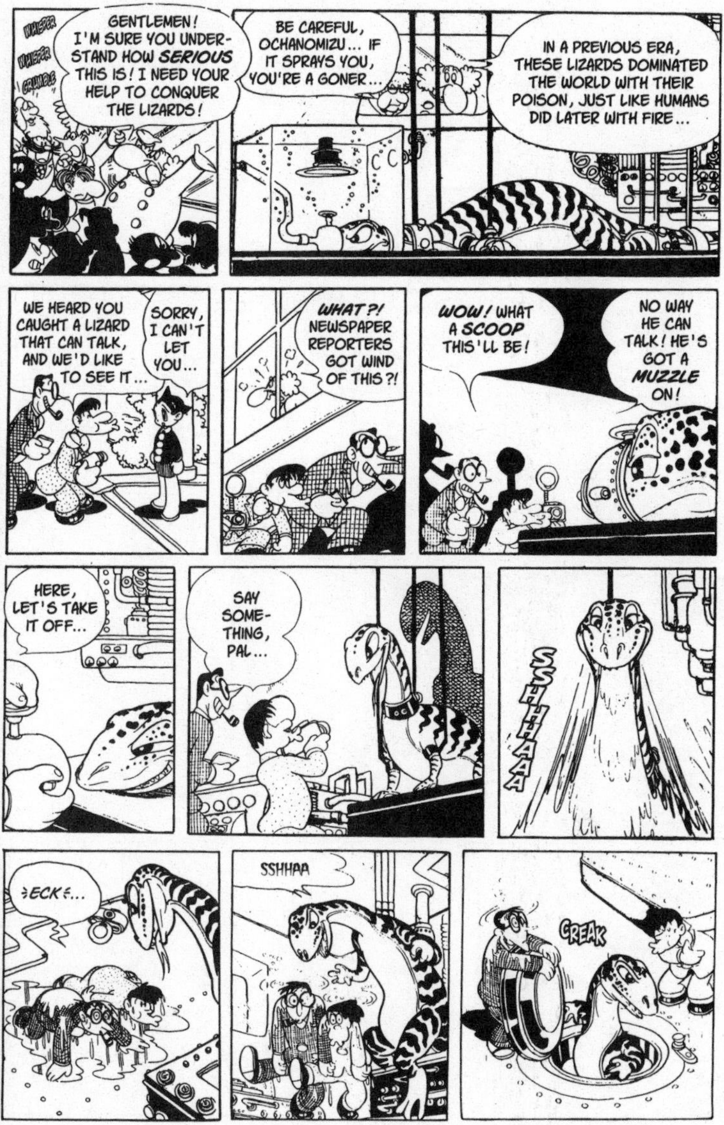
WHISPER
WHISPER
GRUMBLE
GENTLEMEN! I'M SURE YOU UNDERSTAND HOW SERIOUS THIS IS! I NEED YOUR HELP TO CONQUER THE LIZARDS!
BE CAREFUL, OCHANOMIZU... IF IT SPRAYS YOU, YOU'RE A GONER...
IN A PREVIOUS ERA, THESE LIZARDS DOMINATED THE WORLD WITH THEIR POISON, JUST LIKE HUMANS DID LATER WITH FIRE...
WE HEARD YOU CAUGHT A LIZARD THAT CAN TALK, AND WE'D LIKE TO SEE IT...
SORRY, I CAN'T LET YOU...
WHAT?! NEWSPAPER REPORTERS GOT WIND OF THIS?!
WOW! WHAT A SCOOP THIS'LL BE!
NO WAY HE CAN TALK! HE'S GOT A MUZZLE ON!
HERE, LET'S TAKE IT OFF...
SAY SOMETHING, PAL...
SSHHHAAA
ECK...
SSHHAA
CREAK

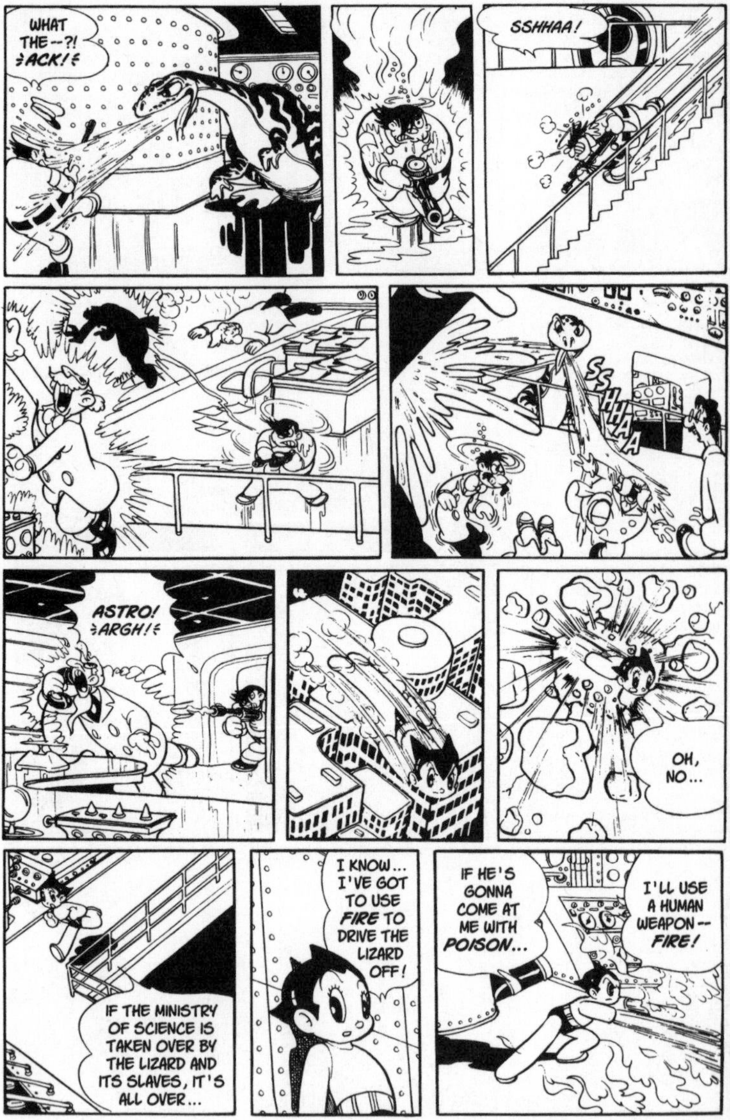
WHAT THE--?! ACK!
SSHHAA!
SSHHAA
ASTRO! ARGH!
OH, NO...
IF THE MINISTRY OF SCIENCE IS TAKEN OVER BY THE LIZARD AND ITS SLAVES, IT'S ALL OVER...
I KNOW... I'VE GOT TO USE FIRE TO DRIVE THE LIZARD OFF!
IF HE'S GONNA COME AT ME WITH POISON...
I'LL USE A HUMAN WEAPON-- FIRE!

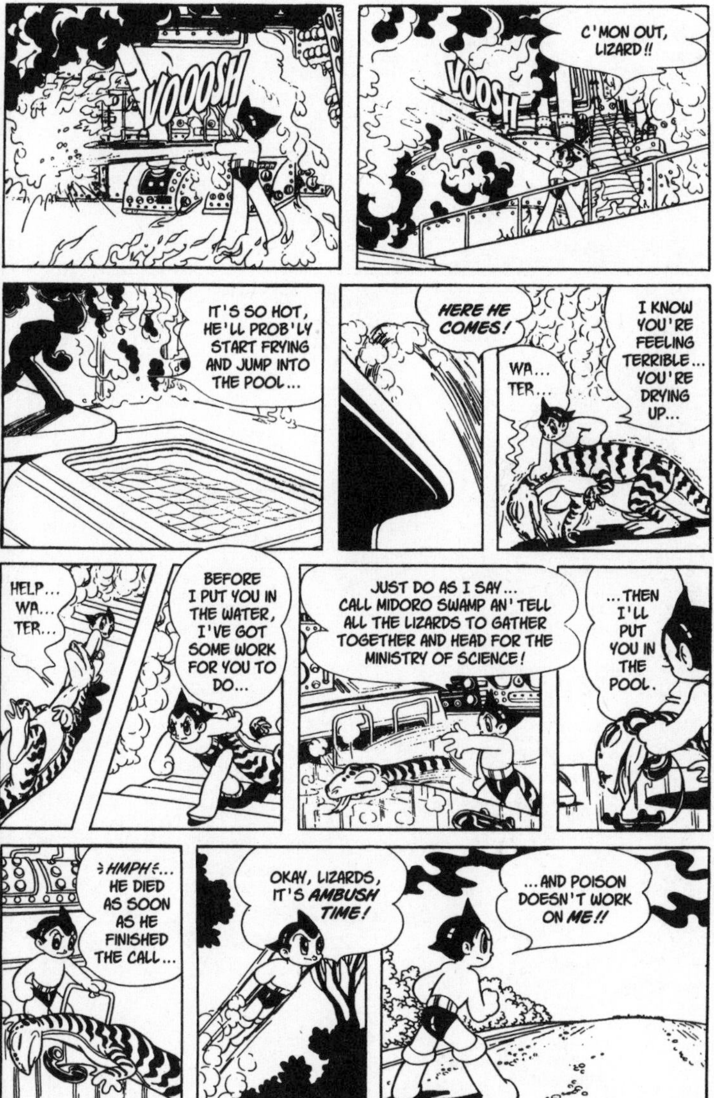
VOOOSH
VOOSH
C'MON OUT, LIZARD!!
IT'S SO HOT, HE'LL PROB'LY START FRYING AND JUMP INTO THE POOL...
HERE HE COMES!
WA... TER...
I KNOW YOU'RE FEELING TERRIBLE... YOU'RE DRYING UP...
HELP... WA... TER...
BEFORE I PUT YOU IN THE WATER, I'VE GOT SOME WORK FOR YOU TO DO...
JUST DO AS I SAY... CALL MIDORO SWAMP AN' TELL ALL THE LIZARDS TO GATHER TOGETHER AND HEAD FOR THE MINISTRY OF SCIENCE!
...THEN I'LL PUT YOU IN THE POOL.
HMPH... HE DIED AS SOON AS HE FINISHED THE CALL...
OKAY, LIZARDS, IT'S AMBUSH TIME!
...AND POISON DOESN'T WORK ON ME!!

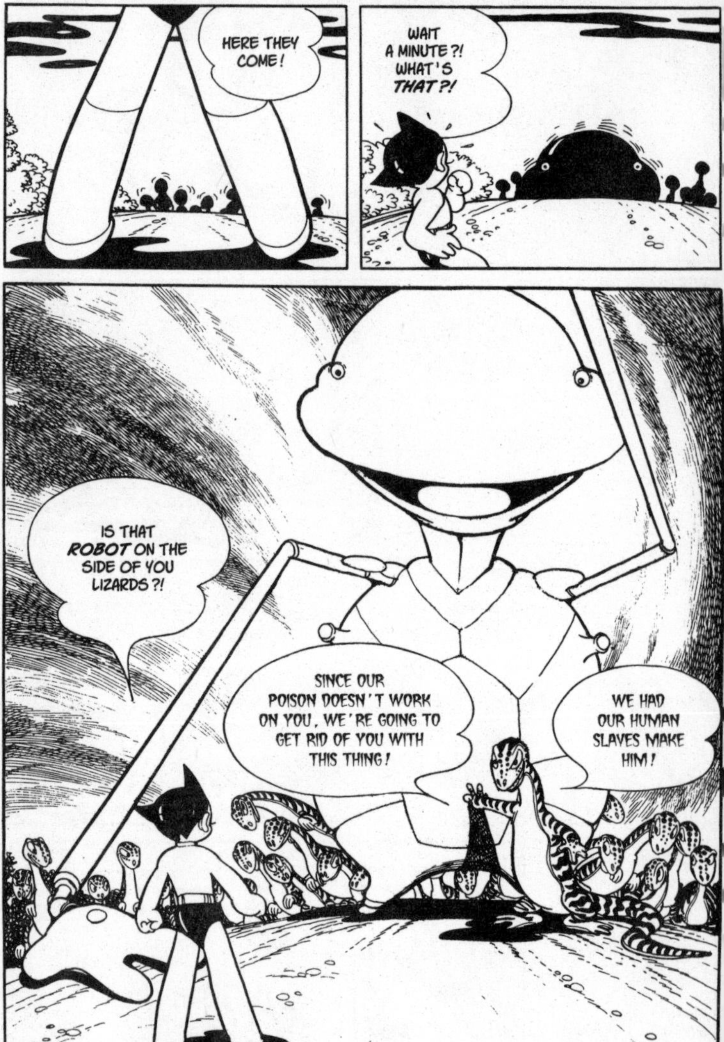
HERE THEY COME!
WAIT A MINUTE?! WHAT'S THAT?!
IS THAT ROBOT ON THE SIDE OF YOU LIZARDS?!
SINCE OUR POISON DOESN'T WORK ON YOU, WE'RE GOING TO GET RID OF YOU WITH THIS THING!
WE HAD OUR HUMAN SLAVES MAKE HIM!

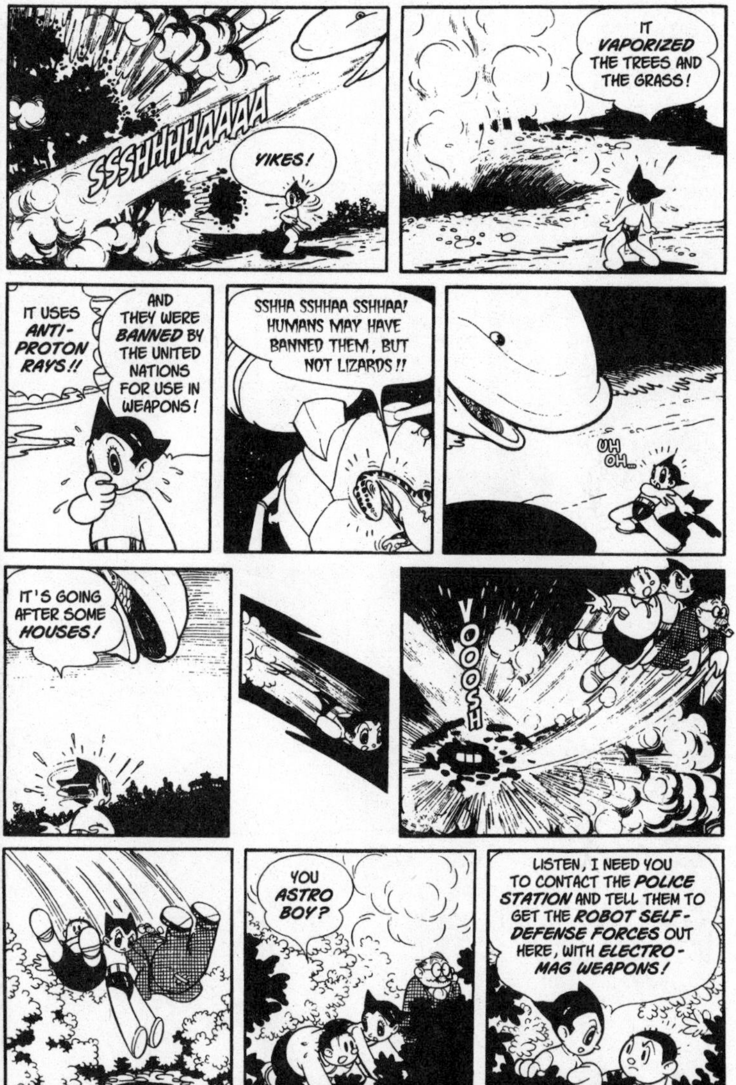
SSSHHHHAAAA
YIKES!
IT VAPORIZED THE TREES AND THE GRASS!
IT USES ANTI-PROTON RAYS!!
AND THEY WERE BANNED BY THE UNITED NATIONS FOR USE IN WEAPONS!
SSHHA SSHHAA SSHHAA! HUMANS MAY HAVE BANNED THEM, BUT NOT LIZARDS!!
UH OH...
IT'S GOING AFTER SOME HOUSES!
VOOOSH
YOU ASTRO BOY?
LISTEN, I NEED YOU TO CONTACT THE POLICE STATION AND TELL THEM TO GET THE ROBOT SELF-DEFENSE FORCES OUT HERE, WITH ELECTRO-MAG WEAPONS!

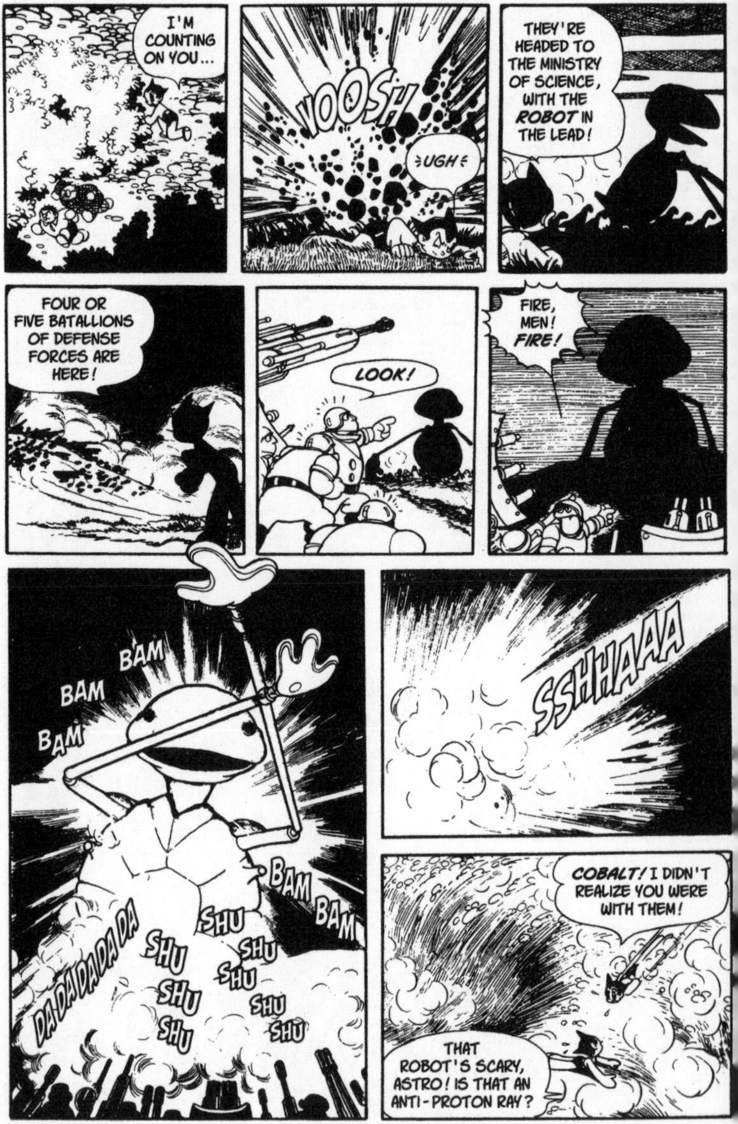
I'M COUNTING ON YOU...
VOOSH
UGH
THEY'RE HEADED TO THE MINISTRY OF SCIENCE, WITH THE ROBOT IN THE LEAD!
FOUR OR FIVE BATALLIONS OF DEFENSE FORCES ARE HERE!
LOOK!
FIRE, MEN! FIRE!
BAM
BAM
BAM
BAM
BAM
DA DA DA DA DA DA
SHU
SHU
SHU
SHU
SHU
SHU
SHU
SHU
SSHHAAA
COBALT! I DIDN'T REALIZE YOU WERE WITH THEM!
THAT ROBOT'S SCARY, ASTRO! IS THAT AN ANTI-PROTON RAY?

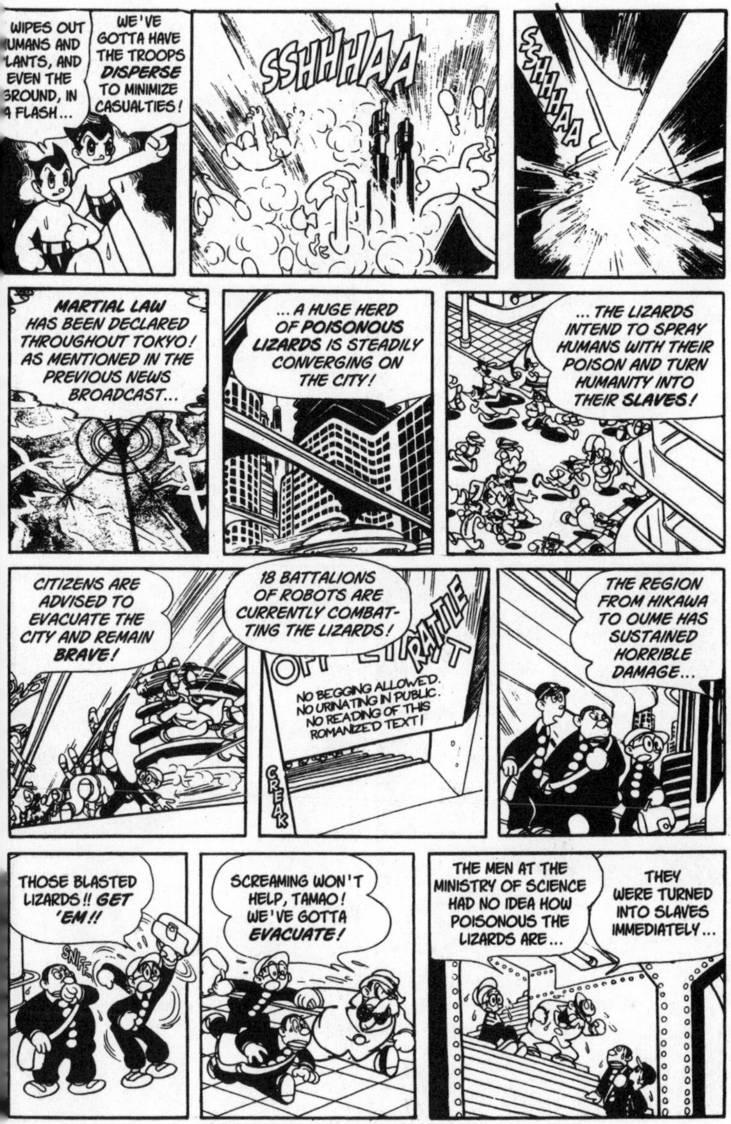

WIPES OUT UMANS AND LANTS, AND EVEN THE GROUND, IN A FLASH...
WE'VE GOTTA HAVE THE TROOPS DISPERSE TO MINIMIZE CASUALTIES!
SSHHHAA
SSHHHAA
MARTIAL LAW HAS BEEN DECLARED THROUGHOUT TOKYO! AS MENTIONED IN THE PREVIOUS NEWS BROADCAST...
...A HUGE HERD OF POISONOUS LIZARDS IS STEADILY CONVERGING ON THE CITY!
...THE LIZARDS INTEND TO SPRAY HUMANS WITH THEIR POISON AND TURN HUMANITY INTO THEIR SLAVES!
CITIZENS ARE ADVISED TO EVACUATE THE CITY AND REMAIN BRAVE!
18 BATTALIONS OF ROBOTS ARE CURRENTLY COMBAT-TING THE LIZARDS!
RATTLE
NO BEGGING ALLOWED. NO URINATING IN PUBLIC. NO READING OF THIS ROMANIZED TEXT!
CREAK
THE REGION FROM HIKAWA TO OUME HAS SUSTAINED HORRIBLE DAMAGE...
THOSE BLASTED LIZARDS!! GET 'EM!!
SNIFF
SCREAMING WON'T HELP, TAMAO! WE'VE GOTTA EVACUATE!
THE MEN AT THE MINISTRY OF SCIENCE HAD NO IDEA HOW POISONOUS THE LIZARDS ARE...
THEY WERE TURNED INTO SLAVES IMMEDIATELY...

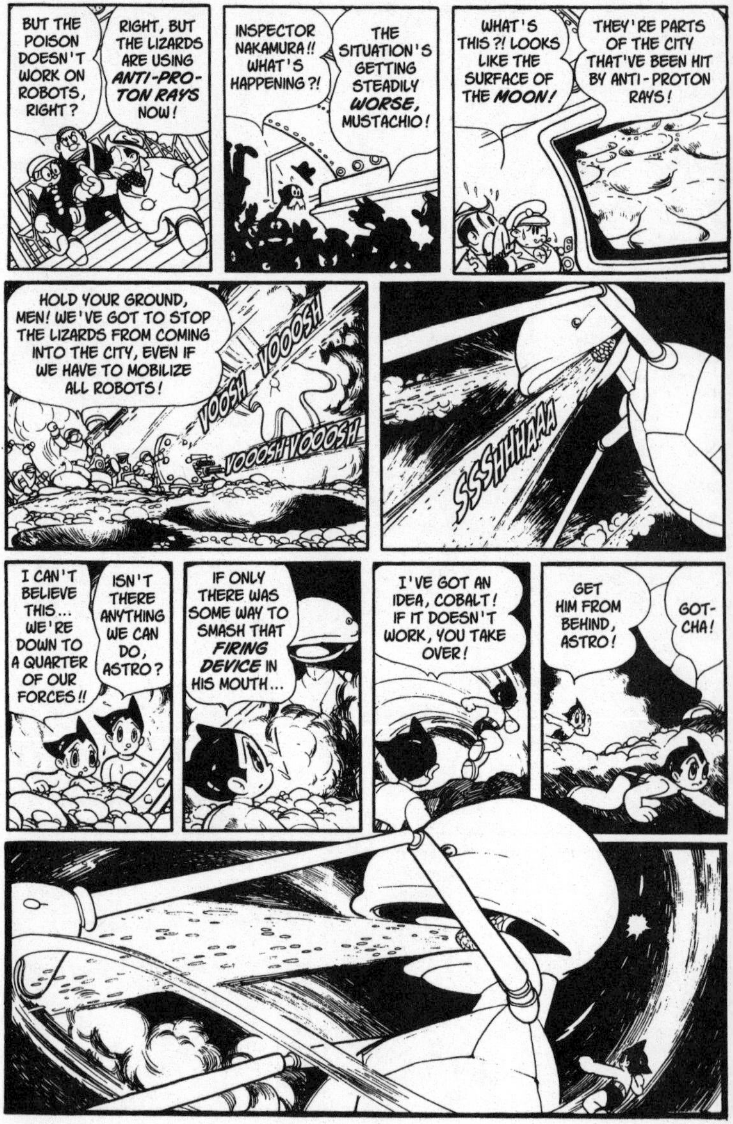
BUT THE POISON DOESN'T WORK ON ROBOTS, RIGHT?
RIGHT, BUT THE LIZARDS ARE USING *ANTI-PROTON RAYS* NOW!
INSPECTOR NAKAMURA!! WHAT'S HAPPENING?!
THE SITUATION'S GETTING STEADILY *WORSE,* MUSTACHIO!
WHAT'S THIS?! LOOKS LIKE THE SURFACE OF THE *MOON!*
THEY'RE PARTS OF THE CITY THAT'VE BEEN HIT BY ANTI-PROTON RAYS!
HOLD YOUR GROUND, MEN! WE'VE GOT TO STOP THE LIZARDS FROM COMING INTO THE CITY, EVEN IF WE HAVE TO MOBILIZE ALL ROBOTS!
VOOOSH
VOOSH
VOOSH
VOOOSH VOOOSH
SSSHHHAAA
I CAN'T BELIEVE THIS... WE'RE DOWN TO A QUARTER OF OUR FORCES!!
ISN'T THERE ANYTHING WE CAN DO, ASTRO?
IF ONLY THERE WAS SOME WAY TO SMASH THAT *FIRING DEVICE* IN HIS MOUTH...
I'VE GOT AN IDEA, COBALT! IF IT DOESN'T WORK, YOU TAKE OVER!
GET HIM FROM BEHIND, ASTRO!
GOT-CHA!

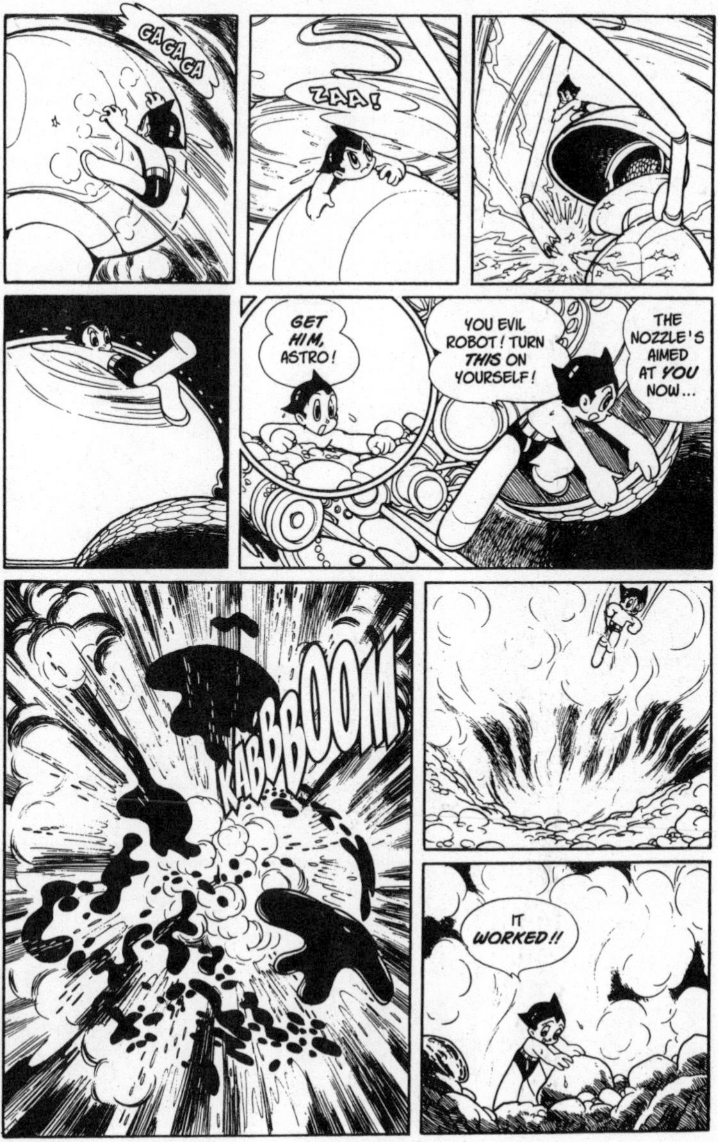
GAGAGA
ZAA!
GET HIM, ASTRO!
YOU EVIL ROBOT! TURN THIS ON YOURSELF!
THE NOZZLE'S AIMED AT YOU NOW...
KABBOOM
IT WORKED!!

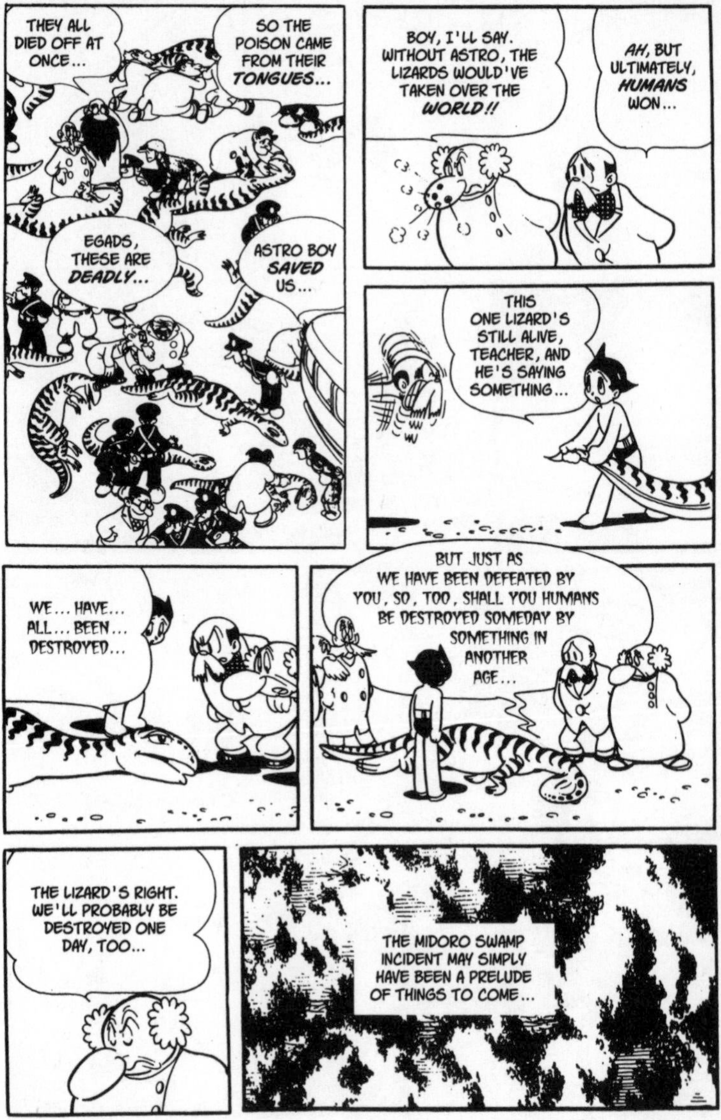
THEY ALL DIED OFF AT ONCE...
SO THE POISON CAME FROM THEIR *TONGUES*...
EGADS, THESE ARE *DEADLY*...
ASTRO BOY *SAVED* US...
BOY, I'LL SAY. WITHOUT ASTRO, THE LIZARDS WOULD'VE TAKEN OVER THE *WORLD!!*
AH, BUT ULTIMATELY, *HUMANS* WON...
THIS ONE LIZARD'S STILL ALIVE, TEACHER, AND HE'S SAYING SOMETHING...
WE... HAVE... ALL... BEEN... DESTROYED...
BUT JUST AS WE HAVE BEEN DEFEATED BY YOU, SO, TOO, SHALL YOU HUMANS BE DESTROYED SOMEDAY BY SOMETHING IN ANOTHER AGE...
THE LIZARD'S RIGHT. WE'LL PROBABLY BE DESTROYED ONE DAY, TOO...
THE MIDORO SWAMP INCIDENT MAY SIMPLY HAVE BEEN A PRELUDE OF THINGS TO COME...

ROBIO AND ROBIETTE

First serialized from May to September 1965
in *Shonen* magazine.

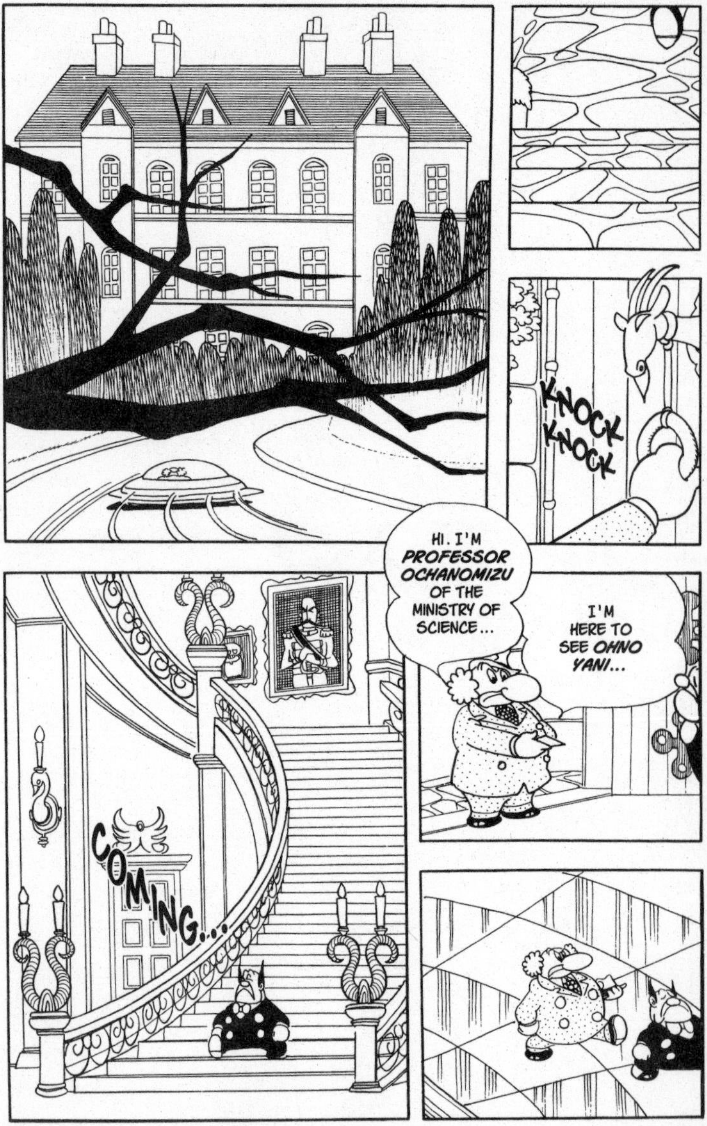
KNOCK KNOCK
COMING...
HI. I'M PROFESSOR OCHANOMIZU OF THE MINISTRY OF SCIENCE...
I'M HERE TO SEE OHNO YANI...

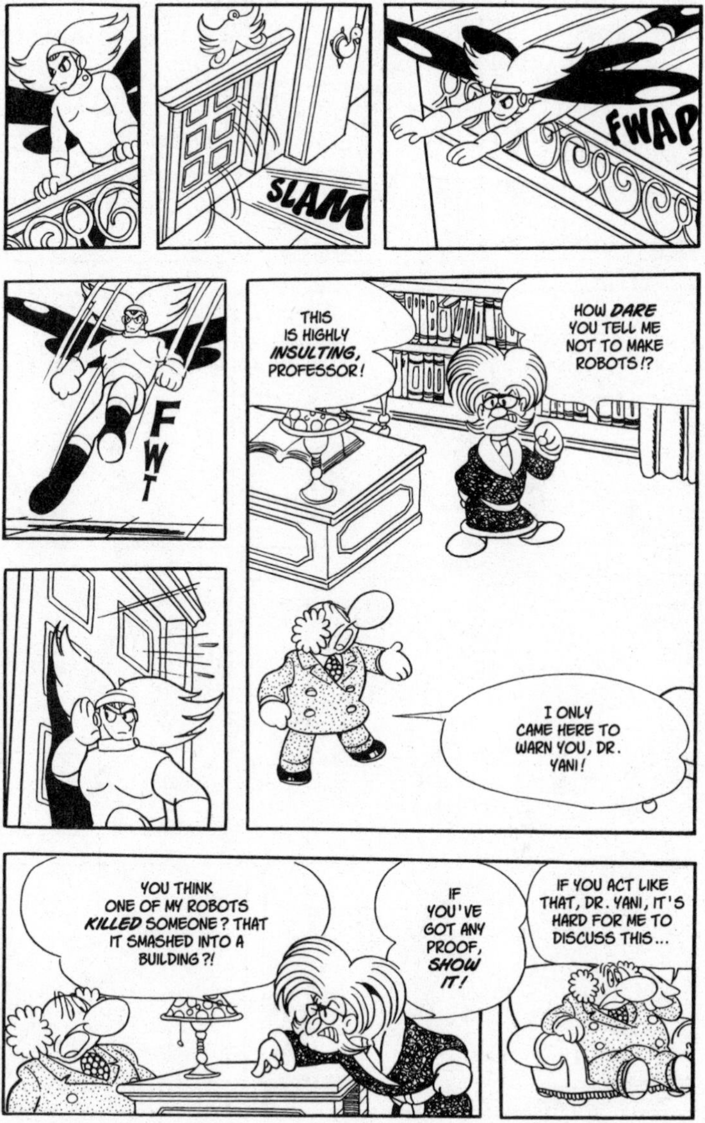
SLAM
FWAP
FWT
THIS IS HIGHLY *INSULTING*, PROFESSOR!
HOW *DARE* YOU TELL ME NOT TO MAKE ROBOTS!?
I ONLY CAME HERE TO WARN YOU, DR. YANI!
YOU THINK ONE OF MY ROBOTS *KILLED* SOMEONE? THAT IT SMASHED INTO A BUILDING?!
IF YOU'VE GOT ANY PROOF, *SHOW IT!*
IF YOU ACT LIKE THAT, DR. YANI, IT'S HARD FOR ME TO DISCUSS THIS...

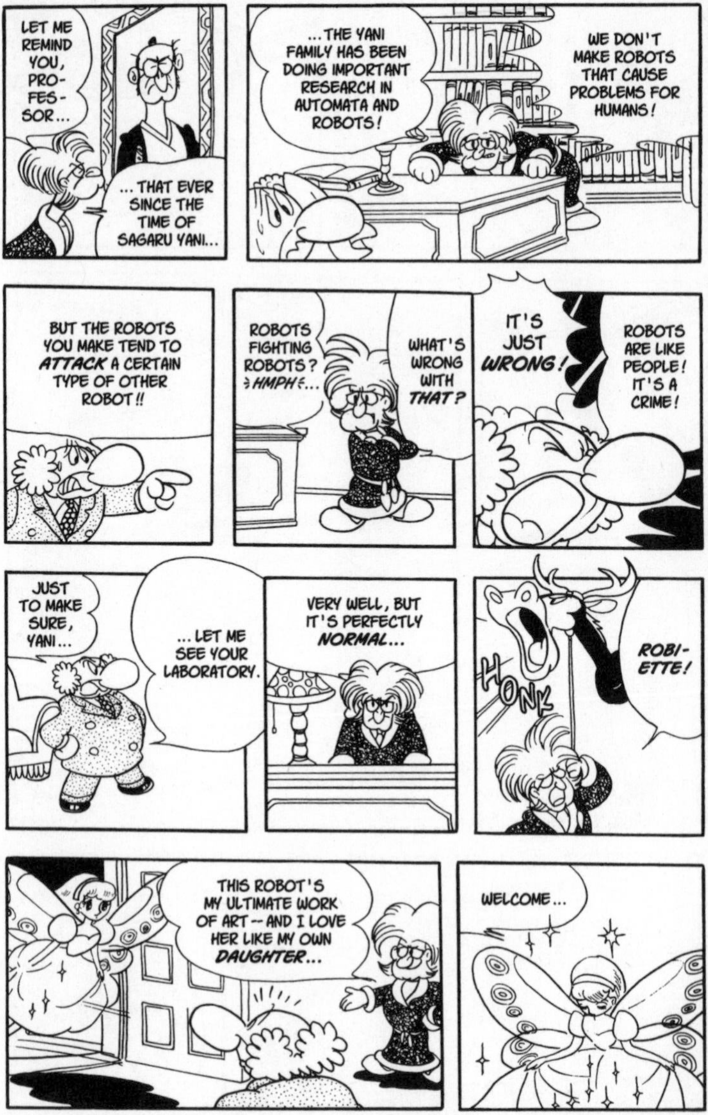
LET ME REMIND YOU, PRO-FES-SOR...
... THAT EVER SINCE THE TIME OF SAGARU YANI...
...THE YANI FAMILY HAS BEEN DOING IMPORTANT RESEARCH IN AUTOMATA AND ROBOTS!
WE DON'T MAKE ROBOTS THAT CAUSE PROBLEMS FOR HUMANS!
BUT THE ROBOTS YOU MAKE TEND TO ATTACK A CERTAIN TYPE OF OTHER ROBOT!!
ROBOTS FIGHTING ROBOTS? HMPH...
WHAT'S WRONG WITH THAT?
IT'S JUST WRONG!
ROBOTS ARE LIKE PEOPLE! IT'S A CRIME!
JUST TO MAKE SURE, YANI...
... LET ME SEE YOUR LABORATORY.
VERY WELL, BUT IT'S PERFECTLY NORMAL...
HONK
ROBI-ETTE!
THIS ROBOT'S MY ULTIMATE WORK OF ART -- AND I LOVE HER LIKE MY OWN DAUGHTER...
WELCOME...

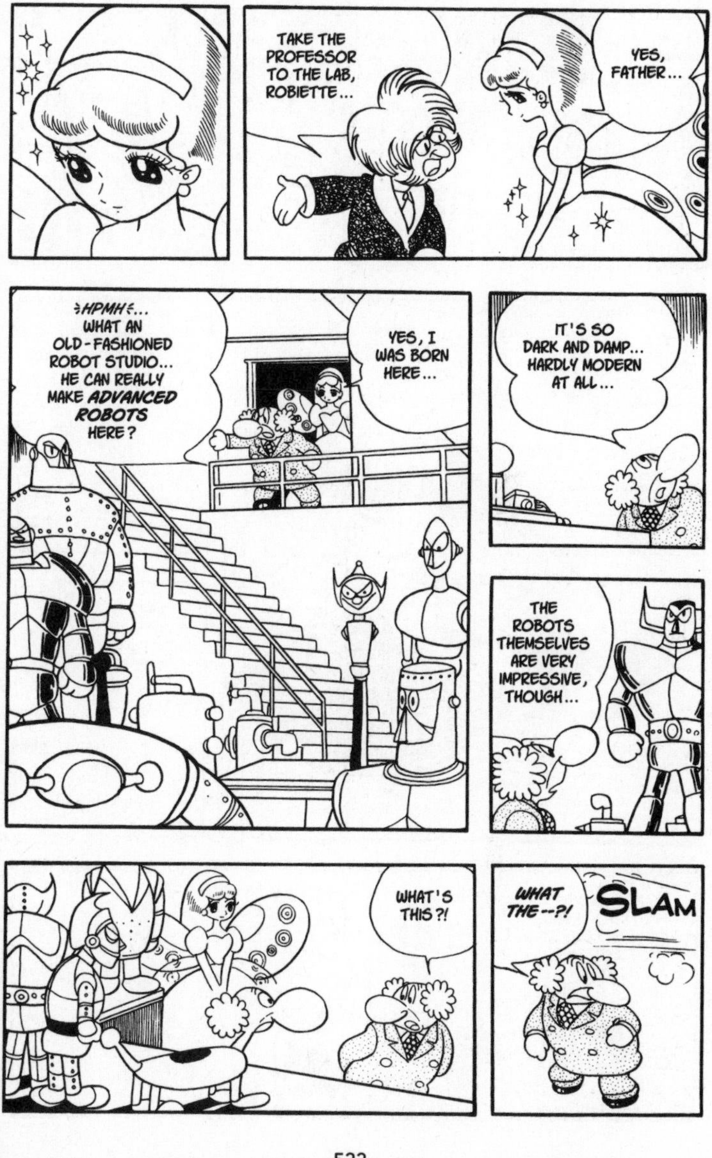
TAKE THE PROFESSOR TO THE LAB, ROBIETTE...
YES, FATHER...
≶HPMH≶... WHAT AN OLD-FASHIONED ROBOT STUDIO... HE CAN REALLY MAKE *ADVANCED ROBOTS* HERE?
YES, I WAS BORN HERE...
IT'S SO DARK AND DAMP... HARDLY MODERN AT ALL...
THE ROBOTS THEMSELVES ARE VERY IMPRESSIVE, THOUGH...
WHAT'S THIS?!
WHAT THE--?!
SLAM

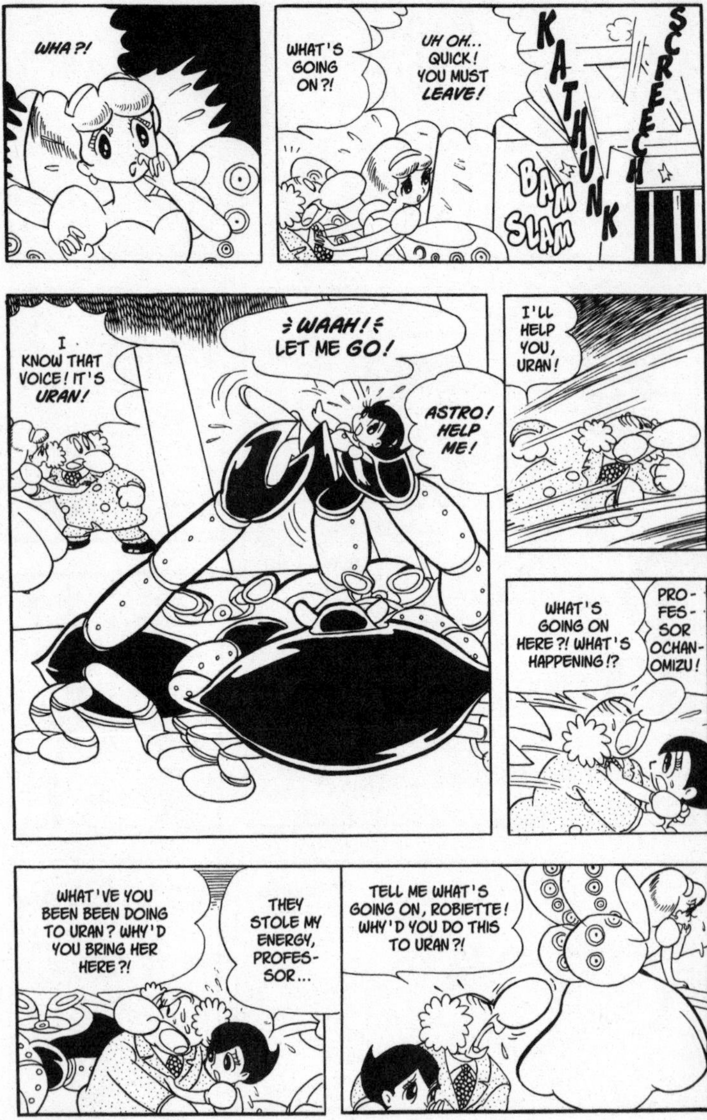
WHA?!
WHAT'S GOING ON?!
UH OH... QUICK! YOU MUST LEAVE!
KATHUNK
SCREECH
BAM
SLAM
I KNOW THAT VOICE! IT'S URAN!
WAAH! LET ME GO!
ASTRO! HELP ME!
I'LL HELP YOU, URAN!
WHAT'S GOING ON HERE?! WHAT'S HAPPENING!?
PRO-FES-SOR OCHAN-OMIZU!
WHAT'VE YOU BEEN BEEN DOING TO URAN? WHY'D YOU BRING HER HERE?!
THEY STOLE MY ENERGY, PROFES-SOR...
TELL ME WHAT'S GOING ON, ROBIETTE! WHY'D YOU DO THIS TO URAN?!

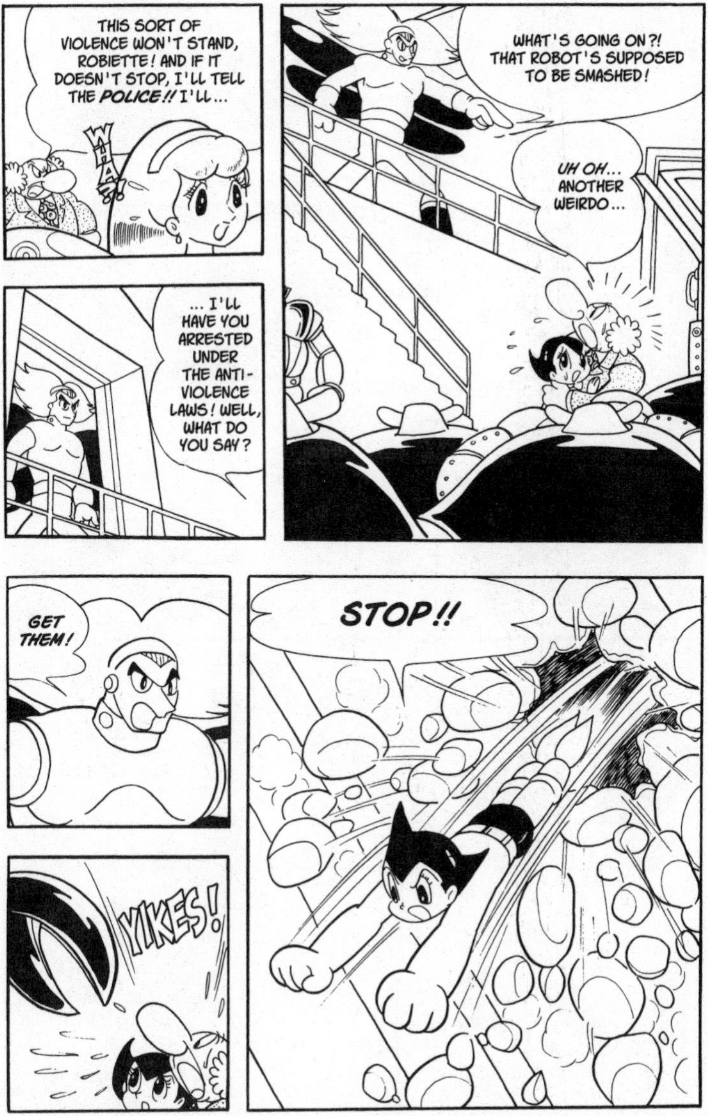
THIS SORT OF VIOLENCE WON'T STAND, ROBIETTE! AND IF IT DOESN'T STOP, I'LL TELL THE POLICE!! I'LL...
WHAP!
... I'LL HAVE YOU ARRESTED UNDER THE ANTI-VIOLENCE LAWS! WELL, WHAT DO YOU SAY?
WHAT'S GOING ON?! THAT ROBOT'S SUPPOSED TO BE SMASHED!
UH OH... ANOTHER WEIRDO...
GET THEM!
YIKES!
STOP!!

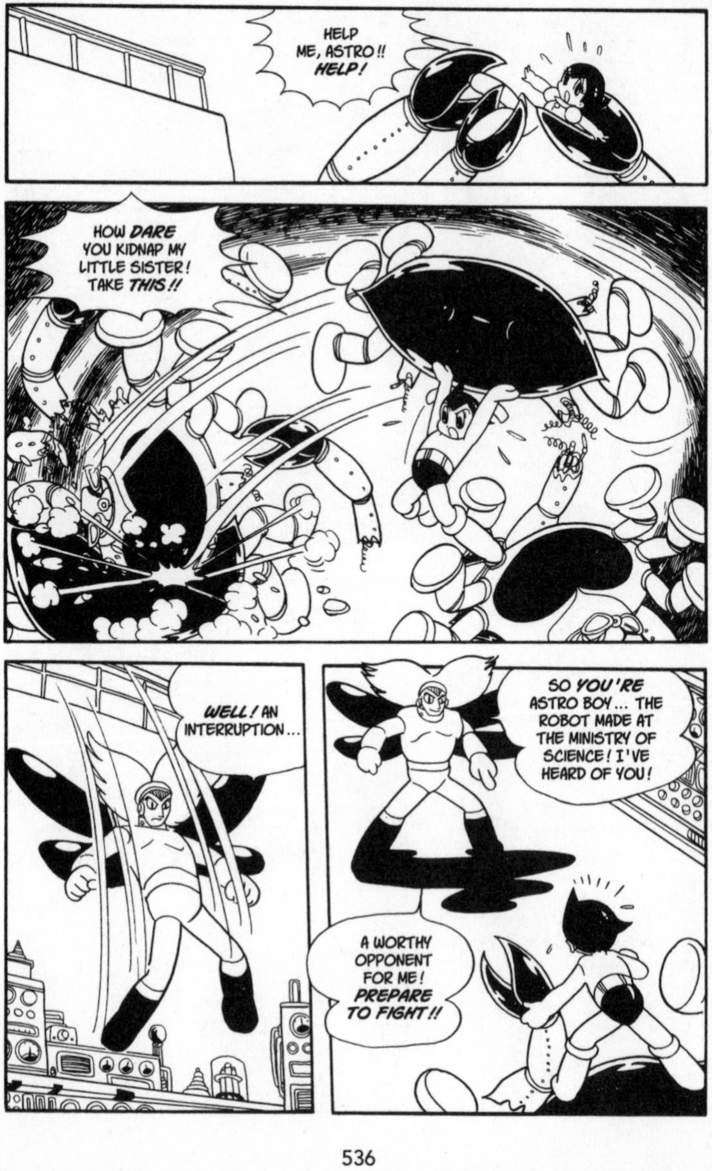
HELP ME, ASTRO!! HELP!
HOW DARE YOU KIDNAP MY LITTLE SISTER! TAKE THIS!!
WELL! AN INTERRUPTION...
SO YOU'RE ASTRO BOY... THE ROBOT MADE AT THE MINISTRY OF SCIENCE! I'VE HEARD OF YOU!
A WORTHY OPPONENT FOR ME! PREPARE TO FIGHT!!

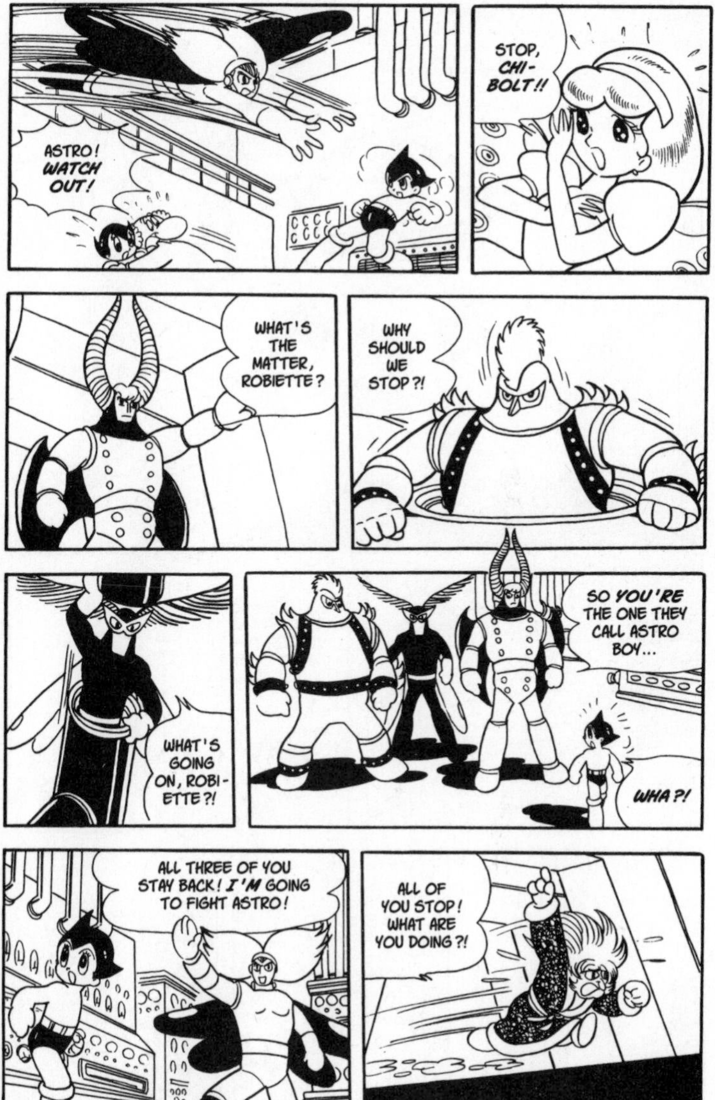
ASTRO! WATCH OUT!
STOP, CHI-BOLT!!
WHAT'S THE MATTER, ROBIETTE?
WHY SHOULD WE STOP?!
WHAT'S GOING ON, ROBI-ETTE?!
SO YOU'RE THE ONE THEY CALL ASTRO BOY...
WHA?!
ALL THREE OF YOU STAY BACK! I'M GOING TO FIGHT ASTRO!
ALL OF YOU STOP! WHAT ARE YOU DOING?!

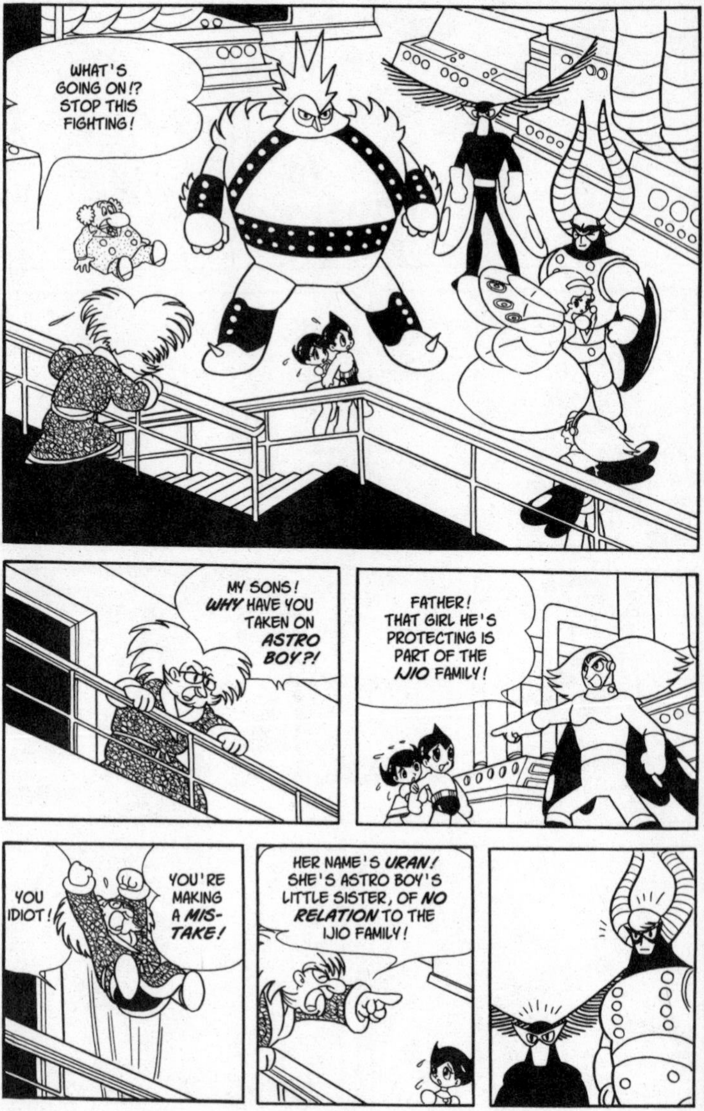
WHAT'S GOING ON!? STOP THIS FIGHTING!
MY SONS! WHY HAVE YOU TAKEN ON ASTRO BOY?!
FATHER! THAT GIRL HE'S PROTECTING IS PART OF THE IJIO FAMILY!
YOU IDIOT!
YOU'RE MAKING A MIS-TAKE!
HER NAME'S URAN! SHE'S ASTRO BOY'S LITTLE SISTER, OF NO RELATION TO THE IJIO FAMILY!

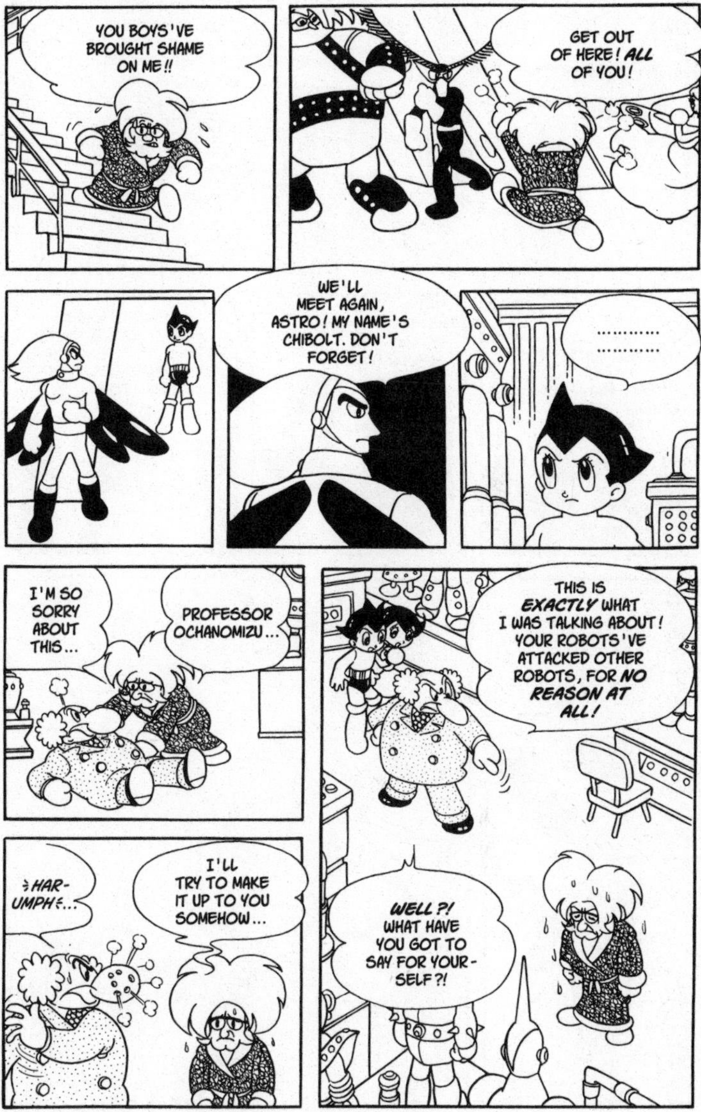
YOU BOYS'VE BROUGHT SHAME ON ME!!
GET OUT OF HERE! ALL OF YOU!
WE'LL MEET AGAIN, ASTRO! MY NAME'S CHIBOLT. DON'T FORGET!
....
I'M SO SORRY ABOUT THIS...
PROFESSOR OCHANOMIZU...
HAR-UMPH...
I'LL TRY TO MAKE IT UP TO YOU SOMEHOW...
THIS IS EXACTLY WHAT I WAS TALKING ABOUT! YOUR ROBOTS'VE ATTACKED OTHER ROBOTS, FOR NO REASON AT ALL!
WELL?! WHAT HAVE YOU GOT TO SAY FOR YOURSELF?!

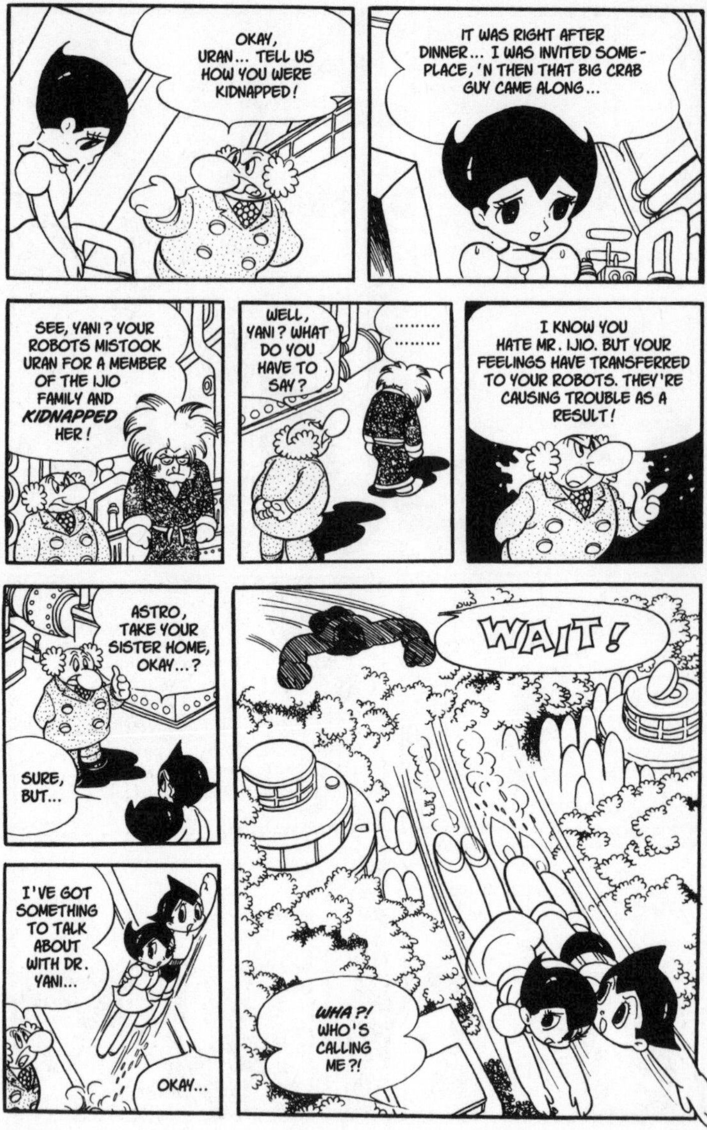

OKAY, URAN... TELL US HOW YOU WERE KIDNAPPED!
IT WAS RIGHT AFTER DINNER... I WAS INVITED SOME-PLACE, 'N THEN THAT BIG CRAB GUY CAME ALONG...
SEE, YANI? YOUR ROBOTS MISTOOK URAN FOR A MEMBER OF THE IJIO FAMILY AND ***KIDNAPPED*** HER!
WELL, YANI? WHAT DO YOU HAVE TO SAY?
....
....
I KNOW YOU HATE MR. IJIO. BUT YOUR FEELINGS HAVE TRANSFERRED TO YOUR ROBOTS. THEY'RE CAUSING TROUBLE AS A RESULT!
ASTRO, TAKE YOUR SISTER HOME, OKAY...?
SURE, BUT...
I'VE GOT SOMETHING TO TALK ABOUT WITH DR. YANI...
OKAY...
WAIT!
WHA?! WHO'S CALLING ME?!

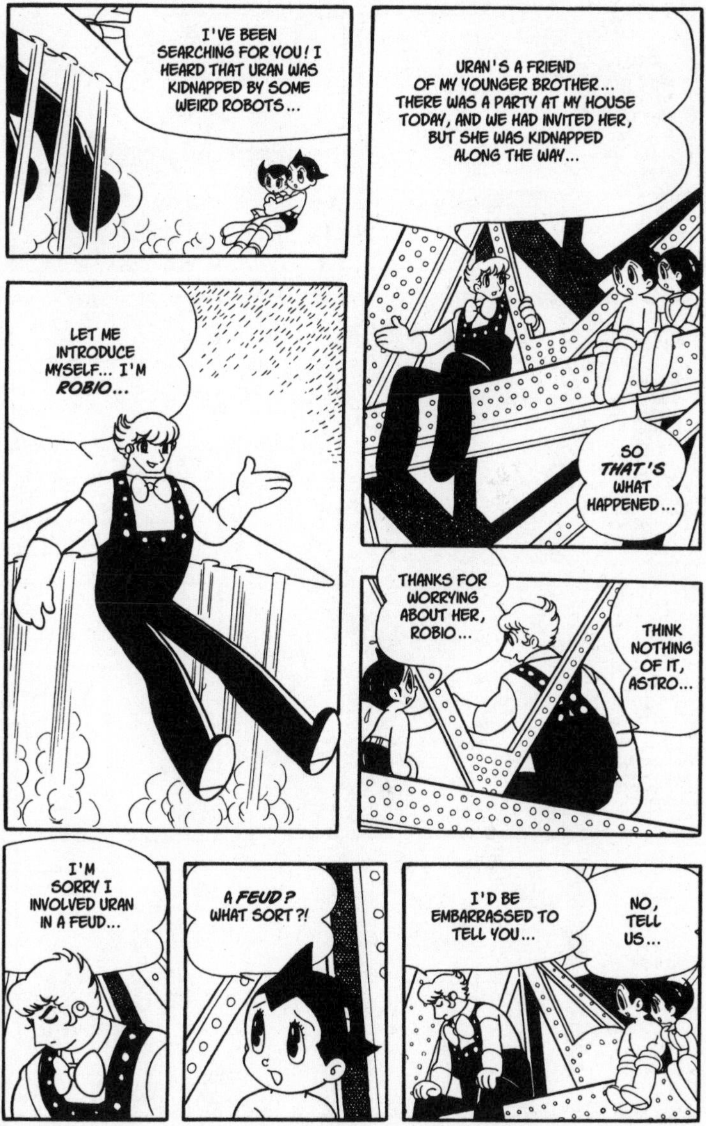
I'VE BEEN SEARCHING FOR YOU! I HEARD THAT URAN WAS KIDNAPPED BY SOME WEIRD ROBOTS...
URAN'S A FRIEND OF MY YOUNGER BROTHER... THERE WAS A PARTY AT MY HOUSE TODAY, AND WE HAD INVITED HER, BUT SHE WAS KIDNAPPED ALONG THE WAY...
SO THAT'S WHAT HAPPENED...
LET ME INTRODUCE MYSELF... I'M ROBIO...
THANKS FOR WORRYING ABOUT HER, ROBIO...
THINK NOTHING OF IT, ASTRO...
I'M SORRY I INVOLVED URAN IN A FEUD...
A FEUD? WHAT SORT?!
I'D BE EMBARRASSED TO TELL YOU...
NO, TELL US...

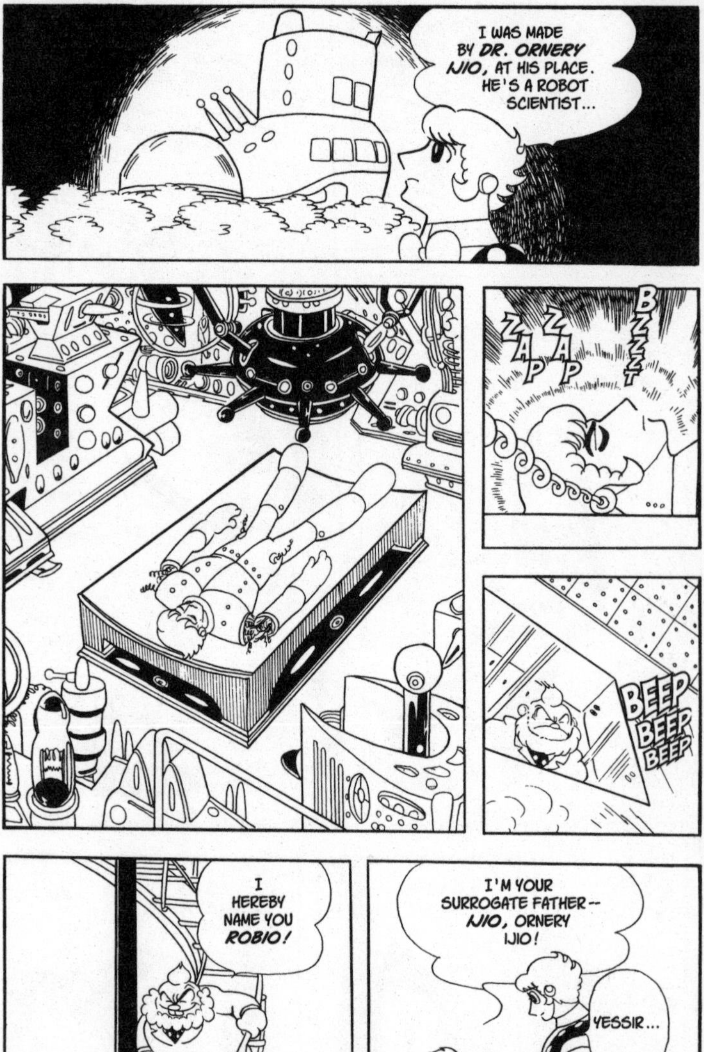
I WAS MADE BY DR. ORNERY IJIO, AT HIS PLACE. HE'S A ROBOT SCIENTIST...
ZAPP ZAPP
BZZZT
BEEP BEEP BEEP
I HEREBY NAME YOU ROBIO!
I'M YOUR SURROGATE FATHER-- IJIO, ORNERY IJIO!
YESSIR...

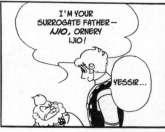

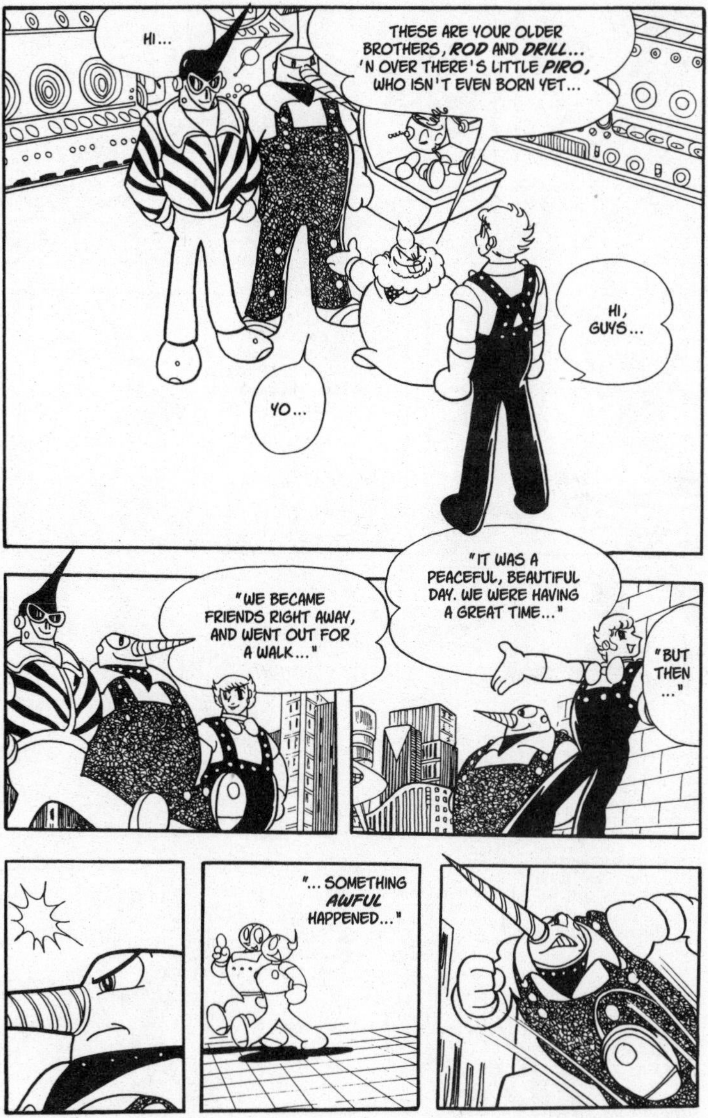
HI...
THESE ARE YOUR OLDER BROTHERS, ROD AND DRILL... 'N OVER THERE'S LITTLE PIRO, WHO ISN'T EVEN BORN YET...
YO...
HI, GUYS...
"WE BECAME FRIENDS RIGHT AWAY, AND WENT OUT FOR A WALK..."
"IT WAS A PEACEFUL, BEAUTIFUL DAY. WE WERE HAVING A GREAT TIME..."
"BUT THEN..."
"...SOMETHING AWFUL HAPPENED..."
...

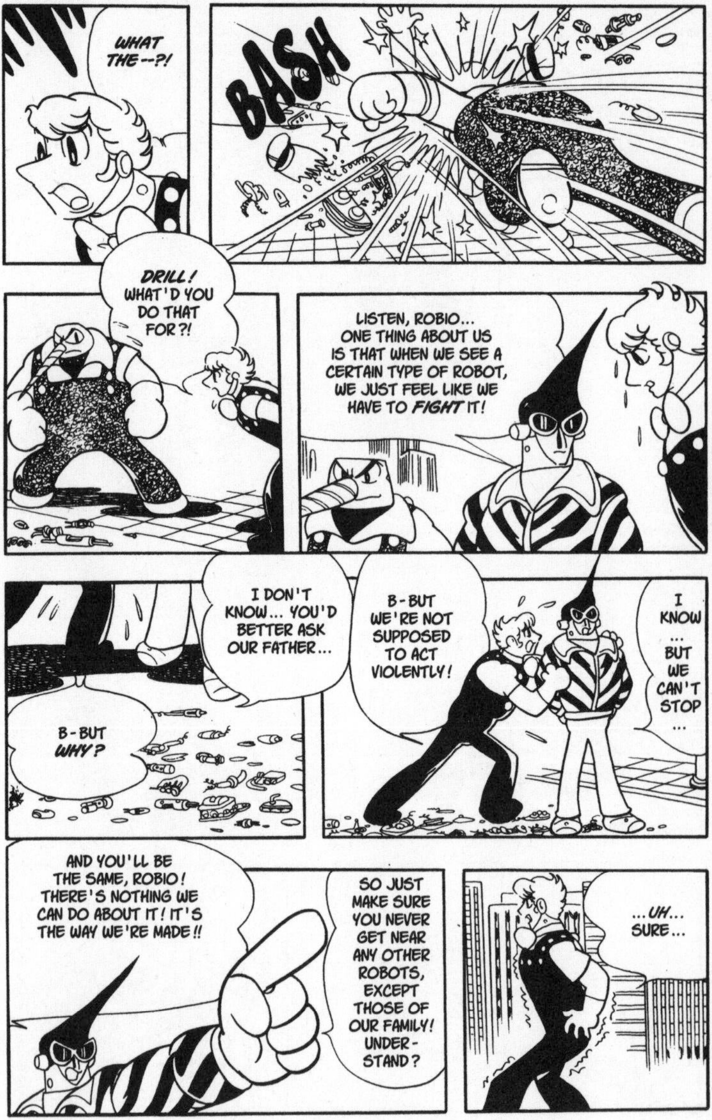
WHAT THE--?!
BASH
DRILL! WHAT'D YOU DO THAT FOR?!
LISTEN, ROBIO... ONE THING ABOUT US IS THAT WHEN WE SEE A CERTAIN TYPE OF ROBOT, WE JUST FEEL LIKE WE HAVE TO FIGHT IT!
B-BUT WHY?
I DON'T KNOW... YOU'D BETTER ASK OUR FATHER...
B-BUT WE'RE NOT SUPPOSED TO ACT VIOLENTLY!
I KNOW ... BUT WE CAN'T STOP ...
AND YOU'LL BE THE SAME, ROBIO! THERE'S NOTHING WE CAN DO ABOUT IT! IT'S THE WAY WE'RE MADE!!
SO JUST MAKE SURE YOU NEVER GET NEAR ANY OTHER ROBOTS, EXCEPT THOSE OF OUR FAMILY! UNDER-STAND?
...UH... SURE...

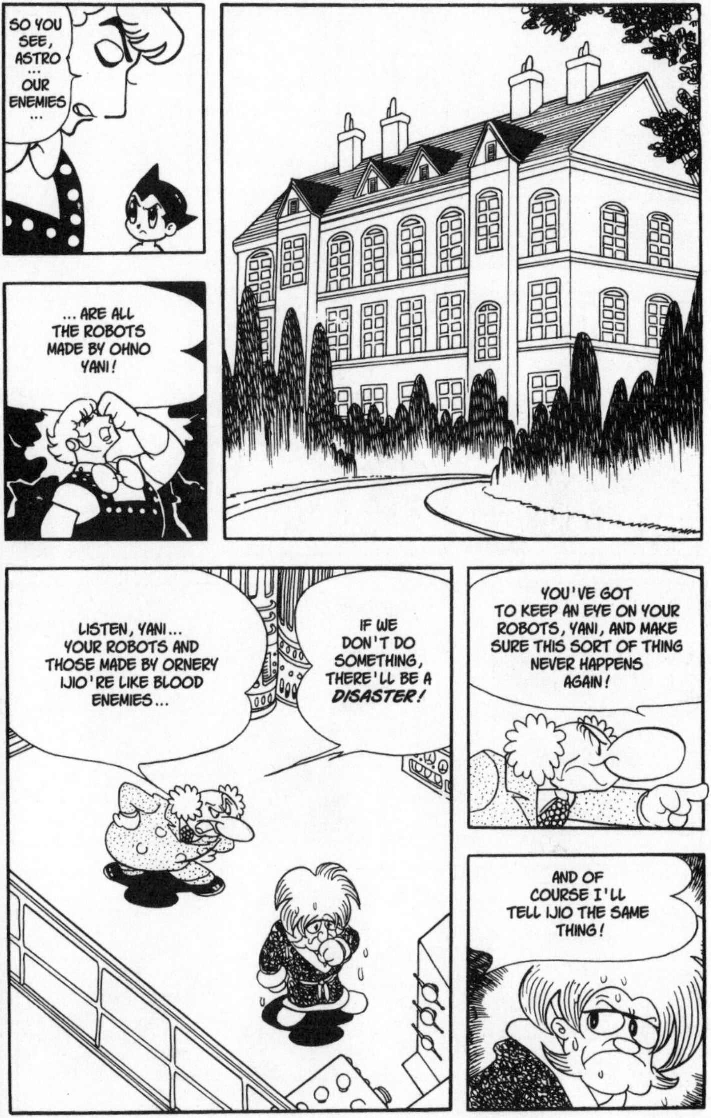
SO YOU SEE, ASTRO ... OUR ENEMIES ...
... ARE ALL THE ROBOTS MADE BY OHNO YANI!
LISTEN, YANI... YOUR ROBOTS AND THOSE MADE BY ORNERY IJIO'RE LIKE BLOOD ENEMIES...
IF WE DON'T DO SOMETHING, THERE'LL BE A *DISASTER!*
YOU'VE GOT TO KEEP AN EYE ON YOUR ROBOTS, YANI, AND MAKE SURE THIS SORT OF THING NEVER HAPPENS AGAIN!
AND OF COURSE I'LL TELL IJIO THE SAME THING!

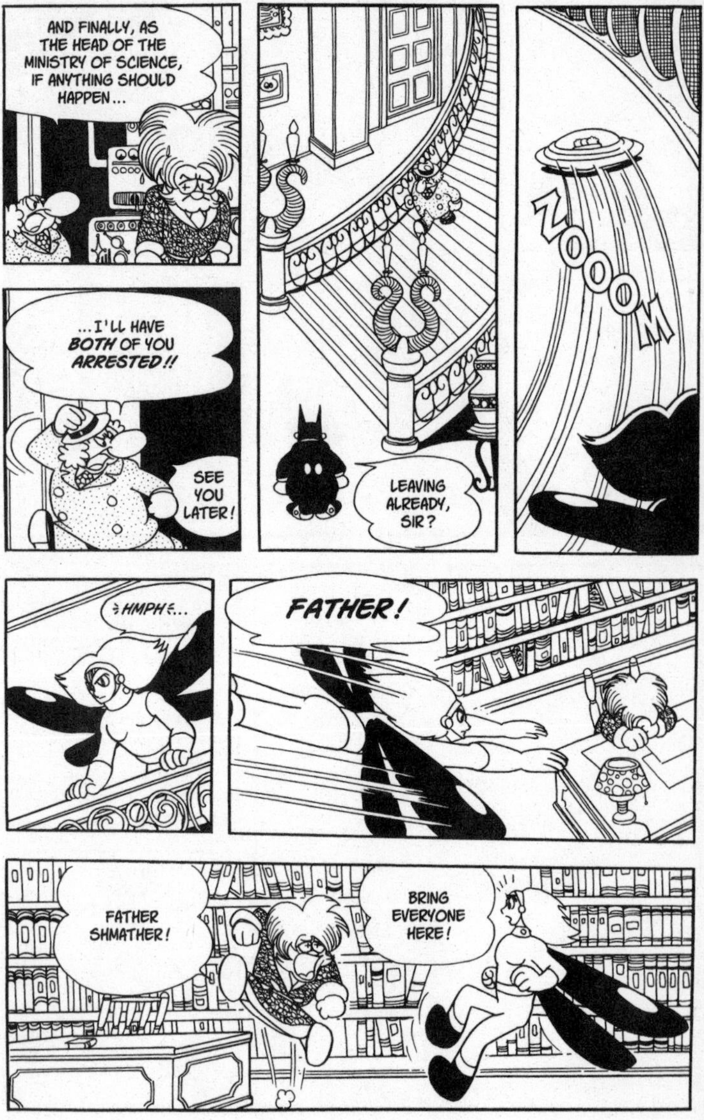
AND FINALLY, AS THE HEAD OF THE MINISTRY OF SCIENCE, IF ANYTHING SHOULD HAPPEN...
...I'LL HAVE BOTH OF YOU ARRESTED!!
SEE YOU LATER!
LEAVING ALREADY, SIR?
ZOOOM
HMPH...
FATHER!
FATHER SHMATHER!
BRING EVERYONE HERE!

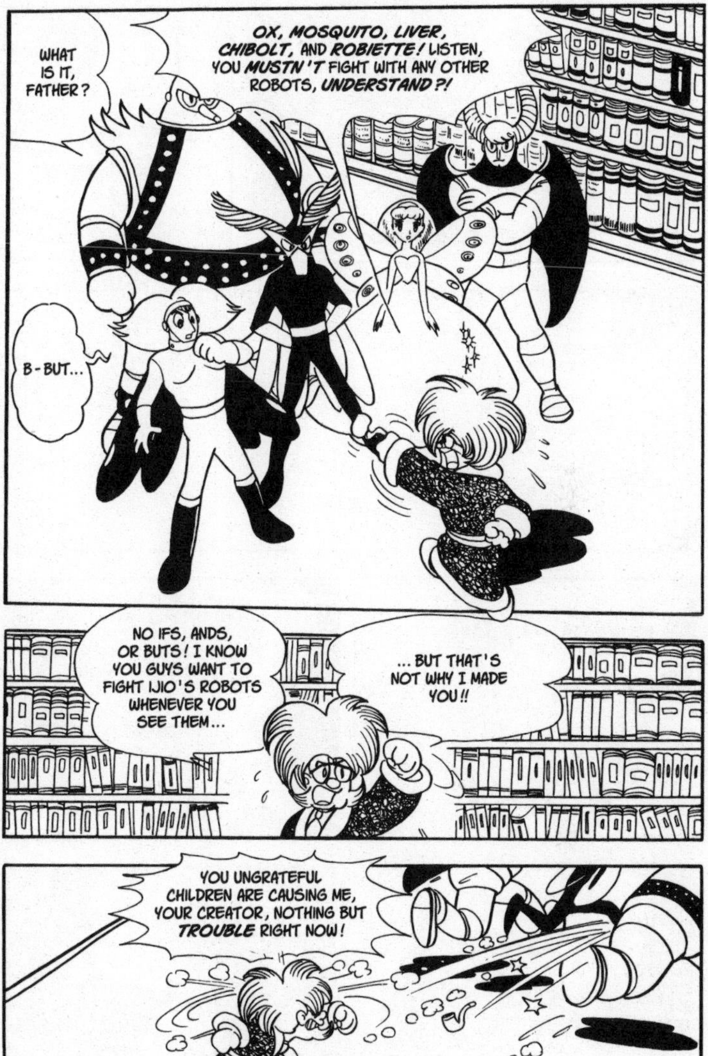
WHAT IS IT, FATHER?
OX, MOSQUITO, LIVER, CHIBOLT, AND ROBIETTE! LISTEN, YOU MUSTN'T FIGHT WITH ANY OTHER ROBOTS, UNDERSTAND?!
B-BUT...
NO IFS, ANDS, OR BUTS! I KNOW YOU GUYS WANT TO FIGHT IJIO'S ROBOTS WHENEVER YOU SEE THEM...
... BUT THAT'S NOT WHY I MADE YOU!!
YOU UNGRATEFUL CHILDREN ARE CAUSING ME, YOUR CREATOR, NOTHING BUT TROUBLE RIGHT NOW!

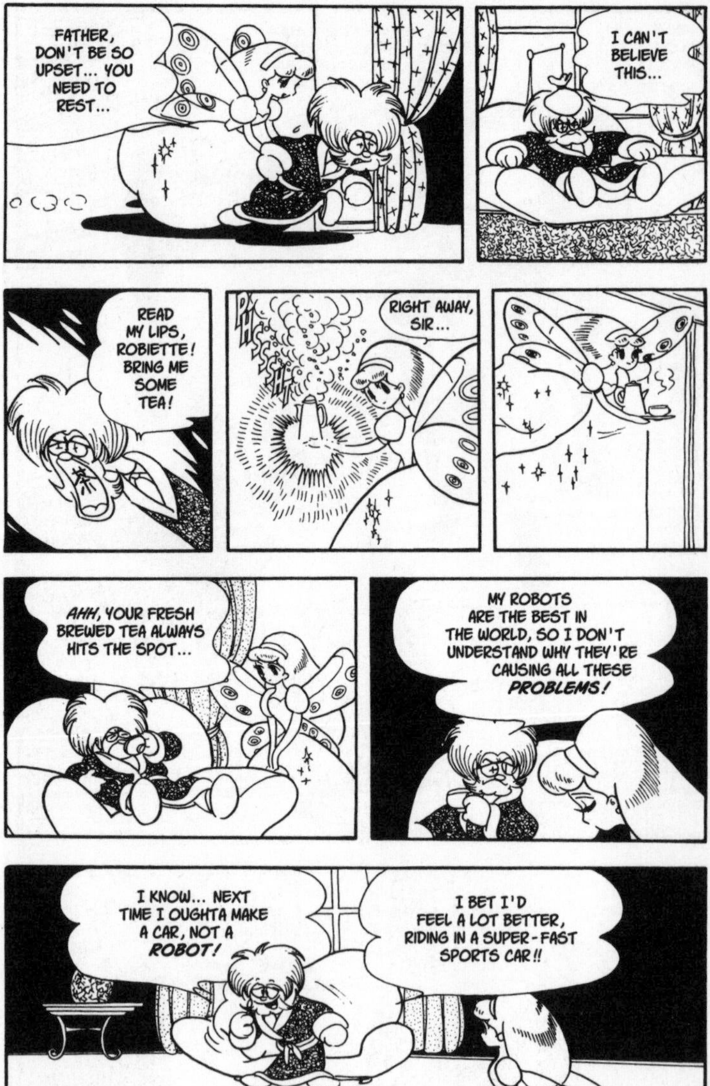
FATHER, DON'T BE SO UPSET... YOU NEED TO REST...
I CAN'T BELIEVE THIS...
READ MY LIPS, ROBIETTE! BRING ME SOME TEA!
RIGHT AWAY, SIR...
AHH, YOUR FRESH BREWED TEA ALWAYS HITS THE SPOT...
MY ROBOTS ARE THE BEST IN THE WORLD, SO I DON'T UNDERSTAND WHY THEY'RE CAUSING ALL THESE PROBLEMS!
I KNOW... NEXT TIME I OUGHTA MAKE A CAR, NOT A ROBOT!
I BET I'D FEEL A LOT BETTER, RIDING IN A SUPER-FAST SPORTS CAR!!

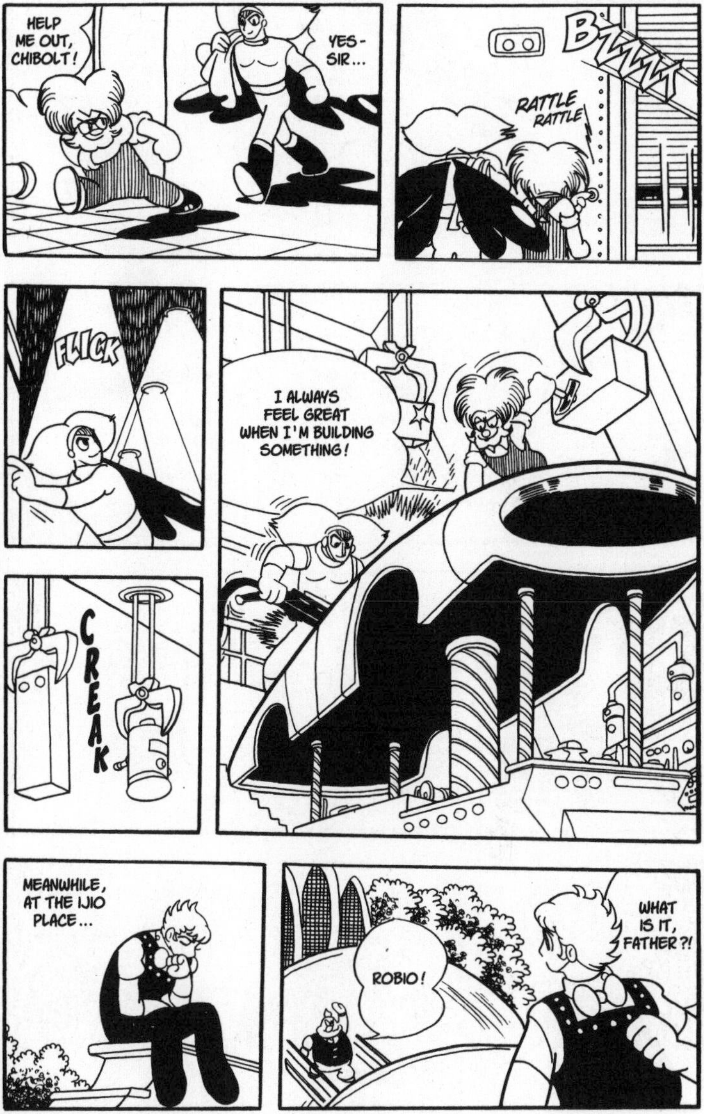
HELP ME OUT, CHIBOLT!
YES-SIR...
BZZZT
RATTLE RATTLE
FLICK
I ALWAYS FEEL GREAT WHEN I'M BUILDING SOMETHING!
CREAK
MEANWHILE, AT THE IJIO PLACE...
ROBIO!
WHAT IS IT, FATHER?!

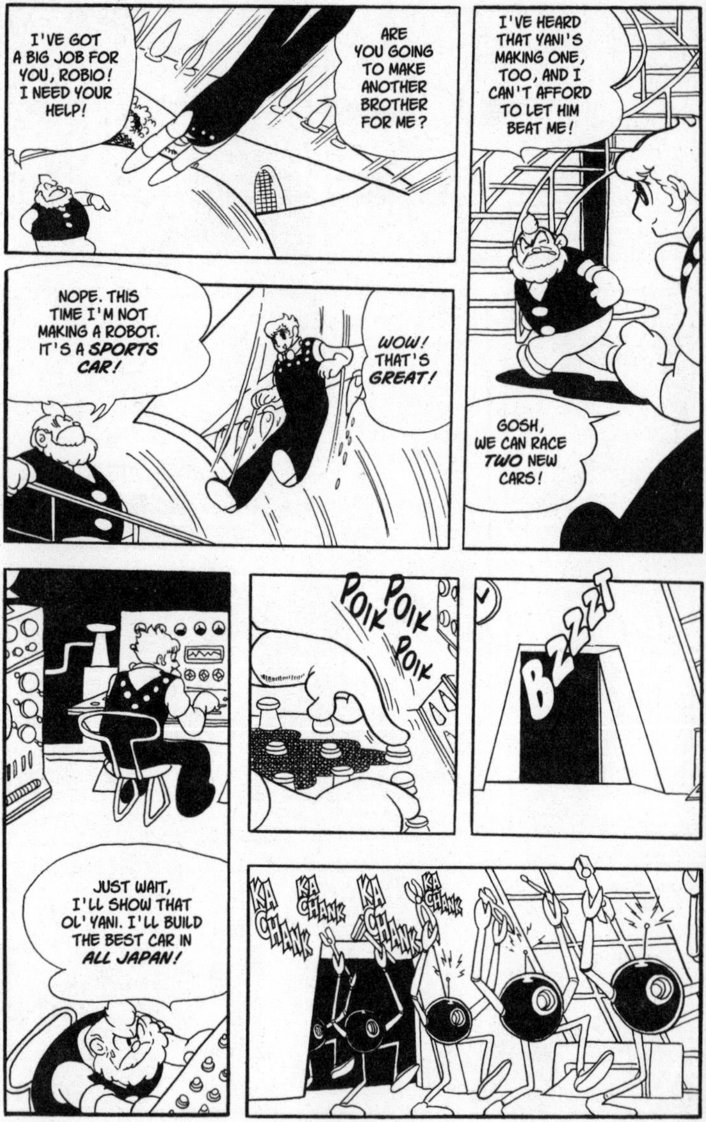
I'VE GOT A BIG JOB FOR YOU, ROBIO! I NEED YOUR HELP!
ARE YOU GOING TO MAKE ANOTHER BROTHER FOR ME?
I'VE HEARD THAT YANI'S MAKING ONE, TOO, AND I CAN'T AFFORD TO LET HIM BEAT ME!
NOPE. THIS TIME I'M NOT MAKING A ROBOT. IT'S A SPORTS CAR!
WOW! THAT'S GREAT!
GOSH, WE CAN RACE TWO NEW CARS!
JUST WAIT, I'LL SHOW THAT OL' YANI. I'LL BUILD THE BEST CAR IN ALL JAPAN!
POIK POIK POIK POIK
BZZZZT
KA CHANK KA CHANK KA CHANK KA CHANK

BAM BAM

RRRRING

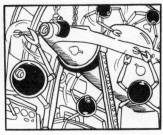

'ELLO... IJIO HERE...

WHAT?! YANI? WHAT THE --?!

I MEAN, GOSH, SURE IS NICE WEATHER... TOMORROW, TOO, *HUH*... DUNNO 'BOUT THE DAY AFTER TOMORROW, THOUGH...

DID OCHANOMIZU VISIT YOUR PLACE, TOO, DR. YANI? REALLY? WELL, HE CAME HERE, TOO...

HE SAID WE WERE *SWORN ENEMIES*... EVER HEAR OF SUCH NONSENSE?!

BY THE WAY, I'VE HEARD YOU'RE MAKING A *SPORTS CAR*...

SO YOU'VE HEARD ALREADY, *EH*? WELL, IT'S TRUE. I *AM* MAKING ONE, THE *BEST* IN *ALL* JAPAN!

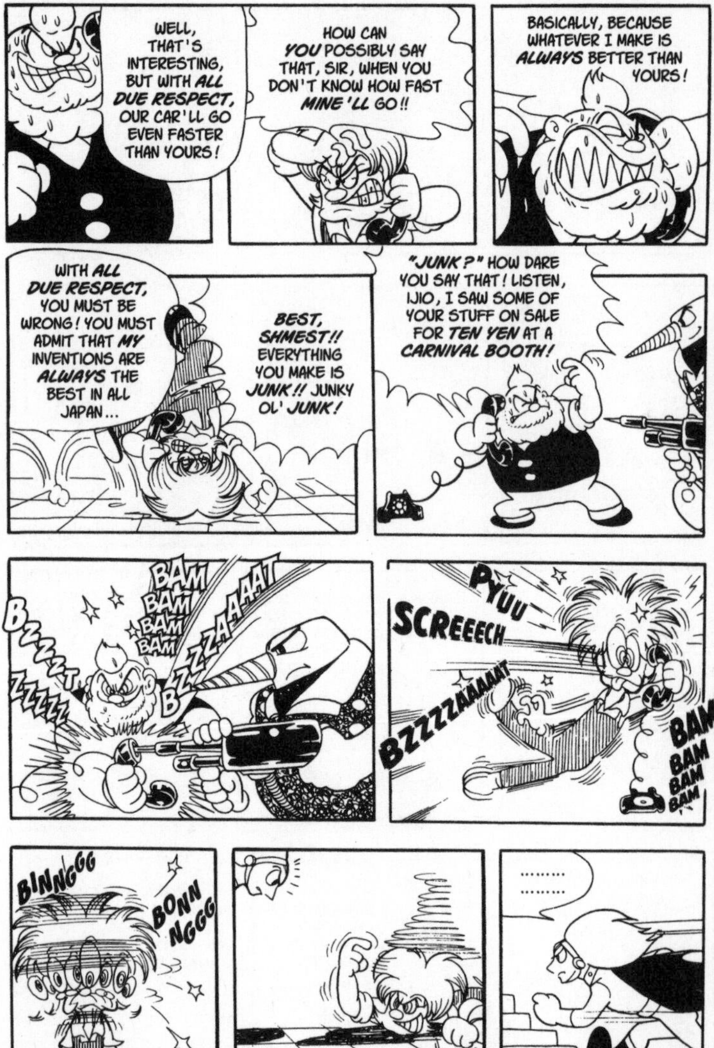
WELL, THAT'S INTERESTING, BUT WITH ALL DUE RESPECT, OUR CAR'LL GO EVEN FASTER THAN YOURS!
HOW CAN YOU POSSIBLY SAY THAT, SIR, WHEN YOU DON'T KNOW HOW FAST MINE'LL GO!!
BASICALLY, BECAUSE WHATEVER I MAKE IS ALWAYS BETTER THAN YOURS!
WITH ALL DUE RESPECT, YOU MUST BE WRONG! YOU MUST ADMIT THAT MY INVENTIONS ARE ALWAYS THE BEST IN ALL JAPAN...
BEST, SHMEST!! EVERYTHING YOU MAKE IS JUNK!! JUNKY OL' JUNK!
"JUNK?" HOW DARE YOU SAY THAT! LISTEN, IJIO, I SAW SOME OF YOUR STUFF ON SALE FOR TEN YEN AT A CARNIVAL BOOTH!
BZZZZT
ZZZZZ
BAM
BAM
BAM
BAM
BZZZZAAAAT
PYUU
SCREEECH
BZZZZAAAAAT
BAM
BAM
BAM
BAM
BAM
BINNGGG
BONN NGGG
....
....

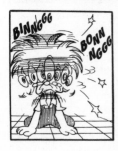

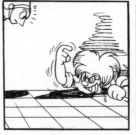

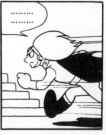

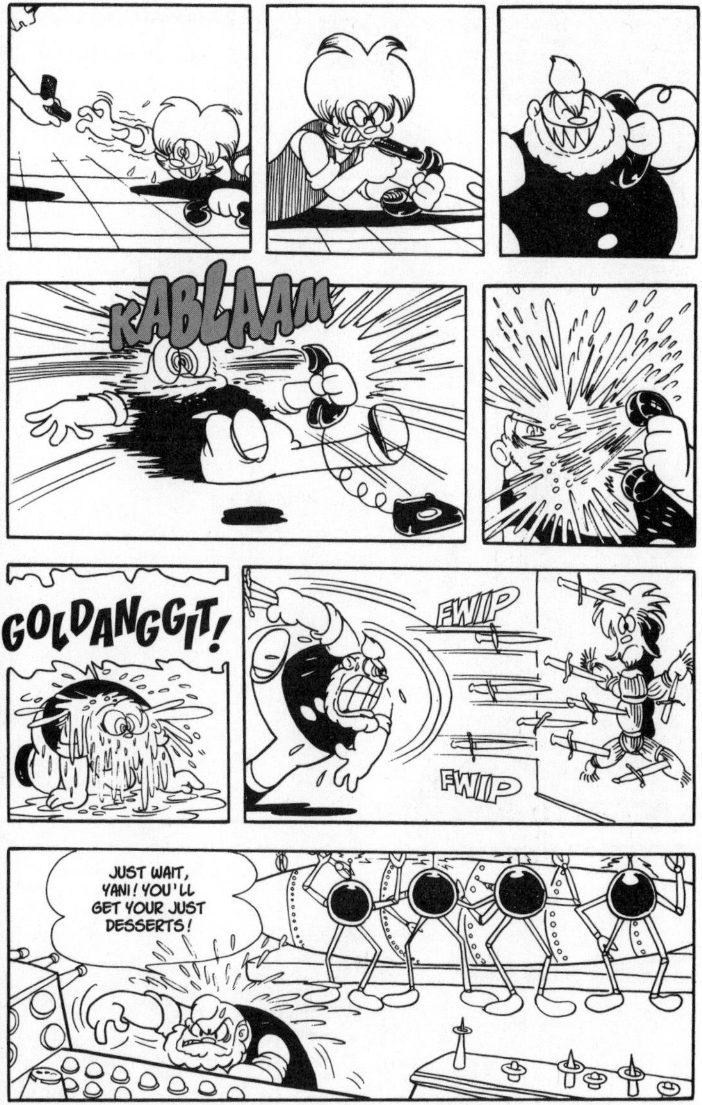
KABLAAM
GOLDANGGIT!
FWIP
FWIP
JUST WAIT, YANI! YOU'LL GET YOUR JUST DESSERTS!

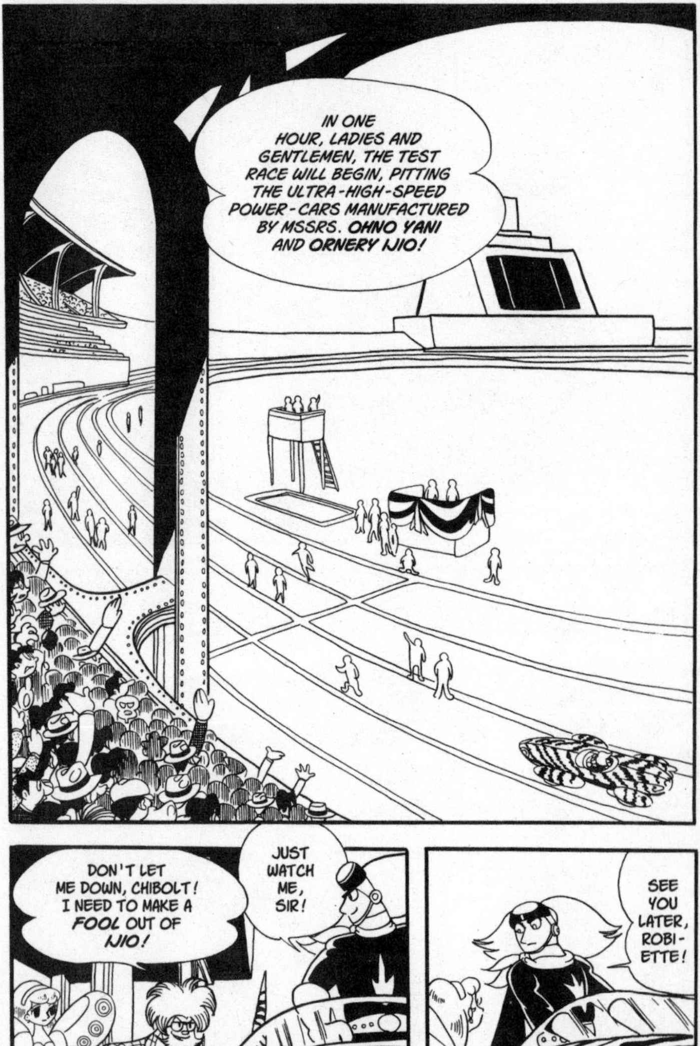
IN ONE HOUR, LADIES AND GENTLEMEN, THE TEST RACE WILL BEGIN, PITTING THE ULTRA-HIGH-SPEED POWER-CARS MANUFACTURED BY MSSRS. **OHNO YANI** AND **ORNERY IJIO!**
DON'T LET ME DOWN, CHIBOLT! I NEED TO MAKE A ***FOOL*** OUT OF ***IJIO!***
JUST WATCH ME, SIR!
SEE YOU LATER, ROBI-ETTE!

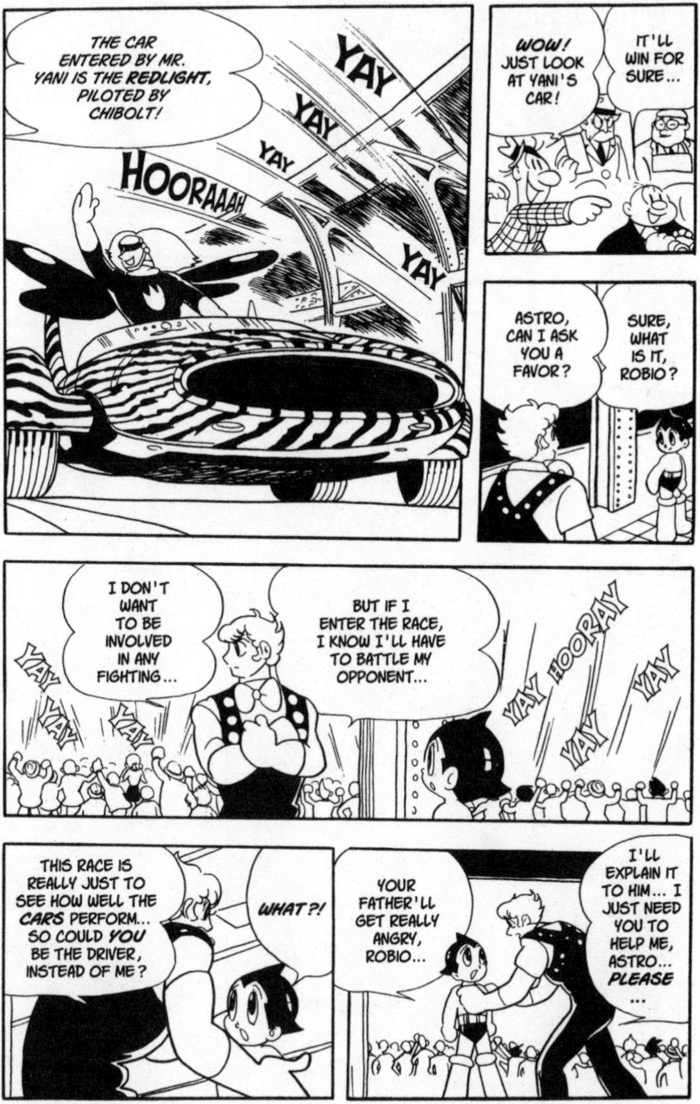

THE CAR ENTERED BY MR. YANI IS THE REDLIGHT, PILOTED BY CHIBOLT!
YAY
YAY
YAY
HOORAAAH
YAY
WOW! JUST LOOK AT YANI'S CAR!
IT'LL WIN FOR SURE...
ASTRO, CAN I ASK YOU A FAVOR?
SURE, WHAT IS IT, ROBIO?
I DON'T WANT TO BE INVOLVED IN ANY FIGHTING...
YAY
YAY
YAY
BUT IF I ENTER THE RACE, I KNOW I'LL HAVE TO BATTLE MY OPPONENT...
YAY
HOORAY
YAY
YAY
THIS RACE IS REALLY JUST TO SEE HOW WELL THE CARS PERFORM... SO COULD YOU BE THE DRIVER, INSTEAD OF ME?
WHAT?!
YOUR FATHER'LL GET REALLY ANGRY, ROBIO...
I'LL EXPLAIN IT TO HIM... I JUST NEED YOU TO HELP ME, ASTRO... PLEASE ...

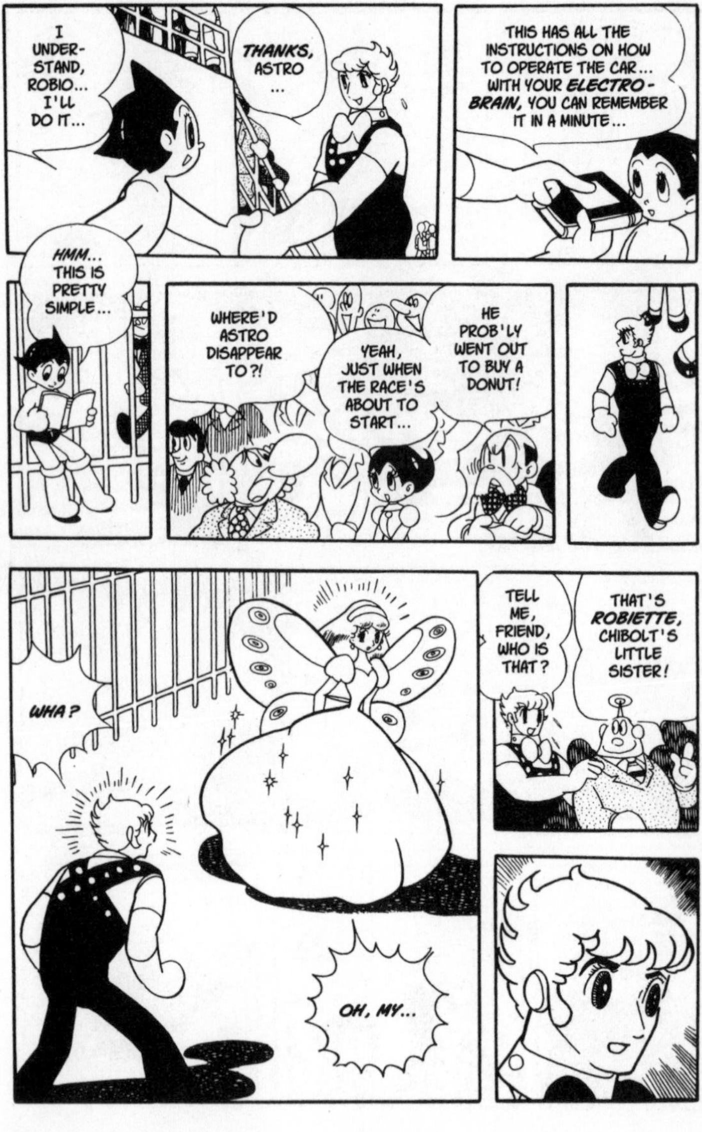
I UNDERSTAND, ROBIO... I'LL DO IT...
THANKS, ASTRO ...
THIS HAS ALL THE INSTRUCTIONS ON HOW TO OPERATE THE CAR... WITH YOUR ELECTRO-BRAIN, YOU CAN REMEMBER IT IN A MINUTE...
HMM... THIS IS PRETTY SIMPLE...
WHERE'D ASTRO DISAPPEAR TO?!
YEAH, JUST WHEN THE RACE'S ABOUT TO START...
HE PROB'LY WENT OUT TO BUY A DONUT!
WHA?
OH, MY...
TELL ME, FRIEND, WHO IS THAT?
THAT'S ROBIETTE, CHIBOLT'S LITTLE SISTER!

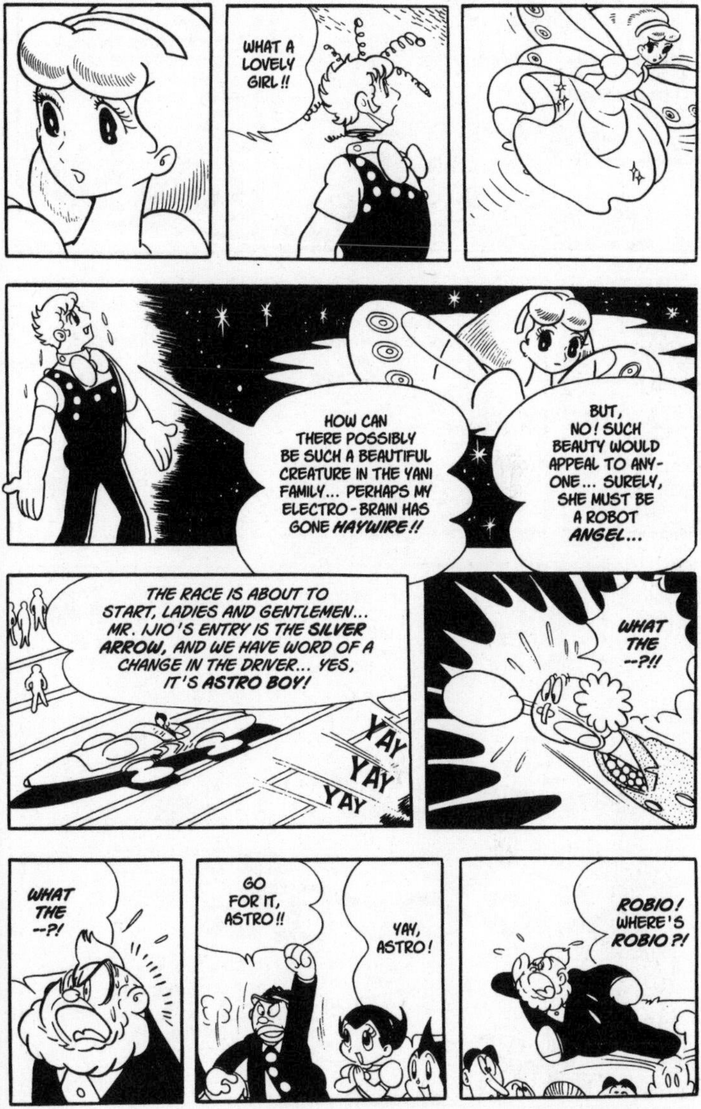
WHAT A LOVELY GIRL!!
HOW CAN THERE POSSIBLY BE SUCH A BEAUTIFUL CREATURE IN THE YANI FAMILY... PERHAPS MY ELECTRO-BRAIN HAS GONE HAYWIRE!!
BUT, NO! SUCH BEAUTY WOULD APPEAL TO ANY-ONE... SURELY, SHE MUST BE A ROBOT ANGEL...
THE RACE IS ABOUT TO START, LADIES AND GENTLEMEN... MR. IJIO'S ENTRY IS THE SILVER ARROW, AND WE HAVE WORD OF A CHANGE IN THE DRIVER... YES, IT'S ASTRO BOY!
YAY
YAY
YAY
WHAT THE --?!!
WHAT THE --?!
GO FOR IT, ASTRO!!
YAY, ASTRO!
ROBIO! WHERE'S ROBIO?!

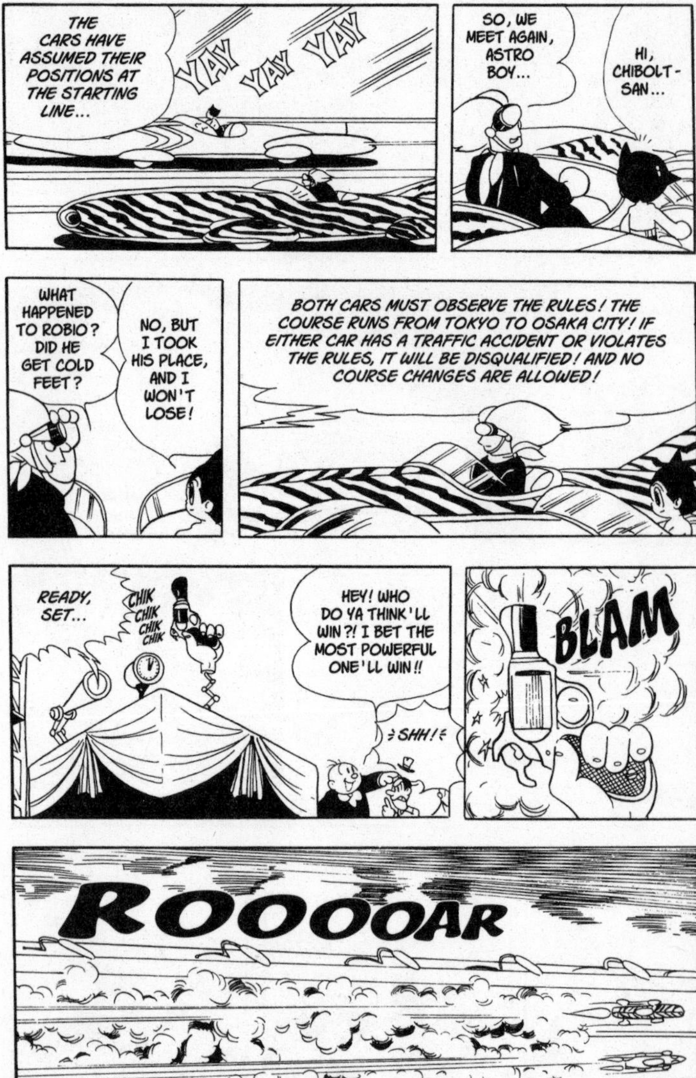
THE CARS HAVE ASSUMED THEIR POSITIONS AT THE STARTING LINE...
YAY YAY YAY
SO, WE MEET AGAIN, ASTRO BOY...
HI, CHIBOLT-SAN...
WHAT HAPPENED TO ROBIO? DID HE GET COLD FEET?
NO, BUT I TOOK HIS PLACE, AND I WON'T LOSE!
BOTH CARS MUST OBSERVE THE RULES! THE COURSE RUNS FROM TOKYO TO OSAKA CITY! IF EITHER CAR HAS A TRAFFIC ACCIDENT OR VIOLATES THE RULES, IT WILL BE DISQUALIFIED! AND NO COURSE CHANGES ARE ALLOWED!
READY, SET...
CHIK CHIK CHIK CHIK
HEY! WHO DO YA THINK'LL WIN?! I BET THE MOST POWERFUL ONE'LL WIN!!
SHH!
BLAM
ROOOOAR

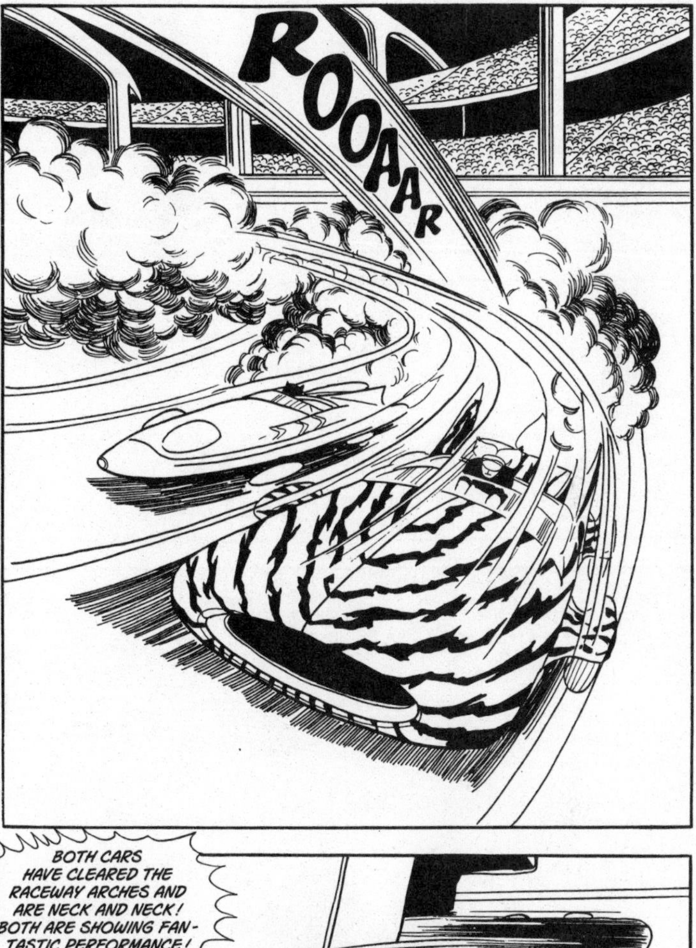
ROOOAAAR

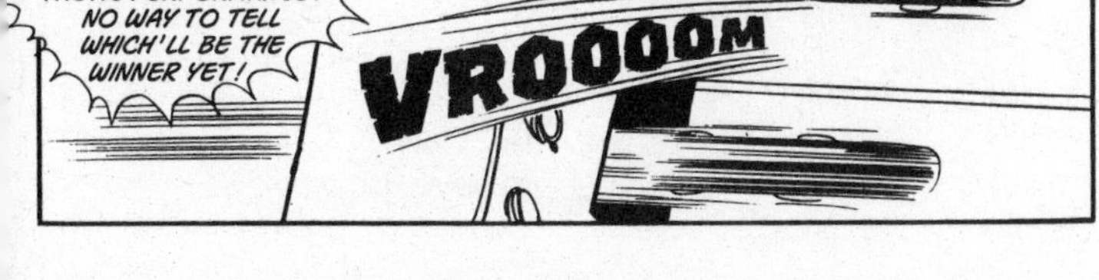
BOTH CARS HAVE CLEARED THE RACEWAY ARCHES AND ARE NECK AND NECK! BOTH ARE SHOWING FAN-TASTIC PERFORMANCE! NO WAY TO TELL WHICH'LL BE THE WINNER YET!
VROOOOM

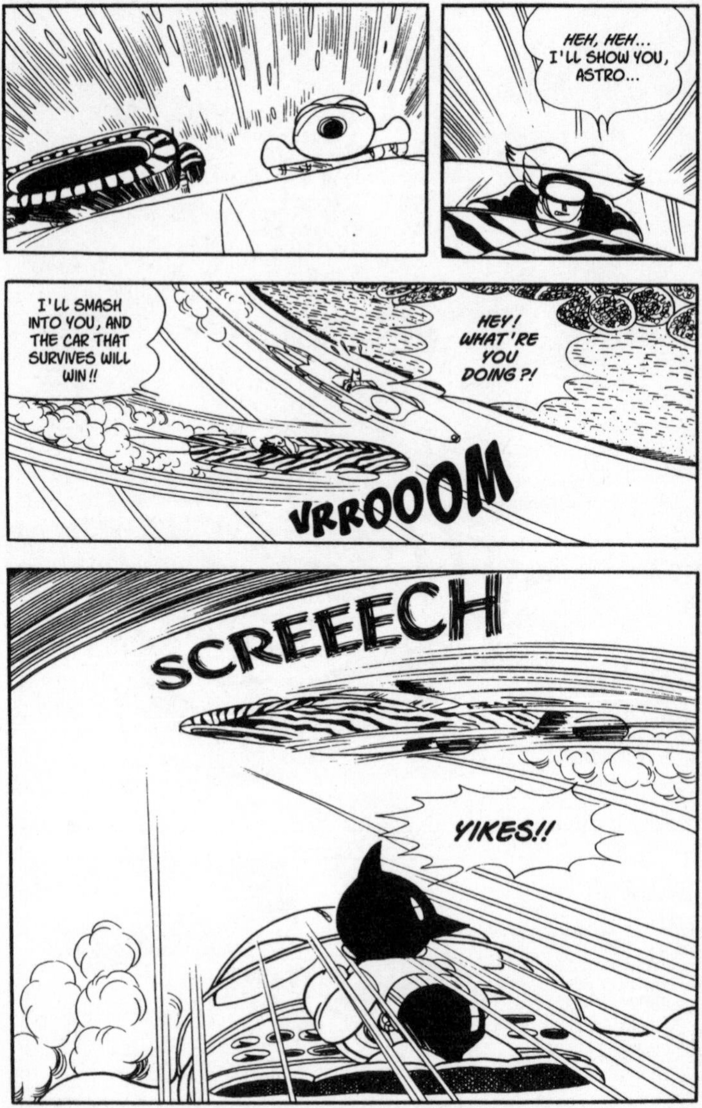
HEH, HEH... I'LL SHOW YOU, ASTRO...
I'LL SMASH INTO YOU, AND THE CAR THAT SURVIVES WILL WIN!!
HEY! WHAT'RE YOU DOING?!
VRROOOM
SCREEECH
YIKES!!

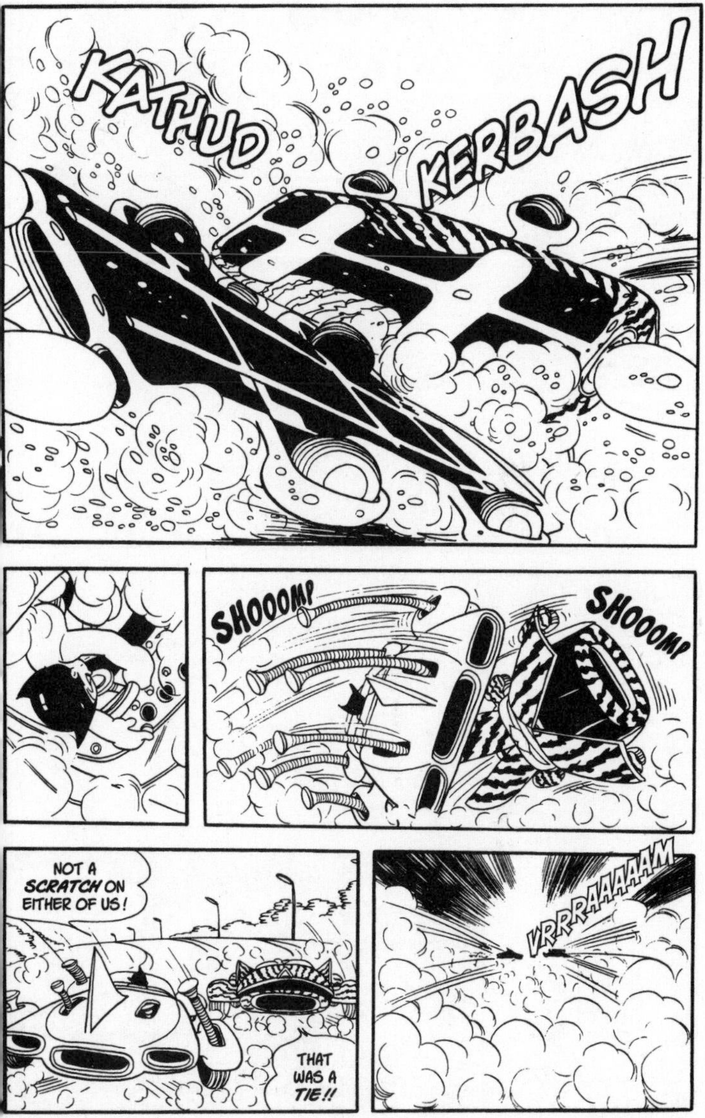
KATHUD
KERBASH
SHOOOMP
SHOOOMP
NOT A SCRATCH ON EITHER OF US!
THAT WAS A TIE!!
VRRRAAAAAM

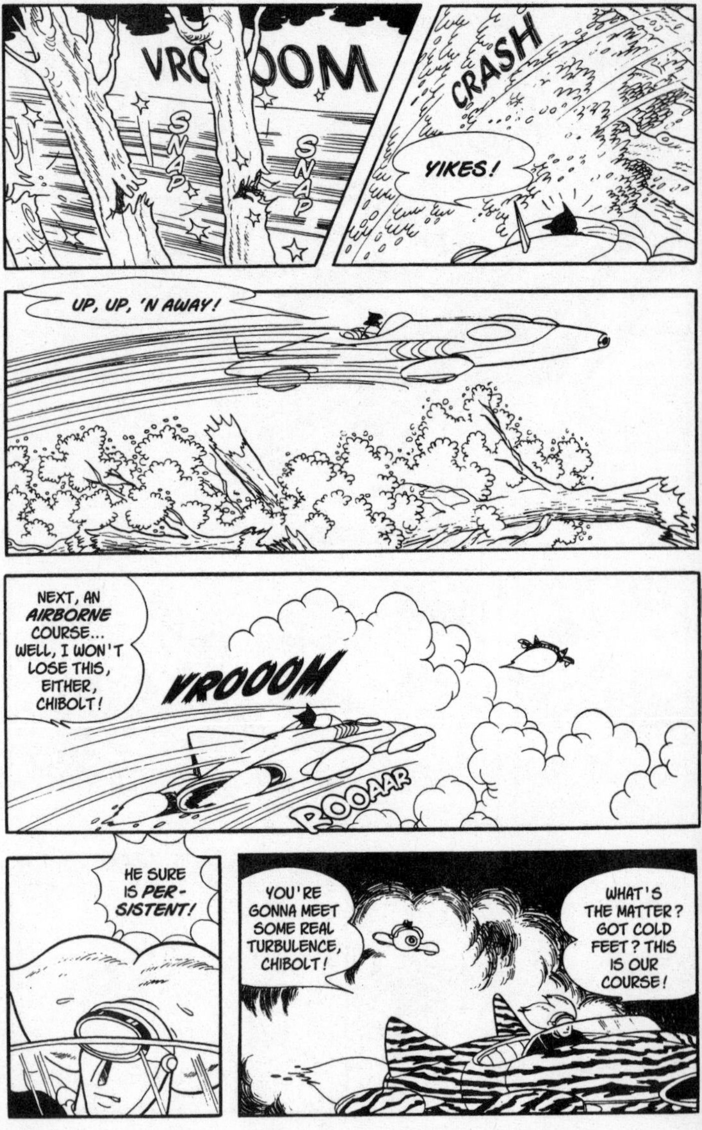
VROOOM
SNAP
SNAP
CRASH
YIKES!
UP, UP, 'N AWAY!
NEXT, AN AIRBORNE COURSE... WELL, I WON'T LOSE THIS, EITHER, CHIBOLT!
VROOOM
ROOAAR
HE SURE IS PERSISTENT!
YOU'RE GONNA MEET SOME REAL TURBULENCE, CHIBOLT!
WHAT'S THE MATTER? GOT COLD FEET? THIS IS OUR COURSE!

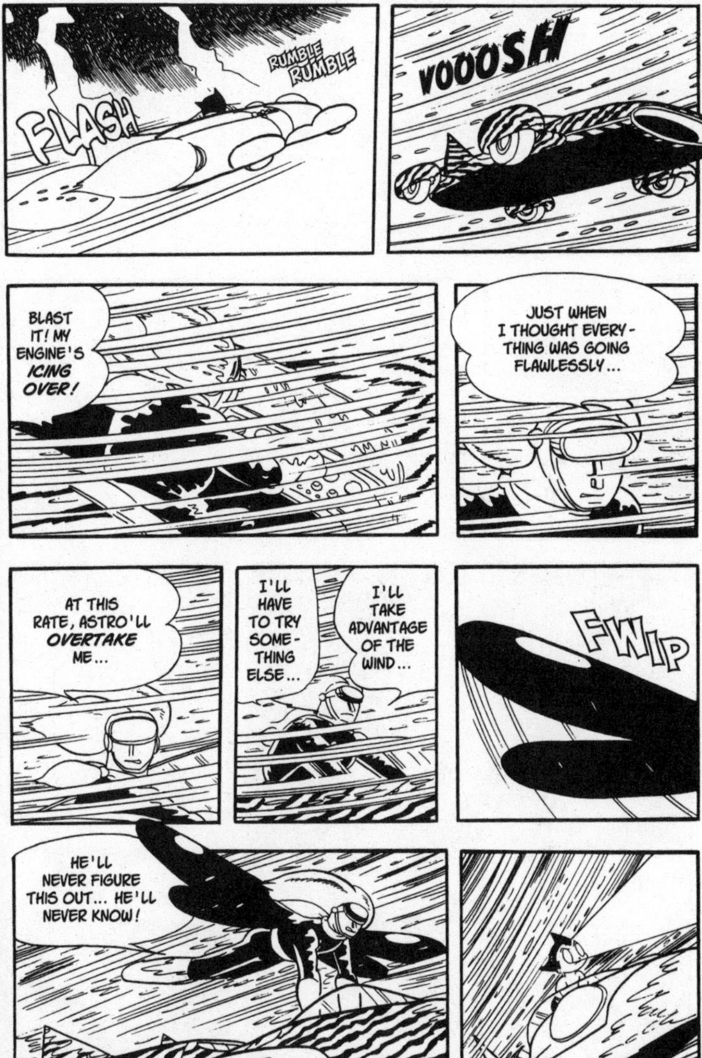
RUMBLE RUMBLE
FLASH
VOOOSH
BLAST IT! MY ENGINE'S *ICING OVER!*
JUST WHEN I THOUGHT EVERY-THING WAS GOING FLAWLESSLY...
AT THIS RATE, ASTRO'LL *OVERTAKE* ME...
I'LL HAVE TO TRY SOME-THING ELSE...
I'LL TAKE ADVANTAGE OF THE WIND...
FWIP
HE'LL NEVER FIGURE THIS OUT... HE'LL NEVER KNOW!

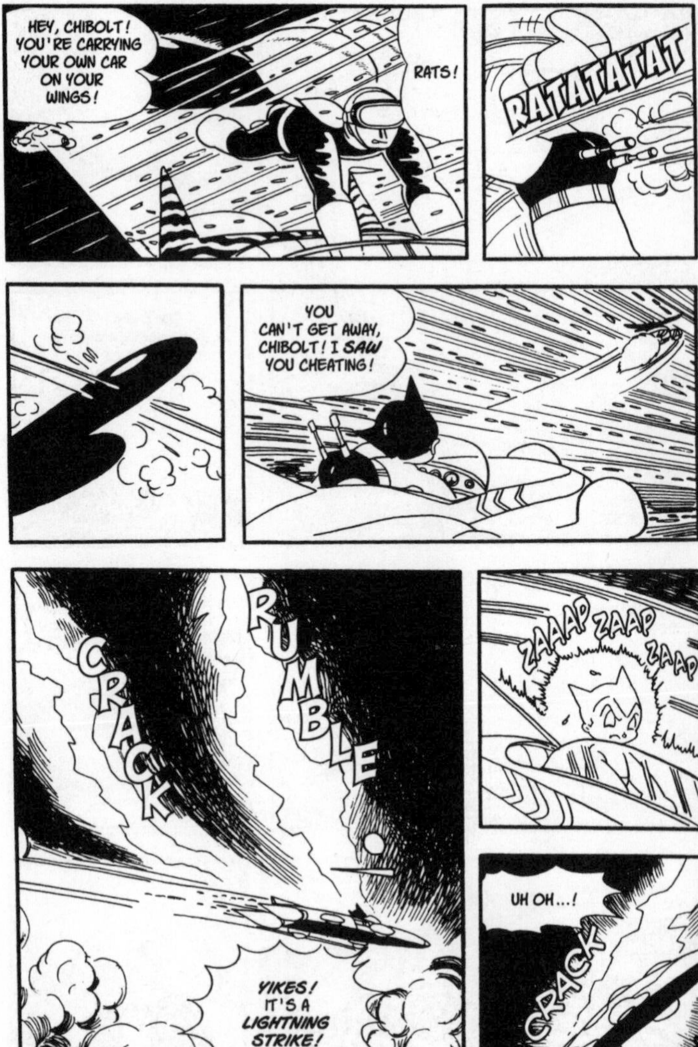
HEY, CHIBOLT! YOU'RE CARRYING YOUR OWN CAR ON YOUR WINGS!
RATS!
RATATATAT
YOU CAN'T GET AWAY, CHIBOLT! I SAW YOU CHEATING!
CRACK
RUMBLE
YIKES! IT'S A LIGHTNING STRIKE!
ZAAAP ZAAP ZAAP
UH OH...!
CRACK

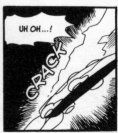

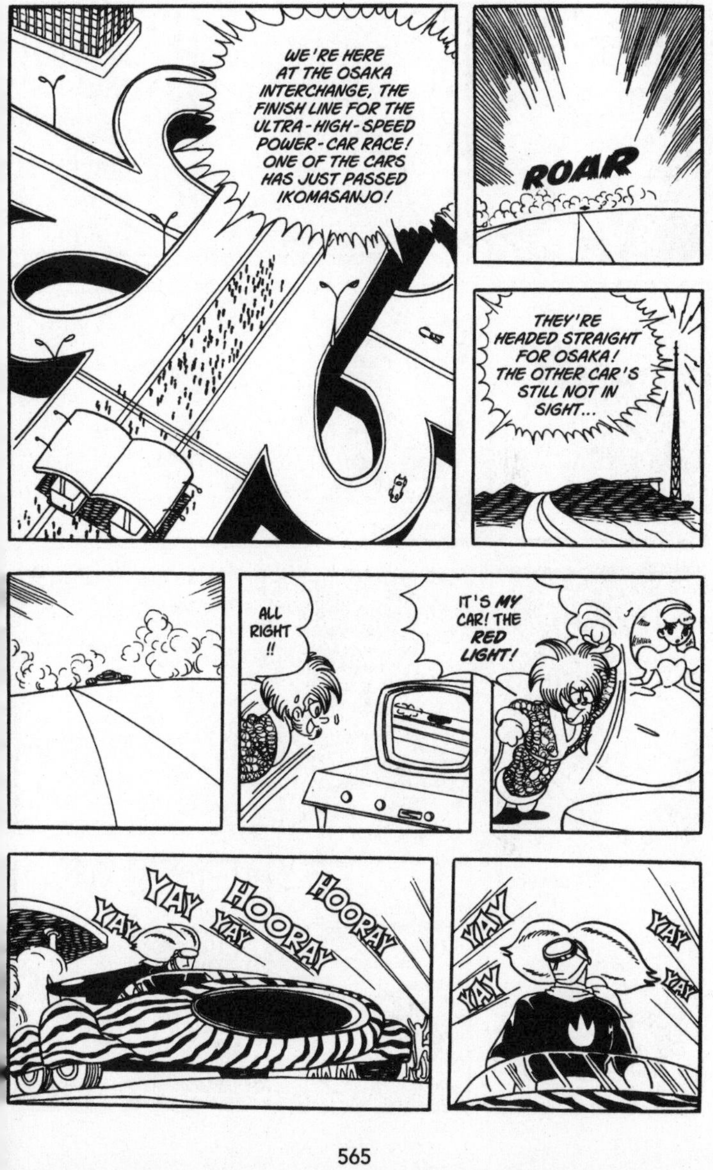
WE'RE HERE AT THE OSAKA INTERCHANGE, THE FINISH LINE FOR THE ULTRA-HIGH-SPEED POWER-CAR RACE! ONE OF THE CARS HAS JUST PASSED IKOMASANJO!
ROAR
THEY'RE HEADED STRAIGHT FOR OSAKA! THE OTHER CAR'S STILL NOT IN SIGHT...
ALL RIGHT !!
IT'S *MY* CAR! THE *RED LIGHT!*
YAY
YAY
YAY
HOORAY
HOORAY
YAY
YAY
YAY
YAY

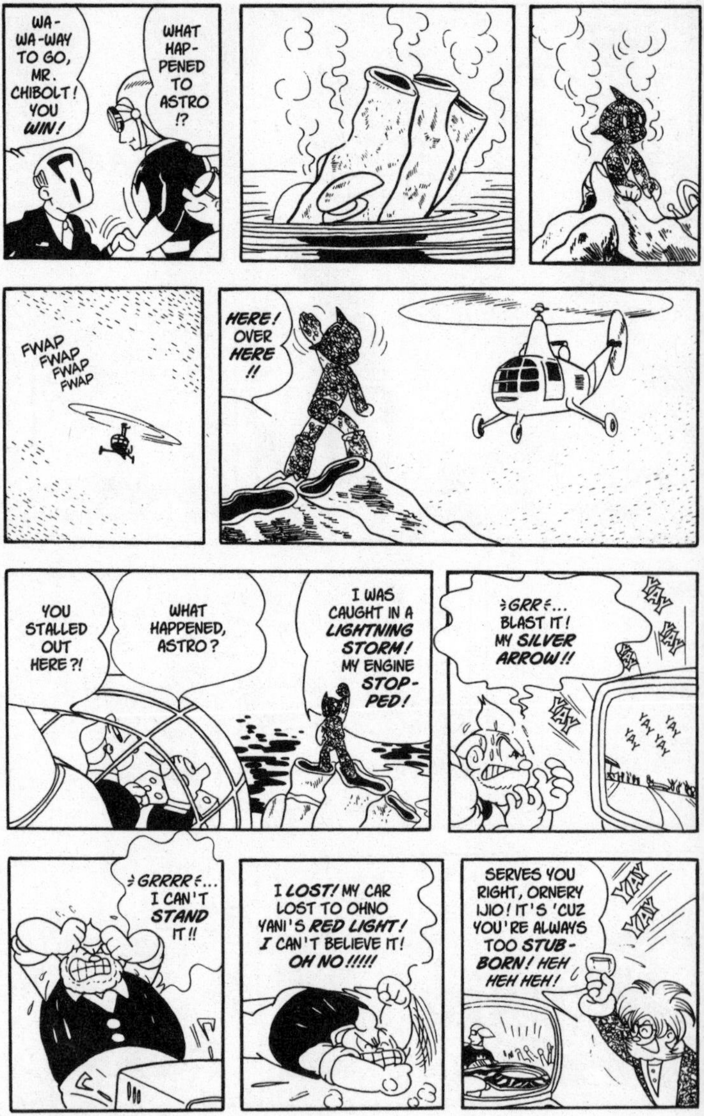

WA-WA-WAY TO GO, MR. CHIBOLT! YOU WIN!
WHAT HAPPENED TO ASTRO!?
FWAP FWAP FWAP FWAP
HERE! OVER HERE!!
YOU STALLED OUT HERE?!
WHAT HAPPENED, ASTRO?
I WAS CAUGHT IN A LIGHTNING STORM! MY ENGINE STOPPED!
GRR... BLAST IT! MY SILVER ARROW!!
YAY YAY YAY YAY
YAY YAY YAY YAY
GRRRR... I CAN'T STAND IT!!
I LOST! MY CAR LOST TO OHNO YANI'S RED LIGHT! I CAN'T BELIEVE IT! OH NO!!!!!
SERVES YOU RIGHT, ORNERY IJIO! IT'S 'CUZ YOU'RE ALWAYS TOO STUBBORN! HEH HEH HEH!
YAY YAY

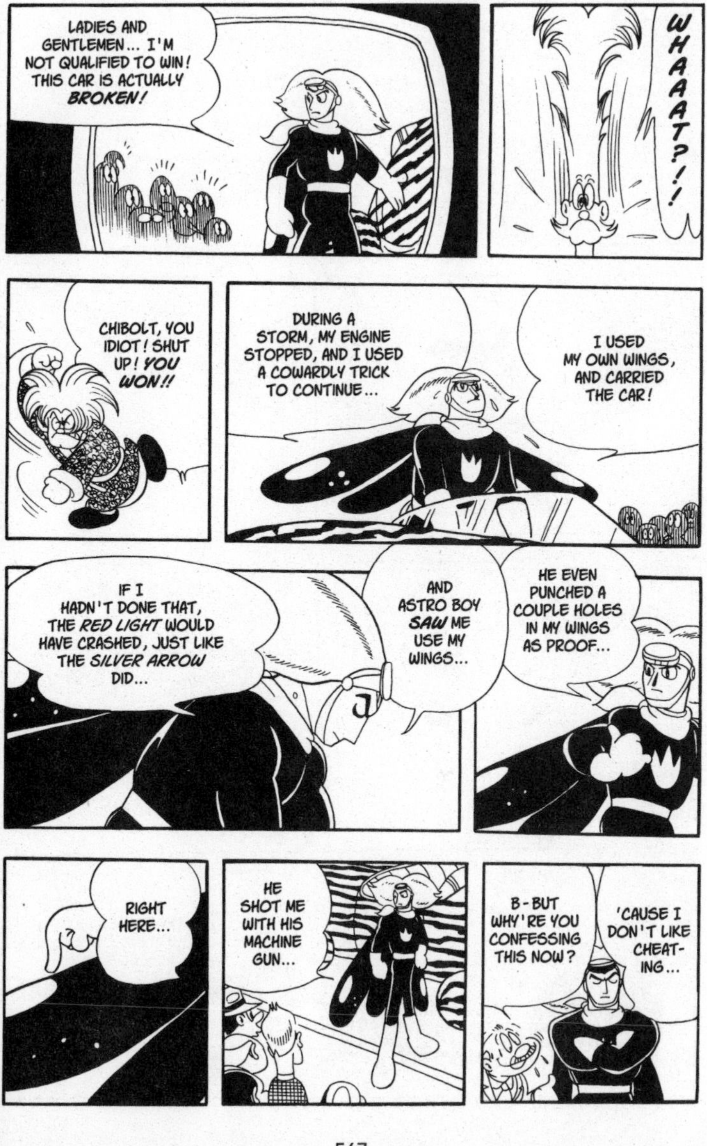

LADIES AND GENTLEMEN... I'M NOT QUALIFIED TO WIN! THIS CAR IS ACTUALLY BROKEN!
WHAAAT?!!
CHIBOLT, YOU IDIOT! SHUT UP! YOU WON!!
DURING A STORM, MY ENGINE STOPPED, AND I USED A COWARDLY TRICK TO CONTINUE...
I USED MY OWN WINGS, AND CARRIED THE CAR!
IF I HADN'T DONE THAT, THE RED LIGHT WOULD HAVE CRASHED, JUST LIKE THE SILVER ARROW DID...
AND ASTRO BOY SAW ME USE MY WINGS...
HE EVEN PUNCHED A COUPLE HOLES IN MY WINGS AS PROOF...
RIGHT HERE...
HE SHOT ME WITH HIS MACHINE GUN...
B-BUT WHY'RE YOU CONFESSING THIS NOW?
'CAUSE I DON'T LIKE CHEAT-ING...

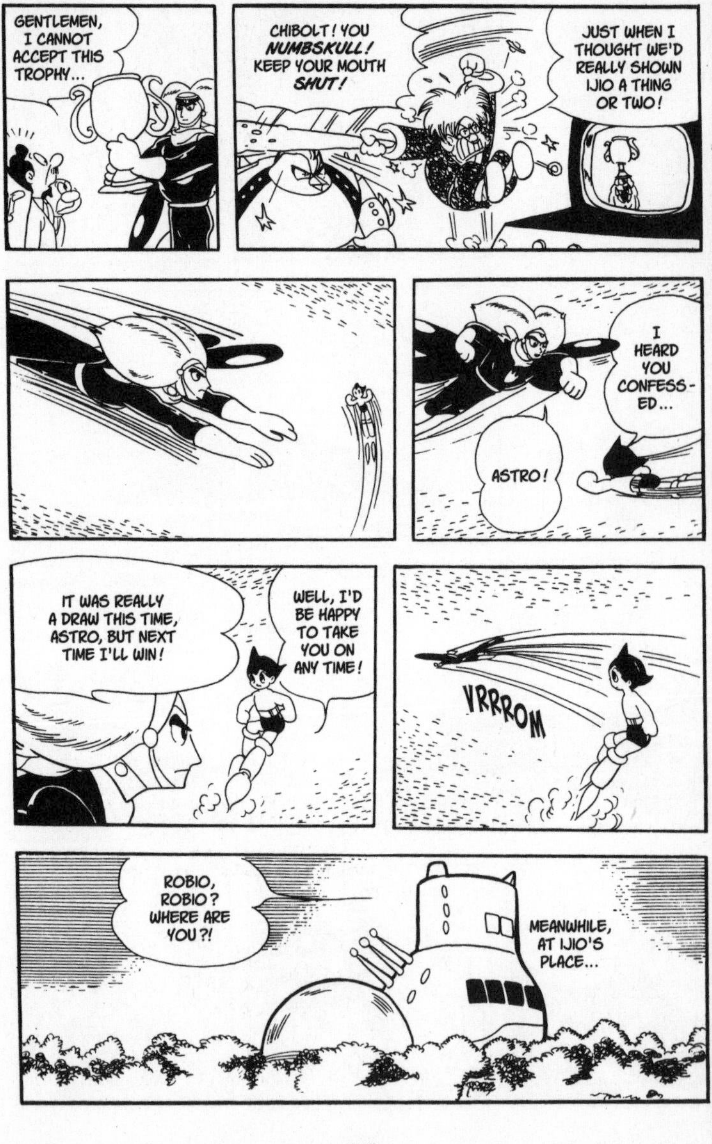
GENTLEMEN, I CANNOT ACCEPT THIS TROPHY...
CHIBOLT! YOU NUMBSKULL! KEEP YOUR MOUTH SHUT!
JUST WHEN I THOUGHT WE'D REALLY SHOWN IJIO A THING OR TWO!
I HEARD YOU CONFESS-ED...
ASTRO!
IT WAS REALLY A DRAW THIS TIME, ASTRO, BUT NEXT TIME I'LL WIN!
WELL, I'D BE HAPPY TO TAKE YOU ON ANY TIME!
VRRROM
ROBIO, ROBIO? WHERE ARE YOU?!
MEANWHILE, AT IJIO'S PLACE...

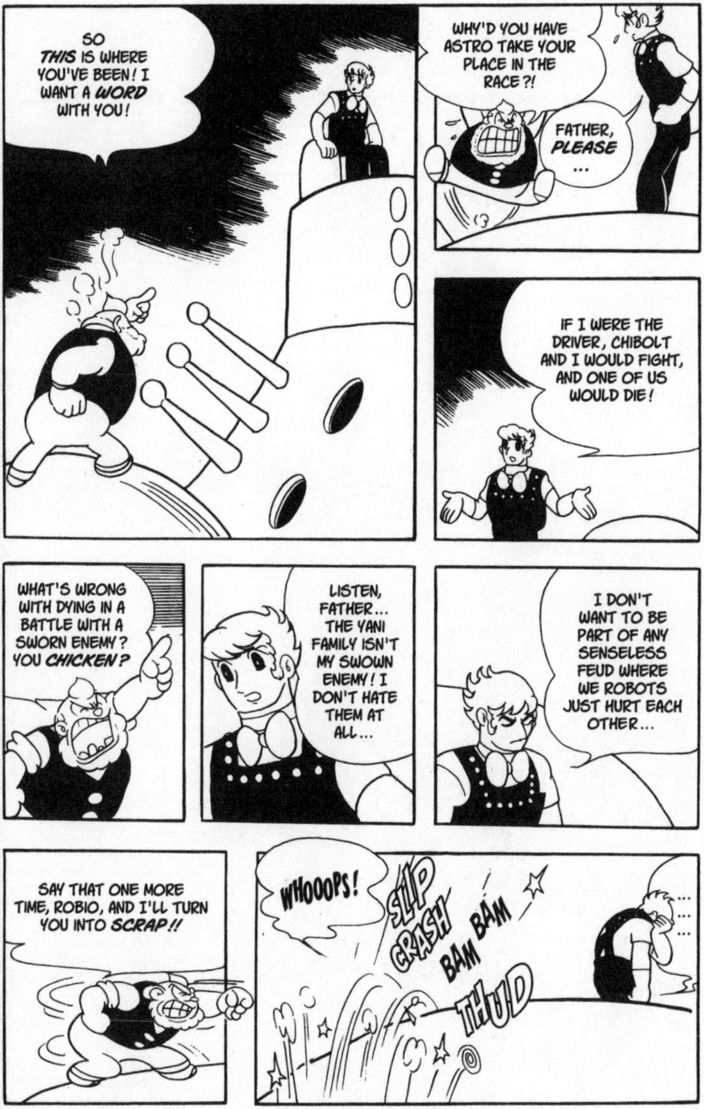
SO THIS IS WHERE YOU'VE BEEN! I WANT A WORD WITH YOU!
WHY'D YOU HAVE ASTRO TAKE YOUR PLACE IN THE RACE?!
FATHER, PLEASE ...
IF I WERE THE DRIVER, CHIBOLT AND I WOULD FIGHT, AND ONE OF US WOULD DIE!
WHAT'S WRONG WITH DYING IN A BATTLE WITH A SWORN ENEMY? YOU CHICKEN?
LISTEN, FATHER... THE YANI FAMILY ISN'T MY SWOWN ENEMY! I DON'T HATE THEM AT ALL...
I DON'T WANT TO BE PART OF ANY SENSELESS FEUD WHERE WE ROBOTS JUST HURT EACH OTHER...
SAY THAT ONE MORE TIME, ROBIO, AND I'LL TURN YOU INTO SCRAP!!
WHOOOPS!
SLIP
CRASH
BAM BAM
THUD
...
...
...

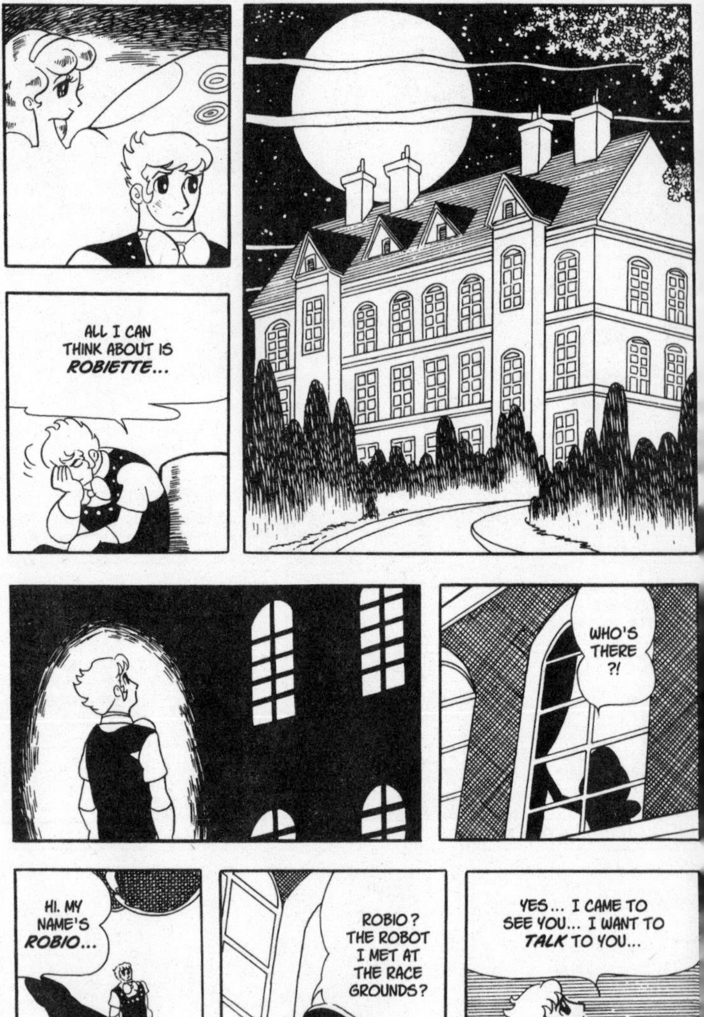
ALL I CAN THINK ABOUT IS *ROBIETTE*...
WHO'S THERE ?!
HI. MY NAME'S *ROBIO*...
ROBIO? THE ROBOT I MET AT THE RACE GROUNDS?
YES... I CAME TO SEE YOU... I WANT TO *TALK* TO YOU...

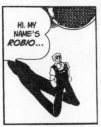

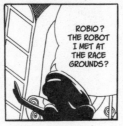

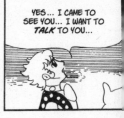

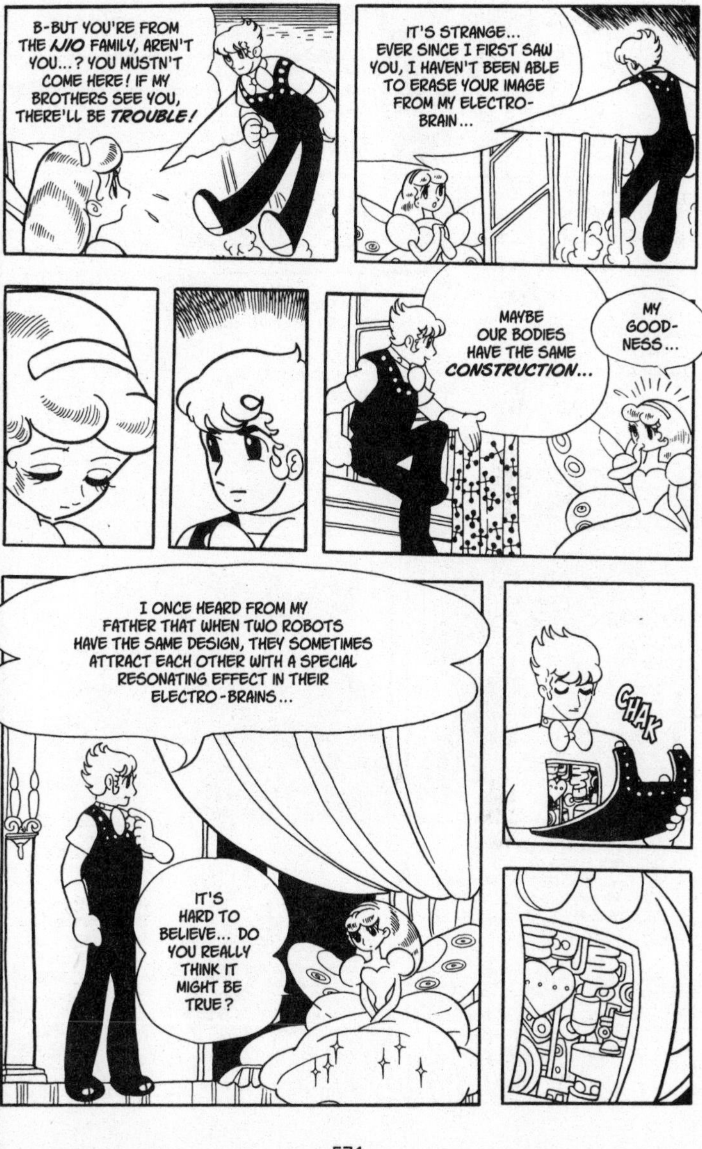
B-BUT YOU'RE FROM THE *NIO* FAMILY, AREN'T YOU...? YOU MUSTN'T COME HERE! IF MY BROTHERS SEE YOU, THERE'LL BE *TROUBLE!*
IT'S STRANGE... EVER SINCE I FIRST SAW YOU, I HAVEN'T BEEN ABLE TO ERASE YOUR IMAGE FROM MY ELECTRO-BRAIN...
MAYBE OUR BODIES HAVE THE SAME *CONSTRUCTION...*
MY GOODNESS...
I ONCE HEARD FROM MY FATHER THAT WHEN TWO ROBOTS HAVE THE SAME DESIGN, THEY SOMETIMES ATTRACT EACH OTHER WITH A SPECIAL RESONATING EFFECT IN THEIR ELECTRO-BRAINS...
IT'S HARD TO BELIEVE... DO YOU REALLY THINK IT MIGHT BE TRUE?
CHAK

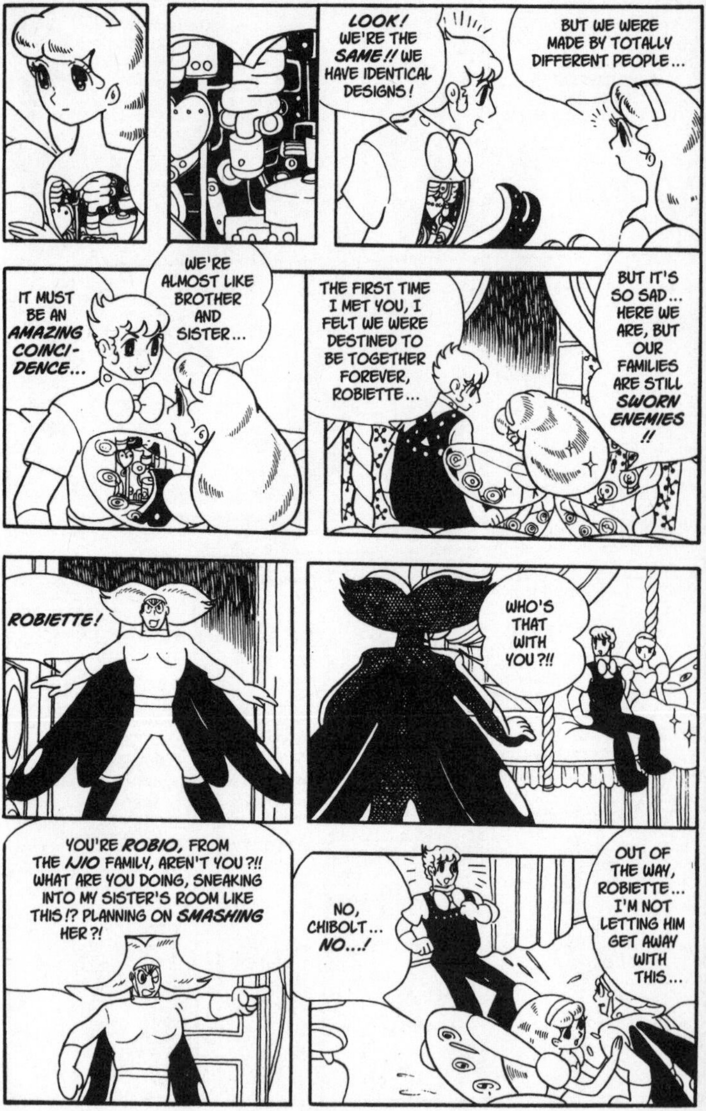
LOOK! WE'RE THE SAME!! WE HAVE IDENTICAL DESIGNS!
BUT WE WERE MADE BY TOTALLY DIFFERENT PEOPLE...
IT MUST BE AN AMAZING COINCI-DENCE...
WE'RE ALMOST LIKE BROTHER AND SISTER...
THE FIRST TIME I MET YOU, I FELT WE WERE DESTINED TO BE TOGETHER FOREVER, ROBIETTE...
BUT IT'S SO SAD... HERE WE ARE, BUT OUR FAMILIES ARE STILL SWORN ENEMIES!!
ROBIETTE!
WHO'S THAT WITH YOU?!!
YOU'RE ROBIO, FROM THE AJIO FAMILY, AREN'T YOU?!! WHAT ARE YOU DOING, SNEAKING INTO MY SISTER'S ROOM LIKE THIS!? PLANNING ON SMASHING HER?!
NO, CHIBOLT... NO...!
OUT OF THE WAY, ROBIETTE... I'M NOT LETTING HIM GET AWAY WITH THIS...

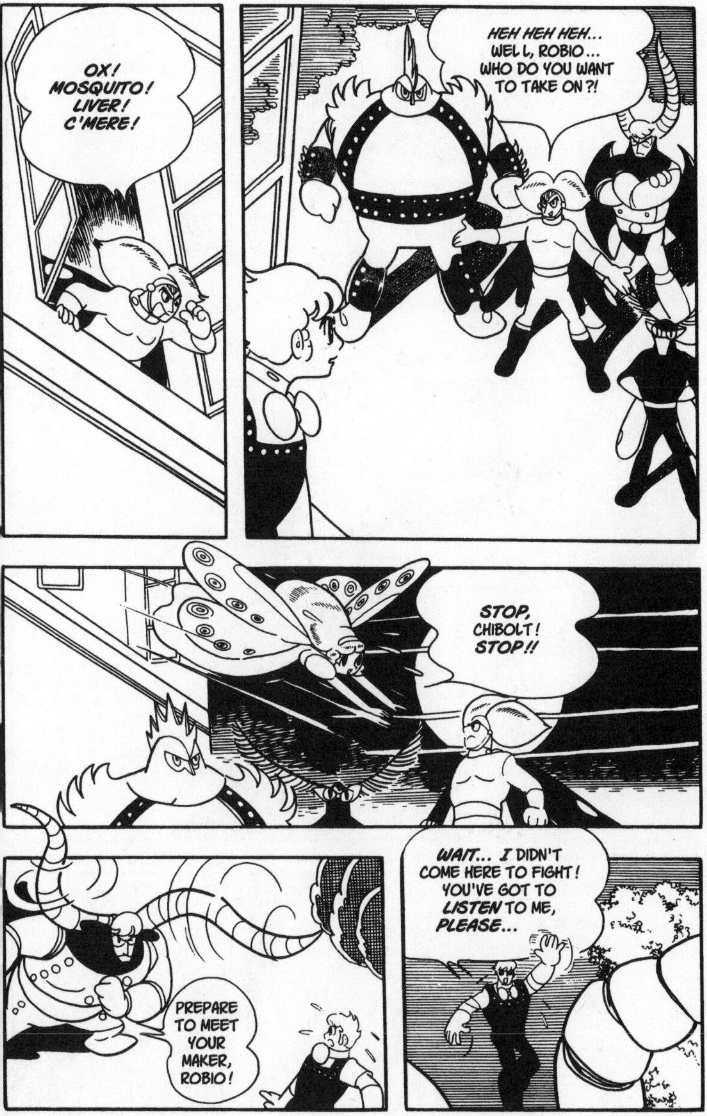
OX! MOSQUITO! LIVER! C'MERE!
HEH HEH HEH... WELL, ROBIO... WHO DO YOU WANT TO TAKE ON?!
STOP, CHIBOLT! STOP!!
PREPARE TO MEET YOUR MAKER, ROBIO!
WAIT... I DIDN'T COME HERE TO FIGHT! YOU'VE GOT TO LISTEN TO ME, PLEASE...

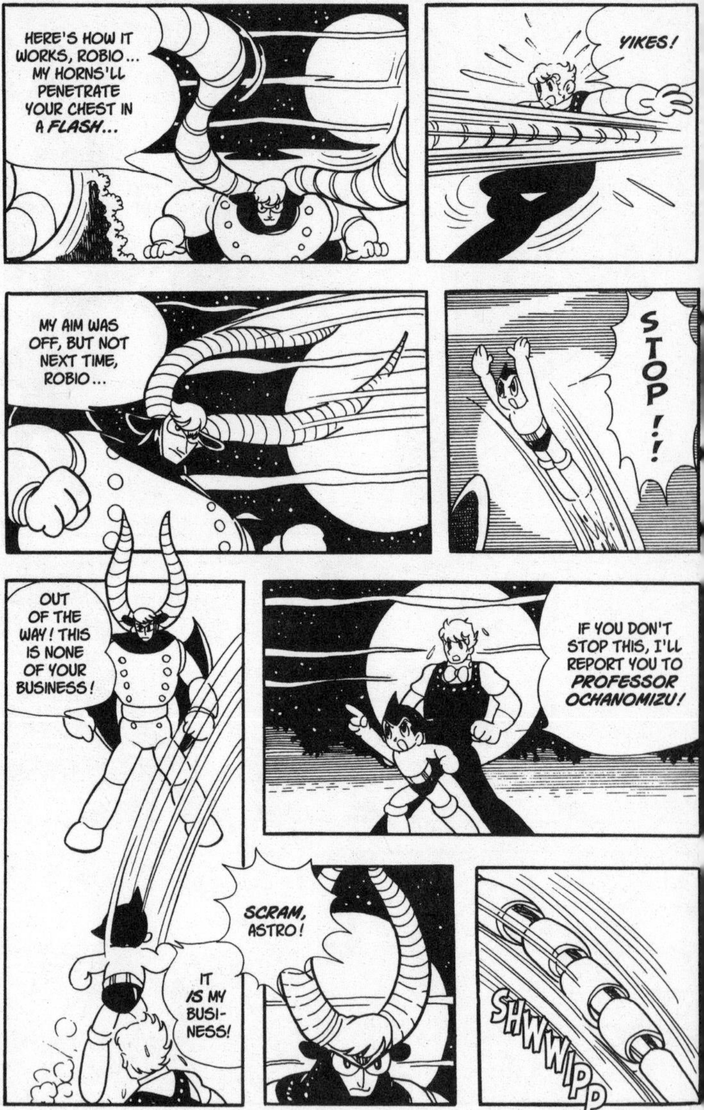
HERE'S HOW IT WORKS, ROBIO... MY HORNS'LL PENETRATE YOUR CHEST IN A *FLASH*...
YIKES!
MY AIM WAS OFF, BUT NOT NEXT TIME, ROBIO...
STOP!!
OUT OF THE WAY! THIS IS NONE OF YOUR BUSINESS!
IT *IS* MY BUSI-NESS!
IF YOU DON'T STOP THIS, I'LL REPORT YOU TO *PROFESSOR OCHANOMIZU!*
SCRAM, ASTRO!
SHWWIPP

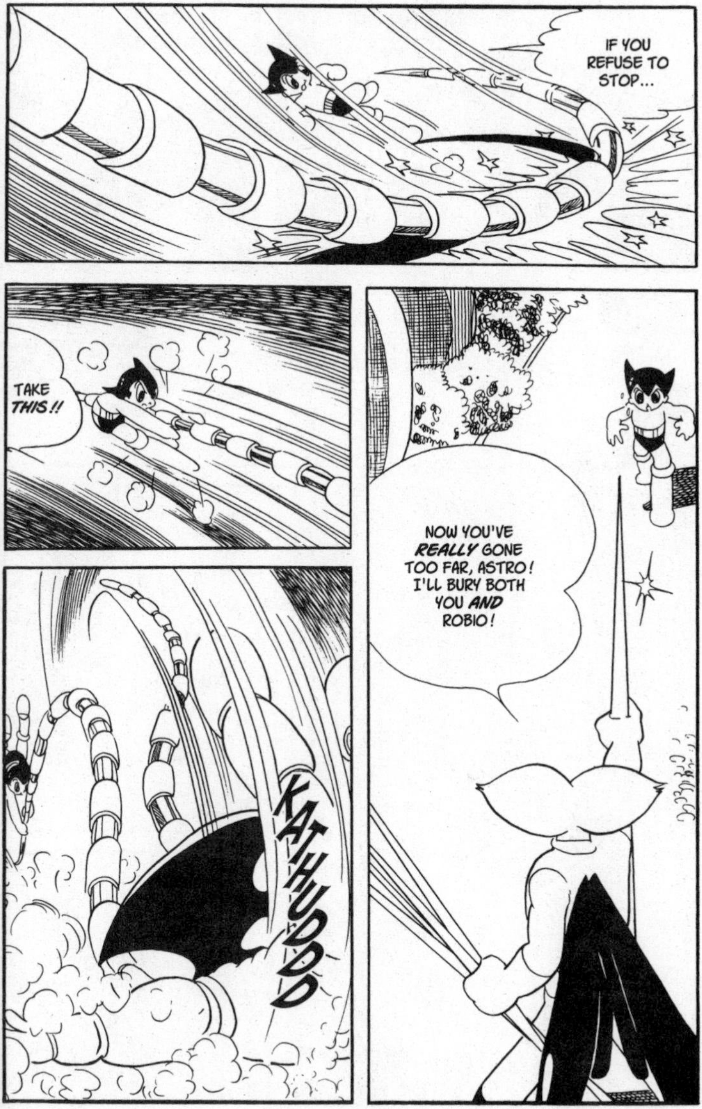
IF YOU REFUSE TO STOP...
TAKE *THIS!!*
KATHUDDD
NOW YOU'VE *REALLY* GONE TOO FAR, ASTRO! I'LL BURY BOTH YOU *AND* ROBIO!

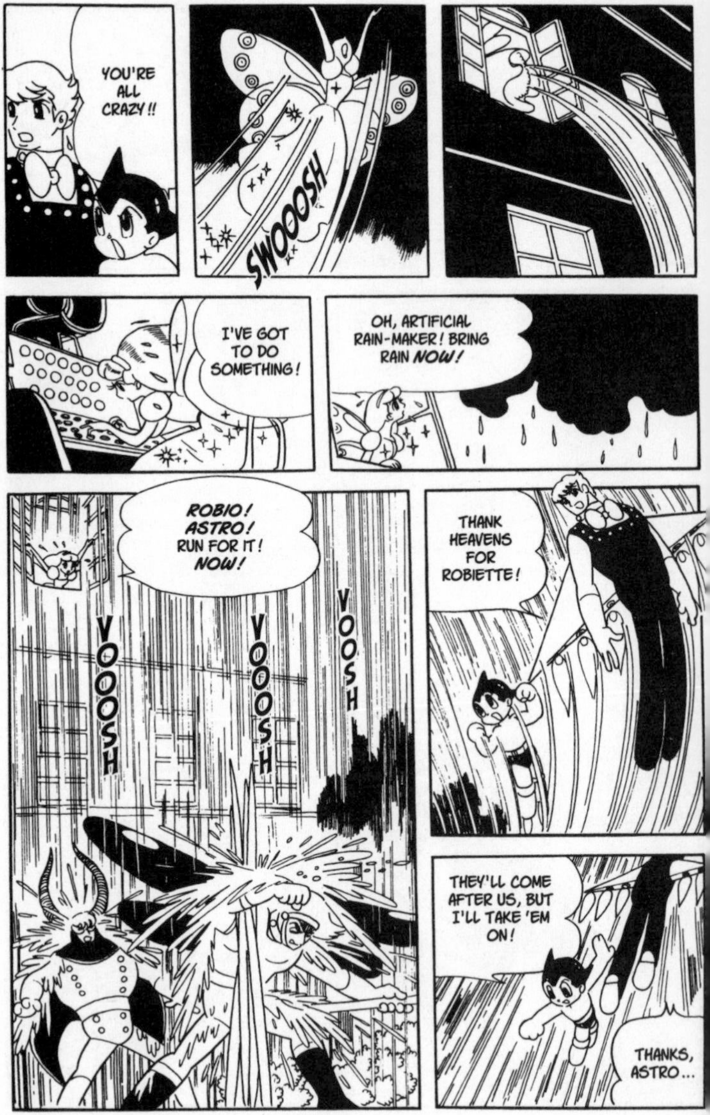
YOU'RE ALL CRAZY!!
SWOOOSH
I'VE GOT TO DO SOMETHING!
OH, ARTIFICIAL RAIN-MAKER! BRING RAIN NOW!
ROBIO! ASTRO! RUN FOR IT! NOW!
VOOOSH
VOOOSH
VOOSH
THANK HEAVENS FOR ROBIETTE!
THEY'LL COME AFTER US, BUT I'LL TAKE 'EM ON!
THANKS, ASTRO...

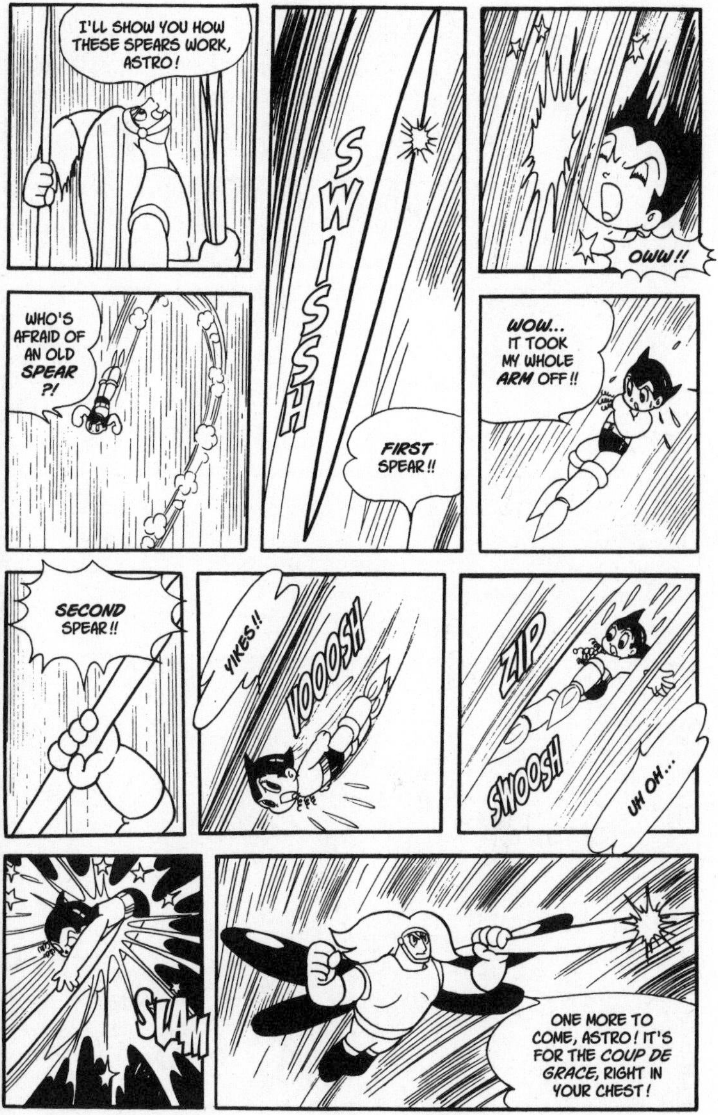
I'LL SHOW YOU HOW THESE SPEARS WORK, ASTRO!
SWISSH
FIRST SPEAR!!
OWW!!
WHO'S AFRAID OF AN OLD SPEAR ?!
WOW... IT TOOK MY WHOLE ARM OFF!!
SECOND SPEAR!!
YIKES!!
VOOOSH
ZIP
SWOOSH
UH OH...
SLAM
ONE MORE TO COME, ASTRO! IT'S FOR THE COUP DE GRACE, RIGHT IN YOUR CHEST!

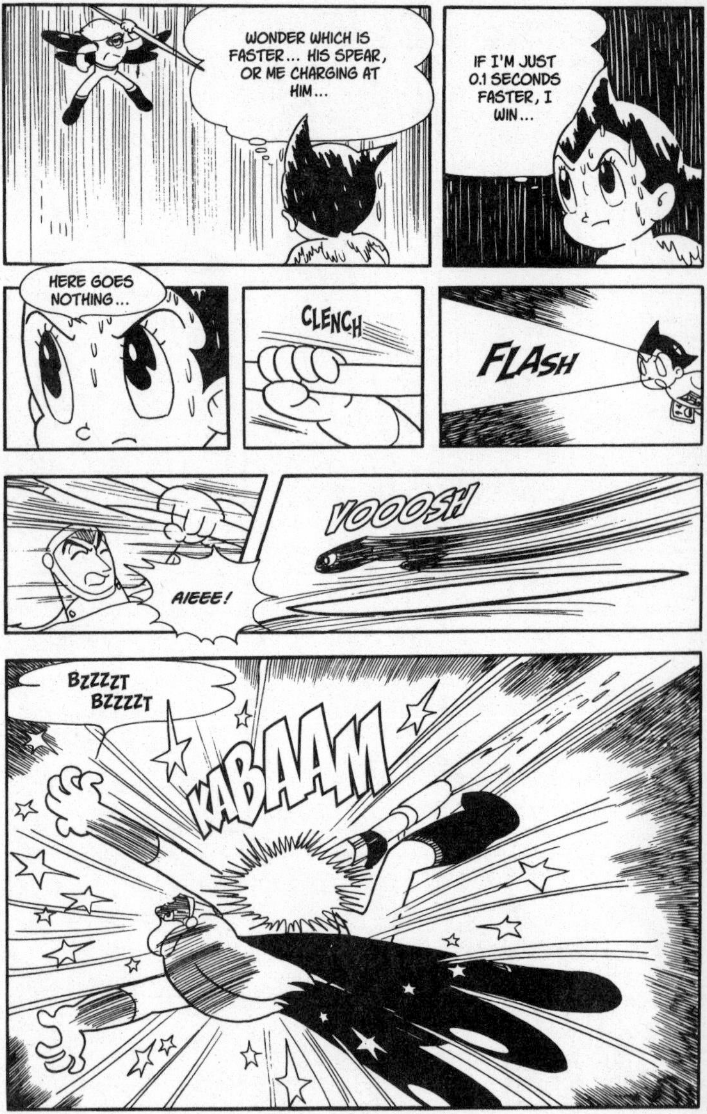
WONDER WHICH IS FASTER... HIS SPEAR, OR ME CHARGING AT HIM...
IF I'M JUST 0.1 SECONDS FASTER, I WIN...
HERE GOES NOTHING...
CLENCH
FLASH
AIEEE!
VOOOSH
BZZZZT BZZZZT
KABAAM

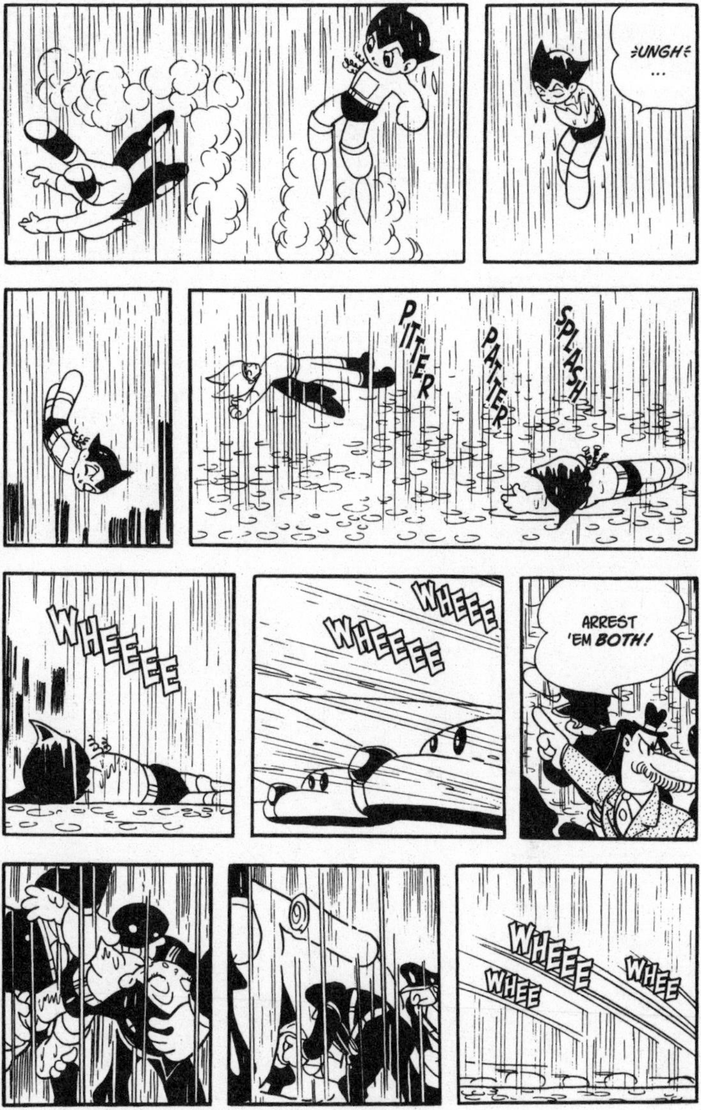
UNGH
...
PITTER
PATTER
SPLASH
WHEEEE
WHEEEE
WHEEE
ARREST 'EM BOTH!
WHEE
WHEEE
WHEE

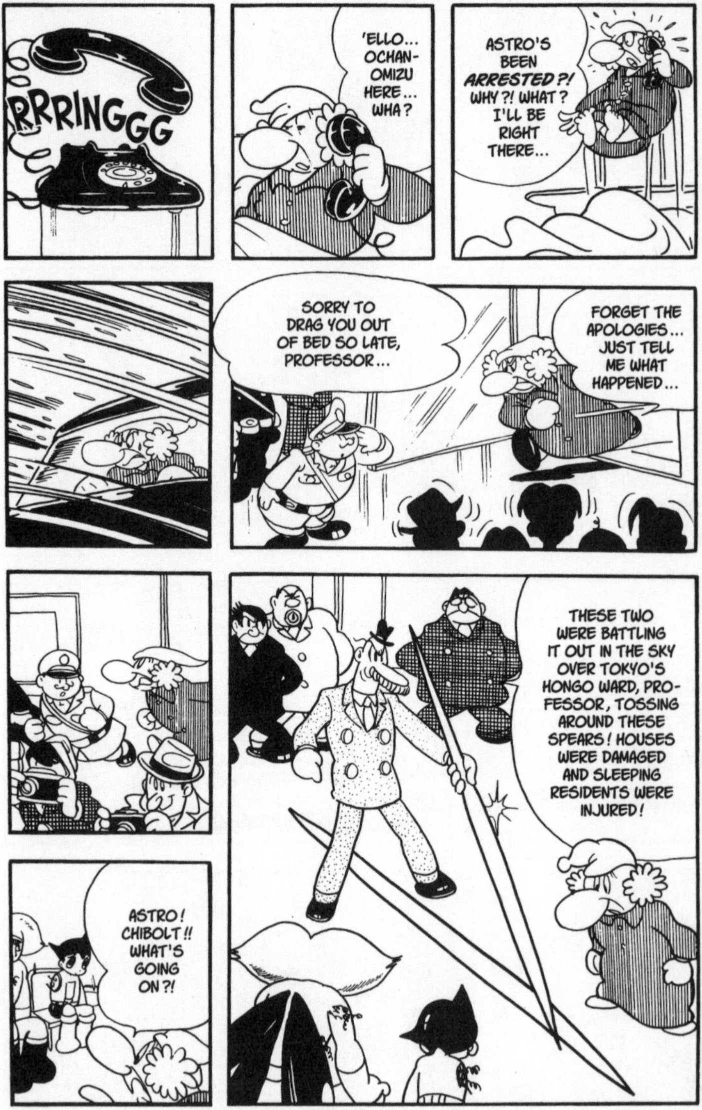
RRRINGGG
'ELLO... OCHAN-OMIZU HERE... WHA?
ASTRO'S BEEN ARRESTED?! WHY?! WHAT? I'LL BE RIGHT THERE...
SORRY TO DRAG YOU OUT OF BED SO LATE, PROFESSOR...
FORGET THE APOLOGIES... JUST TELL ME WHAT HAPPENED...
THESE TWO WERE BATTLING IT OUT IN THE SKY OVER TOKYO'S HONGO WARD, PRO-FESSOR, TOSSING AROUND THESE SPEARS! HOUSES WERE DAMAGED AND SLEEPING RESIDENTS WERE INJURED!
ASTRO! CHIBOLT!! WHAT'S GOING ON?!

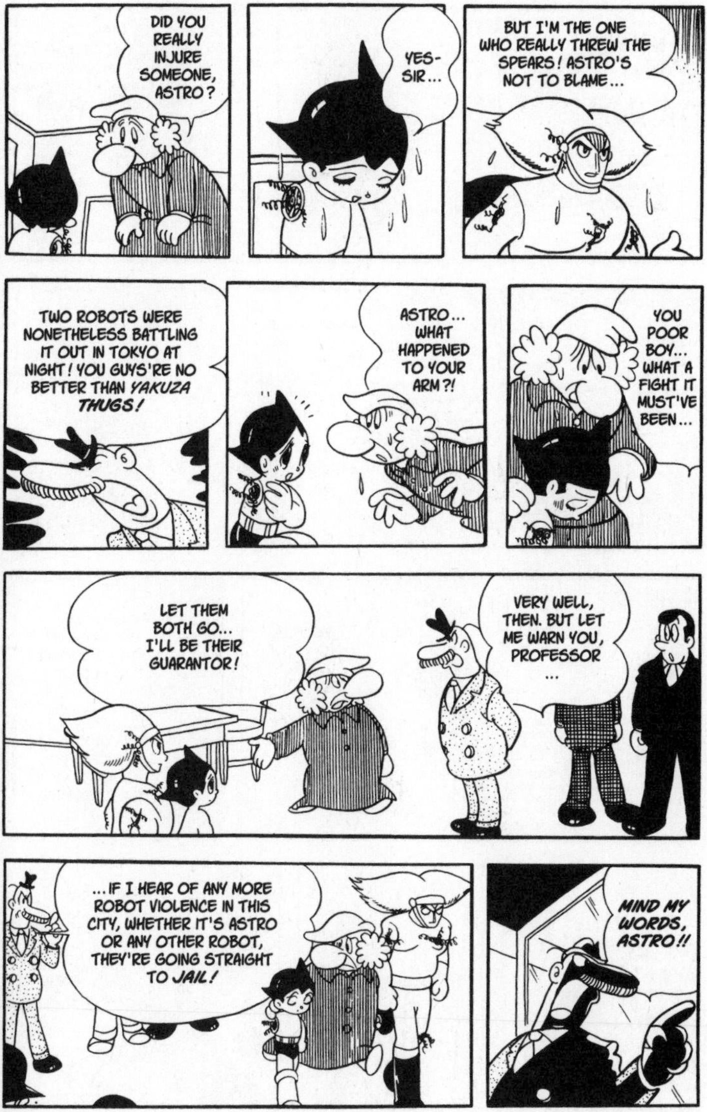
DID YOU REALLY INJURE SOMEONE, ASTRO?
YES-SIR...
BUT I'M THE ONE WHO REALLY THREW THE SPEARS! ASTRO'S NOT TO BLAME...
TWO ROBOTS WERE NONETHELESS BATTLING IT OUT IN TOKYO AT NIGHT! YOU GUYS'RE NO BETTER THAN *YAKUZA THUGS!*
ASTRO... WHAT HAPPENED TO YOUR ARM?!
YOU POOR BOY... WHAT A FIGHT IT MUST'VE BEEN...
LET THEM BOTH GO... I'LL BE THEIR GUARANTOR!
VERY WELL, THEN. BUT LET ME WARN YOU, PROFESSOR ...
...IF I HEAR OF ANY MORE ROBOT VIOLENCE IN THIS CITY, WHETHER IT'S ASTRO OR ANY OTHER ROBOT, THEY'RE GOING STRAIGHT TO *JAIL!*
MIND MY WORDS, ASTRO!!

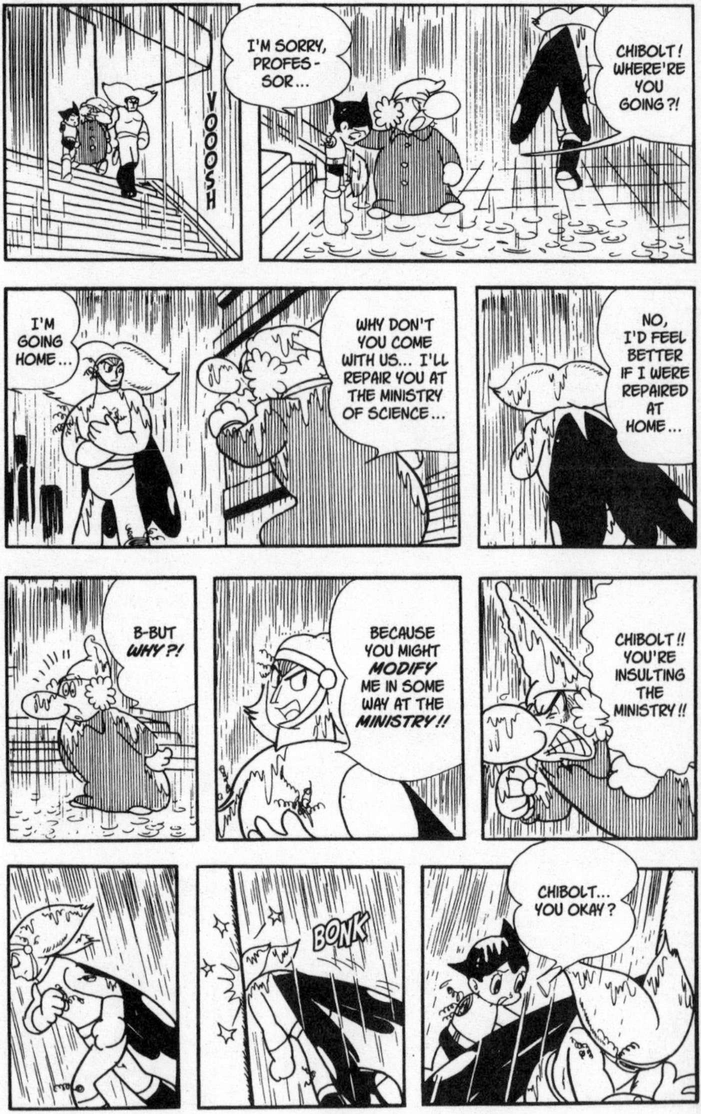
VOOOSH
I'M SORRY, PROFES-SOR...
CHIBOLT! WHERE'RE YOU GOING?!
I'M GOING HOME...
WHY DON'T YOU COME WITH US... I'LL REPAIR YOU AT THE MINISTRY OF SCIENCE...
NO, I'D FEEL BETTER IF I WERE REPAIRED AT HOME...
B-BUT *WHY?!*
BECAUSE YOU MIGHT *MODIFY* ME IN SOME WAY AT THE *MINISTRY!!*
CHIBOLT!! YOU'RE INSULTING THE MINISTRY!!
BONK
CHIBOLT... YOU OKAY?

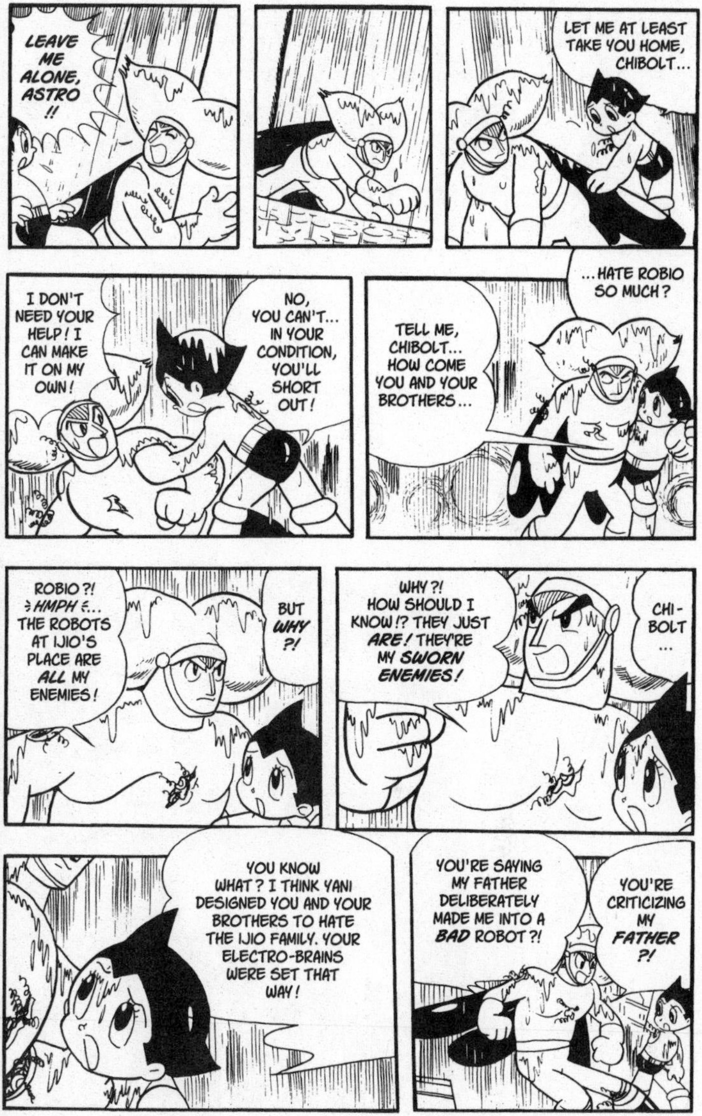
LEAVE ME ALONE, ASTRO !!
LET ME AT LEAST TAKE YOU HOME, CHIBOLT...
I DON'T NEED YOUR HELP! I CAN MAKE IT ON MY OWN!
NO, YOU CAN'T... IN YOUR CONDITION, YOU'LL SHORT OUT!
TELL ME, CHIBOLT... HOW COME YOU AND YOUR BROTHERS...
...HATE ROBIO SO MUCH?
ROBIO?! HMPH... THE ROBOTS AT IJIO'S PLACE ARE ALL MY ENEMIES!
BUT WHY ?!
WHY?! HOW SHOULD I KNOW!? THEY JUST ARE! THEY'RE MY SWORN ENEMIES!
CHI-BOLT ...
YOU KNOW WHAT? I THINK YANI DESIGNED YOU AND YOUR BROTHERS TO HATE THE IJIO FAMILY. YOUR ELECTRO-BRAINS WERE SET THAT WAY!
YOU'RE SAYING MY FATHER DELIBERATELY MADE ME INTO A BAD ROBOT?!
YOU'RE CRITICIZING MY FATHER ?!

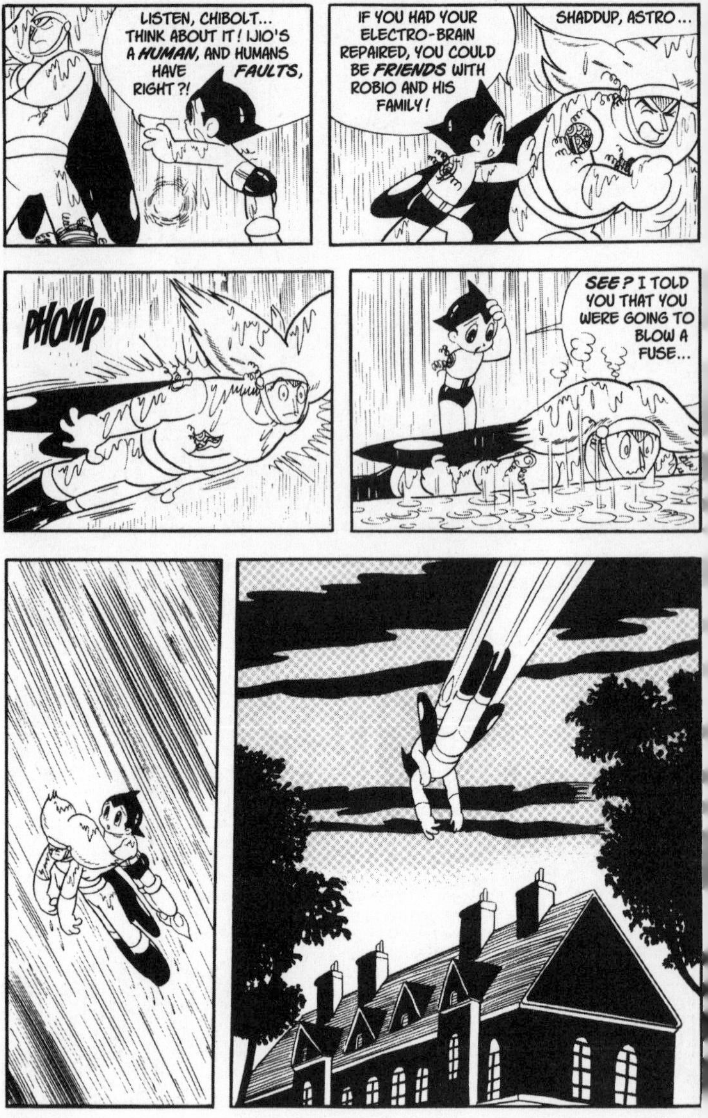

LISTEN, CHIBOLT... THINK ABOUT IT! IJIO'S A HUMAN, AND HUMANS HAVE FAULTS, RIGHT?!
IF YOU HAD YOUR ELECTRO-BRAIN REPAIRED, YOU COULD BE FRIENDS WITH ROBIO AND HIS FAMILY!
SHADDUP, ASTRO...
PHOMP
SEE? I TOLD YOU THAT YOU WERE GOING TO BLOW A FUSE...

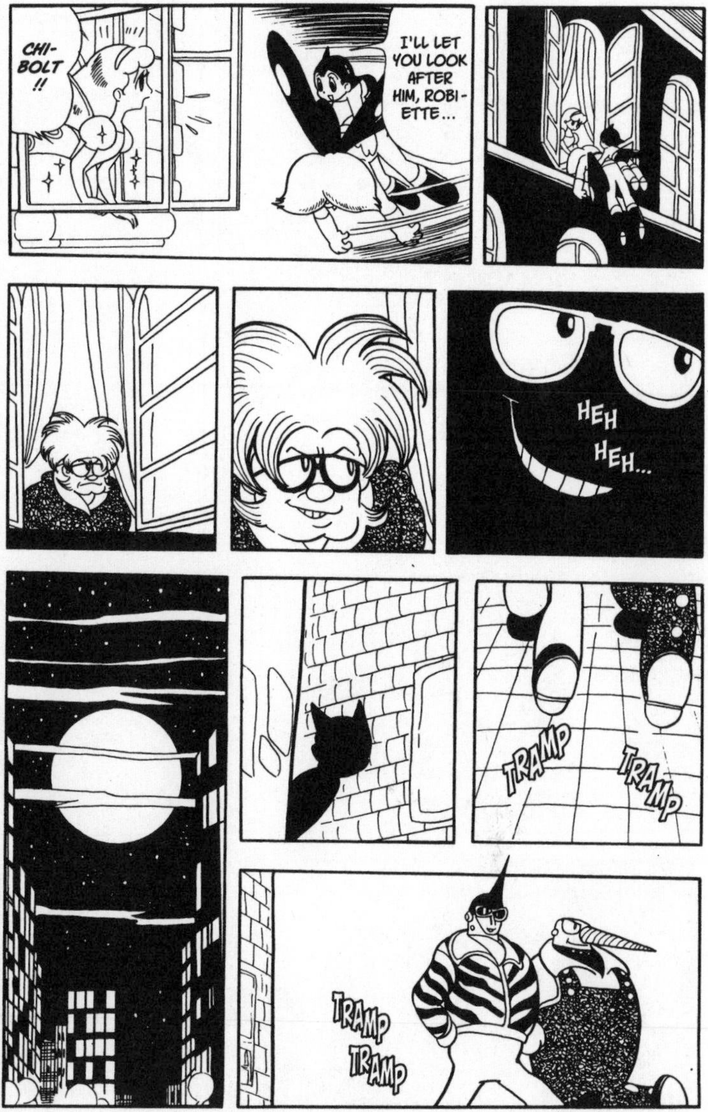

CHI-BOLT !!
I'LL LET YOU LOOK AFTER HIM, ROBI-ETTE...
HEH HEH...
TRAMP
TRAMP
TRAMP
TRAMP

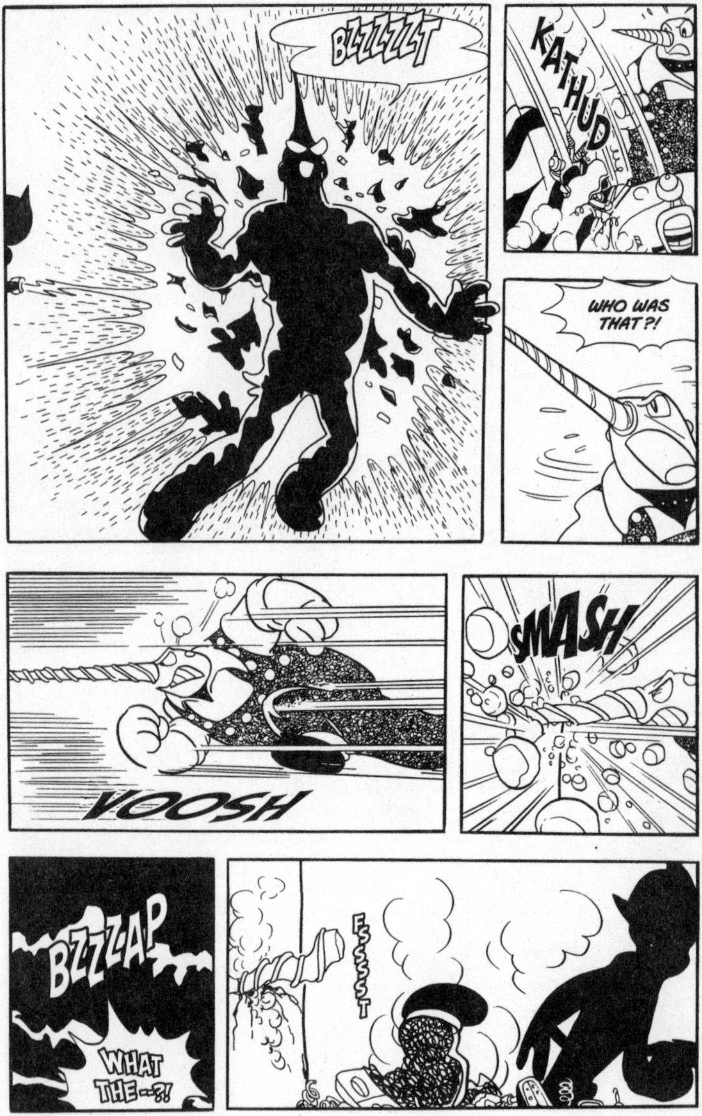
BZZZZZZT
KATHUD
WHO WAS THAT?!
VOOSH
SMASH
BZZZAP
WHAT THE--?!
FSSSST

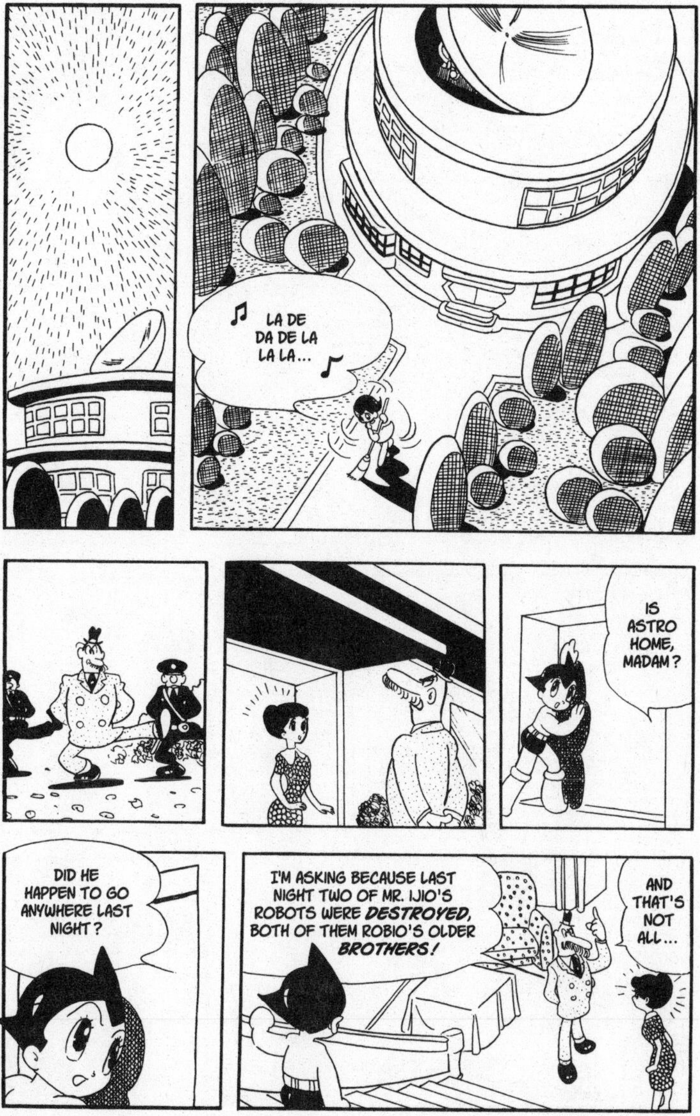
♫ LA DE DA DE LA LA LA... ♪
IS ASTRO HOME, MADAM?
DID HE HAPPEN TO GO ANYWHERE LAST NIGHT?
I'M ASKING BECAUSE LAST NIGHT TWO OF MR. IJIO'S ROBOTS WERE *DESTROYED*, BOTH OF THEM ROBIO'S OLDER *BROTHERS!*
AND THAT'S NOT ALL...

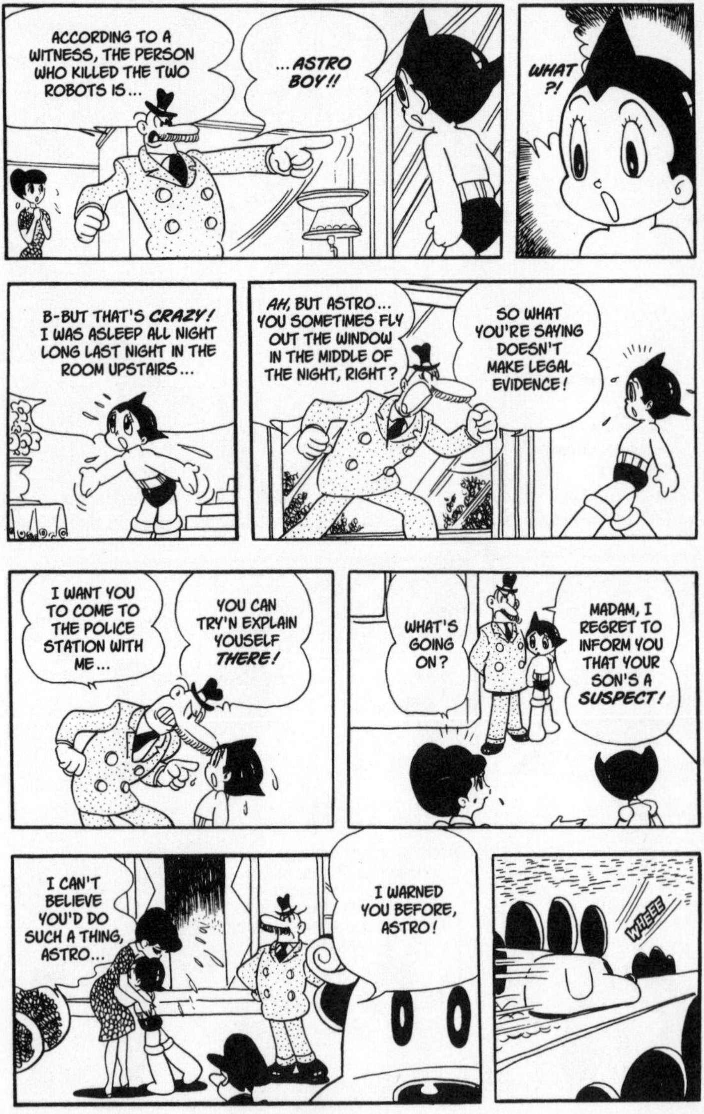

ACCORDING TO A WITNESS, THE PERSON WHO KILLED THE TWO ROBOTS IS...
...ASTRO BOY!!
WHAT ?!
B-BUT THAT'S CRAZY! I WAS ASLEEP ALL NIGHT LONG LAST NIGHT IN THE ROOM UPSTAIRS...
AH, BUT ASTRO... YOU SOMETIMES FLY OUT THE WINDOW IN THE MIDDLE OF THE NIGHT, RIGHT?
SO WHAT YOU'RE SAYING DOESN'T MAKE LEGAL EVIDENCE!
I WANT YOU TO COME TO THE POLICE STATION WITH ME...
YOU CAN TRY'N EXPLAIN YOUSELF THERE!
WHAT'S GOING ON?
MADAM, I REGRET TO INFORM YOU THAT YOUR SON'S A SUSPECT!
I CAN'T BELIEVE YOU'D DO SUCH A THING, ASTRO...
I WARNED YOU BEFORE, ASTRO!
WHEEE

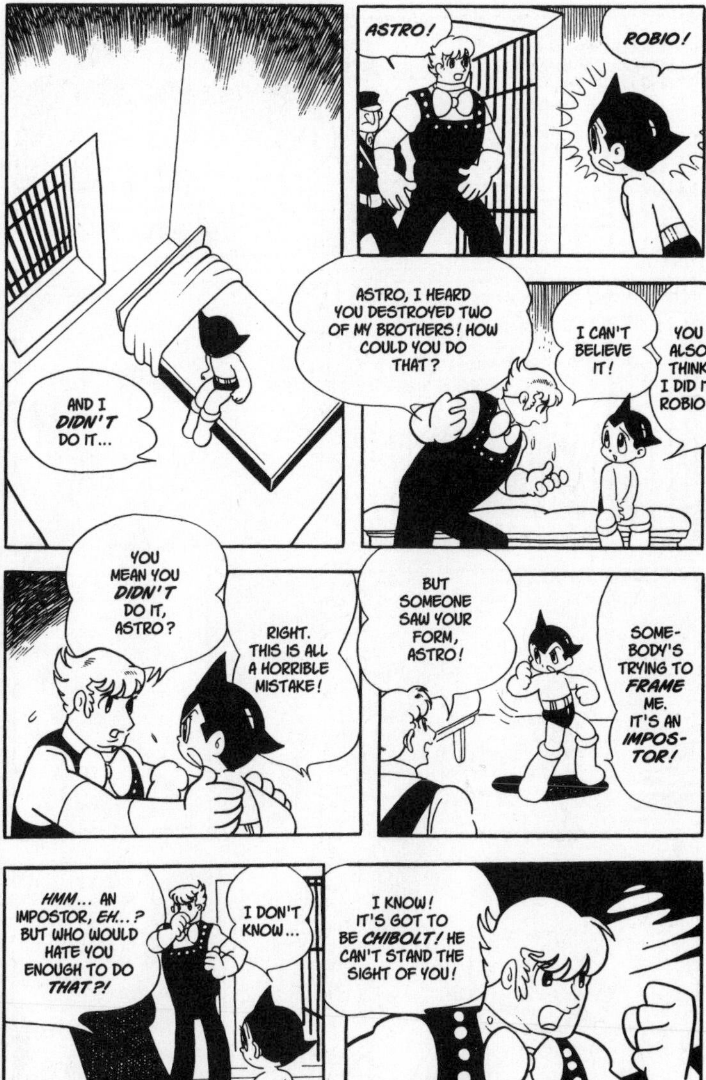
AND I *DIDN'T* DO IT...
ASTRO!
ROBIO!
ASTRO, I HEARD YOU DESTROYED TWO OF MY BROTHERS! HOW COULD YOU DO THAT?
I CAN'T BELIEVE IT!
YOU ALSO THINK I DID IT, ROBIO?
YOU MEAN YOU *DIDN'T* DO IT, ASTRO?
RIGHT. THIS IS ALL A HORRIBLE MISTAKE!
BUT SOMEONE SAW YOUR FORM, ASTRO!
SOME-BODY'S TRYING TO *FRAME* ME. IT'S AN *IMPOSTOR!*
HMM... AN IMPOSTOR, *EH...?* BUT WHO WOULD HATE YOU ENOUGH TO DO *THAT?!*
I DON'T KNOW...
I KNOW! IT'S GOT TO BE *CHIBOLT!* HE CAN'T STAND THE SIGHT OF YOU!

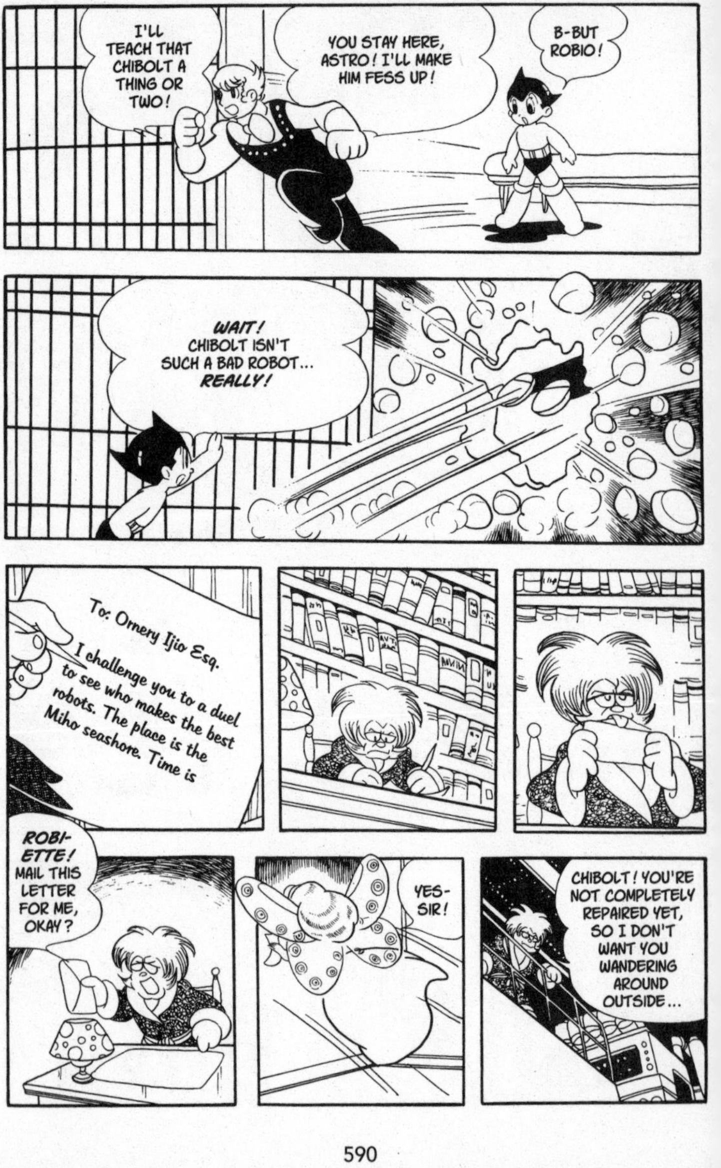
I'LL TEACH THAT CHIBOLT A THING OR TWO!
YOU STAY HERE, ASTRO! I'LL MAKE HIM FESS UP!
B-BUT ROBIO!
WAIT! CHIBOLT ISN'T SUCH A BAD ROBOT... REALLY!
To: Ornery Ijio Esq.
I challenge you to a duel to see who makes the best robots. The place is the Miho seashore. Time is
ROBI-ETTE! MAIL THIS LETTER FOR ME, OKAY?
YES-SIR!
CHIBOLT! YOU'RE NOT COMPLETELY REPAIRED YET, SO I DON'T WANT YOU WANDERING AROUND OUTSIDE...

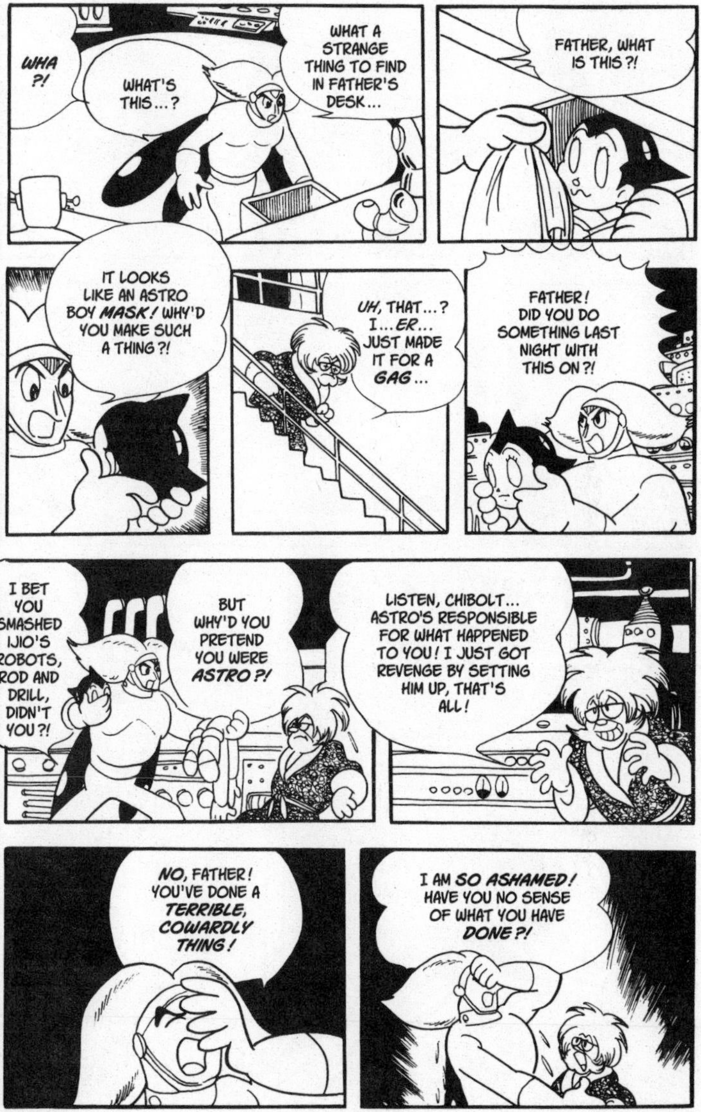
WHA ?!
WHAT'S THIS...?
WHAT A STRANGE THING TO FIND IN FATHER'S DESK...
FATHER, WHAT IS THIS ?!
IT LOOKS LIKE AN ASTRO BOY MASK! WHY'D YOU MAKE SUCH A THING ?!
UH, THAT...? I...ER... JUST MADE IT FOR A GAG...
FATHER! DID YOU DO SOMETHING LAST NIGHT WITH THIS ON ?!
I BET YOU SMASHED IJIO'S ROBOTS, ROD AND DRILL, DIDN'T YOU ?!
BUT WHY'D YOU PRETEND YOU WERE ASTRO ?!
LISTEN, CHIBOLT... ASTRO'S RESPONSIBLE FOR WHAT HAPPENED TO YOU! I JUST GOT REVENGE BY SETTING HIM UP, THAT'S ALL!
NO, FATHER! YOU'VE DONE A TERRIBLE, COWARDLY THING!
I AM SO ASHAMED! HAVE YOU NO SENSE OF WHAT YOU HAVE DONE ?!

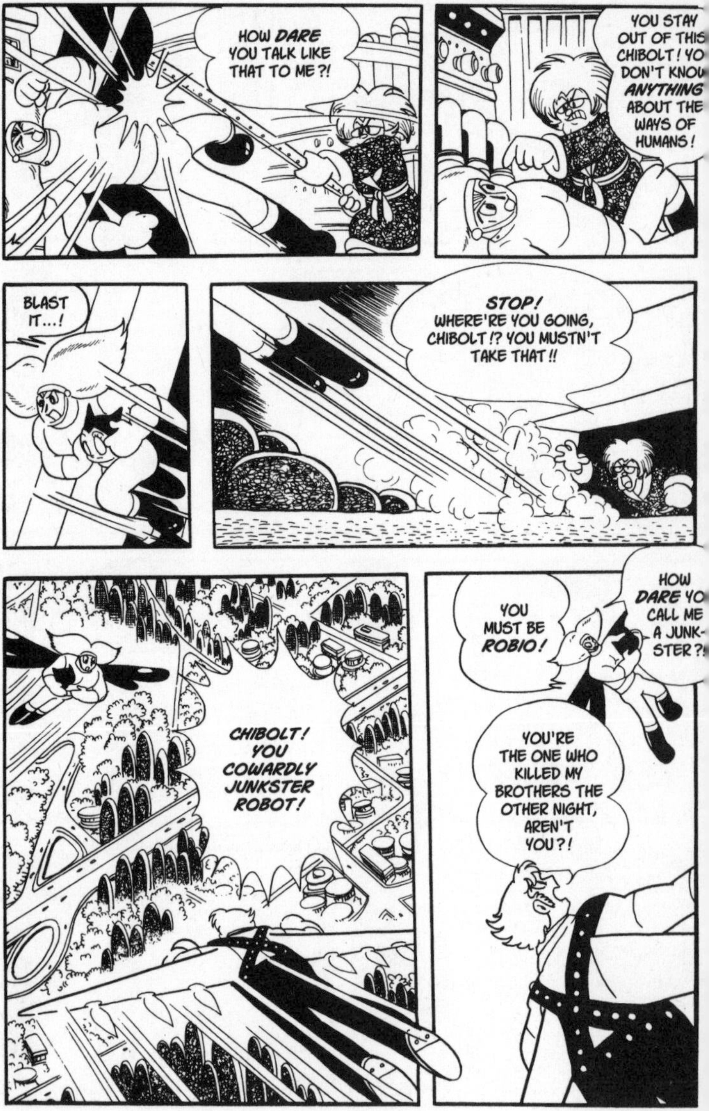
HOW DARE YOU TALK LIKE THAT TO ME?!
YOU STAY OUT OF THIS CHIBOLT! YO DON'T KNOW ANYTHING ABOUT THE WAYS OF HUMANS!
BLAST IT...!
STOP! WHERE'RE YOU GOING, CHIBOLT!? YOU MUSTN'T TAKE THAT!!
CHIBOLT! YOU COWARDLY JUNKSTER ROBOT!
YOU MUST BE ROBIO!
HOW DARE YO CALL ME A JUNK-STER?
YOU'RE THE ONE WHO KILLED MY BROTHERS THE OTHER NIGHT, AREN'T YOU?!

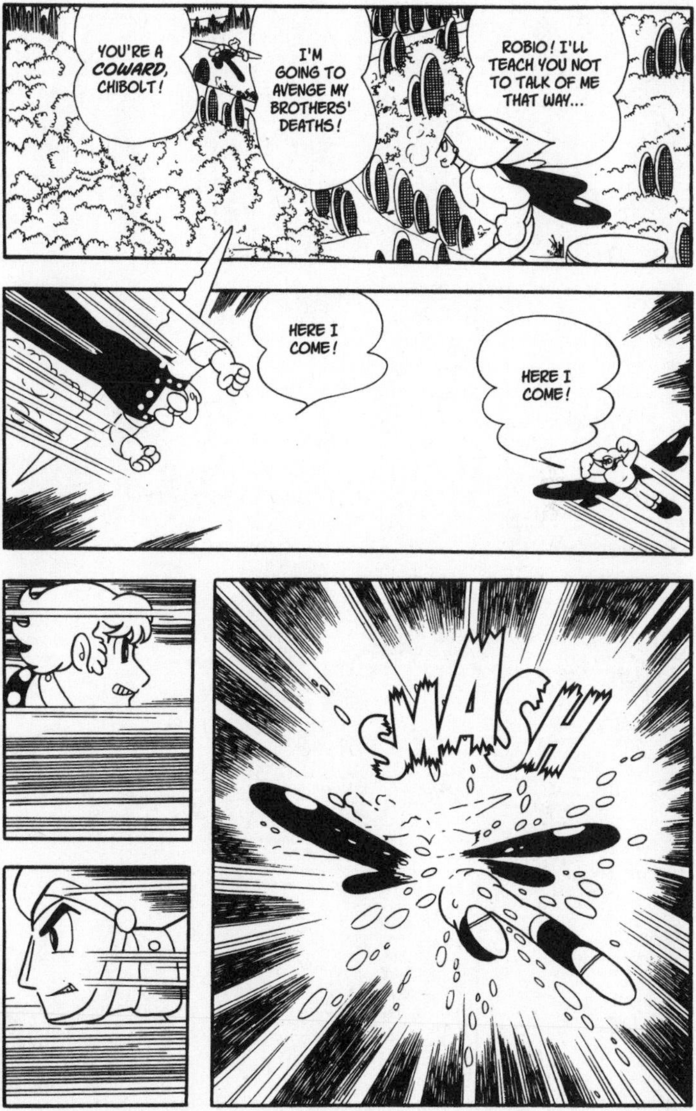
YOU'RE A **COWARD**, CHIBOLT!
I'M GOING TO AVENGE MY BROTHERS' DEATHS!
ROBIO! I'LL TEACH YOU NOT TO TALK OF ME THAT WAY...
HERE I COME!
HERE I COME!
SMASH

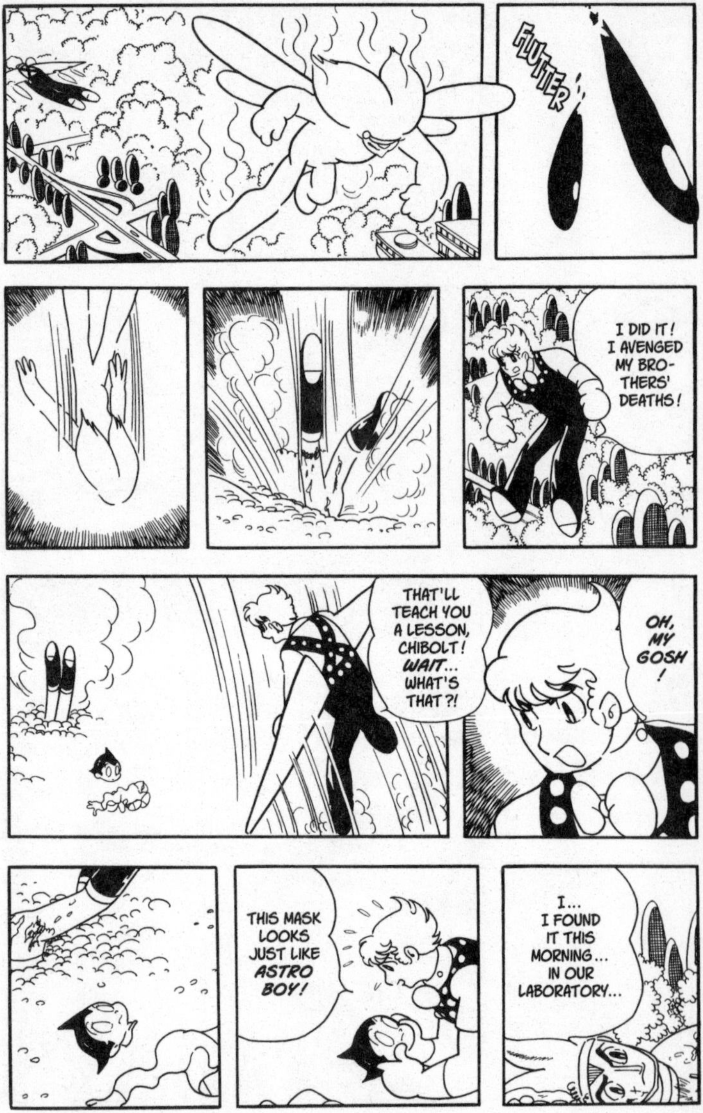
FLUTTER
I DID IT! I AVENGED MY BRO- THERS' DEATHS!
THAT'LL TEACH YOU A LESSON, CHIBOLT! *WAIT*... WHAT'S THAT?!
OH, MY GOSH!
THIS MASK LOOKS JUST LIKE *ASTRO BOY!*
I... I FOUND IT THIS MORNING... IN OUR LABORATORY...

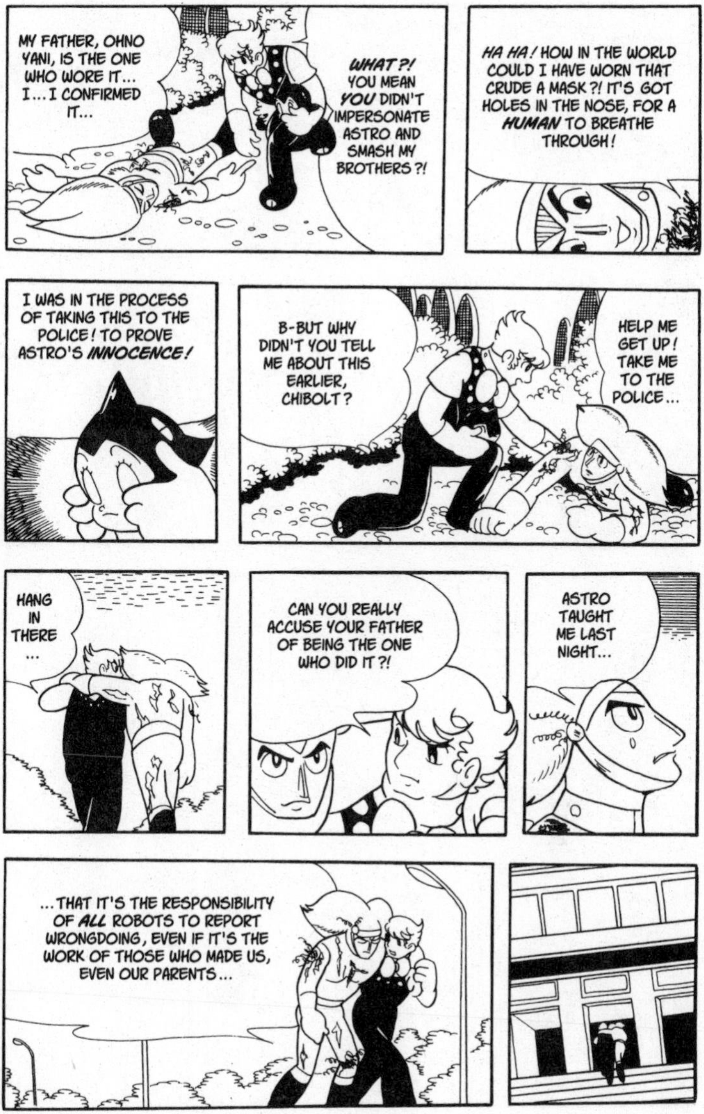
MY FATHER, OHNO YANI, IS THE ONE WHO WORE IT... I... I CONFIRMED IT...
WHAT?! YOU MEAN YOU DIDN'T IMPERSONATE ASTRO AND SMASH MY BROTHERS?!
HA HA! HOW IN THE WORLD COULD I HAVE WORN THAT CRUDE A MASK?! IT'S GOT HOLES IN THE NOSE, FOR A HUMAN TO BREATHE THROUGH!
I WAS IN THE PROCESS OF TAKING THIS TO THE POLICE! TO PROVE ASTRO'S INNOCENCE!
B-BUT WHY DIDN'T YOU TELL ME ABOUT THIS EARLIER, CHIBOLT?
HELP ME GET UP! TAKE ME TO THE POLICE...
HANG IN THERE ...
CAN YOU REALLY ACCUSE YOUR FATHER OF BEING THE ONE WHO DID IT?!
ASTRO TAUGHT ME LAST NIGHT...
...THAT IT'S THE RESPONSIBILITY OF ALL ROBOTS TO REPORT WRONGDOING, EVEN IF IT'S THE WORK OF THOSE WHO MADE US, EVEN OUR PARENTS...

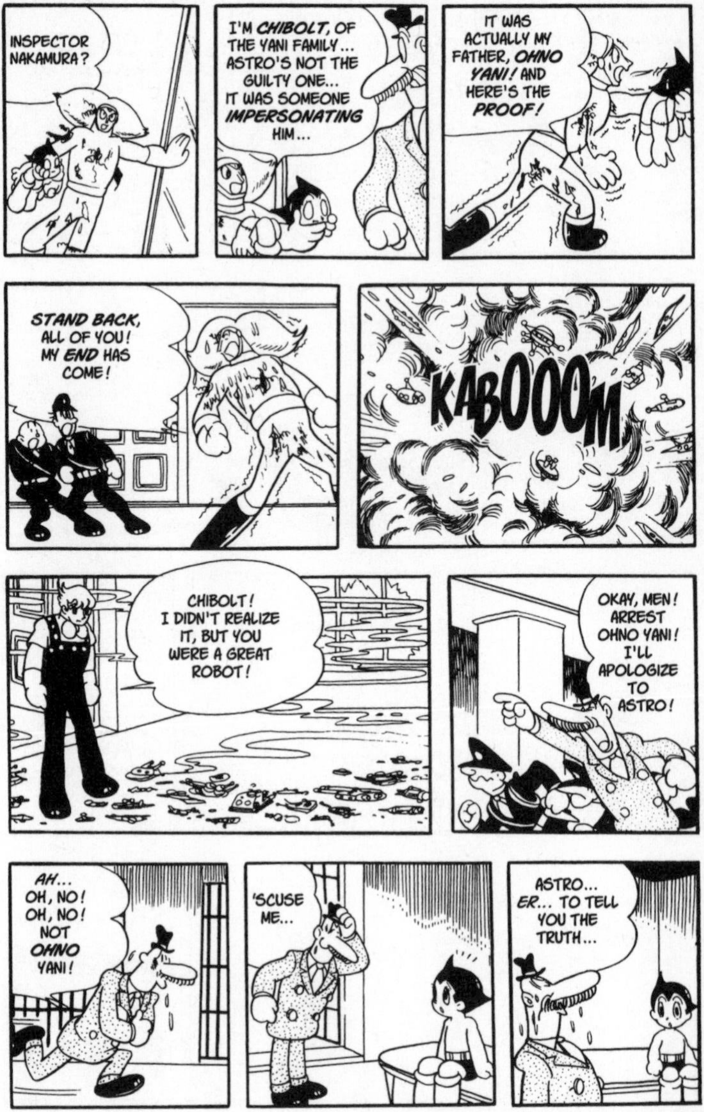
INSPECTOR NAKAMURA?
I'M CHIBOLT, OF THE YANI FAMILY... ASTRO'S NOT THE GUILTY ONE... IT WAS SOMEONE IMPERSONATING HIM...
IT WAS ACTUALLY MY FATHER, OHNO YANI! AND HERE'S THE PROOF!
STAND BACK, ALL OF YOU! MY END HAS COME!
KABOOOM
CHIBOLT! I DIDN'T REALIZE IT, BUT YOU WERE A GREAT ROBOT!
OKAY, MEN! ARREST OHNO YANI! I'LL APOLOGIZE TO ASTRO!
AH... OH, NO! OH, NO! NOT OHNO YANI!
'SCUSE ME...
ASTRO... ER... TO TELL YOU THE TRUTH...

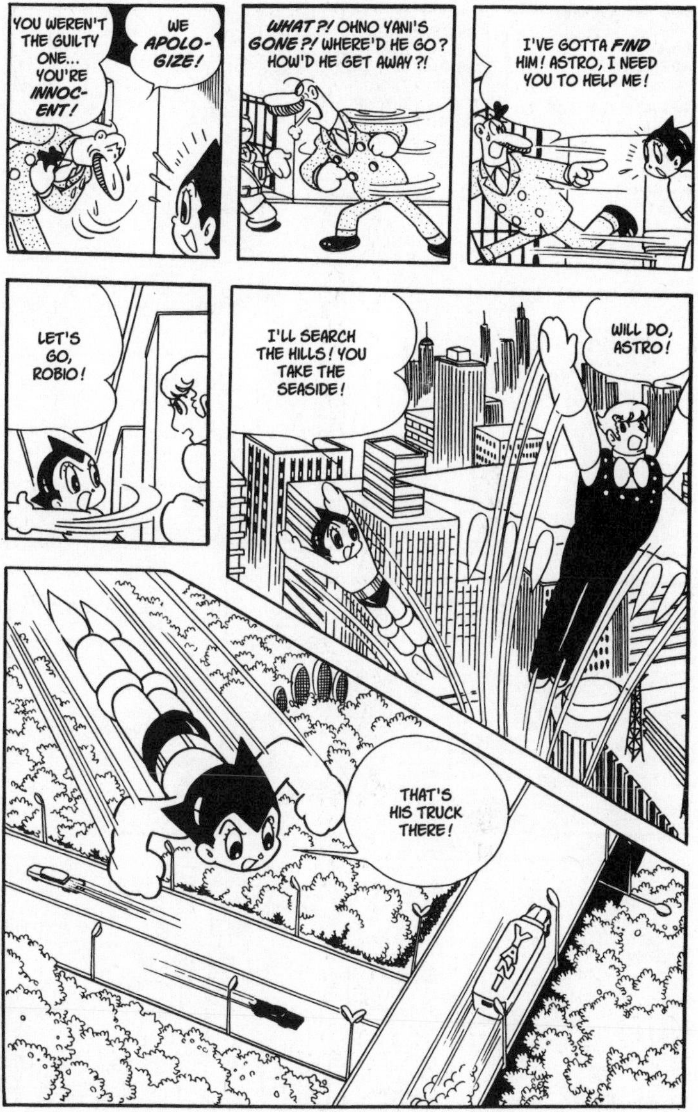
YOU WEREN'T THE GUILTY ONE... YOU'RE INNOCENT!
WE APOLOGIZE!
WHAT?! OHNO YANI'S GONE?! WHERE'D HE GO? HOW'D HE GET AWAY?!
I'VE GOTTA FIND HIM! ASTRO, I NEED YOU TO HELP ME!
LET'S GO, ROBIO!
I'LL SEARCH THE HILLS! YOU TAKE THE SEASIDE!
WILL DO, ASTRO!
THAT'S HIS TRUCK THERE!

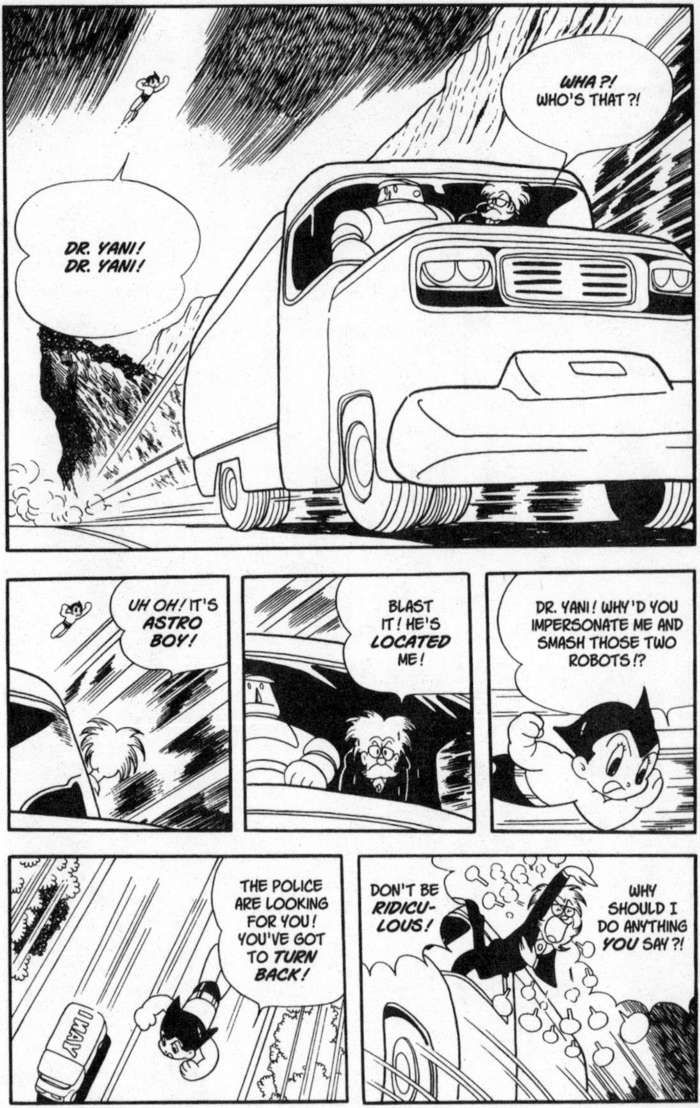
DR. YANI! DR. YANI!
WHA?! WHO'S THAT?!
UH OH! IT'S ASTRO BOY!
BLAST IT! HE'S LOCATED ME!
DR. YANI! WHY'D YOU IMPERSONATE ME AND SMASH THOSE TWO ROBOTS!?
THE POLICE ARE LOOKING FOR YOU! YOU'VE GOT TO TURN BACK!
DON'T BE RIDICULOUS!
WHY SHOULD I DO ANYTHING YOU SAY?!

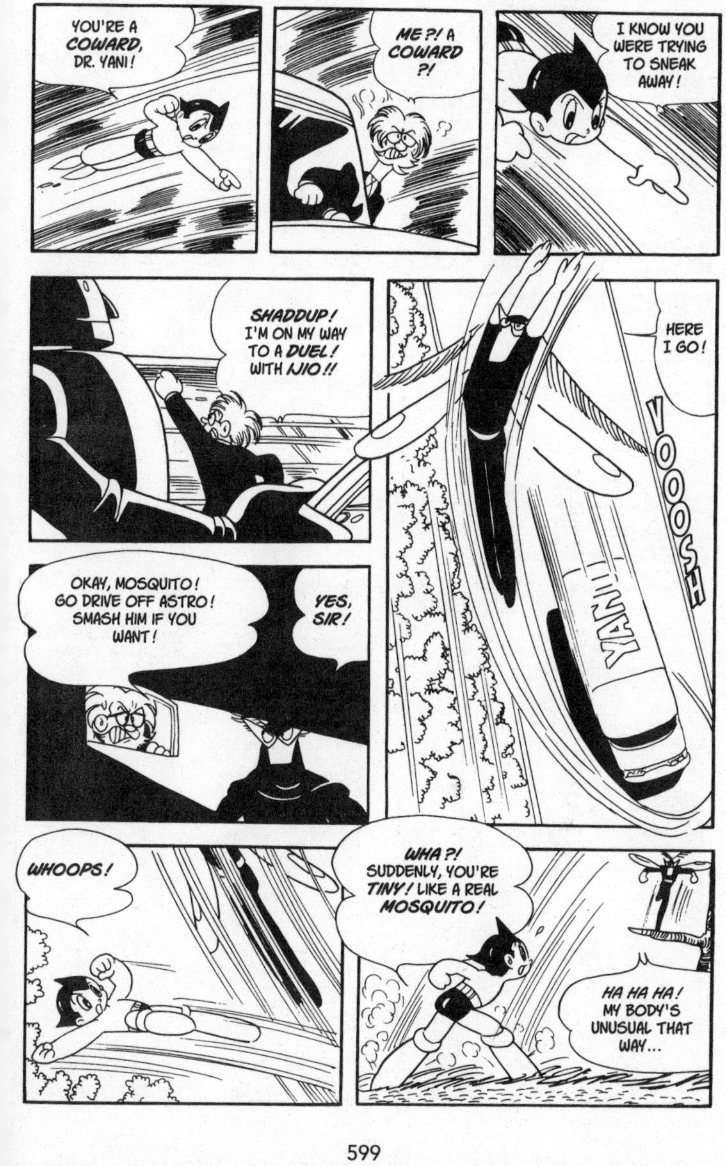
YOU'RE A COWARD, DR. YANI!
ME?! A COWARD ?!
I KNOW YOU WERE TRYING TO SNEAK AWAY!
SHADDUP! I'M ON MY WAY TO A DUEL! WITH IJIO!!
OKAY, MOSQUITO! GO DRIVE OFF ASTRO! SMASH HIM IF YOU WANT!
YES, SIR!
HERE I GO!
VOOOOSH
YANI
WHOOPS!
WHA?! SUDDENLY, YOU'RE TINY! LIKE A REAL MOSQUITO!
HA HA HA! MY BODY'S UNUSUAL THAT WAY...

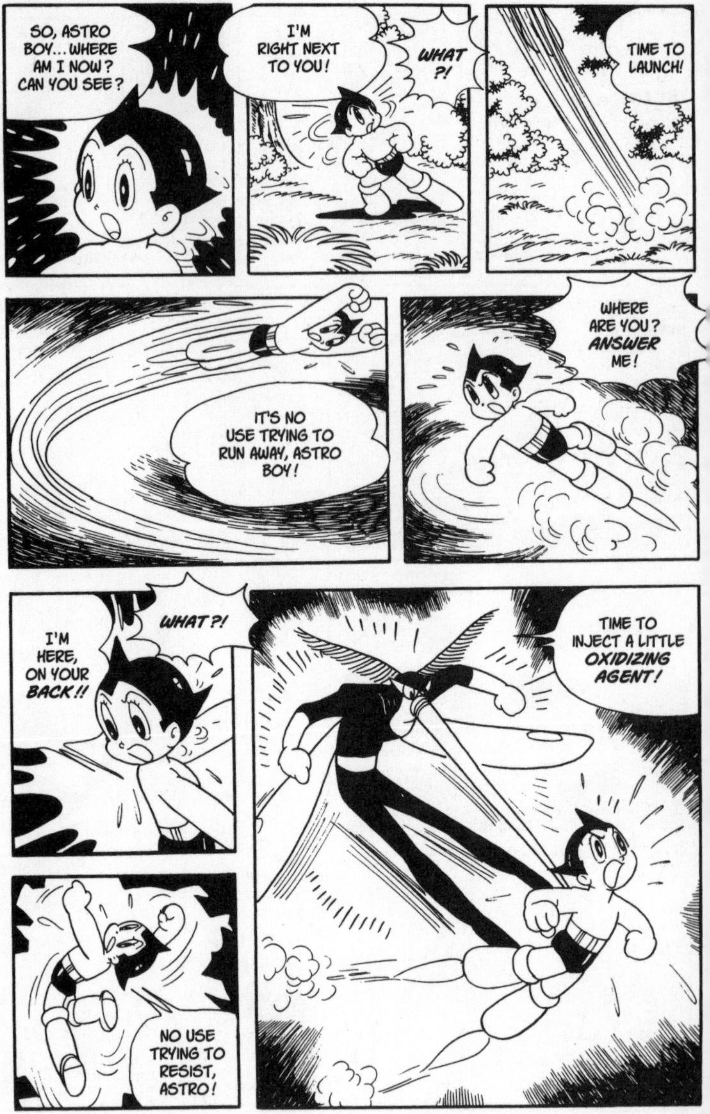
SO, ASTRO BOY... WHERE AM I NOW? CAN YOU SEE?
I'M RIGHT NEXT TO YOU!
WHAT ?!
TIME TO LAUNCH!
IT'S NO USE TRYING TO RUN AWAY, ASTRO BOY!
WHERE ARE YOU? ANSWER ME!
I'M HERE, ON YOUR BACK!!
WHAT?!
NO USE TRYING TO RESIST, ASTRO!
TIME TO INJECT A LITTLE OXIDIZING AGENT!

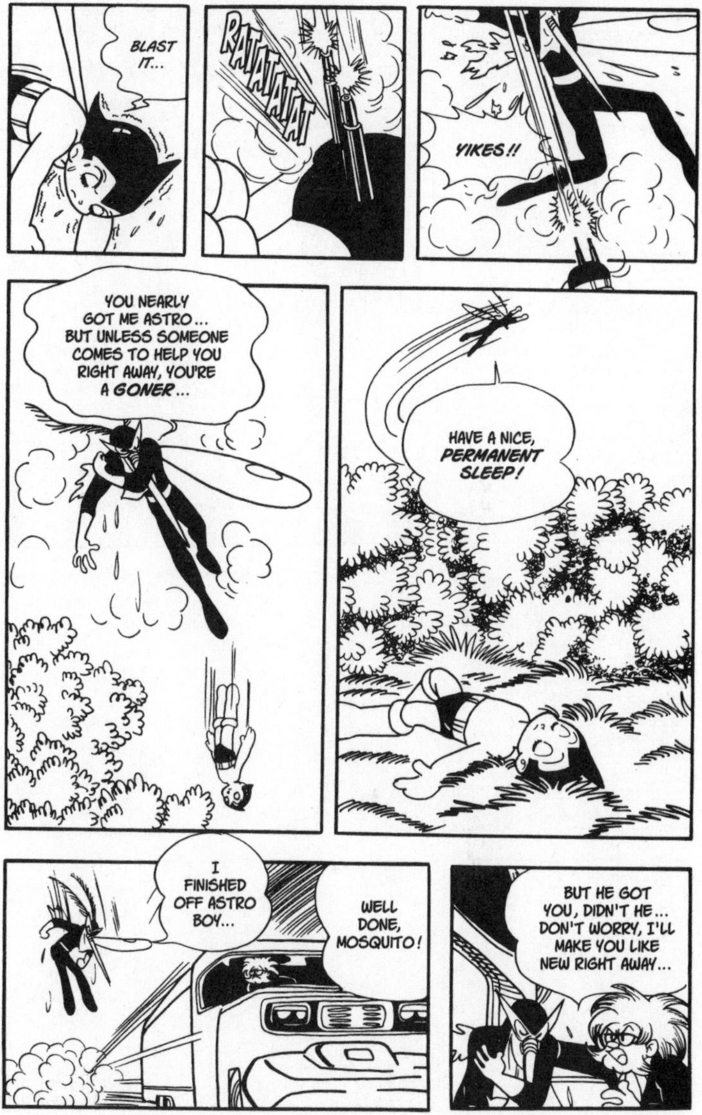
BLAST IT...
RATATATATAT
YIKES!!
YOU NEARLY GOT ME ASTRO... BUT UNLESS SOMEONE COMES TO HELP YOU RIGHT AWAY, YOU'RE A GONER...
HAVE A NICE, PERMANENT SLEEP!
I FINISHED OFF ASTRO BOY...
WELL DONE, MOSQUITO!
BUT HE GOT YOU, DIDN'T HE... DON'T WORRY, I'LL MAKE YOU LIKE NEW RIGHT AWAY...

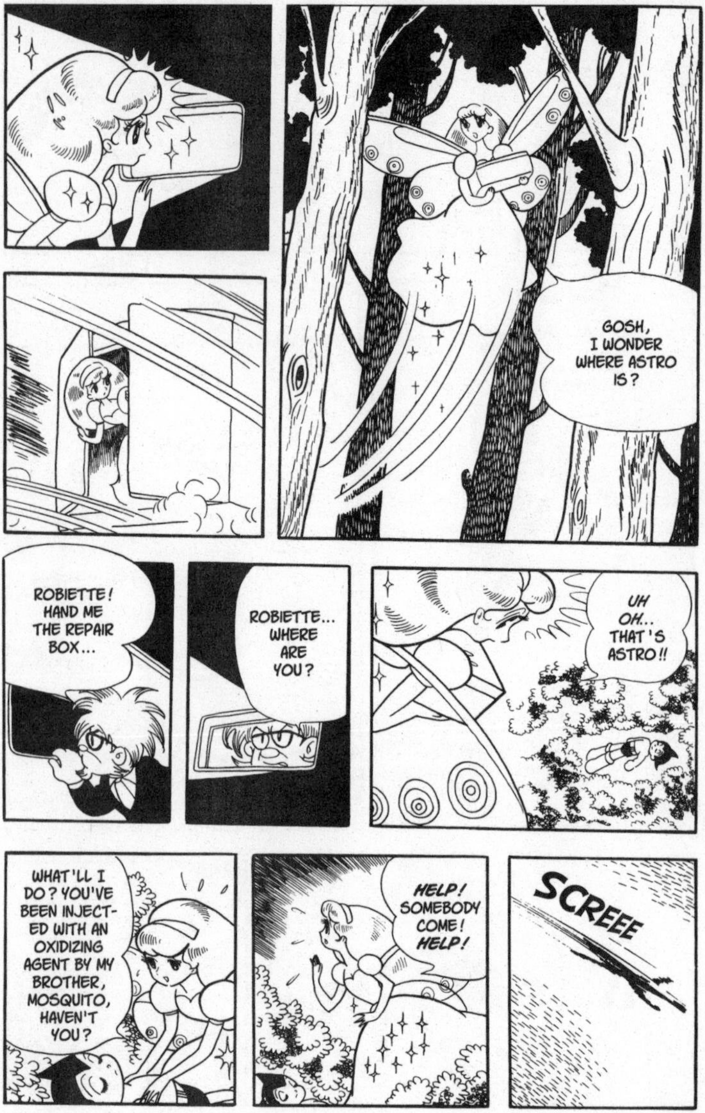
GOSH, I WONDER WHERE ASTRO IS?
ROBIETTE! HAND ME THE REPAIR BOX...
ROBIETTE... WHERE ARE YOU?
UH OH... THAT'S ASTRO!!
WHAT'LL I DO? YOU'VE BEEN INJECTED WITH AN OXIDIZING AGENT BY MY BROTHER, MOSQUITO, HAVEN'T YOU?
HELP! SOMEBODY COME! HELP!
SCREEE

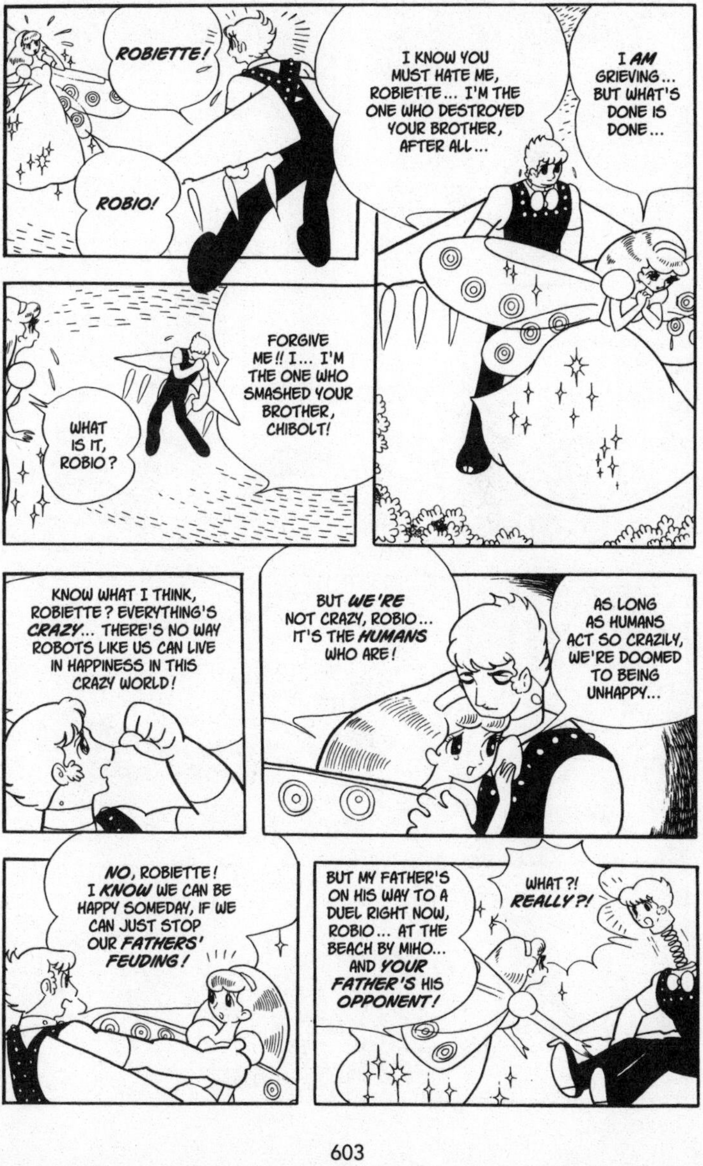
ROBIETTE!
ROBIO!
WHAT IS IT, ROBIO?
FORGIVE ME!! I... I'M THE ONE WHO SMASHED YOUR BROTHER, CHIBOLT!
I KNOW YOU MUST HATE ME, ROBIETTE... I'M THE ONE WHO DESTROYED YOUR BROTHER, AFTER ALL...
I *AM* GRIEVING... BUT WHAT'S DONE IS DONE...
KNOW WHAT I THINK, ROBIETTE? EVERYTHING'S *CRAZY*... THERE'S NO WAY ROBOTS LIKE US CAN LIVE IN HAPPINESS IN THIS CRAZY WORLD!
BUT *WE'RE* NOT CRAZY, ROBIO... IT'S THE *HUMANS* WHO ARE!
AS LONG AS HUMANS ACT SO CRAZILY, WE'RE DOOMED TO BEING UNHAPPY...
NO, ROBIETTE! I *KNOW* WE CAN BE HAPPY SOMEDAY, IF WE CAN JUST STOP OUR *FATHERS' FEUDING*!
BUT MY FATHER'S ON HIS WAY TO A DUEL RIGHT NOW, ROBIO... AT THE BEACH BY MIHO... AND *YOUR FATHER'S* HIS *OPPONENT*!
WHAT?! *REALLY?!*

WE'VE GOT TO HURRY AND STOP THEM, ROBIETTE!

THEY'RE BOTH SO STUBBORN, ROBIO...

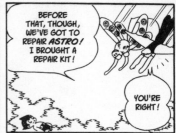

BEFORE THAT, THOUGH, WE'VE GOT TO REPAIR *ASTRO*! I BROUGHT A REPAIR KIT!

YOU'RE RIGHT!

THINK YOU CAN FIX HIM? HE'S BADLY HURT...

I CAN REPAIR MOST ROBOTS...

BLAST IT... ASTRO'S BODY DESIGN IS TOO *COMPLICATED!*

I NEED YOU TO TAKE ASTRO TO THE MINISTRY OF SCIENCE, ROBIETTE. I'LL GO TO THE SITE OF THE DUEL AT MIHO...

I'LL JOIN YOU LATER, ROBIO!

TAKE CARE OF ASTRO!

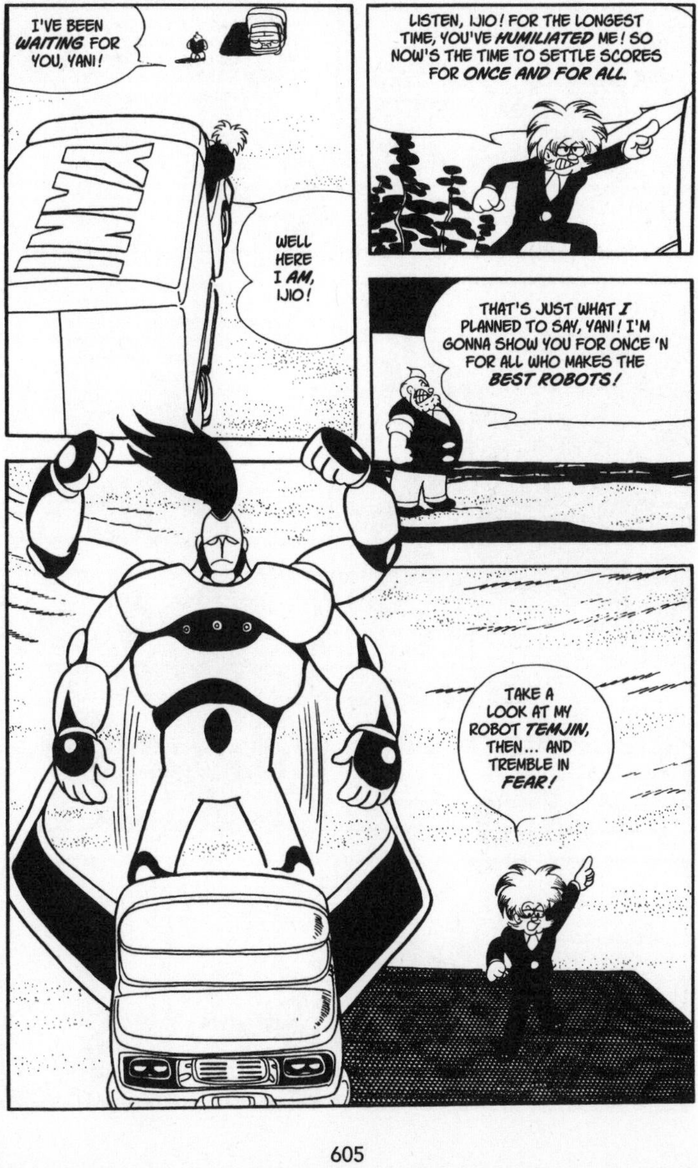
I'VE BEEN WAITING FOR YOU, YANI!
WELL HERE I AM, IJIO!
LISTEN, IJIO! FOR THE LONGEST TIME, YOU'VE HUMILIATED ME! SO NOW'S THE TIME TO SETTLE SCORES FOR ONCE AND FOR ALL.
THAT'S JUST WHAT I PLANNED TO SAY, YANI! I'M GONNA SHOW YOU FOR ONCE 'N FOR ALL WHO MAKES THE BEST ROBOTS!
TAKE A LOOK AT MY ROBOT TEMJIN, THEN... AND TREMBLE IN FEAR!

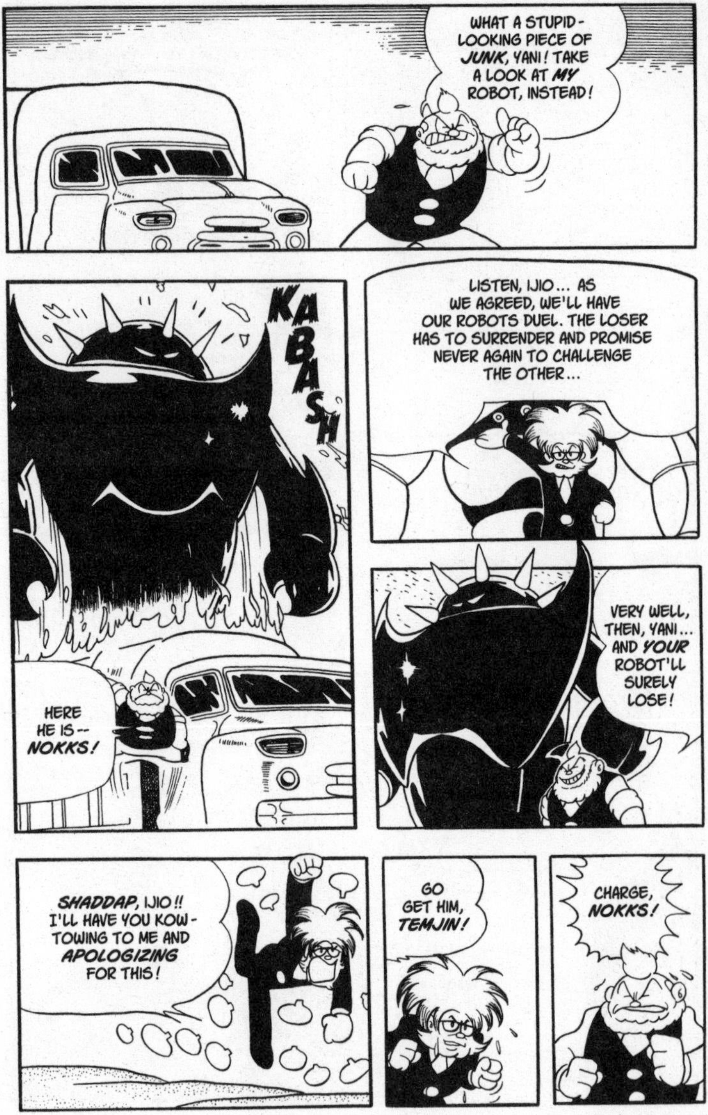
WHAT A STUPID-LOOKING PIECE OF JUNK, YANI! TAKE A LOOK AT MY ROBOT, INSTEAD!
KABASH
HERE HE IS -- NOKKS!
LISTEN, IJIO... AS WE AGREED, WE'LL HAVE OUR ROBOTS DUEL. THE LOSER HAS TO SURRENDER AND PROMISE NEVER AGAIN TO CHALLENGE THE OTHER...
VERY WELL, THEN, YANI... AND YOUR ROBOT'LL SURELY LOSE!
SHADDAP, IJIO!! I'LL HAVE YOU KOW-TOWING TO ME AND APOLOGIZING FOR THIS!
GO GET HIM, TEMJIN!
CHARGE, NOKKS!

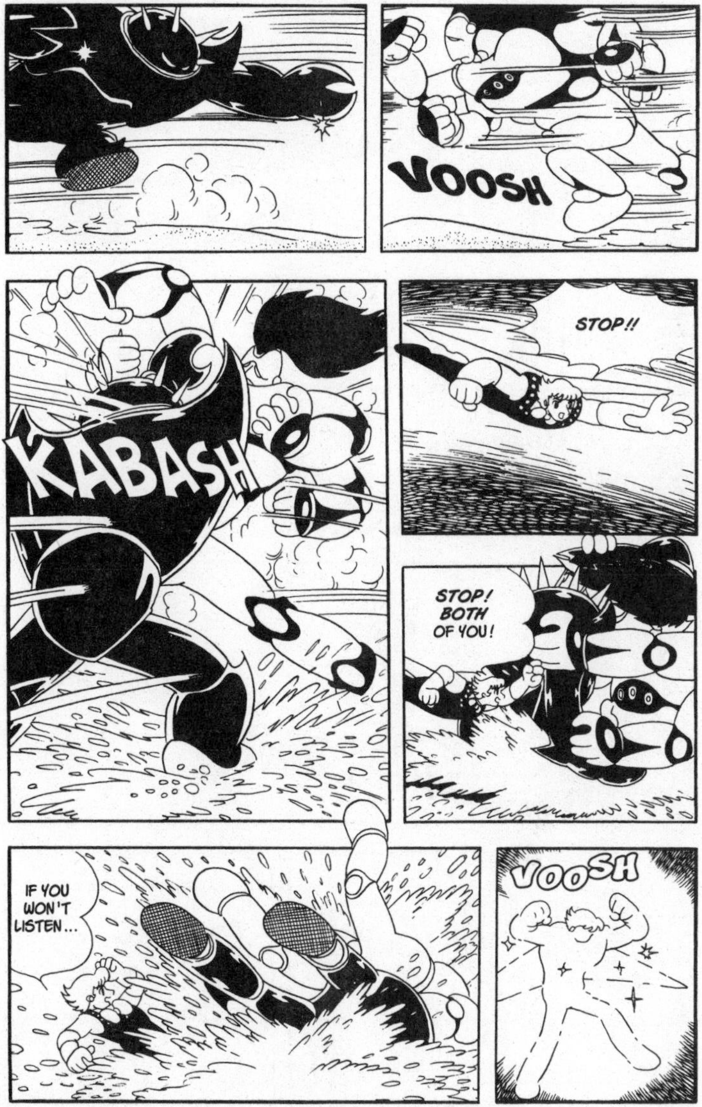
VOOSH
KABASH
STOP!!
STOP! BOTH OF YOU!
IF YOU WON'T LISTEN...
VOOSH

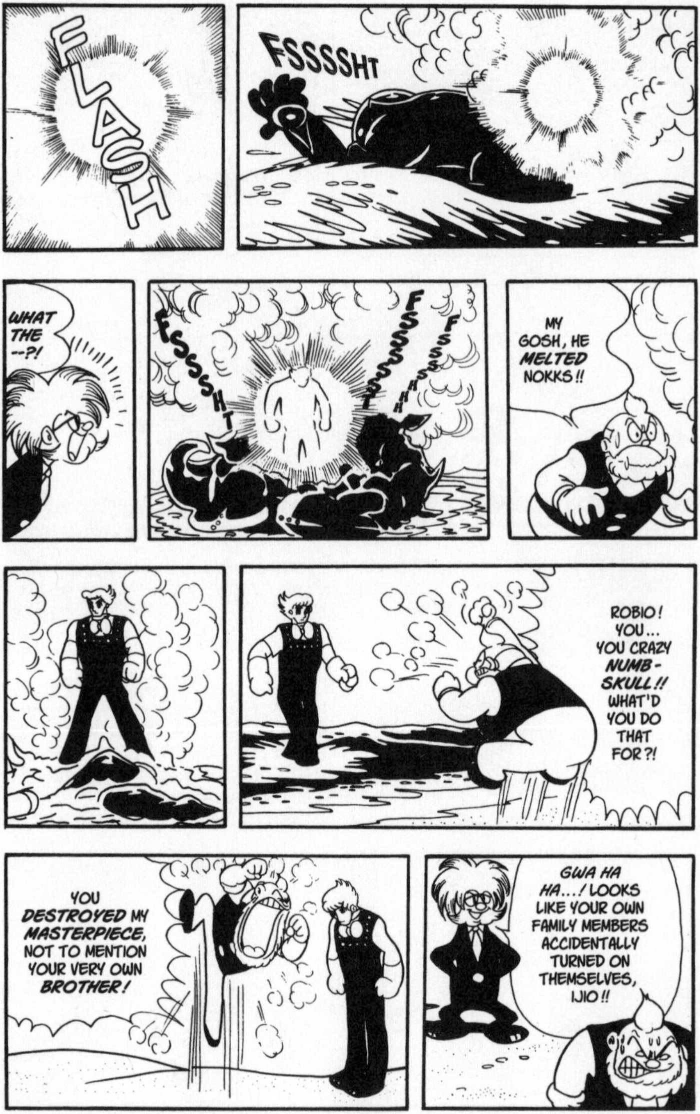
FLASH
FSSSSHT
WHAT THE --?!
FSSSSHT
FSSSSHT
FSSSSHT
MY GOSH, HE MELTED NOKKS!!
ROBIO! YOU... YOU CRAZY NUMB-SKULL!! WHAT'D YOU DO THAT FOR?!
YOU DESTROYED MY MASTERPIECE, NOT TO MENTION YOUR VERY OWN BROTHER!
GWA HA HA...! LOOKS LIKE YOUR OWN FAMILY MEMBERS ACCIDENTALLY TURNED ON THEMSELVES, IJIO!!

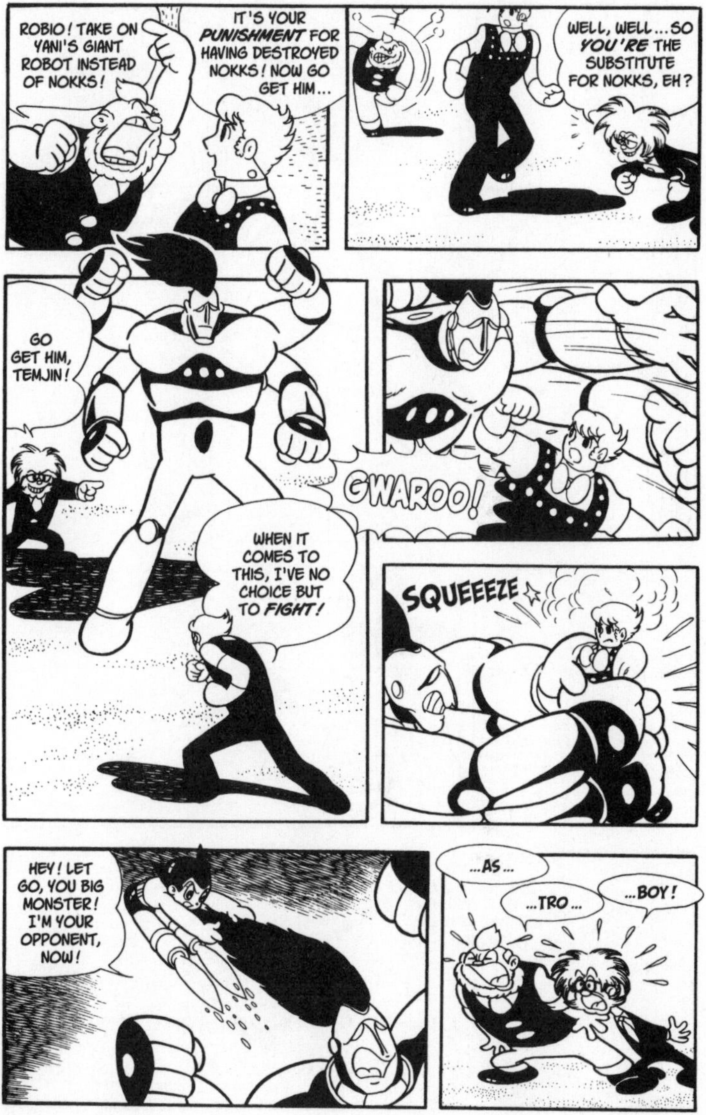

ROBIO! TAKE ON YANI'S GIANT ROBOT INSTEAD OF NOKKS!
IT'S YOUR PUNISHMENT FOR HAVING DESTROYED NOKKS! NOW GO GET HIM...
WELL, WELL...SO YOU'RE THE SUBSTITUTE FOR NOKKS, EH?
GO GET HIM, TEMJIN!
WHEN IT COMES TO THIS, I'VE NO CHOICE BUT TO FIGHT!
GWAROO!
SQUEEEZE
HEY! LET GO, YOU BIG MONSTER! I'M YOUR OPPONENT, NOW!
...AS...
...TRO...
...BOY!

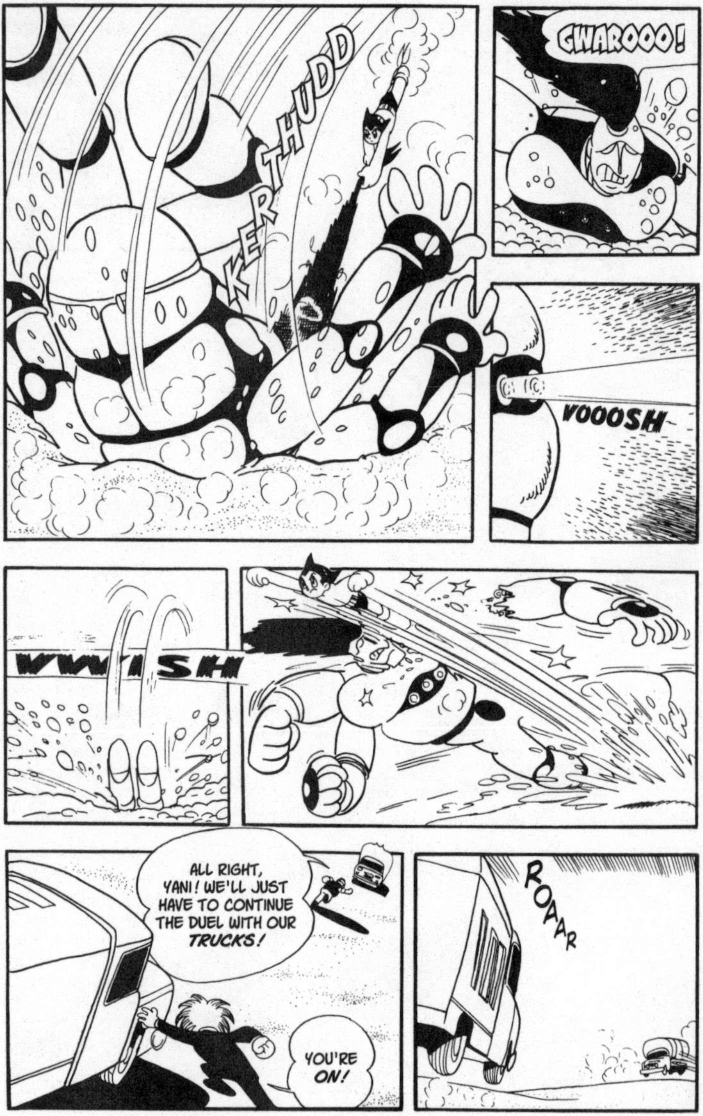
KERTHUDD
GWAROOO!
VOOOSH
WWWISH
ALL RIGHT, YANI! WE'LL JUST HAVE TO CONTINUE THE DUEL WITH OUR TRUCKS!
YOU'RE ON!
ROAAR

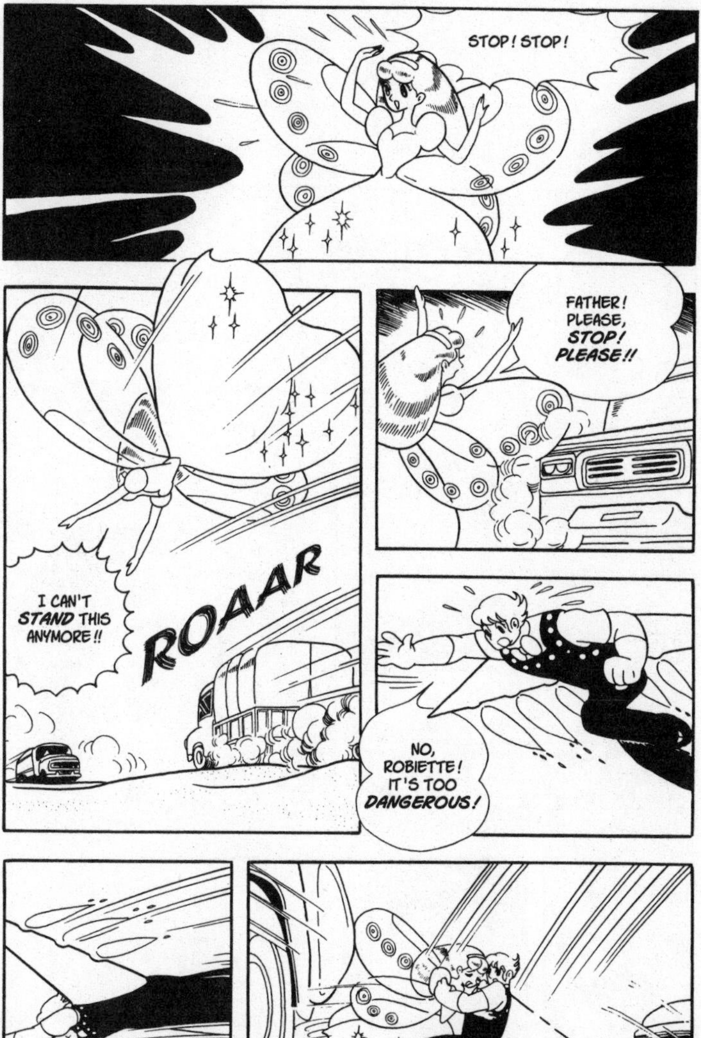
STOP! STOP!
I CAN'T STAND THIS ANYMORE!!
ROAAR
FATHER! PLEASE, STOP! PLEASE!!
NO, ROBIETTE! IT'S TOO DANGEROUS!
ROBIETTE!

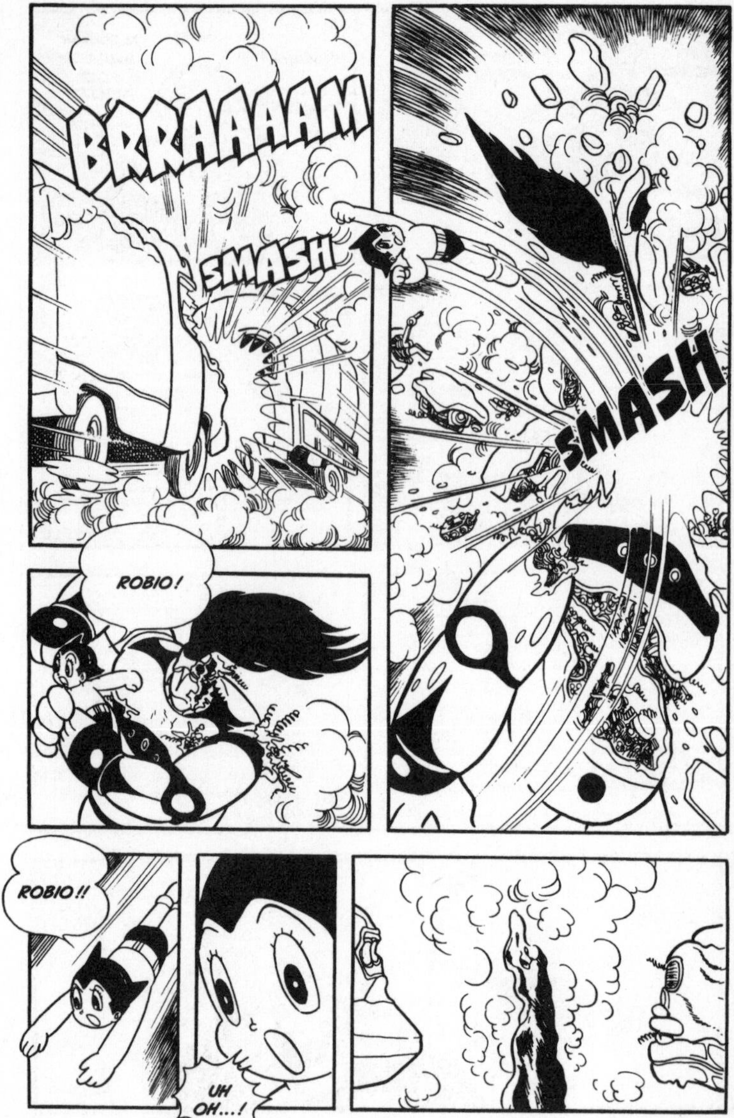
BRRAAAAM
SMASH
SMASH
ROBIO!
ROBIO!!
UH OH...!

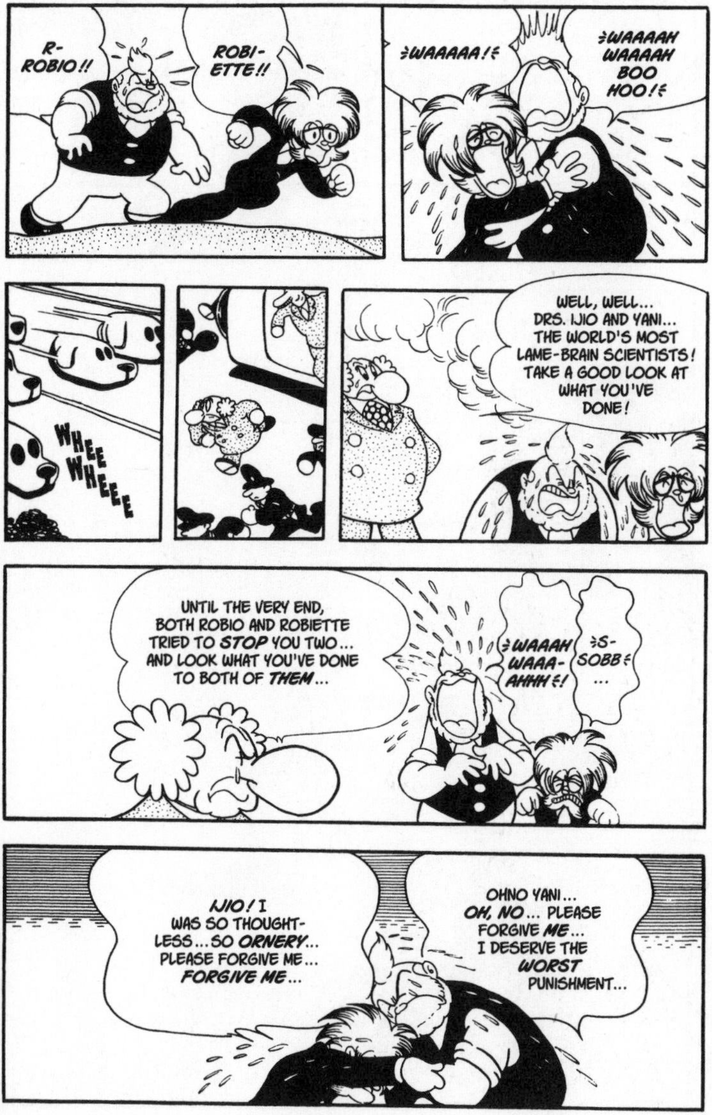
R-
ROBIO!!
ROBI-
ETTE!!
WAAAAA!
WAAAAH
WAAAAH
BOO
HOO!
WHEE
WHEEE
WELL, WELL...
DRS. IJIO AND YANI...
THE WORLD'S MOST
LAME-BRAIN SCIENTISTS!
TAKE A GOOD LOOK AT
WHAT YOU'VE
DONE!
UNTIL THE VERY END,
BOTH ROBIO AND ROBIETTE
TRIED TO STOP YOU TWO...
AND LOOK WHAT YOU'VE DONE
TO BOTH OF THEM...
WAAAH
WAAA-
AHHH!
S-
SOBB
...
IJIO! I
WAS SO THOUGHT-
LESS...SO ORNERY...
PLEASE FORGIVE ME...
FORGIVE ME...
OHNO YANI...
OH, NO... PLEASE
FORGIVE ME...
I DESERVE THE
WORST
PUNISHMENT...

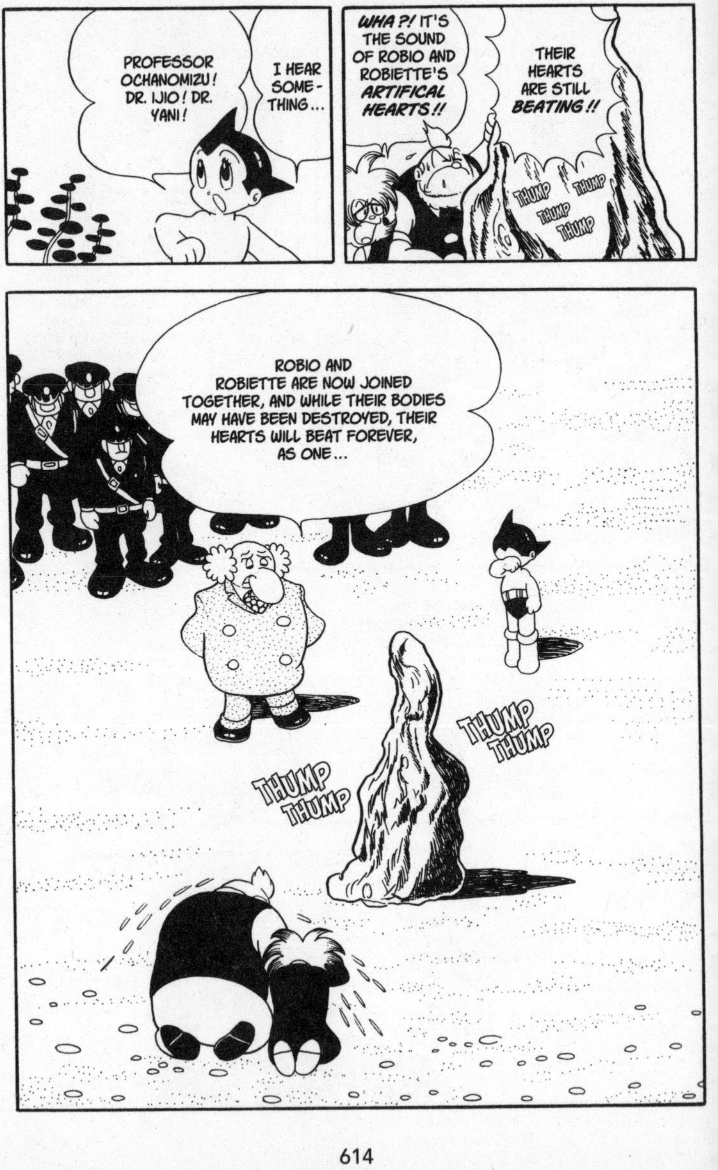
PROFESSOR OCHANOMIZU! DR. IJIO! DR. YANI!
I HEAR SOME-THING...
WHA?! IT'S THE SOUND OF ROBIO AND ROBIETTE'S ARTIFICAL HEARTS!!
THEIR HEARTS ARE STILL BEATING!!
THUMP
THUMP
THUMP
THUMP
ROBIO AND ROBIETTE ARE NOW JOINED TOGETHER, AND WHILE THEIR BODIES MAY HAVE BEEN DESTROYED, THEIR HEARTS WILL BEAT FOREVER, AS ONE...
THUMP THUMP
THUMP THUMP

THE DEVIL'S
BALLOONS

First serialized from December 1963 to February 1964
in the supplement editions of *Shonen* magazine.

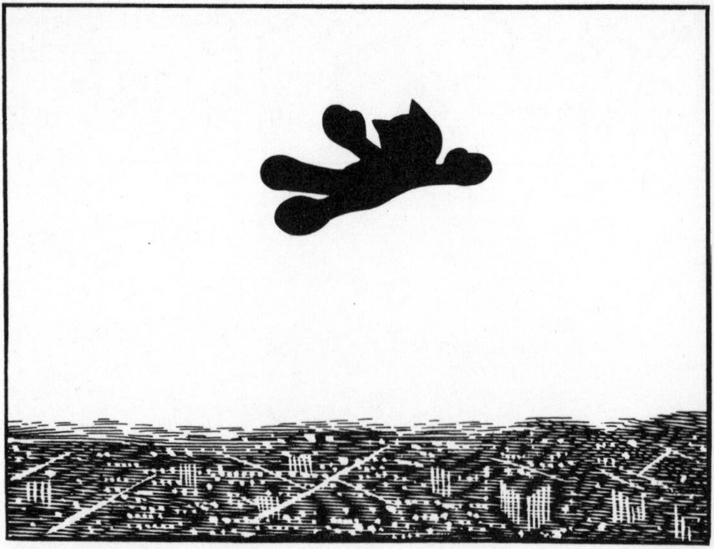

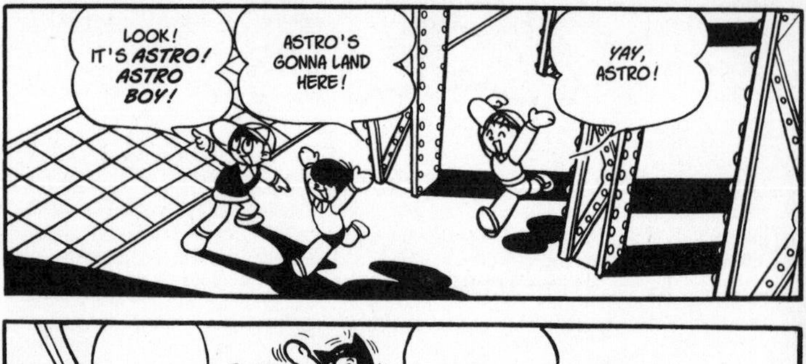
LOOK! IT'S ASTRO! ASTRO BOY!
ASTRO'S GONNA LAND HERE!
YAY, ASTRO!

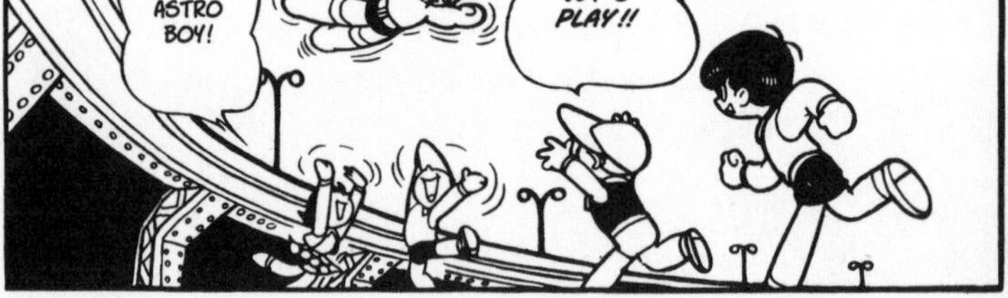
ASTRO BOY!
LET'S PLAY!!

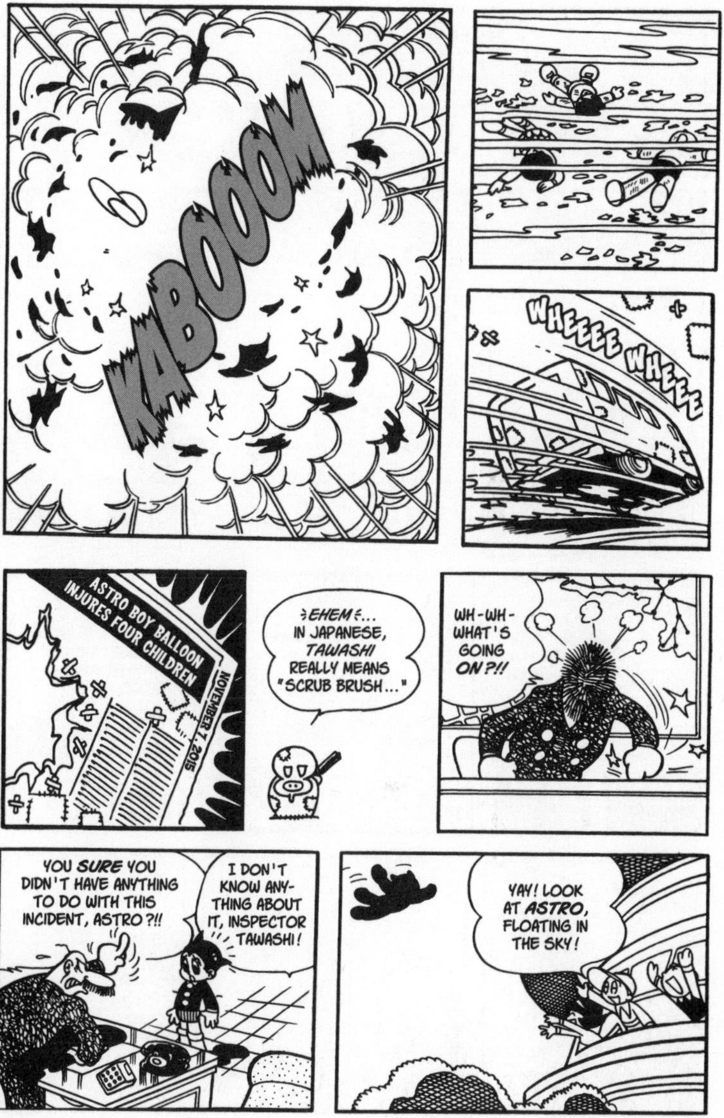
KABOOOM
WHEEEE WHEEEE
ASTRO BOY BALLOON INJURES FOUR CHILDREN
NOVEMBER 7, 2015
≶EHEM≶... IN JAPANESE, TAWASHI REALLY MEANS "SCRUB BRUSH..."
WH-WH-WHAT'S GOING ON?!!
YOU SURE YOU DIDN'T HAVE ANYTHING TO DO WITH THIS INCIDENT, ASTRO?!!
I DON'T KNOW ANYTHING ABOUT IT, INSPECTOR TAWASHI!
YAY! LOOK AT ASTRO, FLOATING IN THE SKY!

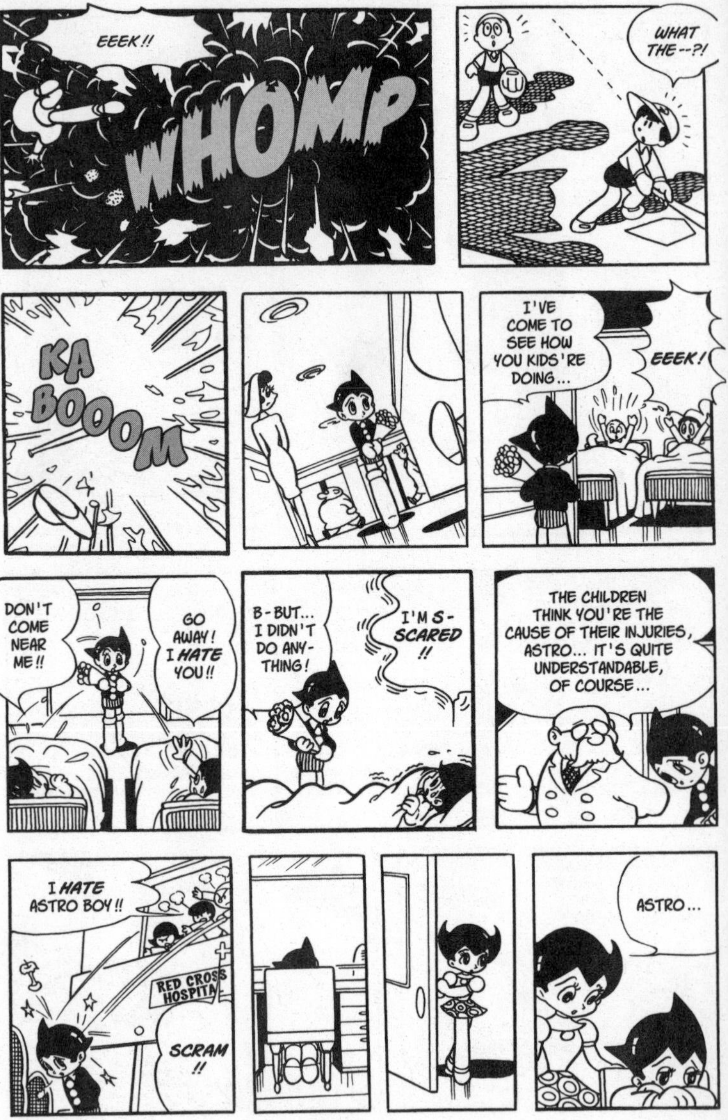
EEEK!!
WHOMP
WHAT THE--?!
KA BOOOM
I'VE COME TO SEE HOW YOU KIDS'RE DOING...
EEEK!
DON'T COME NEAR ME!!
GO AWAY! I HATE YOU!!
B-BUT... I DIDN'T DO ANY-THING!
I'M S-SCARED!!
THE CHILDREN THINK YOU'RE THE CAUSE OF THEIR INJURIES, ASTRO... IT'S QUITE UNDERSTANDABLE, OF COURSE...
I HATE ASTRO BOY!!
RED CROSS HOSPITA
SCRAM!!
ASTRO...

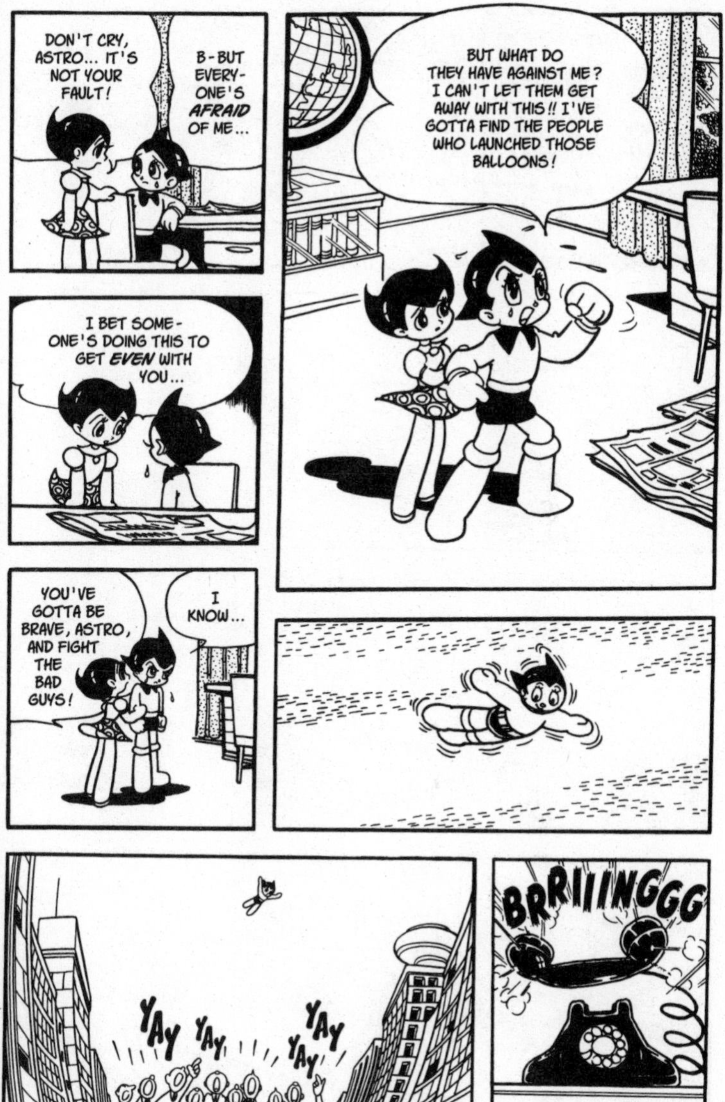
DON'T CRY, ASTRO... IT'S NOT YOUR FAULT!
B-BUT EVERY-ONE'S *AFRAID* OF ME...
BUT WHAT DO THEY HAVE AGAINST ME? I CAN'T LET THEM GET AWAY WITH THIS!! I'VE GOTTA FIND THE PEOPLE WHO LAUNCHED THOSE BALLOONS!
I BET SOME-ONE'S DOING THIS TO GET *EVEN* WITH YOU...
YOU'VE GOTTA BE BRAVE, ASTRO, AND FIGHT THE BAD GUYS!
I KNOW...
YAY YAY YAY YAY
BRRIIINGGG

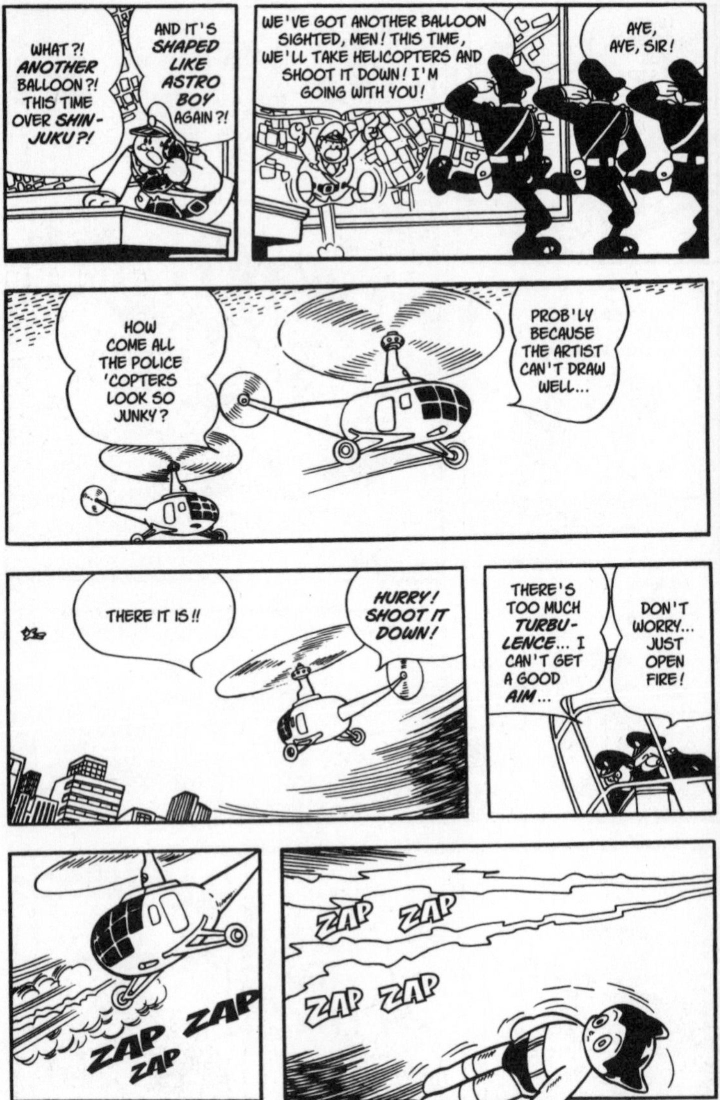
WHAT?! ANOTHER BALLOON?! THIS TIME OVER SHINJUKU?!
AND IT'S SHAPED LIKE ASTRO BOY AGAIN?!
WE'VE GOT ANOTHER BALLOON SIGHTED, MEN! THIS TIME, WE'LL TAKE HELICOPTERS AND SHOOT IT DOWN! I'M GOING WITH YOU!
AYE, AYE, SIR!
HOW COME ALL THE POLICE 'COPTERS LOOK SO JUNKY?
PROB'LY BECAUSE THE ARTIST CAN'T DRAW WELL...
THERE IT IS!!
HURRY! SHOOT IT DOWN!
THERE'S TOO MUCH TURBULENCE... I CAN'T GET A GOOD AIM...
DON'T WORRY... JUST OPEN FIRE!
ZAP ZAP
ZAP
ZAP ZAP
ZAP ZAP

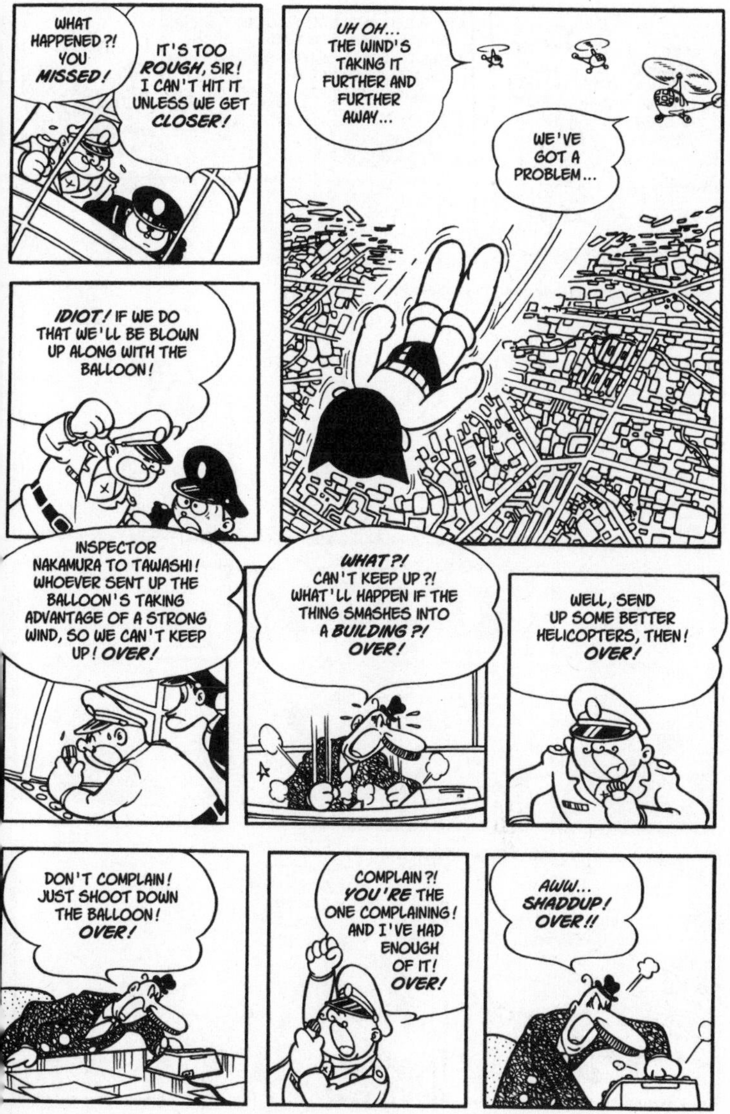

WHAT HAPPENED?! YOU MISSED!
IT'S TOO ROUGH, SIR! I CAN'T HIT IT UNLESS WE GET CLOSER!
UH OH... THE WIND'S TAKING IT FURTHER AND FURTHER AWAY...
WE'VE GOT A PROBLEM...
IDIOT! IF WE DO THAT WE'LL BE BLOWN UP ALONG WITH THE BALLOON!
INSPECTOR NAKAMURA TO TAWASHI! WHOEVER SENT UP THE BALLOON'S TAKING ADVANTAGE OF A STRONG WIND, SO WE CAN'T KEEP UP! OVER!
WHAT?! CAN'T KEEP UP?! WHAT'LL HAPPEN IF THE THING SMASHES INTO A BUILDING?! OVER!
WELL, SEND UP SOME BETTER HELICOPTERS, THEN! OVER!
DON'T COMPLAIN! JUST SHOOT DOWN THE BALLOON! OVER!
COMPLAIN?! YOU'RE THE ONE COMPLAINING! AND I'VE HAD ENOUGH OF IT! OVER!
AWW... SHADDUP! OVER!!

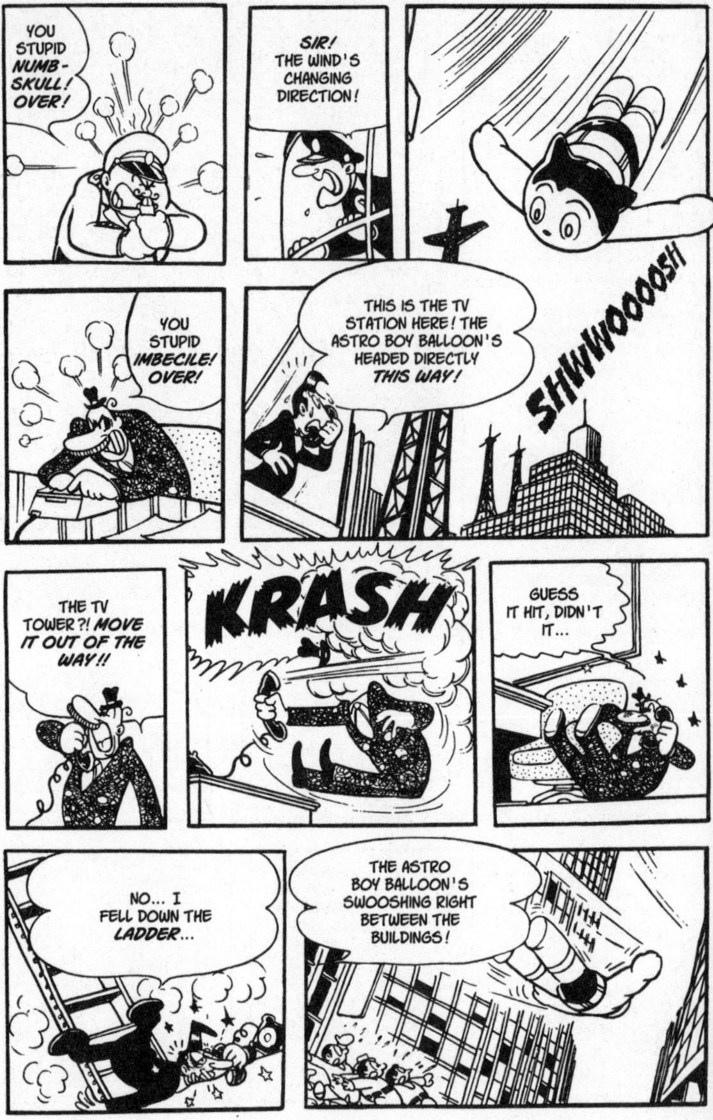
YOU STUPID NUMB-SKULL! OVER!
SIR! THE WIND'S CHANGING DIRECTION!
YOU STUPID IMBECILE! OVER!
THIS IS THE TV STATION HERE! THE ASTRO BOY BALLOON'S HEADED DIRECTLY THIS WAY!
SHWWOOOOSH
THE TV TOWER?! MOVE IT OUT OF THE WAY!!
KRASH
GUESS IT HIT, DIDN'T IT...
NO... I FELL DOWN THE LADDER...
THE ASTRO BOY BALLOON'S SWOOSHING RIGHT BETWEEN THE BUILDINGS!

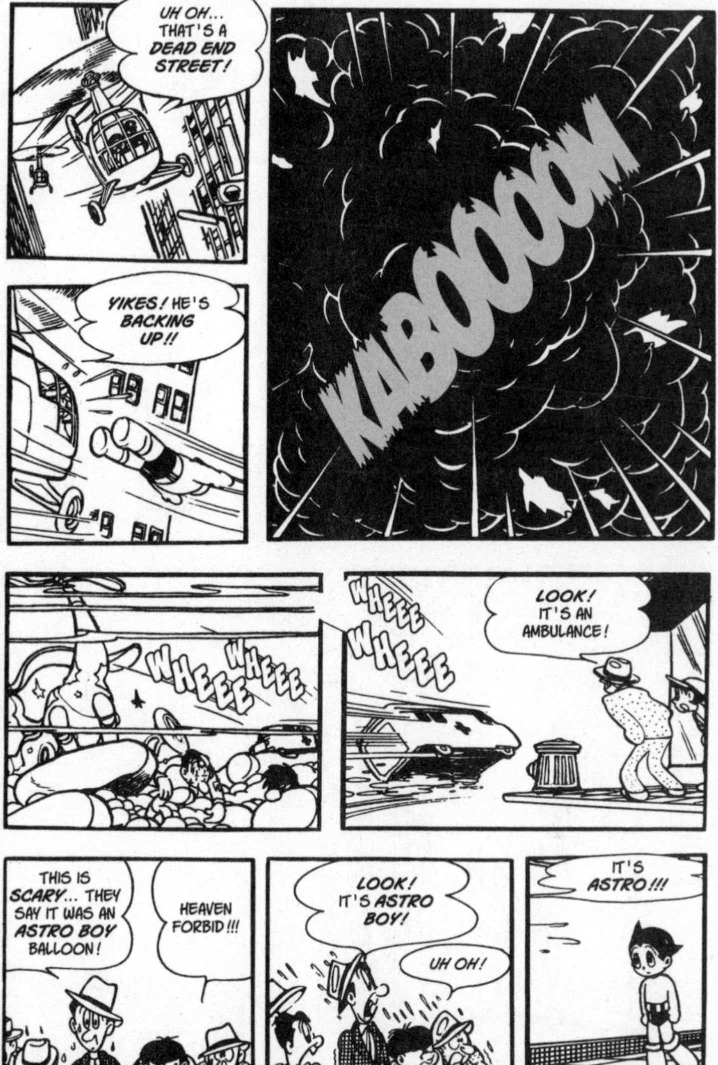
UH OH... THAT'S A DEAD END STREET!
YIKES! HE'S BACKING UP!!
KABOOOOM
WHEEE WHEEE
WHEEE WHEEE
LOOK! IT'S AN AMBULANCE!
THIS IS SCARY... THEY SAY IT WAS AN ASTRO BOY BALLOON!
HEAVEN FORBID!!!
LOOK! IT'S ASTRO BOY!
UH OH!
IT'S ASTRO!!!

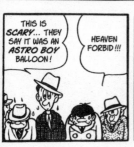

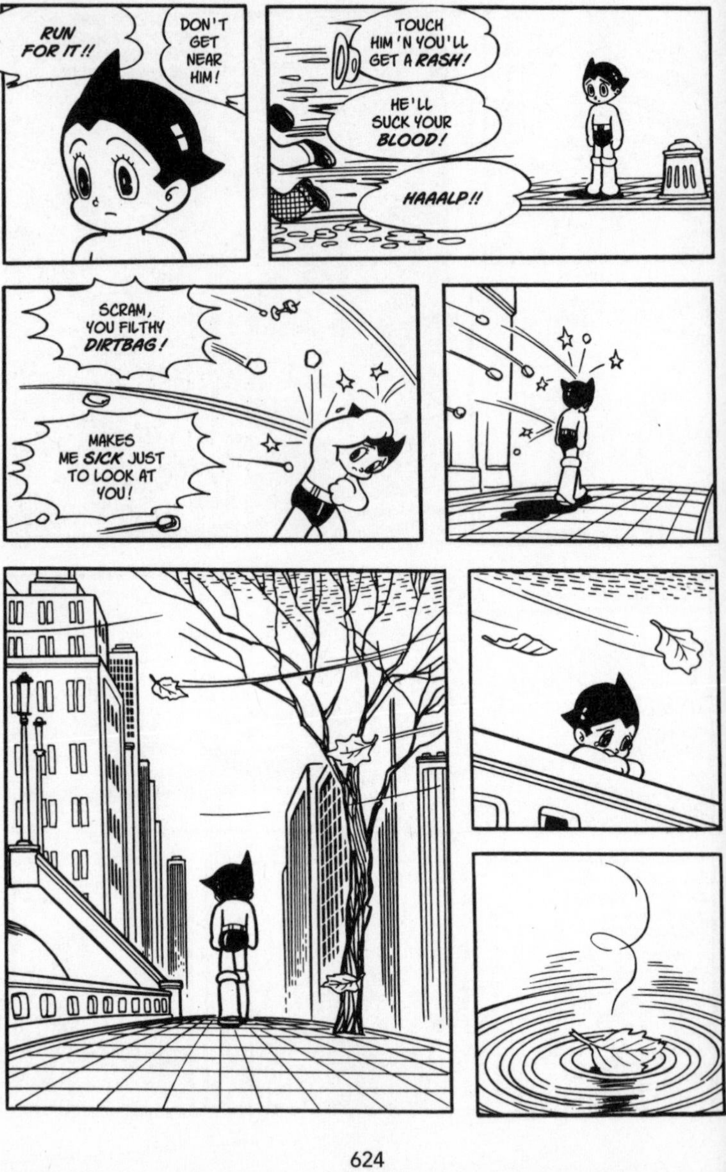

RUN FOR IT!!
DON'T GET NEAR HIM!
TOUCH HIM 'N YOU'LL GET A RASH!
HE'LL SUCK YOUR BLOOD!
HAAALP!!
SCRAM, YOU FILTHY DIRTBAG!
MAKES ME SICK JUST TO LOOK AT YOU!

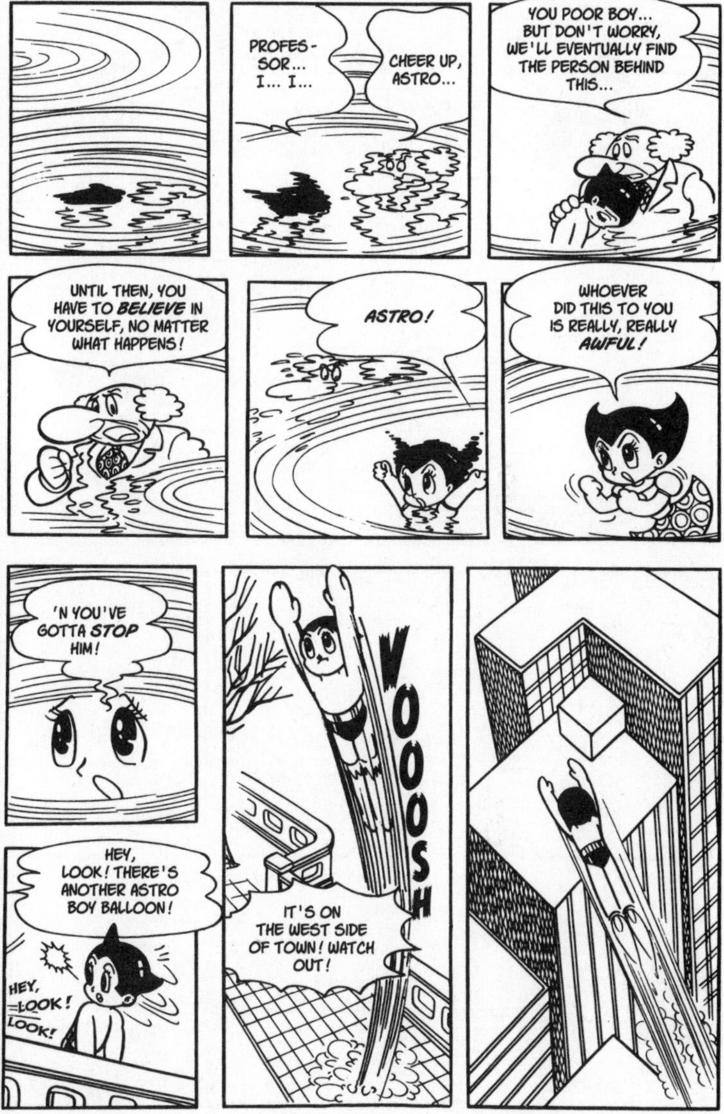
PROFES-SOR... I... I...
CHEER UP, ASTRO...
YOU POOR BOY... BUT DON'T WORRY, WE'LL EVENTUALLY FIND THE PERSON BEHIND THIS...
UNTIL THEN, YOU HAVE TO BELIEVE IN YOURSELF, NO MATTER WHAT HAPPENS!
ASTRO!
WHOEVER DID THIS TO YOU IS REALLY, REALLY AWFUL!
'N YOU'VE GOTTA STOP HIM!
HEY, LOOK! THERE'S ANOTHER ASTRO BOY BALLOON!
HEY, LOOK!
LOOK!
VOOOOSH
IT'S ON THE WEST SIDE OF TOWN! WATCH OUT!

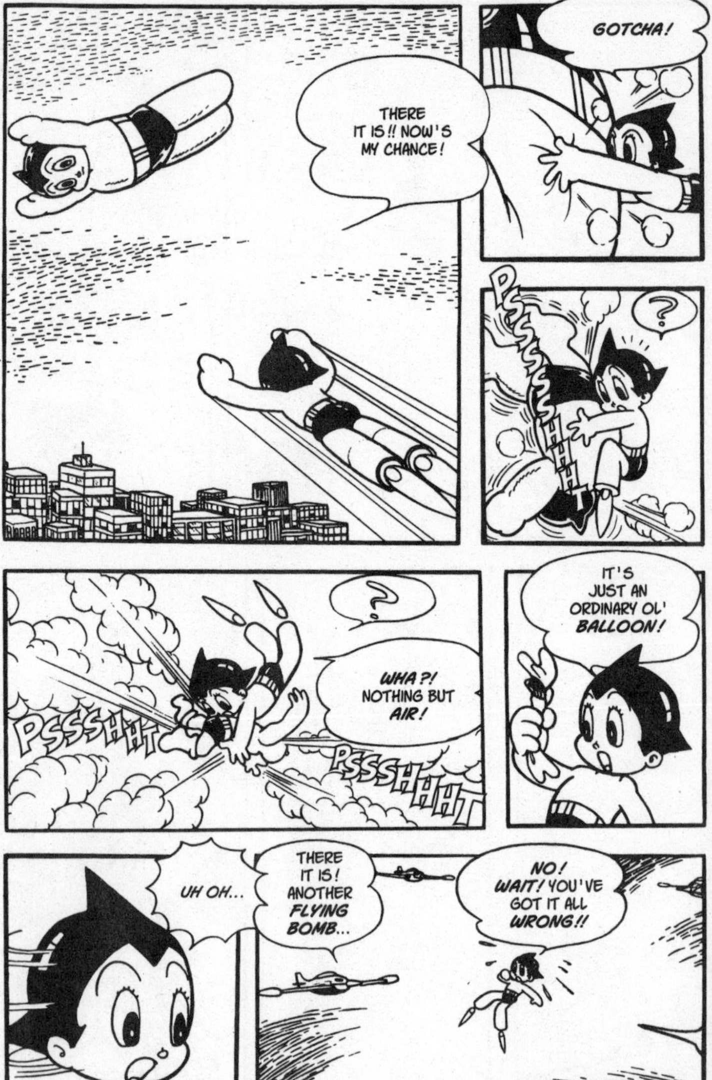
THERE IT IS!! NOW'S MY CHANCE!
GOTCHA!
PSSSSSHHHT
?
?
PSSSHHT
WHA?! NOTHING BUT AIR!
PSSSHHHT
IT'S JUST AN ORDINARY OL' BALLOON!
UH OH...
THERE IT IS! ANOTHER FLYING BOMB...
NO! WAIT! YOU'VE GOT IT ALL WRONG!!

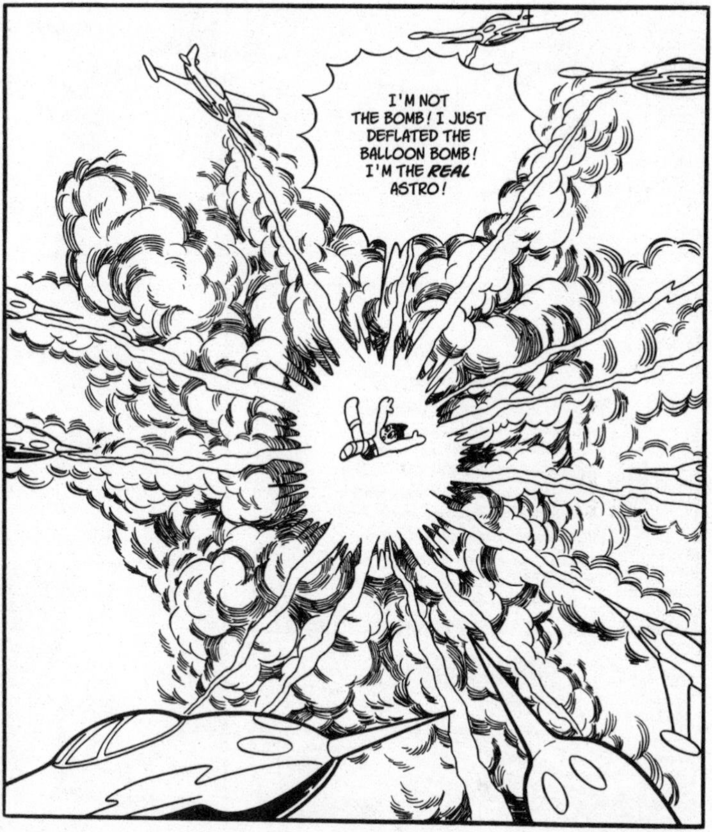
I'M NOT THE BOMB! I JUST DEFLATED THE BALLOON BOMB! I'M THE *REAL* ASTRO!

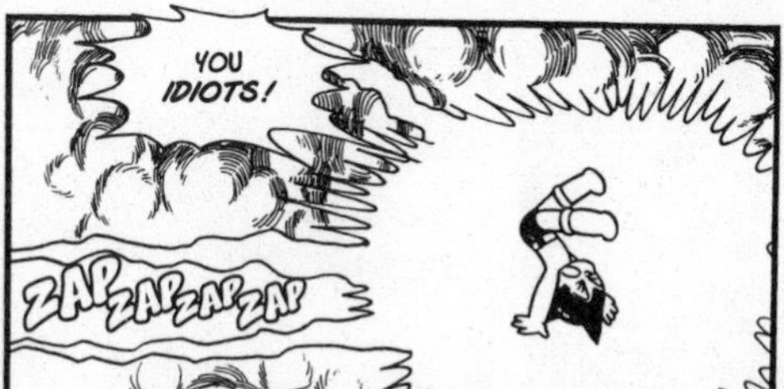
YOU *IDIOTS!*
ZAP ZAP ZAP ZAP

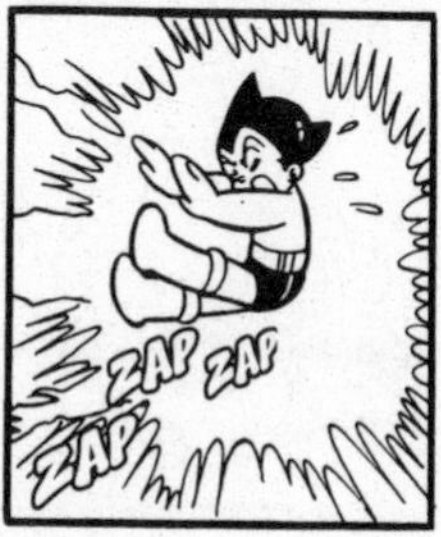
ZAP ZAP ZAP

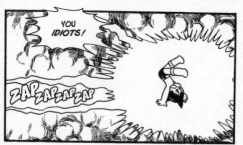

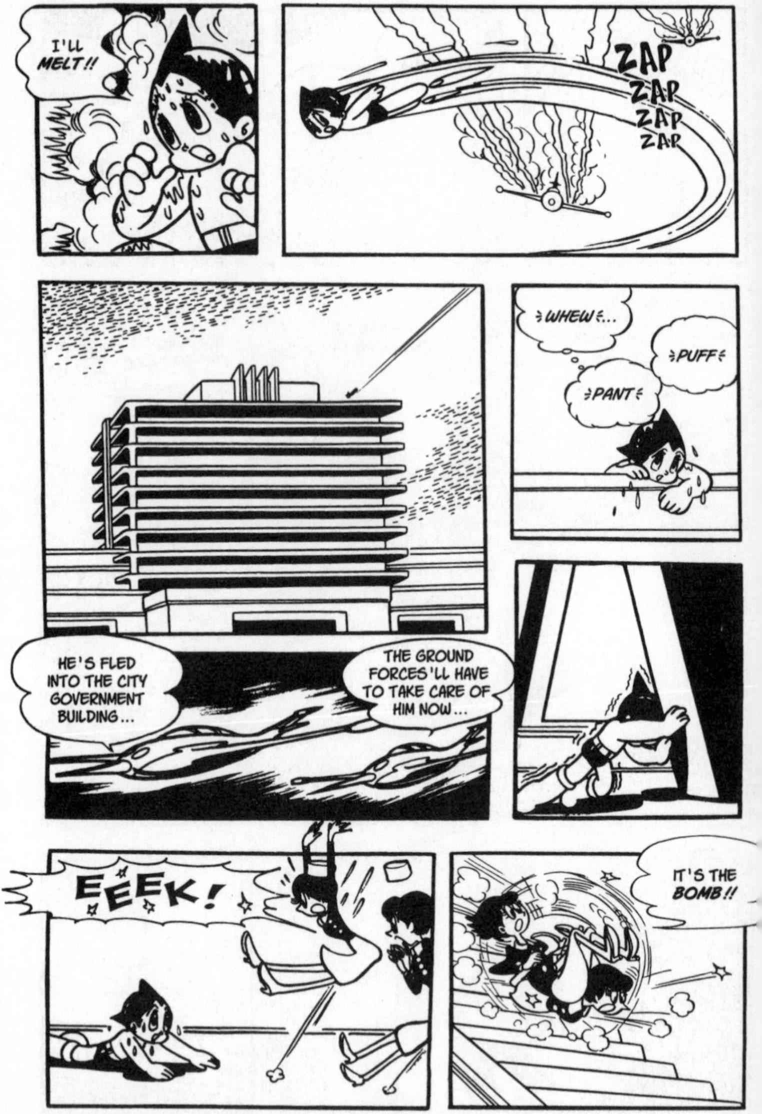
I'LL MELT!!
ZAP
ZAP
ZAP
ZAP
WHEW...
PUFF
PANT
HE'S FLED INTO THE CITY GOVERNMENT BUILDING...
THE GROUND FORCES'LL HAVE TO TAKE CARE OF HIM NOW...
EEEK!
IT'S THE BOMB!!

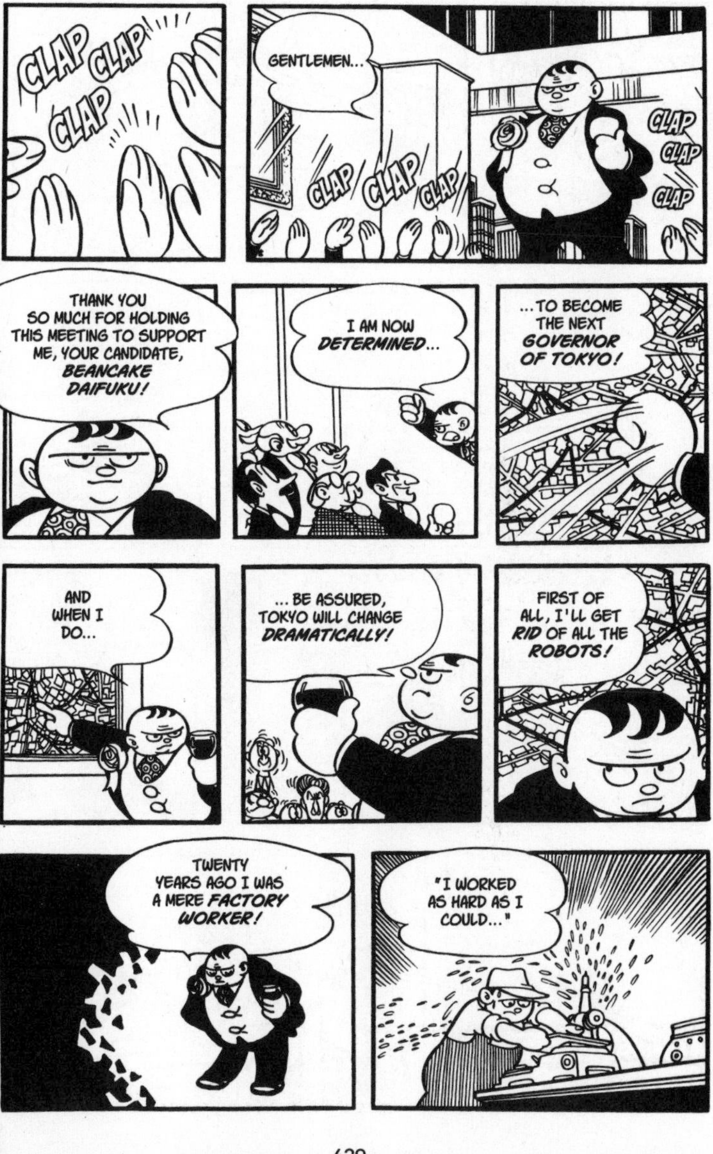
CLAP CLAP
CLAP
GENTLEMEN...
CLAP CLAP CLAP
CLAP
CLAP
CLAP
THANK YOU SO MUCH FOR HOLDING THIS MEETING TO SUPPORT ME, YOUR CANDIDATE, BEANCAKE DAIFUKU!
I AM NOW DETERMINED...
...TO BECOME THE NEXT GOVERNOR OF TOKYO!
AND WHEN I DO...
... BE ASSURED, TOKYO WILL CHANGE DRAMATICALLY!
FIRST OF ALL, I'LL GET RID OF ALL THE ROBOTS!
TWENTY YEARS AGO I WAS A MERE FACTORY WORKER!
"I WORKED AS HARD AS I COULD..."

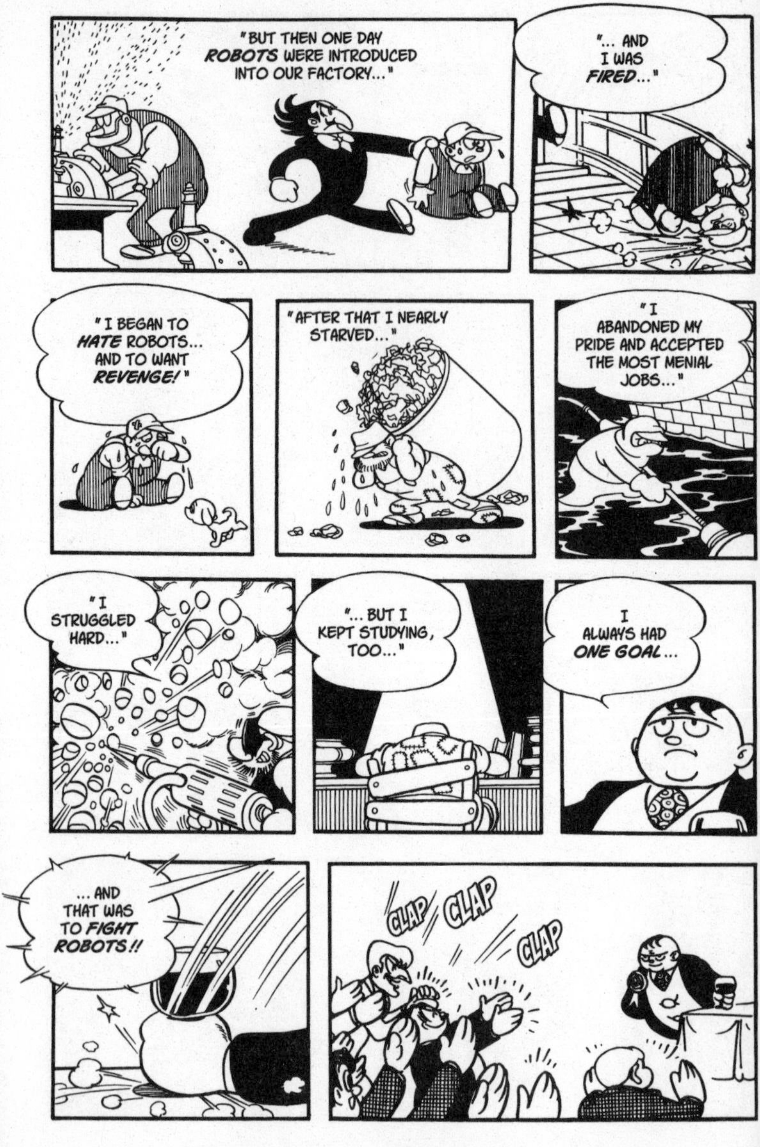
"BUT THEN ONE DAY ROBOTS WERE INTRODUCED INTO OUR FACTORY..."
"... AND I WAS FIRED..."
"I BEGAN TO HATE ROBOTS... AND TO WANT REVENGE!"
"AFTER THAT I NEARLY STARVED..."
"I ABANDONED MY PRIDE AND ACCEPTED THE MOST MENIAL JOBS..."
"I STRUGGLED HARD..."
"... BUT I KEPT STUDYING, TOO..."
I ALWAYS HAD ONE GOAL...
... AND THAT WAS TO FIGHT ROBOTS!!
CLAP CLAP
CLAP

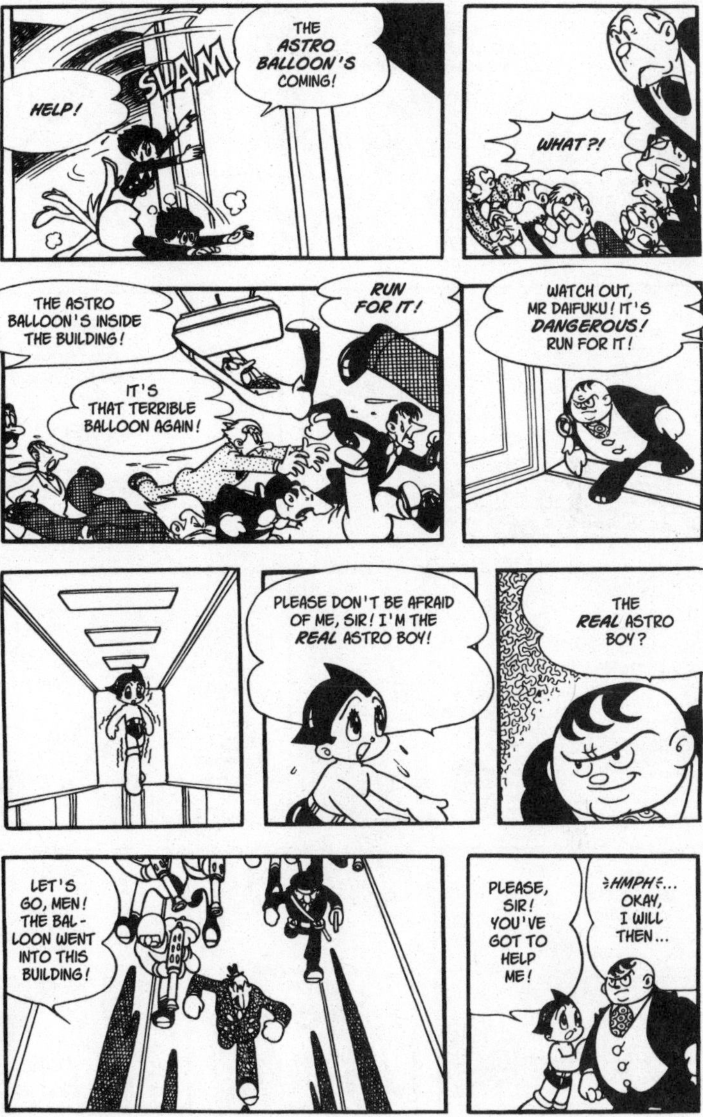
HELP!
SLAM
THE ASTRO BALLOON'S COMING!
WHAT?!
THE ASTRO BALLOON'S INSIDE THE BUILDING!
IT'S THAT TERRIBLE BALLOON AGAIN!
RUN FOR IT!
WATCH OUT, MR DAIFUKU! IT'S DANGEROUS! RUN FOR IT!
PLEASE DON'T BE AFRAID OF ME, SIR! I'M THE REAL ASTRO BOY!
THE REAL ASTRO BOY?
LET'S GO, MEN! THE BAL- LOON WENT INTO THIS BUILDING!
PLEASE, SIR! YOU'VE GOT TO HELP ME!
HMPH... OKAY, I WILL THEN...

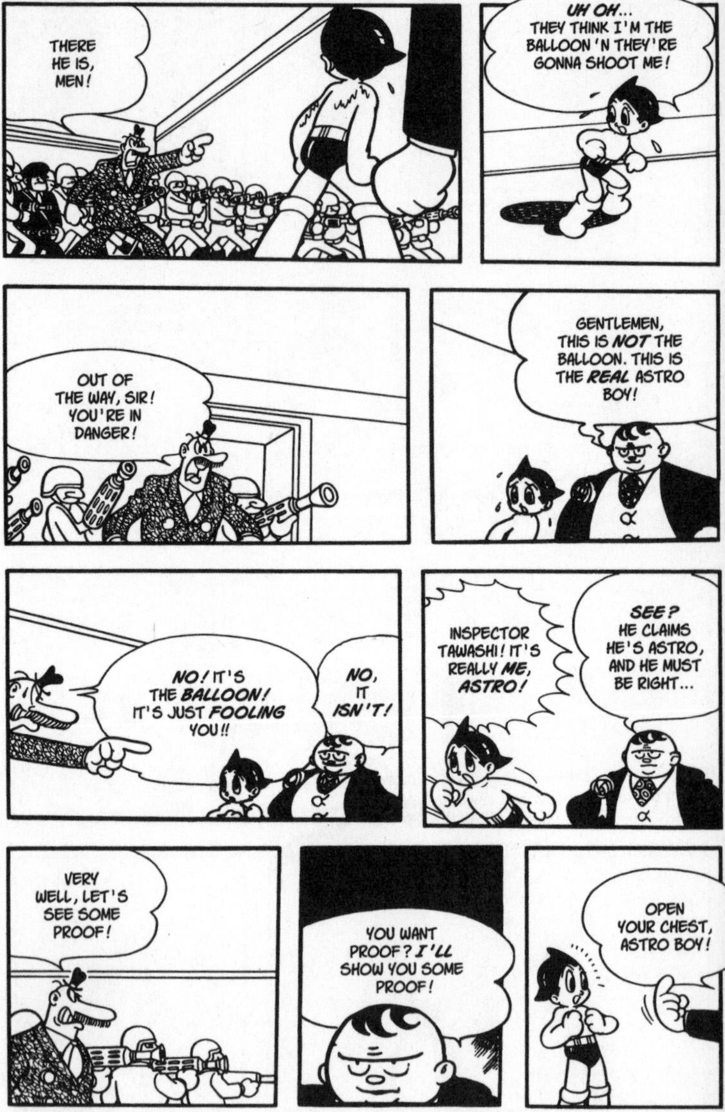
THERE HE IS, MEN!
UH OH... THEY THINK I'M THE BALLOON 'N THEY'RE GONNA SHOOT ME!
OUT OF THE WAY, SIR! YOU'RE IN DANGER!
GENTLEMEN, THIS IS NOT THE BALLOON. THIS IS THE REAL ASTRO BOY!
NO! IT'S THE BALLOON! IT'S JUST FOOLING YOU!!
NO, IT ISN'T!
INSPECTOR TAWASHI! IT'S REALLY ME, ASTRO!
SEE? HE CLAIMS HE'S ASTRO, AND HE MUST BE RIGHT...
VERY WELL, LET'S SEE SOME PROOF!
YOU WANT PROOF? I'LL SHOW YOU SOME PROOF!
OPEN YOUR CHEST, ASTRO BOY!

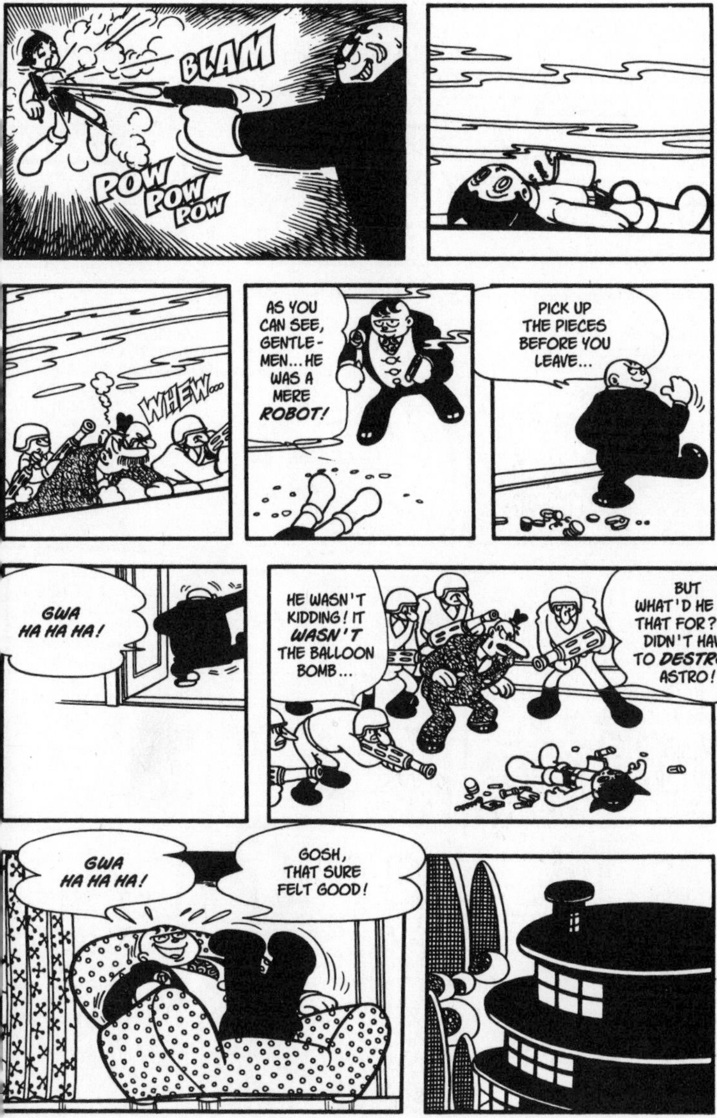
BLAM
POW POW POW
WHEW...
AS YOU CAN SEE, GENTLE-MEN... HE WAS A MERE *ROBOT!*
PICK UP THE PIECES BEFORE YOU LEAVE...
GWA HA HA HA!
HE WASN'T KIDDING! IT *WASN'T* THE BALLOON BOMB...
BUT WHAT'D HE DO THAT FOR? HE DIDN'T HAVE TO *DESTROY* ASTRO!
GWA HA HA HA!
GOSH, THAT SURE FELT GOOD!

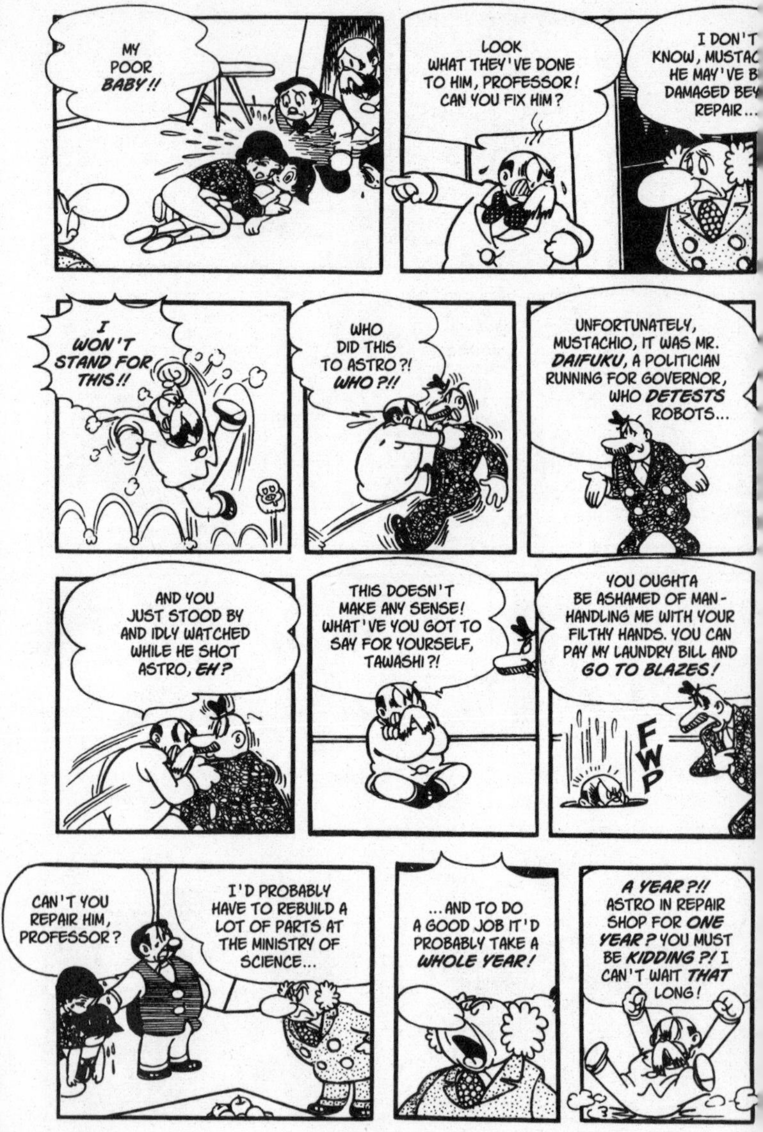

MY POOR BABY!!
LOOK WHAT THEY'VE DONE TO HIM, PROFESSOR! CAN YOU FIX HIM?
I DON'T KNOW, MUSTAC HE MAY'VE B DAMAGED BEY REPAIR...
I WON'T STAND FOR THIS!!
WHO DID THIS TO ASTRO?! WHO?!!
UNFORTUNATELY, MUSTACHIO, IT WAS MR. DAIFUKU, A POLITICIAN RUNNING FOR GOVERNOR, WHO DETESTS ROBOTS...
AND YOU JUST STOOD BY AND IDLY WATCHED WHILE HE SHOT ASTRO, EH?
THIS DOESN'T MAKE ANY SENSE! WHAT'VE YOU GOT TO SAY FOR YOURSELF, TAWASHI?!
YOU OUGHTA BE ASHAMED OF MAN-HANDLING ME WITH YOUR FILTHY HANDS. YOU CAN PAY MY LAUNDRY BILL AND GO TO BLAZES!
FWP
CAN'T YOU REPAIR HIM, PROFESSOR?
I'D PROBABLY HAVE TO REBUILD A LOT OF PARTS AT THE MINISTRY OF SCIENCE...
...AND TO DO A GOOD JOB IT'D PROBABLY TAKE A WHOLE YEAR!
A YEAR?!! ASTRO IN REPAIR SHOP FOR ONE YEAR? YOU MUST BE KIDDING?! I CAN'T WAIT THAT LONG!

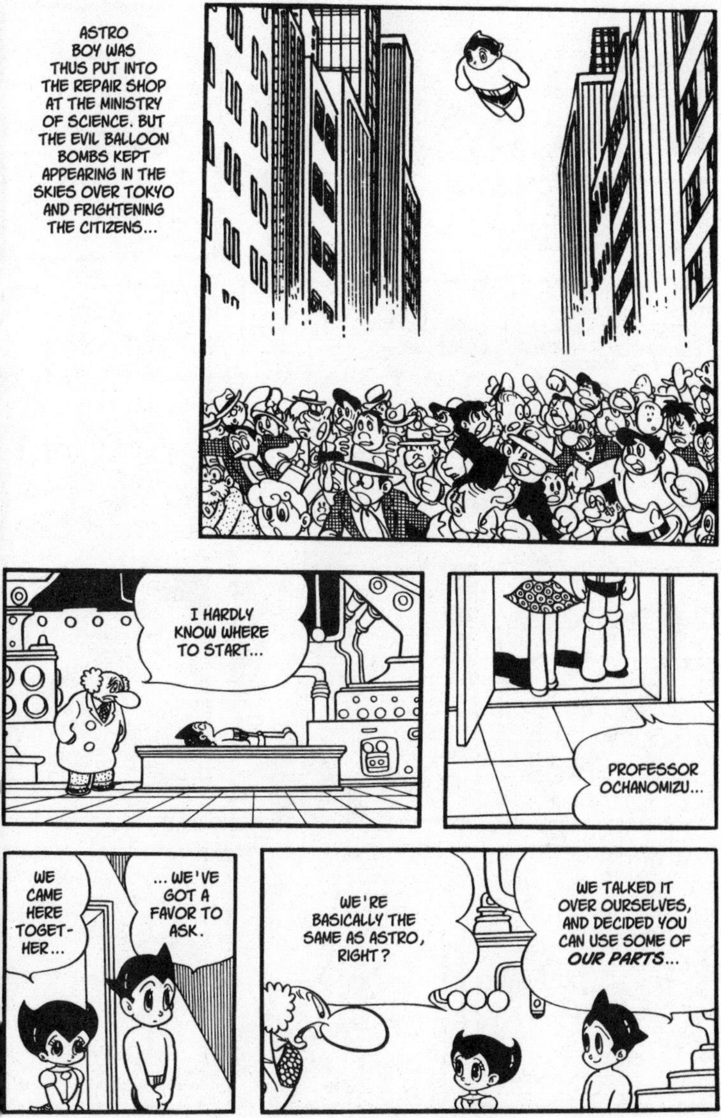
ASTRO BOY WAS THUS PUT INTO THE REPAIR SHOP AT THE MINISTRY OF SCIENCE. BUT THE EVIL BALLOON BOMBS KEPT APPEARING IN THE SKIES OVER TOKYO AND FRIGHTENING THE CITIZENS...
I HARDLY KNOW WHERE TO START...
PROFESSOR OCHANOMIZU...
WE CAME HERE TOGET-HER...
... WE'VE GOT A FAVOR TO ASK.
WE'RE BASICALLY THE SAME AS ASTRO, RIGHT?
WE TALKED IT OVER OURSELVES, AND DECIDED YOU CAN USE SOME OF ***OUR PARTS***...

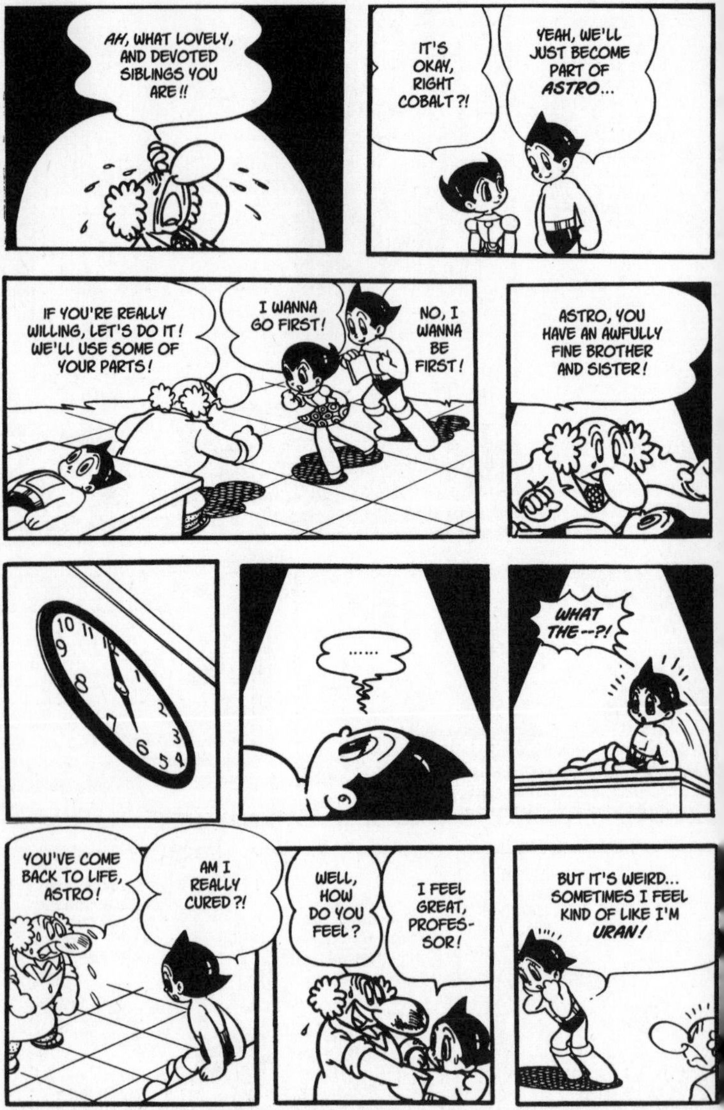
AH, WHAT LOVELY, AND DEVOTED SIBLINGS YOU ARE!!
IT'S OKAY, RIGHT COBALT?!
YEAH, WE'LL JUST BECOME PART OF ASTRO...
IF YOU'RE REALLY WILLING, LET'S DO IT! WE'LL USE SOME OF YOUR PARTS!
I WANNA GO FIRST!
NO, I WANNA BE FIRST!
ASTRO, YOU HAVE AN AWFULLY FINE BROTHER AND SISTER!
......
WHAT THE--?!
YOU'VE COME BACK TO LIFE, ASTRO!
AM I REALLY CURED?!
WELL, HOW DO YOU FEEL?
I FEEL GREAT, PROFES-SOR!
BUT IT'S WEIRD... SOMETIMES I FEEL KIND OF LIKE I'M URAN!

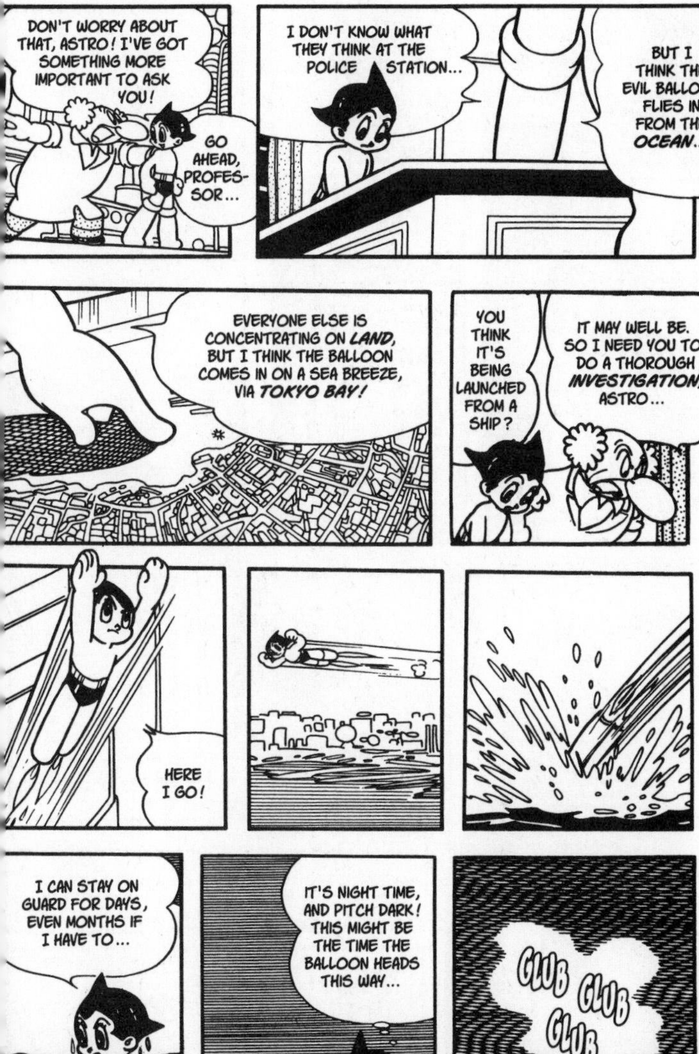
DON'T WORRY ABOUT THAT, ASTRO! I'VE GOT SOMETHING MORE IMPORTANT TO ASK YOU!
GO AHEAD, PROFES-SOR...
I DON'T KNOW WHAT THEY THINK AT THE POLICE STATION...
BUT I THINK THE EVIL BALLOON FLIES IN FROM THE OCEAN...
EVERYONE ELSE IS CONCENTRATING ON LAND, BUT I THINK THE BALLOON COMES IN ON A SEA BREEZE, VIA TOKYO BAY!
YOU THINK IT'S BEING LAUNCHED FROM A SHIP?
IT MAY WELL BE. SO I NEED YOU TO DO A THOROUGH INVESTIGATION, ASTRO...
HERE I GO!
I CAN STAY ON GUARD FOR DAYS, EVEN MONTHS IF I HAVE TO...
IT'S NIGHT TIME, AND PITCH DARK! THIS MIGHT BE THE TIME THE BALLOON HEADS THIS WAY...
GLUB GLUB GLUB

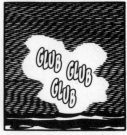

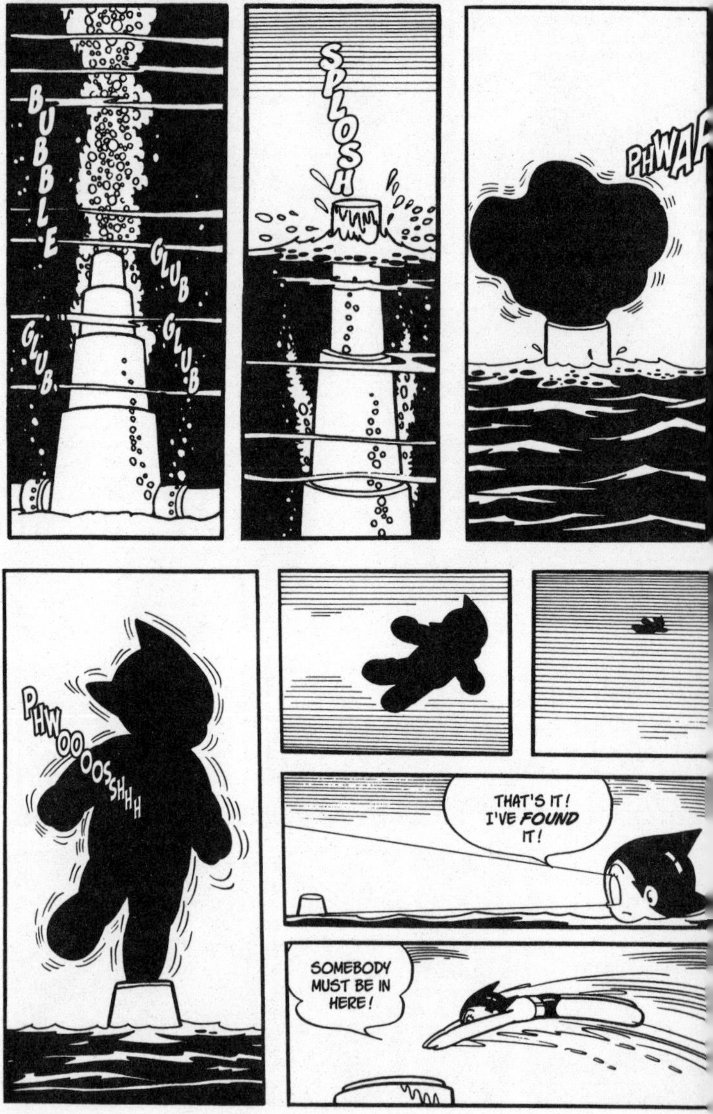
BUBBLE
GLUB
GLUB
GLUB
GLUB
SPLOSH
PHWAP
PHWOOOOOSSHHH
THAT'S IT! I'VE *FOUND* IT!
SOMEBODY MUST BE IN HERE!

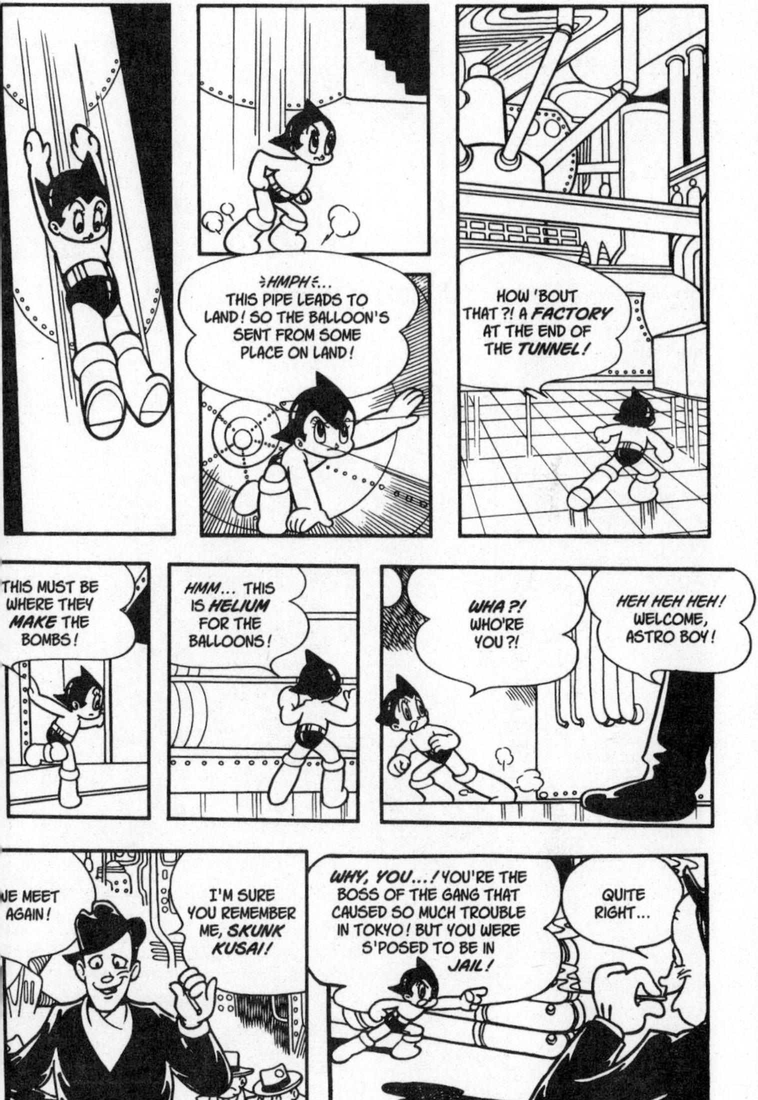

HMPH...
THIS PIPE LEADS TO LAND! SO THE BALLOON'S SENT FROM SOME PLACE ON LAND!
HOW 'BOUT THAT?! A FACTORY AT THE END OF THE TUNNEL!
THIS MUST BE WHERE THEY MAKE THE BOMBS!
HMM... THIS IS HELIUM FOR THE BALLOONS!
WHA?! WHO'RE YOU?!
HEH HEH HEH! WELCOME, ASTRO BOY!
WE MEET AGAIN!
I'M SURE YOU REMEMBER ME, SKUNK KUSAI!
WHY, YOU...! YOU'RE THE BOSS OF THE GANG THAT CAUSED SO MUCH TROUBLE IN TOKYO! BUT YOU WERE S'POSED TO BE IN JAIL!
QUITE RIGHT...

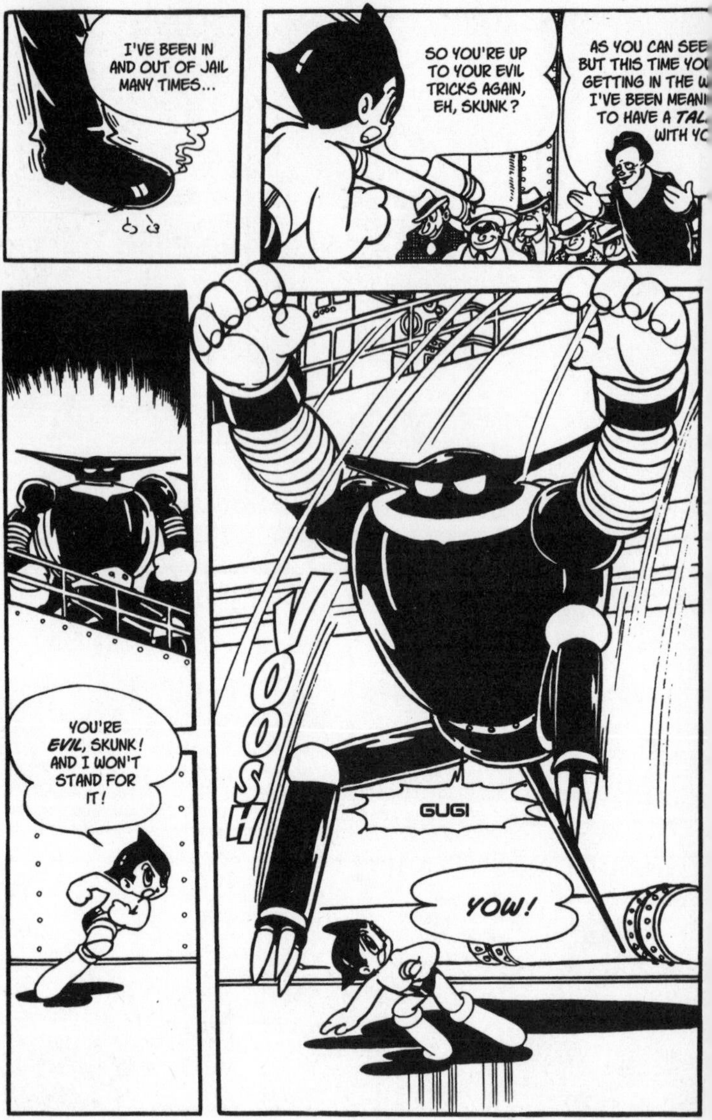
I'VE BEEN IN AND OUT OF JAIL MANY TIMES...
SO YOU'RE UP TO YOUR EVIL TRICKS AGAIN, EH, SKUNK?
AS YOU CAN SEE BUT THIS TIME YO GETTING IN THE W I'VE BEEN MEANI TO HAVE A *TAL* WITH YO
YOU'RE *EVIL*, SKUNK! AND I WON'T STAND FOR IT!
VOOOSH
GUGI
YOW!

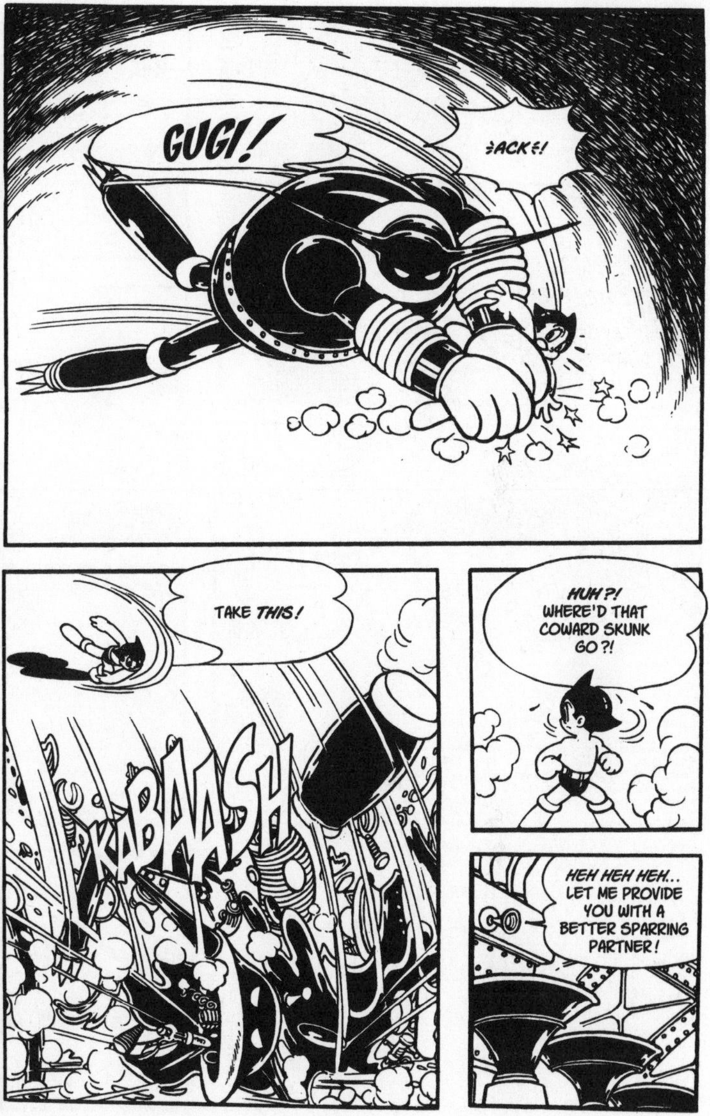
GUGI!
ACK!
TAKE THIS!
KABAASH
HUH?! WHERE'D THAT COWARD SKUNK GO?!
HEH HEH HEH... LET ME PROVIDE YOU WITH A BETTER SPARRING PARTNER!

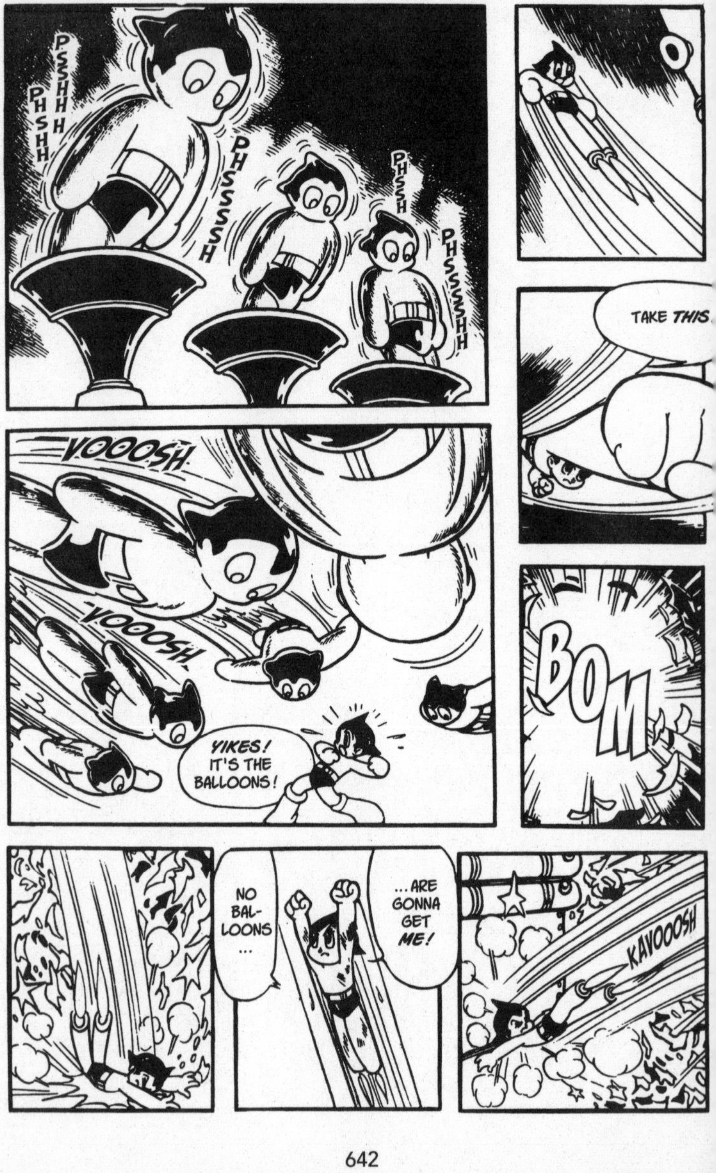
PSSHHH
PHSHH
PHSSSSSH
PHSSH
PHSSSSHH
VOOOSH
VOOOSH
YIKES! IT'S THE BALLOONS!
TAKE THIS
BOM
NO BAL-LOONS ...
...ARE GONNA GET ME!
KAVOOOSH

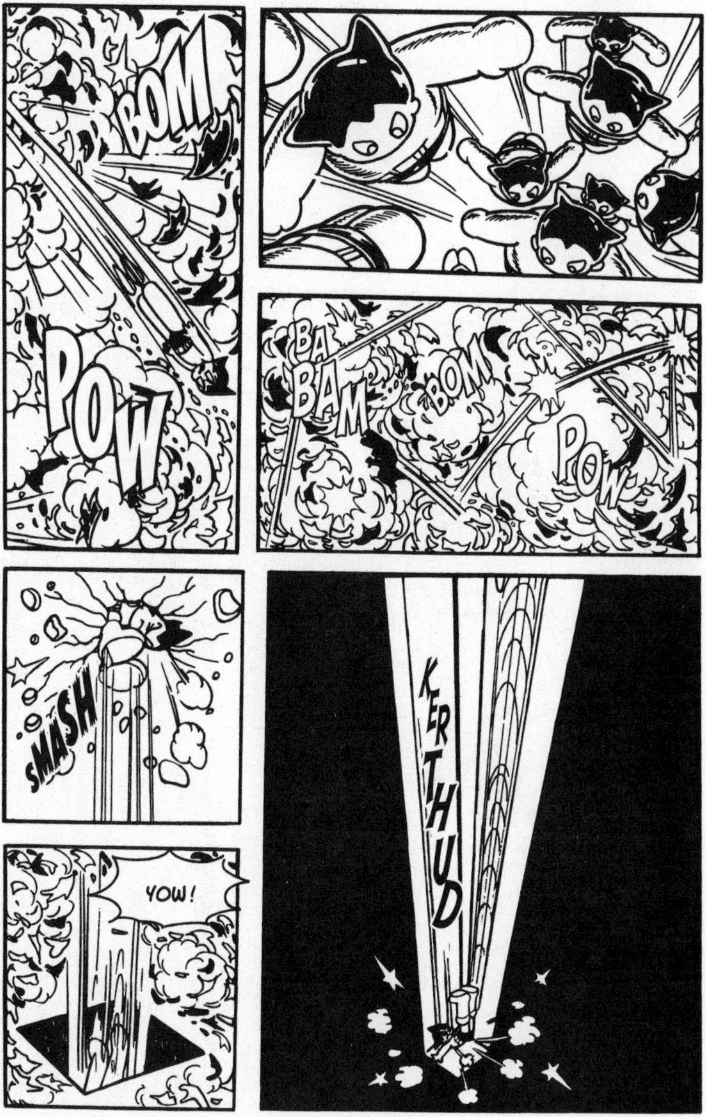
BOM
POW
BA
BAM
BOM
POW
SMASH
YOW!
KERTHUD

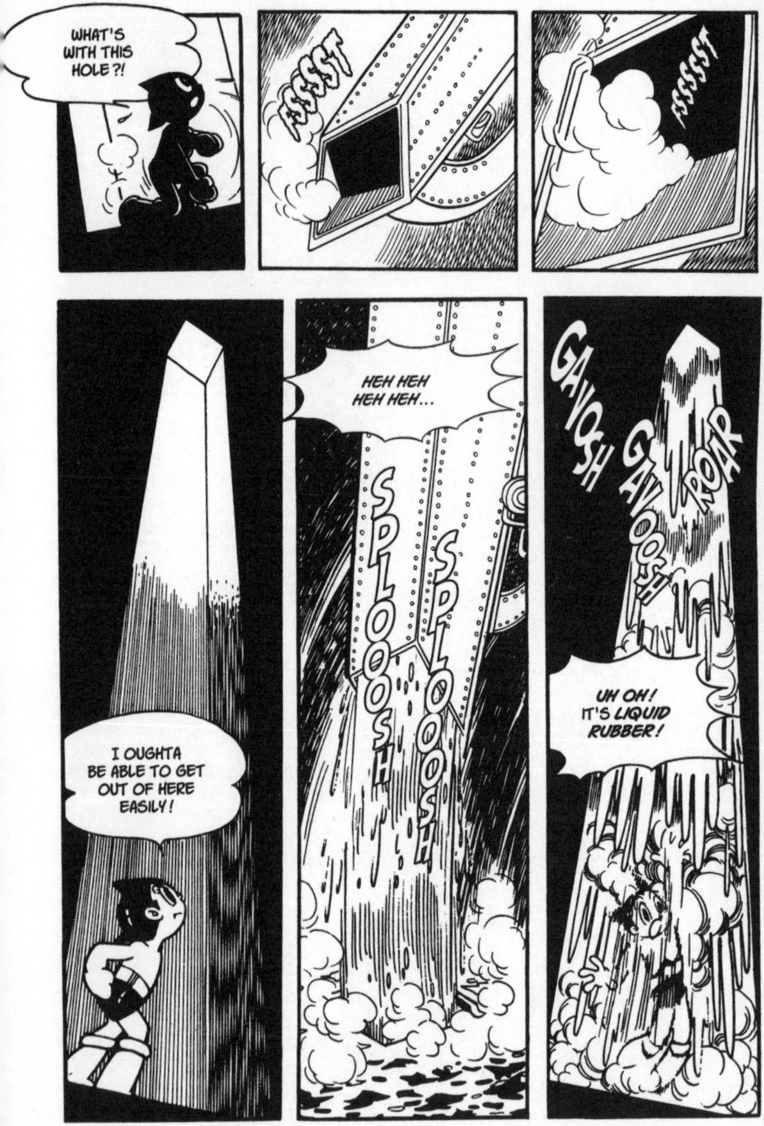

WHAT'S WITH THIS HOLE?!
FSSSST
FSSSST
I OUGHTA BE ABLE TO GET OUT OF HERE EASILY!
HEH HEH HEH HEH...
SPLOOOOSH
SPLOOOOSH
GAVOOSH
GAVOOSH
ROAR
UH OH! IT'S LIQUID RUBBER!

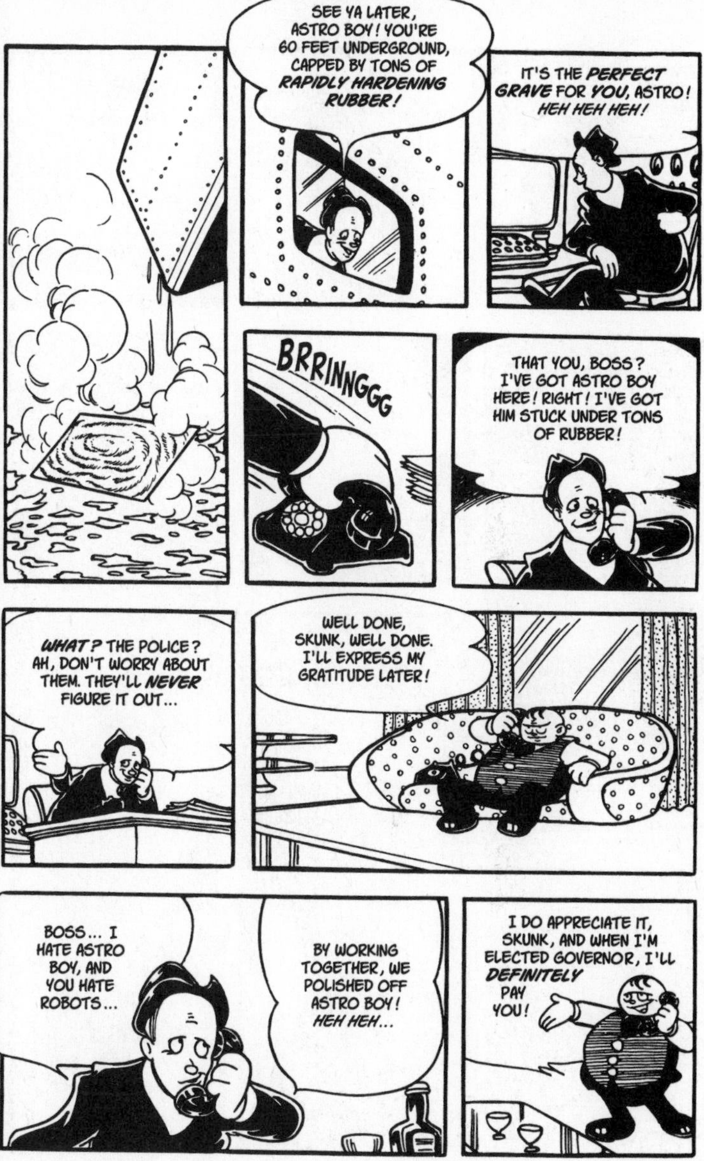
SEE YA LATER, ASTRO BOY! YOU'RE 60 FEET UNDERGROUND, CAPPED BY TONS OF *RAPIDLY HARDENING RUBBER!*
IT'S THE *PERFECT GRAVE* FOR *YOU,* ASTRO! *HEH HEH HEH!*
BRRINNGGG
THAT YOU, BOSS? I'VE GOT ASTRO BOY HERE! RIGHT! I'VE GOT HIM STUCK UNDER TONS OF RUBBER!
WHAT? THE POLICE? AH, DON'T WORRY ABOUT THEM. THEY'LL *NEVER* FIGURE IT OUT...
WELL DONE, SKUNK, WELL DONE. I'LL EXPRESS MY GRATITUDE LATER!
BOSS... I HATE ASTRO BOY, AND YOU HATE ROBOTS...
BY WORKING TOGETHER, WE POLISHED OFF ASTRO BOY! *HEH HEH...*
I DO APPRECIATE IT, SKUNK, AND WHEN I'M ELECTED GOVERNOR, I'LL *DEFINITELY* PAY YOU!

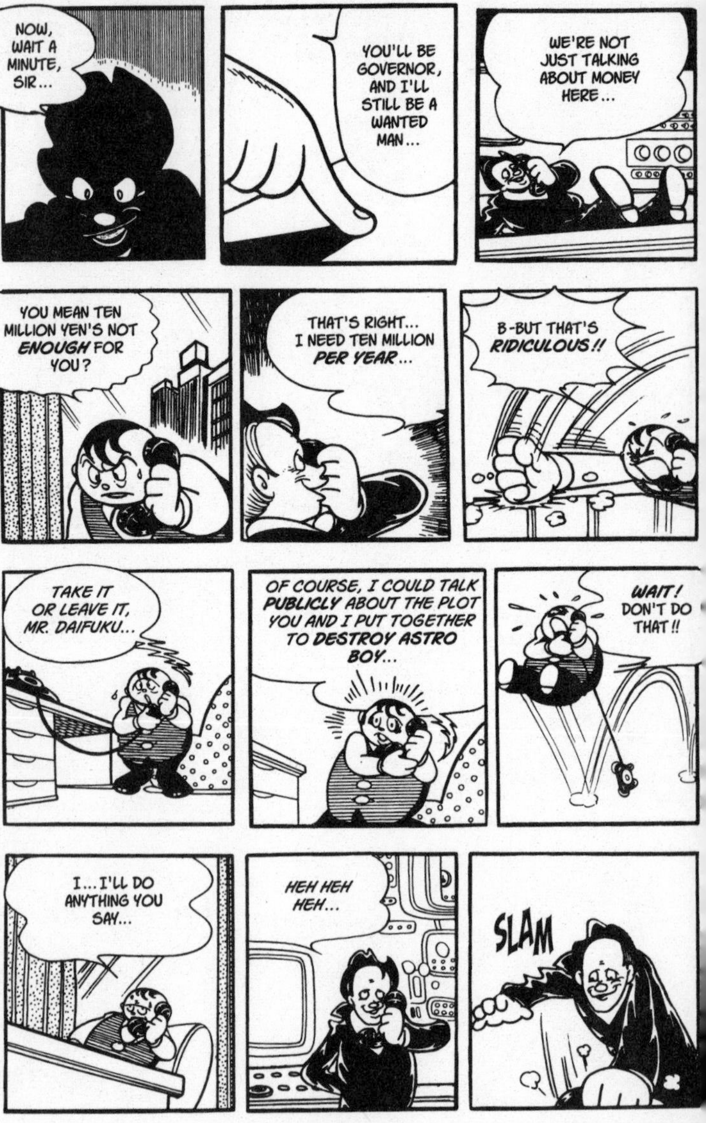
NOW, WAIT A MINUTE, SIR...
YOU'LL BE GOVERNOR, AND I'LL STILL BE A WANTED MAN...
WE'RE NOT JUST TALKING ABOUT MONEY HERE...
YOU MEAN TEN MILLION YEN'S NOT *ENOUGH* FOR YOU?
THAT'S RIGHT... I NEED TEN MILLION *PER YEAR*...
B-BUT THAT'S *RIDICULOUS!!*
TAKE IT OR LEAVE IT, MR. DAIFUKU...
OF COURSE, I COULD TALK ***PUBLICLY*** *ABOUT THE PLOT YOU AND I PUT TOGETHER TO* ***DESTROY ASTRO BOY****...*
WAIT! DON'T DO THAT!!
I... I'LL DO ANYTHING YOU SAY...
HEH HEH HEH...
SLAM

HEH HEH HEH...

WELL, ASTRO... HOW'S IT FEEL TO TAKE A PERMANENT SLEEP IN A HOLE FILLED WITH RUBBER?! HEH HEH...

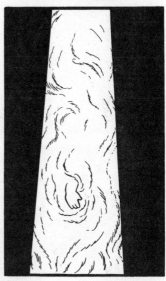

I WANT MORE OF THOSE BALLOONS LAUNCHED, MEN!

WE NEED 'EM TO TERRIFY *EVERY CITIZEN* OF *TOKYO*...

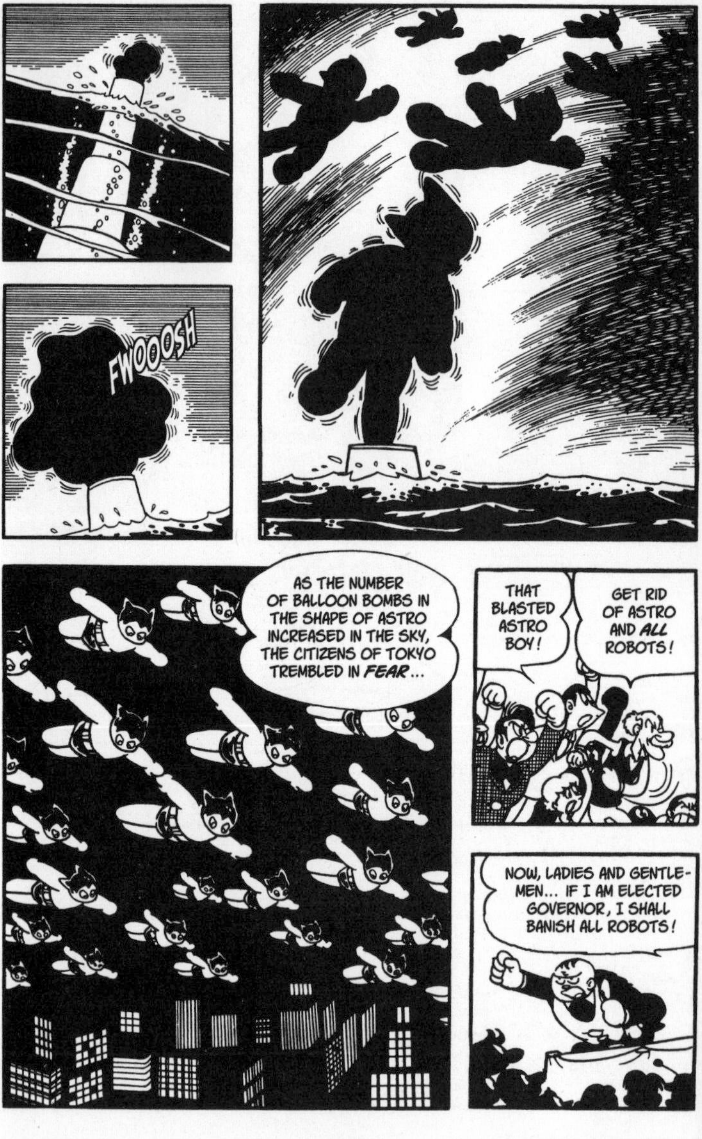
FWOOOSH
AS THE NUMBER OF BALLOON BOMBS IN THE SHAPE OF ASTRO INCREASED IN THE SKY, THE CITIZENS OF TOKYO TREMBLED IN FEAR...
THAT BLASTED ASTRO BOY!
GET RID OF ASTRO AND ALL ROBOTS!
NOW, LADIES AND GENTLE-MEN... IF I AM ELECTED GOVERNOR, I SHALL BANISH ALL ROBOTS!

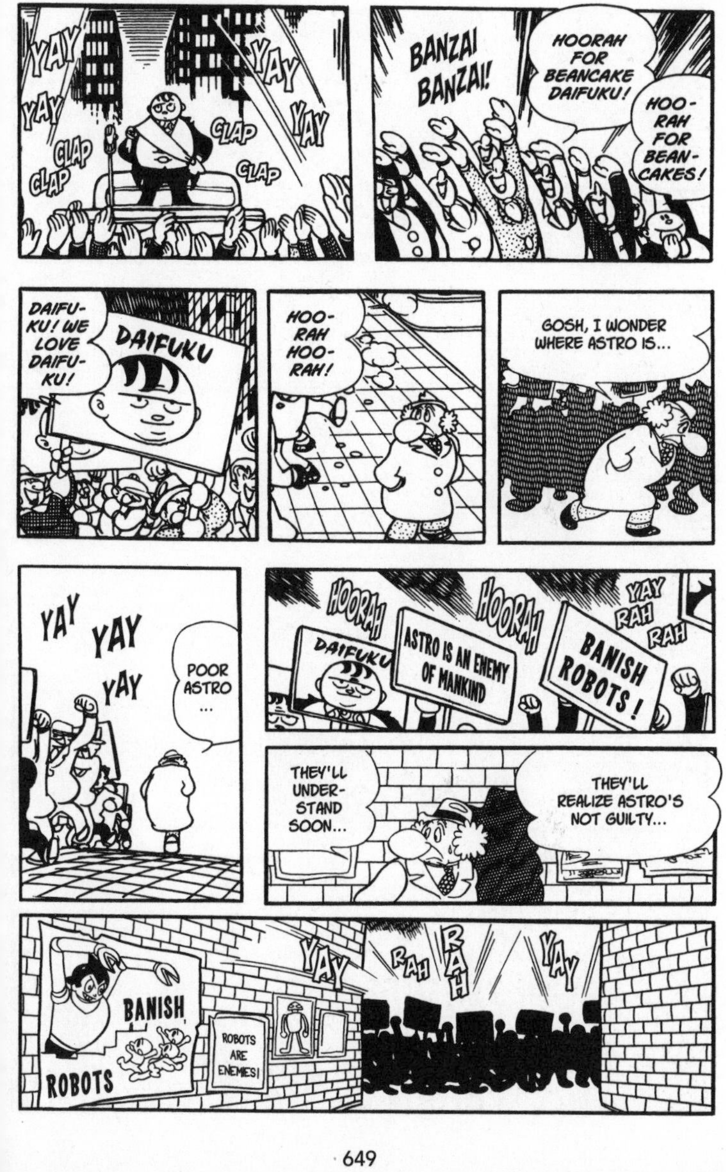
YAY
YAY
YAY
YAY
CLAP
CLAP
CLAP
CLAP
BANZAI BANZAI!
HOORAH FOR BEANCAKE DAIFUKU!
HOO-RAH FOR BEAN-CAKES!
DAIFU-KU! WE LOVE DAIFU-KU!
DAIFUKU
HOO-RAH HOO-RAH!
GOSH, I WONDER WHERE ASTRO IS...
YAY
YAY
YAY
POOR ASTRO ...
HOORAH
DAIFUKU
ASTRO IS AN ENEMY OF MANKIND
HOORAH
YAY RAH RAH
BANISH ROBOTS!
THEY'LL UNDER-STAND SOON...
THEY'LL REALIZE ASTRO'S NOT GUILTY...
BANISH ROBOTS
ROBOTS ARE ENEMIES!
YAY
RAH
RAH
YAY

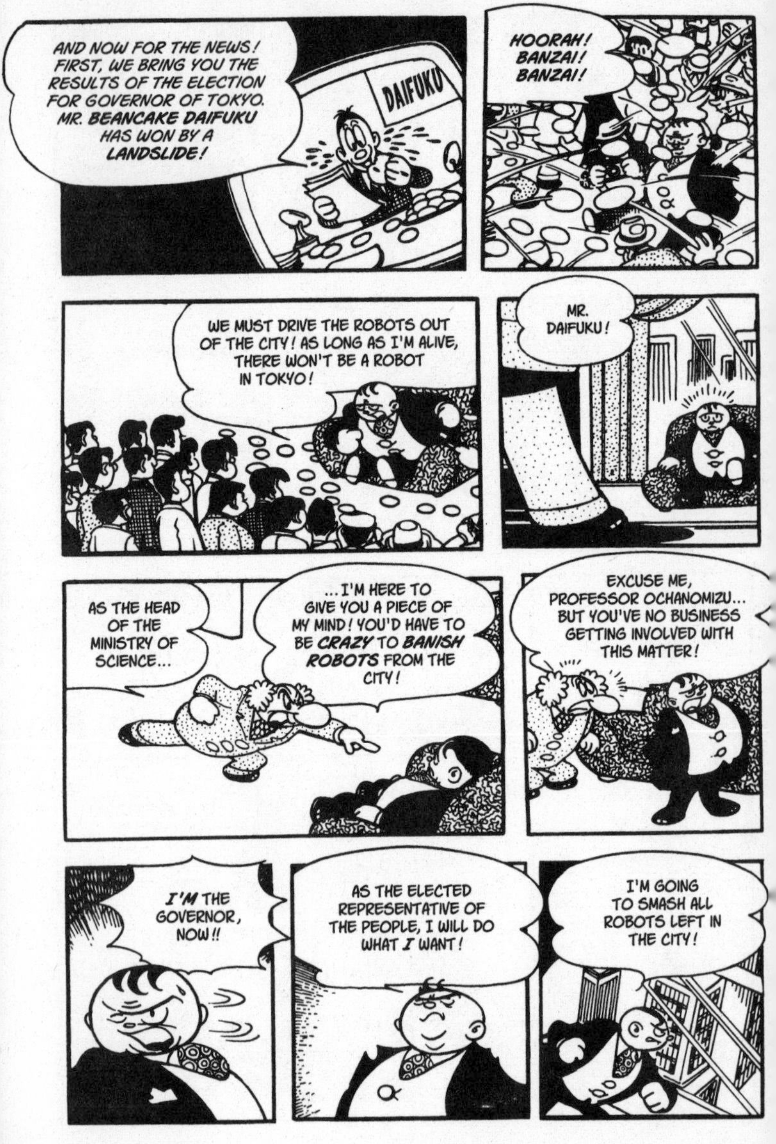
AND NOW FOR THE NEWS! FIRST, WE BRING YOU THE RESULTS OF THE ELECTION FOR GOVERNOR OF TOKYO. MR. **BEANCAKE DAIFUKU** HAS WON BY A **LANDSLIDE!**
DAIFUKU
HOORAH! BANZAI! BANZAI!
WE MUST DRIVE THE ROBOTS OUT OF THE CITY! AS LONG AS I'M ALIVE, THERE WON'T BE A ROBOT IN TOKYO!
MR. DAIFUKU!
AS THE HEAD OF THE MINISTRY OF SCIENCE...
...I'M HERE TO GIVE YOU A PIECE OF MY MIND! YOU'D HAVE TO BE ***CRAZY*** TO ***BANISH ROBOTS*** FROM THE CITY!
EXCUSE ME, PROFESSOR OCHANOMIZU... BUT YOU'VE NO BUSINESS GETTING INVOLVED WITH THIS MATTER!
I'M THE GOVERNOR, NOW!!
AS THE ELECTED REPRESENTATIVE OF THE PEOPLE, I WILL DO WHAT ***I*** WANT!
I'M GOING TO SMASH ALL ROBOTS LEFT IN THE CITY!

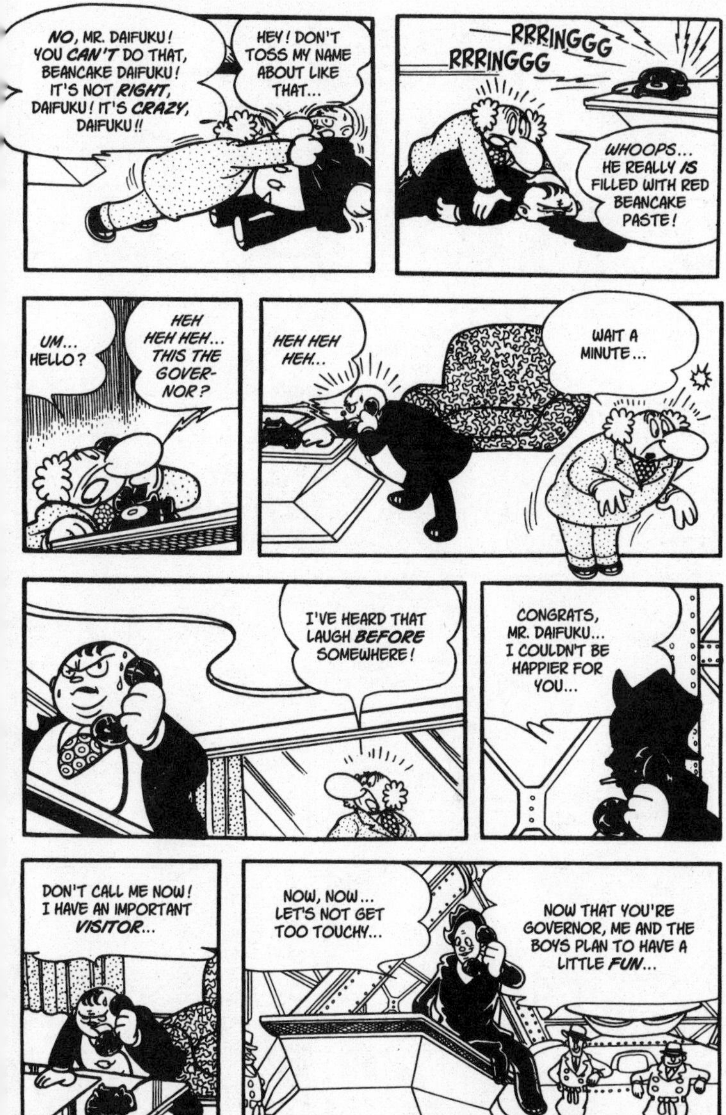
NO, MR. DAIFUKU! YOU CAN'T DO THAT, BEANCAKE DAIFUKU! IT'S NOT RIGHT, DAIFUKU! IT'S CRAZY, DAIFUKU!!
HEY! DON'T TOSS MY NAME ABOUT LIKE THAT...
RRRINGGG
RRRINGGG
WHOOPS... HE REALLY IS FILLED WITH RED BEANCAKE PASTE!
UM... HELLO?
HEH HEH HEH... THIS THE GOVERNOR?
HEH HEH HEH...
WAIT A MINUTE...
I'VE HEARD THAT LAUGH BEFORE SOMEWHERE!
CONGRATS, MR. DAIFUKU... I COULDN'T BE HAPPIER FOR YOU...
DON'T CALL ME NOW! I HAVE AN IMPORTANT VISITOR...
NOW, NOW... LET'S NOT GET TOO TOUCHY...
NOW THAT YOU'RE GOVERNOR, ME AND THE BOYS PLAN TO HAVE A LITTLE FUN...

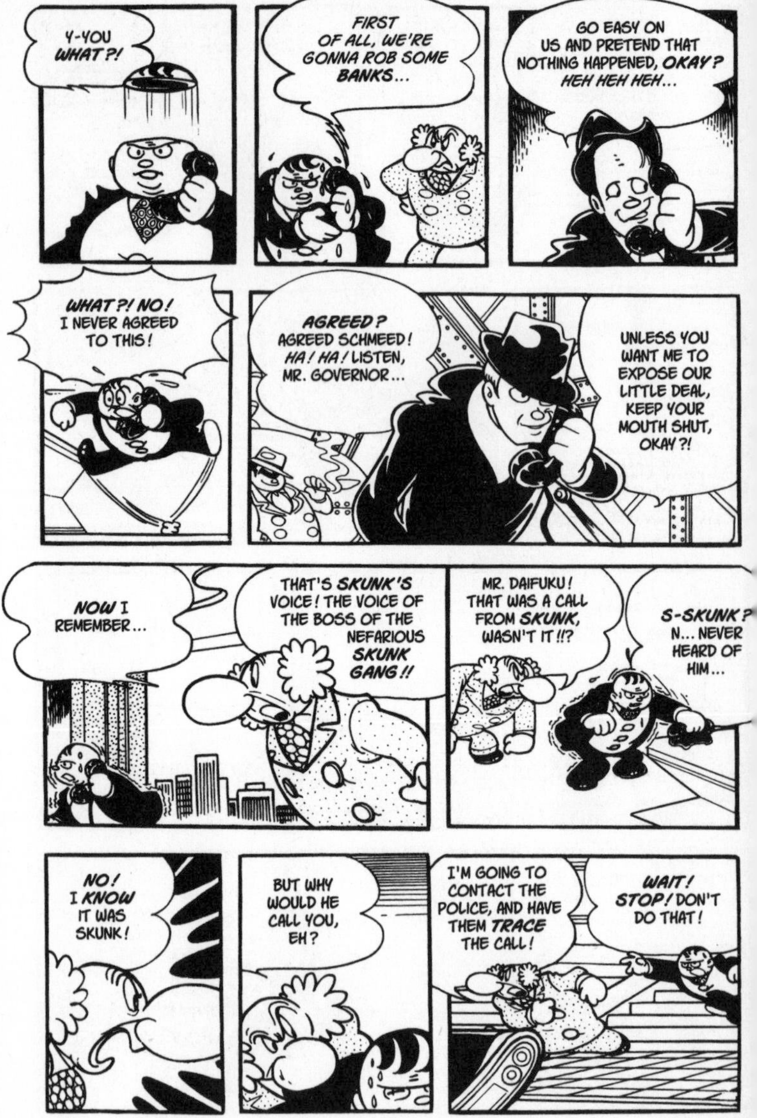
Y-YOU WHAT?!
FIRST OF ALL, WE'RE GONNA ROB SOME BANKS...
GO EASY ON US AND PRETEND THAT NOTHING HAPPENED, OKAY? HEH HEH HEH...
WHAT?! NO! I NEVER AGREED TO THIS!
AGREED? AGREED SCHMEED! HA! HA! LISTEN, MR. GOVERNOR...
UNLESS YOU WANT ME TO EXPOSE OUR LITTLE DEAL, KEEP YOUR MOUTH SHUT, OKAY?!
NOW I REMEMBER...
THAT'S SKUNK'S VOICE! THE VOICE OF THE BOSS OF THE NEFARIOUS SKUNK GANG!!
MR. DAIFUKU! THAT WAS A CALL FROM SKUNK, WASN'T IT!!?
S-SKUNK? N... NEVER HEARD OF HIM...
NO! I KNOW IT WAS SKUNK!
BUT WHY WOULD HE CALL YOU, EH?
I'M GOING TO CONTACT THE POLICE, AND HAVE THEM TRACE THE CALL!
WAIT! STOP! DON'T DO THAT!

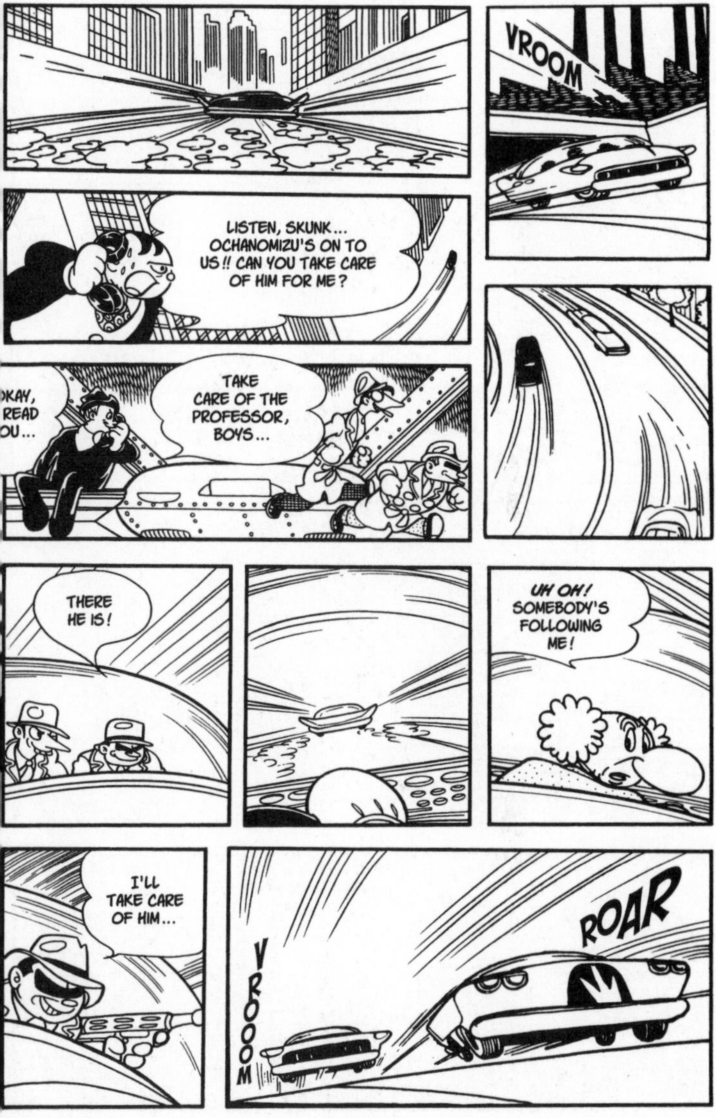
VROOM
LISTEN, SKUNK... OCHANOMIZU'S ON TO US!! CAN YOU TAKE CARE OF HIM FOR ME?
OKAY, READ YOU...
TAKE CARE OF THE PROFESSOR, BOYS...
THERE HE IS!
UH OH! SOMEBODY'S FOLLOWING ME!
I'LL TAKE CARE OF HIM...
VROOOM
ROAR

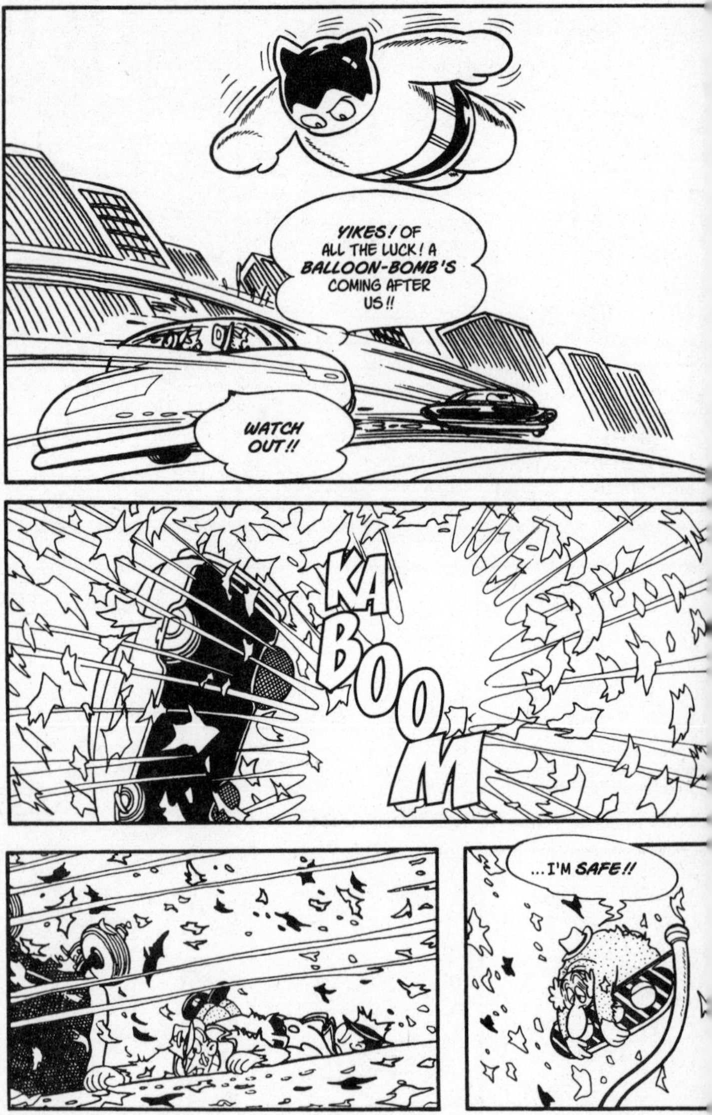
YIKES! OF ALL THE LUCK! A BALLOON-BOMB'S COMING AFTER US!!
WATCH OUT!!
KABOOM
...I'M SAFE!!

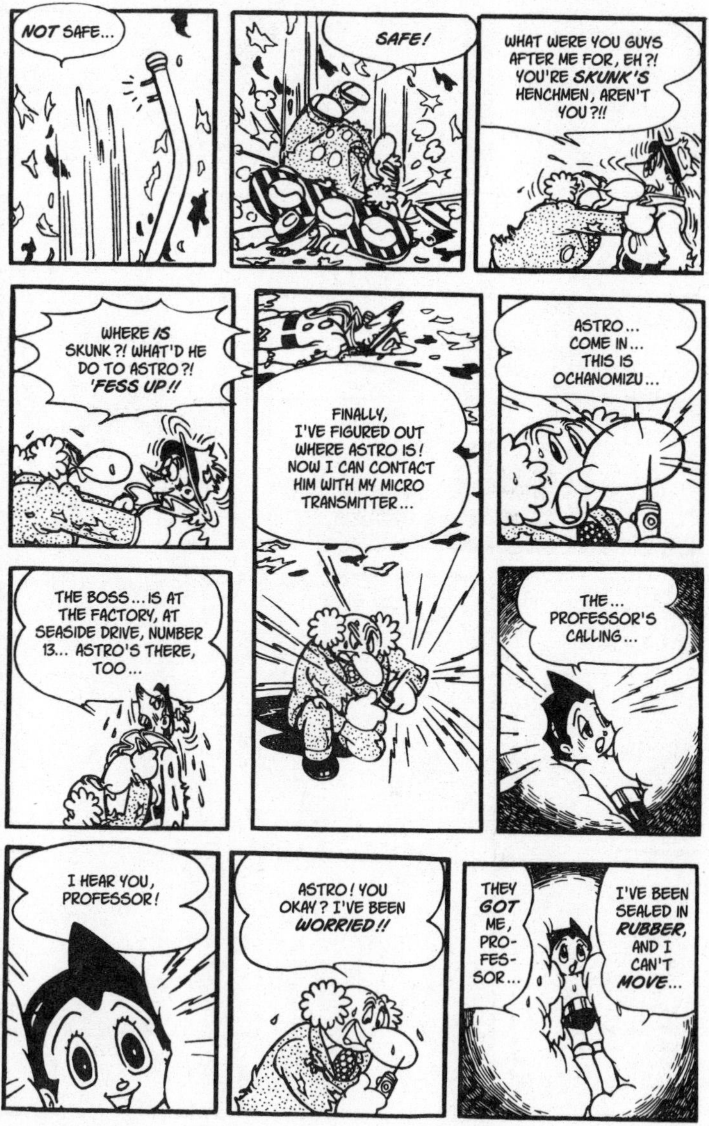
NOT SAFE...
SAFE!
WHAT WERE YOU GUYS AFTER ME FOR, EH?! YOU'RE SKUNK'S HENCHMEN, AREN'T YOU?!!
WHERE IS SKUNK?! WHAT'D HE DO TO ASTRO?! 'FESS UP!!
THE BOSS... IS AT THE FACTORY, AT SEASIDE DRIVE, NUMBER 13... ASTRO'S THERE, TOO...
FINALLY, I'VE FIGURED OUT WHERE ASTRO IS! NOW I CAN CONTACT HIM WITH MY MICRO TRANSMITTER...
ASTRO... COME IN... THIS IS OCHANOMIZU...
THE... PROFESSOR'S CALLING...
I HEAR YOU, PROFESSOR!
ASTRO! YOU OKAY? I'VE BEEN WORRIED!!
THEY GOT ME, PRO-FES-SOR...
I'VE BEEN SEALED IN RUBBER, AND I CAN'T MOVE...

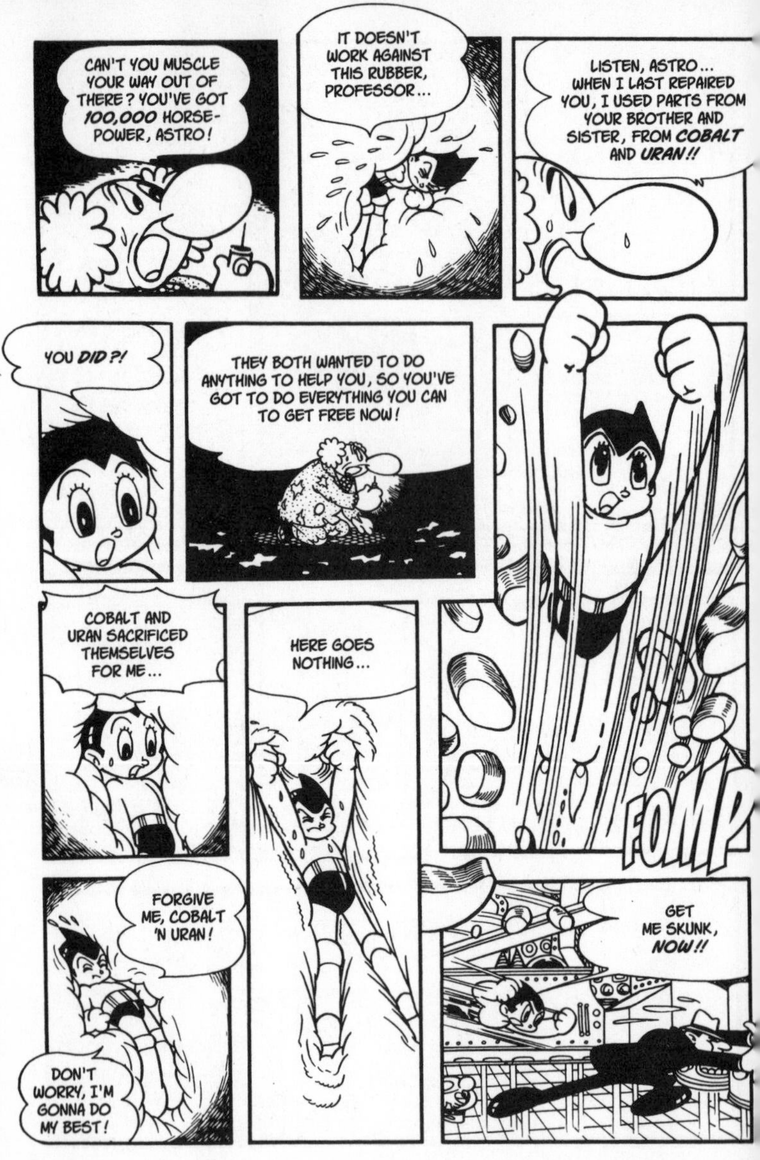

CAN'T YOU MUSCLE YOUR WAY OUT OF THERE? YOU'VE GOT *100,000* HORSE-POWER, ASTRO!
IT DOESN'T WORK AGAINST THIS RUBBER, PROFESSOR...
LISTEN, ASTRO... WHEN I LAST REPAIRED YOU, I USED PARTS FROM YOUR BROTHER AND SISTER, FROM *COBALT* AND *URAN!!*
YOU *DID?!*
THEY BOTH WANTED TO DO ANYTHING TO HELP YOU, SO YOU'VE GOT TO DO EVERYTHING YOU CAN TO GET FREE NOW!
COBALT AND URAN SACRIFICED THEMSELVES FOR ME...
HERE GOES NOTHING...
FOMP
FORGIVE ME, COBALT 'N URAN!
DON'T WORRY, I'M GONNA DO MY BEST!
GET ME SKUNK, *NOW!!*

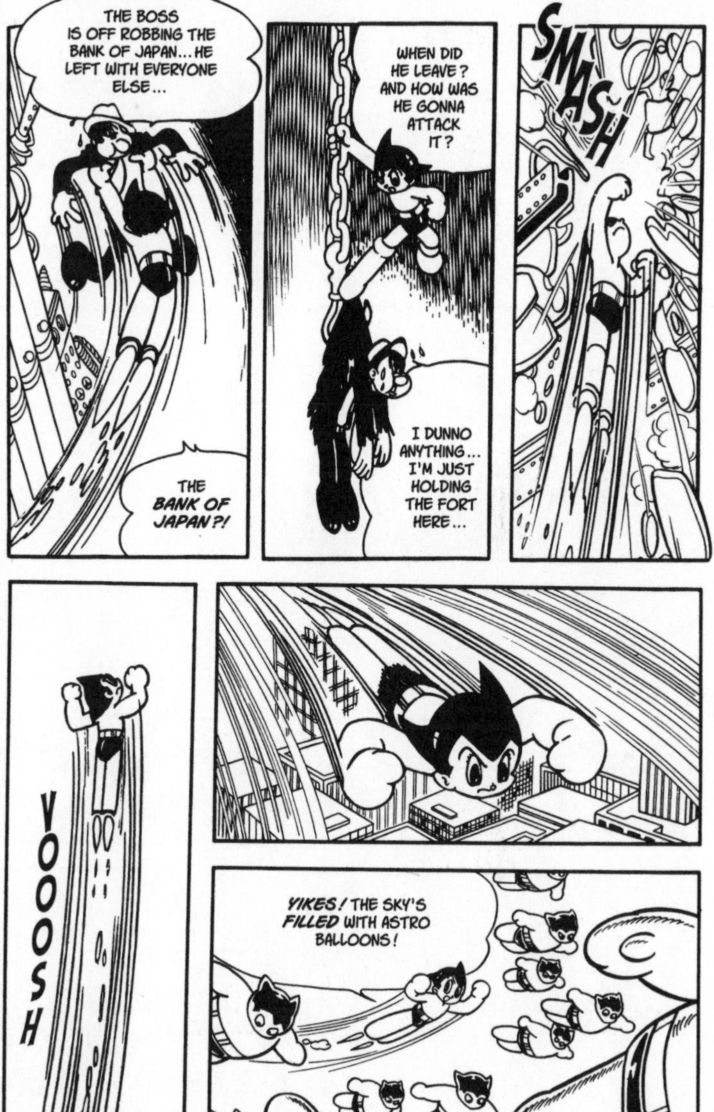
THE BOSS IS OFF ROBBING THE BANK OF JAPAN... HE LEFT WITH EVERYONE ELSE...
THE *BANK OF JAPAN?!*
WHEN DID HE LEAVE? AND HOW WAS HE GONNA ATTACK IT?
I DUNNO ANYTHING... I'M JUST HOLDING THE FORT HERE...
SMASH
VOOOOSH
YIKES! THE SKY'S *FILLED* WITH ASTRO BALLOONS!

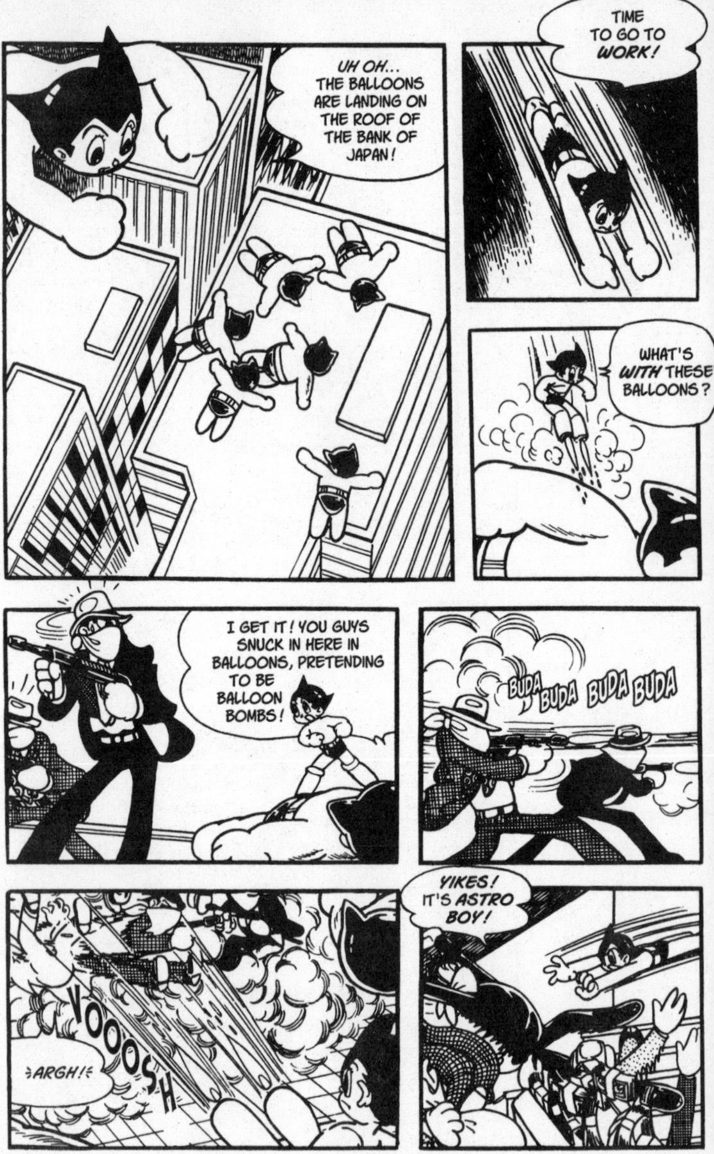
UH OH... THE BALLOONS ARE LANDING ON THE ROOF OF THE BANK OF JAPAN!
TIME TO GO TO WORK!
WHAT'S WITH THESE BALLOONS?
I GET IT! YOU GUYS SNUCK IN HERE IN BALLOONS, PRETENDING TO BE BALLOON BOMBS!
BUDA BUDA BUDA BUDA
VOOOSH
ARGH!
YIKES! IT'S ASTRO BOY!

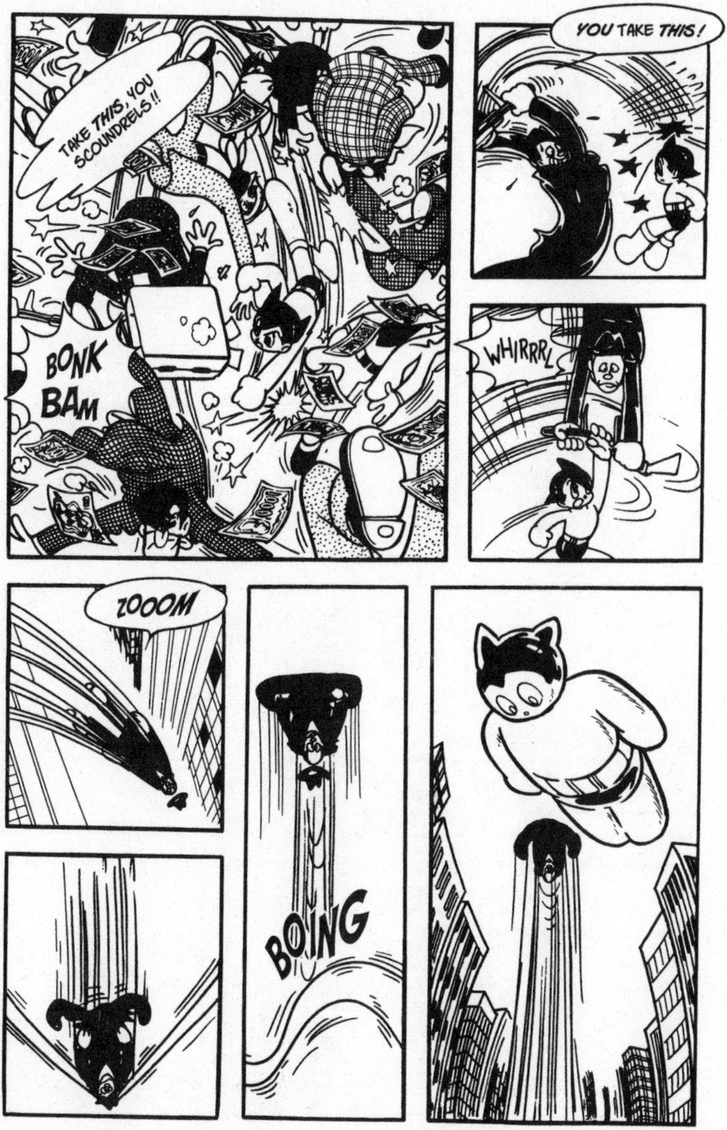

TAKE THIS, YOU SCOUNDRELS!!
BONK
BAM
YOU TAKE THIS!
WHIRRRL
ZOOOM
BOING

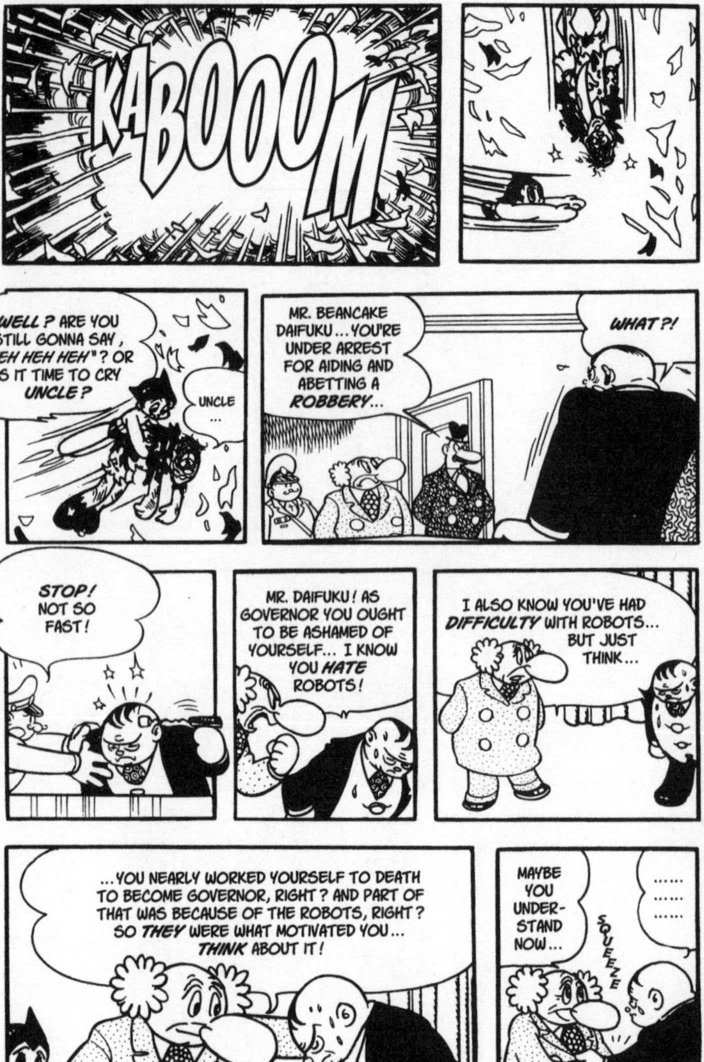
KABOOOM
WELL? ARE YOU STILL GONNA SAY, "HEH HEH HEH"? OR IS IT TIME TO CRY UNCLE?
UNCLE...
MR. BEANCAKE DAIFUKU... YOU'RE UNDER ARREST FOR AIDING AND ABETTING A ROBBERY...
WHAT?!
STOP! NOT SO FAST!
MR. DAIFUKU! AS GOVERNOR YOU OUGHT TO BE ASHAMED OF YOURSELF... I KNOW YOU HATE ROBOTS!
I ALSO KNOW YOU'VE HAD DIFFICULTY WITH ROBOTS... BUT JUST THINK...
...YOU NEARLY WORKED YOURSELF TO DEATH TO BECOME GOVERNOR, RIGHT? AND PART OF THAT WAS BECAUSE OF THE ROBOTS, RIGHT? SO THEY WERE WHAT MOTIVATED YOU... THINK ABOUT IT!
MAYBE YOU UNDER-STAND NOW...
SQUEEZE
......
......
......

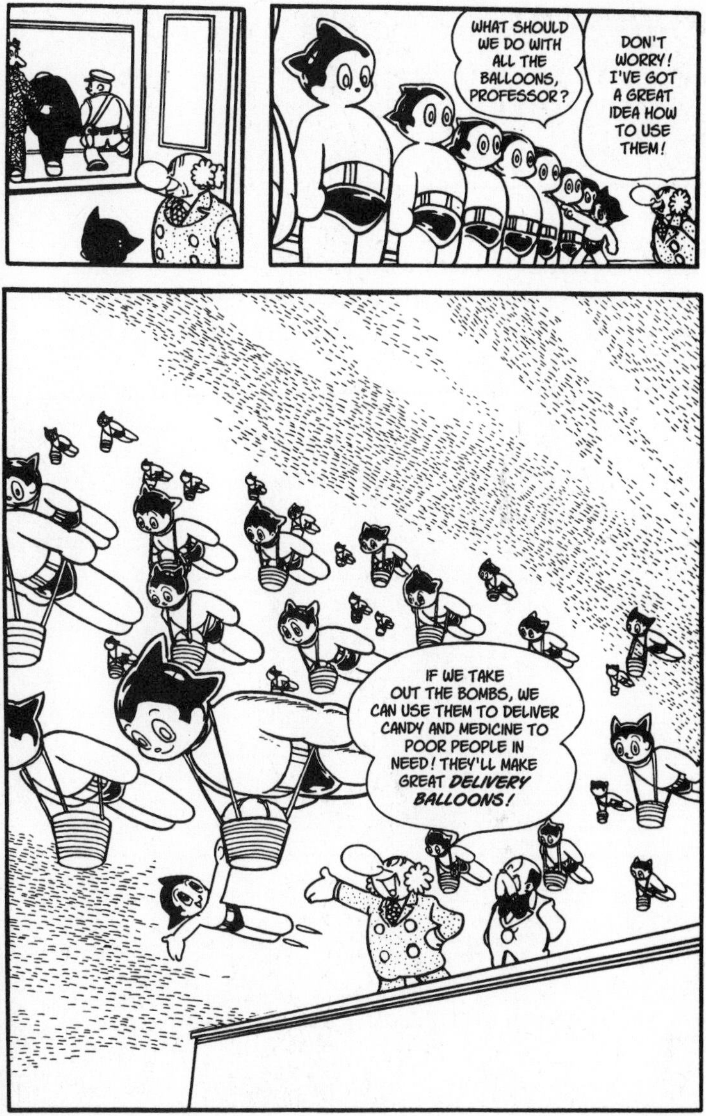
WHAT SHOULD WE DO WITH ALL THE BALLOONS, PROFESSOR?
DON'T WORRY! I'VE GOT A GREAT IDEA HOW TO USE THEM!
IF WE TAKE OUT THE BOMBS, WE CAN USE THEM TO DELIVER CANDY AND MEDICINE TO POOR PEOPLE IN NEED! THEY'LL MAKE GREAT *DELIVERY BALLOONS!*

THE END

THE FROZEN HUMAN

First appeared in the July 1955 supplement
edition of *Shonen* magazine.

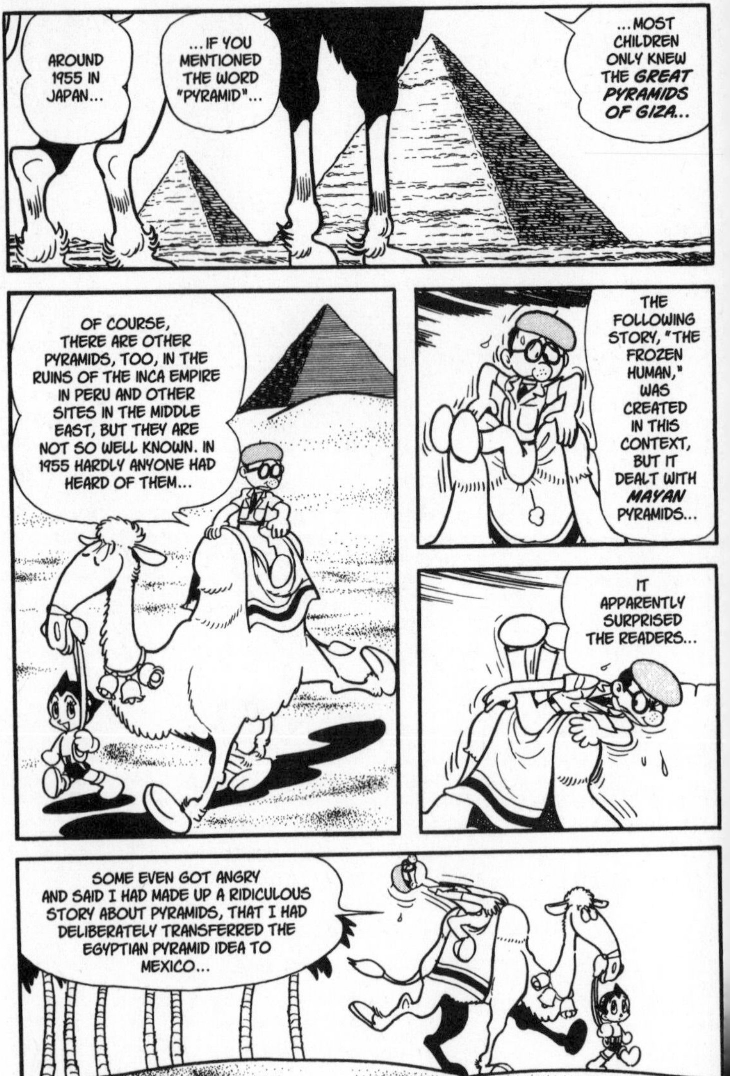
AROUND 1955 IN JAPAN...
...IF YOU MENTIONED THE WORD "PYRAMID"...
...MOST CHILDREN ONLY KNEW THE *GREAT PYRAMIDS OF GIZA*...
OF COURSE, THERE ARE OTHER PYRAMIDS, TOO, IN THE RUINS OF THE INCA EMPIRE IN PERU AND OTHER SITES IN THE MIDDLE EAST, BUT THEY ARE NOT SO WELL KNOWN. IN 1955 HARDLY ANYONE HAD HEARD OF THEM...
THE FOLLOWING STORY, "THE FROZEN HUMAN," WAS CREATED IN THIS CONTEXT, BUT IT DEALT WITH *MAYAN* PYRAMIDS...
IT APPARENTLY SURPRISED THE READERS...
SOME EVEN GOT ANGRY AND SAID I HAD MADE UP A RIDICULOUS STORY ABOUT PYRAMIDS, THAT I HAD DELIBERATELY TRANSFERRED THE EGYPTIAN PYRAMID IDEA TO MEXICO...

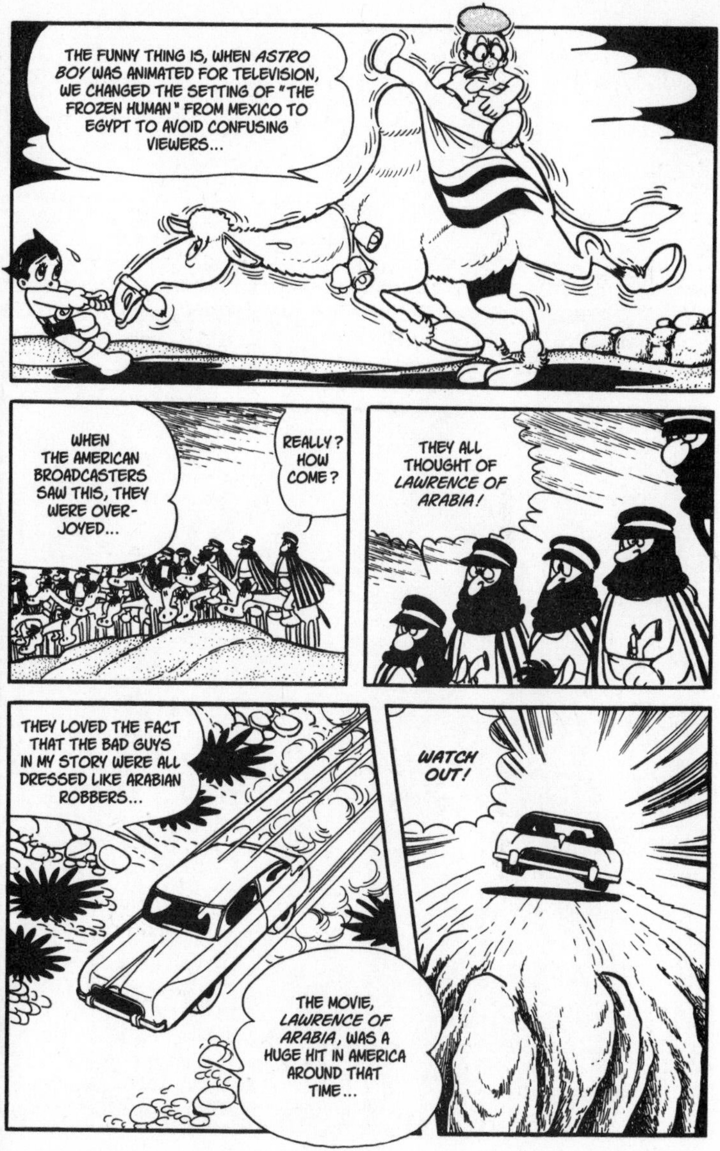
THE FUNNY THING IS, WHEN ASTRO BOY WAS ANIMATED FOR TELEVISION, WE CHANGED THE SETTING OF "THE FROZEN HUMAN" FROM MEXICO TO EGYPT TO AVOID CONFUSING VIEWERS...
WHEN THE AMERICAN BROADCASTERS SAW THIS, THEY WERE OVER-JOYED...
REALLY? HOW COME?
THEY ALL THOUGHT OF LAWRENCE OF ARABIA!
THEY LOVED THE FACT THAT THE BAD GUYS IN MY STORY WERE ALL DRESSED LIKE ARABIAN ROBBERS...
THE MOVIE, LAWRENCE OF ARABIA, WAS A HUGE HIT IN AMERICA AROUND THAT TIME...
WATCH OUT!

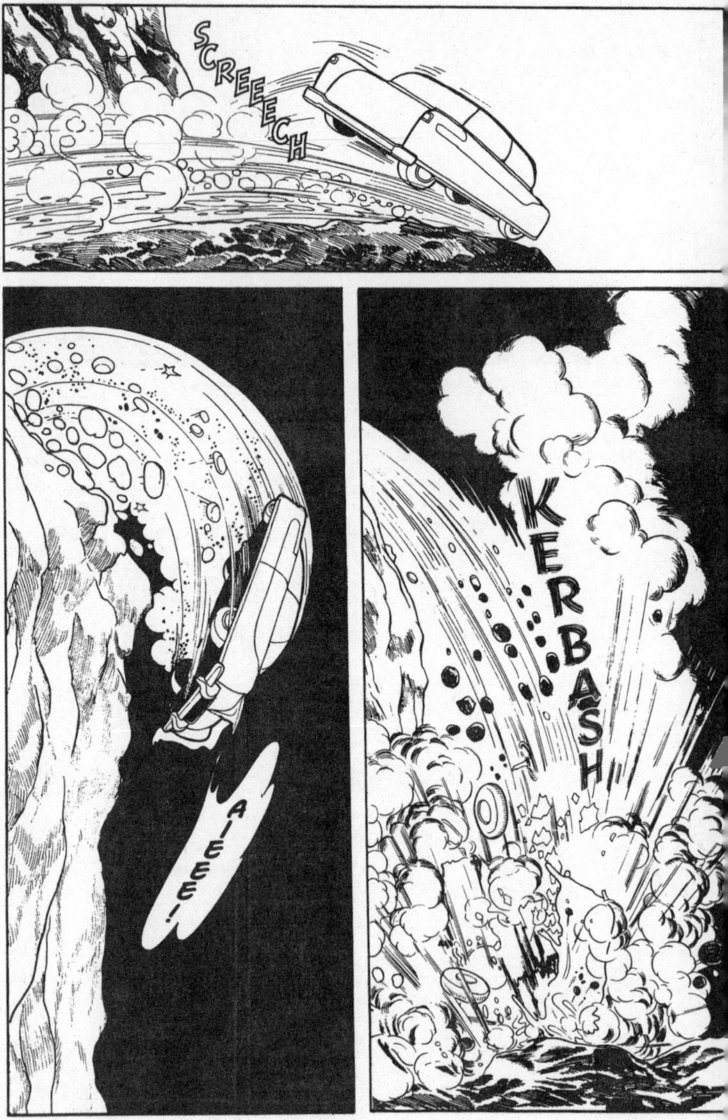
SCREEECH
AIEEEE!
KERBASH

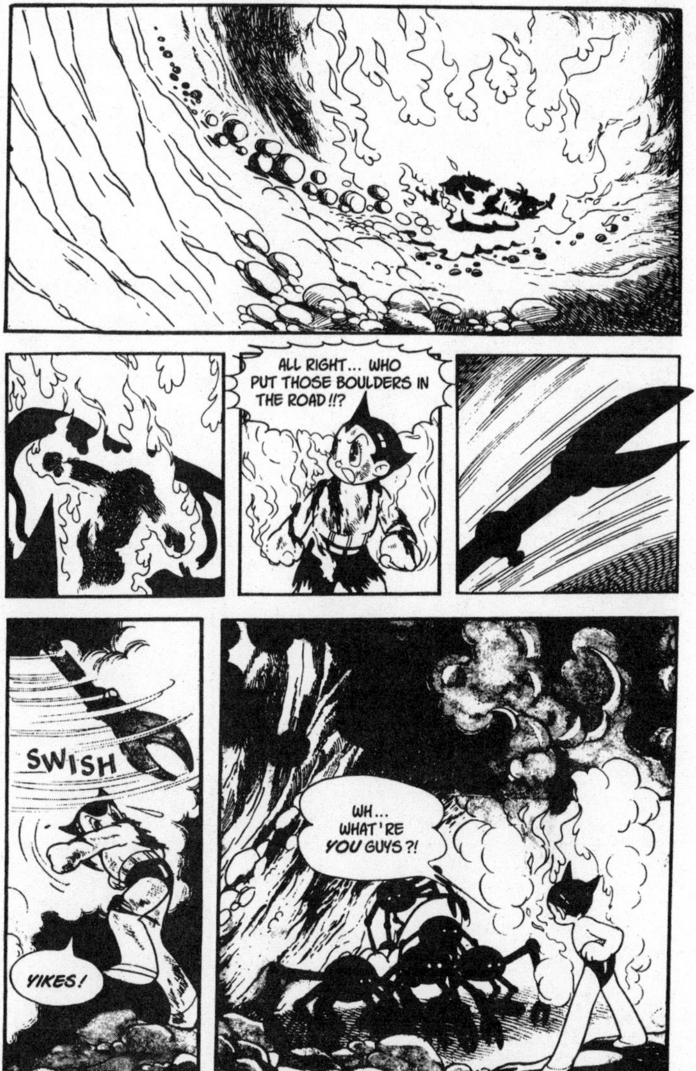
ALL RIGHT... WHO PUT THOSE BOULDERS IN THE ROAD!!?
SWISH
YIKES!
WH... WHAT'RE YOU GUYS?!

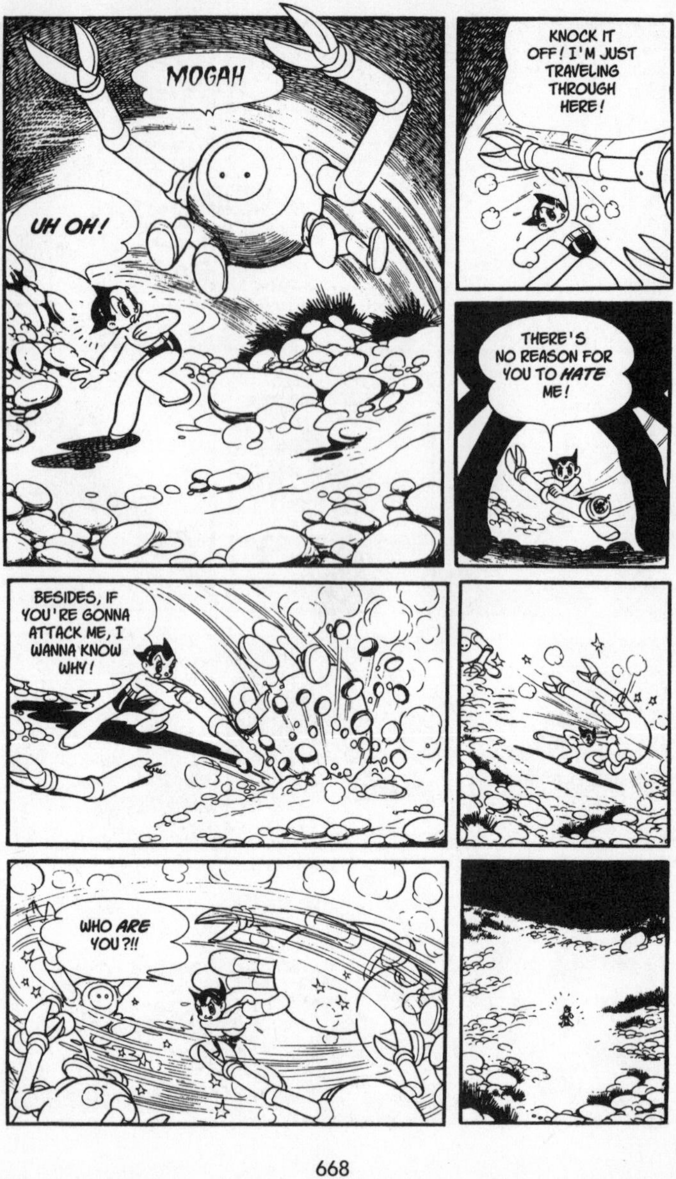
MOGAH
UH OH!
KNOCK IT OFF! I'M JUST TRAVELING THROUGH HERE!
THERE'S NO REASON FOR YOU TO HATE ME!
BESIDES, IF YOU'RE GONNA ATTACK ME, I WANNA KNOW WHY!
WHO ARE YOU?!!

CHIRP CHIRP CHIRP CHIRP CHIRP CHIRP

I'VE ONLY BEEN IN MEXICO FOR *THREE DAYS*...

... AND I'M ALREADY BEING FOLLOWED AND ATTACKED BY WEIRDOS LIKE THAT.

LOOKS LIKE A *TENT* OVER THERE...

EXCUSE ME... I WONDER IF YOU COULD LEND ME SOME CLOTHES YOU DON'T NEED...

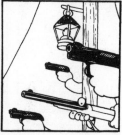

WHAT'RE YOU DOING HERE, KID?

YOU DESERVE TO *DANCE*!

BLAM

PLEASE, MISTER... I'M *ASTRO BOY*... I'M FROM *JAPAN*!

MY CLOTHES WERE ALL BURNED IN A CAR ACCIDENT EARLIER...

BLAM BLAM

A ROBOT?! WELL, I'VE HAD ENOUGH OF *THEM*!

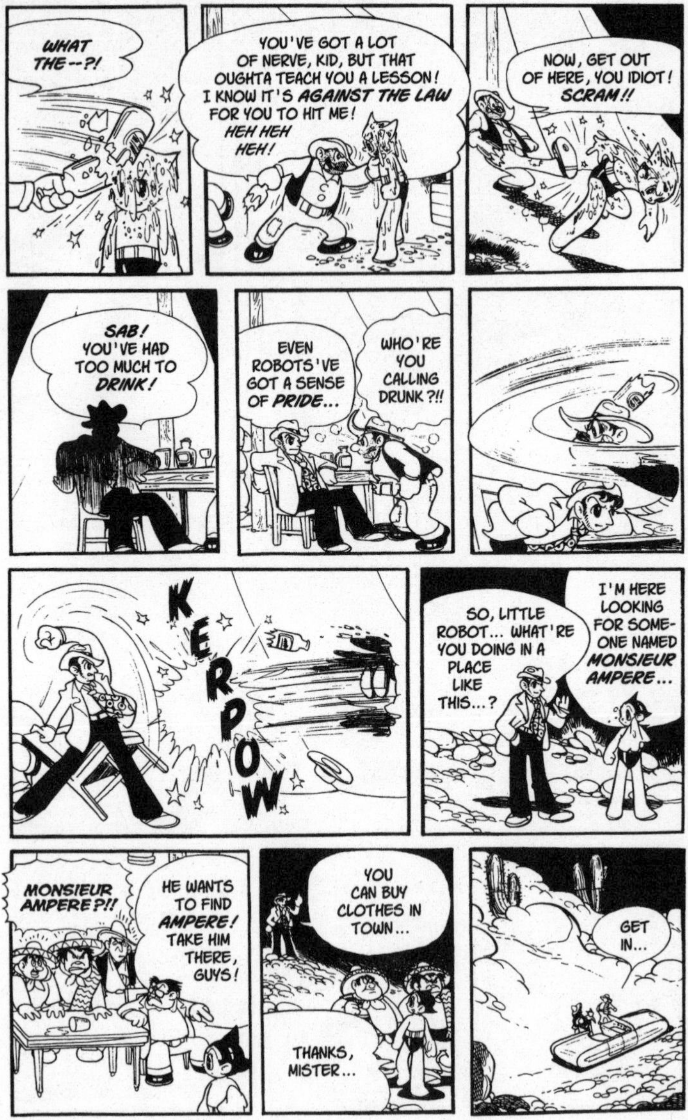
WHAT THE--?!
YOU'VE GOT A LOT OF NERVE, KID, BUT THAT OUGHTA TEACH YOU A LESSON! I KNOW IT'S AGAINST THE LAW FOR YOU TO HIT ME!
HEH HEH HEH!
NOW, GET OUT OF HERE, YOU IDIOT! SCRAM!!
SAB! YOU'VE HAD TOO MUCH TO DRINK!
EVEN ROBOTS'VE GOT A SENSE OF PRIDE...
WHO'RE YOU CALLING DRUNK?!!
KERPOW
SO, LITTLE ROBOT... WHAT'RE YOU DOING IN A PLACE LIKE THIS...?
I'M HERE LOOKING FOR SOMEONE NAMED MONSIEUR AMPERE...
MONSIEUR AMPERE?!!
HE WANTS TO FIND AMPERE! TAKE HIM THERE, GUYS!
YOU CAN BUY CLOTHES IN TOWN...
THANKS, MISTER...
GET IN...

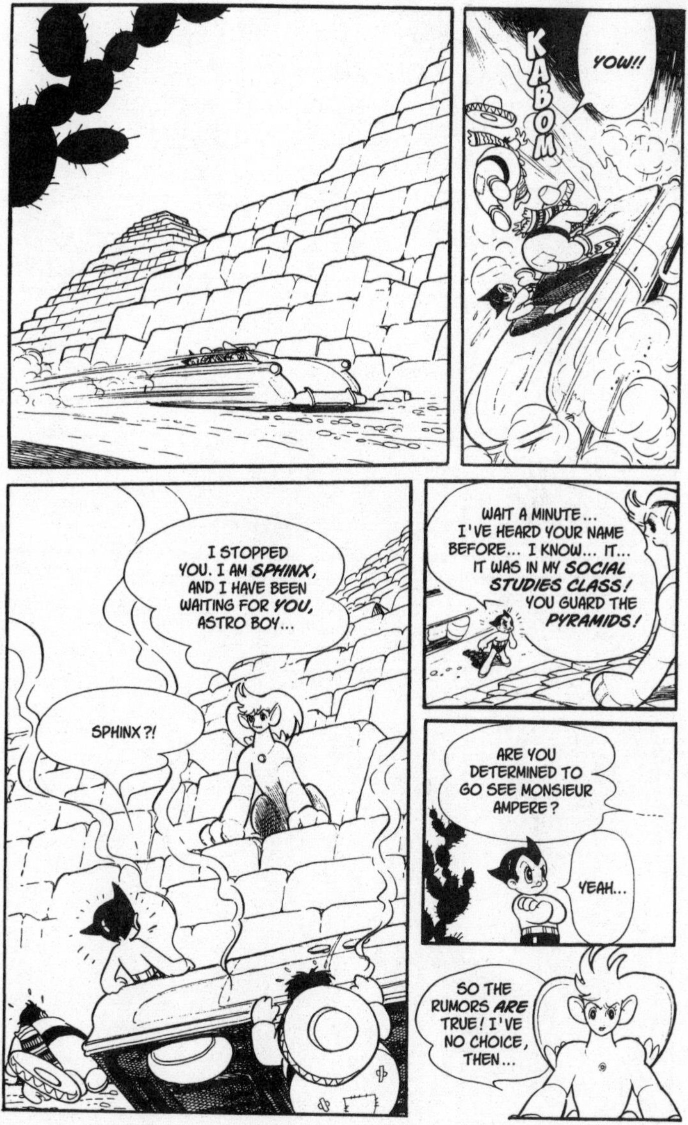
KABOOM
YOW!!
I STOPPED YOU. I AM *SPHINX*, AND I HAVE BEEN WAITING FOR *YOU*, ASTRO BOY...
SPHINX?!
WAIT A MINUTE... I'VE HEARD YOUR NAME BEFORE... I KNOW... IT... IT WAS IN MY *SOCIAL STUDIES CLASS!* YOU GUARD THE *PYRAMIDS!*
ARE YOU DETERMINED TO GO SEE MONSIEUR AMPERE?
YEAH...
SO THE RUMORS *ARE* TRUE! I'VE NO CHOICE, THEN...

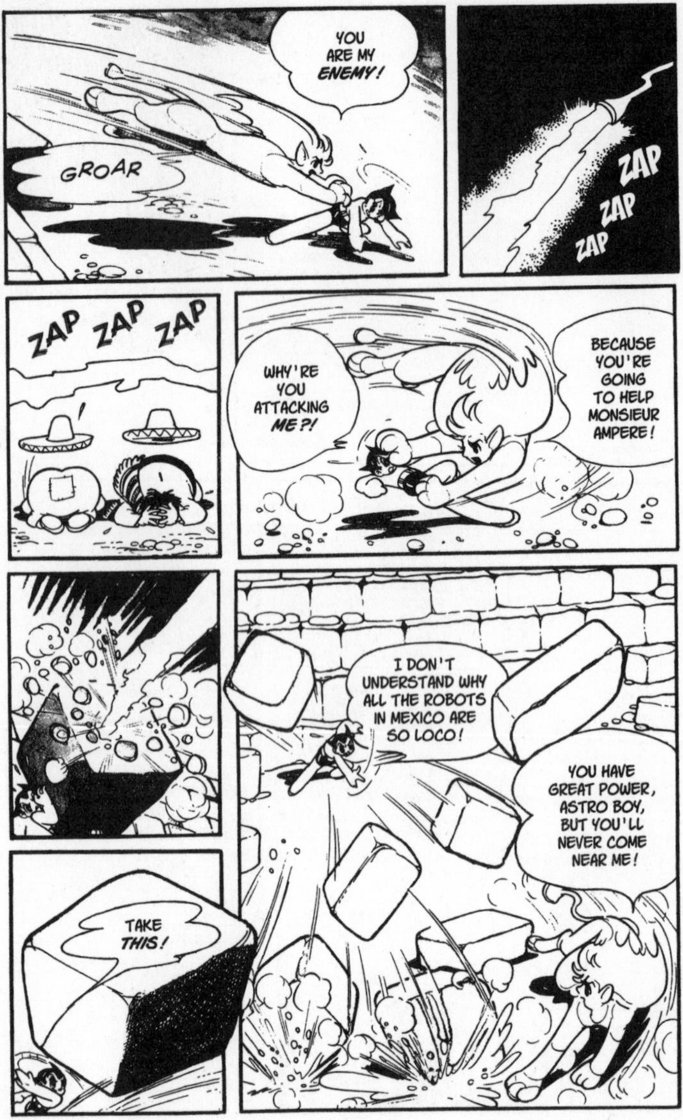
YOU ARE MY ENEMY!
GROAR
ZAP ZAP ZAP
ZAP ZAP ZAP
WHY'RE YOU ATTACKING ME?!
BECAUSE YOU'RE GOING TO HELP MONSIEUR AMPERE!
I DON'T UNDERSTAND WHY ALL THE ROBOTS IN MEXICO ARE SO LOCO!
YOU HAVE GREAT POWER, ASTRO BOY, BUT YOU'LL NEVER COME NEAR ME!
TAKE THIS!

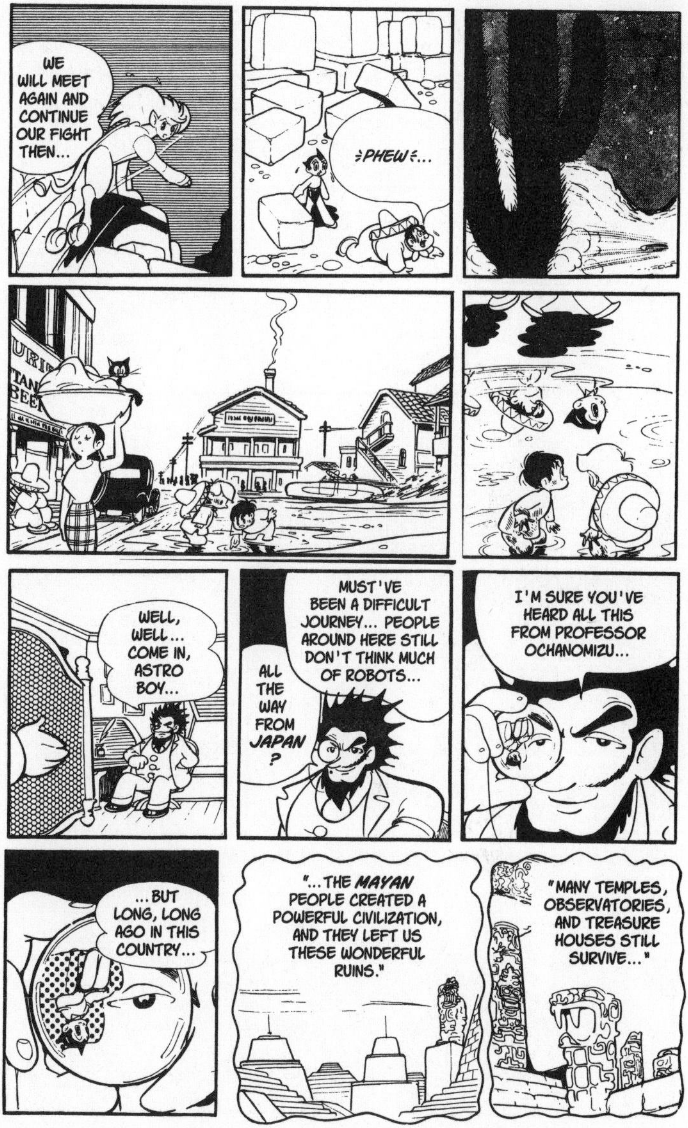
WE WILL MEET AGAIN AND CONTINUE OUR FIGHT THEN...
PHEW...
WELL, WELL... COME IN, ASTRO BOY...
ALL THE WAY FROM JAPAN?
MUST'VE BEEN A DIFFICULT JOURNEY... PEOPLE AROUND HERE STILL DON'T THINK MUCH OF ROBOTS...
I'M SURE YOU'VE HEARD ALL THIS FROM PROFESSOR OCHANOMIZU...
...BUT LONG, LONG AGO IN THIS COUNTRY...
"...THE MAYAN PEOPLE CREATED A POWERFUL CIVILIZATION, AND THEY LEFT US THESE WONDERFUL RUINS."
"MANY TEMPLES, OBSERVATORIES, AND TREASURE HOUSES STILL SURVIVE..."

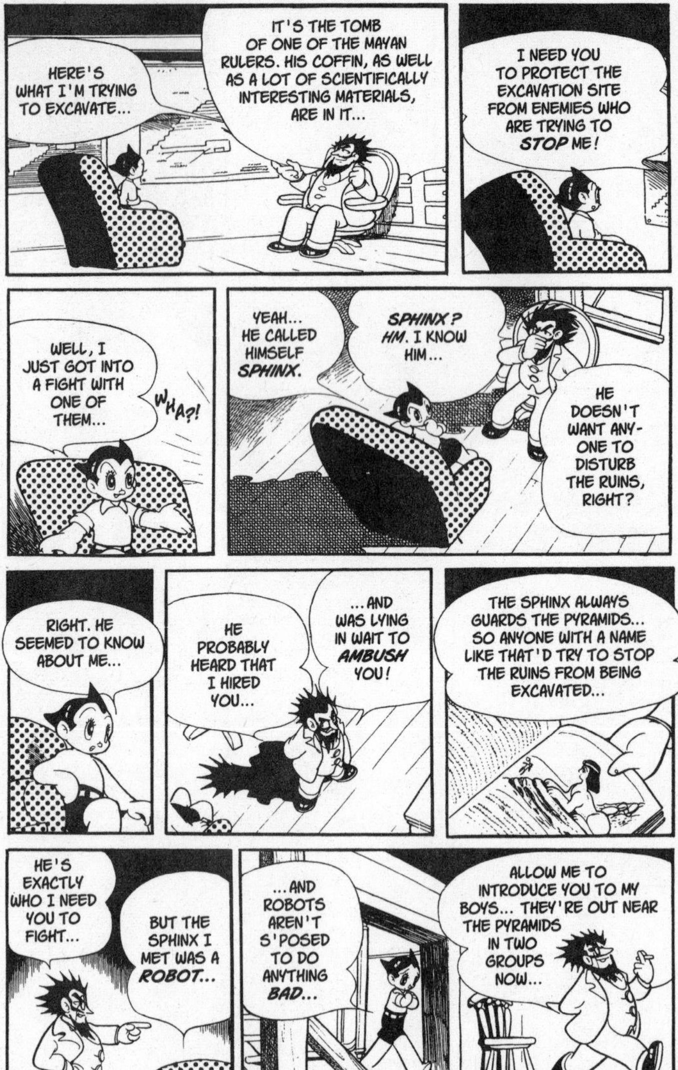
HERE'S WHAT I'M TRYING TO EXCAVATE...
IT'S THE TOMB OF ONE OF THE MAYAN RULERS. HIS COFFIN, AS WELL AS A LOT OF SCIENTIFICALLY INTERESTING MATERIALS, ARE IN IT...
I NEED YOU TO PROTECT THE EXCAVATION SITE FROM ENEMIES WHO ARE TRYING TO STOP ME!
WELL, I JUST GOT INTO A FIGHT WITH ONE OF THEM...
WHA?!
YEAH... HE CALLED HIMSELF SPHINX.
SPHINX? HM. I KNOW HIM...
HE DOESN'T WANT ANY-ONE TO DISTURB THE RUINS, RIGHT?
RIGHT. HE SEEMED TO KNOW ABOUT ME...
HE PROBABLY HEARD THAT I HIRED YOU...
...AND WAS LYING IN WAIT TO AMBUSH YOU!
THE SPHINX ALWAYS GUARDS THE PYRAMIDS... SO ANYONE WITH A NAME LIKE THAT'D TRY TO STOP THE RUINS FROM BEING EXCAVATED...
HE'S EXACTLY WHO I NEED YOU TO FIGHT...
BUT THE SPHINX I MET WAS A ROBOT...
...AND ROBOTS AREN'T S'POSED TO DO ANYTHING BAD...
ALLOW ME TO INTRODUCE YOU TO MY BOYS... THEY'RE OUT NEAR THE PYRAMIDS IN TWO GROUPS NOW...

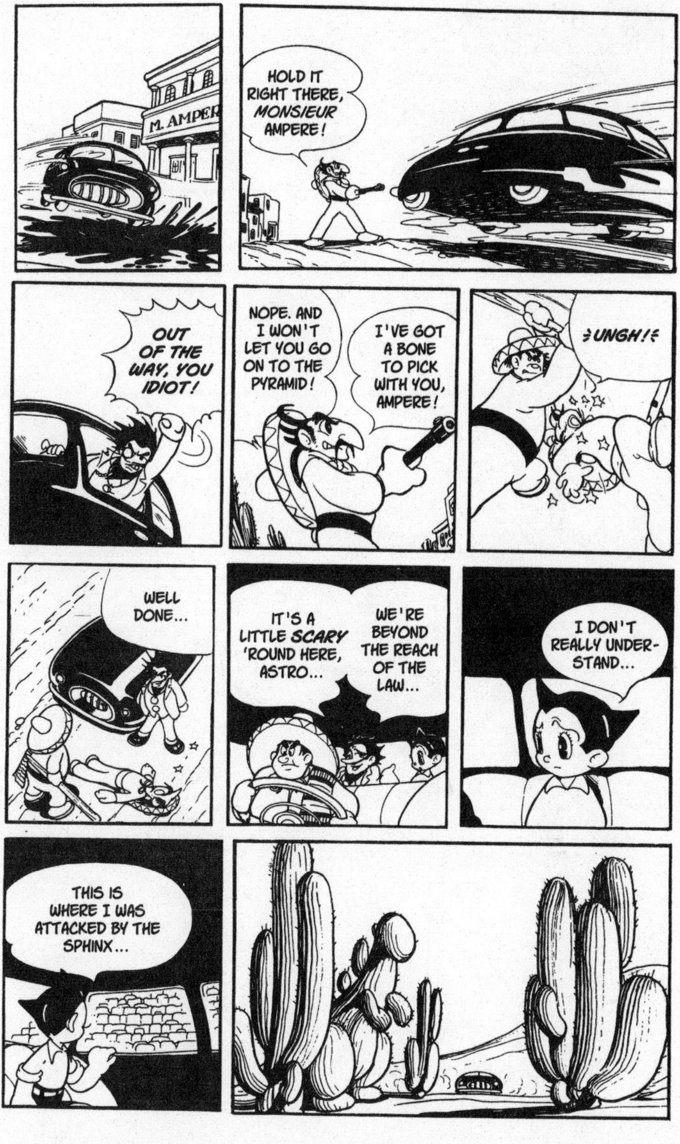
M. AMPER
HOLD IT RIGHT THERE, *MONSIEUR* AMPERE!
OUT OF THE WAY, YOU IDIOT!
NOPE. AND I WON'T LET YOU GO ON TO THE PYRAMID!
I'VE GOT A BONE TO PICK WITH YOU, AMPERE!
UNGH!
WELL DONE...
IT'S A LITTLE *SCARY* 'ROUND HERE, ASTRO...
WE'RE BEYOND THE REACH OF THE LAW...
I DON'T REALLY UNDER-STAND...
THIS IS WHERE I WAS ATTACKED BY THE SPHINX...

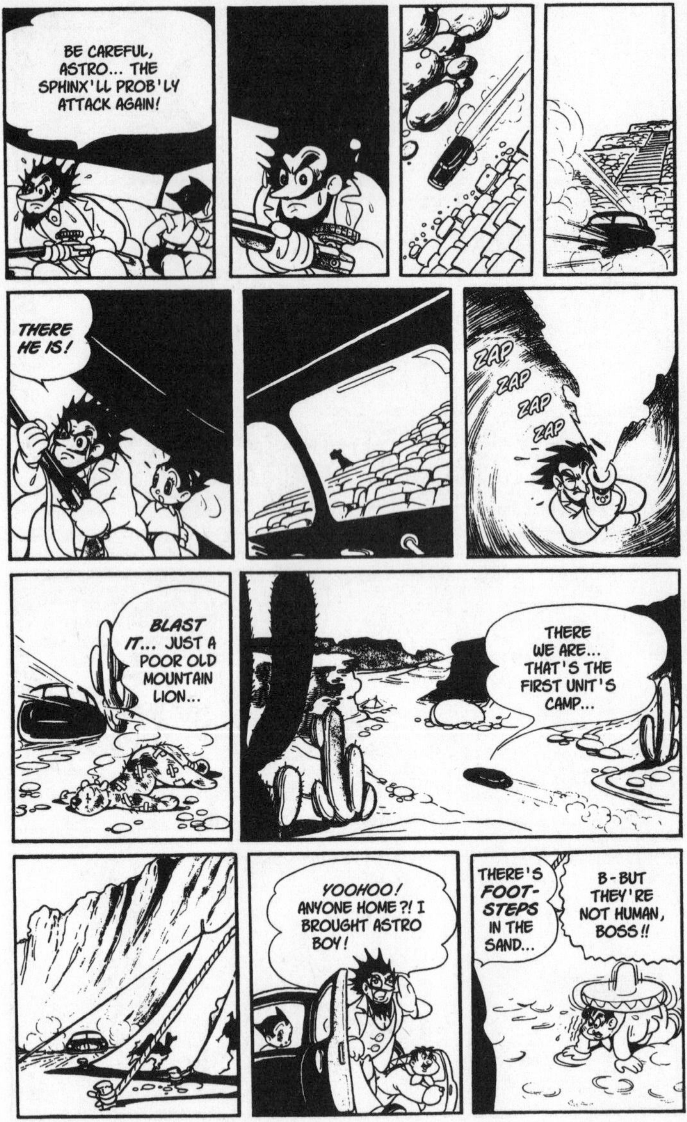
BE CAREFUL, ASTRO... THE SPHINX'LL PROB'LY ATTACK AGAIN!
THERE HE IS!
ZAP
ZAP
ZAP
ZAP
BLAST IT... JUST A POOR OLD MOUNTAIN LION...
THERE WE ARE... THAT'S THE FIRST UNIT'S CAMP...
YOOHOO! ANYONE HOME?! I BROUGHT ASTRO BOY!
THERE'S FOOT-STEPS IN THE SAND...
B-BUT THEY'RE NOT HUMAN, BOSS!!

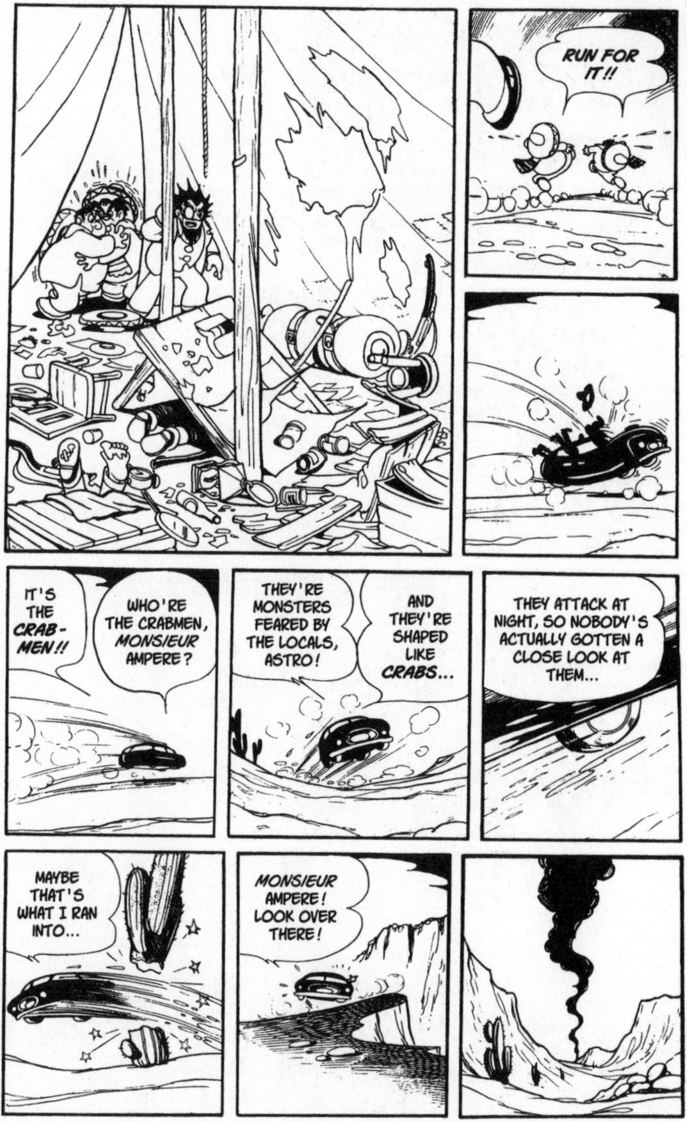
RUN FOR IT!!
IT'S THE CRAB-MEN!!
WHO'RE THE CRABMEN, MONSIEUR AMPERE?
THEY'RE MONSTERS FEARED BY THE LOCALS, ASTRO!
AND THEY'RE SHAPED LIKE CRABS...
THEY ATTACK AT NIGHT, SO NOBODY'S ACTUALLY GOTTEN A CLOSE LOOK AT THEM...
MAYBE THAT'S WHAT I RAN INTO...
MONSIEUR AMPERE! LOOK OVER THERE!

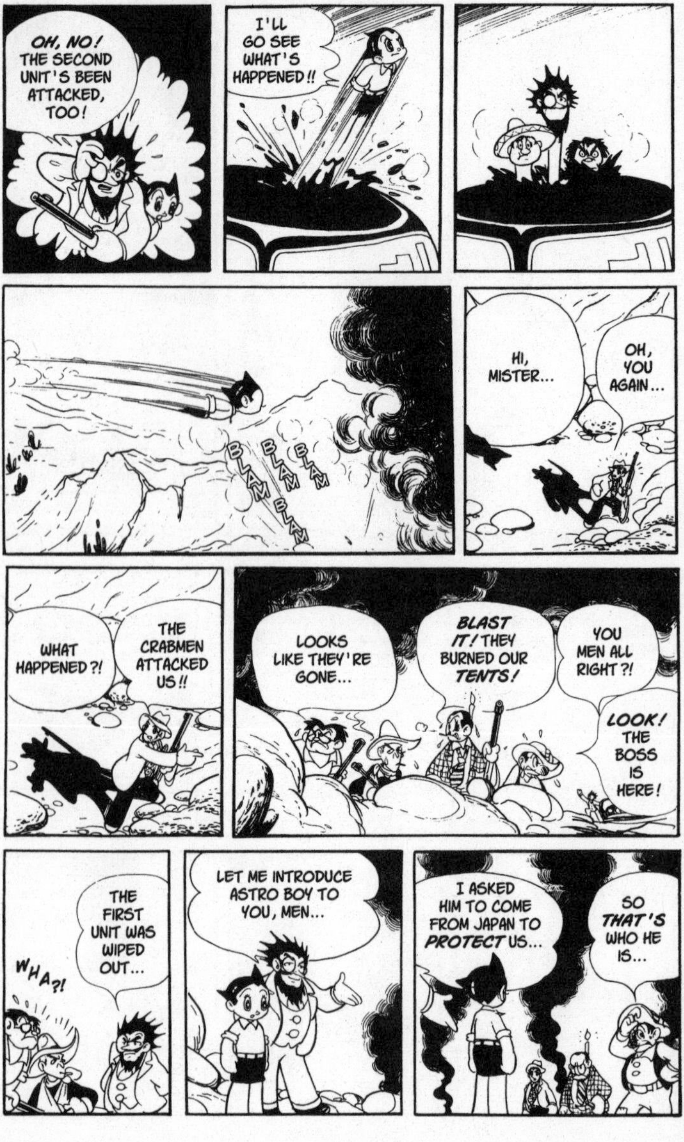
OH, NO! THE SECOND UNIT'S BEEN ATTACKED, TOO!
I'LL GO SEE WHAT'S HAPPENED!!
BLAM
BLAM
BLAM
BLAM
BLAM
HI, MISTER...
OH, YOU AGAIN...
WHAT HAPPENED?!
THE CRABMEN ATTACKED US!!
LOOKS LIKE THEY'RE GONE...
BLAST IT! THEY BURNED OUR TENTS!
YOU MEN ALL RIGHT?!
LOOK! THE BOSS IS HERE!
WHA?!
THE FIRST UNIT WAS WIPED OUT...
LET ME INTRODUCE ASTRO BOY TO YOU, MEN...
I ASKED HIM TO COME FROM JAPAN TO PROTECT US...
SO THAT'S WHO HE IS...

WE CAN'T WASTE ANY TIME HERE, PROFESSOR... WE'VE GOT TO START THE *EXCAVATIONS*...

...BEFORE THE SECOND UNIT'S WIPED OUT, TOO...

I'D FEEL A LOT BETTER IF THE ROBOTS WERE HERE...

SO LET ME EXPLAIN, BOYS. HERE'S THE PYRAMID...

IT HAS ENTRANCES ON THE EAST AND SOUTH SIDES...

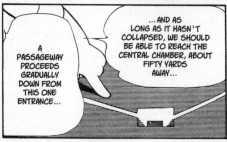

A PASSAGEWAY PROCEEDS GRADUALLY DOWN FROM THIS ONE ENTRANCE...

...AND AS LONG AS IT HASN'T COLLAPSED, WE SHOULD BE ABLE TO REACH THE CENTRAL CHAMBER, ABOUT FIFTY YARDS AWAY...

THIS CHAMBER IS ALSO THE *BURIAL* CHAMBER.

AND IT SHOULD HAVE WHAT WE'RE LOOKING FOR...

IF OUR PATH'S BLOCKED BY ANY FALLEN MATERIAL, WE CAN HAVE ASTRO BOY CLEAR IT FOR US...

SO GET YOUR SHOVELS AND LET'S GO, MEN!

I WONDER WHAT THEIR *REAL* GOAL IS...

THERE ARE TOO MANY *SHADY CHARACTERS* INVOLVED FOR THIS TO BE AN *ORDINARY* EXCAVATION...

679

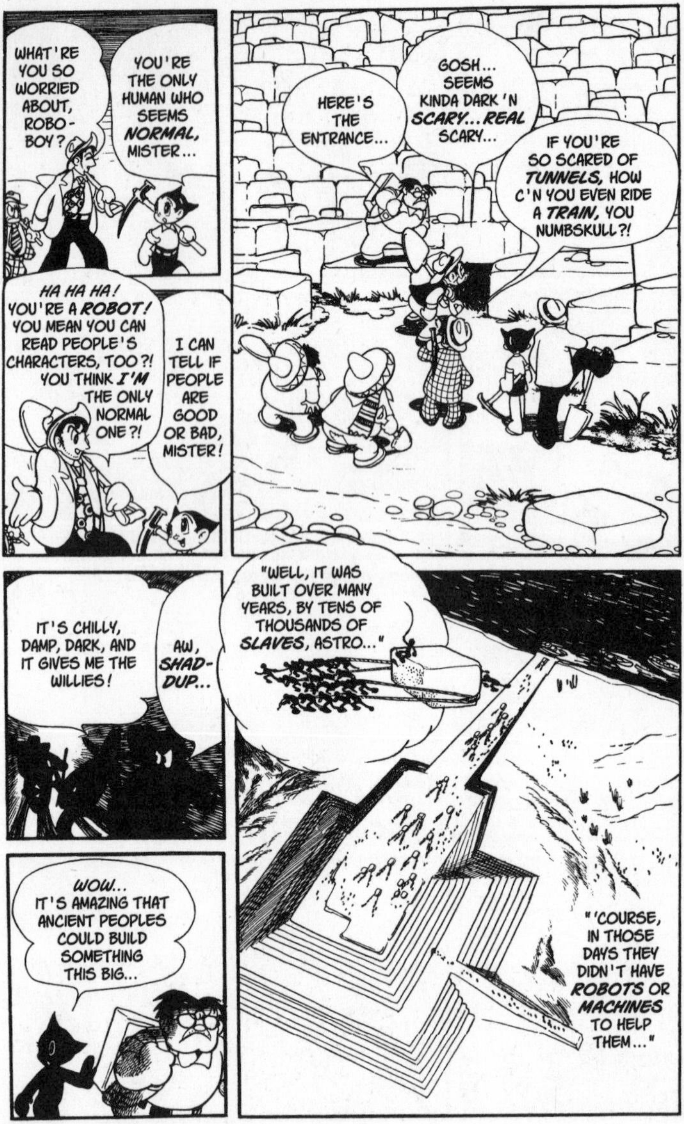
WHAT'RE YOU SO WORRIED ABOUT, ROBO-BOY?
YOU'RE THE ONLY HUMAN WHO SEEMS NORMAL, MISTER...
HERE'S THE ENTRANCE...
GOSH... SEEMS KINDA DARK 'N SCARY... REAL SCARY...
IF YOU'RE SO SCARED OF TUNNELS, HOW C'N YOU EVEN RIDE A TRAIN, YOU NUMBSKULL?!
HA HA HA! YOU'RE A ROBOT! YOU MEAN YOU CAN READ PEOPLE'S CHARACTERS, TOO?! YOU THINK I'M THE ONLY NORMAL ONE?!
I CAN TELL IF PEOPLE ARE GOOD OR BAD, MISTER!
IT'S CHILLY, DAMP, DARK, AND IT GIVES ME THE WILLIES!
AW, SHAD-DUP...
WOW... IT'S AMAZING THAT ANCIENT PEOPLES COULD BUILD SOMETHING THIS BIG...
"WELL, IT WAS BUILT OVER MANY YEARS, BY TENS OF THOUSANDS OF SLAVES, ASTRO..."
"'COURSE, IN THOSE DAYS THEY DIDN'T HAVE ROBOTS OR MACHINES TO HELP THEM..."

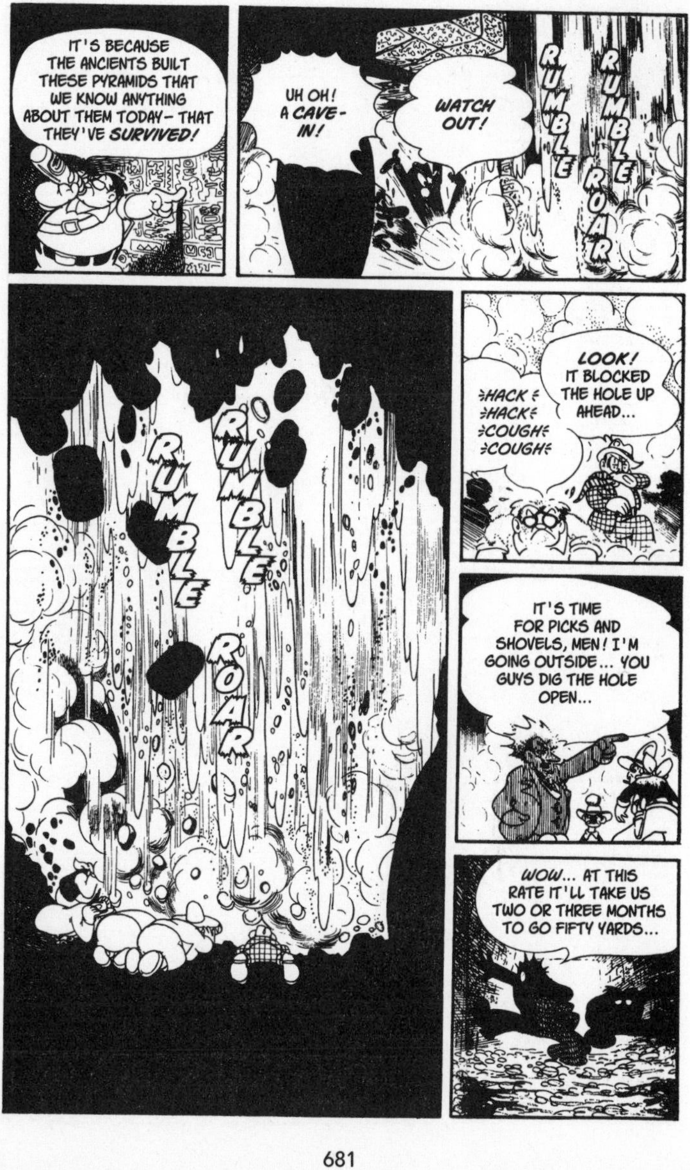
IT'S BECAUSE THE ANCIENTS BUILT THESE PYRAMIDS THAT WE KNOW ANYTHING ABOUT THEM TODAY— THAT THEY'VE SURVIVED!
UH OH! A CAVE-IN!
WATCH OUT!
RUMBLE
RUMBLE ROAR
RUMBLE
RUMBLE
ROAR
HACK HACK COUGH COUGH
LOOK! IT BLOCKED THE HOLE UP AHEAD...
IT'S TIME FOR PICKS AND SHOVELS, MEN! I'M GOING OUTSIDE... YOU GUYS DIG THE HOLE OPEN...
WOW... AT THIS RATE IT'LL TAKE US TWO OR THREE MONTHS TO GO FIFTY YARDS...

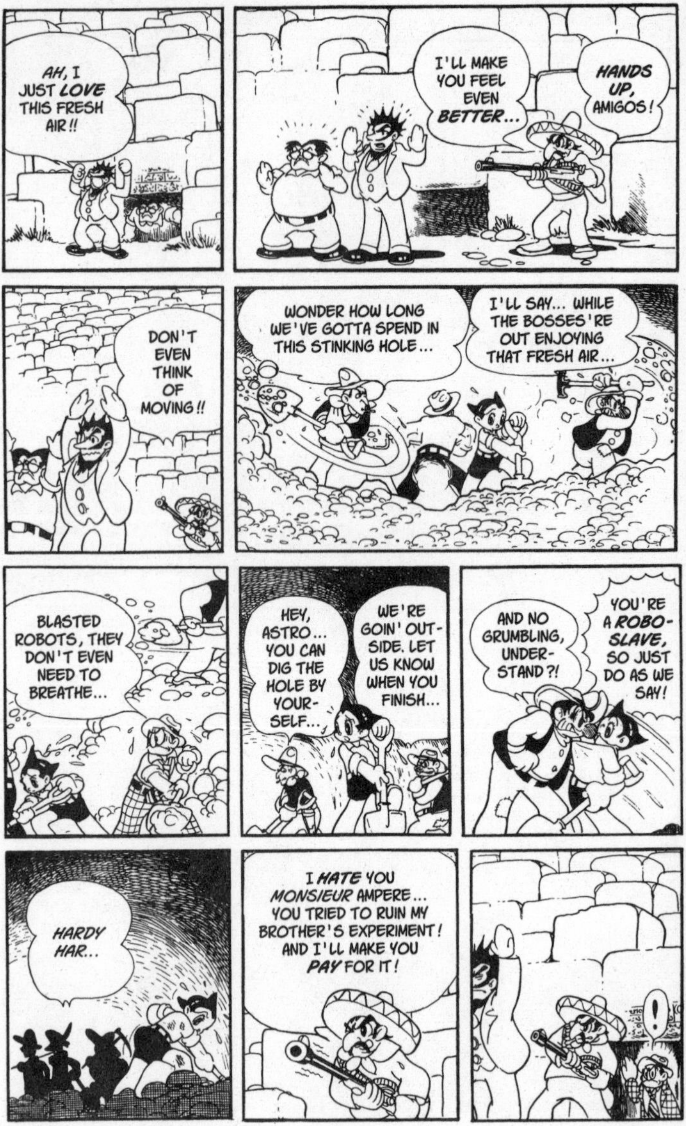
AH, I JUST LOVE THIS FRESH AIR!!
I'LL MAKE YOU FEEL EVEN BETTER...
HANDS UP, AMIGOS!
DON'T EVEN THINK OF MOVING!!
WONDER HOW LONG WE'VE GOTTA SPEND IN THIS STINKING HOLE...
I'LL SAY... WHILE THE BOSSES'RE OUT ENJOYING THAT FRESH AIR...
BLASTED ROBOTS, THEY DON'T EVEN NEED TO BREATHE...
HEY, ASTRO... YOU CAN DIG THE HOLE BY YOURSELF...
WE'RE GOIN' OUTSIDE. LET US KNOW WHEN YOU FINISH...
AND NO GRUMBLING, UNDERSTAND?!
YOU'RE A ROBO-SLAVE, SO JUST DO AS WE SAY!
HARDY HAR...
I HATE YOU MONSIEUR AMPERE... YOU TRIED TO RUIN MY BROTHER'S EXPERIMENT! AND I'LL MAKE YOU PAY FOR IT!
!

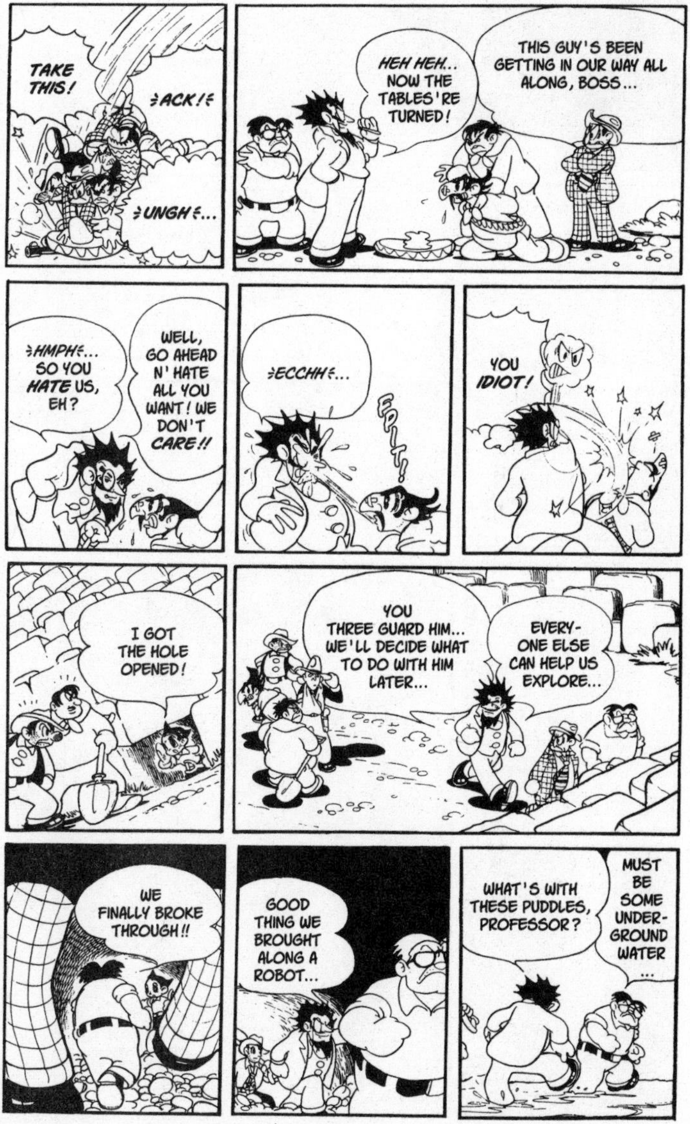

TAKE THIS!
ACK!
UNGH...
HEH HEH... NOW THE TABLES'RE TURNED!
THIS GUY'S BEEN GETTING IN OUR WAY ALL ALONG, BOSS...
HMPH... SO YOU HATE US, EH?
WELL, GO AHEAD N' HATE ALL YOU WANT! WE DON'T CARE!!
ECCHH...
PTIT!
YOU IDIOT!
I GOT THE HOLE OPENED!
YOU THREE GUARD HIM... WE'LL DECIDE WHAT TO DO WITH HIM LATER...
EVERY-ONE ELSE CAN HELP US EXPLORE...
WE FINALLY BROKE THROUGH!!
GOOD THING WE BROUGHT ALONG A ROBOT...
WHAT'S WITH THESE PUDDLES, PROFESSOR?
MUST BE SOME UNDER-GROUND WATER...

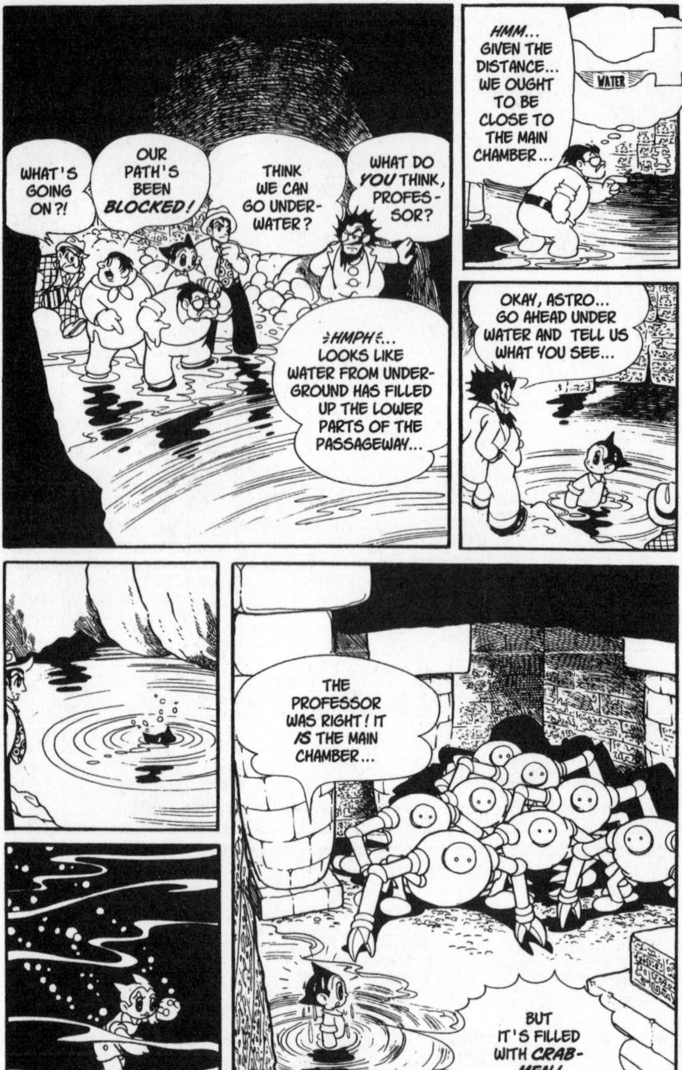
WHAT'S GOING ON?!
OUR PATH'S BEEN BLOCKED!
THINK WE CAN GO UNDER-WATER?
WHAT DO YOU THINK, PROFES-SOR?
HMPH... LOOKS LIKE WATER FROM UNDER-GROUND HAS FILLED UP THE LOWER PARTS OF THE PASSAGEWAY...
HMM... GIVEN THE DISTANCE... WE OUGHT TO BE CLOSE TO THE MAIN CHAMBER...
WATER
OKAY, ASTRO... GO AHEAD UNDER WATER AND TELL US WHAT YOU SEE...
THE PROFESSOR WAS RIGHT! IT IS THE MAIN CHAMBER...
BUT IT'S FILLED WITH CRAB-MEN!

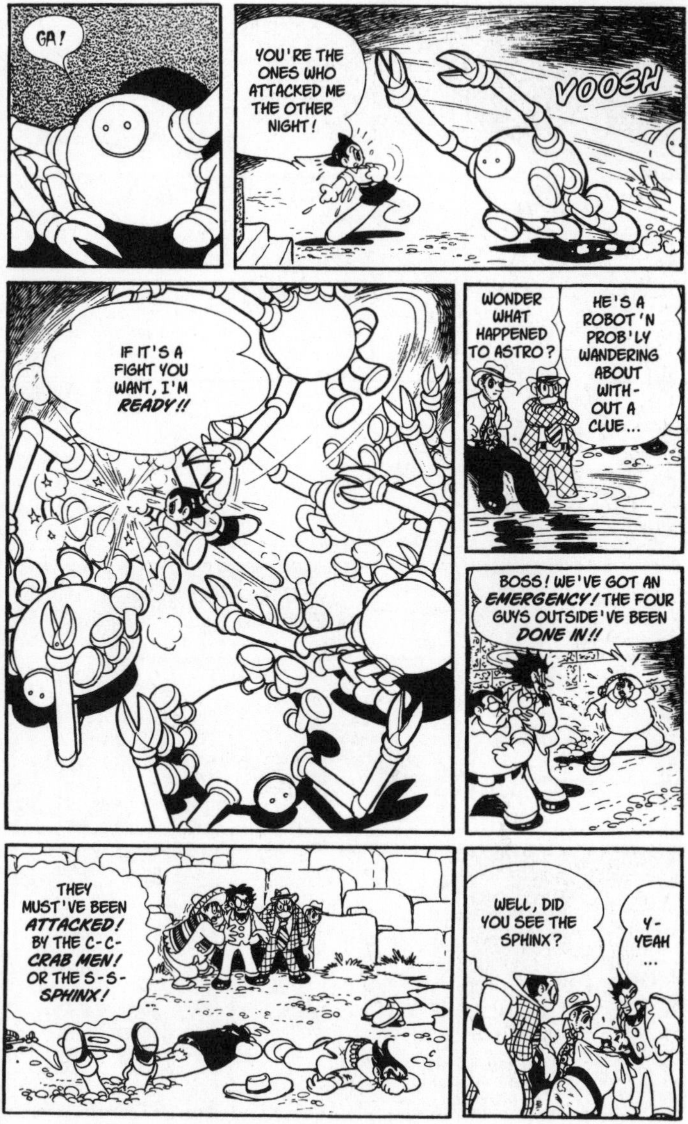
GA!
YOU'RE THE ONES WHO ATTACKED ME THE OTHER NIGHT!
VOOSH
IF IT'S A FIGHT YOU WANT, I'M *READY!!*
WONDER WHAT HAPPENED TO ASTRO?
HE'S A ROBOT 'N PROB'LY WANDERING ABOUT WITH-OUT A CLUE...
BOSS! WE'VE GOT AN *EMERGENCY!* THE FOUR GUYS OUTSIDE'VE BEEN *DONE IN!!*
THEY MUST'VE BEEN *ATTACKED!* BY THE C-C-*CRAB MEN!* OR THE S-S-*SPHINX!*
WELL, DID YOU SEE THE SPHINX?
Y-YEAH ...

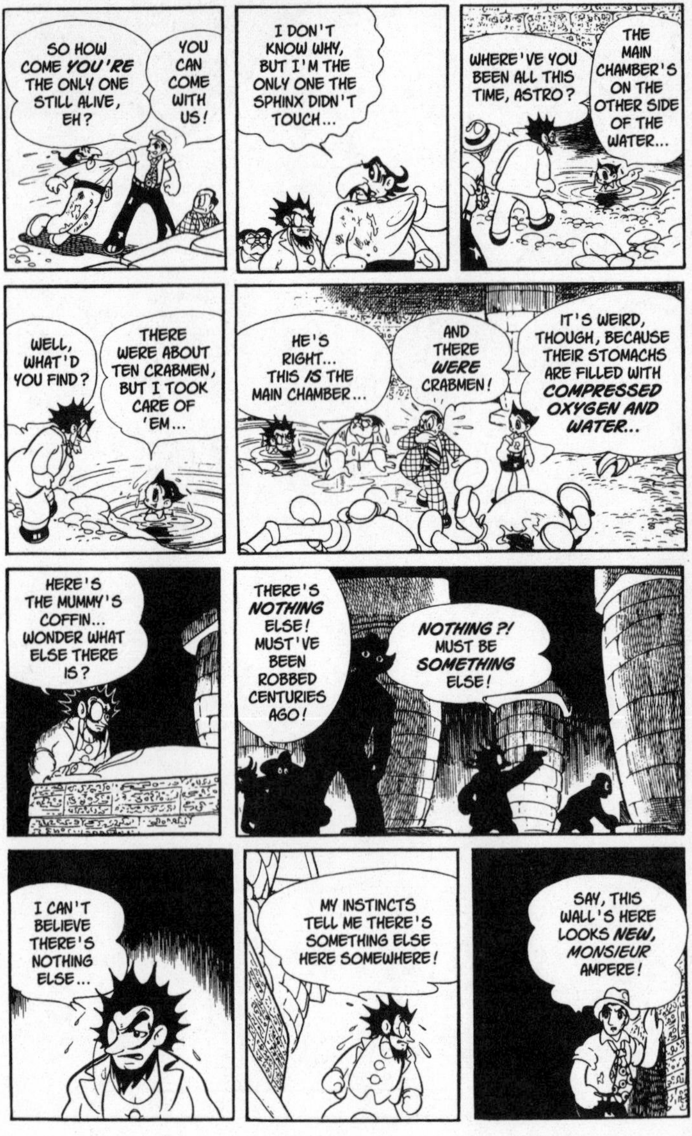
SO HOW COME YOU'RE THE ONLY ONE STILL ALIVE, EH?
YOU CAN COME WITH US!
I DON'T KNOW WHY, BUT I'M THE ONLY ONE THE SPHINX DIDN'T TOUCH...
WHERE'VE YOU BEEN ALL THIS TIME, ASTRO?
THE MAIN CHAMBER'S ON THE OTHER SIDE OF THE WATER...
WELL, WHAT'D YOU FIND?
THERE WERE ABOUT TEN CRABMEN, BUT I TOOK CARE OF 'EM...
HE'S RIGHT... THIS IS THE MAIN CHAMBER...
AND THERE WERE CRABMEN!
IT'S WEIRD, THOUGH, BECAUSE THEIR STOMACHS ARE FILLED WITH COMPRESSED OXYGEN AND WATER...
HERE'S THE MUMMY'S COFFIN... WONDER WHAT ELSE THERE IS?
THERE'S NOTHING ELSE! MUST'VE BEEN ROBBED CENTURIES AGO!
NOTHING?! MUST BE SOMETHING ELSE!
I CAN'T BELIEVE THERE'S NOTHING ELSE...
MY INSTINCTS TELL ME THERE'S SOMETHING ELSE HERE SOMEWHERE!
SAY, THIS WALL'S HERE LOOKS NEW, MONSIEUR AMPERE!

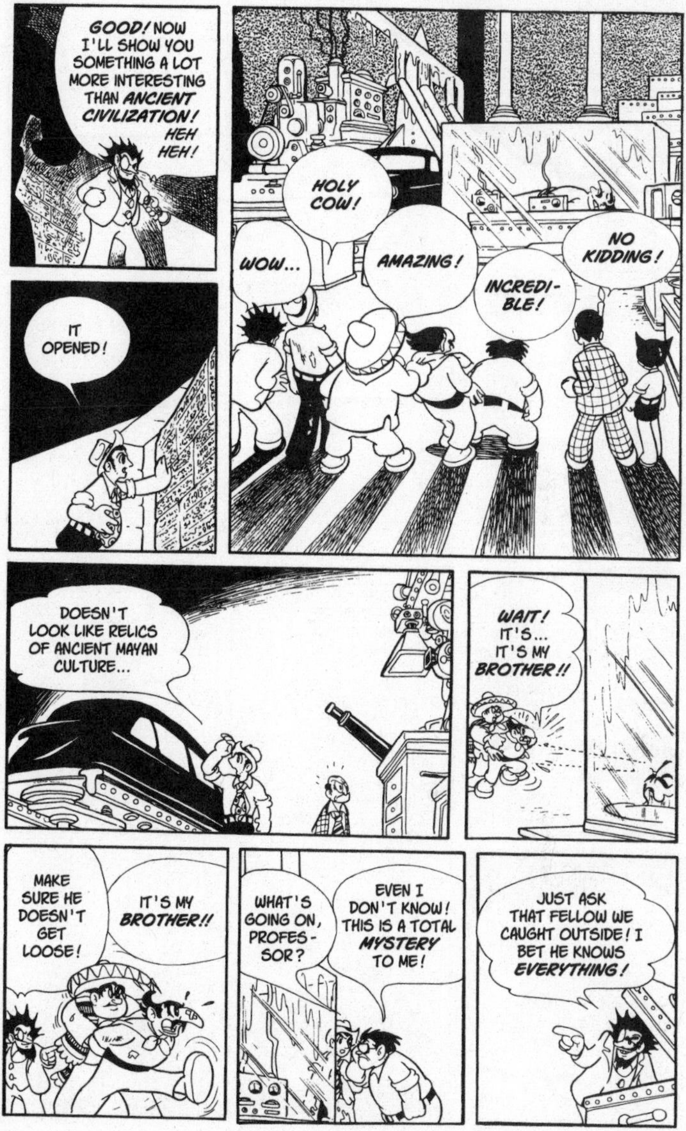
GOOD! NOW I'LL SHOW YOU SOMETHING A LOT MORE INTERESTING THAN ANCIENT CIVILIZATION! HEH HEH!
IT OPENED!
HOLY COW!
WOW...
AMAZING!
INCREDI-BLE!
NO KIDDING!
DOESN'T LOOK LIKE RELICS OF ANCIENT MAYAN CULTURE...
WAIT! IT'S... IT'S MY BROTHER!!
MAKE SURE HE DOESN'T GET LOOSE!
IT'S MY BROTHER!!
WHAT'S GOING ON, PROFES-SOR?
EVEN I DON'T KNOW! THIS IS A TOTAL MYSTERY TO ME!
JUST ASK THAT FELLOW WE CAUGHT OUTSIDE! I BET HE KNOWS EVERYTHING!

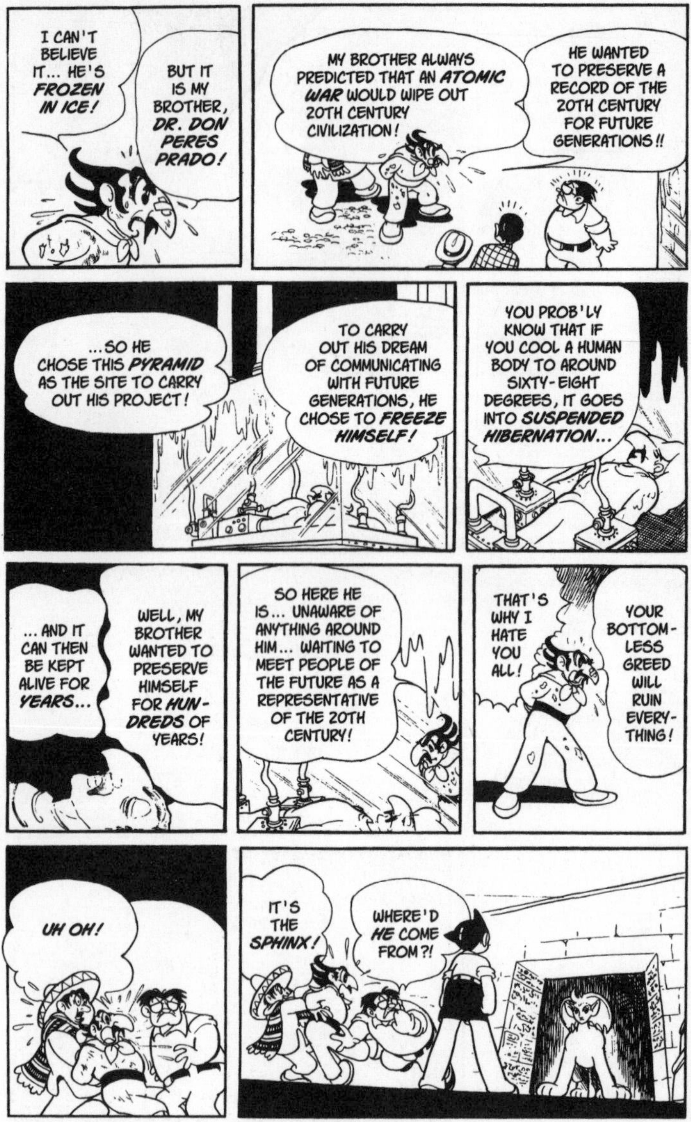
I CAN'T BELIEVE IT... HE'S FROZEN IN ICE!
BUT IT IS MY BROTHER, DR. DON PERES PRADO!
MY BROTHER ALWAYS PREDICTED THAT AN ATOMIC WAR WOULD WIPE OUT 20TH CENTURY CIVILIZATION!
HE WANTED TO PRESERVE A RECORD OF THE 20TH CENTURY FOR FUTURE GENERATIONS!!
...SO HE CHOSE THIS PYRAMID AS THE SITE TO CARRY OUT HIS PROJECT!
TO CARRY OUT HIS DREAM OF COMMUNICATING WITH FUTURE GENERATIONS, HE CHOSE TO FREEZE HIMSELF!
YOU PROB'LY KNOW THAT IF YOU COOL A HUMAN BODY TO AROUND SIXTY-EIGHT DEGREES, IT GOES INTO SUSPENDED HIBERNATION...
...AND IT CAN THEN BE KEPT ALIVE FOR YEARS...
WELL, MY BROTHER WANTED TO PRESERVE HIMSELF FOR HUN-DREDS OF YEARS!
SO HERE HE IS... UNAWARE OF ANYTHING AROUND HIM... WAITING TO MEET PEOPLE OF THE FUTURE AS A REPRESENTATIVE OF THE 20TH CENTURY!
THAT'S WHY I HATE YOU ALL!
YOUR BOTTOM-LESS GREED WILL RUIN EVERY-THING!
UH OH!
IT'S THE SPHINX!
WHERE'D HE COME FROM?!

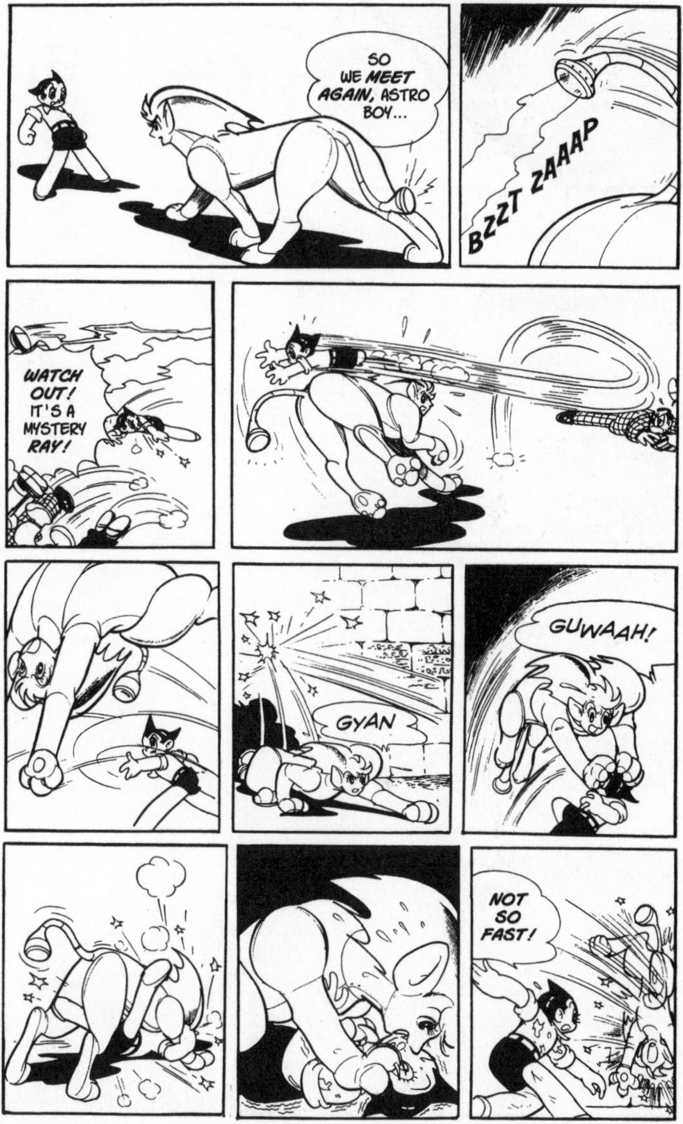
SO WE MEET AGAIN, ASTRO BOY...
BZZT ZAAAP
WATCH OUT! IT'S A MYSTERY RAY!
GYAN
GUWAAH!
NOT SO FAST!

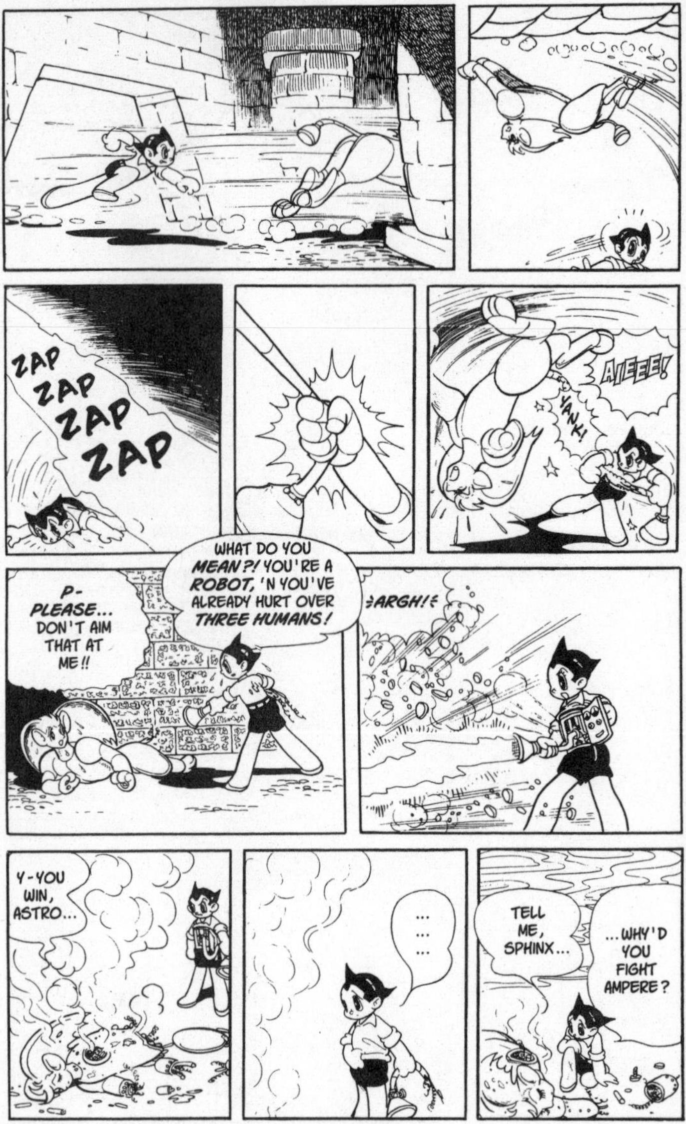

ZAP
ZAP
ZAP
ZAP
AIEEE!
YANK!
WHAT DO YOU MEAN?! YOU'RE A ROBOT, 'N YOU'VE ALREADY HURT OVER THREE HUMANS!
P-PLEASE... DON'T AIM THAT AT ME!!
ARGH!
Y-YOU WIN, ASTRO...
... ...
TELL ME, SPHINX...
...WHY'D YOU FIGHT AMPERE?

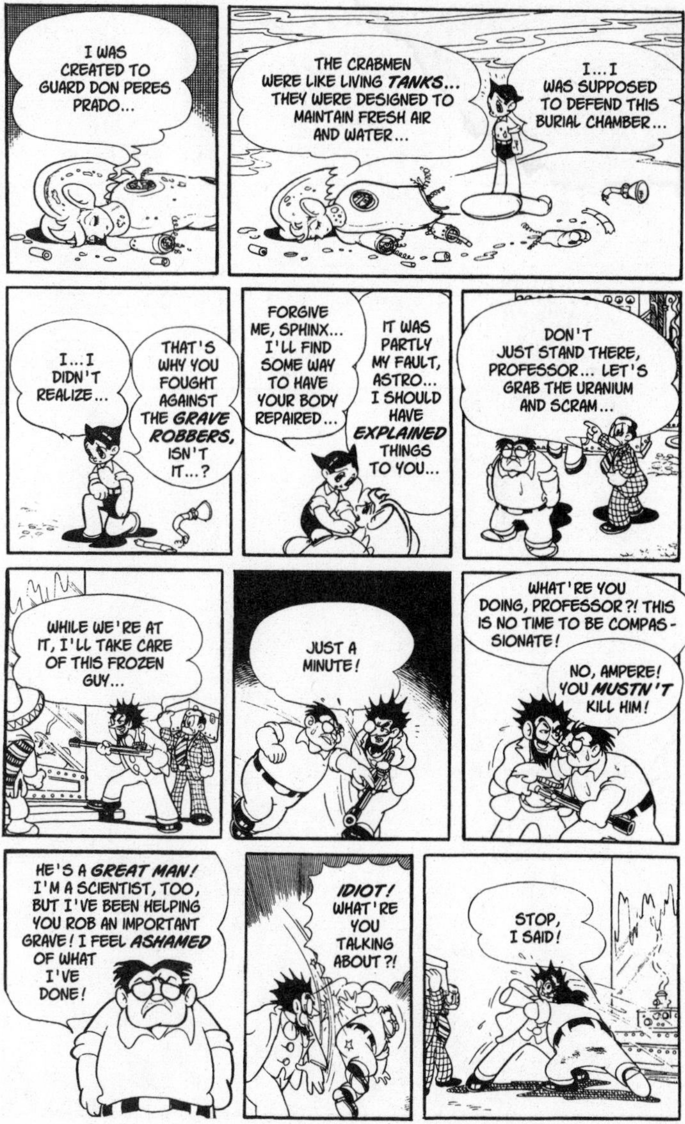

I WAS CREATED TO GUARD DON PERES PRADO...
THE CRABMEN WERE LIKE LIVING TANKS... THEY WERE DESIGNED TO MAINTAIN FRESH AIR AND WATER...
I...I WAS SUPPOSED TO DEFEND THIS BURIAL CHAMBER...
I...I DIDN'T REALIZE...
THAT'S WHY YOU FOUGHT AGAINST THE GRAVE ROBBERS, ISN'T IT...?
FORGIVE ME, SPHINX... I'LL FIND SOME WAY TO HAVE YOUR BODY REPAIRED...
IT WAS PARTLY MY FAULT, ASTRO... I SHOULD HAVE EXPLAINED THINGS TO YOU...
DON'T JUST STAND THERE, PROFESSOR... LET'S GRAB THE URANIUM AND SCRAM...
WHILE WE'RE AT IT, I'LL TAKE CARE OF THIS FROZEN GUY...
JUST A MINUTE!
WHAT'RE YOU DOING, PROFESSOR?! THIS IS NO TIME TO BE COMPAS-SIONATE!
NO, AMPERE! YOU MUSTN'T KILL HIM!
HE'S A GREAT MAN! I'M A SCIENTIST, TOO, BUT I'VE BEEN HELPING YOU ROB AN IMPORTANT GRAVE! I FEEL ASHAMED OF WHAT I'VE DONE!
IDIOT! WHAT'RE YOU TALKING ABOUT?!
STOP, I SAID!

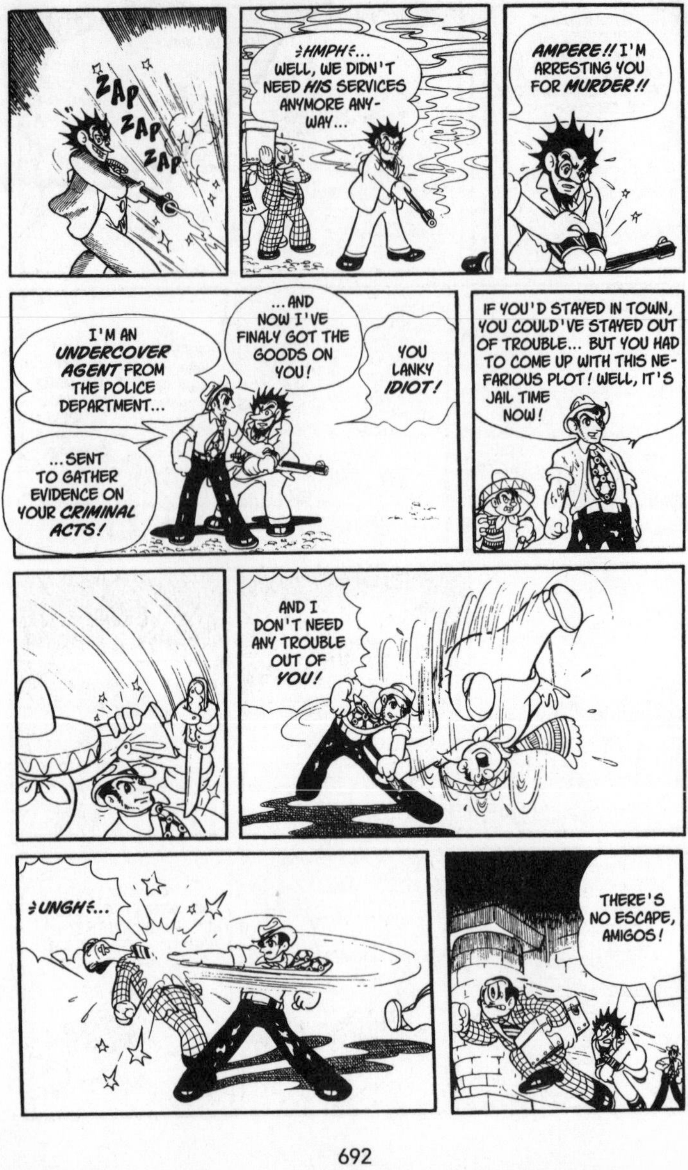
ZAP ZAP ZAP
≑HMPH≑... WELL, WE DIDN'T NEED HIS SERVICES ANYMORE ANY-WAY...
AMPERE!! I'M ARRESTING YOU FOR MURDER!!
I'M AN UNDERCOVER AGENT FROM THE POLICE DEPARTMENT...
...SENT TO GATHER EVIDENCE ON YOUR CRIMINAL ACTS!
...AND NOW I'VE FINALY GOT THE GOODS ON YOU!
YOU LANKY IDIOT!
IF YOU'D STAYED IN TOWN, YOU COULD'VE STAYED OUT OF TROUBLE... BUT YOU HAD TO COME UP WITH THIS NE-FARIOUS PLOT! WELL, IT'S JAIL TIME NOW!
AND I DON'T NEED ANY TROUBLE OUT OF YOU!
≑UNGH≑...
THERE'S NO ESCAPE, AMIGOS!

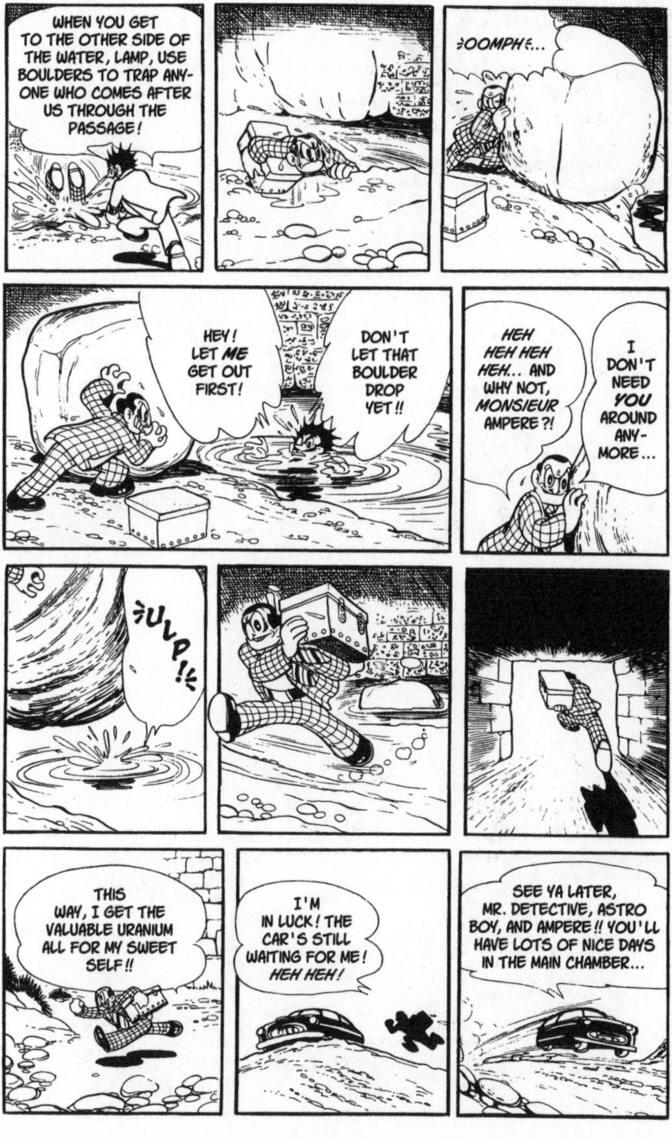
WHEN YOU GET TO THE OTHER SIDE OF THE WATER, LAMP, USE BOULDERS TO TRAP ANY-ONE WHO COMES AFTER US THROUGH THE PASSAGE!
OOMPH...
HEY! LET ME GET OUT FIRST!
DON'T LET THAT BOULDER DROP YET!!
HEH HEH HEH HEH... AND WHY NOT, MONSIEUR AMPERE?!
I DON'T NEED YOU AROUND ANY-MORE...
ULP!!
THIS WAY, I GET THE VALUABLE URANIUM ALL FOR MY SWEET SELF!!
I'M IN LUCK! THE CAR'S STILL WAITING FOR ME! HEH HEH!
SEE YA LATER, MR. DETECTIVE, ASTRO BOY, AND AMPERE!! YOU'LL HAVE LOTS OF NICE DAYS IN THE MAIN CHAMBER...

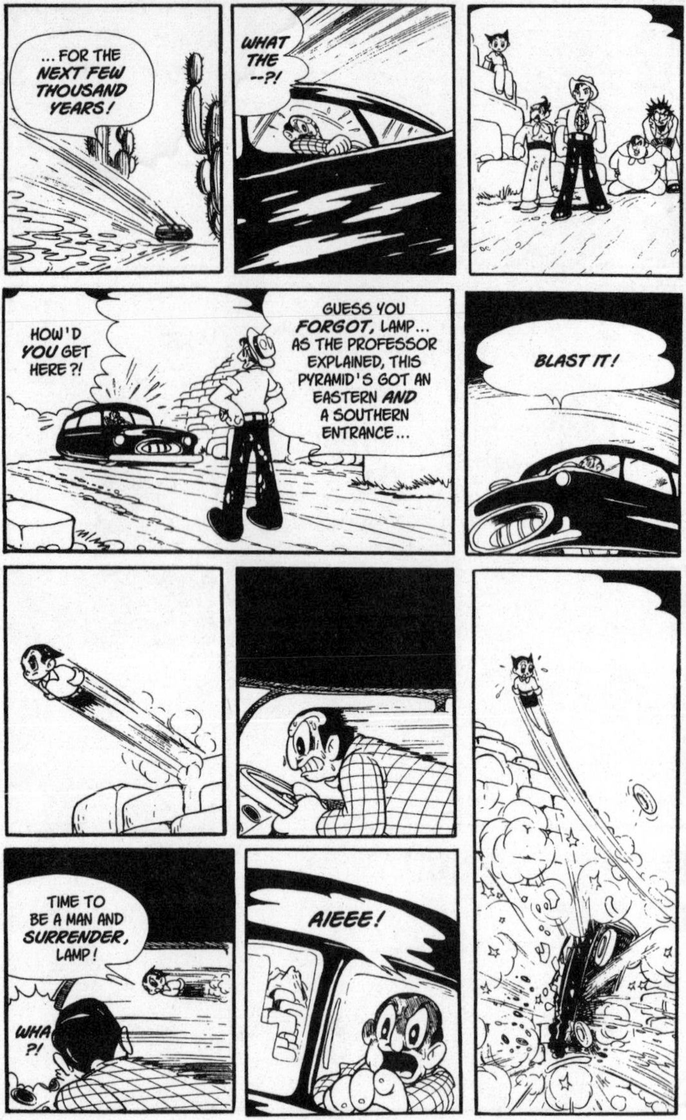
... FOR THE NEXT FEW THOUSAND YEARS!
WHAT THE --?!
HOW'D YOU GET HERE?!
GUESS YOU FORGOT, LAMP... AS THE PROFESSOR EXPLAINED, THIS PYRAMID'S GOT AN EASTERN AND A SOUTHERN ENTRANCE...
BLAST IT!
TIME TO BE A MAN AND SURRENDER, LAMP!
WHA ?!
AIEEE!

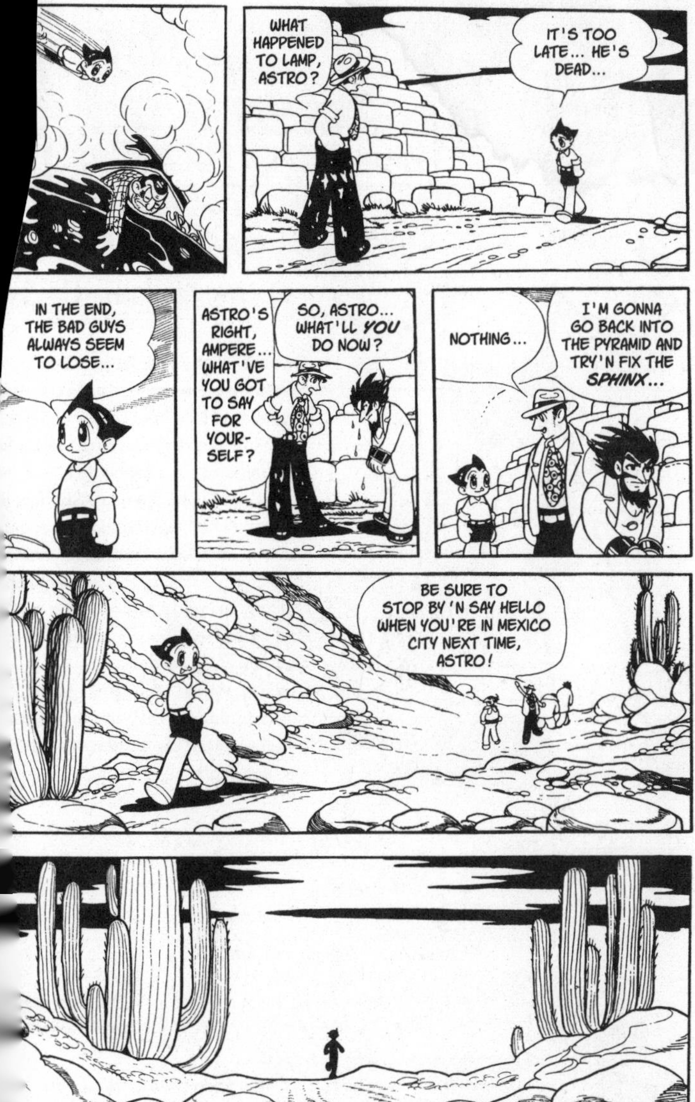
WHAT HAPPENED TO LAMP, ASTRO?
IT'S TOO LATE... HE'S DEAD...
IN THE END, THE BAD GUYS ALWAYS SEEM TO LOSE...
ASTRO'S RIGHT, AMPERE... WHAT'VE YOU GOT TO SAY FOR YOURSELF?
SO, ASTRO... WHAT'LL YOU DO NOW?
NOTHING...
I'M GONNA GO BACK INTO THE PYRAMID AND TRY'N FIX THE SPHINX...
BE SURE TO STOP BY 'N SAY HELLO WHEN YOU'RE IN MEXICO CITY NEXT TIME, ASTRO!

OSAMU TEKUZ

ASTRO BOY

OMNIBUS

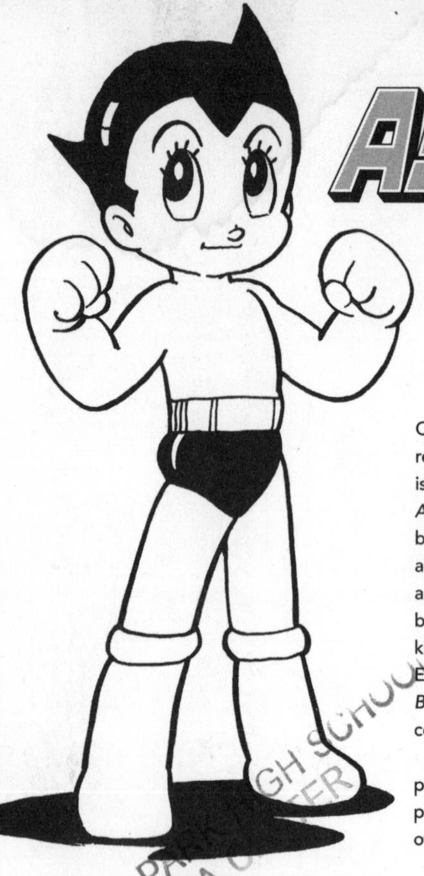

Created by the late Osamu Tezuka, a revered animator and cartoonist who is considered the Walt Disney of Japan, *Astro Boy* was the first manga series to be adapted to animation and became a worldwide phenomenon! Astro Boy is a jet-powered, superstrong, evil-robot bashing, alien-invasion-smashing robo kid with a great story and a lot of hear Exciting, whimsical, and touching, *Astr Boy* harks back to the classic era o comics and animation.

Dark Horse Manga is proud t present these classic tales in bargai priced omnibus volumes, each containin over 600 pages!

VOLUME 1
ISBN 978-1-61655-860-4
$19.99

VOLUME 2
ISBN 978-1-61655-861-1
$19.99

VOLUME 3
ISBN 978-1-61655-893-2
$19.99

VOLUME 4
ISBN 978-1-61655-956-4
$19.99

VOLUME 5
ISBN 978-1-50670-016-8
$19.99

AVAILABLE AT YOUR LOCAL COMICS SHOP OR BOOKSTOR
TO FIND A COMICS SHOP IN YOUR AREA, CALL 1-888-266-422

For more information or to order direct:

- **On the web:** DarkHorse.com • **E-mail:** mailorder@darkhorse.com
- **Phone:** 1-800-862-0052 Mon.–Fri. 9 AM to 5 PM Pacific Time

DARK HORSE MANGA

DarkHorse.com